Guide for Occupational Exploration

Third Edition

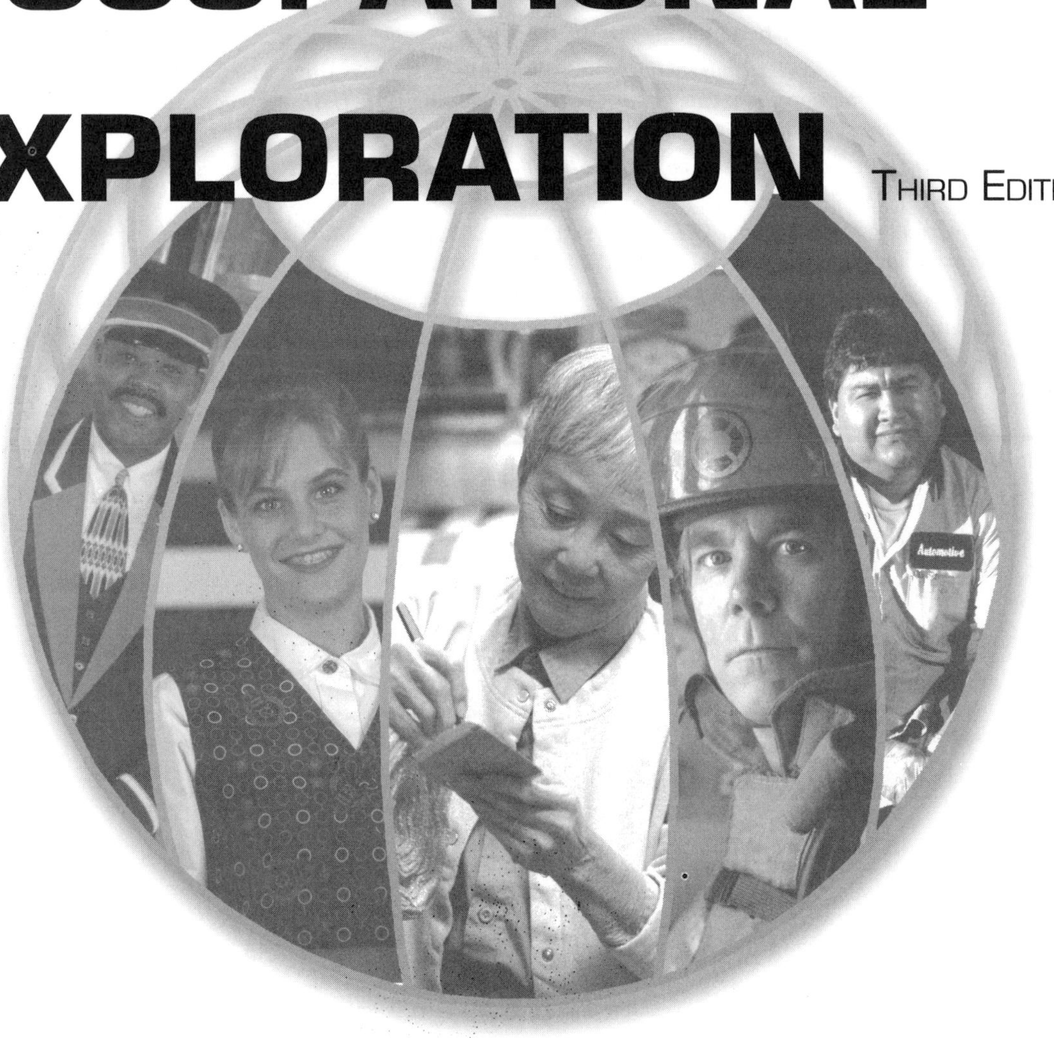

J. Michael Farr
LaVerne L. Ludden, Ed.D.
Laurence Shatkin, Ph.D.

JIST Works

Guide for Occupational Exploration, Third Edition

Published by JIST Works, an imprint of JIST Publishing, Inc.
8902 Otis Avenue
Indianapolis, IN 46216-1033

Phone: 1-800-648-JIST Fax: 1-800-JIST-FAX
E-mail: info@jist.com Web site: www.jist.com

Editors: Susan Pines, Veda Dickerson, Lori Cates
Cover and Interior Designer: Aleata Howard
Interior Layout: Carolyn J. Newland
Proofreaders: Rebecca York, David Faust

Printed in the United States of America

05 04 03 02 9 8 7 6 5 4 3 2

Library of Congress Cataloging-in-Publication Data

Guide for occupational exploration / [compiled by] J. Michael Farr, LaVerne L. Ludden, Laurence Shatkin.— 3rd ed.
p. cm.
Rev. ed. of: Guide for occupational exploration / edited by Thomas F. Harrington, Arthur J. O'Shea. 2nd ed. c1984.
Includes index.
ISBN 1-56370-826-4 — ISBN 1-56370-636-9 (soft)
1. Occupations—United States. 2. Vocational interests—United States. 3. Vocational guidance—United States. I. Farr, J. Michael. II. Ludden, LaVerne, 1949- III. Shatkin, Laurence.

HF5382.5.U5 G83 2001
331.7'02'0973—dc21

2001029100

We have been careful to provide accurate information throughout this book, but it is possible that errors and omissions have been introduced. Please consider this in making any career plans or other important decisions. Trust your own judgment above all else and in all things.

ISBN 1-56370-636-9 Softcover
ISBN 1-56370-826-4 Hardcover

This is a Big Book, But It's Easy to Use

Despite its size, this is an easy book to use. It does contain lots of information, and this makes it look complicated. But, like a dictionary or encyclopedia, it's not meant to be read all the way through. Although the introduction explains the book in detail, here are three suggestions for getting started without delay:

1. **Read the Quick Summary of Major Sections on page v.** It includes short descriptions of the major parts and tips on how to use them.
2. **Identify One or More Interest Areas.** This book organizes all major jobs (and many not-so-major jobs) into just 14 Interest Areas. The Interest Areas and the jobs are listed in a table immediately following the Quick Summary of Major Sections. Use this table to quickly find jobs related to your interests. For example, do you have an interest in art? The table will help you identify numerous job possibilities. Easy.
3. **Dig in As Deeply As You Want.** Part 2 provides information-packed descriptions for almost 1,000 jobs, and a large amount of additional information throughout the book helps you explore career, education, learning, and other options.

This Edition Introduces the First Revision of the GOE Structure Since 1979

The original *Guide for Occupational Exploration* was developed in the 1970s by the U.S. Department of Labor to provide a user-friendly way to help people explore career options based on their interests. The first-edition GOE was published in 1979. A second edition, which included major additional content, was released in 1984 by Thomas Harrington and Arthur O'Shea. Related books, titled *The Complete Guide for Occupational Exploration* and *The Enhanced Guide for Occupational Exploration,* improved on the first two editions of the GOE. These books, by J. Michael Farr, Marilyn Maze, and Donald Mayall, used the original GOE structure. As GOE fans, we decided that someone needed to update the GOE's basic structure to reflect the many changes in jobs and our economy since the 1970s.

This, the third edition of the *Guide for Occupational Exploration,* builds on the strengths of the well-done original and includes many changes to make it easier to understand and use. It also introduces the first revision to the GOE **structure** in over 20 years. Our changes were made to reflect the new jobs and job groupings that did not exist in the 1970s. For example, the original job groupings did not mention computer-related occupations. We have also used an all-new information source on jobs—the O*NET (for Occupational Information Network), which was recently released by the U.S. Department of Labor. These O*NET jobs form the basis for this edition's job descriptions. The original GOE did not include job descriptions, so including them is an enormous improvement. We think that these and many other changes make this the most useful GOE edition ever.

(continues)

(continued)

If you have any suggestions for the next revision (which we will consider, once we recover from this one), please contact us through the publisher at editorial@jist.com or via mail to JIST's address on page ii.

We wish you well in your career and your life.

Mike Farr
LaVerne Ludden
Laurence Shatkin

To Occupational Systems Developers Who Want to Use the New GOE Structure

This edition introduces many changes to the GOE's original structure of Interest Areas, Work Groups, and Subgroups. If you want to use this revised structure in your own publications or databases, we encourage you to do so and are making it easy for you to use. Please refer to the appendix for additional details.

Table of Contents

Quick Summary of Major Sections

Table A and Table B. These important tables are included as part of the table of contents. Table A begins in the right column and lists the GOE's major Interest Areas and Work Groups. Table B follows Table A and lists the almost 1,000 job titles described in this book, within GOE Work Groups.

Introduction. The introduction provides a brief history of the GOE, explains how to understand the major parts of the book, and gives tips on how best to use it for exploring career options. *The introduction begins on page 1.*

Part 1. GOE Interest Areas and Work Groups: Essential Information for Exploring Career Options. Start with this part, because it provides useful information for exploring career and learning options including Interest Area and Work Group descriptions, kinds of work done, things about you that point to this work, skills and knowledge needed, and specific job titles along with courses, education, and training options. *Part 1 begins on page 23.*

Part 2. The Job Descriptions. Read brief, information-packed descriptions for the nearly 1,000 jobs listed in Part 1. *Part 2 begins on page 285.*

Part 3. Crosswalks to Careers by Work Values, Leisure Activities, Home Activities, School Subjects, Work Settings, Skills, Abilities, and Knowledges. These tables help you explore career options by work values, leisure and home activities, school subjects, work settings, skills, abilities, and knowledges. Use these cross-references to find jobs that best suit your interests and past experiences. *Part 3 begins on page 447.*

Appendix. Information for Vocational Counselors and Other Professionals. The appendix contains the following material: information for developers who want to use the new GOE structure in their products; the development background and research support behind the GOE groupings; and tips for career counselors using the GOE. *The appendix begins on page 501.*

Index. Use this alphabetic listing to locate the jobs, Interest Areas, and Work Groups described in this book. *The index begins on page 513.*

Table A: GOE Interest Areas and Work Groups

This table displays the structure of the GOE's 14 Interest Areas and their Work Groups. It provides a quick way to identify Work Groups that are most likely to interest you. The 14 GOE Interest Areas are in large, bold letters and preceded by a two-digit code number. Indented in bold letters below each Interest Area are its related Work Groups. Work Groups have four-digit code numbers, with the first two numbers referring to the Interest Area. If a four-digit Work Group has distinctly different types of jobs within it, it is further divided into two or more groupings that share the first four digits but have an additional two digits to identify them. These six-digit groupings are presented in normal type in the table that follows.

You can use this table to quickly identify Interest Areas and Work Groups for further exploration. Part 1 provides helpful descriptions of each Interest Area and Work Group, and this is where we suggest you begin. Interest Areas and Work Groups are presented in Part 1 in order of their GOE numbers. The job descriptions in Part 2 are also organized within the GOE numbering system. Since the GOE numbering system is used in both Parts 1 and 2, we do not provide page numbers here. You can read more on the GOE structure and numbering system in the book's introduction.

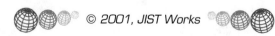

Table B: O*NET Jobs Listed Within GOE Interest Areas and Work Groups

This table presents all of the job titles described in Part 2. The jobs are arranged within related GOE Interest Areas and Work Groups. This arrangement allows you to quickly identify specific job titles that interest you most. Simply write those job titles down, along with their Work Group names and numbers, and you will be able to easily look them up in Part 2. All job descriptions in Part 2 are arranged within Work Groups in the same order as presented in this table.

Note that some Work Groups in Table A were presented with four-digit GOE numbers while in this table they have six digits. We did this to increase the clarity of the GOE's Work Group structure in Table A.

In this table, the four-digit Work Groups have an additional two digits to allow for the future addition of more specific divisions. For example, the first Work Group—"01.01.01 Managerial Work in Arts, Entertainment, and Media"—was presented in the simple four-digit form (01.01) in Table A. The number after each job title is its O*NET number as assigned by the U.S. Department of Labor. This number allows you to cross-reference jobs in other information systems based on the O*NET. More details on the GOE numbering system are provided in Table A and in the book's introduction.

01 Arts, Entertainment, and Media

01.01.01 Managerial Work in Arts, Entertainment, and Media

Agents and Business Managers of Artists, Performers, and Athletes 13-1011.00
Art Directors 27-1011.00
Producers 27-2012.01
Program Directors 27-2012.03
Technical Directors/Managers 27-2012.05

01.02.01 Writing and Editing

Editors 27-3041.00
Technical Writers 27-3042.00
Poets and Lyricists 27-3043.01
Creative Writers 27-3043.02
Copy Writers 27-3043.04

01.03.01 News, Broadcasting, and Public Relations

Broadcast News Analysts 27-3021.00
Reporters and Correspondents 27-3022.00
Public Relations Specialists 27-3031.00
Caption Writers 27-3043.03
Interpreters and Translators 27-3091.00

01.04.01 Visual Arts: Studio Art

Painters and Illustrators 27-1013.01
Sketch Artists 27-1013.02
Cartoonists 27-1013.03
Sculptors 27-1013.04

01.04.02 Visual Arts: Design

Multi-Media Artists and Animators 27-1014.00
Commercial and Industrial Designers 27-1021.00
Fashion Designers 27-1022.00
Floral Designers 27-1023.00
Graphic Designers 27-1024.00
Interior Designers 27-1025.00
Merchandise Displayers and Window Trimmers 27-1026.00
Set Designers 27-1027.01
Exhibit Designers 27-1027.02

01.05.01 Performing Arts, Drama: Directing, Performing, Narrating, and Announcing

Actors 27-2011.00
Directors—Stage, Motion Pictures, Television, and Radio 27-2012.02
Radio and Television Announcers 27-3011.00
Public Address System and Other Announcers 27-3012.00

01.05.02 Performing Arts, Music: Directing, Composing and Arranging, and Performing

Talent Directors 27-2012.04
Music Directors 27-2041. 01
Music Arrangers and Orchestrators 27-2041.02
Composers 27-2041.03
Singers 27-2042.01
Musicians, Instrumental 27-2042.02

01.05.03 Performing Arts, Dance: Performing and Choreography

Dancers 27-2031.00
Choreographers 27-2032.00

01.06.01 Craft Arts

Craft Artists 27-1012.00
Glass Blowers, Molders, Benders, and Finishers 51-9195.04
Potters 51-9195.05

01.07.01 Graphic Arts

Desktop Publishers 43-9031.00
Paste-Up Workers 51-5022.02
Photoengravers 51-5022.03
Camera Operators 51-5022.04
Dot Etchers 51-5022.08
Electronic Masking System Operators 51-5022.09
Precision Etchers and Engravers, Hand or Machine 51-9194.01
Engravers/Carvers 51-9194.02
Etchers 51-9194.03
Pantograph Engravers 51-9194.04
Etchers, Hand 51-9194.05
Engravers, Hand 51-9194.06

01.08.01 Media Technology

Audio and Video Equipment Technicians 27-4011.00
Broadcast Technicians 27-4012.00
Radio Operators 27-4013.00
Sound Engineering Technicians 27-4014.00
Professional Photographers 27-4021.01
Camera Operators, Television, Video, and Motion Picture 27-4031.00
Film and Video Editors 27-4032.00

01.09.01 Modeling and Personal Appearance

Costume Attendants 39-3092.00
Makeup Artists, Theatrical and Performance 39-5091.00
Models 41-9012.00

01.10.01 Sports: Coaching, Instructing, Officiating, and Performing

Athletes and Sports Competitors 27-2021.00
Coaches and Scouts 27-2022.00
Umpires, Referees, and Other Sports Officials 27-2023.00
Fitness Trainers and Aerobics Instructors 39-9031.00

02 Science, Math, and Engineering

02.01.01 Managerial Work in Science, Math, and Engineering

Computer and Information Systems Managers 11-3021.00

Materials Engineers 17-2131.00

Mining and Geological Engineers, Including Mining Safety Engineers 17-2151.00

02.07.03 Engineering: Design

Architects, Except Landscape and Naval 17-1011.00

Landscape Architects 17-1012.00

Marine Engineers and Naval Architects 17-2121.00

Marine Architects 17-2121.02

02.07.04 Engineering: General Engineering

Aerospace Engineers 17-2011.00

Biomedical Engineers 17-2031.00

Civil Engineers 17-2051.00

Electrical Engineers 17-2071.00

Electronics Engineers, Except Computer 17-2072.00

Environmental Engineers 17-2081.00

Health and Safety Engineers, Except Mining Safety Engineers and Inspectors 17-2111.00

Mechanical Engineers 17-2141.00

Petroleum Engineers 17-2171.00

Sales Engineers 41-9031.00

02.08.01 Engineering Technology: Surveying

Surveyors 17-1022.00

Surveying Technicians 17-3031.01

Mapping Technicians 17-3031.02

02.08.02 Engineering Technology: Industrial and Safety

Pressure Vessel Inspectors 13-1041.05

Industrial Engineering Technicians 17-3026.00

Construction and Building Inspectors 47-4011.00

02.08.03 Engineering Technology: Design

Cartographers and Photogrammetrists 17-1021.00

Architectural Drafters 17-3011.01

Civil Drafters 17-3011.02

Electronic Drafters 17-3012.01

Electrical Drafters 17-3012.02

Mechanical Drafters 17-3013.00

02.08.04 Engineering Technology: General

Aerospace Engineering and Operations Technicians 17-3021.00

Civil Engineering Technicians 17-3022.00

Electronics Engineering Technicians 17-3023.01

Calibration and Instrumentation Technicians 17-3023.02

Electrical Engineering Technicians 17-3023.03

Electro-Mechanical Technicians 17-3024.00

Environmental Engineering Technicians 17-3025.00

Mechanical Engineering Technicians 17-3027.00

Numerical Tool and Process Control Programmers 51-4012.00

03 Plants and Animals

03.01.01 Managerial Work: Farming and Fishing

Agricultural Crop Farm Managers 11-9011.02

Fish Hatchery Managers 11-9011.03

Farmers and Ranchers 11-9012.00

Forest and Conservation Technicians 19-4093.00

First-Line Supervisors and Manager/Supervisors—Agricultural Crop Workers 45-1011.01

First-Line Supervisors and Manager/Supervisors—Animal Husbandry Workers 45-1011.02

First-Line Supervisors and Manager/Supervisors—Animal Care Workers, Except Livestock 45-1011.03

First-Line Supervisors and Manager/Supervisors—Fishery Workers 45-1011.06

Farm Labor Contractors 45-2031.00

03.01.02 Managerial Work: Nursery, Groundskeeping, and Logging

Nursery and Greenhouse Managers 11-9011.01

Lawn Service Managers 37-1012.01

First-Line Supervisors and Manager/Supervisors—Landscaping Workers 37-1012.02

First-Line Supervisors and Manager/Supervisors—Horticultural Workers 45-1011.04

First-Line Supervisors and Manager/Supervisors—Logging Workers 45-1011.05

03.02.01 Animal Care and Training

Veterinarians 29-1131.00

Veterinary Technologists and Technicians 29-2056.00

Veterinary Assistants and Laboratory Animal Caretakers 31-9096.00

Animal Trainers 39-2011.00

Nonfarm Animal Caretakers 39-2021.00

Animal Breeders 45-2021.00

03.03.01 Hands-on Work: Farming

Agricultural Equipment Operators 45-2091.00

Farmworkers and Laborers, Crop, Nursery, and Greenhouse 45-2092.00

General Farmworkers 45-2092.02

Farmworkers, Farm and Ranch Animals 45-2093.00

03.03.02 Hands-on Work: Forestry and Logging

Forest and Conservation Workers 45-4011.00

Fallers 45-4021.00

Logging Equipment Operators 45-4022.00

Logging Tractor Operators 45-4022.01

03.03.03 Hands-on Work: Hunting and Fishing

Fishers and Related Fishing Workers 45-3011.00

Hunters and Trappers 45-3021.00

First-Line Supervisors/Managers of Air Crew Members 55-2011.00

First-Line Supervisors/Managers of Weapons Specialists/Crew Members 55-2012.00

First-Line Supervisors/Managers of All Other Tactical Operations Specialists 55-2013.00

04.05.02 Military: Specialists

Air Crew Members 55-3011.00

Aircraft Launch and Recovery Specialists 55-3012.00

Armored Assault Vehicle Crew Members 55-3013.00

Artillery and Missile Crew Members 55-3014.00

Command and Control Center Specialists 55-3015.00

Infantry 55-3016.00

Radar and Sonar Technicians 55-3017.00

Special Forces 55-3018.00

05 Mechanics, Installers, and Repairers

05.01.01 Managerial Work in Mechanics, Installers, and Repairers

First-Line Supervisors/Managers of Mechanics, Installers, and Repairers 49-1011.00

05.02.01 Electrical and Electronic Systems: Installation and Repair

Elevator Installers and Repairers 47-4021.00

Central Office and PBX Installers and Repairers 49-2022.01

Frame Wirers, Central Office 49-2022.02

Communication Equipment Mechanics, Installers, and Repairers 49-2022.03

Telecommunications Facility Examiners 49-2022.04

Station Installers and Repairers, Telephone 49-2022.05

Avionics Technicians 49-2091.00

Electrical and Electronics Installers and Repairers, Transportation Equipment 49-2093.00

Electrical and Electronics Repairers, Commercial and Industrial Equipment 49-2094.00

Electronic Equipment Installers and Repairers, Motor Vehicles 49-2096.00

Home Appliance Installers 49-9031.01

Electrical Power-Line Installers and Repairers 49-9051.00

Telecommunications Line Installers and Repairers 49-9052.00

Signal and Track Switch Repairers 49-9097.00

05.02.02 Electrical and Electronic Systems: Equipment Repair

Data Processing Equipment Repairers 49-2011.02

Office Machine and Cash Register Servicers 49-2011.03

Radio Mechanics 49-2021.00

Electric Home Appliance and Power Tool Repairers 49-2092.01

Electric Motor and Switch Assemblers and Repairers 49-2092.02

Battery Repairers 49-2092.03

Transformer Repairers 49-2092.04

Electrical Parts Reconditioners 49-2092.05

Electrical and Electronics Repairers, Powerhouse, Substation, and Relay 49-2095.00

Electronic Home Entertainment Equipment Installers and Repairers 49-2097.00

Electric Meter Installers and Repairers 49-9012.01

05.03.01 Mechanical Work: Vehicles and Facilities

Airframe-and-Power-Plant Mechanics 49-3011.01

Aircraft Engine Specialists 49-3011.02

Aircraft Body and Bonded Structure Repairers 49-3011.03

Automotive Body and Related Repairers 49-3021.00

Automotive Glass Installers and Repairers 49-3022.00

Automotive Master Mechanics 49-3023.01

Automotive Specialty Technicians 49-3023.02

Bus and Truck Mechanics and Diesel Engine Specialists 49-3031.00

Farm Equipment Mechanics 49-3041.00

Mobile Heavy Equipment Mechanics, Except Engines 49-3042.00

Rail Car Repairers 49-3043.00

Motorboat Mechanics 49-3051.00

Motorcycle Mechanics 49-3052.00

Outdoor Power Equipment and Other Small Engine Mechanics 49-3053.00

Recreational Vehicle Service Technicians 49-3092.00

Heating and Air Conditioning Mechanics 49-9021.01

Refrigeration Mechanics 49-9021.02

Maintenance and Repair Workers, General 49-9042.00

Millwrights 49-9044.00

Locksmiths and Safe Repairers 49-9094.00

Painters, Transportation Equipment 51-9122.00

Bridge and Lock Tenders 53-6011.00

Railroad Inspectors 53-6051.04

05.03.02 Mechanical Work: Machinery Repair

Hand and Portable Power Tool Repairers 49-2092.06

Bicycle Repairers 49-3091.00

Mechanical Door Repairers 49-9011.00

Control and Valve Installers and Repairers, Except Mechanical Door 49-9012.00

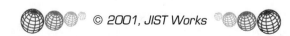

06.03.01 Mining and Drilling

Derrick Operators, Oil and Gas 47-5011.00
Rotary Drill Operators, Oil and Gas 47-5012.00
Service Unit Operators, Oil, Gas, and Mining 47-5013.00
Construction Drillers 47-5021.01
Well and Core Drill Operators 47-5021.02
Continuous Mining Machine Operators 47-5041.00
Mine Cutting and Channeling Machine Operators 47-5042.00
Rock Splitters, Quarry 47-5051.00
Roof Bolters, Mining 47-5061.00
Roustabouts, Oil and Gas 47-5071.00
Excavating and Loading Machine Operators 53-7032.01
Loading Machine Operators, Underground Mining 53-7033.00
Shuttle Car Operators 53-7111.00

06.04.01 Hands-on Work in Construction, Extraction, and Maintenance

Carpenter Assemblers and Repairers 47-2031.03
Construction Laborers 47-2061.00
Helpers—Brickmasons, Blockmasons, Stonemasons, and Tile and Marble Setters 47-3011.00
Helpers—Carpenters 47-3012.00
Helpers—Painters, Paperhangers, Plasterers, and Stucco Masons 47-3014.00
Helpers—Pipelayers, Plumbers, Pipefitters, and Steamfitters 47-3015.00
Helpers—Roofers 47-3016.00
Highway Maintenance Workers 47-4051.00
Septic Tank Servicers and Sewer Pipe Cleaners 47-4071.00
Helpers—Extraction Workers 47-5081.00
Grips and Set-Up Workers, Motion Picture Sets, Studios, and Stages 53-7062.02

07 Transportation

07.01.01 Managerial Work in Transportation

Transportation Managers 11-3071.01
First-Line Supervisors/Managers of Transportation and Material-Moving Machine and Vehicle Operators 53-1031.00
Railroad Conductors and Yardmasters 53-4031.00

07.02.01 Vehicle Expediting and Coordinating

Air Traffic Controllers 53-2021.00
Airfield Operations Specialists 53-2022.00
Railroad Brake, Signal, and Switch Operators 53-4021.00
Traffic Technicians 53-6041.00

07.03.01 Air Vehicle Operation

Airline Pilots, Copilots, and Flight Engineers 53-2011.00
Commercial Pilots 53-2012.00

07.04.01 Water Vehicle Operation

Able Seamen 53-5011.01
Ordinary Seamen and Marine Oilers 53-5011.02
Ship and Boat Captains 53-5021.01
Mates—Ship, Boat, and Barge 53-5021.02
Pilots, Ship 53-5021.03
Motorboat Operators 53-5022.00
Dredge Operators 53-7031.00

07.05.01 Truck Driving

Truck Drivers, Heavy 53-3032.01
Tractor-Trailer Truck Drivers 53-3032.02
Truck Drivers, Light or Delivery Services 53-3033.00

07.06.01 Rail Vehicle Operation

Locomotive Engineers 53-4011.00
Locomotive Firers 53-4012.00
Rail Yard Engineers, Dinkey Operators, and Hostlers 53-4013.00
Subway and Streetcar Operators 53-4041.00

07.07.01 Other Services Requiring Driving

Ambulance Drivers and Attendants, Except Emergency Medical Technicians 53-3011.00
Bus Drivers, Transit and Intercity 53-3021.00
Bus Drivers, School 53-3022.00
Driver/Sales Workers 53-3031.00
Taxi Drivers and Chauffeurs 53-3041.00
Parking Lot Attendants 53-6021.00

07.08.01 Support Work in Transportation

Train Crew Members 53-4021.01
Railroad Yard Workers 53-4021.02
Transportation Inspectors 53-6051.00
Freight Inspectors 53-6051.06
Stevedores, Except Equipment Operators 53-7062.01

08 Industrial Production

08.01.01 Managerial Work in Industrial Production

Industrial Production Managers 11-3051.00
First-Line Supervisors/Managers of Production and Operating Workers 51-1011.00
First-Line Supervisors/Managers of Helpers, Laborers, and Material Movers, Hand 53-1021.00

08.02.01 Production Technology: Machine Set-up and Operation

Extruding and Drawing Machine Setters, Operators, and Tenders, Metal and Plastic 51-4021.00
Forging Machine Setters, Operators, and Tenders, Metal and Plastic 51-4022.00
Rolling Machine Setters, Operators, and Tenders, Metal and Plastic 51-4023.00

Sawing Machine Setters and Set-Up Operators 51-7041.01

Sawing Machine Operators and Tenders 51-7041.02

Woodworking Machine Operators and Tenders, Except Sawing 51-7042.02

Crushing, Grinding, and Polishing Machine Setters, Operators, and Tenders 51-9021.00

Fiber Product Cutting Machine Setters and Set-Up Operators 51-9032.01

Stone Sawyers 51-9032.02

Glass Cutting Machine Setters and Set-Up Operators 51-9032.03

Cutting and Slicing Machine Operators and Tenders 51-9032.04

Extruding, Forming, Pressing, and Compacting Machine Operators and Tenders 51-9041.02

Packaging and Filling Machine Operators and Tenders 51-9111.00

Coating, Painting, and Spraying Machine Operators and Tenders 51-9121.02

Cementing and Gluing Machine Operators and Tenders 51-9191.00

08.03.02 Production Work: Equipment Operation, Assorted Materials Processing

Bakers, Manufacturing 51-3011.02

Meat, Poultry, and Fish Cutters and Trimmers 51-3022.00

Slaughterers and Meat Packers 51-3023.00

Food and Tobacco Roasting, Baking, and Drying Machine Operators and Tenders 51-3091.00

Food Cooking Machine Operators and Tenders 51-3093.00

Metal-Refining Furnace Operators and Tenders 51-4051.00

Pourers and Casters, Metal 51-4052.00

Heaters, Metal and Plastic 51-4191.03

Pressing Machine Operators and Tenders-Textile, Garment, and Related Materials 51-6021.02

Textile Bleaching and Dyeing Machine Operators and Tenders 51-6061.00

Chemical Equipment Controllers and Operators 51-9011.01

Chemical Equipment Tenders 51-9011.02

Separating, Filtering, Clarifying, Precipitating, and Still Machine Setters, Operators, and Tenders 51-9012.00

Mixing and Blending Machine Setters, Operators, and Tenders 51-9023.00

Furnace, Kiln, Oven, Drier, and Kettle Operators and Tenders 51-9051.00

Semiconductor Processors 51-9141.00

Cleaning, Washing, and Metal Pickling Equipment Operators and Tenders 51-9192.00

Cooling and Freezing Equipment Operators and Tenders 51-9193.00

Production Laborers 51-9198.01

Production Helpers 51-9198.02

08.03.03 Production Work: Equipment Operation, Welding, Brazing, and Soldering

Metal Fabricators, Structural Metal Products 51-2041.01

Fitters, Structural Metal—Precision 51-2041.02

Welders, Production 51-4121.01

Welders and Cutters 51-4121.02

Welder-Fitters 51-4121.03

Solderers 51-4121.04

Brazers 51-4121.05

Welding Machine Operators and Tenders 51-4122.02

Soldering and Brazing Machine Operators and Tenders 51-4122.04

08.03.04 Production Work: Plating and Coating

Electrolytic Plating and Coating Machine Setters and Set-Up Operators, Metal and Plastic 51-4193.01

Electrolytic Plating and Coating Machine Operators and Tenders, Metal and Plastic 51-4193.02

Nonelectrolytic Plating and Coating Machine Setters and Set-Up Operators, Metal and Plastic 51-4193.03

Nonelectrolytic Plating and Coating Machine Operators and Tenders, Metal and Plastic 51-4193.04

08.03.05 Production Work: Printing and Reproduction

Bindery Machine Operators and Tenders 51-5011.02

Job Printers 51-5021.00

Hand Compositors and Typesetters 51-5022.01

Scanner Operators 51-5022.05

Strippers 51-5022.06

Platemakers 51-5022.07

Electrotypers and Stereotypers 51-5022.10

Plate Finishers 51-5022.11

Photoengraving and Lithographing Machine Operators and Tenders 51-5022.13

Precision Printing Workers 51-5023.01

Offset Lithographic Press Setters and Set-Up Operators 51-5023.02

Letterpress Setters and Set-Up Operators 51-5023.03

Design Printing Machine Setters and Set-Up Operators 51-5023.04

Marking and Identification Printing Machine Setters and Set-Up Operators 51-5023.05

Embossing Machine Set-Up Operators 51-5023.07

09.02.03 Administrative Detail: Interviewing

Claims Takers, Unemployment Benefits 43-4061.01

Welfare Eligibility Workers and Interviewers 43-4061.02

Interviewers, Except Eligibility and Loan 43-4111.00

Loan Interviewers and Clerks 43-4131.00

09.03.01 Bookkeeping, Auditing, and Accounting

Tax Preparers 13-2082.00

Statement Clerks 43-3021.01

Billing, Cost, and Rate Clerks 43-3021.02

Bookkeeping, Accounting, and Auditing Clerks 43-3031.00

Payroll and Timekeeping Clerks 43-3051.00

Brokerage Clerks 43-4011.00

09.04.01 Material Control

Meter Readers, Utilities 43-5041.00

Production, Planning, and Expediting Clerks 43-5061.00

09.05.01 Customer Service

Cashiers 41-2011.00

Gaming Change Persons and Booth Cashiers 41-2012.00

Counter and Rental Clerks 41-2021.00

Bill and Account Collectors 43-3011.00

Gaming Cage Workers 43-3041.00

Tellers 43-3071.00

Adjustment Clerks 43-4051.01

Customer Service Representatives, Utilities 43-4051.02

New Accounts Clerks 43-4141.00

Order Clerks 43-4151.00

Receptionists and Information Clerks 43-4171.00

Travel Clerks 43-4181.01

09.06.01 Communications

Switchboard Operators, Including Answering Service 43-2011.00

Telephone Operators 43-2021.00

Directory Assistance Operators 43-2021.01

Central Office Operators 43-2021.02

Police, Fire, and Ambulance Dispatchers 43-5031.00

Dispatchers, Except Police, Fire, and Ambulance 43-5032.00

09.07.01 Records Processing: Verification and Proofing

Credit Authorizers 43-4041.01

Credit Checkers 43-4041.02

Insurance Claims Clerks 43-9041.01

Insurance Policy Processing Clerks 43-9041.02

Proofreaders and Copy Markers 43-9081.00

09.07.02 Records Processing: Preparation and Maintenance

Court Reporters 23-2091.00

Medical Records and Health Information Technicians 29-2071.00

Medical Transcriptionists 31-9094.00

Procurement Clerks 43-3061.00

Correspondence Clerks 43-4021.00

File Clerks 43-4071.00

Human Resources Assistants, Except Payroll and Timekeeping 43-4161.00

Office Clerks, General 43-9061.00

09.08.01 Records and Materials Processing

Cargo and Freight Agents 43-5011.00

Couriers and Messengers 43-5021.00

Postal Service Mail Carriers 43-5052.00

Postal Service Mail Sorters, Processors, and Processing Machine Operators 43-5053.00

Shipping, Receiving, and Traffic Clerks 43-5071.00

Marking Clerks 43-5081.02

Stock Clerks- Stockroom, Warehouse, or Storage Yard 43-5081.03

Order Fillers, Wholesale and Retail Sales 43-5081.04

Weighers, Measurers, Checkers, and Samplers, Recordkeeping 43-5111.00

Mail Clerks, Except Mail Machine Operators and Postal Service 43-9051.02

09.09.01 Clerical Machine Operation

Billing, Posting, and Calculating Machine Operators 43-3021.03

Postal Service Clerks 43-5051.00

Computer Operators 43-9011.00

Data Entry Keyers 43-9021.00

Word Processors and Typists 43-9022.00

Mail Machine Operators, Preparation and Handling 43-9051.01

Office Machine Operators, Except Computer 43-9071.00

Duplicating Machine Operators 43-9071.01

Automatic Teller Machine Servicers 49-2011.01

Typesetting and Composing Machine Operators and Tenders 51-5022.12

10 Sales and Marketing

10.01.01 Managerial Work in Sales and Marketing

Advertising and Promotions Managers 11-2011.00

Marketing Managers 11-2021.00

Sales Managers 11-2022.00

First-Line Supervisors/Managers of Retail Sales Workers 41-1011.00

First-Line Supervisors/Managers of Non-Retail Sales Workers 41-1012.00

Laundry and Dry-Cleaning Workers 51-6011.00

Spotters, Dry Cleaning 51-6011.01

Precision Dyers 51-6011.02

Laundry and Drycleaning Machine Operators and Tenders, Except Pressing 51-6011.03

Pressers, Delicate Fabrics 51-6021.01

Pressers, Hand 51-6021.03

Shoe and Leather Workers and Repairers 51-6041.00

Shop and Alteration Tailors 51-6052.01

Custom Tailors 51-6052.02

Upholsterers 51-6093.00

11.07.01 Cleaning and Building Services

Janitors and Cleaners, Except Maids and Housekeeping Cleaners 37-2011.00

Maids and Housekeeping Cleaners 37-2012.00

Locker Room, Coatroom, and Dressing Room Attendants 39-3093.00

11.08.01 Other Personal Services

Cooks, Private Household 35-2013.00

Embalmers 39-4011.00

Funeral Attendants 39-4021.00

Personal and Home Care Aides 39-9021.00

Cleaners of Vehicles and Equipment 53-7061.00

12 Education and Social Service

12.01.01 Managerial Work in Education and Social Service

Education Administrators, Preschool and Child Care Center/Program 11-9031.00

Education Administrators, Elementary and Secondary School 11-9032.00

Education Administrators, Postsecondary 11-9033.00

Social and Community Service Managers 11-9151.00

Park Naturalists 19-1031.03

Instructional Coordinators 25-9031.00

12.02.01 Social Services: Religious

Clergy 21-2011.00

Directors, Religious Activities and Education 21-2021.00

12.02.02 Social Services: Counseling and Social Work

Clinical Psychologists 19-3031.02

Counseling Psychologists 19-3031.03

Substance Abuse and Behavioral Disorder Counselors 21-1011.00

Marriage and Family Therapists 21-1013.00

Mental Health Counselors 21-1014.00

Rehabilitation Counselors 21-1015.00

Child, Family, and School Social Workers 21-1021.00

Medical and Public Health Social Workers 21-1022.00

Mental Health and Substance Abuse Social Workers 21-1023.00

Probation Officers and Correctional Treatment Specialists 21-1092.00

Social and Human Service Assistants 21-1093.00

Residential Advisors 39-9041.00

12.03.01 Educational Services: Counseling and Evaluation

Personal Financial Advisors 13-2052.00

Educational Psychologists 19-3031.01

Educational, Vocational, and School Counselors 21-1012.00

12.03.02 Educational Services: Postsecondary and Adult Teaching and Instructing

Business Teachers, Postsecondary 25-1011.00

Computer Science Teachers, Postsecondary 25-1021.00

Mathematical Science Teachers, Postsecondary 25-1022.00

Architecture Teachers, Postsecondary 25-1031.00

Engineering Teachers, Postsecondary 25-1032.00

Agricultural Sciences Teachers, Postsecondary 25-1041.00

Biological Science Teachers, Postsecondary 25-1042.00

Forestry and Conservation Science Teachers, Postsecondary 25-1043.00

Atmospheric, Earth, Marine, and Space Sciences Teachers, Postsecondary 25-1051.00

Chemistry Teachers, Postsecondary 25-1052.00

Environmental Science Teachers, Postsecondary 25-1053.00

Physics Teachers, Postsecondary 25-1054.00

Anthropology and Archeology Teachers, Postsecondary 25-1061.00

Area, Ethnic, and Cultural Studies Teachers, Postsecondary 25-1062.00

Economics Teachers, Postsecondary 25-1063.00

Geography Teachers, Postsecondary 25-1064.00

Political Science Teachers, Postsecondary 25-1065.00

Psychology Teachers, Postsecondary 25-1066.00

Sociology Teachers, Postsecondary 25-1067.00

Health Specialties Teachers, Postsecondary 25-1071.00

Nursing Instructors and Teachers, Postsecondary 25-1072.00

Education Teachers, Postsecondary 25-1081.00

Library Science Teachers, Postsecondary 25-1082.00

Criminal Justice and Law Enforcement Teachers, Postsecondary 25-1111.00

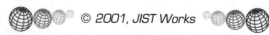

Insurance Adjusters, Examiners, and Investigators 13-1031.02
Insurance Appraisers, Auto Damage 13-1032.00
Cost Estimators 13-1051.00
Logisticians 13-1081.00
Management Analysts 13-1111.00
Appraisers and Assessors of Real Estate 13-2021.00
Assessors 13-2021.01
Appraisers, Real Estate 13-2021.02
Budget Analysts 13-2031.00
Credit Analysts 13-2041.00
Financial Analysts 13-2051.00
Insurance Underwriters 13-2053.00
Loan Counselors 13-2071.00
Loan Officers 13-2072.00
Market Research Analysts 19-3021.00

14 Medical and Health Services

14.01.01 Managerial Work in Medical and Health Services

Medical and Health Services Managers 11-9111.00
Coroners 13-1041.06

14.02.01 Medicine and Surgery

Pharmacists 29-1051.00
Anesthesiologists 29-1061.00
Family and General Practitioners 29-1062.00
Internists, General 29-1063.00
Obstetricians and Gynecologists 29-1064.00
Pediatricians, General 29-1065.00
Psychiatrists 29-1066.00
Surgeons 29-1067.00
Physician Assistants 29-1071.00
Registered Nurses 29-1111.00
Pharmacy Technicians 29-2052.00
Surgical Technologists 29-2055.00
Medical Assistants 31-9092.00
Pharmacy Aides 31-9095.00

14.03.01 Dentistry

Dentists, General 29-1021.00
Oral and Maxillofacial Surgeons 29-1022.00
Orthodontists 29-1023.00
Prosthodontists 29-1024.00
Dental Hygienists 29-2021.00
Dental Assistants 31-9091.00

14.04.01 Health Specialties

Chiropractors 29-1011.00
Optometrists 29-1041.00
Podiatrists 29-1081.00
Opticians, Dispensing 29-2081.00

14.05.01 Medical Technology

Medical and Clinical Laboratory Technologists 29-2011.00
Medical and Clinical Laboratory Technicians 29-2012.00
Cardiovascular Technologists and Technicians 29-2031.00
Diagnostic Medical Sonographers 29-2032.00
Nuclear Medicine Technologists 29-2033.00
Radiologic Technologists 29-2034.01
Radiologic Technicians 29-2034.02
Orthotists and Prosthetists 29-2091.00
Medical Equipment Preparers 31-9093.00

14.06.01 Medical Therapy

Audiologists 29-1121.00
Occupational Therapists 29-1122.00
Physical Therapists 29-1123.00
Radiation Therapists 29-1124.00
Recreational Therapists 29-1125.00
Respiratory Therapists 29-1126.00
Speech-Language Pathologists 29-1127.00
Respiratory Therapy Technicians 29-2054.00
Occupational Therapist Assistants 31-2011.00
Occupational Therapist Aides 31-2012.00
Physical Therapist Assistants 31-2021.00
Physical Therapist Aides 31-2022.00
Massage Therapists 31-9011.00

14.07.01 Patient Care and Assistance

Psychiatric Technicians 29-2053.00
Licensed Practical and Licensed Vocational Nurses 29-2061.00
Home Health Aides 31-1011.00
Nursing Aides, Orderlies, and Attendants 31-1012.00
Psychiatric Aides 31-1013.00

14.08.01 Health Protection and Promotion

Health Educators 21-1091.00
Dietitians and Nutritionists 29-1031.00
Dietetic Technicians 29-2051.00
Athletic Trainers 29-9091.00

Introduction

But First, a Few Words to People Who Do Not Read Introductions

We assume that most people will not read this entire introduction, so we worked hard to make the book easy to understand. Even so, we encourage you to skim the following material.

To avoid complexity, we decided to not address the introduction to technical users, such as labor market experts. Instead, it is written to someone using the book for career exploration, although we include some boring technical details. We use headings and bold type to help you skip information that doesn't interest you and more quickly identify information that does.

If you are a counselor or technical user, additional information on the GOE's background and validity—and tips on using the book as a counseling tool—are included in the appendix. So, without further ado, we present the introduction to this book and ask that you at least skim it for the information you need.

Overview

The GOE was originally developed by the U.S. Department of Labor to help people explore career and learning options based on their interests. It remains an important tool for students, career changers, job seekers, educators, counselors, and other career development professionals. The GOE has an extensive history that is rooted in research into how people can most effectively explore career options based on their interests. There is a lot of validity to this approach, and Part 1 is designed to help you explore career and education options based on your interests. Another major section, Part 2, provides descriptions for almost 1,000 jobs, covering well over 90 percent of the labor market. These features make the GOE a unique and valuable tool for exploring career, education, and other life options.

Exploring career and learning options based on interests makes sense, and it is something you have been doing most of your life. For example, when you were a child, you were probably asked, "What do you want to be when you grow up?" Children often respond to this question by mentioning careers of people who are easily recognized and understood, like a police officer, doctor, or teacher. Older children often change their responses to careers of heroes, such as astronaut, professional athlete, musician, or movie actor. These responses are based on what interests us at that time. As we mature, our career interests often change based on what we learn and as our personalities and interests develop.

Too often, however, people make career decisions based on interests, but without good information on the occupations or learning options that most closely match those interests. For example, a hotel management career would sound interesting to some people, but a decision to get a four-year college degree in that field (and there is such a degree) or to change careers to this field would best be made knowing that pay is often modest and that weekend and night work is the norm. Those details could make a big difference to you. You need to know as many facts as you can before making important decisions—and the GOE is one of the best places to start.

The GOE helps you quickly pinpoint jobs that match your interests by first asking you to choose from among 14 major Interest Areas. It then provides substantial information on groups of jobs within these 14 areas and cross-references almost 1,000 job descriptions.

While it sounds complicated, the GOE is very easy to use. The table of contents is the best place to start, because it offers a quick overview of the major sections as well as tables listing GOE Interest Areas, Work Groups, and specific job titles.

A Quick Review of the Acronyms Used in This Introduction

Government programs and vocational experts use a variety of systems to name, organize, and code occupations. Many of these systems can be cross-referenced so that information from one database can be used with another. For clarification, here are the systems we refer to most often in this introduction.

- **O*NET:** This is short for the Occupational Information Network, a database of information on occupations that was developed by the U.S. Department of Labor.
- **OES:** This refers to the Occupational Employment Statistics survey classification system.
- **SOC:** This refers to the Standard Occupational Classification, yet another system of organizing and coding jobs. The SOC provides a standard for naming and numbering all jobs that every other occupational system plans to use. The O*NET has already adopted this system.
- **DOT:** This refers to a book, the *Dictionary of Occupational Titles,* published by the U.S. Department of Labor. The DOT used a system to organize and code occupations that has been replaced by the newer O*NET system.
- **GOE:** This refers to a book titled the *Guide for Occupational Exploration,* originally published by the U.S. Department of Labor. The GOE presents a way of organizing jobs within groupings based on interests.

Quick Tips on Using the GOE for Career Exploration

The GOE is a unique and valuable book for career exploration because it provides the most often wanted information for all major jobs in one location. If you need help in deciding what kind of work you should choose or switch to, you can use the GOE to help you plan your career, identify jobs you qualify for, or consider jobs requiring additional training or education. Your task is to find not just any job, but one you can do well and that will be satisfying to you.

To find the right kind of job, you need two types of information:

1. **Information about yourself.** You need to know the kind of work you would like to do and whether you are able to do such work. If you can't do it now, can you learn it through an educational or training program?
2. **Information about occupations that sound interesting to you.** What does the worker do on such jobs? What knowledge and skills must the worker have? What training is required?

The GOE helps you locate and learn about occupations that relate to your interests and abilities. When you use it properly, you will be better prepared to plan your career or seek employment. You will learn about many jobs, including some you never knew existed.

The GOE clusters occupations into major Interest Areas that are further divided into Work Groups. Specific jobs are then listed within each Work Group. Rather than trying to explore the impossibly large world of job options, the GOE allows you to identify groups of similar jobs. It begins with broad areas of interest and then narrows down to job groupings that are most closely related to your interests, skills, aptitudes, education, training, and physical abilities. Following are some suggestions for how to use this book to explore career alternatives.

Step 1. Identify Your Interests

What kind of work would you most like to do? Did you know that all jobs have been organized into groups according to workers' interests? Some workers like to help others. Some would rather work with their hands or tools. Others prefer writing, selling, or clerical work. This new GOE edition is based on the original GOE's approach, which organizes all jobs within what are called Interest Areas. These groupings organize jobs into clusters based on the interests of workers. The original GOE had 12 Interest Areas, while this revision uses 14. Each Interest Area has been given a name, a code number, and a brief description, and we will provide more details on them later in this introduction.

Step 2. Select One or More Work Groups to Explore

After you identify one or more major Interest Areas, your next task is to review Work Groups of jobs within the Interest Areas that appeal to you. To know what jobs to explore, you need to decide whether you would enjoy work activities required by the occupations within these groupings. The table of contents includes listings (Table A and Table B) of GOE Interest Areas, Work Groups, and related job titles. Take a few minutes to get familiar with how these lists work.

As you identify GOE Work Groups you would like to learn more about, note the numbers listed next to each. Simply look for the narrative descriptions for each Work Group in Part 1. All descriptions are in numerical order within each Interest Area.

Work Groups that require the most experience, education, or training are usually listed first. Within many Interest Areas are Work Groups and jobs that fit your interests and that you can do or can learn to do quickly. You will also likely find options that interest you but that may require knowledge and skills that you do not have or would have difficulty acquiring. Do not exclude these options too quickly. Depending on your interest level, you may want to consider getting the education or training you need to enter these jobs.

Part 3 provides very helpful "Crosswalks" for identifying job groupings related to your values, leisure activities, preferred work settings, and other characteristics. These cross-references may help you identify career options that you may otherwise overlook, so consider using them to discover Work Groups to explore in more detail.

Step 3. Explore the Work Groups You Selected

Once you identify Work Groups that interest you, look up their descriptions in Part 1 and read them very carefully. As you read about a group, you may discover that it is not what you thought it would be and that you are not interested in it. Or you may find that the training or other requirements are more difficult than you wish to undertake. As you discover more, you can drop some groups from consideration and go on to others.

Step 4: Read the Descriptions for Jobs That Interest You

The information on Work Groups found in Part 1 includes tables with specific job titles. Once you have learned more about the Work Groups that most interest you, you can read the Part 2 information on specific jobs within the Work Group.

Step 5. Create a Plan of Action

Once you have identified job titles that interest you most, you need to decide what to do next. Perhaps you can obtain some of these jobs with your present qualifications, while other jobs will demand additional training, education, or experience. Your next step may be clear to you. If, however, you are still not sure about what you want to do, you can get career planning help in a variety of ways.

Check for career-planning assistance often available to students and graduates at many schools. Also, most areas have government-funded programs that provide similar services, as do local colleges and universities. Look in the yellow pages under Vocational or Career Counseling or ask your librarian for help in locating these resources.

Because the descriptions in this book are brief, you may want additional information on one or more jobs before you make a decision on what to do. Many good books and Internet resources can help you in your career planning. A resource list appears at the end of this introduction.

A Brief History of the Guide for Occupational Exploration

The idea of exploring career options based on interests is surely thousands of years old. For example: "I'd rather work on making really good arrows than killing mastodons." Interests, you see, don't exist in isolation from those things we are good at—they are often one and the same.

So people have been making career decisions based on interests for a long, long time. But the GOE was the result of the first concerted "scientific" effort to create a systematic process using interests for exploring career, learning, and life options. The research for the GOE began in the 1950s and 1960s when researchers worked on coming up with a simple, intuitive way for people to explore careers. They did this under the direction of the U.S. Department of Labor, in response to many requests from career counselors and others who wanted a more user-friendly system than the complex approach used in the *Dictionary of Occupational Titles* (DOT).

In the mid-1970s, these researchers organized all 12,741 job titles in the DOT into 12 broad areas of interests. These original 12 "Interest Areas" were Artistic; Scientific; Plants and Animals; Protective; Mechanical; Industrial; Business Detail; Selling; Accommodating; Humanitarian; Leading-Influencing; and Physical Performing. Each Interest Area was further divided into increasingly specific Work Groups and Subgroups of related jobs. This arrangement made a complex system easy to understand and use.

The new arrangement was called the Guide for Occupational Exploration, and a book with this name was first published in 1979. That first edition presented substantial information on the 12 GOE Interest Areas and their groupings of related jobs, as well as listings of related jobs within each grouping. The original GOE was well received, widely used, and became a standard career reference that was cross-referenced in most major career information systems. The major limitation of this 1979 edition was that you had to use the separate DOT to obtain descriptions for listed jobs—an awkward process.

Drs. Thomas Harrington and Arthur O'Shea released the first major revision of the GOE in 1984. This included the original GOE Interest Areas but added important content developed from research by the Labor Department. One of its important additions was the "Crosswalks" that allowed you to look up jobs related to work values, leisure activities, home activities, school subjects, work settings, and military occupational specialties.

In 1991, a book titled *The Enhanced Guide for Occupational Exploration* by Marilyn Maze and J. Michael Farr was released. Its inclusion of descriptions of the 2,500 largest occupations made the GOE much easier to use. Another book followed in 1993 by J. Michael Farr that included many of the improvements from the Harrington and O'Shea edition. Titled *The Complete Guide for Occupational Exploration,* it added newer occupations from a revised DOT and other improvements. *The Enhanced Guide for Occupational Exploration* was revised in 1995 (by Marilyn Maze and Donald Mayall) and included newer data on occupations and other changes. JIST published all of these editions.

Since the first GOE edition was released in 1979, it has been an important career information source. Many career information systems use its structure to cross-reference occupational information. The basic structure of Interest Areas and increasingly specific Work Groups and Subgroups had not changed in over 20 years, and a change was clearly needed. For those who are interested, an appendix provides additional information on the original research supporting the GOE and its development.

This Edition Presents a Completely Revised Classification System

The GOE classification structure, developed in the mid-1970s, clearly needed revision to reflect the many changes in our economy. The concept of Interest Areas and more specific job groupings within them remained valid, but the original system did not handle the many changes made in our transition from an industrial to an information- and service-based economy.

For example, the original GOE structure put computer programmers in the Subgroup "Data Processing Design," which belonged in the "Mathematics and Statistics" Work Group, which is assigned to the "Leading-Influencing" Interest Area. Not only is the word "computer" absent at any group level, but "Leading-Influencing" seems a poor way of describing what most computer programmers do. The many computer-related jobs that have evolved since the 1970s simply had no logical place within the original GOE's structure. Another example is the engineering occupations, which fit poorly in the "Mechanical" Interest Area in the old GOE, since some engineering fields (for example, electrical engineering) have little or no job tasks that can be considered mechanical.

It was clear to us that the original GOE Interest Areas and related job groupings needed to be updated, but the Department of Labor did not have funding allocated for this project.

So JIST Publishing decided to undertake this project. It was a big task, but we created an entirely new GOE classification system. While we made many changes, we also kept or modified many elements from the old GOE that still made sense. For example, the old "Leading-Influencing" field has been redefined and renamed "General Management and Support," and occupations have been redistributed to where they most make sense.

We also eliminated the old GOE's "Subgroups" in the new structure and now use only the simpler structure of just Work Groups. This was made possible by the use of the new O*NET database, which uses far fewer job titles than the old DOT it replaced. This change made the use of Subgroups within Work Groups unnecessary. (O*NET, as mentioned earlier, stands for the Department of Labor's Occupational Information Network.)

The following table compares the 12 old GOE Interest Areas with the 14 new ones used in this edition. The new arrangement of Work Groups within the Interest Areas are best seen in Table A in the table of contents.

The 12 Old Compared to the 14 New GOE Interest Areas

Original GOE Interest Structure	New GOE Interest Structure
01 Artistic	01 Arts, Entertainment, and Media
02 Scientific	02 Science, Math, and Engineering
03 Plants and Animals	03 Plants and Animals
04 Protective	04 Law, Law Enforcement, and Public Safety
05 Mechanical	05 Mechanics, Installers, and Repairers
	06 Construction, Mining, and Drilling
	07 Transportation
06 Industrial	08 Industrial Production
07 Business Detail	09 Business Detail
08 Selling	10 Sales and Marketing
09 Accommodating	11 Recreation, Travel, and Other Personal Services
10 Humanitarian	12 Education and Social Service
11 Leading-Influencing	13 General Management and Support
12 Physical Performing	14 Medical and Health Services

This Edition Also Introduces the New O*NET Job Descriptions

The original GOE used job titles from the Department of Labor's DOT. The DOT used a system to classify jobs that had been developed in the 1930s and that was updated over the years. But the DOT had numerous flaws that could not be easily corrected, so the Department of Labor abandoned the system, making the 1991 edition of the DOT its final one. A new system to replace the DOT was developed by the U.S. Department of Labor. Called the O*NET, it is the new standard used for collecting and organizing job information. The new O*NET classification system is not only much more compact—using under 1,000 job titles instead of over 12,000 in the old DOT—but it also provides a much better reflection of the American economy than the occupation mix in the DOT.

Many of the changes we made in the new GOE classification system were done to support the new O*NET job groupings and to reflect our current labor market. The older DOT classification was based on the industry where an occupation belonged. For example, the DOT includes large numbers of similar jobs whose only difference is the industry where the job occurs. For example: MODEL MAKER (pottery & porcelain); MODEL MAKER (brick & tile); MODEL MAKER (aircraft manufacturing); MODEL MAKER (automobile manufacturing); and many other model makers in other industries.

The O*NET classification, by contrast, includes only three kinds of model makers: Model Makers, Metal and Plastic; Model Makers, Wood; and Model and Mold Makers, Jewelry. This simplified arrangement demanded changes to the Work Group and Subgroup structure of the original GOE, which included large numbers of Subgroups for the thousands of DOT occupations. The revised GOE has eliminated Subgroups with a simpler system consisting only of Work Groups.

The older DOT and GOE also emphasized industrial occupations, jobs that were much more important when those systems were first developed. For example, the "Industrial" Interest Area in the original GOE included 79 Subgroups of related jobs, with 40 of these groupings in the "Elemental Work: Industrial" group alone, including "Machine Work, Metal and Plastics"; "Machine Work, Wood"; "Machine Work, Paper"; "Machine Work, Fabric and Leather"; and "Machine Work, Textiles." The O*NET classification makes such level of detail unnecessary, so we reduced the number of groupings within the "Industrial Production" Work Group from 79 to a paltry 15.

The new O*NET provided another major advantage over the DOT in that the O*NET offers data on far fewer jobs. This allowed us to include descriptions for all O*NET jobs in this new edition—an enormous advantage over the original GOE, which had listings but no descriptions of 12,741 DOT job titles.

Tips to Understand and Use the Major Parts of This Book

The "Quick Summary of Major Sections" in the table of contents provides brief descriptions for the book's main sections:

- **Part 1.** GOE Interest Areas and Work Groups: Essential Information for Exploring Career Options
- **Part 2.** The Job Descriptions
- **Part 3.** Crosswalks to Careers by Work Values, Leisure Activities, Home Activities, School Subjects, Work Settings, Skills, Abilities, and Knowledges
- **Appendix.** Information for Vocational Counselors and Other Professionals

Following are more detailed descriptions of each section.

Part 1. GOE Interest Areas and Work Groups

This section is more interesting than it sounds. Table A following the "Quick Summary of Major Sections" at the beginning of this book will show you how the GOE organizes jobs into 14 broad Interest Areas and more specific Work Groups of related jobs. You can use Table A to identify Interest Areas and Work Groups that appeal to you, and then turn to the appropriate pages in Part 1 to learn more about them. There you will identify specific jobs within the groupings. If you choose, you can then read the descriptions for these jobs in Part 2. Think of this process as a funnel that narrows your job choices until you are left with those that best match your interests. This process is illustrated below.

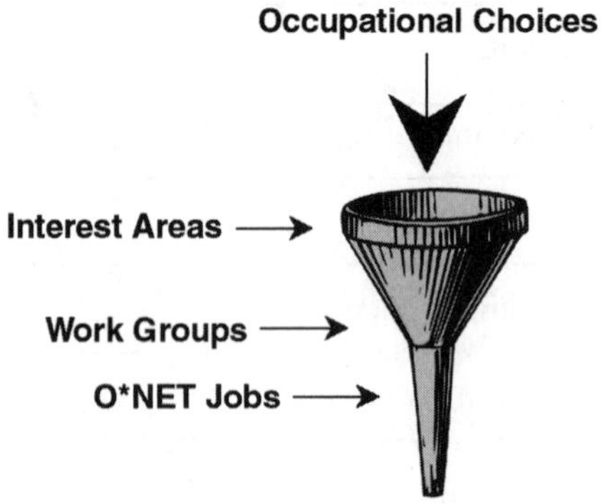

There is a lot of helpful information in Part 1, and it is easier to use than to describe, so please bear with us in this explanation.

Part 1 gives useful details for exploring career options based on interests. It presents information on the GOE's 14 Interest Areas and their related Work Groups so that you know what sorts of jobs they include, the skills required, and the typical education and training needed. It also provides you with information related to school courses, leisure activities, work environments, and other points that may support exploring jobs in certain groups more carefully.

The 14 GOE Interest Areas

Let's begin with the basis for the GOE, the 14 Interest Areas. Remember that the GOE organizes all jobs within one of these Interest Areas:

01 Arts, Entertainment, and Media

02 Science, Math, and Engineering

03 Plants and Animals

04 Law, Law Enforcement, and Public Safety

05 Mechanics, Installers, and Repairers

06 Construction, Mining, and Drilling

07 Transportation

08 Industrial Production

09 Business Detail

10 Sales and Marketing

11 Recreation, Travel, and Other Personal Services

12 Education and Social Service

13 General Management and Support

14 Medical and Health Services

Brief descriptions for each Interest Area follow. As you read them, try to identify the ones that appeal to you most. These are the ones you should explore in more detail in Part 1.

01 Arts, Entertainment, and Media. An interest in creatively expressing feelings or ideas, in communicating news or information, or in performing. You can satisfy this interest in several creative, verbal, or performing activities. For example, if you enjoy literature, perhaps writing or editing would appeal to you. Do you prefer to work in the performing arts? If so, you could direct or perform in drama, music, or dance. If you especially enjoy the visual arts, you could become a critic in painting, sculpture, or ceramics. You may want to use your hands to create or decorate products. You may prefer to model clothes or develop sets for entertainment. Or you may want to participate in sports professionally, as an athlete or coach.

02 Science, Math, and Engineering. An interest in discovering, collecting, and analyzing information about the natural world; in applying scientific research findings to problems in medicine, the life sciences, and the natural sciences; in imagining and manipulating quantitative data; and in applying technology to manufacturing, transportation, mining, and other economic activities. You can satisfy this interest by working with the knowledge and processes of the sciences. You may enjoy researching and developing new knowledge in mathematics, or perhaps solving problems in the physical or life sciences would appeal to you. You may wish to study engineering and help create new machines, processes, and structures. If you want to work with scientific equipment and procedures, you could seek a job in a research or testing laboratory.

03 Plants and Animals. An interest in working with plants and animals, usually outdoors. You can satisfy this interest by working in farming, forestry, fishing, and related fields. You may like doing physical work outdoors, such as on a farm. You may enjoy animals; perhaps training or taking care of animals would appeal to you. If you have management ability, you could own, operate, or manage a farm or related business.

04 Law, Law Enforcement, and Public Safety. An interest in upholding people's rights, or in protecting people and property by using authority, inspecting, or monitoring. You can satisfy this interest by working in law, law enforcement, fire fighting, and related fields. For example, if you enjoy mental challenge and intrigue, you could investigate crimes or fires for a living. If you enjoy working with verbal skills, you may want to defend citizens in court or research deeds, wills, and other legal documents. You may prefer to fight fires and respond to other emergencies. Or, if you want more routine work, perhaps a job in guarding or patrolling would appeal to you; if you have management ability, you could seek a leadership position in law enforcement and the protective services. Many positions in the various military branches are also related to this interest and give you the chance to learn technical and leadership skills while serving your country.

05 Mechanics, Installers, and Repairers. An interest in applying mechanical and electrical/electronic principles to practical situations by use of machines or hand tools. You can satisfy this interest working with a variety of tools, technologies, materials, and settings. If you enjoy making machines run efficiently or fixing them when they break down, you could seek a job installing or repairing such devices as copiers, aircraft engines, automobiles, or watches. You may instead prefer to deal directly with certain materials, and find work cutting and shaping metal or wood. Or if electricity and electronics interest you, you could install cables, troubleshoot telephone networks, or repair videocassette recorders. If you prefer routine or physical work in settings other than factories, perhaps work repairing tires or batteries would appeal to you.

06 Construction, Mining, and Drilling. An interest in assembling components of buildings and other structures, or in using mechanical devices to drill or excavate. If construction interests you, you can find fulfillment in the many building projects that are being undertaken at all times. If you like to organize and plan, you can find careers in management. On the other hand, you can play a more direct role in putting up and finishing buildings by doing jobs such as plumbing, carpentry, masonry, painting, or roofing. You may like working at a mine or oilfield, operating the powerful drilling or digging equipment. There are also several jobs that let you put your hands to the task.

07 Transportation. An interest in operations that move people or materials. You can satisfy this interest by managing a transportation service, by helping vehicles keep on their assigned schedules and routes, or by driving or piloting a vehicle. If you enjoy taking responsibility, perhaps managing a rail line would appeal to you. If you work well with details and can take pressure on the job, you might consider being an air traffic controller. Or would you rather get out on the highway, on the water, or up in the air? If so, then you could drive a truck from state to state, sail down the Mississippi on a barge, or fly a crop duster over a cornfield. If you prefer to stay closer to home, you could drive a delivery van, taxi, or school bus. You can use your physical strength to load freight and arrange it so it gets to its destination in one piece.

08 Industrial Production. An interest in repetitive, concrete, organized activities most often done in a factory setting. You can satisfy this interest by working in one of many industries that mass-produce goods, or for a utility that distributes electric power, gas, and so on. You may enjoy manual work, using your hands or hand tools. Perhaps you prefer to operate machines. You may like to inspect, sort, count, or weigh products. Using your training and experience to set up machines or supervise other workers may appeal to you.

09 Business Detail. An interest in organized, clearly defined activities requiring accuracy and attention to details, primarily in an office setting. You can satisfy this interest in a variety of jobs in which you attend to the details of a business operation. You may enjoy using your math skills; if so, perhaps a job in billing, computing, or financial record-keeping would satisfy you. If you prefer to deal with people, you may want a job in which you meet the public, talk on the telephone, or supervise other workers. You may like to do word processing on a computer, turn out copies on a duplicating machine, or work out sums on a calculator. Perhaps a job in filing or recording would satisfy you. Or you may wish to use your training and experience to manage an office.

10 Sales and Marketing. An interest in bringing others to a particular point of view by personal persuasion, using sales and promotional techniques. You can satisfy this interest in a variety of sales and marketing jobs. If you like using technical knowledge of science or agriculture, you may enjoy selling technical products or services. Or perhaps you are more interested in selling business-related services such as insurance coverage, advertising space, or investment opportunities. Real estate offers several kinds of sales jobs. Perhaps you'd rather work with something you can pick up and show to people. You may work in stores, sales offices, or customers' homes.

11 Recreation, Travel, and Other Personal Services. An interest in catering to the personal wishes and needs of others, so that they may enjoy cleanliness, good food and drink, comfortable lodging away from home, and enjoyable recreation. You can satisfy this interest by providing services for the convenience, feeding, and pampering of others in hotels, restaurants, airplanes, and so on. If you enjoy improving the appearance of others, perhaps working in the hair and beauty care field would satisfy you. You may wish to provide personal services such as taking care of small children, tailoring garments, or ushering. Or you may use your knowledge of the field to manage workers who are providing these services.

12 Education and Social Service. An interest in teaching people or improving their social or spiritual wellbeing. You can satisfy this interest by teaching students, who may be preschoolers, retirees, or any age between. Or if you are interested in helping people sort out their complicated lives, you may find fulfillment as a counselor, social worker, or religious worker. Working in a museum or library may give you opportunities to expand people's understanding of the world. If you also have an interest in business, you may find satisfaction in managerial work in this field.

13 General Management and Support. An interest in making an organization run smoothly. You can satisfy this interest by working in a position of leadership, or by specializing in a function that contributes to the overall effort. The organization may be a profit-making business, a nonprofit, or a government agency. If you especially enjoy working with people, you may find fulfillment from working in human resources. An interest in numbers may cause you to consider accounting, finance, budgeting, or purchasing. Or perhaps you would enjoy managing the organization's physical resources (for example, land, buildings, equipment, and utilities).

14 Medical and Health Services. An interest in helping people be healthy. You can satisfy this interest by working in a health-care team as a doctor, therapist, or nurse. You might specialize in one of the many different parts of the body or types of care, or you might be a generalist who deals with the whole patient. If you like technology, you might find satisfaction working with X rays, one of the electronic means of diagnosis, or clinical laboratory testing. You might work with healthy people, helping them stay in condition through exercise and eating right. If you like to organize, analyze, and plan, a managerial role might be right for you.

Interest Areas Are Divided into More Specific Work Groups

The 14 GOE Interest Areas are divided into more specific Work Groups of related jobs. This process allows you to more clearly see the types of more specific interests within each GOE Interest Area. For example, the "Arts, Entertainment, and Media" Interest Area has the following Work Groups.

01.01 Managerial Work in Arts, Entertainment, and Media

01.02 Writing and Editing

01.03 News, Broadcasting, and Public Relations

01.04 Visual Arts—01.04.01 Visual Arts: Studio Art; 01.04.02 Visual Arts: Design

01.05 Performing Arts—01.05.01 Performing Arts, Drama: Directing, Performing, Narrating, and Announcing; 01.05.02 Performing Arts, Music: Directing, Composing and Arranging, and Performing; 01.05.03 Performing Arts, Dance: Performing and Choreography

01.06 Craft Arts

01.07 Graphic Arts

01.08 Media Technology

01.09 Modeling and Personal Appearance

01.10 Sports: Coaching, Instructing, Officiating, and Performing

In reviewing the list above, note that each Work Group has a four-digit identification number. The first two digits designate the GOE Interest Area (which is "01" for the Arts, Entertainment, and Media Interest Area). The third and fourth digits provide a unique number for each Work Group within that Interest Area. For example, 01.05 is the Work Group titled Performing Arts.

When a Work Group has distinctly different types of jobs, the fifth and sixth digits are used to subdivide a Work Group into more specific groupings. For example, Performing Arts (01.05) is divided into three more specific groupings of 01.05.01 (Performing Arts, Drama: Directing, Performing, Narrating, and Announcing); 01.05.02 (Performing Arts, Music: Directing, Composing and Arranging, and Performing); and 01.05.03 (Performing Arts, Dance: Performing and Choreography). A complete list of the GOE Work Groups is included in Table A of the table of contents.

Helpful Career Planning Information Is Provided for Each Work Group

Part 1 gives a substantial amount of information on each GOE Work Group. This material is carefully selected to help you determine if you are likely to be interested in or good at the jobs within that Work Group. The information is presented in an easy-to-use format that includes details to help you understand and evaluate the career opportunities within that group. Following are the details provided for each Work Group.

GOE number and Work Group name. As described previously, each Work Group is assigned a four-digit number. This number is listed before the name of the Work Group. For example, under the Arts, Entertainment, and Media Interest Area is the Work Group "01.01 Managerial Work in Arts, Entertainment, and Media." (We will continue to use examples from this Work Group throughout this overview.)

Brief definition. This is a short statement that defines the Work Group, and it appears directly following the GOE Work Group number and name. The definition also provides examples of the types of jobs in the group and where they might occur. Here is the Brief Definition statement for 01.01 Managerial Work in Arts, Entertainment, and Media:

Workers in this group manage people who work in the field of arts, entertainment, and media. They oversee performers and performances in the arts and sports. They work for radio, television, and motion picture production companies, and for artists and athletes.

What kind of work would you do? This is a list of typical work activities people do in jobs related to the Work Group. Some of the tasks might be similar to things that you have done in school, at another job, at home, in leisure activities, or as a volunteer. Take into consideration how attractive these activities are when evaluating your interest in this Work Group. Here are just three of the entries for our sample Work Group:

Your work activities would depend on your job. For example, you might

- Evaluate length, content, and suitability of programs for broadcast.

- Assign and direct staff members to develop design concepts into art layouts
- Compose and edit a script, or outline a story for a screenwriter to write the script.

What things about you point to this kind of work? This portion of the Work Group description deals with personal preferences. Information is provided in response to five questions that are helpful to consider in exploring career and life options. Each of these questions are presented below, along with brief explanations and examples.

Is it important for you to...? This question is followed by items that deal with a person's temperament or style of behavior. Sometimes these are referred to as work values —meaning the content of work that is most important to you. If you feel that most items listed are important to you, then this Work Group probably contains occupations that would be a good fit for you. For example:

Is it important to you to

- Plan your work with little supervision?
- Get a feeling of accomplishment?
- Make use of your individual abilities?

Have you enjoyed any of the following as a hobby or leisure-time activity? A list of hobbies, leisure activities, and extracurricular activities follows this question. Pastimes that you engage in as a hobby or leisure activity are an important measure of the appeal jobs in the Work Group might have for you. For example:

- Developing publicity fliers for a school or community event
- Drawing posters for an organization or political campaign
- Planning and arranging programs for school or community organizations

Have you liked and done well in any of the following school subjects? A list of school subjects that are related to this work follows this question. If you like these school subjects, then you probably would do well in studying the knowledges and skills needed for entry into the jobs found in the Work Group. Some school subjects related to our example include the following:

Management • Accounting • Editing • Theater Arts • Business Law • Creative Writing

Are you able to...? This question is followed by a list of basic abilities. Abilities are mental, social, and physical traits used to accomplish tasks. Typically, abilities don't change over a long period of time. The more your abilities match those on the list, the more likely you are to do well in the related jobs. Some abilities listed for our example include the following:

- Listen to and understand information and ideas presented through spoken words and sentences?
- Speak clearly so that it is understandable to a listener?
- Read and understand information and ideas presented in writing?

Would you work in places such as...? A list of workplaces follows this question. The place where people work is important in how well they like the job. If you are not sure what some of the workplaces are like, you might want to visit them. Here are a few of the entries for our example:

Motion picture and recording studios? • Business offices? • Theaters? • Sports stadiums? • Artists' studios and craft workshops?

What skills and knowledges do you need for this kind of work? This part of the Work Group's description has two items, skills and knowledges, which are covered separately. A brief explanation and examples follow.

For most of these jobs, you need these skills. Skills are what you need to perform a task, and we all have thousands of them. Some seem so simple that we take them for granted. For example, riding a bicycle is a skill, but it is so complicated that no one has been able to develop a robot that can perform this task. Each job has skills that are important to perform the work effectively. The skills you find in this section are ones important to the jobs in the Work Group. You should consider whether you have these skills or could acquire them to decide if the related jobs are a good match. Here are some skills listed for our example:

- Coordination—adjusting actions in relation to others' actions
- Management of Personnel Resources—motivating, developing, and directing people as they work, identifying the best people for the job
- Speaking—talking to others to effectively convey information

These knowledges are important in most of these jobs. Knowledge about a job comes through education, experience, or training. The entries here often include topics that are presented as areas of learning, such as a high school course, a training program, or a college course or major. Some entries for our example include the following:

- Administration and Management—principles and processes involved in business and organizational planning, coordination, and execution
- Communications—the science and art of delivering information

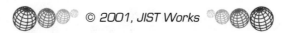

What else should you consider about this kind of work? This entry identifies other issues that are important to

consider when choosing a career. This includes typical ways to enter the occupation, opportunities for promotions, competition for job openings, working conditions, and advantages or disadvantages to the occupation. Here is a partial entry for our example:

Those who manage artists and performers feel some of the same competitive pressure as the artists and performers themselves and must have creativity; and the knowledge of what makes for artists and athletic success.

Nevertheless, managers need to think just as much (or more) in terms of business success. As the media business is becoming more concentrated into large companies, opportunities to artistic risks may be decreasing. The trend also tends to concentrate media jobs in larger cities.

How can you prepare for jobs of this kind? This entry provides information on the type of training, education, or experience that is typically needed for entry into jobs within the Work Group. Since there are often many jobs within each Work Group, the information is general but helpful. Here is what it says for the example Work Group we have been using:

Occupations in this group usually require education and/or training ranging from two to as much as ten years.

Generally it helps to have some mastery of the skill of the workers you will manage. At the very least you need to know what makes the difference between good work and bad work.

Specific Jobs and Their Required Training Are Listed Under Each Work Group

The last bit of information provided for each Work Group in Part 1's description is an important one. The information is provided in the "Specialized Training" table at the end of the description. This table lists the specific jobs that fall within each Work Group (broken down further into six digits), along with the training or education that job typically requires and where you can obtain it. For example, under "01.04.02 Visual Arts: Design" are listed these job titles:

Multi-media Artists and Animators

Commercial and Industrial Designers

Fashion Designers

Floral Designers

Graphic Designers

Interior Designers

Merchandise Displayers and Window Trimmers

Set Designers

Exhibit Designers

The good news is that each and every job listed under the Work Groups have descriptions you can read in Part 2. Here is more detail on the information in the Specialized Training tables:

- In front of each job title is that job's O*NET number. This number allows you to cross-reference other sources of information that use the O*NET classification system, which was developed by the U.S. Department of Labor.
- After the job title comes information on the education or training programs used to enter the occupation. This will include work experience as well as courses, classes, or majors typically required.
- This is followed with information on where the education or training for the job can be found. The options might include trade/technical school, on-the-job training, experience in a related job, military experience, two-year colleges (often referred to as community colleges and junior colleges), four-year colleges, and graduate schools.

We've provided a sample of a Specialized Training table to show you its format.

SPECIALIZED TRAINING

JOBS	EDUCATION/TRAINING	WHERE OBTAINED
01.04.01 Visual Arts: Studio Art		
All in Visual Arts: Studio Art	Experience	Related jobs within the same industry
27-1013.01 Painters and Illustrators	Graphic Design, Commercial Art, and Illustration; Drama/Theater Arts, General; Technical Theater/Theater Design and Stagecraft; Art, General; Drawing; Painting; Printmaking; Medical Illustrating; Fine/Studio Arts	Two-year college, four-year college, art school, military (Army, Navy, Air Force, Marine Corps)

Part 2. The Job Descriptions

Part 2 provides job descriptions for all jobs listed in the Part 1 tables. Table B in the table of contents lists these jobs within GOE Work Groups. There are about 1,000 jobs described in Part 2, including all that are listed in the current O*NET database maintained by the U.S. Department of Labor. The job descriptions are presented in Part 2, in numerical order within GOE Interest Areas and Work Groups.

How the Job Descriptions Are Derived from the Data

Technical and other users of this book will want to know the process we used to get to the information we include in the job descriptions, so we've provided a brief explanation here. The O*NET is a database that offers an enormous amount of data on hundreds of measures for each job. We set out to provide descriptions that were both brief and useful. To do this we had to be flexible in the criteria we used. For example, numeric measures are used for many criteria, such as Occupational Values, Abilities, and Skills Required. Since it is impractical and boring to give you numerical values for such measures, we used some fancy database work to include more useful information.

Following is a brief review of where the information in the descriptions comes from and the criteria we used to include or exclude information. If you want the specific numerical ratings on each measure for a specific job, you can find them in the O*NET database on the Internet at www.onetcenter.org.

The **O*NET numbers, titles, and job descriptions** are derived directly from the newest O*NET database. Earlier versions of the O*NET used different titles and numbers.

The **Education** statement is based on information we obtained from the U.S. Bureau of Labor Statistics. We did this by using their Industry-Occupation Employment Matrix and crosswalking from it to the O*NET occupations via an OES (Occupational Employment Statistics) code provided in the matrix. We did this first to the original O*NET and then to the new O*NET version.

The **Occupational Type** is based on the value for the field called "First Interest High-Point" in the Interest table from O*NET 3.0. This is the highest rated of the six Holland personality types. We'll provide more information on the Holland system later in this introduction.

Job Zone is based on the Job Zone ratings of equivalent occupations in the older O*NET version released in 1998. This crosswalking was necessary because–through an oversight–the newer O*NET 3.0 database lacks these ratings, although it does include definitions of what the Job Zone ratings mean. More information on Job Zone ratings appears later in the introduction.

Average Salary is derived from the OES wage database of the Bureau of Labor Statistics. The most recent OES database available provided 1998 earnings. We accomplished this by starting with O*NET occupations, which we then crosswalked to SOC (Standard Occupational Classification) occupations, which in turn were crosswalked to OES occupations. This method created many instances where an O*NET occupation crosswalked to several OES occupations, and in some cases it was possible to create a better one-to-one match. For example, O*NET occupation number 49-9031.02, Gas Appliance Repairers, crosswalked to the SOC occupation 49-9031 Home Appliance Repairers, which in turn crosswalked to the two OES occupations: 85711 Electric home appliance & power tool repairers and 85944 Gas appliance repairers. In this case, it made sense to use the wage figure for only the latter OES occupation. In other cases, where a one-to-many match was appropriate, multiple OES wages were combined by means of weighted sums. (For example, Occupation #1's salary was multiplied by Occupation #1's employment; Occupation #2's salary was multiplied by Occupation #2's employment; the two products were added together; and then the sum was divided by the total employment for both occupations.)

Projected Growth is derived from the Industry-Occupation Employment Matrix, which is crosswalked from its OES codes to O*NET version 98 and, in turn, to O*NET 3.0.

Occupational Values were determined by rank-ordering the ratings given for values, so that for each occupation the values were listed from highest rated to lowest rated. Then all values not rated more than 3 (midpoint on the 1 to 5 scale) were discarded. If an occupation had no value rated more than 3, the one highest rated value was used.

Skills Required were determined by a similar approach, except that the cutoff score was 3.5, because the rating scale is 0 to 7. Each occupation in the database is rated on both level and importance of the skill, but the two ratings are so highly correlated that either rating could have been used. In this case, the rating for importance was used. The approach for Skills Required was also used for **Abilities** and for the **Interacting with Others** tasks. The latter consisted of those generalized work tasks listed in the O*NET 3.0 table called Work Activity with an identity code beginning with "4.A.4."

The approach for Skills Required was also used for **Physical Work Conditions**, except the cutoff score was set at 2. Even though this is far below the midpoint of the 0-7 rating scale, this level produces a reasonable distribution of characteristics for occupations, ranging from a minimum of 1 to a maximum of 7. The features used were those provided in an O*NET database table called Work Context with an identity code beginning with "4.C.2,"and the ratings for frequency were used.

The job descriptions are brief but packed with useful information. We selected information that we think you will find most helpful. Note that if we included all information in the O*NET database, it would require about 20 pages for each job. The O*NET database includes data on hundreds of measures that would probably have little interest to you. It was impossible to print a book of over 20,000 pages, and most people would not want all that information. Here is a sample job description from Part 2.

A Sample Job Description

This description is listed under

- GOE Interest Area: 01 Arts, Entertainment, and Media
- Work Group 01.01.01: Managerial Work in Arts, Entertainment, and Media

The elements of this job description are pointed out by name for illustration purposes. Each element is explained in detail in the next section.

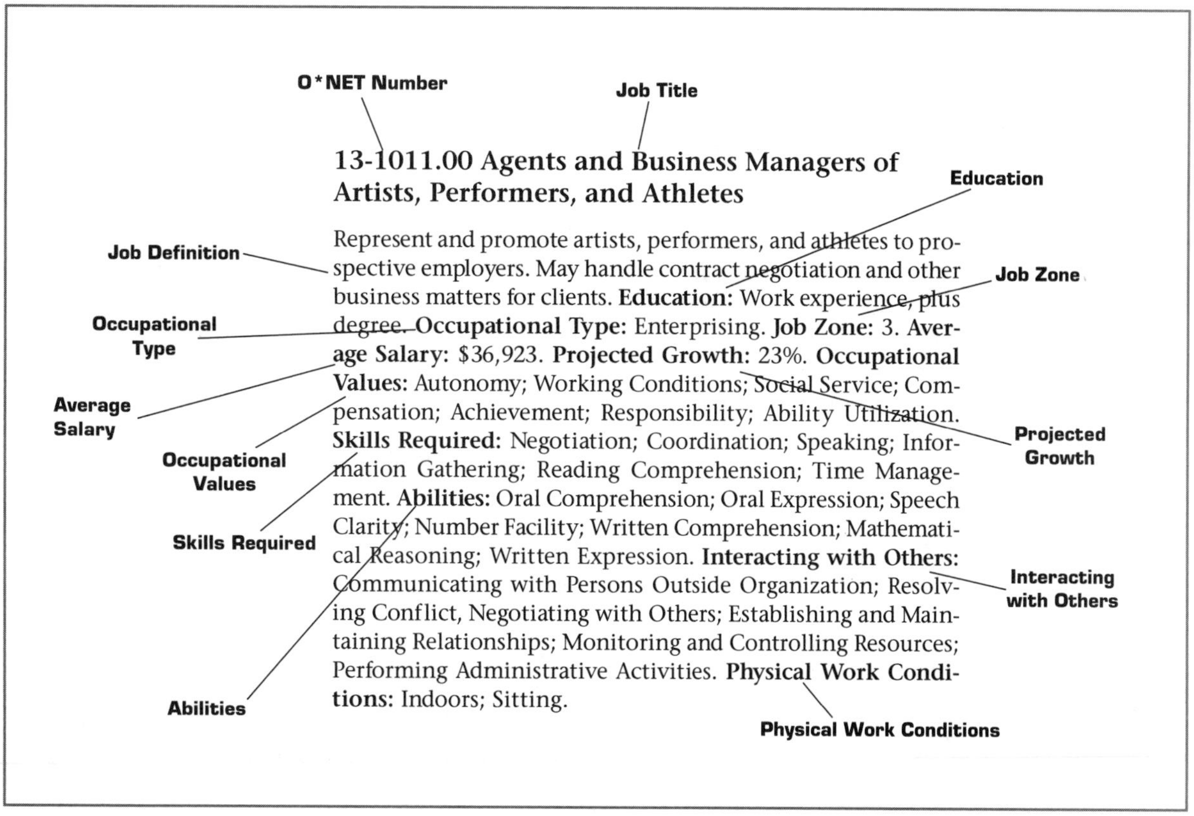

What Each Job Description Includes

We wanted to include lots of useful information in each job description yet keep it short and easy-to-understand. To do this, we had to make some compromises such as providing codes for the "Job Zone" information. The descriptions are pretty easy to understand, with the exception of Job Zone information. Here are descriptions of each component.

O*NET Number. Each job title includes a unique number assigned to it in the U.S. Department of Labor's O*NET database. This number can be used to look up a job in any system using the O*NET number. Note that we use the new O*NET number here, first released in 2000, and not the O*NET number used in the earlier release.

Job Title. This is the official title given to the job by the Department of Labor. Some organizations may use a different job title, but the tasks performed by workers in the job are quite similar.

Job Definition. This is a short one- or two-sentence statement that describes the job.

> **Note**
>
> The O*NET database includes several occupations for which the Department of Labor has not collected a full set of data. For these occupations, the database provides only a job definition. After the definition you will see a note that says "No other data currently available."

Education. While this section of the O*NET description is titled "Education" for simplicity, it includes information on the education, training, or experience typically required for entry into the job. Please note, however, that some (or many) who work in the job may have higher or lower levels than indicated. Certification or licensing also may be required for some jobs, but accurate information on these requirements was not available from the O*NET database. There are 11 levels of education used to classify the education, training, and experience needs of each job:

- *Short-term O-J-T* (on-the-job training). It is possible to work in these occupations and achieve an average level of performance within a few days or weeks through on-the-job training.
- *Moderate-term O-J-T.* Occupations that require this type of training can be performed adequately after a 1- to 12-month period of combined on-the-job

and informal training. Typically, untrained workers observe experienced workers perform tasks and are gradually moved into progressively more difficult assignments.

- *Long-term O-J-T.* This type of training requires more than 12 months of on-the-job training or combined work experience and formal classroom instruction. This includes occupations that use formal apprenticeships for training workers that may take up to four years. It also includes intensive occupation-specific, employer-sponsored training like police academies. Furthermore, it includes occupations that require natural talent that must be developed over many years.
- *Work experience in a related occupation.* This type of job requires a worker to have experience in a related occupation. For example, police detectives are selected based on their experience as police patrol officers.
- *Postsecondary vocational training.* This requirement can vary from training that involves a few months but is usually less than one year. In a few instances there may be as many as four years of training.
- *Associate degree.* This degree usually requires two years of full-time academic work beyond high school.
- *Bachelor's degree.* This is a degree that requires approximately four-to-five years of full-time academic work beyond high school.
- *Work experience, plus degree.* Jobs in this category are often management-related and require some experience in a related nonmanagerial position.
- *Master's degree.* Completion of a master's degree usually requires one-to-two years of full-time study beyond the bachelor's degree.
- *Doctor's degree.* This degree normally requires two or more years of full-time academic work beyond the bachelor's degree.
- *First professional degree.* This type of degree normally requires a minimum of two years of education beyond the bachelor's degree and frequently requires three years.

Occupational Type. This provides a cross-reference to a system used in a variety of career assessment tests and information systems. Called "Holland" codes, the system organizes all occupations into six personality types: Artistic, Conventional, Enterprising, Investigative, Realistic, and Social. The Self-Directed Search (SDS), a career interest inventory published by Psychological Assessment Resources, Inc., uses this system to help people explore occupations. The SDS and other instruments, like the Strong Campbell Interest Inventory and Armed Services Vocational Battery, identify interest areas using the Holland model. Many counselors and educators use these instruments, so you may have taken one. If so, you might recall your type and can use that information in identifying jobs that match. It is also possible to use this information even though you haven't taken one of the assessments. Simply read the personality's definition and determine the one that most closely describes jobs that would interest you. Following are brief descriptions of the six Holland groupings.

The Six "Holland" Personality Types in the Occupational Type Entry

Artistic. These occupations frequently involve working with forms, designs, and patterns. They often require self-expression, and the work can be done without following a clear set of rules.

Conventional. These occupations frequently involve following set procedures and routines. These occupations can include working with data and details more than with ideas. Usually there is a clear line of authority to follow.

Enterprising. These occupations frequently involve starting up and carrying out projects. These occupations can involve leading people and making many decisions. Sometimes they require risk taking and often deal with business.

Investigative. These occupations frequently involve working with ideas and require an extensive amount of thinking. These occupations can involve searching for facts and figuring out problems mentally.

Realistic. These occupations frequently involve work activities that include practical, hands-on problems and solutions. They often deal with plants, animals, and real-world materials like wood, tools, and machinery. Many of the occupations require working outside and do not involve a lot of paperwork or working closely with others.

Social. These occupations frequently involve working with, communicating with, and teaching people. These occupations often involve helping or providing service to others.

GOE Interest Areas Related to Holland Categories

The GOE Interest Areas are easily cross-referenced to Holland categories. Here is a table that shows this relationship.

GOE Interest Area	Holland Occupational Category
01 Arts, Entertainment, and Media	Artistic
02 Science, Math, and Engineering	Investigative
03 Plants and Animals	Realistic
04 Law, Law Enforcement, and Public Safety	Realistic, Social

GOE Interest Area	Holland Occupational Category
05 Mechanics, Installers, and Repairers	Realistic
06 Construction, Mining, and Drilling	Realistic
07 Transportation	Realistic
08 Industrial Production	Realistic
09 Business Detail	Conventional
10 Sales and Marketing	Enterprising
11 Recreation, Travel, and Other Personal Services	Social, Conventional
12 Education and Social Service	Social
13 General Management and Support	Enterprising, Social
14 Medical and Health Services	Investigative, Social

Job Zone. The concept of "Job Zones" takes a bit of explaining. In the descriptions, we use number codes for this since providing text to describe each one would take too much space, as you will soon see. This is the only coded item in the job descriptions, so please forgive us.

Job Zone information is included in the O*NET database, and we decided it was useful enough to include in the job descriptions. Job Zones provide information that is related to and expands on the "Education" entry in the description. In general, the higher the Job Zone number, the more education, training, or experience is required. Jobs within each Job Zone are similar in terms of the following:

- The overall experience needed to do the job
- The general range of education needed to do the job
- On-the-job training needed to do the job

Job Zone information includes a measure that represents the months or years of education, training, and experience needed to become fully competent in performing the job. This measure is called the Standard Vocational Preparation or SVP. You will see the SVP measure used in the following.

Job Zone Definitions

Job Zone 1
Experience: Little or no preparation needed. No previous work-related skill, knowledge, or experience is needed for these occupations. For example, a person can become a general office clerk even if the person has never worked in an office before.

Education: These occupations may require a high school diploma or GED certificate. Some may require a formal training course to obtain a license.

Training: Employees in these occupations need anywhere from a few days to a few months of training. Usually, an experienced worker could show you how to do the job.

Examples: These occupations involve following instructions and helping others. Examples include bus drivers, forest and conservation workers, general office clerks, home health aides, and waiters/waitresses.

SVP Range: Below 4.0—less than six months.

Job Zone 2
Experience: Some preparation needed. Some previous work-related skill, knowledge, or experience may be helpful in these occupations but usually is not needed. For example, a drywall installer might benefit from experience installing drywall, but an inexperienced person could still learn to be an installer with little difficulty.

Education: These occupations usually require a high school diploma and may require some vocational training or job-related course work. In some cases, an associate or bachelor's degree could be needed.

Training: Employees in these occupations need anywhere from a few months to one year of working with experienced employees.

Examples: These occupations often involve using your knowledge and skills to help others. Examples include drywall installers, fire inspectors, flight attendants, pharmacy technicians, salespersons (retail), and tellers.

SVP Range: 4.00 to 5.99—six months to less than two years.

Job Zone 3
Experience: Medium preparation needed. Previous work-related skill, knowledge, or experience is required for these occupations. For example, an electrician must have completed three or four years of apprenticeship or several years of vocational training and often must have passed a licensing exam to perform the job.

Education: Most occupations in this zone require training in vocational schools, related on-the-job experience, or an associate degree. Some may require a bachelor's degree.

Training: Employees in these occupations usually need one or two years of training involving both on-the-job experience and informal training with experienced workers.

Examples: These occupations usually involve using communication and organizational skills to coordinate, supervise, manage, or train others to accomplish goals. Examples include dental assistants, electricians, fish and game wardens, legal secretaries, personnel recruiters, and recreation workers.

SVP Range: 6.0 to less than 7.0—more than one year and less than four years.

(continues)

(continued)

Job Zone 4
Experience: Considerable preparation needed. A minimum of two to four years of work-related skill, knowledge, or experience is needed for these occupations. For example, an accountant must complete four years of college and work for several years in accounting to be considered qualified.

Education: Most of these occupations require a four-year bachelor's degree, but some do not.

Training: Employees in these occupations usually need several years of work-related experience, on-the-job training, and/or vocational training.

Examples: Many of these occupations involve coordinating, supervising, managing, or training others. Examples include accountants, chefs and head cooks, computer programmers, historians, pharmacists, and police detectives.

SVP Range: 7.0 to less than 8.0—two years to less than ten years.

Job Zone 5
Experience: Extensive preparation needed. Extensive skill, knowledge, and experience are needed for these occupations. Many require more than five years of experience. For example, surgeons must complete four years of college and an additional five to seven years of specialized medical training to be able to do their job.

Education: A bachelor's degree is the minimum formal education required for these occupations. However, many also require graduate school. For example, they may require a master's degree, and some require a Ph.D., M.D., or J.D. law degree.

Training: Employees may need some on-the-job training, but most of these occupations assume that the person will already have the required skills, knowledge, work-related experience, and/or training.

Examples: These occupations often involve coordinating, training, supervising, or managing the activities of others to accomplish goals. Very advanced communication and organizational skills are required. Examples include athletic trainers, lawyers, managing editors, physicists, social psychologists, and surgeons.

SVP Range: 8.0 and above—four years to more than ten years.

Average Salary. The average salary is obtained from data collected by the Bureau of Labor Statistics. We used the most recently available data, which was based on information collected for 1998. While this may sound like old information, it takes a few years of analysis before it is released by the government, so this is as good as it gets. The salary is based on the "mean" for all workers in this occupation. This means that half earn more and half less. Keep in mind that new workers usually make much less than the mean when starting in an occupation. Wages also vary from one part of the United States to another. Workers in larger cities often make more than those in rural areas, and workers in larger organizations typically earn more than those in smaller ones.

Projected Growth. The projected growth rate is obtained from the Bureau of Labor Statistics and is estimated for the 1998 to 2008 time period. Again, due to delays in analysis and release, this is the most recent data available. The growth figure represents the percent of new jobs that are projected to be created during this 10-year period. This figure provides some indication of the demand for this occupation in the years to come. The average growth rate for all jobs during this time is projected to be about 14 percent.

Occupational Values. Occupational (or work) values are things that can be very important to you. While there are hundreds of work values, the O*NET database includes 21 occupational values organized into six major categories. While the O*NET provides numeric measures on each value, we only listed those with higher measures for each job. We think this results in a more useful description.

All 21 occupational values are described in the list that follows, arranged within groups of related values. One or more of these work values are likely to be important for you to include in the jobs you should consider. You might want to write down values that are of particular importance and look for jobs where these values exist.

The 21 Occupational Values Used in the Job Descriptions

Achievement. Occupations that satisfy these work values are results-oriented and allow employees to use their strongest abilities, giving them a feeling of accomplishment.

Ability Utilization. Workers on this job make use of their individual abilities.

Achievement. Workers on this job get a feeling of accomplishment.

Comfort. Occupations that satisfy these work values offer job security and good working conditions.

Activity. Workers on this job are busy all the time.

Independence. Workers on this job do their work alone.

Variety. Workers on this job have something different to do every day.

Compensation. Workers on this job are paid well in comparison with other workers.

Security. Workers on this job have steady employment.

Working Conditions. Workers on this job have good working conditions.

Status. Occupations that satisfy these work values offer advancement, potential for leadership, and are often considered prestigious.

Advancement. Workers on this job have opportunities for advancement.

Recognition. Workers on this job receive recognition for the work they do.

Authority. Workers on this job give directions and instructions to others.

Social Status. Workers on this job are looked up to by others in their company and their community.

Altruism. Occupations that satisfy these work values allow employees to provide service to others and work with coworkers in a friendly noncompetitive environment.

Coworkers. Workers on this job have coworkers who are easy to get along with.

Social Service. Workers on this job have work where they do things for other people.

Moral Values. Workers on this job are never pressured to do things that go against their sense of right and wrong.

Safety. Occupations that satisfy these work values offer supportive management that stands behind employees and provides a predictable and stable work environment.

Company Policies and Practices. Workers on this job are treated fairly by the company.

Supervision, Human Relations. Workers on this job have supervisors who back up their workers with management.

Supervision, Technical. Workers on this job have supervisors who train their workers well.

Autonomy. Occupations that satisfy this work value allow employees to work on their own and make decisions.

Creativity. Workers on this job try out their own ideas.

Responsibility. Workers on this job make decisions on their own.

Autonomy. Workers on this job plan their work with little supervision.

Skills Required. A skill is a person's capacity to perform a task. Skills are typically developed through education, training, and experience, although they also interact with abilities. In developing the job descriptions, we had data from the O*NET database on 46 skills for each job. That was too much information to be useful, so we included only those skills with higher numerical ratings for each job. The skills that are included in a description are, therefore, those that are particularly important for that job. Descriptions for the 46 skills follow, organized into two major groupings.

The 46 Skills Used in the Job Descriptions

Basic Skills. These capacities facilitate the acquisition of new knowledge and skills.

Reading Comprehension. Understanding written sentences and paragraphs in work-related documents.

Active Listening. Listening to what other people are saying and asking questions as appropriate.

Writing. Communicating effectively with others in writing as indicated by the needs of the audience.

Speaking. Talking to others to effectively convey information.

Mathematics. Using mathematics to solve problems.

Science. Using scientific methods to solve problems.

Critical Thinking. Using logic and analysis to identify the strengths and weaknesses of different approaches.

Active Learning. Working with new material or information to grasp its implications.

Learning Strategies. Using multiple approaches when learning or teaching new things.

Monitoring. Assessing how well one is doing when learning or doing something.

Cross-Functional Skills. These skills facilitate performance in a variety of job settings.

Social Perceptiveness. Being aware of others' reactions and understanding why they react the way they do.

Coordination. Adjusting actions in relation to others' actions.

Persuasion. Persuading others to approach things differently.

Negotiation. Bringing others together and trying to reconcile differences.

Instructing. Teaching others how to do something.

Service Orientation. Actively looking for ways to help people.

Problem Identification. Identifying the nature of problems.

Information Gathering. Knowing how to find information and identifying essential information.

Information Organization. Finding ways to structure or classify multiple pieces of information.

Synthesis/Reorganization. Reorganizing information to get a better approach to problems or tasks.

Idea Generation. Generating a number of different approaches to problems.

Idea Evaluation. Evaluating the likely success of an idea in relation to the demands of the situation.

Implementation Planning. Developing approaches for implementing an idea.

Solution Appraisal. Observing and evaluating the outcomes of a problem solution to identify lessons learned or redirect efforts.

Operations Analysis. Analyzing needs and product requirements to create a design.

Technology Design. Generating or adapting equipment and technology to serve user needs.

Equipment Selection. Determining the kind of tools and equipment needed to do a job.

Installation. Installing equipment, machines, wiring, or programs to meet specifications.

Programming. Writing computer programs for various purposes.

Testing. Conducting tests to determine whether equipment, software, or procedures are operating as expected.

Operation Monitoring. Watching gauges, dials, or other indicators to make sure a machine is working properly.

Operation and Control. Controlling operations of equipment or systems.

Product Inspection. Inspecting and evaluating the quality of products.

Equipment Maintenance. Performing routine maintenance and determining when and what kind of maintenance is needed.

Troubleshooting. Determining what is causing an operating error and deciding what to do about it.

Repairing. Repairing machines or systems using the needed tools.

Visioning. Developing an image of how a system should work under ideal conditions.

Systems Perception. Determining when important changes have occurred in a system or are likely to occur.

Identifying Downstream Consequences. Determining the long-term outcomes of a change in operations.

Identification of Key Causes. Identifying the things that must be changed to achieve a goal.

(continues)

(continued)

Judgment and Decision Making. Weighing the relative costs and benefits of a potential action.

Systems Evaluation. Looking at many indicators of system performance, taking into account their accuracy.

Time Management. Managing one's own time and the time of others.

Management of Financial Resources. Determining how money will be spent to get the work done, and accounting for these expenditures.

Management of Material Resources. Obtaining and seeing to the appropriate use of equipment, facilities, and materials needed to do certain work.

Management of Personnel Resources. Motivating, developing, and directing people as they work, identifying the best people for the job.

Abilities. Abilities are general traits we have or don't have that allow us to learn or do other things. When someone says you are "good at" or "talented in" something they are often referring to your basic abilities. An example is someone who has the ability to write well. Your basic abilities tend to be stable over time, although you can develop your basic abilities with learning and practice.

The descriptions include one or more abilities from a set of 52 used in the O*NET database. The O*NET provides numeric measures on all of them, but space limitations and common sense helped us decide only to include abilities that were rated highly for the job described. The 52 abilities are organized into four categories. Following are brief descriptions for each, organized within the categories.

The 52 Abilities Used in the Job Descriptions

Cognitive Abilities. These are mental processes that influence the acquisition and application of knowledge in problem solving.

Oral Comprehension. The ability to listen to and understand information and ideas presented through spoken words and sentences.

Written Comprehension. The ability to read and understand information and ideas presented in writing.

Oral Expression. The ability to communicate information and ideas in speaking so others will understand.

Written Expression. The ability to communicate information and ideas in writing so others will understand.

Fluency of Ideas. The ability to come up with a number of ideas about a given topic. It concerns the number of ideas produced and not the quality, correctness, or creativity of the ideas.

Originality. The ability to come up with unusual or clever ideas about a given topic or situation, or to develop creative ways to solve a problem.

Problem Sensitivity. The ability to tell when something is wrong or is likely to go wrong. It does not involve solving the problem, only recognizing there is a problem.

Deductive Reasoning. The ability to apply general rules to specific problems to come up with logical answers. It involves deciding if an answer makes sense or provides a logical explanation for why a series of seemingly unrelated events occur together.

Inductive Reasoning. The ability to combine separate pieces of information, or specific answers to problems, to form general rules or conclusions. It includes coming up with a logical explanation for why a series of seemingly unrelated events occur together.

Information Ordering. The ability to correctly follow a given rule or set of rules in order to arrange things or actions in a certain order. The things or actions can include numbers, letters, words, pictures, procedures, sentences, and mathematical or logical operations.

Category Flexibility. The ability to produce many rules so that each rule tells how to group (or combine) a set of things in a different way.

Mathematical Reasoning. The ability to understand and organize a problem and then to select a mathematical method or formula to solve the problem.

Number Facility. The ability to add, subtract, multiply, or divide quickly and correctly.

Memorization. The ability to remember information such as words, numbers, pictures, and procedures.

Speed of Closure. The ability to quickly make sense of information that seems to be without meaning or organization. It involves quickly combining and organizing different pieces of information into a meaningful pattern.

Flexibility of Closure. The ability to identify or detect a known pattern (a figure, object, word, or sound) that is hidden in other distracting material.

Perceptual Speed. The ability to quickly and accurately compare letters, numbers, objects, pictures, or patterns. The things to be compared may be presented at the same time or one after the other. This ability also includes comparing a presented object with a remembered object.

Spatial Orientation. The ability to know one's location in relation to the environment, or to know where other objects are in relation to one's self.

Visualization. The ability to imagine how something will look after it is moved around or when its parts are moved or rearranged.

Selective Attention. The ability to concentrate and not be distracted while performing a task over a period of time.

Time Sharing. The ability to efficiently shift back and forth between two or more activities or sources of information (such as speech, sounds, touch, or other sources).

Psychomotor Abilities. These abilities influence the capacity to manipulate and control objects primarily using fine motor skills.

Arm-Hand Steadiness. The ability to keep the hand and arm steady while making an arm movement or while holding the arm and hand in one position.

Manual Dexterity. The ability to quickly make coordinated movements of one hand, a hand together with its arm, or two hands to grasp, manipulate, or assemble objects.

Finger Dexterity. The ability to make precisely coordinated movements of the fingers of one or both hands to grasp, manipulate, or assemble very small objects.

Control Precision. The ability to quickly and repeatedly make precise adjustments in moving the controls of a machine or vehicle to exact positions.

Multilimb Coordination. The ability to coordinate movements of two or more limbs together (for example, two arms, two legs, or one leg and one arm) while sitting, standing, or lying down. It does not involve performing the activities while the body is in motion.

Response Orientation. The ability to choose quickly and correctly between two or more movements in response to two or more signals (lights, sounds, pictures, and so on). It includes the speed with which the correct response is started with the hand, foot, or other body parts.

Rate Control. The ability to time the adjustments of a movement or equipment control in anticipation of changes in the speed and/or direction of a continuously moving object or scene.

Reaction Time. The ability to quickly respond (with the hand, finger, or foot) to one signal (sound, light, picture, and so on) when it appears.

Wrist-Finger Speed. The ability to make fast, simple, repeated movements of the fingers, hands, and wrists.

Speed of Limb Movement. The ability to quickly move the arms or legs.

Physical Strength Abilities. These abilities influence strength, endurance, flexibility, balance, and coordination.

Static Strength. The ability to exert maximum muscle force to lift, push, pull, or carry objects.

Explosive Strength. The ability to use short bursts of muscle force to propel oneself (as in jumping or sprinting), or to throw an object.

Dynamic Strength. The ability to exert muscle force repeatedly or continuously over time. This involves muscular endurance and resistance to muscle fatigue.

Trunk Strength. The ability to use one's abdominal and lower back muscles to support part of the body repeatedly or continuously over time without giving out or fatiguing.

Stamina. The ability to exert one's self physically over long periods of time without getting winded or out of breath.

Extent Flexibility. The ability to bend, stretch, twist, or reach out with the body, arms, and/or legs.

Dynamic Flexibility. The ability to quickly and repeatedly bend, stretch, twist, or reach out with the body, arms, and/or legs.

Gross Body Coordination. The ability to coordinate the movement of the arms, legs, and torso together in activities where the whole body is in motion.

Gross Body Equilibrium. The ability to keep or regain one's body balance or stay upright when in an unstable position.

Sensory Abilities. These abilities influence visual, auditory, and speech perception.

Near Vision. The ability to see details of objects at a close range (within a few feet of the observer).

Far Vision. The ability to see details at a distance.

Visual Color Discrimination. The ability to match or detect differences between colors, including shades of color and brightness.

Night Vision. The ability to see under low light conditions.

Peripheral Vision. The ability to see objects or movement of objects to one's side when the eyes are focused forward.

Depth Perception. The ability to judge which of several objects is closer or farther away from the observer, or to judge the distance between an object and the observer.

Glare Sensitivity. The ability to see objects in the presence of glare or bright lighting.

Hearing Sensitivity. The ability to detect or tell the difference between sounds that vary over broad ranges of pitch and loudness.

Auditory Attention. The ability to focus on a single source of auditory (hearing) information in the presence of other distracting sounds.

Sound Localization. The ability to tell the direction from which a sound originated.

Speech Recognition. The ability to identify and understand the speech of another person.

Speech Clarity. The ability to speak clearly so that it is understandable to a listener.

Interacting with Others. Almost all jobs require at least some interaction with others. The O*NET database provides data on 17 measures related to interacting with others, organized into three categories. As with abilities and skills, we only include those with higher ratings for each job. Following are brief descriptions for each measure.

The 17 Measures Used in the Job Descriptions for Interacting with Others

Communicating and Interacting

Interpreting Meaning of Information to Others. Translating or explaining what information means and how it can be understood or used to support responses or feedback to others.

Communicating with Other Workers. Providing information to supervisors, fellow workers, and subordinates. This information can be exchanged face-to-face, in writing, or via telephone/electronic transfer.

Communicating with Persons Outside. Communicating with persons outside the organization, representing the organization to customers, the public, government, the organization, and other external sources. This information can be exchanged face-to-face, in writing, or via telephone/electronic transfer.

Establishing and Maintaining Relationships. Developing constructive and cooperative working relationships with others.

Assisting and Caring for Others. Providing assistance or personal care to others.

Selling or Influencing Others. Convincing others to buy merchandise/goods, or otherwise changing their minds or actions.

Resolving Conflict, Negotiating with Others. Handling complaints, arbitrating disputes, and resolving grievances, or otherwise negotiating with others.

Performing for/Working with Public. Performing for people or dealing directly with the public, including serving persons in restaurants and stores, and receiving clients or guests.

Coordinating, Developing, Managing, and Advising Others

Coordinating Work and Activities of Others. Coordinating members of a work group to accomplish tasks.

Developing and Building Teams. Encouraging and building mutual trust, respect, and cooperation among team members.

(continues)

(continued)

Teaching Others. Identifying educational needs, developing formal training programs or classes, and teaching or instructing others.

Guiding, Directing, and Motivating Subordinates. Providing guidance and direction to subordinates, including setting performance standards and monitoring subordinates.

Coaching and Developing Others. Identifying developmental needs of others and coaching or otherwise helping others to improve their knowledge or skills.

Provide Consultation and Advice to Others. Providing consultation and expert advice to management or other groups on technical, systems-related, or process related topics.

Administering

Performing Administrative Activities. Approving requests, handling paperwork, and performing day-to-day administrative tasks.

Staffing Organizational Units. Recruiting, interviewing, selecting, hiring, and promoting persons for the organization.

Monitoring and Controlling Resources. Monitoring and controlling resources and overseeing the spending of money.

Physical Work Conditions. This category describes the work context as it relates to the interactions between the worker and the physical job environment. This includes work setting, environmental conditions, job hazards, body positioning, and work attire. The O*NET provides measures on 26 items that evaluate each occupation's physical work conditions. We found that many physical work conditions received a low rating in the O*NET database even though it was obvious they were an important part of the workplace where the job is typically found. That is why we set the rating at about 30 for the cutoff point. We included the highest rated physical condition if none were rated higher than 30. Brief descriptions for each measure follow.

The 26 Physical Work Conditions Used in the Descriptions

Indoors. Amount job requires working indoors.

Outdoors. Amount job requires working outdoors.

Distracting Sounds and Noise Levels. Sounds and noise levels that are distracting and uncomfortable.

Very Hot. Very hot (above 90°F) or very cold (under 32°F) temperatures.

Extremely Bright or Inadequate Lighting. Extremely bright or inadequate lighting conditions.

Contaminants. Contaminants present like pollutants, gases, dust, odors, and so on.

Cramped Work Space, Awkward Positions. Cramped work space that requires getting into awkward positions.

Whole Body Vibration. For example, operating a jackhammer or earthmoving equipment.

Radiation. Potential exposure to radiation.

Diseases/Infections. Potential diseases/infections (for example, patient care, some laboratory work, and sanitation control).

High Places. For example, heights above 8 feet on ladders, poles, scaffolding, and catwalks.

Hazardous Conditions. For example, high-voltage electricity, combustibles, explosives, chemicals; does not include hazardous equipment or situations.

Hazardous Equipment. For example, saws and machinery/ mechanical parts. Includes exposure to vehicular traffic but not driving a vehicle.

Hazardous Situations. Situations involving likely cuts, bites, stings, or minor burns.

Sitting. Amount of sitting required.

Standing. Amount of standing required.

Climbing Ladders, Scaffolds, Poles, etc. Covers all climbing to elevated locations.

Walking or Running. Amount of walking or running.

Kneeling, Crouching, or Crawling. Amount of kneeling, stooping, crouching, or crawling.

Keeping or Regaining Balance. Amount of keeping or regaining balance.

Using Hands on Objects, Tools, Controls. Using hands to handle, control, or feel objects, tools, or controls.

Bending or Twisting the Body. Amount of bending or twisting the body.

Making Repetitive Motions. Need to make repetitive motions.

Special Uniform. Examples are that of a commercial pilot, nurse, police officer, or military personnel.

Common Protective or Safety Attire. Examples are safety shoes, glasses, gloves, hearing protection, hard hat, or personal flotation device.

Specialized Protective or Safety Attire. Examples are breathing apparatus, safety harness, full protection suit, or radiation protection.

Whew! You now should understand why, when we said the job descriptions were packed with information, we were not exaggerating. We hope you understand why we did not and could not include all available information. We tried our best to create useful and easily understood job descriptions, but doing so required some compromise.

Part 3. Crosswalks to Careers

Think of this section of the book as a series of career assessment inventories. It consists of eight tables called "Crosswalks" because they allow you to cross-reference jobs that are related to the things they list. They are very useful for exploring career options based on your interests, values, previous experiences, and other factors. You can use one or more of the eight tables to explore your career options in a variety of interesting ways.

Crosswalk A: Work Values with Corresponding Work Groups

Crosswalk B: Leisure Activities with Corresponding Work Groups

Crosswalk C: Home Activities with Corresponding Work Groups

Crosswalk D: School Subjects with Corresponding Work Groups

Crosswalk E: Work Settings with Corresponding Work Groups

Crosswalk F: Skills with Corresponding Work Groups

Crosswalk G: Abilities with Corresponding Work Groups

Crosswalk H: Knowledges with Corresponding Work Groups

These Crosswalks were designed to help you identify possible career options based on interests and other factors. Using one or more of the Crosswalks in this way is likely to help you discover career options you may not have previously considered. For example, if you like to cook for your friends or family, using the Crosswalks would help you identify the possibility of becoming a chef even though you had not seriously considered that option before.

The first five Crosswalks were originally developed by staff under the direction of the U.S. Department of Labor and first presented in the 1984 edition of GOE by Thomas Harrington and Arthur O'Shea. We have updated them in a number of ways. We also added the last three Crosswalks, based on the data we have developed. Unfortunately, the new O*NET database did not crosswalk to military careers, and we could not include this Crosswalk in the new edition. All Crosswalks now use the new GOE groupings and relate to the new O*NET occupations. This means you can look up information on any of the listed GOE Work Groups in Part 1.

The Appendix and Index

We considered a variety of additional appendices but ended up with just one titled "Information for Vocational Counselors and Other Professionals." It includes information for developers interested in using the new GOE structure in their own products; technical information on the research behind the original GOE; and tips for using the GOE to assist others explore career options.

We also included an index that arranges all the job titles, Interest Areas, and Work Groups in this book in alphabetical order.

The Top Sources of Additional Information

If you have read the introduction thus far, you know that there is a ton of information in this book (or, more accurately, pounds). This book is intended to help you identify career options, and we hope you will understand that you will need additional information before jumping into a new career or educational program.

Thousands of career resources are available in books, Internet sites, magazines, and more, providing endless information on careers, jobs, education, training, earnings, and many related topics. Many resources are not worth your time to read or, for Internet sites, change almost daily. So we decided that we would not try to provide you with a long list of printed and Internet resources but, rather, with a few that are particularly good or that can lead you to other resources. Here are our suggestions for places to begin your search for additional information.

The resources here are those that cross-reference the O*NET job titles we've included in this GOE or that we consider will be most useful as supplements to those who use the GOE. We admit that our selection is subjective, and that we could not include many worthy resources, but we hope that the quality and usefulness of our listed resources will make up for the brevity of the list.

People you already know or can come to know. If you want to know more about a particular job or place of employment, ask the people who do that kind of work or who work in that particular place. This is often the only source of information for small organizations.

Occupational Outlook Handbook (OOH). Updated every two years by the U.S. Department of Labor, this book is the most widely used of all career references. It provides excellent descriptions for about 250 major jobs, covering about 85 percent of the workforce. It includes well-written information on skills required, working conditions, duties, qualifications, pay, and advancement. Very helpful for preparing for interviews by identifying key skills to emphasize.

Career Guide to Industries. Another excellent book from the U.S. Department of Labor. Similar to the *OOH,* but it covers major industries, an important but often overlooked issue to consider in making career decisions.

The O*NET Dictionary of Occupational Titles. This is the only book (besides this new GOE) to include descriptions for all jobs from the government's O*NET database. Its descriptions provide more details than we could include in the GOE, so it is a useful resource.

Best Jobs for the 21st Century. Provides lots of job lists including fastest growing, highest pay, and many others by age, gender, education level, and other criteria. It also provides descriptions for the hundreds of jobs included in the various lists. There are also several variations of this book including *Best Jobs for the 21st Century for College Graduates* and *Best Jobs for the 21st Century That Don't Require a Degree.*

The Very Quick Job Search. If you need one job search book, this is the one to have. Very thorough and has won multiple awards.

JIST's Web site (www.jist.com). You can buy any book mentioned here at this site, but it is much more than a bookstore. For example, you can download a free book on job seeking (the *Quick Job Search*); read summaries of recommended Internet career and education sites (with instant links to them); use an interactive job search workshop; and get lots of career information.

The O*NET Web site. If you want to see more of the O*NET data, go to www.onetcenter.org. You can also get lots of other information on the O*NET at www.acinet.org.

You. That's right. We believe that your very best career exploration resource is yourself. So plan to spend more time on learning about yourself and your many strengths and options. As always, you are your own best resource.

Part 1

GOE Interest Areas and Work Groups

Essential Information for Exploring Career Options

This part provides helpful information on each GOE Interest Area and its related Work Groups. The introduction gives a good overview of the content, but here is a brief review.

Each of the GOE's 14 Interest Areas is divided into Work Groups of related jobs. Since the jobs within groupings are similar, this will help you quickly identify the major jobs that are most likely to meet your interests.

(continues)

(continued)

Each Interest Area is given a two-digit code number. For example, the Arts, Entertainment, and Media Interest Area is given the code 01. Major groupings of jobs within each Interest Area are given a four-digit code number. For example 01.01 is for the jobs in the "Managerial Work in Arts, Entertainment, and Media" area. Some four-digit Work Groups are further divided into two or more Work Groups whose jobs have similar characteristics but are likely to interest different people. These Work Groups are given six-digit codes such as

- 01.05.01 Performing Arts, Drama: Directing, Performing, Narrating, and Announcing
- 01.05.02 Performing Arts, Music: Directing, Composing and Arranging, and Performing

Work Groups that do not have divisions are often presented with six digits, such as 01.01.01 Managerial Work in Arts, Entertainment, and Media. The fifth and sixth digits allow for future Work Groups that may be added to the GOE.

Part 1 provides a brief description of each Work Group, followed by questions that will help you decide if the grouping is worthy of more exploration. The approach is simple to use and will help you quickly identify groups of jobs you should consider in more detail. Training and education usually needed for the jobs in each grouping are also listed. You can then go to Part 2 for more information on specific jobs. For more details on the contents of Part 1, please read this book's introduction.

The 14 GOE Interest Areas

Here are the 14 major Interest Areas covered in Part 1. Information is presented in numeric order by two-digit Interest Area code and four-digit Work Group code.

01—Arts, Entertainment, and Media

02—Science, Math, and Engineering

03—Plants and Animals

04—Law, Law Enforcement, and Public Safety

05—Mechanics, Installers, and Repairers

06—Construction, Mining, and Drilling

07—Transportation

08—Industrial Production

09—Business Detail

10—Sales and Marketing

11—Recreation, Travel, and Other Personal Services

12—Education and Social Service

13—General Management and Support

14—Medical and Health Services

01 Arts, Entertainment, and Media

An interest in creatively expressing feelings or ideas, in communicating news or information, or in performing.

You can satisfy this interest in several creative, verbal, or performing activities. For example, if you enjoy literature, perhaps writing or editing would appeal to you. Do you prefer to work in the performing arts? If so, you could direct or perform in drama, music, or dance. If you especially enjoy the visual arts, you could become a critic in painting, sculpture, or ceramics. You may want to use your hands to create or decorate products. You may prefer to model clothes or develop sets for entertainment. Or you may want to participate in sports professionally, as an athlete or coach.

01.01 Managerial Work in Arts, Entertainment, and Media

01.02 Writing and Editing

01.03 News, Broadcasting, and Public Relations

01.04 Visual Arts

01.05 Performing Arts

01.06 Craft Arts

01.07 Graphic Arts

01.08 Media Technology

01.09 Modeling and Personal Appearance

01.10 Sports: Coaching, Instructing, Officiating, and Performing

01.01 Managerial Work in Arts, Entertainment, and Media

Workers in this group manage people who work in the field of arts, entertainment, and media. They oversee performers and performances in the arts and sports. They work for radio, television, and motion picture production companies, and for artists and athletes.

What kind of work would you do?

Your work activities would depend on your job. For example, you might

- Evaluate length, content, and suitability of programs for broadcast.
- Assign and direct staff members to develop design concepts into art layouts.
- Compose and edit a script, or outline a story for a screenwriter to write the script.
- Assign research, writing, and editorial duties to staff members and review work products.
- Edit copy or review edited copy to ensure that writing meets establishment standards.
- Read novels, stories, and plays and prepare synopses for review by an editorial department or a film, radio, or television producer.
- Write leading or policy editorials, headlines, articles, and other materials.

What things about you point to this kind of work?

Is it important for you to

- Plan your work with little supervision?
- Get a feeling of accomplishment?
- Make use of your individual abilities?
- Make decisions on your own?

Have you enjoyed any of the following as a hobby or leisure-time activity?

- Developing publicity fliers for a school or community event
- Drawing posters for an organization or political campaign
- Planning and arranging programs for school or community organizations
- Designing stage sets for school or other amateur theater
- Making videos of family activities
- Writing articles, stories, or plays
- Editing or proofreading a school or organizational newspaper, yearbook, or magazine
- Designing your own greeting cards and writing original verses

Have you liked and done well in any of the following school subjects?

- Management
- Accounting
- Editing
- Cinematography
- Theater Arts
- Contract Law
- Business Law
- Creative Writing
- Personnel Management

Are you able to

- Listen to and understand information and ideas presented through spoken words and sentences?
- Speak clearly so that it is understandable to a listener?
- Communicate information and ideas in speaking so others will understand?
- Read and understand information and ideas presented in writing?
- Communicate information and ideas in writing so others will understand?
- Come up with unusual or clever ideas about a given topic or situation, or develop creative ways to solve a problem?
- See details of objects at close range (within a few feet)?

Would you work in places such as

- Motion picture and recording studios?
- Television studios?
- Business offices?
- Theaters?
- Sports stadiums?
- Artists' studios and craft workshops?

What skills and knowledges do you need for this kind of work?

For most of these jobs, you need these skills:

- Coordination—adjusting actions in relation to others' actions
- Management of Personnel Resources—motivating, developing, and directing people as they work, identifying the best people for the job
- Speaking—talking to others to effectively convey information
- Reading Comprehension—understanding written sentences and paragraphs in work-related documents
- Writing—communicating effectively with others in writing as indicated by their needs

These knowledges are important in most of these jobs:

- Administration and Management—principles and processes involved in business and organizational planning, coordination, and execution
- Communications—the science and art of delivering information

What else should you consider about this kind of work?

Those who manage artists and performers feel some of the same competitive pressure as the artists and performers themselves, and must have creativity and the knowledge of what makes for artistic and athletic success.

Nevertheless, managers need to think just as much (or more) in terms of business success. As the media business is becoming more concentrated into large companies, opportunities to take artistic risks may be decreasing. This trend also tends to concentrate media jobs in larger cities.

Professionalism in sports, on the other hand, is reaching smaller cities, and much newspaper and television production will always be done at the local level.

How can you prepare for jobs of this kind?

Occupations in this group usually require education and/or training ranging from two to as much as ten years.

Generally it helps to have some mastery of the skill of the workers you will manage. At the very least you need to know what makes the difference between good work and bad work.

For example, a television producer is expected to be able to evaluate the quality of a script, the talent of a director, and the skill of a video editor—competencies that are usually acquired in school and college courses in literature and film studies, plus experience in the television industry. An art director needs to know about art, layout design, and copy writing, probably from college courses in commercial art and writing.

Business managers of artists and performers need some knowledge of an art form or sport, which they may acquire either formally through education, possibly college-level, or informally through training and practice.

All jobs in this group require knowledge of business management. This is best learned through college courses in accounting, personnel management, and finance. Specialized courses and even majors in arts or media production and management are available at some colleges.

SPECIALIZED TRAINING

JOBS	EDUCATION/TRAINING	WHERE OBTAINED
01.01.01 Managerial Work in Arts, Entertainment, and Media		
All in Managerial Work in Arts, Entertainment, and Media	Experience	Related jobs within the same industry
13-1011.00 Agents and Business Managers of Artists, Performers, and Athletes	Music, General; Business and Personal Services Marketing Operations, Other; Hospitality and Recreation Marketing Operations, General; Public Relations and Organizational Communications; Music Business Management and Merchandising; Recreation Products/Services Marketing Operations	Four-year college, business school

(continues)

(continued)

SPECIALIZED TRAINING

JOBS	EDUCATION/TRAINING	WHERE OBTAINED
01.01.01 Managerial Work in Arts, Entertainment, and Media		
27-1011.00 Art Directors	Graphic Design, Commercial Art, and Illustration; Advertising	Four-year college, art school, military (Army, Navy, Air Force, Marine Corps)
27-2012.01 Producers	Radio and Television Broadcasting; Drama/Theater Arts, General; Technical Theater/Theater Design and Stagecraft; Film-Video Making/Cinematography and Production; Acting and Directing	On the job, four-year college, school for performing arts, military (Army, Navy, Marine Corps)
27-2012.03 Program Directors	Film-Video Making/Cinematography and Production; Acting and Directing; Drama/Theater Arts, General	On the job, four-year college, school for performing arts, military (Army, Navy, Air Force, Marine Corps)
27-2012.05 Technical Directors/Managers	Film-Video Making/Cinematography and Production; Radio and Television Broadcasting	On the job, four-year college, school for performing arts, military (Army, Navy)

01.02 Writing and Editing

Workers in this group write or edit prose or poetry. Some use knowledge of a technical field to write manuals. Most work for publishers, in radio and television studios, and in the theater and motion picture industries. Some are self-employed and sell their stories and plays directly to publishers.

What kind of work would you do?

Your work activities would depend on your job. For example, you might

- Review submitted book manuscripts and determine market demand based on consumer trends and personal knowledge.
- Prepare recommended editorial revisions in the script, using a computer or typewriter.
- Write narrative, dramatic, lyric, or other types of poetry for publication.
- Coordinate book design and production activities.
- Draw sketches to illustrate specified materials or assembly sequence.
- Recommend purchasing material for use in developing scripts.
- Write articles, bulletins, sales letters, speeches, and other related informative and promotional material.

What things about you point to this kind of work?

Is it important for you to

- Plan your work with little supervision?
- Make use of your individual abilities?
- Try out your own ideas?
- Get a feeling of accomplishment?

Have you enjoyed any of the following as a hobby or leisure-time activity?

- Writing articles, stories, or plays
- Editing or proofreading a school or organizational newspaper, yearbook, or magazine
- Belonging to a literary or book club
- Designing your own greeting cards and writing original verses
- Doing crossword puzzles
- Doing desktop publishing for a school or community publication
- Planning advertisements for a school or community newspaper

Have you liked and done well in any of the following school subjects?

- Grammar
- Spelling
- Creative Writing
- Literature
- Technical Writing
- Psychology
- Abstract Writing
- Fiction Writing
- Editing
- Copy Writing

Are you able to

- Read and understand information and ideas presented in writing?
- Communicate information and ideas in writing so others will understand?
- See details of objects at close range (within a few feet)?
- Communicate information and ideas in speaking so others will understand?
- Listen to and understand information and ideas presented through spoken words and sentences?
- Come up with unusual or clever ideas about a given topic or situation, or develop creative ways to solve a problem?
- Come up with a number of ideas about a given topic?
- Correctly follow a given rule or set of rules in order to arrange things or actions in a certain order?

Would you work in places such as

- Business offices?
- Television studios?
- Motion picture and recording studios?
- Theaters?

What skills and knowledges do you need for this kind of work?

For most of these jobs, you need these skills:

- Writing—communicating effectively with others in writing as indicated by their needs
- Reading Comprehension—understanding written sentences and paragraphs in work-related documents

These knowledges are important in most of these jobs:

- English Language—the structure and content of the English language, including the meaning and spelling of words, rules of composition, and grammar
- Communications—the science and art of delivering information

What else should you consider about this kind of work?

There is keen competition for most jobs in this group. Although some work is available in cities all over the country, most jobs are found in cities where large publishing companies have their headquarters. Copy writers work for advertising agencies, mostly in cities.

Many creative writers are self-employed. They write stories, poetry, and other materials and submit them to publishers or producers for consideration. Many hire agents who help them sell their work. Well-known writers are asked to take assignments to write about specific subjects.

Technical writing jobs are not as competitive and may be found anywhere there are technology companies. They require a different kind of creativity, in that they require you to translate complicated concepts and procedures into terms your readers can understand. Some technical writers do freelance work.

When applying for writing jobs, you should bring samples of your work with you.

How can you prepare for jobs of this kind?

Occupations in this group usually require education and/or training ranging from two to more than six years. All jobs in the group require spelling, grammar, punctuation, and composition skills, which are usually acquired in school and college courses in English, journalism, and creative writing.

Experience with minor publishers is helpful in getting positions with major publishers and advertising agencies.

For technical writing, a college degree or course work in a technical field such as computer programming or engineering is usually necessary.

SPECIALIZED TRAINING

JOBS	EDUCATION/TRAINING	WHERE OBTAINED
	01.02.01 Writing and Editing	
All in Writing and Editing	Experience; practice; competition; publication	Related jobs within the same industry, writing or editing for school and amateur publications
27-3041.00 Editors	English Technical and Business Writing; Journalism; Broadcast Journalism; English Creative Writing; Business Communications; Radio and Television Broadcasting	Four-year college, military (Army, Navy, Air Force, Marine Corps)
27-3042.00 Technical Writers	English Creative Writing; English Technical and Business Writing; Business Communications	Four-year college
27-3043.01 Poets and Lyricists	English Creative Writing	Four-year college
27-3043.02 Creative Writers	Journalism; English Technical and Business Writing; English Creative Writing; Drama/Theater Arts, General; Playwriting and Screenwriting; Broadcast Journalism; Radio and Television Broadcasting	Four-year college, military (Air Force, Navy)
27-3043.04 Copy Writers	Advertising	Four-year college

01.03 News, Broadcasting, and Public Relations

Workers in this group write, edit, translate, and report factual or persuasive information. They use their language skills and knowledge of special writing techniques to communicate facts or convince people of a point of view. They find employment with radio and television stations, newspapers, publishing firms, and advertising agencies. Some translators travel with visiting foreign businesspeople or diplomats; others work in courtrooms and law firms.

What kind of work would you do?

Your work activities would depend on your job. For example, you might

- Examine news items to determine selection.
- Gather and verify factual information regarding a story through interviews, observation, and research.
- Organize material and determine slant or emphasis.
- Revise text to meet editorial approval or to fit time or space requirements.
- Purchase advertising space to promote client's product.
- Take photographs or shoot video to illustrate stories.
- Translate foreign-language dialogue into English-language captions.

What things about you point to this kind of work?

Is it important for you to

- Make use of your individual abilities?
- Get a feeling of accomplishment?
- Have good working conditions?

Have you enjoyed any of the following as a hobby or leisure-time activity?

- Planning advertisements for a school or community newspaper
- Announcing or emceeing a program
- Speaking on radio or television
- Developing publicity fliers for a school or community event

- Doing desktop publishing for a school or community publication
- Writing articles, stories, or plays
- Teaching immigrants or other individuals to speak, write, or read English

Have you liked and done well in any of the following school subjects?

- Grammar
- Spelling
- News Writing
- Abstract Writing
- Economics
- Journalism
- Public Speaking
- Editing
- Broadcast Journalism
- Newscasting

Are you able to

- Communicate information and ideas in writing so others will understand?
- Communicate information and ideas in speaking so others will understand?
- Listen to and understand information and ideas presented through spoken words and sentences?
- Read and understand information and ideas presented in writing?
- Speak clearly so that it is understandable to a listener?
- See details of objects at close range (within a few feet)?
- Identify and understand the speech of another person?

Would you work in places such as

- Business offices?
- Radio studios?
- Television studios?
- Courthouses?

What skills and knowledges do you need for this kind of work?

For most of these jobs, you need these skills:

- Writing—communicating effectively with others in writing as indicated by their needs
- Reading Comprehension—understanding written sentences and paragraphs in work-related documents
- Speaking—talking to others to effectively convey information
- Active Listening—listening to what other people are saying and asking questions as appropriate
- Information Gathering—knowing how to find information and identifying essential information

These knowledges are important in most of these jobs:

- English Language—the structure and content of the English language, including the meaning and spelling of words, rules of composition, and grammar
- Communications—the science and art of delivering information

What else should you consider about this kind of work?

Competition is keen for jobs in journalism and public relations. An internship while you are in college can be very valuable for getting your first job. The trend in public relations is toward more work being done by public relations firms rather than by an in-house PR staff. Expect to start with a small PR firm or small city newspaper and advance your career by moving to larger employers as you gain experience and a portfolio of your work.

News analysts and specialized correspondents must have a background in what they are writing about, such as music, art, economics, or technology. They are hired by large newspapers and publishing companies.

The growth in international trade and immigration is increasing the need for interpreters and translators, but also the availability of multilingual people. The best opportunities are in languages not widely known in the U.S. Freelancers may find many opportunities.

When applying for writing jobs, you should bring samples of your work with you.

How can you prepare for jobs of this kind?

Most of these jobs require at least four years of education and/or training, and some require six years or more. You should have good skills with spelling, grammar, punctuation, and composition, usually acquired in school and college courses in English, journalism, and creative writing.

Experience with minor publications is helpful in getting positions with major publications and public relations agencies.

For interpreting or translating, experience living in a foreign country is very valuable, partly to hone your language skills and partly to improve your understanding of the culture.

SPECIALIZED TRAINING

JOBS	EDUCATION/TRAINING	WHERE OBTAINED
01.03.01 News, Broadcasting, and Public Relations		
All in News, Broadcasting, and Public Relations	Experience	Related jobs within the same industry
27-3021.00 Broadcast News Analysts	English Creative Writing; Broadcast Journalism; Journalism	On the job, four-year college, graduate school, military (Army, Navy, Air Force)
27-3022.00 Reporters and Correspondents	Journalism; Broadcast Journalism	Four-year college, military (all branches)
27-3031.00 Public Relations Specialists	Business Services Marketing Operations; Public Relations and Organizational Communications	Four-year college, military (all branches)
27-3043.03 Caption Writers	English Creative Writing	Four-year college
27-3091.00 Interpreters and Translators	Foreign Languages and Literatures, General; Foreign Language Interpretation and Translation; Communication Disorders, General; Sign Language Interpreter	Four-year college, graduate school, living in foreign cultures, military (Army, Navy, Air Force, Marine Corps)

01.04 Visual Arts

Workers in this group draw, paint, or sculpt works of art, or design consumer goods in which visual appeal is important. They work for advertising agencies, printing and publishing firms, television and motion picture studios, museums, and restoration laboratories. They also work for manufacturers and in retail and wholesale trade. Many operate their own commercial art studios or do freelance work.

What kind of work would you do?

Your work activities would depend on your job. For example, you might

- Construct artistic forms from metal, using metalworking or welding tools.
- Design packaging and containers for products, such as foods, beverages, or medicines.
- Develop drawings, paintings, diagrams, and models of medical or biological subjects.
- Dress mannequins for use in displays.
- Plan floral arrangements according to client's requirements, utilizing knowledge of design and properties of materials.
- Install finished stained glass in window or doorframe.
- Select furniture, draperies, pictures, lamps, and rugs for decorative quality and appearance.

What things about you point to this kind of work?

Is it important for you to

- Make use of your individual abilities?
- Get a feeling of accomplishment?
- Try out your own ideas?

Have you enjoyed any of the following as a hobby or leisure-time activity?

- Drawing posters for an organization or political campaign
- Taking photographs
- Designing and making costumes for school plays, festivals, and other events

- Painting landscapes, seascapes, or portraits
- Designing stage sets for school or other amateur theater
- Illustrating the school yearbook

Have you liked and done well in any of the following school subjects?

- Art
- Computer Graphics
- Arts and Crafts
- Sculpture/Sculpting
- Fashion Illustration
- Ceramics
- Floral Arranging
- Photography
- Painting, Fine Arts and Applied

Are you able to

- Imagine how something will look after it is moved around or when its parts are moved or rearranged?
- Come up with unusual or clever ideas about a given topic or situation, or to develop creative ways to solve a problem?
- Come up with a number of ideas about a given topic?
- See details of objects at close range (within a few feet)?
- Listen to and understand information and ideas presented through spoken words and sentences?
- Keep your hand and arm steady while making an arm movement or while holding your arm and hand in one position?
- Communicate information and ideas in speaking so others will understand?
- Match or detect differences between colors, including shades of color and brightness?

Would you work in places such as

- Artists' studios and craft workshops?
- Business offices?
- Motion picture and recording studios?
- Private homes?
- Stores and shopping malls?
- Television studios?

What skills and knowledges do you need for this kind of work?

For most of these jobs, you need these skills:

- Idea Generation—generating a number of different approaches to problems
- Product Inspection—inspecting and evaluating the quality of products

These knowledges are important in most of these jobs:

- Fine Arts—theory and techniques required to produce, compose, and perform works of music, dance, visual arts, drama, and sculpture
- Design—design techniques, principles, tools, and instruments involved in the production and use of precision technical plans, blueprints, drawings, and models

What else should you consider about this kind of work?

If you are interested in this kind of work, your chances for employment will be greater if you do many kinds of artwork rather than specializing in one or two.

When applying for either full-time or freelance work in this field, you should bring samples of your work with you to interviews.

Art dealers and commercial art galleries exhibit and sell the work of artists, taking a commission on sales prices.

People who are just getting started in the field may have their work exhibited in community centers, hospitals, hotels, and other public places. They may show and sell their work at craft and community fairs.

How can you prepare for jobs of this kind?

Education and training required for jobs in this group ranges from two to ten years. Many persons obtain a four-year degree with a major in fine or commercial art. Others earn an art institute certificate in two or three years.

Smaller companies sometimes hire workers with vocational school or junior college backgrounds and provide on-the-job training to improve their skills.

Successful freelance visual artists must have established their reputations as illustrators, designers, or art restorers.

SPECIALIZED TRAINING

JOBS	EDUCATION/TRAINING	WHERE OBTAINED
01.04.01 Visual Arts: Studio Art		
All in Visual Arts: Studio Art	Experience	Related jobs within the same industry
27-1013.01 Painters and Illustrators	Graphic Design, Commercial Art, and Illustration; Drama/Theater Arts, General; Technical Theater/Theater Design and Stagecraft; Art, General; Drawing; Painting; Printmaking; Medical Illustrating; Fine/Studio Arts	Two-year college, four-year college, art school, military (Army, Navy, Air Force, Marine Corps)
27-1013.02 Sketch Artists	Painting; Forensic Technology/Technician; Graphic Design, Commercial Art, and Illustration; Art, General; Drawing	Two-year college, four-year college, art school
27-1013.03 Cartoonists	Graphic Design, Commercial Art, and Illustration; Crafts, Folk Art, and Artisanry	Four-year college, art school, on the job
27-1013.04 Sculptors	Sculpture; Art, General; Fine/Studio Arts	Two-year college, four-year college, art school
01.04.02 Visual Arts: Design		
All in Visual Arts: Design	Experience	Related jobs within the same industry
27-1014.00 Multi-Media Artists and Animators	Metal and Jewelry Arts; Painting; Fine Arts and Art Studies, Other; Fiber, Textile, and Weaving Arts; Ceramics Arts and Ceramics; Printmaking; Sculpture; Drawing; Fine/Studio Arts; Art, General; Technical Theater/Theater Design and Stagecraft; Crafts, Folk Art, and Artisanry; Graphic Design, Commercial Art, and Illustration; Medical Illustrating; Intermedia	Four-year college, art school, on the job; military data not yet available
27-1021.00 Commercial and Industrial Designers	Home Furnishings and Equipment Installers and Consultants, General; Graphic Design, Commercial Art, and Illustration; Industrial Design; Fashion Design and Illustration	Four-year college
27-1022.00 Fashion Designers	Clothing, Apparel, and Textile Workers and Managers, General; Fashion Design and Illustration; Graphic Design, Commercial Art, and Illustration; Custom Tailor	Four-year college, two-year college, trade/technical school, on the job
27-1023.00 Floral Designers	Floristry Marketing Operations; Home Furnishings and Equipment Installers and Consultants, General	Four-year college, two-year college, trade/technical school, on the job
27-1024.00 Graphic Designers	Art, General; Graphic Design, Commercial Art, and Illustration; Printmaking	Two-year college, four-year college, art school, on the job, military (Army, Navy, Air Force, Marine Corps)
27-1025.00 Interior Designers	Interior Design; Interior Environments; Housing Studies, General; Interior Architecture; Home Furnishings and Equipment Installers and Consultants, General	Four-year college, two-year college, trade/technical school, on the job

JOBS	EDUCATION/TRAINING	WHERE OBTAINED
	01.04.02 Visual Arts: Design	
27-1026.00 Merchandise Displayers and Window Trimmers	Design and Visual Communications; Home Furnishings and Equipment Installers and Consultants, General	Four-year college, two-year college, trade/technical school, on the job
27-1027.01 Set Designers	Technical Theater/Theater Design and Stagecraft; Dramatic/Theater Arts and Stagecraft, Other; Drama/Theater Arts, General; Interior Design	Four-year college, on the job
27-1027.02 Exhibit Designers	Home Furnishings and Equipment Installers and Consultants, General; Technical Theater/Theater Design and Stagecraft; Interior Design; Graphic Design, Commercial Art, and Illustration; Drama/Theater Arts, General	Four-year college, two-year college, on the job

01.05 Performing Arts

Workers in this group direct or perform for the public in works of drama, music, dance, or spectacle. They are employed by motion picture, television, and radio studios, stock companies, nightclubs, theaters, orchestras, bands, choral groups, music publishing and recording companies, traveling carnivals or circuses, and permanently located amusement parks. They may compose, arrange, or orchestrate musical compositions, choreograph dance routines, or plan the presentation of performances. Besides the time spent on stage, performers must spend a large portion of their time practicing their craft, auditioning for parts, and rehearsing their performances.

What kind of work would you do?

Your work activities would depend on your job. For example, you might

- Direct cast, crew, and technicians during production or recording and filming in a studio or on location.
- Portray and interpret role, using speech, gestures, and body movements, to entertain television audience.
- Compose new musical scores.
- Improvise music during a performance.
- Practice performance on a musical instrument to maintain and improve skills.
- Coordinate dancing with that of a partner or dance ensemble.
- Harmonize body movements to the rhythm of musical accompaniment.
- Work with a choreographer to refine or modify dance steps.

What things about you point to this kind of work?

Is it important for you to

- Make use of your individual abilities?
- Get a feeling of accomplishment?
- Never be pressured to do things that go against your sense of right and wrong?

Have you enjoyed any of the following as a hobby or leisure-time activity?

- Acting in a play or amateur variety show
- Directing school or other amateur plays or musicals
- Entertaining at parties or other events
- Planning and arranging programs for school or community organizations
- Playing a musical instrument
- Singing in a choir or other group
- Creating dance steps for school or other amateur musicals
- Being a cheerleader
- Taking ballet or other dancing lessons
- Taking lessons in singing or in playing a musical instrument
- Doing impersonations

- Writing songs for club socials or amateur plays
- Teaching dancing as a volunteer in an after-school center
- Performing magic tricks for friends

Have you liked and done well in any of the following school subjects?

- Dance
- Public Speaking
- Drama
- Theater Arts
- Directing
- Band
- Choir/Chorus
- Voice
- Music: Theory and History

Are you able to

- Communicate information and ideas in speaking so others will understand?
- Come up with unusual or clever ideas about a given topic or situation, or to develop creative ways to solve a problem?
- Remember information such as words, numbers, pictures, and procedures?
- Listen to and understand information and ideas presented through spoken words and sentences?
- Speak clearly so that it is understandable to a listener?
- Read and understand information and ideas presented in writing?
- Detect or tell the difference between sounds that vary over broad ranges of pitch and loudness?

Would you work in places such as

- Amusement parks, circuses, and carnivals?
- Radio studios?
- Television studios?
- Motion picture and recording studios?
- Theaters?
- Gambling casinos and card clubs?
- Nightclubs?
- Ships and boats?
- Business offices?

What skills and knowledges do you need for this kind of work?

For most of these jobs, you need these skills:

- Speaking—talking to others to effectively convey information
- Coordination—adjusting actions in relation to others' actions
- Reading Comprehension—understanding written sentences and paragraphs in work-related documents
- Monitoring—assessing how well you are doing when learning or doing something
- Active Listening—listening to what other people are saying and asking questions as appropriate

These knowledges are important in most of these jobs:

- Fine Arts—theory and techniques required to produce, compose, and perform works of music, dance, visual arts, drama, and sculpture
- English Language—the structure and content of the English language, including the meaning and spelling of words, rules of composition, and grammar

What else should you consider about this kind of work?

You should take part in amateur performances to improve your skills. In most disciplines, it is to your advantage to gain as broad a background as possible in a variety of performing styles. The more versatile you are, the better your opportunities for full-time employment will be. Although many jobs in this field are found in large cities, people can find employment in smaller communities. Most performing artists are not permanently employed and must audition for roles.

Performers are often required to meet demanding schedules with early and late hours for rehearsals and performances. Frequent travel may be necessary. Performing careers may be short, because there may be more roles for young people or (in some cases) because the physical demands are great. Some performers make career changes to teaching their craft, or to directing the performances of others.

How can you prepare for jobs of this kind?

Occupations in this group usually require education and/or training ranging from one to more than ten years. Experience is also necessary to get a career started and is a vital part of the educational program.

For jobs in drama, initial training and experience are available in speech classes, debate classes, and school or community plays. Colleges and schools for the performing arts offer drama and communications programs with courses in speech, theater, pantomime, directing, and acting. These programs also provide experience in acting, announcing, and directing. Because acting careers are sometimes short and often never get beyond the amateur level, it helps to get an education that will also prepare you for another kind of work.

Although some persons with great natural talent may find work without formal instruction and even achieve great success as rock, country, or jazz singers or instrumental musicians, they are the rare exceptions. Professional instrumental musicians and singers usually begin their training while in elementary school and continue training throughout their working lives, with several hours of practice each day necessary for the development and maintenance of required skills. Courses in music theory and voice are offered in high schools, colleges, and music academies and by private instructors. Membership in a musical or singing group is valuable experience and preparation.

Initial dance training is often found in elementary and high schools. However, instruction in a dance studio, beginning at a very early age and continuing while employed, is usually needed to develop and maintain skills. Daily practice is essential. Liberal arts colleges, community dance companies, ethnic culture societies, dance academies, and theatre arts schools offer two- to four-year programs in dancing techniques, interpretation, and the history of dance. Many of these organizations cooperate with professional ballet and interpretive dance companies to provide experience as well as instruction. Private dance teachers must be able to demonstrate the techniques of many different types of dancing. Choreographers usually need to start as dancers and may take special college coursework in choreography.

SPECIALIZED TRAINING

JOBS	EDUCATION/TRAINING	WHERE OBTAINED
01.05.01 Performing Arts, Drama: Directing, Performing, Narrating, and Announcing		
All in Performing Arts, Drama: Directing, Performing, Narrating, and Announcing	Experience; Speech; Grammar; Voice; Oral Interpretation	On the job, high school, two-year or four-year college, school and amateur theatrical performances
27-2011.00 Actors	Drama/Theater Arts, General; Acting and Directing	On the job, two-year college, four-year college, school of performing arts
27-2012.02 Directors—Stage, Motion Pictures, Television, and Radio	Drama/Theater Arts, General; Radio and Television Broadcasting; Parks, Recreation, and Leisure Facilities Management; Technical Theater/Theater Design and Stagecraft; Film-Video Making/Cinematography and Production; Acting and Directing	On the job, four-year college, school of performing arts, military (Army, Navy, Air Force, Marine Corps)
27-3011.00 Radio and Television Announcers	Radio and Television Broadcasting; Broadcast Journalism	On the job, two-year college, four-year college, military (Army, Navy, Air Force, Coast Guard)
27-3012.00 Public Address System and Other Announcers	Communications, General	On the job, two-year college
01.05.02 Performing Arts, Music: Directing, Composing and Arranging, and Performing		
All in Performing Arts, Music: Directing, Composing and Arranging, and Performing	Composition, Arranging	On the job, music academy, four-year college, school and amateur musical performances
27-2012.04 Talent Directors	Drama/Theater Arts, General; Acting and Directing	On the job, four-year college, school of performing arts

(continues)

(continued)

SPECIALIZED TRAINING

JOBS	EDUCATION/TRAINING	WHERE OBTAINED
01.05.02 Performing Arts, Music: Directing, Composing and Arranging, and Performing		
27-2041.01 Music Directors	Music–Voice and Choral/Opera Performance; Music Conducting; Religious/Sacred Music; Musicology and Ethnomusicology; Music–General Performance; Music, General	On the job, two-year college, four-year college, music conservatory, military (all branches)
27-2041.02 Music Arrangers and Orchestrators	Music, General; Music Theory and Composition	On the job, two-year college, four-year college, music conservatory, military (Army, Navy, Air Force)
27-2041.03 Composers	Music, General; Music Theory and Composition	On the job, four-year college, music conservatory, military (Army, Navy)
27-2042.01 Singers	Music, General; Music–General Performance; Music–Voice and Choral/Opera Performance	On the job, two-year college, four-year college, music conservatory, military (Army, Navy, Air Force)
27-2042.02 Musicians, Instrumental	Music, General; Music–General Performance; Religious/Sacred Music; Music–Piano and Organ Performance	On the job, two-year college, four-year college, music conservatory, military (all branches)
01.05.03 Performing Arts, Dance: Performing and Choreography		
All in Performing Arts, Dance: Performing and Choreography	Experience	School and amateur dance performances
27-2031.00 Dancers	Dance	Private dance instruction, two-year college, four-year college, school of performing arts
27-2032.00 Choreographers	Dance	Private dance instruction, four-year college, school of performing arts

01.06 Craft Arts

Workers in this group create visually appealing objects from clay, glass, fabric, and other materials. Their jobs demand considerable skill. Some are employed by manufacturing firms, but many are self-employed, selling items they have made through galleries and gift shops.

What kind of work would you do?

Your work activities would depend on your job. For example, you might

- Shape, bend, or join sections of glass, using paddles, pressing and flattening hand tools, or cork.
- Raise and shape clay into ware, such as vases and pitchers, on a revolving wheel, using hands, fingers, and thumbs.
- Blow melted glass tubing into specified shapes, using compressed air or your own breath.
- Smooth surfaces of finished pottery pieces, using rubber scrapers and wet sponges.
- Preheat or melt glass pieces or anneal or cool glass products and components, using ovens and refractory powder.

- Position ball of clay in the center of a potter's wheel.

What things about you point to this kind of work?

Is it important for you to

- Never be pressured to do things that go against your sense of right and wrong?
- Do your work alone?
- Get a feeling of accomplishment?

Have you enjoyed any of the following as a hobby or leisure-time activity?

- Making ceramic objects
- Carving small wooden objects
- Designing and making costumes for school plays, festivals, and other events
- Doing needlework
- Weaving rugs or making quilts
- Mounting and framing pictures

Have you liked and done well in any of the following school subjects?

- Arts and Crafts
- Graphic Arts
- Commercial Art
- Design Graphics
- Design Media
- Painting, Fine Arts and Applied
- Crafts Shop
- Moldmaking

Are you able to

- Keep your hand and arm steady while making an arm movement or while holding your arm and hand in one position?
- Imagine how something will look after it is moved around or when its parts are moved or rearranged?
- Quickly make coordinated movements of one hand, a hand together with its arm, or two hands to grasp, manipulate, or assemble objects?
- Make fast, simple, repeated movements of the fingers, hands, and wrists?
- Quickly and repeatedly make precise adjustments in moving the controls of a machine or vehicle to exact positions?
- Bend, stretch, twist, or reach out with the body, arms, and/or legs?
- Coordinate movements of two or more limbs together?

Would you work in places such as

- Artists' studios and craft workshops?
- Factories and plants?

What skills and knowledges do you need for this kind of work?

For most of these jobs, you need these skills:

- Product Inspection—inspecting and evaluating the quality of products
- Operation and Control—controlling operations of equipment or systems

These knowledges are important in most of these jobs:

- Production and Processing—inputs, outputs, raw materials, waste, quality control, costs, and techniques for maximizing the manufacture and distribution of goods
- Fine Arts—theory and techniques required to produce, compose, and perform works of music, dance, visual arts, drama, and sculpture

What else should you consider about this kind of work?

Work of this type is found in large and small communities all over the country. Some jobs (particularly for glass blowers) are located where there are manufacturing plants; others are in towns and city neighborhoods that have reputations for encouraging the visual arts.

These jobs are often performed in small workshops, where workers create their crafts either alone or with a few other craft artists who share the costs of the facilities.

How can you prepare for jobs of this kind?

Occupations in this group usually require education and/or training ranging from one to more than ten years. Courses in art or craft work may provide initial preparation. Trade unions and employers sometimes cooperate to offer apprenticeship training. In some crafts it may also be possible to arrange for an informal apprenticeship with a master craft artist.

Specialized Training

JOBS	EDUCATION/TRAINING	WHERE OBTAINED
01.06.01 Craft Arts		
All in Craft Arts	Experience	Related jobs within the same industry
27-1012.00 Craft Artists	Metal and Jewelry Arts; Painting; Fine Arts and Art Studies, Other; Fiber, Textile and Weaving Arts; Ceramics Arts and Ceramics; Printmaking; Sculpture; Drawing; Fine/Studio Arts; Art, General; Technical Theater/Theater Design and Stagecraft; Crafts, Folk Art and Artisanry; Graphic Design, Commercial Art and Illustration; Medical Illustrating; Intermedia	Two-year college, trade/technical school, on the job
51-9195.04 Glass Blowers, Molders, Benders, and Finishers	Laser and Optical Technology/Technician; Crafts, Folk Art, and Artisanry	Two-year college, trade/technical school, on the job
51-9195.05 Potters	Art, General; Ceramics Arts and Ceramics	Two-year college, art school, on the job

01.07 Graphic Arts

Workers in this group produce printed materials, specializing in text, pictures, or combining both. Some of them use precision engraving and etching equipment and use considerable manual dexterity. Others use computerized or photographic equipment and rely more on technical skills. All of them have a good sense of what is visually appealing. They are employed by manufacturing firms, printing and publishing companies, and the publications departments in businesses of all kinds.

What kind of work would you do?

Your work activities would depend on your job. For example, you might

- Enter data, such as coordinates of images and color specifications, into a desktop publishing system to retouch and make color corrections.
- Compare measurements, using a ruler and proportion wheel, to determine the proportions needed to make reduced or enlarged photographic prints for paste-up.
- Etch designs on metal rollers and plates, using etching machines, hand tools, and acidic chemicals, to produce printing plates and rollers.
- Adjust camera settings, lights, and lens.
- Apply opaque to defective areas of film to block out blemishes and pinholes.
- Position artist's layout on digitizing tables of electronic masking system to prepare for data entry in system memory.
- Sandblast exposed area of glass, using spray gun, to cut design in surface.

What things about you point to this kind of work?

Is it important for you to

- Never be pressured to do things that go against your sense of right and wrong?
- Do your work alone?
- Have good working conditions?

Have you enjoyed any of the following as a hobby or leisure-time activity?

- Doing desktop publishing for a school or community publication
- Illustrating the school yearbook
- Belonging to a computer club
- Developing film
- Developing publicity fliers for a school or community event
- Taking photographs

Have you liked and done well in any of the following school subjects?

- Arts and Crafts

- Graphic Arts
- Commercial Art
- Computer Graphics
- Computer Concept/Methods
- Design Graphics
- Design Media
- Advertising Art/Production
- Offset Printing
- Photography

Are you able to

- See details of objects at close range (within a few feet)?
- Keep your hand and arm steady while making an arm movement or while holding your arm and hand in one position?
- Imagine how something will look after it is moved around or when its parts are moved or rearranged?
- Quickly make coordinated movements of one hand, a hand together with its arm, or two hands to grasp, manipulate, or assemble objects?
- Correctly follow a given rule or set of rules in order to arrange things or actions in a certain order?
- Make precisely coordinated movements of the fingers of one or both hands to grasp, manipulate, or assemble very small objects?
- Quickly and repeatedly make precise adjustments in moving the controls of a machine or vehicle to exact positions?

Would you work in places such as

- Artists' studios and craft workshops?
- Business offices?
- Factories and plants?
- Photographers' studios?

What skills and knowledges do you need for this kind of work?

For most of these jobs, you need these skills:

- Product Inspection—inspecting and evaluating the quality of products
- Operation and Control—controlling operations of equipment or systems
- Equipment Selection—determining the kind of tools and equipment needed to do a job

These knowledges are important in most of these jobs:

- Fine Arts—theory and techniques required to produce, compose, and perform works of music, dance, visual arts, drama, and sculpture
- Design—design techniques, principles, tools, and instruments involved in the production and use of precision technical plans, blueprints, drawings, and models

What else should you consider about this kind of work?

Work of this type is found in large and small communities all over the country. Most of these jobs are located where there are publishing companies and manufacturing plants.

People interested in art who prefer working under the direction of others, rather than strictly on their own, will find many job opportunities in this work group. Although much of the work is artistic in nature, these workers do not have to spend as much time or money on training as they would to prepare for other visual arts jobs.

Demand for paste-up workers is decreasing as they are being replaced by high-tech workers such as desktop publishers and electronic masking system operators. On the other hand, the most highly skilled and artistic etchers and engravers will probably always find work.

Some jobs, such as those in printing and publishing companies, may require evening or night-shift work. People who are skilled in their crafts and have a good reputation in their communities may open their own businesses, or freelance.

How can you prepare for jobs of this kind?

Occupations in this group usually require education and/or training ranging from one to more than ten years. Courses in industrial art, drafting, art, or craft work may provide initial preparation. Trade unions and employers sometimes cooperate to offer apprenticeship training.

Some employers will give on-the-job training to workers who possess manual skill or experience. Many of these jobs are highly specialized and require two or more years of training and experience. Desktop publishing can be learned through certification programs at community colleges or technical schools, or sometimes (for those already skilled at word processing) in a few months of on-the-job training.

SPECIALIZED TRAINING

JOBS	EDUCATION/TRAINING	WHERE OBTAINED
	01.07.01 Graphic Arts	
All in Graphic Arts	Experience; Graphic Processes; Graphic Arts; Math Computing (Fractions)	High school, two-year college, four-year college, community center, trade school, related jobs within the same industry
43-9031.00 Desktop Publishers	Computer Typography and Composition Equipment Operator; Lithographer and Platemaker; Mechanical Typesetter and Composer; Graphic and Printing Equipment Operator, General	On the job, two-year college, trade/technical school, business college, military (Army, Navy, Marine Corps)
51-5022.02 Paste-Up Workers	Graphic Design, Commercial Art, and Illustration	On the job, two-year college, trade/technical school
51-5022.03 Photoengravers	Lithographer and Platemaker; Graphic and Printing Equipment Operator, Other; Graphic and Printing Equipment Operator, General	On the job, two-year college, trade/technical school
51-5022.04 Camera Operators	Commercial Photography; Graphic and Printing Equipment Operator, General; Lithographer and Platemaker	On the job, two-year college, trade/technical school, military (Army, Navy, Air Force)
51-5022.08 Dot Etchers	Graphic and Printing Equipment Operator, General; Lithographer and Platemaker	On the job, two-year college, trade/technical school
51-5022.09 Electronic Masking System Operators	Graphic and Printing Equipment Operator, General; Lithographer and Platemaker	On the job, two-year college, trade/technical school
51-9194.01 Precision Etchers and Engravers, Hand or Machine	Watch, Clock, and Jewelry Repairer; Graphic and Printing Equipment Operator, General; Mechanical Typesetter and Composer	On the job, trade/technical school
51-9194.02 Engravers/Carvers	Crafts, Folk Art, and Artisanry; Graphic Design, Commercial Art, and Illustration	Two-year college, trade/technical school, on the job
51-9194.03 Etchers	Art, General; Ceramics Arts and Ceramics	Two-year college, trade/technical school, on the job
51-9194.04 Pantograph Engravers	Graphic Design, Commercial Art, and Illustration	On the job
51-9194.05 Etchers, Hand	Industrial Electronics Installer and Repairer; Optical Technician/Assistant; Optometric/Ophthalmic Laboratory Technician; Graphic and Printing Equipment Operator, General; Electrical and Electronics Equipment Installer and Repairer; Lithographer and Platemaker	On the job, two-year college, trade/technical school
51-9194.06 Engravers, Hand	Graphic Design, Commercial Art, and Illustration	On the job, two-year college, trade/technical school

01.08 Media Technology

Workers in this group perform the technical tasks that create the photographs, movies and videos, radio and television broadcasts, and sound recordings that provide entertainment and information for all of us. They are employed by local and network broadcasters, film studios and independent film or video production companies, recording studios, and photography studios.

What kind of work would you do?

Your work activities would depend on your job. For example, you might

- Set up, adjust, and operate equipment, such as cameras, sound mixers, and recorders, during audio or video production.
- Preview a scheduled radio or TV program to ensure that the signal is functioning and the program is ready for transmission.
- Turn controls or throw switches to activate power, adjust voice volume and modulation, and set radio transmitter on specified frequency.
- Synchronize and equalize prerecorded dialogue, music, and sound effects with the visual action of a motion picture or television production, using control console.
- Focus camera and adjust settings based on lighting, subject material, distance, and film speed.
- Read charts and compute ratios to determine variables, such as lighting, shutter angles, filter factors, and camera distance.
- Trim film segments to specified lengths and reassemble segments in a sequence that presents the story with maximum effect.

What things about you point to this kind of work?

Is it important for you to

- Make use of your individual abilities?
- Never be pressured to do things that go against your sense of right and wrong?
- Have good working conditions?
- Get a feeling of accomplishment?

Have you enjoyed any of the following as a hobby or leisure-time activity?

- Creating unusual lighting effects for school or other amateur plays
- Developing film
- Belonging to a computer club
- Operating a CB or ham radio
- Taking photographs
- Building or repairing radios or television sets
- Making videos of family activities

Have you liked and done well in any of the following school subjects?

- Art
- Photography
- Computer Graphics
- Computer Concept/Methods
- Electricity/Electronics
- Advertising Art/Production
- Acoustics
- Radio/TV Operations
- Theater Arts

Are you able to

- Listen to and understand information and ideas presented through spoken words and sentences?
- Communicate information and ideas in speaking so others will understand?
- Quickly and repeatedly make precise adjustments in moving the controls of a machine or vehicle to exact positions?
- Correctly follow a given rule or set of rules in order to arrange things or actions in a certain order?
- See details of objects at close range?
- Imagine how something will look after it is moved around or when its parts are moved or rearranged?

Would you work in places such as

- Motion picture and recording studios?
- Photographers' studios?
- Radio studios?
- Television studios?
- Theaters?

What skills and knowledges do you need for this kind of work?

For most of these jobs, you need these skills:

- Operation and Control—controlling operations of equipment or systems

- Speaking—talking to others to effectively convey information
- Product Inspection—inspecting and evaluating the quality of products
- Equipment Selection—determining the kind of tools and equipment needed to do a job
- Active Listening—listening to what other people are saying and asking questions as appropriate
- Monitoring—assessing how well one is doing when learning or doing something

These knowledges are important in most of these jobs:

- Telecommunications—knowledge of transmission, broadcasting, switching, control, and operation of telecommunications systems
- Communications—the science and art of delivering information

What else should you consider about this kind of work?

Work of this type is mostly found in cities, where broadcasting stations, film and video production companies, and recording studios are located. Photographers' studios are located in large and small communities throughout the country.

Because of the glamour associated with show business, there is keen competition for some of these jobs. In some fields, beginners can assemble a portfolio of amateur or student work (e.g., photographs, videos, and sound recordings) to interest employers in their skills and creativity, and thus may gain entry to at least an apprenticeship if not a first job.

Many of these jobs involve working under pressure or during evening or night hours because the production is "live" or because of deadlines. Some of these jobs, such as film editor or professional photographer, offer opportunities for freelancers who have established a reputation.

How can you prepare for jobs of this kind?

Occupations in this group usually require education and/or training ranging from six months to more than ten years, but for most the preparation takes two to four years. Courses in the technical aspects of the job (e.g., photography or electronics) are important preparation at both the high school and post-secondary levels. Since computers are increasingly being used in all the media technologies, post-secondary and on-the-job training will usually include learning the particular applications that are used for editing film, digitizing sound, touching up photographs, etc. Education and training should also include background in the artistic aspects of the medium—for example, history of film, photography as an art form, or music.

Radio operators need two to four years of education and training. They need some technical knowledge to operate and occasionally repair their equipment. High school or technical school courses in electronics and math are helpful. These workers also must know enough about the federal laws that affect their work to pass a licensing exam.

Specialized Training

JOBS	EDUCATION/TRAINING	WHERE OBTAINED
01.08.01 Media Technology		
All in Media Technology	Experience	Related jobs within the same industry
27-4011.00 Audio and Video Equipment Technicians	Educational/Instructional Media Technology/ Technician; Educational/Instructional Media Design	On the job, two-year college, four-year college, military (all branches)
27-4012.00 Broadcast Technicians	Radio and Television Broadcasting Technology/ Technician	Two-year college, trade/technical school
27-4013.00 Radio Operators	Communication Systems Installer and Repairer; Electrical and Electronics Equipment Installer and Repairer	Two-year college, trade/technical school, on the job, military (all branches)
27-4014.00 Sound Engineering Technicians	Radio and Television Broadcasting Technology/ Technician	Two-year college, trade/technical school

JOBS	EDUCATION/TRAINING	WHERE OBTAINED
01.08.01 Media Technology		
27-4021.01 Professional Photographers	Commercial Photography; Photography	On the job, two-year college, four-year college, military (all branches)
27-4031.00 Camera Operators, Television, Video, and Motion Picture	Film-Video Making/Cinematography and Production; Commercial Photography; Photography; Photographic Technology/Technician	On the job, four-year college, art school, military (all branches)
27-4032.00 Film and Video Editors	Radio and Television Broadcasting Technology/ Technician; Film-Video Making/Cinematography and Production	On the job, four-year college, military (Marine Corps)

01.09 Modeling and Personal Appearance

Workers in this group pose before a camera or a live audience, or they prepare the makeup or costuming for models or performers. Models display clothing, hairstyles, and commercial products; appear in fashion shows and other public or private product exhibitions; and pose for artists and photographers. They and their makeup artists work for manufacturers, wholesalers, and retailers. Some are employed by motion picture and television studios; others work in nightclubs. Many models are self-employed, or get jobs through model agencies or unions. Makeup artists and costume attendants who attend to performers work for theaters and motion picture and television studios.

What kind of work would you do?

Your work activities would depend on your job. For example, you might

- Apply makeup to performers to alter their appearance to accord with their roles.
- Study production information, such as character, period settings, and situations, to determine makeup requirements.
- Dress in sample or completed garments and select own accessories.
- Pose as directed or strike suitable interpretive poses for promoting and selling merchandise or fashions during photo sessions.
- Design and construct costume or send it to a tailor for construction or major repairs and alterations.
- Examine costume fit on a cast member, and sketch or write notes for alterations.

What things about you point to this kind of work?

Is it important for you to

- Never be pressured to do things that go against your sense of right and wrong?
- Receive recognition for the work you do?
- Try out your own ideas?
- Get a feeling of accomplishment?
- Have good working conditions?

Have you enjoyed any of the following as a hobby or leisure-time activity?

- Acting in a play or amateur variety show
- Modeling clothes for a fashion show
- Posing for an artist or photographer
- Applying makeup for amateur theater
- Creating or styling hairdos for friends
- Being a cheerleader
- Doing needlework

Have you liked and done well in any of the following school subjects?

- Personal Grooming
- Acting Techniques
- Clothing
- Cosmetology
- Costuming
- Drama

- Fashion Illustration
- Modeling, Personal

Are you able to

- Keep your hand and arm steady while making an arm movement or while holding your arm and hand in one position?
- Match or detect differences between colors, including shades of color and brightness?
- Imagine how something will look after it is moved around or when its parts are moved or rearranged?

Would you work in places such as

- Convention and trade show centers?
- Television studios?
- Photographers' studios?
- Stores and shopping malls?
- Motion picture and recording studios?

What skills and knowledges do you need for this kind of work?

For most of these jobs, you need these skills:

- Idea Generation—generating a number of different approaches to problems
- Speaking—talking to others to effectively convey information
- Coordination—adjusting actions in relation to others' actions
- Information Organization—finding ways to structure or classify multiple pieces of information

These knowledges are important in most of these jobs:

- Fine Arts—theory and techniques required to produce, compose, and perform works of music, dance, visual arts, drama, and sculpture
- Customer and Personal Service—knowledge of principles and processes for providing customer and personal services

What else should you consider about this kind of work?

There is a good deal of competition for modeling work, since many people feel that it can lead to careers in motion picture or television acting.

To find a job, you can register at motion picture and television personnel offices and model agencies, or audition for jobs advertised in trade magazines.

Some models find permanent employment with manufacturing firms or model agencies and schools, but most work on a freelance basis. Many are registered with model and talent agencies, which refer them to job interviews for a small fee. A small number earn large salaries; many, however, hold other jobs to support themselves. Since the demand is greatest for young models, careers in the field are likely to be short.

Costume attendants and makeup artists often work irregular hours and face pressure to make quick alterations to costumes and makeup just before a performance. They may face periods of unemployment between productions.

How can you prepare for jobs of this kind?

Occupations in this group usually require education and/or training ranging from a short demonstration to more than two years.

Training for modeling is usually brief and given on the job. Modeling schools offer courses in graceful movement and personal grooming. Workers are often hired because of their appearance or size. Models may get only part-time work until the quality of their work is recognized. Because modeling careers are often short, it is helpful to get some education or training that will prepare you for other kinds of work.

Costume attendants and makeup artists usually learn their skills through vocational training in fashion design or cosmetology, often with a component of apprenticeship or more informal on-the-job learning.

SPECIALIZED TRAINING

JOBS	EDUCATION/TRAINING	WHERE OBTAINED
01.09.01 Modeling and Personal Appearance		
All in Modeling and Personal Appearance	Knowledge of fashion	Related jobs within the same industry

JOBS	EDUCATION/TRAINING	WHERE OBTAINED
01.09.01 Modeling and Personal Appearance		
39-3092.00 Costume Attendants	Custom Tailor; Clothing, Apparel, and Textile Workers and Managers, General	Apprenticeship, on the job
39-5091.00 Makeup Artists, Theatrical and Performance	Make-Up Artist; Cosmetologist	Trade/technical school, on the job
41-9012.00 Models	Fashion Modeling; Fashion Merchandising; Apparel and Accessories Marketing Operations, General	On the job, two-year college, modeling school

01.10 Sports: Coaching, Instructing, Officiating, and Performing

Workers in this group participate in professional sporting events such as football, baseball, and horse racing. Included are contestants, trainers, coaches, referees, and umpires. Some work at private recreational facilities such as ski resorts, tennis courts, and gymnasiums.

What kind of work would you do?

Your work activities would depend on your job. For example, you might

- Demonstrate skill in bronco riding, calf roping, steer wrestling, or other rodeo events.
- Evaluate team and opposition capabilities to develop and plan game strategy.
- Exercise and practice under the direction of an athletic trainer or professional coach to prepare and train for competitive events.
- Instruct athletes, individually or in groups, demonstrating sport techniques and game strategies.
- Organize and conduct competition and tournaments.
- Prepare reports to regulating organizations concerning sporting activities, complaints, and actions taken or needed, such as fines or other disciplinary actions.
- Teach and demonstrate use of gymnastic and training apparatuses, such as trampolines and weights.

What things about you point to this kind of work?

Is it important for you to

- Make use of your individual abilities?
- Get a feeling of accomplishment?
- Receive recognition for the work you do?

Have you enjoyed any of the following as a hobby or leisure-time activity?

- Coaching children or youth in sports activities
- Handling equipment for a local athletic team
- Keeping score for athletic events
- Participating in gymnastics
- Racing midget or stock cars
- Umpiring or refereeing amateur sporting events
- Playing baseball, basketball, football, or other sports

Have you liked and done well in any of the following school subjects?

- Physical Education
- Coaching
- Officiating

Are you able to

- See objects or movement of objects to your side when your eyes are focused forward?
- Quickly respond (with your hand, finger, or foot) to one signal (sound, light, picture, etc.) when it appears?
- See details at a distance?
- Coordinate the movement of your arms, legs, and torso together in activities where your whole body is in motion?
- Coordinate movements of two or more limbs together?

- Judge which of several objects is closer or farther away from you, or judge the distance between an object and you?
- Use your abdominal and lower-back muscles to support part of your body repeatedly or continuously over time?
- Listen to and understand information and ideas presented through spoken words and sentences?

Would you work in places such as

- Amusement parks, circuses, and carnivals?
- Bowling alleys?
- Country clubs and resorts?
- Gymnasiums and health clubs?
- Racetracks?
- Ships and boats?
- Sports stadiums?
- Elementary schools?
- High schools?
- Colleges and universities?

What skills and knowledges do you need for this kind of work?

For most of these jobs, you need these skills:

- Monitoring—assessing how well you are doing when learning or doing something
- Speaking—talking to others to effectively convey information
- Coordination—adjusting actions in relation to others' actions

These knowledges are important in most of these jobs:

- Education and Training—instructional methods and training techniques including curriculum design principles, learning theory, group and individual teaching techniques, design of individual development plans, and test design principles
- Biology—plant and animal living tissue, cells, organisms, and entities, including their functions, interdependencies, and interactions with each other and the environment

What else should you consider about this kind of work?

People in this group work at racetracks, golf courses, speedways, ball parks, gymnasiums, and other places where people watch sports events or participate in sports and fitness activities.

If you're interested in this kind of career, you should take part in as many school and amateur sports as possible and keep to a strict training schedule. Most coaches, scouts, and instructors have some experience as players.

Many of these jobs are seasonal. For example, most of the people who work at racetracks have other jobs when the tracks are not in session. Golf and tennis pros may do other work during the off-season, or they may contract to work at clubs in several parts of the country in order to work year-round.

A career in professional sports sounds like an exciting and glamorous way to earn a living. But there's a lot of hard work and constant competition. Frequent travel is common. The risk of physical injury is great, especially in the contact sports. Some injuries may shorten or end a player's sports career. Also, after reaching a certain age, many competitive players must find work in areas other than team play. For these reasons, expertise in a second area besides sports is desirable.

One possible career move is to instructing, officiating, coaching, or scouting. Because of the increase in professionalism and the role of women in sports such as soccer and basketball, there are more jobs in these fields, but competition remains keen.

Fitness trainers and aerobics instructors are in demand, but they often work irregular hours—part-time, evenings, and weekends.

How can you prepare for jobs of this kind?

Occupations in this group usually require education and/or training ranging from six months to more than ten years.

Professional coaches and officials often obtain the necessary training and experience by working with high school and college athletic teams. Umpires in major-league baseball usually receive training in special umpire schools and must have experience in the minor leagues. Officials in horse racing usually have some type of related work experience and receive on-the-job training.

Professional athletes often receive initial training while on high school or college teams. They are recruited by professional clubs or teams and work under a contract. Training continues as long as they remain in active competition.

Fitness trainers and aerobics instructors typically prepare by taking extensive lessons in the activity that interests them, perhaps as part of a college program in physical education. Often they need to be certified as instructors before they can teach others. Certification requirements may include knowledge of CPR.

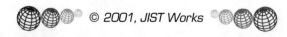

SPECIALIZED TRAINING

JOBS	EDUCATION/TRAINING	WHERE OBTAINED
01.10.01 Sports: Coaching, Instructing, Officiating, and Performing		
All in Sports: Coaching, Instructing, Officiating, and Performing	Experience; rules and techniques of sport	School and amateur athletic competitions
27-2021.00 Athletes and Sports Competitors	Health and Physical Education, General	On the job, four-year college, private lessons
27-2022.00 Coaches and Scouts	Physical Education Teaching and Coaching	On the job, four-year college
27-2023.00 Umpires, Referees, and Other Sports Officials	Umpires and Other Sports Officials; Equestrian/Equine Studies, Horse Management, and Training; Animal Trainer	On the job, two-year college
39-9031.00 Fitness Trainers and Aerobics Instructors	Education Administration and Supervision, General; Health and Physical Education, General; Physical Education Teaching and Coaching; Education, General; Adult and Continuing Teacher Education; Educational Supervision	On the job, private lessons, four-year college, military (Navy, Marine Corps, Air Force)

02 Science, Math, and Engineering

An interest in discovering, collecting, and analyzing information about the natural world; in applying scientific research findings to problems in medicine, the life sciences, and the natural sciences; in imagining and manipulating quantitative data; and in applying technology to manufacturing, transportation, mining, and other economic activities.

You can satisfy this interest by working with the knowledge and processes of the sciences. You may enjoy researching and developing new knowledge in mathematics, or perhaps solving problems in the physical or life sciences would appeal to you. You may wish to study engineering and help create new machines, processes, and structures. If you want to work with scientific equipment and procedures, you could seek a job in a research or testing laboratory.

02.01 Managerial Work in Science, Math, and Engineering

02.02 Physical Sciences

02.03 Life Sciences

02.04 Social Sciences

02.05 Laboratory Technology

02.06 Mathematics and Computers

02.07 Engineering

02.08 Engineering Technology

02.01 Managerial Work in Science, Math, and Engineering

Workers in this group manage scientists who are doing research and engineers who are applying scientific principles to solve real-world problems. They set goals, oversee financial and technical resources, and evaluate outcomes. They work for industries, government agencies, universities, and hospitals.

What kind of work would you do?

Your work activities would depend on your job. For example, you might

- Direct engineering of water control, treatment, and distribution projects.
- Establish procedures and direct testing, operation, maintenance, and repair of transmitter equipment.
- Plan and direct oilfield development, gas and oil production, and geothermal drilling.
- Prepare and administer budgets, approve and review expenditures, and prepare financial reports.
- Schedule, direct, and assign duties to engineers, technicians, researchers, and other staff.
- Provide technical assistance to agencies conducting environmental studies.

What things about you point to this kind of work?

Is it important for you to

- Have good working conditions?
- Plan your work with little supervision?
- Give directions and instructions to others?

Have you enjoyed any of the following as a hobby or leisure-time activity?

- Conducting experiments involving plants
- Experimenting with a chemistry set
- Serving as president of a club or other organization
- Using a pocket calculator or spreadsheet to figure out income and expenses for an organization
- Budgeting the family income
- Helping run a school or community fair or carnival
- Reading about technological developments, such as computer science or aerospace

Have you liked and done well in any of the following school subjects?

- Management
- Biology
- Physics
- Accounting
- Personnel Management
- Physical Science

Are you able to

- Listen to and understand information and ideas presented through spoken words and sentences?
- Read and understand information and ideas presented in writing?
- Communicate information and ideas in writing so others will understand?
- Communicate information and ideas in speaking so others will understand?
- Apply general rules to specific problems to come up with logical answers?
- Combine separate pieces of information, or specific answers to problems, to form general rules or conclusions?
- Speak clearly so that it is understandable to a listener?

Would you work in places such as

- Colleges and universities?
- Factories and plants?
- Business offices?
- Fish hatcheries?
- Laboratories?
- Forests?
- Oil fields?
- Computer centers?
- Waterworks and light and power plants?
- Government offices?

What skills and knowledges do you need for this kind of work?

For most of these jobs, you need these skills:

- Coordination—adjusting actions in relation to others' actions

- Implementation Planning—developing approaches for implementing an idea
- Reading Comprehension—understanding written sentences and paragraphs in work-related documents
- Critical Thinking—using logic and analysis to identify the strengths and weaknesses of different approaches
- Speaking—talking to others to effectively convey information
- Judgment and Decision Making—weighing the relative costs and benefits of a potential action

These knowledges are important in most of these jobs:

- Administration and Management—principles and processes involved in business and organizational planning, coordination, and execution
- Mathematics—numbers, their operations, and interrelationships including arithmetic, algebra, geometry, calculus, statistics, and their applications

What else should you consider about this kind of work?

Engineering and science managers are employed by government agencies, industry, and colleges throughout the country.

Generally they work most often in business offices, classrooms, or research laboratories, but they sometimes need to visit such sites as the floor of a plant where manufacturing is being done, a remote natural setting where research is being conducted, or an urban neighborhood where surveying is being done.

How can you prepare for jobs of this kind?

Occupations in engineering and science management usually require education and/or training ranging from four years to more than ten years.

The most common route to management is by first preparing to be a scientist, programmer, engineer, or some other worker in science, math, or engineering. After gaining experience and expertise in this kind of job, you might get formal or informal training in management that prepares you to deal with setting goals, measuring outcomes, accounting for financial resources, and managing human resources. Another possible route is to major in management in college, with a minor or second degree in a field related to science, math, or engineering.

SPECIALIZED TRAINING

JOBS	EDUCATION/TRAINING	WHERE OBTAINED
02.01.01 Managerial Work in Science, Math, and Engineering		
All in Managerial Work in Science, Math, and Engineering	Experience; Budgeting; Personnel; Oral and Written Communications	Four-year college, graduate school, related jobs within the same industry
11-3021.00 Computer and Information Systems Managers	Management Information Systems and Business Data Processing, General	Four-year college, military (all branches)
11-9041.00 Engineering Managers	Water Resources Engineering; Engineering/Industrial Management; Surveying; Civil Engineering, General	Four-year college, graduate school, military (Army, Navy, Air Force, Coast Guard)
11-9121.00 Natural Sciences Managers	Natural Resources Conservation, General; Environmental Science/Studies	Four-year college, graduate school, military (Marine Corps)

02.02 Physical Sciences

Workers in this group are concerned mostly with nonliving things, such as chemicals, rocks, metals, and movements of the earth and stars. They conduct scientific studies and perform other activities requiring a knowledge of math, physics, or chemistry. Some workers investigate, discover, and test new theories. Some develop new or improved materials or processes for use in production and construction. Some do research in such fields as geology, astronomy, oceanography, and meteorology. Workers base their conclusions on information that can be measured or proved. Industries, government agencies, and large universities employ most of these workers in research facilities.

What kind of work would you do?

Your work activities would depend on your job. For example, you might

- Analyze and interpret meteorological data gathered by surface and upper-air stations, satellites, and radar to prepare reports and forecasts.
- Construct and interpret maps, graphs, and diagrams.
- Compute positions of sun, moon, planets, stars, nebulae, and galaxies.
- Investigate origin and activity of glaciers, volcanoes, and earthquakes.
- Perform computations and apply methods of numerical analysis.
- Prepare environmental impact reports based on results of study.
- Study and test hypotheses and alternative theories.

What things about you point to this kind of work?

Is it important for you to

- Plan your work with little supervision?
- Make use of your individual abilities?
- Never be pressured to do things that go against your sense of right and wrong?
- Make decisions on your own?

Have you enjoyed any of the following as a hobby or leisure-time activity?

- Experimenting with a chemistry set
- Performing experiments for a science fair
- Reading about technological developments such as computer science or aerospace
- Reading medical or scientific magazines
- Belonging to a computer club
- Collecting rocks or minerals

Have you liked and done well in any of the following school subjects?

- Research Methods
- Physics
- Geography
- Astronomy
- Geology, Specialized/Advanced
- Chemistry, Advanced/Specialized
- Calculus
- Ecology/Environmental Science
- Meteorology
- Physical Science

Are you able to

- Read and understand information and ideas presented in writing?
- Communicate information and ideas in writing so others will understand?
- Understand and organize a problem and then select a mathematical method or formula to solve the problem?
- Apply general rules to specific problems to come up with logical answers?
- Combine separate pieces of information, or specific answers to problems, to form general rules or conclusions?
- Add, subtract, multiply, or divide quickly and correctly?
- Listen to and understand information and ideas presented through spoken words and sentences?
- Communicate information and ideas in speaking so others will understand?

Would you work in places such as

- Laboratories?
- Colleges and universities?
- Business offices?
- Mines and quarries?
- Ships and boats?
- Computer centers?

What skills and knowledges do you need for this kind of work?

For most of these jobs, you need these skills:

- Science—using scientific methods to solve problems
- Mathematics—using mathematics to solve problems
- Information Gathering—knowing how to find information and identifying essential information
- Reading Comprehension—understanding written sentences and paragraphs in work-related documents
- Active Learning—working with new material or information to grasp its implications
- Critical Thinking—using logic and analysis to identify the strengths and weaknesses of different approaches
- Programming—writing computer programs for various purposes

These knowledges are important in most of these jobs:

- Mathematics—numbers, their operations, and interrelationships including arithmetic, algebra, geometry, calculus, statistics, and their applications
- Physics—physical principles, laws, and applications including air, water, material dynamics, light, atomic principles, heat, electric theory, earth formations, and meteorological and related natural phenomena

What else should you consider about this kind of work?

Workers in this group are employed in large and small communities across the country.

Some of the jobs require traveling to conduct field trips, during which workers must live without the usual domestic comforts. Physical scientists may be required to work long hours to meet research deadlines or to complete experiments. They must keep informed of the most recent developments in their fields by attending seminars, reading professional journals, and being active in professional organizations.

Job outlook is mixed, with some specializations in greater demand, especially those that have direct, practical applications other than defense.

How can you prepare for jobs of this kind?

Occupations in the physical sciences usually require education and/or training ranging from four years to more than ten years. A bachelor's degree with a major in mathematics or a specific physical science is the minimum requirement for entrance into this field. Graduate degrees are needed for most research work and college teaching. A master's degree may qualify an individual for work in laboratory teaching or applied research in a college, university, or industrial setting. Advanced studies or a Ph.D. are usually required for work in basic research. Important courses include algebra, geometry, advanced math, physics, and earth and space science. Chemistry and technical writing courses are helpful and in some cases required.

SPECIALIZED TRAINING

JOBS	EDUCATION/TRAINING	WHERE OBTAINED
02.02.01 Physical Sciences		
All in Physical Sciences	Data Processing; Programming Language; Analytic Geometry; Calculus; experience	Four-year college, graduate school, related jobs within the same industry
19-2011.00 Astronomers	Earth and Planetary Sciences; Astrophysics; Astronomy	Four-year college, graduate school, military (Navy)
19-2012.00 Physicists	Nuclear Physics; Chemistry, General; Earth and Planetary Sciences; Physics, General; Chemical and Atomic/Molecular Physics; Plasma and High-Temperature Physics; Astrophysics; Optics; Solid State and Low-Temperature Physics; Acoustics; Theoretical and Mathematical Physics; Health Physics/Radiologic Health; Astronomy; Elementary Particle Physics; Physical and Theoretical Chemistry	Four-year college, graduate school, military (Army, Navy, Coast Guard)

JOBS	EDUCATION/TRAINING	WHERE OBTAINED
	02.02.01 Physical Sciences	
19-2021.00 Atmospheric and Space Scientists	Atmospheric Sciences and Meteorology	Four-year college, graduate school, military (Navy, Air Force, Marine Corps, Coast Guard)
19-2031.00 Chemists	Chemical and Atomic/Molecular Physics; Physics, General; Physical and Theoretical Chemistry; Medicinal/Pharmaceutical Chemistry; Organic Chemistry; Inorganic Chemistry; Analytical Chemistry; Chemistry, General	Four-year college, graduate school, military (Army, Navy, Air Force, Marine Corps)
19-2032.00 Materials Scientists	Materials Science	Four-year college, graduate school
19-2042.01 Geologists	Geology; Geochemistry; Geophysics and Seismology; Paleontology; Oceanography; Anthropology; Geography; Mining Technology/Technician	Four-year college, graduate school, military (Navy, Coast Guard)
19-2043.00 Hydrologists	Geology; Geophysics and Seismology; Oceanography	Four-year college, graduate school, military (Navy, Coast Guard)
19-3092.00 Geographers	Geography	Four-year college, graduate school

02.03 Life Sciences

Workers in this group do research and conduct experiments to find out more about plants, animals, and other living things. Some study methods of producing better species of plants or animals; some work to find ways of preserving the natural balance in the environment. Others conduct research to improve medicine, health, and living conditions for human beings. These jobs are found in manufacturing plants, government agencies, universities, and hospitals.

What kind of work would you do?

Your work activities would depend on your job. For example, you might

- Collect and analyze biological data about relationships among and between organisms and their environment.
- Conduct public educational programs on forest care and conservation.
- Develop improved manufacturing methods for natural and synthetic fibers.
- Develop methods of extracting drugs from aquatic plants and animals.
- Investigate transmission of electrical impulses along nerves and muscles.
- Observe action of microorganisms upon living tissues of plants.
- Provide advice on rural or urban land use.

What things about you point to this kind of work?

Is it important for you to

- Plan your work with little supervision?
- Make use of your individual abilities?
- Make decisions on your own?

Have you enjoyed any of the following as a hobby or leisure-time activity?

- Studying the habits of wildlife
- Conducting experiments involving plants
- Experimenting with a chemistry set
- Nursing sick pets
- Performing experiments for a science fair
- Reading medical or scientific magazines
- Studying plants in gardens, parks, or forests

Have you liked and done well in any of the following school subjects?

- Biology
- Research Methods
- Biochemistry
- Soil Science
- Zoology
- Veterinary Sciences
- Physiology
- Microbiology
- Genetics
- Food Science

Are you able to

- Apply general rules to specific problems to come up with logical answers?
- Combine separate pieces of information, or specific answers to problems, to form general rules or conclusions?
- Read and understand information and ideas presented in writing?
- See details of objects at close range (within a few feet)?
- Communicate information and ideas in writing so others will understand?
- Tell when something is wrong or is likely to go wrong?
- Correctly follow a given rule or set of rules in order to arrange things or actions in a certain order?

Would you work in places such as

- Laboratories?
- Colleges and universities?
- Fish hatcheries?
- Farms?
- Forests?
- Zoos and aquariums?
- Hospitals and nursing homes?
- Animal hospitals, boarding kennels, and grooming parlors?
- Factories and plants?

What skills and knowledges do you need for this kind of work?

For most of these jobs, you need these skills:

- Science–using scientific methods to solve problems
- Reading Comprehension–understanding written sentences and paragraphs in work-related documents
- Information Gathering–knowing how to find information and identifying essential information
- Critical Thinking–using logic and analysis to identify the strengths and weaknesses of different approaches
- Active Learning–working with new material or information to grasp its implications
- Programming–writing computer programs for various purposes

These knowledges are important in most of these jobs:

- Biology–plant and animal living tissue, cells, organisms, and entities, including their functions, interdependencies, and interactions with each other and the environment
- Chemistry–the composition, structure, and properties of substances and of the chemical processes and transformations that they undergo.
- Mathematics–numbers, their operations, and interrelationships including arithmetic, algebra, geometry, calculus, statistics, and their applications

What else should you consider about this kind of work?

Some students and workers in this field must handle tissues and waste products of humans and animals. Some work in remote areas such as forests and deserts.

Life scientists must keep informed of developments in their fields by attending seminars, reading professional books and magazines, and being active in professional organizations. Chances of employment are best for those with advanced degrees in life sciences along with some experience in a related field.

How can you prepare for jobs of this kind?

Occupations in this group usually call for education and/or training ranging from four years to more than ten years. Important academic courses include algebra, geometry, advanced math, chemistry, and physics.

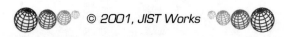

Technical writing and composition courses are helpful. A bachelor's degree with a major in biology or another life science is generally required; graduate degrees are needed for most research work and college teaching. A master's degree may qualify a person for laboratory teaching. Advanced studies or a Ph.D. are usually required for basic research positions.

SPECIALIZED TRAINING

JOBS	EDUCATION/TRAINING	WHERE OBTAINED
02.03.01 Life Sciences: Animal Specialization		
All in Life Sciences: Animal Specialization	Chemistry; Statistics; Biology; Chordate Anatomy	Four-year college, graduate school
19-1011.00 Animal Scientists	Agricultural Animal Health; Poultry Science; Agricultural Animal Nutrition; Agricultural Animal Breeding and Genetics; Animal Sciences, General; Agriculture/Agricultural Sciences, General; Dairy Science	Four-year college, graduate school
19-1023.00 Zoologists and Wildlife Biologists	Zoology, General	Four-year college, graduate school
19-1041.00 Epidemiologists	Epidemiology; Environmental Health; Health Physics/Radiologic Health; Biophysics; Biotechnology Research; Toxicology; Parasitology; Anatomy; Biological Immunology; Zoology, General; Pharmacology, Human and Animal; Microbiology/Bacteriology; Biochemistry; Medical Anatomy; Medical Pathology; Medical Physics/Biophysics; Medical Pharmacology and Pharmaceutical Sciences; Basic Medical Sciences, Other	Four-year college, graduate school, medical school, military (Army, Navy, Air Force)
19-1042.00 Medical Scientists, Except Epidemiologists	Medical Pharmacology and Pharmaceutical Sciences; Toxicology; Epidemiology; Parasitology; Anatomy; Basic Medical Sciences, Other; Biological Immunology; Biophysics; Zoology, General; Medical Anatomy; Pharmacology, Human and Animal; Microbiology/Bacteriology; Environmental Health; Medical Physics/Biophysics; Biotechnology Research; Biochemistry; Health Physics/Radiologic Health; Medical Pathology	Four-year college, graduate school, medical school
02.03.02 Life Sciences: Plant Specialization		
All in Life Sciences: Plant Specialization	Botany; Agricultural Systems; Taxonomy; Zoology; Horticulture; Plant Pathology; Quantitative Analysis; Soil Chemistry; Statistics	Four-year college, graduate school
19-1013.01 Plant Scientists	Plant Breeding and Genetics; Agricultural Plant Pathology; Agricultural Plant Physiology; Plant Protection (Pest Management); Range Science and Management; Plant Sciences, Other; Agriculture/Agricultural Sciences, Other; Horticulture Science; Entomology; Plant Sciences, General; Agronomy and Crop Science; Agricultural Extension; Agriculture/Agricultural Sciences, General	Four-year college, graduate school

(continues)

(continued)

SPECIALIZED TRAINING

JOBS	EDUCATION/TRAINING	WHERE OBTAINED
02.03.02 Life Sciences: Plant Specialization		
19-1013.02 Soil Scientists	Range Science and Management; Soil Sciences; Agricultural Extension; Agriculture/Agricultural Sciences, General	Four-year college, graduate school
19-1031.01 Soil Conservationists	Forestry Sciences; Forest Management; Natural Resources Conservation, General; Soil Sciences; Forestry, General	Four-year college, graduate school
19-1031.02 Range Managers	Plant Sciences, General; Range Science and Management; Natural Resources Conservation, General	Four-year college, graduate school
19-1032.00 Foresters	Horticulture Services Operations and Management, General; Natural Resources Conservation, General; Forest Harvesting and Production Technology/Technician; Nursery Operations and Management; Forestry Sciences; Forest Management; Forestry, General	Four-year college, graduate school
02.03.03 Life Sciences: Plant and Animal Specialization		
All in Life Sciences: Plant and Animal Specialization	Chemistry; Statistics; Biology; Botany; Chordate Anatomy	Four-year college, graduate school
19-1020.01 Biologists	Marine/Aquatic Biology; Basic Medical Sciences, Other; Zoology, General	Four-year college, graduate school, medical school
19-1021.00 Biochemists and Biophysicists	Medical Microbiology; Biostatistics; Entomology; Biotechnology Research; Evolutionary Biology; Biological Immunology; Virology; Biometrics; Miscellaneous Biological Specializations, Other; Zoology, General; Pathology, Human and Animal; Pharmacology, Human and Animal; Physiology, Human and Animal; Zoology, Other; Medical Cell Biology; Medical Physiology; Medical Toxicology; Basic Medical Sciences, Other; Environmental Health; Marine/Aquatic Biology; Genetics, Plant and Animal; Medical Physics/Biophysics; Botany, General; Toxicology; Plant Sciences, General; Agricultural Plant Pathology; Agricultural Plant Physiology; Biology, General; Nutritional Sciences; Biophysics; Plant Pathology; Plant Physiology; Botany, Other; Parasitology; Molecular Biology; Cell and Molecular Biology, Other; Radiation Biology/Radiobiology; Microbiology/Bacteriology; Anatomy; Ecology; Neuroscience; Cell Biology; Biochemistry	Four-year college, graduate school

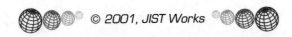

JOBS	EDUCATION/TRAINING	WHERE OBTAINED
02.03.03 Life Sciences: Plant and Animal Specialization		
19-1021.01 Biochemists	Zoology, General; Pharmacology, Human and Animal; Biotechnology Research; Biophysics; Biochemistry; Medical Biochemistry	Four-year college, graduate school, medical school, military (Army, Navy, Air Force)
19-1021.02 Biophysicists	Medical Physics/Biophysics; Biochemistry; Biophysics	Four-year college, graduate school, medical school
19-1022.00 Microbiologists	Biochemistry; Microbiology/Bacteriology; Virology; Medical Microbiology; Cell Biology	Four-year college, graduate school, medical school, military (Army, Navy, Air Force)
19-1031.00 Conservation Scientists	Natural Resources Law Enforcement and Protective Services; Forestry Sciences; Conservation and Renewable Natural Resources, Other; Forestry and Related Sciences, Other; Wood Science and Pulp/Paper Technology; Forest Management; Natural Resources Management and Protective Services, Other; Natural Resources Management and Policy; Natural Resources Conservation, General; Soil Sciences; Range Science and Management; Forestry, General	Four-year college, graduate school
19-2041.00 Environmental Scientists and Specialists, Including Health	Natural Resources Law; Enforcement and Protective Services; Forestry Sciences; Conservation and Renewable Natural Resources, Other; Forestry and Related Sciences, Other; Wood Science and Pulp/Paper Technology; Forest Management; Natural Resources Management and Protective Services, Other; Natural Resources Management and Policy; Natural Resources Conservation, General; Soil Sciences; Range Science and Management; Forestry, General	Four-year college, graduate school
02.03.04 Life Sciences: Food Research		
All in Life Sciences: Food Research	Quantitative Analysis; Genetics; Bacteriology; Human Nutrition; Food Toxicology	Four-year college, graduate school
19-1012.00 Food Scientists and Technologists	Agriculture/Agricultural Sciences, General; Food Sciences and Technology; Foods and Nutrition Studies, General; Foods and Nutrition Science	Four-year college, graduate school
19-4011.01 Agricultural Technicians	Animal Sciences, General; Dairy Science; Biological Technology/Technician	Two-year college, graduate school
19-4011.02 Food Science Technicians	Chemical Technology/Technician; Food Sciences and Technology; Occupational Safety and Health Technology/Technician	Two-year college, trade/technical school

02.04 Social Sciences

Workers in this group gather, study, and analyze information about individuals, groups, or entire societies. They conduct research into all aspects of human behavior, including abnormal behavior, language, work, politics, lifestyle, and cultural expression. They are employed by schools and colleges, government agencies, businesses, museums, and private research foundations.

What kind of work would you do?

Your work activities would depend on your job. For example, you might

- Reconstruct and decipher ancient languages from examples found in archeological remains of past civilizations.
- Develop research designs on the basis of existing knowledge and evolving theory.
- Gather, analyze, and report data on human physique, social customs, and artifacts such as weapons, tools, pottery, and clothing.
- Organize and conduct public-opinion surveys and interpret results.
- Supervise research projects and students' study projects.
- Study consumer reaction to new products and package designs, using surveys and tests, and measure the effectiveness of advertising media.
- Teach theories, principles, and methods of economics.

What things about you point to this kind of work?

Is it important for you to

- Plan your work with little supervision?
- Have good working conditions?
- Make use of your individual abilities?
- Get a feeling of accomplishment?

Have you enjoyed any of the following as a hobby or leisure-time activity?

- Belonging to a political science club
- Campaigning for political candidates or issues
- Conducting house-to-house or telephone surveys for a PTA or other organization
- Reading business magazines and newspapers
- Visiting museums or historic sites

Have you liked and done well in any of the following school subjects?

- Research Methods
- Psychology, Advanced/Specialized
- Social Anthropology
- Sociology
- History
- Archeology
- Political Science
- Human Growth and Development
- Economics

Are you able to

- Read and understand information and ideas presented in writing?
- Communicate information and ideas in writing so others will understand?
- Listen to and understand information and ideas presented through spoken words and sentences?
- Communicate information and ideas in speaking so others will understand?
- Combine separate pieces of information, or specific answers to problems, to form general rules or conclusions?
- Apply general rules to specific problems to come up with logical answers?
- See details of objects at close range (within a few feet)?

Would you work in places such as

- Business offices?
- Doctors' and dentists' offices and clinics?
- Colleges and universities?
- Factories and plants?
- Jails and reformatories?
- Laboratories?
- Government offices?

What skills and knowledges do you need for this kind of work?

For most of these jobs, you need these skills:

- Information Gathering—knowing how to find information and identifying essential information
- Writing—communicating effectively with others in writing as indicated by their needs

- Reading Comprehension—understanding written sentences and paragraphs in work-related documents
- Information Organization—finding ways to structure or classify multiple pieces of information
- Programming—writing computer programs for various purposes

These knowledges are important in most of these jobs:

- English Language—the structure and content of the English language including the meaning and spelling of words, rules of composition, and grammar
- Mathematics—numbers, their operations, and interrelationships including arithmetic, algebra, geometry, calculus, statistics, and their applications

What else should you consider about this kind of work?

Many people in this group work for government agencies of one kind or another. Some work for private businesses, and others for museums and other nonprofit institutions, or for colleges and universities. You can apply directly for some of the government jobs, but for most you have to go through civil-service channels.

Some of these workers are self-employed. They may get grants from the government or private groups to do research, or they may do special studies for business, industry, or government.

Most of this work is done during regular business hours. Archeologists and anthropologists make field trips to distant places in this country and abroad.

How can you prepare for jobs of this kind?

Almost all occupations in this group require four or more years of college study in the social sciences. Some jobs call for specialization in a particular field such as government, sociology, history, economics, or psychology. Courses in computer science and statistics are important for use in handling research data. Coursework in English and math is also very helpful.

Employers expect workers in this group to keep up with developments and trends in their area. This is done by reading journals, attending seminars and workshops, and studying for advanced degrees.

SPECIALIZED TRAINING

JOBS	EDUCATION/TRAINING	WHERE OBTAINED
02.04.01 Social Sciences: Psychology, Sociology, and Anthropology		
All in Social Sciences: Psychology, Sociology, and Anthropology	Psychology; Statistics; Writing	Four-year college, graduate school
19-3032.00 Industrial-Organizational Psychologists	Social Psychology; Psychology, General; Industrial and Organizational Psychology	Four-year college, graduate school, military (Navy, Air Force)
19-3041.00 Sociologists	Sociology; Criminal Justice Studies; Anthropology; Criminology; Political Science, General; Urban Affairs/Studies; Demography/Population Studies	Four-year college, graduate school
19-3091.01 Anthropologists	International Relations and Affairs; Demography/Population Studies; Archeology; Anthropology; Music, General; Musicology and Ethnomusicology; Sociology	Four-year college, graduate school
19-3091.02 Archeologists	Anthropology; Archeology	Four-year college, graduate school

(continues)

(continued)

SPECIALIZED TRAINING

JOBS	EDUCATION/TRAINING	WHERE OBTAINED
02.04.02 Social Sciences: Economics, Public Policy, and History		
All in Social Sciences: Economics, Public Policy, and History	Economics; History; Government; Statistics; Writing	Four-year college, graduate school
19-3011.00 Economists	Business/Managerial Economics; Agricultural Economics; Economics, General; Applied and Resource Economics; Econometrics and Quantitative Economics; Development Economics and International Development; International Economics; Economics, Other; Agricultural Business and Management, General	Four-year college, graduate school
19-3022.00 Survey Researchers	Business/Managerial Economics; Agricultural Economics; Economics, General; Applied and Resource Economics; Econometrics and Quantitative Economics; Development Economics and International Development; International Economics; Economics, Other	Four-year college, graduate school
19-3051.00 Urban and Regional Planners	Architectural Urban Design and Planning; Public Policy Analysis; City/Urban, Community, and Regional Planning	Four-year college, graduate school
19-3093.00 Historians	Political Science, General; European History; American (United States) History; Business Administration and Management, General; Drama/Theater Literature, History, and Criticism; Drama/Theater Arts, General; History and Philosophy of Science and Technology; Public/Applied History and Archival Administration; International Relations and Affairs; History, General	Four-year college, graduate school, military (Navy, Air Force, Marine Corps)
19-3094.00 Political Scientists	Political Science and Government, Other; American Government and Politics; Political Science, General; International Relations and Affairs	Four-year college, graduate school
19-4061.00 Social Science Research Assistants	Education, General	Four-year college
19-4061.01 City Planning Aides	Civil Engineering/Civil Technology/Technician	Four-year college

02.05 Laboratory Technology

Workers in this group use special laboratory techniques and equipment to perform tests in such fields as chemistry, biology, and physics; then they record information resulting from their experiments and tests. These reports are used by scientists, medical doctors, researchers, and engineers. Hospitals, government agencies, universities, and private industries employ these workers in their laboratories and research activities.

What kind of work would you do?

Your work activities would depend on your job. For example, you might

- Analyze samples of toxic materials to identify compounds and develop treatment.
- Calibrate microscopes and test instruments.
- Dissect, trim, and stain sections of plants or animals to display desired features.
- Evaluate and interpret core samples and cuttings, and other geological data used in prospecting for oil or gas.
- Inspect engines for wear and defective parts, using equipment and measuring devices.
- Taste or smell food or beverages to ensure flavor meets specifications or to select samples with specific characteristics.
- Water and feed rations to livestock and laboratory animals.

What things about you point to this kind of work?

Is it important for you to

- Never be pressured to do things that go against your sense of right and wrong?
- Have steady employment?

Have you enjoyed any of the following as a hobby or leisure-time activity?

- Conducting experiments involving plants
- Developing film
- Experimenting with a chemistry set
- Performing experiments for a science fair
- Reading about technological developments, such as computer science or aerospace
- Reading medical or scientific magazines
- Studying plants in gardens, parks, or forests

Have you liked and done well in any of the following school subjects?

- Laboratory Science
- Chemistry
- Chemical Safety
- Research Methods
- Biology
- Math Computing, Standard Formula
- Photography
- Physical Science

Are you able to

- See details of objects at close range (within a few feet)?
- Correctly follow a given rule or set of rules in order to arrange things or actions in a certain order?
- Communicate information and ideas in writing so others will understand?
- Apply general rules to specific problems to come up with logical answers?
- Read and understand information and ideas presented in writing?
- Quickly and repeatedly make precise adjustments in moving the controls of a machine or vehicle to exact positions?

Would you work in places such as

- Laboratories?
- Animal hospitals, boarding kennels, and grooming parlors?
- Colleges and universities?
- Factories and plants?
- Farms?
- Fish hatcheries?
- Hospitals and nursing homes?
- Waterworks and light and power plants?
- Zoos and aquariums?

What skills and knowledges do you need for this kind of work?

For most of these jobs, you need these skills:

- Science—using scientific methods to solve problems

- Information Gathering—knowing how to find information and identifying essential information

These knowledges are important in most of these jobs:

- Mathematics—numbers, their operations, and interrelationships including arithmetic, algebra, geometry, calculus, statistics, and their applications
- Chemistry—the composition, structure, and properties of substances and of the chemical processes and transformations that they undergo

What else should you consider about this kind of work?

Laboratory technology workers are hired by hospitals; medical, commercial, and industrial testing laboratories; water-treatment and power-distribution facilities; and funeral homes.

Hospital laboratories may require that you work evening or night shifts, or weekends and holidays. Most other work is done on a regular schedule. Occasional-to-frequent travel is required on jobs with oil-producing and mining companies.

There are usually openings for beginners in medical laboratory work in all parts of the country.

How can you prepare for jobs of this kind?

Occupations in this group usually require education and/or training ranging from one year to more than ten years. Most of the jobs are entry positions requiring a two- to four-year degree. Some workers move into laboratory or testing work from production areas. On-the-job training is sometimes available to applicants who have appropriate skills or work-related/military experience. Some jobs are offered to those who have taken scientific or technical courses in high school or a post-high-school program. Courses in chemistry, physical science, math, and report writing are helpful.

SPECIALIZED TRAINING

JOBS	EDUCATION/TRAINING	WHERE OBTAINED
02.05.01 Laboratory Technology: Physical Sciences		
All in Laboratory Technology: Physical Sciences	Physical Science; Algebra; Shop Math	High school, two-year college, trade/technical school
19-4031.00 Chemical Technicians	Medical Laboratory Assistant; Chemical Technology/Technician; Petroleum Technology/Technician; Quality Control Technology/Technician; Food Sciences and Technology; Automotive Engineering Technology/Technician	Two-year college, trade/technical school, military (Army, Navy)
19-4041.00 Geological and Petroleum Technicians	Hydraulic Technology/Technician; Industrial Production Technology/Technicians, Other; Aeronautical and Aerospace Engineering Technology/Technician; Mechanical Engineering-Related Technology/Technicians, Other; Mining Technology/Technician; Engineering-Related Technology/Technicians, Other; Mining and Petroleum Technology/Technicians, Other; Engineering-Related Technology/Technician, General; Metallurgical Technology/Technician; Environmental Control Technology/Technicians, Other; Environmental and Pollution Control Technology/Technician; Water Quality and Wastewater Treatment Technology/Technician; Energy Management and Systems Technology/Technician; Petroleum Technology/Technician; Physical Science Technology/Technicians, Other	Two-year college, trade/technical school; military data not yet available

JOBS	EDUCATION/TRAINING	WHERE OBTAINED
	02.05.01 Laboratory Technology: Physical Sciences	
19-4041.01 Geological Data Technicians	Petroleum Technology/Technician	Two-year college, trade/technical school
19-4041.02 Geological Sample Test Technicians	Petroleum Technology/Technician; Chemical Technology/Technician; Physical Science Technology/ Technicians, Other	Two-year college, trade/technical school, military (Coast Guard)
19-4051.00 Nuclear Technicians	Industrial Radiologic Technology/Technician; Nuclear and Industrial Radiologic Technology/Technicians, Other; Nuclear/Nuclear Power Technology/Technician	Two-year college, trade/technical school
19-4051.01 Nuclear Equipment Operation Technicians	Industrial Radiologic Technology/Technician; Nuclear and Industrial Radiologic Technology/Technicians, Other	Two-year college, trade/technical school
	02.05.02 Laboratory Technology: Life Sciences	
All in Laboratory Technology: Life Sciences	Life Science; Chemistry; Biology; Math Computing (Fractions and Decimals); Report Writing	High school, two-year college, four-year college
19-4021.00 Biological Technicians	Agricultural Animal Nutrition; Agricultural Production Workers and Managers, General; Agricultural Animal Husbandry and Production Management; Animal Sciences, General; Plant Sciences, General; Agronomy and Crop Science; Biological Technology/Technician; Crop Production Operations and Management	Two-year college, trade/technical school
19-4091.00 Environmental Science and Protection Technicians, Including Health	Environmental Control Technology/Technicians, Other; Chemical Technology/Technician	Two-year college, trade/technical school, military (Air Force, Coast Guard)
27-4021.02 Photographers, Scientific	Commercial Photography; Photography; Ophthalmic Medical Technologist	On the job, two-year college, trade/ technical school, military (Navy, Air Force, Coast Guard)

02.06 Mathematics and Computers

Workers in this group use advanced math, statistics, and computer programs to solve problems and conduct research. They analyze and interpret numerical data for planning and decision making. Some of these workers determine how computers may best be used to solve problems or process information. Businesses and industries, colleges, research organizations, and government agencies hire these workers. Some programmers work as consultants on changing assignments.

What kind of work would you do?

Your work activities would depend on your job. For example, you might

- Assist users to identify and solve data communication problems.
- Design or review insurance and pension plans and calculate premiums.
- Develop statistical methodology.
- Direct programmers and analysts to make changes to database management systems.
- Meet with users to develop system or project requirements.
- Translate data into numerical values, equations, flowcharts, graphs, or other media.
- Write instructions to guide operating personnel during production runs.

What things about you point to this kind of work?

Is it important for you to

- Make use of your individual abilities?
- Plan your work with little supervision?
- Have good working conditions?

Have you enjoyed any of the following as a hobby or leisure-time activity?

- Belonging to a computer club
- Budgeting the family income
- Creating a Web page for an organization
- Performing experiments for a science fair
- Programming computer games
- Reading about technological developments, such as computer science or aerospace
- Upgrading hardware in a personal computer

Have you liked and done well in any of the following school subjects?

- Computer Programming
- Computer Concept/Methods
- Database Theory/Design
- Data Retrieval Techniques
- Statistics, Advanced/Specialized
- Math Computing, Advanced/Specialized
- Computer Network Management
- Geographic Information Systems
- Systems Analysis

Are you able to

- Understand and organize a problem and then select a mathematical method or formula to solve the problem?
- Read and understand information and ideas presented in writing?
- Communicate information and ideas in speaking so others will understand?
- Add, subtract, multiply, or divide quickly and correctly?
- Apply general rules to specific problems to come up with logical answers?
- Listen to and understand information and ideas presented through spoken words and sentences?
- Communicate information and ideas in writing so others will understand?

Would you work in places such as

- Computer centers?
- Colleges and universities?
- Factories and plants?
- Business offices?
- Government offices?
- Hospitals and nursing homes?
- Motion picture and recording studios?

What skills and knowledges do you need for this kind of work?

For most of these jobs, you need these skills:

- Reading Comprehension—understanding written sentences and paragraphs in work-related documents

- Critical Thinking—using logic and analysis to identify the strengths and weaknesses of different approaches
- Programming—writing computer programs for various purposes

These knowledges are important in most of these jobs:

- Computers and Electronics—electric circuit boards, processors, chips, and computer hardware and software, including applications and programming
- Mathematics—numbers, their operations, and interrelationships including arithmetic, algebra, geometry, calculus, statistics, and their applications

What else should you consider about this kind of work?

People are hired for data-processing work for all kinds of businesses and industries, government agencies, and service firms. Those trained in financial analysis are most likely to have jobs with such places as banks, insurance companies, and government offices. Those trained in scientific analysis are most likely to work in colleges and in industrial research centers.

There are many openings for well-trained beginners in this group. People in government jobs are sometimes appointed, but usually must pass civil-service tests. If you're interested in working in data processing design, you can improve your chances of getting a job by learning about as many different kinds of equipment and knowing as many computer languages as possible.

Beginners usually start as trainees even though they have the required education, because the technology changes so fast that previous education or work may not be fully relevant to the new job. New hires are promoted to higher-level work after getting experience on the job. Actuaries and some other workers must continue to take tests after employment to upgrade their accreditation in the field. The tests are prepared by national professional organizations.

How can you prepare for jobs of this kind?

Occupations in this group usually require education and/or training ranging from two years to more than ten years. Coursework in math concepts, technical writing, economics, computer science, programming languages, and accounting are useful for jobs in this group. Most of the jobs call for four or more years of study in mathematics and statistics at the college level.

Experience in banking, accounting, or a related field is helpful for some jobs. Other jobs call for experience and training in a scientific or technical area.

Workers in this group are expected to keep up with developments and trends in their areas (the computer field in particular is very fast moving). They attend seminars and workshops, or study for advanced degrees.

SPECIALIZED TRAINING

JOBS	EDUCATION/TRAINING	WHERE OBTAINED
02.06.01 Mathematics and Computers: Data Processing		
All in Mathematics and Computers: Data Processing	Programming Languages; Algebra; Keyboarding	High school, two- or four-year college, hobbyist experience
15-1011.00 Computer and Information Scientists, Research	Data Processing Technology/Technician; Business Information and Data Processing Services, Other; Business Systems Networking and Telecommunications; Business Systems Analysis and Design; Business Computer Programming/Programmer; Computer and Information Sciences, Other; Information Sciences and Systems; Computer Systems Analysis; Computer Programming; Computer and Information Sciences, General; Computer Science	Four-year college; military data not yet available
15-1021.00 Computer Programmers	Computer Programming; Management Information Systems and Business Data Processing, General; Business Computer Programming/Programmer	Two-year college, four-year college, military (all branches)

(continues)

(continued)

SPECIALIZED TRAINING

JOBS	EDUCATION/TRAINING	WHERE OBTAINED
02.06.01 Mathematics and Computers: Data Processing		
15-1041.00 Computer Support Specialists	Management Information Systems and Business Data Processing, General; Computer Installer and Repairer; Computer Science; Electrical and Electronics Equipment Installer and Repairer, General; Information Sciences and Systems; Business Systems Analysis and Design; Business Systems Networking and Telecommunications	Two-year college, four-year college, military (all branches)
15-1051.00 Computer Systems Analysts	Computer Programming; Computer Systems Analysis; Management Information Systems and Business Data Processing, General; Business Computer Programming/Programmer; Business Systems Analysis and Design; Computer and Information Sciences, General	Four-year college, military (all branches)
15-1061.00 Database Administrators	Management Information Systems and Business Data Processing, General; Computer and Information Sciences, General; Information Sciences and Systems; Business Computer Programming/Programmer; Business Systems Analysis and Design; Computer Programming	Four-year college, military (all branches)
15-1071.01 Computer Security Specialists	Business Systems Analysis and Design; Computer and Information Sciences, General; Management Information Systems and Business Data Processing; Business Systems Networking and Telecommunications; Computer Systems Analysis; Business Computer Facilities Operator	Two-year college, trade/technical school, four-year college, military (Army, Navy, Marine Corps, Coast Guard)
15-1081.00 Network Systems and Data Communications Analysts	Business Systems Networking and Telecommunications; Data Processing Technology/Technician; Management Information Systems and Business Data Processing, General	Four-year college, military (Army, Navy, Air Force, Marine Corps)
02.06.02 Mathematics and Computers: Data Analysis		
All in Mathematics and Computers: Data Analysis	Programming Languages; College Algebra; Statistics	Four-year college
15-2011.00 Actuaries	Actuarial Science; Finance, General	Four-year college, continuing professional study
15-2021.00 Mathematicians	Theoretical and Mathematical Physics; Physics, General; Applied Mathematics, General; Mathematics	Four-year college, graduate school, military (Army, Navy, Air Force)
15-2031.00 Operations Research Analysts	Applied Mathematics, General; Management Science; Operations Research	Four-year college, graduate school, military (Army, Navy, Air Force, Marine Corps)

JOBS	EDUCATION/TRAINING	WHERE OBTAINED
02.06.02 Mathematics and Computers: Data Analysis		
15-2041.00 Statisticians	Mathematics; Applied Mathematics, General; Mathematical Statistics; Demography/Population Studies; Econometrics and Quantitative Economics; Biostatistics; Business Statistics; Economics, General; Health and Medical Biostatistics; Medical Biomathematics and Biometrics	Four-year college, graduate school, military (Army, Navy, Air Force, Marine Corps)
15-3011.00 Mathematical Technicians	Applied Mathematics, General	Two-year college
43-9111.00 Statistical Assistants	Accounting Technician	On the job

02.07 Engineering

Workers in this group plan, design, and direct the development and construction of buildings, bridges, roads, airports, dams, sewage systems, air-conditioning systems, mining machinery, and other structures and equipment. They utilize scientific principles to develop processes and techniques for generating and transmitting electrical power, for manufacturing chemicals, for extracting metals from ores, and for controlling the quality of products being made. Workers specialize in one or more kinds of engineering, such as civil, electrical, mechanical, mining, and safety. Some are hired by industrial plants, petroleum and mining companies, research laboratories, and construction companies. Others find employment with federal, state, and local governments.

What kind of work would you do?

Your work activities would depend on your job. For example, you might

- Assist in the development of custom-made machinery.
- Conduct research to evaluate safety levels for products.
- Consult with customers concerning maintenance of software systems.
- Design and oversee the construction and operation of nuclear fuels reprocessing systems and reclamation systems.
- Write technical reports and submit findings.
- Lay out and direct mine construction operations.
- Plan the layout of electric power generating plants and distribution lines and stations.

What things about you point to this kind of work?

Is it important for you to

- Make use of your individual abilities?
- Try out your own ideas?
- Plan your work with little supervision?

Have you enjoyed any of the following as a hobby or leisure-time activity?

- Belonging to a computer club
- Experimenting with a chemistry set
- Installing and repairing home stereo equipment
- Performing experiments for a science fair
- Reading about technological developments, such as computer science or aerospace
- Reading medical or scientific magazines
- Upgrading hardware in a personal computer
- Designing and building an addition or remodeling the interior of a home

Have you liked and done well in any of the following school subjects?

- Calculus
- Physics
- Math Computing, Advanced/Specialized
- Computer Science
- Naval Architecture
- Architectural History

- Metallurgy/Metal Properties
- Mechanics/Mechanics of Materials
- Physical Science

Are you able to

- Read and understand information and ideas presented in writing?
- Apply general rules to specific problems to come up with logical answers?
- Communicate information and ideas in speaking so others will understand?
- Communicate information and ideas in writing so others will understand?
- Listen to and understand information and ideas presented through spoken words and sentences?
- Combine separate pieces of information, or specific answers to problems, to form general rules or conclusions?
- Understand and organize a problem and then select a mathematical method or formula to solve the problem?
- Add, subtract, multiply, or divide quickly and correctly?

Would you work in places such as

- Laboratories?
- Business offices?
- Colleges and universities?
- Construction sites?
- Factories and plants?
- Farms?
- Government offices?
- Mines and quarries?
- Oil fields?
- Waterworks and light and power plants?
- Streets and highways?

What skills and knowledges do you need for this kind of work?

For most of these jobs, you need these skills:

- Mathematics—using mathematics to solve problems
- Critical Thinking—using logic and analysis to identify the strengths and weaknesses of different approaches
- Reading Comprehension—understanding written sentences and paragraphs in work-related documents
- Science—using scientific methods to solve problems
- Programming—writing computer programs for various purposes

These knowledges are important in most of these jobs:

- Engineering and Technology—equipment, tools, mechanical devices, and their uses to produce motion, light, power, technology, and other applications
- Mathematics—numbers, their operations, and interrelationships including arithmetic, algebra, geometry, calculus, statistics, and their applications
- Design—design techniques, principles, tools, and instruments involved in the production and use of precision technical plans, blueprints, drawings, and models

What else should you consider about this kind of work?

Most types of engineering jobs are found in every large city. A few are available only in places where there are mines, quarries, or oil fields. Cutbacks in defense spending have reduced openings in some fields and regions, but well-trained beginners can usually find openings in most regions of the country.

If you're interested in engineering but not sure which branch to specialize in, look into several branches to learn more about them. You can do this by talking to people in the field, by working as an intern, and by getting information from engineering societies, teachers, and job counselors.

In most places, beginners work with more experienced engineers and later advance to higher-level work in research, design, or management. Many top executives and CEOs began as engineers.

Most engineers work in clean, quiet offices or laboratories. A few spend considerable time in factories or in production areas outdoors.

Some jobs, especially those in sales, require regular travel. Many engineers who specialize in forestry, marine equipment, and metallurgy also spend a lot of time away from their home offices.

How can you prepare for jobs of this kind?

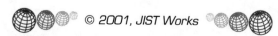

Work in this group usually requires education and/or training ranging from four years to more than ten years. Most workers entering this field have a bachelor's degree in engineering, and in many colleges this program is expected to take five years. College graduates trained in one of the natural sciences or mathematics qualify for a few beginning jobs. Experienced technicians with some engineering education may advance to engineering jobs.

Coursework for engineering includes English composition for technical writing skills, algebra, geometry, trigonometry, chemistry, physics, drafting or design graphics, computer programming, and social sciences (for example, government and economics). Most engineers study calculus, differential equations or numerical analysis, statics, dynamics, heat transfer, thermodynamics, and fluid dynamics or fluid mechanics. Specialized engineering courses are taken in the last two years of college.

Several engineering schools have agreements with liberal arts colleges to allow students to spend three years in the college and two years in the engineering school. A bachelor's degree is then granted by each school. Some engineering schools offer a five or six-year cooperative work-study program in which the students alternate periods in school with employment in related jobs. These students earn part of their tuition costs and get on-the-job experience as they learn.

Architects and landscape architects may prepare with a five-year first professional degree, or by completing a master's degree in the field after a bachelor's in another (perhaps related) field. These degree programs include both technical and design courses. In architecture, the trend is toward an advanced degree, and the program must be accredited for you to become licensed.

SPECIALIZED TRAINING

JOBS	EDUCATION/TRAINING	WHERE OBTAINED
	02.07.01 Engineering: Research and Systems Design	
All in Engineering: Research and Systems Design	Calculus; Physics; Programming Languages; Mechanics; Thermodynamics	Four-year college, graduate school
15-1031.00 Computer Software Engineers, Applications	Information Sciences and Systems; Computer Engineering	Four-year college, graduate school, military (Army, Navy, Air Force, Marine Corps)
15-1032.00 Computer Software Engineers, Systems Software	Computer Engineering; Information Sciences and Systems	Four-year college, graduate school, military (Army, Navy, Air Force, Marine Corps)
17-2021.00 Agricultural Engineers	Engineering, General; Agricultural Engineering	Four-year college, graduate school
17-2041.00 Chemical Engineers	Polymer/Plastics Engineering; Textile Sciences and Engineering; Chemical Engineering	Four-year college, graduate school
17-2061.00 Computer Hardware Engineers	Information Sciences and Systems; Computer Engineering	Four-year college, graduate school, military (Army, Navy, Air Force, Marine Corps)
17-2121.01 Marine Engineers	Engineering, General; Naval Architecture and Marine Engineering	Four-year college, graduate school, military (Army, Navy, Coast Guard)
17-2161.00 Nuclear Engineers	Nuclear Engineering; Geotechnical Engineering; Civil Engineering, General	Four-year college, graduate school, military (Army, Navy, Air Force, Marine Corps)

(continues)

SPECIALIZED TRAINING

JOBS	EDUCATION/TRAINING	WHERE OBTAINED
02.07.02 Engineering: Industrial and Safety		
All in Engineering: Industrial and Safety	Calculus; Physics; Programming Language; Mechanics	Four-year college, graduate school
17-2111.01 Industrial Safety and Health Engineers	Environmental/Environmental Health Engineering; Engineering, General	Four-year college, graduate school, military (Army, Navy, Air Force, Marine Corps)
17-2111.02 Fire-Prevention and Protection Engineers	Engineering, General	Four-year college, graduate school, military (Navy, Coast Guard)
17-2111.03 Product Safety Engineers	Engineering, General	Four-year college, graduate school
17-2112.00 Industrial Engineers	Engineering/Industrial Management; Industrial/ Manufacturing Engineering	Four-year college, graduate school, military (all branches)
17-2131.00 Materials Engineers	Materials Science	Four-year college, graduate school, military (Navy)
17-2151.00 Mining and Geological Engineers, Including Mining Safety Engineers	Mining and Mineral Engineering; Petroleum Engineering	Four-year college, graduate school
02.07.03 Engineering: Design		
All in Engineering: Design	Calculus; Physics; Programming Languages; Mechanics	Four-year college, graduate school
17-1011.00 Architects, Except Landscape and Naval	Architecture; Architectural Environmental Design	Four-year college, graduate school, school of design, military (Air Force)
17-1012.00 Landscape Architects	Architectural Environmental Design; Landscape Architecture	Four-year college, certificate program
17-2121.00 Marine Engineers and Naval Architects	Naval Architecture and Marine Engineering	Four-year college, graduate school; military data not yet available
17-2121.02 Marine Architects	Engineering, General; Naval Architecture and Marine Engineering	Four-year college, graduate school, military (Navy, Coast Guard)
02.07.04 Engineering: General Engineering		
All in Engineering: General Engineering	Calculus; Physics; Programming Languages; Mechanics	Four-year college, graduate school
17-2011.00 Aerospace Engineers	Aerospace, Aeronautical, and Astronautical Engineering	Four-year college, graduate school, military (Navy, Air Force, Marine Corps, Coast Guard)

JOBS	EDUCATION/TRAINING	WHERE OBTAINED
	02.07.04 Engineering: General Engineering	
17-2031.00 Biomedical Engineers	Geophysical Engineering; Systems Engineering; Textile Sciences and Engineering; Engineering Design; Polymer/Plastics Engineering; Geological Engineering; Engineering, Other; Engineering/Industrial Management; Engineering Science; Engineering Physics; Engineering Mechanics; Bioengineering and Biomedical Engineering; Architectural Engineering; Engineering, General; Environmental Health Engineering; Ocean Engineering	Four-year college, graduate school; military data not yet available
17-2051.00 Civil Engineers	Transportation and Highway Engineering; Civil Engineering, General; Water Resources Engineering; Geotechnical Engineering; Architectural Engineering; Agricultural Mechanization, General; Structural Engineering	Four-year college, graduate school, military (Army, Navy, Air Force)
17-2071.00 Electrical Engineers	Electrical, Electronics, and Communication Engineering; Computer Engineering	Four-year college, graduate school, military (all branches)
17-2072.00 Electronics Engineers, Except Computer	Electrical, Electronics, and Communication Engineering	Four-year college, graduate school, military (all branches)
17-2081.00 Environmental Engineers	Geophysical Engineering; Systems Engineering; Textile Sciences and Engineering; Engineering Design; Polymer/Plastics Engineering; Geological Engineering; Engineering, Other; Engineering/Industrial Management; Engineering Science; Engineering Physics; Engineering Mechanics; Bioengineering and Biomedical Engineering; Architectural Engineering; Engineering, General; Environmental Health Engineering; Ocean Engineering	Four-year college, graduate school; military data not yet available
17-2111.00 Health and Safety Engineers, Except Mining Safety Engineers and Inspectors	Natural Resources Law Enforcement and Protective Services; Occupational Safety and Health Technology/Technician; Engineering, General	Four-year college, graduate school; military data not yet available
17-2141.00 Mechanical Engineers	Textile Sciences and Engineering; Mechanical Engineering	Four-year college, graduate school, military (Navy, Air Force)
17-2171.00 Petroleum Engineers	Mining and Mineral Engineering; Petroleum Engineering	Four-year college, graduate school
41-9031.00 Sales Engineers	Agricultural Engineering; Electrical, Electronics, and Communication Engineering; Naval Architecture and Marine Engineering; Systems Engineering; Mining and Mineral Engineering; Mechanical Engineering; Nuclear Engineering; Ceramic Sciences and Engineering; Aerospace, Aeronautical, and Astronautical Engineering; Chemical Engineering	On the job, four-year college

02.08 Engineering Technology

Workers in this group perform a variety of technical tasks. They make detailed drawings and work plans; measure and prepare maps of land and water areas; operate complex communications equipment; inspect buildings and equipment for structural, mechanical, or electrical problems; and schedule and control production and transportation operations. Many work in industrial plants, oil fields and mines, research laboratories, and construction sites. Engineering firms, manufacturers, and federal, state, and local governments hire these workers.

What kind of work would you do?

Your work activities would depend on your job. For example, you might

- Conduct tests of an elevator's speed, brakes, and safety devices.
- Draft maps of survey data.
- Inspect bridges, dams, highways, buildings, wiring, plumbing, electrical circuits, sewers, heating systems, and foundations for conformance to specifications and codes.
- Maintain and repair testing equipment.
- Prepare graphs or charts of data or enter data into a computer for analysis.
- Examine permits and inspection records to determine that inspection schedule and remedial actions conform to procedures and regulations.
- Test aircraft systems under simulated operational conditions using test instrumentation and equipment.

What things about you point to this kind of work?

Is it important for you to

- Never be pressured to do things that go against your sense of right and wrong?
- Make use of your individual abilities?

Have you enjoyed any of the following as a hobby or leisure-time activity?

- Building or repairing radios or television sets
- Doing electrical wiring and repairs in the home
- Installing and repairing home stereo equipment
- Operating a CB or ham radio
- Performing experiments for a science fair
- Reading about technological developments, such as computer science or aerospace
- Reading medical or scientific magazines

Have you liked and done well in any of the following school subjects?

- Math Computing, Advanced/Specialized
- Surveying
- Drafting
- Architectural Drafting
- Electric/Electronic Theory
- Mechanical Drawing
- Laser Electronics/Optics
- Radio/TV Operations
- Computerized Drafting and Design
- Physical Science

Are you able to

- Read and understand information and ideas presented in writing?
- See details of objects at close range (within a few feet)?
- Communicate information and ideas in writing so others will understand?
- Add, subtract, multiply, or divide quickly and correctly?
- Apply general rules to specific problems to come up with logical answers?
- Correctly follow a given rule or set of rules in order to arrange things or actions in a certain order?
- Understand and organize a problem and then select a mathematical method or formula to solve the problem?
- Communicate information and ideas in speaking so others will understand?
- Listen to and understand information and ideas presented through spoken words and sentences?

Would you work in places such as

- Laboratories?
- Business offices?
- Construction sites?
- Factories and plants?
- Farms?
- Mines and quarries?

- Oil fields?
- Waterworks and light and power plants?
- Streets and highways?

What skills and knowledges do you need for this kind of work?

For most of these jobs, you need these skills:

- Mathematics—using mathematics to solve problems
- Information Gathering—knowing how to find information and identifying essential information
- Programming—writing computer programs for various purposes

These knowledges are important in most of these jobs:

- Engineering and Technology—equipment, tools, mechanical devices, and their uses to produce motion, light, power, technology, and other applications
- Mathematics—numbers, their operations, and interrelationships including arithmetic, algebra, geometry, calculus, statistics, and their applications

What else should you consider about this kind of work?

Many industries and businesses hire engineering technologists. They can also find jobs with federal, state, and local government agencies.

Generally, there are many openings for newcomers with good training. Cutbacks on defense spending have reduced job openings in a few specialties and regions, or have increased competition from out-of-work engineers. Civil-service tests are required for most government jobs. For those in industry, you may have to start out as a trainee.

Opportunity for advancement varies. Additional schooling may be necessary for promotion in fields such as drafting and surveying, but promotions are made in production planning and testing jobs without more training.

Most workers have regular daytime hours; those in communications may have to work nights or evenings.

Some of these jobs require frequent travel. You might have to spend time in remote areas with a surveying team. In inspecting jobs, both with the government and private industry, you might have to make regular visits to various work sites. Drafters generally work in offices and at times are under pressure to meet deadlines.

Some of the jobs require that you be on your feet and physically active most of the time, and may require a physical exam. Some industrial jobs (e.g., with lasers or high-voltage electricity) require extra safety precautions.

How can you prepare for jobs of this kind?

Work in this group usually requires education and/or training ranging from two years to more than ten years. The most common way to prepare for this kind of work is through related post-high-school courses, on-the-job training, and work experience. Many technical and vocational schools and two-year colleges offer programs in surveying. With some classroom instruction in surveying, beginners can start as instrument workers, but they will need a two- or possibly four-year degree to become licensed or registered. Advancement may be based on experience, additional education, and/or written examinations.

Basic preparation for jobs in drafting includes high school and two-year college courses in algebra, geometry, trigonometry, physical sciences, industrial arts, and mechanical drawing. Trade/technical school courses in structural design and layout provide the knowledge and skills needed for advanced drafting jobs. A three- to four-year apprenticeship is another method for entering drafting work. This program offers workers the advantages of classroom instruction and on-the-job training while they earn regular wages.

Technicians usually begin work as trainees in routine jobs under close supervision of an experienced technician or engineer. With added training and experience they may advance to supervisory or engineering positions.

College courses in business administration or industrial engineering provide the most common preparation for jobs in production and material coordination. People with a high school education and work experience in a production firm may be admitted to on-the-job training programs. High school courses in industrial arts and bookkeeping or accounting are helpful. English courses are also important to develop verbal skills for report writing.

SPECIALIZED TRAINING

JOBS	EDUCATION/TRAINING	WHERE OBTAINED
02.08.01 Engineering Technology: Surveying		
All in Engineering Technology: Surveying	Trigonometry; Physics; Computer Applications	Two-year college, trade/technical school, military
17-1022.00 Surveyors	Geography; Cartography; Surveying; Mechanical Engineering/Mechanical Technology/Technician	Two-year college, trade/technical school, military (all branches)
17-3031.01 Surveying Technicians	Surveying	Two-year college, trade/technical school, military (Army, Navy, Air Force, Marine Corps)
17-3031.02 Mapping Technicians	Surveying; Cartography; Civil/Structural Drafting; Drafting, General	Two-year college, trade/technical school, military (Army, Navy, Air Force, Marine Corps)
02.08.02 Engineering Technology: Industrial and Safety		
All in Engineering Technology: Industrial and Safety	Trigonometry; Physics	Two-year college; trade/technical school, military
13-1041.05 Pressure Vessel Inspectors	Industrial Machinery Maintenance and Repairer; Stationary Energy Sources Installer and Operator	Work experience in a related occupation, two-year college, trade/technical school, military (Navy, Air Force)
17-3026.00 Industrial Engineering Technicians	Industrial/Manufacturing Technology/Technician; Quality Control Technology/Technician	Two-year college, trade/technical school, military (Air Force)
47-4011.00 Construction and Building Inspectors	Architectural Engineering Technology/Technician; Electrical, Electronic, and Communications Engineering Technology/Technician; Fire Protection and Safety Technology/Technician; Electrical and Power Transmission Installer, General; Electrician; Construction/Building Inspector; Plumber and Pipefitter; Heating, Air Conditioning, and Refrigeration Mechanic and Repairer; Construction/Building Technology/Technician	Work experience in a related occupation, two-year college, trade/technical school, military (Army, Navy, Air Force)
02.08.03 Engineering Technology: Design		
All in Engineering Technology: Design	Trigonometry; Physics; Computer Applications	Two-year college, trade/technical school, military
17-1021.00 Cartographers and Photogrammetrists	Surveying; Cartography; Drafting, General; Civil/Structural Drafting	Two-year college, trade/technical school, military (Army, Navy, Air Force, Marine Corps)
17-3011.01 Architectural Drafters	Civil/Structural Drafting; Architectural Drafting; Drafting, General; Heating, Air Conditioning, and Refrigeration Technology/Technician	Two-year college, trade/technical school, military (Army, Air Force, Marine Corps)

JOBS	EDUCATION/TRAINING	WHERE OBTAINED
02.08.03 Engineering Technology: Design		
17-3011.02 Civil Drafters	Civil/Structural Drafting; Drafting, General	Two-year college, trade/technical school, military (Army, Navy, Air Force, Marine Corps)
17-3012.01 Electronic Drafters	Drafting, General; Operations Management and Supervision; Electrical/Electronics Drafting; Electrical, Electronic, and Communications Engineering Technology/Technician; Computer Engineering Technology/Technician	Two-year college, trade/technical school
17-3012.02 Electrical Drafters	Electrical/Electronics Drafting; Civil/Structural Drafting; Drafting, General	Two-year college, trade/technical school
17-3013.00 Mechanical Drafters	Instrumentation Technology/Technician; Mechanical Drafting; Electrical/Electronics Drafting; Mechanical Engineering/Mechanical Technology/Technician; Electromechanical Technology/Technician; Drafting, General	Two-year college, trade/technical school
02.08.04 Engineering Technology: General		
All in Engineering Technology: General	Trigonometry; Physics; Computer Applications	Two-year college, trade/technical school, military
17-3021.00 Aerospace Engineering and Operations Technicians	Mechanical Engineering/Mechanical Technology/Technician; Aeronautical and Aerospace Engineering Technology/Technician	Two-year college, trade/technical school, military (Army, Air Force)
17-3022.00 Civil Engineering Technicians	Civil Engineering/Civil Technology/Technician; Architectural Engineering Technology/Technician; Construction/Building Technology/Technician; Interior Architecture	Two-year college, trade/technical school, military (Navy, Air Force)
17-3023.01 Electronics Engineering Technicians	Computer Engineering Technology/Technician; Computer Maintenance Technology/Technician; Robotics Technology/Technician; Electrical and Electronics Equipment Installer and Repairer; Industrial Electronics Installer and Repairer; Electromechanical Technology/Technician; Electrical, Electronic, and Communications Engineering Technology/Technician	Two-year college, trade/technical school, four-year college
17-3023.02 Calibration and Instrumentation Technicians	Instrument Calibration and Repairer; Aeronautical and Aerospace Engineering Technology/Technician; Instrumentation Technology/Technician; Electromechanical Technology/Technician; Electrical, Electronic, and Communications Engineering Technology/Technician	Two-year college, trade/technical school
17-3023.03 Electrical Engineering Technicians	Electrical, Electronic, and Communications Engineering Technology/Technician	Two-year college, trade/technical school

(continues)

(continued)

SPECIALIZED TRAINING

JOBS	EDUCATION/TRAINING	WHERE OBTAINED
02.08.04 Engineering Technology: General		
17-3024.00 Electro-Mechanical Technicians	Electromechanical Technology/Technician; Robotics Technology/Technician; Aircraft Mechanic/Technician, Powerplant	Work experience in a related occupation, two-year college, trade/technical school
17-3025.00 Environmental Engineering Technicians	Hydraulic Technology/Technician; Industrial Production Technology/Technicians, Other; Aeronautical and Aerospace Engineering Technology/Technician; Mechanical Engineering-Related Technology/Technicians, Other; Mining Technology/Technician; Engineering-Related Technology/Technicians, Other; Mining and Petroleum Technology/Technicians, Other; Engineering-Related Technology/Technician, General; Metallurgical Technology/Technician; Architectural Engineering Technology/Technician; Environmental Control Technology/Technicians, Other; Environmental and Pollution Control Technology/Technician; Water Quality and Wastewater Treatment Technology/Technician; Solar Technology/Technician; Laser and Optical Technology/Technician; Communications Technology/Technicians, Other; Radio and Television Broadcasting Technology/Technician; Plastics Technology/Technician; Energy Management and Systems Technology/Technician	Two-year college, trade/technical school; military data not yet available
17-3027.00 Mechanical Engineering Technicians	Automotive Engineering Technology/Technician; Mechanical Engineering/Mechanical Technology/Technician; Heating, Air Conditioning, and Refrigeration Technology/Technician; Mechanical Drafting; Drafting, General; Energy Management and Systems Technology/Technician	Two-year college, trade/technical school, military (Coast Guard)
51-4012.00 Numerical Tool and Process Control Programmers	Business Computer Programming/Programmer; Management Information Systems and Business; Data Processing; Machinist/Machine Technologist; Computer Systems Analysis; Data Processing Technology/Technician; Computer Programming	Work experience in a related occupation, two-year college, trade/technical school, military (Navy)

03 Plants and Animals

An interest in working with plants and animals, usually outdoors.

You can satisfy this interest by working in farming, forestry, fishing, and related fields. You may like doing physical work outdoors, such as on a farm. You may enjoy animals; perhaps training or taking care of animals would appeal to you. If you have management ability, you could own, operate, or manage a farm or related business.

03.01 Managerial Work in Plants and Animals

Workers in this group operate or manage farms, ranches, hatcheries, nurseries, forests, and other plant and animal businesses. Some breed specialty plants and animals. Others provide services to increase production or beautify land areas. Many work in rural areas or woodlands and on farms, ranches, and forest preserves. Others find employment with commercial nurseries, landscaping firms, business services, or government agencies located in large and small communities all over the country. Many are self-employed, operating their own large or small businesses.

What kind of work would you do?

Your work activities would depend on your job. For example, you might

- Analyze market conditions to determine acreage allocations.
- Arrange with buyers for sale and shipment of crops.
- Change logging operations or methods to eliminate unsafe conditions.
- Hire and direct workers engaged in planting, cultivating, irrigating, harvesting, and marketing crops and raising livestock.
- Negotiate with bank officials to obtain credit from bank.
- Oversee movement of mature fish to lakes, ponds, streams, or commercial tanks.
- Select and purchase seed, plant nutrients, and disease-control chemicals.

What things about you point to this kind of work?

Is it important for you to

- Plan your work with little supervision?
- Make decisions on your own?
- Never be pressured to do things that go against your sense of right and wrong?

Have you enjoyed any of the following as a hobby or leisure-time activity?

- Belonging to a 4-H or garden club
- Breeding animals
- Designing and landscaping a flower garden
- Raising vegetables in a home garden
- Raising or caring for animals
- Serving as president of a club or other organization
- Studying plants in gardens, parks, or forests
- Reading farm magazines

Have you liked and done well in any of the following school subjects?

- Management
- Dairy Science/Technology
- Plant Pest Management/Pathology
- Agriculture, Mechanized
- Agricultural Systems
- Agribusiness
- Animal Breeding
- Animal Grooming
- Animal Science
- Farm and Ranch Management

Are you able to

- Communicate information and ideas in speaking so others will understand?
- Correctly follow a given rule or set of rules in order to arrange things or actions in a certain order?
- Apply general rules to specific problems to come up with logical answers?
- Tell when something is wrong or is likely to go wrong?
- Read and understand information and ideas presented in writing?
- Listen to and understand information and ideas presented through spoken words and sentences?
- See details of objects at close range (within a few feet)?

Would you work in places such as

- Farms?
- Fish hatcheries?
- Forests?
- Ships and boats?
- Plant nurseries?
- Golf courses and tennis courts?
- Parks and campgrounds?

What skills and knowledges do you need for this kind of work?

For most of these jobs, you need these skills:

- Speaking—talking to others to effectively convey information
- Product Inspection—inspecting and evaluating the quality of products
- Coordination—adjusting actions in relation to others' actions
- Problem Identification—identifying the nature of problems

These knowledges are important in most of these jobs:

- Administration and Management—principles and processes involved in business and organizational planning, coordination, and execution
- Biology—plant and animal living tissue, cells, organisms, and entities, including their functions, interdependencies, and interactions with each other and the environment

What else should you consider about this kind of work?

Many workers in this group are in business for themselves. They run plant nurseries, plan and care for lawns and trees, or have their own large or small farms. They raise a variety of plants and animals, from soybeans to peanuts, from cattle to canaries. Many of these businesses are small, with few employees.

Others in this group work for someone else, managing a farm, ranch, or stand of timber; or providing services to help the owners with production or harvesting. Some jobs are available with state government agencies.

It is hard for newcomers to start their own farming businesses. Many people in farming have been in it most of their lives. The cost of land and equipment makes it almost impossible for most people to start from scratch in this field. Federal loans are available, however, to qualified people who wish to start their own farming businesses.

Openings are more plentiful for people who want to manage farms for others. Many large farms are owned by large companies that hire well-trained managers to take responsibility for day-to-day operations. Competition for jobs is increasing as these agricultural companies merge.

People in this kind of work put in long hours. Whether they own or manage the business, doing all the work themselves or having many people work under them, most spend much more than eight hours a day on the job. Work in landscaping or other "city farming" is not likely to take as much time.

In most of these jobs, workers spend a lot of time outside in all kinds of weather. For some jobs these managers have to be physically strong and active.

In addition to being experts in raising plants and animals, people who do well in this kind of work are knowledgeable about business and government regulations and skilled in marketing their products and managing their money.

How can you prepare for jobs of this kind?

Occupations in this group usually require education and/or training ranging from one year to more than ten years. Most jobs in this group are open only to people with work experience. Growing up on a farm is good initial preparation for many of these jobs. Formal training for management jobs is available at the high school and higher levels. For example, vocational agriculture courses are offered in many high schools to high school students during the day and to adults at night and on weekends. Programs in agribusiness, agronomy, animal science, forest management, poultry science, dairy science, mechanized agriculture, and small-business management are provided by colleges and trade/technical schools. Each state has at least one college that offers four- or five-year programs in agricultural fields.

Workers with management training and farm experience qualify for jobs with farm cooperatives, corporations, and owners of large farms. Some workers form companies that contract to provide farm services.

Courses in horticulture, gardening, and turf management provide preparation for jobs in nurseries, tree services, and landscaping firms.

SPECIALIZED TRAINING

JOBS	EDUCATION/TRAINING	WHERE OBTAINED
03.01.01 Managerial Work: Farming and Fishing		
All in Managerial Work: Farming and Fishing	Experience; Agribusiness	Related jobs within the same industry or growing up on a farm, two-year college, trade/technical school, four-year college
11-9011.02 Agricultural Crop Farm Managers	Agricultural Supplies Retailing and Wholesaling	Two-year college, trade/technical school, four-year college
11-9011.03 Fish Hatchery Managers	Agricultural Business/Agribusiness Operations; Fishing and Fisheries Sciences and Management; Aquaculture Operations and Production Management; Agricultural Business and Management, General; Farm and Ranch Management; Agricultural Production Workers and Managers, General	Two-year college, trade/technical school, four-year college
11-9012.00 Farmers and Ranchers	Agricultural Production Workers and Managers, General; Agricultural Animal Husbandry and Production Management; Crop Production Operations and Management	On the job, two-year college, trade/technical school, four-year college
19-4093.00 Forest and Conservation Technicians	Harvesting and Production Technology; Disease and Pest Control; Equipment Maintenance and Repair; Selection and Identification of Trees; Forest Management; Safety Procedures	Two-year college, trade/technical school, on the job
45-1011.01 First-Line Supervisors and Manager/Supervisors—Agricultural Crop Workers	Agricultural Animal Husbandry and Production Management; Agricultural Production Workers and Managers, General; Agricultural Mechanization, Other; Crop Production Operations and Management; Horticulture Science; Plant Sciences, General; Agricultural Supplies Retailing and Wholesaling; Plant Protection (Pest Management)	Two-year college, trade/technical school, four-year college, on the job
45-1011.02 First-Line Supervisors and Manager/Supervisors—Animal Husbandry Workers	Agricultural Production Workers and Managers, General; Range Science and Management; Agricultural Animal Husbandry and Production Management; Agricultural Supplies Retailing and Wholesaling; Equestrian/Equine Studies, Horse Management and Training; Animal Sciences, General; Dairy Science; Plant Sciences, General	Two-year college, trade/technical school, four-year college, on the job
45-1011.03 First-Line Supervisors and Manager/Supervisors—Animal Care Workers, Except Livestock	Agricultural Production Workers and Managers, General; Agricultural Animal Husbandry and Production Management; Animal Sciences, General; Agricultural Animal Nutrition	Two-year college, trade/technical school, on the job
45-1011.06 First-Line Supervisors and Manager/Supervisors—Fishery Workers	Aquaculture Operations and Production Management; Agricultural Production Workers and Managers, General; Fishing and Fisheries Sciences and Management	Two-year college, trade/technical school, on the job

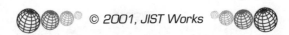

JOBS	EDUCATION/TRAINING	WHERE OBTAINED
	03.01.01 Managerial Work: Farming and Fishing	
45-2031.00 Farm Labor Contractors	Agricultural Supplies and Related Services, Other; Agricultural Supplies Retailing and Wholesaling; Agricultural Animal Breeding and Genetics; Crop Production Operations and Management; Range Science and Management; Agronomy and Crop Science; Plant Sciences, General; Poultry Science; Dairy Science; Agricultural Animal Nutrition; Farm and Ranch Management; Agricultural Production Workers and Managers, Other; Agricultural Business and Production, Other; Agricultural Animal Husbandry and Production Management; Agricultural Production Workers and Managers, General; Agricultural Business and Management, Other; Animal Sciences, General	Two-year college, trade/technical school, four-year college, on the job
	03.01.02 Managerial Work: Nursery, Groundskeeping, and Logging	
All in Managerial Work: Nursery, Groundskeeping, and Logging	Experience; Horticultural Operations	Related jobs within the same industry
11-9011.01 Nursery and Greenhouse Managers	Horticulture Science; Plant Sciences, General; Farm and Ranch Management; Horticulture Services Operations and Management, General; Agricultural Business and Management, General; Nursery Operations and Management; Greenhouse Operations and Management; Agricultural Business/Agribusiness Operations	Two-year college, trade/technical school, four-year college
37-1012.01 Lawn Service Managers	Horticulture Services Operations and Management, General; Turf Management; Ornamental Horticulture Operations and Management	Two-year college, trade/technical school, on the job
37-1012.02 First-Line Supervisors and Manager/Supervisors—Landscaping Workers	Turf Management; Horticulture Services Operations and Management, General; Ornamental Horticulture Operations and Management; Landscaping Operations and Management; Horticulture Services Operations and Management, Other	Two-year college, trade/technical school, on the job
45-1011.04 First-Line Supervisors and Manager/Supervisors—Horticultural Workers	Forest Harvesting and Production Technology/Technician; Agricultural Production Workers and Managers, General; Horticulture Services Operations and Management, General; Plant Sciences, General; Nursery Operations and Management; Greenhouse Operations and Management; Ornamental Horticulture Operations and Management; Crop Production Operations and Management; Horticulture Science	Two-year college, trade/technical school, on the job
45-1011.05 First-Line Supervisors and Manager/Supervisors—Logging Workers	Agricultural Business and Management, General; Forest Harvesting and Production Technology; Logging/Timber Harvesting; Forest Products Technology	Two-year college, trade/technical school, on the job

03.02 Animal Care and Training

Workers in this group care for and train animals of many kinds. They work in pet shops, pet grooming parlors, testing laboratories, animal shelters, and veterinary offices. Some are employed by zoos, aquariums, circuses, and other places where animals are exhibited or used in entertainment acts. Others work for animal training or obedience schools, stables, kennels, racetracks, or riding academies. This group does not include workers employed on farms, ranches, or other places where animals are raised for food.

What kind of work would you do?

Your work activities would depend on your job. For example, you might

- Cue or signal animals during performance.
- Groom and feed horses.
- Clean barns, stables, pens, and kennels.
- Observe fish and aquatic life to detect and treat disease, injury, and illness according to instructions.
- Order, unload, and store feed and supplies.
- Record information about animals such as weight, size, physical condition, diet, medications, and food intake.
- Train guard dog to protect property and teach guide dog and its handler to function as a team.

What things about you point to this kind of work?

Is it important for you to

- Never be pressured to do things that go against your sense of right and wrong?
- Do your work alone?
- Be busy all the time?
- Have steady employment?

Have you enjoyed any of the following as a hobby or leisure-time activity?

- Belonging to a 4-H or garden club
- Breeding animals
- Nursing sick pets
- Raising or caring for animals
- Training dogs or other animals to perform on command
- Reading farm magazines

Have you liked and done well in any of the following school subjects?

- Biology
- Animal Obedience Training
- Horseshoeing
- Farm and Ranch Management
- Veterinary Sciences

Are you able to

- Tell when something is wrong or is likely to go wrong?
- Listen to and understand information and ideas presented through spoken words and sentences?

Would you work in places such as

- Amusement parks, circuses, and carnivals?
- Animal hospitals, boarding kennels, and grooming parlors?
- Farms?
- Fish hatcheries?
- Laboratories?
- Zoos and aquariums?

What skills and knowledges do you need for this kind of work?

For most of these jobs, you need these skills:

- Problem Identification—identifying the nature of problems
- Speaking—talking to others to effectively convey information
- Active Listening—listening to what other people are saying and asking questions as appropriate

These knowledges are important in most of these jobs:

- Biology—plant and animal living tissue, cells, organisms, and entities, including their functions, interdependencies, and interactions with each other and the environment
- Medicine and Dentistry—the information and techniques needed to diagnose and treat injuries, diseases, and deformities

What else should you consider about this kind of work?

Carnivals, zoos, and pet shops hire many of the workers in this group. They are also employed by veterinarians, racetracks, boarding kennels, and laboratories that use animals in testing. Some workers have their own pet grooming businesses.

Most veterinarians work in private practice, but some work for farms taking care of livestock, while others work in research or meat inspection jobs.

Expansion in the testing of food and drugs by government agencies will increase the need for people to care for laboratory animals, and increasing numbers of household pets will create jobs for animal groomers, veterinary hospital helpers, and other pet caretakers. Best opportunities for veterinarians will be in small towns and rural communities, and for those who have acquired specialized training beyond the veterinary degree.

Many places hire beginners for these jobs. Persons who have cared for animals at home or have farm experience are more likely to be hired.

Most of this work is done at a fixed location on a regular schedule. Many jobs require cleaning up after animals. Jobs with carnivals or circuses require frequent travel.

Temporary work is sometimes available at racetracks and zoos, and with traveling carnivals that hire people to help care for their animals in the towns where they perform.

Depending on the animals involved, physical requirements vary. Caring for guinea pigs in a testing laboratory takes much less strength and activity than caring for lions and tigers at a zoo.

How can you prepare for jobs of this kind?

Occupations in this group usually require education and/or training ranging from a short demonstration (e.g., for some animal caretaker jobs) to six or more years for (e.g., for a veterinarian). Most beginning workers are given a few simple duties; more responsibility is added as these workers gain experience. Some high schools, vocational schools, and junior colleges have courses in animal care. These courses cover the housing and feeding of animals, basic zoology and anatomy, and methods of treating sick or injured animals. Also helpful are training in animal grooming and coursework in animal science and vocational agriculture.

Some of these jobs require special skills. For instance, workers who train or exercise horses must know how to ride, and those who work for aquariums must know how to swim.

Jobs in training guide dogs, saddle horses, or animal performers are given to workers who have at least six months of experience in the care of animals.

Veterinarians usually complete a four-year degree before getting four years of professional instruction in a veterinary college. Experience working with animals, and perhaps a standardized test, may also be required for admission to veterinary school.

SPECIALIZED TRAINING

JOBS	EDUCATION/TRAINING	WHERE OBTAINED
	03.02.01 Animal Care and Training	
All in Animal Care and Training	Experience	Related jobs within the same industry, volunteer work at a veterinary hospital
29-1131.00 Veterinarians	Veterinary Ophthalmology; Veterinary Nutrition; Veterinary Anesthesiology; Veterinary Practice; Laboratory Animal Medicine; Veterinary Internal Medicine; Veterinary Emergency and Critical Care Medicine; Theriogenology; Veterinary Dentistry; Veterinary Medicine (D.V.M.); Veterinary Radiology; Veterinary Surgery; Veterinary Toxicology; Zoological Medicine; Veterinary Dermatology	Four-year college, veterinary school, military (Army, Air Force)
29-2056.00 Veterinary Technologists and Technicians	Veterinarian Assistant/Animal Health Technician	On the job, two-year college, trade/ technical school

(continues)

(continued)

SPECIALIZED TRAINING

JOBS	EDUCATION/TRAINING	WHERE OBTAINED
03.02.01 Animal Care and Training		
31-9096.00 Veterinary Assistants and Laboratory Animal Caretakers	Veterinarian Assistant/Animal Health Technician	On the job, two-year college, trade/technical school
39-2011.00 Animal Trainers	Equestrian/Equine Studies, Horse Management and Training; Animal Trainer	Four-year college, on the job
39-2021.00 Nonfarm Animal Caretakers	Agricultural Supplies Retailing and Wholesaling; Agricultural Animal Husbandry and Production Management; Agricultural Production Workers and Managers, General	On the job, two-year college, trade/technical school, military (Army)
45-2021.00 Animal Breeders	Agricultural Production Workers and Managers, General; Agricultural Animal Husbandry and Production Management	Two-year college, trade/technical school, four-year college, on the job

03.03 Hands-on Work in Plants and Animals

Workers in this group perform strenuous tasks with plants or animals, usually outdoors in a nonfactory setting. They work with their hands, use tools and equipment, or operate machinery. They work on farms or ranches; at logging camps or fish hatcheries; in forests or game preserves; or with commercial fishing businesses, onshore or in fishing boats. In cities and towns they usually work in parks, gardens, or nurseries.

What kind of work would you do?

Your work activities would depend on your job. For example, you might

- Collect, inspect, pack, or place eggs in an incubator.
- Control equipment to load, unload, or stack logs; pull stumps; and clear brush.
- Cultivate grass or lawn, using power aerator and thatcher.
- Herd livestock to pasture for grazing, or to scales, trucks, or other enclosures.
- Move containerized shrubs, plants, and trees using a wheelbarrow.
- Plant, transplant, fertilize, spray with pesticides, prune, cultivate, and water flowers, shrubbery, and trees.
- Remove catch from fishing equipment and use measuring equipment to ensure compliance with legal size.

What things about you point to this kind of work?

Is it important for you to

- Never be pressured to do things that go against your sense of right and wrong?
- Do your work alone?
- Be busy all the time?

Have you enjoyed any of the following as a hobby or leisure-time activity?

- Belonging to a 4-H or garden club
- Camping, hiking, or engaging in other outdoor activities
- Driving a truck and tractor to harvest crops on a family farm
- Gardening
- Mowing the lawn with a riding lawnmower
- Raising vegetables in a home garden
- Trimming shrubs and hedges

Have you liked and done well in any of the following school subjects?

- Horticulture
- Vocational Agriculture
- Food and Fiber Crops
- Forestry
- Plant Pest Management/Pathology
- Agriculture, Mechanized
- Landscaping
- Agronomy

Are you able to

- Exert maximum muscle force to lift, push, pull, or carry objects?
- Quickly make coordinated movements of one hand, a hand together with its arm, or two hands to grasp, manipulate, or assemble objects?
- Use your abdominal and lower-back muscles to support part of your body repeatedly or continuously over time?

Would you work in places such as

- Country clubs and resorts?
- Farms?
- Forests?
- Golf courses and tennis courts?
- Parks and campgrounds?
- Plant nurseries?
- Private homes?
- Ships and boats?
- Hotels and motels?

What skills and knowledges do you need for this kind of work?

For most of these jobs, you need these skills:

- Equipment Selection—determining the kind of tools and equipment needed to do a job
- Operation and Control—controlling operations of equipment or systems

These knowledges are important in most of these jobs:

- Mechanical—machines and tools, including their designs, uses, benefits, repair, and maintenance
- Biology—plant and animal living tissue, cells, organisms, and entities, including their functions, interdependencies, and interactions with each other and the environment

What else should you consider about this kind of work?

Many of the workers in this group are hired by farmers, ranchers, lumber companies, and commercial fisheries. Some work for businesses that provide services to farms, corporate campuses, and private homes. A few of the jobs are with parks operated by state or local governments. Some workers are self-employed as hunters, trappers, or fishers. Many of these jobs are open to beginners and some offer chances for advancement to supervisory work.

Much of this work is seasonal. If you live in a farming or fishing area, temporary work is available at certain times of the year. In towns and cities, groundskeeping companies and parks often hire extra workers in the spring and summer.

This is active physical work. You have to be out in all kinds of weather and willing to put in a full day's work to succeed. Farm work can be dangerous because of the power equipment used, so safety precautions must be observed. Many of these jobs require long hours of hard work at certain times of the year, such as during planting or harvesting of crops. Persons wanting full-time work must look for other jobs in the "off" season.

How can you prepare for jobs of this kind?

Occupations in this group usually require education and/or training ranging from a short demonstration to more than three months. Prior training is not required for most jobs in this group. In some jobs, training is given by the employer when workers are hired or when their duties are changed. Most employers require job applicants to be in good physical condition, and for jobs on fishing boats, commercial fisheries hire only persons who can swim. To be eligible for jobs in local, state, or national parks or with other government agencies, applicants must pass civil-service examinations.

Some vocational high schools offer courses in general farming, farm animal care, and equipment operation, and a few participate in work/study projects. This experience can be helpful in obtaining a job because employers prefer to hire workers who need less on-the-job training.

Many vocational schools and training programs offer courses in landscaping, animal science, dairy science, forest management, and wildlife and fisheries management.

SPECIALIZED TRAINING

JOBS	EDUCATION/TRAINING	WHERE OBTAINED
03.03.01 Hands-on Work: Farming		
All in Hands-on Work: Farming	Experience	Related jobs within the same industry, growing up on a farm
45-2091.00 Agricultural Equipment Operators	Agricultural Supplies Retailing and Wholesaling; Crop Production Operations and Management; Agricultural Production Workers and Managers, General; Agricultural Power Machinery Operator	On the job, trade/technical school
45-2092.00 Farmworkers and Laborers, Crop, Nursery, and Greenhouse	Agricultural Production Workers and Managers, General; Agricultural Animal Husbandry and Production Management; Crop Production Operations and Management; Agricultural Power Machinery Operator	On the job
45-2092.02 General Farmworkers	Agricultural Production Workers and Managers, General; Agricultural Animal Husbandry and Production Management; Crop Production Operations and Management; Agricultural Power Machinery Operator	On the job, trade/technical school
45-2093.00 Farmworkers, Farm and Ranch Animals	Agricultural Production Workers and Managers, General; Agricultural Animal Husbandry and Production Management; Agricultural Supplies Retailing and Wholesaling	On the job, trade/technical school
03.03.02 Hands-on Work: Forestry and Logging		
All in Hands-on Work: Forestry and Logging	Experience; Logging Procedures	Related jobs within the same industry
45-4011.00 Forest and Conservation Workers	Forest Harvesting and Production Technology/ Technician	On the job, trade/technical school
45-4021.00 Fallers	Logging/Timber Harvesting	On the job, trade/technical school
45-4022.00 Logging Equipment Operators	Logging/Timber Harvesting	On the job
45-4022.01 Logging Tractor Operators	Logging/Timber Harvesting	On the job, trade/technical school
03.03.03 Hands-on Work: Hunting and Fishing		
All in Hands-on Work: Hunting and Fishing	Experience	Hunting and fishing for sport, related jobs within the same industry
45-3011.00 Fishers and Related Fishing Workers	Fishing Technology/Commercial Fishing; Aquaculture Operations and Production Management; Agricultural Production Workers and Managers, General; Fishing and Fisheries Sciences and Management	On the job, trade/technical school

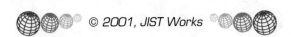

JOBS	EDUCATION/TRAINING	WHERE OBTAINED
03.03.03 Hands-on Work: Hunting and Fishing		
45-3021.00 Hunters and Trappers	Agricultural Supplies Retailing and Wholesaling	On the job, trade/technical school
03.03.04 Hands-on Work: Nursery, Groundskeeping, and Pest Control		
All in Hands-on Work: Nursery, Groundskeeping, and Pest Control	Experience	Gardening as a hobby, related jobs within the same industry
37-2021.00 Pest Control Workers	Agricultural Supplies Retailing and Wholesaling	On the job, trade/technical school, military (Air Force)
37-3011.00 Landscaping and Groundskeeping Workers	Greenhouse Operations and Management; Nursery Operations and Management; Ornamental Horticulture Operations and Management; Horticulture Services Operations and Management, General	On the job, trade/technical school
37-3012.00 Pesticide Handlers, Sprayers, and Applicators, Vegetation	Crop Production Operations and Management; Agricultural Production Workers and Managers, General; Horticulture Services Operations and Management, General; Landscaping Operations and Management; Agricultural Power Machinery Operator; Turf Management; Nursery Operations and Management	On the job, trade/technical school
37-3013.00 Tree Trimmers and Pruners	Agricultural Production Workers and Managers, General; Crop Production Operations and Management; Horticulture Services Operations and Management, Other	On the job, trade/technical school
45-2092.01 Nursery Workers	Ornamental Horticulture Operations and Management; Horticulture Services Operations and Management, General; Nursery Operations and Management; Greenhouse Operations and Management	On the job, trade/technical school

04 Law, Law Enforcement, and Public Safety

An interest in upholding people's rights or in protecting people and property by using authority, inspecting, or monitoring.

You can satisfy this interest by working in law, law enforcement, fire fighting, and related fields. For example, if you enjoy mental challenge and intrigue, you could investigate crimes or fires for a living. If you enjoy working with verbal skills, you may want to defend citizens in court or research deeds, wills, and other legal documents. You may prefer to fight fires and respond to other emergencies. Or, if you want more routine work, perhaps a job in guarding or patrolling would appeal to you; if you have management ability, you could seek a leadership position in law enforcement and the protective services. Work in the military gives you the chance to use technical and/or leadership skills while serving your country.

04.01 Managerial Work in Law, Law Enforcement, and Public Safety

04.02 Law

04.03 Law Enforcement

04.04 Public Safety

04.05 Military

04.01 Managerial Work in Law, Law Enforcement, and Public Safety

Workers in this group manage fire and police departments. They set goals and policies, oversee financial and human resources, evaluate outcomes, and represent their departments to the public and the governments of the jurisdictions they serve. They work for cities and towns. Supervisors of forest fire fighters mostly work for the federal government.

What kind of work would you do?

Your work activities would depend on your job. For example, you might

- Direct building inspections to ensure compliance with fire and safety regulations.
- Discipline staff for violation of department rules and regulations.
- Monitor and evaluate job performance of subordinates.
- Prepare budgets and manage expenditures of department funds.
- Supervise and coordinate investigation of criminal cases.
- Write and submit proposals for new equipment or modification of existing equipment.
- Direct collection, preparation, and handling of evidence and personal property of prisoners.

What things about you point to this kind of work?

Is it important for you to

- Give directions and instructions to others?
- Get a feeling of accomplishment?
- Have coworkers who are easy to get along with?
- Be treated fairly by the company?

Have you enjoyed any of the following as a hobby or leisure-time activity?

- Directing traffic at community events
- Instructing family members in observing traffic regulations
- Reading detective stories; watching television detective shows
- Serving as a volunteer in a fire department or emergency rescue squad
- Serving as president of a club or other organization

Have you liked and done well in any of the following school subjects?

- Management
- Fire Fighting
- Police Science
- Accounting
- Personnel Management
- Government

Are you able to

- Communicate information and ideas in speaking so others will understand?
- Listen to and understand information and ideas presented through spoken words and sentences?
- Communicate information and ideas in writing so others will understand?
- Combine separate pieces of information, or specific answers to problems, to form general rules or conclusions?
- Tell when something is wrong or is likely to go wrong?
- Speak clearly so that it is understandable to a listener?
- Efficiently shift back and forth between two or more activities or sources of information?

Would you work in places such as

- Fire stations?
- Police headquarters?
- Government offices?
- Forests?

What skills and knowledges do you need for this kind of work?

For most of these jobs, you need these skills:

- Coordination—adjusting actions in relation to others' actions
- Management of Personnel Resources—motivating, developing, and directing people as they work, identifying the best people for the job
- Speaking—talking to others to effectively convey information
- Critical Thinking—using logic and analysis to identify the strengths and weaknesses of different approaches

- Judgment and Decision Making—weighing the relative costs and benefits of a potential action
- Implementation Planning—developing approaches for implementing an idea
- Writing—communicating effectively with others in writing as indicated by their needs
- Problem Identification—identifying the nature of problems

These knowledges are important in most of these jobs:

- Public Safety and Security—weaponry, public safety, and security operations; rules, regulations, precautions, prevention; and the protection of people, data, and property
- Administration and Management—principles and processes involved in business and organizational planning, coordination, and execution

What else should you consider about this kind of work?

These workers are hired by police and fire departments in cities and towns throughout the U.S. They may have to take a civil-service exam to qualify.

These jobs carry considerable responsibility. Workers are responsible not only for budgets, facilities, equipment, and staff, but also for the safety and security of hundreds or maybe thousands of citizens. Because they are on the public payroll, these jobs are also political, especially in the higher levels. They may be helped by an alliance with a popular political figure, but they may be threatened if that person loses power. They also require sensitivity to local neighborhood and ethnic interests and concerns.

Advancement proceeds up a series of ranks that vary from one jurisdiction to another. In addition to experience, some training or exams may be required for promotion. At the highest levels, many advance by taking a position in another town or city.

How can you prepare for jobs of this kind?

Occupations in this group usually require from four to six years of education and/or training. Less education is necessary initially, because almost all managers of police and fire fighting agencies begin as police detectives or fire fighters and work up through the ranks. They may complete a two-year college major in fire science or a two- or four-year major in law enforcement, then get training to advance in rank.

Specialized training in an area such as juvenile crime or fire inspection helps early in the career; later, training in management is helpful to move up from the street to a managerial position.

SPECIALIZED TRAINING

JOBS	EDUCATION/TRAINING	WHERE OBTAINED
04.01.01 Managerial Work in Law, Law Enforcement, and Public Safety		
All in Managerial Work in Law, Law Enforcement, and Public Safety	Experience; Budgeting; Personnel; Oral and Written Communications	Two-year college, four-year college, military, related jobs within the same industry
13-1061.00 Emergency Management Specialists	Administrative Assistant/Secretarial Science, General; Executive Assistant/Secretary; Public Policy Analysis	Four-year college; military data not yet available
33-1011.00 First-Line Supervisors/Managers of Correctional Officers	Corrections/Correctional Administration; Criminal Justice/Law Enforcement Administration	Two-year college, four-year college; military data not yet available
33-1012.00 First-Line Supervisors/Managers of Police and Detectives	Corrections/Correctional Administration; Criminal Justice/Law Enforcement Administration	Two-year college, four-year college, military (all branches)
33-1021.01 Municipal Fire Fighting and Prevention Supervisors	Fire Protection and Safety Technology/Technician; Fire Services Administration	Two-year college, four-year college, military (Army, Navy, Air Force, Marine Corps)
33-1021.02 Forest Fire Fighting and Prevention Supervisors	Fire Services Administration; Natural Resources Law Enforcement and Protective Services; Fire Science/ Firefighting	Two-year college, four-year college

04.02 Law

Workers in this group provide legal advice and representation to clients, hear and make decisions on court cases, help individuals and groups reach agreements, and conduct investigations into legal matters. Although they specialize in many different fields, all of them apply knowledge of laws and regulations to the problems they must solve. They work for law firms, courts, businesses, government agencies, and legislators.

What kind of work would you do?

Your work activities would depend on your job. For example, you might

- Arbitrate disputes between parties and assist in the real estate closing process.
- Attend committee meetings to obtain information on proposed legislation.
- Examine legal data to determine the advisability of defending or prosecuting a lawsuit.
- Interview clients and witnesses to ascertain facts of a case.
- Prepare and draft legal documents such as wills, deeds, patent applications, mortgages, leases, and contracts.
- Research laws, regulations, policies, and precedent decisions to prepare for hearings.
- Rule on exceptions, motions, and admissibility of evidence.

What things about you point to this kind of work?

Is it important for you to

- Have good working conditions?
- Plan your work with little supervision?
- Have steady employment?

Have you enjoyed any of the following as a hobby or leisure-time activity?

- Doing public speaking or debating
- Writing articles, stories, or plays
- Belonging to a literary or book club
- Campaigning for political candidates or issues
- Helping persuade people to sign petitions for a PTA or other organization
- Advising family members on their personal problems
- Serving as president of a club or other organization
- Belonging to a political science club

Have you liked and done well in any of the following school subjects?

- Legal Terminology
- Law, Comprehensive
- Grammar
- Public Speaking
- Arbitration/Negotiation

Are you able to

- Read and understand information and ideas presented in writing?
- Communicate information and ideas in writing so others will understand?
- Listen to and understand information and ideas presented through spoken words and sentences?
- Communicate information and ideas in speaking so others will understand?
- Speak clearly so that it is understandable to a listener?
- See details of objects at close range (within a few feet)?
- Apply general rules to specific problems to come up with logical answers?

Would you work in places such as

- Business offices?
- Courthouses?
- Government offices?
- Police headquarters?
- Libraries?

What skills and knowledges do you need for this kind of work?

For most of these jobs, you need these skills:

- Reading Comprehension—understanding written sentences and paragraphs in work-related documents
- Information Gathering—knowing how to find information and identifying essential information

These knowledges are important in most of these jobs:

- Law, Government, and Jurisprudence—laws, legal codes, court procedures, precedents, government regulations, executive orders, agency rules, and the democratic political process

- English Language—the structure and content of the English language, including the meaning and spelling of words, rules of composition, and grammar

What else should you consider about this kind of work?

People in this group either work for others or set up private law practices. Many find work in private businesses or with government agencies. New lawyers and other workers in this group have better employment opportunities in large cities than in small communities.

Lawyers in small towns and cities conduct civil or criminal cases in court, draw up wills and other legal papers, and perform related activities. Those in large cities usually specialize in one kind of law, such as criminal, civil, tax, labor, or patent.

If you want a private practice you must do research before setting up your office to be sure you will have enough business. Joining an existing law firm is often a good idea.

Some government workers in this group are elected or appointed to office. Others get jobs through civil-service channels. Many of these jobs are in county seats or state capitals.

Newcomers with good training in such fields as investigating can usually find work with private law firms. Many lawyers go into politics or take management jobs with businesses. They have a chance to use their training to solve many kinds of problems.

Most workers in this group have regular office hours, but many put in much more than the usual eight hours a day. They spend evenings and weekends doing things related to their work, or get involved in social and community activities that will help their careers. People in private practice have to get and keep clients. Many of them try to get agreements with businesses and individuals to handle all their legal problems so they can be sure of a steady income.

How can you prepare for jobs of this kind?

Occupations in this group usually require education and/or training ranging from four years to more than ten years.

Lawyers must pass the bar exam to practice law. Educational requirements vary. In some states proof of graduation from an approved law school is necessary. A four-year college degree and completion of a program for law clerks is acceptable in some states. Other states allow persons who study law with a licensed lawyer to take the bar examination. Correspondence courses in law are accepted as preparation for the bar examination in some states.

Most law schools require a four-year college degree. The major does not matter, as long as it prepares you with skills for logic, critical thinking, library research, writing, and speaking.

Law students take courses in constitutional law, legal procedures, criminal law, torts, wills and estates, real estate law, labor law, criminal versus civil procedure, etc.

Some jobs in this group call for legal education but not a license. For example, paralegal assistants and legal investigators need legal knowledge but do not practice law. Many of them enter the field with a two- or four-year degree in paralegal studies; some get a certificate in paralegal studies after a degree in another field.

SPECIALIZED TRAINING

JOBS	EDUCATION/TRAINING	WHERE OBTAINED
04.02.01 Law: Legal Practice and Justice Administration		
All in Law: Legal Practice and Justice Administration	Legal Procedure and Principles; Oral and Written Communication	Four-year college, law school
23-1011.00 Lawyers	Law (LL.B., J.D.); Juridical Science/Legal Specialization (LL.M., M.C.L., J.S.D./S.)	Four-year college, law school, military (all branches)
23-1021.00 Administrative Law Judges, Adjudicators, and Hearing Officers	Law (LL.B., J.D.); Social Work	Four-year college, law school, work experience

JOBS	EDUCATION/TRAINING	WHERE OBTAINED
04.02.01 Law: Legal Practice and Justice Administration		
23-1022.00 Arbitrators, Mediators, and Conciliators	Law (LL.B., J.D.); Social Work	Four-year college, law school, work experience
23-1023.00 Judges, Magistrate Judges, and Magistrates	Law (LL.B., J.D.)	Four-year college, law school, work experience, military (Army, Navy, Air Force, Marine Corps)
04.02.02 Law: Legal Support		
All in Law: Legal Support	Legal Procedure; Oral and Written Communication	Two-year college, four-year college
23-2011.00 Paralegals and Legal Assistants	Paralegal/Legal Assistant	Two-year college, four-year college, military (Army, Navy, Air Force, Marine Corps)
23-2092.00 Law Clerks	Paralegal/Legal Assistant	Two-year college, military (Army, Navy Air Force, Marine Corps)
23-2093.01 Title Searchers	Paralegal/Legal Assistant	On the job, two-year college, business college
23-2093.02 Title Examiners and Abstractors	Office Supervision and Management; Business Administration and Management, General; Paralegal/Legal Assistant	On the job, two-year college, four-year college

04.03 Law Enforcement

Workers in this group enforce laws and regulations to protect people, animals, and property. They investigate suspicious persons and acts, prevent crimes, and identify the causes of fires, working for federal, state, and local governments. Some are hired by private businesses, such as factories and stores. They operate in a variety of settings, such as railroads, hotels, lumberyards, industrial plants, and amusement establishments.

What kind of work would you do?

Your work activities would depend on your job. For example, you might

- Arrest or assist in the arrest of criminals or suspects.
- Collect and preserve criminal evidence used to solve cases.
- Escort prisoners to and from jails and courts.
- Drive and guard armored vehicles to transport money and valuables to prevent theft and ensure safe delivery.
- Inspect campsites to ensure camper compliance with forest use regulations.
- Photograph crime or accident scenes.
- Keep records and write reports of activities, findings, transactions, violations, discrepancies, and decisions.

What things about you point to this kind of work?

Is it important for you to

- Have steady employment?
- Get a feeling of accomplishment?
- Have supervisors who back up the workers with management?
- Be treated fairly by the company?

Have you enjoyed any of the following as a hobby or leisure-time activity?

- Being a member of the school safety patrol
- Directing traffic at community events
- Instructing family members in observing traffic regulations

- Reading detective stories; watching television detective shows
- Serving as a volunteer in a fire department or emergency rescue squad
- Hunting or target shooting

Have you liked and done well in any of the following school subjects?

- Law Enforcement
- Police Science
- Human Growth and Development
- Criminology
- Criminal Investigating
- Customs Law
- Penology

Are you able to

- Communicate information and ideas in speaking so others will understand?
- Listen to and understand information and ideas presented through spoken words and sentences?
- Combine separate pieces of information, or specific answers to problems, to form general rules or conclusions?
- Tell when something is wrong or is likely to go wrong?
- Speak clearly so that it is understandable to a listener?
- Communicate information and ideas in writing so others will understand?
- See details of objects at close range (within a few feet)?

Would you work in places such as

- Police headquarters?
- Ports and harbors?
- Airports?
- Construction sites?
- Factories and plants?
- Forests?
- Gambling casinos and card clubs?
- Jails and reformatories?
- Laboratories?
- Stores and shopping malls?
- Streets and highways?
- Courthouses?
- Private homes?

What skills and knowledges do you need for this kind of work?

For most of these jobs, you need these skills:

- Speaking—talking to others to effectively convey information
- Information Gathering—knowing how to find information and identifying essential information

These knowledges are important in most of these jobs:

- Public Safety and Security—weaponry, public safety, and security operations, rules, regulations, precautions, prevention, and the protection of people, data, and property
- Law, Government, and Jurisprudence—laws, legal codes, court procedures, precedents, government regulations, executive orders, agency rules, and the democratic political process

What else should you consider about this kind of work?

Most jobs in this group are with federal, state, and local government agencies. Workers usually must pass civil-service tests and meet certain physical and personal requirements to be hired.

Applicants for jobs with government agencies can usually take the required tests at any time. The names of those who pass are kept on file for consideration when jobs open.

Shift work is standard, and sometimes overtime work is required. Most workers in these jobs are on call at all times to respond to emergencies.

Jobs in investigating can be physically demanding and dangerous, but the workers are trained to handle problems in the safest and most practical way possible.

How can you prepare for jobs of this kind?

Occupations in this group usually require education and/or training ranging from one to more than ten years.

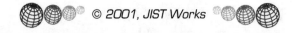

Local civil-service regulations usually control the selection of police officers. Workers must be U.S. citizens, and their height and weight must be within certain ranges. In addition, these workers may be required to take written, oral, and physical examinations. The physical examinations often include tests of strength and ability to move quickly and easily. To work in these jobs, persons should be in good physical condition to use firearms and work on dangerous missions. Background investigations are made of all applicants.

Many jobs in this group require knowledge of government, psychology, sociology, and law enforcement. Most police departments prefer to hire people with a high school education or its equal, and some require some college. However, some departments hire people if they have worked in related activities, for example, as guards or volunteer police officers.

Jobs with federal law enforcement agencies usually require a college degree. For example, customs enforcement officers must have a degree or three years of related work experience; FBI Special Agents are required to have a degree in law, or an accounting degree plus a year of related work experience. Promotions are usually based on written examinations and job performance and are usually subject to civil service laws.

SPECIALIZED TRAINING

JOBS	EDUCATION/TRAINING	WHERE OBTAINED
04.03.01 Law Enforcement: Investigation and Protection		
All in Law Enforcement: Investigation and Protection	Law; Criminology; Police Science or Fire Fighting; First Aid	Two-year college, four-year college, military
33-2021.02 Fire Investigators	Security and Loss Prevention Services; Fire Protection and Safety Technology/Technician; Fire Science/Firefighting; Fire Services Administration	Work experience in a related occupation, two-year college, four-year college
33-3011.00 Bailiffs	Law Enforcement/Police Science	On the job, two-year college, four-year college
33-3012.00 Correctional Officers and Jailers	Law Enforcement/Police Science; Criminal Justice and Corrections, Other; Corrections/Correctional Administration	On the job, two-year college, four-year college, military (Army, Navy, Air Force, Marine Corps)
33-3021.01 Police Detectives	Law Enforcement/Police Science	Work experience in a related occupation, two-year college, four-year college, military (all branches)
33-3021.03 Criminal Investigators and Special Agents	Law Enforcement/Police Science	Work experience in a related occupation, two-year college, four-year college, military (all branches)
33-3021.04 Child Support, Missing Persons, and Unemployment Insurance Fraud Investigators	Law Enforcement/Police Science; Social Work	On the job, two-year college, four-year college
33-3021.05 Immigration and Customs Inspectors	Law Enforcement/Police Science; Security and Loss Prevention Services; International Business Marketing	Work experience in a related occupation, two-year college
33-3031.00 Fish and Game Wardens	Natural Resources Law Enforcement and Protective Services; Fishing and Fisheries Sciences and Management; Wildlife and Wildlands Management	On the job, two-year college, four-year college
33-3041.00 Parking Enforcement Workers	Law Enforcement/Police Science	On the job, two-year college, four-year college

(continues)

(continued)

SPECIALIZED TRAINING

JOBS	EDUCATION/TRAINING	WHERE OBTAINED
04.03.01 Law Enforcement: Investigation and Protection		
33-3051.01 Police Patrol Officers	Law Enforcement/Police Science	Two-year college, four-year college, military (Army, Air Force, Marine Corps, Coast Guard)
33-3051.02 Highway Patrol Pilots	Aircraft Pilot and Navigator (Professional)	On the job, two-year college, four-year college, flight school
33-3051.03 Sheriffs and Deputy Sheriffs	Law Enforcement/Police Science	On the job, two-year college, four-year college, military (Army, Air Force, Marine Corps)
33-3052.00 Transit and Railroad Police	Security and Loss Prevention Services	On the job, two-year college, four-year college
04.03.02 Law Enforcement: Technology		
All in Law Enforcement: Technology	Law; Criminal Justice System	Work experience in a related occupation
19-4092.00 Forensic Science Technicians	Forensic Technology/Technician; Criminology	Two-year college, four-year college
33-3021.02 Police Identification and Records Officers	Law Enforcement/Police Science	Work experience in a related occupation, two-year college, four-year college
04.03.03 Law Enforcement: Security		
All in Law Enforcement: Security	Experience	Related jobs within the same industry
33-9011.00 Animal Control Workers	Law Enforcement/Police Science; Criminal Justice and Corrections, Other; Animal Trainer; Protective Services, Other	On the job, two-year college, trade/technical school
33-9021.00 Private Detectives and Investigators	Security and Loss Prevention Services	On the job, two-year college, four-year college, military (Army, Navy, Air Force, Marine Corps)
33-9031.00 Gaming Surveillance Officers and Gaming Investigators	Security and Loss Prevention Services	On the job, two-year college, four-year college
33-9032.00 Security Guards	Security and Loss Prevention Services	On the job
33-9091.00 Crossing Guards	Security and Loss Prevention Services	On the job
33-9092.00 Lifeguards, Ski Patrol, and Other Recreational Protective Service Workers	Criminal Justice and Corrections, Other	On the job, two-year college, four-year college

04.04 Public Safety

Workers in this group protect the public by responding to emergencies and by ensuring that people are not exposed to unsafe products or facilities. Some respond hastily to emergencies, stabilizing sick or injured people en route to a hospital, or acting quickly to put out fires and evacuate people from burning buildings. Dealing with sudden crises requires them to have both technical skills and the ability keep a cool head. Others investigate business practices, examine records, and inspect materials, products, workplaces, utilities, and transportation equipment for compliance with government regulations or conformance to company policies. They may impound records, close down businesses, or bring other pressures to bear against individuals or organizations they find to be in violation of rules. Although they are not involved directly with construction, installation, or processing operations, they must know the technical principles to be able to measure and evaluate the quality of the materials and equipment they inspect.

What kind of work would you do?

Your work activities would depend on your job. For example, you might

- Confer with management or other personnel to resolve or settle equal opportunity issues and disputes.
- Drive and operate fire-fighting vehicles and equipment.
- Give first aid in emergencies.
- Investigate animal bites and alleged violations, interview witnesses, and report violations to police or request arrest of violators.
- Measure density of lead shielding in walls, using radiometric equipment.
- Prepare report of findings and recommendations for corrective action.
- Recommend changes in policies and procedures to prevent accidents and illness.

What things about you point to this kind of work?

Is it important for you to

- Have steady employment?
- Make decisions on your own?
- Be treated fairly by the company?
- Get a feeling of accomplishment?

Have you enjoyed any of the following as a hobby or leisure-time activity?

- Being a member of the school safety patrol
- Directing traffic at community events
- Instructing family members in observing traffic regulations
- Reading detective stories; watching television detective shows
- Serving as a volunteer counselor at a youth camp or center
- Hunting or target shooting
- Serving as a volunteer in a fire department or emergency rescue squad
- Applying first aid in emergencies as a volunteer

Have you liked and done well in any of the following school subjects?

- Fire Fighting
- Fire Safety
- Safety Regulations
- Emergency Care/Rescue
- First Aid

Are you able to

- Communicate information and ideas in speaking so others will understand?
- Tell when something is wrong or is likely to go wrong?
- Listen to and understand information and ideas presented through spoken words and sentences?
- Read and understand information and ideas presented in writing?
- Apply general rules to specific problems to come up with logical answers?
- Communicate information and ideas in writing so others will understand?
- See details of objects at a close range (within a few feet)?

Would you work in places such as

- Forests?
- Streets and highways?
- Airports?
- Bus and train stations?
- Construction sites?
- Factories and plants?
- Farms?

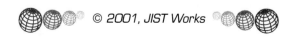

- Gambling casinos and card clubs?
- Hospitals and nursing homes?
- Mines and quarries?
- Ports and harbors?
- Waterworks and light and power plants?
- Schools and homes for people with disabilities?

What skills and knowledges do you need for this kind of work?

For most of these jobs, you need these skills:

- Information Gathering—knowing how to find information and identifying essential information
- Speaking—talking to others to effectively convey information
- Problem Identification—identifying the nature of problems
- Critical Thinking—using logic and analysis to identify the strengths and weaknesses of different approaches

These knowledges are important in most of these jobs:

- Public Safety and Security—weaponry, public safety, and security operations; rules, regulations, precautions, prevention; and the protection of people, data, and property
- English Language—the structure and content of the English language, including the meaning and spelling of words, rules of composition, and grammar

What else should you consider about this kind of work?

Many jobs in this group are with local, state, and federal governments. For most government jobs you must pass civil-service examinations. Some jobs are with private industry and nonprofit organizations.

Most jobs in the group have regular working hours, although some involve evening or night-shift work. Some require travel, usually within the state or metropolitan area. Some workers are required to wear uniforms.

Some work in an office all day; others must go from place to place to inspect licenses and determine compliance of beauty shop operators, food service workers, etc. Others are stationed at inspection locations, such as port-of-entry and border crossings. Fire fighters sometimes face life-threatening situations but are trained in safety procedures.

How can you prepare for jobs of this kind?

Occupations in this group usually require education and/or training ranging from one to more than ten years. Some jobs call for prior knowledge of the regulations to be enforced and the procedures to be used. Others demand special training such as insurance underwriting. Clerical and other workers within a company or government agency are sometimes promoted to positions in this group. Other jobs require skills and knowledge that are identified by special tests. Fire fighters must also past tests of physical strength and agility. Emergency medical technicians must know CPR, among other first-aid techniques. College-level coursework in English (especially composition, reporting, and technical writing), government, and history is useful.

Many of the jobs in this group are in government agencies and are filled by those who qualify through civil-service examinations. Some jobs are filled through appointments made by governors, mayors, and other political leaders.

SPECIALIZED TRAINING

JOBS	EDUCATION/TRAINING	WHERE OBTAINED
	04.04.01 Public Safety: Emergency Responding	
All in Public Safety: Emergency Responding	First Aid and Artificial Respiration; Fire Fighting and Rescue Techniques	Two-year college, trade/technical school, military, related jobs within the same industry
29-2041.00 Emergency Medical Technicians and Paramedics	Emergency Medical Technology/Technician	Two-year college, trade/technical school, military (Army, Navy, Air Force, Coast Guard)

JOBS	EDUCATION/TRAINING	WHERE OBTAINED
	04.04.01 Public Safety: Emergency Responding	
33-2011.00 Fire Fighters	Fire Science/Firefighting; Fire Protection, Other	Two-year college, trade/technical school; military data not yet available
33-2011.01 Municipal Fire Fighters	Fire Science/Firefighting	On the job, two-year college, trade/technical school, military (all branches)
33-2011.02 Forest Fire Fighters	Natural Resources Law Enforcement and Protective Services; Fire Science/Firefighting	On the job, two-year college, trade/technical school
	04.04.02 Public Safety: Regulations Enforcement	
All in Public Safety Regulations Enforcement	Experience	Related jobs within the same industry
13-1041.00 Compliance Officers, Except Agriculture, Construction, Health and Safety, and Transportation	Natural Resources Law Enforcement and Protective Services; Occupational Safety and Health Technician/Technician; Taxation	Two-year college, trade/technical school; military data not yet available
13-1041.01 Environmental Compliance Inspectors	Environmental and Pollution Control Technician/Technician; Plant Protection (Pest Management); Plant Sciences, General; Food Sciences and Technology; Agricultural Supplies Retailing and Wholesaling; Agricultural and Food Products Processing Operations and Management; Water Quality and Wastewater Treatment Technology/Technician	Two-year college, trade/technical school, military (Air Force, Marine Corps)
13-1041.02 Licensing Examiners and Inspectors	Public Administration; Law Enforcement/Police Science; Driver and Safety Teacher Education	Two-year college, trade/technical school, military (Marine Corps, Coast Guard)
13-1041.03 Equal Opportunity Representatives and Officers	Human Resources Management; Community Organization, Resources, and Services; Public Administration	Two-year college, trade/technical school, military (all branches)
13-1041.04 Government Property Inspectors and Investigators	Quality Control Technology/Technician; Law Enforcement/Police Science	Two-year college, trade/technical school, military (Coast Guard)
13-2061.00 Financial Examiners	Finance, General	Two-year college, trade/technical school
19-4051.02 Nuclear Monitoring Technicians	Health Physics/Radiologic Health; Nuclear and Industrial Radiologic Technology/Technicians, Other; Nuclear/Nuclear Power Technology/Technician	Two-year college, trade/technical school, military (Army, Navy, Marine Corps)
29-9011.00 Occupational Health and Safety Specialists	Occupational Safety and Health Technology/Technician	Two-year college, military (Army, Navy, Air Force)

(continues)

(continued)

SPECIALIZED TRAINING

JOBS	EDUCATION/TRAINING	WHERE OBTAINED
04.04.02 Public Safety: Regulations Enforcement		
29-9012.00 Occupational Health and Safety Technicians	Natural Resources Law Enforcement and Protective Services; Occupational Safety and Health Technology/Technician; Taxation; Health Aide; Orthoptics; Health and Medical Diagnostic and Treatment Services, Other; Health and Medical Assistants, Other; Health Professions and Related Sciences, Other; Diagnostic Medical Sonography	Two-year college, trade/technical school; military data not yet available
33-2021.01 Fire Inspectors	Fire Protection and Safety Technology/Technician	Two-year college, trade/technical school, military (Army, Air Force, Marine Corps)
33-2022.00 Forest Fire Inspectors and Prevention Specialists	Natural Resources Law Enforcement and Protective Services; Fire Services Administration; Fire Science/Firefighting	Two-year college, four-year college
45-2011.00 Agricultural Inspectors	Plant Sciences, General; Agricultural and Food Products Processing Operations and Management; Plant Protection (Pest Management)	Two-year college, trade/technical school
53-6051.01 Aviation Inspectors	Occupational Safety and Health Technology	Two-year college, trade/technical school, military (Coast Guard)
53-6051.02 Public Transportation Inspectors	Transportation and Highway Engineering; Civil Engineering, General	Two-year college, trade/technical school
53-6051.03 Marine Cargo Inspectors	Occupational Safety and Health Technology; Taxation	Two-year college, trade/technical school, military (Coast Guard)

04.05 Military

Workers in this group serve in the Armed Forces of the United States: the Air Force, Army, Coast Guard, Marines, Navy, and National Guard. Although workers in the Armed Forces perform almost every occupation found in the civilian workforce, the occupations in this subgroup are unique to the military and have no civilian counterparts. The purpose of workers in the military is to ensure peace and protect the nation in times of war. In unusual cases, the military must assist in national emergencies or to restore order in events of civil disobedience.

What kind of work would you do?

Your work activities would depend on your job. For example, you might

- Confer with management or other personnel to plan strategy.
- Fly aircraft to attack or defend against the enemy.
- Use military vehicles such as tanks to engage the enemy.
- Maintain missile defense systems.
- Monitor radar and other devices to identify enemy positions.

What things about you point to this kind of work?

Is it important for you to

- Have steady employment?
- Make decisions on your own?
- Be treated fairly by the company?
- Get a feeling of accomplishment?

Have you enjoyed any of the following as a hobby or leisure-time activity?

- Being a member of the school safety patrol
- Directing traffic at community events
- Instructing family members in observing traffic regulations
- Reading military stories; watching television shows and movies about the military
- Hiking and camping
- Hunting or target shooting
- Serving as a volunteer in a fire department or emergency rescue squad
- Applying first aid in emergencies as a volunteer

Have you liked and done well in any of the following school subjects?

- Political Science
- History
- Mathematics
- Mechanics
- First Aid

Are you able to

- Communicate information and ideas in speaking so others will understand?
- Tell when something is wrong or is likely to go wrong?
- Listen to and understand information and ideas presented through spoken words and sentences?
- Read and understand information and ideas presented in writing?
- Apply general rules to specific problems to come up with logical answers?
- Communicate information and ideas in writing so others will understand?
- See details of objects at close range (within a few feet)?

Would you work in places such as

- Military bases?
- Foreign countries?
- Forests?
- Airports?
- Ports and harbors?

What skills and knowledges do you need for this kind of work?

For most of these jobs, you need these skills:

- Information Gathering—knowing how to find information and identifying essential information
- Speaking—talking to others to effectively convey information
- Problem Identification—identifying the nature of problems
- Critical Thinking—using logic and analysis to identify the strengths and weaknesses of different approaches

These knowledges are important in most of these jobs:

- Public Safety and Security—weaponry, public safety, and security operations, rules, regulations, precautions, prevention, and the protection of people, data, and property
- English Language—the structure and content of the English language, including the meaning and spelling of words, rules of composition, and grammar

What else should you consider about this kind of work?

You must pass physical and mental tests and be within certain age limits to qualify for military occupations. Women are excluded from jobs that involve direct exposure to combat.

The jobs require a high degree of physical conditioning. Usually, workers are assigned for short periods and must move frequently. The work environment is highly structured, and you must be able to understand and follow orders. You are required to wear uniforms and obey some regulations not found in civilian life. The work schedule can vary a great deal.

Military personnel who engage the enemy are under a great deal of physical and mental stress. Jobs can be highly dangerous, even during peacetime.

Although the military has done a lot of downsizing in recent years, there are many opportunities for new recruits. Military service can be a stepping stone to many good careers in civilian life.

How can you prepare for jobs of this kind?

Occupations in this group usually require a high school education. Officers and senior personnel are normally required to have a college education. Promotion to higher ranks in the officer corps usually requires graduate education. All jobs require several months to several years of specialized military training, including physical conditioning.

The O*NET currently doesn't have data on the characteristics of the new military jobs that have been added. However, we have included the following job titles and numbers.

04.05.01 Military: Officers and Supervisors

55-1011.00	Air Crew Officers
55-1012.00	Aircraft Launch and Recovery Officers
55-1013.00	Armored Assault Vehicle Officers
55-1014.00	Artillery and Missile Officers
55-1015.00	Command and Control Center Officers
55-1016.00	Infantry Officers
55-1017.00	Special Forces Officers
55-2011.00	First-Line Supervisors/Managers of Air Crew Members
55-2012.00	First-Line Supervisors/Managers of Weapons Specialists/Crew Members
55-2013.00	First-Line Supervisors/Managers of All Other Tactical Operations Specialists

04.05.02 Military: Specialists

55-3011.00	Air Crew Members
55-3012.00	Aircraft Launch and Recovery Specialists
55-3013.00	Armored Assault Vehicle Crew Members
55-3014.00	Artillery and Missile Crew Members
55-3015.00	Command and Control Center Specialists
55-3016.00	Infantry
55-3017.00	Radar and Sonar Technicians
55-3018.00	Special Forces

05 Mechanics, Installers, and Repairers

An interest in applying mechanical and electrical/electronic principles to practical situations by use of machines or hand tools.

You can satisfy this interest working with a variety of tools, technologies, materials, and settings. If you enjoy making machines run efficiently or fixing them when they break down, you could seek a job installing or repairing such devices as copiers, aircraft engines, automobiles, or watches. You may instead prefer to deal directly with certain materials, and find work cutting and shaping metal or wood. Or if electricity and electronics interest you, you could install cables, troubleshoot telephone networks, or repair videocassette recorders. If you prefer routine or physical work in settings other than factories, perhaps work repairing tires or batteries would appeal to you.

05.01 Managerial Work in Mechanics, Installers, and Repairers

05.02 Electrical and Electronic Systems

05.03 Mechanical Work

05.04 Hands-on Work in Mechanics, Installers, and Repairers

05.01 Managerial Work in Mechanics, Installers, and Repairers

Workers in this group directly supervise and coordinate activities of mechanics, repairers, and installers and their helpers. They are generally found in smaller establishments where they perform both supervisory and management functions, such as accounting, marketing, and personnel work, and may also engage in the same repair and installation work as the workers they supervise.

What kind of work would you do?

Your work activities would depend on your job. For example, you might

- Assign workers to perform activities such as service appliances, repair and maintain vehicles, and install machinery and equipment.
- Compute estimates and actual costs of factors, such as materials, labor, and outside contractors, and prepare budgets.
- Establish or adjust work methods and procedures to meet production schedules, using knowledge of capacities of machines, equipment, and personnel.
- Patrol work area and examine tools and equipment to detect unsafe conditions or violations of safety rules.
- Recommend or initiate personnel actions, such as employment, performance evaluations, promotions, transfers, discharges, and disciplinary measures.

What things about you point to this kind of work?

Is it important for you to

- Give directions and instructions to others?
- Make decisions on your own?
- Plan your work with little supervision?

Have you enjoyed any of the following as a hobby or leisure-time activity?

- Building or repairing radios or television sets
- Building model airplanes, automobiles, or boats
- Building cabinets or furniture
- Designing and building an addition or remodeling the interior of a home
- Doing electrical wiring and repairs in the home
- Installing and repairing home stereo equipment
- Reading mechanical or automotive magazines
- Serving as a leader of a scouting or other group

Have you liked and done well in any of the following school subjects?

- Management
- Industrial Organization
- Industrial Safety
- Personnel Management
- Blueprint/Schematic Reading

Are you able to

- Communicate information and ideas in speaking so others will understand?
- See details of objects at close range (within a few feet)?
- Correctly follow a given rule or set of rules in order to arrange things or actions in a certain order?
- Listen to and understand information and ideas presented through spoken words and sentences?
- Read and understand information and ideas presented in writing?
- Apply general rules to specific problems to come up with logical answers?

Would you work in places such as

- Factories and plants?
- Business offices?
- Auto service stations and repair shops?
- Mines and quarries?
- Farms?
- Oil fields?
- Ports and harbors?
- Radio studios?
- Television studios?
- Motion picture and recording studios?
- Ships and boats?

What skills and knowledges do you need for this kind of work?

For most of these jobs, you need these skills:

- Management of Personnel Resources—motivating, developing, and directing people as they work, identifying the best people for the job

- Coordination—adjusting actions in relation to others' actions
- Time Management—managing your own time and the time of others

These knowledges are important in most of these jobs:

- Mechanical—machines and tools, including their designs, uses, benefits, repair, and maintenance
- Administration and Management—principles and processes involved in business and organizational planning, coordination, and execution

What else should you consider about this kind of work?

Opportunities for these managers/supervisors are good, although somewhat sensitive to the business cycle. The best opportunities are likely to be in supervising workers who repair, service, or install equipment used for purposes other than manufacturing, which is in decline in the United States. Fortunately, many other kinds of mechanical, electrical, and electronic equipment are gaining in use—in businesses of all kinds, hospitals, malls, and private homes. In electronics, the trend toward "works-on-a-chip" makes mechanics and servicers less necessary for some equipment, but the field as a whole is growing as new devices are invented and marketed.

These workers must think quickly to make policy and operational decisions that conform to overall company policy.

Most of these managers work a regular eight-hour day, but some have to work overtime without additional pay. However, they often receive benefits such as bonuses, stock options, and participation in profit-sharing plans.

Although they spend much of their time in an office doing paperwork, they frequently tour work sites to observe operations, monitor progress, detect possible problems, and give directions to workers. They also may spend a small amount of time doing the same work as the people they supervise.

How can you prepare for jobs of this kind?

Managers/supervisors of mechanics, installers, and repairers may require as much as four to six years of education and/or training. Many work their way up from jobs as mechanics, installers, or repairers and enter these initial jobs with only two years of education or training, gained in a college or apprenticeship program. Later they acquire the managerial skills they need with coursework in accounting, personnel, and finance.

Others begin their preparation with a two- or four-year degree in industrial management. Through coursework or work experience they gain knowledge of the tasks performed by the people whose work they oversee.

SPECIALIZED TRAINING

JOBS	EDUCATION/TRAINING	WHERE OBTAINED
05.01.01 Managerial Work in Mechanics, Installers, and Repairers		
49-1011.00 First-Line Supervisors/Managers of Mechanics, Installers, and Repairers	Logistics and Materials Management; Business Administration and Management, General; Vehicle Parts and Accessories Marketing Operations; Operations Management and Supervision	Work experience in a related occupation, two-year college, trade/technical school, on the job, military (all branches)

05.02 Electrical and Electronic Systems

Workers in this group repair and install electrical devices and systems such as motors, transformers, appliances, and power lines; and electronic devices and systems such as radios, computers, and telephone networks. They work for manufacturers, utilities, and service companies. Since electrical and electronic equipment is used almost everywhere, they may work in almost any kind of location, as well as in repair shops.

What kind of work would you do?

Your work activities would depend on your job. For example, you might

- Assemble electrical parts, such as alternators, generators, starting devices, and switches, following schematic drawings, using hand, machine, and power tools.
- Install safety and control devices, cables, drives, rails, motors, and elevator cars.
- Connect electrical wiring to control panels and electric motors.
- Maintain records of repairs, calibrations, and tests.
- Position loudspeakers and microphones.
- Read blueprints, wiring diagrams, schematic drawings, and engineering instructions for assembling electronics units, applying knowledge of electronic theory and components.
- Test installed equipment for conformance to specifications, using test equipment.

What things about you point to this kind of work?

Is it important for you to

- Never be pressured to do things that go against your sense of right and wrong?
- Have steady employment?
- Be treated fairly by the company?

Have you enjoyed any of the following as a hobby or leisure-time activity?

- Building or repairing radios or television sets
- Doing electrical wiring and repairs in the home
- Operating a CB or ham radio
- Building model airplanes, automobiles, or boats
- Creating unusual lighting effects for school or other amateur plays
- Installing and repairing home stereo equipment
- Upgrading hardware in a personal computer

Have you liked and done well in any of the following school subjects?

- Electricity/Electronics
- Blueprint/Schematic Reading
- Electric/Electronic Shop
- Electric/Electronic Theory
- Electrical Circuits
- Electronic Devices
- Electrical Systems
- Power Systems/Technology
- Math Computing, Standard Formula
- Business Machine Repair

Are you able to

- Quickly make coordinated movements of one hand, a hand together with its arm, or two hands to grasp, manipulate, or assemble objects?
- Tell when something is wrong or is likely to go wrong?
- Correctly follow a given rule or set of rules in order to arrange things or actions in a certain order?
- Make precisely coordinated movements of the fingers of one or both hands to grasp, manipulate, or assemble very small objects?
- See details of objects at close range (within a few feet)?

Would you work in places such as

- Airports?
- Streets and highways?
- Business offices?
- Computer centers?
- Construction sites?
- Factories and plants?
- Waterworks and light and power plants?
- Hospitals and nursing homes?
- Railroad tracks and yards?

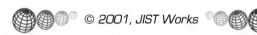

- Motion picture and recording studios?
- Radio studios?
- Television studios?

What skills and knowledges do you need for this kind of work?

For most of these jobs, you need these skills:

- Repairing—repairing machines or systems using the needed tools
- Installation—installing equipment, machines, wiring, or programs to meet specifications

These knowledges are important in most of these jobs:

- Computers and Electronics—electric circuit boards, processors, chips, and computer hardware and software, including applications and programming
- Mechanical—machines and tools, including their designs, uses, benefits, repair, and maintenance

What else should you consider about this kind of work?

Some jobs in this group are found in almost every large and small city. Others are available only where certain industries are located. Best opportunities are in installation, service, and repair of equipment used for purposes other than manufacturing. High-tech fields, such as the technology of data-processing equipment or lasers, are in especially high demand. Because of miniaturization and better quality control, some products need fewer repairs and service calls. Nevertheless, so many new electronic devices are being created that the field as a whole is growing.

Factories, service companies, and large companies with an in-house service staff hire many of these workers. Others are self-employed, working full-time or part-time. Work schedules vary. Factories, hospitals, and radio and TV studios, for instance, have rotating shifts.

Some equipment repairs or adjustments are made in a repair shop; others are made in the customer's office or home. Some jobs require climbing or crawling to reach wiring and components.

Careful safety procedures must be observed for some jobs because of the chance of electric shock. Good color vision is usually needed, since electronic parts are often color-coded.

How can you prepare for jobs of this kind?

Work in this group usually requires education and/or training ranging from two to six years, depending on the type of equipment. Colleges and technical schools offer two-year programs in electronics technology or electrical engineering technology. Courses in electricity, electronics, mathematics, and blueprint reading are especially helpful.

A few companies provide extensive training to prepare workers for repair jobs. Correspondence courses in such fields as electricity and electronics are often helpful. Apprenticeships are also available, and military experience can be a start.

Technology in this field is changing constantly, so workers need to take courses and get training to keep their skills current.

SPECIALIZED TRAINING

JOBS	EDUCATION/TRAINING	WHERE OBTAINED
05.02.01 Electrical and Electronic Systems: Installation and Repair		
All in Electrical and Electronic Systems: Installation and Repair	Electronics; Algebra; Shop Safety; experience	High school, two-year college, trade/technical school, four-year college, related jobs within the same industry
47-4021.00 Elevator Installers and Repairers	Industrial Machinery Maintenance and Repair	Two-year college, trade/technical school, on the job, military (Navy)
49-2022.01 Central Office and PBX Installers and Repairers	Communication Systems Installer and Repairer; Electrical and Electronics Equipment Installer and Repairer, General	Two-year college, trade/technical school, four-year college, military (all branches)
49-2022.02 Frame Wirers, Central Office	Electrical and Electronics Equipment Installer and Repairer, General; Communication Systems Installer and Repairer	Two-year college, trade/technical school, on the job

(continues)

(continued)

SPECIALIZED TRAINING

JOBS	EDUCATION/TRAINING	WHERE OBTAINED
05.02.01 Electrical and Electronic Systems: Installation and Repair		
49-2022.03 Communication Equipment Mechanics, Installers, and Repairers	Communication Systems Installer and Repairer; Electrical and Electronics Equipment Installer and Repairer, General	Two-year college, trade/technical school, four-year college, military (all branches)
49-2022.04 Telecommunications Facility Examiners	Electrical and Electronics Equipment Installer and Repairer, General; Computer Installer and Repairer; Communication Systems Installer and Repairer; Electrician; Lineworker; Electrical and Power Transmission Installer, General	Two-year college, trade/technical school, four-year college, military (Army, Navy, Marine Corps)
49-2022.05 Station Installers and Repairers, Telephone	Electrical and Electronics Equipment Installer and Repairer, General; Communication Systems Installer and Repairer	Two-year college, trade/technical school
49-2091.00 Avionics Technicians	Electrical and Power Transmission Installer, General; Aircraft Mechanic/Technician, Airframe; Aircraft Mechanic/Technician, Powerplant; Electrician	Two-year college, trade/technical school, on the job, military (all branches)
49-2093.00 Electrical and Electronics Installers Repairers, Transportation Equipment	Auto/Automotive Mechanic/Technician; Electrical and Power Transmission Installer, General; Electrician	Two-year college, trade/technical school, on the job, military (Army, Marine Corps)
49-2094.00 Electrical and Electronics Repairers, Commercial and Industrial Equipment	Electrical and Electronics Equipment Installer and Repairer, General; Business Machine Repairer; Communication Systems Installer and Repairer; Computer Installer and Repairer; Aviation Systems and Avionics Maintenance Technologist/Technician; Computer Maintenance Technology/Technician; Industrial Electronics Installer and Repairer; Industrial Radiologic Technology/Technician	Two-year college, trade/technical school, military (all branches)
49-2096.00 Electronic Equipment Installers and Repairers, Motor Vehicles	Electrical and Power Transmission Installer, General; Electrician; Auto/Automotive Mechanic/Technician	Two-year college, trade/technical school, on the job, military (Army, Marine Corps)
49-9031.01 Home Appliance Installers	Major Appliance Installer and Repairer; Electrical and Electronics Equipment Installer and Repairer, General	Two-year college, trade/technical school, on the job
49-9051.00 Electrical Power-Line Installers and Repairers	Lineworker; Electrical and Power Transmission Installer, General	Two-year college, trade/technical school, on the job, military (Army, Navy, Air Force, Marine Corps)
49-9052.00 Telecommunications Line Installers and Repairers	Lineworker; Electrical and Power Transmission Installer, General	Two-year college, trade/technical school, on the job, military (Army, Navy, Marine Corps, Coast Guard)
49-9097.00 Signal and Track Switch Repairers	Electrician; Lineworker; Electrical and Power Transmission Installer, General	Two-year college, trade/technical school, on the job

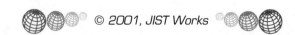

JOBS	EDUCATION/TRAINING	WHERE OBTAINED
05.02.02 Electrical and Electronic Systems: Equipment Repair		
All in Electrical and Electronic Systems: Equipment Repair	Electronics; Algebra; Shop Safety; experience	Two-year college, trade/technical school, four-year college, related jobs within the same industry
49-2011.02 Data Processing Equipment Repairers	Computer Maintenance Technology/Technician	Two-year college, trade/technical school, military (all branches)
49-2011.03 Office Machine and Cash Register Servicers	Business Machine Repairer; Electrical and Electronics Equipment Installer and Repairer, General; Computer Installer and Repairer	Trade/technical school, on the job, military (Navy)
49-2021.00 Radio Mechanics	Communication Systems Installer and Repairer; Electrical and Electronics Equipment Installer and Repairer, General	Two-year college, trade/technical school, military (all branches)
49-2092.01 Electric Home Appliance and Power Tool Repairers	Electrical and Electronics Equipment Installer and Repairer, General; Major Appliance Installer and Repairer; Electrical and Electronics Equipment Installer and Repairer, General; Heating, Air Conditioning, and Refrigeration Mechanic and Repairer	Two-year college, trade/technical school, military (Navy)
49-2092.02 Electric Motor and Switch Assemblers and Repairers	Electrical and Power Transmission Installer, General; Electrical and Electronics Equipment Installer and Repairer, General; Electrician; Auto/Automotive Mechanic/Technician; Stationary Energy Sources Installer and Operator; Electrical and Electronics Equipment Installer and Repairer, General; Industrial Electronics Installer and Repairer	Two-year college, trade/technical school, on the job, military (all branches)
49-2092.03 Battery Repairers	Electrical and Electronics Equipment Installer and Repairer, General; Electrical and Power Transmission Installer, General; Electrician	On the job
49-2092.04 Transformer Repairers	Electrician; Electrical and Electronics Equipment Installer and Repairer, General; Stationary Energy Sources Installer and Operator; Electrical and Power Transmission Installer, General	Two-year college, trade/technical school, on the job
49-2092.05 Electrical Parts Reconditioners	Electrical and Electronics Equipment Installer and Repairer, General; Electrical and Electronics Equipment Installer and Repairer, Other	Two-year college, trade/technical school, on the job
49-2095.00 Electrical and Electronics Repairers, Power-house, Substation, and Relay	Electrician; Stationary Energy Sources Installer and Operator; Electrical and Power Transmission Installer, General	Two-year college, trade/technical school, on the job, military (Army, Navy, Coast Guard)
49-2097.00 Electronic Home Entertainment Equipment Installers and Repairers	Electrical and Electronics Equipment Installer and Repairer, General; Musical Instrument Repairer; Communication Systems Installer and Repairer	Two-year college, trade/technical school, military (Army, Navy, Air Force, Marine Corps)
49-9012.01 Electric Meter Installers and Repairers	Instrument Calibration and Repairer	On the job, two-year college, trade/technical school

05.03 Mechanical Work

Workers in this group install, service, and repair various kinds of machinery. Some are large, such as bodies and engines of cars, trucks, buses, airplanes, and ships; furnaces and air conditioners; office machines; and home appliances. Others are small, such as locks, watches, medical instruments, power tools, and musical instruments. These workers are hired by manufacturers, service companies, and businesses that use machines.

What kind of work would you do?

Your work activities would depend on your job. For example, you might

- Assemble new or reconditioned appliances.
- Clean equipment with solvent, brushes, and air hoses to remove dirt, lint, oil, and rust.
- Fasten components together with screws, nails, or glue, using hand tools or portable power tools.
- Grind and polish optics, using hand tools and polishing cloths.
- Inspect and test machinery and equipment to diagnose machine malfunctions.
- Install door frames, door closers, and electronic-eye mechanisms using power tools, hand tools, and electronic test equipment.
- Repair watch cases, surface defects of clocks, and watchbands.

What things about you point to this kind of work?

Is it important for you to

- Never be pressured to do things that go against your sense of right and wrong?
- Do your work alone?
- Be treated fairly by the company?

Have you enjoyed any of the following as a hobby or leisure-time activity?

- Building model airplanes, automobiles, or boats
- Repairing or assembling bicycles or tricycles
- Making sketches of machines or other mechanical equipment
- Operating a model train layout
- Reading airplane or boat magazines
- Reading mechanical or automotive magazines
- Repairing plumbing in the home

Have you liked and done well in any of the following school subjects?

- Industrial Arts
- Blueprint/Schematic Reading
- Shop Math
- Auto Body Repair/Shop
- Auto Mechanics
- Diesel Mechanics/Diesels
- Aircraft Mechanics
- Locksmithing/Lock Repair
- Hydraulics/Hydraulic Shop
- Watchmaking/Watch Repair Shop
- Instrument Repair

Are you able to

- Quickly make coordinated movements of one hand, a hand together with its arm, or two hands to grasp, manipulate, or assemble objects?
- Make precisely coordinated movements of the fingers of one or both hands to grasp, manipulate, or assemble very small objects?
- See details of objects at close range (within a few feet)?
- Correctly follow a given rule or set of rules in order to arrange things or actions in a certain order?
- Quickly and repeatedly make precise adjustments in moving the controls of a machine or vehicle to exact positions?
- Tell when something is wrong or is likely to go wrong?
- Keep your hand and arm steady while making an arm movement or while holding your arm and hand in one position?

Would you work in places such as

- Airplanes?
- Auto service stations and repair shops?
- Bowling alleys?
- Buses and trolleys?
- Construction sites?
- Factories and plants?
- Business offices?
- Waterworks and light and power plants?

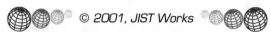

- Hospitals and nursing homes?
- Mines and quarries?
- Ships and boats?
- Trains?
- Farms?

What skills and knowledges do you need for this kind of work?

For most of these jobs, you need these skills:

- Repairing—repairing machines or systems using the needed tools
- Equipment Selection—determining the kind of tools and equipment needed to do a job

These knowledges are important in most of these jobs:

- Mechanical—machines and tools, including their designs, uses, benefits, repair, and maintenance
- Engineering and Technology—equipment, tools, mechanical devices, and their uses to produce motion, light, power, technology, and other applications

What else should you consider about this kind of work?

Workers in this group do fabrication, installation, servicing, and repairs for manufacturers, merchandisers of appliances, specialized repair shops (such as auto repair garages), and service companies. Some are self-employed and market their skills directly to consumers or businesses.

As some devices (such as watches) become more electronic and cheaper, opportunities will decline in some specialties. In other cases (such as automobiles), the demand for repairs will continue or grow, but workers will need to upgrade their skills to stay employable as technology changes. The American love of gadgets and of labor-saving devices guarantees that many of these jobs will long be in demand, but some (such as bridge and lock tenders) may decline because of advances in technology. In addition, the export of manufacturing capability from the U.S. is likely to reduce the need for certain machinery maintenance jobs.

How can you prepare for jobs of this kind?

For work in this group, education and/or training requirements vary from six months to six years, depending on the sophistication of the machinery being worked on.

Some of these jobs (for example, motorcycle mechanics and repairers) are taught by a training program at the repair shop, lasting six months to two years.

Most automobile mechanics also learn their skills on the job. They usually start as helpers, lubrication workers, or gasoline station attendants. However, formal training programs are available. Three to four years of experience are required to become a general automobile mechanic.

A few of these jobs (for example, some musical instrument repairers) require a long apprenticeship to learn skills of working with precision tools and delicate materials.

In almost all of the jobs, high school courses in blueprint reading and mechanical drawing are a good first step. Since keeping up with new technology is the key to continued employment and good income, high school courses in mathematics should go beyond shop math.

SPECIALIZED TRAINING

JOBS	EDUCATION/TRAINING	WHERE OBTAINED
05.03.01 Mechanical Work: Vehicles and Facilities		
All in Mechanical Work: Vehicles and Facilities	Shop Math; Shop Safety; experience	High school, trade/technical school, military, related jobs within the same industry
49-3011.01 Airframe-and-Power-Plant Mechanics	Aircraft Mechanic/Technician, Airframe; Aircraft Mechanic/Technician, Powerplant	Trade/technical school, on the job, military (all branches)
49-3011.02 Aircraft Engine Specialists	Aircraft Mechanic/Technician, Airframe; Aircraft Mechanic/Technician, Powerplant	Trade/technical school, on the job, military (all branches)

(continues)

(continued)

SPECIALIZED TRAINING

JOBS	EDUCATION/TRAINING	WHERE OBTAINED
05.03.01 Mechanical Work: Vehicles and Facilities		
49-3011.03 Aircraft Body and Bonded Structure Repairers	Aircraft Mechanic/Technician, Airframe	Trade/technical school, on the job, military (all branches)
49-3021.00 Automotive Body and Related Repairers	Auto/Automotive Body Repairer	Trade/technical school, on the job, military (Army, Navy, Air Force, Marine Corps)
49-3022.00 Automotive Glass Installers and Repairers	Auto/Automotive Body Repairer	Trade/technical school, on the job
49-3023.01 Automotive Master Mechanics	Auto/Automotive Mechanic/Technician	Trade/technical school, on the job, military (all branches)
49-3023.02 Automotive Specialty Technicians	Heating, Air Conditioning, and Refrigeration Mechanic and Repairer; Auto/Automotive Mechanic/Technician; Machinist/Machine Technologist	Trade/technical school, on the job, military (Army, Navy, Marine Corps)
49-3031.00 Bus and Truck Mechanics and Diesel Engine Specialists	Agricultural Power Machinery Operator; Heavy Equipment Maintenance and Repair; Auto/Automotive Mechanic/Technician; Diesel Engine Mechanic and Repairer	Trade/technical school, on the job, military (all branches)
49-3041.00 Farm Equipment Mechanics	Agricultural Power Machinery Operator	Trade/technical school, on the job
49-3042.00 Mobile Heavy Equipment Mechanics, Except Engines	Heavy Equipment Maintenance and Repairer	Trade/technical school, on the job, military (all branches)
49-3043.00 Rail Car Repairers	Instrument Calibration and Repairer; Heavy Equipment Maintenance and Repairer	Trade/technical school, on the job
49-3051.00 Motorboat Mechanics	Marine Maintenance and Ship Repairer	Trade/technical school, on the job, military (Army, Marine Corps, Coast Guard)
49-3052.00 Motorcycle Mechanics	Motorcycle Mechanic and Repairer	Trade/technical school, on the job
49-3053.00 Outdoor Power Equipment and Other Small Engine Mechanics	Agricultural Power Machinery Operator; Electrical and Electronics Equipment Installer and Repairer, General; Small Engine Mechanic and Repairer; Agricultural Mechanization, General	Trade/technical school, on the job, military (Army)
49-3092.00 Recreational Vehicle Service Technicians	Auto/Automotive Mechanic/Technician	Trade/technical school, on the job; military data not yet available
49-9021.01 Heating and Air Conditioning Mechanics	Heating, Air Conditioning, and Refrigeration Mechanic and Repairer	Two-year college, trade/technical school, on the job, military (Army, Navy, Air Force, Marine Corps)

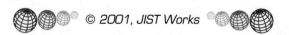

JOBS	EDUCATION/TRAINING	WHERE OBTAINED
	05.03.01 Mechanical Work: Vehicles and Facilities	
49-9021.02 Refrigeration Mechanics	Heating, Air Conditioning, and Refrigeration Mechanic and Repairer	Two-year college, trade/technical school, on the job, military (all branches)
49-9042.00 Maintenance and Repair Workers, General	Agricultural Mechanization, General; Building/ Property Maintenance and Manager; Mechanics and Repairers, Other	Trade/technical school, on the job, military (Air Force)
49-9044.00 Millwrights	Industrial Machinery Maintenance and Repair	Trade/technical school, on the job
49-9094.00 Locksmiths and Safe Repairers	Locksmith and Safe Repairer	Two-year college, trade/technical school, on the job, military (Navy)
51-9122.00 Painters, Transportation Equipment	Painter and Wall Coverer; Auto/Automotive Body Repairer	Trade/technical school, on the job, military (Army)
53-6011.00 Bridge and Lock Tenders	Bridge and Lock Tender Training	On the job
53-6051.04 Railroad Inspectors	Heavy Equipment Maintenance and Repairer	On the job, military (Army)
	05.03.02 Mechanical Work: Machinery Repair	
All in Mechanical Work: Machinery Repair	Shop Math; Shop Safety; experience	High school, trade/technical school, military, related jobs within the same industry
49-2092.06 Hand and Portable Power Tool Repairers	Agricultural Mechanization, General; Instrument Calibration and Repairer; Precision Metal Workers, Other	Trade/technical school, on the job
49-3091.00 Bicycle Repairers	Bicycle Mechanic and Repairer	On the job
49-9011.00 Mechanical Door Repairers	Industrial Machinery Maintenance and Repair	Trade/technical school, on the job
49-9012.00 Control and Valve Installers and Repairers, Except Mechanical Door	Instrument Calibration and Repairer; Industrial Machinery Maintenance and Repair	Trade/technical school, on the job; military data not yet available
49-9012.02 Valve and Regulator Repairers	Stationary Energy Sources Installer and Operator; Instrument Calibration and Repairer; Industrial Equipment Maintenance and Repair, Other; Industrial Machinery Maintenance and Repair	Trade/technical school, on the job
49-9012.03 Meter Mechanics	Instrument Calibration and Repairer	Trade/technical school, on the job
49-9031.02 Gas Appliance Repairers	Major Appliance Installer and Repairer; Electrical and Electronics Equipment Installer and Repairer, General	Trade/technical school, on the job

(continues)

(continued)

SPECIALIZED TRAINING

JOBS	EDUCATION/TRAINING	WHERE OBTAINED
05.03.02 Mechanical Work: Machinery Repair		
49-9041.00 Industrial Machinery Mechanics	Industrial Equipment Maintenance and Repair, Other; Agricultural Power Machinery Operator; Stationary Energy Sources Installer and Operator; Industrial Machinery Maintenance and Repair; Heating, Air Conditioning, and Refrigeration Mechanic and Repairer; Tool and Die Maker/Technologist	Trade/technical school, on the job, military (all branches)
49-9043.00 Maintenance Workers, Machinery	Electrical and Electronics Equipment Installer and Repairer, General; Industrial Machinery Maintenance and Repair; Industrial Electronics Installer and Repairer	Trade/technical school, on the job, military (Army, Air Force)
49-9091.00 Coin, Vending, and Amusement Machine Servicers and Repairers	Electrical and Electronics Equipment Installer and Repairer, Other	Trade/technical school, on the job
05.03.03 Mechanical Work: Medical and Technical Equipment Fabrication and Repair		
All in Mechanical Work: Medical and Technical Equipment Fabrication and Repair	Shop Math; Shop Safety; experience	High school, trade/technical school, military, related jobs within the same industry
49-9061.00 Camera and Photographic Equipment Repairers	Electrical and Electronics Equipment Installer and Repairer, General; Industrial Electronics Installer and Repairer; Miscellaneous Mechanics and Repairers, Other; Computer Installer and Repairer	On the job, two-year college, trade/technical school, military (Navy, Air Force, Marine Corps)
49-9062.00 Medical Equipment Repairers	Biomedical Engineering-Related Technology/Technician	On the job, two-year college, trade/technical school, military (Army, Navy, Air Force)
49-9064.00 Watch Repairers	Watch, Clock, and Jewelry Repairer	On the job, trade/technical school
51-9082.00 Medical Appliance Technicians	Orthotics/Prosthetics	Four-year college, military (Air Force)
51-9083.00 Ophthalmic Laboratory Technicians	Ophthalmic Medical Technologist; Optometric/Ophthalmic Laboratory Technician; Optical Technician/Assistant	Trade/technical school, on the job; military data not yet available
51-9083.02 Optical Instrument Assemblers	Optical Technician/Assistant; Opticianry/Dispensing Optician; Laser and Optical Technology/Technician	On the job, trade/technical school
05.03.04 Mechanical Work: Musical Instrument Fabrication and Repair		
All in Mechanical Work: Musical Instrument Fabrication and Repair	Shop Math; Shop Safety; experience	High school, trade/technical school, related jobs within the same industry

JOBS	EDUCATION/TRAINING	WHERE OBTAINED
05.03.04 Mechanical Work: Musical Instrument Fabrication and Repair		
49-9063.01 Keyboard Instrument Repairers and Tuners	Musical Instrument Repairer	On the job, technical school
49-9063.02 Stringed Instrument Repairers and Tuners	Musical Instrument Repairer	On the job, technical school
49-9063.03 Reed or Wind Instrument Repairers and Tuners	Musical Instrument Repairer	On the job, technical school, military (Marine Corps)
49-9063.04 Percussion Instrument Repairers and Tuners	Musical Instrument Repairer	On the job, technical school

05.04 Hands-on Work in Mechanics, Installers, and Repairers

Workers in this group perform a variety of tasks requiring little skill, such as moving materials, repairing simple machines and equipment, and helping skilled workers. These jobs are found in a variety of settings, mostly other than in factories.

What kind of work would you do?

Your work activities would depend on your job. For example, you might

- Break up concrete to facilitate installation or repair of equipment, using an air hammer.
- Clean or lubricate vehicles, machinery, equipment, instruments, tools, work areas, and other objects using hand tools, power tools, and cleaning equipment.
- Assemble and disassemble machinery, equipment, components, and other parts, using hand tools and power tools.
- Locate punctures in tubeless tires by visual inspection or by immersing inflated tires in a water bath and observing air bubbles.
- Place wheel on balancing machine to determine the counterweights required to balance the wheel.
- Apply protective materials to equipment, components, and parts to prevent defects and corrosion.
- Rig scaffolds, hoists, and shoring; erect barricades; and dig trenches.

What things about you point to this kind of work?

Is it important for you to

- Never be pressured to do things that go against your sense of right and wrong?
- Be busy all the time?
- Have steady employment?
- Have supervisors who train workers well?

Have you enjoyed any of the following as a hobby or leisure-time activity?

- Building model airplanes, automobiles, or boats
- Building cabinets or furniture
- Building or repairing radios or television sets
- Carving small wooden objects
- Doing electrical wiring and repairs in the home
- Repairing electrical household appliances
- Repairing or assembling bicycles or tricycles

Have you liked and done well in any of the following school subjects?

- Industrial Arts

Are you able to

- Quickly make coordinated movements of one hand, a hand together with its arm, or two hands to grasp, manipulate, or assemble objects?
- Correctly follow a given rule or set of rules in order to arrange things or actions in a certain order?

Would you work in places such as

- Auto service stations and repair shops?
- Factories and plants?
- Construction sites?
- Waterworks and light and power plants?
- Streets and highways?
- Mines and quarries?
- Oil fields?

What skills and knowledges do you need for this kind of work?

For most of these jobs, you need these skills:

- Repairing—repairing machines or systems using the needed tools
- Equipment Selection—determining the kind of tools and equipment needed to do a job

These knowledges are important in most of these jobs:

- Mechanical—machines and tools, including their designs, uses, benefits, repair, and maintenance
- Engineering and Technology—equipment, tools, mechanical devices, and their uses to produce motion, light, power, technology, and other applications

What else should you consider about this kind of work?

People in this group work for many kinds of businesses, ranging from automobile service shops to factories. Many of the jobs are open to beginners. If you are in a job helping a skilled worker, you might be able to learn the trade from that person. Those with a high school education or its equal may qualify for apprenticeship programs leading to more skilled jobs.

Evening or night-shift jobs and overtime work are common in this group. Working conditions vary. Some jobs are hot or dirty; others are done mostly outdoors, in all kinds of weather.

Workers are often required to wear safety clothing to protect themselves from common job hazards such as falling objects, extreme temperatures, and exposure to dangerous chemicals. Because of the physical labor inherent in some jobs, applicants often must pass a physical examination.

How can you prepare for jobs of this kind?

Work in this group usually requires education and/or training ranging from a short demonstration or brief explanation to more than three months. The most important hiring consideration is usually the physical ability of the applicant. Some of these jobs are available through union hiring halls.

SPECIALIZED TRAINING

JOBS	EDUCATION/TRAINING	WHERE OBTAINED
05.04.01 Hands-on Work in Mechanics, Installers, and Repairers		
All in Hands-on Work in Mechanics, Installers, and Repairers	Shop Safety; experience	High school, related jobs within the same industry
47-3013.00 Helpers—Electricians	Miscellaneous Repair Operations	On the job
49-3093.00 Tire Repairers and Changers	Miscellaneous Repair Operations	On the job
49-9098.00 Helpers—Installation, Maintenance, and Repair Workers	Electrical and Power Transmission Installer, General; Electrician; Heating, Air Conditioning, and Refrigeration Mechanic and Repairer; Heavy Equipment Maintenance and Repair; Industrial Machinery Maintenance and Repair	On the job, military (Navy)

06 Construction, Mining, and Drilling

An interest in assembling components of buildings and other structures,or in using mechanical devices to drill or excavate.

If construction interests you, you can find fulfillment in the many building projects that are being undertaken at all times. If you like to organize and plan, you can find careers in management. On the other hand, you can play a more direct role in putting up and finishing buildings by doing jobs such as plumbing, carpentry, masonry, painting, or roofing. You may like working at a mine or oil field, operating the powerful drilling or digging equipment. There are also several jobs that let you put your hands to the task.

06.01 Managerial Work in Construction, Mining, and Drilling

06.02 Construction

06.03 Mining and Drilling

06.04 Hands-on Work in Construction, Extraction, and Maintenance

06.01 Managerial Work in Construction, Mining, and Drilling

Workers in this group directly supervise and coordinate activities of the workers who construct buildings, roads, or other structures, or who drill or dig for oil and minerals. They are responsible for setting and meeting goals, and for bringing together the people and equipment needed to get the work done.

What kind of work would you do?

Your work activities would depend on your job. For example, you might

- Analyze and resolve worker problems and recommend motivational plans.
- Direct and supervise workers on construction sites to ensure projects meet specifications.
- Negotiate with workers, supervisors, union personnel, and other parties to resolve grievances or settle complaints.
- Record information, such as personnel, production, and operational data, on specified forms.
- Train workers in construction methods and the operation of equipment.
- Suggest and initiate personnel actions such as promotions, transfers, and hires.
- Recommend measures to improve production methods to increase efficiency and safety.

What things about you point to this kind of work?

Is it important for you to

- Give directions and instructions to others?
- Plan your work with little supervision?
- Make decisions on your own?

Have you enjoyed any of the following as a hobby or leisure-time activity?

- Building cabinets or furniture
- Constructing stage sets for school or other amateur theater
- Designing and building an addition or remodeling the interior of a home
- Serving as a leader of a scouting or other group
- Doing electrical wiring and repairs in the home
- Collecting rocks or minerals
- Repairing plumbing in the home

Have you liked and done well in any of the following school subjects?

- Management
- Construction Technology
- Accounting
- Personnel Management
- Geology

Are you able to

- Communicate information and ideas in speaking so others will understand?
- Listen to and understand information and ideas presented through spoken words and sentences?
- Tell when something is wrong or is likely to go wrong?
- Read and understand information and ideas presented in writing?
- Apply general rules to specific problems to come up with logical answers?
- See details of objects at close range (within a few feet)?
- Correctly follow a given rule or set of rules in order to arrange things or actions in a certain order?
- Speak clearly so that it is understandable to a listener?

Would you work in places such as

- Construction sites?
- Mines and quarries?
- Oil fields?
- Business offices?

What skills and knowledges do you need for this kind of work?

For most of these jobs, you need these skills:

- Coordination—adjusting actions in relation to others' actions
- Management of Personnel Resources—motivating, developing, and directing people as they work, identifying the best people for the job

These knowledges are important in most of these jobs:

- Administration and Management—principles and processes involved in business and organizational planning, coordination, and execution
- Personnel and Human Resources—policies and practices involved in personnel/human resource functions

What else should you consider about this kind of work?

Construction managers work in all parts of the country. Some work for government agencies, such as the public works department. Others work for construction firms that may relocate workers frequently. Management jobs in petroleum production and mining are available only where the natural resources are located, but because these sites are often scattered, these workers also may be moved frequently. In addition, both types of workers tend to be specialists who can transfer to another firm in the same or a related industry.

Most of these managers work a regular eight-hour day, but some have to work overtime without additional pay, especially to meet construction deadlines.

Workers divide their time between the office, where they do paperwork, and the worksite, where they observe operations, monitor progress, detect possible problems, and give directions to workers.

Job opportunities are good for construction managers, although there is some sensitivity to the business cycle. Opportunities fluctuate even more sharply in the petroleum industry, although some mining industries are more stable.

How can you prepare for jobs of this kind?

Work in this group usually requires education and/or training ranging from four to six years. Generally, these workers must have college-level courses in management, business math, business writing, record keeping, data processing, and industrial safety, plus technical competence in most or all of the jobs they supervise. This is acquired through college course work and on-the-job training. Most jobs call for supervisory experience. Some industries offer on-the-job training in data processing and management techniques.

SPECIALIZED TRAINING

JOBS	EDUCATION/TRAINING	WHERE OBTAINED
06.01.01 Managerial Work in Construction, Mining, and Drilling		
All in Managerial Work in Construction, Mining, and Drilling	Experience; Budgeting; Personnel; Oral and Written Communications	Two-year college, trade/technical school, four-year college, related jobs within the same industry
11-9021.00 Construction Managers	Construction Management; Construction Engineering; Civil Engineering; Construction and Building Technology; Civil Technology	Four-year college, trade/technical school, two-year college, on the job, military (Army, Navy, Air Force, Marine Corps)
47-1011.01 First-Line Supervisors and Manager/Supervisors—Construction Trades Workers	Operations Management and Supervision; Business Administration and Management, General	Two-year college, trade/technical school, on the job, military (all branches)
47-1011.02 First-Line Supervisors and Manager/Supervisors—Extractive Workers	Mining Technology; Petroleum Engineering Technology	Two-year college, trade/technical school, on the job

06.02 Construction

Workers in this group construct buildings and other large structures. Besides laying the foundations and putting up the framework, walls, floors, and roof, they also install plumbing and electric conduits, windows, and insulation, and finish interior surfaces with paint, paper, and carpeting. Outside they may install driveways, parking lots, fences, and swimming pools. They may also apply their skills to servicing or refurbishing components of buildings. General construction companies and specialized installation and service firms employ these workers.

What kind of work would you do?

Your work activities would depend on your job. For example, you might

- Apply alternate layers of hot asphalt or tar and roofing paper until roof covering is completed as specified.
- Descend into water with the aid of a diver helper, using scuba gear or a diving suit.
- Install structures and fixtures such as windows, frames, floorings, and trim; or hardware, using carpenter's hand and power tools.
- Load and unload trucks and move and position materials and equipment for other workers.
- Maintain and repair or replace wiring, equipment, and fixtures using hand and power tools.
- Measure and mark surfaces to be tiled and lay out work, following blueprints.
- Verify depth of alignment of trenches, roads, or bridges, using gauging instruments such as a tape measure or level.

What things about you point to this kind of work?

Is it important for you to

- Never be pressured to do things that go against your sense of right and wrong?
- Do your work alone?

Have you enjoyed any of the following as a hobby or leisure-time activity?

- Building cabinets or furniture
- Constructing stage sets for school or other amateur theater
- Designing and building an addition or remodeling the interior of a home
- Designing stage sets for school or other amateur theater
- Doing electrical wiring and repairs in the home
- Painting the interior or exterior of a home
- Repairing plumbing in the home

Have you liked and done well in any of the following school subjects?

- Construction Shop
- Shop Math
- Bricklaying
- Plumbing
- Carpentry
- Blueprint/Schematic Reading
- Heavy Equipment Operating

Are you able to

- Quickly make coordinated movements of one hand, a hand together with its arm, or two hands to grasp, manipulate, or assemble objects?
- Correctly follow a given rule or set of rules in order to arrange things or actions in a certain order?
- Bend, stretch, twist, or reach out with your body, arms, and/or legs?
- Exert maximum muscle force to lift, push, pull, or carry objects?

Would you work in places such as

- Construction sites?
- Airports?
- Factories and plants?
- Farms?
- Mines and quarries?
- Oil fields?
- Ports and harbors?
- Streets and highways?
- Waterworks and light and power plants?

What skills and knowledges do you need for this kind of work?

For most of these jobs, you need these skills:

- Equipment Selection—determining the kind of tools and equipment needed to do a job

- Product Inspection—inspecting and evaluating the quality of products
- Operation and Control—controlling operations of equipment or systems

These knowledges are important in most of these jobs:

- Building and Construction—materials, methods, and the appropriate tools to construct objects, structures, and buildings
- Mechanical—machines and tools, including their designs, uses, benefits, repair, and maintenance

What else should you consider about this kind of work?

Construction jobs are affected by varying local labor market conditions and by periodic downturns in the business cycle, but over the long run many of the jobs in this group are in high demand in most locations. Skilled workers can usually find employment almost anywhere.

Many construction workers have their own businesses, subcontracting for specialized work (for example, drywalling, roofing, or plumbing) within a larger construction project. Those who branch out on their own usually have gained experience working for someone else.

Almost all of these jobs are associated with craft unions, and in some regions you may have to join a union to be hired. For many jobs you must provide your own hand tools. Usually you are required to wear a hard hat and safety glasses, and sometimes must also wear a safety strap and steel-toed shoes.

Regular working hours can be expected, with some overtime to meet construction deadlines. People who enjoy the outdoors often prefer construction work; however, the weather and seasons affect the availability of such work.

How can you prepare for jobs of this kind?

Work in this group usually requires education and/or training ranging from six months to six years. The best way to acquire the skills required in the construction trades is a formal apprenticeship lasting three to four years. Apprentices generally must be at least 18 years old and in good physical condition. High school or vocational courses in mathematics (including computing fractions), mechanical drawing, carpentry, and electricity are helpful. Many people acquire construction skills by working as laborers and helpers and observing skilled workers.

SPECIALIZED TRAINING

JOBS	EDUCATION/TRAINING	WHERE OBTAINED
06.02.01 Construction: Masonry, Stone, and Brick Work		
All in Construction: Masonry, Stone, and Brick Work	Masonry Shop; Shop Math; Construction Site Safety; experience	High school, trade/technical school, on the job, related jobs within the same industry
47-2021.00 Brickmasons and Blockmasons	Mason and Tile Setter	On the job, trade/technical school, military (Army, Navy, Air Force, Marine Corps)
47-2022.00 Stonemasons	Mason and Tile Setter	Trade/technical school, on the job
47-2042.00 Floor Layers, Except Carpet, Wood, and Hard Tiles	Mason and Tile Setter; Construction Trades, Other	On the job, trade/technical school
47-2044.00 Tile and Marble Setters	Mason and Tile Setter	On the job, trade/technical school
47-2051.00 Cement Masons and Concrete Finishers	Construction and Building Finishers and Managers, Other	Trade/technical school, military (Army, Navy, Air Force, Marine Corps)

(continues)

SPECIALIZED TRAINING

JOBS	EDUCATION/TRAINING	WHERE OBTAINED
06.02.01 Construction: Masonry, Stone, and Brick Work		
47-2053.00 Terrazzo Workers and Finishers	Construction and Building Finishers and Managers, Other	Trade/technical school, on the job, military (Army, Navy, Air Force, Marine Corps)
51-9195.03 Stone Cutters and Carvers	Crafts, Folk Art and Artisanry; Mason and Tile Setter	On the job, trade/technical school
06.02.02 Construction: Construction and Maintenance		
All in Construction: Construction and Maintenance	Wood Shop; Carpentry; Shop Math; Construction Site Safety; experience	High school, trade/technical school, on the job, related jobs within the same industry
47-2011.00 Boilermakers	Industrial Machinery Maintenance and Repairer	On the job, trade/technical school, military (Navy)
47-2031.01 Construction Carpenters	Carpenter	On the job, trade/technical school, military (Army, Navy, Air Force, Marine Corps)
47-2031.02 Rough Carpenters	Carpenter; Agricultural Mechanization, General	On the job, trade/technical school
47-2031.04 Ship Carpenters and Joiners	Marine Maintenance and Ship Repairer; Carpenter	On the job, trade/technical school
47-2031.05 Boat Builders and Shipwrights	Carpenter; Marine Maintenance and Ship Repairer	On the job, trade/technical school
47-2041.00 Carpet Installers	Construction Trades, Other	On the job, trade/technical school
47-2043.00 Floor Sanders and Finishers	Painter and Wall Coverer; Construction Trades, Other; Heating, Air Conditioning, and Refrigeration Mechanic and Repairer	On the job, trade/technical school, military (Army, Navy)
47-2081.01 Ceiling Tile Installers	Carpenter	On the job, trade/technical school
47-2081.02 Drywall Installers	Construction Trades, Other	On the job, trade/technical school
47-2111.00 Electricians	Marine Maintenance and Ship Repairer; Electrical and Power Transmission Installer, General; Electrician	On the job, trade/technical school, military (all branches)
47-2121.00 Glaziers	Construction Trades, Other	On the job, trade/technical school
47-2131.00 Insulation Workers, Floor, Ceiling, and Wall	Construction Trades, Other	On the job, trade/technical school
47-2132.00 Insulation Workers, Mechanical	Construction Trades, Other	On the job, trade/technical school

JOBS	EDUCATION/TRAINING	WHERE OBTAINED
06.02.02 Construction: Construction and Maintenance		
47-2141.00 Painters, Construction and Maintenance	Painter and Wall Coverer; Marine Maintenance and Ship Repairer	On the job, trade/technical school, military (Navy)
47-2142.00 Paperhangers	Painter and Wall Coverer	On the job, trade/technical school
47-2152.01 Pipe Fitters	Plumber and Pipefitter	On the job, trade/technical school, military (Army, Navy, Coast Guard)
47-2152.02 Plumbers	Plumber and Pipefitter	On the job, trade/technical school, military (Army, Navy)
47-2161.00 Plasterers and Stucco Masons	Construction Trades, Other	On the job, trade/technical school, military (Air Force)
47-2181.00 Roofers	Construction Trades, Other	On the job, trade/technical school
47-2211.00 Sheet Metal Workers	Sheet Metal Worker; Construction Trades, Other	On the job, trade/technical school, military (Navy)
49-2098.00 Security and Fire Alarm Systems Installers	Electromechanical Instrumentation and Maintenance Technology/Technicians, Other; Electrical and Electronics Equipment Installer and Repairer, General; Instrument Calibration and Repairer; Lineworker; Marine Maintenance and Ship Repairer; Electrician	On the job, trade/technical school; military data not yet available
06.02.03 Construction: General		
All in Construction: General	Shop Math; Construction Site Safety; experience	High school, on the job, trade/technical school, related jobs within the same industry
47-2031.06 Brattice Builders	Carpenter	On the job, trade/technical school
47-2071.00 Paving, Surfacing, and Tamping Equipment Operators	Construction Equipment Operator	On the job, trade/technical school, military (Army, Navy, Air Force)
47-2072.00 Pile-Driver Operators	Construction Equipment Operator	On the job, trade/technical school
47-2073.01 Grader, Bulldozer, and Scraper Operators	Construction Equipment Operator	On the job, trade/technical school, military (Army)
47-2073.02 Operating Engineers	Vehicle and Equipment Operators, Other; Construction Equipment Operator	On the job, trade/technical school, military (Army, Navy, Air Force, Marine Corps)
47-2082.00 Tapers	Construction Trades, Other	On the job, trade/technical school
47-2151.00 Pipelayers	Heating, Air Conditioning, and Refrigeration Mechanic and Repairer; Agricultural Power Machinery Operator; Painter and Wall Coverer; Construction Trades, Other	On the job, trade/technical school, military (Army, Navy)

(continues)

(continued)

SPECIALIZED TRAINING

JOBS	EDUCATION/TRAINING	WHERE OBTAINED
06.02.03 Construction: General		
47-2152.03 Pipelaying Fitters	Painter and Wall Coverer; Construction Trades, Other; Heating, Air Conditioning, and Refrigeration Mechanic and Repairer	On the job, trade/technical school, military (Army, Navy)
47-2171.00 Reinforcing Iron and Rebar Workers	Construction and Building Finishers and Managers, Other	On the job, trade/technical school, military (Navy)
47-2221.00 Structural Iron and Steel Workers	Construction Trades, Other	On the job, trade/technical school, military (Navy)
47-4031.00 Fence Erectors	Construction Trades, Other	On the job, trade/technical school; military data not yet available
47-4041.00 Hazardous Materials Removal Workers	Construction Trades, Other	On the job, trade/technical school; military data not yet available
47-4061.00 Rail-Track Laying and Maintenance Equipment Operators	Construction Equipment Operator	On the job, trade/technical school
47-4091.00 Segmental Pavers	Mason and Tile Setter; Construction and Building Finishers and Managers, Other	On the job, trade/technical school; military data not yet available
47-5031.00 Explosives Workers, Ordnance Handling Experts, and Blasters	Construction Trades, Other	On the job, trade/technical school, military (Army, Navy, Air Force, Marine Corps)
49-9045.00 Refractory Materials Repairers, Except Brickmasons	Construction Trades, Other	On the job, trade/technical school
49-9092.00 Commercial Divers	Diver (Professional)	On the job, trade/technical school, military (Navy, Marine Corps, Coast Guard)
49-9095.00 Manufactured Building and Mobile Home Installers	Building/Property Maintenance and Management	On the job, trade/technical school
49-9096.00 Riggers	Construction Equipment Operator; Marine Maintenance and Ship Repair; Logging/Timber Harvesting	On the job, trade/technical school, military (Army, Navy, Marine Corps)

06.03 Mining and Drilling

Workers in this group operate drilling or other excavating and pumping equipment, usually in oil fields, quarries, and mines. They are hired by large energy or extractive companies, or by small drilling contractors that do work for the large companies.

What kind of work would you do?

Your work activities would depend on your job. For example, you might

- Adjust pipes between pumps and wells, using hand tools.
- Clean, maintain, and repair tools and equipment.
- Examine drillings or core samples from the bottom of wells to determine the nature of the strata.
- Lower and explode charges in boreholes to start the flow of oil from the well.
- Observe meters and gauges to control pump pressure.
- Position a truck-mounted derrick at the drilling area specified on the field map.
- Record drilling progress and geological data.

What things about you point to this kind of work?

Is it important for you to

- Never be pressured to do things that go against your sense of right and wrong?
- Have supervisors who back up the workers with management?
- Be treated fairly by the company?

Have you enjoyed any of the following as a hobby or leisure-time activity?

- Building model airplanes, automobiles, or boats
- Collecting rocks or minerals
- Driving a bus as a volunteer for an organization
- Making sketches of machines or other mechanical equipment
- Mowing the lawn with a riding lawnmower
- Reading mechanical or automotive magazines

Have you liked and done well in any of the following school subjects?

- Oil Field Practices
- Mining Practices
- Earth Science
- Heavy Equipment Operating
- Pump Operation

Are you able to

- Quickly and repeatedly make precise adjustments in moving the controls of a machine or vehicle to exact positions?
- Quickly make coordinated movements of one hand, a hand together with its arm, or two hands to grasp, manipulate, or assemble objects?
- Coordinate movements of two or more limbs together?

Would you work in places such as

- Mines and quarries?
- Oil fields?
- Construction sites?
- Streets and highways?

What skills and knowledges do you need for this kind of work?

For most of these jobs, you need these skills:

- Operation and Control—controlling operations of equipment or systems
- Operation Monitoring—watching gauges, dials, or other indicators to make sure a machine is working properly

These knowledges are important in most of these jobs:

- Mechanical—machines and tools, including their designs, uses, benefits, repair, and maintenance
- Engineering and Technology—equipment, tools, mechanical devices, and their uses to produce motion, light, power, technology, and other applications

What else should you consider about this kind of work?

Workers in this group are mostly hired by small mining and drilling contractors or by the extraction departments of large mineral or petroleum companies.

Sites of rich deposits are scattered around the world, and not necessarily in the most comfortable climates or the most familiar cultures. As the resources are depleted or when the political and economic climates change, workers in this group often are relocated by their employers.

The oil industry has fluctuated greatly for over a generation, but the long-term demand for petroleum is likely to continue, creating opportunities in this field over the long term. Many other mining industries are more stable, although some may experience boom or bust because of economic, political, or technological changes that affect supply and demand. Mining workers with good skills can often change industries in search of better opportunities.

How can you prepare for jobs of this kind?

Work in this group usually requires education and/or training ranging from six months to two years, although some jobs require more. The skills are usually learned from on-the-job training programs offered by the employer.

SPECIALIZED TRAINING

JOBS	EDUCATION/TRAINING	WHERE OBTAINED
06.03.01 Mining and Drilling		
All in Mining and Drilling	Shop Math; Work Site Safety; experience	High school, on the job, trade/technical school, related jobs within the same industry
47-5011.00 Derrick Operators, Oil and Gas	Vehicle and Equipment Operators, Other	On the job, trade/technical school
47-5012.00 Rotary Drill Operators, Oil and Gas	Vehicle and Equipment Operators, Other	On the job, trade/technical school
47-5013.00 Service Unit Operators, Oil, Gas, and Mining	Vehicle and Equipment Operators, Other	On the job, trade/technical school
47-5021.01 Construction Drillers	Vehicle and Equipment Operators, Other; Construction Equipment Operator	On the job, trade/technical school, on the job, military (Army)
47-5021.02 Well and Core Drill Operators	Construction Equipment Operator	On the job, trade/technical school, military (Army, Navy)
47-5041.00 Continuous Mining Machine Operators	Vehicle and Equipment Operators, Other	On the job, trade/technical school
47-5042.00 Mine Cutting and Channeling Machine Operators	Vehicle and Equipment Operators, Other; Construction Equipment Operator	On the job, trade/technical school
47-5051.00 Rock Splitters, Quarry	Vehicle and Equipment Operators, Other	Trade/technical school, on the job
47-5061.00 Roof Bolters, Mining	Vehicle and Equipment Operators, Other	On the job, trade/technical school
47-5071.00 Roustabouts, Oil and Gas	Industrial Equipment Maintenance and Repair, Other	On the job, trade/technical school
53-7032.01 Excavating and Loading Machine Operators	Construction Equipment Operator; Vehicle and Equipment Operators, Other	On the job, trade/technical school, military (Army)

JOBS	EDUCATION/TRAINING	WHERE OBTAINED
	06.03.01 Mining and Drilling	
53-7033.00 Loading Machine Operators, Underground Mining	Vehicle and Equipment Operators, Other	On the job, trade/technical school
53-7111.00 Shuttle Car Operators	Vehicle and Equipment Operators, Other	On the job, trade/technical school

06.04 Hands-on Work in Construction, Extraction, and Maintenance

Workers in this group perform a variety of tasks requiring little skill, such as moving materials, cleaning work areas, doing routine installations, operating simple tools, and helping skilled workers. They work at construction sites, oil fields, quarries, and mines.

What kind of work would you do?

Your work activities would depend on your job. For example, you might

- Apply grout between joints of bricks or tiles, using a grouting trowel.
- Clean construction sites to eliminate possible hazards.
- Cut tile or linoleum to fit.
- Drill holes in timbers or lumber.
- Load and unload trucks, and haul and hoist materials.
- Mix concrete using a portable mixer.
- Set signs and cones around work areas to divert traffic.

What things about you point to this kind of work?

Is it important for you to

- Never be pressured to do things that go against your sense of right and wrong?
- Be busy all the time?

Have you enjoyed any of the following as a hobby or leisure-time activity?

- Building cabinets or furniture
- Building model airplanes, automobiles, or boats
- Constructing stage sets for school or other amateur theater
- Designing and building an addition or remodeling the interior of a home
- Operating a model train layout
- Painting the interior or exterior of a home
- Repairing plumbing in the home

Have you liked and done well in any of the following school subjects?

- Industrial Arts
- Carpentry
- Bricklaying
- Plumbing
- Construction Shop

Are you able to

- Exert maximum muscle force to lift, push, pull, or carry objects?
- Quickly make coordinated movements of one hand, a hand together with its arm, or two hands to grasp, manipulate, or assemble objects?

Would you work in places such as

- Construction sites?
- Motion picture and recording studios?
- Streets and highways?
- Railroad tracks and yards?
- Private homes?
- Parks and campgrounds?

What skills and knowledges do you need for this kind of work?

For most of these jobs, you need these skills:

- Equipment Selection—determining the kind of tools and equipment needed to do a job

- Installation–installing equipment, machines, wiring, or programs to meet specifications

These knowledges are important in most of these jobs:

- Building and Construction–materials, methods, and the appropriate tools to construct objects, structures, and buildings
- Mechanical–machines and tools, including their designs, uses, benefits, repair, and maintenance

What else should you consider about this kind of work?

People in this group work for construction companies and subcontractors, or for energy or mineral companies and their drilling or mining subcontractors. Many of the jobs are open to beginners. If you are in a job helping a skilled worker, you might be able to learn the trade from that person. Those with a high school education or its equal may qualify for apprenticeship programs leading to more skilled jobs.

Evening or night-shift jobs and overtime work are common in this group. Working conditions vary. Some jobs are hot or dirty; others are done mostly outdoors, in all kinds of weather.

You are likely to need to wear safety clothing as protection against common job hazards such as falling or flying objects. Your hiring may depend on your passing a physical exam that shows you can handle the physical labor required.

How can you prepare for jobs of this kind?

Work in this group usually requires education and/or training ranging from a short demonstration or brief explanation to more than six months. The most important hiring consideration is usually the physical ability of the applicant. Some of these jobs are available through union hiring halls.

SPECIALIZED TRAINING

JOBS	EDUCATION/TRAINING	WHERE OBTAINED
06.04.01 Hands-on Work in Construction, Extraction, and Maintenance		
All in Hands-on Work in Construction, Extraction, and Maintenance	Construction Site Safety; experience	High school, on the job, related jobs within the same industry
47-2031.03 Carpenter Assemblers and Repairers	Carpenter	On the job, trade/technical school, military (Marine Corps)
47-2061.00 Construction Laborers	Stationary Energy Sources Installer and Operator; Custodial, Housekeeping, and Home Services Workers and Managers; Custodian/Caretaker; Painter and Wall Coverer; Construction Trades, Other; Heating, Air Conditioning, and Refrigeration Mechanic and Repairer	On the job, military (Army, Navy)
47-3011.00 Helpers—Brickmasons, Blockmasons, Stonemasons, and Tile and Marble Setters	Miscellaneous Construction Trade Training	On the job
47-3012.00 Helpers—Carpenters	Miscellaneous Construction Trade Training	On the job, military (Army, Navy)
47-3014.00 Helpers–Painters, Paperhangers, Plasterers, and Stucco Masons	Miscellaneous Construction Trade Training	On the job
47-3015.00 Helpers–Pipelayers, Plumbers, Pipefitters, and Steamfitters	Miscellaneous Construction Trade Training	On the job

JOBS	EDUCATION/TRAINING	WHERE OBTAINED
06.04.01 Hands-on Work in Construction, Extraction, and Maintenance		
47-3016.00 Helpers—Roofers	Miscellaneous Construction Trade Training	On the job
47-4051.00 Highway Maintenance Workers	Miscellaneous Construction Trade Training	On the job
47-4071.00 Septic Tank Servicers and Sewer Pipe Cleaners	Plumber and Pipefitter	On the job
47-5081.00 Helpers—Extraction Workers	Mining Equipment Operator Training	On the job
53-7062.02 Grips and Set-Up Workers, Motion Picture Sets, Studios, and Stages	Miscellaneous Construction Trade Training	On the job

07 Transportation

An interest in operations that move people or materials.

You can satisfy this interest by managing a transportation service, by helping vehicles keep on their assigned schedules and routes, or by driving or piloting a vehicle. If you enjoy taking responsibility, perhaps managing a rail line would appeal to you. If you work well with details and can take pressure on the job, you might consider being an air traffic controller. Or would you rather get out on the highway, on the water, or up in the air? If so, then you could drive a truck from state to state, sail down the Mississippi on a barge, or fly a crop duster over a cornfield. If you prefer to stay closer to home, you could drive a delivery van, taxi, or school bus. You can use your physical strength to load freight and arrange it so it gets to its destination in one piece.

07.01 Managerial Work in Transportation

07.02 Vehicle Expediting and Coordinating

07.03 Air Vehicle Operation

07.04 Water Vehicle Operation

07.05 Truck Driving

07.06 Rail Vehicle Operation

07.07 Other Services Requiring Driving

07.08 Support Work in Transportation

07.01 Managerial Work in Transportation

Workers in this group manage transportation services. They may be responsible for a whole airline, rail line, bus line, or subway system; they may oversee a fleet of trucks or cargo vessels; or they may coordinate the activities of the crew on one large train. They have a good knowledge of the transportation equipment for which they are responsible, and they understand how to plan for and react to factors that might affect whether the vehicles complete their routes safely, on schedule, and within budget. Most of them work within basic guidelines of policy and goals set by their employers.

What kind of work would you do?

Your work activities would depend on your job. For example, you might

- Analyze expenditures and other financial reports to develop plans, policies, and budgets for increasing profits and improving services.
- Explain and demonstrate work tasks to new workers or assign workers to experienced workers for further training.
- Interpret transportation and tariff regulations, shipping orders, safety regulations, and company policies and procedures for workers.
- Negotiate and authorize contracts with equipment and materials suppliers.
- Oversee the process of investigation and response to customer or shipper complaints relating to the operations department.
- Review transportation schedules, worker assignments, and routes to ensure compliance with standards for personnel selection, safety, and union contract terms.
- Signal an engineer to begin a train run, stop the train, or change speed, using a radiotelephone, lantern, teletypewriter, or hand movement.

What things about you point to this kind of work?

Is it important for you to

- Give directions and instructions to others?
- Plan your work with little supervision?
- Make decisions on your own?

Have you enjoyed any of the following as a hobby or leisure-time activity?

- Chauffeuring special groups, such as children, older people, or people with disabilities
- Serving as a leader of a scouting or other group
- Driving a bus as a volunteer for an organization
- Driving an ambulance as a volunteer
- Reading airplane or boat magazines
- Operating a model train layout
- Operating a motorboat or other pleasure boat

Have you liked and done well in any of the following school subjects?

- Management
- Accounting
- Personnel Management
- Airport Safety

Are you able to

- Communicate information and ideas in speaking so others will understand?
- Read and understand information and ideas presented in writing?
- Listen to and understand information and ideas presented through spoken words and sentences?
- Tell when something is wrong or is likely to go wrong?
- Speak clearly so that it is understandable to a listener?
- Communicate information and ideas in writing so others will understand?
- Apply general rules to specific problems to come up with logical answers?

Would you work in places such as

- Business offices?
- Airports?
- Bus and train stations?
- Freight terminals?
- Ports and harbors?
- Railroad tracks and yards?
- Ships and boats?

What skills and knowledges do you need for this kind of work?

For most of these jobs, you need these skills:

- Coordination—adjusting actions in relation to others' actions
- Speaking—talking to others to effectively convey information

These knowledges are important in most of these jobs:

- Transportation—principles and methods for moving people or goods by air, rail, sea, or road, including their relative costs, advantages, and limitations
- Administration and Management—principles and processes involved in business and organizational planning, coordination, and execution

What else should you consider about this kind of work?

Workers in this group are hired by transportation companies such as airlines, bus lines, railroads, and trucking firms. They also manage the transportation services within large companies or government agencies that move around a lot of people, equipment, supplies, or products.

Success depends largely on getting vehicles to run on time, which means that the work can be stressful. Because government regulations on the industry are decreasing, some aspects of the job are becoming less complex, but competition among transportation service companies is also increasing. Among the high-level management jobs, the trend toward international trade and just-in-time inventory will create many opportunities, especially for those who have good computer skills. Among the lower-level supervisory jobs, increasing competition and consolidation among transportation providers are likely to limit growth of new jobs, but many replacements will be needed as existing workers retire.

How can you prepare for jobs of this kind?

Work in this group usually requires education and/or training ranging from two to six years.

Transportation managers can learn management skills and the practices of the industry in college majors such as logistics or aviation management.

Managers and supervisors of vehicle operations generally learn accounting and personnel skills in two- and four-year college programs, although a few may begin as vehicle operators and work their way up to management with additional training.

Railroad conductors and yardmasters mostly learn their skills through employers' training programs and on the job, although some formal study of clerical skills in business college can be helpful.

SPECIALIZED TRAINING

JOBS	EDUCATION/TRAINING	WHERE OBTAINED
07.01.01 Managerial Work in Transportation		
All in Managerial Work in Transportation	Budgeting; Personnel; Oral and Written Communications	Two-year college, four-year college, work experience in a related occupation
11-3071.01 Transportation Managers	Logistics and Materials Management; Business Administration and Management, General; Aviation Management; Fire Protection and Safety Technology/Technician; General Distribution Operations; Agricultural Supplies Retailing and Wholesaling; Crop Production Operations and Management; Agricultural Production Workers and Managers, General	Four-year college, on the job, military (all branches)
53-1031.00 First-Line Supervisors/Managers of Transportation and Material-Moving Machine and Vehicle Operators	Marine Science/Merchant Marine Officer; Business Administration and Management, General; Logistics and Materials Management; General Distribution Operations	Work experience in a related occupation, two-year college, four-year college, on the job, military (Air Force)
53-4031.00 Railroad Conductors and Yardmasters	Business Administration and Management, General	Work experience in a related occupation, on the job

07.02 Vehicle Expediting and Coordinating

Workers in this group monitor and control the movements of vehicles. They work at airports or along rail lines, routing vehicles so that they keep on schedule but also keep a safe distance from other vehicles. Traffic technicians work under the direction of a traffic engineer to conduct field studies of traffic volume, signals, lighting, and other factors that influence the flow of vehicles.

What kind of work would you do?

Your work activities would depend on your job. For example, you might

- Complete daily activity reports and keep records of messages from aircraft.
- Inspect, adjust, and control radio equipment and airport lights.
- Issue landing and take-off authorizations and instructions, and communicate other information to aircraft.
- Observe moving trains and control track switches and car-retarder systems to couple freight cars.
- Recommend changes in traffic-control devices and regulations on the basis of findings.
- Relay air traffic information such as altitudes, expected times of arrival, and courses of aircraft to control centers.

What things about you point to this kind of work?

Is it important for you to

- Never be pressured to do things that go against your sense of right and wrong?
- Be treated fairly by the company?
- Have supervisors who back up the workers with management?
- Have steady employment?

Have you enjoyed any of the following as a hobby or leisure-time activity?

- Directing traffic at community events
- Driving a bus as a volunteer for an organization
- Driving an ambulance as a volunteer
- Operating a model train layout
- Planning family recreational activities
- Reading airplane or boat magazines

Have you liked and done well in any of the following school subjects?

- Scheduling
- Airport Safety
- Shipping Regulations
- Transportation Engineering/Technology
- Traffic Control/Management
- Industrial Distribution

Are you able to

- Listen to and understand information and ideas presented through spoken words and sentences?
- See details of objects at close range (within a few feet)?
- Read and understand information and ideas presented in writing?
- Speak clearly so that it is understandable to a listener?
- Communicate information and ideas in speaking so others will understand?
- See details at a distance?

Would you work in places such as

- Airports?
- Streets and highways?
- Railroad tracks and yards?

What skills and knowledges do you need for this kind of work?

For most of these jobs, you need these skills:

- Active Listening—listening to what other people are saying and asking questions as appropriate
- Speaking—talking to others to effectively convey information

These knowledges are important in most of these jobs:

- Transportation—principles and methods for moving people or goods by air, rail, sea, or road, including their relative costs, advantages, and limitations
- Telecommunications—transmission, broadcasting, switching, control, and operation of telecommunications systems

What else should you consider about this kind of work?

Workers in this group are hired by government agencies, airlines, or railroads. Because traffic moves both day and night, most of these workers have to work occasional or frequent night shifts.

Air traffic controllers and airfield operations specialists work at airports and at control centers that guide planes in mid-flight. These workers are under considerable pressure to maintain passenger safety while keeping air traffic flowing on schedule, often at a brisk pace. Nevertheless, job turnover is low, and therefore new job opportunities will be limited. Automation is streamlining some monotonous tasks. For air traffic controllers, yearly physical exams are required, and at age 56 they must transfer to a position where they do not directly control airplane traffic.

Traffic technicians work for government transportation departments and for consulting firms in cities and towns, where they support the work of traffic engineers. Opportunities will probably be better than for most technician jobs, because the need for traffic planning is not very sensitive to economic trends. Best opportunities will be for those who keep up with technological change.

Workers who control the movement of railcars are hired by railroad companies throughout the country. They are responsible for the safety of the railcars and also for keeping them on schedule. Rail activity is growing slowly, and there will be continued need to replace workers who retire.

How can you prepare for jobs of this kind?

Requirements for education and/or training in this group vary, from six months to six years.

Air traffic controllers usually take two to four years of college before qualifying to be hired by the federal government. Then they enroll in a rigorous six-month training program. Airfield operations specialists may complete four years of college in a transportation-related curriculum; training on the job is also required.

Traffic technicians are usually graduates of a two-year civil engineering technology program.

Workers who control railcar switching and braking generally learn their skills in training programs provided by their employers.

SPECIALIZED TRAINING

JOBS	EDUCATION/TRAINING	WHERE OBTAINED
07.02.01 Vehicle Expediting and Coordinating		
All in Vehicle Expediting and Coordinating	Oral Communications	High school
53-2021.00 Air Traffic Controllers	Air Traffic Controller	Two-year college, four-year college, FAA training program, on the job, military (Air Force)
53-2022.00 Airfield Operations Specialists	Air Traffic Controller	Two-year college, four-year college, FAA training program, on the job; military data not yet available
53-4021.00 Railroad Brake, Signal, and Switch Operators	Railroad Operations	On the job
53-6041.00 Traffic Technicians	Civil Engineering/Civil Technology/Technician	Two-year college, four-year college

07.03 Air Vehicle Operation

Workers in this group pilot airplanes or helicopters, or train or supervise pilots. Most are hired by commercial airlines. Some find jobs piloting planes for private companies, such as package-delivery services or crop-dusting services, or for individuals.

What kind of work would you do?

Your work activities would depend on your job. For example, you might

- Direct the course of airplanes and deviations from course required by weather conditions, such as wind drifts and forecasted atmospheric conditions.
- Conduct preflight checks and read gauges to verify that fluids and pressure are at prescribed levels.
- Give training and instruction in aircraft operations for students and other pilots.
- Keep a log of the rate of fuel consumption, engine performance, and uncorrected malfunctions.
- Pilot an airplane or helicopter to photograph areas of the earth's surface or to dust or spray fields.
- Study maps to become acquainted with topography, obstacles, or hazards, such as air turbulence, hedgerows, and hills.
- Utilize navigation aids, such as radio beams and beacons, to locate the position and direct course of an airplane.

What things about you point to this kind of work?

Is it important for you to

- Make use of your individual abilities?
- Get a feeling of accomplishment?
- Never be pressured to do things that go against your sense of right and wrong?
- Be paid well in comparison with other workers?

Have you enjoyed any of the following as a hobby or leisure-time activity?

- Operating a CB or ham radio
- Racing midget or stock cars
- Reading airplane or boat magazines
- Building model airplanes, automobiles, or boats

Have you liked and done well in any of the following school subjects?

- Flight Safety
- Flight Training/Pilot Training
- Math Computing, Standard Formula
- Meteorology
- Navigation
- Aeronautical Charts

Are you able to

- See details of objects at close range (within a few feet)?
- Quickly and repeatedly make precise adjustments in moving the controls of a machine or vehicle to exact positions?
- Know your location in relation to the environment, or know where other objects are in relation to yourself?
- Tell when something is wrong or is likely to go wrong?
- Communicate information and ideas in speaking so others will understand?
- See details at a distance?

Would you work in places such as

- Airplanes?
- Airports?

What skills and knowledges do you need for this kind of work?

For most of these jobs, you need these skills:

- Operation Monitoring—watching gauges, dials, or other indicators to make sure a machine is working properly
- Operation and Control—controlling the operations of equipment or systems
- Judgment and Decision Making—weighing the relative costs and benefits of a potential action
- Problem Identification—identifying the nature of problems
- Information Gathering—knowing how to find information and identifying essential information
- Monitoring—assessing how well you are doing when learning or doing something

These knowledges are important in most of these jobs:

- Transportation—principles and methods for moving people or goods by air, rail, sea, or road, including their relative costs, advantages, and limitations
- Physics—physical principles, laws, and applications including air, water, material dynamics, light, atomic principles, heat, electric theory, earth formations, and meteorological and related natural phenomena

What else should you consider about this kind of work?

Most of the jobs in flying are found in and around cities where there are major airports, although some are available in smaller towns.

Commercial airlines and air-charter services hire most of the pilots. Airlines hire only pilots with extensive experience. Pilots also get jobs with flying schools, private companies, and government agencies. Competition for jobs is expected to be keen.

For most of these jobs, work schedules change frequently. Pilots often work under mental stress and must always be alert and ready to make decisions quickly. They are given routine physical exams.

How can you prepare for jobs of this kind?

Work in this group usually requires education and/or training ranging from four to six years. Flight training is available in the military and in civilian flight schools approved by the Federal Aviation Administration. A high school education or its equal is the minimum requirement for acceptance.

Most major airlines have their own programs to provide additional specialized training before assigning pilots to service. Some airlines require that a pilot have two years of college; many prefer college graduates. Employers require that pilots have a certain amount of accumulated flying time—1,000 to 2,000 hours for airlines and helicopter services, less for crop dusting. One way to gain hours is by working as a flight instructor.

SPECIALIZED TRAINING

JOBS	EDUCATION/TRAINING	WHERE OBTAINED
	07.03.01 Air Vehicle Operation	
All in Air Vehicle Operation	Aircraft Pilot and Navigator (Professional) Training; Aircraft Pilot (Private) Training	Trade/technical school, flight school, military (all branches)
53-2011.00 Airline Pilots, Copilots, and Flight Engineers	Aircraft Pilot and Navigator (Professional)	On the job, trade/technical school, flight school, military (all branches)
53-2012.00 Commercial Pilots	Aircraft Pilot and Navigator (Professional)	On the job, trade/technical school, flight school, military (all branches)

07.04 Water Vehicle Operation

Workers in this group operate ships, boats, and barges. They steer them, operate motor equipment, maintain the vessel, and see that passengers and/or cargo and handled well. Most are hired by freight-shipping companies, although some work for cruise lines, fishing fleets, or individuals.

What kind of work would you do?

Your work activities would depend on your job. For example, you might

- Collect fares from customers or signal ferryboat the helper to collect fares.
- Examine machinery for specified pressure and flow of lubricants.
- Interview, hire, and instruct the crew, and assign watches and living quarters.
- Observe the water from the masthead and advise navigational direction.
- Record data in ship's log such as weather conditions and distance traveled.
- Steer the ship and maintain visual communication with other ships.
- Supervise the crew in cleaning and maintaining the decks, superstructure, and bridge.

What things about you point to this kind of work?

Is it important for you to

- Never be pressured to do things that go against your sense of right and wrong?
- Plan your work with little supervision?

Have you enjoyed any of the following as a hobby or leisure-time activity?

- Reading airplane or boat magazines
- Building model airplanes, automobiles, or boats
- Camping, hiking, or engaging in other outdoor activities
- Driving a bus as a volunteer for an organization
- Operating a CB or ham radio
- Operating a motorboat or other pleasure boat

Have you liked and done well in any of the following school subjects?

- Water Safety
- Navigation
- Ship Systems
- Shipping Regulations
- Engine Mechanics
- Diesel Mechanics/Diesels

Are you able to

- See details at a distance?
- Know your location in relation to the environment, or know where other objects are in relation to yourself?
- Quickly and repeatedly make precise adjustments in moving the controls of a machine or vehicle to exact positions?
- Communicate information and ideas in speaking so others will understand?
- See objects in the presence of glare or bright lighting?
- See details of objects at close range (within a few feet)?

Would you work in places such as

- Ships and boats?
- Ports and harbors?

What skills and knowledges do you need for this kind of work?

For most of these jobs, you need these skills:

- Operation and Control—controlling operations of equipment or systems
- Operation Monitoring—watching gauges, dials, or other indicators to make sure a machine is working properly

These knowledges are important in most of these jobs:

- Transportation—principles and methods for moving people or goods by air, rail, sea, or road, including their relative costs, advantages, and limitations
- Mechanical—machines and tools, including their designs, uses, benefits, repair, and maintenance

What else should you consider about this kind of work?

Work in water transportation is found in seaports, around the Great Lakes, and in cities along navigable rivers such as the Mississippi and the Ohio.

People in water transportation work for barge lines, passenger-ship lines, construction companies, and the government agencies in charge of port and harbor operation.

Because ship pilots and other workers in water transportation are promoted from lower-level work on the same kind of craft, getting a job in water vehicle operation is difficult.

Ship officers are usually away from home for long periods and have to adjust to frequent changes in work schedules. Workers in this group face the possibility of injury through fires, collisions, and other disasters.

How can you prepare for jobs of this kind?

Work in this group usually requires education and/or training ranging from six months to as much as six years.

Ship captains advance through several officer ranks, beginning with third mate. Most third mate positions are earned by completing a training course at a marine academy.

Some marine trade unions offer programs to train seamen (that word is used for both men and women) to become third mates. U.S. citizens who have been approved by the U.S. Public Health Service for vision and general health are eligible to become trainees. They must also pass Coast Guard tests on navigation, freight handling, and deck operations.

SPECIALIZED TRAINING

JOBS	EDUCATION/TRAINING	WHERE OBTAINED
07.04.01 Water Vehicle Operation		
All in Water Vehicle Operation	Experience	Boating as a hobby, related jobs within the same industry, military
53-5011.01 Able Seamen	Water Transportation Workers, Other	On the job, trade/technical school, military (Army, Navy, Coast Guard)
53-5011.02 Ordinary Seamen and Marine Oilers	Water Transportation Workers, Other; Marine Maintenance and Ship Repair	On the job, trade/technical school, military (Army, Navy, Coast Guard)
53-5021.01 Ship and Boat Captains	Marine Science/Merchant Marine Officer; Water Transportation Workers, Other; Fishing Technology/Commercial Fishing	Marine Academy, trade/technical school, on the job, military (Army, Navy, Coast Guard)
53-5021.02 Mates—Ship, Boat, and Barge	Marine Science/Merchant Marine Officer; Fishing Technology/Commercial Fishing; Water Transportation Workers, Other	Marine Academy, trade/technical school, on the job, military (Coast Guard)
53-5021.03 Pilots, Ship	Marine Science/Merchant Marine Officer	Marine Academy, trade/technical school, on the job, military (Army, Navy, Coast Guard)
53-5022.00 Motorboat Operators	Water Transportation Workers, Other	On the job, trade/technical school, military (Army, Navy, Coast Guard)
53-7031.00 Dredge Operators	Water Transportation Workers, Other; Construction Equipment Operator	On the job, trade/technical school

07.05 Truck Driving

Workers in this group drive large trucks, small trucks, or delivery vans. They may cover long distances or a familiar local route. Most of these jobs are found with trucking companies, or with wholesale and retail companies that do deliveries.

What kind of work would you do?

Your work activities would depend on your job. For example, you might

- Clean, inspect, and service vehicles.
- Communicate with the base or other vehicles using a telephone or radio.
- Drive a tractor-trailer combination, applying knowledge of commercial driving regulations to transport and deliver products, livestock, or materials, usually over long distances.
- Fasten chains or binders to secure the load on the trailer during transit.
- Keep a record of the materials and products transported.
- Load and unload trucks, vans, or automobiles.
- Obtain the customer's signature or collect payment for services.

What things about you point to this kind of work?

Is it important for you to

- Be paid well in comparison with other workers?
- Do your work alone?
- Be treated fairly by the company?

Have you enjoyed any of the following as a hobby or leisure-time activity?

- Driving a truck and tractor to harvest crops on a family farm

- Driving a bus as a volunteer for an organization
- Driving an ambulance as a volunteer
- Instructing family members in observing traffic regulations
- Racing midget or stock cars
- Repairing the family car

Have you liked and done well in any of the following school subjects?

- Truck Mechanics
- Truck Operating
- Diesel Mechanics/Diesels
- Driver Education

Are you able to

- Quickly respond (with your hand, finger, or foot) to one signal (sound, light, picture, etc.) when it appears?
- See details at a distance?
- Know your location in relation to the environment, or know where other objects are in relation to yourself?
- Exert maximum muscle force to lift, push, pull, or carry objects?
- Choose quickly and correctly between two or more movements in response to two or more signals?
- See details of objects at close range (within a few feet)?
- Bend, stretch, twist, or reach out with your body, arms, and/or legs?

Would you work in places such as

- Streets and highways?
- Freight terminals?

What skills and knowledges do you need for this kind of work?

For most of these jobs, you need these skills:

- Operation and Control—controlling operations of equipment or systems
- Equipment Maintenance—performing routine maintenance and determining when and what kind of maintenance is needed

These knowledges are important in most of these jobs:

- Transportation—principles and methods for moving people or goods by air, rail, sea, or road, including their relative costs, advantages, and limitations
- Geography—various methods for describing the location and distribution of land, sea, and air masses including their physical locations, relationships, and characteristics

What else should you consider about this kind of work?

Beginners are more likely to be hired for local driving jobs than for long-distance operations. If you'd like to get into long-distance truck driving eventually, experience in local driving can be a big help. Many full-time drivers start by getting part-time and temporary work driving locally.

A regular eight-hour day is standard in some of the jobs, but for others you work evenings, nights, on call, weekends, or holidays, and may often have to spend nights away from home.

Some truck drivers are self-employed. They do local or long-distance hauling or deliveries on their own, or accept contracts to deliver mail for the Postal Service or merchandise for private businesses.

Some must load and unload their trucks. Many companies require that workers undergo a physical exam before they are hired and once each year after being hired.

Although advancement in trucking is limited, some drivers become supervisors or managers.

Other forms of transportation are not likely to replace trucking for a long time, so job opportunities are expected to be good.

How can you prepare for jobs of this kind?

Work in this group usually requires education and/or training ranging from 30 days to more than a year. Driver education courses offered by high schools and private schools are helpful. Truck driving courses are offered by some private vocational schools. Passing a driving test, and sometimes a physical, is required. A good driving record is also necessary.

Requirements for local drivers vary with the type of truck driven and the business of the employer. New workers may learn by riding with a veteran driver, but more training is given if a special type of truck is used. The requirements are similar for the long-haul truckers. Some firms give classes on general duties, operating and loading procedures, and company rules and records.

The U.S. Department of Transportation sets standards for truckers driving from state to state. Long-distance truckers must take a written test on the Motor Carrier Safety Regulations. They must also pass a driving test with the type of truck they will drive on the job. Many firms have height and weight limits for their drivers. Others hire only those with several years of long-distance trucking experience.

SPECIALIZED TRAINING

JOBS	EDUCATION/TRAINING	WHERE OBTAINED
07.05.01 Truck Driving		
All in Truck Driving	Road Safety; Driver Education; experience	High school, on the job, related jobs within the same industry, military
53-3032.01 Truck Drivers, Heavy	Agricultural Power Machinery Operator; Truck, Bus, and Other Commercial Vehicle Operator	On the job, trade/technical school, military (all branches)
53-3032.02 Tractor-Trailer Truck Drivers	Logging/Timber Harvesting; Truck, Bus, and Other Commercial Vehicle Operator	On the job, trade/technical school, military (Army, Air Force, Marine Corps, Coast Guard)
53-3033.00 Truck Drivers, Light or Delivery Services	Truck, Bus, and Other Commercial Vehicle Operator	On the job, trade/technical school, military (Army, Air Force, Marine Corps, Coast Guard)

07.06 Rail Vehicle Operation

Workers in this group drive locomotives, subways, and streetcars. Most of these jobs are found with railroads and city transit authorities.

What kind of work would you do?

Your work activities would depend on your job. For example, you might

- Answer questions from passengers concerning fares, schedules, and routings.
- Drive locomotives to and from various stations in a roundhouse to have locomotives cleaned, serviced, repaired, or supplied.
- Inspect the engine at the start and end of a shift, and refuel and lubricate the engine as needed.
- Observe train signals along the route and verify their meaning for the engineer.
- Observe the track from left side of the locomotive to detect obstructions on the tracks.
- Receive the starting signal from the conductor and move the controls, such as the throttle and air brakes, to drive the locomotive.
- Prepare reports to explain accidents, unscheduled stops, or delays.

What things about you point to this kind of work?

Is it important for you to

- Never be pressured to do things that go against your sense of right and wrong?
- Have supervisors who back up the workers with management?
- Be treated fairly by the company?

Have you enjoyed any of the following as a hobby or leisure-time activity?

- Driving a bus as a volunteer for an organization
- Driving an ambulance as a volunteer
- Operating a model train layout
- Reading mechanical or automotive magazines

Have you liked and done well in any of the following school subjects?

- Diesel Mechanics/Diesels
- Engine Mechanics
- Safety Regulations
- Locomotive Equipment/Operating

- Railroad Safety

Are you able to

- See details at a distance?
- Quickly and repeatedly make precise adjustments in moving the controls of a machine or vehicle to exact positions?
- See details of objects at close range (within a few feet)?
- Quickly respond (with your hand, finger, or foot) to one signal (sound, light, picture, etc.) when it appears?

Would you work in places such as

- Trains?
- Railroad tracks and yards?
- Bus and train stations?
- Buses and trolleys?

What skills and knowledges do you need for this kind of work?

For most of these jobs, you need these skills:

- Operation and Control—controlling operations of equipment or systems
- Operation Monitoring—watching gauges, dials, or other indicators to make sure a machine is working properly

These knowledges are important in most of these jobs:

- Transportation—principles and methods for moving people or goods by air, rail, sea, or road, including their relative costs, advantages, and limitations
- Mechanical—machines and tools, including their designs, uses, benefits, repair, and maintenance

What else should you consider about this kind of work?

Workers in this group are hired by railroad lines that crisscross the nation or by subway lines in the largest cities.

Railroad jobs are usually filled through a seniority system: You have to start in a lower-level job and work your way up. A regular eight-hour day is standard in some of the jobs, but for others you work evenings, nights, on call, weekends, or holidays. Frequent nights away from home may be required.

How can you prepare for jobs of this kind?

Work in this group usually requires education and/or training ranging from 30 days to more than a year.

Railroads prefer that engineer helpers have a high school education or its equal. Helpers are eligible for promotion when they pass tests on locomotive equipment and operation. They generally learn these skills on the job over several years.

SPECIALIZED TRAINING

JOBS	EDUCATION/TRAINING	WHERE OBTAINED
07.06.01 Rail Vehicle Operation		
All in Rail Vehicle Operation	Experience	Related jobs within the same industry
53-4011.00 Locomotive Engineers	Railroad Operations Training	On the job, military (Army)
53-4012.00 Locomotive Firers	Railroad Operations Training	On the job, military (Army)
53-4013.00 Rail Yard Engineers, Dinkey Operators, and Hostlers	Vehicle and Equipment Operators, Other	On the job, military (Army)
53-4041.00 Subway and Streetcar Operators	Vehicle and Equipment Operators, Other	On the job

07.07 Other Services Requiring Driving

Workers in this group drive ambulances, taxis, buses (city, intercity, or school), or other small vehicles, mostly to take people from place to place. Some drive a route to sell or deliver items, such as ice cream bars, take-out food, or newspapers. Some park cars on parking lots.

What kind of work would you do?

Your work activities would depend on your job. For example, you might

- Collect coins from vending machines, refill machines, and remove aged merchandise.
- Assist passengers with baggage and collect tickets or cash fares.
- Comply with local traffic regulations.
- Inspect vehicles to detect damage.
- Service vehicles with gas, oil, and water.
- Transport sick or injured persons to a hospital, or convalescents to their destinations.
- Vacuum, sweep, and clean the interior, and wash and polish the exterior, of an automobile.

What things about you point to this kind of work?

Is it important for you to

- Never be pressured to do things that go against your sense of right and wrong?
- Do your work alone?
- Have supervisors who back up the workers with management?
- Have work where you do things for other people?

Have you enjoyed any of the following as a hobby or leisure-time activity?

- Chauffeuring special groups, such as children, older people, or people with disabilities
- Driving a bus as a volunteer for an organization
- Driving an ambulance as a volunteer
- Directing traffic at community events
- Instructing family members in observing traffic regulations
- Racing midget or stock cars

Have you liked and done well in any of the following school subjects?

- Driver Education
- Traffic Control/Management
- Emergency Care/Rescue

Are you able to

- Quickly respond (with your hand, finger, or foot) to one signal (sound, light, picture, etc.) when it appears?
- Communicate information and ideas in speaking so others will understand?

Would you work in places such as

- Streets and highways?
- Bus and train stations?
- Buses and trolleys?
- Hospitals and nursing homes?
- Country clubs and resorts?

What skills and knowledges do you need for this kind of work?

For most of these jobs, you need these skills:

- Operation and Control—controlling operations of equipment or systems
- Service Orientation—actively looking for ways to help people
- Equipment Maintenance—performing routine maintenance and determining when and what kind of maintenance is needed

These knowledges are important in most of these jobs:

- Customer and Personal Service—principles and processes for providing customer and personal services including needs assessment techniques, quality service standards, alternative delivery systems, and customer satisfaction evaluation techniques
- Transportation—principles and methods for moving people or goods by air, rail, sea, or road, including their relative costs, advantages, and limitations

What else should you consider about this kind of work?

These drivers work for bus, taxi, limousine, and ambulance services, for school districts, for food and parts supply companies that distribute their goods locally using vans, and for parking lots.

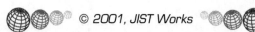

Most of the jobs are for a standard eight-hour day, but some require evening or weekend work, and for others you must be on call. Some jobs require you to wear a uniform. For most of these jobs you need to deal with the public and show tact and politeness, as well as good driving skills.

Some of the jobs are sensitive to the business cycle, but the outlook is generally good.

How can you prepare for jobs of this kind?

Work in this group sometimes requires only a brief demonstration of the tasks and rarely more than six months of training. In almost every case you need to have a good driving record.

For jobs in which you drive passengers, you generally need a special driver's license. Bus and taxi companies often have in-house training programs for new hires.

SPECIALIZED TRAINING

JOBS	EDUCATION/TRAINING	WHERE OBTAINED
07.07.01 Other Services Requiring Driving		
All in Other Services Requiring Driving	Road Safety; Driver Education; experience	High school, on the job, related jobs within the same industry
53-3011.00 Ambulance Drivers and Attendants, Except Emergency Medical Technicians	Emergency Medical Technology	On the job, two-year college, military (Coast Guard)
53-3021.00 Bus Drivers, Transit and Intercity	Truck, Bus, and Other Commercial Vehicle Operator	On the job, trade/technical school, military (Air Force, Coast Guard)
53-3022.00 Bus Drivers, School	Truck, Bus, and Other Commercial Vehicle Operator	On the job, trade/technical school, military (Air Force, Coast Guard)
53-3031.00 Driver/Sales Workers	General Retailing Operations	On the job
53-3041.00 Taxi Drivers and Chauffeurs	Truck, Bus, and Other Commercial Vehicle Operator	On the job, trade/technical school, military (Army)
53-6021.00 Parking Lot Attendants	Parking Lot Operations	On the job

07.08 Support Work in Transportation

Workers in this group provide support for routine operations at airports, railroads, and docks. They load and unload cargo, secure cargo inside vehicles, and refuel and clean vehicles.

What kind of work would you do?

Your work activities would depend on your job. For example, you might

- Assist passengers to board and leave trains.
- Pull or push track switches to reroute train cars.
- Collect tickets, fares, and passes from passengers.
- Inspect shipments to ascertain that freight is securely braced and blocked.
- Monitor the temperature and humidity of the freight storage area.
- Signal the locomotive engineer to start or stop the train when coupling or uncoupling cars.
- Watch for and relay traffic signals to start and stop train cars during shunting, using your arm or a lantern.

What things about you point to this kind of work?

Is it important for you to

- Never be pressured to do things that go against your sense of right and wrong?

- Have supervisors who back up the workers with management?
- Be treated fairly by the company?
- Have supervisors who train workers well?

Have you enjoyed any of the following as a hobby or leisure-time activity?

- Building model airplanes, automobiles, or boats
- Operating a CB or ham radio
- Operating a model train layout
- Reading airplane or boat magazines
- Repairing or assembling bicycles or tricycles

Have you liked and done well in any of the following school subjects?

- Airport Safety
- Safety Regulations

Are you able to

- Bend, stretch, twist, or reach out with your body, arms, and/or legs?
- Correctly follow a given rule or set of rules in order to arrange things or actions in a certain order?
- Exert maximum muscle force to lift, push, pull, or carry objects?

Would you work in places such as

- Airports?
- Freight terminals?
- Ports and harbors?
- Railroad tracks and yards?
- Trains?
- Ships and boats?

What skills and knowledges do you need for this kind of work?

For most of these jobs, you need these skills:

- Coordination—adjusting actions in relation to others' actions
- Problem Identification—identifying the nature of problems
- Active Listening—listening to what other people are saying and asking questions as appropriate

These knowledges are important in most of these jobs:

- Transportation—principles and methods for moving people or goods by air, rail, sea, or road, including their relative costs, advantages, and limitations
- Mechanical—machines and tools, including their designs, uses, benefits, repair, and maintenance

What else should you consider about this kind of work?

Workers in this group are hired by railroad lines and shipping lines. They perform a variety of tasks, often using physical labor, to keep vehicles running smoothly and see that their cargo is loaded and stored properly.

Job opportunities will be mixed and fluctuate over time. The amount of traffic and the volume of goods being shipped depend on the health of the economy. Containerizing of cargo and mechanization of some routine tasks will eliminate certain jobs.

Many of these jobs involve movement of large vehicles and loads of freight, and therefore safety precautions must be taken. Because vehicles arrive and depart at all hours, night or weekend work is sometimes required.

How can you prepare for jobs of this kind?

Work in this group sometimes requires less than six months of training, and occasionally as much as two years. Usually no formal education beyond high school is required.

Some of the jobs are associated with unions. For most of them you start with simpler tasks and learn more complex tasks by observing experienced workers on the job.

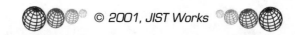

SPECIALIZED TRAINING

JOBS	EDUCATION/TRAINING	WHERE OBTAINED
07.08.01 Support Work in Transportation		
All in Support Work in Transportation	Experience	Related jobs within the same industry
53-4021.01 Train Crew Members	Heavy Equipment Maintenance and Repair	Trade/technical school, on the job, military (Army)
53-4021.02 Railroad Yard Workers	Heavy Equipment Maintenance and Repair; Railroad Operations Training	Trade/technical school, on the job
53-6051.00 Transportation Inspectors	Civil Engineering/Civil Technology/Technician; Heavy Equipment Maintenance and Repair	Trade/technical school, on the job
53-6051.06 Freight Inspectors	Business Administration and Management, General; Logistics and Materials Management	Trade/technical school, on the job
53-7062.01 Stevedores, Except Equipment Operators	Miscellaneous Transportation Operations	On the job, military (Army, Navy, Marine Corps)

08 Industrial Production

An interest in repetitive, concrete, organized activities most often done in a factory setting.

You can satisfy this interest by working in one of many industries that mass-produce goods, or for a utility that distributes electric power, gas, and so on. You may enjoy manual work, using your hands or hand tools. Perhaps you prefer to operate machines. You may like to inspect, sort, count, or weigh products. Using your training and experience to set up machines or supervise other workers may appeal to you.

08.01 Managerial Work in Industrial Production

08.02 Production Technology

08.03 Production Work

08.04 Metal and Plastics Machining Technology

08.05 Woodworking Technology

08.06 Systems Operation

08.07 Hands-on Work: Loading, Moving, Hoisting, and Conveying

08.01 Managerial Work in Industrial Production

Workers in this group manage industrial processing and manufacturing plants. They make decisions about policy and operation in accordance with overall company policy and goals. They must have a working knowledge of the equipment and methods for the activity that they direct.

What kind of work would you do?

Your work activities would depend on your job. For example, you might

- Assign duties and work schedules.
- Direct and coordinate the activities of employees engaged in the production or processing of goods.
- Inspect materials, products, or equipment to detect defects or malfunctions.
- Inventory and order supplies.
- Negotiate materials prices with suppliers.
- Resolve customer complaints.
- Review plans and confer with research and support staff to develop new products and processes or improve the quality of existing products.

What things about you point to this kind of work?

Is it important for you to

- Give directions and instructions to others?
- Plan your work with little supervision?
- Make decisions on your own?

Have you enjoyed any of the following as a hobby or leisure-time activity?

- Building cabinets or furniture
- Making sketches of machines or other mechanical equipment
- Reading mechanical or automotive magazines
- Repairing or assembling bicycles or tricycles
- Serving as a leader of a scouting or other group

Have you liked and done well in any of the following school subjects?

- Industrial Safety
- Industrial Organization
- Manufacturing Processes
- Management
- Personnel Management
- Accounting
- Quality Control

Are you able to

- Communicate information and ideas in speaking so others will understand?
- Listen to and understand information and ideas presented through spoken words and sentences?
- Read and understand information and ideas presented in writing?
- Tell when something is wrong or is likely to go wrong?
- Speak clearly so that it is understandable to a listener?
- Communicate information and ideas in writing so others will understand?

Would you work in places such as

- Factories and plants?
- Business offices?

What skills and knowledges do you need for this kind of work?

For most of these jobs, you need these skills:

- Coordination—adjusting actions in relation to others' actions
- Management of Personnel Resources—motivating, developing, and directing people as they work, identifying the best people for the job
- Problem Identification—identifying the nature of problems

These knowledges are important in most of these jobs:

- Production and Processing—inputs, outputs, raw materials, waste, quality control, costs, and techniques for maximizing the manufacture and distribution of goods
- Administration and Management—principles and processes involved in business and organizational planning, coordination, and execution

What else should you consider about this kind of work?

Workers in this group are hired by manufacturing plants in cities and towns throughout the country.

Production work in most industries is moving outside of the United States, so demand for these occupations is growing only slightly or even shrinking. The ups and downs of the business cycle also affect job openings in this group. Nevertheless, there is a continuing need for workers to replace those who retire, and in a select few industries (especially those that produce exports) jobs are being added. If an industry goes into decline, managers may be able to find work in a related or even very different industry, particularly if they have special skills that are portable, such as knowledge of computer applications.

Most of these managers work a regular eight-hour day, with occasional overtime. They divide their time between the office, where they do paperwork, and the work floor, where they observe production, monitor progress, detect possible problems, and give directions to workers. They also may spend a small amount of time doing the same work as the people whom they supervise.

How can you prepare for jobs of this kind?

Work in this group typically requires from two to six years of education and/or training.

Some workers study industrial management in college, then learn the particular methods and materials of an industry mostly on the job. Others begin as production workers, learning their skills largely on the job, and move up into management by taking college-level classes, perhaps getting a degree.

SPECIALIZED TRAINING

JOBS	EDUCATION/TRAINING	WHERE OBTAINED
08.01.01 Managerial Work in Industrial Production		
All in Managerial Work in Industrial Production	Experience; Budgeting; Personnel; Oral and Written Communications	Two-year college, four-year college, military, related jobs within the same industry
11-3051.00 Industrial Production Managers	Agricultural and Food Products Processing Operations and Management; Education Administration and Supervision, General; Adult and Continuing Education Administration; Textile Sciences and Engineering; Corrections/Correctional Administration; Operations Management and Supervision; Food Sciences and Technology; Business Administration and Management, General; Education, General	Two-year college, four-year college, on the job, military (Air Force, Navy)
51-1011.00 First-Line Supervisors/Managers of Production and Operating Workers	Custom Tailor; Operations Management and Supervision; Clothing, Apparel, and Textile Workers and Managers, General; Quality Control Technology/Technician; Food Sciences and Technology; Drycleaner and Launderer (Commercial); Electrical and Electronics Equipment Installer and Repairer; Business Machine Repairer; Machinist/Machine Technologist; Business Administration and Management, General; Logistics and Materials Management; Agricultural and Food Products Processing Operations and Management	Two-year college, on the job, military (all branches)
53-1021.00 First-Line Supervisors/Managers of Helpers, Laborers, and Material Movers, Hand	Business Administration and Management, General; Operations Management and Supervision	Two-year college, on the job, military (Army)

08.02 Production Technology

Workers in this group perform highly skilled hand and/or machine work requiring special techniques, training, and experience. Some set up machines for others to operate, or they set up and perform a variety of machine operations on their own. Some do precision handwork. Some inspect and test the work of others to make sure it meets standards of quality. Production technology workers mostly are employed on assembly lines, but the materials they work with may be as big as airplane bodies or as small as gemstones.

What kind of work would you do?

Your work activities would depend on your job. For example, you might

- Add components, chemicals, and solutions to a welding machine, using hand tools.
- Clean and lubricate a casting machine and dies, using air hose and brushes.
- Disassemble and repair machinery and equipment.
- Immerse jewelry in cleaning solution or acid to remove stains, or in a solution of gold or other metal to color jewelry.
- Maintain stock of machine parts and machining tools.
- Polish engravings using felt and cork wheels.
- Use or operate a product to test its functional performance.

What things about you point to this kind of work?

Is it important for you to

- Never be pressured to do things that go against your sense of right and wrong?
- Do your work alone?
- Be busy all the time?
- Be treated fairly by the company?

Have you enjoyed any of the following as a hobby or leisure-time activity?

- Building model airplanes, automobiles, or boats
- Making sketches of machines or other mechanical equipment
- Operating a model train layout
- Repairing the family car

Have you liked and done well in any of the following school subjects?

- Industrial Shop
- Industrial Safety
- Bookbinding
- Bookkeeping
- Botany
- Manufacturing Processes
- Tool Design
- Jewelry
- Industrial Materials
- Shop Math
- Machine Operating

Are you able to

- Quickly make coordinated movements of one hand, a hand together with its arm, or two hands to grasp, manipulate, or assemble objects?
- Quickly and repeatedly make precise adjustments in moving the controls of a machine or vehicle to exact positions?
- See details of objects at close range (within a few feet)?
- Correctly follow a given rule or set of rules in order to arrange things or actions in a certain order?
- Keep your hand and arm steady while making an arm movement or while holding your arm and hand in one position?

Would you work in places such as

- Factories and plants?

What skills and knowledges do you need for this kind of work?

For most of these jobs, you need these skills:

- Product Inspection–inspecting and evaluating the quality of products
- Operation and Control–controlling operations of equipment or systems

These knowledges are important in most of these jobs:

- Mechanical–machines and tools, including their designs, uses, benefits, repair, and maintenance

- Production and Processing—inputs, outputs, raw materials, waste, quality control, costs, and techniques for maximizing the manufacture and distribution of goods

What else should you consider about this kind of work?

Workers in this group are hired by manufacturing plants in many different industries. Manufacturing is generally in decline in the United States, so comparatively few new jobs are likely to open in these occupations. However, a few industries are exceptions and are growing, especially those that export to foreign markets. Also, in some highly skilled occupations there are many opportunities because retiring workers are not being replaced by young workers in sufficient numbers. Young workers seem unwilling to undergo the long training necessary for learning the skills, or they think that even highly skilled jobs lack prestige if you work with your hands. Many of these jobs offer great satisfaction from seeing concrete results, the products of skilled work that few people can do.

How can you prepare for jobs of this kind?

Work in this group requires as little as six months of education and/or training, or as much as four years.

Some of the jobs involve fairly simple machinery or materials and can be learned through relatively rapid on-the-job training. Other machines or materials are more complex, or the tolerances are more demanding, so a formal apprenticeship is required, with probably four years of classroom instruction and increasingly responsible (paid) work. Many of these jobs (and their apprenticeships) are associated with unions.

As industrial technology advances, it is important to keep learning in order to stay employable.

SPECIALIZED TRAINING

JOBS	EDUCATION/TRAINING	WHERE OBTAINED
08.02.01 Production Technology: Machine Set-up and Operation		
All in Production Technology: Machine Set-up and Operation	Machine Operating; Machine Shop; Math Computing (Fractions); experience	High school, trade school, related jobs within the same industry
51-4021.00 Extruding and Drawing Machine Setters, Operators, and Tenders, Metal and Plastic	Plastics Technology/Technician; Machinist/Machine Technologist	On the job, trade/technical school
51-4022.00 Forging Machine Setters, Operators, and Tenders, Metal and Plastic	Machinist/Machine Technologist; Tool and Die Maker/ Technologist	On the job, trade/technical school
51-4023.00 Rolling Machine Setters, Operators, and Tenders, Metal and Plastic	Machinist/Machine Technologist; Sheet Metal Worker; Precision Metal Workers, Other	On the job, trade/technical school
51-4031.01 Sawing Machine Tool Setters and Set-Up Operators, Metal and Plastic	Plastics Technology/Technician; Machinist/Machine Technologist	On the job, trade/technical school
51-4031.02 Punching Machine Setters and Set-Up Operators, Metal and Plastic	Machinist/Machine Technologist; Sheet Metal Worker	On the job, trade/technical school
51-4031.03 Press and Press Brake Machine Setters and Set-Up Operators, Metal and Plastic	Sheet Metal Worker; Machinist/Machine Technologist	On the job, trade/technical school

JOBS	EDUCATION/TRAINING	WHERE OBTAINED
08.02.01 Production Technology: Machine Set-up and Operation		
51-4031.04 Shear and Slitter Machine Setters and Set-Up Operators, Metal and Plastic	Machinist/Machine Technologist; Sheet Metal Worker	On the job, trade/technical school
51-4032.00 Drilling and Boring Machine Tool Setters, Operators, and Tenders, Metal and Plastic	Machinist/Machine Technologist	On the job, trade/technical school
51-4033.01 Grinding, Honing, Lapping, and Deburring Machine Set-Up Operators	Tool and Die Maker/Technologist; Watch, Clock and Jewelry Repairer; Machinist/Machine Technologist	On the job, trade/technical school
51-4033.02 Buffing and Polishing Set-Up Operators	Machinist/Machine Technologist	On the job, trade/technical school
51-4034.00 Lathe and Turning Machine Tool Setters, Operators, and Tenders, Metal and Plastic	Machinist/Machine Technologist; Watch, Clock, and Jewelry Repairer	On the job, trade/technical school
51-4035.00 Milling and Planing Machine Setters, Operators, and Tenders, Metal and Plastic	Machinist/Machine Technologist; Watch, Clock, and Jewelry Repairer	On the job, trade/technical school
51-4072.01 Plastic Molding and Casting Machine Setters and Set-Up Operators	Plastics Technology/Technician	On the job, trade/technical school
51-4072.02 Plastic Molding and Casting Machine Operators and Tenders	Plastics Technology/Technician	On the job, trade/technical school
51-4072.03 Metal Molding, Coremaking, and Casting Machine Setters and Set-Up Operators	Precision Metal Workers, Other	On the job, trade/technical school
51-4072.04 Metal Molding, Coremaking, and Casting Machine Operators and Tenders	Precision Metal Workers, Other	On the job, trade/technical school
51-4072.05 Casting Machine Set-Up Operators	Precision Metal Workers, Other	On the job, trade/technical school
51-4081.01 Combination Machine Tool Setters and Set-Up Operators, Metal and Plastic	Watch, Clock, and Jewelry Repairer; Machinist/Machine Technologist; Tool and Die Maker/Technologist	On the job, trade/technical school
51-4122.01 Welding Machine Setters and Set-Up Operators	Welder/Welding Technologist	On the job, trade/technical school

(continues)

(continued)

SPECIALIZED TRAINING

JOBS	EDUCATION/TRAINING	WHERE OBTAINED
08.02.01 Production Technology: Machine Set-up and Operation		
51-4122.03 Soldering and Brazing Machine Setters and Set-Up Operators	Welder/Welding Technologist	On the job, trade/technical school
51-4191.01 Heating Equipment Setters and Set-Up Operators, Metal and Plastic	Machinist/Machine Technologist	On the job, trade/technical school
51-4191.02 Heat Treating, Annealing, and Tempering Machine Operators and Tenders, Metal and Plastic	Precision Metal Workers, Other	On the job, trade/technical school
51-5011.01 Bindery Machine Setters and Set-Up Operators	Graphic and Printing Equipment Operators, Other	On the job, trade/technical school
51-5023.06 Screen Printing Machine Setters and Set-Up Operators	Graphic and Printing Equipment Operators, Other; Graphic and Printing Equipment Operator, General; Printing Press Operator	On the job, trade/technical school
51-6062.00 Textile Cutting Machine Setters, Operators, and Tenders	Industrial Machinery Maintenance and Repair	On the job, trade/technical school
51-6063.00 Textile Knitting and Weaving Machine Setters, Operators, and Tenders	Industrial Machinery Maintenance and Repair	On the job, trade/technical school
51-6064.00 Textile Winding, Twisting, and Drawing Out Machine Setters, Operators, and Tenders	Industrial Machinery Maintenance and Repair	On the job, trade/technical school
51-7042.01 Woodworking Machine Setters and Set-Up Operators, Except Sawing	Gunsmith; Cabinet Maker and Millworker; Woodworkers, General	On the job, trade/technical school
51-9041.01 Extruding, Forming, Pressing, and Compacting Machine Setters and Set-Up Operators	Industrial Machinery Maintenance and Repair; Precision Production Trades, Other	On the job, trade/technical school
51-9121.01 Coating, Painting, and Spraying Machine Setters and Set-Up Operators	Industrial Machinery Maintenance and Repair; Machinist/Machine Technologist; Precision Production Trades, Other; Precision Metal Workers, Other	On the job, trade/technical school
51-9196.00 Paper Goods Machine Setters, Operators, and Tenders	Industrial Machinery Maintenance and Repair	On the job, trade/technical school

JOBS	EDUCATION/TRAINING	WHERE OBTAINED
08.02.02 Production Technology: Precision Hand Work		
All in Production Technology: Precision Hand Work	Math Computing (Fractions); knowledge of specific materials, tools, and operations in manufacturing process	High school, trade school, related jobs within the same industry
51-2011.01 Aircraft Structure Assemblers, Precision	Aircraft Mechanic/Technician, Airframe	Two-year college, trade/technical school, on the job
51-2011.02 Aircraft Systems Assemblers, Precision	Aircraft Mechanic/Technician, Airframe; Aircraft Mechanic/Technician, Powerplant	Two-year college, trade/technical school, on the job, military (Air Force)
51-2011.03 Aircraft Rigging Assemblers	Aeronautical and Aerospace Engineering Technology/ Technician; Aircraft Mechanic/Technician, Airframe	Two-year college, trade/technical school, on the job
51-2022.00 Electrical and Electronic Equipment Assemblers	Industrial Machinery Maintenance and Repair; Musical Instrument Repairer; Electrical and Electronics Equipment Installer and Repairer, General; Business Machine Repairer; Communication Systems Installer and Repairer; Electrical and Electronics Equipment Installer and Repairer, Other; Instrument Calibration and Repair; Industrial Electronics Installer and Repairer	Two-year college, trade/technical school, on the job
51-2023.00 Electromechanical Equipment Assemblers	Business Machine Repairer; Electrical and Electronics Equipment Installer and Repairer, General; Aircraft Mechanic/Technician, Powerplant; Electrical and Electronics Equipment Installer and Repairer, Other	Two-year college, trade/technical school, on the job
51-2031.00 Engine and Other Machine Assemblers	Industrial Machinery Maintenance and Repair	Trade/technical school, on the job
51-2093.00 Timing Device Assemblers, Adjusters, and Calibrators	Watch, Clock, and Jewelry Repairer	Trade/technical school, on the job
51-4071.00 Foundry Mold and Coremakers	Precision Metal Workers, Other	On the job, trade/technical school, military (Navy)
51-5012.00 Bookbinders	Graphic and Printing Equipment Operators, Other	On the job, trade/technical school
51-9071.01 Jewelers	Crafts, Folk Art, and Artisanry; Metal and Jewelry Arts; Art, General; Watch, Clock, and Jewelry Repairer	On the job, trade/technical school
51-9071.02 Silversmiths	Crafts, Folk Art, and Artisanry	On the job, trade/technical school
51-9071.03 Model and Mold Makers, Jewelry	Watch, Clock, and Jewelry Repairer; Metal and Jewelry Arts; Art, General; Machinist/Machine Technologist	On the job, trade/technical school
51-9071.04 Bench Workers, Jewelry	Metal and Jewelry Arts; Ceramics Arts and Ceramics; Art, General; Watch, Clock, and Jewelry Repairer	On the job, trade/technical school
51-9071.05 Pewter Casters and Finishers	Machinist/Machine Technologist; Metal and Jewelry Arts; Art, General	On the job, trade/technical school

(continues)

(continued)

SPECIALIZED TRAINING

JOBS	EDUCATION/TRAINING	WHERE OBTAINED
08.02.02 Production Technology: Precision Hand Work		
51-9071.06 Gem and Diamond Workers	Watch, Clock, and Jewelry Repairer; Art, General; Metal and Jewelry Arts	Two-year college, on the job, trade/technical school
51-9081.00 Dental Laboratory Technicians	Dental Laboratory Technician	On the job, trade/technical school, military (Navy, Air Force)
51-9083.01 Precision Lens Grinders and Polishers	Optical Technician/Assistant; Opticianry/Dispensing Optician; Optometric/Ophthalmic Laboratory Technician	On the job, two-year college, trade/technical school, military (Army, Navy)
51-9195.01 Precision Mold and Pattern Casters, except Nonferrous Metals	Construction Trades, Other; Mason and Tile Setter	On the job, trade/technical school
51-9195.02 Precision Pattern and Die Casters, Nonferrous Metals	Machinist/Machine Technologist; Precision Metal Workers, Other	On the job, trade/technical school
08.02.03 Production Technology: Inspection		
All in Production Technology: Inspection	Knowledge of specific operations in manufacturing process	Related jobs within the same industry
45-4023.00 Log Graders and Scalers	Forest Products Technology/Technician	On the job, trade/technical school
51-9061.00 Inspectors, Testers, Sorters, Samplers, and Weighers	Instrument Calibration and Repair; Precision Metal Workers, Other; Sheet Metal Worker; Machinist/Machine Technologist; Quality Control Technology/Technician; Electromechanical Technology/Technician; Machine Shop Assistant; Quality Control Technology/Technician; Precision Metal Workers, Other; Sheet Metal Worker; Machine Shop Assistant; Clothing, Apparel, and Textile Workers and Managers, General; Commercial Garment and Apparel Worker; Industrial Production Technology/Technicians, Other; Machinist/Machine Technologist; Sheet Metal Worker	Trade/technical school, on the job
51-9061.01 Materials Inspectors	Electrical and Electronics Equipment Installer and Repairer, General; Auto/Automotive Mechanic/Technician; Construction/Building Inspector; Marine Maintenance and Ship Repair; Precision Production Trades, Other; Precision Metal Workers, Other; Welder/Welding Technologist; Tool and Die Maker/Technologist; Machine Shop Assistant; Machinist/Machine Technologist; Food Sciences and Technology; Diesel Engine Mechanic and Repairer; Watch, Clock, and Jewelry Repairer; Petroleum Technology/Technician; Industrial/Manufacturing Technology/Technician; Plastics Technology/Technician; Aircraft Mechanic/	Trade/technical school, on the job, military (Army, Navy, Air Force, Marine Corps)

JOBS	EDUCATION/TRAINING	WHERE OBTAINED
08.02.03 Production Technology: Inspection		
	Technician, Airframe; Aeronautical and Aerospace Engineering Technology/Technician; Gunsmith; Carpenter; Plumber and Pipefitter; Business Machine Repairer; Heating, Air Conditioning, and Refrigeration Mechanic and Repair; Industrial Machinery Maintenance and Repair; Metallurgical Technology/Technician	
51-9061.02 Mechanical Inspectors	Motorcycle Mechanic and Repairer; Aircraft Mechanic/Technician, Powerplant; Auto/Automotive Mechanic/Technician; Diesel Engine Mechanic and Repairer; Aeronautical and Aerospace Engineering Technology/Technician; Agricultural Power Machinery Operator; Agricultural Mechanization, General; Aircraft Mechanic/Technician, Airframe; Auto/Automotive Body Repairer	Trade/technical school, on the job, military (all branches)
51-9061.03 Precision Devices Inspectors and Testers	Watch, Clock, and Jewelry Repairer; Machine Shop Assistant; Miscellaneous Mechanics and Repairers, Other; Instrument Calibration and Repairer; Aeronautical and Aerospace Engineering Technology/Technician; Industrial Production Technology/Technicians, Other; Electromechanical Technology/Technician; Biomedical Engineering-Related Technology/Technician; Aviation Systems and Avionics Maintenance Technologist/Technician	Trade/technical school, on the job, military (Army, Navy, Air Force, Marine Corps)
51-9061.04 Electrical and Electronic Inspectors and Testers	Electromechanical Technology/Technician; Electrical and Electronics Equipment Installer and Repairer, General; Aviation Systems and Avionics Maintenance Technologist/Technician; Aircraft Mechanic/Technician, Airframe; Stationary Energy Sources Installer and Operator; Instrument Calibration and Repairer; Industrial Electronics Installer and Repairer; Communication Systems Installer and Repairer; Electrical and Electronics Equipment Installer and Repairer, Other; Lineworker; Electrician; Quality Control Technology/Technician; Electrical and Power Transmission Installer, General	Trade/technical school, on the job, military (Army, Air Force, Marine Corps)
51-9061.05 Production Inspectors, Testers, Graders, Sorters, Samplers, Weighers	Printing Press Operator; Shoe, Boot, and Leather Repairer; Heating, Air Conditioning, and Refrigeration Mechanic and Repair; Heavy Equipment Maintenance and Repair; Industrial Machinery Maintenance and Repair; Instrument Calibration and Repairer; Gunsmith; Musical Instrument Repairer; Watch, Clock, and Jewelry Repairer; Miscellaneous Mechanics and Repairers, Other; Stationary Energy Sources Installer and Operator; Auto/Automotive Body Repairer; Auto/Automotive Mechanic/Technician; Aircraft Mechanic/Technician, Powerplant; Lithographer and Platemaker; Electrical and Electronics Equipment Installer and Repairer, General;	Trade/technical school, on the job, military (Navy, Air Force, Marine Corps, Coast Guard)

(continues)

(continued)

SPECIALIZED TRAINING

JOBS	EDUCATION/TRAINING	WHERE OBTAINED
08.02.03 Production Technology: Inspection		
51-9061.05 Production Inspectors, Testers, Graders, Sorters, Samplers, Weighers *(continued)*	Welder/Welding Technologist; Graphic and Printing Equipment Operator, General; Optometric/Ophthalmic Laboratory Technician; Marine Maintenance and Ship Repair; Precision Production Trades, Other; Furniture Designer and Maker; Graphic and Printing Equipment Operators, Other; Precision Metal Workers, Other; Upholsterer; Tool and Die Maker/Technologist; Sheet Metal Worker; Machine Shop Assistant; Machinist/Machine Technologist; Leatherworkers and Upholsterers, Other; Small Engine Mechanic and Repairer; Woodworkers, General; Barber/Hairstylist; Clothing, Apparel, and Textile Workers and Managers, General; Petroleum Technology/Technician; Automotive Engineering Technology/Technician; Aeronautical and Aerospace Engineering Technology/Technician; Quality Control Technology/Technician; Industrial Production Technology/Technicians, Other; Commercial Garment and Apparel Worker; Baker/Pastry Chef; Wood Science and Pulp/Paper Technology; Photographic Technology/Technician; Industrial Electronics Installer and Repairer; Forestry, General; Motorcycle Mechanic and Repairer; Agricultural and Food Products Processing Operations and Management; Agricultural Power Machinery Operator; Plastics Technology/Technician; Plumber and Pipefitter; Forest Products Technology/Technician; Construction Trades, Other; Construction and Building Finishers and Managers, Other; Painter and Wall Coverer; Construction/Building Inspector; Lineworker; Electrical and Power Transmission Installer, General; Chemical Technology/Technician; Nuclear/Nuclear Power Technology/Technician; Drycleaner and Launderer (Commercial); Custom Tailor; Business Machine Repairer; Electrical and Electronics Equipment Installer and Repairer, Other; Mason and Tile Setter	
53-6051.05 Motor Vehicle Inspectors	Diesel Engine Mechanic and Repairer; Auto/Automotive Mechanic/Technician	Trade/technical school, on the job

08.03 Production Work

Workers in this group use hands and hand tools with skill to make or process materials, products, and parts. They follow established procedures and techniques. Although their jobs are found most often in manufacturing plants, they are also found in places we might not ordinarily think of as factories, such as printing and publishing companies, slaughterhouses, and canneries.

What kind of work would you do?

Your work activities would depend on your job. For example, you might

- Adjust a machine to apply a specified amount of glue, cement, or adhesive.
- Clean and maintain tools and equipment, using solvent, brushes, and rags.
- Estimate the weight of a product visually and by feel.
- Hang, fold, package, and tag finished articles for delivery to customer.
- Maintain a log of instrument readings, test results, and shift production.
- Remove parts such as skin, feathers, scales, or bones from carcasses.
- Read work orders and job specifications to select ink and paper stock.
- Weld metal parts or components together, using brazing, gas, or arc-welding equipment.

What things about you point to this kind of work?

Is it important for you to

- Never be pressured to do things that go against your sense of right and wrong?
- Do your work alone?
- Be busy all the time?

Have you enjoyed any of the following as a hobby or leisure-time activity?

- Cooking large quantities of food for community events
- Making sketches of machines or other mechanical equipment
- Repairing the family car
- Canning and preserving food
- Doing desktop publishing for a school or community publication

Have you liked and done well in any of the following school subjects?

- Industrial Shop
- Industrial Safety
- Industrial Materials
- Machine Operating
- Model Making
- Print Shop/Printing
- Printmaking
- Offset Printing
- Lithography
- Welding

Are you able to

- Quickly make coordinated movements of one hand, a hand together with its arm, or two hands to grasp, manipulate, or assemble objects?
- See details of objects at close range (within a few feet)?
- Correctly follow a given rule or set of rules in order to arrange things or actions in a certain order?
- Quickly and repeatedly make precise adjustments in moving the controls of a machine or vehicle to exact positions?
- Keep your hand and arm steady while making an arm movement or while holding your arm and hand in one position?

Would you work in places such as

- Factories and plants?

What skills and knowledges do you need for this kind of work?

For most of these jobs, you need these skills:

- Operation and Control—controlling operations of equipment or systems
- Product Inspection—inspecting and evaluating the quality of products

These knowledges are important in most of these jobs:

- Production and Processing—inputs, outputs, raw materials, waste, quality control, costs, and techniques for maximizing the manufacture and distribution of goods

- Mechanical—machines and tools, including their designs, uses, benefits, repair, and maintenance

What else should you consider about this kind of work?

Workers in this group are hired by manufacturers and processors in many different industries—e.g., automobile manufacturing, baking, garment sewing, printing, and computer chip fabrication, to name just a few.

The outlook for jobs will depend partly on the health of the particular industry, and also will probably vary with the amount of economic activity in general. But on the whole, manufacturing and processing are in decline in the United States, so in many industries most of the job openings will be to replace retiring workers. In addition, some of these occupations are becoming automated, replacing workers with robots. Best opportunities will be for higher-skilled occupations in certain industries that are growing, such as those that serve an aging population (dental laboratory technicians, to cite just one example) or those that export to foreign markets.

Some of these jobs involve working with hazardous materials, or in environments that are noisy, hot, or bad-smelling; safety precautions may be necessary.

How can you prepare for jobs of this kind?

Work in this group requires education and/or training that may last less than six months or as much as six years.

Occupations with "precision" in the title generally require the most formal education and training, usually requiring classroom studies (perhaps a two-year degree) and on-the-job training (probably a formal apprenticeship). The same is true for many of the jobs in printing and reproduction. On the other hand, many other jobs require only on-the-job training, perhaps no more than observing and following directions of experienced workers. Many of these jobs (and their training programs) are associated with unions.

As industrial technology advances, it is important to keep learning to stay employable.

SPECIALIZED TRAINING

JOBS	EDUCATION/TRAINING	WHERE OBTAINED
08.03.01 Production Work: Machine Work, Assorted Materials		
All in Production Work: Machine Work, Assorted Materials	Production Machine Operation	On the job
51-4011.01 Numerical Control Machine Tool Operators and Tenders, Metal and Plastic	Machine Shop Assistant	On the job, trade/technical school, military (Army, Navy, Air Force, Marine Corps)
51-4081.02 Combination Machine Tool Operators and Tenders, Metal and Plastic	Machine Shop Assistant	On the job, trade/technical school
51-6031.01 Sewing Machine Operators, Garment	Commercial Garment and Apparel Worker; Clothing, Apparel, and Textile Workers and Managers, General	On the job
51-6031.02 Sewing Machine Operators, Non-Garment	Window Treatment Maker and Installer; Clothing, Apparel and Textile Workers and Managers, General; Commercial Garment and Apparel Worker; Home Furnishings and Equipment Installers and Consultants, General; Upholsterer	On the job
51-6042.00 Shoe Machine Operators and Tenders	Shoe, Boot, and Leather Repairer	On the job

JOBS	EDUCATION/TRAINING	WHERE OBTAINED
08.03.01 Production Work: Machine Work, Assorted Materials		
51-6091.01 Extruding and Forming Machine Operators and Tenders, Synthetic or Glass Fibers	Manufacturing Operations, Miscellaneous Materials	On the job
51-7041.01 Sawing Machine Setters and Set-Up Operators	Woodworkers, General; Cabinet Maker and Millworker	On the job, trade/technical school
51-7041.02 Sawing Machine Operators and Tenders	Woodworkers, General; Cabinet Maker and Millworker	On the job, trade/technical school
51-7042.02 Woodworking Machine Operators and Tenders, Except Sawing	Woodworkers, General; Gunsmith; Cabinet Maker and Millworker	On the job
51-9021.00 Crushing, Grinding, and Polishing Machine Setters, Operators, and Tenders	Agricultural and Food Products Processing Operations and Management	On the job, trade/technical school
51-9032.01 Fiber Product Cutting Machine Setters and Set-Up Operators	Precision Production Trades, Other; Industrial Machinery Maintenance and Repair	On the job, trade/technical school
51-9032.02 Stone Sawyers	Industrial Machinery Maintenance and Repair	On the job, trade/technical school
51-9032.03 Glass Cutting Machine Setters and Set-Up Operators	Industrial Machinery Maintenance and Repair	On the job, trade/technical school
51-9032.04 Cutting and Slicing Machine Operators and Tenders	Industrial Machinery Maintenance and Repair	On the job, trade/technical school
51-9041.02 Extruding, Forming, Pressing, and Compacting Machine Operators and Tenders	Industrial Machinery Maintenance and Repair; Machine Shop Assistant	On the job, military (Navy)
51-9111.00 Packaging and Filling Machine Operators and Tenders	Industrial Machinery Maintenance and Repair	On the job, trade/technical school, military (Marine Corps)
51-9121.02 Coating, Painting, and Spraying Machine Operators and Tenders	Production Machine Operation	On the job
51-9191.00 Cementing and Gluing Machine Operators and Tenders	Graphic and Printing Equipment Operators, Other	On the job, trade/technical school

(continues)

(continued)

SPECIALIZED TRAINING

JOBS	EDUCATION/TRAINING	WHERE OBTAINED
08.03.02 Production Work: Equipment Operation, Assorted Materials Processing		
All in Production Work: Equipment Operation, Assorted Materials Processing	Production Machine Operation	On the job
51-3011.02 Bakers, Manufacturing	Baker/Pastry Chef; Agricultural and Food Products Processing Operations	On the job, trade/technical school
51-3022.00 Meat, Poultry, and Fish Cutters and Trimmers	Meatcutter; Agricultural and Food Products Processing Operations	On the job
51-3023.00 Slaughterers and Meat Packers	Meatcutter	On the job, trade/technical school
51-3091.00 Food and Tobacco Roasting, Baking, and Drying Machine Operators and Tenders	Agricultural and Food Products Processing Operations	On the job
51-3093.00 Food Cooking Machine Operators and Tenders	Agricultural and Food Products Processing Operations	On the job
51-4051.00 Metal-Refining Furnace Operators and Tenders	Manufacturing Operations, Miscellaneous Materials; Miscellaneous Precision Metal Worker Training	On the job
51-4052.00 Pourers and Casters, Metal	Manufacturing Operations, Miscellaneous Materials; Miscellaneous Precision Metal Worker Training	On the job
51-4191.03 Heaters, Metal and Plastic	Precision Metal Workers, Other	On the job, trade/technical school
51-6021.02 Pressing Machine Operators and Tenders–Textile, Garment, and Related Materials	Clothing, Apparel, and Textile Workers and Managers, General; Commercial Garment and Apparel Worker	On the job
51-6061.00 Textile Bleaching and Dyeing Machine Operators and Tenders	Manufacturing Operations, Miscellaneous Materials	On the job
51-9011.01 Chemical Equipment Controllers and Operators	Chemical Technology/Technician	On the job, trade/technical school
51-9011.02 Chemical Equipment Tenders	Chemical Technology/Technician	On the job, trade/technical school
51-9012.00 Separating, Filtering, Clarifying, Precipitating, and Still Machine Setters, Operators, and Tenders	Agricultural and Food Products Processing Operations and Management	On the job, military (Army)

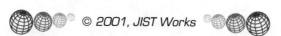

JOBS	EDUCATION/TRAINING	WHERE OBTAINED
08.03.02 Production Work: Equipment Operation, Assorted Materials Processing		
51-9023.00 Mixing and Blending Machine Setters, Operators, and Tenders	Agricultural and Food Products Processing Operations and Management	On the job, trade/technical school
51-9051.00 Furnace, Kiln, Oven, Drier, and Kettle Operators and Tenders	Agricultural and Food Products Processing Operations; Manufacturing Operations, Miscellaneous Materials	On the job
51-9141.00 Semiconductor Processors	Industrial Electronics Installer and Repairer; Electrical and Electronics Equipment Installer and Repairer	On the job
51-9192.00 Cleaning, Washing, and Metal Pickling Equipment Operators and Tenders	Manufacturing Operations, Miscellaneous Materials; Agricultural and Food Products Processing Operations	On the job
51-9193.00 Cooling and Freezing Equipment Operators and Tenders	Manufacturing Operations, Miscellaneous Materials; Agricultural and Food Products Processing Operations	On the job
51-9198.01 Production Laborers	Manufacturing Operations, Miscellaneous Materials	On the job
51-9198.02 Production Helpers	Manufacturing Operations, Miscellaneous Materials	On the job
08.03.03 Production Work: Equipment Operation, Welding, Brazing, and Soldering		
All in Production Work: Equipment Operation, Welding, Brazing, and Soldering	Experience	Related jobs within the same industry
51-2041.01 Metal Fabricators, Structural Metal Products	Machinist/Machine Technologist; Machine Shop Assistant; Sheet Metal Worker; Marine Maintenance and Ship Repairer	Two-year college, trade/technical school, apprenticeship; military data not yet available
51-2041.02 Fitters, Structural Metal—Precision	Machine Shop Assistant	On the job, trade/technical school
51-4121.01 Welders, Production	Welder/Welding Technologist	Trade/technical school, on the job
51-4121.02 Welders and Cutters	Welder/Welding Technologist	Trade/technical school, on the job, military (all branches)
51-4121.03 Welder-Fitters	Welder/Welding Technologist	Trade/technical school, on the job, military (Navy, Air Force)
51-4121.04 Solderers	Gunsmith; Welder/Welding Technologist	On the job
51-4121.05 Brazers	Welder/Welding Technologist	Trade/technical school, on the job
51-4122.02 Welding Machine Operators and Tenders	Welder/Welding Technologist	On the job, trade/technical school

(continues)

(continued)

SPECIALIZED TRAINING

JOBS	EDUCATION/TRAINING	WHERE OBTAINED
08.03.03 Production Work: Equipment Operation, Welding, Brazing, and Soldering		
51-4122.04 Soldering and Brazing Machine Operators and Tenders	Welder/Welding Technologist	On the job
08.03.04 Production Work: Plating and Coating		
All in Production Work: Plating and Coating	Production Machine Operation	On the job
51-4193.01 Electrolytic Plating and Coating Machine Setters and Set-Up Operators, Metal and Plastic	Precision Metal Workers, Other	On the job, trade/technical school
51-4193.02 Electrolytic Plating and Coating Machine Operators and Tenders, Metal and Plastic	Precision Metal Workers, Other	On the job, trade/technical school, military (Air Force)
51-4193.03 Nonelectrolytic Plating and Coating Machine Setters and Set-Up Operators, Metal and Plastic	Precision Metal Workers, Other	On the job, trade/technical school, military (Air Force)
51-4193.04 Nonelectrolytic Plating and Coating Machine Operators and Tenders, Metal and Plastic	Precision Metal Workers, Other	On the job, trade/technical school, military (Air Force)
08.03.05 Production Work: Printing and Reproduction		
All in Production Work: Printing and Reproduction	Production Machine Operation	On the job
51-5011.02 Bindery Machine Operators and Tenders	Graphic and Printing Equipment Operators, Other	On the job, military (Navy, Air Force, Marine Corps)
51-5021.00 Job Printers	Mechanical Typesetter and Composer; Graphic and Printing Equipment Operator, General	On the job, trade/technical school
51-5022.01 Hand Compositors and Typesetters	Graphic and Printing Equipment Operator, General; Mechanical Typesetter and Composer	On the job, trade/technical school
51-5022.05 Scanner Operators	Graphic and Printing Equipment Operator, General; Lithographer and Platemaker	On the job, trade/technical school
51-5022.06 Strippers	Lithographer and Platemaker; Graphic and Printing Equipment Operator, General	On the job, trade/technical school

JOBS	EDUCATION/TRAINING	WHERE OBTAINED
08.03.05 Production Work: Printing and Reproduction		
51-5022.07 Platemakers	Graphic and Printing Equipment Operator, General; Lithographer and Platemaker	On the job, trade/technical school, military (Army, Navy, Air Force, Marine Corps)
51-5022.10 Electrotypers and Stereotypers	Mechanical Typesetter and Composer; Graphic and Printing Equipment Operator, General	On the job, trade/technical school
51-5022.11 Plate Finishers	Lithographer and Platemaker; Graphic and Printing Equipment Operator, General	On the job, trade/technical school
51-5022.13 Photoengraving and Lithographing Machine Operators and Tenders	Graphic and Printing Equipment Operators, Other; Lithographer and Platemaker; Graphic and Printing Equipment Operator, General; Photographic Technology/Technician	On the job, trade/technical school
51-5023.01 Precision Printing Workers	Desktop Publishing Equipment Operator; Photographic Technology/Technician; Graphic and Printing Equipment Operator, General; Mechanical Typesetter and Composer; Lithographer and Platemaker; Computer Typography and Composition Equipment Operator; Graphic Design, Commercial Art, and Illustration; Printing Press Operator	On the job, trade/technical school, military (Army, Navy, Air Force, Marine Corps)
51-5023.02 Offset Lithographic Press Setters and Set-Up Operators	Graphic and Printing Equipment Operator, General; Printing Press Operator	On the job, trade/technical school, military (Navy, Air Force, Marine Corps)
51-5023.03 Letterpress Setters and Set-Up Operators	Printing Press Operator; Graphic and Printing Equipment Operator, General	On the job, trade/technical school
51-5023.04 Design Printing Machine Setters and Set-Up Operators	Graphic and Printing Equipment Operator, General; Printing Press Operator	On the job, trade/technical school
51-5023.05 Marking and Identification Printing Machine Setters and Set-Up Operators	Graphic and Printing Equipment Operator, General; Printing Press Operator	On the job
51-5023.07 Embossing Machine Set-Up Operators	Mechanical Typesetter and Composer; Printing Press Operator; Graphic and Printing Equipment Operator, General	On the job, trade/technical school
51-5023.08 Engraver Set-Up Operators	Lithographer and Platemaker; Graphic and Printing Equipment Operator, General	On the job, trade/technical school
51-5023.09 Printing Press Machine Operators and Tenders	Graphic and Printing Equipment Operators, Other; Printing Press Operator; Graphic and Printing Equipment Operator, General	On the job
51-9131.01 Photographic Retouchers and Restorers	Photographic Technology/Technician; Graphic Design, Commercial Art, and Illustration	Trade/technical school, two-year college, on the job

(continues)

(continued)

SPECIALIZED TRAINING

JOBS	EDUCATION/TRAINING	WHERE OBTAINED
08.03.05 Production Work: Printing and Reproduction		
51-9131.02 Photographic Reproduction Technicians	Photographic Technology/Technician	On the job, trade/technical school, military (Army)
51-9131.03 Photographic Hand Developers	Photographic Technology/Technician	On the job, trade/technical school, military (Navy)
51-9131.04 Film Laboratory Technicians	Photographic Technology/Technician	On the job, two-year college, trade/technical school
51-9132.00 Photographic Processing Machine Operators	Graphic and Printing Equipment Operator, General; Photographic Technology/Technician; Lithographer and Platemaker	On the job, trade/technical school, military (Army, Navy)
08.03.06 Production Work: Hands-on Work, Assorted Materials		
All in Production Work: Hands-on Work, Assorted Materials	Knowledge of materials and processes of the industry	On the job
45-2041.00 Graders and Sorters, Agricultural Products	Agricultural and Food Products Processing Operations and Management	On the job
51-2021.00 Coil Winders, Tapers, and Finishers	Industrial Electronics Installer and Repairer; Electrical and Electronics Equipment Installer and Repairer, General; Electrical and Electronics Equipment Installer and Repairer, Other	On the job, trade/technical school
51-2091.00 Fiberglass Laminators and Fabricators	Furniture Designer and Maker	On the job, trade/technical school
51-2092.00 Team Assemblers	Furniture Designer and Maker; Window Treatment Maker and Installer; Shoe, Boot, and Leather Repairer; Sheet Metal Worker	On the job
51-3092.00 Food Batchmakers	Agricultural and Food Products Processing Operations and Management; Institutional Food Workers and Administrators, General	On the job, trade/technical school
51-6051.00 Sewers, Hand	Graphic and Printing Equipment Operators, Other; Clothing, Apparel, and Textile Workers and Managers, General	On the job
51-6092.00 Fabric and Apparel Patternmakers	Clothing, Apparel, and Textile Workers and Managers, General; Commercial Garment and Apparel Worker; Shoe, Boot, and Leather Repairer; Home Furnishings and Equipment Installers and Consultants, General; Window Treatment Maker and Installer; Fashion Design and Illustration; Marine Maintenance and Ship Repair	On the job, trade/technical school

JOBS	EDUCATION/TRAINING	WHERE OBTAINED
08.03.06 Production Work: Hands-on Work, Assorted Materials		
51-9022.00 Grinding and Polishing Workers, Hand	Watch, Clock, and Jewelry Repairer; Woodworkers, Other; Musical Instrument Repairer; Gunsmith; Mason and Tile Setter; Tool and Die Maker/Technologist; Machine Shop Assistant; Welder/Welding Technologist; Precision Metal Workers, Other; Woodworkers, General; Furniture Designer and Maker; Auto/Automotive Body Repairer	On the job
51-9031.00 Cutters and Trimmers, Hand	Machine Shop Assistant; Marine Maintenance and Ship Repair; Leatherworkers and Upholsterers, Other; Shoe, Boot, and Leather Repairer; Musical Instrument Repairer; Window Treatment Maker and Installer; Home Furnishings and Equipment Installers and Consultants, General; Commercial Garment and Apparel Worker; Clothing, Apparel, and Textile Workers and Managers, General	On the job
51-9123.00 Painting, Coating, and Decorating Workers	Dental Laboratory Technician; Metal and Jewelry Arts; Painter and Wall Coverer; Watch, Clock, and Jewelry Repairer; Auto/Automotive Body Repairer; Machine Shop Assistant; Graphic Design, Commercial Art, and Illustration; Art, General; Photographic Technology/Technician; Ceramics Arts and Ceramics	On the job
51-9195.06 Mold Makers, Hand	Precision Production Trades, Other; Dental Laboratory Technician	On the job, trade/technical school
51-9195.07 Molding and Casting Workers	Dental Laboratory Technician; Plastics Technology/Technician; Construction and Building Finishers and Managers, Other; Electrical and Electronics Equipment Installer and Repairer, General; Industrial Electronics Installer and Repairer; Aviation Systems and Avionics Maintenance Technologist/Technician; Machinist/Machine Technologist; Precision Production Trades, Other; Crafts, Folk Art, and Artisanry	On the job, trade/technical school
51-9197.00 Tire Builders	Manufacturing Operations, Miscellaneous Materials	On the job

08.04 Metal and Plastics Machining Technology

Workers in this group cut and grind metal and plastic parts to desired shapes and measurements, usually following specifications that require very precise work. They create the patterns, molds, and models that manufacturers then use to mass-produce products of all kinds. Most work in machine shops of manufacturing plants.

What kind of work would you do?

Your work activities would depend on your job. For example, you might

- Align, fit, and join parts using bolts or screws, or by welding or gluing.
- Compute the number, width, and angle of cutting tools, micrometers, scales, and gauges; and adjust tools to produce specified cuts.
- Cut and shape sheet metal, and heat and bend metal to the specified shape.
- Inspect and test a model or other product to verify conformance to specifications, using precision measuring instruments or a circuit tester.

- Operate plate curving machine to cut plates to fit a printing press.
- Set up and operate machines such as lathes, drill presses, punch presses, or bandsaws to fabricate prototypes or models.
- Study blueprints, drawings, or sketches, and compute the dimensions for laying out materials and planning model production.

What things about you point to this kind of work?

Is it important for you to

- Never be pressured to do things that go against your sense of right and wrong?
- Have supervisors who back up the workers with management?

Have you enjoyed any of the following as a hobby or leisure-time activity?

- Building model airplanes, automobiles, or boats
- Making sketches of machines or other mechanical equipment
- Repairing plumbing in the home
- Repairing or assembling bicycles or tricycles

Have you liked and done well in any of the following school subjects?

- Blueprint/Schematic Reading
- Metal Forming and Fabrication/Technology
- Tool Design
- Model Making
- Shop Math

Are you able to

- Correctly follow a given rule or set of rules in order to arrange things or actions in a certain order?
- Quickly make coordinated movements of one hand, a hand together with its arm, or two hands to grasp, manipulate, or assemble objects?
- See details of objects at close range (within a few feet)?
- Imagine how something will look after it is moved around or when its parts are moved or rearranged?
- Quickly and repeatedly make precise adjustments in moving the controls of a machine or vehicle to exact positions?
- Keep your hand and arm steady while making an arm movement or while holding your arm and hand in one position?
- Read and understand information and ideas presented in writing?

Would you work in places such as

- factories and plants?

What skills and knowledges do you need for this kind of work?

For most of these jobs, you need these skills:

- Product Inspection–inspecting and evaluating the quality of products
- Operation and Control–controlling operations of equipment or systems

These knowledges are important in most of these jobs:

- Mechanical–machines and tools, including their designs, uses, benefits, repair, and maintenance
- Production and Processing–inputs, outputs, raw materials, waste, quality control, costs, and techniques for maximizing the manufacture and distribution of goods

What else should you consider about this kind of work?

Workers in this group are hired by manufacturers of automobiles, machine tools, and durable consumer goods. Many work for machine shops that contract for work from the manufacturers.

Employment in this field is not growing, because manufacturing is in decline in this country. Nevertheless, many older workers are retiring and will need to be replaced, and employers are having trouble finding young people with mechanical and mathematical abilities who are willing to undergo the training for these highly skilled jobs. Therefore, there actually are lots of job opportunities.

Safety precautions are necessary when working around high-speed machines and razor-sharp metal edges.

How can you prepare for jobs of this kind?

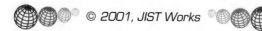

Work in this group usually requires education and/or training ranging from two years to six years. A four-year formal apprenticeship is the best way to become a general machinist. Training includes learning proper machine speeds and feeds and the operation of various machine tools. Apprentices are also trained in the use of hand tools and assembly procedures. They study blueprint reading, shop math, shop practices, and mechanical drawing. High school or vocational courses in these areas are helpful. Many mechanics and repairers acquire their skills by working with experienced workers for several years. Other sources of training are apprenticeships, vocational or technical schools, the armed services, and correspondence schools.

SPECIALIZED TRAINING

JOBS	EDUCATION/TRAINING	WHERE OBTAINED
08.04.01 Metal and Plastics Machining Technology		
All in Metal and Plastics Machining Technology	Shop Math; Shop Safety; experience	High school, on the job, trade/technical school, related jobs within the same industry
51-4041.00 Machinists	Machinist/Machine Technologist; Machine Shop Assistant	On the job, trade/technical school, military (all branches)
51-4061.00 Model Makers, Metal and Plastic	Watch, Clock, and Jewelry Repairer; Machinist/Machine Technologist; Instrument Calibration and Repairer; Machine Shop Assistant	On the job, trade/technical school
51-4062.00 Patternmakers, Metal and Plastic	Tool and Die Maker/Technologist; Plastics Technology/Technician; Machinist/Machine Technologist	On the job, trade/technical school, military (Navy)
51-4111.00 Tool and Die Makers	Tool and Die Maker/Technologist; Machinist/Machine Technologist	On the job, trade/technical school
51-4192.00 Lay-Out Workers, Metal and Plastic	Machine Shop Assistant; Machinist/Machine Technologist	On the job, trade/technical school
51-4194.00 Tool Grinders, Filers, and Sharpeners	Tool and Die Maker/Technologist; Machine Shop Assistant; Gunsmith; Agricultural Mechanization, General	On the job, trade/technical school, military (Navy)

08.05 Woodworking Technology

Workers in this group follow specifications as they cut, shape, and finish wood products such as furniture and cabinets. Some create wooden models of products that will be mass-produced out of wood, metal, or plastic. Although most work in manufacturing plants, some work in homes and offices to custom-make cabinets.

What kind of work would you do?

Your work activities would depend on your job. For example, you might

- Apply varnish, stain, oil, or lacquer to finish surfaces.
- Cut and shape wood stock to desired dimensions using woodworking machines such as a bandsaw or lathe.
- Inspect finished work pieces for irregularities and conformance to specifications or patterns.
- Glue, fit, and clamp parts and subassemblies together to form complete units.
- Read blueprints, drawings, or written specifications to determine the size and shape of the pattern and the required machine setup.
- Sharpen and maintain woodworking tools.
- Sand and scrape work pieces to prepare for finishing.

What things about you point to this kind of work?

Is it important for you to

- Never be pressured to do things that go against your sense of right and wrong?
- Do your work alone?

Have you enjoyed any of the following as a hobby or leisure-time activity?

- Building cabinets or furniture
- Designing and building an addition or remodeling the interior of a home
- Refinishing or reupholstering furniture
- Building model airplanes, automobiles, or boats
- Carving small wooden objects

Have you liked and done well in any of the following school subjects?

- Wood Shop/Woodworking
- Blueprint/Schematic Reading
- Wood Machining
- Cabinetmaking
- Shop Math

Are you able to

- Keep your hand and arm steady while making an arm movement or while holding your arm and hand in one position?
- Imagine how something will look after it is moved around or when its parts are moved or rearranged?
- Quickly make coordinated movements of one hand, a hand together with its arm, or two hands to grasp, manipulate, or assemble objects?
- Quickly and repeatedly make precise adjustments in moving the controls of a machine or vehicle to exact positions?
- See details of objects at close range (within a few feet)?

Would you work in places such as

- Factories and plants?

What skills and knowledges do you need for this kind of work?

For most of these jobs, you need these skills:

- Equipment Selection—determining the kind of tools and equipment needed to do a job
- Product Inspection—inspecting and evaluating the quality of products

These knowledges are important in most of these jobs:

- Building and Construction—materials, methods, and the appropriate tools to construct objects, structures, and buildings
- Design—design techniques, principles, tools, and instruments involved in the production and use of precision technical plans, blueprints, drawings, and models

What else should you consider about this kind of work?

Workers in this group are employed by furniture manufacturers in various locations; by manufacturers of automobiles, boats, and other products that use wooden models as part of the design process; and by small, perhaps one-person, businesses that custom-make cabinets, bookshelves, and other built-in kinds of furniture in clients' homes and offices.

Opportunities in these jobs are generally expected to be fair, with a need for replacement of older workers who are retiring.

These workers generally have a love of working with wood, although the amount of hand work versus machine work that they do varies from job to job. Safety precautions are necessary when working with power cutting tools and flammable finishes.

How can you prepare for jobs of this kind?

Work in this group usually requires education and/or training ranging from two to four years. Workers train in formal and informal apprenticeships, where they learn how to operate the various hand and machine tools, how to use various finishes, and the properties of various kinds of wood. These training programs are offered by manufacturers and by skilled, self-employed workers who are interested in expanding their businesses. Some useful high school courses are blueprint reading, shop math, woodshop practices, and mechanical drawing.

SPECIALIZED TRAINING

JOBS	EDUCATION/TRAINING	WHERE OBTAINED
08.05.01 Woodworking Technology		
All in Woodworking Technology	Wood Shop; Shop Math; Shop Safety; experience	High school, on the job, trade/technical school, related jobs within the same industry
51-7011.00 Cabinetmakers and Bench Carpenters	Cabinet Maker and Millworker; Woodworkers, General	On the job, trade/technical school
51-7021.00 Furniture Finishers	Crafts, Folk Art, and Artisanry; Furniture Designer and Maker; Woodworkers, General	On the job, trade/technical school
51-7031.00 Model Makers, Wood	Woodworkers, General; Furniture Designer and Maker; Cabinet Maker and Millworker	On the job, trade/technical school
51-7032.00 Patternmakers, Wood	Woodworkers, General; Furniture Designer and Maker; Cabinet Maker and Millworker	On the job, trade/technical school

08.06 Systems Operation

Workers in this group operate and maintain equipment in systems that generate and distribute electricity, provide water and process wastewater, and pump oil and gas from oil fields to storage tanks. These jobs are found in utility companies, refineries, ships, industrial plants, and large apartment houses.

What kind of work would you do?

Your work activities would depend on your job. For example, you might

- Adjust controls on equipment to generate the specified electrical power.
- Examine pipelines for leaks.
- Inspect engines and other equipment.
- Note malfunctions of equipment, instruments, or controls.
- Test electrical systems to determine voltage, using a voltage meter.
- Start the motor that pumps water through the system and open valves to direct water.
- Report major breakdowns and problems with oil wells.

What things about you point to this kind of work?

Is it important for you to

- Never be pressured to do things that go against your sense of right and wrong?
- Be treated fairly by the company?
- Have supervisors who back up the workers with management?

Have you enjoyed any of the following as a hobby or leisure-time activity?

- Doing electrical wiring and repairs in the home
- Making sketches of machines or other mechanical equipment
- Reading about technological developments such as computer science or aerospace
- Repairing electrical household appliances
- Repairing plumbing in the home

Have you liked and done well in any of the following school subjects?

- Shop Math
- Power Systems/Technology
- Irrigation
- Oil Field Practices
- Engine Mechanics
- Diesel Mechanics/Diesels
- Wastewater/Water Treatment Processes

Are you able to

- Quickly and repeatedly make precise adjustments in moving the controls of a machine or vehicle to exact positions?
- Tell when something is wrong or is likely to go wrong?

Would you work in places such as

- Factories and plants?
- Waterworks and light and power plants?
- Farms?
- Ships and boats?
- Hospitals and nursing homes?
- Airports?
- Ports and harbors?

What skills and knowledges do you need for this kind of work?

For most of these jobs, you need these skills:

- Operation and Control—controlling operations of equipment or systems
- Operation Monitoring—watching gauges, dials, or other indicators to make sure a machine is working properly

These knowledges are important in most of these jobs:

- Mechanical—machines and tools, including their designs, uses, benefits, repair, and maintenance
- Engineering and Technology—equipment, tools, mechanical devices, and their uses to produce motion, light, power, technology, and other applications

What else should you consider about this kind of work?

Energy companies, utilities, industrial plants, farms, and shipping companies hire the workers in this group. Because energy is generated and distributed around the clock, many of these occupations require shift work.

The boom-and-bust cycle of the energy industry over the past generation seems likely to continue, making an uncertain outlook for jobs related to oil and gas production and transmission. In general, the outlook is better in transmission than in production. Most jobs related to power generation are on a downward turn, especially in nuclear power, although there is a need to replace workers who retire.

Many of the jobs in this group are with city and county governments that operate their own power plants, water systems, and wastewater processing facilities. In most places, to qualify for these jobs you must pass a civil-service examination.

Many of these workers are surrounded by extremely hot, high-pressure, or explosive liquids and gases and must observe safety precautions. Most of them have to be able to think and act quickly in case of emergencies. Some of them have to crawl inside boilers and work in cramped spaces to inspect, clean, or repair interiors.

How can you prepare for jobs of this kind?

Requirements for education and/or training in this group vary. The most common requirement is from four to six years, but some occupations require less. High school and vocational school courses in machine shop, mechanical drawing, mathematics (including computing fractions and decimals), and physics are helpful. Workers in atomic-powered plants must have special training.

Boiler operators usually enter through apprenticeship programs lasting up to four years. It is also possible to become an operator after several years of preparation as an assistant; however, this usually takes longer than an apprenticeship.

Operators of systems that transmit oil or natural gas usually start as helpers. Operators of generating or distributing systems for electricity usually start as manual workers, advancing with experience. One to four years of experience is usually required to develop the necessary knowledge and skills.

SPECIALIZED TRAINING

JOBS	EDUCATION/TRAINING	WHERE OBTAINED
08.06.01 Systems Operation: Utilities and Power Plant		
All in Systems Operation: Utilities and Power Plant	Utility and Plant Operations	Related jobs within the same industry
51-8011.00 Nuclear Power Reactor Operators	Nuclear/Nuclear Power Technology/Technician	On the job, two-year college, four-year college, trade/technical school, military (Navy)
51-8012.00 Power Distributors and Dispatchers	Stationary Energy Sources Installer and Operator	On the job, two-year college, four-year college, trade/technical school
51-8013.01 Power Generating Plant Operators, Except Auxiliary Equipment Operators	Stationary Energy Sources Installer and Operator	On the job, two-year college, four-year college, trade/technical school, military (Navy)
51-8013.02 Auxiliary Equipment Operators, Power	Stationary Energy Sources Installer and Operator	On the job, trade/technical school, military (Navy)
51-8021.01 Boiler Operators and Tenders, Low Pressure	Stationary Energy Sources Installer and Operator	On the job, trade/technical school, military (Navy)
51-8021.02 Stationary Engineers	Stationary Energy Sources Installer and Operator; Heating, Air Conditioning, and Refrigeration Mechanic and Repairer	On the job, trade/technical school, military (Army, Navy, Air Force, Coast Guard)
51-8031.00 Water and Liquid Waste Treatment Plant and System Operators	Water Quality and Wastewater Treatment Technology/Technician	On the job, two-year college, trade/technical school, military (Army, Navy, Air Force, Coast Guard)
53-5031.00 Ship Engineers	Marine Science/Merchant Marine Officer	Work experience in a related occupation, Merchant Marine Academy, four-year college, military (Army, Navy, Coast Guard)
08.06.02 Systems Operation: Oil, Gas, and Water Distribution		
All in Systems Operation: Oil, Gas, and Water Distribution	Experience	On the job, related jobs within the same industry
51-8091.00 Chemical Plant and System Operators	Chemical Technology/Technician; Plastics Technology/Technician	On the job, trade/technical school
51-8092.01 Gas Processing Plant Operators	Chemical Technology/Technician; Stationary Energy Sources Installer and Operator	On the job, trade/technical school, military (Navy, Marine Corps)
51-8092.02 Gas Distribution Plant Operators	Stationary Energy Sources Installer and Operator	On the job, two-year college, trade/technical school
51-8093.01 Petroleum Pump System Operators	Stationary Energy Sources Installer and Operator	On the job, two-year college, trade/technical school

(continues)

(continued)

SPECIALIZED TRAINING

JOBS	EDUCATION/TRAINING	WHERE OBTAINED
08.06.02 Systems Operation: Oil, Gas, and Water Distribution		
51-8093.02 Petroleum Refinery and Control Panel Operators	Stationary Energy Sources Installer and Operator	On the job, two-year college, trade/technical school
51-8093.03 Gaugers	Stationary Energy Sources Installer and Operator	On the job, two-year college, trade/technical school, military (Navy, Air Force)
53-7071.01 Gas Pumping Station Operators	Stationary Energy Sources Installer and Operator	On the job, trade/technical school
53-7071.02 Gas Compressor Operators	Stationary Energy Sources Installer and Operator	On the job, trade/technical school
53-7073.00 Wellhead Pumpers	Industrial Equipment Maintenance and Repairs, Other	On the job, two-year college, trade/technical school

08.07 Hands-on Work: Loading, Moving, Hoisting, and Conveying

Workers in this group use their hands, machinery, tools, and other equipment to package or move products or materials. They work in a variety of settings, including offices, mailrooms, manufacturing plants, water treatment plants, and construction sites. They may work with small packages or computer chips, or with huge containers or structural components of buildings.

What kind of work would you do?

Your work activities would depend on your job. For example, you might

- Assemble product containers and crates, using hand tools and precut lumber.
- Attach, fasten, and disconnect cables or lines to loads and materials, using hand tools.
- Identify and mark materials, products, and samples, following instructions.
- Read meter to verify the content, temperature, and volume of liquid loads.
- Turn valves and start pumps to commence or regulate the flow of substances, such as gases, liquids, slurries, or powdered materials.
- Measure, weigh, and count products and materials, using equipment.
- Operate blenders and heaters to mix, blend, and heat products.
- Record product and packaging information on specified forms and records.
- Repair, maintain, and adjust equipment using hand tools.

What things about you point to this kind of work?

Is it important for you to

- Never be pressured to do things that go against your sense of right and wrong?
- Have supervisors who back up the workers with management?
- Do your work alone?
- Be busy all the time?

Have you enjoyed any of the following as a hobby or leisure-time activity?

- Handling equipment for a local athletic team
- Operating a model train layout
- Reading mechanical or automotive magazines
- Building model airplanes, automobiles, or boats
- Carving small wooden objects

Have you liked and done well in any of the following school subjects?

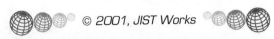

- Industrial Shop
- Industrial Safety

Are you able to

- Quickly make coordinated movements of one hand, a hand together with its arm, or two hands to grasp, manipulate, or assemble objects?
- Quickly and repeatedly make precise adjustments in moving the controls of a machine or vehicle to exact positions?

Would you work in places such as

- Factories and plants?
- Warehouses?
- Airports?
- Bus and train stations?
- Freight terminals?
- Ports and harbors?
- Mines and quarries?
- Oil fields?
- Waterworks and light and power plants?

What skills and knowledges do you need for this kind of work?

For most of these jobs, you need these skills:

- Operation and Control—controlling operations of equipment or systems
- Operation Monitoring—watching gauges, dials, or other indicators to make sure a machine is working properly

These knowledges are important in most of these jobs:

- Mechanical—machines and tools, including their designs, uses, benefits, repair, and maintenance
- Production and Processing—inputs, outputs, raw materials, waste, quality control, costs, and techniques for maximizing the manufacture and distribution of goods

What else should you consider about this kind of work?

A variety of different industries hire the workers in this group. Heavier industries and shipping companies need workers to move materials and large containers, and many machines used in manufacturing and processing need workers to feed in materials and take away the output. Many manufacturers employ packers.

Some industries are doing better than others, and as a result the outlook for jobs varies. In general, manufacturing is on the decline in the United States. One serious concern for hands-on workers even in prosperous industries is the possibility that human workers may be needed less for some jobs because of automation and robotics. Best opportunities are probably for the more skilled hand workers who are doing something that a machine cannot do.

Most of these jobs require a 40-hour work week, with some overtime or shift work. Some of the loading and moving jobs are noisy and/or dirty, and because of the presence of heavy machinery they often require safety precautions.

How can you prepare for jobs of this kind?

Most of these occupations require less than six months of education and/or training. A few require as much as two years.

Often the tasks can be learned by observing experienced workers or through brief on-the-job training. Some of the more complex machines for moving and loading require a more involved training program. Irradiated-fuel handlers must have special training because of the hazardous materials they work with.

SPECIALIZED TRAINING

JOBS	EDUCATION/TRAINING	WHERE OBTAINED
08.07.01 Hands-on Work: Loading, Moving, Hoisting, and Conveying		
All in Hands-on Work: Loading, Moving, Hoisting, and Conveying	Experience	On the job, related jobs within the same industry
47-4041.01 Irradiated-Fuel Handlers	Nuclear/Nuclear Power Technology/Technician	On the job, trade/technical school

(continues)

(continued)

SPECIALIZED TRAINING

JOBS	EDUCATION/TRAINING	WHERE OBTAINED
08.07.01 Hands-on Work: Loading, Moving, Hoisting, and Conveying		
53-7011.00 Conveyor Operators and Tenders	Vehicle and Equipment Operators, Other	On the job
53-7021.00 Crane and Tower Operators	Construction Equipment Operator; Vehicle and Equipment Operators, Other	On the job, military (Army, Navy)
53-7032.00 Excavating and Loading Machine and Dragline Operators	Construction Equipment Operator	On the job
53-7032.02 Dragline Operators	Vehicle and Equipment Operators, Other; Construction Equipment Operator	On the job
53-7041.00 Hoist and Winch Operators	Logging/Timber Harvesting; Industrial Equipment Maintenance and Repairs, Other; Construction Equipment Operator; Vehicle and Equipment Operators, Other	On the job, military (Army)
53-7051.00 Industrial Truck and Tractor Operators	Materials Moving Operations, Miscellaneous Materials	On the job, military (Air Force)
53-7062.00 Laborers and Freight, Stock, and Material Movers, Hand	Materials Moving Operations, Miscellaneous Materials	On the job
53-7062.03 Freight, Stock, and Material Movers, Hand	Materials Moving Operations, Miscellaneous Materials	On the job, military (Army, Navy, Air Force)
53-7063.00 Machine Feeders and Offbearers	Manufacturing Operations, Miscellaneous Materials	On the job
53-7064.00 Packers and Packagers, Hand	Manufacturing Operations, Miscellaneous Materials	On the job, military (Marine Corps)
53-7072.00 Pump Operators, Except Wellhead Pumpers	Stationary Energy Sources Installer and Operator; Vehicle and Equipment Operators, Other; Industrial Equipment Maintenance and Repairs, Other; Chemical Technology/Technician	On the job
53-7081.00 Refuse and Recyclable Material Collectors	Truck, Bus, and Other Commercial Vehicle Operator	On the job
53-7121.00 Tank Car, Truck, and Ship Loaders	Materials Moving Operations, Miscellaneous Materials	On the job; military data not yet available

09 Business Detail

An interest in organized, clearly defined activities requiring accuracy and attention to details, primarily in an office setting.

You can satisfy this interest in a variety of jobs in which you attend to the details of a business operation. You may enjoy using your math skills; if so, perhaps a job in billing, computing, or financial record-keeping would satisfy you. If you prefer to deal with people, you may want a job in which you meet the public, talk on the telephone, or supervise other workers. You may like to do word processing on a computer, turn out copies on a duplicating machine, or work out sums on a calculator. Perhaps a job in filing or recording would satisfy you. Or you may wish to use your training and experience to manage an office.

09.01 Managerial Work in Business Detail

09.02 Administrative Detail

09.03 Bookkeeping, Auditing, and Accounting

09.04 Material Control

09.05 Customer Service

09.06 Communications

09.07 Records Processing

09.08 Records and Materials Processing

09.09 Clerical Machine Operation

09.01 Managerial Work in Business Detail

Workers in this group supervise and coordinate certain high-level business activities: contracts for buying or selling goods and services, office support services, facilities planning and maintenance, customer service, or administrative support. Within the general policies and goals of their organization they make plans, oversee financial and technical resources, and evaluate outcomes. They work in the offices of every kind of business, government agency, and school.

What kind of work would you do?

Your work activities would depend on your job. For example, you might

- Analyze the financial activities of an establishment or department and assist in planning a budget.
- Consult with a supervisor and other personnel to resolve problems such as equipment performance, output quality, and work schedules.
- Help workers in resolving problems and completing work.
- Inspect equipment for defects and notify maintenance personnel or outside service contractors for repairs.
- Maintain records of such matters as inventory, personnel, orders, supplies, and machine maintenance.
- Plan, prepare, and devise work schedules according to budgets and workloads.
- Supervise and coordinate the activities of workers engaged in customer service activities.

What things about you point to this kind of work?

Is it important for you to

- Give directions and instructions to others?
- Have good working conditions?
- Plan your work with little supervision?

Have you enjoyed any of the following as a hobby or leisure-time activity?

- Addressing letters for an organization
- Balancing checkbooks for family members
- Budgeting the family income
- Conducting house-to-house or telephone surveys for a PTA or other organization
- Using a pocket calculator or spreadsheet to figure out income and expenses for an organization
- Helping run a school or community fair or carnival
- Serving as a leader of a scouting or other group

Have you liked and done well in any of the following school subjects?

- Management
- Business Organization
- Business Analysis
- Business Math
- Clerical Practices/Office Practices
- Business Computer Applications

Are you able to

- Communicate information and ideas in speaking so others will understand?
- Communicate information and ideas in writing so others will understand?
- Read and understand information and ideas presented in writing?
- See details of objects at a close range (within a few feet)?
- Speak clearly so that it is understandable to a listener?
- Add, subtract, multiply, or divide quickly and correctly?

Would you work in places such as

- Business offices?
- Government offices?
- Auto service stations and repair shops?
- Colleges and universities?
- Courthouses?
- Libraries?
- Stores and shopping malls?
- Travel agencies?

What skills and knowledges do you need for this kind of work?

For most of these jobs, you need these skills:

- Coordination—adjusting actions in relation to others' actions

- Speaking—talking to others to effectively convey information
- Reading Comprehension—understanding written sentences and paragraphs in work-related documents
- Management of Personnel Resources—motivating, developing, and directing people as they work, identifying the best people for the job
- Writing—communicating effectively with others in writing as indicated by their needs

These knowledges are important in most of these jobs:

- Administration and Management—principles and processes involved in business and organizational planning, coordination, and execution
- Customer and Personal Service—principles and processes for providing customer and personal services including needs-assessment techniques, quality service standards, alternative delivery systems, and customer satisfaction evaluation techniques

What else should you consider about this kind of work?

Workers in this group are employed in cities and towns throughout the United States. They work a standard 40-hour week most of the time, in offices that are clean, air-conditioned, and well-lighted.

The outlook for these occupations is good—even though these managers are often the first workers to be let go when a business is downsizing, and even though automation is cutting into certain routine parts of their work. They may not have secure employment in one business, but if they lose their position they can usually find one in another office, provided they keep their skills up to date (especially with computer productivity applications).

How can you prepare for jobs of this kind?

Work in this group requires education and/or training that lasts from two to four years.

Some workers enter directly after getting a two- or four-year college degree in office supervision and management, or perhaps in a specialization such as administrative support or customer service. Through experiences on the job, they learn the issues and procedures of their particular industry.

Workers with less formal education start by taking a job in administrative support or customer service, then may work their way up to management after gaining experience and taking courses in office management.

Both kinds of workers benefit from high school classes in writing and math that go beyond the "business" level, and in speech. It is also important to know how to work with computer applications such as word processing and spreadsheets. Continuous learning is the key to staying employable.

SPECIALIZED TRAINING

JOBS	EDUCATION/TRAINING	WHERE OBTAINED
09.01.01 Managerial Work in Business Detail		
All in Managerial Work in Business Detail	Budgeting; Personnel; Oral and Written Communications; Office Procedures	Two-year college, four-year college, on the job, military (all branches)
11-3011.00 Administrative Services Managers	Office Supervision and Management; Health System/Health Services Administration; Business Administration and Management, General	Four-year college, military (all branches)
43-1011.01 First-Line Supervisors, Customer Service	Logistics and Materials Management; Travel-Tourism Management; Hotel/Motel and Restaurant Management; Office Supervision and Management; Business Administration and Management, General; Health Unit Manager/Ward Supervisor; Criminal Justice/Law Enforcement Administration; Food and Beverage/Restaurant Operations Manager; Travel Services Marketing Operations; Tourism Promotion Operations; General Distribution Operations; Operations Management and Supervision	Two-year college, four-year college, on the job, military (all branches)

(continues)

(continued)

SPECIALIZED TRAINING

JOBS	EDUCATION/TRAINING	WHERE OBTAINED
09.01.01 Managerial Work in Business Detail		
43-1011.02 First-Line Supervisors, Administrative Support	Data Processing Technology/Technician; Office Supervision and Management; Business Computer Facilities Operator; Management Information Systems and Business Data Processing, General; Operations Management and Supervision; Logistics and Materials Management; Business Administration and Management, General; Criminal Justice/Law Enforcement Administration; General Distribution Operations	Two-year college, four-year college, on the job, military (all branches)

09.02 Administrative Detail

Workers in this group do high-level clerical work requiring special skills and knowledge, as well as some low-level managerial work. They work in the offices of businesses, industries, courts of law, and government agencies, as well as in medicine, law, and other professions.

What kind of work would you do?

Your work activities would depend on your job. For example, you might

- Answer questions and advise customers regarding loans and transactions.
- Compile and type statistical reports, using a typewriter or computer.
- Study management methods to improve workflow, simplify reporting procedures, or implement cost reductions.
- File correspondence and other records.
- Collect court fees or fines and record amounts collected.
- Prepare and process legal documents and papers such as summonses, subpoenas, complaints, appeals, motions, and pretrial agreements.
- Answer the telephone and give information to callers, take messages, or transfer calls to appropriate individuals.

What things about you point to this kind of work?

Is it important for you to

- Be treated fairly by the company?
- Be busy all the time?
- Have good working conditions?

Have you enjoyed any of the following as a hobby or leisure-time activity?

- Serving as president of a club or other organization
- Collecting and arranging stamps or coins
- Doing desktop publishing for a school or community publication
- Keying in text for a school or community publication
- Reading business magazines and newspapers
- Serving as secretary of a club or other organization

Have you liked and done well in any of the following school subjects?

- Clerical Practices/Office Practices
- Business Law
- Business Math
- Business Writing
- Accounting
- Record-Keeping
- Insurance Law

Are you able to

- Listen to and understand information and ideas presented through spoken words and communicate information and ideas in speaking so others will understand?
- Read and understand information and ideas presented in writing?
- Communicate information and ideas in writing so others will understand?

- See details of objects at close range (within a few feet)?
- Add, subtract, multiply, or divide quickly and correctly?
- Speak clearly so that it is understandable to a listener?
- Correctly follow a given rule or set of rules in order to arrange things or actions in a certain order?

Would you work in places such as

- Business offices?
- Government offices?
- Courthouses?
- High schools?
- Elementary schools?
- Doctors' and dentists' offices and clinics?
- Drugstores?
- Hospitals and nursing homes?
- Schools and homes for people with disabilities?
- Streets and highways?
- Travel agencies?

What skills and knowledges do you need for this kind of work?

For most of these jobs, you need these skills:

- Reading Comprehension—understanding written sentences and paragraphs in work-related documents
- Writing—communicating effectively with others in writing as indicated by their needs

These knowledges are important in most of these jobs:

- Clerical—administrative and clerical procedures and systems such as word processing systems, filing and records management systems, stenography and transcription, forms design principles, and other office procedures and terminology
- English Language—the structure and content of the English language, including the meaning and spelling of words, rules of composition, and grammar

What else should you consider about this kind of work?

Beginners with training are hired for many of the jobs in this group. Higher-level jobs, such as managing an office or being responsible for a complete activity, are obtained through promotion. For government jobs with local, state, or federal agencies, a civil-service test is often required.

Regular business hours apply in most of these jobs. If you work for a local government you may have to attend meetings on weekends or at night.

The outlook for these jobs is mixed. Some workers in more managerial roles may lose jobs because automation has reduced the number of people they supervise. Job opportunities in the financial industries will be fair, with ups and downs as the economy fluctuates, and some erosion of jobs to automation. Secretaries who do not specialize in legal or medical work will face competition from automation.

Some positions require workers who can be trusted with confidential information. Workers in small offices often perform a variety of tasks. They may serve as bookkeeper, clerk, and receptionist. Working conditions are usually pleasant, often in a modern, well-lighted office building.

How can you prepare for jobs of this kind?

Occupations in this group usually require education and/or training ranging from six months to six years.

People who have a good working knowledge of English, grammar, spelling, and basic math can qualify for beginning jobs in this group. These workers receive training on the job. Some must have special training such as shorthand, stenotype, legal stenography, or medical terminology.

SPECIALIZED TRAINING

JOBS	EDUCATION/TRAINING	WHERE OBTAINED
	09.02.01 Administrative Detail: Administration	
All in Administrative Detail: Administration	Experience; Office Procedures; Speech Communications	High school, two- or four-year college, related jobs within the same industry

(continues)

(continued)

SPECIALIZED TRAINING

JOBS	EDUCATION/TRAINING	WHERE OBTAINED
09.02.01 Administrative Detail: Administration		
43-4031.01 Court Clerks	Court Reporter; Administrative Assistant/Secretarial Science, General	On the job, two-year college, business college, military (Navy, Air Force, Marine Corps, Coast Guard)
43-4031.02 Municipal Clerks	Administrative Assistant/Secretarial Science, General; Executive Assistant/Secretary	On the job, two-year college, business college
43-4031.03 License Clerks	General Office/Clerical and Typing Services; Administrative Assistant/Secretarial Science, General	On the job, business college
09.02.02 Administrative Detail: Secretarial Work		
All in Administrative Detail: Secretarial Work	Experience; Office Procedures; Keyboarding; Word Processing; Speech Communications; Business Math	High school, two-year college, business college, related jobs within the same industry
43-6011.00 Executive Secretaries and Administrative Assistants	Business Administration and Management, General; Office Supervision and Management; Administrative Assistant/Secretarial Science, General; Executive Assistant/Secretary	Four-year college, business college, military (Army, Navy, Marine Corps, Coast Guard)
43-6012.00 Legal Secretaries	Legal Administrative Assistant/Secretary; Administrative Assistant/Secretarial Science, General	Two-year college, business college, military (Army, Navy, Marine Corps, Coast Guard)
43-6013.00 Medical Secretaries	Medical Administrative Assistant/Secretary; Administrative Assistant/Secretarial Science, General; Medical Transcription; Medical Office Management	Two-year college, business college
43-6014.00 Secretaries, Except Legal, Medical, and Executive	Administrative Assistant/Secretarial Science, General	Two-year college, business college, military (Navy)
09.02.03 Administrative Detail: Interviewing		
All in Administrative Detail: Interviewing	Experience; Office Procedures; Speech Communications; Business Math	High school, on the job, two-year college, business college, related jobs within the same industry
43-4061.01 Claims Takers, Unemployment Benefits	Public Administration; Human Resources Management	On the job, business college
43-4061.02 Welfare Eligibility Workers and Interviewers	Social Work; Community Organization, Resources and Services; Administrative Assistant/Secretarial Science, General	On the job, two-year college, military (Air Force)
43-4111.00 Interviewers, Except Eligibility and Loan	Receptionist; Administrative Assistant/Secretarial Science, General	On the job, military (Army, Navy, Air Force)
43-4131.00 Loan Interviewers and Clerks	Finance, General; Banking and Financial Support Services	On the job, business college

09.03 Bookkeeping, Auditing, and Accounting

Workers in this group collect, organize, compute, and record the numerical information used in business and financial transactions. They use both clerical and math skills, and some use machines. They work in banks, finance companies, accounting firms, payroll and inventory control departments in business and government agencies, and other places.

What kind of work would you do?

Your work activities would depend on your job. For example, you might

- Calculate amounts due, costs, discounts, dividends, equity, interest, net charges, outstanding balances, principal, profits, ratios, taxes, or wages.
- Identify and note, or correct, discrepancies in records.
- Compute taxes owed, using an adding machine or personal computer, and complete entries on forms, following tax form instructions and tax tables.
- Prepare reports and graphs to show comparisons or survey results of statistical information obtained.
- Record financial data such as receipts, expenditures, accounts payable, accounts receivable, and profit and loss.
- Review timesheets, work charts, timecards, and union agreements for completeness and to determine payroll factors and pay rates.
- Verify totals on forms prepared by others to detect errors in arithmetic or procedure, as needed.

What things about you point to this kind of work?

Is it important for you to

- Have good working conditions?
- Do your work alone?
- Be busy all the time?

Have you enjoyed any of the following as a hobby or leisure-time activity?

- Balancing checkbooks for family members
- Budgeting the family income
- Operating a calculator or adding machine for an organization
- Preparing family income tax returns
- Helping friends and relatives with their tax reports
- Serving as treasurer of a club or other organization
- Using a pocket calculator or spreadsheet to figure out income and expenses for an organization

Have you liked and done well in any of the following school subjects?

- Math Computing, Standard Formula
- Bookkeeping
- Accounting
- Business Computer Applications
- Statistics
- Calculating Machine Operating
- Clerical Practices/Office Practices
- Record-Keeping
- Financial Information Systems
- Production/Inventory Control

Are you able to

- Add, subtract, multiply, or divide quickly and correctly?
- Understand and organize a problem and then select a mathematical method or formula to solve the problem?
- Read and understand information and ideas presented in writing?
- See details of objects at close range (within a few feet)?
- Communicate information and ideas in writing so others will understand?
- Correctly follow a given rule or set of rules in order to arrange things or actions in a certain order?
- Listen to and understand information and ideas presented through spoken words and sentences?
- Communicate information and ideas in speaking so others will understand?

Would you work in places such as

- Business offices?
- Factories and plants?
- Doctors' and dentists' offices and clinics?

- Government offices?
- Hotels and motels?
- Hospitals and nursing homes?
- Warehouses?
- Freight terminals?
- Gambling casinos and card clubs?
- Stores and shopping malls?
- Travel agencies?
- Colleges and universities?
- Racetracks?

What skills and knowledges do you need for this kind of work?

For most of these jobs, you need these skills:

- Mathematics—using mathematics to solve problems
- Information Gathering—knowing how to find information and identifying essential information
- Reading Comprehension—understanding written sentences and paragraphs in work-related documents

These knowledges are important in most of these jobs:

- Mathematics—numbers, their operations, and interrelationships including arithmetic, algebra, geometry, calculus, statistics, and their applications
- Clerical—administrative and clerical procedures and systems such as word processing systems, filing and records management systems, stenography and transcription, forms design principles, and other office procedures and terminology

What else should you consider about this kind of work?

Most jobs in this group are in business offices. Many of these people work for banks, savings and loan institutions, and insurance companies. Some have jobs with freight terminals, where they keep track of the costs of shipping by water, land, or air. Trained beginners are hired for many of these jobs.

Workers in small offices may do a variety of tasks. Some may keep all records for a business or agency. Usually experience is necessary for such positions.

In large offices, workers may have only certain tasks to do, and may repeat these tasks every day. Most jobs of this nature are entry-level jobs requiring little or no experience.

Most of the work is done during regular daytime working hours. You might have to work the evening or night shift in freight terminals and hotels. Some jobs can lead to supervisory or management positions.

Automation is replacing many of the routine tasks handled by these workers. As a result, job opportunities in most of these occupations will be found mostly in replacing retiring workers. Workers in this group should make an effort to upgrade their skills so they can stay employable or move into a more managerial or technical role.

How can you prepare for jobs of this kind?

Occupations in this group usually require education and/or training ranging from 30 days to two years.

People with basic math skills can enter many of the jobs in this group. They receive on-the-job training for specific tasks. For entry to some jobs, training in bookkeeping or other business subjects such as word processing is required. Business training is offered by high schools, business colleges, and two-year colleges.

SPECIALIZED TRAINING

JOBS	EDUCATION/TRAINING	WHERE OBTAINED
09.03.01 Bookkeeping, Auditing, and Accounting		
All in Bookkeeping, Auditing, and Accounting	Speech Communications, Business Math, Bookkeeping, Spreadsheet Applications	On the job, two-year college, business college
13-2082.00 Tax Preparers	Taxation; Accounting Technician	On the job, two-year college, business college
43-3021.01 Statement Clerks	Accounting Technician	On the job, two-year college, business college

JOBS	EDUCATION/TRAINING	WHERE OBTAINED
09.03.01 Bookkeeping, Auditing, and Accounting		
43-3021.02 Billing, Cost, and Rate Clerks	International Business Marketing; Banking and Financial Support Services; Administrative Assistant/Secretarial Science, General; General Distribution Operations; Accounting Technician; Finance, General; Administrative and Secretarial Services, Other; General Office/Clerical and Typing Services	On the job, two-year college, business college, military (Navy, Air Force)
43-3031.00 Bookkeeping, Accounting, and Auditing Clerks	Accounting Technician; Accounting, Other	On the job, two-year college, business college; military data not yet available
43-3051.00 Payroll and Time-keeping Clerks	Accounting Technician	On the job, two-year college, business college, military (Army, Navy, Air Force, Marine Corps)
43-4011.00 Brokerage Clerks	Accounting Technician; Accounting, Other	On the job, two-year college, business college; military data not yet available

09.04 Material Control

Workers in this group monitor the production of a business or the use of utilities. They examine documents or meters and maintain records of consumption or production. Some order raw materials and supplies and arrange for shipping of output. Workers find jobs for waterworks, electricity and gas suppliers, institutions, industrial plants, government agencies, factories, transportation companies, department stores, hotels, restaurants, hospitals, laundries, and dry-cleaning plants.

What kind of work would you do?

Your work activities would depend on your job. For example, you might

- Calculate figures, such as labor and materials amounts, manufacturing costs, and wages, using pricing schedules, an adding machine, or a calculator.
- Collect bills in arrears.
- Inspect meters for defects, damage, and unauthorized connections
- Maintain files such as maintenance records, bills of lading, and cost reports.
- Read electric meters.
- Review documents such as production schedules, staffing tables, and specifications, to obtain information such as materials, priorities, and personnel requirements.
- Walk or drive a truck over an established route and take readings of meter dials.

What things about you point to this kind of work?

Is it important for you to

- Never be pressured to do things that go against your sense of right and wrong?
- Have supervisors who back up the workers with management?
- Be treated fairly by the company?

Have you enjoyed any of the following as a hobby or leisure-time activity?

- Balancing checkbooks for family members
- Buying large quantities of food or other products for an organization
- Collecting and arranging stamps or coins
- Keeping score for athletic events
- Keying in text for a school or community publication
- Operating a calculator or adding machine for an organization

Have you liked and done well in any of the following school subjects?

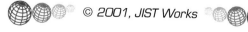

- Business Computer Applications
- Business Math
- Clerical Practices/Office Practices

- Record-Keeping

Are you able to

- Add, subtract, multiply, or divide quickly and correctly?
- See details of objects at close range (within a few feet)?
- Communicate information and ideas in writing so others will understand?

Would you work in places such as

- Factories and plants?
- Private homes?
- Waterworks and light and power plants?
- Freight terminals?

What skills and knowledges do you need for this kind of work?

For most of these jobs, you need these skills:

- Reading Comprehension—understanding written sentences and paragraphs in work-related documents
- Writing—communicating effectively with others in writing as indicated by their needs
- Mathematics—using mathematics to solve problems

These knowledges are important in most of these jobs:

- Clerical—administrative and clerical procedures and systems such as word processing systems, filing and records management systems, stenography and transcription, forms design principles, and other office procedures and terminology
- Mathematics—numbers, their operations, and interrelationships including arithmetic, algebra, geometry, calculus, statistics, and their applications

What else should you consider about this kind of work?

People in this group work for a variety of businesses. Many production, planning, and expediting clerks are hired by factories and distributing warehouses; others find jobs in such establishments as stores, hospitals, libraries, laundries, and movie studios. A few jobs are found on ships and in train depots. Meter readers work for utilities companies.

Beginners are hired for many of the jobs. Some of this work can lead to supervisory jobs. The outlook for these jobs is good, although automation is possibly a threat to meter readers.

You might have to work an evening or night shift; however, most jobs in this group are done during a regular eight-hour day. Most of the work is done indoors.

How can you prepare for jobs of this kind?

Work as a utilities meter reader usually requires education and/or training of less than six months, often only a short demonstration. Evidence of basic reading, writing, and mathematics skills, such as multiplying and dividing fractions, may be required by employers. These skills should be learned in high school. On-the-job training is provided to teach workers the procedures used in each job.

Production, planning, and expediting clerks may be required to have as much as two years of education and/or training to acquire the reading, writing, and mathematics skills needed on the job.

SPECIALIZED TRAINING

JOBS	EDUCATION/TRAINING	WHERE OBTAINED
	09.04.01 Material Control	
All in Material Control	Business Math; Record-Keeping	High school, on the job
43-5041.00 Meter Readers, Utilities	Meter Reading Procedures	On the job
43-5061.00 Production, Planning, and Expediting Clerks	Business Computer Facilities Operator; Clothing, Apparel, and Textile Workers and Managers, General; Commercial Garment and Apparel Worker; Watch, Clock, and Jewelry Repairer; Graphic and Printing	On the job, two-year college, business college, military (all branches)

JOBS	EDUCATION/TRAINING	WHERE OBTAINED
	09.04.01 Material Control	
	Equipment Operator, General; Mechanical Typesetter and Composer; Business Administration and Management, General; Purchasing, Procurement, and Contracts Management; Accounting Technician; Logistics and Materials Management; Management Information Systems and Business Data Processing; Administrative Assistant/Secretarial Science, General; Information Processing/Data Entry Technician; General Office/Clerical and Typing Services	

09.05 Customer Service

Workers in this group deal with people in person, often standing behind a window or in a booth. They may receive payment; collect information; give out change, cash, or merchandise; provide information in answer to questions; or help customers fill out forms. Many keep written records of the information or money they receive, or perform other clerical duties. Private businesses, banks, institutions such as schools and hospitals, and government agencies hire them to work in offices and reception areas.

What kind of work would you do?

Your work activities would depend on your job. For example, you might

- Answer the telephone and receive orders by phone.
- Trace delinquent customers to new addresses by inquiring at the post office or questioning neighbors.
- Cash checks and pay out money after verification of signatures and customer balances.
- Provide customers with travel suggestions and information such as guides, directories, brochures, and maps.
- Receive, examine, and tag articles to be altered, cleaned, stored, or repaired.
- Remove deposits from automated teller machines and night depositories, and count and balance the cash in them.
- Compute the total charge for merchandise or services and shipping charges.

What things about you point to this kind of work?

Is it important for you to

- Have supervisors who back up the workers with management?
- Have good working conditions?
- Never be pressured to do things that go against your sense of right and wrong?

Have you enjoyed any of the following as a hobby or leisure-time activity?

- Collecting and arranging stamps or coins
- Conducting house-to-house or telephone surveys for a PTA or other organization
- Helping out in the school library or other library
- Serving as a salesperson or clerk in a store run by a charity
- Serving as a volunteer interviewer in a social-service organization

Have you liked and done well in any of the following school subjects?

- Public Speaking
- Business Math
- Business Machine Operating
- Clerical Practices/Office Practices
- Record-Keeping

Are you able to

- Communicate information and ideas in speaking so others will understand?
- Listen to and understand information and ideas presented through spoken words and sentences?
- Speak clearly so that it is understandable to a listener?
- See details of objects at close range (within a few feet)?

- Read and understand information and ideas presented in writing?
- Communicate information and ideas in writing so others will understand?
- Add, subtract, multiply, or divide quickly and correctly?

Would you work in places such as

- Auto service stations and repair shops?
- Bus and train stations?
- Airports?
- Country clubs and resorts?
- Doctors' and dentists' offices and clinics?
- Drugstores?
- Gambling casinos and card clubs?
- Hotels and motels?
- Restaurants, cafeterias, and other eating places?
- Stores and shopping malls?
- Theaters?
- Travel agencies?
- Racetracks?

What skills and knowledges do you need for this kind of work?

For most of these jobs, you need these skills:

- Speaking—talking to others to effectively convey information
- Active Listening—listening to what other people are saying and asking questions as appropriate

These knowledges are important in most of these jobs:

- Clerical—administrative and clerical procedures and systems such as word processing systems, filing and records management systems, stenography and transcription, forms design principles, and other office procedures and terminology
- Customer and Personal Service—principles and processes for providing customer and personal services, including needs assessment techniques, quality service standards, alternative delivery systems, and customer satisfaction evaluation techniques

What else should you consider about this kind of work?

The occupations in this group are found in a variety of places, such as hotels, banks, hospitals, retail stores, police departments, business offices, airlines, railroad stations, gambling casinos, and government agencies. Inexperienced people are hired for many of these jobs.

A number of government jobs are in this group. Most are with local agencies, such as tourist information centers and police departments, but others are with state and federal agencies.

Some workers are hired for regular daytime hours; others work from noon until about eight, or late into the night. A few have to be on the job on weekends and holidays. People who work for airports, hospitals, hotels, and fire and police departments may have to work rotating shifts. Some workers in this group have to ask strangers for information that is considered personal or confidential and may encounter resistance.

Temporary jobs at state and national parks, sports stadiums, and amusement parks are available. If you're interested in this kind of work as a summer job, apply for it as early in the year as possible. Some places have all their summer hiring done by late winter.

A few of these jobs require uniforms. Employers usually provide these, but you have to keep them fresh and clean.

The overall outlook for this group is good, especially for jobs that deal with information and require good people skills. One exception is tellers; many jobs are being lost because of the consolidation of banks and the growth of ATM use.

How can you prepare for jobs of this kind?

Almost all these jobs require less than six months of training.

People who like contact with the public usually enter these jobs. Some jobs require typing or other clerical skills. On-the-job training is usually provided. Many employers prefer workers with a high school education or its equal, with courses in speech, English, and math especially useful. Chances for promotion are improved with additional education and training. Jobs in the federal government usually require a civil-service examination.

SPECIALIZED TRAINING

JOBS	EDUCATION/TRAINING	WHERE OBTAINED
09.05.01 Customer Service		
All in Customer Service	Experience; Record-Keeping	High school, on the job, related jobs within the same industry
41-2011.00 Cashiers	Banking and Financial Support Services; Food Products Retailing and Wholesaling Operations; General Retailing Operations; Finance, General	On the job
41-2012.00 Gaming Change Persons and Booth Cashiers	Hospitality and Recreation Marketing Operations, General	On the job
41-2021.00 Counter and Rental Clerks	General Selling Skills and Sales Operations; Watch, Clock, and Jewelry Repairer; Vehicle and Petroleum Products Marketing Operations, Other; Drycleaner and Launderer (Commercial); Clothing, Apparel, and Textile Workers and Managers, General; Travel Services Marketing Operations; General Retailing Operations	On the job
43-3011.00 Bill and Account Collectors	Finance, General; General Office/Clerical and Typing Services; Administrative Assistant/Secretarial Science, General; Banking and Financial Support Services	On the job, business college, on the job
43-3041.00 Gaming Cage Workers	General Retailing Operations; Banking and Financial Support Services	On the job
43-3071.00 Tellers	Financial Services Marketing Operations; Finance, General; Banking and Financial Support Services; International Business Marketing	On the job, business college
43-4051.01 Adjustment Clerks	Administrative Assistant/Secretarial Science, General; Vehicle Parts and Accessories Marketing Operations; General Office/Clerical and Typing Services	On the job, business college
43-4051.02 Customer Service Representatives, Utilities	Administrative Assistant/Secretarial Science, General; Receptionist	On the job
43-4141.00 New Accounts Clerks	Finance, General; Banking and Financial Support Services	Work experience in a related occupation
43-4151.00 Order Clerks	General Office/Clerical and Typing Services; Administrative Assistant/Secretarial Science, General	On the job, business college
43-4171.00 Receptionists and Information Clerks	Tourism Promotion Operations; General Office/Clerical and Typing Services; Information Processing/Data Entry Technician; Receptionist; Administrative Assistant/Secretarial Science, General	On the job
43-4181.01 Travel Clerks	Travel Services Marketing Operations; Tourism Promotion Operations	On the job, business college, military (Army, Navy, Air Force, Marine Corps)

09.06 Communications

Workers in this group talk with people by telephone or using other communication equipment to give and receive information. Some deal with the public; some interact only with fellow workers. Many keep written records of the information they receive or perform other clerical duties. Private businesses, hotels, telephone companies, institutions such as schools and hospitals, and government agencies hire them to work in offices.

What kind of work would you do?

Your work activities would depend on your job. For example, you might

- Greet callers, furnish information to callers or visitors, and relay calls.
- Give information regarding subscribers' telephone numbers.
- Operate a communication system, such as telephone, switchboard, intercom, two-way radio, or public address.
- Provide instructions to callers, utilizing knowledge of emergency medical care.
- Record details of calls, dispatches, and messages and maintain logs and files, using a computer.
- Consult charts to determine the charges for pay-telephone calls.
- Question callers to determine the nature of a problem and the type and number of personnel and equipment needed.

What things about you point to this kind of work?

Is it important for you to

- Never be pressured to do things that go against your sense of right and wrong?
- Have supervisors who back up the workers with management?
- Do your work alone?

Have you enjoyed any of the following as a hobby or leisure-time activity?

- Doing public speaking or debating
- Operating a CB or ham radio
- Recruiting members for a club or other organization
- Serving as a volunteer interviewer in a social-service organization
- Speaking on radio or television

Have you liked and done well in any of the following school subjects?

- Traffic Control/Management
- Clerical Practices/Office Practices
- Business Math
- Record-Keeping

Are you able to

- Listen to and understand information and ideas presented through spoken words and sentences?
- Communicate information and ideas in speaking so others will understand?
- Speak clearly so that it is understandable to a listener?
- Identify and understand the speech of another person?

Would you work in places such as

- Police headquarters?
- Fire stations?
- Freight terminals?

What skills and knowledges do you need for this kind of work?

For most of these jobs, you need these skills:

- Active Listening—listening to what other people are saying and asking questions as appropriate
- Speaking—talking to others to effectively convey information

These knowledges are important in most of these jobs:

- Telecommunications—transmission, broadcasting, switching, control, and operation of telecommunications systems
- English Language—the structure and content of the English language, including the meaning and spelling of words, rules of composition, and grammar

What else should you consider about this kind of work?

Workers in this group are all employed in offices, from which they communicate with the public or with other workers. Inexperienced people are hired for many of these jobs.

A number of government jobs are in this group. Most are with local agencies, such as fire and police departments, but others are with state and federal agencies. In cases of fires, crimes, or other emergencies, people's lives may depend on how fast and accurately information is transmitted.

Airports, hospitals, hotels, and fire and police departments never close, so people who work there may have to work rotating shifts.

The outlook for jobs in this group is mixed. Telephone operators are being replaced by automation and will have fewer opportunities. Dispatchers will have more opportunities, although these will vary depending on the type of employer. Fire and police departments are tending to centralize their dispatching offices, thus limiting job growth. Jobs for taxi dispatchers will generally be more plentiful, although demand will vary with the state of the economy. Tow-truck dispatchers can count on steadier demand, because breakdowns and accidents happen steadily.

How can you prepare for jobs of this kind?

Occupations in this group usually require education and/or training ranging from 30 days to two years.

Telephone operators get brief on-the-job training. Many employers prefer workers with a high school education. Courses in speech and English can be helpful.

Dispatchers may need as much as two years of training, most of it on the job. Jobs in the federal government usually require a civil-service examination.

SPECIALIZED TRAINING

JOBS	EDUCATION/TRAINING	WHERE OBTAINED
	09.06.01 Communications	
All in Communications	Speech Communications; Record-Keeping; experience	High school, on the job, related jobs within the same industry
43-2011.00 Switchboard Operators, Including Answering Service	Administrative Assistant/Secretarial Science, General; Receptionist	On the job
43-2021.00 Telephone Operators	Receptionist	On the job
43-2021.01 Directory Assistance Operators	Operator Training	On the job
43-2021.02 Central Office Operators	Administrative Assistant/Secretarial Science, General; Receptionist	On the job, military (Army, Navy, Marine Corps)
43-5031.00 Police, Fire, and Ambulance Dispatchers	Administrative Assistant/Secretarial Science, General; Receptionist	On the job
43-5032.00 Dispatchers, Except Police, Fire, and Ambulance	General Distribution Operations; Nuclear/Nuclear Power Technology/Technician; Receptionist; Stationary Energy Sources Installer and Operator; Water Transportation Workers, Other; Administrative Assistant/Secretarial Science, General	On the job, military (Army, Air Force, Marine Corps)

09.07 Records Processing

Workers in this group prepare, review, file, and coordinate recorded information. Some check records and schedules for accuracy. Some schedule the activities of people or the use of equipment. Jobs in this group are found in most businesses, institutions, and government agencies.

What kind of work would you do?

Your work activities would depend on your job. For example, you might

- Calculate and compile statistics and prepare reports for management.
- Compile and analyze credit information gathered by investigation.
- Examine engineering drawings, blueprints, orders, and other documentation for completeness and accuracy.
- Prepare reports for the Federal Aviation Administration on schedule delays caused by mechanical difficulties.
- Sort or classify information according to content; purpose; user criteria; or chronological, alphabetical, or numerical order.
- Prepare folders and maintain records of newly admitted hospital patients.
- Write or type information on forms to record customer's requests and specifications.

What things about you point to this kind of work?

Is it important for you to

- Never be pressured to do things that go against your sense of right and wrong?
- Have good working conditions?

Have you enjoyed any of the following as a hobby or leisure-time activity?

- Addressing letters for an organization
- Collecting and arranging stamps or coins
- Buying large quantities of food or other products for an organization

Have you liked and done well in any of the following school subjects?

- Accounting
- Clerical Practices/Office Practices
- Medical Record Science
- Medical Terminology
- Insurance
- Business Math
- Record-Keeping

Are you able to

- Read and understand information and ideas presented in writing?
- See details of objects at close range (within a few feet)?
- Listen to and understand information and ideas presented through spoken words and sentences?
- Communicate information and ideas in writing so others will understand?
- Communicate information and ideas in speaking so others will understand?

Would you work in places such as

- Government offices?
- Business offices?
- Libraries?
- Hospitals and nursing homes?
- Doctors' and dentists' offices and clinics?
- High schools?
- Elementary schools?
- Colleges and universities?
- Jails and reformatories?
- Computer centers?

What skills and knowledges do you need for this kind of work?

For most of these jobs, you need these skills:

- Reading Comprehension—understanding written sentences and paragraphs in work-related documents
- Information Gathering—knowing how to find information and identifying essential information
- Writing—communicating effectively with others in writing as indicated by their needs

These knowledges are important in most of these jobs:

- Clerical—administrative and clerical procedures and systems such as word processing systems, filing and records management systems, stenography and transcription, forms design principles, and other office procedures and terminology

- English Language—the structure and content of the English language, including the meaning and spelling of words, rules of composition, and grammar

What else should you consider about this kind of work?

Many jobs in this group, such as file clerk, are found in almost every office and every locality. Others, such as medical transcriptionist, court reporter, insurance policy processing clerk, and proofreader, are available only in certain kinds of businesses.

Many of the jobs are open to newcomers. For some of them, your chances of finding work are improved if you type well. For others, employers look at your math and reading abilities. You can be promoted to higher-level jobs from many of these positions.

Almost all of this work is done during a regular eight-hour day. You might have to work evening or night shifts or weekends with establishments such as airlines, railroads, freight terminals, and shipping companies. Part-time or temporary work is usually available. Most of this work is done in a comfortable indoor setting and is considered "office work," although many jobs are done outside the office, for example, in a mailroom or library.

Usually, opportunities for promotion are good. As better jobs open up, many employers like to promote people who already work for them rather than hire from the outside. This is one reason it is a good idea to take courses in bookkeeping, computer applications, or other office skills while you're in these jobs. When openings occur, you will be qualified.

The overall employment outlook for this group is mixed. Many clerical jobs formerly done by workers are being eliminated because automation can do them more cheaply. Yet some of these occupations employ so many workers that there will be many openings to replace retiring workers, even if the total number of jobs declines. Also, medical records technicians should find many new job openings at hospitals. In general, opportunities will be better in occupations where the work is nonroutine, involves specialized knowledge or training, or brings the worker in contact with the public.

How can you prepare for jobs of this kind?

Occupations in this group usually require education and/or training ranging from 30 days to two years. A high school education or its equivalent is generally required. It is helpful to have coursework in language skills such as punctuation, grammar, and spelling, in basic math, and in record-keeping. Some employers prefer workers who have completed general business or clerical courses. Many employers provide on-the-job training, ranging from a short demonstration to a one-year program. Sometimes applicants are tested to determine their ability to do or learn to do the tasks. Workers entering federal government jobs generally are required to take civil-service examinations.

SPECIALIZED TRAINING

JOBS	EDUCATION/TRAINING	WHERE OBTAINED
09.07.01 Records Processing: Verification and Proofing		
All in Records Processing: Verification and Proofing	Speech Communications; Record-Keeping	High school, on the job, related jobs within the same industry
43-4041.01 Credit Authorizers	Finance, General; Banking and Financial Support Services	On the job
43-4041.02 Credit Checkers	Banking and Financial Support Services Training	On the job
43-9041.01 Insurance Claims Clerks	Insurance Marketing Operations; Insurance and Risk Management; General Office/Clerical and Typing Services	On the job, business college
43-9041.02 Insurance Policy Processing Clerks	Administrative Assistant/Secretarial Science, General; Banking and Financial Support Services; General Office/Clerical and Typing Services; Finance, General	On the job, business college

(continues)

(continued)

SPECIALIZED TRAINING

JOBS	EDUCATION/TRAINING	WHERE OBTAINED
09.07.01 Records Processing: Verification and Proofing		
43-9081.00 Proofreaders and Copy Markers	Business Communications; General Office/Clerical and Typing Services; Administrative Assistant/Secretarial Science, General	On the job, two-year college, business college
09.07.02 Records Processing: Preparation and Maintenance		
All in Records Processing: Preparation and Maintenance	Record-Keeping; Keyboarding	High school, related jobs within the same industry
23-2091.00 Court Reporters	Court Reporter	Two-year college, business college; military data not yet available
29-2071.00 Medical Records and Health Information Technicians	Medical Records Technology/Technician; Health and Medical Diagnostic and Treatment Services, Other	Two-year college, business college, military (Army, Navy, Air Force)
31-9094.00 Medical Transcriptionists	Medical Transcription	Two-year college, business college; military data not yet available
43-3061.00 Procurement Clerks	Administrative and Secretarial Services, Other	On the job, military (Air Force, Marine Corps)
43-4021.00 Correspondence Clerks	Administrative Assistant/Secretarial Science, General; General Office/Clerical and Typing Services	Business college, on the job
43-4071.00 File Clerks	General Office/Clerical and Typing Services; Administrative Assistant/Secretarial Science, General	On the job
43-4161.00 Human Resources Assistants, Except Payroll and Timekeeping	Human Resources Management	On the job, business college, military (all branches)
43-9061.00 Office Clerks, General	Health Unit Coordinator/Ward Clerk; General Office/Clerical and Typing Services; Administrative Assistant/Secretarial Science, General	On the job, military (all branches)

09.08 Records and Materials Processing

Workers in this group routinely file, sort, route, or deliver items such as letters, packages, or messages. Some of their work may be done with machines and computer terminals. Their jobs are found in most businesses, factories, government agencies, and in the U.S. Postal Service and various private courier services.

What kind of work would you do?

Your work activities would depend on your job. For example, you might

- Sort letters or packages into sacks or bins, and place identifying tags on sacks or bins according to the destination and type.
- Deliver mail to residences and business establishments along a route.
- Obtain signatures, receipts, or payments from recipients for articles delivered.
- Read orders for merchandise to ascertain a catalog number, size, color, and quantity.
- Pack, seal, label, and affix postage to prepare materials for shipping, using work devices such as hand tools, power tools, and postage meters.
- Receive, count, and store stock items and record data, manually or using a computer.

What things about you point to this kind of work?

Is it important for you to

- Never be pressured to do things that go against your sense of right and wrong?
- Do your work alone?
- Have steady employment?
- Have supervisors who back up the workers with management?

Have you enjoyed any of the following as a hobby or leisure-time activity?

- Addressing letters for an organization
- Keying in text for a school or community publication
- Doing desktop publishing for a school or community publication
- Operating a calculator or adding machine for an organization
- Using a pocket calculator or spreadsheet to figure out income and expenses for an organization

Have you liked and done well in any of the following school subjects?

- Business Machine Operating
- Data Entry
- Business Math
- Typing
- Record-Keeping
- Calculating Machine Operating

Are you able to

- Read and understand information and ideas presented in writing?
- See details of objects at close range (within a few feet)?
- Acquire and organize visual information?

Would you work in places such as

- Business offices?
- Government offices?
- Freight terminals?
- Factories and plants?
- Courthouses?

What skills and knowledges do you need for this kind of work?

For most of these jobs, you need these skills:

- Reading Comprehension—understanding written sentences and paragraphs in work-related documents
- Active Listening—listening to what other people are saying and asking questions as appropriate
- Mathematics—using mathematics to solve problems

These knowledges are important in most of these jobs:

- Clerical—administrative and clerical procedures and systems such as word processing systems, filing and records management systems, stenography and transcription, forms design principles, and other office procedures and terminology
- Mathematics—numbers, their operations, and interrelationships including arithmetic, algebra, geometry, calculus, statistics, and their applications

What else should you consider about this kind of work?

Much of the work in these jobs is done during a regular eight-hour day, although the U.S. Postal Service and private courier services may require some work on evening or night shifts or weekends. Part-time or temporary work is often available. Most of the work is done indoors, in comfortable offices, stockrooms, and mailrooms, but some delivery jobs are done at least partly outdoors and may involve driving vehicles. During certain hours and seasons (such as the pre-Christmas rush), the work may become very intense and require extra hours and a faster pace.

The employment outlook for this group is mixed. Many records-processing jobs are being eliminated as businesses covert to computerized ordering systems, bar code readers, faxes, and other forms of automation. Also, keen competition is expected for jobs with the U.S. Postal Service. Nevertheless, many job openings will still be available in some of these occupations to replace retiring workers. In addition, the growth of catalog and Internet sales will increase jobs for order fillers and shipping clerks despite automation. Your chances for being hired or promoted are better if you have taken courses in bookkeeping, computer applications, or other office skills.

How can you prepare for jobs of this kind?

Occupations in this group usually require education and/or training ranging from three months to two years. A high school education or its equal is usually expected of new hires. Useful high school courses include spelling, grammar, typing, business math, and business machine operation.

Many employers provide on-the-job training, ranging from a short demonstration to a few weeks. Some employers, including the U.S. Postal Service, require one or more examinations that measure speed and accuracy doing clerical tasks.

SPECIALIZED TRAINING

JOBS	EDUCATION/TRAINING	WHERE OBTAINED
09.08.01 Records and Materials Processing		
All in Records and Materials Processing	Experience	On the job, related jobs within the same industry
43-5011.00 Cargo and Freight Agents	General Distribution Operations; General Office/Clerical and Typing Services	On the job; military data not yet available
43-5021.00 Couriers and Messengers	General Office/Clerical and Typing Services	On the job, military (Air Force)
43-5052.00 Postal Service Mail Carriers	Mail Delivery Procedures	On the job
43-5053.00 Postal Service Mail Sorters, Processors, and Processing Machine Operators	General Office/Clerical and Typing Services	On the job
43-5071.00 Shipping, Receiving, and Traffic Clerks	Administrative and Secretarial Services, Other	On the job, military (Army, Navy, Air Force, Marine Corps)
43-5081.02 Marking Clerks	General Retailing Operations; General Office/Clerical and Typing Services; General Distribution Operations	On the job; military data not yet available
43-5081.03 Stock Clerks—Stockroom, Warehouse, or Storage Yard	Vehicle Parts and Accessories Marketing Operations; General Distribution Operations; Administrative and Secretarial Services, Other	On the job, business college, military (all branches)

JOBS	EDUCATION/TRAINING	WHERE OBTAINED
09.08.01 Records and Materials Processing		
43-5081.04 Order Fillers, Wholesale and Retail Sales	General Office/Clerical and Typing Services	On the job, business college
43-5111.00 Weighers, Measurers, Checkers, and Samplers, Recordkeeping	Administrative Assistant/Secretarial Science, General; General Office/Clerical and Typing Services; General Retailing Operations	On the job, military (Army, Navy, Marine Corps)
43-9051.02 Mail Clerks, Except Mail Machine Operators and Postal Service	General Office/Clerical and Typing Services; Administrative Assistant/Secretarial Science, General	On the job

09.09 Clerical Machine Operation

Workers in this group use business machines to record or process data. They operate machines that type, print, sort, compute, send, or receive information. Their jobs are found in businesses, factories, government agencies, and wherever else large amounts of data are handled.

What kind of work would you do?

Your work activities would depend on your job. For example, you might

- Compile, sort, and verify the accuracy of data to be entered.
- Enter commands using a computer terminal, and activate controls on a computer and peripheral equipment to integrate and operate equipment.
- Fill reservoirs with paint or ink.
- Keep a record of completed work.
- Place original copies in feed trays, feed originals into feed rolls, or position originals on the table beneath a camera lens.
- Type from recorded dictation.
- Store completed documents on a computer hard drive or data storage medium, such as a disk.

What things about you point to this kind of work?

Is it important for you to

- Never be pressured to do things that go against your sense of right and wrong?
- Do your work alone?
- Have supervisors who back up the workers with management?

Have you enjoyed any of the following as a hobby or leisure-time activity?

- Operating a calculator or adding machine for an organization
- Addressing letters for an organization
- Keying in text for a school or community publication
- Doing desktop publishing for a school or community publication
- Using a pocket calculator or spreadsheet to figure out income and expenses for an organization

Have you liked and done well in any of the following school subjects?

- Business Machine Operating
- Data Entry
- Data Applications
- Business Math
- Typing
- Record-Keeping
- Calculating Machine Operating

Are you able to

- See details of objects at close range (within a few feet)?
- Read and understand information and ideas presented in writing?
- Make fast, simple, repeated movements of your fingers, hands, and wrists?

Would you work in places such as

- Computer centers?
- Business offices?
- Government offices?
- Freight terminals?
- Hospitals and nursing homes?
- Courthouses?

What skills and knowledges do you need for this kind of work?

For most of these jobs, you need these skills:

- Operation and Control—controlling operations of equipment or systems
- Reading Comprehension—understanding written sentences and paragraphs in work-related documents

These knowledges are important in most of these jobs:

- Computers and Electronics—electric circuit boards, processors, chips, and computer hardware and software, including applications and programming
- Clerical—administrative and clerical procedures and systems such as word processing systems, filing and records management systems, stenography and transcription, forms design principles, and other office procedures and terminology

What else should you consider about this kind of work?

This kind of work can be found in almost every kind of business and industry. A few jobs, such as typesetting machine operators and automatic teller machine servicers, are found only in certain industries. Job opportunities are usually available for well-trained newcomers in this field. If you've been trained to operate many different kinds of equipment rather than just one, your chances of finding a job are better. However, advances in technology are causing declining demand for computer operators (users now tend to operate their own computer equipment), billing machine operators, typesetters, and data-entry keyers. On the other hand, ATM servicers can expect many opportunities as use of these machines grows.

In many places, these jobs can lead to higher-level work in the same field. However, you usually need more education to qualify for managerial or supervisory jobs. Workers in supervisory jobs should enjoy dealing with people because they often train new workers, interview job applicants, and assign workers to jobs.

Most of these jobs are done on a regular eight-hour daytime schedule in a comfortable office setting.

Because office equipment is constantly changing, you might have to learn to operate new machines from time to time. Some employers send you to training sessions given by equipment manufacturers to learn the new methods. In small firms, machine operators may also do a variety of other office tasks.

How can you prepare for jobs of this kind?

Occupations in this group usually require education and/or training ranging from three months to two years. Most employers require that an applicant have a high school education or its equal. Courses in spelling, grammar, typing, and business machine operation are important preparation for jobs in this group. Basic arithmetic skills are required for some jobs.

Some employers provide machine instruction and on-the-job training. However, graduation from a business college can be an advantage.

SPECIALIZED TRAINING

JOBS	EDUCATION/TRAINING	WHERE OBTAINED
	09.09.01 Clerical Machine Operation	
All in Clerical Machine Operation	Business Machine Operation; Office Procedures	High school, related jobs within the same industry
43-3021.03 Billing, Posting, and Calculating Machine Operators	Finance, General; Banking and Financial Support Services; Accounting Technician	On the job

JOBS	EDUCATION/TRAINING	WHERE OBTAINED
09.09.01 Clerical Machine Operation		
43-5051.00 Postal Service Clerks	General Office/Clerical and Typing Services	On the job
43-9011.00 Computer Operators	Management Information Systems and Business Data Processing, General; Business Computer Facilities Operator; Data Processing Technology/Technician	On the job, two-year college, trade/ technical school, business college, military (all branches)
43-9021.00 Data Entry Keyers	Information Processing/Data Entry Technician; Mechanical Typesetter and Composer; Computer Typography and Composition Equipment Operator; Graphic and Printing Equipment Operator, General	Business college, on the job; military data not yet available
43-9022.00 Word Processors and Typists	General Office/Clerical and Typing Services; Administrative Assistant/Secretarial Science, General; Court Reporter	On the job, business college, military (all branches)
43-9051.01 Mail Machine Operators, Preparation and Handling	Administrative Assistant/Secretarial Science, General; General Office/Clerical and Typing Services	On the job
43-9071.00 Office Machine Operators, Except Computer	General Office/Clerical and Typing Services; Banking and Financial Support Services	On the job; military data not yet available
43-9071.01 Duplicating Machine Operators	General Office/Clerical and Typing Services; Administrative Assistant/Secretarial Science, General	On the job
49-2011.01 Automatic Teller Machine Servicers	Miscellaneous Protective Services; ATM Service	On the job, trade/technical school
51-5022.12 Typesetting and Composing Machine Operators and Tenders	Graphic and Printing Equipment Operator, General; Mechanical Typesetter and Composer; Computer Typography and Composition Equipment Operator	On the job, trade/technical school

10 Sales and Marketing

An interest in bringing others to a particular point of view by personal persuasion, using sales and promotional techniques.

You can satisfy this interest in a variety of sales and marketing jobs. If you like using technical knowledge of science or agriculture, you may enjoy selling technical products or services. Or perhaps you are more interested in selling business-related services such as insurance coverage, advertising space, or investment opportunities. Real estate offers several kinds of sales jobs. Perhaps you'd rather work with something you can pick up and show to people. You may work in stores, sales offices, or customers' homes.

10.01 Managerial Work in Sales and Marketing

10.02 Sales Technology

10.03 General Sales

10.04 Personal Soliciting

10.01 Managerial Work in Sales and Marketing

Workers in this group direct or manage various kinds of selling and/or advertising operations—either a department within a business or a specialized business firm that contracts to provide selling and/or advertising services. These workers usually carry out their activities according to policies and procedures determined by owners, boards of directors, administrators, and other persons with higher authority.

What kind of work would you do?

Your work activities would depend on your job. For example, you might

- Analyze business developments and consult trade journals to monitor market trends and determine market opportunities for products.
- Coordinate promotional activities and shows to market products and services.
- Direct the activities of workers engaged in developing and producing advertisements.
- Assist a sales staff in completing complicated and difficult sales.
- Plan and prepare advertising and promotional material.
- Supervise and train service representatives.

What things about you point to this kind of work?

Is it important for you to

- Have good working conditions?
- Try out your own ideas?
- Give directions and instructions to others?

Have you enjoyed any of the following as a hobby or leisure-time activity?

- Conducting house-to-house or telephone surveys for a PTA or other organization
- Developing publicity flyers for a school or community event
- Helping persuade people to sign petitions for a PTA or other organization
- Planning advertisements for a school or community newspaper
- Reading business magazines and newspapers
- Selling advertising space in a school yearbook, newspaper, or magazine
- Serving as a leader of a scouting or other group
- Soliciting funds for community organizations

Have you liked and done well in any of the following school subjects?

- Management
- Marketing/Merchandising
- Business Writing
- Personnel Management
- Accounting
- Consumer Behavior
- Advertising
- Selling

Are you able to

- Communicate information and ideas in speaking so others will understand?
- Listen to and understand information and ideas presented through spoken words and sentences?
- Read and understand information and ideas presented in writing?
- Communicate information and ideas in writing so others will understand?
- Come up with unusual or clever ideas about a given topic or situation, or develop creative ways to solve a problem?
- Come up with a number of ideas about a given topic?
- Speak clearly so that it is understandable to a listener?

Would you work in places such as

- Business offices?
- Stores and shopping malls?
- Convention and trade show centers?

What skills and knowledges do you need for this kind of work?

For most of these jobs, you need these skills:

- Speaking—talking to others to effectively convey information
- Coordination—adjusting actions in relation to others' actions
- Information Gathering—knowing how to find information and identifying essential information

These knowledges are important in most of these jobs:

- Administration and Management—principles and processes involved in business and organizational planning, coordination, and execution
- Sales and Marketing—principles and methods involved in showing, promoting, and selling products or services

What else should you consider about this kind of work?

Employment for workers in this group may be found in cities and towns throughout the United States. The jobs are located in comfortable offices and usually require a standard 40-hour work week, with occasional late nights under the pressure of a marketing campaign.

Competition for these jobs is likely to be keen. The best opportunities will be for college graduates with business experience, a high level of creativity, and good communications skills. Knowledge of how to work in new media such as the Internet can also be very valuable. Job openings related to service industries, including business services, will be more plentiful than those related to manufactured goods.

The overall trend is away from in-house sales and marketing staffs and toward outsourcing these functions to specialized firms.

How can you prepare for jobs of this kind?

Work in this group generally requires four years of education and/or training. First-line supervisors and manager/supervisors may enter with less preparation.

A bachelor's degree in advertising or marketing is good preparation for most of these occupations. Courses in writing and speech communication can be very helpful. If you want to work in a particular industry (for example, financial services), you may want to take relevant coursework.

Workers with less formal education may start by taking a job selling advertising space or doing clerical work in support of marketing, then may be able to work their way up to management after gaining experience and taking courses in management.

Advances in technology continue to have great impact on how marketing and advertising are done, so it is important to learn new skills throughout a career in this field.

SPECIALIZED TRAINING

JOBS	EDUCATION/TRAINING	WHERE OBTAINED
10.01.01 Managerial Work in Sales and Marketing		
All in Managerial Work in Sales and Marketing	Experience; Budgeting; Personnel; Oral and Written Communications	Two-year college, four-year college
11-2011.00 Advertising and Promotions Managers	Hospitality and Recreation Marketing Operations, General; Hotel/Motel Services Marketing Operations; Advertising; Radio and Television Broadcasting; Film-Video Making/Cinematography and Production; Hotel/Motel and Restaurant Management; Business Marketing and Marketing Management	Work experience in a related occupation, four-year college
11-2021.00 Marketing Managers	Business Marketing and Marketing Management; Fashion and Fabric Consultant; International Business Marketing; Clothing, Apparel, and Textile Workers and Managers, General; Apparel and Accessories Marketing Operations, General; Fashion Merchandising; Business Services Marketing Operations	Work experience in a related occupation, four-year college
11-2022.00 Sales Managers	International Business Marketing; Vehicle Marketing Operations; Advertising; Business Marketing and Marketing Management; General Retailing Operations	Work experience in a related occupation, four-year college

JOBS	EDUCATION/TRAINING	WHERE OBTAINED
	10.01.01 Managerial Work in Sales and Marketing	
41-1011.00 First-Line Supervisors/Managers of Retail Sales Workers	General Marketing Operations; General Retailing Operations; Clothing/Apparel and Textile Studies; Clothing, Apparel, and Textile Workers and Managers, General; Hotel/Motel and Restaurant Management; General Selling Skills and Sales Operations; International Business Marketing; General Distribution Operations; Home Products Marketing Operations; Office Products Marketing Operations; Hospitality and Recreation Marketing Operations, General; Recreation Products/Services Marketing Operations; Insurance Marketing Operations; Vehicle Parts and Accessories Marketing Operations; Petroleum Products Retailing Operations; International Business; Agricultural Power Machinery Operator; Health Products and Services Marketing Operations; Food and Beverage/Restaurant Operations Manager; Agricultural Mechanization, General; Food Products Retailing and Wholesaling Operations; Apparel and Accessories Marketing Operations, General; Business and Personal Services Marketing Operations, Other; Business Services Marketing Operations; Agricultural Supplies Retailing and Wholesaling	Work experience in a related occupation, two-year college, four-year college, military (all branches)
41-1012.00 First-Line Supervisors/Managers of Non-Retail Sales Workers	Hospitality and Recreation Marketing Operations, General; Business and Personal Services Marketing Operations, Other; Office Products Marketing Operations; Food Products Retailing and Wholesaling Operations; General Distribution Operations; General Marketing Operations; General Retailing Operations; General Selling Skills and Sales Operations; Home Products Marketing Operations; Recreation Products/Services Marketing Operations; Health Products and Services Marketing Operations; Insurance Marketing Operations; Vehicle Parts and Accessories Marketing Operations; Apparel and Accessories Marketing Operations, General; Petroleum Products Retailing Operations; Agricultural Supplies Retailing and Wholesaling; International Business Marketing; International Business; Agricultural Power Machinery Operator; Hotel/Motel and Restaurant Management; Clothing, Apparel, and Textile Workers and Managers, General; Agricultural Mechanization, General; Clothing/Apparel and Textile Studies; Business Services Marketing Operations; Food and Beverage/Restaurant Operations Manager	Work experience in a related occupation, two-year college, four-year college, military (all branches)

10.02 Sales Technology

Workers in this group sell products such as industrial machinery, data processing equipment, and pharmaceuticals, plus services such as investment counseling, insurance, and advertising. They advise customers of the capabilities, uses, and other important features of these products and services, and help customers choose those best suited to their needs. They work for manufacturers, wholesalers, insurance companies, financial institutions, and business service establishments. Some are self-employed.

What kind of work would you do?

Your work activities would depend on your job. For example, you might

- Assist customers with product selection, utilizing knowledge of engineering specifications.
- Demonstrate the use of agricultural equipment or machines.
- Interview clients to determine their assets, liabilities, cash flow, insurance coverage, tax status, and financial objectives.
- Negotiate terms of sale and services with customers.
- Plan and sketch layouts to meet customer needs.
- Sell electrical or electronic equipment such as computers, data processing equipment, and radiographic equipment to businesses and industrial establishments.
- Solicit orders from customers in person or by phone.

What things about you point to this kind of work?

Is it important for you to

- Have good working conditions?
- Plan your work with little supervision?

Have you enjoyed any of the following as a hobby or leisure-time activity?

- Doing public speaking or debating
- Helping persuade people to sign petitions for a PTA or other organization
- Reading business magazines and newspapers
- Selling advertising space in a school yearbook, newspaper, or magazine
- Conducting experiments involving plants
- Performing experiments for a science fair

Have you liked and done well in any of the following school subjects?

- Selling
- Business Law
- Business Math
- Advertising Art/Production
- Marketing/Merchandising
- Consumer Behavior
- Advertising

Are you able to

- Communicate information and ideas in speaking so others will understand?
- Listen to and understand information and ideas presented through spoken words and sentences?
- Read and understand information and ideas presented in writing?
- Speak clearly so that it is understandable to a listener?
- Communicate information and ideas in writing so others will understand?
- Add, subtract, multiply, or divide quickly and correctly?

Would you work in places such as

- Farms?
- Factories and plants?
- Doctors' and dentists' offices and clinics?
- Hospitals and nursing homes?
- Laboratories?
- Business offices?
- Private homes?
- Stores and shopping malls?
- Restaurants, cafeterias, and other eating places?

What skills and knowledges do you need for this kind of work?

For most of these jobs, you need these skills:

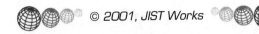

- Speaking—talking to others to effectively convey information
- Persuasion—persuading others to approach things differently

These knowledges are important in most of these jobs:

- Sales and Marketing—principles and methods involved in showing, promoting, and selling products or services
- Mathematics—numbers, their operations, and interrelationships including arithmetic, algebra, geometry, calculus, statistics, and their applications

What else should you consider about this kind of work?

Many of the jobs in this group require frequent travel. Workers may be on the road, calling on customers in various communities, for as long as two or three weeks at a time. The "territories" of sales representatives may be as large as several states or as small as a single metropolitan area.

Sales representatives who cover a single metropolitan area use company (or sometimes their own) cars. Those whose territories include several states usually fly or use other public transportation.

Most of these jobs entail meeting new people and many require working under pressure, making decisions that affect sales or investments involving large sums of money.

Some workers receive a salary; others work on a commission, usually a percentage of the selling price. Some workers receive a combination of salary and commission; some own their own businesses.

In many sales occupations there is great competition at the beginning to establish a clientele, and many beginners drop out because they are not successful (especially in nontechnical fields where they have not invested a lot of time in learning the subject). On the other hand, those who can get past the first rung of this career will generally have good opportunities. In addition, the high turnover rate means that there will always be a large number of openings for beginners to try their luck and apply their skills.

Sales jobs in most fields are sensitive to the ups and downs of the economy. Automation is not likely to replace the person-to-person contact that is required for these jobs, but it may increase workers' productivity and thus reduce the overall number of jobs. Opportunities representing manufacturers will be better in fast-growing industries (such as medical equipment) than in some others. There will also be better than average growth of jobs that involve selling services.

How can you prepare for jobs of this kind?

Occupations in this group usually require education and/or training ranging from six months to more than six years. A common way to prepare is to obtain a two- or four-year degree with a major in business administration, marketing, or a similar field. Many jobs require a knowledge of accounting, psychology, composition, business law, speech, and economics. For jobs in technical sales, a degree in a field such as engineering, chemistry, or physics is helpful. Sometimes workers in other sales groups advance after obtaining related work experience.

Some employers prefer to hire persons who have sales experience and some technical or scientific education. The company then provides training, through classes or work in other jobs, to familiarize the employee with the products. All companies provide formal or informal training to explain company sales policies and procedures. Insurance companies, brokerage firms, and equipment manufacturers frequently send employees to training centers and universities for extensive training.

SPECIALIZED TRAINING

JOBS	EDUCATION/TRAINING	WHERE OBTAINED
10.02.01 Sales Technology: Technical Sales		
All in Sales Technology: Technical Sales	Technical knowledge of product and industry; Computer Applications; Technical Writing; Oral Communications; Sales Technique	On the job, four-year college, related jobs within the same industry
41-4011.01 Sales Representatives, Agricultural	Veterinarian Assistant/Animal Health Technician; Agricultural Supplies Retailing and Wholesaling; Animal Sciences, General; Agricultural Animal Nutrition; Poultry Science; General Selling Skills and Sales Operations	On the job, two-year college, business college

(continues)

(continued)

SPECIALIZED TRAINING

JOBS	EDUCATION/TRAINING	WHERE OBTAINED
10.02.01 Sales Technology: Technical Sales		
41-4011.02 Sales Representatives, Chemical and Pharmaceutical	Chemical Technology/Technician; Pharmacy Technician/Assistant; Water Quality and Wastewater Treatment Technology/Technician; General Selling Skills and Sales Operations; Agricultural Supplies Retailing and Wholesaling	On the job, four-year college, two-year college, business college
41-4011.03 Sales Representatives, Electrical/Electronic	Computer Maintenance Technology/Technician; General Selling Skills and Sales Operations; Instrumentation Technology/Technician; Electrical, Electronic, and Communications Engineering Technology/Technician; Computer Engineering Technology/Technician; Office Products Marketing Operations; Metallurgical Technology/Technician	On the job, two-year college, business college
41-4011.04 Sales Representatives, Mechanical Equipment and Supplies	Agricultural Supplies Retailing and Wholesaling; Construction/Building Technology/Technician; Petroleum Technology/Technician; Aeronautical and Aerospace Engineering Technology/Technician; Metallurgical Technology/Technician; Plastics Technology/Technician; General Selling Skills and Sales Operations; Welder/Welding Technologist; Construction Equipment Operator; Machinist/Machine Technologist; Industrial Machinery Maintenance and Repair; Industrial/Manufacturing Technology/Technician	On the job, two-year college, business college
41-4011.05 Sales Representatives, Medical	Health Products and Services Marketing Operations; Biomedical Engineering-Related Technology/Technician; General Selling Skills and Sales Operations	On the job, four-year college, two-year college, business college
41-4011.06 Sales Representatives, Instruments	Instrumentation Technology/Technician; General Selling Skills and Sales Operations	On the job, four-year college, two-year college, business college
10.02.02 Sales Technology: Intangible Sales		
All in Sales Technology: Intangible Sales	Technical knowledge of subject matter or product; Sales Technique; Oral Communications	On the job, two-year college, company training program or seminars, related jobs within the same industry
41-3011.00 Advertising Sales Agents	General Selling Skills and Sales Operations; Business Services Marketing Operations; Advertising	On the job, two-year college, four-year college, business college
41-3021.00 Insurance Sales Agents	Finance, General; Insurance and Risk Management; Insurance Marketing Operations	On the job, two-year college, four-year college, business college
41-3031.01 Sales Agents, Securities and Commodities	Financial Services Marketing Operations; Finance, General; Financial Planning; Investments and Securities; Taxation	On the job, four-year college
41-3031.02 Sales Agents, Financial Services	Financial Services Marketing Operations; Finance, General; Business Services Marketing Operations; Financial Planning	On the job, two-year college, four-year college, business college

10.03 General Sales

Workers in this group sell, demonstrate, and solicit orders for products and services of many kinds. They are hired by retail and wholesale firms, manufacturers and distributors, business services, and nonprofit organizations. Some spend all their time in a single location, such as a department store or automobile agency. Others call on businesses or individuals to sell products or services, or follow up on earlier sales.

What kind of work would you do?

Your work activities would depend on your job. For example, you might

- Advise customers on variables and options to assist customers in making decisions.
- Assemble and stock product displays in retail stores.
- Compute the sales price of merchandise.
- Contact utility companies for a service hookup to a client's property.
- Estimate delivery dates and arrange delivery schedules.
- Rent merchandise to customers.
- Take inventory of stock.

What things about you point to this kind of work?

Is it important for you to

- Have good working conditions?
- Plan your work with little supervision?
- Never be pressured to do things that go against your sense of right and wrong?
- Get a feeling of accomplishment?

Have you enjoyed any of the following as a hobby or leisure-time activity?

- Helping persuade people to sign petitions for a PTA or other organization
- Helping run a school or community fair or carnival
- Soliciting clothes, food, and other supplies for needy people
- Recruiting members for a club or other organization
- Using a pocket calculator or spreadsheet to figure out income and expenses for an organization
- Serving as a salesperson or clerk in a store run by a charity

Have you liked and done well in any of the following school subjects?

- Selling
- Marketing/Merchandising
- Business Math
- Retailing
- Real Estate Laws/Regulations
- Consumer Behavior
- Record-Keeping
- Advertising
- Cashiering

Are you able to

- Communicate information and ideas in speaking so others will understand?
- Listen to and understand information and ideas presented through spoken words and sentences?
- Add, subtract, multiply, or divide quickly and correctly?
- Read and understand information and ideas presented in writing?
- Speak clearly so that it is understandable to a listener?
- See details of objects at close range (within a few feet)?
- Communicate information and ideas in writing so others will understand?

Would you work in places such as

- Stores and shopping malls?
- Travel agencies?
- Private homes?
- Convention and trade show centers?
- Country clubs and resorts?
- Factories and plants?

What skills and knowledges do you need for this kind of work?

For most of these jobs, you need these skills:

- Speaking—talking to others to effectively convey information
- Active Listening—listening to what other people are saying and asking questions as appropriate
- Service Orientation—actively looking for ways to help people

These knowledges are important in most of these jobs:

- Sales and Marketing—principles and methods involved in showing, promoting, and selling products or services
- Customer and Personal Service—principles and processes for providing customer and personal services including needs-assessment techniques, quality service standards, alternative delivery systems, and customer satisfaction evaluation techniques

What else should you consider about this kind of work?

Many of the people in this group have jobs in retail stores. Others are hired by companies that make or distribute various products. Some work for real estate companies, travel agencies, freight lines, and other businesses.

In many retail stores, part-time or temporary work is easier to get than a full-time job. Because so many stores are open nights and Sundays, they often hire part-time help for these hours. At Christmas and other busy shopping times, extra workers are hired.

People who do door-to-door selling, or represent a company that does "party plan" sales, usually are self-employed. They may have to meet certain quotas set by the companies that make the things they sell; but apart from that, they're on their own.

Many of the people in this group earn the same salary no matter how much or how little they sell. Others get a base salary plus a commission on sales. A few depend only on commissions for their income.

Travel is necessary for many of these jobs. Some salespersons are away from home, on the road for weeks at a time, but others call on businesses only in the local area. Many of these jobs require use of a personal car.

The outlook for jobs in this group varies. In some occupations, such as real estate sales agent and travel agent, many beginners drop out because they are not successful at building a clientele and closing sales, but the rewards are good for those with the skills and drive to overcome the early hurdles. The high turnover rate in most of these occupations will provide many openings for beginners, although there will sometimes be a lot of competition, especially for the jobs that require the least amount of education or training.

Sales jobs often are at risk when the economy slows down. Technology will limit job openings in some fields where buyers can use the Internet to view merchandise and make purchases directly from manufacturers and other sellers. Much of the work of service station attendants is now being done by self-service pumps that can read credit cards.

How can you prepare for jobs of this kind?

Occupations in this group usually require education and/or training ranging from three months to more than two years. Most employers require that applicants have a high school education or its equal. Coursework in math computation, speech, English grammar, selling, and retailing is helpful. Many high schools, junior colleges, and community colleges offer courses and programs in this field. Some schools provide work-study programs in which students work part-time as well as attend classes. Selling experience during vacations is also helpful in preparing for this kind of work.

Employers usually provide on-the-job training to teach new workers about the company policies and the products or services to be sold. These training programs may last from one week to three months. Certain workers must have special skills, such as driving a truck or playing a musical instrument. Other workers are required to make minor repairs or adjustments on equipment they sell.

Real estate sales agents need a good background of knowledge about the communities where they show properties. Travel agents benefit from a good knowledge of world geography and cultures.

SPECIALIZED TRAINING

JOBS	EDUCATION/TRAINING	WHERE OBTAINED
10.03.01 General Sales		
All in General Sales	Product knowledge; Sales Technique; Oral Communications	Two-year college, company training, related jobs within the same industry

JOBS	EDUCATION/TRAINING	WHERE OBTAINED
	10.03.01 General Sales	
41-2022.00 Parts Salespersons	General Retailing Operations; Agricultural Supplies Retailing and Wholesaling; General Selling Skills and Sales Operations; Vehicle Parts and Accessories Marketing Operations	On the job, two-year college, business college
41-2031.00 Retail Salespersons	Hospitality and Recreation Marketing Operations, General; Greenhouse Operations and Management; Nursery Operations and Management; Apparel and Accessories Marketing Operations, General; Fashion Merchandising; Apparel and Accessories Marketing Operations, Other; Floristry Marketing Operations; General Selling Skills and Sales Operations; Recreation Products/Services Marketing Operations; Vehicle Parts and Accessories Marketing Operations; Vehicle Marketing Operations; Health Products and Services Marketing Operations; Marketing Operations/Marketing and Distribution, Other; Clothing, Apparel, and Textile Workers and Managers, General; Ornamental Horticulture Operations and Management; Home Furnishings and Equipment Installers and Consultants, General; General Retailing Operations; Fashion and Fabric Consultant; Agricultural Supplies Retailing and Wholesaling; Home Products Marketing Operations; Horticulture Services Operations and Management, General	On the job, two-year college, business college, military (Navy, Air Force, Marine Corps)
41-3041.00 Travel Agents	Travel Services Marketing Operations	Two-year college, business college, on the job
41-4012.00 Sales Representatives, Wholesale and Manufacturing, Except Technical and Scientific Products	Office Products Marketing Operations; Fashion Merchandising; Apparel and Accessories Marketing Operations, Other; Business and Personal Services Marketing Operations, Other; Floristry Marketing Operations; Food Products Retailing and Wholesaling Operations; Agricultural Supplies Retailing and Wholesaling; Apparel and Accessories Marketing Operations, General; General Selling Skills and Sales Operations; General Retailing Operations; Hospitality and Recreation Marketing Operations, General; Recreation Products/Services Marketing Operations; Marketing Operations/Marketing and Distribution, Other; Architectural Engineering Technology/Technician; Clothing, Apparel, and Textile Workers and Managers, General; Fashion and Fabric Consultant	On the job, two-year college, business college
41-9021.00 Real Estate Brokers	Real Estate	Two-year college, business college, on the job
41-9022.00 Real Estate Sales Agents	Real Estate; General Selling Skills and Sales Operations	Two-year college, business college, on the job

(continues)

(continued)

SPECIALIZED TRAINING

JOBS	EDUCATION/TRAINING	WHERE OBTAINED
10.03.01 General Sales		
43-5081.01 Stock Clerks, Sales Floor	Food Products Retailing and Wholesaling Operations; General Retailing Operations; Marketing Operations/ Marketing and Distribution, Other	On the job, military (Air Force, Marine Corps)
53-6031.00 Service Station Attendants	Heavy Equipment Maintenance and Repair; Petroleum Products Retailing Operations	On the job

10.04 Personal Soliciting

Workers in this group appeal to people directly and sell them merchandise or services. In most cases they do not build a long-term relationship with the buyer. They may sell products on the street, staying in one location or moving through business and residential areas. They may call potential buyers by telephone. They may demonstrate a product in a mall or other place with a lot of foot traffic.

What kind of work would you do?

Your work activities would depend on your job. For example, you might

- Circulate among potential customers or travel by foot, truck, automobile, or bicycle to deliver or sell merchandise or services.
- Solicit new organization membership.
- Explain products or services and prices and demonstrate the use of products.
- Instruct customers in the alteration of products.
- Maintain records of accounts and orders and develop prospect lists.
- Set up and arrange displays to attract the attention of prospective customers.
- Distribute product samples or literature that details products or services.

What things about you point to this kind of work?

Is it important for you to

- Do your work alone?
- Get a feeling of accomplishment?
- Never be pressured to do things that go against your sense of right and wrong?

Have you enjoyed any of the following as a hobby or leisure-time activity?

- Soliciting clothes, food, and other supplies for needy people
- Soliciting funds for community organizations
- Campaigning for political candidates or issues
- Conducting house-to-house or telephone surveys for a PTA or other organization
- Doing public speaking or debating
- Developing publicity flyers for a school or community event
- Helping persuade people to sign petitions for a PTA or other organization
- Recruiting members for a club or other organization

Have you liked and done well in any of the following school subjects?

- Selling
- Marketing/Merchandising
- Business Math
- Psychology
- Consumer Behavior
- Advertising
- Copy Writing
- Promotion

Are you able to

- Communicate information and ideas in speaking so others will understand?
- Speak clearly so that it is understandable to a listener?
- Listen to and understand information and ideas presented through spoken words and sentences?

- Communicate information and ideas in writing so others will understand?

Would you work in places such as

- Business offices?
- Private homes?
- Stores and shopping malls?

What skills and knowledges do you need for this kind of work?

For most of these jobs, you need these skills:

- Persuasion—persuading others to approach things differently
- Speaking—talking to others to effectively convey information
- Social Perceptiveness—being aware of others' reactions and understanding why they react the way they do

These knowledges are important in most of these jobs:

- Sales and Marketing—principles and methods involved in showing, promoting, and selling products or services
- English Language—the structure and content of the English language, including the meaning and spelling of words, rules of composition, and grammar

What else should you consider about this kind of work?

Workers in the sales occupations in this group are employed by a wide variety of businesses that need person-to-person selling. People in these jobs feel comfortable talking with strangers, are persistent and persuasive, and do not take rejection personally.

The general outlook for these occupations is good. Jobs are constantly being created because of turnover. Automation is not likely to diminish the need for motivated people who know how to appeal personally to others. Telemarketing seems to be growing as a way to reach buyers.

Workers in these jobs may be paid a straight salary but often are paid at least in part based on the volume of sales. Occasionally workers may be under considerable pressure to close a lot of sales. Usually many part-time openings are available.

How can you prepare for jobs of this kind?

Occupations in this group usually require very little education and/or training. Employers give trainee workers a brief demonstration of the tasks and strategies.

Although it may not be required, a high school education or its equal is usually helpful. Coursework in speech, selling, and retailing is particularly relevant. Selling experience during school vacations is probably the best preparation for this kind of work.

SPECIALIZED TRAINING

JOBS	EDUCATION/TRAINING	WHERE OBTAINED
	10.04.01 Personal Soliciting	
All in Personal Soliciting	Sales Technique; Oral Communication; experience	On the job, related jobs within the same industry
41-9011.00 Demonstrators and Product Promoters	General Retailing Operations; Fiber, Textile, and Weaving Arts; Painting; Art, General; Home Furnishings and Equipment Installers and Consultants, General; Fashion and Fabric Consultant; Clothing, Apparel, and Textile Workers and Managers, General; General Selling Skills and Sales Operations; Business and Personal Services Marketing Operations, Other; Home Products Marketing Operations	On the job
41-9041.00 Telemarketers	General Retailing Operations; General Marketing Operations; Home Products Marketing Operations	On the job
41-9091.00 Door-To-Door Sales Workers, News and Street Vendors, and Related Workers	General Marketing Operations; Home Products Marketing Operations; General Retailing Operations	On the job

11 Recreation, Travel, and Other Personal Services

An interest in catering to the personal wishes and needs of others, so that they may enjoy cleanliness, good food and drink, comfortable lodging away from home, and enjoyable recreation.

You can satisfy this interest by providing services for the convenience, feeding, and pampering of others in hotels, restaurants, airplanes, and so on. If you enjoy improving the appearance of others, perhaps working in the hair and beauty care field would satisfy you. You may wish to provide personal services such as taking care of small children, tailoring garments, or ushering. Or you may use your knowledge of the field to manage workers who are providing these services.

11.01 Managerial Work in Recreation, Travel, and Other Personal Services

11.02 Recreational Services

11.03 Transportation and Lodging Services

11.04 Barber and Beauty Services

11.05 Food and Beverage Services

11.06 Apparel, Shoes, Leather, and Fabric Care

11.07 Cleaning and Building Services

11.08 Other Personal Services

11.01 Managerial Work in Recreation, Travel, and Other Personal Services

Workers in this group manage, through lower-level personnel, all or part of the activities in restaurants, hotels, resorts, and other places where people expect good personal service. Some of them manage services that keep a building clean. Within the guidelines of their organization, they set goals, monitor resources, and evaluate the work of others.

What kind of work would you do?

Your work activities would depend on your job. For example, you might

- Inspect guestrooms, public areas, and grounds for cleanliness and appearance.
- Assign duties to workers and schedule shifts.
- Confer with staff to resolve production and personnel problems.
- Greet and register guests.
- Interview and hire workers.
- Select and purchase new furnishings.
- Test cooked food by tasting and smelling to ensure palatability and flavor conformity.

What things about you point to this kind of work?

Is it important for you to

- Give directions and instructions to others?
- Plan your work with little supervision?
- Make decisions on your own?

Have you enjoyed any of the following as a hobby or leisure-time activity?

- Budgeting the family income
- Planning family recreational activities
- Serving as a host or hostess for houseguests
- Setting the table and serving family meals
- Buying large quantities of food or other products for an organization
- Serving as a leader of a scouting or other group
- Ushering for school or community events

Have you liked and done well in any of the following school subjects?

- Management
- Recreation
- Hotel Administration
- Accounting
- Personnel Management
- Business Math
- Consumer Behavior

Are you able to

- Communicate information and ideas in speaking so others will understand?
- Listen to and understand information and ideas presented through spoken words and sentences?
- Speak clearly so that it is understandable to a listener?

Would you work in places such as

- Hotels and motels?
- Restaurants, cafeterias, and other eating places?
- Hospitals and nursing homes?
- Schools and homes for people with disabilities?
- Country clubs and resorts?
- Jails and reformatories?
- Business offices?
- Gambling casinos and card clubs?
- Recreation centers and playgrounds?
- Gymnasiums and health clubs?

What skills and knowledges do you need for this kind of work?

For most of these jobs, you need these skills:

- Coordination—adjusting actions in relation to others' actions
- Management of Personnel Resources—motivating, developing, and directing people as they work, identifying the best people for the job

These knowledges are important in most of these jobs:

- Administration and Management—principles and processes involved in business and organizational planning, coordination, and execution
- Customer and Personal Service—principles and processes for providing customer and personal services including needs-assessment techniques, quality service standards, alternative delivery systems, and customer satisfaction evaluation techniques

What else should you consider about this kind of work?

Workers in this group are employed by restaurants, hotels, casinos, resorts, and large office complexes. Most of them work some evening and/or weekend hours. They may occasionally come under pressure because of an unexpected turnout of customers, a mechanical malfunction, or some other problem.

Opportunities in this field are generally very good, although the occupations have some sensitivity to the business cycle or to competition within the leisure industry. Dining out and travel for tourism, family vacations, and business conferences are all on the increase. As restaurants are increasingly owned by chains, owner-managers will increasingly be replaced by hired managers. In hotels the trend is toward budget hotels with fewer services and thus a smaller staff of managers. In many settings there is a trend toward outsourcing housekeeping and janitorial management to specialized service companies rather than keeping managers on staff, so many opportunities can be expected in those firms.

How can you prepare for jobs of this kind?

Work in this group requires education and/or training that lasts from two to four years.

Two- or four-year degrees in food service management, hotel management, or related subjects provide an entry route for some workers. Courses in bookkeeping, marketing, and personnel can be especially helpful.

Other workers begin by taking a job providing direct service to the public or clerical support to management, then may work their way up to management after gaining experience and taking courses in management.

High school classes in business, math, and speech can be good background. Knowledge of computer applications such as word processing and spreadsheets is growing in importance. Continuous learning is the key to staying employable.

SPECIALIZED TRAINING

JOBS	EDUCATION/TRAINING	WHERE OBTAINED
11.01.01 Managerial Work in Recreation, Travel, and Other Personal Services		
All in Managerial Work in Recreation, Travel, and Other Personal Services	Experience; Budgeting; Personnel; Oral and Written Communications; knowledge of the industry	Two-year college, business college, four-year college, related jobs within the same industry
11-9051.00 Food Service Managers	Food Systems Administration; Foods and Nutrition Studies, General; Institutional Food Workers and Administrators, General; Food and Beverage/Restaurant Operations Manager; Culinary Arts/Chef Training; Food Caterer; Hotel/Motel and Restaurant Management; Waiter/Waitress and Dining Room Manager; Hospitality and Recreation Marketing Operations, General; Food Sales Operations; Hospitality/Administration Management; Franchise Operation; Institutional Food Services Administrator	Two-year college, business college, four-year college, military (all branches)
11-9071.00 Gaming Managers	Business Administration and Management, General; Hospitality/Administration Management	Two-year college, business college, four-year college
11-9081.00 Lodging Managers	Food and Beverage/Restaurant Operations Manager; Franchise Operation; Hospitality/Administration Management; Hotel/Motel and Restaurant Management	Two-year college, business college, four-year college, military (Navy, Air Force)
13-1121.00 Meeting and Convention Planners	Institutional Food Workers and Administrators, General; Travel-Tourism Management; Hotel/Motel and Restaurant Management; Foods and Nutrition Studies, General; Food Systems Administration; Food Caterer	Two-year college, business college, four-year college

JOBS	EDUCATION/TRAINING	WHERE OBTAINED
11.01.01 Managerial Work in Recreation, Travel, and Other Personal Services		
35-1012.00 First-Line Supervisors/Managers of Food Preparation and Serving Workers	Food Caterer; Food Systems Administration; Institutional Food Workers and Administrators, General; Waiter/Waitress and Dining Room Manager; Dietician Assistant; Foods and Nutrition Studies, General; Institutional Food Services Administrator	Two-year college, business college, military (all branches)
37-1011.01 Housekeeping Supervisors	Custodial, Housekeeping, and Home Services Workers and Managers; Executive Housekeeper	Two-year college, business college, four-year college, military (Navy)
37-1011.02 Janitorial Supervisors	Custodial, Housekeeping, and Home Services Workers and Managers; Custodian/Caretaker	Two-year college, business college, military (Marine Corps)
39-1011.00 Gaming Supervisors	Business Administration and Management, General; Hospitality/Administration Management	Two-year college, business college, four-year college
39-1021.00 First-Line Supervisors/Managers of Personal Service Workers	Custodian/Caretaker; Tourism Promotion Operations; Executive Housekeeper; Hotel/Motel and Restaurant Management; Custodial, Housekeeping, and Home Services Workers and Managers; Flight Attendant	Two-year college, business college
53-1011.00 Aircraft Cargo Handling Supervisors	Materials Moving Operations, Miscellaneous Materials	On the job; military data not yet available

11.02 Recreational Services

Workers in this group provide services to help people enjoy their leisure activities. They may lead people in recreational activities such as exercise, crafts, music, or camping. Or they may help people engage in recreation by performing such services as dealing cards, guiding tourists, taking tickets, or operating thrill rides.

What kind of work would you do?

Your work activities would depend on your job. For example, you might

- Assist patrons on and off amusement rides, boats, or ski lifts, and in mounting and riding animals, and fasten or direct patrons to fasten safety belts.
- Collect admission tickets and passes from patrons at entertainment events.
- Explain hunting and fishing laws to groups to ensure compliance.
- Monitor patrons' activities to prevent disorderly conduct and rowdiness.
- Plan tour itineraries, applying knowledge of travel routes and destination sites.
- Speak a foreign language to communicate with foreign visitors.
- Verify, compute, and pay out winnings.

What things about you point to this kind of work?

Is it important for you to

- Never be pressured to do things that go against your sense of right and wrong?
- Have work where you do things for other people?
- Have good working conditions?

Have you enjoyed any of the following as a hobby or leisure-time activity?

- Announcing or emceeing a program
- Chauffeuring special groups, such as children, older people, or people with disabilities
- Serving as a volunteer counselor at a youth camp or center
- Helping run a school or community fair or carnival
- Ushering for school or community events
- Planning family recreational activities
- Serving as a host or hostess for houseguests

Have you liked and done well in any of the following school subjects?

- Recreation
- Public Speaking

Are you able to

- Communicate information and ideas in speaking so others will understand?
- Speak clearly so that it is understandable to a listener?
- Listen to and understand information and ideas presented through spoken words and sentences?
- See details of objects at close range (within a few feet)?
- Efficiently shift back and forth between two or more activities or sources of information?

Would you work in places such as

- Recreation centers and playgrounds?
- Gambling casinos and card clubs?
- Nightclubs?
- Theaters?
- Amusement parks, circuses, and carnivals?
- Bowling alleys?

What skills and knowledges do you need for this kind of work?

For most of these jobs, you need these skills:

- Speaking—talking to others to effectively convey information
- Service Orientation—actively looking for ways to help people

These knowledges are important in most of these jobs:

- Customer and Personal Service—principles and processes for providing customer and personal services including needs-assessment techniques, quality service standards, alternative delivery systems, and customer satisfaction evaluation techniques
- English Language—the structure and content of the English language, including the meaning and spelling of words, rules of composition, and grammar

What else should you consider about this kind of work?

These workers are employed by resorts, cruise ships, casinos, theme parks, movie theaters, municipal recreation departments, and government agencies throughout the United States. Some of them work part-time. Weekend or evening work often is required. Some of the work may be seasonal. Travel and tour guides may spend weeks away from home.

As Americans increase their spending on leisure, these occupations will provide many job opportunities, although downturns in the economy may slow the demand for workers at times. Because these occupations require little specific education or training, there will be keen competition for jobs in some fields. Best opportunities will be for those who have gained some experience in the job, perhaps through part-time work while in school.

How can you prepare for jobs of this kind?

Work in this group requires education and/or training that lasts from a few hours to four years.

Some of these jobs (for example, taking tickets) can be learned from a brief demonstration. In general, a high school diploma or its equivalent is sometimes necessary, but for part-time work it may not be needed. Gambling dealers and motion picture projectionists receive training from their employers in situations that simulate work with the public.

Full-time recreation workers are generally expected to have a college degree. Although degrees in recreation are available, graduates seeking jobs as recreation workers do not need special coursework as much as they need experience in part-time, volunteer, or temporary work.

Travel and tour guides often will have an advantage if they speak a foreign language and are familiar with a foreign culture.

SPECIALIZED TRAINING

JOBS	EDUCATION/TRAINING	WHERE OBTAINED
11.02.01 Recreational Services		
All in Recreational Services	Skill and knowledge in specialty area	Hobbies, related jobs within the same industry

JOBS	EDUCATION/TRAINING	WHERE OBTAINED
	11.02.01 Recreational Services	
39-1012.00 Slot Key Persons	Recreation Products/Services Marketing Operations	On the job
39-3011.00 Gaming Dealers	Card Dealer	On the job, Proprietary school
39-3012.00 Gaming and Sports Book Writers and Runners	Card Dealer	On the job, Proprietary school
39-3021.00 Motion Picture Projectionists	Miscellaneous Mechanics and Repairers, Other; Educational/Instructional Media Technology/ Technician	On the job, military (Navy, Air Force)
39-3031.00 Ushers, Lobby Attendants, and Ticket Takers	Hospitality and Recreation Marketing Operations, General	On the job
39-3091.00 Amusement and Recreation Attendants	Amusement Mechanical Maintenance and Operation	On the job
39-6021.00 Tour Guides and Escorts	Recreation Products/Services Marketing Operations; Hospitality and Recreation Marketing Operations, General; Parks, Recreation, and Leisure Studies; Tourism Promotion Operations	Two-year college, on the job
39-6022.00 Travel Guides	Parks, Recreation, and Leisure Facilities Management; Travel Services Marketing Operations; Recreation Products/Services Marketing Operations; Hospitality and Recreation Marketing Operations, General	Two-year college, on the job
39-9032.00 Recreation Workers	Parks, Recreation, and Leisure Facilities Management; Hospitality/Administration Management; Child Care and Guidance Workers and Managers, General; Child Care Provider/Assistant; Parks, Recreation, and Leisure Studies	Four-year college, two-year college, on the job, military (all branches)

11.03 Transportation and Lodging Services

Workers in this group help visitors, travelers, and customers get acquainted with and feel at ease in an unfamiliar setting. They are charged with the safety and comfort of people who are traveling or vacationing. They may register travelers at hotels, book trips for passengers, or carry travelers' luggage. These workers find employment with air, rail, and water transportation companies; hotels and restaurants; retirement homes; and related establishments.

What kind of work would you do?

Your work activities would depend on your job. For example, you might

- Administer first aid to passengers in distress, when needed.
- Deliver, carry, or transfer luggage, trunks, and packages to/from rooms, loading areas, vehicles, or transportation terminals.
- Greet, register, and assign rooms to guests of hotels or motels.
- Issue and collect passenger boarding passes and tear or punch tickets to prevent reuse.
- Record and review a client's activities to assure that a program is followed.
- Transport customers and baggage, using a motor vehicle.
- Walk the aisle of a plane to verify that passengers have complied with federal regulations prior to takeoff.

What things about you point to this kind of work?

Is it important for you to

- Have work where you do things for other people?
- Never be pressured to do things that go against your sense of right and wrong?
- Have co-workers who are easy to get along with?
- Have supervisors who back up the workers with management?

Have you enjoyed any of the following as a hobby or leisure-time activity?

- Mixing drinks for family or friends
- Serving as a host or hostess for houseguests
- Chauffeuring special groups such as children, older people, or people with disabilities
- Serving as a salesperson or clerk in a store run by a charity organization
- Planning family recreational activities
- Setting tables for club or organizational functions

Have you liked and done well in any of the following school subjects?

- Record-Keeping
- Flight Safety

Are you able to

- Communicate information and ideas in speaking so others will understand?
- Listen to and understand information and ideas presented through spoken words and sentences?
- Speak clearly so that it is understandable to a listener?
- Add, subtract, multiply, or divide quickly and correctly?

Would you work in places such as

- Hotels and motels?
- Airplanes?
- Ships and boats?
- Trains?
- Country clubs and resorts?

What skills and knowledges do you need for this kind of work?

For most of these jobs, you need these skills:

- Service Orientation—actively looking for ways to help people
- Speaking—talking to others to effectively convey information

These knowledges are important in most of these jobs:

- Customer and Personal Service—principles and processes for providing customer and personal services including needs-assessment techniques, quality service standards, alternative delivery systems, and customer satisfaction evaluation techniques
- Transportation—principles and methods for moving people or goods by air, rail, sea, or road, including their relative costs, advantages, and limitations

What else should you consider about this kind of work?

Workers in this group are employed throughout the country wherever travelers visit or pass through. Because travelers expect services around the clock, these workers sometimes work nights or weekends. Flight attendants and other transportation attendants have to spend nights away from home, but some enjoy the opportunities for free or low-cost travel.

Work associated with travel is partly sensitive to economic downturns, but in the long run travel seems to be increasing. These jobs also have fairly high turnover, so there are usually many job openings. Automation is likely to cut into the demand for some of the more routine clerical functions of ticket agents and desk clerks. On the other hand, flight attendants are required by federal law, and some of the other occupations will continue to be in demand because travelers expect personal service.

How can you prepare for jobs of this kind?

Education and/or training requirements for this group vary from a few days to six months. Most training is done on the job.

Flight attendants, other travel attendants, desk clerks, and ticket agents are expected to have high school diplomas, and some college or experience working with the public is a plus. They are given from one to several weeks of intensive training by their employers. Flight attendants start with four to six weeks of training and need to take several hours of training in safety and other procedures each year. The ability to speak a foreign language can be very useful.

The other occupations require only a brief period of training on the job.

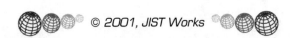

SPECIALIZED TRAINING

JOBS	EDUCATION/TRAINING	WHERE OBTAINED
11.03.01 Transportation and Lodging Services		
All in Transportation and Lodging Services	Scheduling; Company Policies; Government Regulations	Related jobs within the same industry
39-6011.00 Baggage Porters and Bellhops	Travel Services Operations	On the job
39-6012.00 Concierges	Hospitality and Recreation Marketing Operations, General; Hospitality and Recreation Marketing Operations, Other	On the job
39-6031.00 Flight Attendants	Flight Attendant	On the job, two-year college, business college, airline school, military (Navy, Air Force)
39-6032.00 Transportation Attendants, Except Flight Attendants and Baggage Porters	Travel Services Marketing Operations	On the job
43-4081.00 Hotel, Motel, and Resort Desk Clerks	Hotel/Motel Services Marketing Operations; Hospitality and Recreation Marketing Operations, General	On the job, two-year college, business college, military (Navy, Air Force)
43-4181.02 Reservation and Transportation Ticket Agents	Travel Services Marketing Operations; Flight Attendant	On the job, two-year college, business college

11.04 Barber and Beauty Services

Workers in this group cut and style hair and provide a variety of other services to improve people's appearance or physical condition. They may specialize in one activity or perform many different duties.

What kind of work would you do?

Your work activities would depend on your job. For example, you might

- Apply clear or colored liquid polish onto nails with a brush.
- Clean work area and tools.
- Comb, brush, and spray hair or wigs to set styles.
- Order supplies.
- Question patrons regarding services and style of haircuts desired.
- Record services on tickets or receive payment.
- Shape and color eyebrows or eyelashes and remove facial hair, using depilatory cream and tweezers.

What things about you point to this kind of work?

Is it important for you to

- Have work where you do things for other people?
- Never be pressured to do things that go against your sense of right and wrong?
- Plan your work with little supervision?

Have you enjoyed any of the following as a hobby or leisure-time activity?

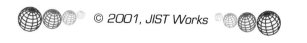

- Cutting and trimming hair for other members of the family
- Applying makeup for amateur theater
- Creating or styling hairdos for friends

Have you liked and done well in any of the following school subjects?

- Cosmetology
- Personal Grooming

Are you able to

- Keep your hand and arm steady while making an arm movement or while holding your arm and hand in one position?
- Quickly make coordinated movements of one hand, a hand together with its arm, or two hands to grasp, manipulate, or assemble objects?
- Make precisely coordinated movements of the fingers of one or both hands to grasp, manipulate, or assemble very small objects?
- See details of objects at a close range (within a few feet)?
- Make fast, simple, repeated movements of your fingers, hands, and wrists?
- Communicate information and ideas in speaking so others will understand?

Would you work in places such as

- Barber shops and beauty salons?

What skills and knowledges do you need for this kind of work?

For most of these jobs, you need these skills:

- Active Listening—listening to what other people are saying and asking questions as appropriate
- Service Orientation—actively looking for ways to help people

These knowledges are important in most of these jobs:

- Customer and Personal Service—principles and processes for providing customer and personal services including needs-assessment techniques, quality service standards, alternative delivery systems, and customer satisfaction evaluation techniques
- Sales and Marketing—principles and methods involved in showing, promoting, and selling products or services

What else should you consider about this kind of work?

Many people in this field are self-employed, either in their own shops or in their homes. Most have had experience working for someone else. If you are considering this kind of work because you want your own business, you should realize that it's not done overnight. First you have to get regular customers and save enough money to buy your own equipment. Shops often hire well-trained beginners. Some schools help their graduates to find jobs.

Working hours depend on shop policy. You may have to work Saturdays, Sundays, and evenings.

In some jobs you are on a salary. However, most employers set the prices for the services offered and the worker receives a percentage of these prices. The amount the worker is paid may vary and may depend on the supplies and tools provided by the employer. For example, some employers provide the needed towels, shampoo, or lotions and keep a larger share of the money collected. You usually receive tips from customers. You may be expected to join a union and pay membership dues.

In this kind of work you stand and use your hands and arms all day. Some people are bothered by odors and fumes from the chemicals used in hair care.

In many of these jobs you have to wear uniforms, which may or may not be furnished by the shop.

The outlook is generally very good for these occupations. Demand is increasing over the long run, turnover produces a steady number of job openings, and automation is not likely to replace the human touch anytime soon. Opportunities will be better at unisex hair salons than in traditional male barbershops.

How can you prepare for jobs of this kind?

Occupations in this group usually require education and/or training ranging from six months to more than two years. Both public and private vocational schools offer courses in cosmetology, barbering, electrolysis, and manicure. In a few areas, apprenticeships in cosmetology are available. Manufacturers of barbering and cosmetology equipment and materials offer training courses about the use of their products.

Formal training requirements vary according to the occupation and state. Studies usually include anatomy, bacteriology, dermatology, and physiology. Techniques such as hair cutting, permanent waving, electrolysis, and hair and scalp analysis are also included.

Students of cosmetology or barbering schools get supervised practical experience. Trainees and workers develop further expertise by attending seminars and participating in contests sponsored by schools, trade associations, and manufacturers. Changing hair styles, new products, and new techniques make frequent attendance at training and demonstration classes necessary.

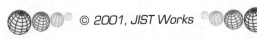

SPECIALIZED TRAINING

JOBS	EDUCATION/TRAINING	WHERE OBTAINED
11.04.01 Barber and Beauty Services		
All in Barber and Beauty Services	Skill and knowledge in specialty area	Trade/technical school
39-5011.00 Barbers	Barber/Hairstylist	Trade/technical school, military (Navy, Coast Guard)
39-5012.00 Hairdressers, Hairstylists, and Cosmetologists	Cosmetologist; Barber/Hairstylist; Funeral Services and Mortuary Science	Trade/technical school
39-5092.00 Manicurists and Pedicurists	Cosmetologist	Trade/technical school
39-5093.00 Shampooers	Cosmetologist	Trade/technical school
39-5094.00 Skin Care Specialists	Cosmetic Services, General; Cosmetologist; Electrolysis Technician	Trade/technical school

11.05 Food and Beverage Services

Workers in this group prepare and serve food. Some of them cook or do other tasks to prepare food in kitchens of restaurants or institutional cafeterias. Others aid in the preparation process by cutting meat, baking bread and pastries, or decorating cakes. The various kinds of workers who serve food and drink may wait on tables, serve diners at a counter, bring meals outside at drive-ins, or tend bar. Other workers play a supporting role by greeting diners as they enter a restaurant, by washing dishes, or by keeping the dining room set up with clean linens and silverware.

What kind of work would you do?

Your work activities would depend on your job. For example, you might

- Bake bread, rolls, cakes, and pastry.
- Carve meat.
- Compute the cost of meals or beverages.
- Clean food preparation equipment, work areas, and counters or tables.
- Dip candy centers, fruit, or nuts into coatings to coat, decorate, and identify products.
- Order items to replace stocks.
- Plan menus, taking advantage of foods in season and local availability.

What things about you point to this kind of work?

Is it important for you to

- Never be pressured to do things that go against your sense of right and wrong?
- Have co-workers who are easy to get along with?
- Be busy all the time?

Have you enjoyed any of the following as a hobby or leisure-time activity?

- Baking and decorating cakes
- Canning and preserving food
- Cooking large quantities of food for community events
- Mixing drinks for family or friends
- Planning and cooking meals
- Setting tables for club or organizational functions
- Setting the table and serving family meals
- Waiting on tables at club or organizational functions

Have you liked and done well in any of the following school subjects?

- Food Preparation/Service

- Cookery, Quantity
- Cooking
- Culinary Arts
- Baking
- Cake Decorating
- Menu Planning

Are you able to

- Quickly make coordinated movements of one hand, a hand together with its arm, or two hands to grasp, manipulate, or assemble objects?
- Make fast, simple, repeated movements of your fingers, hands, and wrists?
- Listen to and understand information and ideas presented through spoken words and sentences?
- Correctly follow a given rule or set of rules in order to arrange things or actions in a certain order?
- Communicate information and ideas in speaking so others will understand?

Would you work in places such as

- Restaurants, cafeterias, and other eating places?
- Nightclubs?
- Country clubs and resorts?
- Gambling casinos and card clubs?
- Sports stadiums?
- Ships and boats?

What skills and knowledges do you need for this kind of work?

For most of these jobs, you need these skills:

- Service Orientation—actively looking for ways to help people
- Active Listening—listening to what other people are saying and asking questions as appropriate

These knowledges are important in most of these jobs:

- Customer and Personal Service—principles and processes for providing customer and personal services including needs-assessment techniques, quality service standards, alternative delivery systems, and customer satisfaction evaluation techniques
- Mathematics—numbers, their operations, and interrelationships including arithmetic, algebra, geometry, calculus, statistics, and their applications

What else should you consider about this kind of work?

Restaurants, institutional cafeterias, and catering services employ these workers. Jobs may be found in cities and towns everywhere. Many workers are employed part-time.

Many of these jobs require work on evenings and weekends. Kitchen workers often have to stand for hours, endure a hot working environment, lift heavy pots, and take safety precautions against burns and cuts from sharp knives. Servers are also constantly on their feet and must humor a sometimes-demanding public. In restaurants, a dining room full of hungry customers can put all staff under considerable pressure.

The increase in meals eaten out makes for a good outlook for these occupations, especially in restaurants and bakeries. Many jobs also will be created by turnover.

Bartenders usually must be over 21, and employers often prefer to hire people over 25. Workers must have a knowledge of the laws applying to the sale of alcoholic beverages.

How can you prepare for jobs of this kind?

These occupations require education and/or training ranging from a few days to four years or more.

Chefs and head cooks typically learn through an apprenticeship program that takes several years. Many begin by studying in a culinary arts program at a vocational school, community college, or specialized culinary school. Restaurant cooks may go through a similar but somewhat shorter training program, but some simply start out as short-order or cafeteria cooks and improve their skills through on-the-job training, sometimes provided in cooperation with the local school district. Butchers and bakers also apprentice for their jobs. A high school diploma or its equivalent is usually required for admission to an apprenticeship program. High school or community college coursework in business math and management can be especially useful, and it is very important to have experience in part-time and summer jobs in the food industry.

Some bartenders learn their skills at a vocational or bartending school.

The other occupations in this group require only a few days or weeks of training, usually provided by the employer.

SPECIALIZED TRAINING

JOBS	EDUCATION/TRAINING	WHERE OBTAINED
11.05.01 Food and Beverage Services: Preparing		
All in Food and Beverage Services: Preparing	Health; Food Preparation; Business Math	High school, on the job, related jobs within the same industry
35-1011.00 Chefs and Head Cooks	Culinary Arts/Chef Training; Baker/Pastry Chef; Institutional Food Workers and Administrators, General	On the job, two-year college, culinary institute, trade/technical school, military (all branches)
35-2011.00 Cooks, Fast Food	Kitchen Personnel/Cook and Assistant Training	On the job, vocational school
35-2012.00 Cooks, Institution and Cafeteria	Kitchen Personnel/Cook and Assistant Training; Baker/Pastry Chef	On the job, vocational school, two-year college, trade/technical school, military (all branches)
35-2014.00 Cooks, Restaurant	Kitchen Personnel/Cook and Assistant Training; Culinary Arts/Chef Training	On the job, vocational school, two-year college, culinary institute, trade/technical school, military (all branches)
35-2015.00 Cooks, Short Order	Kitchen Personnel/Cook and Assistant Training	On the job, vocational school
35-2021.00 Food Preparation Workers	Institutional Food Workers and Administrators, General; Meat Cutter; Food Caterer; Kitchen Personnel/Cook and Assistant Training	On the job, vocational school
35-9021.00 Dishwashers	Institutional Food Workers and Administrators, General	On the job
51-3011.01 Bakers, Bread and Pastry	Baker/Pastry Chef	On the job, two-year college, culinary institute, trade/technical school, military (Army, Navy, Marine Corps, Coast Guard)
51-3021.00 Butchers and Meat Cutters	Meat Cutter	On the job, two-year college, trade/technical school
11.05.02 Food and Beverage Services: Serving		
All in Food and Beverage Services: Serving	Food Preparation and Service; Catering; Health	High school, on the job, related jobs within the same industry
35-3011.00 Bartenders	Bartender/Mixologist	On the job, vocational school, bartending school
35-3021.00 Combined Food Preparation and Serving Workers, Including Fast Food	Food Sales Operations; Hospitality and Recreation Marketing Operations, General	On the job, military (Marine Corps)
35-3022.00 Counter Attendants, Cafeteria, Food Concession, and Coffee Shop	Hospitality and Recreation Marketing Operations, General; Food Sales Operations; Waiter/Waitress and Dining Room Manager	On the job

(continues)

(continued)

SPECIALIZED TRAINING

JOBS	EDUCATION/TRAINING	WHERE OBTAINED
11.05.02 Food and Beverage Services: Serving		
35-3031.00 Waiters and Waitresses	Waiter/Waitress and Dining Room Manager	On the job, vocational school
35-3041.00 Food Servers, Nonrestaurant	Waiter/Waitress and Dining Room Manager	On the job, vocational school
35-9011.00 Dining Room and Cafeteria Attendants and Bartender Helpers	Waiter/Waitress and Dining Room Procedures; Bartender/Mixologist	On the job
35-9031.00 Hosts and Hostesses, Restaurant, Lounge, and Coffee Shop	Waiter/Waitress and Dining Room Manager	On the job, trade/technical school

11.06 Apparel, Shoes, Leather, and Fabric Care

Workers in this group clean, alter, restore, and repair clothing, shoes, or other items made from fabric or leather. Their jobs are found in clothing stores, manufacturing plants, and specialty cleaning, alteration, and repair shops.

What kind of work would you do?

Your work activities would depend on your job. For example, you might

- Align and stitch or glue materials such as fabric, fleece, leather, or wood to join parts.
- Compute dimensions of patterns according to size, considering stretching of material, and measure and mark patterns.
- Draw individual patterns or alter existing patterns to fit customers' measurements.
- Examine upholstery to locate defects.
- Measure and mark alteration lines.
- Press garments, using a hand iron or pressing machine.
- Mix bleaching agent with hot water in vats and soak material until it is bleached.

What things about you point to this kind of work?

Is it important for you to

- Never be pressured to do things that go against your sense of right and wrong?
- Do your work alone?
- Be busy all the time?
- Have steady employment?

Have you enjoyed any of the following as a hobby or leisure-time activity?

- Designing and making costumes for school plays, festivals, and other events
- Doing needlework
- Making belts or other leather articles
- Refinishing or reupholstering furniture
- Weaving rugs or making quilts

Have you liked and done well in any of the following school subjects?

- Leathercraft
- Costuming
- Clothing
- Bookbinding
- Botany
- Sewing

Are you able to

- Keep your hand and arm steady while making an arm movement or while holding your arm and hand in one position?

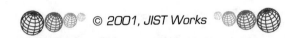

- See details of objects at close range (within a few feet)?
- Quickly make coordinated movements of one hand, a hand together with its arm, or two hands to grasp, manipulate, or assemble objects?
- Make precisely coordinated movements of the fingers of one or both hands to grasp, manipulate, or assemble very small objects?
- Make fast, simple, repeated movements of your fingers, hands, and wrists?
- Imagine how something will look after it is moved around or when its parts are moved or rearranged?

Would you work in places such as

- Factories and plants?
- Laundries and dry cleaners?
- Motion picture and recording studios?
- Theaters?
- Television studios?

What skills and knowledges do you need for this kind of work?

For most of these jobs, you need these skills:

- Product Inspection—inspecting and evaluating the quality of products
- Equipment Selection—determining the kind of tools and equipment needed to do a job
- Operation and Control—controlling operations of equipment or systems

These knowledges are important in most of these jobs:

- Production and Processing—inputs, outputs, raw materials, waste, quality control, costs, and techniques for maximizing the manufacture and distribution of goods
- Design—design techniques, principles, tools, and instruments involved in the production and use of precision technical plans, blueprints, drawings, and models

What else should you consider about this kind of work?

These workers are employed throughout the United States. Most of them work a regular 40-hour week. Working conditions in some jobs are hot, noisy, or in the presence of bad-smelling chemicals.

The overall outlook for jobs in this group is only fair. The trend is toward importing clothing and shoes made or assembled abroad rather than producing or repairing clothing in the United States. Ready-made clothing is also reducing the demand for tailoring services. Dry cleaning will offer better opportunities, partly because of job turnover.

How can you prepare for jobs of this kind?

These jobs require education and/or training ranging from a few days to four or more years.

Many of these trades are learned on the job. Workers begin as helpers and receive instruction from experienced workers, advancing to more skilled tasks over time. Formal apprenticeships are available for some of these trades, such as tailoring and upholstering. These combine classroom instruction with on-the-job training and take several years. A high school education is usually expected of new recruits. High school or vocational school classes in sewing are very helpful.

The dry-cleaning occupations can generally be learned in only a few days or weeks.

SPECIALIZED TRAINING

JOBS	EDUCATION/TRAINING	WHERE OBTAINED
11.06.01 Apparel, Shoes, Leather, and Fabric Care		
All in Apparel, Shoes, Leather, and Fabric Care	Knowledge of materials, tools, and processes in the industry	On the job, related jobs within the same industry
49-9093.00 Fabric Menders, Except Garment	Clothing, Apparel and Textile Workers and Managers, General; Commercial Garment and Apparel Worker	On the job; military data not yet available
51-6011.00 Laundry and Dry-Cleaning Workers	Clothing, Apparel, and Textile Workers and Managers, General; Dry Cleaner and Launderer (Commercial)	On the job

(continues)

(continued)

SPECIALIZED TRAINING

JOBS	EDUCATION/TRAINING	WHERE OBTAINED
	11.06.01 Apparel, Shoes, Leather, and Fabric Care	
51-6011.01 Spotters, Dry Cleaning	Dry Cleaner and Launderer (Commercial); Clothing, Apparel, and Textile Workers and Managers, General	On the job
51-6011.02 Precision Dyers	Dry Cleaner and Launderer (Commercial); Clothing, Apparel, and Textile Workers and Managers, General	Apprenticeship, trade/technical school, on the job
51-6011.03 Laundry and Dry Cleaning Machine Operators and Tenders, Except Pressing	Clothing, Apparel, and Textile Workers and Managers, General; Dry Cleaner and Launderer (Commercial)	On the job, military (Army, Navy)
51-6021.01 Pressers, Delicate Fabrics	Dry Cleaner and Launderer (Commercial); Clothing, Apparel, and Textile Workers and Managers, General	Apprenticeship, trade/technical school, on the job
51-6021.03 Pressers, Hand	Dry Cleaner and Launderer (Commercial); Clothing, Apparel, and Textile Workers and Managers, General	Apprenticeship, trade/technical school, on the job
51-6041.00 Shoe and Leather Workers and Repairers	Shoe, Boot, and Leather Repairer; Leatherworkers and Upholsterers, Other; Crafts, Folk Art, and Artisanry	Apprenticeship, on the job
51-6052.01 Shop and Alteration Tailors	Custom Tailor; Commercial Garment and Apparel Worker; Clothing, Apparel, and Textile Workers and Managers, General; Fashion and Fabric Consultant	Work experience in a related occupation, apprenticeship, on the job, military (Army, Navy, Marine Corps)
51-6052.02 Custom Tailors	Clothing, Apparel, and Textile Workers and Managers, General; Custom Tailor	Work experience in a related occupation, apprenticeship, on the job
51-6093.00 Upholsterers	Home Furnishings and Equipment Installers and Consultants, General; Upholsterer	Apprenticeship, on the job

11.07 Cleaning and Building Services

Workers in this group maintain the cleanliness of houses, various kinds of buildings, vehicles, and large equipment. They use detergents and other cleaning agents, vacuum cleaners, brushes, and specialized equipment to remove dirt, spills, and trash so the living or working environment is healthy, safe, and pleasant to be in. Some cleaners also do minor repairs, such as fixing leaky faucets. In hospitals, they may disinfect equipment and supplies. Some of these workers provide other services for the convenience of people working or seeking recreation in a building, such as retrieving people's personal items in a locker room.

What kind of work would you do?

Your work activities would depend on your job. For example, you might

- Clean and remove debris from driveways and garage areas.
- Clean swimming pools with a vacuum.
- Gather and empty trash.
- Mix cleaning solutions and abrasive compositions and other compounds according to a formula.
- Mow and trim lawns and shrubbery using mowers and hand and power trimmers, and clear debris from grounds.
- Polish metalwork, such as fixtures and fittings.
- Turn controls to regulate temperatures or room environments.

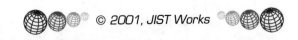

What things about you point to this kind of work?

Is it important for you to

- Never be pressured to do things that go against your sense of right and wrong?
- Do your work alone?
- Be busy all the time?
- Have work where you do things for other people?

Have you enjoyed any of the following as a hobby or leisure-time activity?

- Washing and waxing the family car
- Serving as a host or hostess for houseguests

Have you liked and done well in any of the following school subjects?

- Home Management

Are you able to

- Quickly make coordinated movements of one hand, a hand together with its arm, or two hands to grasp, manipulate, or assemble objects?
- Use your abdominal and lower-back muscles to support part of your body repeatedly or continuously over time?

Would you work in places such as

- Hotels and motels?
- Hospitals and nursing homes?
- Schools and homes for people with disabilities?
- Elementary schools?
- High schools?
- Business offices?
- Government offices?
- Stores and shopping malls?
- Country clubs and resorts?
- Airports?
- Convention and trade show centers?
- Factories and plants?
- Gambling casinos and card clubs?

What skills and knowledges do you need for this kind of work?

For most of these jobs, you need these skills:

- Operation and Control—controlling the operations of equipment or systems
- Service Orientation—actively looking for ways to help people

These knowledges are important in most of these jobs:

- Customer and Personal Service—principles and processes for providing customer and personal services including needs-assessment techniques, quality service standards, alternative delivery systems, and customer satisfaction evaluation techniques
- Mechanical—machines and tools, including their designs, uses, benefits, repair, and maintenance

What else should you consider about this kind of work?

These workers are employed in every kind of building, including private homes. The work may not have a lot of prestige, but it is vital to making our living and working environments comfortable and safe.

Many of these jobs are performed at night or on weekends, when buildings are empty of other workers and cleaning will not disrupt business functions. In some situations, however, the large amount of cleaning and attention to supplies also requires a daylight shift for some cleaners and attendants. Many jobs are part-time.

Cleaning work can be physically strenuous, so workers need to learn how to lift and bend safely. Some workers may be expected to shovel snow.

The employment outlook for cleaners is good, partly because these jobs have a high turnover rate. The trend is toward outsourcing janitorial work to cleaning services rather than maintaining an in-house cleaning staff. Experienced workers with an interest in management may be able to start their own cleaning businesses.

How can you prepare for jobs of this kind?

These occupations require only a short period of training, perhaps a few days at most.

Employers train new workers in how to operate and maintain the equipment, how to select and handle cleansers, and what standards of work are expected. No special education is required, but it helps to be able to do simple arithmetic and read directions that come with detergents. Some shop courses in high school may be helpful in jobs that include repair work.

SPECIALIZED TRAINING

JOBS	EDUCATION/TRAINING	WHERE OBTAINED
11.07.01 Cleaning and Building Services		
All in Cleaning and Building Services	Basic Math; experience	High school, related jobs within the same industry
37-2011.00 Janitors and Cleaners, Except Maids and Housekeeping Cleaners	Custodian/Caretaker; Custodial, Housekeeping, and Home Services Workers and Managers; Building/Property Maintenance and Management	On the job
37-2012.00 Maids and Housekeeping Cleaners	Custodian/Caretaker Training	On the job
39-3093.00 Locker Room, Coatroom, and Dressing Room Attendants	Institutional Food Workers and Administrators, General; Dietician Assistant; Massage; Foods and Nutrition Studies, General; Dietetics/Human Nutritional Services	Work experience in a related occupation, on the job

11.08 Other Personal Services

Workers in this group provide personal services to people who need a lot of attention: young children, people with chronic health problems, people in mourning, or very busy people. They provide such services as companionship, bathing and grooming, simple meal preparation, organizing the household, running errands, and basic emotional support.

What kind of work would you do?

Your work activities would depend on your job. For example, you might

- Assist mourners in and out of limousines.
- Assist parents in establishing good study habits for children.
- Drive motor vehicles to transport clients to specified locations.
- Groom, exercise, or feed pets.
- Perform errands or handle an employer's social or business affairs.
- Purchase or order foodstuffs and household supplies and record expenditures.
- Sort clothing and other articles, load washing machines, and iron and fold dried items.
- Dress and place bodies in caskets.

What things about you point to this kind of work?

Is it important for you to

- Have work where you do things for other people?
- Never be pressured to do things that go against your sense of right and wrong?
- Have steady employment?
- Do your work alone?

Have you enjoyed any of the following as a hobby or leisure-time activity?

- Baby-sitting for younger children
- Chauffeuring special groups, such as children, older people, or people with disabilities
- Doing volunteer work for the Red Cross
- Helping conduct physical exercises for people with disabilities
- Helping people with disabilities take walks
- Nursing sick relatives and friends
- Serving as a host or hostess for houseguests
- Serving as a volunteer aide in a hospital, nursing home, or retirement home

Have you liked and done well in any of the following school subjects?

- Home Management
- Home/Consumer Economics

- Human Growth and Development
- Child Development/Care
- Cooking
- Driver Education

Are you able to

- Communicate information and ideas in speaking so others will understand?
- Listen to and understand information and ideas presented through spoken words and sentences?

Would you work in places such as

- Private homes?
- Kindergartens and day-care centers?

What skills and knowledges do you need for this kind of work?

For most of these jobs, you need these skills:

- Service Orientation—actively looking for ways to help people
- Social Perceptiveness—being aware of others' reactions and understanding why they react the way they do

These knowledges are important in most of these jobs:

- Customer and Personal Service—principles and processes for providing customer and personal services including needs-assessment techniques, quality service standards, alternative delivery systems, and customer satisfaction evaluation techniques
- Psychology—human behavior and performance, mental processes, psychological research methods, and the assessment and treatment of behavioral and affective disorders

What else should you consider about this kind of work?

These workers are mostly employed by individuals or families. Funeral attendants and embalmers work for funeral homes.

Many workers have a 40-hour week, but others work evenings or weekends, and live-in workers can expect longer hours. The working environment is usually pleasant, but work tasks can involve lifting, stooping, and a lot of time on your feet. Because the work usually requires close contact with people who may be very dependent, it can be emotionally draining. The people for whom you are responsible may be pleasant or difficult and demanding. These jobs offer few routes for advancement. Some workers may advance to similar but better-paying jobs in institutional or office settings.

Embalmers have to work with bodies that may be disfigured by injury or disease.

The outlook for jobs in this group is excellent. Demand continues to outpace the number of available workers. Automation cannot supply the personal touch that these jobs require.

How can you prepare for jobs of this kind?

These jobs generally do not require formal education or training, but a few weeks of training will be helpful.

Because some jobs require workers to handle money, manage household budgets, or do simple meal preparation, basic arithmetic and/or home economics can be useful high school courses. Certification courses at community colleges and vocational schools are available for child monitors and home-health-care aides. Some workers receive training from organizations that recruit volunteers for this kind of work. Part-time baby-sitting jobs and care for your own family members can also be valuable experience.

Embalmers usually get two to four years of college training and perhaps also an apprenticeship. All states require them to be licensed. In some states this is the same license as for a funeral director.

SPECIALIZED TRAINING

JOBS	EDUCATION/TRAINING	WHERE OBTAINED
11.08.01 Other Personal Services		
All in Other Personal Services	Basic Math; experience	High school, related jobs within the same industry
35-2013.00 Cooks, Private Household	Custodial, Housekeeping, and Home Services Workers and Managers; Homemaker's Aide	On the job

(continues)

(continued)

SPECIALIZED TRAINING

JOBS	EDUCATION/TRAINING	WHERE OBTAINED
11.08.01 Other Personal Services		
39-4011.00 Embalmers	Funeral Services and Mortuary Science	On the job, two-year college, mortuary school, military (Army, Navy)
39-4021.00 Funeral Attendants	Funeral Procedures	Work experience in a related occupation, on the job
39-9021.00 Personal and Home Care Aides	Child Care and Guidance Workers and Managers, General; Child Care Provider/Assistant; Custodial, Housekeeping, and Home Services Workers and Managers; Elder Care Provider/Companion; Homemaker's Aide	High school, vocational school, on the job
53-7061.00 Cleaners of Vehicles and Equipment	Cleaning Services	On the job, military (Army)

12 Education and Social Service

An interest in teaching people or improving their social or spiritual well-being.

You can satisfy this interest by teaching students, who may be preschoolers, retirees, or any age between. Or if you are interested in helping people sort out their complicated lives, you may find fulfillment as a counselor, social worker, or religious worker. Working in a museum or library may give you opportunities to expand people's understanding of the world. If you also have an interest in business, you may find satisfaction in managerial work in this field.

12.01 Managerial Work in Education and Social Service

12.02 Social Services

12.03 Educational Services

12.01 Managerial Work in Education and Social Service

Workers in this group are employed at colleges, school districts, corporations, parks, and social-service agencies. They are responsible for planning, budgeting, evaluating results, and supervising workers. They need to balance their financial responsibilities against the educational and social-service goals of their organizations and sometimes must make trade-offs. They enjoy helping people achieve their learning and social goals, but they are content to do so behind the scenes.

What kind of work would you do?

Your work activities would depend on your job. For example, you might

- Advise teaching and administrative staff in assessment, curriculum development, management of student behavior, and use of materials and equipment.
- Confer with park staff to determine subjects to be presented to the public.
- Coordinate volunteer service programs, such as the Red Cross, hospital volunteers, or vocational training for disabled individuals.
- Interview, recruit, or hire volunteers and staff.
- Organize and develop training procedure manuals and guides.
- Prepare and submit budget requests or grant proposals to solicit program funding.
- Train instructors and supervisors in effective training techniques.

What things about you point to this kind of work?

Is it important for you to

- Get a feeling of accomplishment?
- Give directions and instructions to others?
- Plan your work with little supervision?

Have you enjoyed any of the following as a hobby or leisure-time activity?

- Helping members of the family with their English lessons
- Instructing family members in observing traffic regulations
- Camping, hiking, or engaging in other outdoor activities
- Planning and arranging programs for school or community organizations
- Serving as a leader of a scouting or other group
- Teaching immigrants or other individuals to speak, write, or read English
- Teaching games to children as a volunteer aide in a nursery school

Have you liked and done well in any of the following school subjects?

- Management
- Education
- Educational Psychology
- Accounting
- Personnel Management

Are you able to

- Communicate information and ideas in speaking so others will understand?
- Listen to and understand information and ideas presented through spoken words and sentences?
- Speak clearly so that it is understandable to a listener?
- Read and understand information and ideas presented in writing?
- Communicate information and ideas in writing so others will understand?
- Apply general rules to specific problems to come up with logical answers?
- See details of objects at a close range (within a few feet)?

Would you work in places such as

- Elementary schools?
- High schools?
- Colleges and universities?
- Kindergartens and day-care centers?
- Parks and campgrounds?
- Laboratories?
- Business offices?
- Government offices?

What skills and knowledges do you need for this kind of work?

For most of these jobs, you need these skills:

- Speaking—talking to others to effectively convey information
- Reading Comprehension—understanding written sentences and paragraphs in work-related documents

These knowledges are important in most of these jobs:

- Education and Training—instructional methods and training techniques including curriculum design principles, learning theory, group and individual teaching techniques, design of individual development plans, and test-design principles
- Administration and Management—principles and processes involved in business and organizational planning, coordination, and execution

What else should you consider about this kind of work?

Many of these workers are on the public payroll and therefore have to please several parties with possibly conflicting goals: students or social-service clients, parents or family members, employers, employees, elected officials, governing boards, and taxpayers. Policy and personnel changes that an administrator makes may not show results for many years, yet there is often pressure to justify budgets. Workdays often include evening hours for attending meetings. Some school administrators get long summer vacations, but others do not. The overall outlook for educational and social-service managers is good, although competition can be intense in some fields, especially at the university level.

How can you prepare for jobs of this kind?

Occupations in this group require a minimum of four years of post-secondary education, and often six or more.

Workers typically hold at least the same degree as the people they are supervising—for example, a bachelor's or master's in education for those who supervise teachers, a master's for those who supervise social workers, and a doctorate for college and university administrators. Many hold a master's degree in administration or management in addition, or instead.

Like all managers, these people must keep abreast of technological change to stay employable.

SPECIALIZED TRAINING

JOBS	EDUCATION/TRAINING	WHERE OBTAINED
12.01.01 Managerial Work in Education and Social Service		
All in Managerial Work in Education and Social Service	Experience; Budgeting; Personnel; Oral and Written Communications; Educational Methods	Four-year college, graduate school
11-9031.00 Education Administrators, Preschool and Child Care Center/Program	Educational/Instructional Media Design; Educational Evaluation and Research; Education of the Mentally Handicapped; Education of the Multiple Handicapped; Education of the Physically Handicapped; Education of the Speech Impaired; Education of the Specific Learning Disabled; Counselor Education Counseling and Guidance Services; Educational Assessment, Testing, and Measurement; Special Education, General; Education of the Emotionally Handicapped; Child Care Services Manager; Child Care and Guidance Workers and Managers, General; Education of the Deaf and Hearing Impaired; Pre-Elementary/Early Childhood/Kindergarten Teacher Education; Curriculum and Instruction; Education Administration and Supervision, General; Administration of Special Education; Education, General; Educational Supervision	Work experience in a related occupation, four-year college, graduate school, military (Army, Navy, Air Force)

(continues)

(continued)

SPECIALIZED TRAINING

JOBS	EDUCATION/TRAINING	WHERE OBTAINED
12.01.01 Managerial Work in Education and Social Service		
11-9032.00 Education Administrators, Elementary and Secondary School	Home Economics Teacher Education (Vocational) Education, General; Curriculum and Instruction; Clothing/Apparel and Textile Studies; Education of the Deaf and Hearing Impaired; Agricultural Extension; Administration of Special Education; Special Education, General; Educational Evaluation and Research; Education of the Specific Learning Disabled; Education of the Speech Impaired; Counselor Education Counseling and Guidance Services; Educational Supervision; Education of the Multiple Handicapped; Education of the Physically Handicapped; Education Administration and Supervision, General; Educational/Instructional Media Design; Education of the Mentally Handicapped; Education of the Emotionally Handicapped; Elementary, Middle, and Secondary Education Administration; Educational Assessment, Testing, and Measurement; Agricultural Teacher Education (Vocational)	Work experience in a related occupation, four-year college, graduate school, military (Army, Navy, Air Force)
11-9033.00 Education Administrators, Postsecondary	Education Administration and Supervision, General; Community and Junior College Administration; Educational Statistics and Research Methods; Higher Education Administration; College/Postsecondary Student Counseling and Personnel Services; Adult and Continuing Education Administration; Education, General	Work experience in a related occupation, four-year college, graduate school, military (Army, Navy, Air Force)
11-9151.00 Social and Community Service Managers	Public Administration; Social Work; Health System/Health Services Administration; Hospital/Health Facilities Administration; Nursing Administration (Post–R.N.); Business Administration and Management, General; Community Organization, Resources, and Services	Work experience in a related occupation, four-year college, graduate school, military (Army, Navy, Air Force)
19-1031.03 Park Naturalists	Plant Sciences, General; Range Science and Management	Four-year college, graduate school
25-9031.00 Instructional Coordinators	Education of the Deaf and Hearing Impaired; Educational/Instructional Media Design; Educational Evaluation and Research; Educational Statistics and Research Methods; Educational Assessment, Testing, and Measurement; Education of the Physically Handicapped; Education of the Multiple Handicapped; Elementary, Middle, and Secondary Education Administration; International and Comparative Education; Education of the Specific Learning Disabled; Education of the Gifted and Talented; Education of the Speech Impaired; Education of the Emotionally Handicapped; Education of the Blind and Visually Handicapped; Special Education, General; Education	Work experience in a related occupation, four-year college, graduate school, military (Navy, Air Force)

JOBS	EDUCATION/TRAINING	WHERE OBTAINED
12.01.01 Managerial Work in Education and Social Service		
	of the Mentally Handicapped; Administration of Special Education; Education Administration and Supervision, General; Curriculum and Instruction; Bilingual/Bicultural Education; Education, General; Educational Supervision	

12.02 Social Services

Workers in this group help people deal with their problems and major life events. They may work on a person-to-person basis or with groups of people. Workers sometimes specialize in problems that are personal, social, vocational, physical, educational, or spiritual in nature. Schools, rehabilitation centers, mental health clinics, guidance centers, and religious institutions employ these workers. Jobs are also found in public and private welfare and employment services, juvenile courts, and vocational rehabilitation programs.

What kind of work would you do?

Your work activities would depend on your job. For example, you might

- Assist and advise groups in promoting interfaith understanding.
- Counsel clients and patients, individually and in group sessions, to assist in overcoming dependencies, adjusting to life, and making changes.
- Lead congregations in worship services.
- Maintain case history records and prepare reports.
- Oversee day-to-day group activities of residents in an institution.
- Utilize treatment methods such as psychotherapy, hypnosis, behavior modification, stress reduction therapy, psychodrama, and play therapy.
- Write proposals to obtain government or private funding for projects designed to meet the needs of a community.

What things about you point to this kind of work?

Is it important for you to

- Have work where you do things for other people?
- Plan your work with little supervision?
- Get a feeling of accomplishment?

Have you enjoyed any of the following as a hobby or leisure-time activity?

- Baby-sitting for younger children
- Coaching children or youth in sports activities
- Helping people with disabilities take walks
- Serving as a leader of a scouting or other group
- Serving as a volunteer aide in a hospital, nursing home, or retirement home
- Serving as a volunteer counselor at a youth camp or center
- Teaching in a religious school

Have you liked and done well in any of the following school subjects?

- Human Growth and Development
- Social Problems
- Social Psychology
- Social Work
- Religion
- Rescue
- Abnormal Psychology
- Psychology, Advanced/Specialized
- Public Speaking
- Guidance
- Philosophy

Are you able to

- Communicate information and ideas in speaking so others will understand?
- Listen to and understand information and ideas presented through spoken words and sentences?
- Tell when something is wrong or is likely to go wrong?
- Speak clearly so that it is understandable to a listener?

- Communicate information and ideas in writing so others will understand?
- Read and understand information and ideas presented in writing?

Would you work in places such as

- Government offices?
- Hospitals and nursing homes?
- Schools and homes for people with disabilities?
- Elementary schools?
- High schools?
- Jails and reformatories?
- Factories and plants?
- Business offices?

What skills and knowledges do you need for this kind of work?

For most of these jobs, you need these skills:

- Speaking—talking to others to effectively convey information
- Social Perceptiveness—being aware of others' reactions and understanding why they react the way they do
- Active Listening—listening to what other people are saying and asking questions as appropriate

These knowledges are important in most of these jobs:

- Therapy and Counseling—information and techniques needed to rehabilitate physical and mental ailments and to provide career guidance
- Psychology—human behavior and performance, mental processes, psychological research methods, and the assessment and treatment of behavioral and affective disorders

What else should you consider about this kind of work?

Workers in this group want to make a difference in people's lives, and they often get many satisfactions of that kind, which can offset the occasional failures, bureaucratic roadblocks, people's natural resistance to change, emotionally draining situations, and (in some cases) low pay.

These occupations differ greatly in their hours and working environments. Counseling psychologists and social workers in private practice may have office hours on some evenings for the convenience of their clients, but they usually can balance that by taking off time during the day. On the other hand, clergy, social workers on the public payroll, probation officers, residential advisors, and social and human services workers often must see clients in the evening and/or on weekends, may often be "on call" or work extra hours, and may need to travel to crime-ridden neighborhoods.

Residential advisors often are short-term or part-time workers who are gaining experience and some income before or while they work on a higher degree in a counseling occupation.

In general, the employment outlook in this field is good. For clergy, there is a great need for Roman Catholic priests; opportunities in the other faiths are best outside of cities. Probation officers and correctional treatment specialists, despite tight budgets, will be needed to relieve prison overcrowding. Clinical and counseling psychologists will have mixed opportunities, depending on specialty; those with doctorates will fare best. Managed care is making counseling affordable for more people, but policy on what is covered can change. Private insurance is beginning to cover some services provided by social workers and human services workers; many new jobs will be created in the private sector.

How can you prepare for jobs of this kind?

Work in this group generally requires from two to six or more years of education and/or training.

Most clergy need a bachelor's degree plus some education and training in seminary. Clinical and counseling psychologists need at least a master's in psychology, and in most cases a doctorate plus clinical training is advisable. Social workers generally need a bachelor's in the subject, plus a master's if they want to do counseling.

Probation officers and correctional treatment specialists can sometimes begin with a two-year degree, but a bachelor's is an advantage, and for jobs with the federal government it is necessary. Human services workers usually enter with a two-year degree.

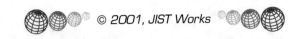

SPECIALIZED TRAINING

JOBS	EDUCATION/TRAINING	WHERE OBTAINED
12.02.01 Social Services: Religious		
All in Social Services: Religious	Foreign Languages; Music; Philosophy; Psychology; Sociology; Comparative Religion; Religious History; Education; Public Speaking	Four-year college, seminary
21-2011.00 Clergy	Missions/Missionary Studies and Misology; Divinity/ Ministry (B.D., M.Div.); Pastoral Counseling and Specialized Ministries; Bible/Biblical Studies	Four-year college, seminary, military (Army, Navy, Air Force)
21-2021.00 Directors, Religious Activities and Education	Missions/Missionary Studies and Misology; Religious Education; Bible/Biblical Studies; Pastoral Counseling and Specialized Ministries	Four-year college, seminary, military (Army, Navy, Air Force)
12.02.02 Social Services: Counseling and Social Work		
All in Social Services: Counseling and Social Work	Psychology; Sociology; Biology; Anthropology; Interviewing Techniques	Four-year college, graduate school
19-3031.02 Clinical Psychologists	Clinical Psychology; Psychology, General; Psychoanalysis; Counseling Psychology	Four-year college, graduate school, clinical training, military (Army, Navy, Air Force)
19-3031.03 Counseling Psychologists	Counselor Education; Counseling and Guidance Services; College/Postsecondary Student Counseling and Personnel Services; Psychology, General; Clinical Psychology; Psychoanalysis; Counseling Psychology	Four-year college, graduate school, clinical training, military (Army, Navy, Air Force)
21-1011.00 Substance Abuse and Behavioral Disorder Counselors	Clinical Psychology; Social Work; Clinical and Medical Social Work; Alcohol/Drug Abuse Counseling; Counseling Psychology	Four-year college, graduate school, military (all branches)
21-1013.00 Marriage and Family Therapists	Social Work; Community Organization, Resources, and Services; Community Health Liaison; Alcohol/ Drug Abuse Counseling; Mental Health Services, Other	Four-year college, graduate school
21-1014.00 Mental Health Counselors	Clinical Psychology; Alcohol/Drug Abuse Counseling; Counseling Psychology; Social Work; Clinical and Medical Social Work	Four-year college, graduate school, military (all branches)
21-1015.00 Rehabilitation Counselors	Social Work; Clinical and Medical Social Work; Community Health Liaison; Alcohol/Drug Abuse Counseling; Mental Health Services, Other	Four-year college, graduate school, clinical training; military data not yet available
21-1021.00 Child, Family, and School Social Workers	Social Work; Community Organization, Resources, and Services	Four-year college, graduate school
21-1022.00 Medical and Public Health Social Workers	Alcohol/Drug Abuse Counseling; Clinical and Medical Social Work; Social Work; Counseling Psychology; Clinical Psychology	Four-year college, graduate school, military (all branches)

(continues)

(continued)

SPECIALIZED TRAINING

JOBS	EDUCATION/TRAINING	WHERE OBTAINED
12.02.02 Social Services: Counseling and Social Work		
21-1023.00 Mental Health and Substance Abuse Social Workers	Clinical and Medical Social Work; Social Work; Clinical Psychology; Alcohol/Drug Abuse Counseling; Counseling Psychology	Four-year college, graduate school, military (all branches)
21-1092.00 Probation Officers and Correctional Treatment Specialists	Social Work	Two-year college, four-year college, military (Army, Navy, Marine Corps)
21-1093.00 Social and Human Service Assistants	Custodial, Housekeeping and Home Services Workers and Managers; Elder Care Provider/Companion; Homemaker's Aide	On the job, two-year college, military (Navy, Air Force, Marine Corps, Coast Guard)
39-9041.00 Residential Advisors	Child Care Provider/Assistant; Child Care Services Manager; Child Care and Guidance Workers and Managers, General	Four-year college, military (Navy)

12.03 Educational Services

Workers in this group do general and specialized teaching, vocational training, and advising about education, career planning, or finances. Some provide library and museum services. Jobs are found in schools, colleges, libraries, and museums.

What kind of work would you do?

Your work activities would depend on your job. For example, you might

- Advise students on academic and vocational curricula.
- Develop and administer tests.
- Direct the research of other teachers or graduate students working for advanced academic degrees.
- Grade examinations and papers.
- Keep attendance records.
- Organize collections of books, publications, documents, audiovisual aids, and other reference materials for convenient access.
- Prepare and deliver lectures to students.

What things about you point to this kind of work?

Is it important for you to

- Have good working conditions?
- Get a feeling of accomplishment?
- Have work where you do things for other people?

Have you enjoyed any of the following as a hobby or leisure-time activity?

- Teaching games to children as a volunteer aide in a nursery school
- Teaching immigrants or other individuals to speak, write, or read English
- Tutoring pupils in school subjects
- Doing public speaking or debating
- Helping members of the family with their English lessons
- Helping out in the school library or other library
- Instructing family members in observing traffic regulations

Have you liked and done well in any of the following school subjects?

- Education
- Guidance
- Physical Science
- Biology
- Foreign Languages

- Psychology
- Human Growth and Development
- Public Speaking
- Child Development/Care

Are you able to

- Communicate information and ideas in speaking so others will understand?
- Read and understand information and ideas presented in writing?
- Speak clearly so that it is understandable to a listener?
- Listen to and understand information and ideas presented through spoken words and sentences?
- Communicate information and ideas in writing so others will understand?

Would you work in places such as

- Elementary schools?
- High schools?
- Kindergartens and day-care centers?
- Colleges and universities?
- Schools and homes for people with disabilities?
- Libraries?
- Laboratories?
- Computer centers?
- Zoos and aquariums?

What skills and knowledges do you need for this kind of work?

For most of these jobs, you need these skills:

- Speaking—talking to others to effectively convey information
- Reading Comprehension—understanding written sentences and paragraphs in work-related documents

These knowledges are important in most of these jobs:

- Education and Training—instructional methods and training techniques including curriculum design principles, learning theory, group and individual teaching techniques, design of individual development plans, and test-design principles
- English Language—the structure and content of the English language, including the meaning and spelling of words, rules of composition, and grammar

What else should you consider about this kind of work?

Almost all of these occupations offer opportunities for part-time or volunteer work. This is often a good way to get experience and decide whether you enjoy the work. Most of these workers take great satisfaction from improving people's lives by opening them to new ideas and skills. These rewards offset the occasional feelings of burnout.

One special reward that many college faculty enjoy is tenure, which means that they cannot be fired without due cause (this is designed to guarantee academic freedom). To qualify, they work under limited-term contracts for several years, during which time they demonstrate their ability at teaching, research, and general contribution to the college. They are evaluated on these matters by a faculty committee, and if they are not granted tenure they usually must find work elsewhere. Public school teachers also may be awarded tenure, based on achievement of a graduate degree and a good record of teaching.

Teachers are employed by school districts, private and parochial schools, and colleges. They teach in classrooms, lecture halls, labs, simulated or real work situations (for example, a garage or kitchen); meet in offices with fellow teachers, parents, students, and administrators; and often correct papers at home on evenings and weekends. Most teachers are hired for only nine months of each year, giving them time to further their education or find summer employment.

The outlook for teachers varies greatly, depending on specialty and location. Best opportunities will be in urban and rural areas, and in special education, math, science, computers, and bilingual education. Adult education also appears to be a growing area. The outlook for college faculty offers keen competition that will gradually ease early in the 21st century as many older faculty retire; in certain disciplines, however, many workers will continue to be hired only as temporary or part-time faculty. There tends to be less competition for college teaching when there are more job openings in industry.

Teacher assistants may help with instruction, often offering one-on-one help with remedial or special education; or they may be limited to noninstructional roles such as monitoring hallways, lunchrooms, and playgrounds, recording grades and attendance, and handling instructional equipment. Some workers do both. The outlook for jobs is very good, partly because of the large turnover in this occupation. The same applies to child-care workers, with an additional boost caused by welfare-to-work legislation.

Many archivists work for corporations and federal and state governments. They generally work a 40-hour week in comfortable surroundings. In museums and archives, the best opportunities will be for those with advanced or dual specialties and those who are skilled with computer applications.

Librarians and library assistants may have to work evenings and/or weekends. Automation is allowing library assistants to do much of the work formerly done by professional librarians, thus improving the job outlook for one occupation at the expense of the other. Best opportunities for professional librarians will be in nontraditional settings such as corporations and consulting firms. Computer skills are a must in this field.

How can you prepare for jobs of this kind?

Occupations in this group usually require education and/or training ranging from four to six years. A few require only two years or less.

Teachers in public schools qualify for their teacher's licenses by getting a bachelor's degree, most often with certain required coursework and with supervised classroom experience. (The same may not apply in some private or parochial schools, and in some states there are procedures by which experienced workers can begin teaching with only a college degree provided they meet other requirements later.) A master's degree is often useful for beginning teachers, especially in some fields such as special education, and it may be a requirement for pay increases or tenure. Vocational teachers are often required to have extensive work experience in their teaching field. A good high school academic record is a helpful beginning for a teaching career, and some states require that teachers accumulate a certain minimal grade-point average while in college.

Educational psychologists and counselors are usually expected to have a master's. College faculty at four-year institutions need to have a doctoral degree in their field, except for temporary or part-time positions. At two-year colleges, a master's degree is usually acceptable, but the pressure of competition makes a doctorate important in most fields.

Requirements vary greatly for child-care workers and preschool teachers. In some states, a Child Development Associate credential is helpful or required. To earn it, you need a high school diploma or its equal, 120 hours of training, and 480 hours of experience, and evaluation by a team of child-care professionals.

SPECIALIZED TRAINING

JOBS	EDUCATION/TRAINING	WHERE OBTAINED
12.03.01 Educational Services: Counseling and Evaluation		
All in Educational Services: Counseling and Evaluation	Psychology; Educational Methods	Four-year college, graduate school
13-2052.00 Personal Financial Advisors	Finance, General; Financial Planning	Work experience in a related occupation, four-year college
19-3031.01 Educational Psychologists	School Psychology; Clinical Psychology; Cognitive Psychology and Psycholinguistics; Social Psychology; Counseling Psychology; Educational Assessment, Testing, and Measurement; Educational Psychology; Psychology, General; Industrial and Organizational Psychology	Four-year college plus graduate school, military (Army, Navy, Air Force)
21-1012.00 Educational, Vocational, and School Counselors	Community and Junior College Administration; School Psychology; College/Postsecondary Student Counseling and Personnel Services; Counselor Education Counseling and Guidance Services; Bilingual/Bicultural Education; Education Administration and Supervision, General; Higher Education Administration	Four-year college plus graduate school, military (Army, Navy, Air Force, Coast Guard)

JOBS	EDUCATION/TRAINING	WHERE OBTAINED
12.03.02 Educational Services: Postsecondary and Adult Teaching and Instructing		
All in Educational Services: Postsecondary and Adult Teaching and Instructing	Research Methods; Educational Methods	Four-year college
25-1011.00 Business Teachers, Postsecondary	Business Education; Entrepreneurship; Business, General; Business Administration and Management; Business Administration and Management, General; Purchasing, Procurement and Contracts Management; Logistics and Materials Management; Operations Management and Supervision; Business Administration and Management, Other; Accounting; Financial Management and Services; Human Resources Management; International Business; Management Information Systems; Marketing Management and Research; Real Estate	Four-year college, graduate school of business; military data not yet available
25-1021.00 Computer Science Teachers, Postsecondary	Business Computer Programming/Programmer; Management Information Systems and Business Data Processing, General; Mathematics and Computer Science; Computer Science; Computer Programming; Information Sciences and Systems; Computer and Information Sciences, General; Business Systems Analysis and Design; Computer Systems Analysis; Business Systems Networking and Telecommunications	Four-year college, plus graduate school, military (Army, Navy, Air Force, Marine Corps)
25-1022.00 Mathematical Science Teachers, Postsecondary	Health and Medical Biostatistics; Biostatistics; Mathematics; Applied Mathematics, General; Operations Research; Mathematical Statistics; Mathematics and Computer Science; Medical Biomathematics and Biometrics; Finance, General; Actuarial Science; Business Statistics	Four-year college plus graduate school, military (Army, Navy, Air Force, Marine Corps)
25-1031.00 Architecture Teachers, Postsecondary	Architectural Design; Architectural History and Theory; Building Structures and Environmental Systems; Site Planning; Construction; Professional Responsibilities and Standards; Cultural, Social, Economic and Environmental Issues Relating to Architectural Practice; Heating and Cooling Systems; Safety and Health Standards; Interior Design Principles and Standards; Site Engineering; Legal Codes and Zoning Development; Environmental Impact; Garden and Landscape Art and Design	Four-year college, graduate school
25-1032.00 Engineering Teachers, Postsecondary	Material Engineering; Industrial/Manufacturing Engineering; Engineering/Industrial Management; Engineering Design; Textile Sciences and Engineering; Systems Engineering; Petroleum Engineering; Engineering Science; Mining and Mineral Engineering; Geophysical Engineering; Mechanical Engineering; Metallurgical Engineering; Materials Science; Ocean Engineering; Polymer/Plastics Engineering; Nuclear Engineering; Naval Architecture and Marine Engineering; Environmental Health Engineering; Architectural Engineering; Engineering-Related Technology/	Four-year college plus graduate school, military (Army, Navy, Air Force, Marine Corps)

(continues)

(continued)

SPECIALIZED TRAINING

JOBS	EDUCATION/TRAINING	WHERE OBTAINED
12.03.02 Educational Services: Postsecondary and Adult Teaching and Instructing		
25-1032.00 Engineering Teachers, Postsecondary *(continued)*	Technician, General; Geological Engineering; Agricultural Engineering; Bioengineering and Biomedical Engineering; Ceramic Sciences and Engineering; Chemical Engineering; Civil Engineering, General; Geotechnical Engineering; Engineering Mechanics; Engineering Physics; Transportation and Highway Engineering; Water Resources Engineering; Computer Engineering; Electrical, Electronics, and Communication Engineering; Engineering, General; Aerospace, Aeronautical, and Astronautical Engineering; Structural Engineering	
25-1041.00 Agricultural Sciences Teachers, Postsecondary	Entomology; Pathology, Human and Animal; Zoology, General; Pharmacology, Human and Animal; Virology; Genetics, Plant and Animal; Physiology, Human and Animal; Neuroscience; Nutritional Sciences; Parasitology; Radiation Biology/Radiobiology; Biometrics; Biological and Physical Sciences; Biotechnology Research; Evolutionary Biology; Biological Immunology; Toxicology; Natural Resources Management and Policy; Plant Protection (Pest Management); Agronomy and Crop Science; Horticulture Science; Plant Breeding and Genetics; Agricultural Plant Pathology; Range Science and Management; Ecology; Environmental Science/Studies; Marine/Aquatic Biology; Agricultural Plant Physiology; Agricultural Animal Nutrition; Agriculture/Agricultural Sciences, General; Animal Sciences, General; Agricultural Animal Breeding and Genetics; Plant Sciences, General; Agricultural Animal Physiology; Dairy Science; Poultry Science; Food Sciences and Technology; Natural Resources Conservation, General; Agricultural Animal Health; Plant Pathology; Botany, General; Soil Sciences; Cell Biology; Biochemistry; Plant Physiology; Biology, General; Biophysics; Microbiology/Bacteriology; Wildlife and Wildlands Management; Fishing and Fisheries Sciences and Management; Forest Management; Forestry Sciences; Molecular Biology; Anatomy; Forestry, General	Four-year college plus graduate school, military (Army, Navy, Air Force, Marine Corps)
25-1042.00 Biological Science Teachers, Postsecondary	Medical Pathology; Epidemiology; Medical Physiology; Basic Medical Sciences, Other; Medical Toxicology; Medical Clinical Sciences (M.S., Ph.D.); Wildlife and Wildlands Management; Marine/Aquatic Biology; Natural Resources Conservation, General; Environmental Science/Studies; Natural Resources Management and Policy; Fishing and Fisheries Sciences and Management; Forestry, General; Range Science and Management; Forest Management; Plant Protection (Pest Management); Biology, General; Biochemistry;	Four-year college plus graduate school, military (Army, Navy, Air Force, Marine Corps)

JOBS	EDUCATION/TRAINING	WHERE OBTAINED
12.03.02 Educational Services: Postsecondary and Adult Teaching and Instructing		
	Biophysics; Botany, General; Plant Pathology; Plant Physiology; Forestry Sciences; Food Sciences and Technology; Agriculture/Agricultural Sciences, General; Animal Sciences, General; Agricultural Animal Breeding and Genetics; Agricultural Animal Health; Agricultural Animal Nutrition; Agricultural Animal Physiology; Soil Sciences; Poultry Science; Microbiology/Bacteriology; Plant Sciences, General; Agronomy and Crop Science; Horticulture Science; Plant Breeding and Genetics; Agricultural Plant Pathology; Agricultural Plant Physiology; Dairy Science; Medical Physics/Biophysics; Physiology, Human and Animal; Biological and Physical Sciences; Biopsychology; Medicine (M.D.); Medical Anatomy; Cell Biology; Medical Biomathematics and Biometrics; Entomology; Medical Cell Biology; Medical Genetics; Medical Immunology; Medical Microbiology; Medical Molecular Biology; Medical Neurobiology; Medical Biochemistry; Genetics, Plant and Animal; Medical Nutrition; Anatomy; Ecology; Neuroscience; Nutritional Sciences; Parasitology; Pharmacology, Human and Animal; Toxicology; Pathology, Human and Animal; Biometrics; Biotechnology Research; Evolutionary Biology; Biological Immunology; Virology; Zoology, General; Molecular Biology	
25-1043.00 Forestry and Conservation Science Teachers, Postsecondary	Evolutionary Biology; Biological and Physical Sciences; Zoology, General; Entomology; Forestry Sciences; Soil Sciences; Natural Resources Conservation, General; Ecology; Natural Resources Management and Policy; Fishing and Fisheries Sciences and Management; Forestry, General; Range Science and Management; Plant Protection (Pest Management); Forest Management; Environmental Science/Studies; Wildlife and Wildlands Management; Biology, General; Botany, General; Agricultural Animal Breeding and Genetics; Biometrics; Marine/Aquatic Biology; Plant Sciences, General; Plant Breeding and Genetics; Genetics, Plant and Animal; Plant Pathology	Four-year college plus graduate school, military (Army, Navy, Air Force, Marine Corps)
25-1051.00 Atmospheric, Earth, Marine, and Space Sciences Teachers, Postsecondary	Geophysics and Seismology; Oceanography; Paleontology; Earth and Planetary Sciences; Geochemistry; Geology; Physical Sciences, General; Metallurgy	Four-year college plus graduate school; military data not yet available
25-1052.00 Chemistry Teachers, Postsecondary	Polymer Chemistry; Physical Sciences, General; Analytical Chemistry; Medicinal/Pharmaceutical Chemistry; Chemistry, General; Physical and Theoretical Chemistry; Inorganic Chemistry; Organic Chemistry	Four-year college plus graduate school, military (Army, Navy, Air Force, Marine Corps)
25-1053.00 Environmental Science Teachers, Postsecondary	Geophysics and Seismology; Oceanography; Paleontology; Earth and Planetary Sciences; Geochemistry; Geology; Physical Sciences, General; Metallurgy	Four-year college plus graduate school; military data not yet available

(continues)

(continued)

SPECIALIZED TRAINING

JOBS	EDUCATION/TRAINING	WHERE OBTAINED
12.03.02 Educational Services: Postsecondary and Adult Teaching and Instructing		
25-1054.00 Physics Teachers, Postsecondary	Nuclear Physics; Biological and Physical Sciences; Plasma and High-Temperature Physics; Physical Sciences, General; Solid State and Low-Temperature Physics; Elementary Particle Physics; Acoustics; Theoretical and Mathematical Physics; Physics, General; Chemical and Atomic/Molecular Physics; Optics	Four-year college plus graduate school, military (Army, Navy, Air Force, Marine Corps)
25-1061.00 Anthropology and Archeology Teachers, Post-secondary	History, General; Demography/Population Studies; Social Sciences, General; Anthropology; Archeology; American Indian/Native American Studies	Four-year college plus graduate school, military (Army, Navy, Air Force, Marine Corps)
25-1062.00 Area, Ethnic, and Cultural Studies Teachers, Postsecondary	Canadian Studies; Demography/Population Studies; Islamic Studies; South Asian Studies; Pacific Area Studies; Afro-American (Black) Studies; American Indian/Native American Studies; Social Sciences, General; Western European Studies; Russian and Slavic Area Studies; Hispanic-American Studies; Southeast Asian Studies; Criminal Justice Studies; Scandinavian Area Studies; Middle Eastern Studies; African Studies; American Studies/Civilization; Political Science, General; Eastern European Area Studies; Women's Studies; European History; East Asian Studies; European Studies; Asian Studies; Peace and Conflict Studies; Economics, General; Jewish/Judaic Studies; Medieval and Renaissance Studies; Urban Affairs/Studies; Science, Technology, and Society; Latin American Studies; Sociology; Asian-American Studies; History, General	Four-year college plus graduate school, military (Army, Navy, Air Force, Marine Corps)
25-1063.00 Economics Teachers, Postsecondary	Economics, General; Applied and Resource Economics; Econometrics and Quantitative Economics; International Economics; Demography/Population Studies; Development Economics and International Development; Agricultural Economics; Urban Affairs/Studies; Agricultural Business and Management, General; Business/Managerial Economics	Four-year college plus graduate school, military (Army, Navy, Air Force, Marine Corps)
25-1064.00 Geography Teachers, Postsecondary	Geography; Cartography	Four-year college plus graduate school; military data not yet available
25-1065.00 Political Science Teachers, Postsecondary	Political Science, General; American Government and Politics; Social Sciences, General; Urban Affairs/Studies; Demography/Population Studies; International Relations and Affairs; Peace and Conflict Studies	Four-year college plus graduate school, military (Army, Navy, Air Force, Marine Corps)
25-1066.00 Psychology Teachers, Postsecondary	Counseling Psychology; Developmental and Child Psychology; Experimental Psychology; Social Sciences, General; Social Psychology; Criminology; Physiological Psychology/Psychobiology; Industrial	Four-year college plus graduate school, military (Army, Navy, Air Force, Marine Corps)

JOBS	EDUCATION/TRAINING	WHERE OBTAINED
12.03.02 Educational Services: Postsecondary and Adult Teaching and Instructing		
	and Organizational Psychology; School Psychology; Psychology, General; Clinical Psychology; Gerontology; Socio-Psychological Sports Studies; Cognitive Psychology and Psycholinguistics; Community Psychology	
25-1067.00 Sociology Teachers, Postsecondary	Sociology; Criminal Justice Studies; Social Sciences, General; Demography/Population Studies; European Studies; Criminology; Corrections/Correctional Administration; Social Psychology; Socio-Psychological Sports Studies; Peace and Conflict Studies; Gerontology	Four-year college plus graduate school, military (Army, Navy, Air Force, Marine Corps)
25-1071.00 Health Specialties Teachers, Postsecondary	Hypnotherapy; Speech-Language Pathology and Audiology; Zoological Medicine; Sign Language Interpreter; Osteopathic Medicine (D.O.); Movement Therapy; Physical Therapy; Veterinary Pathology; Veterinary Medicine (D.V.M.); Veterinary Nutrition; Gerontology; Veterinary Microbiology; Laboratory Animal Medicine; Dance Therapy; Community Health Liaison; Dentistry (D.D.S., D.M.D.); Health and Physical Education, General; Theriogenology; Veterinary Preventive Medicine; Chiropractic (D.C., D.C.M.); Occupational Therapy; Veterinary Practice; Exercise Sciences/Physiology and Movement Studies; Vocational Rehabilitation Counseling; Communication Disorders, General; Veterinary Ophthalmology; Veterinary Surgery; Audiology/Hearing Sciences; Recreational Therapy; Rehabilitation/Therapeutic Services, Other; Veterinary Toxicology; Athletic Training and Sports Medicine; Speech-Language Pathology; Adapted Physical Education/Therapeutic Recreation; Veterinary Radiology; Orthotics/Prosthetics; Music Therapy; Medical Radiologic Technology/Technician; Orthodontics Specialty; Environmental Health; Electrocardiograph Technology/Technician; Psychoanalysis; Public Health, General; Oral Pathology Specialty; Endodontics Specialty; Podiatry (D.P.M., D.P., Pod.D.); Emergency Medical Technology/Technician; Dental Clinical Sciences/Graduate Dentistry (M.S., Ph.D.); Perfusion Technology/Technician; Epidemiology; Respiratory Therapy Technician; Medical Pharmacology and Pharmaceutical Sciences; Dental/Oral Surgery Specialty; Surgical/Operating Room Technician; Diagnostic Medical Sonography; Medical Technology; Psychiatric/Mental Health Services Technician; Clinical and Medical Social Work; Pharmacy (B.Pharm., Pharm.D.); Dental Public Health Specialty; Nuclear Medical Technology/Technician; Occupational Health and Industrial Hygiene; Veterinary Internal Medicine; Veterinary Emergency and Critical Care Medicine; Veterinary Dermatology; Veterinary Clinical Sciences (M.S., Ph.D.); Electroencephalograph Technology/Technician; Dental Hygienist; Optometry (O.D.);	Four-year college plus graduate school, military (Army, Navy, Air Force, Marine Corps)

(continues)

(continued)

SPECIALIZED TRAINING

JOBS	EDUCATION/TRAINING	WHERE OBTAINED
12.03.02 Educational Services: Postsecondary and Adult Teaching and Instructing		
25-1071.00 Health Specialties Teachers, Postsecondary *(continued)*	Veterinary Dentistry; Public Health Education and Promotion; Dental Laboratory Technician; Pedodontics Specialty; Acupuncture and Oriental Medicine; Naturopathic Medicine; Health System/Health Services Administration; Medical Dietician; Prosthodontics Specialty; Hospital/Health Facilities Administration; Health Physics/Radiologic Health; Periodontics Specialty; Physician Assistant; Medical Illustrating; Cardiovascular Technology/Technician; Art Therapy; Veterinary Anesthesiology; Pharmacy Administration and Pharmaceutics	
25-1072.00 Nursing Instructors and Teachers, Postsecondary	Nursing, Surgical (Post–R.N.); Nursing Anesthetist (Post–R.N.); Nursing, Psychiatric/Mental Health (Post–R.N.); Nursing (R.N. Training); Nursing, Pediatric (Post–R.N.); Nursing Science (Post–R.N.); Nursing Midwifery (Post–R.N.); Nursing, Maternal/Child Health (Post–R.N.); Nursing, Adult Health (Post–R.N.); Nursing, Family Practice (Post–R.N.); Nursing, Public Health (Post–R.N.)	Four-year college or nursing school plus graduate school, military (Air Force)
25-1081.00 Education Teachers, Postsecondary	Education, General; Bilingual/Bicultural Education; Curriculum and Instruction; Education Administration and Supervision; Educational/Instructional Media Design; Educational Evaluation, Research and Statistics; International and Comparative Education; Educational Psychology; Social and Philosophical Foundations of Education; Special Education; Student Counseling and Personnel Services; Teacher Education; Teaching English as a Second Language/Foreign Language	Four-year college plus graduate school; military data not yet available
25-1082.00 Library Science Teachers, Postsecondary	Library Science; Library Science/Librarianship; Library Science, Other	Four-year college plus graduate school; military data not yet available
25-1111.00 Criminal Justice and Law Enforcement Teachers, Postsecondary	Criminal Justice and Corrections; Corrections/Correctional Administration; Criminal Justice Studies; Law Enforcement/Police Science; Criminal Justice and Corrections, Other; Fire Services Administration	Four-year college plus graduate school; military data not yet available
25-1112.00 Law Teachers, Postsecondary	Law and Legal Studies; Law (LL.B., J.D.); Juridical Science/Legal Specialization (LL.M., M.C.L., J.S.D./S.); Law and Legal Studies, Other	Four-year college plus law school; military data not yet available
25-1113.00 Social Work Teachers, Postsecondary	Social Work; Public Administration	Four-year college plus graduate school; military data not yet available
25-1121.00 Art, Drama, and Music Teachers, Postsecondary	Ceramics Arts and Ceramics; Acting and Directing; Painting; Playwriting and Screenwriting; Drama/Theater Literature, History and Criticism; Metal and Jewelry Arts; Art History, Criticism, and Conservation; Sculpture; Printmaking; Intermedia; Music Business	Four-year college plus graduate school, military (Army, Navy, Air Force, Marine Corps)

JOBS	EDUCATION/TRAINING	WHERE OBTAINED
12.03.02 Educational Services: Postsecondary and Adult Teaching and Instructing		
	Management and Merchandising; Music—Voice and Choral/Opera Performance; Drawing; Fiber, Textile, and Weaving Arts; Arts Management; Film/Cinema Studies; Fine/Studio Arts; Art, General; Photography; Music History and Literature; Film-Video Making/Cinematography and Production; Technical Theater/Theater Design and Stagecraft; Music—Piano and Organ Performance; Music Theory and Composition; Music Conducting; Dance; Music—General Performance; Crafts, Folk Art, and Artisanry; Drama/Theater Arts, General; Music, General; Musicology and Ethnomusicology	
25-1122.00 Communications Teachers, Postsecondary	Communications, General; Advertising; Journalism and Mass Communications; Public Relations and Organizational Communications; Radio and Television Broadcasting; Communications, Other	Four-year college plus graduate school; military data not yet available
25-1123.00 English Language and Literature Teachers, Postsecondary	Comparative Literature; English Technical and Business Writing; English Language and Literature, General; English Composition; English Literature (British and Commonwealth); Linguistics; English Creative Writing; American Literature (United States); Speech and Rhetorical Studies; Journalism	Four-year college plus graduate school, military (Army, Navy, Air Force, Marine Corps)
25-1124.00 Foreign Language and Literature Teachers, Postsecondary	Chinese Language and Literature; Germanic Languages and Literatures, Other; Scandinavian Languages and Literatures; German Language and Literature; Greek Language and Literature (Modern); South Asian Languages and Literatures; French Language and Literature; Italian Language and Literature; Portuguese Language and Literature; Spanish Language and Literature; East European Languages and Literatures, Other; Slavic Languages and Literatures (Other Than Russian); Russian Language and Literature; Classics and Classical Languages and Literatures; Japanese Language and Literature; Romance Languages and Literatures, Other; Arabic Language and Literature; Hebrew Language and Literature; Middle Eastern Languages and Literatures, Other; Greek Language and Literature (Ancient and Medieval); Foreign Language Interpretation and Translation; Latin Language and Literature (Ancient and Medieval); Classical and Ancient Near Eastern Languages and Literatures; Comparative Literature; Linguistics; East and Southeast Asian Languages and Literatures, Other; Foreign Languages and Literatures, General	Four-year college plus graduate school, military (Army, Navy, Air Force, Marine Corps)
25-1125.00 History Teachers, Postsecondary	American (United States) History; History, General; Latin American Studies; Scandinavian Area Studies; Middle Eastern Studies; Eastern European Area Studies; Pacific Area Studies; Demography/Population Studies; Russian and Slavic Area Studies; Archeology; Urban	Four-year college plus graduate school, military (Army, Navy, Air Force, Marine Corps)

(continues)

(continued)

SPECIALIZED TRAINING

JOBS	EDUCATION/TRAINING	WHERE OBTAINED
12.03.02 Educational Services: Postsecondary and Adult Teaching and Instructing		
25-1125.00 History Teachers, Postsecondary *(continued)*	Affairs/Studies; African Studies; European Studies; American Studies/Civilization; European History; Asian Studies; Public/Applied History and Archival Administration; East Asian Studies; History and Philosophy of Science and Technology; Medieval and Renaissance Studies; Jewish/Judaic Studies; Asian-American Studies; Women's Studies; Science, Technology, and Society; Western European Studies; South Asian Studies; Southeast Asian Studies; Criminal Justice Studies; Islamic Studies; Canadian Studies; Hispanic-American Studies; Afro-American (Black) Studies; American Indian/Native American Studies	
25-1126.00 Philosophy and Religion Teachers, Postsecondary	Philosophy; Religion/Religious Studies; Philosophy and Religion, Other	Four-year college plus graduate school or seminary; military data not yet available
25-1191.00 Graduate Teaching Assistants	Bachelor's degree in a relevant field	Four-year college
25-1192.00 Home Economics Teachers, Postsecondary	Home Economics, General; Business Home Economics; Home Economics Communications; Family and Community Studies; Foods and Nutrition Studies; Housing Studies; Individual and Family Development Studies; Clothing/Apparel and Textile Studies; Home Economics, Other	Four-year college plus graduate school; military data not yet available
25-1193.00 Recreation and Fitness Studies Teachers, Postsecondary	Parks, Recreation, and Leisure Studies; Parks, Recreation, and Leisure Facilities Management; Health and Physical Education/Fitness; Parks, Recreation, Leisure, and Fitness Studies, Other; Leisure and Recreational Activities	Four-year college plus graduate school; military data not yet available
25-1194.00 Vocational Education Teachers, Postsecondary	Business Teacher Education (Vocational); Law Enforcement/Police Science; Education Administration and Supervision, General; Educational Supervision; Education, General; Teacher Education, Multiple Levels; Home Economics Teacher Education (Vocational); Adult and Continuing Teacher Education; Agricultural Teacher Education (Vocational); Watch, Clock, and Jewelry Repairer; Technical Teacher Education (Vocational); Trade and Industrial Teacher Education (Vocational); Health Occupations Teacher Education (Vocational); Marketing Operations Teacher Education/Marketing and Distribution Teacher; Aircraft Mechanic/Technician, Powerplant; Truck, Bus, and Other Commercial Vehicle Operator; Human Resources Management; Agricultural and Food Products Processing Operations and Management; Secondary Teacher Education	Work experience in a related occupation, four-year college, graduate school, military (all branches)

JOBS	EDUCATION/TRAINING	WHERE OBTAINED
12.03.02 Educational Services: Postsecondary and Adult Teaching and Instructing		
25-3011.00 Adult Literacy, Remedial Education, and GED Teachers and Instructors	Teacher Education, Multiple Levels; Teaching English as a Second Language/Foreign Language; Adult and Continuing Teacher Education; Bilingual/Bicultural Education; Education, General	Work experience in a related occupation, four-year college, graduate school, military (Navy, Air Force, Marine Corps, Coast Guard)
25-3021.00 Self-Enrichment Education Teachers	Acting and Directing; Drama/Theater Arts, General; Fire Science/Firefighting; Music—General Performance; Teaching English as a Second Language/Foreign Language; Teacher Education, Specific Academic and Vocational Programs; Music, General; Marketing Operations Teacher Education/Marketing and Distribution Teacher Education; Education, General; Drama and Dance Teacher Education; Music Teacher Education; Art Teacher Education; Bilingual/Bicultural Education; Adult and Continuing Teacher Education; Driver and Safety Teacher Education; Teacher Education, Multiple Levels	Work experience in a related occupation, four-year college, graduate school, military (Navy, Air Force, Marine Corps, Coast Guard)
25-9021.00 Farm and Home Management Advisors	Agricultural Supplies Retailing and Wholesaling; Agricultural Teacher Education (Vocational); Animal Sciences, General; Agricultural Business and Management, General; Agricultural Production Workers and Managers, General; Agricultural Animal Husbandry and Production Management; Crop Production Operations and Management; Education, General; Agricultural Animal Nutrition; Agricultural Extension; Farm and Ranch Management; Clothing/Apparel and Textile Studies; Foods and Nutrition Studies, General; Dietetics/Human Nutritional Services; Home Economics Teacher Education (Vocational)	Four-year college, graduate school
12.03.03 Educational Services: Preschool, Elementary, and Secondary Teaching and Instructing		
All in Educational Services: Preschool, Elementary, and Secondary Teaching and Instructing	Educational Methods	Education courses in four-year college, teaching experience
25-2011.00 Preschool Teachers, Except Special Education	Art Teacher Education; Teacher Education, Multiple Levels; Pre-Elementary/Early Childhood/Kindergarten Teacher Education; Educational Supervision; Education Administration and Supervision, General; Education, General; Bilingual/Bicultural Education; Child Care Services Manager; Child Care and Guidance Workers and Managers, General; Speech Teacher Education; Drama and Dance Teacher Education; English Teacher Education; Reading Teacher Education; Physical Education Teaching and Coaching; Music Teacher Education	Two-year college, four-year college
25-2012.00 Kindergarten Teachers, Except Special Education	Education Administration and Supervision, General; Physical Education Teaching and Coaching; Music Teacher Education; Drama and Dance Teacher Education; Mathematics Teacher Education; English Teacher	Four-year college, graduate school

(continues)

(continued)

SPECIALIZED TRAINING

JOBS	EDUCATION/TRAINING	WHERE OBTAINED
12.03.03 Educational Services: Preschool, Elementary, and Secondary Teaching and Instructing		
25-2021.00 Kindergarten Teachers, Except Special Education *(continued)*	Education; Teacher Education, Multiple Levels; Pre-Elementary/Early Childhood/Kindergarten Teacher Education; Reading Teacher Education; Educational Supervision; Bilingual/Bicultural Education; Speech Teacher Education; Art Teacher Education; Education, General	
25-2021.00 Elementary School Teachers, Except Special Education	Music Teacher Education; Health Teacher Education; Foreign Languages Teacher Education; English Teacher Education; Art Teacher Education; Social Science Teacher Education; Spanish Language Teacher Education; History Teacher Education; German Language Teacher Education; French Language Teacher Education; Drama and Dance Teacher Education; Social Studies Teacher Education; Science Teacher Education, General; Reading Teacher Education; Physical Education Teaching and Coaching; Education Administration and Supervision, General; Mathematics Teacher Education; Teacher Education, Multiple Levels; Computer Teacher Education; Educational Supervision; Speech Teacher Education; Bilingual/Bicultural Education; Education, General; Elementary Teacher Education; Teacher Education, Specific Academic and Vocational Programs	Four-year college, graduate school
25-2022.00 Middle School Teachers, Except Special and Vocational Education	Teacher Education, Specific Academic and Vocational Programs; Secondary Teacher Education; Junior High/ Intermediate/Middle School Teacher Education; Teacher Education, Multiple Levels; Spanish Language Teacher Education; Speech Teacher Education; German Language Teacher Education; Education Administration and Supervision, General; Educational Supervision; Health Teacher Education; French Language Teacher Education; Drama and Dance Teacher Education; English Teacher Education; Driver and Safety Teacher Education; Art Teacher Education; Education, General; Science Teacher Education, General; Social Studies Teacher Education; Reading Teacher Education; Social Science Teacher Education; Physical Education Teaching and Coaching; Music Teacher Education; Mathematics Teacher Education; Bilingual/Bicultural Education; History Teacher Education; Physics Teacher Education; Chemistry Teacher Education; Biology Teacher Education; Foreign Languages Teacher Education; Computer Teacher Education	Four-year college, graduate school, military (Navy, Air Force)
25-2023.00 Vocational Education Teachers, Middle School	Teacher Education, Specific Academic and Vocational Programs; Education, General; Educational Supervision; Health Occupations Teacher Education (Vocational); Bilingual/Bicultural Education; Education	Four-year college, graduate school, military (Navy, Air Force)

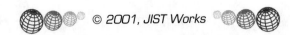

JOBS	EDUCATION/TRAINING	WHERE OBTAINED
12.03.03 Educational Services: Preschool, Elementary, and Secondary Teaching and Instructing		
	Administration and Supervision, General; Junior High/Intermediate/Middle School Teacher Education; Technical Teacher Education (Vocational); Marketing Operations Teacher Education/Marketing and Distribution Teacher Education; Trade and Industrial Teacher Education (Vocational); Computer Teacher Education; Teacher Education, Multiple Levels; Agricultural Teacher Education (Vocational); Technology Teacher Education/Industrial Arts Teacher Education; Home Economics Teacher Education (Vocational); Business Teacher Education (Vocational)	
25-2031.00 Secondary School Teachers, Except Special and Vocational Education	Speech Teacher Education; French Language Teacher Education; Spanish Language Teacher Education; Physics Teacher Education; German Language Teacher Education; Teacher Education, Specific Academic and Vocational Programs; History Teacher Education; Education Administration and Supervision, General; Physical Education Teaching and Coaching; Educational Supervision; Music Teacher Education; Mathematics Teacher Education; Secondary Teacher Education; Science Teacher Education, General; Teacher Education, Multiple Levels; Reading Teacher Education; Art Teacher Education; Health Teacher Education; Driver and Safety Teacher Education; Foreign Languages Teacher Education; English Teacher Education; Biology Teacher Education; Social Science Teacher Education; Computer Teacher Education; Chemistry Teacher Education; Education, General; Drama and Dance Teacher Education; Social Studies Teacher Education; Bilingual/Bicultural Education	Four-year college, graduate school, military (Navy, Air Force)
25-2032.00 Vocational Education Teachers, Secondary School	Home Economics Teacher Education (Vocational); Technology Teacher Education/Industrial Arts Teacher Education; Computer Teacher Education; Trade and Industrial Teacher Education (Vocational); Technical Teacher Education (Vocational); Marketing Operations Teacher Education/Marketing and Distribution Teacher Education; Secondary Teacher Education; Bilingual/Bicultural Education; Education Administration and Supervision, General; Educational Supervision; Education, General; Health Occupations Teacher Education (Vocational); Teacher Education, Specific Academic and Vocational Programs; Agricultural Teacher Education (Vocational); Business Teacher Education (Vocational); Teacher Education, Multiple Levels	Four-year college, graduate school, military (Navy, Air Force)
25-2041.00 Special Education Teachers, Preschool, Kindergarten, and Elementary School	Special Education, General; Education of the Deaf and Hearing Impaired; Education of the Gifted and Talented; Education of the Emotionally Handicapped; Education of the Mentally Handicapped; Education of the Multiple Handicapped; Education of the Physically Handicapped; Education of the Blind and Visually	Four-year college, graduate school; military data not available

(continues)

(continued)

SPECIALIZED TRAINING

JOBS	EDUCATION/TRAINING	WHERE OBTAINED
12.03.03 Educational Services: Preschool, Elementary, and Secondary Teaching and Instructing		
25-2041.00 Special Education Teachers, Preschool, Kindergarten, and Elementary School *(continued)*	Handicapped; Education of the Specific Learning Disabled; Education of the Speech Impaired; Education of the Autistic; Special Education, Other	
25-2042.00 Special Education Teachers, Middle School	Special Education, General; Education of the Deaf and Hearing Impaired; Education of the Gifted and Talented; Education of the Emotionally Handicapped; Education of the Mentally Handicapped; Education of the Multiple Handicapped; Education of the Physically Handicapped; Education of the Blind and Visually Handicapped; Education of the Specific Learning Disabled; Education of the Speech Impaired; Education of the Autistic; Special Education, Other	Four-year college, graduate school; military data not available
25-2043.00 Special Education Teachers, Secondary School	Special Education, General; Education of the Deaf and Hearing Impaired; Education of the Gifted and Special Education, General; Education of the Deaf and Talented; Education of the Emotionally Handicapped; Education of the Mentally Handicapped; Education of the Multiple Handicapped; Education of the Physically Handicapped; Education of the Blind and Visually Handicapped; Education of the Specific Learning Disabled; Education of the Speech Impaired; Education of the Autistic; Special Education, Other	Four-year college, graduate school; military data not available
25-9041.00 Teacher Assistants	Education, General; Bilingual/Bicultural Education; Teacher Assistant/Aide	On the job, two-year college, four-year college
39-9011.00 Child Care Workers	Child Care and Guidance Workers and Managers, General; Child Care Provider/Assistant	On the job, vocational school, community college
12.03.04 Educational Services: Library and Museum		
All in Educational Services: Library and Museum	Research Methods	Two-year college, four-year college, on the job
25-4011.00 Archivists	Museology/Museum Studies; Public/Applied History and Archival Administration; History, General; Art History, Criticism and Conservation; Art, General	Four-year college plus graduate school
25-4012.00 Curators	Education, General; Curriculum and Instruction; Educational/Instructional Media Design; Museology/Museum Studies; History, General; Art, General; Art History, Criticism and Conservation; Public/Applied History and Archival Administration	Four-year college plus graduate school

JOBS	EDUCATION/TRAINING	WHERE OBTAINED
12.03.04 Educational Services: Library and Museum		
25-4013.00 Museum Technicians and Conservators	Public/Applied History and Archival Administration; Ceramics Arts and Ceramics; Art History, Criticism and Conservation; History, General; Art, General; Museology/Museum Studies; Crafts, Folk Art, and Artisanry	Four-year college plus graduate school
25-4021.00 Librarians	Library Science/Librarianship; Educational/ Instructional Media Design	Four-year college plus graduate school, military (Army, Navy, Air Force)
25-4031.00 Library Technicians	Library Assistant	On the job, two-year college
25-9011.00 Audio-Visual Collections Specialists	Educational/Instructional Media Technology/ Technician; Educational/Instructional Media Design	On the job, four-year college, military (all branches)
43-4121.00 Library Assistants, Clerical	Administrative Assistant/Secretarial Science, General; General Office/Clerical and Typing Services; Library Assistant	On the job, trade/technical school

13 General Management and Support

An interest in making an organization run smoothly.

You can satisfy this interest by working in a position of leadership, or by specializing in a function that contributes to the overall effort. The organization may be a profit-making business, a nonprofit, or a government agency. If you especially enjoy working with people, you may find fulfillment from working in human resources. An interest in numbers may cause you to consider accounting, finance, budgeting, or purchasing. Or perhaps you would enjoy managing the organization's physical resources (for example, land, buildings, equipment, and utilities).

13.01 General Management Work and Management of Support Functions

13.02 Management Support

13.01 General Management Work and Management of Support Functions

Workers in this group are top-level and middle-level administrators who direct, through lower-level personnel, all or part of the activities in business establishments, government agencies, and labor unions. They set policies, make important decisions, and determine priorities. They use a variety of skills, including math, critical thinking, communications, insight into human nature, and computer applications. They have a good knowledge of how their industry operates and what laws and regulations they must follow.

What kind of work would you do?

Your work activities would depend on your job. For example, you might

- Analyze and classify risks as to the frequency and financial impact of risks on a company.
- Direct and coordinate the activities of a business involved with buying and selling investment products and financial services.
- Examine, evaluate, and process loan applications.
- Formulate, implement, and interpret policies and procedures.
- Arrange and direct funeral services.
- Search public records for transactions such as sales, leases, and assessments.
- Transfer or discharge employees according to work performance.
- Plan work activities and prepare schedules.
- Settle claims for property or crop damage.

What things about you point to this kind of work?

Is it important for you to

- Give directions and instructions to others?
- Plan your work with little supervision?
- Have good working conditions?

Have you enjoyed any of the following as a hobby or leisure-time activity?

- Balancing checkbooks for family members
- Budgeting the family income
- Helping run a school or community fair or carnival
- Planning and arranging programs for school or community organizations
- Reading business magazines and newspapers
- Serving as a leader of a scouting or other group
- Serving as president of a club or other organization
- Serving as treasurer of a club or other organization

Have you liked and done well in any of the following school subjects?

- Management
- Accounting
- Personnel Management
- Finance
- Labor and Industry
- Business Analysis
- Business Law
- Business Organization
- Business Writing
- Arbitration/Negotiation
- Operations Management

Are you able to

- Communicate information and ideas in speaking so others will understand?
- Listen to and understand information and ideas presented through spoken words and sentences?
- Read and understand information and ideas presented in writing?
- Communicate information and ideas in writing so others will understand?
- Speak clearly so that it is understandable to a listener?
- Tell when something is wrong or is likely to go wrong?
- Apply general rules to specific problems to come up with logical answers?

Would you work in places such as

- Business offices?
- Government offices?

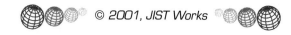

What skills and knowledges do you need for this kind of work?

For most of these jobs, you need these skills:

- Speaking—talking to others to effectively convey information
- Coordination—adjusting actions in relation to others' actions
- Reading Comprehension—understanding written sentences and paragraphs in work-related documents
- Management of Personnel Resources—motivating, developing, and directing people as they work, identifying the best people for the job
- Writing—communicating effectively with others in writing as indicated by their needs
- Information Gathering—knowing how to find information and identifying essential information

These knowledges are important in most of these jobs:

- Administration and Management—principles and processes involved in business and organizational planning, coordination, and execution
- Mathematics—numbers, their operations, and interrelationships including arithmetic, algebra, geometry, calculus, statistics, and their applications
- Personnel and Human Resources—policies and practices involved in personnel/human resource functions

What else should you consider about this kind of work?

Many jobs in this group are found in large cities, or in towns that are county seats, are state capitals, or have industrial parks.

Some of these workers play managerial roles within businesses and industries of all kinds. Others manage a particular type of business, such as a funeral home or community association. Some jobs are with local, state, and federal government agencies.

In a few jobs, well-trained beginners are given consideration. This is more likely to happen in small businesses than in large ones. In most companies and government agencies, people start out in lower-level positions and work their way up.

Workers in this group have heavy responsibilities. They may have to work long hours to meet specific situations or to solve problems such as shortages of materials or financial losses. They may have to travel to distant parts of the country or to foreign countries to attend meetings and conduct business. In order to move up the promotion ladder, these workers sometimes change employers and therefore must relocate.

The overall outlook for this group is for many opportunities (with ups and downs caused by economic trends) but keen competition. For managers of specific businesses, the outlook depends on the particular industry. Best opportunities will be for those with graduate degrees and those who are skilled with computers and verbal and written communication.

How can you prepare for jobs of this kind?

Occupations in this group usually require education and/or training ranging from two years to more than ten years. Most jobs in this group call for experience in related positions, usually within the same industry or specialization. Degrees in business administration or law provide preparation for many jobs in this group. However, some administrative jobs require training and experience in such fields as engineering, chemistry, or sociology. Liberal arts graduates who take advantage of opportunities for management training or coursework sometimes parlay their communications and critical thinking skills into a very successful career. College coursework in the following subjects is helpful: management, business law, business math, speech or public speaking, government, finance, accounting, economics, history, and English (especially writing).

Some businesses offer management-trainee programs to advance employees to management positions. Some employers accept inexperienced college graduates with business degrees and place them in these training programs.

SPECIALIZED TRAINING

JOBS	EDUCATION/TRAINING	WHERE OBTAINED
13.01.01 General Management Work and Management of Support Functions		
All in General Management Work and Management of Support Functions	Experience; Budgeting; Personnel; Oral and Written Communications	Four-year college, graduate school of business
11-1011.01 Government Service Executives	Counseling Psychology; Alcohol/Drug Abuse Counseling; General Retailing Operations; Hospitality/Administration Management; Environmental Health; Community Health Liaison; Arts Management; Art, General; International Relations and Affairs; International Economics; Development Economics and International Development; Economics, General; Public Administration; Community Organization, Resources and Services; Fire Services Administration; Law Enforcement/Police Science; Corrections/Correctional Administration; Parks, Recreation, and Leisure Facilities Management; Wildlife and Wildlands Management; Natural Resources Law Enforcement and Protective Services; Environmental Science/Studies; Natural Resources Conservation, General; Range Science and Management; Plant Sciences, General; Business Administration and Management, General; Criminal Justice/Law Enforcement Administration	Work experience in a related occupation, four-year college, graduate school of business, military (all branches)
11-1011.02 Private Sector Executives	General Retailing Operations; Business Administration and Management, General; Enterprise Management and Operation, General; Finance, General; Investments and Securities	Work experience in a related occupation, four-year college, graduate school of business, military (Army, Navy, Air Force, Marine Corps)
11-1021.00 General and Operations Managers	Public Administration and Services, Other; Public Policy Analysis; Community Organization, Resources and Services; Public Administration; Arts Management; Business Administration and Management, General; Enterprise Management and Operation, General; International Business	Work experience in a related occupation, four-year college, graduate school of business
11-1031.00 Legislators	Public Administration and Services, Other; Public Policy Analysis; Community Organization, Resources and Services; Public Administration	Work experience in a related occupation, four-year college
11-2031.00 Public Relations Managers	Public Relations and Organizational Communications; Business Administration and Management, General; Advertising; Marketing Management and Research, Other; International Business Marketing; Marketing Research; Business Marketing and Marketing Management; Apparel and Accessories Marketing Operations, General; Arts Management; Vehicle Marketing Operations; Hotel/Motel Services Marketing Operations; Business Services Marketing Operations; Fashion Merchandising	Work experience in a related occupation, four-year college, graduate school of business

(continues)

SPECIALIZED TRAINING

JOBS	EDUCATION/TRAINING	WHERE OBTAINED
13.01.01 General Management Work and Management of Support Functions		
11-3031.00 Financial Managers	Finance, General; International Finance; Investments and Securities; Public Finance; Financial Management and Services, Other	Work experience in a related occupation, four-year college, graduate school of business
11-3031.01 Treasurers, Controllers, and Chief Financial Officers	Investments and Securities; Finance, General	Work experience in a related occupation, four-year college, graduate school of business, military (all branches)
11-3031.02 Financial Managers, Branch or Department	Finance, General; Investments and Securities	Work experience in a related occupation, four-year college, graduate school of business
11-3040.00 Human Resources Managers	Labor/Personnel Relations and Studies; Human Resources Management	Work experience in a related occupation, four-year college, graduate school of business, military (all branches)
11-3041.00 Compensation and Benefits Managers	Labor/Personnel Relations and Studies; Human Resources Management	Work experience in a related occupation, four-year college, graduate school of business, military (all branches)
11-3042.00 Training and Development Managers	Human Resources Management; Public Administration	Work experience in a related occupation, four-year college, graduate school, military (Navy, Air Force, Marine Corps, Coast Guard)
11-3061.00 Purchasing Managers	Purchasing, Procurement, and Contracts Management; Business Administration and Management, General; General Retailing Operations	Work experience in a related occupation, four-year college, graduate school of business, military (Army, Navy, Air Force, Coast Guard)
11-3071.02 Storage and Distribution Managers	International Business; Business Administration and Management, General; General Distribution Operations; International Business Marketing	Work experience in a related occupation, four-year college, graduate school of business, military (all branches)
11-9061.00 Funeral Directors	Funeral Services and Mortuary Science	On the job, two-year college, four-year college, trade/technical school, apprenticeship
11-9131.00 Postmasters and Mail Superintendents	Public Administration; Business Administration and Management, General	Work experience in a related occupation, four-year college, graduate school of business, military (Navy, Marine Corps)
11-9141.00 Property, Real Estate, and Community Association Managers	Real Estate	Four-year college, graduate school of business, military (Marine Corps)

13.02 Management Support

Workers in this group plan, manage, analyze, evaluate, and make decisions about personnel, purchases, and financial transactions and records. They use mathematics, logic, psychology, computerized tools, and knowledge of industry practices and government regulations that apply to their specific fields. They provide information and recommendations that help higher management accomplish the goals of the organization. They supervise clerical and sometimes technical staff that support them.

What kind of work would you do?

Your work activities would depend on your job. For example, you might

- Arrange for employee physical examinations, first aid, and other medical attention.
- Collect data on customer preferences and buying habits.
- Conduct staff meetings with sales personnel to introduce new merchandise.
- Interview job applicants to select people who meet employer qualifications.
- Maintain records of business transactions.
- Supervise clerical or administrative personnel.

What things about you point to this kind of work?

Is it important for you to

- Have good working conditions?
- Be treated fairly by the company?
- Make decisions on your own?

Have you enjoyed any of the following as a hobby or leisure-time activity?

- Balancing checkbooks for family members
- Buying large quantities of food or other products for an organization
- Budgeting the family income
- Reading business magazines and newspapers
- Serving as a volunteer interviewer in a social-service organization
- Serving as treasurer of a club or other organization
- Using a pocket calculator or spreadsheet to figure income and expenses for an organization

Have you liked and done well in any of the following school subjects?

- Business Organization
- Accounting
- Auditing Procedures
- Business Analysis
- Business Writing
- Personnel Management
- Data Applications
- Business Law
- Money and Banking

Are you able to

- Read and understand information and ideas presented in writing?
- Communicate information and ideas in speaking so others will understand?
- Listen to and understand information and ideas presented through spoken words and sentences?
- Communicate information and ideas in writing so others will understand?
- Add, subtract, multiply, or divide quickly and correctly?
- Understand and organize a problem and then select a mathematical method or formula to solve the problem?
- See details of objects at close range (within a few feet)?

Would you work in places such as

- Business offices?
- Government offices?
- Farms?
- Factories and plants?

What skills and knowledges do you need for this kind of work?

For most of these jobs, you need these skills:

- Information Gathering—knowing how to find information and identifying essential information
- Judgment and Decision Making—weighing the relative costs and benefits of a potential action

- Reading Comprehension—understanding written sentences and paragraphs in work-related documents

These knowledges are important in most of these jobs:

- Mathematics—numbers, their operations, and interrelationships including arithmetic, algebra, geometry, calculus, statistics, and their applications
- Economics and Accounting—economic and accounting principles and practices, financial markets, banking, and the analysis and reporting of financial data

What else should you consider about this kind of work?

Most of the jobs in this group are in and around large cities. All kinds of businesses and industries hire these workers. In some fields it is common to work for several clients simultaneously or one after the other, either as a self-employed professional or as a contractor working for a consulting firm.

In most of these fields there are many openings for new workers when the economy is not on a downturn. Most new workers start as trainees, but in many jobs they can advance rapidly. However, in many specializations automation is allowing clerical and higher-level staff to handle some tasks that used to be assigned to middle managers. Therefore, best opportunities will be for those who have skills with computer-based applications and also have the interpersonal and communications skills required for advancement. Workers may not have long-term security with one company, but those with up-to-date skills and flexibility will remain employable.

Some of the people in government jobs are elected or appointed to office. Others must pass civil-service tests.

In some specialties, frequent travel or occasional overtime work is required.

How can you prepare for jobs of this kind?

Occupations in this group usually require education and/or training ranging from four years to more than ten years. For some human resource jobs, two years may be acceptable but not preferable. Work experience is a major consideration in preparing for jobs in this group. Experience in related positions for the same employer is often required. However, courses in accounting, human resources, business law, economics, investments, writing, math, government, and computer science are helpful. Some of these courses are available in high schools, but most are offered by business schools, colleges, and graduate schools of business.

SPECIALIZED TRAINING

JOBS	EDUCATION/TRAINING	WHERE OBTAINED
13.02.01 Management Support: Human Resources		
All in Management Support: Human Resources	Human Resources Management; Speech Communication	Four-year college, two-year college, business school
13-1071.01 Employment Interviewers, Private or Public Employment Service	Human Resources Management	Four-year college, business school, two-year college, military (Navy, Air Force, Marine Corps)
13-1071.02 Personnel Recruiters	Human Resources Management; Education, General; Education Administration and Supervision, General; Elementary, Middle, and Secondary Education Administration; Educational Statistics and Research Methods; Educational Evaluation and Research; Educational Assessment, Testing, and Measurement	Four-year college, business school, two-year college, military (all branches)
13-1072.00 Compensation, Benefits, and Job Analysis Specialists	Human Resources Management	Four-year college, graduate school, military (Army, Navy, Air Force, Coast Guard)

JOBS	EDUCATION/TRAINING	WHERE OBTAINED
13.02.01 Management Support: Human Resources		
13-1073.00 Training and Development Specialists	Adult and Continuing Education Administration; Public Administration; Education Administration and Supervision, General; Human Resources Management	Four-year college, graduate school
13.02.02 Management Support: Purchasing		
All in Management Support: Purchasing	Oral and Written Communications; Algebra; Accounting; Budgeting; Spreadsheet Applications	Four-year college, graduate school of business
13-1021.00 Purchasing Agents and Buyers, Farm Products	International Business Marketing; Agricultural Animal Husbandry and Production Management; Agricultural Supplies Retailing and Wholesaling; Forest Harvesting and Production Technology/Technician; General Selling Skills and Sales Operations; Agricultural Production Workers and Managers, General; General Buying Operations	Four-year college, graduate school of business, military (all branches)
13-1022.00 Wholesale and Retail Buyers, Except Farm Products	Home Furnishings and Equipment Installers and Consultants, General; Agricultural Supplies Retailing and Wholesaling; General Buying Operations; International Business Marketing; Fashion and Fabric Consultant; Clothing, Apparel, and Textile Workers and Managers, General; General Retailing Operations	Four-year college, graduate school of business
13-1023.00 Purchasing Agents, Except Wholesale, Retail, and Farm Products	Institutional Food Services Administrator; Agricultural Supplies Retailing and Wholesaling; Institutional Food Workers and Administrators, General; Business Administration and Management, General; Purchasing, Procurement and Contracts Management; General Buying Operations	Four-year college, graduate school of business
13.02.03 Management Support: Accounting and Auditing		
All in Management Support: Accounting and Auditing	Accounting; Oral and Written Communications; Algebra; Budgeting; Spreadsheet Applications	Four-year college, graduate school of business
13-2011.00 Accountants and Auditors	Accounting; Taxation	Four-year college, graduate school of business; military data not yet available
13-2011.01 Accountants	Accounting	Four-year college, graduate school of business, military (all branches)
13-2011.02 Auditors	Accounting; Finance, General	Four-year college, graduate school of business, military (all branches)
13-2081.00 Tax Examiners, Collectors, and Revenue Agents	Accounting	Four-year college, graduate school of business

(continues)

(continued)

SPECIALIZED TRAINING

JOBS	EDUCATION/TRAINING	WHERE OBTAINED
13.02.04 Management Support: Investigation and Analysis		
All in Management Support: Investigation and Analysis	Accounting; Oral and Written Communications; Algebra; Budgeting; Spreadsheet Applications	Four-year college, graduate school of business
13-1031.01 Claims Examiners, Property and Casualty Insurance	Insurance and Risk Management; Finance, General	Four-year college, two-year college
13-1031.02 Insurance Adjusters, Examiners, and Investigators	Real Estate; Insurance Marketing Operations; Finance, General; Insurance and Risk Management; Banking and Financial Support Services	On the job, two-year college, business college
13-1032.00 Insurance Appraisers, Auto Damage	Insurance Marketing Operations	On the job, two-year college, business college
13-1051.00 Cost Estimators	Business Administration and Management, General; Purchasing, Procurement, and Contracts Management	Work experience in a related occupation, two-year college, trade/technical school, military (Navy)
13-1081.00 Logisticians	Engineering/Industrial Management; Logistics and Materials Management	Two-year college, four-year college
13-1111.00 Management Analysts	Business Administration and Management, General	Four-year college plus graduate school of business, military (all branches)
13-2021.00 Appraisers and Assessors of Real Estate	Real Estate	Work experience in a related occupation, four-year college
13-2021.01 Assessors	Real Estate	Work experience in a related occupation, four-year college
13-2021.02 Appraisers, Real Estate	Real Estate	Work experience in a related occupation, four-year college, graduate school of business
13-2031.00 Budget Analysts	Finance, General; Accounting; Non-Profit and Public Management; Business Administration and Management, General; Public Administration; Public Finance	Four-year college, graduate school of business, military (all branches)
13-2041.00 Credit Analysts	Finance, General; Banking and Financial Support Services	Four-year college, graduate school of business
13-2051.00 Financial Analysts	Finance, General; Investments and Securities; Insurance and Risk Management; Financial Planning	Four-year college, graduate school of business
13-2053.00 Insurance Underwriters	Finance, General; Insurance and Risk Management	Four-year college, graduate school of business
13-2071.00 Loan Counselors	International Finance; Financial Services Marketing Operations; Finance, General; Banking and Financial Support Services	Four-year college, graduate school of business

JOBS	EDUCATION/TRAINING	WHERE OBTAINED
13.02.04 Management Support: Investigation and Analysis		
13-2072.00 Loan Officers	Finance, General; Banking and Financial Support Services; International Finance; Financial Services Marketing Operations	Four-year college, graduate school of business
19-3021.00 Market Research Analysts	Economics, General; Econometrics and Quantitative Economics; Applied and Resource Economics; Marketing Research	Four-year college, graduate school of business

14 Medical and Health Services

An interest in helping people be healthy.

You can satisfy this interest by working in a health-care team as a doctor, therapist, or nurse. You might specialize in one of the many different parts of the body or types of care, or you might be a generalist who deals with the whole patient. If you like technology, you might find satisfaction working with X rays, one of the electronic means of diagnosis, or clinical laboratory testing. You might work with healthy people, helping them stay in condition through exercise and eating right. If you like to organize, analyze, and plan, a managerial role might be right for you.

14.01 Managerial Work in Medical and Health Services

14.02 Medicine and Surgery

14.03 Dentistry

14.04 Health Specialties

14.05 Medical Technology

14.06 Medical Therapy

14.07 Patient Care and Assistance

14.08 Health Protection and Promotion

14.01 Managerial Work in Medical and Health Services

Workers in this group manage medical activities. Some primarily supervise doctors, nurses, therapists, and other health-care workers. Others provide leadership for all aspects of a hospital or nursing home, including finance and physical facilities. Some make decisions about how an autopsy is to be conducted. They do planning, budgeting, staffing, and evaluation of outcomes. They work for hospitals, health insurers, and government agencies.

What kind of work would you do?

Your work activities would depend on your job. For example, you might

- Recruit, hire, and evaluate the performance of medical staff and auxiliary personnel.
- Develop instructional materials and conduct in-service and community-based educational programs.
- Direct and coordinate the activities of medical, nursing, technical, clerical, service, and maintenance personnel of a health-care facility or mobile unit.
- Establish work schedules and assignments for a staff, according to workload, space, and equipment availability.
- Direct the activities of physicians and technologists conducting autopsies and pathological and toxicological analyses to determine the cause of deaths.
- Direct investigations into circumstances of deaths to fix responsibility for accidental, violent, or unexplained deaths.
- Testify at inquests, hearings, and court trials.

What things about you point to this kind of work?

Is it important for you to

- Have steady employment?
- Plan your work with little supervision?

Have you enjoyed any of the following as a hobby or leisure-time activity?

- Applying first aid in emergencies as a volunteer
- Budgeting the family income
- Doing volunteer work for the Red Cross
- Helping run a school or community fair or carnival
- Nursing sick relatives and friends
- Reading medical or scientific magazines
- Serving as a volunteer aide in a hospital, nursing home, or retirement home

Have you liked and done well in any of the following school subjects?

- Management
- Patient and Health Care
- Pathology
- Health
- Medical Terminology
- Personnel Management
- Accounting
- Business Organization
- Health Law

Are you able to

- Communicate information and ideas in speaking so others will understand?
- Listen to and understand information and ideas presented through spoken words and sentences?
- Read and understand information and ideas presented in writing?
- Communicate information and ideas in writing so others will understand?
- Tell when something is wrong or is likely to go wrong?
- Combine separate pieces of information, or specific answers to problems, to form general rules or conclusions?

Would you work in places such as

- Hospitals and nursing homes?
- Schools and homes for people with disabilities?
- Business offices?
- Government offices?

What skills and knowledges do you need for this kind of work?

For most of these jobs, you need these skills:

- Active Listening—listening to what other people are saying and asking questions as appropriate
- Information Gathering—knowing how to find information and identifying essential information

- Reading Comprehension—understanding written sentences and paragraphs in work-related documents
- Critical Thinking—using logic and analysis to identify the strengths and weaknesses of different approaches
- Judgment and Decision-Making—weighing the relative costs and benefits of a potential action
- Problem Identification—identifying the nature of problems

These knowledges are important in most of these jobs:

- Administration and Management—principles and processes involved in business and organizational planning, coordination, and execution
- Biology—plant and animal living tissue, cells, organisms, and entities, including their functions, interdependencies, and interactions with each other and the environment

What else should you consider about this kind of work?

These workers implement policies set by governing bodies and try to keep medical services excellent while containing costs. Sometimes they are under a lot of pressure from different parties—such as governing bodies, health-care workers, patients, government officials—who have conflicting goals. Health care goes on around the clock, and these workers may be "on call" for emergency situations. The work can give great satisfaction because it contributes to health and even saves lives.

The overall outlook for these occupations is good. The growth of managed care and the development of expensive high-tech procedures such as organ transplantation have increased the need for good management. Although most of the jobs are in hospitals, consolidation and centralization of hospitals and the aging of the population will mean that the greatest growth will be in home health agencies and long-term care facilities.

Like any managers, these managers need to keep abreast of new management technologies, especially those using computer applications. In addition, the workers need to keep their medical knowledge and skills up to date.

How can you prepare for jobs of this kind?

Occupations in this group usually require education and/or training ranging from four to six or more years.

For most generalist jobs in this field, standard preparation is a master's degree in health services administration, public health, public administration, or business management. The master's program may include supervised experience working in administration. Some workers get this managerial degree after getting a professional degree as a doctor, nurse, or therapist, but others do their undergraduate work in business or the liberal arts. Health services managers may begin with a bachelor's degree in health services administration or business management.

Coroners usually go to medical or osteopathic school to become physicians, take special coursework in pathology, then do a residency training program with a coroner to learn how to perform medical autopsies, analyze human remains and crime scenes, and present findings to the criminal justice system.

High school courses in math, chemistry, biology, and writing are very useful.

SPECIALIZED TRAINING

JOBS	EDUCATION/TRAINING	WHERE OBTAINED
14.01.01 Managerial Work in Medical and Health Services		
All in Managerial Work in Medical and Health Services	Biology; Chemistry; Health Care System; Budgeting; Personnel; Oral and Written Communications	Volunteer work in a hospital or health-care facility, four-year college, graduate school
11-9111.00 Medical and Health Services Managers	Medical Records Administration; Communication Disorders Sciences and Services, Other; Hospital/Health Facilities Administration; Nursing Administration (Post-R.N.); Emergency Medicine Residency; Business Administration and Management, General; Health System/Health Services Administration	Work experience in a related occupation, four-year college, graduate school, military (Army, Navy, Air Force, Coast Guard)

JOBS	EDUCATION/TRAINING	WHERE OBTAINED
14.01.01 Managerial Work in Medical and Health Services		
13-1041.06 Coroners	Forensic Pathology Residency	Four-year college, medical school, residency in a coroner's office

14.02 Medicine and Surgery

Workers in this group diagnose and treat human diseases, disorders, and injuries. They work in such places as hospitals, clinics, health facilities, industrial plants, pharmacies, and government agencies. Some are professionals who make life-and-death decisions, perform invasive procedures, and prescribe drugs. They may specialize or work in general practice. Many are self-employed and have their own offices. Other workers in this group provide care under the supervision of professionals.

What kind of work would you do?

Your work activities would depend on your job. For example, you might

- Administer anesthetic or sedation during medical procedures, using local, intravenous, spinal, or caudal methods.
- Assist a pharmacist to prepare and dispense medication.
- Clean and sterilize instruments.
- Lift and turn patients.
- Operate on patients to correct deformities, repair injuries, prevent diseases, or improve or restore patients' functions.
- Put dressings on patients following surgery.
- Prescribe or recommend drugs or other forms of treatment such as physical therapy, inhalation therapy, or related therapeutic procedures.

What things about you point to this kind of work?

Is it important for you to

- Have work where you do things for other people?
- Get a feeling of accomplishment?
- Make use of your individual abilities?

Have you enjoyed any of the following as a hobby or leisure-time activity?

- Applying first aid in emergencies as a volunteer
- Doing volunteer work for the Red Cross
- Nursing sick relatives and friends
- Reading medical or scientific magazines
- Serving as a volunteer aide in a hospital, nursing home, or retirement home
- Advising family members on their personal problems

Have you liked and done well in any of the following school subjects?

- Patient and Health Care
- Pathology
- Health
- Nursing Care
- Physiology
- Anatomy, Specialized/Advanced
- Pharmacology
- Psychology, Advanced/Specialized
- Human Growth and Development
- Biology
- Anesthesia

Are you able to

- Listen to and understand information and ideas presented through spoken words and sentences?
- Read and understand information and ideas presented in writing?
- Communicate information and ideas in speaking so others will understand?
- Correctly follow a given rule or set of rules to arrange things or actions in a certain order?
- Tell when something is wrong or is likely to go wrong?
- Communicate information and ideas in writing so others will understand?

- See details of objects at close range (within a few feet)?

Would you work in places such as

- Doctors' and dentists' offices and clinics?
- Drugstores?
- Hospitals and nursing homes?
- Schools and homes for people with disabilities?

What skills and knowledges do you need for this kind of work?

For most of these jobs, you need these skills:

- Reading Comprehension—understanding written sentences and paragraphs in work-related documents
- Active Listening—listening to what other people are saying and asking questions as appropriate
- Information Gathering—knowing how to find information and identifying essential information

These knowledges are important in most of these jobs:

- Medicine and Dentistry—the information and techniques needed to diagnose and treat injuries, diseases, and deformities
- Biology—plant and animal living tissue, cells, organisms, and entities, including their functions, interdependencies, and interactions with each other and the environment

What else should you consider about this kind of work?

People have medical needs at all hours of the day or night, so physicians, physician assistants, and surgical technologists are commonly "on call" for nights and weekends on a rotating basis. Registered nurses working in hospitals and long-term care facilities usually are expected to work evening, night, and weekend shifts. (In industrial and educational settings and doctor's offices, they usually have more conventional hours.) Many pharmacists and pharmacy aides also do shift work. All of the workers in this group need to take precautions in dealing with infectious agents and controlled substances. Most of them often deal with people in pain or dying. Despite the emotional drain, there is great satisfaction from relieving pain and helping people recover their health.

The educational and training program for physicians is extremely long, highly stressful at times, and leaves most new physicians burdened with years of debt. Paperwork is increasing in all medical fields, and HMOs sometimes limit the therapies that physicians can apply. The outlook for physicians is mixed, because HMOs and hospital mergers are limiting the need for some specialists; best opportunities will be for primary care physicians in general and family medicine, internal medicine, and general pediatrics.

Registered nurses often spend a lot of time standing and walking, and sometimes must raise patients from beds. The greatest demand for nurses will be for home health care and in nursing homes.

The outlook for physician assistants is very good, because they are seen as a way of keeping down health-care costs. The aging of the population and the development of new surgical procedures and drugs will cause a steady demand for surgical technologists, pharmacists, and pharmacy aides. Best opportunities for pharmacists will be in long-term and home care settings, and in research.

How can you prepare for jobs of this kind?

Education and/or training requirements for occupations in this group vary widely, from two years to ten or more years. These educational programs include supervised work with patients, especially toward the later parts of the curriculum.

Physicians typically complete a bachelor's degree, plus four years of medical school, plus three to eight years of internship and residency, depending on the specialty selected.

Most registered nurses take a two-year associate degree program at a community college or technical school. Some get a bachelor of science in nursing. A small number enter through a two- to three-year diploma program at a hospital. Studies in all programs include biological, physical, and social sciences as well as nursing theory and practice. Two- and three-year programs prepare graduates for general and private-duty nursing. Graduates of four-year baccalaureate programs qualify for general-duty nursing, positions in public health agencies, or advancement to supervisory and administrative work.

Physician assistants prepare with a program that typically lasts two years. Usually they already have a previous two- or four-year degree, and many have experience working in the health-care field.

Pharmacists obtain at least five years of education beyond high school. Most get a five-year bachelor of science in pharmacy, while others enter a six-year doctor of pharmacy program. Most colleges of pharmacy require applicants to have one or two years of college education, with coursework in science, math, and other subjects.

Pharmacy aides are trained in programs that vary from six months to two years. In drugstores, on-the-job training may be sufficient. In hospitals and government agencies, a longer and more formal program is usually required.

Surgical technologists get nine months to two years of training—less if they have a background in nursing or military training.

Medical assistants may learn their skills several ways, including on-the-job training or a program at a technical school or community college lasting from six months to two years.

For most jobs in this group, high school coursework in math concepts; English literature and composition; biological, social, and behavioral sciences; health; first aid; and cardiopulmonary resuscitation are useful. Volunteer work in a hospital or health-care facility is also recommended.

SPECIALIZED TRAINING

JOBS	EDUCATION/TRAINING	WHERE OBTAINED
	14.02.01 Medicine and Surgery	
All in Medicine and Surgery	Anatomy (Chordate, Microscopic, Gross); Physiology; Biochemistry; Microbiology; Chemistry	Volunteer work at a hospital or health-care facility, two- or four-year college
29-1051.00 Pharmacists	Pharmacy Administration and Pharmaceutics; Pharmacy (B.Pharm., Pharm.D.)	College of pharmacy, military (Army, Navy, Air Force, Coast Guard)
29-1061.00 Anesthesiologists	Critical Care Anesthesiology Residency; Medical Clinical Sciences (M.S., Ph.D.); Anesthesiology Residency	Four-year college plus medical school, internship, residency, military (Army, Navy, Air Force)
29-1062.00 Family and General Practitioners	Internal Medicine Residency; Medicine (M.D.); Family Medicine Residency; Geriatric Medicine Residency; Pediatrics Residency	Four-year college plus medical school, internship, residency, military (Army, Navy, Air Force, Coast Guard)
29-1063.00 Internists, General	Medicine (M.D.); Internal Medicine Residency	Four-year college plus medical school, internship, residency, military (Army, Navy, Air Force, Coast Guard)
29-1064.00 Obstetricians and Gynecologists	Medicine (M.D.); Obstetrics and Gynecology Residency; Neonatal-Perinatal Medicine Residency; Family Medicine Residency	Four-year college plus medical school, internship, residency, military (Army, Navy, Air Force, Coast Guard)
29-1065.00 Pediatricians, General	Medicine (M.D.); Family Medicine Residency; Neonatal-Perinatal Medicine Residency; Pediatrics Residency	Four-year college plus medical school, internship, residency, military (Army, Navy, Air Force, Coast Guard)
29-1066.00 Psychiatrists	Medicine (M.D.); Psychiatry Residency; Child Psychiatry Residency; Psychoanalysis	Four-year college plus medical school, internship, residency, military (Army, Navy, Air Force, Coast Guard)
29-1067.00 Surgeons	Critical Care Surgery Residency; General Surgery Residency; Hand Surgery Residency; Orthopedics/Orthopedic Surgery Residency; Pediatric Orthopedics Residency; Pediatric Surgery Residency; Thoracic Surgery Residency; Vascular Surgery Residency; Plastic Surgery Residency	Four-year college plus medical school, internship, residency, military (Army, Navy, Air Force, Coast Guard)

(continues)

(continued)

SPECIALIZED TRAINING

JOBS	EDUCATION/TRAINING	WHERE OBTAINED
14.02.01 Medicine and Surgery		
29-1071.00 Physician Assistants	Physician Assistant	Four-year college, technical school, military (Army, Navy, Air Force, Coast Guard)
29-1111.00 Registered Nurses	Nursing, Pediatric (Post-R.N.); Nursing Administration (Post-R.N.); Nursing (R.N. Training); Nursing, Public Health (Post-R.N.); Nursing, Other; Nursing, Surgical (Post-R.N.); Nursing, Psychiatric/Mental Health (Post-R.N.); Nursing Science (Post-R.N.); Nursing Midwifery (Post-R.N.); Nursing, Maternal/Child Health (Post-R.N.); Nursing, Family Practice (Post-R.N.); Nursing Anesthetist (Post-R.N.); Nursing, Adult Health (Post-R.N.)	Two-year college, four-year college, school of nursing, hospital (diploma program), graduate school, military (Army, Navy, Air Force)
29-2052.00 Pharmacy Technicians	Pharmacy Technician/Assistant Training	On the job, two-year college, hospital, military (Army, Navy, Air Force)
29-2055.00 Surgical Technologists	Surgical/Operating Room Technician	Two-year college, technical school, hospital, military (Army, Navy, Air Force)
31-9092.00 Medical Assistants	Medical Assistant; Health and Medical Assistants, Other; Medical Office Management	On the job, two-year college, technical school, military (Army, Navy, Air Force, Coast Guard)
31-9095.00 Pharmacy Aides	Pharmacy Technician/Assistant	On the job, two-year college, hospital; military data not yet available

14.03 Dentistry

Workers in this group provide health care for patients' teeth and mouth tissues. Most dentists are general practitioners, performing a variety of oral-care tasks. Others specialize: orthodontists straighten teeth; prosthodontists make artificial teeth and dentures; oral and maxillofacial surgeons operate on the mouth and jaws. Dental hygienists clean teeth and teach people how to take care of their teeth. Dental assistants provide chairside help, get the patient and equipment ready, and keep records.

What kind of work would you do?

Your work activities would depend on your job. For example, you might

- Clean teeth using dental instruments.
- Determine the nature and cause of oral conditions.
- Expose and develop X-ray film.
- Instruct patients in oral hygiene and plaque-control programs.
- Record treatment information in patient records.
- Restore the natural color of teeth by bleaching, cleaning, and polishing.
- Schedule appointments, prepare bills and receive payment for dental services, complete insurance forms, and maintain records.

What things about you point to this kind of work?

Is it important for you to

- Have work where you do things for other people?
- Get a feeling of accomplishment?
- Make use of your individual abilities?

Have you enjoyed any of the following as a hobby or leisure-time activity?

- Applying first aid in emergencies as a volunteer
- Carving small wooden objects
- Doing needlework
- Nursing sick relatives and friends
- Reading medical or scientific magazines
- Serving as a volunteer aide in a hospital, nursing home, or retirement home
- Doing volunteer work for the Red Cross

Have you liked and done well in any of the following school subjects?

- Dental Anatomy
- Patient and Health Care
- Oral Anatomy
- Oral Communication
- Oral Hygiene
- Health
- Physiology
- Anatomy
- Pharmacology
- Human Growth and Development
- Child Development/Care
- Biology
- Oral Development
- Anesthesia

Are you able to

- Keep your hand and arm steady while making an arm movement or while holding your arm and hand in one position?
- See details of objects at close range (within a few feet)?
- Make precisely coordinated movements of the fingers of one or both hands to grasp, manipulate, or assemble very small objects?
- Tell when something is wrong or is likely to go wrong?
- Quickly and repeatedly make precise adjustments in moving the controls of a machine or vehicle to exact positions?
- Communicate information and ideas in speaking so others will understand?
- Listen to and understand information and ideas presented through spoken words and sentences?

Would you work in places such as

- Doctors' and dentists' offices and clinics?

What skills and knowledges do you need for this kind of work?

For most of these jobs, you need these skills:

- Reading Comprehension—understanding written sentences and paragraphs in work-related documents
- Problem Identification—identifying the nature of problems

These knowledges are important in most of these jobs:

- Medicine and Dentistry—the information and techniques needed to diagnose and treat injuries, diseases, and deformities
- Biology—plant and animal living tissue, cells, organisms, and entities, including their functions, interdependencies, and interactions with each other and the environment

What else should you consider about this kind of work?

Some dentists work in hospitals and research, but most dentists are solo practitioners with a small staff of dental hygienists and assistants. They may work evenings or weekends to suit their patients' schedules. They may go into considerable debt to obtain their education and set up a practice. They need emotional stability to deal with patients who are in pain or discomfort. The job outlook for dentists is unclear. An aging population will need more dental services, but there may be increased competition from new graduates of dentistry school. In addition, an increasing number of routine and less profitable tasks are likely to be given to hygienists and assistants.

Dentists and dental hygienists sometimes find chairside work physically demanding. Both need to take precautions to protect themselves from X rays and from communicable diseases.

Many dental hygienists' jobs are for only a few days a week, perhaps including weekends, so many workers hold jobs at more than one dental practice. Most work in private dental offices, but some are hired by school systems, HMOs, and long-term health-care facilities. The employment outlook is probably good, provided that competition from new graduates does not increase. Many jobs will open because of turnover.

The dental assistant is sometimes called the dentist's "third hand." These workers often have a wide variety of duties, ranging from developing X rays to accepting payment for services. Job turnover will provide many openings in the occupation, and the outlook for employment is very good.

How can you prepare for jobs of this kind?

Education and/or training requirements for occupations in this group vary widely, from a few months to ten years.

Dentists qualify for their licenses by graduating from an accredited dental school and passing exams. Students usually get a bachelor's degree before being admitted to dental school, which takes about four years. It begins with classroom study and laboratory work and involves increasing amounts of supervised practice on patients. Specializing in orthodontics, etc., requires additional years of education and perhaps another licensing exam.

Dental hygienists are also licensed and must have an accredited education and pass an exam. Most dental hygiene programs take two years and grant an associate degree. Some prefer applicants to have a prior year of college. Bachelor's degree programs, which are usually needed for those who want to go into research, teaching, or clinical practice in an educational setting, may require two years of college beforehand. These educational programs offer a mix of classroom study and supervised clinical practice.

Most dental assistants learn on the job, but certification programs are available, lasting six months or less.

For all of these occupations, high school courses in biology and chemistry are useful. Those planning to be dentists should also study math, and those planning to be dental assistants will be helped by learning office procedures either in class or through a part-time clerical job.

SPECIALIZED TRAINING

JOBS	EDUCATION/TRAINING	WHERE OBTAINED
14.03.01 Dentistry		
All in Dentistry	Anatomy (Chordate, Microscopic, Gross); Physiology; Biochemistry; Microbiology; Chemistry	Volunteer work at a hospital or health-care facility, two- or four-year college
29-1021.00 Dentists, General	Dentistry (D.D.S., D.M.D.); Dental Clinical Sciences/Graduate Dentistry (M.S., Ph.D.); Periodontics Specialty; Pedodontics Specialty; Endodontics Specialty; Dental Public Health Specialty	Four-year college plus dental school, military (Army, Navy, Air Force, Coast Guard)
29-1022.00 Oral and Maxillo-facial Surgeons	Dentistry (D.D.S., D.M.D.); Dental/Oral Surgery Specialty	Four-year college plus dental school, post-graduate clinical training, military (Army, Navy, Air Force)
29-1023.00 Orthodontists	Dentistry (D.D.S., D.M.D.); Orthodontics Specialty	Four-year college plus dental school, post-graduate clinical training, military (Army, Navy, Air Force)
29-1024.00 Prosthodontists	Dentistry (D.D.S., D.M.D.); Prosthodontics Specialty	Four-year college plus dental school, post-graduate clinical training, military (Army, Navy, Air Force)
29-2021.00 Dental Hygienists	Dental Hygienist	Two-year college, military (Army, Navy, Air Force, Coast Guard)
31-9091.00 Dental Assistants	Dental Assistant	On the job, trade/technical school, military (Army, Navy, Air Force, Coast Guard)

14.04 Health Specialties

Workers in this group are health professionals and technicians who specialize in certain parts of the human body. They are employed in private practices, vision-care chains, hospitals, and long-term health-care facilities. Optometrists diagnose various diseases, disorders, and injuries of the eye, but opticians specialize in using lenses to correct imperfections in how the eye focuses. Podiatrists maintain the health of the feet and lower extremities. Chiropractors adjust the spinal column and other joints to prevent disease and correct abnormalities of the human body believed to be caused by interference with the nervous system.

What kind of work would you do?

Your work activities would depend on your job. For example, you might

- Examine eyes to determine visual acuity and perception and to diagnose diseases and other abnormalities, such as glaucoma and color blindness.
- Fabricate lenses to prescription specifications.
- Maintain an inventory of materials and clean instruments.
- Prescribe corrective footwear.
- Treat conditions such as corns, calluses, ingrown nails, tumors, shortened tendons, bunions, cysts, and abscesses by surgical methods.
- Instruct patients in eye care and the use of glasses or contact lenses.

What things about you point to this kind of work?

Is it important for you to

- Have work where you do things for other people?
- Get a feeling of accomplishment?
- Make use of your individual abilities?

Have you enjoyed any of the following as a hobby or leisure-time activity?

- Applying first aid in emergencies as a volunteer
- Doing volunteer work for the Red Cross
- Helping conduct physical exercises for people with disabilities
- Helping people with disabilities take walks
- Nursing sick relatives and friends
- Reading medical or scientific magazines
- Serving as a volunteer aide in a hospital, nursing home, or retirement home

Have you liked and done well in any of the following school subjects?

- Patient and Health Care
- Health
- Optics
- Anatomy
- Physiology
- Pharmacology
- Anesthesia
- Kinesiology

Are you able to

- Communicate information and ideas in speaking so others will understand?
- Tell when something is wrong or is likely to go wrong?
- See details of objects at close range (within a few feet)?

Would you work in places such as

- Doctors' and dentists' offices and clinics?
- Stores and shopping malls?

What skills and knowledges do you need for this kind of work?

For most of these jobs, you need these skills:

- Active Listening—listening to what other people are saying and asking questions as appropriate
- Speaking—talking to others to effectively convey information

These knowledges are important in most of these jobs:

- Medicine and Dentistry—the information and techniques needed to diagnose and treat injuries, diseases, and deformities
- Biology—plant and animal living tissue, cells, organisms, and entities, including their functions, interdependencies, and interactions with each other and the environment

What else should you consider about this kind of work?

The professional occupations in this group require a long education that can create considerable debt. To avoid the added expense of setting up a solo practice, an increasing number of new professionals go into partnerships or work as salaried employees of existing practices, HMOs, retail optical stores, and so on. All workers in this group work in fairly comfortable surroundings, although they may have to spend some time on their feet. The work week is about 40 hours, but it may include evening and weekend hours for the convenience of patients.

Optometrists should not be confused with ophthalmologists, who are MDs who specialize in the eye and may do surgery. They are also to be distinguished from opticians, who follow the prescriptions of optometrists and ophthalmologists to fit and adjust lenses and frames for eyeglasses, and in some states may also fit contact lenses. Dispensing opticians may begin as an employee of a practice and eventually set up their own business, perhaps a franchise of a chain. The aging of the population will increase job opportunities for optometrists, optometric technicians, and opticians.

Podiatrists diagnose and treat a wide variety of foot problems, but some may specialize in surgery, orthopedics, or sports medicine. Most work in private practice and supervise a small staff. The outlook for jobs is fair, because although an aging and physically active population will need more care for their feet, the occupation has a low turnover. Another way of looking at this is that the work is satisfying and few workers retire early. Podiatrists often see results more quickly than other medical practitioners, and they are more likely to work fairly normal hours.

Chiropractors follow a holistic philosophy that treats the whole patient, emphasizes the body's ability to restore itself, and aims to encourage a healthful lifestyle. As the baby boomers age and need more health care, their interest in alternative health therapies will mean a good job outlook for chiropractors.

How can you prepare for jobs of this kind?

Education and/or training requirements for occupations in this group vary widely, from two years to eight or ten years.

Optometrists, podiatrists, and chiropractors all qualify for their state licensing exams by completing a long educational and training process. First they complete some undergraduate work that emphasizes biology, chemistry, math, and perhaps physics. For optometrists and podiatrists, usually a bachelor's degree is expected; for chiropractors, at least two years must be completed, and a few states require a bachelor's degree. The professional program at a school of optometry, podiatric medicine, or chiropractic medicine takes about four years and is a combination of classroom and laboratory instruction, with supervised work with patients in the last two years. Most states also require podiatrists to complete one to three years of a hospital residency program with extensive clinical work. Continuing education may also be required to maintain a license.

Many opticians learn through an apprenticeship or on-the-job training, but a two-year associate degree is becoming a requirement. Some obtain a bachelor's degree that combines study of opticianry and business management.

SPECIALIZED TRAINING

JOBS	EDUCATION/TRAINING	WHERE OBTAINED
14.04.01 Health Specialties		
All in Health Specialties	Anatomy (Chordate, Microscopic, Gross); Physiology; Biochemistry; Microbiology; Chemistry	Volunteer work at a hospital or health-care facility, two- or four-year college
29-1011.00 Chiropractors	Chiropractic (D.C., D.C.M.)	Two-year college or four-year college plus college of chiropractic medicine, military (Air Force)
29-1041.00 Optometrists	Optometry (O.D.)	Four-year college plus college of optometry, military (Army, Navy, Air Force)

JOBS	EDUCATION/TRAINING	WHERE OBTAINED
14.04.01 Health Specialties		
29-1081.00 Podiatrists	Podiatry (D.P.M., D.P., Pod.D.)	Four-year college plus college of podiatric medicine, residency, military (Navy, Air Force)
29-2081.00 Opticians, Dispensing	Opticianry/Dispensing Optician	Apprenticeship, on the job, two-year college, military (Navy, Air Force)

14.05 Medical Technology

Workers in this group use technology mostly to detect signs of disease. They are employed by hospitals, long-term health-care facilities, HMOs, physicians' offices, and specialized diagnostic laboratories and practices. They perform tests requested by physicians, and the findings they report help the physicians to diagnose disease and formulate a therapy.

What kind of work would you do?

Your work activities would depend on your job. For example, you might

- Adjust equipment settings for blood collection or replacement.
- Attach electrodes to specified locations on patients, such as chests, arms, and legs.
- Conduct chemical analysis of body fluids, including blood, urine, and spinal fluid, to determine the presence of normal and abnormal components.
- Draw blood from patients, observing principles of asepsis, to obtain blood samples.
- Enter analyses of medical tests and clinical results into a computer for storage.
- Perform blood counts using a microscope.
- Prepare and position patients for testing.

What things about you point to this kind of work?

Is it important for you to

- Never be pressured to do things that go against your sense of right and wrong?
- Have work where you do things for other people?
- Have steady employment?

Have you enjoyed any of the following as a hobby or leisure-time activity?

- Applying first aid in emergencies as a volunteer
- Doing volunteer work for the Red Cross
- Experimenting with a chemistry set
- Installing and repairing home stereo equipment
- Nursing sick relatives and friends
- Performing experiments for a science fair
- Reading medical or scientific magazines
- Serving as a volunteer aide in a hospital, nursing home, or retirement home

Have you liked and done well in any of the following school subjects?

- Patient and Health Care
- Pathology
- Health
- X-Ray Technology
- Anatomy
- Physiology
- Human Growth and Development
- Nuclear Safety
- Auditory Development
- Hematology

Are you able to

- Communicate information and ideas in speaking so others will understand?
- Listen to and understand information and ideas presented through spoken words and sentences?
- Read and understand information and ideas presented in writing?
- Correctly follow a given rule or set of rules in order to arrange things or actions in a certain order?

- See details of objects at close range (within a few feet)?
- Communicate information and ideas in writing so others will understand?
- Tell when something is wrong or is likely to go wrong?

Would you work in places such as

- Doctors' and dentists' offices and clinics?
- Hospitals and nursing homes?
- Elementary schools?

What skills and knowledges do you need for this kind of work?

For most of these jobs, you need these skills:

- Operation and Control—controlling the operations of equipment or systems
- Speaking—talking to others to effectively convey information

These knowledges are important in most of these jobs:

- Medicine and Dentistry—the information and techniques needed to diagnose and treat injuries, diseases, and deformities
- Biology—plant and animal living tissue, cells, organisms, and entities, including their functions, interdependencies, and interactions with each other and the environment

What else should you consider about this kind of work?

Like most health-care workers, the workers in this group put in about a 40-hour week, with some availability on evenings and weekends to fit patients' schedules. The surroundings are generally pleasant, although some of them have to work with unpleasant chemicals or body fluids. Most of them need to take precautions to avoid exposing themselves or patients to infection or unintended radiation. They may deal with patients who are in pain or seriously ill. They find satisfaction in being part of the health-care team that enables people to live longer and fuller lives.

The outlook is generally good. As the American population grows older, the need for medical tests will increase. Some of the occupations have a large number of workers and therefore will create many jobs through turnover. Jobs are also being created as new technologies permit testing procedures for signs that previously were not detectable. On the other hand, technology is automating some routine laboratory procedures so that they can be done by robots or by fewer workers.

How can you prepare for jobs of this kind?

Occupations in this group usually require education and/or training ranging from a few weeks to six years. The preparatory programs typically begin with classroom and laboratory work, and for those occupations that involve working directly with patients, there is supervised clinical work.

Clinical laboratory technologists usually prepare with a bachelor's degree in medical technology or a life science, whereas technicians may have a two-year degree or learn on the job. Radiologic technologists and technicians both get similar amounts of training—two to four years—but some radiologic technologists specialize in ultrasound, CAT scanning, or other forms of noninvasive diagnosis. Cardiovascular technologists (who test pulmonary and cardiovascular systems) usually get two or four years of education and training, whereas cardiovascular technicians (who usually record only the heart) get six months to a year. Nuclear medicine technologists and diagnostic medical sonographers prepare with a two- or four-year program.

High school courses in math, chemistry, biology, algebra, and health are very useful for all of these occupations. For those that involve nuclear or electronic technologies, a course in physics is also recommended.

SPECIALIZED TRAINING

JOBS	EDUCATION/TRAINING	WHERE OBTAINED
	14.05.01 Medical Technology	
All in Medical Technology	Anatomy; Physiology; Biochemistry; Microbiology; Chemistry; Physics	Volunteer work at a hospital or health-care facility, two- or four-year college

JOBS	EDUCATION/TRAINING	WHERE OBTAINED
14.05.01 Medical Technology		
29-2011.00 Medical and Clinical Laboratory Technologists	Cytotechnologist; Medical Laboratory Technician; Medical Technology; Health and Medical Laboratory Technology/Technicians, Other	Four-year college, military (Army, Navy, Air Force)
29-2012.00 Medical and Clinical Laboratory Technicians	Hematology Technology/Technician; Medical Laboratory Technician	Four-year college, trade/technical school, hospital, on the job, military (Army, Navy, Air Force)
29-2031.00 Cardiovascular Technologists and Technicians	Diagnostic Medical Sonography; Cardiovascular Technology/Technician	Two-year college, four-year college, on the job, military (Navy, Air Force)
29-2032.00 Diagnostic Medical Sonographers	Diagnostic Medical Sonography	Two-year college, trade/technical school, hospital, on the job, military (Navy, Air Force)
29-2033.00 Nuclear Medicine Technologists	Nuclear Medical Technology/Technician; Medical Radiologic Technology/Technician	Two-year college, four-year college; military data not yet available
29-2034.01 Radiologic Technologists	Medical Radiologic Technology/Technician; Health and Medical Diagnostic and Treatment Services, Other	Two-year college, four-year college, military (Army, Navy, Air Force)
29-2034.02 Radiologic Technicians	Medical Radiologic Technology/Technician	Two-year college, four-year college, military (Army, Navy, Air Force)
29-2091.00 Orthotists and Prosthetists	Medical Assistant; Orthotics/Prosthetics	Two-year college, military (Navy, Air Force)
31-9093.00 Medical Equipment Preparers	Biomedical Engineering-Related Technology/ Technician; Respiratory Therapy Technician	On the job, trade/technical school, hospital, two-year college, military (Army)

14.06 Medical Therapy

Workers in this group care for, treat, or train people to improve their physical and emotional well-being. Most persons in this group work with people who are sick, injured, or disabled. Hospitals, nursing homes, and rehabilitation centers hire workers in this group, as do schools, industrial plants, doctors' offices, and sports organizations.

What kind of work would you do?

Your work activities would depend on your job. For example, you might

- Administer massage, applying knowledge of massage techniques and body physiology.
- Conduct individual and group aerobic, strength, and flexibility exercises.
- Design and construct special equipment, such as splints and braces.
- Instruct patients and families in treatment procedures to be continued at home.
- Maintain patient charts, which contain pertinent identification and therapy information.
- Select activities that will help individuals learn work skills within the limits of their mental and physical capabilities.
- Teach clients personal skills such as eating, grooming, dressing, and using bathroom facilities.

What things about you point to this kind of work?

Is it important for you to

- Have work where you do things for other people?
- Get a feeling of accomplishment?
- Have coworkers who are easy to get along with?

Have you enjoyed any of the following as a hobby or leisure-time activity?

- Applying first aid in emergencies as a volunteer
- Chauffeuring special groups such as children, older people, or people with disabilities
- Doing volunteer work for the Red Cross
- Helping conduct physical exercises for people with disabilities
- Helping people with disabilities take walks
- Nursing sick relatives and friends

Have you liked and done well in any of the following school subjects?

- Patient and Health Care
- Pathology
- Health
- Anatomy
- Physiology
- Human Growth and Development
- Kinesiology
- Physical Therapy

Are you able to

- Communicate information and ideas in speaking so others will understand?
- Listen to and understand information and ideas presented through spoken words and sentences?
- Tell when something is wrong or is likely to go wrong?
- Read and understand information and ideas presented in writing?
- Communicate information and ideas in writing so others will understand?
- Speak clearly so that it is understandable to a listener?
- Apply general rules to specific problems to come up with logical answers?

Would you work in places such as

- Doctors' and dentists' offices and clinics?
- Hospitals and nursing homes?
- Schools and homes for people with disabilities?
- Recreation centers and playgrounds?

What skills and knowledges do you need for this kind of work?

For most of these jobs, you need these skills:

- Speaking–talking to others to effectively convey information
- Active Listening–listening to what other people are saying and asking questions as appropriate

These knowledges are important in most of these jobs:

- Therapy and Counseling–information and techniques needed to rehabilitate physical and mental ailments and to provide career guidance
- Education and Training–instructional methods and training techniques including curriculum-design principles, learning theory, group and individual teaching techniques, design of individual development plans, and test-design principles

What else should you consider about this kind of work?

Some of these workers are part-time employees, some are self-employed, and some open their own therapy facilities. The trend, however, is that large health-care organizations are buying up practices and contracting their services to HMOs.

Many workers in this field have to do some evening or night-shift work and work on weekends. This is especially true for jobs in hospitals or other around-the-clock health-care places. You may be on call or have to work overtime. Workers with seniority usually can be selective about the days and shifts they work.

The outlook for jobs in this group is generally good because an aging population needs more health care, and these services cannot be performed by machines. However, there may be keen competition for jobs (or even for admission to training programs), and cost-control measures by HMOs and Medicare may limit growth.

How can you prepare for jobs of this kind?

Occupations in this group usually require education and/or training ranging from two to six years, although some jobs as aides require as little as six months of training. Many of these occupations are licensed, and workers qualify for the licensing exam by getting a college degree in a specialized field such as speech, music, recreation, art, or physical education. The program usually includes supervised work with patients. In some fields many workers get a degree in another field, such as a life science, before taking the necessary academic and clinical courses in a master's program.

SPECIALIZED TRAINING

JOBS	EDUCATION/TRAINING	WHERE OBTAINED
	14.06.01 Medical Therapy	
All in Medical Therapy	Anatomy; Physiology; Biochemistry; Microbiology; Chemistry; Psychology	Volunteer work at a hospital or health-care facility, two- or four-year college
29-1121.00 Audiologists	Communication Disorders, General; Speech-Language Pathology and Audiology; Audiology/Hearing Sciences	Four-year college plus graduate school, military (Army, Navy, Air Force, Coast Guard)
29-1122.00 Occupational Therapists	Occupational Therapy	Four-year college, graduate school, military (Army, Navy, Air Force)
29-1123.00 Physical Therapists	Physical Therapy; Movement Therapy; Exercise Sciences/Physiology and Movement Studies; Health and Physical Education, General	Four-year college, graduate school, military (Army, Navy, Air Force, Coast Guard)
29-1124.00 Radiation Therapists	Nuclear Medical Technology/Technician	Two-year college, graduate school, military (Army, Navy, Air Force)
29-1125.00 Recreational Therapists	Music Therapy; Health and Physical Education, General; Recreational Therapy; Adapted Physical Education/Therapeutic Recreation; Art Therapy; Dance Therapy	Four-year college, graduate school
29-1126.00 Respiratory Therapists	Respiratory Therapy Technician	Two-year college, four-year college, military (Army, Navy, Air Force)
29-1127.00 Speech-Language Pathologists	Speech-Language Pathology; Speech-Language Pathology and Audiology; Communication Disorders, General	Four-year college plus graduate school, military (Army, Navy, Air Force, Coast Guard)
29-2054.00 Respiratory Therapy Technicians	Respiratory Therapy Technician	Two-year college, four-year college; military data not yet available
31-2011.00 Occupational Therapist Assistants	Health Aide; Occupational Therapy Assistant	On the job, two-year college, military (Navy, Air Force)
31-2012.00 Occupational Therapist Aides	Health Aide; Occupational Therapy Assistant	On the job, two-year college, military (Navy, Air Force)
31-2021.00 Physical Therapist Assistants	Health Aide; Physical Therapy Assistant	On the job, two-year college, military (Navy, Air Force)
31-2022.00 Physical Therapist Aides	Health Aide; Physical Therapy Assistant	On the job, two-year college, military (Navy, Air Force)
31-9011.00 Massage Therapists	Hospitality and Recreation Marketing Operations, General; Hospitality and Recreation Marketing Operations, Other; Massage	Two-year college; military data not yet available

14.07 Patient Care and Assistance

Workers in this group are concerned with the physical needs and welfare of others. They may assist professional workers. These workers care for people who are very old, very young, or have handicaps, frequently helping people do the things they cannot do for themselves. Jobs are found in hospitals, clinics, day-care centers, nurseries, schools, private homes, and centers for disabled people.

What kind of work would you do?

Your work activities would depend on your job. For example, you might

- Assist patients to walk.
- Administer medication as directed by a physician or nurse.
- Demonstrate and assist patients in bathing, dressing, and grooming.
- Measure and record vital signs.
- Sterilize equipment and supplies, using germicides, a sterilizer, or an autoclave.
- Serve meals and feed patients who need assistance.
- Collect samples, such as urine, blood, and sputum, from patients for testing and perform routine laboratory tests on samples.

What things about you point to this kind of work?

Is it important for you to

- Have work where you do things for other people?
- Never be pressured to do things that go against your sense of right and wrong?
- Have steady employment?

Have you enjoyed any of the following as a hobby or leisure-time activity?

- Applying first aid in emergencies as a volunteer
- Chauffeuring special groups such as children, older people, or people with disabilities
- Driving an ambulance as a volunteer
- Helping conduct physical exercises for people with disabilities
- Helping people with disabilities take walks
- Nursing sick relatives and friends
- Serving as a volunteer in a fire department or emergency rescue squad

Have you liked and done well in any of the following school subjects?

- Patient and Health Care
- Pathology
- Health
- Nursing Care
- Psychology
- Nutrition
- Human Growth and Development

Are you able to

- Listen to and understand information and ideas presented through spoken words and sentences?
- Communicate information and ideas in speaking so others will understand?
- Tell when something is wrong or is likely to go wrong?
- Read and understand information and ideas presented in writing?
- Exert maximum muscle force to lift, push, pull, or carry objects?

Would you work in places such as

- Hospitals and nursing homes?
- Doctors' and dentists' offices and clinics?
- Schools and homes for people with disabilities?
- Elementary schools?
- High schools?
- Factories and plants?
- Colleges and universities?

What skills and knowledges do you need for this kind of work?

For most of these jobs, you need these skills:

- Service Orientation—actively looking for ways to help people
- Active Listening—listening to what other people are saying and asking questions as appropriate
- Social Perceptiveness—being aware of others' reactions and understanding why they react the way they do

These knowledges are important in most of these jobs:

- Customer and Personal Service—principles and processes for providing customer and personal services including needs-assessment techniques, quality service standards, alternative delivery systems, and customer satisfaction evaluation techniques
- Medicine and Dentistry—the information and techniques needed to diagnose and treat injuries, diseases, and deformities

What else should you consider about this kind of work?

Some workers in this group, such as practical nurses and home health aides, often work in temporary or part-time jobs.

There are usually many openings for well-trained newcomers in this field. Many of these jobs are with places operated by federal, state, or local governments. You may have to pass a civil-service test to qualify for some of them. The outlook is mostly very good because of job turnover and the growing health-care needs of a graying population.

If you take a job caring for someone in that person's home, you might have to be on duty 24 hours a day. People who work for places that provide around-the-clock patient care usually have to work evening or night shifts and weekends. An advantage of some of these jobs is that they include room and board as part of the wages.

Some of these jobs involve close physical contact with people. Workers may have to help lift, bathe, groom, or feed people.

Additional schooling is necessary to advance to higher-level work.

How can you prepare for jobs of this kind?

Occupations in this group usually require education and/or training ranging from 30 days to more than two years. Employers usually require that applicants have a high school education or its equal. Coursework in health, first aid, English grammar, and speech for interpersonal communication is useful. Hospitals, community agencies, colleges, and public vocational schools offer training courses for many of these jobs. The average program requires about one year to complete. Some jobs in this group require state licenses.

Hospitals and clinics provide on-the-job training for many of these jobs. This training usually includes classroom instruction, demonstration of skills and techniques, and practice. The length of training depends on the job.

Interest and experience in home management, child care, or adult care provide a good background for working with aged, blind, or very young people.

SPECIALIZED TRAINING

JOBS	EDUCATION/TRAINING	WHERE OBTAINED
14.07.01 Patient Care and Assistance		
All in Patient Care and Assistance	Medical Terminology; Math Computing (Fractions and Decimals)	High school, volunteer work at a hospital or health-care facility
29-2053.00 Psychiatric Technicians	Psychiatric/Mental Health Services Technician	Trade/technical school, hospital, two-year college, four-year college, military (Army, Navy, Air Force)
29-2061.00 Licensed Practical and Licensed Vocational Nurses	Practical Nurse (L.P.N. Training)	Trade/technical school, hospital, two-year college, four-year college, military (Army)
31-1011.00 Home Health Aides	Nurse Assistant/Aide; Custodial, Housekeeping, and Home Services Workers and Managers; Elder Care Provider/Companion; Homemaker's Aide; Home Health Aide; Health Aide	On the job, vocational school
31-1012.00 Nursing Aides, Orderlies, and Attendants	Nurse Assistant/Aide; Home Health Aide; Health Aide	On the job, vocational school, hospital, military (Army, Navy, Air Force)

(continues)

SPECIALIZED TRAINING

JOBS	EDUCATION/TRAINING	WHERE OBTAINED
14.07.01 Patient Care and Assistance		
31-1013.00 Psychiatric Aides	Nurse Assistant/Aide; Health Aide; Mental Health Services, Other; Psychiatric/Mental Health Services Technician	On the job, vocational school, military (Navy, Air Force)

14.08 Health Protection and Promotion

Workers in this group help people maintain good health and fitness. They educate and advise people to help them live healthier lifestyles, eat well, and get into better physical condition.

What kind of work would you do?

Your work activities would depend on your job. For example, you might

- Collaborate with health specialists and civic groups to ascertain community health needs, determine the availability of services, and develop goals.
- Evaluate the physical condition of athletes and advise or prescribe routines and corrective exercises to strengthen muscles.
- Inspect facilities, equipment, accommodations, operating procedures, and staff competence to ensure health and sanitation regulation compliance.
- Investigate complaints concerning violations of public health laws or substandard products or service.
- Prepare and disseminate educational and informational materials.
- Supervise the activities of workers engaged in planning, preparing, and serving meals.
- Write research reports and other publications to document and communicate research findings.

What things about you point to this kind of work?

Is it important for you to

- Have work where you do things for other people?
- Get a feeling of accomplishment?
- Make use of your individual abilities?

Have you enjoyed any of the following as a hobby or leisure-time activity?

- Developing publicity fliers for a school or community event
- Doing public speaking or debating
- Doing volunteer work for the Red Cross
- Campaigning for political candidates or issues
- Helping persuade people to sign petitions for a PTA or other organization
- Reading medical or scientific magazines
- Planning and cooking meals

Have you liked and done well in any of the following school subjects?

- Health
- Diet and Therapy
- Nutrition
- Physical Education
- Public Health
- Health Law
- Biostatistics and Epidemiology
- Industrial Hygiene
- Menu Planning

Are you able to

- Communicate information and ideas in speaking so others will understand?
- Speak clearly so that it is understandable to a listener?
- Tell when something is wrong or is likely to go wrong?
- Listen to and understand information and ideas presented through spoken words and sentences?

- Read and understand information and ideas presented in writing?
- Communicate information and ideas in writing so others will understand?
- Combine separate pieces of information, or specific answers to problems, to form general rules or conclusions?
- See details of objects at close range (within a few feet)?

Would you work in places such as

- Business offices?
- Government offices?
- Hospitals and nursing homes?
- Gymnasiums and health clubs?
- Sports stadiums?
- Colleges and universities?
- Schools and homes for people with disabilities?

What skills and knowledges do you need for this kind of work?

For most of these jobs, you need these skills:

- Speaking—talking to others to effectively convey information
- Information Gathering—knowing how to find information and identifying essential information
- Active Listening—listening to what other people are saying and asking questions as appropriate

These knowledges are important in most of these jobs:

- Education and Training—instructional methods and training techniques including curriculum-design principles, learning theory, group and individual teaching techniques, design of individual development plans, and test-design principles
- Biology—plant and animal living tissue, cells, organisms, and entities, including their functions, interdependencies, and interactions with each other and the environment

What else should you consider about this kind of work?

Many jobs in this group involve working with healthy, rather than sick, people; this is unusual in the health-care field. In addition, many of these workers are responsible for the health of a large number of people. That can be a reason for great satisfaction, but occasionally a source of stress.

Health educators work mainly for government agencies. Workers may have to take a civil-service exam.

Dietitians may practice clinical dietetics, working with individual patients in such settings as a hospital or nursing home; community dietetics, working to educate a large group or the public in such settings as a public health agency or HMO; management dietetics, planning meals for a food service; or consulting dietetics, contracting to offer their services to any of these employers or perhaps to individuals. Dietetic technicians work under the direction of dietitians in the same settings.

Athletic trainers help athletes maintain fitness and recover from injury. Most work with college athletic teams; others work for high schools, sports medicine clinics, and fitness centers.

The job outlook for this group is generally good. Positions in public health depend partly on government spending, which may go up or down. Best opportunities for dietitians will be in commercial food services and the food industry. Athletic trainers will have increased opportunities because of the growth of professional sports and the fear of lawsuits, but they also are likely to face keen competition.

How can you prepare for jobs of this kind?

Occupations in this group usually require education and/or training ranging from two to six years.

Health educators often have a master's or even doctoral degree. They need to know not only about public health issues, but also about educational techniques.

Dietitians usually get a bachelor's degree to enter the occupation and to be licensed in those states that require it. Programs accredited by the American Dietetics Association include some supervised clinical work. A master's degree is sometimes needed to go into management, public health, or teaching. Dietetic technicians may have less than a bachelor's degree.

Athletic trainers may have a bachelor's degree in athletic training, a program that includes supervised clinical experience. Some get a bachelor's degree in another field and complete an internship.

For all of the occupations, high school courses in biology, chemistry, health, and speech communication are useful. For those in dietetics, home economics may also be a good choice.

SPECIALIZED TRAINING

JOBS	EDUCATION/TRAINING	WHERE OBTAINED
14.08.01 Health Protection and Promotion		
21-1091.00 Health Educators	Curriculum and Instruction; Community Health Liaison	Four-year college plus graduate school, military (Air Force)
29-1031.00 Dietitians and Nutritionists	Dietetics/Human Nutritional Services; Food Systems Administration; Foods and Nutrition Science; Foods and Nutrition Studies, General; Institutional Food Services Administrator; Institutional Food Workers and Administrators, General; Medical Dietician; Medical Nutrition; Medical Pathology	Four-year college, graduate school, military (Army, Navy, Air Force, Coast Guard)
29-2051.00 Dietetic Technicians	Dietetics/Human Nutritional Services; Dietician Assistant; Foods and Nutrition Science; Foods and Nutrition Studies, General; Institutional Food Workers and Administrators, General	Two-year college, four-year college
29-9091.00 Athletic Trainers	Health and Physical Education, General; Athletic Training and Sports Medicine	On the job, four-year college, internship

Part 2

The Job Descriptions

The original edition of the *Guide for Occupational Exploration* cross-referenced so many jobs titles—over 12,000—that their descriptions simply could not be included. The newest release of the U.S. Department of Labor's O*NET database, however, provides information on almost 1,000 job titles—a more manageable number.

We've included brief but information-packed descriptions for every job in the most recent O*NET database. The introduction gives additional details on how we created the descriptions, but we designed them to be easy to understand. The one exception is the coded information in the "Job Zone." This is described in the introduction, so you'll have to refer to it to understand this one measure.

The jobs are arranged within Interest Areas in GOE number order. This numbering system is also explained in the introduction, but you can quickly see how it works by reviewing the table of contents. There you will see the GOE's system of Interest Areas followed by groupings of related jobs. Simply use the table of contents to identify groups of jobs that sound interesting, learn more about the groups in Part 1, and then look up their job descriptions in Part 2. If you want more information than provided in the descriptions that follow, the introduction lists print, Internet, and other resources.

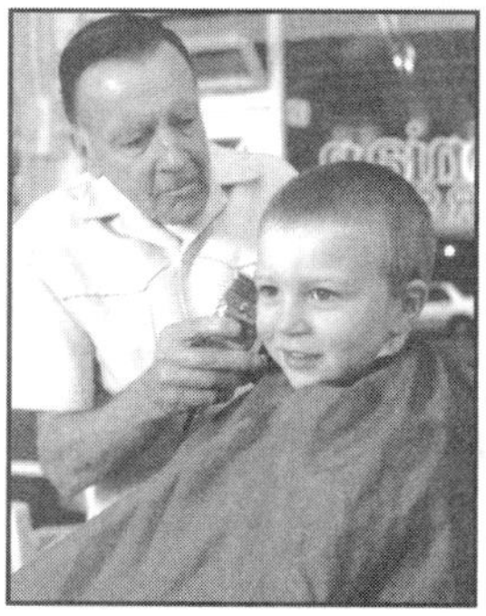

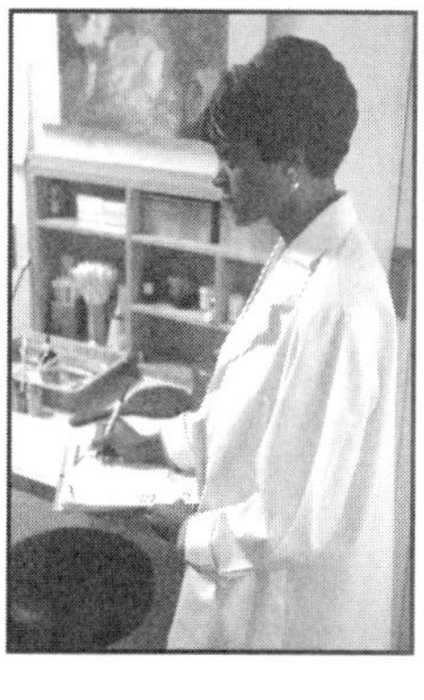

01 Arts, Entertainment, and Media

01.01 Managerial Work in Arts, Entertainment, and Media

01.02 Writing and Editing

01.03 News, Broadcasting, and Public Relations

01.04 Visual Arts

01.05 Performing Arts

01.06 Craft Arts

01.07 Graphic Arts

01.08 Media Technology

01.09 Modeling and Personal Appearance

01.10 Sports: Coaching, Instructing, Officiating, and Performing

01.01.01 Managerial Work in Arts, Entertainment, and Media

13-1011.00 Agents and Business Managers of Artists, Performers, and Athletes

Represent and promote artists, performers, and athletes to prospective employers. May handle contract negotiation and other business matters for clients. **Education:** Work experience, plus degree. **Occupational Type:** Enterprising. **Job Zone:** 3. **Average Salary:** $36,923. **Projected Growth:** 23%. **Occupational Values:** Autonomy; Working Conditions; Social Service; Compensation; Achievement; Responsibility; Ability Utilization. **Skills Required:** Negotiation; Coordination; Speaking; Information Gathering; Reading Comprehension; Time Management. **Abilities:** Oral Comprehension; Oral Expression; Speech Clarity; Number Facility; Written Comprehension; Mathematical Reasoning; Written Expression. **Interacting with Others:** Communicating with Persons Outside Organization; Resolving Conflict, Negotiating with Others; Establishing and Maintaining Relationships; Monitoring and Controlling Resources; Performing Administrative Activities. **Physical Work Conditions:** Indoors; Sitting.

27-1011.00 Art Directors

Formulate design concepts and presentation approaches, and direct workers engaged in art work, layout design, and copy writing for visual communications media, such as magazines, books, newspapers, and packaging. **Education:** Bachelor's degree. **Occupational Type:** Artistic. **Job Zone:** 4. **Average Salary:** $31,690. **Projected Growth:** 27.1%. **Occupational Values:** Ability Utilization; Creativity; Achievement; Autonomy; Responsibility; Recognition; Working Conditions. **Skills Required:** Product Inspection; Coordination; Operations Analysis; Management of Personnel Resources; Writing; Idea Evaluation; Time Management. **Abilities:** Originality; Speech Clarity; Fluency of Ideas; Oral Expression; Visualization; Oral Comprehension; Written Expression. **Interacting with Others:** Communicating with Other Workers; Communicating with Persons Outside Organization; Coordinating Work and Activities of Others. **Physical Work Conditions:** Indoors; Sitting; Using Hands on Objects, Tools, Controls.

27-2012.01 Producers

Plan and coordinate various aspects of radio, television, stage, or motion picture production, such as selecting script, coordinating writing, directing and editing, and arranging financing. **Education:** Long-term O-J-T. **Occupational Type:** Artistic. **Job Zone:** 4. **Average Salary:** $27,370. **Projected Growth:** 23.8%. **Occupational Values:** Achievement; Autonomy; Responsibility; Ability Utilization; Authority; Creativity; Recognition. **Skills Required:** Coordination; Reading Comprehension; Speaking; Idea Generation; Management of Material Resources; Management of Financial Resources; Writing. **Abilities:** Oral Expression; Written Comprehension; Originality; Written Expression; Oral Comprehension; Problem Sensitivity; Deductive Reasoning. **Interacting with Others:** Coordinating Work and Activities of Others; Communicating with Other Workers; Resolving Conflict, Negotiating with Others; Staffing Organizational Units; Establishing and Maintaining Relationships; Guiding, Directing, and Motivating Subordinates; Monitoring and Controlling Resources. **Physical Work Conditions:** Indoors; Sitting.

27-2012.03 Program Directors

Direct and coordinate activities of personnel engaged in preparation of radio or television station program schedules and programs, such as sports or news. **Education:** Long-term O-J-T. **Occupational Type:** Enterprising. **Job Zone:** 5. **Average Salary:** $27,370. **Projected Growth:** 23.8%. **Occupational Values:** Authority; Autonomy; Responsibility; Variety; Achievement; Creativity; Working Conditions. **Skills Required:** Coordination; Writing; Management of Personnel Resources; Reading Comprehension; Implementation Planning; Time Management; Idea Evaluation. **Abilities:** Oral Expression; Near Vision; Oral Comprehension; Written Comprehension; Written Expression; Deductive Reasoning; Speech Clarity. **Interacting with Others:** Guiding, Directing, and Motivating Subordinates; Monitoring and Controlling Resources; Coordinating Work and Activities of Others; Communicating with Other Workers; Staffing Organizational Units; Providing Consultation and Advice to Others; Establishing and Maintaining Relationships. **Physical Work Conditions:** Indoors; Sitting.

27-2012.05 Technical Directors/Managers

Coordinate activities of technical departments, such as taping, editing, engineering, and maintenance, to produce radio or television programs. **Education:** Long-term O-J-T. **Occupational Type:** Realistic. **Job Zone:** 4. **Average Salary:** $27,370. **Projected Growth:** 23.8%. **Occupational Values:** Autonomy; Authority; Ability Utilization; Responsibility; Achievement; Creativity; Variety. **Skills Required:** Coordination; Management of Personnel Resources; Speaking; Operation Monitoring; Operation and Control; Monitoring; Instructing. **Abilities:** Speech Clarity; Oral Comprehension; Oral Expression. **Interacting with Others:** Coordinating Work and Activities of Others; Guiding, Directing and Motivating Subordinates; Communicating with Other Workers; Teaching Others; Coaching and Developing Others. **Physical Work Conditions:** Indoors; Sitting; Using Hands on Objects, Tools, Controls.

01.02.01 Writing and Editing

27-3041.00 Editors

Perform variety of editorial duties, such as laying out, indexing, and revising content of written materials, in preparation for final publication. **Education:** Bachelor's degree. **Occupational Type:** Artistic. **Job Zone:** 4. **Average Salary:** $36,325. **Projected Growth:** 24.4%. **Occupational Values:** Creativity; Achievement; Ability Utilization; Responsibility; Autonomy; Recognition; Security. **Skills Required:** Writing; Reading Comprehension; Product Inspection; Monitoring; Coordination; Information Organization. **Abilities:** Written Comprehension; Written Expression; Near Vision; Deductive Reasoning; Information Ordering; Oral Comprehension; Oral Expression. **Interacting with Others:** Communicating with Other Workers;

Providing Consultation and Advice to Others. **Physical Work Conditions:** Indoors; Sitting.

27-3042.00 Technical Writers

Write technical materials, such as equipment manuals, appendices, or operating and maintenance instructions. May assist in layout work. **Education:** Bachelor's degree. **Occupational Type:** Artistic. **Job Zone:** 5. **Average Salary:** $41,080. **Projected Growth:** 24.4%. **Occupational Values:** Ability Utilization; Achievement; Creativity; Responsibility; Working Conditions; Company Policies and Practices; Autonomy. **Skills Required:** Information Gathering; Writing; Reading Comprehension; Synthesis/Reorganization; Information Organization; Active Listening; Active Learning. **Abilities:** Written Expression; Written Comprehension; Near Vision. **Interacting with Others:** Interpreting Meaning of Information to Others; Communicating with Other Workers; Communicating with Persons Outside Organization. **Physical Work Conditions:** Indoors; Sitting; Using Hands on Objects, Tools, Controls.

27-3043.01 Poets and Lyricists

Write poetry or song lyrics for publication or performance. **Education:** Bachelor's degree. **Occupational Type:** Artistic. **Job Zone:** 4. **Average Salary:** $34,570. **Projected Growth:** 24.4%. **Occupational Values:** Creativity; Ability Utilization; Independence; Achievement; Autonomy; Responsibility; Recognition. **Skills Required:** Writing; Reading Comprehension. **Abilities:** Originality; Written Expression; Fluency of Ideas. **Interacting with Others:** Communicating with Persons Outside Organization. **Physical Work Conditions:** Indoors; Sitting.

27-3043.02 Creative Writers

Create original written works, such as plays or prose, for publication or performance. **Education:** Bachelor's degree. **Occupational Type:** Artistic. **Job Zone:** 4. **Average Salary:** $34,570. **Projected Growth:** 24.4%. **Occupational Values:** Creativity; Ability Utilization; Achievement; Autonomy; Working Conditions; Independence; Recognition. **Skills Required:** Writing; Reading Comprehension; Idea Generation; Information Gathering; Monitoring. **Abilities:** Written Expression; Originality; Written Comprehension; Fluency of Ideas; Near Vision. **Interacting with Others:** Communicating with Other Workers; Communicating with Persons Outside Organization. **Physical Work Conditions:** Indoors; Sitting.

27-3043.04 Copy Writers

Write advertising copy for use by publication or broadcast media to promote sale of goods and services. **Education:** Bachelor's degree. **Occupational Type:** Artistic. **Job Zone:** 4. **Average Salary:** $34,570. **Projected Growth:** 24.4%. **Occupational Values:** Creativity; Ability Utilization; Working Conditions; Responsibility; Achievement; Recognition; Autonomy. **Skills Required:** Writing; Reading Comprehension; Idea Generation; Monitoring; Information Gathering; Active Learning; Critical Thinking. **Abilities:** Written Expression; Written Comprehension; Oral Comprehension; Fluency of Ideas; Near Vision; Oral Expression; Originality. **Interacting with Others:** Communicating with Other Workers; Providing Consultation and Advice to Others. **Physical Work Conditions:** Indoors; Sitting; Using Hands on Objects, Tools, Controls.

01.03.01 News, Broadcasting, and Public Relations

27-3021.00 Broadcast News Analysts

Analyze, interpret, and broadcast news received from various sources. **Education:** Long-term O-J-T. **Occupational Type:** Artistic. **Job Zone:** 4. **Average Salary:** $31,580. **Projected Growth:** 2.8%. **Occupational Values:** Achievement; Ability Utilization; Working Conditions; Creativity; Recognition; Social Status; Company Policies and Practices. **Skills Required:** Information Gathering; Information Organization; Speaking; Writing; Reading Comprehension; Active Listening; Synthesis/Reorganization. **Abilities:** Oral Expression; Oral Comprehension; Speech Clarity; Written Expression; Written Comprehension; Inductive Reasoning. **Interacting with Others:** Interpreting Meaning of Information to Others; Performing for/Working with Public. **Physical Work Conditions:** Indoors; Sitting.

27-3022.00 Reporters and Correspondents

Collect and analyze facts about newsworthy events by interview, investigation, or observation. Report and write stories for newspaper, news magazine, radio, or television. **Education:** Bachelor's degree. **Occupational Type:** Artistic. **Job Zone:** 4. **Average Salary:** $26,040. **Projected Growth:** 2.8%. **Occupational Values:** Ability Utilization; Achievement; Creativity; Recognition; Variety; Advancement; Security. **Skills Required:** Information Gathering; Active Listening; Writing; Reading Comprehension; Information Organization; Speaking; Synthesis/Reorganization. **Abilities:** Oral Expression; Oral Comprehension; Written Expression; Speech Clarity; Written Comprehension; Fluency of Ideas. **Interacting with Others:** Communicating with Persons Outside Organization; Performing for/Working with Public. **Physical Work Conditions:** Standing; Indoors; Outdoors; Sitting.

27-3031.00 Public Relations Specialists

Engage in promoting or creating good will for individuals, groups, or organizations by writing or selecting favorable publicity material and releasing it through various communications media. May prepare and arrange displays and make speeches. **Education:** Bachelor's degree. **Occupational Type:** Enterprising. **Job Zone:** 4. **Average Salary:** $34,550. **Projected Growth:** 24.6%. **Occupational Values:** Creativity; Achievement; Ability Utilization; Recognition; Responsibility; Working Conditions; Compensation. **Skills Required:** Writing; Speaking; Persuasion; Information Gathering; Identification of Key Causes; Critical Thinking; Implementation Planning. **Abilities:** Oral Expression; Written Expression; Oral Comprehension; Speech Clarity; Fluency of Ideas; Near Vision; Originality. **Interacting with Others:** Communicating with Persons Outside Organization; Establishing and Maintaining Relationships; Communicating with Other Workers; Selling or Influencing Others. **Physical Work Conditions:** Indoors; Sitting.

27-3043.03 Caption Writers

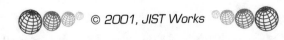

Write caption phrases of dialogue for hearing-impaired and foreign language speaking viewers of movie or television productions. **Education:** Bachelor's degree. **Occupational Type:** Artistic. **Job Zone:** 3. **Average Salary:** $34,570. **Projected Growth:** 24.4%. **Occupational Values:** Ability Utilization; Working Conditions; Moral Values; Achievement; Autonomy; Independence; Variety. **Skills Required:** Writing; Reading Comprehension; Active Listening. **Abilities:** Written Expression; Oral Comprehension; Written Comprehension; Near Vision. **Interacting with Others:** Interpreting Meaning of Information to Others; Communicating with Other Workers. **Physical Work Conditions:** Indoors; Sitting.

27-3091.00 Interpreters and Translators

Translate or interpret written, oral, or sign language text into another language for others. **Education:** Bachelor's degree. **Occupational Type:** Artistic. **Job Zone:** 3. **Average Salary:** $36,790. **Projected Growth:** 21.2%. **Occupational Values:** Ability Utilization; Achievement; Working Conditions; Social Service; Autonomy; Moral Values; Social Status. **Skills Required:** Active Listening; Speaking; Reading Comprehension; Writing. **Abilities:** Oral Comprehension; Oral Expression; Written Comprehension; Speech Recognition; Speech Clarity; Written Expression; Memorization. **Interacting with Others:** Interpreting Meaning of Information to Others. **Physical Work Conditions:** Indoors; Sitting.

01.04.01 Visual Arts: Studio Art

27-1013.01 Painters and Illustrators

Paint or draw subject material to produce original artwork or illustrations, using watercolors, oils, acrylics, tempera, or other paint mediums. **Education:** Work experience, plus degree. **Occupational Type:** Artistic. **Job Zone:** 4. **Average Salary:** $31,690. **Projected Growth:** 25.7%. **Occupational Values:** Ability Utilization; Creativity; Autonomy; Achievement; Independence; Responsibility; Moral Values. **Skills Required:** Idea Generation; Product Inspection. **Abilities:** Originality; Visualization; Visual Color Discrimination. **Interacting with Others:** Communicating with Persons Outside Organization. **Physical Work Conditions:** Indoors; Using Hands on Objects, Tools, Controls; Sitting; Making Repetitive Motions; Standing.

27-1013.02 Sketch Artists

Sketch likenesses of subjects according to observation or descriptions to assist law enforcement agencies in identifying suspects, to depict courtroom scenes, or to entertain patrons, using mediums such as pencil, charcoal, and pastels. **Education:** Work experience, plus degree. **Occupational Type:** Artistic. **Job Zone:** 3. **Average Salary:** $31,690. **Projected Growth:** 25.7%. **Occupational Values:** Ability Utilization; Achievement; Creativity; Moral Values; Autonomy; Working Conditions; Responsibility. **Skills Required:** Active Listening; Information Organization; Synthesis/Reorganization; Speaking. **Abilities:** Visualization. **Interacting with Others:** Communicating with Persons Outside Organization. **Physical Work Conditions:** Indoors; Sitting; Using Hands on Objects, Tools, Controls; Making Repetitive Motions.

27-1013.03 Cartoonists

Create original artwork using any of a wide variety of mediums and techniques, such as painting and sculpture. **Education:** Work experience, plus degree. **Occupational Type:** Artistic. **Job Zone:** 4. **Average Salary:** $31,690. **Projected Growth:** 25.7%. **Occupational Values:** Creativity; Ability Utilization; Autonomy; Achievement; Independence; Working Conditions; Recognition. **Skills Required:** Idea Generation; Idea Evaluation; Reading Comprehension. **Abilities:** Originality; Fluency of Ideas; Visual Color Discrimination; Visualization; Arm-Hand Steadiness; Oral Comprehension; Written Comprehension. **Interacting with Others:** Communicating with Other Workers. **Physical Work Conditions:** Indoors; Sitting.

27-1013.04 Sculptors

Design and construct three-dimensional art works, using materials such as stone, wood, plaster, and metal and employing various manual and tool techniques. **Education:** Work experience, plus degree. **Occupational Type:** Artistic. **Job Zone:** 5. **Average Salary:** $31,690. **Projected Growth:** 25.7%. **Occupational Values:** Creativity; Ability Utilization; Independence; Autonomy; Achievement; Responsibility; Moral Values. **Skills Required:** Idea Generation; Equipment Selection. **Abilities:** Originality; Visualization; Manual Dexterity. **Interacting with Others:** Monitoring and Controlling Resources. **Physical Work Conditions:** Using Hands on Objects, Tools, Controls; Indoors; Standing.

01.04.02 Visual Arts: Design

27-1014.00 Multi-Media Artists and Animators

Create special effects, animation, or other visual images using film, video, computers, or other electronic tools and media for use in products or creations such as computer games, movies, music videos, and commercials. No other data currently available.

27-1021.00 Commercial and Industrial Designers

Develop and design manufactured products, such as cars, home appliances, and children's toys. Combine artistic talent with research on product use, marketing, and materials to create the most functional and appealing product design. **Education:** Bachelor's degree. **Occupational Type:** Artistic. **Job Zone:** 4. **Average Salary:** $29,190. **Projected Growth:** 27.1%. **Occupational Values:** Ability Utilization; Creativity; Achievement; Autonomy; Working Conditions; Compensation; Responsibility. **Skills Required:** Operations Analysis; Identification of Key Causes; Idea Evaluation; Active Listening; Idea Generation; Product Inspection; Critical Thinking. **Abilities:** Originality; Written Comprehension; Fluency of Ideas; Oral Comprehension; Oral Expression; Visualization; Written Expression. **Interacting with Others:** Communicating with Persons Outside Organization; Communicating with Other Workers. **Physical Work Conditions:** Indoors; Using Hands on Objects, Tools, Controls; Sitting; Standing.

27-1022.00 Fashion Designers

Design clothing and accessories. Create original garments or design garments that follow well established fashion trends. May develop the line of color and kinds of materials. **Education:** Bachelor's degree. **Occupational Type:** Artistic. **Job Zone:** 3. **Average Salary:** $29,190. **Projected Growth:** 27.1%. **Occupational Values:** Creativity; Achievement; Ability Utilization; Autonomy; Responsibility; Moral Values; Recognition. **Skills Required:** Idea Generation; Active Learning; Operations Analysis; Visioning; Coordination; Identification of Key Causes; Information Gathering. **Abilities:** Fluency of Ideas; Originality; Visual Color Discrimination; Visualization; Finger Dexterity; Near Vision; Oral Comprehension. **Interacting with Others:** Communicating with Other Workers. **Physical Work Conditions:** Indoors; Using Hands on Objects, Tools, Controls; Sitting.

27-1023.00 Floral Designers

Design, cut, and arrange live, dried, or artificial flowers and foliage. **Education:** Bachelor's degree. **Occupational Type:** Artistic. **Job Zone:** 2. **Average Salary:** $29,190. **Projected Growth:** 27.1%. **Occupational Values:** Creativity; Achievement; Moral Values; Ability Utilization; Autonomy; Responsibility; Independence. **Skills Required:** Active Listening; Service Orientation; Speaking; Mathematics; Idea Generation; Operations Analysis; Product Inspection. **Abilities:** Oral Comprehension; Originality; Visual Color Discrimination; Visualization; Fluency of Ideas; Oral Expression; Wrist-Finger Speed. **Interacting with Others:** Communicating with Persons Outside Organization. **Physical Work Conditions:** Using Hands on Objects, Tools, Controls; Indoors; Standing; Sitting.

27-1024.00 Graphic Designers

Design or create graphics to meet a client's specific commercial or promotional needs, such as packaging, displays, or logos. May use a variety of mediums to achieve artistic or decorative effects. **Education:** Work experience, plus degree. **Occupational Type:** Artistic. **Job Zone:** 4. **Average Salary:** $29,190. **Projected Growth:** 25.7%. **Occupational Values:** Ability Utilization; Achievement; Creativity; Working Conditions; Autonomy; Recognition; Independence. **Skills Required:** Information Organization; Operation and Control; Idea Generation. **Abilities:** Originality; Fluency of Ideas; Visualization; Oral Expression; Visual Color Discrimination. **Interacting with Others:** Communicating with Persons Outside Organization. **Physical Work Conditions:** Indoors; Sitting; Using Hands on Objects, Tools, Controls.

27-1025.00 Interior Designers

Plan, design, and furnish interiors of residential, commercial, or industrial buildings. Formulate design which is practical, aesthetic, and conducive to intended purposes, such as raising productivity, selling merchandise, or improving lifestyle. May specialize in a particular field, style, or phase of interior design. **Education:** Bachelor's degree. **Occupational Type:** Artistic. **Job Zone:** 4. **Average Salary:** $31,760. **Projected Growth:** 27.2%. **Occupational Values:** Creativity; Ability Utilization; Achievement; Autonomy; Recognition; Responsibility; Working Conditions. **Skills Required:** Idea Generation; Speaking; Coordination; Active Listening; Judgment and Decision Making; Operations Analysis. **Abilities:** Visualization; Fluency of Ideas; Originality; Oral Expression; Oral Comprehension; Visual Color Discrimination. **Interacting with Others:** Establishing and Maintaining Relationships. **Physical Work Conditions:** Indoors; Sitting.

27-1026.00 Merchandise Displayers and Window Trimmers

Plan and erect commercial displays, such as those in windows and interiors of retail stores and at trade exhibitions. **Education:** Bachelor's degree. **Occupational Type:** Artistic. **Job Zone:** 3. **Average Salary:** $18,180. **Projected Growth:** 12.7%. **Occupational Values:** Ability Utilization; Creativity; Moral Values; Achievement; Working Conditions; Independence; Responsibility. **Skills Required:** Idea Generation; Installation; Idea Evaluation; Product Inspection; Implementation Planning. **Abilities:** Visualization. **Interacting with Others:** Communicating with Other Workers. **Physical Work Conditions:** Using Hands on Objects, Tools, Controls; Indoors; Standing; Bending or Twisting the Body; Hazardous Situations.

27-1027.01 Set Designers

Design sets for theatrical, motion picture, and television productions. **Education:** Bachelor's degree. **Occupational Type:** Artistic. **Job Zone:** 5. **Average Salary:** $29,190. **Projected Growth:** 27.1%. **Occupational Values:** Ability Utilization; Creativity; Achievement; Autonomy; Moral Values; Recognition; Responsibility. **Skills Required:** Coordination; Management of Material Resources; Implementation Planning; Management of Financial Resources; Operations Analysis; Product Inspection; Time Management. **Abilities:** Visualization; Oral Comprehension; Oral Expression; Originality; Written Comprehension; Fluency of Ideas; Visual Color Discrimination. **Interacting with Others:** Communicating with Other Workers; Coordinating Work and Activities of Others. **Physical Work Conditions:** Indoors; Standing; Using Hands on Objects, Tools, Controls; Sitting; Walking or Running.

27-1027.02 Exhibit Designers

Plan, design, and oversee construction and installation of permanent and temporary exhibits and displays. **Education:** Bachelor's degree. **Occupational Type:** Artistic. **Job Zone:** 4. **Average Salary:** $29,190. **Projected Growth:** 27.1%. **Occupational Values:** Creativity; Ability Utilization; Achievement; Autonomy; Moral Values; Working Conditions; Responsibility. **Skills Required:** Operations Analysis; Idea Generation; Coordination; Idea Evaluation; Implementation Planning; Active Listening; Monitoring. **Abilities:** Originality; Oral Expression; Visualization; Fluency of Ideas; Oral Comprehension; Wrist-Finger Speed; Visual Color Discrimination. **Interacting with Others:** Coordinating Work and Activities of Others. **Physical Work Conditions:** Indoors; Standing; Using Hands on Objects, Tools, Controls; Walking or Running.

01.05.01 Performing Arts, Drama: Directing, Performing, Narrating, and Announcing

27-2011.00 Actors

Play parts in stage, television, radio, video, or motion picture productions for entertainment, information, or instruction. Interpret serious or comic role by speech, gesture, and body movement to entertain or inform audience. May dance and sing. **Education:** Long-term O-J-T. **Occupational Type:** Artistic. **Job Zone:** 3. **Average Salary:** $27,370. **Projected Growth:** 23.8%. **Occupational Values:** Ability Utilization; Achievement; Recognition; Creativity; Variety; Moral Values; Social Status. **Skills Required:** Speaking; Monitoring; Reading Comprehension; Social Perceptiveness. **Abilities:** Oral Expression; Memorization; Originality; Speech Clarity; Written Comprehension; Fluency of Ideas. **Interacting with Others:** Performing for/Working with Public; Communicating with Other Workers; Communicating with Persons Outside Organization. **Physical Work Conditions:** Indoors; Special Uniform; Standing; Outdoors; Sitting.

27-2012.02 Directors—Stage, Motion Pictures, Television, and Radio

Interpret script, conduct rehearsals, and direct activities of cast and technical crew for stage, motion pictures, television, or radio programs. **Education:** Long-term O-J-T. **Occupational Type:** Artistic. **Job Zone:** 4. **Average Salary:** $27,370. **Projected Growth:** 23.8%. **Occupational Values:** Authority; Achievement; Responsibility; Creativity; Ability Utilization; Recognition; Autonomy. **Skills Required:** Speaking; Coordination; Reading Comprehension; Idea Evaluation; Management of Personnel Resources; Idea Generation; Social Perceptiveness. **Abilities:** Speech Clarity; Oral Comprehension; Oral Expression; Written Comprehension. **Interacting with Others:** Communicating with Other Workers; Coordinating Work and Activities of Others; Staffing Organizational Units; Guiding, Directing, and Motivating Subordinates; Coaching and Developing Others; Monitoring and Controlling Resources; Establishing and Maintaining Relationships. **Physical Work Conditions:** Indoors; Outdoors.

27-3011.00 Radio and Television Announcers

Talk on radio or television. May interview guests, act as master of ceremonies, read news flashes, identify station by giving call letters, or announce song title and artist. **Education:** Long-term O-J-T. **Occupational Type:** Artistic. **Job Zone:** 2. **Average Salary:** $17,950. **Projected Growth:** -4.3%. **Occupational Values:** Working Conditions; Recognition; Ability Utilization; Supervision, Human Relations; Creativity; Achievement; Autonomy. **Skills Required:** Speaking; Active Listening; Reading Comprehension; Information Gathering; Time Management. **Abilities:** Oral Expression; Speech Clarity; Oral Comprehension; Memorization; Written Comprehension. **Interacting with Others:** Communicating with Persons Outside Organization; Performing for/Working with Public. **Physical Work Conditions:** Indoors; Sitting; Using Hands on Objects, Tools, Controls.

27-3012.00 Public Address System and Other Announcers

Make announcements over loud speaker at sporting or other public events. May act as master of ceremonies or disc jockey at weddings, parties, clubs, or other gathering places. **Education:** Long-term O-J-T. **Occupational Type:** Social. **Job Zone:** 3. **Average Salary:** $17,100. **Projected Growth:** 23.8%. **Occupational Values:** Recognition; Working Conditions; Responsibility; Moral Values; Achievement; Variety; Company Policies and Practices. **Skills Required:** Speaking; Reading Comprehension; Social Perceptiveness; Coordination; Monitoring; Active Listening. **Abilities:** Speech Clarity; Oral Expression; Far Vision; Selective Attention; Written Comprehension; Near Vision. **Interacting with Others:** Performing for/Working with Public; Communicating with Persons Outside Organization. **Physical Work Conditions:** Sitting; Indoors; Outdoors.

01.05.02 Performing Arts, Music: Directing, Composing and Arranging, and Performing

27-2012.04 Talent Directors

Audition and interview performers to select most appropriate talent for parts in stage, television, radio, or motion picture productions. **Education:** Long-term O-J-T. **Occupational Type:** Artistic. **Job Zone:** 3. **Average Salary:** $27,370. **Projected Growth:** 23.8%. **Occupational Values:** Responsibility; Autonomy; Working Conditions; Variety; Ability Utilization; Authority; Achievement. **Skills Required:** Speaking; Negotiation; Active Listening. **Abilities:** Oral Expression; Speech Clarity. **Interacting with Others:** Communicating with Persons Outside Organization; Establishing and Maintaining Relationships; Resolving Conflict, Negotiating with Others; Communicating with Other Workers; Providing Consultation and Advice to Others; Selling or Influencing Others; Staffing Organizational Units. **Physical Work Conditions:** Indoors; Sitting; Standing.

27-2041.01 Music Directors

Direct and conduct instrumental or vocal performances by musical groups, such as orchestras or choirs. **Education:** Long-term O-J-T. **Occupational Type:** Artistic. **Job Zone:** 5. **Average Salary:** $22,440. **Projected Growth:** 14.8%. **Occupational Values:** Ability Utilization; Responsibility; Achievement; Autonomy; Creativity; Moral Values; Recognition. **Skills Required:** Coordination; Monitoring; Management of Personnel Resources; Instructing; Implementation Planning; Speaking. **Abilities:** Oral Comprehension; Oral Expression; Hearing Sensitivity; Written Comprehension; Auditory Attention; Originality; Memorization. **Interacting with Others:** Coordinating Work and Activities of Others. **Physical Work Conditions:** Indoors; Standing; Sitting.

27-2041.02 Music Arrangers and Orchestrators

Write and transcribe musical scores. **Education:** Long-term O-J-T. **Occupational Type:** Artistic. **Job Zone:** 4. **Average Salary:** $22,440. **Projected Growth:** 14.8%. **Occupational Values:** Ability Utilization; Autonomy; Achievement; Creativity; Moral Values; Independence; Responsibility. **Skills Required:** Idea Generation; Synthesis/Reorganization; Writing; Coordination. **Abilities:** Originality; Hearing Sensitivity; Auditory Attention; Fluency of Ideas; Written Expression. **Interacting with Others:** Interpreting Meaning of Information to Others. **Physical Work Conditions:** Indoors; Sitting.

27-2041.03 Composers

Compose music for orchestra, choral group, or band. **Education:** Long-term O-J-T. **Occupational Type:** Artistic. **Job Zone:** 5. **Average Salary:** $22,440. **Projected Growth:** 14.8%. **Occupational Values:** Ability Utilization; Creativity; Autonomy; Moral Values; Independence; Achievement; Responsibility. **Skills Required:** Idea Generation. **Abilities:** Hearing Sensitivity; Originality; Fluency of Ideas; Auditory Attention; Sound Localization; Written Comprehension; Written Expression. **Interacting with Others:** Interpreting Meaning of Information to Others. **Physical Work Conditions:** Indoors; Sitting.

27-2042.01 Singers

Sing songs on stage, radio, television, or motion pictures. **Education:** Long-term O-J-T. **Occupational Type:** Artistic. **Job Zone:** 2. **Average Salary:** $22,440. **Projected Growth:** 14.8%. **Occupational Values:** Ability Utilization; Achievement; Moral Values; Recognition; Creativity; Autonomy; Working Conditions. **Skills Required:** Coordination. **Abilities:** Hearing Sensitivity; Memorization. **Interacting with Others:** Performing for/Working with Public. **Physical Work Conditions:** Indoors; Standing; Sitting.

27-2042.02 Musicians, Instrumental

Play one or more musical instruments in recital, in accompaniment, or as members of an orchestra, band, or other musical group. **Education:** Long-term O-J-T. **Occupational Type:** Artistic. **Job Zone:** 5. **Average Salary:** $32,120. **Projected Growth:** 14.8%. **Occupational Values:** Ability Utilization; Achievement; Moral Values; Recognition; Creativity; Autonomy; Working Conditions. **Skills Required:** Coordination. **Abilities:** Hearing Sensitivity; Auditory Attention; Memorization; Wrist-Finger Speed; Speed of Closure; Sound Localization; Finger Dexterity. **Interacting with Others:** Performing for/Working with Public; Developing and Building Teams; Teaching Others. **Physical Work Conditions:** Indoors; Using Hands on Objects, Tools, Controls; Sitting; Making Repetitive Motions.

01.05.03 Performing Arts, Dance: Performing and Choreography

27-2031.00 Dancers

Perform dances. May also sing or act. **Education:** Postsecondary vocational training. **Occupational Type:** Artistic. **Job Zone:** 4. **Average Salary:** $21,420. **Projected Growth:** 13.6%. **Occupational Values:** Moral Values; Ability Utilization; Achievement; Recognition; Creativity; Autonomy; Social Status. **Skills Required:** Active Learning. **Abilities:** Gross Body Coordination; Speed of Limb Movement; Dynamic Strength; Stamina; Dynamic Flexibility; Spatial Orientation; Trunk Strength. **Interacting with Others:** Performing for/Working with Public; Coordinating Work and Activities of Others. **Physical Work Conditions:** Indoors; Standing; Walking or Running; Bending or Twisting the Body; Making Repetitive Motions; Keeping or Regaining Balance; Kneeling, Crouching, or Crawling.

27-2032.00 Choreographers

Create and teach dance. May direct and stage presentations. **Education:** Postsecondary vocational training. **Occupational Type:** Artistic. **Job Zone:** 5. **Average Salary:** $21,420. **Projected Growth:** 13.6%. **Occupational Values:** Creativity; Ability Utilization; Authority; Responsibility; Autonomy; Moral Values; Achievement. **Skills Required:** Instructing; Coordination; Idea Generation; Reading Comprehension; Speaking. **Abilities:** Originality; Fluency of Ideas; Gross Body Coordination; Oral Expression; Spatial Orientation; Dynamic Flexibility; Dynamic Strength. **Interacting with Others:** Coordinating Work and Activities of Others; Teaching Others. **Physical Work Conditions:** Indoors; Standing; Bending or Twisting the Body; Walking or Running; Making Repetitive Motions; Keeping or Regaining Balance.

01.06.01 Craft Arts

27-1012.00 Craft Artists

Create or reproduce handmade objects for sale and exhibition using a variety of techniques such as welding, weaving, pottery, and needlecraft. No other data currently available.

51-9195.04 Glass Blowers, Molders, Benders, and Finishers

Shape molten glass according to patterns. **Education:** Work experience, plus degree. **Occupational Type:** Realistic. **Job Zone:** 4. **Average Salary:** $19,847. **Projected Growth:** 25.7%. **Occupational Values:** Moral Values; Independence; Ability Utilization; Achievement; Recognition; Compensation; Autonomy. **Skills Required:** Equipment Selection. **Abilities:** Visualization; Arm-Hand Steadiness; Manual Dexterity. **Interacting with Others:** Coaching and Developing Others. **Physical Work Conditions:** Indoors; Using Hands on Objects, Tools, Controls; Standing; Making Repetitive Motions; Common Protective or Safety Attire; Hazardous Situations; Very Hot.

51-9195.05 Potters

Mold clay into ware as clay revolves on potter's wheel. **Education:** Work experience, plus degree. **Occupational Type:** Realistic. **Job Zone:** 4. **Average Salary:** $19,847. **Projected Growth:** 25.7%. **Occupational Values:** Moral Values; Independence; Autonomy; Achievement; Creativity; Variety; Responsibility. **Skills Required:** Operation and Control. **Abilities:** Arm-Hand Steadiness; Manual Dexterity; Visualization; Wrist-Finger Speed. **Interacting with Others:** Monitoring and Controlling Resources. **Physical Work Conditions:** Using Hands on Objects, Tools, Controls; Indoors; Making Repetitive Motions; Sitting; Bending or Twisting the Body.

01.07.01 Graphic Arts

43-9031.00 Desktop Publishers

Format typescript and graphic elements using computer software to produce publication-ready material. **Education:** Long-term O-J-T. **Occupational Type:** Realistic. **Job Zone:** 4. **Average Salary:** $29,130. **Projected Growth:** 72.6%. **Occupational Values:** Working Conditions; Moral Values; Independence; Security; Supervision, Human Relations; Company Policies and Practices; Autonomy. **Skills Required:** Reading Comprehension; Equipment Selection; Operation and Control. **Abilities:** Near Vision; Wrist-Finger Speed. **Interacting with Others:** Communicating with Other Workers. **Physical Work Conditions:** Indoors; Sitting; Using Hands on Objects, Tools, Controls.

51-5022.02 Paste-Up Workers

Arrange and mount typeset material and illustrations into pasteup for printing reproduction, based on artist's or editor's layout. **Education:** Long-term O-J-T. **Occupational Type:** Realistic. **Job Zone:** 4. **Average Salary:** $19,820. **Projected Growth:** -51.2%. **Occupational Values:** Moral Values; Independence; Working Conditions; Activity; Security; Supervision, Human Relations; Autonomy. **Skills Required:** Product Inspection. **Abilities:** Manual Dexterity; Near Vision. **Interacting with Others:** Communicating with Other Workers. **Physical Work Conditions:** Indoors; Using Hands on Objects, Tools, Controls; Sitting; Contaminants; Hazardous Situations; Standing.

51-5022.03 Photoengravers

Photograph copy, develop negatives, and prepare photosensitized metal plates for use in letterpress and gravure printing. **Education:** Long-term O-J-T. **Occupational Type:** Realistic. **Job Zone:** 4. **Average Salary:** $28,430. **Projected Growth:** –51.5%. **Occupational Values:** Moral Values; Independence; Achievement; Autonomy; Working Conditions; Supervision, Human Relations; Ability Utilization. **Skills Required:** Product Inspection. **Abilities:** Visual Color Discrimination; Near Vision; Finger Dexterity; Night Vision. **Interacting with Others:** Communicating with Other Workers. **Physical Work Conditions:** Indoors; Using Hands on Objects, Tools, Controls; Contaminants; Sitting; Standing.

51-5022.04 Camera Operators

Operate process camera and related darkroom equipment to photograph and develop negatives of material to be printed. **Education:** Long-term O-J-T. **Occupational Type:** Realistic. **Job Zone:** 4. **Average Salary:** $24,350. **Projected Growth:** –31.4%. **Occupational Values:** Moral Values; Independence; Autonomy; Creativity; Social Status; Ability Utilization; Working Conditions. **Skills Required:** Operation and Control. **Abilities:** Information Ordering; Visualization. **Interacting with Others:** Communicating with Other Workers. **Physical Work Conditions:** Indoors; Using Hands on Objects, Tools, Controls; Standing.

51-5022.08 Dot Etchers

Increase or reduce size of photographic dots by chemical or photomechanical methods to make color corrections on halftone negatives or positives to be used in preparation of lithographic printing plates. **Education:** Long-term O-J-T. **Occupational Type:** Realistic. **Job Zone:** 5. **Average Salary:** $29,141. **Projected Growth:** 0.2%. **Occupational Values:** Moral Values; Independence; Working Conditions; Autonomy; Security; Responsibility. **Skills Required:** Product Inspection. **Abilities:** Visual Color Discrimination; Near Vision. **Interacting with Others:** Communicating with Other Workers. **Physical Work Conditions:** Indoors; Using Hands on Objects, Tools, Controls; Sitting.

51-5022.09 Electronic Masking System Operators

Operate computerized masking system to produce stripping masks used in production of offset lithographic printing plates. **Education:** Long-term O-J-T. **Occupational Type:** Realistic. **Job Zone:** 4. **Average Salary:** $29,141. **Projected Growth:** 0.2%. **Occupational Values:** Moral Values; Independence; Working Conditions; Security; Supervision, Technical; Compensation; Company Policies and Practices. **Skills Required:** Operation and Control. **Abilities:** Near Vision. **Interacting with Others:** Communicating with Other Workers. **Physical Work Conditions:** Indoors; Sitting; Using Hands on Objects, Tools, Controls.

51-9194.01 Precision Etchers and Engravers, Hand or Machine

Engrave or etch flat or curved metal, wood, rubber, or other materials by hand or machine for printing, identification, or decorative purposes. Includes etchers and engravers of both hard and soft metals or materials, and jewelry and seal engravers. **Education:** Long-term O-J-T. **Occupational Type:** Realistic. **Job Zone:** 3. **Average Salary:** $18,148. **Projected Growth:** 0.2%. **Occupational Values:** Moral Values; Independence; Activity; Working Conditions; Achievement; Ability Utilization; Autonomy. **Skills Required:** Operation and Control. **Abilities:** Arm-Hand Steadiness. **Interacting with Others:** Communicating with Other Workers. **Physical Work Conditions:** Indoors; Using Hands on Objects, Tools, Controls; Standing; Making Repetitive Motions; Sitting.

51-9194.02 Engravers/Carvers

Engrave or carve designs or lettering onto objects, using hand-held power tools. **Education:** Work experience, plus degree. **Occupational Type:** Realistic. **Job Zone:** 3. **Average Salary:** $18,148. **Projected Growth:** 25.7%. **Occupational Values:** Moral Values; Independence; Working Conditions; Ability Utilization; Achievement; Creativity; Autonomy. **Skills Required:** Product Inspection. **Abilities:** Arm-Hand Steadiness; Manual Dexterity; Near Vision; Control Precision; Visualization; Finger Dexterity. **Interacting with Others:** Communicating with Persons Outside Organization. **Physical Work Conditions:** Indoors; Using Hands on Objects, Tools, Controls; Hazardous Equipment; Sitting; Making Repetitive Motions; Common Protective or Safety Attire.

51-9194.03 Etchers

Etch or cut artistic designs in glass articles, using acid solutions, sandblasting equipment, and design patterns. **Education:**

Work experience, plus degree. **Occupational Type:** Realistic. **Job Zone:** 3. **Average Salary:** $18,148. **Projected Growth:** 25.7%. **Occupational Values:** Independence; Moral Values; Creativity; Achievement; Autonomy; Ability Utilization; Working Conditions. **Skills Required:** Product Inspection. **Abilities:** Manual Dexterity; Arm-Hand Steadiness; Information Ordering. **Interacting with Others:** Communicating with Other Workers. **Physical Work Conditions:** Indoors; Using Hands on Objects, Tools, Controls; Common Protective or Safety Attire; Hazardous Equipment; Making Repetitive Motions; Sitting; Contaminants.

51-9194.04 Pantograph Engravers

Affix identifying information onto a variety of materials and products, using engraving machines or equipment. **Education:** Short-term O-J-T. **Occupational Type:** Realistic. **Job Zone:** 1. **Average Salary:** $16,450. **Projected Growth:** 0.2%. **Occupational Values:** Moral Values; Independence; Supervision, Technical; Activity. **Skills Required:** Product Inspection; Equipment Selection; Operation and Control. **Abilities:** Arm-Hand Steadiness; Control Precision; Near Vision; Manual Dexterity. **Interacting with Others:** Communicating with Other Workers. **Physical Work Conditions:** Indoors; Using Hands on Objects, Tools, Controls; Hazardous Equipment; Sitting; Standing; Hazardous Situations.

51-9194.05 Etchers, Hand

Etch patterns, designs, lettering, or figures onto a variety of materials and products. **Education:** Short-term O-J-T. **Occupational Type:** Realistic. **Job Zone:** 1. **Average Salary:** $18,148. **Projected Growth:** 0.2%. **Occupational Values:** Moral Values; Independence; Company Policies and Practices; Supervision, Technical. **Skills Required:** Product Inspection; Equipment Selection. **Abilities:** Manual Dexterity; Arm-Hand Steadiness; Near Vision. **Interacting with Others:** Communicating with Other Workers. **Physical Work Conditions:** Indoors; Using Hands on Objects, Tools, Controls; Hazardous Conditions; Sitting; Contaminants; Hazardous Situations.

51-9194.06 Engravers, Hand

Engrave designs and identifying information onto rollers or plates used in printing. **Education:** Short-term O-J-T. **Occupational Type:** Realistic. **Job Zone:** 3. **Average Salary:** $18,148. **Projected Growth:** 0.2%. **Occupational Values:** Moral Values; Independence; Supervision, Technical; Activity. **Skills Required:** Product Inspection. **Abilities:** Manual Dexterity; Near Vision; Arm-Hand Steadiness; Visual Color Discrimination. **Interacting with Others:** Coordinating Work and Activities of Others. **Physical Work Conditions:** Indoors; Using Hands on Objects, Tools, Controls; Sitting; Making Repetitive Motions.

01.08.01 Media Technology

27-4011.00 Audio and Video Equipment Technicians

Set up, or set up and operate, audio and video equipment including microphones, sound speakers, video screens, projectors, video monitors, recording equipment, connecting wires and cables, sound and mixing boards, and related electronic equipment for concerts, sports events, meetings and conventions, presentations, and news conferences. May also set up and operate associated spotlights and other custom lighting systems. **Education:** Short-term O-J-T. **Occupational Type:** Conventional. **Job Zone:** 4. **Average Salary:** $32,067. **Projected Growth:** 18.2%. **Occupational Values:** Working Conditions; Moral Values; Ability Utilization; Authority; Coworkers; Autonomy; Achievement. **Skills Required:** Idea Generation; Implementation Planning; Speaking; Synthesis/Reorganization; Writing; Reading Comprehension; Idea Evaluation. **Abilities:** Speech Clarity; Oral Expression; Visualization. **Interacting with Others:** Establishing and Maintaining Relationships; Teaching Others; Communicating with Other Workers; Coordinating Work and Activities of Others. **Physical Work Conditions:** Indoors; Using Hands on Objects, Tools, Controls; Sitting; Standing.

27-4012.00 Broadcast Technicians

Set up, operate, and maintain the electronic equipment used to transmit radio and television programs. Control audio equipment to regulate volume level and quality of sound during radio and television broadcasts. Operate radio transmitter to broadcast radio and television programs. **Education:** Postsecondary vocational training. **Occupational Type:** Realistic. **Job Zone:** 4. **Average Salary:** $28,933. **Projected Growth:** 6%. **Occupational Values:** Moral Values; Company Policies and Practices; Ability Utilization; Working Conditions; Supervision, Human Relations; Security; Achievement. **Skills Required:** Operation and Control; Monitoring; Information Organization; Operation Monitoring; Instructing; Equipment Maintenance; Coordination. **Abilities:** Information Ordering; Written Comprehension; Written Expression; Control Precision; Oral Comprehension; Oral Expression; Manual Dexterity. **Interacting with Others:** Communicating with Other Workers. **Physical Work Conditions:** Standing; Using Hands on Objects, Tools, Controls; Indoors; Outdoors.

27-4013.00 Radio Operators

Receive and transmit communications using radiotelegraph or radiotelephone equipment in accordance with government regulations. May repair equipment. **Education:** Associate degree. **Occupational Type:** Realistic. **Job Zone:** 3. **Average Salary:** $21,350. **Projected Growth:** 16.8%. **Occupational Values:** Company Policies and Practices; Moral Values; Supervision, Human Relations; Achievement; Security; Working Conditions; Independence. **Skills Required:** Operation Monitoring; Active Listening; Operation and Control; Speaking; Information Gathering. **Abilities:** Oral Comprehension; Oral Expression; Auditory Attention; Control Precision; Speech Clarity; Written Comprehension. **Interacting with Others:** Communicating with Other Workers. **Physical Work Conditions:** Indoors; Sitting; Using Hands on Objects, Tools, Controls.

27-4014.00 Sound Engineering Technicians

Operate machines and equipment to record, synchronize, mix, or reproduce music, voices, or sound effects in sporting arenas, theater productions, recording studios, or movie and video productions. **Education:** Associate degree. **Occupational Type:** Realistic. **Job Zone:** 3. **Average Salary:** $36,790. **Projected Growth:** 15.9%. **Occupational Values:** Moral Values; Working Conditions; Company Policies and Practices; Ability Utilization; Security; Activity; Achievement. **Skills Required:** Operation and Control; Operation Monitoring; Equipment Selection. **Abilities:** Control Precision; Hearing Sensitivity. **Interacting with Others:** Communicating with Other Workers. **Physical Work Conditions:** Indoors; Using Hands on Objects, Tools, Controls; Sitting.

27-4021.01 Professional Photographers

Photograph subjects or news-worthy events, using still cameras, color or black-and-white film, and various photographic accessories. **Education:** Moderate-term O-J-T. **Occupational Type:** Artistic. **Job Zone:** 3. **Average Salary:** $20,940. **Projected Growth:** 7.7%. **Occupational Values:** Creativity; Ability Utilization; Achievement; Autonomy; Responsibility; Recognition; Variety. **Skills Required:** Equipment Selection; Operation and Control. **Abilities:** Visualization; Arm-Hand Steadiness; Control Precision; Far Vision; Fluency of Ideas; Depth Perception; Information Ordering. **Interacting with Others:** Communicating with Persons Outside Organization. **Physical Work Conditions:** Standing; Using Hands on Objects, Tools, Controls; Indoors.

27-4031.00 Camera Operators, Television, Video, and Motion Picture

Operate television, video, or motion picture camera to photograph images or scenes for various purposes, such as TV broadcasts, advertising, video production, or motion pictures. **Education:** Long-term O-J-T. **Occupational Type:** Artistic. **Job Zone:** 4. **Average Salary:** $21,520. **Projected Growth:** 29%. **Occupational Values:** Ability Utilization; Achievement; Moral Values; Recognition; Working Conditions; Variety; Supervision, Human Relations. **Skills Required:** Operation and Control. **Abilities:** Visualization; Oral Comprehension; Written Comprehension; Control Precision; Far Vision; Oral Expression; Arm-Hand Steadiness. **Interacting with Others:** Communicating with Other Workers. **Physical Work Conditions:** Indoors; Using Hands on Objects, Tools, Controls; Standing; Outdoors; Sitting.

27-4032.00 Film and Video Editors

Edit motion picture soundtracks, film, and video. **Education:** Long-term O-J-T. **Occupational Type:** Artistic. **Job Zone:** 4. **Average Salary:** $38,770. **Projected Growth:** 23.8%. **Occupational Values:** Autonomy; Creativity; Achievement; Recognition; Social Status; Responsibility; Compensation. **Skills Required:** Synthesis/Reorganization; Information Organization; Monitoring; Product Inspection; Solution Appraisal; Reading Comprehension; Speaking. **Abilities:** Visualization; Near Vision; Information Ordering. **Interacting with Others:** Communicating with Other Workers. **Physical Work Conditions:** Indoors; Sitting; Using Hands on Objects, Tools, Controls.

01.09.01 Modeling and Personal Appearance

39-3092.00 Costume Attendants

Select, fit, and take care of costumes for cast members, and aid entertainers. **Education:** Work experience in a related occupation. **Occupational Type:** Artistic. **Job Zone:** 4. **Average Salary:** $15,330. **Projected Growth:** 19.3%. **Occupational Values:** Moral Values; Creativity; Autonomy; Responsibility; Working Conditions; Ability Utilization; Social Service. **Skills Required:** Product Inspection; Information Gathering; Information Organization; Reading Comprehension. **Abilities:** Arm-Hand Steadiness. **Interacting with Others:** Monitoring and Controlling Resources. **Physical Work Conditions:** Indoors; Standing; Using Hands on Objects, Tools, Controls.

39-5091.00 Makeup Artists, Theatrical and Performance

Apply makeup to performers to reflect period, setting, and situation of their role. **Education:** Postsecondary vocational training. **Occupational Type:** Artistic. **Job Zone:** 2. **Average Salary:** $15,150. **Projected Growth:** 10.2%. **Occupational Values:** Social Service; Moral Values; Creativity; Ability Utilization; Achievement; Autonomy; Independence. **Skills Required:** Information Gathering. **Abilities:** Originality; Visual Color Discrimination; Arm-Hand Steadiness; Visualization; Manual Dexterity; Near Vision; Finger Dexterity. **Interacting with Others:** Assisting and Caring for Others. **Physical Work Conditions:** Using Hands on Objects, Tools, Controls; Indoors; Sitting; Standing.

41-9012.00 Models

Model garments and other apparel to display clothing before photographers or prospective buyers at fashion shows, private showings, or retail establishments. May pose for photos to be used for advertising purposes. May pose as subject for paintings, sculptures, and other types of artistic expression. **Education:** Long-term O-J-T. **Occupational Type:** Artistic. **Job Zone:** 1. **Average Salary:** $17,310. **Projected Growth:** 23.8%. **Occupational Values:** Recognition; Compensation; Moral Values; Social Status. **Skills Required:** Social Perceptiveness. **Abilities:** Oral Comprehension. **Interacting with Others:** Performing for/Working with Public; Communicating with Persons Outside Organization; Establishing and Maintaining Relationships. **Physical Work Conditions:** Standing; Indoors; Walking or Running; Special Uniform.

01.10.01 Sports: Coaching, Instructing, Officiating, and Performing

27-2021.00 Athletes and Sports Competitors

Compete in athletic events. **Education:** Long-term O-J-T. **Occupational Type:** Enterprising. **Job Zone:** 3. **Average Salary:** $22,210. **Projected Growth:** 27.9%. **Occupational Values:** Ability Utilization; Recognition; Compensation; Social Status; Achievement; Coworkers; Company Policies and Practices. **Skills Required:** Coordination; Monitoring; Active Listening. **Abilities:** Speed of Limb Movement; Stamina; Explosive Strength; Gross Body Coordination; Dynamic Strength; Extent Flexibility; Oral Comprehension. **Interacting with Others:** Communicating with Other Workers. **Physical Work Conditions:**

Special Uniform; Standing; Walking or Running; Hazardous Situations; Outdoors; Bending or Twisting the Body; Common Protective or Safety Attire.

27-2022.00 Coaches and Scouts

Instruct or coach groups or individuals in the fundamentals of sports. Demonstrate techniques and methods of participation. May evaluate athletes' strengths and weaknesses as possible recruits or to improve the athletes' techniques to prepare them for competition. **Education:** Long-term O-J-T. **Occupational Type:** Enterprising. **Job Zone:** 5. **Average Salary:** $22,228. **Projected Growth:** 27.9%. **Occupational Values:** Responsibility; Autonomy; Achievement; Recognition; Authority; Social Status; Working Conditions. **Skills Required:** Instructing; Management of Personnel Resources; Judgment and Decision Making; Identification of Key Causes; Speaking; Negotiation; Idea Generation. **Abilities:** Oral Expression; Far Vision; Problem Sensitivity; Visualization; Deductive Reasoning; Speech Clarity. **Interacting with Others:** Coaching and Developing Others; Communicating with Other Workers; Developing and Building Teams; Communicating with Persons Outside Organization. **Physical Work Conditions:** Outdoors; Standing; Walking or Running; Indoors; Sitting.

27-2023.00 Umpires, Referees, and Other Sports Officials

Officiate at competitive athletic or sporting events. Detect infractions of rules and decide penalties according to established regulations. **Education:** Long-term O-J-T. **Occupational Type:** Enterprising. **Job Zone:** 3. **Average Salary:** $22,210. **Projected Growth:** 27.9%. **Occupational Values:** Responsibility; Authority; Achievement; Ability Utilization; Autonomy; Company Policies and Practices; Recognition. **Skills Required:** Coordination. **Abilities:** Oral Expression; Far Vision; Selective Attention; Near Vision; Oral Comprehension; Speech Clarity; Time Sharing. **Interacting with Others:** Communicating with Other Workers. **Physical Work Conditions:** Special Uniform; Standing; Walking or Running; Outdoors; Indoors.

39-9031.00 Fitness Trainers and Aerobics Instructors

Instruct or coach groups or individuals in exercise activities and the fundamentals of sports. Demonstrate techniques and methods of participation. Observe participants and inform them of corrective measures necessary to improve their skills. **Education:** Moderate-term O-J-T. **Occupational Type:** Social. **Job Zone:** 3. **Average Salary:** $20,671. **Projected Growth:** 28.4%. **Occupational Values:** Creativity; Authority; Social Service; Responsibility; Achievement; Company Policies and Practices; Autonomy. **Skills Required:** Speaking; Instructing; Coordination; Learning Strategies; Monitoring; Social Perceptiveness. **Abilities:** Oral Expression; Speech Clarity; Time Sharing; Gross Body Coordination; Multilimb Coordination; Stamina; Information Ordering. **Interacting with Others:** Coaching and Developing Others; Establishing and Maintaining Relationships; Teaching Others; Developing and Building Teams; Providing Consultation and Advice to Others; Guiding, Directing, and Motivating Subordinates; Interpreting Meaning of Information to Others. **Physical Work Conditions:** Standing; Outdoors; Indoors; Walking or Running.

02 Science, Math, and Engineering

02.01.01 Managerial Work in Science, Math, and Engineering

11-3021.00 Computer and Information Systems Managers

Plan, direct, or coordinate activities in such fields as electronic data processing, information systems, systems analysis, and computer programming. **Education:** Work experience, plus degree. **Occupational Type:** Enterprising. **Job Zone:** 5. **Average Salary:** $75,320. **Projected Growth:** 43.5%. **Occupational Values:** Working Conditions; Authority; Responsibility; Ability Utilization; Security; Autonomy; Compensation. **Skills Required:** Problem Identification; Coordination; Reading Comprehension; Active Learning; Speaking; Writing; Judgment and Decision Making. **Abilities:** Oral Comprehension; Oral Expression; Written Comprehension; Written Expression; Mathematical Reasoning; Number Facility; Speech Clarity. **Interacting with Others:** Guiding, Directing, and Motivating Subordinates; Coordinating Work and Activities of Others; Establishing and Maintaining Relationships; Communicating with Other Workers; Developing and Building Teams; Performing Administrative Activities; Monitoring and Controlling Resources. **Physical Work Conditions:** Indoors; Sitting.

11-9041.00 Engineering Managers

Plan, direct, or coordinate activities in such fields as architecture and engineering, or manage research and development in these fields. **Education:** Work experience, plus degree. **Occupational Type:** Enterprising. **Job Zone:** 5. **Average Salary:** $75,320. **Projected Growth:** 43.5%. **Occupational Values:** Autonomy; Compensation; Authority; Working Conditions; Company Policies and Practices; Working Conditions; Ability Utilization; Achievement. **Skills Required:** Implementation Planning; Coordination; Operations Analysis; Reading Comprehension; Speaking; Management of Material Resources; Judgment and Decision Making. **Abilities:** Oral Comprehension; Oral Expression; Written Comprehension; Written Expression; Deductive Reasoning; Inductive Reasoning; Speech Clarity. **Interacting with Others:** Guiding, Directing, and Motivating Subordinates; Coordinating Work and Activities of Others; Providing Consultation and Advice to Others; Communicating with Other Workers; Developing and Building Teams; Establishing and Maintaining Relationships; Communicating with Persons Outside Organization. **Physical Work Conditions:** Indoors; Sitting.

11-9121.00 Natural Sciences Managers

Plan, direct, or coordinate activities in such fields as life sciences, physical sciences, mathematics, statistics, and manage research and development in these fields. **Education:** Work experience, plus degree. **Occupational Type:** Investigative. **Job Zone:** 5. **Average Salary:** $75,320. **Projected Growth:** 43.5%. **Occupational Values:** Working Conditions; Responsibility; Autonomy; Authority; Ability Utilization; Creativity; Company Policies and Practices. **Skills Required:** Coordination; Reading Comprehension; Critical Thinking; Time Management; Judgment and Decision Making; Implementation Planning; Speaking. **Abilities:** Oral Comprehension; Written Comprehension; Oral Expression; Written Expression; Fluency of Ideas; Number Facility; Deductive Reasoning. **Interacting with Others:** Communicating with Other Workers; Providing Consultation and Advice to Others; Developing and Building Teams; Communicating with Persons Outside Organization; Establishing and Maintaining Relationships; Coordinating Work and Activities of Others; Interpreting Meaning of Information to Others. **Physical Work Conditions:** Indoors; Sitting.

02.02.01 Physical Sciences

19-2011.00 Astronomers

Observe, research, and interpret celestial and astronomical phenomena to increase basic knowledge and apply such information to practical problems. **Education:** Doctor's degree. **Occupational Type:** Investigative. **Job Zone:** 5. **Average Salary:** $73,240. **Projected Growth:** 2.2%. **Occupational Values:** Autonomy; Independence; Moral Values; Ability Utilization; Creativity; Responsibility; Achievement. **Skills Required:** Mathematics; Science; Information Gathering; Active Learning; Critical Thinking; Reading Comprehension; Technology Design. **Abilities:** Inductive Reasoning; Mathematical Reasoning; Written Comprehension; Deductive Reasoning; Number Facility; Written Expression. **Interacting with Others:** Interpreting Meaning of Information to Others. **Physical Work Conditions:** Sitting; Indoors; Outdoors; Standing; Using Hands on Objects, Tools, Controls.

19-2012.00 Physicists

Conduct research into the phases of physical phenomena, develop theories and laws on the basis of observation and experiments, and devise methods to apply laws and theories to industry and other fields. **Education:** Doctor's degree. **Occupational Type:** Investigative. **Job Zone:** 5. **Average Salary:** $73,240. **Projected Growth:** 2.2%. **Occupational Values:** Autonomy; Ability Utilization; Creativity; Achievement; Recognition; Working Conditions; Social Status. **Skills Required:** Science; Mathematics; Active Learning; Writing; Reading Comprehension; Critical Thinking; Idea Generation. **Abilities:** Written Comprehension; Oral Comprehension; Written Expression; Deductive Reasoning; Inductive Reasoning; Mathematical Reasoning; Oral Expression. **Interacting with Others:** Interpreting Meaning of Information to Others. **Physical Work Conditions:** Indoors; Sitting.

19-2021.00 Atmospheric and Space Scientists

Investigate atmospheric phenomena and interpret meteorological data gathered by surface and air stations, satellites, and radar to prepare reports and forecasts for public and other uses. **Education:** Bachelor's degree. **Occupational Type:** Investigative. **Job Zone:** 4. **Average Salary:** $54,430. **Projected Growth:** 14.6%. **Occupational Values:** Moral Values; Security; Autonomy; Ability Utilization; Responsibility; Social Status; Achievement. **Skills Required:** Information Gathering; Critical Thinking; Information Organization; Active Learning; Reading Comprehension; Speaking; Science. **Abilities:** Speech Clarity; Oral Expression; Written Comprehension. **Interacting**

with Others: Interpreting Meaning of Information to Others; Communicating with Other Workers; Communicating with Persons Outside Organization; Performing for/Working with Public. **Physical Work Conditions:** Indoors; Sitting.

19-2031.00 Chemists

Conduct qualitative and quantitative chemical analyses or chemical experiments in laboratories for quality or process control or to develop new products or knowledge. **Education:** Bachelor's degree. **Occupational Type:** Investigative. **Job Zone:** 4. **Average Salary:** $46,220. **Projected Growth:** 13.9%. **Occupational Values:** Ability Utilization; Creativity; Security; Responsibility; Achievement; Autonomy; Moral Values. **Skills Required:** Science; Information Gathering; Active Learning; Critical Thinking; Reading Comprehension; Writing; Judgment and Decision Making. **Abilities:** Deductive Reasoning; Mathematical Reasoning; Oral Expression; Written Comprehension; Written Expression; Near Vision; Oral Comprehension. **Interacting with Others:** Communicating with Other Workers; Coordinating Work and Activities of Others; Interpreting Meaning of Information to Others. **Physical Work Conditions:** Indoors; Hazardous Conditions; Contaminants; Common Protective or Safety Attire; Using Hands on Objects, Tools, Controls; Standing.

19-2032.00 Materials Scientists

Research and study the structures and chemical properties of various natural and manmade materials, including metals, alloys, rubber, ceramics, semiconductors, polymers, and glass. Determine ways to strengthen or combine materials or develop new materials with new or specific properties for use in a variety of products and applications. **Education:** Bachelor's degree. **Occupational Type:** Investigative. **Job Zone:** 4. **Average Salary:** $48,990. **Projected Growth:** 22.7%. **Occupational Values:** Autonomy; Creativity; Ability Utilization; Responsibility; Working Conditions; Moral Values; Security. **Skills Required:** Science; Writing; Reading Comprehension; Mathematics; Information Gathering; Active Learning; Speaking. **Abilities:** Written Comprehension; Written Expression; Mathematical Reasoning; Originality; Deductive Reasoning; Fluency of Ideas; Oral Expression. **Interacting with Others:** Guiding, Directing, and Motivating Subordinates. **Physical Work Conditions:** Indoors; Sitting; Using Hands on Objects, Tools, Controls.

19-2042.01 Geologists

Study composition, structure, and history of the earth's crust. Examine rocks, minerals, and fossil remains to identify and determine the sequence of processes affecting the development of the earth. **Education:** Bachelor's degree. **Occupational Type:** Investigative. **Job Zone:** 5. **Average Salary:** $53,890. **Projected Growth:** 15.5%. **Occupational Values:** Moral Values; Ability Utilization; Responsibility; Autonomy; Achievement; Creativity; Independence. **Skills Required:** Science; Mathematics; Critical Thinking; Information Gathering; Writing; Active Learning; Equipment Selection. **Abilities:** Written Expression; Written Comprehension; Inductive Reasoning; Deductive Reasoning; Mathematical Reasoning; Number Facility; Oral Expression. **Interacting with Others:** Communicating with Other Workers; Interpreting Meaning of Information to Others. **Physical Work Conditions:** Outdoors; Sitting; Indoors.

19-2043.00 Hydrologists

Research the distribution, circulation, and physical properties of underground and surface waters. Study the form and intensity of precipitation, its rate of infiltration into the soil, its movement through the earth, and its return to the ocean and atmosphere. **Education:** Bachelor's degree. **Occupational Type:** Investigative. **Job Zone:** 5. **Average Salary:** $53,890. **Projected Growth:** 15.5%. **Occupational Values:** Autonomy; Ability Utilization; Moral Values; Responsibility; Independence; Achievement; Creativity. **Skills Required:** Critical Thinking; Mathematics; Science; Information Gathering; Writing; Information Organization; Active Learning. **Abilities:** Written Comprehension; Deductive Reasoning; Mathematical Reasoning; Inductive Reasoning; Number Facility; Oral Comprehension. **Interacting with Others:** Interpreting Meaning of Information to Others. **Physical Work Conditions:** Indoors; Sitting; Outdoors; Standing; Using Hands on Objects, Tools, Controls.

19-3092.00 Geographers

Study nature and use of areas of earth's surface, relating and interpreting interactions of physical and cultural phenomena. Conduct research on physical aspects of a region, including land forms, climates, soils, plants and animals, and conduct research on the spatial implications of human activities within a given area, including social characteristics, economic activities, and political organization, as well as researching interdependence between regions at scales ranging from local to global. **Education:** Master's degree. **Occupational Type:** Investigative. **Job Zone:** 4. **Average Salary:** $38,990. **Projected Growth:** 22.7%. **Occupational Values:** Autonomy; Ability Utilization; Moral Values; Responsibility; Independence; Achievement; Creativity. **Skills Required:** Writing; Information Gathering; Speaking; Information Organization; Reading Comprehension. **Abilities:** Oral Expression; Written Expression; Written Comprehension. **Interacting with Others:** Communicating with Other Workers. **Physical Work Conditions:** Outdoors; Indoors; Sitting.

02.03.01 Life Sciences: Animal Specialization

19-1011.00 Animal Scientists

Conduct research in the genetics, nutrition, reproduction, growth, and development of domestic farm animals. **Education:** Bachelor's degree. **Occupational Type:** Investigative. **Job Zone:** 5. **Average Salary:** $42,340. **Projected Growth:** 10.9%. **Occupational Values:** Autonomy; Independence; Responsibility; Creativity; Ability Utilization; Achievement; Security. **Skills Required:** Information Gathering; Science; Information Organization; Active Learning; Critical Thinking; Solution Appraisal; Implementation Planning. **Abilities:** Deductive Reasoning; Inductive Reasoning; Written Comprehension; Mathematical Reasoning; Oral Comprehension; Written Expression; Number Facility. **Interacting with Others:** Interpreting Meaning of Information to Others. **Physical Work Conditions:** Indoors; Sitting.

19-1023.00 Zoologists and Wildlife Biologists

Study the origins, behavior, diseases, genetics, and life processes of animals and wildlife. May specialize in wildlife research and management, including the collection and analysis of biological data to determine the environmental effects of present and potential use of land and water areas. **Education:** Doctor's degree. **Occupational Type:** Investigative. **Job Zone:** 5. **Average Salary:** $46,140. **Projected Growth:** 35%. **Occupational Values:** Autonomy; Achievement; Ability Utilization; Creativity; Responsibility; Security; Activity. **Skills Required:** Science; Information Gathering; Reading Comprehension; Information Organization; Active Learning; Critical Thinking; Problem Identification. **Abilities:** Deductive Reasoning; Category Flexibility; Inductive Reasoning; Near Vision. **Interacting with Others:** Interpreting Meaning of Information to Others. **Physical Work Conditions:** Using Hands on Objects, Tools, Controls; Indoors; Common Protective or Safety Attire; Hazardous Situations; Outdoors.

19-1041.00 Epidemiologists

Investigate and describe the determinants and distribution of disease, disability, and other health outcomes, and develop the means for prevention and control. **Education:** Doctor's degree. **Occupational Type:** Investigative. **Job Zone:** 4. **Average Salary:** $50,410. **Projected Growth:** 24.6%. **Occupational Values:** Social Status; Achievement; Ability Utilization; Security; Autonomy; Compensation; Responsibility. **Skills Required:** Active Learning; Science; Instructing; Idea Evaluation; Critical Thinking; Information Gathering; Speaking. **Abilities:** Oral Expression; Inductive Reasoning; Speech Clarity; Oral Comprehension; Written Expression; Near Vision; Problem Sensitivity. **Interacting with Others:** Communicating with Other Workers; Interpreting Meaning of Information to Others; Communicating with Persons Outside Organization; Teaching Others. **Physical Work Conditions:** Indoors; Diseases/Infections; Sitting; Using Hands on Objects, Tools, Controls; Common Protective or Safety Attire; Special Uniform.

19-1042.00 Medical Scientists, Except Epidemiologists

Conduct research dealing with the understanding of human diseases and the improvement of human health. Engage in clinical investigation or other research, production, technical writing, or related activities. **Education:** Doctor's degree. **Occupational Type:** Investigative. **Job Zone:** 4. **Average Salary:** $50,410. **Projected Growth:** 24.6%. **Occupational Values:** Achievement; Social Status; Security; Ability Utilization; Compensation; Autonomy; Responsibility. **Skills Required:** Active Learning; Instructing; Information Gathering; Science; Critical Thinking; Idea Evaluation; Speaking. **Abilities:** Oral Expression; Inductive Reasoning; Speech Clarity; Oral Comprehension; Written Expression; Near Vision; Problem Sensitivity. **Interacting with Others:** Communicating with Other Workers; Interpreting Meaning of Information to Others; Communicating with Persons Outside Organization; Teaching Others. **Physical Work Conditions:** Indoors; Diseases/Infections; Sitting; Using Hands on Objects, Tools, Controls; Common Protective or Safety Attire; Special Uniform.

02.03.02 Life Sciences: Plant Specialization

19-1013.01 Plant Scientists

Conduct research in breeding, production, and yield of plants or crops, and in control of pests. **Education:** Bachelor's degree. **Occupational Type:** Investigative. **Job Zone:** 5. **Average Salary:** $42,340. **Projected Growth:** 10.9%. **Occupational Values:** Autonomy; Independence; Responsibility; Creativity; Ability Utilization; Achievement; Moral Values. **Skills Required:** Science; Information Gathering; Reading Comprehension; Information Organization; Problem Identification; Writing; Critical Thinking. **Abilities:** Written Comprehension; Deductive Reasoning; Oral Comprehension; Inductive Reasoning; Information Ordering. **Interacting with Others:** Interpreting Meaning of Information to Others. **Physical Work Conditions:** Indoors; Sitting; Outdoors.

19-1013.02 Soil Scientists

Research or study soil characteristics, map soil types, and investigate responses of soils to known management practices to determine use capabilities of soils and effects of alternative practices on soil productivity. **Education:** Bachelor's degree. **Occupational Type:** Investigative. **Job Zone:** 5. **Average Salary:** $42,340. **Projected Growth:** 10.9%. **Occupational Values:** Autonomy; Independence; Creativity; Moral Values; Ability Utilization; Responsibility; Security. **Skills Required:** Science; Critical Thinking; Information Gathering; Reading Comprehension; Information Organization; Problem Identification; Testing. **Abilities:** Deductive Reasoning; Inductive Reasoning; Written Comprehension. **Interacting with Others:** Interpreting Meaning of Information to Others. **Physical Work Conditions:** Indoors; Sitting; Outdoors; Using Hands on Objects, Tools, Controls.

19-1031.01 Soil Conservationists

Plan and develop coordinated practices for soil erosion control, soil and water conservation, and sound land use. **Education:** Bachelor's degree. **Occupational Type:** Investigative. **Job Zone:** 4. **Average Salary:** $42,750. **Projected Growth:** 17.9%. **Occupational Values:** Autonomy; Responsibility; Ability Utilization; Creativity; Achievement; Independence; Security. **Skills Required:** Implementation Planning; Solution Appraisal; Science; Information Gathering; Idea Evaluation; Mathematics; Monitoring. **Abilities:** Deductive Reasoning. **Interacting with Others:** Providing Consultation and Advice to Others; Communicating with Persons Outside Organization; Interpreting Meaning of Information to Others. **Physical Work Conditions:** Outdoors; Using Hands on Objects, Tools, Controls; Indoors; Sitting; Standing.

19-1031.02 Range Managers

Research or study range land management practices to provide sustained production of forage, livestock, and wildlife. **Education:** Bachelor's degree. **Occupational Type:** Investigative. **Job Zone:** 5. **Average Salary:** $42,750. **Projected Growth:** 17.9%. **Occupational Values:** Autonomy; Independence; Responsibility; Ability Utilization; Creativity; Achievement; Security. **Skills**

Required: Judgment and Decision Making; Implementation Planning; Information Gathering; Identification of Key Causes; Idea Evaluation; Identifying Downstream Consequences; Critical Thinking. **Abilities:** Inductive Reasoning; Oral Expression; Problem Sensitivity. **Interacting with Others:** Communicating with Other Workers. **Physical Work Conditions:** Outdoors; Walking or Running; Standing.

19-1032.00 Foresters

Manage forested lands for economic, recreational, and conservation purposes. May inventory the type, amount, and location of standing timber, appraise the timber's worth, negotiate the purchase, and draw up contracts for procurement. May determine how to conserve wildlife habitats, creek beds, water quality, and soil stability, and how best to comply with environmental regulations. May devise plans for planting and growing new trees, monitor trees for healthy growth, and determine the best time for harvesting. Develop forest management plans for public and privately-owned forested lands. **Education:** Bachelor's degree. **Occupational Type:** Realistic. **Job Zone:** 4. **Average Salary:** $42,750. **Projected Growth:** 17.9%. **Occupational Values:** Autonomy; Responsibility; Ability Utilization; Achievement; Creativity; Independence; Activity. **Skills Required:** Reading Comprehension; Solution Appraisal; Systems Perception; Implementation Planning; Information Gathering; Visioning; Identifying Downstream Consequences. **Abilities:** Oral Expression. **Interacting with Others:** Providing Consultation and Advice to Others. **Physical Work Conditions:** Outdoors; Special Uniform; Standing; Hazardous Situations.

02.03.03 Life Sciences: Plant and Animal Specialization

19-1020.01 Biologists

Research or study basic principles of plant and animal life, such as origin, relationship, development, anatomy, and functions. **Education:** Doctor's degree. **Occupational Type:** Investigative. **Job Zone:** 5. **Average Salary:** $46,140. **Projected Growth:** 35%. **Occupational Values:** Ability Utilization; Autonomy; Achievement; Creativity; Independence; Responsibility; Activity. **Skills Required:** Science; Reading Comprehension; Writing; Critical Thinking; Active Learning; Mathematics; Information Organization. **Abilities:** Deductive Reasoning; Inductive Reasoning; Information Ordering; Written Comprehension; Written Expression; Oral Expression. **Interacting with Others:** Providing Consultation and Advice to Others; Communicating with Persons Outside Organization; Communicating with Other Workers; Interpreting Meaning of Information to Others. **Physical Work Conditions:** Indoors; Common Protective or Safety Attire; Using Hands on Objects, Tools, Controls.

19-1021.00 Biochemists and Biophysicists

Study the chemical composition and physical principles of living cells and organisms, their electrical and mechanical energy, and related phenomena. May conduct research to further understanding of the complex chemical combinations and reactions involved in metabolism, reproduction, growth, and heredity. May determine the effects of foods, drugs, serums, hormones, and other substances on tissues and vital processes of living organisms. No other data currently available.

19-1021.01 Biochemists

Research or study chemical composition and processes of living organisms that affect vital processes such as growth and aging to determine chemical actions and effects on organisms such as the action of foods, drugs, or other substances on body functions and tissues. **Education:** Doctor's degree. **Occupational Type:** Investigative. **Job Zone:** 5. **Average Salary:** $46,140. **Projected Growth:** 35%. **Occupational Values:** Ability Utilization; Creativity; Autonomy; Responsibility; Security; Independence; Achievement. **Skills Required:** Science; Information Gathering; Active Learning; Reading Comprehension; Writing; Mathematics; Critical Thinking. **Abilities:** Inductive Reasoning; Deductive Reasoning; Written Comprehension; Information Ordering; Written Expression; Near Vision; Problem Sensitivity. **Interacting with Others:** Interpreting Meaning of Information to Others; Providing Consultation and Advice to Others; Communicating with Other Workers. **Physical Work Conditions:** Indoors; Using Hands on Objects, Tools, Controls; Sitting; Common Protective or Safety Attire.

19-1021.02 Biophysicists

Research or study physical principles of living cells and organisms, their electrical and mechanical energy, and related phenomena. **Education:** Doctor's degree. **Occupational Type:** Investigative. **Job Zone:** 5. **Average Salary:** $46,140. **Projected Growth:** 35%. **Occupational Values:** Autonomy; Ability Utilization; Independence; Responsibility; Security; Moral Values; Achievement. **Skills Required:** Science; Reading Comprehension; Mathematics; Idea Generation; Information Gathering; Writing; Critical Thinking. **Abilities:** Written Comprehension; Deductive Reasoning; Inductive Reasoning; Near Vision; Information Ordering. **Interacting with Others:** Interpreting Meaning of Information to Others. **Physical Work Conditions:** Indoors; Using Hands on Objects, Tools, Controls; Common Protective or Safety Attire.

19-1022.00 Microbiologists

Investigate the growth, structure, development, and other characteristics of microscopic organisms, such as bacteria, algae, or fungi. Includes medical microbiologists who study the relationship between organisms and disease or the effects of antibiotics on microorganisms. **Education:** Doctor's degree. **Occupational Type:** Investigative. **Job Zone:** 5. **Average Salary:** $46,140. **Projected Growth:** 35%. **Occupational Values:** Autonomy; Ability Utilization; Independence; Creativity; Working Conditions; Responsibility; Moral Values. **Skills Required:** Science; Reading Comprehension; Writing; Information Gathering; Critical Thinking; Problem Identification. **Abilities:** Deductive Reasoning; Inductive Reasoning; Near Vision; Written Comprehension. **Interacting with Others:** Interpreting Meaning of Information to Others. **Physical Work Conditions:** Indoors; Diseases/Infections; Common Protective or Safety Attire; Using Hands on Objects, Tools, Controls; Sitting; Standing.

19-1031.00 Conservation Scientists

Manage, improve, and protect natural resources to maximize their use without damaging the environment. May conduct soil surveys and develop plans to eliminate soil erosion or to protect rangelands from fire and rodent damage. May instruct farmers, agricultural production managers, or ranchers in best ways to use crop rotation, contour plowing, or terracing to conserve soil and water; in the number and kind of livestock and forage plants best suited to particular ranges; and in range and farm improvements such as fencing and reservoirs for stock watering. No other data currently available.

19-2041.00 Environmental Scientists and Specialists, Including Health

Conduct research or perform investigation for the purpose of identifying, abating, or eliminating sources of pollutants or hazards that affect either the environment or the health of the population. Utilizing knowledge of various scientific disciplines, may collect, synthesize, study, report, and take action based on data derived from measurements or observations of air, food, soil, water, and other sources. **Education:** Bachelor's degree. **Occupational Type:** Investigative. **Job Zone:** 5. **Average Salary:** No data available. **Projected Growth:** 22.7%. **Occupational Values:** Autonomy; Ability Utilization; Achievement; Creativity; Independence; Responsibility; Security. **Skills Required:** Mathematics; Reading Comprehension; Science; Active Learning; Information Gathering; Idea Generation; Information Organization. **Abilities:** Mathematical Reasoning; Written Expression; Written Comprehension; Problem Sensitivity; Inductive Reasoning; Deductive Reasoning; Number Facility. **Interacting with Others:** Interpreting Meaning of Information to Others. **Physical Work Conditions:** Indoors; Outdoors; Contaminants; Common Protective or Safety Attire; Sitting.

02.03.04 Life Sciences: Food Research

19-1012.00 Food Scientists and Technologists

Use chemistry, microbiology, engineering, and other sciences to study the principles underlying the processing and deterioration of foods. Analyze food content to determine levels of vitamins, fat, sugar, and protein. Discover new food sources. Research ways to make processed foods safe, palatable, and healthful. Apply food science knowledge to determine best ways to process, package, preserve, store, and distribute food. **Education:** Bachelor's degree. **Occupational Type:** Investigative. **Job Zone:** 4. **Average Salary:** $42,340. **Projected Growth:** 10.9%. **Occupational Values:** Autonomy; Security; Responsibility; Ability Utilization; Creativity; Independence; Activity. **Skills Required:** Science; Active Learning; Product Inspection; Information Gathering; Critical Thinking; Implementation Planning; Solution Appraisal. **Abilities:** Written Comprehension; Oral Comprehension. **Interacting with Others:** Providing Consultation and Advice to Others. **Physical Work Conditions:** Indoors; Sitting.

19-4011.01 Agricultural Technicians

Set up and maintain laboratory and collect and record data to assist scientist in biology or related agricultural science experiments. **Education:** Associate degree. **Occupational Type:** Realistic. **Job Zone:** 2. **Average Salary:** $27,430. **Projected Growth:** 7%. **Occupational Values:** Moral Values; Company Policies and Practices; Supervision, Technical; Activity; Supervision, Human Relations; Security. **Skills Required:** Mathematics. **Abilities:** Oral Comprehension. **Interacting with Others:** Communicating with Other Workers. **Physical Work Conditions:** Indoors; Using Hands on Objects, Tools, Controls; Diseases/Infections; Standing; Kneeling, Crouching, or Crawling.

19-4011.02 Food Science Technicians

Perform standardized qualitative and quantitative tests to determine physical or chemical properties of food or beverage products. **Education:** Associate degree. **Occupational Type:** Realistic. **Job Zone:** 2. **Average Salary:** $27,430. **Projected Growth:** 7%. **Occupational Values:** Moral Values; Security; Supervision, Human Relations; Activity; Working Conditions; Company Policies and Practices; Ability Utilization. **Skills Required:** Science; Product Inspection; Reading Comprehension; Information Gathering; Critical Thinking; Mathematics; Writing. **Abilities:** Near Vision; Number Facility; Information Ordering; Written Expression. **Interacting with Others:** Interpreting Meaning of Information to Others. **Physical Work Conditions:** Indoors; Using Hands on Objects, Tools, Controls; Sitting; Standing; Common Protective or Safety Attire.

02.04.01 Social Sciences: Psychology, Sociology, and Anthropology

19-3032.00 Industrial-Organizational Psychologists

Apply principles of psychology to personnel, administration, management, sales, and marketing problems. Activities may include policy planning, employee screening, training and development, and organizational development and analysis. May work with management to reorganize the work setting to improve worker productivity. **Education:** Master's degree. **Occupational Type:** Investigative. **Job Zone:** 5. **Average Salary:** $48,050. **Projected Growth:** 11.4%. **Occupational Values:** Autonomy; Working Conditions; Creativity; Compensation; Ability Utilization; Achievement; Variety. **Skills Required:** Information Gathering; Active Learning; Speaking; Critical Thinking; Problem Identification; Identification of Key Causes; Active Listening. **Abilities:** Oral Comprehension; Oral Expression; Written Comprehension; Written Expression; Mathematical Reasoning; Originality; Inductive Reasoning. **Interacting with Others:** Providing Consultation and Advice to Others; Communicating with Other Workers; Teaching Others; Communicating with Persons Outside Organization. **Physical Work Conditions:** Indoors; Sitting.

19-3041.00 Sociologists

Study human society and social behavior by examining the groups and social institutions that people form, as well as various social, religious, political, and business organizations. May study the behavior and interaction of groups, trace their origin and growth, and analyze the influence of group activities on individual members. **Education:** Master's degree. **Occupational Type:** Investigative. **Job Zone:** 3. **Average Salary:** $38,990. **Pro-**

jected Growth: 12.7%. **Occupational Values:** Autonomy; Creativity; Working Conditions; Responsibility; Ability Utilization; Achievement; Security. **Skills Required:** Information Gathering; Writing; Critical Thinking; Reading Comprehension; Active Learning; Active Listening; Problem Identification. **Abilities:** Written Expression; Oral Comprehension; Written Comprehension; Oral Expression; Deductive Reasoning; Inductive Reasoning; Mathematical Reasoning. **Interacting with Others:** Interpreting Meaning of Information to Others. **Physical Work Conditions:** Indoors; Sitting.

19-3091.01 Anthropologists

Research or study the origins and physical, social, and cultural development and behavior of humans and the cultures and organizations they have created. **Education:** Master's degree. **Occupational Type:** Investigative. **Job Zone:** 4. **Average Salary:** $38,990. **Projected Growth:** 12.7%. **Occupational Values:** Autonomy; Ability Utilization; Creativity; Responsibility; Achievement; Moral Values; Variety. **Skills Required:** Active Learning; Writing; Reading Comprehension; Information Gathering; Information Organization; Science; Critical Thinking. **Abilities:** Oral Comprehension; Written Expression; Inductive Reasoning; Written Comprehension; Fluency of Ideas; Oral Expression; Category Flexibility. **Interacting with Others:** Interpreting Meaning of Information to Others. **Physical Work Conditions:** Indoors; Sitting.

19-3091.02 Archeologists

Conduct research to reconstruct record of past human life and culture from human remains, artifacts, architectural features, and structures recovered through excavation, underwater recovery, or other means of discovery. **Education:** Master's degree. **Occupational Type:** Investigative. **Job Zone:** 4. **Average Salary:** $38,990. **Projected Growth:** 12.7%. **Occupational Values:** Autonomy; Achievement; Responsibility; Creativity; Ability Utilization; Recognition; Social Status. **Skills Required:** Synthesis/Reorganization; Information Gathering; Information Organization; Active Learning; Science; Critical Thinking; Reading Comprehension. **Abilities:** Category Flexibility; Inductive Reasoning; Deductive Reasoning; Information Ordering; Written Comprehension; Oral Comprehension. **Interacting with Others:** Interpreting Meaning of Information to Others. **Physical Work Conditions:** Outdoors; Using Hands on Objects, Tools, Controls; Indoors; Kneeling, Crouching, or Crawling; Sitting; Standing.

02.04.02 Social Sciences: Economics, Public Policy, and History

19-3011.00 Economists

Conduct research, prepare reports, or formulate plans to aid in solution of economic problems arising from production and distribution of goods and services. May collect and process economic and statistical data using econometric and sampling techniques. **Education:** Bachelor's degree. **Occupational Type:** Investigative. **Job Zone:** 5. **Average Salary:** $48,330. **Projected Growth:** 18.4%. **Occupational Values:** Autonomy; Ability Utilization; Working Conditions; Achievement; Security; Responsibility; Independence. **Skills Required:** Problem Identification; Information Gathering; Monitoring; Systems Perception; Reading Comprehension; Writing; Identifying Downstream Consequences. **Abilities:** Mathematical Reasoning; Written Comprehension; Written Expression; Number Facility; Oral Expression; Speech Clarity; Deductive Reasoning. **Interacting with Others:** Communicating with Other Workers; Communicating with Persons Outside Organization; Interpreting Meaning of Information to Others; Providing Consultation and Advice to Others; Teaching Others. **Physical Work Conditions:** Indoors; Sitting.

19-3022.00 Survey Researchers

Design or conduct surveys. May supervise interviewers who conduct the survey in person or over the telephone. May present survey results to client. No other data currently available.

19-3051.00 Urban and Regional Planners

Develop comprehensive plans and programs for use of land and physical facilities of local jurisdictions, such as towns, cities, counties, and metropolitan areas. **Education:** Master's degree. **Occupational Type:** Investigative. **Job Zone:** 4. **Average Salary:** $42,860. **Projected Growth:** 17.4%. **Occupational Values:** Autonomy; Ability Utilization; Achievement; Creativity; Social Status; Working Conditions; Security. **Skills Required:** Implementation Planning; Judgment and Decision Making; Information Gathering; Idea Evaluation; Reading Comprehension; Idea Generation; Systems Perception. **Abilities:** Inductive Reasoning. **Interacting with Others:** Providing Consultation and Advice to Others; Communicating with Persons Outside Organization; Communicating with Other Workers. **Physical Work Conditions:** Indoors; Sitting.

19-3093.00 Historians

Research, analyze, record, and interpret the past as recorded in sources such as government and institutional records, newspapers, and other periodicals, photographs, interviews, films, and unpublished manuscripts such as personal diaries and letters. **Education:** Master's degree. **Occupational Type:** Investigative. **Job Zone:** 4. **Average Salary:** $38,990. **Projected Growth:** 12.7%. **Occupational Values:** Autonomy; Working Conditions; Achievement; Responsibility; Ability Utilization; Independence; Recognition. **Skills Required:** Reading Comprehension; Writing; Information Gathering; Information Organization; Speaking; Active Listening; Critical Thinking. **Abilities:** Written Comprehension; Written Expression; Oral Comprehension; Oral Expression; Memorization; Speech Clarity. **Interacting with Others:** Interpreting Meaning of Information to Others. **Physical Work Conditions:** Indoors; Sitting.

19-3094.00 Political Scientists

Study the origin, development, and operation of political systems. Research a wide range of subjects, such as relations between the United States and foreign countries, the beliefs and institutions of foreign nations, or the politics of small towns or a major metropolis. May study topics such as public opinion, political decision making, and ideology. May analyze the structure and operation of governments, as well as various political entities. May conduct public opinion surveys, analyze election results, or analyze public documents. **Education:**

Master's degree. **Occupational Type:** Investigative. **Job Zone:** 5. **Average Salary:** $38,990. **Projected Growth:** 12.7%. **Occupational Values:** Autonomy; Working Conditions; Responsibility; Ability Utilization; Creativity; Achievement; Security. **Skills Required:** Writing; Information Gathering; Reading Comprehension; Critical Thinking; Speaking; Information Organization; Synthesis/Reorganization. **Abilities:** Written Comprehension; Oral Comprehension; Oral Expression; Written Expression; Deductive Reasoning; Inductive Reasoning. **Interacting with Others:** Providing Consultation and Advice to Others; Communicating with Persons Outside Organization; Communicating with Other Workers. **Physical Work Conditions:** Indoors; Sitting.

19-4061.00 Social Science Research Assistants

Assist social scientists in laboratory, survey, and other social research. May perform publication activities, laboratory analysis, quality control, or data management. Normally these individuals work under the direct supervision of a social scientist and assist in those activities which are more routine. No other data currently available.

19-4061.01 City Planning Aides

Compile data from various sources, such as maps, reports, and field and file investigations, for use by city planner in making planning studies. **Education:** Bachelor's degree. **Occupational Type:** Conventional. **Job Zone:** 3. **Average Salary:** $34,759. **Projected Growth:** 21.2%. **Occupational Values:** Working Conditions; Supervision, Human Relations; Company Policies and Practices; Security; Advancement; Activity; Ability Utilization. **Skills Required:** Information Gathering; Writing; Information Organization; Mathematics; Active Listening; Speaking. **Abilities:** Written Comprehension; Written Expression; Oral Comprehension; Oral Expression; Information Ordering; Mathematical Reasoning; Speech Clarity. **Interacting with Others:** Communicating with Other Workers; Communicating with Persons Outside Organization. **Physical Work Conditions:** Indoors; Sitting.

02.05.01 Laboratory Technology: Physical Sciences

19-4031.00 Chemical Technicians

Conduct chemical and physical laboratory tests to assist scientists in making qualitative and quantitative analyses of solid, liquid, and gaseous materials for purposes such as research and development of new products or processes, quality control, maintenance of environmental standards, and other work involving experimental, theoretical, or practical application of chemistry and related sciences. **Education:** Associate degree. **Occupational Type:** Realistic. **Job Zone:** 3. **Average Salary:** $31,450. **Projected Growth:** 7%. **Occupational Values:** Moral Values; Activity; Security; Supervision, Human Relations; Ability Utilization; Working Conditions; Achievement. **Skills Required:** Science; Critical Thinking; Reading Comprehension; Mathematics. **Abilities:** Information Ordering; Near Vision; Written Comprehension; Written Expression; Control Precision; Deductive Reasoning; Mathematical Reasoning. **Interacting with Others:** Communicating with Other Workers. **Physical Work Conditions:** Indoors; Using Hands on Objects, Tools, Controls; Contaminants; Hazardous Conditions; Sitting; Common Protective or Safety Attire; Standing.

19-4041.00 Geological and Petroleum Technicians

Assist scientists in the use of electrical, sonic, or nuclear measuring instruments in both laboratory and production activities to obtain data indicating potential sources of metallic ore, gas, or petroleum. Analyze mud and drill cuttings. Chart pressure, temperature, and other characteristics of wells or bore holes. Investigate and collect information leading to the possible discovery of new oil fields. No other data currently available.

19-4041.01 Geological Data Technicians

Measure, record, and evaluate geological data, using sonic, electronic, electrical, seismic, or gravity-measuring instruments to prospect for oil or gas. May collect and evaluate core samples and cuttings. **Education:** Associate degree. **Occupational Type:** Realistic. **Job Zone:** 3. **Average Salary:** $37,503. **Projected Growth:** 7%. **Occupational Values:** Moral Values; Company Policies and Practices; Compensation; Security; Ability Utilization; Activity; Autonomy. **Skills Required:** Reading Comprehension; Information Gathering; Mathematics; Information Organization; Writing; Science; Speaking. **Abilities:** Control Precision; Written Comprehension; Information Ordering; Near Vision; Inductive Reasoning; Oral Expression; Written Expression. **Interacting with Others:** Communicating with Other Workers. **Physical Work Conditions:** Outdoors; Using Hands on Objects, Tools, Controls; Standing.

19-4041.02 Geological Sample Test Technicians

Test and analyze geological samples, crude oil, or petroleum products to detect presence of petroleum, gas, or mineral deposits indicating potential for exploration and production, or to determine physical and chemical properties to ensure that products meet quality standards. **Education:** Associate degree. **Occupational Type:** Realistic. **Job Zone:** 3. **Average Salary:** $37,503. **Projected Growth:** 7%. **Occupational Values:** Moral Values; Company Policies and Practices; Security; Advancement; Compensation; Supervision, Human Relations; Coworkers. **Skills Required:** Science. **Abilities:** Information Ordering; Near Vision; Wrist-Finger Speed; Deductive Reasoning; Oral Expression; Problem Sensitivity; Written Expression. **Interacting with Others:** Communicating with Other Workers. **Physical Work Conditions:** Using Hands on Objects, Tools, Controls; Outdoors; Indoors; Standing; Common Protective or Safety Attire; Walking or Running.

19-4051.00 Nuclear Technicians

Assist scientists in both laboratory and production activities by performing technical tasks involving nuclear physics, primarily in operation, maintenance, production, and quality control support activities. No other data currently available.

19-4051.01 Nuclear Equipment Operation Technicians

Operate equipment used for the release, control, and utilization of nuclear energy to assist scientists in laboratory and production activities. **Education:** Associate degree. **Occupational Type:** Realistic. **Job Zone:** 3. **Average Salary:** $45,970. **Projected**

Growth: 7%. **Occupational Values:** Compensation; Company Policies and Practices; Ability Utilization; Supervision, Human Relations; Activity; Independence; Security. **Skills Required:** Science; Reading Comprehension; Operation and Control; Information Gathering; Operation Monitoring; Active Listening. **Abilities:** Problem Sensitivity; Control Precision; Information Ordering; Perceptual Speed; Written Comprehension; Near Vision; Number Facility. **Interacting with Others:** Communicating with Other Workers. **Physical Work Conditions:** Indoors; Using Hands on Objects, Tools, Controls; Common Protective or Safety Attire; Radiation; Contaminants; Hazardous Conditions; Specialized Protective or Safety Attire.

02.05.02 Laboratory Technology: Life Sciences

19-4021.00 Biological Technicians

Assist biological and medical scientists in laboratories. Set up, operate, and maintain laboratory instruments and equipment, monitor experiments, make observations, and calculate and record results. May analyze organic substances, such as blood, food, and drugs. **Education:** Associate degree. **Occupational Type:** Realistic. **Job Zone:** 2. **Average Salary:** $27,430. **Projected Growth:** 7%. **Occupational Values:** Moral Values; Activity; Supervision, Technical; Company Policies and Practices; Supervision, Human Relations; Security. **Skills Required:** Mathematics. **Abilities:** Oral Comprehension. **Interacting with Others:** Communicating with Other Workers. **Physical Work Conditions:** Indoors; Using Hands on Objects, Tools, Controls; Diseases/Infections; Standing; Kneeling, Crouching, or Crawling.

19-4091.00 Environmental Science and Protection Technicians, Including Health

Performs laboratory and field tests to monitor the environment and investigate sources of pollution, including those that affect health. Under direction of an environmental scientist or specialist, may collect samples of gases, soil, water, and other materials for testing and take corrective actions as assigned. **Education:** Associate degree. **Occupational Type:** Investigative. **Job Zone:** 3. **Average Salary:** $34,931. **Projected Growth:** 7%. **Occupational Values:** Security; Independence; Company Policies and Practices; Activity; Supervision, Human Relations; Responsibility; Moral Values. **Skills Required:** Science; Information Gathering; Mathematics; Reading Comprehension; Critical Thinking; Writing; Information Organization. **Abilities:** Information Ordering; Control Precision; Number Facility; Written Comprehension; Deductive Reasoning; Mathematical Reasoning; Near Vision. **Interacting with Others:** Providing Consultation and Advice to Others. **Physical Work Conditions:** Using Hands on Objects, Tools, Controls; Contaminants; Indoors; Outdoors; Sitting; Common Protective or Safety Attire; Hazardous Conditions.

27-4021.02 Photographers, Scientific

Photograph variety of subject material to illustrate or record scientific/medical data or phenomena, utilizing knowledge of scientific procedures and photographic technology and techniques. **Education:** Moderate-term O-J-T. **Occupational Type:** Artistic. **Job Zone:** 3. **Average Salary:** $20,940. **Projected Growth:** 7.7%. **Occupational Values:** Ability Utilization; Achievement; Autonomy; Independence; Creativity; Responsibility; Recognition. **Skills Required:** Equipment Selection; Operation and Control. **Abilities:** Near Vision; Visual Color Discrimination; Far Vision; Information Ordering; Arm-Hand Steadiness; Visualization; Control Precision. **Interacting with Others:** Communicating with Other Workers. **Physical Work Conditions:** Indoors; Using Hands on Objects, Tools, Controls; Standing.

02.06.01 Mathematics and Computers: Data Processing

15-1011.00 Computer and Information Scientists, Research

Conduct research into fundamental computer and information science as theorists, designers, or inventors. Solve or develop solutions to problems in the field of computer hardware and software. No other data currently available.

15-1021.00 Computer Programmers

Convert project specifications and statements of problems and procedures to detailed logical flow charts for coding into computer language. Develop and write computer programs to store, locate, and retrieve specific documents, data, and information. May program web sites. **Education:** Bachelor's degree. **Occupational Type:** Investigative. **Job Zone:** 4. **Average Salary:** $49,570. **Projected Growth:** 29.5%. **Occupational Values:** Ability Utilization; Creativity; Security; Autonomy; Company Policies and Practices; Autonomy; Achievement; Compensation. **Skills Required:** Programming; Writing; Critical Thinking; Reading Comprehension; Information Organization; Testing; Problem Identification. **Abilities:** Oral Expression; Oral Comprehension; Written Comprehension; Written Expression; Deductive Reasoning; Mathematical Reasoning; Near Vision. **Interacting with Others:** Providing Consultation and Advice to Others; Communicating with Other Workers; Guiding, Directing, and Motivating Subordinates; Teaching Others. **Physical Work Conditions:** Indoors; Sitting.

15-1041.00 Computer Support Specialists

Provide technical assistance to computer system users. Answer questions or resolve computer problems for clients in person, via telephone, or from remote location. May provide assistance concerning the use of computer hardware and software, including printing, installation, word processing, electronic mail, and operating systems. **Education:** Bachelor's degree. **Occupational Type:** Investigative. **Job Zone:** 4. **Average Salary:** $37,120. **Projected Growth:** 102.3%. **Occupational Values:** Autonomy; Security; Working Conditions; Company Policies and Practices; Compensation; Activity; Achievement. **Skills Required:** Troubleshooting; Testing; Operations Analysis; Instructing; Problem Identification; Information Gathering; Critical Thinking. **Abilities:** Oral Comprehension; Oral Expression; Written Comprehension; Near Vision; Problem Sensitivity; Speech Clarity; Deductive Reasoning. **Interacting with**

Others: Communicating with Other Workers; Providing Consultation and Advice to Others. **Physical Work Conditions:** Indoors; Sitting; Using Hands on Objects, Tools, Controls.

15-1051.00 Computer Systems Analysts

Analyze science, engineering, business, and all other data processing problems for application to electronic data processing systems. Analyze user requirements, procedures, and problems to automate or improve existing systems and review computer system capabilities, workflow, and scheduling limitations. May analyze or recommend commercially available software. May supervise computer programmers. **Education:** Bachelor's degree. **Occupational Type:** Investigative. **Job Zone:** 3. **Average Salary:** $52,180. **Projected Growth:** 93.6%. **Occupational Values:** Company Policies and Practices; Security; Ability Utilization; Autonomy; Compensation; Creativity; Responsibility. **Skills Required:** Programming; Reading Comprehension; Troubleshooting; Testing; Problem Identification; Operations Analysis; Writing. **Abilities:** Written Comprehension; Mathematical Reasoning; Written Expression; Oral Comprehension; Deductive Reasoning; Near Vision; Fluency of Ideas. **Interacting with Others:** Communicating with Other Workers; Providing Consultation and Advice to Others; Communicating with Persons Outside Organization; Teaching Others. **Physical Work Conditions:** Indoors; Sitting; Using Hands on Objects, Tools, Controls.

15-1061.00 Database Administrators

Coordinate changes to computer databases, test and implement the database applying knowledge of database management systems. May plan, coordinate, and implement security measures to safeguard computer databases. **Education:** Bachelor's degree. **Occupational Type:** Investigative. **Job Zone:** 4. **Average Salary:** $47,980. **Projected Growth:** 77.2%. **Occupational Values:** Security; Company Policies and Practices; Compensation; Working Conditions; Ability Utilization; Responsibility; Creativity. **Skills Required:** Programming; Mathematics; Operations Analysis; Reading Comprehension; Technology Design; Instructing; Testing. **Abilities:** Oral Expression; Written Comprehension; Deductive Reasoning; Information Ordering; Mathematical Reasoning; Category Flexibility; Oral Comprehension. **Interacting with Others:** Communicating with Other Workers. **Physical Work Conditions:** Indoors; Sitting; Using Hands on Objects, Tools, Controls.

15-1071.01 Computer Security Specialists

Plan, coordinate, and implement security measures for information systems to regulate access to computer data files and prevent unauthorized modification, destruction, or disclosure of information. **Education:** Bachelor's degree. **Occupational Type:** Investigative. **Job Zone:** 4. **Average Salary:** $38,822. **Projected Growth:** No data available. **Occupational Values:** Working Conditions; Compensation; Responsibility; Autonomy; Ability Utilization; Creativity; Social Status. **Skills Required:** Programming; Writing; Idea Generation; Implementation Planning; Mathematics; Technology Design. **Abilities:** Deductive Reasoning; Oral Comprehension; Oral Expression; Written Comprehension; Near Vision; Information Ordering; Written Expression. **Interacting with Others:** Providing Consultation and Advice to Others; Communicating with Other Workers. **Physical Work Conditions:** Indoors; Sitting; Standing; Using Hands on Objects, Tools, Controls.

15-1081.00 Network Systems and Data Communications Analysts

Analyze, design, test, and evaluate network systems, such as local area networks (LAN), wide area networks (WAN), Internet, intranet, and other data communications systems. Perform network modeling, analysis, and planning. Research and recommend network and data communications hardware and software. Include telecommunications specialists who deal with the interfacing of computer and communications equipment. May supervise computer programmers. **Education:** Bachelor's degree. **Occupational Type:** Investigative. **Job Zone:** 4. **Average Salary:** $51,344. **Projected Growth:** 117.5%. **Occupational Values:** Ability Utilization; Compensation; Security; Company Policies and Practices; Working Conditions; Autonomy; Achievement. **Skills Required:** Active Learning; Operations Analysis; Testing; Reading Comprehension; Critical Thinking; Judgment and Decision Making; Identification of Key Causes. **Abilities:** Written Comprehension; Oral Expression; Near Vision; Oral Comprehension; Speech Clarity; Written Expression; Information Ordering. **Interacting with Others:** Providing Consultation and Advice to Others. **Physical Work Conditions:** Indoors; Sitting; Using Hands on Objects, Tools, Controls.

02.06.02 Mathematics and Computers: Data Analysis

15-2011.00 Actuaries

Analyze statistical data, such as mortality, accident, sickness, disability, and retirement rates, and construct probability tables to forecast risk and liability for payment of future benefits. May ascertain premium rates required and cash reserves necessary to ensure payment of future benefits. **Education:** Bachelor's degree. **Occupational Type:** Conventional. **Job Zone:** 5. **Average Salary:** $65,560. **Projected Growth:** 7.1%. **Occupational Values:** Autonomy; Working Conditions; Security; Company Policies and Practices; Ability Utilization; Independence; Supervision, Human Relations. **Skills Required:** Mathematics; Information Organization; Information Gathering; Critical Thinking; Solution Appraisal; Reading Comprehension; Synthesis/Reorganization. **Abilities:** Number Facility; Mathematical Reasoning. **Interacting with Others:** Monitoring and Controlling Resources. **Physical Work Conditions:** Sitting; Indoors; Using Hands on Objects, Tools, Controls.

15-2021.00 Mathematicians

Conduct research in fundamental mathematics or in application of mathematical techniques to science, management, and other fields. Solve or direct solutions to problems in various fields by mathematical methods. **Education:** Doctor's degree. **Occupational Type:** Investigative. **Job Zone:** 5. **Average Salary:** $51,829. **Projected Growth:** –5.5%. **Occupational Values:** Autonomy; Ability Utilization; Independence; Working Conditions; Responsibility; Security; Achievement. **Skills Required:** Mathematics; Reading Comprehension; Learning Strategies; Active Learning; Information Gathering; Information Organization; Critical Thinking. **Abilities:** Mathematical Reasoning; Number Facility; Deductive Reasoning; Inductive Reasoning;

Oral Comprehension; Written Comprehension; Information Ordering. **Interacting with Others:** Interpreting Meaning of Information to Others. **Physical Work Conditions:** Indoors; Sitting.

15-2031.00 Operations Research Analysts

Formulate and apply mathematical modeling and other optimizing methods using a computer to develop and interpret information that assists management with decision making, policy formulation, or other managerial functions. May develop related software, service, or products. Frequently concentrates on collecting and analyzing data and developing decision support software. May develop and supply optimal time, cost, or logistics networks for program evaluation, review, or implementation. **Education:** Master's degree. **Occupational Type:** Investigative. **Job Zone:** 4. **Average Salary:** $48,931. **Projected Growth:** 8.7%. **Occupational Values:** Autonomy; Ability Utilization; Creativity; Responsibility; Company Policies and Practices; Responsibility; Working Conditions; Achievement. **Skills Required:** Problem Identification; Critical Thinking; Judgment and Decision Making; Mathematics; Systems Evaluation; Information Gathering; Active Learning. **Abilities:** Mathematical Reasoning; Written Comprehension; Oral Comprehension; Written Expression; Deductive Reasoning; Number Facility; Oral Expression. **Interacting with Others:** Providing Consultation and Advice to Others; Communicating with Other Workers. **Physical Work Conditions:** Indoors; Sitting.

15-2041.00 Statisticians

Engage in the development of mathematical theory or apply statistical theory and methods to collect, organize, interpret, and summarize numerical data to provide usable information. May specialize in fields such as bio-statistics, agricultural statistics, business statistics, economic statistics, or other fields. **Education:** Bachelor's degree. **Occupational Type:** Investigative. **Job Zone:** 4. **Average Salary:** $48,540. **Projected Growth:** 2.3%. **Occupational Values:** Autonomy; Ability Utilization; Independence; Working Conditions; Responsibility; Achievement; Creativity. **Skills Required:** Information Gathering; Mathematics; Critical Thinking; Active Learning; Synthesis/Reorganization; Information Organization; Reading Comprehension. **Abilities:** Mathematical Reasoning; Number Facility; Deductive Reasoning; Inductive Reasoning; Near Vision; Written Expression. **Interacting with Others:** Interpreting Meaning of Information to Others. **Physical Work Conditions:** Indoors; Sitting.

15-3011.00 Mathematical Technicians

Apply standardized mathematical formulas, principles, and methodology to technological problems in engineering and physical sciences in relation to specific industrial and research objectives, processes, equipment, and products. **Education:** Associate degree. **Occupational Type:** Investigative. **Job Zone:** 4. **Average Salary:** $30,460. **Projected Growth:** 7%. **Occupational Values:** Ability Utilization; Working Conditions; Moral Values; Supervision, Human Relations; Advancement; Security; Activity. **Skills Required:** Mathematics; Critical Thinking; Information Organization; Reading Comprehension; Synthesis/Reorganization; Judgment and Decision Making; Active Listening. **Abilities:** Mathematical Reasoning; Number Facility; Deductive Reasoning. **Interacting with Others:** Communicating with Other Workers. **Physical Work Conditions:** Indoors; Sitting; Using Hands on Objects, Tools, Controls.

43-9111.00 Statistical Assistants

Compile and compute data according to statistical formulas for use in statistical studies. May perform actuarial computations and compile charts and graphs for use by actuaries. Includes actuarial clerks. **Education:** Moderate-term O-J-T. **Occupational Type:** Conventional. **Job Zone:** 2. **Average Salary:** $23,380. **Projected Growth:** -4.5%. **Occupational Values:** Independence; Moral Values; Working Conditions; Activity; Supervision, Human Relations; Company Policies and Practices; Security. **Skills Required:** Mathematics; Information Gathering; Information Organization. **Abilities:** Mathematical Reasoning; Number Facility; Written Expression; Written Comprehension; Near Vision. **Interacting with Others:** Interpreting Meaning of Information to Others. **Physical Work Conditions:** Indoors; Sitting; Making Repetitive Motions.

02.07.01 Engineering: Research and Systems Design

15-1031.00 Computer Software Engineers, Applications

Develop, create, and modify general computer applications software or specialized utility programs. Analyze user needs and develop software solutions. Design software or customize software for client use with the aim of optimizing operational efficiency. May analyze and design databases within an application area, working individually or coordinating database development as part of a team. **Education:** Bachelor's degree. **Occupational Type:** Investigative. **Job Zone:** 4. **Average Salary:** $61,910. **Projected Growth:** 107.9%. **Occupational Values:** Ability Utilization; Working Conditions; Responsibility; Creativity; Autonomy; Activity; Social Status. **Skills Required:** Operations Analysis; Mathematics; Science; Programming; Troubleshooting; Information Organization; Information Gathering. **Abilities:** Written Comprehension; Inductive Reasoning; Oral Comprehension; Mathematical Reasoning; Oral Expression; Written Expression; Deductive Reasoning. **Interacting with Others:** Providing Consultation and Advice to Others; Communicating with Other Workers; Communicating with Persons Outside Organization; Teaching Others. **Physical Work Conditions:** Indoors; Sitting; Using Hands on Objects, Tools, Controls.

15-1032.00 Computer Software Engineers, Systems Software

Research, design, develop, and test operating systems-level software, compilers, and network distribution software for medical, industrial, military, communications, aerospace, business, scientific, and general computing applications. Set operational specifications and formulate and analyze software requirements. Apply principles and techniques of computer science, engineering, and mathematical analysis. **Education:** Bachelor's degree. **Occupational Type:** Investigative. **Job Zone:** 4. **Average Salary:** $62,093. **Projected Growth:** 107.9%. **Occupational Values:** Ability Utilization; Working Conditions; Creativity; Responsibility; Activity; Social Status; Achievement. **Skills Required:** Operations Analysis; Mathematics; Troubleshooting; Science; Information Organization; Programming; Information Gathering. **Abilities:** Written Comprehension; Inductive Reasoning; Oral Comprehension; Mathematical Reasoning; Oral Expression; Written Expression; Deductive Reasoning. **Interacting with Others:** Providing Consultation and Advice to Others; Communicating with Other Workers; Communicating with Persons Outside Organization; Teaching Others. **Physical Work Conditions:** Indoors; Sitting; Using Hands on Objects, Tools, Controls.

17-2021.00 Agricultural Engineers

Apply knowledge of engineering technology and biological science to agricultural problems concerned with power and machinery, electrification, structures, soil and water conservation, and processing of agricultural products. **Education:** Bachelor's degree. **Occupational Type:** Investigative. **Job Zone:** 5. **Average Salary:** $52,510. **Projected Growth:** 22.6%. **Occupational Values:** Ability Utilization; Creativity; Responsibility; Autonomy; Achievement; Social Status; Moral Values. **Skills Required:** Technology Design; Idea Evaluation; Idea Generation; Science; Mathematics; Operations Analysis; Implementation Planning. **Abilities:** Deductive Reasoning; Visualization; Information Ordering; Speech Clarity. **Interacting with Others:** Communicating with Other Workers; Coordinating Work and Activities of Others; Providing Consultation and Advice to Others. **Physical Work Conditions:** Indoors; Sitting; Outdoors; Using Hands on Objects, Tools, Controls.

17-2041.00 Chemical Engineers

Design chemical plant equipment and devise processes for manufacturing chemicals and products, such as gasoline, synthetic rubber, plastics, detergents, cement, paper, and pulp, by applying principles and technology of chemistry, physics, and engineering. **Education:** Bachelor's degree. **Occupational Type:** Investigative. **Job Zone:** 5. **Average Salary:** $64,760. **Projected Growth:** 9.5%. **Occupational Values:** Ability Utilization; Creativity; Autonomy; Social Status; Responsibility; Achievement; Security. **Skills Required:** Science; Critical Thinking; Operations Analysis; Operation Monitoring; Testing; Active Learning; Information Organization. **Abilities:** Deductive Reasoning; Written Comprehension; Mathematical Reasoning; Inductive Reasoning; Originality; Written Expression; Information Ordering. **Interacting with Others:** Communicating with Other Workers; Providing Consultation and Advice to Others; Coordinating Work and Activities of Others; Establishing and Maintaining Relationships; Interpreting Meaning of Information to Others. **Physical Work Conditions:** Indoors; Common Protective or Safety Attire; Using Hands on Objects, Tools, Controls; Sitting; Contaminants; Hazardous Conditions; Standing.

17-2061.00 Computer Hardware Engineers

Research, design, develop, and test computer or computer-related equipment for commercial, industrial, military, or scientific use. May supervise the manufacturing and installation of computer or computer-related equipment and components. **Education:** Bachelor's degree. **Occupational Type:** Investigative. **Job Zone:** 4. **Average Salary:** $62,093. **Projected Growth:** 107.9%. **Occupational Values:** Ability Utilization; Working Conditions; Creativity; Responsibility; Activity; Social Status; Autonomy. **Skills Required:** Operations Analysis; Mathematics; Troubleshooting; Science; Programming; Information Organization; Information Gathering. **Abilities:** Written Comprehension; Inductive Reasoning; Oral Comprehension; Mathematical Reasoning; Oral Expression; Written Expression; Deductive Reasoning. **Interacting with Others:** Providing Consultation and Advice to Others; Communicating with Other Workers; Communicating with Persons Outside Organization; Teaching Others. **Physical Work Conditions:** Indoors; Sitting; Using Hands on Objects, Tools, Controls.

17-2121.01 Marine Engineers

Design, develop, and take responsibility for the installation of ship machinery and related equipment including propulsion machines and power supply systems. **Education:** Bachelor's degree. **Occupational Type:** Realistic. **Job Zone:** 5. **Average Salary:** $48,050. **Projected Growth:** 22.6%. **Occupational Values:** Ability Utilization; Autonomy; Creativity; Responsibility; Social Status; Achievement; Activity. **Skills Required:** Reading Comprehension; Mathematics; Critical Thinking; Writing; Equipment Selection; Idea Evaluation; Coordination. **Abilities:** Oral Expression. **Interacting with Others:** Communicating with Other Workers. **Physical Work Conditions:** Sitting; Using Hands on Objects, Tools, Controls; Indoors; Hazardous Equipment.

17-2161.00 Nuclear Engineers

Conduct research on nuclear engineering problems or apply principles and theory of nuclear science to problems concerned with release, control, and utilization of nuclear energy and nuclear waste disposal. **Education:** Bachelor's degree. **Occupational Type:** Investigative. **Job Zone:** 5. **Average Salary:** $71,310. **Projected Growth:** 5.8%. **Occupational Values:** Ability Utilization; Social Status; Creativity; Responsibility; Autonomy; Activity; Security. **Skills Required:** Science; Problem Identification; Critical Thinking; Information Gathering; Judgment and Decision Making; Mathematics; Reading Comprehension. **Abilities:** Mathematical Reasoning; Deductive Reasoning; Problem Sensitivity; Speech Clarity; Written Expression; Inductive Reasoning; Near Vision. **Interacting with Others:** Communicating with Other Workers; Providing Consultation and Advice to Others; Interpreting Meaning of Information to Others; Communicating with Persons Outside Organization; Coordinating Work and Activities of Others. **Physical Work Conditions:** Indoors; Sitting; Hazardous Conditions; Common Protective or Safety Attire; Standing; Using Hands on Objects, Tools, Controls.

02.07.02 Engineering: Industrial and Safety

17-2111.01 Industrial Safety and Health Engineers

Plan, implement, and coordinate safety programs requiring application of engineering principles and technology, to prevent or correct unsafe environmental working conditions. **Education:** Bachelor's degree. **Occupational Type:** Investigative. **Job Zone:** 4. **Average Salary:** $38,409. **Projected Growth:** 22.6%. **Occupational Values:** Autonomy; Ability Utilization; Responsibility; Social Status; Creativity; Achievement; Activity. **Skills Required:** Technology Design; Science; Problem Identification; Operations Analysis; Critical Thinking; Identification of Key Causes; Information Gathering. **Abilities:** Oral Comprehension; Written Comprehension; Deductive Reasoning; Inductive Reasoning; Mathematical Reasoning; Problem Sensitivity; Written Expression. **Interacting with Others:** Providing Consultation and Advice to Others. **Physical Work Conditions:** Indoors; Sitting.

17-2111.02 Fire-Prevention and Protection Engineers

Research causes of fires, determine fire protection methods, and design or recommend materials or equipment such as structural components or fire-detection equipment to assist organizations in safeguarding life and property against fire, explosion, and related hazards. **Education:** Bachelor's degree. **Occupational Type:** Investigative. **Job Zone:** 4. **Average Salary:** $38,409. **Projected Growth:** 22.6%. **Occupational Values:** Responsibility; Autonomy; Achievement; Ability Utilization; Social Status; Creativity; Supervision, Human Relations. **Skills Required:** Instructing; Speaking; Judgment and Decision Making; Problem Identification; Operations Analysis; Technology Design; Critical Thinking. **Abilities:** Oral Expression; Deductive Reasoning; Inductive Reasoning; Problem Sensitivity. **Interacting with Others:** Communicating with Persons Outside Organization. **Physical Work Conditions:** Indoors; Sitting.

17-2111.03 Product Safety Engineers

Develop and conduct tests to evaluate product safety levels and recommend measures to reduce or eliminate hazards. **Education:** Bachelor's degree. **Occupational Type:** Investigative. **Job Zone:** 5. **Average Salary:** $50,990. **Projected Growth:** 22.6%. **Occupational Values:** Achievement; Ability Utilization; Autonomy; Creativity; Responsibility; Activity; Working Conditions. **Skills Required:** Testing; Critical Thinking; Information Gathering; Product Inspection; Writing; Science; Problem Identification. **Abilities:** Written Expression; Deductive Reasoning; Problem Sensitivity; Inductive Reasoning; Oral Comprehension; Oral Expression; Written Comprehension. **Interacting with Others:** Providing Consultation and Advice to Others. **Physical Work Conditions:** Indoors; Sitting; Using Hands on Objects, Tools, Controls.

17-2112.00 Industrial Engineers

Design, develop, test, and evaluate integrated systems for managing industrial production processes including human work factors, quality control, inventory control, logistics and material flow, cost analysis, and production coordination. **Education:** Bachelor's degree. **Occupational Type:** Enterprising. **Job Zone:** 4. **Average Salary:** $52,610. **Projected Growth:** 12.8%. **Occupational Values:** Ability Utilization; Creativity; Autonomy; Responsibility; Activity; Authority; Social Status. **Skills Required:** Mathematics; Reading Comprehension; Information Gathering; Systems Evaluation; Writing; Critical Thinking; Idea Generation. **Abilities:** Written Comprehension; Written Expression; Oral Comprehension; Oral Expression; Deductive Reasoning; Fluency of Ideas; Mathematical Reasoning. **Interacting with Others:** Communicating with Other Workers; Providing Consultation and Advice to Others; Coordinating Work and Activities of Others. **Physical Work Conditions:** Indoors; Sitting.

17-2131.00 Materials Engineers

Evaluate materials and develop machinery and processes to manufacture materials for use in products that must meet specialized design and performance specifications. Develop new uses for known materials. Include those working with composite materials or specializing in one type of material, such as graphite, metal and metal alloys, ceramics and glass, plastics and polymers, and naturally occurring materials. **Education:** Bachelor's degree. **Occupational Type:** Investigative. **Job Zone:** 5. **Average Salary:** $57,970. **Projected Growth:** 9%. **Occupational Values:** Ability Utilization; Creativity; Moral Values; Autonomy; Responsibility; Working Conditions; Achievement. **Skills Required:** Judgment and Decision Making; Information Gathering; Operations Analysis; Critical Thinking; Science; Mathematics; Technology Design. **Abilities:** Deductive Reasoning; Inductive Reasoning; Oral Expression; Problem Sensitivity; Written Comprehension; Written Expression; Mathematical Reasoning. **Interacting with Others:** Providing Consultation and Advice to Others. **Physical Work Conditions:** Indoors; Sitting.

17-2151.00 Mining and Geological Engineers, Including Mining Safety Engineers

Determine the location and plan the extraction of coal, metallic ores, nonmetallic minerals, and building materials, such as stone and gravel. Work involves conducting preliminary surveys of deposits or undeveloped mines and planning their development; examining deposits or mines to determine whether they can be worked at a profit; making geological and topographical surveys; evolving methods of mining best suited to character, type, and size of deposits; and supervising mining operations. **Education:** Bachelor's degree. **Occupational Type:** Investigative. **Job Zone:** 4. **Average Salary:** $56,090. **Projected Growth:** –12.6%. **Occupational Values:** Responsibility; Autonomy; Ability Utilization; Social Status; Achievement; Authority; Creativity. **Skills Required:** Mathematics; Science; Critical Thinking; Information Gathering; Operations Analysis; Idea Evaluation; Judgment and Decision Making. **Abilities:** Oral Expression; Deductive Reasoning. **Interacting with Others:** Communicating with Other Workers; Coordinating Work and Activities of Others. **Physical Work Conditions:** Indoors; Sitting; Common Protective or Safety Attire.

02.07.03 Engineering: Design

17-1011.00 Architects, Except Landscape and Naval

Plan and design structures such as private residences, office buildings, theaters, factories, and other structural property. **Education:** Bachelor's degree. **Occupational Type:** Artistic. **Job**

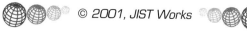

Zone: 4. Average Salary: $47,710. Projected Growth: 18.9%. Occupational Values: Ability Utilization; Creativity; Recognition; Achievement; Social Status; Working Conditions; Compensation. Skills Required: Coordination; Mathematics; Idea Generation; Implementation Planning; Product Inspection; Speaking; Visioning. Abilities: Visualization; Deductive Reasoning; Written Expression; Fluency of Ideas; Information Ordering; Number Facility; Oral Comprehension. Interacting with Others: Communicating with Persons Outside Organization; Providing Consultation and Advice to Others; Establishing and Maintaining Relationships. Physical Work Conditions: Indoors; Sitting; Using Hands on Objects, Tools, Controls.

17-1012.00 Landscape Architects

Plan and design land areas for such projects as parks and other recreational facilities, airports, highways, hospitals, schools, land subdivisions, and commercial, industrial, and residential sites. **Education:** Bachelor's degree. **Occupational Type:** Artistic. **Job Zone:** 5. **Average Salary:** $37,930. **Projected Growth:** 14.5%. **Occupational Values:** Ability Utilization; Creativity; Achievement; Social Status; Moral Values; Autonomy; Recognition. **Skills Required:** Visioning; Idea Generation; Mathematics; Synthesis/Reorganization; Active Listening; Idea Evaluation; Critical Thinking. **Abilities:** Visualization. **Interacting with Others:** Providing Consultation and Advice to Others; Communicating with Persons Outside Organization. **Physical Work Conditions:** Indoors; Sitting; Using Hands on Objects, Tools, Controls; Outdoors.

17-2121.00 Marine Engineers and Naval Architects

Design, develop, and evaluate the operation of marine vessels, ship machinery, and related equipment such as power supply and propulsion systems. No other data currently available.

17-2121.02 Marine Architects

Design and oversee construction and repair of marine craft and floating structures such as ships, barges, tugs, dredges, submarines, torpedoes, floats, and buoys. May confer with marine engineers. **Education:** Bachelor's degree. **Occupational Type:** Realistic. **Job Zone:** 5. **Average Salary:** $67,130. **Projected Growth:** No data available. **Occupational Values:** Ability Utilization; Creativity; Achievement; Social Status; Autonomy; Recognition; Compensation. **Skills Required:** Active Learning; Critical Thinking; Reading Comprehension; Testing; Idea Evaluation; Mathematics; Synthesis/Reorganization. **Abilities:** Deductive Reasoning; Visualization; Written Comprehension. **Interacting with Others:** Communicating with Other Workers. **Physical Work Conditions:** Indoors; Sitting; Using Hands on Objects, Tools, Controls.

02.07.04 Engineering: General Engineering

17-2011.00 Aerospace Engineers

Perform a variety of engineering work in designing, constructing, and testing aircraft, missiles, and spacecraft. May conduct basic and applied research to evaluate adaptability of materials and equipment to aircraft design and manufacture. May recommend improvements in testing equipment and techniques. **Education:** Bachelor's degree. **Occupational Type:** Investigative. **Job Zone:** 5. **Average Salary:** $66,950. **Projected Growth:** 8.8%. **Occupational Values:** Ability Utilization; Social Status; Creativity; Responsibility; Autonomy; Achievement; Security. **Skills Required:** Mathematics; Science; Active Learning; Technology Design; Implementation Planning; Reading Comprehension; Testing. **Abilities:** Written Comprehension; Deductive Reasoning; Mathematical Reasoning; Number Facility; Oral Comprehension; Oral Expression; Written Expression. **Interacting with Others:** Providing Consultation and Advice to Others; Interpreting Meaning of Information to Others; Communicating with Other Workers. **Physical Work Conditions:** Indoors; Sitting.

17-2031.00 Biomedical Engineers

Apply knowledge of engineering, biology, and biomechanical principles to the design, development, and evaluation of biological and health systems and products such as artificial organs, prostheses, instrumentation, medical information systems, and health management and care delivery systems. No other data currently available.

17-2051.00 Civil Engineers

Perform engineering duties in planning, designing, and overseeing construction and maintenance of building structures, and facilities such as roads, railroads, airports, bridges, harbors, channels, dams, irrigation projects, pipelines, power plants, water and sewage systems, and waste disposal units. Includes architectural, structural, traffic, ocean, and geo-technical engineers. **Education:** Bachelor's degree. **Occupational Type:** Realistic. **Job Zone:** 4. **Average Salary:** $53,450. **Projected Growth:** 20.9%. **Occupational Values:** Ability Utilization; Autonomy; Achievement; Creativity; Social Status; Activity; Responsibility. **Skills Required:** Mathematics; Implementation Planning; Reading Comprehension; Operations Analysis; Problem Identification; Writing; Critical Thinking. **Abilities:** Deductive Reasoning; Inductive Reasoning; Oral Expression; Written Comprehension; Information Ordering; Mathematical Reasoning; Near Vision. **Interacting with Others:** Communicating with Other Workers; Coordinating Work and Activities of Others; Providing Consultation and Advice to Others. **Physical Work Conditions:** Indoors; Outdoors; Sitting; Standing.

17-2071.00 Electrical Engineers

Design, develop, test, or supervise the manufacturing and installation of electrical equipment, components, or systems for commercial, industrial, military, or scientific use. **Education:** Bachelor's degree. **Occupational Type:** Investigative. **Job Zone:** 5. **Average Salary:** $62,260. **Projected Growth:** 25.9%. **Occupational Values:** Ability Utilization; Responsibility; Creativity; Autonomy; Social Status; Achievement; Working Conditions. **Skills Required:** Mathematics; Science; Reading Comprehension; Judgment and Decision Making; Critical Thinking; Technology Design; Problem Identification. **Abilities:** Number Facility; Oral Expression; Written Comprehension; Deductive Reasoning; Mathematical Reasoning; Oral Comprehension; Written Expression. **Interacting with Others:** Communicating with Persons Outside Organization. **Physical Work Conditions:** Indoors; Sitting; Using Hands on Objects, Tools, Controls.

17-2072.00 Electronics Engineers, Except Computer

Research, design, develop, and test electronic components and systems for commercial, industrial, military, or scientific use utilizing knowledge of electronic theory and materials properties. Design electronic circuits and components for use in fields such as telecommunications, aerospace guidance and propulsion control, acoustics, or instruments and controls. **Education:** Bachelor's degree. **Occupational Type:** Investigative. **Job Zone:** 5. **Average Salary:** $62,260. **Projected Growth:** 25.9%. **Occupational Values:** Ability Utilization; Responsibility; Creativity; Working Conditions; Autonomy; Social Status; Achievement. **Skills Required:** Judgment and Decision Making; Reading Comprehension; Mathematics; Critical Thinking; Idea Generation; Science; Writing. **Abilities:** Mathematical Reasoning; Oral Comprehension; Oral Expression; Written Comprehension; Deductive Reasoning; Number Facility; Written Expression. **Interacting with Others:** Communicating with Other Workers; Coordinating Work and Activities of Others. **Physical Work Conditions:** Indoors; Using Hands on Objects, Tools, Controls; Sitting; Hazardous Conditions; Standing.

17-2081.00 Environmental Engineers

Design, plan, or perform engineering duties in the prevention, control, and remediation of environmental health hazards, utilizing various engineering disciplines. Work may include waste treatment, site remediation, or pollution control technology. No other data currently available.

17-2111.00 Health and Safety Engineers, Except Mining Safety Engineers and Inspectors

Promote worksite or product safety by applying knowledge of industrial processes, mechanics, chemistry, psychology, and industrial health and safety laws. No other data currently available.

17-2141.00 Mechanical Engineers

Perform engineering duties in planning and designing tools, engines, machines, and other mechanically functioning equipment. Oversee installation, operation, maintenance, and repair of such equipment as centralized heat, gas, water, and steam systems. **Education:** Bachelor's degree. **Occupational Type:** Realistic. **Job Zone:** 4. **Average Salary:** $53,290. **Projected Growth:** 16.4%. **Occupational Values:** Autonomy; Ability Utilization; Responsibility; Creativity; Social Status; Achievement; Activity. **Skills Required:** Mathematics; Technology Design; Science; Operations Analysis; Problem Identification; Reading Comprehension; Active Learning. **Abilities:** Mathematical Reasoning; Deductive Reasoning; Written Comprehension; Number Facility; Near Vision; Visualization; Inductive Reasoning. **Interacting with Others:** Providing Consultation and Advice to Others; Communicating with Other Workers. **Physical Work Conditions:** Indoors; Sitting; Hazardous Equipment; Using Hands on Objects, Tools, Controls.

17-2171.00 Petroleum Engineers

Devise methods to improve oil and gas well production and determine the need for new or modified tool designs. Oversee drilling and offer technical advice to achieve economical and satisfactory progress. **Education:** Bachelor's degree. **Occupational Type:** Realistic. **Job Zone:** 5. **Average Salary:** $74,260. **Projected Growth:** –3.6%. **Occupational Values:** Ability Utilization; Social Status; Autonomy; Responsibility; Creativity; Compensation; Achievement. **Skills Required:** Mathematics; Writing; Science; Critical Thinking; Reading Comprehension; Product Inspection; Problem Identification. **Abilities:** Inductive Reasoning; Oral Expression; Written Comprehension; Deductive Reasoning; Oral Comprehension; Problem Sensitivity; Written Expression. **Interacting with Others:** Communicating with Other Workers; Coordinating Work and Activities of Others; Providing Consultation and Advice to Others. **Physical Work Conditions:** Using Hands on Objects, Tools, Controls; Sitting; Indoors; Standing; Outdoors; Walking or Running.

41-9031.00 Sales Engineers

Sell business goods or services, the selling of which requires a technical background equivalent to a baccalaureate degree in engineering. **Education:** Moderate-term O-J-T. **Occupational Type:** Enterprising. **Job Zone:** 5. **Average Salary:** $54,600. **Projected Growth:** 15.7%. **Occupational Values:** Ability Utilization; Achievement; Responsibility; Working Conditions; Moral Values; Activity; Autonomy. **Skills Required:** Persuasion; Speaking; Service Orientation; Social Perceptiveness; Active Listening; Problem Identification; Operations Analysis. **Abilities:** Oral Comprehension; Oral Expression; Speech Clarity; Written Comprehension; Written Expression; Near Vision; Visualization. **Interacting with Others:** Communicating with Persons Outside Organization; Selling or Influencing Others; Communicating with Other Workers; Establishing and Maintaining Relationships; Providing Consultation and Advice to Others; Interpreting Meaning of Information to Others; Resolving Conflict, Negotiating with Others. **Physical Work Conditions:** Indoors; Sitting; Using Hands on Objects, Tools, Controls; Standing.

02.08.01 Engineering Technology: Surveying

17-1022.00 Surveyors

Make exact measurements and determine property boundaries. Provide data relevant to the shape, contour, gravitation, location, elevation, or dimension of land or land features on or near the earth's surface for engineering, mapmaking, mining, land evaluation, construction, and other purposes. **Education:** Postsecondary vocational training. **Occupational Type:** Investigative. **Job Zone:** 4. **Average Salary:** $37,640. **Projected Growth:** 1.4%. **Occupational Values:** Moral Values; Achievement; Autonomy; Security; Ability Utilization; Responsibility; Compensation. **Skills Required:** Writing; Mathematics; Information Gathering; Science; Reading Comprehension; Coordination; Management of Personnel Resources. **Abilities:** Written Expression; Mathematical Reasoning; Near Vision; Far Vision; Number Facility; Oral Expression; Written Comprehension. **Interacting with Others:** Communicating with Other Workers. **Physical Work Conditions:** Indoors; Outdoors; Standing; Using Hands on Objects, Tools, Controls; Walking or Running.

17-3031.01 Surveying Technicians

Adjust and operate surveying instruments, such as the theodolite and electronic distance-measuring equipment, and compile notes, make sketches, and enter data into computers. **Education:** Postsecondary vocational training. **Occupational Type:** Realistic. **Job Zone:** 4. **Average Salary:** $25,940. **Projected Growth:** 21.8%. **Occupational Values:** Moral Values; Company Policies and Practices; Security; Supervision, Human Relations; Authority; Achievement; Compensation. **Skills Required:** Mathematics. **Abilities:** Written Expression. **Interacting with Others:** Communicating With Other Workers. **Physical Work Conditions:** Outdoors; Standing; Using Hands on Objects, Tools, Controls.

17-3031.02 Mapping Technicians

Calculate mapmaking information from field notes, and draw and verify accuracy of topographical maps. **Education:** Postsecondary vocational training. **Occupational Type:** Conventional. **Job Zone:** 3. **Average Salary:** $25,940. **Projected Growth:** 1.4%. **Occupational Values:** Moral Values; Activity; Achievement; Autonomy; Security; Independence; Company Policies and Practices. **Skills Required:** Mathematics; Information Gathering; Information Organization. **Abilities:** Near Vision; Wrist-Finger Speed; Written Comprehension; Inductive Reasoning; Mathematical Reasoning; Number Facility. **Interacting with Others:** Communicating With Other Workers. **Physical Work Conditions:** Indoors; Using Hands on Objects, Tools, Controls; Sitting.

02.08.02 Engineering Technology: Industrial and Safety

13-1041.05 Pressure Vessel Inspectors

Inspect pressure vessel equipment for conformance with safety laws and standards regulating their design, fabrication, installation, repair, and operation. **Education:** Work experience in a related occupation. **Occupational Type:** Realistic. **Job Zone:** 4. **Average Salary:** $36,820. **Projected Growth:** 10.5%. **Occupational Values:** Independence; Autonomy; Security; Responsibility; Supervision, Human Relations; Moral Values; Company Policies and Practices. **Skills Required:** Mathematics; Product Inspection; Testing. **Abilities:** Problem Sensitivity; Oral Expression; Written Expression; Oral Comprehension; Written Comprehension. **Interacting with Others:** Communicating With Other Workers. **Physical Work Conditions:** Indoors; Standing.

17-3026.00 Industrial Engineering Technicians

Apply engineering theory and principles to problems of industrial layout or manufacturing production, usually under the direction of engineering staff. May study and record time, motion, method, and speed involved in performance of production, maintenance, clerical, and other worker operations for such purposes as establishing standard production rates or improving efficiency. **Education:** Associate degree. **Occupational Type:** Investigative. **Job Zone:** 3. **Average Salary:** $38,320. **Projected Growth:** 15.9%. **Occupational Values:** Moral Values; Supervision, Human Relations; Company Policies and Practices; Ability Utilization; Activity; Achievement; Advancement. **Skills Required:** Testing; Mathematics; Product Inspection; Science; Solution Appraisal; Information Gathering; Idea Evaluation. **Abilities:** Number Facility. **Interacting with Others:** Communicating With Other Workers; Interpreting Meaning of Information to Others. **Physical Work Conditions:** Indoors; Sitting.

47-4011.00 Construction and Building Inspectors

Inspect structures using engineering skills to determine structural soundness and compliance with specifications, building codes, and other regulations. Inspections may be general in nature or may be limited to a specific area, such as electrical systems or plumbing. **Education:** Work experience in a related occupation. **Occupational Type:** Conventional. **Job Zone:** 3. **Average Salary:** $37,540. **Projected Growth:** 15.7%. **Occupational Values:** Responsibility; Autonomy; Security; Independence; Supervision, Human Relations; Company Policies and Practices; Activity. **Skills Required:** Product Inspection; Problem Identification; Judgment and Decision Making; Writing; Identification of Key Causes; Information Gathering; Active Listening. **Abilities:** Problem Sensitivity; Oral Expression; Written Expression; Written Comprehension; Deductive Reasoning; Near Vision; Inductive Reasoning. **Interacting with Others:** Communicating With Persons Outside Organization; Performing Administrative Activities. **Physical Work Conditions:** Standing; Indoors; Outdoors; Common Protective or Safety Attire; Walking or Running.

02.08.03 Engineering Technology: Design

17-1021.00 Cartographers and Photogrammetrists

Collect, analyze, and interpret geographic information provided by geodetic surveys, aerial photographs, and satellite data. Research, study, and prepare maps and other spatial data in digital or graphic form for legal, social, political, educational, and design purposes. May work with Geographic Information Systems (GIS). May design and evaluate algorithms, data structures, and user interfaces for GIS and mapping systems. **Education:** Postsecondary vocational training. **Occupational Type:** Conventional. **Job Zone:** 4. **Average Salary:** $37,640. **Projected Growth:** 1.4%. **Occupational Values:** Autonomy; Ability Utilization; Responsibility; Moral Values; Working Conditions; Achievement; Independence. **Skills Required:** Information Organization; Mathematics; Information Gathering; Product Inspection; Operations Analysis; Reading Comprehension; Synthesis/Reorganization. **Abilities:** Far Vision; Near Vision; Mathematical Reasoning; Written Comprehension; Number Facility. **Interacting with Others:** Interpreting Meaning of Information to Others. **Physical Work Conditions:** Indoors; Sitting; Outdoors.

17-3011.01 Architectural Drafters

Prepare detailed drawings of architectural designs and plans for buildings and structures according to specifications provided by architect. **Education:** Postsecondary vocational training. **Occupational Type:** Realistic. **Job Zone:** 4. **Average Salary:** $32,170. **Projected Growth:** 6.4%. **Occupational Values:** Working Conditions; Moral Values; Independence; Ability Utilization; Compensation; Achievement; Social Status. **Skills Required:** Mathematics; Visioning; Programming; Reading Comprehension. **Abilities:** Visualization; Arm-Hand Steadiness; Written Comprehension; Near Vision; Manual Dexterity; Visual Color Discrimination; Written Expression. **Interacting with Others:** Interpreting Meaning of Information to Others. **Physical Work Conditions:** Indoors; Using Hands on Objects, Tools, Controls; Sitting.

17-3011.02 Civil Drafters

Prepare drawings and topographical and relief maps used in civil engineering projects, such as highways, bridges, pipelines, flood control projects, and water and sewerage control systems. **Education:** Postsecondary vocational training. **Occupational Type:** Realistic. **Job Zone:** 3. **Average Salary:** $32,170. **Projected Growth:** 6.4%. **Occupational Values:** Moral Values; Working Conditions; Ability Utilization; Activity; Achievement; Company Policies and Practices; Independence. **Skills Required:** Mathematics. **Abilities:** Inductive Reasoning; Mathematical Reasoning; Near Vision; Number Facility; Information Ordering; Written Comprehension. **Interacting with Others:** Communicating with Other Workers. **Physical Work Conditions:** Indoors; Sitting; Using Hands on Objects, Tools, Controls.

17-3012.01 Electronic Drafters

Draw wiring diagrams, circuit board assembly diagrams, schematics, and layout drawings used for manufacture, installation, and repair of electronic equipment. **Education:** Postsecondary vocational training. **Occupational Type:** Realistic. **Job Zone:** 3. **Average Salary:** $32,170. **Projected Growth:** 6.4%. **Occupational Values:** Working Conditions; Ability Utilization; Moral Values; Compensation; Company Policies and Practices; Activity; Social Status. **Skills Required:** Mathematics; Reading Comprehension; Operations Analysis; Critical Thinking; Technology Design; Information Gathering; Testing. **Abilities:** Information Ordering; Near Vision; Visualization; Arm-Hand Steadiness; Number Facility; Oral Comprehension; Oral Expression. **Interacting with Others:** Communicating with Other Workers. **Physical Work Conditions:** Indoors; Using Hands on Objects, Tools, Controls; Sitting.

17-3012.02 Electrical Drafters

Develop specifications and instructions for installation of voltage transformers, overhead or underground cables, and related electrical equipment used to conduct electrical energy from transmission lines or high-voltage distribution lines to consumers. **Education:** Postsecondary vocational training. **Occupational Type:** Conventional. **Job Zone:** 4. **Average Salary:** $32,170. **Projected Growth:** 6.4%. **Occupational Values:** Ability Utilization; Moral Values; Autonomy; Company Policies and Practices; Achievement; Authority; Security. **Skills Required:** Mathematics; Operations Analysis; Product Inspection; Information Gathering; Synthesis/Reorganization; Judgment and Decision Making; Reading Comprehension. **Abilities:** Near Vision. **Interacting with Others:** Communicating with Other Workers. **Physical Work Conditions:** Sitting; Hazardous Conditions; Indoors; Using Hands on Objects, Tools, Controls.

17-3013.00 Mechanical Drafters

Prepare detailed working diagrams of machinery and mechanical devices, including dimensions, fastening methods, and other engineering information. **Education:** Postsecondary vocational training. **Occupational Type:** Realistic. **Job Zone:** 4. **Average Salary:** $32,170. **Projected Growth:** 6.4%. **Occupational Values:** Moral Values; Working Conditions; Ability Utilization; Activity; Company Policies and Practices; Achievement; Autonomy. **Skills Required:** Mathematics; Product Inspection; Technology Design; Information Gathering; Information Organization; Problem Identification; Critical Thinking. **Abilities:** Visualization; Arm-Hand Steadiness; Near Vision; Written Comprehension; Oral Comprehension; Deductive Reasoning; Finger Dexterity. **Interacting with Others:** Communicating With Other Workers. **Physical Work Conditions:** Indoors; Sitting; Using Hands on Objects, Tools, Controls.

02.08.04 Engineering Technology: General

17-3021.00 Aerospace Engineering and Operations Technicians

Operate, install, calibrate, and maintain integrated computer or communications systems consoles, simulators, and other data acquisition, test, and measurement instruments and equipment to launch, track, position, and evaluate air and space vehicles. May record and interpret test data. **Education:** Associate degree. **Occupational Type:** Investigative. **Job Zone:** 4. **Average Salary:** $37,420. **Projected Growth:** 15.9%. **Occupational Values:** Activity; Moral Values; Achievement; Working Conditions; Security; Ability Utilization; Compensation. **Skills Required:** Testing; Science; Mathematics; Product Inspection; Installation; Operation Monitoring; Solution Appraisal. **Abilities:** Deductive Reasoning; Information Ordering; Near Vision; Written Comprehension; Inductive Reasoning; Visualization. **Interacting with Others:** Communicating with Other Workers; Interpreting Meaning of Information to Others; Providing Consultation and Advice to Others. **Physical Work Conditions:** Indoors; Using Hands on Objects, Tools, Controls; Sitting; Standing.

17-3022.00 Civil Engineering Technicians

Apply theory and principles of civil engineering in planning, designing, and overseeing construction and maintenance of structures and facilities under the direction of engineering staff or physical scientists. **Education:** Associate degree. **Occupational Type:** Realistic. **Job Zone:** 4. **Average Salary:** $34,420. **Projected Growth:** 15.9%. **Occupational Values:** Moral Values; Working Conditions; Activity; Ability Utilization; Supervision, Human Relations; Achievement; Security. **Skills Required:** Information Gathering; Science; Mathematics; Judgment and Decision Making; Operations Analysis; Active Listening; Critical Thinking. **Abilities:** Number Facility; Problem Sensitivity; Mathematical Reasoning; Oral Comprehension; Written Comprehension; Written Expression; Deductive Reasoning. **Interacting with Others:** Communicating with Other Workers. **Physical Work Conditions:** Indoors; Sitting; Outdoors; Standing.

17-3023.01 Electronics Engineering Technicians

Lay out, build, test, troubleshoot, repair, and modify developmental and production electronic components, parts, equipment, and systems, such as computer equipment, missile control instrumentation, electron tubes, test equipment, and machine tool numerical controls, applying principles and theories of electronics, electrical circuitry, engineering mathematics, electronic and electrical testing, and physics. Usually work under direction of engineering staff. **Education:** Associate degree. **Occupational Type:** Realistic. **Job Zone:** 4. **Average Salary:** $35,970. **Projected Growth:** 16.8%. **Occupational Values:** Moral Values; Working Conditions; Ability Utilization; Activity; Achievement; Advancement; Security. **Skills Required:** Troubleshooting; Testing; Mathematics; Active Learning; Problem Identification; Science; Operations Analysis. **Abilities:** Visualization; Written Comprehension; Deductive Reasoning; Oral Comprehension; Problem Sensitivity; Written Expression. **Interacting with Others:** Communicating with Other Workers. **Physical Work Conditions:** Indoors; Using Hands on Objects, Tools, Controls; Standing; Sitting.

17-3023.02 Calibration and Instrumentation Technicians

Develop, test, calibrate, operate, and repair electrical, mechanical, electromechanical, electrohydraulic, or electronic measuring and recording instruments, apparatus, and equipment. **Education:** Associate degree. **Occupational Type:** Realistic. **Job Zone:** 4. **Average Salary:** $35,970. **Projected Growth:** 16.8%. **Occupational Values:** Moral Values; Supervision, Human Relations; Company Policies and Practices; Working Conditions; Security; Activity; Achievement. **Skills Required:** Information Gathering; Equipment Selection. **Abilities:** Mathematical Reasoning; Deductive Reasoning; Information Ordering; Problem Sensitivity; Written Comprehension. **Interacting with Others:** Communicating with Other Workers. **Physical Work Conditions:** Indoors; Sitting; Standing.

17-3023.03 Electrical Engineering Technicians

Apply electrical theory and related knowledge to test and modify developmental or operational electrical machinery and electrical control equipment and circuitry in industrial or commercial plants and laboratories. Usually work under direction of engineering staff. **Education:** Associate degree. **Occupational Type:** Realistic. **Job Zone:** 4. **Average Salary:** $35,970. **Projected Growth:** 16.8%. **Occupational Values:** Moral Values; Working Conditions; Activity; Ability Utilization; Achievement; Advancement; Company Policies and Practices. **Skills Required:** Technology Design; Troubleshooting; Information Gathering; Problem Identification; Active Learning. **Abilities:** Written Comprehension; Oral Comprehension. **Interacting with Others:** Communicating with Other Workers. **Physical Work Conditions:** Indoors; Sitting.

17-3024.00 Electro-Mechanical Technicians

Operate, test, and maintain unmanned, automated, servo-mechanical, or electromechanical equipment. May operate unmanned submarines, aircraft, or other equipment at worksites such as oil rigs, deep ocean exploration, or hazardous waste removal. May assist engineers in testing and designing robotics equipment. **Education:** Work experience in a related occupation. **Occupational Type:** Realistic. **Job Zone:** 4. **Average Salary:** $35,889. **Projected Growth:** 5.7%. **Occupational Values:** Moral Values; Independence; Company Policies and Practices; Activity; Supervision, Human Relations; Ability Utilization; Compensation. **Skills Required:** Operation Monitoring; Testing; Troubleshooting; Operation and Control; Repairing; Product Inspection; Equipment Maintenance. **Abilities:** Arm-Hand Steadiness; Manual Dexterity; Finger Dexterity; Information Ordering; Near Vision; Visualization. **Interacting with Others:** Communicating with Other Workers. **Physical Work Conditions:** Indoors; Using Hands on Objects, Tools, Controls; Hazardous Equipment; Sitting; Standing; Making Repetitive Motions.

17-3025.00 Environmental Engineering Technicians

Apply theory and principles of environmental engineering to modify, test, and operate equipment and devices used in the prevention, control, and remediation of environmental pollution, including waste treatment and site remediation. May assist in the development of environmental pollution remediation devices under direction of engineer. No other data currently available.

17-3027.00 Mechanical Engineering Technicians

Apply theory and principles of mechanical engineering to modify, develop, and test machinery and equipment under direction of engineering staff or physical scientists. **Education:** Associate degree. **Occupational Type:** Realistic. **Job Zone:** 4. **Average Salary:** $39,170. **Projected Growth:** 15.9%. **Occupational Values:** Moral Values; Activity; Achievement; Security; Advancement; Company Policies and Practices; Supervision, Human Relations. **Skills Required:** Technology Design; Testing; Operation and Control; Reading Comprehension; Mathematics; Judgment and Decision Making; Science. **Abilities:** Written Comprehension; Oral Comprehension; Oral Expression; Written Expression; Mathematical Reasoning; Number Facility; Visualization. **Interacting with Others:** Communicating with Other Workers. **Physical Work Conditions:** Indoors; Using Hands on Objects, Tools, Controls; Hazardous Equipment; Sitting; Common Protective or Safety Attire; Standing.

51-4012.00 Numerical Tool and Process Control Programmers

Develop programs to control machining or processing of parts by automatic machine tools, equipment, or systems. **Education:** Work experience in a related occupation. **Occupational Type:** Realistic. **Job Zone:** 3. **Average Salary:** $40,490. **Projected Growth:** 6.1%. **Occupational Values:** Moral Values; Compensation; Independence; Company Policies and Practices; Autonomy; Ability Utilization; Activity. **Skills Required:** Operations Analysis; Programming; Information Gathering; Mathematics; Information Organization; Product Inspection; Problem Identification. **Abilities:** Information Ordering; Mathematical Reasoning; Number Facility; Written Comprehension; Near Vision; Deductive Reasoning; Written Expression. **Interacting with Others:** Interpreting Meaning of Information to Others. **Physical Work Conditions:** Indoors; Sitting; Using Hands on Objects, Tools, Controls.

03 Plants and Animals

03.01 Managerial Work in Plants and Animals

03.02 Animal Care and Training

03.03 Hands-on Work in Plants and Animals

03.01.01 Managerial Work: Farming and Fishing

11-9011.02 Agricultural Crop Farm Managers

Direct and coordinate, through subordinate supervisory personnel, activities of workers engaged in agricultural crop production for corporations, cooperatives, or other owners. **Education:** Work experience, plus degree. **Occupational Type:** Enterprising. **Job Zone:** 4. **Average Salary:** $25,360. **Projected Growth:** -0.8%. **Occupational Values:** Autonomy; Authority; Responsibility; Creativity; Activity; Ability Utilization; Achievement. **Skills Required:** Management of Personnel Resources; Speaking; Negotiation; Coordination; Management of Financial Resources; Product Inspection; Critical Thinking. **Abilities:** Oral Expression; Deductive Reasoning; Oral Comprehension; Written Comprehension; Written Expression; Inductive Reasoning; Problem Sensitivity. **Interacting with Others:** Coordinating Work and Activities of Others; Communicating with Other Workers; Communicating with Persons Outside Organization; Monitoring and Controlling Resources; Guiding, Directing, and Motivating Subordinates; Performing Administrative Activities; Providing Consultation and Advice to Others. **Physical Work Conditions:** Standing; Indoors; Outdoors.

11-9011.03 Fish Hatchery Managers

Direct and coordinate, through subordinate supervisory personnel, activities of workers engaged in fish hatchery production for corporations, cooperatives, or other owners. **Education:** Work experience, plus degree. **Occupational Type:** Enterprising. **Job Zone:** 4. **Average Salary:** $49,157. **Projected Growth:** -0.8%. **Occupational Values:** Autonomy; Authority; Responsibility; Creativity; Achievement; Variety; Compensation. **Skills Required:** Management of Financial Resources; Management of Personnel Resources; Speaking; Science; Writing. **Abilities:** Oral Comprehension. **Interacting with Others:** Coordinating Work and Activities of Others; Guiding, Directing, and Motivating Subordinates; Monitoring and Controlling Resources; Communicating with Other Workers; Staffing Organizational Units; Performing Administrative Activities; Developing and Building Teams. **Physical Work Conditions:** Outdoors; Sitting; Standing.

11-9012.00 Farmers and Ranchers

On an ownership or rental basis, operate farms, ranches, greenhouses, nurseries, timber tracts, or other agricultural production establishments which produce crops, horticultural specialties, livestock, poultry, finfish, shellfish, or animal specialties. May plant, cultivate, harvest, perform post-harvest activities, and market crops and livestock. May hire, train, and supervise farm workers or supervise a farm labor contractor. May prepare cost, production, and other records. May maintain and operate machinery and perform physical work. **Education:** Long-term O-J-T. **Occupational Type:** Realistic. **Job Zone:** 3. **Average Salary:** $49,157. **Projected Growth:** -13.2%. **Occupational Values:** Autonomy; Responsibility; Creativity; Achievement; Authority; Moral Values; Variety. **Skills Required:** Product Inspection; Operation and Control; Equipment Selection; Science. **Abilities:** Information Ordering; Deductive Reasoning; Manual Dexterity. **Interacting with Others:** Monitoring and Controlling Resources; Coordinating Work and Activities of Others; Teaching Others; Guiding, Directing, and Motivating Subordinates; Selling or Influencing Others; Communicating with Persons Outside Organization; Staffing Organizational Units. **Physical Work Conditions:** Using Hands on Objects, Tools, Controls; Outdoors; Standing; Hazardous Equipment; Hazardous Situations; Common Protective or Safety Attire; Contaminants.

19-4093.00 Forest and Conservation Technicians

Compile data pertaining to size, content, condition, and other characteristics of forest tracts; under direction of foresters, train and lead forest workers in forest propagation, fire prevention and suppression. May assist conservation scientists in managing, improving, and protecting rangelands and wildlife habitats, and help provide technical assistance regarding the conservation of soil, water, and related natural resources. No other data currently available.

45-1011.01 First-Line Supervisors and Manager/Supervisors—Agricultural Crop Workers

Directly supervise and coordinate activities of agricultural crop workers. Manager/Supervisors are generally found in smaller establishments where they perform both supervisory and management functions, such as accounting, marketing, and personnel work, and may also engage in the same agricultural work as the workers they supervise. **Education:** Work experience in a related occupation. **Occupational Type:** Enterprising. **Job Zone:** 3. **Average Salary:** $27,410. **Projected Growth:** 6.2%. **Occupational Values:** Authority; Responsibility; Autonomy; Activity; Moral Values; Achievement; Variety. **Skills Required:** Management of Personnel Resources; Coordination; Speaking; Management of Material Resources; Time Management; Problem Identification; Equipment Selection. **Abilities:** Oral Expression; Oral Comprehension; Near Vision. **Interacting with Others:** Coordinating Work and Activities of Others; Communicating with Other Workers. **Physical Work Conditions:** Outdoors; Standing; Using Hands on Objects, Tools, Controls; Hazardous Equipment.

45-1011.02 First-Line Supervisors and Manager/Supervisors—Animal Husbandry Workers

Directly supervise and coordinate activities of animal husbandry workers. Manager/Supervisors are generally found in smaller establishments where they perform both supervisory and management functions, such as accounting, marketing, and personnel work, and may also engage in the same animal husbandry work as the workers they supervise. **Education:** Work experience in a related occupation. **Occupational Type:** Enterprising. **Job Zone:** 3. **Average Salary:** $27,410. **Projected Growth:** 6.2%. **Occupational Values:** Authority; Responsibility; Activity; Autonomy; Moral Values; Achievement; Security. **Skills Required:** Coordination; Management of Personnel Resources; Speaking; Time Management; Problem Identification; Judgment and Decision Making; Product Inspection. **Abilities:** Oral Expression; Problem Sensitivity; Written Comprehension; Deductive Reasoning; Information Ordering; Memorization; Oral Comprehension. **Interacting with Others:** Communicating with Other Workers; Coordinating Work and Activities of

Others; Guiding, Directing, and Motivating Subordinates. **Physical Work Conditions:** Outdoors; Standing; Using Hands on Objects, Tools, Controls; Contaminants; Indoors; Walking or Running.

45-1011.03 First-Line Supervisors and Manager/ Supervisors—Animal Care Workers, Except Livestock

Directly supervise and coordinate activities of animal care workers. Manager/Supervisors are generally found in smaller establishments where they perform both supervisory and management functions, such as accounting, marketing, and personnel work, and may also engage in the same animal care work as the workers they supervise. **Education:** Work experience in a related occupation. **Occupational Type:** Realistic. **Job Zone:** 3. **Average Salary:** $27,410. **Projected Growth:** 6.2%. **Occupational Values:** Authority; Responsibility; Autonomy; Activity; Security; Achievement; Moral Values. **Skills Required:** Time Management; Speaking; Coordination; Management of Personnel Resources; Problem Identification; Critical Thinking; Writing. **Abilities:** Oral Expression; Problem Sensitivity; Written Comprehension; Oral Comprehension; Written Expression. **Interacting with Others:** Coordinating Work and Activities of Others; Communicating with Other Workers. **Physical Work Conditions:** Standing; Indoors; Hazardous Situations; Outdoors; Using Hands on Objects, Tools, Controls.

45-1011.06 First-Line Supervisors and Manager/ Supervisors—Fishery Workers

Directly supervise and coordinate activities of fishery workers. Manager/Supervisors are generally found in smaller establishments where they perform both supervisory and management functions, such as accounting, marketing, and personnel work, and may also engage in the same fishery work as the workers they supervise. **Education:** Work experience in a related occupation. **Occupational Type:** Realistic. **Job Zone:** 3. **Average Salary:** $27,410. **Projected Growth:** 6.2%. **Occupational Values:** Authority; Responsibility; Activity; Autonomy; Achievement; Moral Values; Security. **Skills Required:** Management of Personnel Resources; Coordination; Implementation Planning; Time Management; Active Listening. **Abilities:** Oral Expression; Problem Sensitivity; Oral Comprehension; Deductive Reasoning; Information Ordering; Near Vision. **Interacting with Others:** Communicating with Other Workers; Coordinating Work and Activities of Others. **Physical Work Conditions:** Outdoors; Sitting; Standing; Using Hands on Objects, Tools, Controls; Indoors; Walking or Running.

45-2031.00 Farm Labor Contractors

Recruit, hire, furnish, and supervise seasonal or temporary agricultural laborers for a fee. May transport, house, and provide meals for workers. No other data currently available.

03.01.02 Managerial Work: Nursery, Groundskeeping, and Logging

11-9011.01 Nursery and Greenhouse Managers

Plan, organize, direct, control, and coordinate activities of workers engaged in propagating, cultivating, and harvesting horticultural specialties, such as trees, shrubs, flowers, mushrooms, and other plants. **Education:** Work experience in a related occupation. **Occupational Type:** Enterprising. **Job Zone:** 4. **Average Salary:** $25,360. **Projected Growth:** 15.1%. **Occupational Values:** Authority; Autonomy; Ability Utilization; Moral Values; Creativity; Responsibility; Achievement. **Skills Required:** Implementation Planning; Management of Personnel Resources; Time Management; Management of Financial Resources; Judgment and Decision Making; Speaking; Coordination. **Abilities:** Oral Expression; Written Comprehension; Oral Comprehension. **Interacting with Others:** Guiding, Directing, and Motivating Subordinates; Communicating with Other Workers; Communicating with Persons Outside Organization; Coordinating Work and Activities of Others; Staffing Organizational Units. **Physical Work Conditions:** Indoors; Standing; Kneeling, Crouching, or Crawling; Outdoors.

37-1012.01 Lawn Service Managers

Plan, direct, and coordinate activities of workers engaged in pruning trees and shrubs, cultivating lawns, and applying pesticides and other chemicals according to service contract specifications. **Education:** Work experience in a related occupation. **Occupational Type:** Enterprising. **Job Zone:** 4. **Average Salary:** $25,410. **Projected Growth:** 20%. **Occupational Values:** Authority; Autonomy; Moral Values; Responsibility; Company Policies and Practices; Ability Utilization. **Skills Required:** Management of Personnel Resources; Time Management; Active Listening; Implementation Planning; Problem Identification; Product Inspection; Mathematics. **Abilities:** Oral Comprehension; Oral Expression; Written Comprehension. **Interacting with Others:** Guiding, Directing and Motivating Subordinates; Coordinating Work and Activities of Others; Establishing and Maintaining Relationships. **Physical Work Conditions:** Outdoors; Standing.

37-1012.02 First-Line Supervisors and Manager/ Supervisors—Landscaping Workers

Directly supervise and coordinate activities of landscaping workers. Manager/Supervisors are generally found in smaller establishments where they perform both supervisory and management functions, such as accounting, marketing, and personnel work, and may also engage in the same landscaping work as the workers they supervise. **Education:** Work experience in a related occupation. **Occupational Type:** Realistic. **Job Zone:** 3. **Average Salary:** $23,628. **Projected Growth:** 6.2%. **Occupational Values:** Authority; Responsibility; Autonomy; Activity; Moral Values; Coworkers; Achievement. **Skills Required:** Management of Personnel Resources; Coordination; Time Management; Speaking; Instructing; Active Listening; Identification of Key Causes. **Abilities:** Oral Expression; Oral Comprehension; Speech Clarity. **Interacting with Others:** Coordinating Work and Activities of Others; Guiding, Directing, and Motivating Subordinates; Communicating with Other Workers. **Physical Work Conditions:** Outdoors; Standing; Contaminants; Walking or Running; Using Hands on Objects, Tools, Controls; Hazardous Situations.

45-1011.04 First-Line Supervisors and Manager/ Supervisors—Horticultural Workers

Directly supervise and coordinate activities of horticultural workers. Manager/Supervisors are generally found in smaller establishments were they perform both supervisory and management functions, such as accounting, marketing, and personnel work, and may also engage in the same horticultural work as the workers they supervise. **Education:** Work experience in a related occupation. **Occupational Type:** Realistic. **Job Zone:** 3. **Average Salary:** $27,410. **Projected Growth:** 6.2%. **Occupational Values:** Authority; Autonomy; Responsibility; Activity; Moral Values; Achievement; Security. **Skills Required:** Coordination; Management of Personnel Resources; Time Management; Reading Comprehension; Instructing; Speaking. **Abilities:** Oral Expression. **Interacting with Others:** Coordinating Work and Activities of Others; Guiding, Directing, and Motivating Subordinates. **Physical Work Conditions:** Outdoors; Standing; Using Hands on Objects, Tools, Controls.

45-1011.05 First-Line Supervisors and Manager/ Supervisors—Logging Workers

Directly supervise and coordinate activities of logging workers. Manager/Supervisors are generally found in smaller establishments where they perform both supervisory and management functions, such as accounting, marketing, and personnel work, and may also engage in the same logging work as the workers they supervise. **Education:** Work experience in a related occupation. **Occupational Type:** Realistic. **Job Zone:** 4. **Average Salary:** $27,410. **Projected Growth:** 6.2%. **Occupational Values:** Authority; Responsibility; Autonomy; Activity; Moral Values; Achievement; Security. **Skills Required:** Coordination; Time Management; Management of Personnel Resources; Speaking; Implementation Planning; Problem Identification; Instructing. **Abilities:** Information Ordering; Oral Expression; Problem Sensitivity; Written Expression; Speech Clarity. **Interacting with Others:** Communicating with Other Workers; Coordinating Work and Activities of Others; Guiding, Directing, and Motivating Subordinates. **Physical Work Conditions:** Outdoors; Standing; Common Protective or Safety Attire; Hazardous Equipment; Hazardous Situations; Distracting Sounds and Noise Levels; Using Hands on Objects, Tools, Controls.

03.02.01 Animal Care and Training

29-1131.00 Veterinarians

Diagnose and treat diseases and dysfunctions of animals. May engage in a particular function such as research and development, consultation, administration, technical writing, sale or production of commercial products, or rendering of technical services to commercial firms or other organizations. Includes veterinarians who inspect livestock. **Education:** First professional degree. **Occupational Type:** Investigative. **Job Zone:** 5. **Average Salary:** $50,950. **Projected Growth:** 24.7%. **Occupational Values:** Achievement; Ability Utilization; Responsibility; Autonomy; Social Status; Recognition; Security. **Skills Required:** Science; Critical Thinking; Judgment and Decision Making; Solution Appraisal; Reading Comprehension; Problem Identification; Active Listening. **Abilities:** Deductive Reasoning; Problem Sensitivity; Inductive Reasoning; Manual Dexterity; Near Vision; Oral Expression; Wrist-Finger Speed. **Interacting with Others:** Assisting and Caring for Others; Interpreting Meaning of Information to Others; Teaching Others; Communicating with Other Workers. **Physical Work Conditions:** Common Protective or Safety Attire; Hazardous Situations; Indoors; Diseases/Infections; Standing; Using Hands on Objects, Tools, Controls; Contaminants.

29-2056.00 Veterinary Technologists and Technicians

Perform medical tests in a laboratory environment for use in the treatment and diagnosis of diseases in animals. Prepare vaccines and serums for prevention of diseases. Prepare tissue samples, take blood samples, and execute laboratory tests, such as urinalysis and blood counts. Clean and sterilize instruments and materials and maintain equipment and machines. No other data currently available.

31-9096.00 Veterinary Assistants and Laboratory Animal Caretakers

Feed, water, and examine pets and other nonfarm animals for signs of illness, disease, or injury in laboratories and animal hospitals and clinics. Clean and disinfect cages and work areas, and sterilize laboratory and surgical equipment. May provide routine post-operative care, administer medication orally or topically, or prepare samples for laboratory examination under the supervision of veterinary or laboratory animal technologists or technicians, veterinarians, or scientists. **Education:** Short-term O-J-T. **Occupational Type:** Realistic. **Job Zone:** 3. **Average Salary:** $16,182. **Projected Growth:** 28%. **Occupational Values:** Moral Values; Security; Variety. **Skills Required:** Science; Information Organization; Active Listening; Equipment Selection; Reading Comprehension; Information Gathering. **Abilities:** Oral Comprehension; Wrist-Finger Speed. **Interacting with Others:** Assisting and Caring for Others. **Physical Work Conditions:** Indoors; Common Protective or Safety Attire; Hazardous Situations; Standing; Using Hands on Objects, Tools, Controls; Diseases/Infections; Special Uniform.

39-2011.00 Animal Trainers

Train animals for riding, harness, security, performance, obedience, or assisting persons with disabilities. Accustom animals to human voice and contact and condition animals to respond to commands. Train animals according to prescribed standards for show or competition. May train animals to carry pack loads or work as part of pack team. **Education:** Bachelor's degree. **Occupational Type:** Social. **Job Zone:** 3. **Average Salary:** $13,416. **Projected Growth:** 21.6%. **Occupational Values:** Responsibility; Autonomy; Independence; Moral Values; Creativity; Achievement; Compensation. **Skills Required:** Instructing; Learning Strategies; Speaking; Monitoring; Solution Appraisal; Idea Evaluation; Judgment and Decision Making. **Abilities:** Oral Expression. **Interacting with Others:** Establishing and Maintaining Relationships. **Physical Work Conditions:** Standing; Hazardous Situations; Indoors; Kneeling, Crouching, or Crawling; Outdoors; Walking or Running; Bending or Twisting the Body.

39-2021.00 Nonfarm Animal Caretakers

Feed, water, groom, bathe, exercise, or otherwise care for pets and other nonfarm animals, such as dogs, cats, ornamental fish or birds, zoo animals, and mice. Work in settings such as kennels, animal shelters, zoos, circuses, and aquariums. May keep records of feedings, treatments, and animals received or discharged. May clean, disinfect, and repair cages, pens, or fish tanks. **Education:** Short-term O-J-T. **Occupational Type:** Realistic. **Job Zone:** 1. **Average Salary:** $14,820. **Projected Growth:** 21.6%. **Occupational Values:** Moral Values; Independence; Activity; Company Policies and Practices; Supervision, Human Relations; Supervision, Technical. **Skills Required:** Problem Identification. **Abilities:** Oral Expression. **Interacting with Others:** Communicating with Persons Outside Organization. **Physical Work Conditions:** Standing; Outdoors; Contaminants; Indoors; Using Hands on Objects, Tools, Controls.

45-2021.00 Animal Breeders

Breed animals, including cattle, goats, horses, sheep, swine, poultry, dogs, cats, or pet birds. Select and breed animals according to their genealogy, characteristics, and offspring. May require a knowledge of artificial insemination techniques and equipment use. May involve keeping records on heats, birth intervals, or pedigree. **Education:** Bachelor's degree. **Occupational Type:** Realistic. **Job Zone:** 3. **Average Salary:** $22,440. **Projected Growth:** 21.6%. **Occupational Values:** Responsibility; Independence; Autonomy; Moral Values; Activity; Compensation; Security. **Skills Required:** Equipment Selection. **Abilities:** Deductive Reasoning. **Interacting with Others:** Communicating with Persons Outside Organization. **Physical Work Conditions:** Hazardous Situations; Outdoors; Standing; Using Hands on Objects, Tools, Controls; Kneeling, Crouching, or Crawling.

03.03.01 Hands-on Work: Farming

45-2091.00 Agricultural Equipment Operators

Drive and control farm equipment to till soil and to plant, cultivate, and harvest crops. May perform tasks such as crop baling or hay bucking. May operate stationary equipment to perform post-harvest tasks such as husking, shelling, threshing, and ginning. **Education:** Short-term O-J-T. **Occupational Type:** Realistic. **Job Zone:** 2. **Average Salary:** $15,740. **Projected Growth:** -6.6%. **Occupational Values:** Moral Values; Independence; Activity; Autonomy. **Skills Required:** Operation and Control; Equipment Maintenance; Product Inspection; Equipment Selection; Operation Monitoring; Repairing; Troubleshooting. **Abilities:** Control Precision; Multilimb Coordination; Static Strength; Far Vision; Manual Dexterity; Extent Flexibility; Hearing Sensitivity. **Interacting with Others:** Communicating with Other Workers. **Physical Work Conditions:** Outdoors; Hazardous Equipment; Using Hands on Objects, Tools, Controls; Hazardous Situations; Contaminants; Sitting; Standing.

45-2092.00 Farmworkers and Laborers, Crop, Nursery, and Greenhouse

Manually plant, cultivate, and harvest vegetables, fruits, nuts, horticultural specialties, and field crops. Use hand tools, such as shovels, trowels, hoes, tampers, pruning hooks, shears, and knives. Duties may include tilling soil and applying fertilizers; transplanting, weeding, thinning, or pruning crops; applying pesticides; cleaning, grading, sorting, packing, and loading harvested products. May construct trellises, repair fences and farm buildings, or participate in irrigation activities. No other data currently available.

45-2092.02 General Farmworkers

Apply pesticides, herbicides, and fertilizer to crops and livestock; plant, maintain, and harvest food crops. **Education:** Short-term O-J-T. **Occupational Type:** Realistic. **Job Zone:** 1. **Average Salary:** $12,580. **Projected Growth:** -6.6%. **Occupational Values:** Moral Values; Independence. **Skills Required:** Operation and Control; Equipment Maintenance; Repairing; Operation Monitoring; Equipment Selection. **Abilities:** Multilimb Coordination; Static Strength; Control Precision; Dynamic Strength; Gross Body Coordination; Manual Dexterity; Trunk Strength. **Interacting with Others:** Monitoring and Controlling Resources. **Physical Work Conditions:** Outdoors; Standing; Contaminants; Hazardous Equipment; Using Hands on Objects, Tools, Controls; Walking or Running; Very Hot.

45-2093.00 Farmworkers, Farm and Ranch Animals

Attend to live farm, ranch, or aquacultural animals that may include cattle, sheep, swine, goats, horses and other equines, poultry, finfish, shellfish, and bees. Attend to animals produced for animal products such as meat, fur, skins, feathers, eggs, milk, and honey. Duties may include feeding, watering, herding, grazing, castrating, branding, de-beaking, weighing, catching, and loading animals. May maintain records on animals; examine animals to detect diseases and injuries; assist in birth deliveries; and administer medications, vaccinations, or insecticides as appropriate. May clean and maintain animal housing areas. **Education:** Short-term O-J-T. **Occupational Type:** Realistic. **Job Zone:** 1. **Average Salary:** $15,360. **Projected Growth:** -6.6%. **Occupational Values:** Moral Values; Independence; Activity. **Skills Required:** Problem Identification. **Abilities:** Static Strength; Manual Dexterity. **Interacting with Others:** Monitoring and Controlling Resources. **Physical Work Conditions:** Outdoors; Standing; Hazardous Situations; Walking or Running; Kneeling, Crouching, or Crawling; Bending or Twisting the Body; Using Hands on Objects, Tools, Controls.

03.03.02 Hands-on Work: Forestry and Logging

45-4011.00 Forest and Conservation Workers

Under supervision, perform manual labor necessary to develop, maintain, or protect forest, forested areas, and woodlands through such activities as raising and transporting tree seedlings; combating insects, pests, and diseases harmful to trees;

and building erosion and water control structures to prevent leaching of forest soil. **Education:** Short-term O-J-T. **Occupational Type:** Realistic. **Job Zone:** 1. **Average Salary:** $23,140. **Projected Growth:** 0.7%. **Occupational Values:** Moral Values; Achievement; Independence; Company Policies and Practices; Activity; Responsibility; Autonomy. **Skills Required:** Science. **Abilities:** Static Strength; Manual Dexterity; Dynamic Strength. **Interacting with Others:** Communicating with Other Workers. **Physical Work Conditions:** Outdoors; Standing; Hazardous Situations; Common Protective or Safety Attire; Using Hands on Objects, Tools, Controls; Walking or Running; Special Uniform.

45-4021.00 Fallers

Use axes or chainsaws to fell trees, using knowledge of tree characteristics and cutting techniques to control direction of fall and minimize tree damage. **Education:** Short-term O-J-T. **Occupational Type:** Realistic. **Job Zone:** 1. **Average Salary:** $23,510. **Projected Growth:** –11.5%. **Occupational Values:** Moral Values; Activity; Company Policies and Practices; Supervision, Technical; Independence; Supervision, Human Relations. **Skills Required:** Equipment Selection; Operation and Control; Judgment and Decision Making; Critical Thinking; Coordination; Identification of Key Causes. **Abilities:** Information Ordering; Multilimb Coordination; Static Strength; Spatial Orientation; Speed of Limb Movement; Trunk Strength; Explosive Strength. **Interacting with Others:** Communicating with Other Workers. **Physical Work Conditions:** Outdoors; Hazardous Equipment; Standing; Hazardous Situations; Using Hands on Objects, Tools, Controls; Distracting Sounds and Noise Levels; Whole Body Vibration.

45-4022.00 Logging Equipment Operators

Drive logging tractor or wheeled vehicle equipped with one or more accessories (such as bulldozer blade, frontal shear, grapple, logging arch, cable winches, hoisting rack, or crane boom) to fell tree; to skid, load, unload, or stack logs; or to pull stumps or clear brush. No other data currently available.

45-4022.01 Logging Tractor Operators

Drive tractor equipped with one or more accessories such as bulldozer blade, frontal hydraulic shear, grapple, logging arch, cable winches, hoisting rack, or crane boom to fell tree, to skid, load and unload, or stack logs, or to pull stumps or clear brush. **Education:** Short-term O-J-T. **Occupational Type:** Realistic. **Job Zone:** 2. **Average Salary:** $22,750. **Projected Growth:** –2%. **Occupational Values:** Moral Values; Coworkers; Company Policies and Practices; Supervision, Human Relations; Activity; Supervision, Technical. **Skills Required:** Operation and Control. **Abilities:** Control Precision; Multilimb Coordination. **Interacting with Others:** Communicating with Other Workers. **Physical Work Conditions:** Outdoors; Using Hands on Objects, Tools, Controls; Sitting; Hazardous Equipment; Whole Body Vibration.

03.03.03 Hands-on Work: Hunting and Fishing

45-3011.00 Fishers and Related Fishing Workers

Use nets, fishing rods, traps, or other equipment to catch and gather fish or other aquatic animals from rivers, lakes, or oceans, for human consumption or other uses. May haul game onto ship. **Education:** Short-term O-J-T. **Occupational Type:** Realistic. **Job Zone:** 1. **Average Salary:** $18,150. **Projected Growth:** 1.7%. **Occupational Values:** Moral Values; Activity. **Skills Required:** Negotiation. **Abilities:** Extent Flexibility; Manual Dexterity; Static Strength. **Interacting with Others:** Communicating with Other Workers; Resolving Conflict, Negotiating with Others; Selling or Influencing Others. **Physical Work Conditions:** Outdoors; Using Hands on Objects, Tools, Controls; Standing; Contaminants; Hazardous Situations.

45-3021.00 Hunters and Trappers

Hunt and trap wild animals for human consumption, fur, feed, bait, or other purposes. **Education:** Short-term O-J-T. **Occupational Type:** Realistic. **Job Zone:** 2. **Average Salary:** $18,150. **Projected Growth:** 1.7%. **Occupational Values:** Independence; Autonomy. **Skills Required:** Equipment Selection. **Abilities:** Manual Dexterity; Speed of Limb Movement; Static Strength. **Interacting with Others:** Monitoring and Controlling Resources. **Physical Work Conditions:** Outdoors; Using Hands on Objects, Tools, Controls; Hazardous Situations; Standing; Common Protective or Safety Attire; Kneeling, Crouching, or Crawling.

03.03.04 Hands-on Work: Nursery, Groundskeeping, and Pest Control

37-2021.00 Pest Control Workers

Spray or release chemical solutions or toxic gases and set traps to kill pests and vermin such as mice, termites, and roaches that infest buildings and surrounding areas. **Education:** Moderate-term O-J-T. **Occupational Type:** Realistic. **Job Zone:** 2. **Average Salary:** $22,490. **Projected Growth:** 25.4%. **Occupational Values:** Independence; Moral Values; Supervision, Technical; Company Policies and Practices; Security. **Skills Required:** Problem Identification; Operation and Control; Mathematics; Equipment Selection. **Abilities:** Information Ordering. **Interacting with Others:** Communicating with Other Workers. **Physical Work Conditions:** Indoors; Contaminants; Hazardous Conditions; Standing; Specialized Protective or Safety Attire; Kneeling, Crouching, or Crawling; Using Hands on Objects, Tools, Controls.

37-3011.00 Landscaping and Groundskeeping Workers

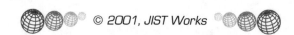

Landscape or maintain grounds of property using hand or power tools or equipment. Workers typically perform a variety of tasks, which may include any combination of the following: sod laying, mowing, trimming, planting, watering, fertilizing, digging, raking, sprinkler installation, and installation of mortarless segmental concrete masonry wall units. **Education:** Short-term O-J-T. **Occupational Type:** Realistic. **Job**

Zone: 1. **Average Salary:** $17,140. **Projected Growth:** 20.7%. **Occupational Values:** Moral Values; Independence. **Skills Required:** Equipment Selection. **Abilities:** Manual Dexterity; Stamina; Static Strength; Dynamic Strength; Trunk Strength. **Interacting with Others:** Communicating with Persons Outside Organization. **Physical Work Conditions:** Outdoors; Using Hands on Objects, Tools, Controls; Standing; Walking or Running; Bending or Twisting the Body; Kneeling, Crouching, or Crawling; Contaminants.

37-3012.00 Pesticide Handlers, Sprayers, and Applicators, Vegetation

Mix or apply pesticides, herbicides, fungicides, or insecticides through sprays, dusts, vapors, soil incorporation, or chemical application on trees, shrubs, lawns, or botanical crops. Usually requires specific training and State or Federal certification. **Education:** Moderate-term O-J-T. **Occupational Type:** Realistic. **Job Zone:** 2. **Average Salary:** $21,650. **Projected Growth:** 23.6%. **Occupational Values:** Moral Values; Independence. **Skills Required:** Operation and Control. **Abilities:** Arm-Hand Steadiness. **Interacting with Others:** Communicating with Other Workers. **Physical Work Conditions:** Outdoors; Contaminants; Standing; Using Hands on Objects, Tools, Controls; Hazardous Conditions.

37-3013.00 Tree Trimmers and Pruners

Cut away dead or excess branches from trees or shrubs to maintain right-of-way for roads, sidewalks, or utilities, or to improve appearance, health, and value of tree. Prune or treat trees or shrubs using handsaws, pruning hooks, sheers, and clippers. May use truck-mounted lifts and power pruners. May fill cavities in trees to promote healing and prevent deterioration. **Education:** Short-term O-J-T. **Occupational Type:** Realistic. **Job Zone:** 2. **Average Salary:** $22,070. **Projected Growth:** 12.1%. **Occupational Values:** Moral Values; Independence. **Skills Required:** Operation and Control. **Abilities:** Extent Flexibility; Multilimb Coordination. **Interacting with Others:** Communicating with Other Workers. **Physical Work Conditions:** Outdoors; Hazardous Situations; High Places; Standing; Using Hands on Objects, Tools, Controls; Climbing Ladders, Scaffolds, Poles, etc.; Keeping or Regaining Balance.

45-2092.01 Nursery Workers

Work in nursery facilities or at customer location planting, cultivating, harvesting, and transplanting trees, shrubs, or plants. **Education:** Short-term O-J-T. **Occupational Type:** Realistic. **Job Zone:** 1. **Average Salary:** $17,140. **Projected Growth:** 1.7%. **Occupational Values:** Moral Values; Company Policies and Practices; Supervision, Technical; Supervision, Human Relations; Independence; Activity. **Skills Required:** Equipment Selection. **Abilities:** Wrist-Finger Speed. **Interacting with Others:** Communicating with Persons Outside Organization. **Physical Work Conditions:** Using Hands on Objects, Tools, Controls; Outdoors; Standing; Common Protective or Safety Attire; Kneeling, Crouching, or Crawling; Bending or Twisting the Body; Hazardous Situations.

04 Law, Law Enforcement, and Public Safety

04.01 Managerial Work in Law, Law Enforcement, and Public Safety

04.02 Law

04.03 Law Enforcement

04.04 Public Safety

04.05 Military

04.01.01 Managerial Work in Law, Law Enforcement, and Public Safety

13-1061.00 Emergency Management Specialists

Coordinate disaster response or crisis management activities; provide disaster preparedness training; and prepare emergency plans and procedures for natural (e.g., hurricanes, floods, earthquakes), wartime, or technological (e.g., nuclear power plant emergencies, hazardous materials spills) disasters or hostage situations. No other data currently available.

33-1011.00 First-Line Supervisors/Managers of Correctional Officers

Supervise and coordinate activities of correctional officers and jailers. No other data currently available.

33-1012.00 First-Line Supervisors/Managers of Police and Detectives

Supervise and coordinate activities of members of police force. **Education:** Work experience in a related occupation. **Occupational Type:** Enterprising. **Job Zone:** 4. **Average Salary:** $48,700. **Projected Growth:** 12%. **Occupational Values:** Authority; Responsibility; Social Status; Achievement; Autonomy; Security; Coworkers. **Skills Required:** Coordination; Management of Personnel Resources; Speaking; Critical Thinking; Judgment and Decision Making; Problem Identification; Social Perceptiveness. **Abilities:** Oral Expression; Inductive Reasoning; Oral Comprehension; Written Expression; Near Vision; Problem Sensitivity; Reaction Time. **Interacting with Others:** Performing for/Working with Public; Communicating with Persons Outside Organization; Resolving Conflict, Negotiating with Others; Coordinating Work and Activities of Others; Establishing and Maintaining Relationships; Guiding, Directing, and Motivating Subordinates; Communicating with Other Workers. **Physical Work Conditions:** Special Uniform; Indoors; Sitting; Outdoors; Standing.

33-1021.01 Municipal Fire Fighting and Prevention Supervisors

Supervise fire fighters who control and extinguish municipal fires, protect life and property, and conduct rescue efforts. **Education:** Work experience in a related occupation. **Occupational Type:** Realistic. **Job Zone:** 4. **Average Salary:** $44,830. **Projected Growth:** 10.7%. **Occupational Values:** Achievement; Authority; Responsibility; Social Status; Coworkers; Security; Autonomy. **Skills Required:** Management of Personnel Resources; Writing; Coordination; Implementation Planning; Speaking; Instructing; Information Gathering. **Abilities:** Oral Expression; Time Sharing; Deductive Reasoning; Oral Comprehension; Problem Sensitivity; Speech Clarity; Inductive Reasoning. **Interacting with Others:** Communicating with Other Workers; Coordinating Work and Activities of Others. **Physical Work Conditions:** Special Uniform; Common Protective or Safety Attire; Outdoors; Very Hot; Hazardous Situations; Standing; Contaminants.

33-1021.02 Forest Fire Fighting and Prevention Supervisors

Supervise fire fighters who control and suppress fires in forests or vacant public land. **Education:** Work experience in a related occupation. **Occupational Type:** Realistic. **Job Zone:** 5. **Average Salary:** $44,830. **Projected Growth:** 10.7%. **Occupational Values:** Authority; Responsibility; Achievement; Autonomy; Social Status; Coworkers; Security. **Skills Required:** Judgment and Decision Making; Coordination; Implementation Planning; Instructing; Identifying Downstream Consequences; Speaking; Management of Personnel Resources. **Abilities:** Oral Expression; Problem Sensitivity; Far Vision; Speech Clarity; Flexibility of Closure; Spatial Orientation; Speed of Closure. **Interacting with Others:** Coordinating Work and Activities of Others; Communicating with Other Workers; Teaching Others; Guiding, Directing, and Motivating Subordinates. **Physical Work Conditions:** Special Uniform; Common Protective or Safety Attire; Outdoors; Specialized Protective or Safety Attire; Hazardous Situations; Very Hot; Distracting Sounds and Noise Levels.

04.02.01 Law: Legal Practice and Justice Administration

23-1011.00 Lawyers

Represent clients in criminal and civil litigation and other legal proceedings, draw up legal documents, and manage or advise clients on legal transactions. May specialize in a single area or may practice broadly in many areas of law. **Education:** First professional degree. **Occupational Type:** Enterprising. **Job Zone:** 5. **Average Salary:** $78,170. **Projected Growth:** 17.2%. **Occupational Values:** Autonomy; Ability Utilization; Compensation; Responsibility; Achievement; Working Conditions; Creativity. **Skills Required:** Speaking; Critical Thinking; Persuasion; Reading Comprehension; Information Gathering; Writing; Synthesis/Reorganization. **Abilities:** Oral Comprehension; Oral Expression; Written Comprehension; Written Expression; Speech Clarity; Deductive Reasoning; Problem Sensitivity. **Interacting with Others:** Interpreting Meaning of Information to Others; Communicating with Persons Outside Organization; Communicating with Other Workers; Providing Consultation and Advice to Others; Selling or Influencing Others. **Physical Work Conditions:** Indoors; Sitting; Standing.

23-1021.00 Administrative Law Judges, Adjudicators, and Hearing Officers

Conduct hearings to decide or recommend decisions on claims concerning government programs or other government-related matters. Prepare decisions. Determine penalties or the existence and the amount of liability, or recommend the acceptance or rejection of claims, or compromise settlements. **Education:** Work experience, plus degree. **Occupational Type:** Enterprising. **Job Zone:** 5. **Average Salary:** $33,870. **Projected Growth:** 2.9%. **Occupational Values:** Autonomy; Security; Working Conditions; Responsibility; Ability Utilization; Achievement; Variety. **Skills Required:** Active Listening; Reading Comprehension; Judgment and Decision Making; Critical Thinking;

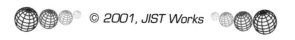

Speaking; Information Gathering; Writing. **Abilities:** Oral Comprehension; Oral Expression; Written Comprehension; Written Expression; Speech Clarity; Inductive Reasoning; Memorization. **Interacting with Others:** Interpreting Meaning of Information to Others; Communicating with Other Workers; Communicating with Persons Outside Organization; Resolving Conflict, Negotiating with Others. **Physical Work Conditions:** Indoors; Sitting.

23-1022.00 Arbitrators, Mediators, and Conciliators

Facilitate negotiation and conflict resolution through dialogue. Resolve conflicts outside of the court system by mutual consent of parties involved. **Education:** Work experience, plus degree. **Occupational Type:** Enterprising. **Job Zone:** 5. **Average Salary:** $33,870. **Projected Growth:** 2.9%. **Occupational Values:** Autonomy; Working Conditions; Security; Responsibility; Ability Utilization; Company Policies and Practices; Variety. **Skills Required:** Active Listening; Reading Comprehension; Judgment and Decision Making; Critical Thinking; Information Gathering; Speaking; Writing. **Abilities:** Oral Comprehension; Oral Expression; Written Comprehension; Written Expression; Speech Clarity; Inductive Reasoning; Memorization. **Interacting with Others:** Interpreting Meaning of Information to Others; Communicating with Other Workers; Communicating with Persons Outside Organization; Resolving Conflict, Negotiating with Others. **Physical Work Conditions:** Indoors; Sitting.

23-1023.00 Judges, Magistrate Judges, and Magistrates

Arbitrate, advise, adjudicate, or administer justice in a court of law. May sentence defendant in criminal cases according to government statutes. May determine liability of defendant in civil cases. May issue marriage licenses and perform wedding ceremonies. **Education:** Work experience, plus degree. **Occupational Type:** Enterprising. **Job Zone:** 5. **Average Salary:** $66,900. **Projected Growth:** 2.9%. **Occupational Values:** Responsibility; Autonomy; Social Status; Security; Working Conditions; Recognition; Ability Utilization. **Skills Required:** Critical Thinking; Judgment and Decision Making; Active Listening; Reading Comprehension; Information Gathering; Speaking; Writing. **Abilities:** Speech Clarity; Inductive Reasoning; Oral Comprehension; Oral Expression; Written Comprehension; Auditory Attention; Deductive Reasoning. **Interacting with Others:** Resolving Conflict, Negotiating with Others; Interpreting Meaning of Information to Others; Performing for/Working with Public; Communicating with Other Workers; Communicating with Persons Outside Organization. **Physical Work Conditions:** Indoors; Special Uniform; Sitting.

04.02.02 Law: Legal Support

23-2011.00 Paralegals and Legal Assistants

Assist lawyers by researching legal precedent, investigating facts, or preparing legal documents. Conduct research to support a legal proceeding, to formulate a defense, or to initiate legal action. **Education:** Associate degree. **Occupational Type:** Enterprising. **Job Zone:** 4. **Average Salary:** $32,638. **Projected Growth:** 62%. **Occupational Values:** Working Conditions; Activity; Security; Autonomy; Ability Utilization; Company Policies and Practices; Variety. **Skills Required:** Information Gathering; Reading Comprehension; Writing; Critical Thinking; Speaking; Information Organization; Negotiation. **Abilities:** Written Comprehension; Oral Comprehension; Written Expression; Oral Expression; Deductive Reasoning. **Interacting with Others:** Communicating with Other Workers. **Physical Work Conditions:** Indoors; Sitting.

23-2092.00 Law Clerks

Assist lawyers or judges by researching or preparing legal documents. May meet with clients or assist lawyers and judges in court. **Education:** Associate degree. **Occupational Type:** Enterprising. **Job Zone:** 4. **Average Salary:** $27,430. **Projected Growth:** 11.6%. **Occupational Values:** Working Conditions; Activity; Company Policies and Practices; Security; Achievement; Ability Utilization; Advancement. **Skills Required:** Information Gathering; Reading Comprehension; Critical Thinking; Writing; Active Listening; Information Organization; Active Learning. **Abilities:** Written Comprehension; Oral Expression; Written Expression; Near Vision; Oral Comprehension; Speech Clarity; Number Facility. **Interacting with Others:** Communicating with Other Workers. **Physical Work Conditions:** Indoors; Sitting.

23-2093.01 Title Searchers

Compile list (chain) of mortgages, deeds, contracts, judgments, and other instruments pertaining to title by searching public and private records of real estate or title insurance company. **Education:** Moderate-term O-J-T. **Occupational Type:** Conventional. **Job Zone:** 2. **Average Salary:** $23,930. **Projected Growth:** –0.6%. **Occupational Values:** Independence; Company Policies and Practices; Working Conditions; Moral Values; Supervision, Human Relations; Security; Autonomy. **Skills Required:** Information Gathering; Reading Comprehension; Writing; Active Listening; Information Organization; Speaking; Product Inspection. **Abilities:** Written Comprehension; Near Vision. **Interacting with Others:** Communicating with Persons Outside Organization. **Physical Work Conditions:** Indoors; Sitting.

23-2093.02 Title Examiners and Abstractors

Search public records and examine titles to determine legal condition of property title. Copy or prepare summaries (abstracts) of recorded documents which affect condition of title to property (e.g., mortgages, trust deeds, and contracts). May prepare and issue policy that guarantees legality of title. Abstractors: Summarize pertinent legal or insurance details or sections of statutes or case law from reference books for purpose of examination, proof, or ready reference. Search out titles to determine if title deed is correct. **Education:** Moderate-term O-J-T. **Occupational Type:** Conventional. **Job Zone:** 3. **Average Salary:** $29,100. **Projected Growth:** –0.6%. **Occupational Values:** Company Policies and Practices; Independence; Supervision, Human Relations; Security; Autonomy; Working Conditions; Activity. **Skills Required:** Information Gathering; Reading Comprehension; Information Organization; Speaking; Mathematics; Active Listening; Writing. **Abilities:** Near Vision; Written Comprehension; Written Expression. **Interacting with Others:** Interpreting Meaning of Information to Others. **Physical Work Conditions:** Indoors; Sitting.

04.03.01 Law Enforcement: Investigation and Protection

33-2021.02 Fire Investigators

Conduct investigations to determine causes of fires and explosions. **Education:** Work experience in a related occupation. **Occupational Type:** Investigative. **Job Zone:** 4. **Average Salary:** $41,110. **Projected Growth:** 17.2%. **Occupational Values:** Achievement; Ability Utilization; Responsibility; Security; Social Status; Variety; Autonomy. **Skills Required:** Judgment and Decision Making; Active Listening; Speaking; Writing; Information Gathering; Problem Identification; Reading Comprehension. **Abilities:** Inductive Reasoning; Oral Expression; Problem Sensitivity; Written Expression; Speech Clarity; Flexibility of Closure; Oral Comprehension. **Interacting with Others:** Communicating with Persons Outside Organization. **Physical Work Conditions:** Special Uniform; Standing; Common Protective or Safety Attire; Indoors; Contaminants; Kneeling, Crouching, or Crawling; Outdoors.

33-3011.00 Bailiffs

Maintain order in courts of law. **Education:** Moderate-term O-J-T. **Occupational Type:** Social. **Job Zone:** 1. **Average Salary:** $23,230. **Projected Growth:** 9.4%. **Occupational Values:** Security; Supervision, Human Relations; Company Policies and Practices; Moral Values; Coworkers; Working Conditions. **Skills Required:** Speaking; Social Perceptiveness. **Abilities:** Speech Clarity; Oral Expression. **Interacting with Others:** Performing for/Working with Public; Communicating with Persons Outside Organization. **Physical Work Conditions:** Indoors; Special Uniform; Standing.

33-3012.00 Correctional Officers and Jailers

Guard inmates in penal or rehabilitative institution in accordance with established regulations and procedures. May guard prisoners in transit between jail, courtroom, prison, or other point. Includes deputy sheriffs and police who spend the majority of their time guarding prisoners in correctional institutions. **Education:** Long-term O-J-T. **Occupational Type:** Realistic. **Job Zone:** 2. **Average Salary:** $28,540. **Projected Growth:** 38.7%. **Occupational Values:** Security; Company Policies and Practices; Supervision, Human Relations; Activity; Coworkers; Authority; Achievement. **Skills Required:** Social Perceptiveness. **Abilities:** Problem Sensitivity; Explosive Strength; Oral Expression; Selective Attention; Far Vision; Reaction Time. **Interacting with Others:** Assisting and Caring for Others; Communicating with Persons Outside Organization. **Physical Work Conditions:** Special Uniform; Indoors; Standing; Walking or Running; Sitting; Using Hands on Objects, Tools, Controls.

33-3021.01 Police Detectives

Conduct investigations to prevent crimes or solve criminal cases. **Education:** Work experience in a related occupation. **Occupational Type:** Enterprising. **Job Zone:** 4. **Average Salary:** $48,029. **Projected Growth:** 21%. **Occupational Values:** Responsibility; Achievement; Ability Utilization; Security; Supervision, Human Relations; Variety; Company Policies and Practices. **Skills Required:** Information Gathering; Active Listening; Speaking; Critical Thinking; Active Learning; Information Organization; Writing. **Abilities:** Inductive Reasoning; Oral Comprehension; Deductive Reasoning; Oral Expression; Written Expression. **Interacting with Others:** Communicating with Other Workers; Performing for/Working with Public. **Physical Work Conditions:** Indoors; Special Uniform; Sitting.

33-3021.03 Criminal Investigators and Special Agents

Investigate alleged or suspected criminal violations of federal, state, or local laws to determine if evidence is sufficient to recommend prosecution. **Education:** Work experience in a related occupation. **Occupational Type:** Enterprising. **Job Zone:** 4. **Average Salary:** $48,029. **Projected Growth:** 21%. **Occupational Values:** Security; Achievement; Ability Utilization; Company Policies and Practices; Social Status; Supervision, Human Relations; Responsibility. **Skills Required:** Information Gathering; Active Listening; Speaking; Critical Thinking; Information Organization; Social Perceptiveness; Writing. **Abilities:** Inductive Reasoning; Oral Comprehension; Oral Expression; Flexibility of Closure; Written Expression; Near Vision; Written Comprehension. **Interacting with Others:** Communicating with Other Workers; Interpreting Meaning of Information to Others. **Physical Work Conditions:** Indoors; Outdoors; Standing; Walking or Running; Sitting.

33-3021.04 Child Support, Missing Persons, and Unemployment Insurance Fraud Investigators

Conduct investigations to locate, arrest, and return fugitives and persons wanted for non-payment of support payments and unemployment insurance fraud, and to locate missing persons. **Education:** Moderate-term O-J-T. **Occupational Type:** Enterprising. **Job Zone:** 4. **Average Salary:** $48,029. **Projected Growth:** 9.4%. **Occupational Values:** Achievement; Security; Ability Utilization; Supervision, Human Relations; Activity; Responsibility; Company Policies and Practices. **Skills Required:** Active Listening; Speaking; Information Gathering; Reading Comprehension; Information Organization. **Abilities:** Oral Comprehension; Written Comprehension; Speech Clarity; Oral Expression; Problem Sensitivity; Written Expression. **Interacting with Others:** Communicating with Persons Outside Organization; Communicating with Other Workers; Establishing and Maintaining Relationships. **Physical Work Conditions:** Indoors; Sitting.

33-3021.05 Immigration and Customs Inspectors

Investigate and inspect persons, common carriers, goods, and merchandise arriving in or departing from the United States or between states to detect violations of immigration and customs laws and regulations. **Education:** Work experience in a related occupation. **Occupational Type:** Conventional. **Job Zone:** 3. **Average Salary:** $36,820. **Projected Growth:** 10.5%. **Occupational Values:** Supervision, Human Relations; Security; Company Policies and Practices; Supervision, Technical; Activity; Responsibility; Coworkers. **Skills Required:** Information Gathering; Problem Identification; Reading Comprehension; Judgment and Decision Making; Active Listening; Writing; Speaking. **Abilities:** Oral Expression; Problem Sensitivity; Near Vision; Oral Comprehension; Written Comprehension; Written Expression; Memorization. **Interacting with Others:** Communicating with Persons Outside Organization; Interpreting Meaning of Information to Others. **Physical Work Conditions:** Indoors; Standing; Using Hands on Objects, Tools, Controls; Special Uniform; Walking or Running.

33-3031.00 Fish and Game Wardens

Patrol assigned area to prevent fish and game law violations. Investigate reports of damage to crops or property by wildlife. Compile biological data. **Education:** Moderate-term O-J-T. **Occupational Type:** Realistic. **Job Zone:** 3. **Average Salary:** $35,040. **Projected Growth:** 9.4%. **Occupational Values:** Responsibility; Security; Achievement; Variety; Ability Utilization; Authority; Autonomy. **Skills Required:** Critical Thinking; Speaking; Information Gathering; Problem Identification; Active Listening; Persuasion; Judgment and Decision Making. **Abilities:** Speech Clarity; Far Vision; Inductive Reasoning; Oral Expression. **Interacting with Others:** Performing for/Working with Public; Communicating with Persons Outside Organization; Resolving Conflict, Negotiating with Others; Providing Consultation and Advice to Others. **Physical Work Conditions:** Special Uniform; Outdoors; Hazardous Situations; Walking or Running; Standing.

33-3041.00 Parking Enforcement Workers

Patrol assigned area such as public parking lot or section of city to issue tickets to overtime parking violators and illegally parked vehicles. **Education:** Moderate-term O-J-T. **Occupational Type:** Conventional. **Job Zone:** 1. **Average Salary:** $24,850. **Projected Growth:** 9.4%. **Occupational Values:** Independence; Security; Supervision, Human Relations; Activity; Company Policies and Practices; Supervision, Technical; Moral Values. **Skills Required:** Writing. **Abilities:** Written Expression. **Interacting with Others:** Communicating with Other Workers. **Physical Work Conditions:** Special Uniform; Outdoors; Standing; Walking or Running; Very Hot.

33-3051.01 Police Patrol Officers

Patrol assigned area to enforce laws and ordinances, regulate traffic, control crowds, prevent crime, and arrest violators. **Education:** Long-term O-J-T. **Occupational Type:** Social. **Job Zone:** 3. **Average Salary:** $37,710. **Projected Growth:** 31.6%. **Occupational Values:** Security; Supervision, Human Relations; Company Policies and Practices; Achievement; Variety; Coworkers; Social Status. **Skills Required:** Problem Identification; Social Perceptiveness; Critical Thinking; Speaking; Active Listening; Judgment and Decision Making; Information Gathering. **Abilities:** Oral Expression; Reaction Time; Inductive Reasoning; Far Vision; Written Expression; Oral Comprehension; Problem Sensitivity. **Interacting with Others:** Performing for/Working with Public; Assisting and Caring for Others; Resolving Conflict, Negotiating with Others; Communicating with Other Workers; Communicating with Persons Outside Organization; Establishing and Maintaining Relationships; Performing Administrative Activities. **Physical Work Conditions:** Special Uniform; Outdoors; Walking or Running; Standing; Common Protective or Safety Attire; Using Hands on Objects, Tools, Controls; Indoors.

33-3051.02 Highway Patrol Pilots

Pilot aircraft to patrol highway and enforce traffic laws. **Education:** Long-term O-J-T. **Occupational Type:** Realistic. **Job Zone:** 3. **Average Salary:** $37,710. **Projected Growth:** 31.6%. **Occupational Values:** Achievement; Security; Company Policies and Practices; Ability Utilization; Responsibility; Supervision, Human Relations; Social Service. **Skills Required:** Operation and Control; Social Perceptiveness; Speaking; Problem Identification; Active Listening; Service Orientation; Critical Thinking. **Abilities:** Far Vision; Oral Comprehension; Oral Expression; Rate Control; Spatial Orientation; Control Precision; Depth Perception. **Interacting with Others:** Communicating with Persons Outside Organization; Performing for/Working with Public; Assisting and Caring for Others; Communicating with Other Workers; Establishing and Maintaining Relationships; Interpreting Meaning of Information to Others; Resolving Conflict, Negotiating with Others. **Physical Work Conditions:** Special Uniform; Outdoors; Sitting; Using Hands on Objects, Tools, Controls; Common Protective or Safety Attire; Distracting Sounds and Noise Levels.

33-3051.03 Sheriffs and Deputy Sheriffs

Enforce law and order in rural or unincorporated districts or serve legal processes of courts. May patrol courthouse, guard court or grand jury, or escort defendants. **Education:** Long-term O-J-T. **Occupational Type:** Social. **Job Zone:** 2. **Average Salary:** $28,270. **Projected Growth:** 34.2%. **Occupational Values:** Security; Achievement; Responsibility; Supervision, Human Relations; Company Policies and Practices; Variety; Social Status. **Skills Required:** Active Listening; Information Gathering; Judgment and Decision Making; Problem Identification; Speaking; Critical Thinking; Social Perceptiveness. **Abilities:** Oral Expression; Inductive Reasoning; Oral Comprehension; Written Comprehension. **Interacting with Others:** Performing for/Working with Public; Communicating with Persons Outside Organization. **Physical Work Conditions:** Special Uniform; Indoors; Outdoors; Sitting; Standing.

33-3052.00 Transit and Railroad Police

Protect and police railroad and transit property, employees, or passengers. **Education:** Moderate-term O-J-T. **Occupational Type:** Enterprising. **Job Zone:** 2. **Average Salary:** $40,360. **Projected Growth:** 9.4%. **Occupational Values:** Responsibility; Security; Achievement; Company Policies and Practices; Ability Utilization; Activity; Authority. **Skills Required:** Information Gathering; Speaking; Active Listening; Coordination; Critical Thinking; Implementation Planning. **Abilities:** Inductive Reasoning; Oral Expression; Problem Sensitivity; Written Expression; Deductive Reasoning. **Interacting with Others:** Communicating with Other Workers. **Physical Work Conditions:** Outdoors; Standing; Walking or Running; Special Uniform.

04.03.02 Law Enforcement: Technology

19-4092.00 Forensic Science Technicians

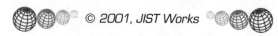

Collect, identify, classify, and analyze physical evidence related to criminal investigations. Perform tests on weapons or substances such as fiber, hair, and tissue to determine significance to investigation. May testify as expert witnesses on evidence or crime laboratory techniques. May serve as specialists in area of expertise such as ballistics, fingerprinting, handwriting, or biochemistry. **Education:** Associate degree. **Occupational Type:** Investigative. **Job Zone:** 4. **Average Salary:** $31,250. **Projected Growth:** 7%. **Occupational Values:** Autonomy; Achievement; Ability Utilization; Security; Variety; Recognition; Creativity. **Skills Required:** Information Organization; Information Gathering; Problem Identification; Reading Comprehension; Critical Thinking; Science; Coordination. **Abilities:** Inductive Reasoning; Information Ordering; Oral Expression; Category Flexibility; Flexibility of Closure; Near Vision; Oral Comprehension. **Interacting with Others:** Communicating with Other Workers. **Physical Work Conditions:** Indoors; Using Hands on Objects, Tools, Controls; Outdoors; Sitting; Standing; Common Protective or Safety Attire.

33-3021.02 Police Identification and Records Officers

Collect evidence at crime scene, classify and identify fingerprints, and photograph evidence for use in criminal and civil cases. **Education:** Work experience in a related occupation. **Occupational Type:** Conventional. **Job Zone:** 3. **Average Salary:** $48,029. **Projected Growth:** 21%. **Occupational Values:** Security; Supervision, Human Relations; Company Policies and Practices; Moral Values; Activity; Coworkers; Achievement. **Skills Required:** Information Gathering; Information Organization; Writing. **Abilities:** Category Flexibility. **Interacting with Others:** Communicating with Other Workers. **Physical Work Conditions:** Indoors; Special Uniform; Standing; Outdoors; Using Hands on Objects, Tools, Controls.

04.03.03 Law Enforcement: Security

33-9011.00 Animal Control Workers

Handle animals for the purpose of investigations of mistreatment or for control of abandoned, dangerous, or unattended animals. **Education:** Moderate-term O-J-T. **Occupational Type:** Social. **Job Zone:** 2. **Average Salary:** $17,470. **Projected Growth:** 9.4%. **Occupational Values:** Security; Moral Values; Achievement; Authority; Supervision, Technical; Company Policies and Practices; Supervision, Human Relations. **Skills Required:** Instructing; Speaking; Problem Identification; Judgment and Decision Making; Critical Thinking; Learning Strategies; Active Listening. **Abilities:** Oral Expression; Written Expression; Oral Comprehension; Speech Clarity. **Interacting with Others:** Assisting and Caring for Others; Teaching Others. **Physical Work Conditions:** Hazardous Situations; Indoors; Standing; Common Protective or Safety Attire; Outdoors; Using Hands on Objects, Tools, Controls; Walking or Running.

33-9021.00 Private Detectives and Investigators

Detect occurrences of unlawful acts or infractions of rules in private establishment. Seek, examine, and compile information for client. **Education:** Moderate-term O-J-T. **Occupational Type:** Enterprising. **Job Zone:** 2. **Average Salary:** $21,020. **Projected Growth:** 24.3%. **Occupational Values:** Ability Utilization; Achievement; Responsibility; Security; Company Policies and Practices; Social Status; Creativity. **Skills Required:** Speaking; Critical Thinking; Problem Identification; Active Listening; Information Gathering; Social Perceptiveness; Writing. **Abilities:** Inductive Reasoning; Oral Comprehension; Oral Expression; Problem Sensitivity; Written Expression; Deductive Reasoning; Speech Clarity. **Interacting with Others:** Communicating with Other Workers; Communicating with Persons Outside Organization. **Physical Work Conditions:** Indoors; Standing; Outdoors; Walking or Running.

33-9031.00 Gaming Surveillance Officers and Gaming Investigators

Act as oversight and security agent for management and customers. Observe casino or casino hotel operation for irregular activities such as cheating or theft by either employees or patrons. May utilize one-way mirrors above the casino floor, in the cashier's cage, and at the desk. Use audio/video equipment to observe operation of the business. Usually required to provide verbal and written reports of all violations and suspicious behavior to supervisor. No other data currently available.

33-9032.00 Security Guards

Guard, patrol, or monitor premises to prevent theft, violence, or infractions of rules. **Education:** Short-term O-J-T. **Occupational Type:** Social. **Job Zone:** 1. **Average Salary:** $15,226. **Projected Growth:** 28.6%. **Occupational Values:** Moral Values; Supervision, Human Relations; Security; Company Policies and Practices; Independence. **Skills Required:** Problem Identification; Speaking; Social Perceptiveness; Active Listening. **Abilities:** Oral Expression; Oral Comprehension; Night Vision; Problem Sensitivity; Selective Attention; Time Sharing; Near Vision. **Interacting with Others:** Performing Administrative Activities. **Physical Work Conditions:** Special Uniform; Indoors; Outdoors; Standing; Walking or Running.

33-9091.00 Crossing Guards

Guide or control vehicular or pedestrian traffic at such places as street and railroad crossings and construction sites. **Education:** Short-term O-J-T. **Occupational Type:** Social. **Job Zone:** 1. **Average Salary:** $14,940. **Projected Growth:** 4%. **Occupational Values:** Moral Values; Independence; Supervision, Human Relations; Security; Supervision, Technical; Company Policies and Practices; Authority. **Skills Required:** Speaking. **Abilities:** Far Vision; Reaction Time; Time Sharing; Depth Perception; Oral Expression; Peripheral Vision; Problem Sensitivity. **Interacting with Others:** Communicating with Persons Outside Organization; Performing for/Working with Public; Assisting and Caring for Others. **Physical Work Conditions:** Outdoors; Standing; Special Uniform; Common Protective or Safety Attire; Making Repetitive Motions; Walking or Running; Contaminants.

33-9092.00 Lifeguards, Ski Patrol, and Other Recreational Protective Service Workers

Monitor recreational areas such as pools, beaches, or ski slopes to provide assistance and protection to participants. Includes lifeguards and ski patrollers. **Education:** Short-term O-J-T. **Occupational Type:** Realistic. **Job Zone:** 2. **Average Salary:** $17,470. **Projected Growth:** 9.4%. **Occupational Values:** Moral Values; Social Service; Achievement; Supervision, Human Relations; Authority; Variety; Supervision, Technical. **Skills Required:** Instructing; Service Orientation; Problem Identification; Judgment and Decision Making; Social Perceptiveness; Critical

Thinking; Product Inspection. **Abilities:** Far Vision; Oral Expression; Problem Sensitivity; Stamina; Gross Body Coordination; Speech Clarity; Dynamic Strength. **Interacting with Others:** Assisting and Caring for Others; Communicating with Persons Outside Organization; Performing for/Working with Public. **Physical Work Conditions:** Outdoors; Special Uniform; Walking or Running; Standing; Common Protective or Safety Attire; Very Hot; Extremely Bright or Inadequate Lighting.

04.04.01 Public Safety: Emergency Responding

29-2041.00 Emergency Medical Technicians and Paramedics

Assess injuries, administer emergency medical care, and extricate trapped individuals. Transport injured or sick persons to medical facilities. **Education:** Postsecondary vocational training. **Occupational Type:** Social. **Job Zone:** 2. **Average Salary:** $20,290. **Projected Growth:** 31.6%. **Occupational Values:** Social Service; Achievement; Ability Utilization; Coworkers; Security; Variety; Responsibility. **Skills Required:** Problem Identification; Coordination; Service Orientation; Speaking; Operation Monitoring; Judgment and Decision Making; Active Listening. **Abilities:** Problem Sensitivity; Oral Comprehension; Oral Expression; Deductive Reasoning; Speed of Closure. **Interacting with Others:** Assisting and Caring for Others; Communicating with Other Workers. **Physical Work Conditions:** Special Uniform; Common Protective or Safety Attire; Diseases/Infections; Using Hands on Objects, Tools, Controls; Indoors; Kneeling, Crouching, or Crawling; Outdoors.

33-2011.00 Fire Fighters

Control and extinguish fires or respond to emergency situations where life, property, or the environment is at risk. Duties may include fire prevention, emergency medical service, hazardous material response, search and rescue, and disaster management. No other data currently available.

33-2011.01 Municipal Fire Fighters

Control and extinguish municipal fires, protect life and property, and conduct rescue efforts. **Education:** Long-term O-J-T. **Occupational Type:** Realistic. **Job Zone:** 2. **Average Salary:** $31,150. **Projected Growth:** 4.7%. **Occupational Values:** Achievement; Moral Values; Social Status; Coworkers; Supervision, Human Relations; Security; Supervision, Technical. **Skills Required:** Equipment Maintenance; Coordination; Operation and Control; Equipment Selection; Judgment and Decision Making; Service Orientation; Problem Identification. **Abilities:** Oral Comprehension; Dynamic Strength; Explosive Strength; Stamina; Response Orientation; Static Strength; Control Precision. **Interacting with Others:** Communicating with Other Workers; Assisting and Caring for Others. **Physical Work Conditions:** Common Protective or Safety Attire; Special Uniform; Hazardous Situations; Specialized Protective or Safety Attire; Using Hands on Objects, Tools, Controls; Hazardous Conditions; Indoors.

33-2011.02 Forest Fire Fighters

Control and suppress fires in forests or vacant public land. **Education:** Long-term O-J-T. **Occupational Type:** Realistic. **Job Zone:** 2. **Average Salary:** $31,150. **Projected Growth:** 4.7%. **Occupational Values:** Achievement; Coworkers; Moral Values; Security; Supervision, Human Relations; Social Status; Ability Utilization. **Skills Required:** Coordination; Monitoring; Idea Evaluation; Critical Thinking; Idea Generation; Judgment and Decision Making; Service Orientation. **Abilities:** Oral Expression; Spatial Orientation; Stamina; Explosive Strength; Gross Body Coordination; Multilimb Coordination; Problem Sensitivity. **Interacting with Others:** Communicating with Other Workers. **Physical Work Conditions:** Common Protective or Safety Attire; Outdoors; Special Uniform; Standing; Very Hot; Hazardous Situations; Specialized Protective or Safety Attire.

04.04.02 Public Safety: Regulations Enforcement

13-1041.00 Compliance Officers, Except Agriculture, Construction, Health and Safety, and Transportation

Examine, evaluate, and investigate eligibility for or conformity with laws and regulations governing contract compliance of licenses and permits, and other compliance and enforcement inspection activities not classified elsewhere. No other data currently available.

13-1041.01 Environmental Compliance Inspectors

Inspect and investigate sources of pollution to protect the public and environment and ensure conformance with federal, state, and local regulations and ordinances. **Education:** Work experience in a related occupation. **Occupational Type:** Investigative. **Job Zone:** 3. **Average Salary:** $36,820. **Projected Growth:** 10.5%. **Occupational Values:** Supervision, Human Relations; Achievement; Company Policies and Practices; Security; Activity; Autonomy; Ability Utilization. **Skills Required:** Reading Comprehension; Information Gathering; Speaking; Science; Critical Thinking; Judgment and Decision Making; Writing. **Abilities:** Written Comprehension; Oral Expression; Problem Sensitivity; Written Expression; Inductive Reasoning; Near Vision; Oral Comprehension. **Interacting with Others:** Communicating with Persons Outside Organization. **Physical Work Conditions:** Indoors; Contaminants; Standing; Using Hands on Objects, Tools, Controls; Walking or Running.

13-1041.02 Licensing Examiners and Inspectors

Examine, evaluate, and investigate eligibility for, conformity with, or liability under licenses or permits. **Education:** Work experience in a related occupation. **Occupational Type:** Conventional. **Job Zone:** 3. **Average Salary:** $36,820. **Projected Growth:** 10.5%. **Occupational Values:** Security; Company Policies and Practices; Supervision, Human Relations; Responsibility; Autonomy; Coworkers; Working Conditions. **Skills Required:** Speaking; Information Gathering; Monitoring; Reading Comprehension. **Abilities:** Oral Expression; Written Comprehension; Oral Comprehension; Speech Clarity; Written Expression. **Interacting with Others:** Communicating with Persons Outside Organization. **Physical Work Conditions:** Indoors; Sitting; Using Hands on Objects, Tools, Controls.

13-1041.03 Equal Opportunity Representatives and Officers

Monitor and evaluate compliance with equal opportunity laws, guidelines, and policies to ensure that employment practices and contracting arrangements give equal opportunity without regard to race, religion, color, national origin, sex, age, or disability. **Education:** Work experience in a related occupation. **Occupational Type:** Social. **Job Zone:** 4. **Average Salary:** $36,820. **Projected Growth:** 10.5%. **Occupational Values:** Working Conditions; Company Policies and Practices; Responsibility; Achievement; Supervision, Human Relations; Autonomy; Security. **Skills Required:** Reading Comprehension; Speaking; Information Gathering; Writing; Active Listening; Problem Identification; Implementation Planning. **Abilities:** Written Comprehension; Oral Comprehension; Oral Expression; Written Expression; Problem Sensitivity; Information Ordering; Deductive Reasoning. **Interacting with Others:** Communicating with Persons Outside Organization; Interpreting Meaning of Information to Others; Communicating with Other Workers; Providing Consultation and Advice to Others. **Physical Work Conditions:** Indoors; Sitting.

13-1041.04 Government Property Inspectors and Investigators

Investigate or inspect government property to ensure compliance with contract agreements and government regulations. **Education:** Work experience in a related occupation. **Occupational Type:** Enterprising. **Job Zone:** 3. **Average Salary:** $36,820. **Projected Growth:** 10.5%. **Occupational Values:** Security; Company Policies and Practices; Supervision, Human Relations; Advancement; Variety; Social Status; Responsibility. **Skills Required:** Reading Comprehension; Judgment and Decision Making; Information Gathering; Speaking; Critical Thinking; Problem Identification; Writing. **Abilities:** Problem Sensitivity; Oral Expression; Written Comprehension; Written Expression; Near Vision; Deductive Reasoning; Oral Comprehension. **Interacting with Others:** Communicating with Persons Outside Organization. **Physical Work Conditions:** Indoors; Standing; Sitting; Using Hands on Objects, Tools, Controls; Walking or Running.

13-2061.00 Financial Examiners

Enforce or ensure compliance with laws and regulations governing financial and securities institutions and financial and real estate transactions. May examine, verify correctness of, or establish authenticity of records. **Education:** Work experience in a related occupation. **Occupational Type:** Enterprising. **Job Zone:** 4. **Average Salary:** $36,820. **Projected Growth:** 10.5%. **Occupational Values:** Working Conditions; Security; Activity; Responsibility; Compensation; Autonomy; Advancement. **Skills Required:** Reading Comprehension; Speaking; Writing; Judgment and Decision Making; Active Listening; Mathematics; Information Gathering. **Abilities:** Written Comprehension; Oral Expression; Problem Sensitivity; Number Facility; Deductive Reasoning; Mathematical Reasoning; Near Vision. **Interacting with Others:** Communicating with Persons Outside Organization; Communicating with Other Workers. **Physical Work Conditions:** Indoors; Sitting; Using Hands on Objects, Tools, Controls.

19-4051.02 Nuclear Monitoring Technicians

Collect and test samples to monitor results of nuclear experiments and contamination of humans, facilities, and environment. **Education:** Associate degree. **Occupational Type:** Realistic. **Job Zone:** 3. **Average Salary:** $45,970. **Projected Growth:** 7%. **Occupational Values:** Compensation; Company Policies and Practices; Security; Supervision, Human Relations; Activity; Supervision, Technical; Ability Utilization. **Skills Required:** Science; Information Gathering; Mathematics; Operation Monitoring; Reading Comprehension; Critical Thinking; Testing. **Abilities:** Problem Sensitivity; Control Precision; Near Vision; Oral Expression; Inductive Reasoning; Number Facility; Written Comprehension. **Interacting with Others:** Communicating with Other Workers. **Physical Work Conditions:** Indoors; Contaminants; Specialized Protective or Safety Attire; Using Hands on Objects, Tools, Controls; Hazardous Conditions; Common Protective or Safety Attire; Standing.

29-9011.00 Occupational Health and Safety Specialists

Review, evaluate, and analyze work environments. Design programs and procedures to control, eliminate, and prevent disease or injury caused by chemical, physical, and biological agents or ergonomic factors. May conduct inspections and enforce adherence to laws and regulations governing the health and safety of individuals. May be employed in the public or private sector. **Education:** Associate degree. **Occupational Type:** Social. **Job Zone:** 5. **Average Salary:** $29,882. **Projected Growth:** 35%. **Occupational Values:** Autonomy; Ability Utilization; Company Policies and Practices; Responsibility; Working Conditions; Achievement; Security. **Skills Required:** Information Gathering; Speaking; Reading Comprehension; Science; Critical Thinking; Active Listening; Mathematics. **Abilities:** Oral Expression; Problem Sensitivity; Written Comprehension; Oral Comprehension; Written Expression; Inductive Reasoning; Number Facility. **Interacting with Others:** Communicating with Other Workers; Communicating with Persons Outside Organization; Providing Consultation and Advice to Others. **Physical Work Conditions:** Indoors; Contaminants; Using Hands on Objects, Tools, Controls; Common Protective or Safety Attire; Walking or Running; Sitting; Standing.

29-9012.00 Occupational Health and Safety Technicians

Collect data on work environments for analysis by occupational health and safety specialists. Implement and conduct evaluation of programs designed to limit chemical, physical, biological, and ergonomic risks to workers. No other data currently available.

33-2021.01 Fire Inspectors

Inspect buildings and equipment to detect fire hazards and enforce state and local regulations. **Education:** Work experience in a related occupation. **Occupational Type:** Conventional. **Job Zone:** 2. **Average Salary:** $41,110. **Projected Growth:** 17.2%. **Occupational Values:** Achievement; Security; Social Status; Ability Utilization; Company Policies and Practices; Moral Values; Responsibility. **Skills Required:** Testing; Problem Identification; Information Gathering; Writing; Troubleshooting; Speaking; Critical Thinking. **Abilities:** Oral Expression; Problem Sensitivity; Inductive Reasoning; Speech Clarity; Written Expression; Oral Comprehension; Near Vision. **Interacting with Others:** Communicating with Persons Outside Organization; Providing Consultation and Advice to Others. **Physical Work Conditions:** Special Uniform; Standing; Indoors; Walking or Running; Kneeling, Crouching, or Crawling; Outdoors; Using Hands on Objects, Tools, Controls.

33-2022.00 Forest Fire Inspectors and Prevention Specialists

Enforce fire regulations and inspect for forest fire hazards. Report forest fires and weather conditions. **Education:** Work experience in a related occupation. **Occupational Type:** Realistic. **Job Zone:** 2. **Average Salary:** $37,430. **Projected Growth:** 17.2%. **Occupational Values:** Achievement; Ability Utilization; Security; Responsibility; Social Status; Moral Values; Authority. **Skills Required:** Speaking; Information Gathering; Critical Thinking; Judgment and Decision Making; Monitoring; Identification of Key Causes; Coordination. **Abilities:** Far Vision; Problem Sensitivity; Oral Expression; Speech Clarity. **Interacting with Others:** Communicating with Other Workers; Communicating with Persons Outside Organization. **Physical Work Conditions:** Outdoors; Special Uniform; Common Protective or Safety Attire; Contaminants; Standing; Very Hot; Walking or Running.

45-2011.00 Agricultural Inspectors

Inspect agricultural commodities, processing equipment and facilities, and fish and logging operations to ensure compliance with regulations and laws governing health, quality, and safety. **Education:** Work experience in a related occupation. **Occupational Type:** Realistic. **Job Zone:** 4. **Average Salary:** $36,820. **Projected Growth:** 10.5%. **Occupational Values:** Responsibility; Security; Autonomy; Independence; Supervision, Human Relations; Activity; Company Policies and Practices. **Skills Required:** Product Inspection; Speaking; Writing; Problem Identification; Reading Comprehension; Information Gathering. **Abilities:** Problem Sensitivity; Oral Expression; Written Comprehension; Written Expression; Deductive Reasoning; Oral Comprehension; Speech Clarity. **Interacting with Others:** Communicating with Persons Outside Organization; Providing Consultation and Advice to Others. **Physical Work Conditions:** Outdoors; Standing; Walking or Running; Indoors; Using Hands on Objects, Tools, Controls.

53-6051.01 Aviation Inspectors

Inspect aircraft, maintenance procedures, air navigational aids, air traffic controls, and communications equipment to ensure conformance with federal safety regulations. **Education:** Work experience in a related occupation. **Occupational Type:** Realistic. **Job Zone:** 4. **Average Salary:** $31,678. **Projected Growth:** 10.5%. **Occupational Values:** Supervision, Human Relations; Responsibility; Security; Company Policies and Practices; Compensation; Autonomy; Supervision, Technical. **Skills Required:** Product Inspection; Information Gathering; Problem Identification; Testing; Reading Comprehension; Operation Monitoring; Critical Thinking. **Abilities:** Problem Sensitivity; Written Expression; Information Ordering; Near Vision; Written Comprehension; Oral Expression; Deductive Reasoning. **Interacting with Others:** Communicating with Other Workers. **Physical Work Conditions:** Standing; Using Hands on Objects, Tools, Controls; Indoors; Outdoors; Distracting Sounds and Noise Levels.

53-6051.02 Public Transportation Inspectors

Monitor operation of public transportation systems to ensure good service and compliance with regulations. Investigate accidents, equipment failures, and complaints. **Education:** Work experience in a related occupation. **Occupational Type:** Enterprising. **Job Zone:** 4. **Average Salary:** $39,560. **Projected Growth:** 10.5%. **Occupational Values:** Supervision, Human Relations; Security; Company Policies and Practices; Responsibility; Independence; Autonomy; Moral Values. **Skills Required:** Identification of Key Causes; Writing; Information Gathering; Product Inspection. **Abilities:** Oral Expression; Problem Sensitivity; Written Expression. **Interacting with Others:** Communicating with Other Workers. **Physical Work Conditions:** Sitting; Indoors; Outdoors.

53-6051.03 Marine Cargo Inspectors

Inspect cargoes of seagoing vessels to certify compliance with health and safety regulations in cargo handling and stowage. **Education:** Work experience in a related occupation. **Occupational Type:** Conventional. **Job Zone:** 5. **Average Salary:** $39,560. **Projected Growth:** 10.5%. **Occupational Values:** Responsibility; Autonomy; Independence; Security; Moral Values; Company Policies and Practices; Compensation. **Skills Required:** Judgment and Decision Making; Mathematics; Information Gathering; Reading Comprehension; Critical Thinking; Product Inspection. **Abilities:** Problem Sensitivity; Number Facility; Written Comprehension; Oral Expression; Deductive Reasoning; Mathematical Reasoning; Near Vision. **Interacting with Others:** Interpreting Meaning of Information to Others. **Physical Work Conditions:** Outdoors; Standing; Using Hands on Objects, Tools, Controls; Walking or Running.

04.05.01 Military: Officers and Supervisors

55-1011.00 Air Crew Officers

Perform and direct in-flight duties to ensure the successful completion of combat, reconnaissance, transport, and search and rescue missions. Duties include operating aircraft communications and radar equipment; establishing satellite linkages and jamming enemy communications capabilities; operating aircraft weapons and defensive systems; conducting pre-flight, in-flight, and post-flight inspections of onboard equipment; and directing cargo and personnel drops. No other data currently available.

55-1012.00 Aircraft Launch and Recovery Officers

Plan and direct the operation and maintenance of catapults, arresting gear, and associated mechanical, hydraulic, and control systems involved primarily in aircraft carrier takeoff and landing operations. Duties include supervision of readiness and safety of arresting gear, launching equipment, barricades, and visual landing aid systems; planning and coordinating the design, development, and testing of launch and recovery systems; preparing specifications for catapult and arresting gear installations; evaluating design proposals; determining handling equipment needed for new aircraft; preparing technical data and instructions for operation of landing aids; and training personnel in carrier takeoff and landing procedures. No other data currently available.

55-1013.00 Armored Assault Vehicle Officers

Direct the operation of tanks, light armor, and amphibious assault vehicle units during combat situations on land or in aquatic environments. Duties include directing crew members in the operation of targeting and firing systems; coordinating the operation of advanced onboard communications and navigation equipment; directing the transport of personnel and equipment during combat; formulating and implementing battle plans, including the tactical employment of armored vehicle units; and coordinating with infantry, artillery, and air support units. No other data currently available.

55-1014.00 Artillery and Missile Officers

Manage personnel and weapons operations to destroy enemy positions, aircraft, and vessels. Duties include planning, targeting, and coordinating the tactical deployment of field artillery and air defense artillery missile systems units; directing the establishment and operation of fire control communications systems; targeting and launching intercontinental ballistic missiles; directing the storage and handling of nuclear munitions and components; overseeing security of weapons storage and launch facilities; and managing maintenance of weapons systems. No other data currently available.

55-1015.00 Command and Control Center Officers

Manage the operation of communications, detection, and weapons systems essential for controlling air, ground, and naval operations. Duties include managing critical communication links between air, naval, and ground forces; formulating and implementing emergency plans for natural and wartime disasters; coordinating emergency response teams and agencies; evaluating command center information and need for high-level military and government reporting; managing the operation of surveillance and detection systems; providing technical information and advice on capabilities and operational readiness; and directing operation of weapons targeting, firing, and launch computer systems. No other data currently available.

55-1016.00 Infantry Officers

Direct, train, and lead infantry units in ground combat operations. Duties include directing deployment of infantry weapons, vehicles, and equipment; directing location, construction, and camouflage of infantry positions and equipment; managing field communications operations; coordinating with armor, artillery, and air support units; performing strategic and tactical planning, including battle plan development; and leading basic reconnaissance operations. No other data currently available.

55-1017.00 Special Forces Officers

Lead elite teams that implement unconventional operations by air, land, or sea during combat or peacetime. These activities include offensive raids, demolitions, reconnaissance, search and rescue, and counterterrorism. In addition to their combat training, special forces officers often have specialized training in swimming, diving, parachuting, survival, emergency medicine, and foreign languages. Duties include directing advanced reconnaissance operations and evaluating intelligence information; recruiting, training, and equipping friendly forces; leading raids and invasions on enemy territories; training personnel to implement individual missions and contingency plans; performing strategic and tactical planning for politically sensitive missions; and operating sophisticated communications equipment. No other data currently available.

55-2011.00 First-Line Supervisors/Managers of Air Crew Members

Supervise and coordinate the activities of air crew members. Supervisors may also perform the same activities as the workers they supervise. No other data currently available.

55-2012.00 First-Line Supervisors/Managers of Weapons Specialists/Crew Members

Supervise and coordinate the activities of weapons specialists/crew members. Supervisors may also perform the same activities as the workers they supervise. No other data currently available.

55-2013.00 First-Line Supervisors/Managers of All Other Tactical Operations Specialists

Supervise and coordinate the activities of all other tactical operations specialists not classified separately above. Supervisors may also perform the same activities as the workers they supervise. No other data currently available.

04.05.02 Military: Specialists

55-3011.00 Air Crew Members

Perform in-flight duties to ensure the successful completion of combat, reconnaissance, transport, and search and rescue missions. Duties include operating aircraft communications and detection equipment, including establishing satellite linkages and jamming enemy communications capabilities; conducting pre-flight, in-flight, and post-flight inspections of onboard equipment; operating and maintaining aircraft weapons and defensive systems; operating and maintaining aircraft in-flight refueling systems; executing aircraft safety and emergency procedures; computing and verifying passenger, cargo, fuel, and emergency and special equipment weight and balance data; and conducting cargo and personnel drops. No other data currently available.

55-3012.00 Aircraft Launch and Recovery Specialists

Operate and maintain catapults, arresting gear, and associated mechanical, hydraulic, and control systems involved primarily in aircraft carrier takeoff and landing operations. Duties include installing and maintaining visual landing aids; testing and maintaining launch and recovery equipment; using electric and mechanical test equipment and hand tools; activating airfield arresting systems such as crash barriers and cables during emergency landing situations; directing aircraft launch and recovery operations; using hand or light signals; and maintaining logs of airplane launches, recoveries, and equipment maintenance. No other data currently available.

55-3013.00 Armored Assault Vehicle Crew Members

Operate tanks, light armor, and amphibious assault vehicles during combat situations on land or in aquatic environments. Duties include driving armored vehicles which require specialized training; operating and maintaining targeting and firing systems; operating and maintaining advanced onboard communications and navigation equipment; transporting personnel and equipment in a combat environment; and operating and maintaining auxiliary weapons, including machine guns and grenade launchers. No other data currently available.

55-3014.00 Artillery and Missile Crew Members

Target, fire, and maintain weapons used to destroy enemy positions, aircraft, and vessels. Field artillery crew members predominantly use guns, cannons, and howitzers in ground combat operations. Air defense artillery crew members predominantly use missiles and rockets. Naval artillery crew members predominantly use torpedoes and missiles launched from a ship or submarine. Duties include testing, inspecting, and storing ammunition, missiles, and torpedoes; conducting preventive and routine maintenance on weapons and related equipment; establishing and maintaining radio and wire communications; and operating weapons targeting, firing, and launch computer systems. No other data currently available.

55-3015.00 Command and Control Center Specialists

Operate and monitor communications, detection, and weapons systems essential for controlling air, ground, and naval operations. Duties include maintaining and relaying critical communications between air, naval, and ground forces; implementing emergency plans for natural and wartime disasters; relaying command center information to high-level military and government decision makers; monitoring surveillance and detection systems such as air defense; interpreting and evaluating tactical situations and making recommendations to superiors; and operating weapons targeting, firing, and launch computer systems. No other data currently available.

55-3016.00 Infantry

Operate weapons and equipment in ground combat operations. Duties include operating and maintaining weapons such as rifles, machine guns, mortars, and hand grenades; locating, constructing, and camouflaging infantry positions and equipment; evaluating terrain and recording topographical information; operating and maintaining field communications equipment; assessing need for and directing supporting fire; placing explosives and performing minesweeping activities on land; and participating in basic reconnaissance operations. No other data currently available.

55-3017.00 Radar and Sonar Technicians

Operate equipment using radio or sound wave technology to identify, track, and analyze objects or natural phenomena of military interest. Includes airborne, shipboard, and terrestrial positions. May perform minor maintenance. No other data currently available.

55-3018.00 Special Forces

Implement unconventional operations by air, land, or sea during combat or peacetime as members of elite teams. These activities include offensive raids, demolitions, reconnaissance, search and rescue, and counterterrorism. In addition to their combat training, Special Forces members often have specialized training in swimming, diving, parachuting, survival, emergency medicine, and foreign languages. Duties include conducting advanced reconnaissance operations and collecting intelligence information; recruiting, training, and equipping friendly forces; conducting raids and invasions on enemy territories; laying and detonating explosives for demolition targets; locating, identifying, defusing, and disposing of ordnance; and operating and maintaining sophisticated communications equipment. No other data currently available.

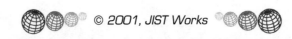

05 Mechanics, Installers, and Repairers

05.01.01 Managerial Work in Mechanics, Installers, and Repairers

49-1011.00 First-Line Supervisors/Managers of Mechanics, Installers, and Repairers

Supervise and coordinate the activities of mechanics, installers, and repairers. **Education:** Work experience in a related occupation. **Occupational Type:** Enterprising. **Job Zone:** 4. **Average Salary:** $39,600. **Projected Growth:** 8.9%. **Occupational Values:** Authority; Responsibility; Autonomy; Security; Activity; Coworkers; Variety. **Skills Required:** Coordination; Management of Personnel Resources; Time Management; Monitoring; Problem Identification; Management of Financial Resources; Speaking. **Abilities:** Oral Expression; Near Vision; Information Ordering; Oral Comprehension. **Interacting with Others:** Coordinating Work and Activities of Others; Guiding, Directing, and Motivating Subordinates; Communicating with Other Workers; Monitoring and Controlling Resources. **Physical Work Conditions:** Indoors; Standing; Common Protective or Safety Attire; Using Hands on Objects, Tools, Controls.

05.02.01 Electrical and Electronic Systems: Installation and Repair

47-4021.00 Elevator Installers and Repairers

Assemble, install, repair, or maintain electric or hydraulic freight or passenger elevators, escalators, or dumbwaiters. **Education:** Long-term O-J-T. **Occupational Type:** Realistic. **Job Zone:** 4. **Average Salary:** $47,860. **Projected Growth:** 12.2%. **Occupational Values:** Moral Values; Independence; Company Policies and Practices; Security; Responsibility; Compensation; Supervision, Technical. **Skills Required:** Installation; Repairing; Product Inspection; Equipment Maintenance; Testing; Troubleshooting; Operation Monitoring. **Abilities:** Deductive Reasoning. **Interacting with Others:** Communicating with Other Workers. **Physical Work Conditions:** Indoors; Using Hands on Objects, Tools, Controls; Hazardous Equipment; Standing; Hazardous Situations; Common Protective or Safety Attire; Hazardous Conditions.

49-2022.01 Central Office and PBX Installers and Repairers

Test, analyze, and repair telephone or telegraph circuits and equipment at a central office location using test meters and hand tools. Analyze and repair defects in communications equipment on customers' premises using circuit diagrams, polarity probes, meters, and a telephone test set. May install equipment. **Education:** Postsecondary vocational training. **Occupational Type:** Realistic. **Job Zone:** 4. **Average Salary:** $43,680. **Projected Growth:** 32.3%. **Occupational Values:** Moral Values; Company Policies and Practices; Security; Supervision, Technical; Supervision, Human Relations; Independence; Compensation. **Skills Required:** Repairing; Installation; Troubleshooting; Testing. **Abilities:** Problem Sensitivity. **Interacting with Others:** Communicating with Other Workers. **Physical Work Conditions:** Indoors; Sitting; Using Hands on Objects, Tools, Controls; Standing.

49-2022.02 Frame Wirers, Central Office

Connect wires from telephone lines and cables to distributing frames in telephone company central office, using soldering iron and other hand tools. **Education:** Postsecondary vocational training. **Occupational Type:** Realistic. **Job Zone:** 2. **Average Salary:** $46,110. **Projected Growth:** –1.4%. **Occupational Values:** Moral Values; Supervision, Technical; Security; Company Policies and Practices; Supervision, Human Relations; Independence. **Skills Required:** Installation; Testing; Problem Identification. **Abilities:** Extent Flexibility. **Interacting with Others:** Communicating with Other Workers. **Physical Work Conditions:** Indoors; Using Hands on Objects, Tools, Controls; Standing.

49-2022.03 Communication Equipment Mechanics, Installers, and Repairers

Install, maintain, test, and repair communication cables and equipment. **Education:** Postsecondary vocational training. **Occupational Type:** Realistic. **Job Zone:** 3. **Average Salary:** $40,731. **Projected Growth:** –13.6%. **Occupational Values:** Moral Values; Variety; Supervision, Technical; Security; Activity; Supervision, Human Relations; Company Policies and Practices. **Skills Required:** Repairing; Testing; Installation; Equipment Maintenance. **Abilities:** Manual Dexterity. **Interacting with Others:** Communicating with Other Workers. **Physical Work Conditions:** Using Hands on Objects, Tools, Controls; Hazardous Conditions; Outdoors; Standing; Common Protective or Safety Attire; High Places; Kneeling, Crouching, or Crawling.

49-2022.04 Telecommunications Facility Examiners

Examine telephone transmission facilities to determine equipment requirements for providing subscribers with new or additional telephone services. **Education:** Postsecondary vocational training. **Occupational Type:** Realistic. **Job Zone:** 3. **Average Salary:** $40,731. **Projected Growth:** –13.6%. **Occupational Values:** Moral Values; Responsibility; Supervision, Technical; Independence; Supervision, Human Relations; Security; Company Policies and Practices. **Skills Required:** Information Gathering. **Abilities:** Gross Body Equilibrium. **Interacting with Others:** Communicating with Persons Outside Organization. **Physical Work Conditions:** Climbing Ladders, Scaffolds, Poles, etc.; High Places; Outdoors; Hazardous Conditions; Standing; Common Protective or Safety Attire; Using Hands on Objects, Tools, Controls.

49-2022.05 Station Installers and Repairers, Telephone

Install and repair telephone station equipment, such as telephones, coin collectors, telephone booths, and switching-key equipment. **Education:** Postsecondary vocational training. **Occupational Type:** Realistic. **Job Zone:** 4. **Average Salary:**

$39,630. **Projected Growth:** 12.7%. **Occupational Values:** Moral Values; Security; Supervision, Technical; Supervision, Human Relations; Company Policies and Practices; Independence; Activity. **Skills Required:** Repairing; Installation; Troubleshooting; Problem Identification; Testing; Equipment Selection. **Abilities:** Problem Sensitivity; Manual Dexterity. **Interacting with Others:** Communicating with Other Workers. **Physical Work Conditions:** Using Hands on Objects, Tools, Controls; Standing; Common Protective or Safety Attire; Climbing Ladders, Scaffolds, Poles, etc.; Indoors; Special Uniform.

49-2091.00 Avionics Technicians

Install, inspect, test, adjust, or repair avionics equipment such as radar, radio, navigation, and missile control systems in aircraft or space vehicles. **Education:** Postsecondary vocational training. **Occupational Type:** Realistic. **Job Zone:** 4. **Average Salary:** $35,172. **Projected Growth:** 12.7%. **Occupational Values:** Moral Values; Supervision, Human Relations; Independence; Company Policies and Practices; Security; Compensation; Activity. **Skills Required:** Troubleshooting; Testing; Operation and Control; Installation; Equipment Maintenance; Repairing; Equipment Selection. **Abilities:** Finger Dexterity; Information Ordering; Near Vision; Problem Sensitivity; Visualization; Written Comprehension; Extent Flexibility. **Interacting with Others:** Communicating with Other Workers. **Physical Work Conditions:** Using Hands on Objects, Tools, Controls; Standing; Hazardous Conditions; Indoors; Common Protective or Safety Attire; Kneeling, Crouching, or Crawling; Distracting Sounds and Noise Levels.

49-2093.00 Electrical and Electronics Installers and Repairers, Transportation Equipment

Install, adjust, or maintain mobile electronics communication equipment, including sound, sonar, security, navigation, and surveillance systems on trains, watercraft, or other mobile equipment. **Education:** Postsecondary vocational training. **Occupational Type:** Realistic. **Job Zone:** 3. **Average Salary:** $33,870. **Projected Growth:** 12.7%. **Occupational Values:** Moral Values; Security; Supervision, Human Relations; Activity; Company Policies and Practices; Independence; Responsibility. **Skills Required:** Repairing; Installation; Problem Identification. **Abilities:** Manual Dexterity; Arm-Hand Steadiness; Finger Dexterity; Control Precision; Near Vision; Extent Flexibility; Information Ordering. **Interacting with Others:** Communicating with Persons Outside Organization. **Physical Work Conditions:** Using Hands on Objects, Tools, Controls; Indoors; Hazardous Equipment; Kneeling, Crouching, or Crawling; Standing; Hazardous Conditions; Bending or Twisting the Body.

49-2094.00 Electrical and Electronics Repairers, Commercial and Industrial Equipment

Repair, test, adjust, or install electronic equipment, such as industrial controls, transmitters, and antennas. **Education:** Postsecondary vocational training. **Occupational Type:** Realistic. **Job Zone:** 3. **Average Salary:** $35,590. **Projected Growth:** –2.4%. **Occupational Values:** Moral Values; Security; Supervision, Human Relations; Company Policies and Practices; Compensation; Variety; Ability Utilization. **Skills Required:** Installation; Troubleshooting; Equipment Maintenance; Repairing; Testing; Operation and Control; Reading Comprehension. **Abilities:** Oral Expression; Oral Comprehension; Written Comprehension; Deductive Reasoning. **Interacting with Others:** Communicating with Other Workers. **Physical Work Conditions:** Indoors; Using Hands on Objects, Tools, Controls; Sitting.

49-2096.00 Electronic Equipment Installers and Repairers, Motor Vehicles

Install, diagnose, or repair communications, sound, security, or navigation equipment in motor vehicles. **Education:** Postsecondary vocational training. **Occupational Type:** Realistic. **Job Zone:** 3. **Average Salary:** $33,870. **Projected Growth:** 12.7%. **Occupational Values:** Moral Values; Security; Supervision, Human Relations; Company Policies and Practices; Activity; Compensation; Independence. **Skills Required:** Repairing; Installation; Problem Identification. **Abilities:** Manual Dexterity; Arm-Hand Steadiness; Finger Dexterity; Control Precision; Near Vision; Extent Flexibility; Information Ordering. **Interacting with Others:** Communicating with Persons Outside Organization. **Physical Work Conditions:** Using Hands on Objects, Tools, Controls; Indoors; Hazardous Equipment; Kneeling, Crouching, or Crawling; Standing; Hazardous Conditions; Bending or Twisting the Body.

49-9031.01 Home Appliance Installers

Install household appliances such as refrigerators, washing machines, and stoves in mobile homes or customers' homes. **Education:** Long-term O-J-T. **Occupational Type:** Realistic. **Job Zone:** 3. **Average Salary:** $26,626. **Projected Growth:** 5.6%. **Occupational Values:** Moral Values; Security; Activity; Company Policies and Practices; Supervision, Human Relations; Working Conditions; Independence. **Skills Required:** Installation. **Abilities:** Static Strength. **Interacting with Others:** Communicating with Persons Outside Organization. **Physical Work Conditions:** Using Hands on Objects, Tools, Controls; Indoors; Standing; Kneeling, Crouching, or Crawling.

49-9051.00 Electrical Power-Line Installers and Repairers

Install or repair cables or wires used in electrical power or distribution systems. May erect poles and light or heavy-duty transmission towers. **Education:** Long-term O-J-T. **Occupational Type:** Realistic. **Job Zone:** 4. **Average Salary:** $42,600. **Projected Growth:** 1.1%. **Occupational Values:** Moral Values; Security; Supervision, Technical; Company Policies and Practices; Supervision, Human Relations; Independence; Compensation. **Skills Required:** Troubleshooting; Installation; Equipment Maintenance; Testing; Repairing; Problem Identification; Equipment Selection. **Abilities:** Manual Dexterity; Multilimb Coordination; Finger Dexterity; Information Ordering; Visualization; Arm-Hand Steadiness; Extent Flexibility. **Interacting with Others:** Communicating with Other Workers. **Physical Work Conditions:** Common Protective or Safety Attire; Outdoors; Using Hands on Objects, Tools, Controls; Hazardous Conditions; High Places; Climbing Ladders, Scaffolds, Poles, etc.; Standing.

49-9052.00 Telecommunications Line Installers and Repairers

String and repair telephone and television cable, including fiber optics and other equipment for transmitting messages or television programming. **Education:** Long-term O-J-T. **Occupational Type:** Realistic. **Job Zone:** 3. **Average Salary:** $32,750.

Projected Growth: 30.3%. **Occupational Values:** Moral Values; Independence; Security; Supervision, Technical; Supervision, Human Relations; Company Policies and Practices; Compensation. **Skills Required:** Installation; Repairing; Troubleshooting; Equipment Maintenance; Testing; Problem Identification. **Abilities:** Manual Dexterity; Control Precision; Oral Comprehension. **Interacting with Others:** Communicating with Other Workers. **Physical Work Conditions:** Outdoors; Using Hands on Objects, Tools, Controls; Kneeling, Crouching, or Crawling; Standing.

49-9097.00 Signal and Track Switch Repairers

Install, inspect, test, maintain, or repair electric gate crossings, signals, signal equipment, track switches, section lines, or intercommunications systems within a railroad system. **Education:** Postsecondary vocational training. **Occupational Type:** Realistic. **Job Zone:** 4. **Average Salary:** $38,440. **Projected Growth:** –13.6%. **Occupational Values:** Moral Values; Supervision, Technical; Security; Company Policies and Practices; Supervision, Human Relations; Achievement; Responsibility. **Skills Required:** Equipment Maintenance; Repairing; Troubleshooting; Testing; Installation; Operation Monitoring; Product Inspection. **Abilities:** Control Precision. **Interacting with Others:** Communicating with Other Workers. **Physical Work Conditions:** Outdoors; Using Hands on Objects, Tools, Controls; Standing; Common Protective or Safety Attire; Hazardous Conditions; Hazardous Equipment; Hazardous Situations.

05.02.02 Electrical and Electronic Systems: Equipment Repair

49-2011.02 Data Processing Equipment Repairers

Repair, maintain, and install computer hardware such as peripheral equipment and word processing systems. **Education:** Postsecondary vocational training. **Occupational Type:** Realistic. **Job Zone:** 4. **Average Salary:** $29,340. **Projected Growth:** 47%. **Occupational Values:** Moral Values; Security; Variety; Working Conditions; Ability Utilization; Independence; Company Policies and Practices. **Skills Required:** Testing; Repairing; Troubleshooting; Operation Monitoring; Problem Identification; Science; Installation. **Abilities:** Inductive Reasoning; Near Vision; Problem Sensitivity; Deductive Reasoning; Information Ordering; Oral Comprehension; Visual Color Discrimination. **Interacting with Others:** Interpreting Meaning of Information to Others. **Physical Work Conditions:** Indoors; Using Hands on Objects, Tools, Controls; Sitting; Standing.

49-2011.03 Office Machine and Cash Register Servicers

Repair and service office machines, such as adding, accounting, calculating, duplicating, and typewriting machines. Include the repair of manual, electrical, and electronic office machines. **Education:** Long-term O-J-T. **Occupational Type:** Realistic. **Job Zone:** 3. **Average Salary:** $27,830. **Projected Growth:** 15.6%. **Occupational Values:** Moral Values; Independence; Supervision, Technical; Security; Supervision, Human Relations; Responsibility; Activity. **Skills Required:** Repairing; Installation; Reading Comprehension; Operation and Control; Troubleshooting; Testing; Instructing. **Abilities:** Finger Dexterity; Near Vision; Written Comprehension; Control Precision; Manual Dexterity; Deductive Reasoning; Information Ordering. **Interacting with Others:** Communicating with Persons Outside Organization. **Physical Work Conditions:** Indoors; Using Hands on Objects, Tools, Controls; Hazardous Equipment; Sitting; Standing.

49-2021.00 Radio Mechanics

Test or repair mobile or stationary radio transmitting and receiving equipment and two-way radio communications systems used in ship-to-shore communications and found in service and emergency vehicles. **Education:** Postsecondary vocational training. **Occupational Type:** Realistic. **Job Zone:** 3. **Average Salary:** $30,590. **Projected Growth:** –1.4%. **Occupational Values:** Moral Values; Independence; Security; Company Policies and Practices; Achievement; Supervision, Technical; Ability Utilization. **Skills Required:** Repairing; Testing; Troubleshooting; Problem Identification; Installation; Product Inspection; Operation Monitoring. **Abilities:** Finger Dexterity. **Interacting with Others:** Providing Consultation and Advice to Others. **Physical Work Conditions:** Using Hands on Objects, Tools, Controls; Indoors; Hazardous Situations; Sitting.

49-2092.01 Electric Home Appliance and Power Tool Repairers

Repair, adjust, and install all types of electric household appliances. **Education:** Long-term O-J-T. **Occupational Type:** Realistic. **Job Zone:** 3. **Average Salary:** $24,160. **Projected Growth:** 5.6%. **Occupational Values:** Moral Values; Variety; Independence; Security; Working Conditions; Compensation; Activity. **Skills Required:** Repairing; Troubleshooting; Problem Identification; Equipment Maintenance; Installation. **Abilities:** Problem Sensitivity. **Interacting with Others:** Communicating with Persons Outside Organization. **Physical Work Conditions:** Indoors; Using Hands on Objects, Tools, Controls; Sitting; Standing.

49-2092.02 Electric Motor and Switch Assemblers and Repairers

Test, repair, rebuild, and assemble electric motors, generators, and equipment. **Education:** Long-term O-J-T. **Occupational Type:** Realistic. **Job Zone:** 3. **Average Salary:** $27,730. **Projected Growth:** 4.4%. **Occupational Values:** Moral Values; Independence; Security; Activity; Compensation; Supervision, Human Relations; Company Policies and Practices. **Skills Required:** Testing; Repairing; Installation; Operation Monitoring; Product Inspection; Troubleshooting; Problem Identification. **Abilities:** Finger Dexterity; Information Ordering; Near Vision; Arm-Hand Steadiness; Manual Dexterity; Visualization; Wrist-Finger Speed. **Interacting with Others:** Communicating with Other Workers. **Physical Work Conditions:** Indoors; Using Hands on Objects, Tools, Controls; Hazardous Equipment; Hazardous Conditions; Standing; Common Protective or Safety Attire; Sitting.

49-2092.03 Battery Repairers

Inspect, repair, recharge, and replace batteries. **Education:** Long-term O-J-T. **Occupational Type:** Realistic. **Job Zone:** 2. Average Salary: $27,730. **Projected Growth:** 4.4%. **Occupational Values:** Moral Values; Security; Supervision, Technical; Supervision, Human Relations; Independence; Activity; Company Policies and Practices. **Skills Required:** Repairing; Product Inspection; Equipment Selection. **Abilities:** Problem Sensitivity. **Interacting with Others:** Communicating with Other Workers. **Physical Work Conditions:** Using Hands on Objects, Tools, Controls; Indoors; Hazardous Situations; Common Protective or Safety Attire; Contaminants; Kneeling, Crouching, or Crawling; Standing.

49-2092.04 Transformer Repairers

Clean and repair electrical transformers. **Education:** Postsecondary vocational training. **Occupational Type:** Realistic. **Job Zone:** 4. **Average Salary:** $27,730. **Projected Growth:** 12.7%. **Occupational Values:** Moral Values; Security; Supervision, Technical; Company Policies and Practices; Activity; Supervision, Human Relations; Independence. **Skills Required:** Repairing; Equipment Maintenance. **Abilities:** Manual Dexterity; Problem Sensitivity. **Interacting with Others:** Communicating with Other Workers. **Physical Work Conditions:** Outdoors; Using Hands on Objects, Tools, Controls; Standing; Common Protective or Safety Attire; Hazardous Conditions; Climbing Ladders, Scaffolds, Poles, etc.; Walking or Running.

49-2092.05 Electrical Parts Reconditioners

Recondition and rebuild salvaged, electrical parts of equipment and wind new coils on armatures of used generators and motors. **Education:** Postsecondary vocational training. **Occupational Type:** Realistic. **Job Zone:** 2. **Average Salary:** $27,730. **Projected Growth:** 12.7%. **Occupational Values:** Moral Values; Independence; Security; Activity; Supervision, Human Relations; Company Policies and Practices; Supervision, Technical. **Skills Required:** Repairing; Equipment Selection. **Abilities:** Finger Dexterity. **Interacting with Others:** Communicating with Other Workers. **Physical Work Conditions:** Indoors; Using Hands on Objects, Tools, Controls; Sitting; Common Protective or Safety Attire; Making Repetitive Motions.

49-2095.00 Electrical and Electronics Repairers, Powerhouse, Substation, and Relay

Inspect, test, repair, or maintain electrical equipment in generating stations, substations, and in-service relays. **Education:** Postsecondary vocational training. **Occupational Type:** Realistic. **Job Zone:** 5. **Average Salary:** $47,100. **Projected Growth:** 12.7%. **Occupational Values:** Moral Values; Security; Company Policies and Practices; Responsibility; Variety; Activity; Compensation. **Skills Required:** Testing; Repairing; Equipment Maintenance; Troubleshooting; Problem Identification. **Abilities:** Deductive Reasoning. **Interacting with Others:** Communicating with Other Workers. **Physical Work Conditions:** Using Hands on Objects, Tools, Controls; Indoors; Hazardous Conditions; Standing; Common Protective or Safety Attire.

49-2097.00 Electronic Home Entertainment Equipment Installers and Repairers

Repair, adjust, or install audio or television receivers, stereo systems, camcorders, video systems, or other electronic home entertainment equipment. **Education:** Postsecondary vocational training. **Occupational Type:** Realistic. **Job Zone:** 3. **Average Salary:** $23,540. **Projected Growth:** –11.9%. **Occupational Values:** Moral Values; Security; Independence; Variety; Compensation; Working Conditions; Ability Utilization. **Skills Required:** Repairing; Troubleshooting; Testing; Problem Identification; Installation; Science; Active Listening. **Abilities:** Finger Dexterity; Oral Comprehension; Arm-Hand Steadiness; Control Precision; Information Ordering; Manual Dexterity; Near Vision. **Interacting with Others:** Communicating with Persons Outside Organization. **Physical Work Conditions:** Indoors; Using Hands on Objects, Tools, Controls; Bending or Twisting the Body; Sitting.

49-9012.01 Electric Meter Installers and Repairers

Install electric meters on customers' premises or on pole. Test meters and perform necessary repairs. Turn current on/off by connecting/disconnecting service drop. **Education:** Long-term O-J-T. **Occupational Type:** Realistic. **Job Zone:** 3. **Average Salary:** $40,850. **Projected Growth:** No data available. **Occupational Values:** Moral Values; Independence; Security; Company Policies and Practices; Supervision, Human Relations; Activity; Supervision, Technical. **Skills Required:** Repairing; Installation; Troubleshooting; Testing; Equipment Maintenance; Problem Identification; Product Inspection. **Abilities:** Information Ordering; Arm-Hand Steadiness; Extent Flexibility; Near Vision; Multilimb Coordination; Problem Sensitivity; Visual Color Discrimination. **Interacting with Others:** Communicating with Other Workers. **Physical Work Conditions:** Hazardous Conditions; Outdoors; Using Hands on Objects, Tools, Controls; Standing; Hazardous Situations; Common Protective or Safety Attire.

05.03.01 Mechanical Work: Vehicles and Facilities

49-3011.01 Airframe-and-Power-Plant Mechanics

Inspect, test, repair, maintain, and service aircraft. **Education:** Postsecondary vocational training. **Occupational Type:** Realistic. **Job Zone:** 4. **Average Salary:** $38,123. **Projected Growth:** 10.4%. **Occupational Values:** Moral Values; Security; Compensation; Company Policies and Practices; Supervision, Human Relations; Achievement; Ability Utilization. **Skills Required:** Testing; Repairing; Equipment Selection; Equipment Maintenance; Troubleshooting; Installation; Mathematics. **Abilities:** Manual Dexterity; Arm-Hand Steadiness; Control Precision; Deductive Reasoning; Finger Dexterity; Information Ordering; Near Vision. **Interacting with Others:** Communicating with Other Workers. **Physical Work Conditions:** Using Hands on Objects, Tools, Controls; Hazardous Equipment; Common Protective or Safety Attire; Indoors; Standing; Kneeling, Crouching, or Crawling; Bending or Twisting the Body.

49-3011.02 Aircraft Engine Specialists

Repair and maintain the operating condition of aircraft engines. Includes helicopter engine mechanics. **Education:** Postsecondary vocational training. **Occupational Type:** Realistic. **Job Zone:** 4. **Average Salary:** $41,650. **Projected Growth:** 10.4%. **Occupational Values:** Moral Values; Security; Ability Utilization; Compensation; Company Policies and Practices; Achievement; Supervision, Human Relations. **Skills Required:** Repairing; Equipment Maintenance; Testing; Troubleshooting;

Operation Monitoring; Equipment Selection; Reading Comprehension. **Abilities:** Problem Sensitivity; Deductive Reasoning; Manual Dexterity; Written Comprehension; Inductive Reasoning; Near Vision. **Interacting with Others:** Communicating with Other Workers. **Physical Work Conditions:** Using Hands on Objects, Tools, Controls; Hazardous Equipment; Standing; Hazardous Situations; Indoors; Common Protective or Safety Attire; Hazardous Conditions.

49-3011.03 Aircraft Body and Bonded Structure Repairers

Repair body or structure of aircraft according to specifications. **Education:** Postsecondary vocational training. **Occupational Type:** Realistic. **Job Zone:** 3. **Average Salary:** $37,630. **Projected Growth:** 10.4%. **Occupational Values:** Moral Values; Security; Compensation; Company Policies and Practices; Supervision, Human Relations; Achievement; Ability Utilization. **Skills Required:** Equipment Selection; Installation; Problem Identification; Repairing; Equipment Maintenance; Product Inspection; Troubleshooting. **Abilities:** Arm-Hand Steadiness; Information Ordering; Manual Dexterity; Control Precision; Extent Flexibility. **Interacting with Others:** Communicating with Other Workers. **Physical Work Conditions:** Using Hands on Objects, Tools, Controls; Hazardous Equipment; Indoors; Standing; Common Protective or Safety Attire; Kneeling, Crouching, or Crawling.

49-3021.00 Automotive Body and Related Repairers

Repair and refinish automotive vehicle bodies and straighten vehicle frames. **Education:** Long-term O-J-T. **Occupational Type:** Realistic. **Job Zone:** 3. **Average Salary:** $27,400. **Projected Growth:** 15.8%. **Occupational Values:** Moral Values; Security; Independence; Activity; Company Policies and Practices; Ability Utilization; Achievement. **Skills Required:** Repairing; Product Inspection; Installation; Equipment Selection; Information Organization; Information Gathering; Problem Identification. **Abilities:** Manual Dexterity; Information Ordering; Multilimb Coordination; Oral Comprehension; Visualization; Arm-Hand Steadiness; Control Precision. **Interacting with Others:** Communicating with Persons Outside Organization. **Physical Work Conditions:** Using Hands on Objects, Tools, Controls; Indoors; Distracting Sounds and Noise Levels; Standing; Common Protective or Safety Attire; Kneeling, Crouching, or Crawling; Cramped Work Space, Awkward Positions.

49-3022.00 Automotive Glass Installers and Repairers

Replace or repair broken windshields and window glass in motor vehicles. **Education:** Long-term O-J-T. **Occupational Type:** Realistic. **Job Zone:** 2. **Average Salary:** $27,400. **Projected Growth:** 15.8%. **Occupational Values:** Moral Values; Independence; Security; Company Policies and Practices; Compensation; Responsibility; Supervision, Human Relations. **Skills Required:** Installation; Product Inspection; Repairing; Equipment Selection; Problem Identification. **Abilities:** Static Strength; Arm-Hand Steadiness; Gross Body Coordination; Extent Flexibility; Multilimb Coordination; Trunk Strength. **Interacting with Others:** Communicating with Other Workers. **Physical Work Conditions:** Using Hands on Objects, Tools, Controls; Standing; Common Protective or Safety Attire; Indoors; Hazardous Situations; Outdoors.

49-3023.01 Automotive Master Mechanics

Repair automobiles, trucks, buses, and other vehicles. Master mechanics repair virtually any part on the vehicle or specialize in the transmission system. **Education:** Long-term O-J-T. **Occupational Type:** Realistic. **Job Zone:** 3. **Average Salary:** $27,360. **Projected Growth:** 16.7%. **Occupational Values:** Moral Values; Ability Utilization; Independence; Compensation; Security; Responsibility; Activity. **Skills Required:** Repairing; Troubleshooting; Problem Identification; Equipment Maintenance; Installation. **Abilities:** Information Ordering; Problem Sensitivity; Extent Flexibility; Hearing Sensitivity; Manual Dexterity; Visualization; Control Precision. **Interacting with Others:** Communicating with Persons Outside Organization. **Physical Work Conditions:** Using Hands on Objects, Tools, Controls; Standing; Indoors; Common Protective or Safety Attire; Hazardous Equipment; Bending or Twisting the Body; Kneeling, Crouching, or Crawling.

49-3023.02 Automotive Specialty Technicians

Repair only one system or component on a vehicle, such as brakes, suspension, or radiator. **Education:** Long-term O-J-T. **Occupational Type:** Realistic. **Job Zone:** 2. **Average Salary:** $27,360. **Projected Growth:** 16.7%. **Occupational Values:** Moral Values; Independence; Responsibility; Security; Ability Utilization; Achievement; Activity. **Skills Required:** Repairing; Troubleshooting; Installation; Testing; Equipment Maintenance; Problem Identification. **Abilities:** Extent Flexibility; Information Ordering; Visualization; Hearing Sensitivity; Manual Dexterity; Near Vision; Problem Sensitivity. **Interacting with Others:** Communicating with Persons Outside Organization. **Physical Work Conditions:** Using Hands on Objects, Tools, Controls; Standing; Common Protective or Safety Attire; Indoors; Contaminants; Kneeling, Crouching, or Crawling; Bending or Twisting the Body.

49-3031.00 Bus and Truck Mechanics and Diesel Engine Specialists

Inspect, repair, and maintain diesel engines used to power machines. **Education:** Long-term O-J-T. **Occupational Type:** Realistic. **Job Zone:** 3. **Average Salary:** $29,340. **Projected Growth:** 9.8%. **Occupational Values:** Moral Values; Independence; Security; Achievement; Compensation; Responsibility; Activity. **Skills Required:** Repairing; Troubleshooting; Equipment Maintenance; Equipment Selection; Product Inspection; Testing; Installation. **Abilities:** Problem Sensitivity; Hearing Sensitivity. **Interacting with Others:** Communicating with Other Workers. **Physical Work Conditions:** Using Hands on Objects, Tools, Controls; Standing; Indoors; Kneeling, Crouching, or Crawling; Hazardous Equipment.

49-3041.00 Farm Equipment Mechanics

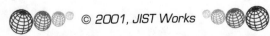

Diagnose, adjust, repair, or overhaul farm machinery and vehicles such as tractors, harvesters, dairy equipment, and irrigation systems. **Education:** Long-term O-J-T. **Occupational Type:** Realistic. **Job Zone:** 3. **Average Salary:** $22,750. **Projected Growth:** –5.2%. **Occupational Values:** Moral Values; Security; Independence; Achievement; Activity; Responsibility; Ability Utilization. **Skills Required:** Equipment Maintenance; Installation; Repairing; Testing; Troubleshooting; Operation and Control; Equipment Selection. **Abilities:** Control Precision; Multilimb Coordination; Hearing Sensitivity; Information Ordering; Extent Flexibility; Problem Sensitivity; Arm-Hand Steadiness. **Interacting with Others:** Communicating with Other Workers. **Physical Work Conditions:** Using Hands on Objects, Tools, Controls; Hazardous Equipment; Outdoors; Standing; Bending or Twisting the Body; Hazardous Situations; Kneeling, Crouching, or Crawling.

49-3042.00 Mobile Heavy Equipment Mechanics, Except Engines

Diagnose, adjust, repair, or overhaul mobile mechanical, hydraulic, and pneumatic equipment such as cranes, bulldozers, graders, and conveyors used in construction, logging, and surface mining. **Education:** Long-term O-J-T. **Occupational Type:** Realistic. **Job Zone:** 4. **Average Salary:** $31,520. **Projected Growth:** 9.3%. **Occupational Values:** Moral Values; Compensation; Ability Utilization; Security; Company Policies and Practices; Activity; Supervision, Human Relations. **Skills Required:** Repairing; Problem Identification; Equipment Maintenance; Operation and Control; Product Inspection; Troubleshooting; Testing. **Abilities:** Problem Sensitivity. **Interacting with Others:** Communicating with Other Workers. **Physical Work Conditions:** Using Hands on Objects, Tools, Controls; Hazardous Equipment; Kneeling, Crouching, or Crawling; Outdoors; Standing; Bending or Twisting the Body; Cramped Work Space, Awkward Positions.

49-3043.00 Rail Car Repairers

Diagnose, adjust, repair, or overhaul railroad rolling stock, mine cars, or mass transit rail cars. **Education:** Long-term O-J-T. **Occupational Type:** Realistic. **Job Zone:** 3. **Average Salary:** $36,330. **Projected Growth:** 14.3%. **Occupational Values:** Moral Values; Independence; Ability Utilization; Supervision, Human Relations; Variety; Security; Company Policies and Practices. **Skills Required:** Repairing; Installation; Equipment Maintenance; Troubleshooting; Equipment Selection. **Abilities:** Manual Dexterity; Finger Dexterity. **Interacting with Others:** Communicating with Other Workers. **Physical Work Conditions:** Using Hands on Objects, Tools, Controls; Outdoors; Hazardous Equipment; Hazardous Situations; Common Protective or Safety Attire; Kneeling, Crouching, or Crawling; Distracting Sounds and Noise Levels.

49-3051.00 Motorboat Mechanics

Repairs and adjusts electrical and mechanical equipment of gasoline or diesel powered inboard or inboard-outboard boat engines. **Education:** Long-term O-J-T. **Occupational Type:** Realistic. **Job Zone:** 3. **Average Salary:** $31,773. **Projected Growth:** No data available. **Occupational Values:** Moral Values; Security; Company Policies and Practices; Compensation; Ability Utilization; Independence; Activity. **Skills Required:** Repairing; Testing; Troubleshooting; Problem Identification; Equipment Maintenance. **Abilities:** Control Precision. **Interacting with Others:** Performing Administrative Activities. **Physical Work Conditions:** Using Hands on Objects, Tools, Controls; Indoors; Standing; Outdoors.

49-3052.00 Motorcycle Mechanics

Diagnose, adjust, repair, or overhaul motorcycles, scooters, mopeds, dirt bikes, or similar motorized vehicles. **Education:** Long-term O-J-T. **Occupational Type:** Realistic. **Job Zone:** 2. **Average Salary:** $23,440. **Projected Growth:** 3.9%. **Occupational Values:** Moral Values; Independence; Security; Activity; Responsibility; Compensation; Achievement. **Skills Required:** Repairing; Problem Identification; Troubleshooting; Equipment Selection; Operation and Control. **Abilities:** Finger Dexterity. **Interacting with Others:** Communicating with Other Workers. **Physical Work Conditions:** Using Hands on Objects, Tools, Controls; Indoors; Kneeling, Crouching, or Crawling; Contaminants; Standing.

49-3053.00 Outdoor Power Equipment and Other Small Engine Mechanics

Diagnose, adjust, repair, or overhaul small engines used to power lawn mowers, chain saws, and related equipment. **Education:** Long-term O-J-T. **Occupational Type:** Realistic. **Job Zone:** 3. **Average Salary:** $21,580. **Projected Growth:** 5%. **Occupational Values:** Moral Values; Company Policies and Practices; Security; Activity; Achievement; Independence; Ability Utilization. **Skills Required:** Repairing; Equipment Maintenance; Problem Identification; Troubleshooting; Product Inspection; Equipment Selection; Installation. **Abilities:** Control Precision. **Interacting with Others:** Communicating with Other Workers. **Physical Work Conditions:** Using Hands on Objects, Tools, Controls; Indoors; Kneeling, Crouching, or Crawling; Standing; Contaminants; Hazardous Equipment.

49-3092.00 Recreational Vehicle Service Technicians

Diagnose, inspect, adjust, repair, or overhaul recreational vehicles including travel trailers. May specialize in maintaining gas, electrical, hydraulic, plumbing, or chassis/towing systems as well as repairing generators, appliances, and interior components. **Education:** Long-term O-J-T. **Occupational Type:** Realistic. **Job Zone:** 2. **Average Salary:** $21,420. **Projected Growth:** 14.3%. **Occupational Values:** Moral Values; Security; Company Policies and Practices; Activity; Supervision, Human Relations; Supervision, Technical; Variety. **Skills Required:** Installation; Troubleshooting; Repairing; Problem Identification. **Abilities:** Control Precision. **Interacting with Others:** Communicating with Persons Outside Organization. **Physical Work Conditions:** Standing; Using Hands on Objects, Tools, Controls; Indoors; Outdoors.

49-9021.01 Heating and Air Conditioning Mechanics

Install, service, and repair heating and air conditioning systems in residences and commercial establishments. **Education:** Long-term O-J-T. **Occupational Type:** Realistic. **Job Zone:** 4. **Average Salary:** $29,160. **Projected Growth:** 16.9%. **Occupational Values:** Moral Values; Independence; Activity; Security; Responsibility; Company Policies and Practices; Compensation. **Skills Required:** Troubleshooting; Installation; Repairing; Testing; Equipment Selection; Equipment Maintenance; Problem Identification. **Abilities:** Deductive Reasoning. **Interacting with Others:** Communicating with Persons Outside Organization. **Physical Work Conditions:** Using Hands on Objects, Tools, Controls; Indoors; Standing; Kneeling, Crouching, or Crawling.

49-9021.02 Refrigeration Mechanics

Install and repair industrial and commercial refrigerating systems. **Education:** Long-term O-J-T. **Occupational Type:** Realistic. **Job Zone:** 4. **Average Salary:** $29,160. **Projected Growth:** 16.9%. **Occupational Values:** Moral Values; Independence;

Security; Activity; Company Policies and Practices; Responsibility; Supervision, Human Relations. **Skills Required:** Installation; Repairing; Troubleshooting; Testing; Problem Identification; Operation Monitoring; Product Inspection. **Abilities:** Control Precision. **Interacting with Others:** Communicating with Other Workers. **Physical Work Conditions:** Indoors; Using Hands on Objects, Tools, Controls; Standing; Hazardous Equipment; Kneeling, Crouching, or Crawling.

49-9042.00 Maintenance and Repair Workers, General

Perform work involving the skills of two or more maintenance or craft occupations to keep machines, mechanical equipment, or the structure of an establishment in repair. Duties may involve pipe fitting; boiler making; insulating; welding; machining; carpentry; repairing electrical or mechanical equipment; installing, aligning, and balancing new equipment; and repairing buildings, floors, or stairs. **Education:** Long-term O-J-T. **Occupational Type:** Realistic. **Job Zone:** 3. **Average Salary:** $23,290. **Projected Growth:** 7.7%. **Occupational Values:** Moral Values; Independence; Supervision, Human Relations; Company Policies and Practices; Activity; Variety; Security. **Skills Required:** Installation; Repairing; Equipment Maintenance; Problem Identification; Troubleshooting; Equipment Selection. **Abilities:** Information Ordering; Visualization; Control Precision; Finger Dexterity; Manual Dexterity; Extent Flexibility; Problem Sensitivity. **Interacting with Others:** Performing Administrative Activities. **Physical Work Conditions:** Using Hands on Objects, Tools, Controls; Common Protective or Safety Attire; Indoors; Standing; Hazardous Equipment; Distracting Sounds and Noise Levels.

49-9044.00 Millwrights

Install, dismantle, or move machinery and heavy equipment according to layout plans, blueprints, or other drawings. **Education:** Long-term O-J-T. **Occupational Type:** Realistic. **Job Zone:** 4. **Average Salary:** $32,382. **Projected Growth:** –1.9%. **Occupational Values:** Moral Values; Activity; Supervision, Human Relations; Company Policies and Practices; Security; Compensation; Independence. **Skills Required:** Installation; Equipment Selection; Repairing; Equipment Maintenance. **Abilities:** Control Precision; Information Ordering; Static Strength; Visualization; Depth Perception; Far Vision; Manual Dexterity. **Interacting with Others:** Communicating with Other Workers. **Physical Work Conditions:** Using Hands on Objects, Tools, Controls; Hazardous Equipment; Common Protective or Safety Attire; Indoors; Distracting Sounds and Noise Levels; Standing; Bending or Twisting the Body.

49-9094.00 Locksmiths and Safe Repairers

Repair and open locks, make keys, change locks and safe combinations, and install and repair safes. **Education:** Moderate-term O-J-T. **Occupational Type:** Realistic. **Job Zone:** 3. **Average Salary:** $24,890. **Projected Growth:** 10%. **Occupational Values:** Independence; Moral Values; Security; Responsibility; Working Conditions; Company Policies and Practices; Compensation. **Skills Required:** Installation; Repairing. **Abilities:** Arm-Hand Steadiness. **Interacting with Others:** Communicating with Persons Outside Organization. **Physical Work Conditions:** Using Hands on Objects, Tools, Controls; Indoors; Standing.

51-9122.00 Painters, Transportation Equipment

Operate or tend painting machines to paint surfaces of transportation equipment, such as automobiles, buses, trucks, trains, boats, and airplanes. **Education:** Moderate-term O-J-T. **Occupational Type:** Realistic. **Job Zone:** 2. **Average Salary:** $29,110. **Projected Growth:** 9%. **Occupational Values:** Moral Values; Company Policies and Practices; Independence; Supervision, Human Relations; Activity; Supervision, Technical; Security. **Skills Required:** Equipment Selection. **Abilities:** Visual Color Discrimination. **Interacting with Others:** Communicating with Other Workers. **Physical Work Conditions:** Making Repetitive Motions; Standing; Bending or Twisting the Body; Common Protective or Safety Attire; Contaminants; Using Hands on Objects, Tools, Controls; Indoors.

53-6011.00 Bridge and Lock Tenders

Operate and tend bridges, canal locks, and lighthouses to permit marine passage on inland waterways, near shores, and at danger points in waterway passages. May supervise such operations. Includes drawbridge operators, lock tenders and operators, and slip bridge operators. **Education:** Moderate-term O-J-T. **Occupational Type:** Realistic. **Job Zone:** 2. **Average Salary:** $30,300. **Projected Growth:** 21.5%. **Occupational Values:** Independence; Moral Values; Security; Supervision, Human Relations; Autonomy. **Skills Required:** Operation and Control; Repairing; Equipment Maintenance; Troubleshooting. **Abilities:** Far Vision; Control Precision; Depth Perception; Manual Dexterity; Written Expression. **Interacting with Others:** Communicating with Persons Outside Organization. **Physical Work Conditions:** Using Hands on Objects, Tools, Controls; Hazardous Equipment; Indoors; Outdoors; Sitting; Special Uniform.

53-6051.04 Railroad Inspectors

Inspect railroad equipment, roadbed, and track to ensure safe transport of people or cargo. **Education:** Work experience in a related occupation. **Occupational Type:** Realistic. **Job Zone:** 2. **Average Salary:** $39,560. **Projected Growth:** –3.2%. **Occupational Values:** Moral Values; Responsibility; Security; Activity; Company Policies and Practices; Coworkers; Supervision, Human Relations. **Skills Required:** Testing; Repairing; Troubleshooting; Problem Identification; Operation Monitoring; Equipment Maintenance; Product Inspection. **Abilities:** Problem Sensitivity; Oral Expression; Written Expression; Control Precision; Deductive Reasoning; Extent Flexibility; Manual Dexterity. **Interacting with Others:** Communicating with Other Workers. **Physical Work Conditions:** Outdoors; Standing; Using Hands on Objects, Tools, Controls; Hazardous Equipment; Walking or Running.

05.03.02 Mechanical Work: Machinery Repair

49-2092.06 Hand and Portable Power Tool Repairers

Repair and adjust hand and power tools. **Education:** Long-term O-J-T. **Occupational Type:** Realistic. **Job Zone:** 2. **Average Salary:** $27,730. **Projected Growth:** 5.6%. **Occupational Values:**

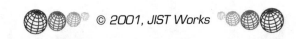

Moral Values; Independence; Activity; Security; Responsibility; Company Policies and Practices; Working Conditions. **Skills Required:** Problem Identification; Repairing. **Abilities:** Manual Dexterity; Finger Dexterity; Visualization; Wrist-Finger Speed; Near Vision. **Interacting with Others:** Monitoring and Controlling Resources. **Physical Work Conditions:** Using Hands on Objects, Tools, Controls; Indoors; Common Protective or Safety Attire; Standing; Hazardous Equipment; Making Repetitive Motions; Sitting.

49-3091.00 Bicycle Repairers

Repair and service bicycles. **Education:** Moderate-term O-J-T. **Occupational Type:** Realistic. **Job Zone:** 2. **Average Salary:** $15,700. **Projected Growth:** 22.6%. **Occupational Values:** Moral Values; Independence; Responsibility; Security; Working Conditions; Autonomy. **Skills Required:** Repairing; Installation; Troubleshooting; Problem Identification; Equipment Selection. **Abilities:** Manual Dexterity. **Interacting with Others:** Performing for/Working with Public. **Physical Work Conditions:** Using Hands on Objects, Tools, Controls; Indoors; Kneeling, Crouching, or Crawling; Standing; Hazardous Equipment.

49-9011.00 Mechanical Door Repairers

Install, service, or repair opening and closing mechanisms of automatic doors and hydraulic door closers. Includes garage door mechanics. **Education:** Postsecondary vocational training. **Occupational Type:** Realistic. **Job Zone:** 3. **Average Salary:** $35,640. **Projected Growth:** 4.4%. **Occupational Values:** Moral Values; Independence; Supervision, Technical; Company Policies and Practices; Security; Supervision, Human Relations; Activity. **Skills Required:** Installation; Equipment Maintenance; Repairing. **Abilities:** Manual Dexterity; Arm-Hand Steadiness; Extent Flexibility; Information Ordering. **Interacting with Others:** Communicating with Persons Outside Organization. **Physical Work Conditions:** Using Hands on Objects, Tools, Controls; Standing; Hazardous Equipment; Indoors; Kneeling, Crouching, or Crawling; Bending or Twisting the Body; Outdoors.

49-9012.00 Control and Valve Installers and Repairers, Except Mechanical Door

Install, repair, and maintain mechanical regulating and controlling devices such as electric meters, gas regulators, thermostats, safety and flow valves, and other mechanical governors. No other data currently available.

49-9012.02 Valve and Regulator Repairers

Test, repair, and adjust mechanical regulators and valves. **Education:** Postsecondary vocational training. **Occupational Type:** Realistic. **Job Zone:** 3. **Average Salary:** $37,600. **Projected Growth:** 4.4%. **Occupational Values:** Moral Values; Independence; Security; Supervision, Technical; Supervision, Human Relations; Responsibility; Activity. **Skills Required:** Repairing; Product Inspection; Testing. **Abilities:** Manual Dexterity; Finger Dexterity; Information Ordering; Near Vision; Wrist-Finger Speed. **Interacting with Others:** Communicating with Persons Outside Organization. **Physical Work Conditions:** Using Hands on Objects, Tools, Controls; Hazardous Equipment; Indoors; Standing; Bending or Twisting the Body; Common Protective or Safety Attire; Contaminants.

49-9012.03 Meter Mechanics

Test, adjust, and repair gas, water, and oil meters. **Education:** Long-term O-J-T. **Occupational Type:** Realistic. **Job Zone:** 2. **Average Salary:** $40,850. **Projected Growth:** 4.4%. **Occupational Values:** Moral Values; Independence; Security; Company Policies and Practices; Supervision, Human Relations; Supervision, Technical; Activity. **Skills Required:** Repairing; Product Inspection; Equipment Maintenance; Testing; Installation. **Abilities:** Arm-Hand Steadiness; Near Vision; Finger Dexterity; Information Ordering; Manual Dexterity. **Interacting with Others:** Performing Administrative Activities. **Physical Work Conditions:** Outdoors; Using Hands on Objects, Tools, Controls; Standing; Kneeling, Crouching, or Crawling; Walking or Running; Hazardous Situations.

49-9031.02 Gas Appliance Repairers

Repair and install gas appliances and equipment such as ovens, dryers, and hot water heaters. **Education:** Long-term O-J-T. **Occupational Type:** Realistic. **Job Zone:** 4. **Average Salary:** $33,140. **Projected Growth:** 5.6%. **Occupational Values:** Moral Values; Independence; Security; Supervision, Human Relations; Company Policies and Practices; Responsibility; Compensation. **Skills Required:** Installation; Repairing; Troubleshooting; Testing; Problem Identification; Operation Monitoring; Identification of Key Causes. **Abilities:** Manual Dexterity. **Interacting with Others:** Performing for/Working with Public. **Physical Work Conditions:** Using Hands on Objects, Tools, Controls; Indoors; Kneeling, Crouching, or Crawling; Contaminants; Hazardous Conditions; Hazardous Situations; Standing.

49-9041.00 Industrial Machinery Mechanics

Repair, install, adjust, or maintain industrial production and processing machinery or refinery and pipeline distribution systems. **Education:** Long-term O-J-T. **Occupational Type:** Realistic. **Job Zone:** 3. **Average Salary:** $21,185. **Projected Growth:** 4.4%. **Occupational Values:** Moral Values; Independence; Activity; Security; Company Policies and Practices; Supervision, Human Relations; Variety. **Skills Required:** Repairing; Equipment Maintenance; Troubleshooting; Problem Identification; Testing; Operation Monitoring; Equipment Selection. **Abilities:** Visualization; Control Precision; Extent Flexibility; Finger Dexterity; Hearing Sensitivity; Information Ordering; Manual Dexterity. **Interacting with Others:** Communicating with Other Workers. **Physical Work Conditions:** Indoors; Using Hands on Objects, Tools, Controls; Common Protective or Safety Attire; Hazardous Equipment; Standing; Distracting Sounds and Noise Levels; Bending or Twisting the Body.

49-9043.00 Maintenance Workers, Machinery

Lubricate machinery, change parts, or perform other routine machinery maintenance. **Education:** Long-term O-J-T. **Occupational Type:** Realistic. **Job Zone:** 1. **Average Salary:** $30,240. **Projected Growth:** 4.4%. **Occupational Values:** Moral Values; Variety; Supervision, Human Relations; Activity; Company Policies and Practices; Security; Coworkers. **Skills Required:** Equipment Maintenance; Repairing; Troubleshooting; Testing; Operation Monitoring; Operation and Control; Installation. **Abilities:** Manual Dexterity; Extent Flexibility; Written Comprehension. **Interacting with Others:** Communicating with Other Workers. **Physical Work Conditions:** Indoors; Using Hands on Objects, Tools, Controls; Common Protective or

Safety Attire; Hazardous Equipment; Standing; Distracting Sounds and Noise Levels; Bending or Twisting the Body.

49-9091.00 Coin, Vending, and Amusement Machine Servicers and Repairers

Install, service, adjust, or repair coin, vending, or amusement machines including video games, juke boxes, pinball machines, or slot machines. **Education:** Long-term O-J-T. **Occupational Type:** Realistic. **Job Zone:** 2. **Average Salary:** $23,260. **Projected Growth:** 15.6%. **Occupational Values:** Moral Values; Independence; Security; Company Policies and Practices; Responsibility; Supervision, Technical; Activity. **Skills Required:** Repairing; Equipment Maintenance. **Abilities:** Manual Dexterity; Finger Dexterity. **Interacting with Others:** Monitoring and Controlling Resources. **Physical Work Conditions:** Indoors; Using Hands on Objects, Tools, Controls; Standing; Bending or Twisting the Body; Kneeling, Crouching, or Crawling; Making Repetitive Motions.

05.03.03 Mechanical Work: Medical and Technical Equipment Fabrication and Repair

49-9061.00 Camera and Photographic Equipment Repairers

Repair and adjust cameras and photographic equipment, including commercial video and motion picture camera equipment. **Education:** Moderate-term O-J-T. **Occupational Type:** Realistic. **Job Zone:** 4. **Average Salary:** $28,320. **Projected Growth:** 8.2%. **Occupational Values:** Moral Values; Working Conditions; Security; Ability Utilization; Independence; Autonomy; Compensation. **Skills Required:** Repairing; Troubleshooting; Testing; Reading Comprehension; Operation Monitoring; Information Gathering; Critical Thinking. **Abilities:** Near Vision; Arm-Hand Steadiness; Deductive Reasoning; Finger Dexterity; Wrist-Finger Speed. **Interacting with Others:** Communicating with Persons Outside Organization. **Physical Work Conditions:** Using Hands on Objects, Tools, Controls; Indoors; Sitting.

49-9062.00 Medical Equipment Repairers

Test, adjust, or repair biomedical or electromedical equipment. **Education:** Long-term O-J-T. **Occupational Type:** Realistic. **Job Zone:** 3. **Average Salary:** $34,190. **Projected Growth:** 13.5%. **Occupational Values:** Moral Values; Security; Activity; Company Policies and Practices; Compensation; Ability Utilization; Achievement. **Skills Required:** Repairing; Equipment Maintenance; Testing; Troubleshooting; Installation; Equipment Selection; Operation Monitoring. **Abilities:** Deductive Reasoning; Problem Sensitivity. **Interacting with Others:** Teaching Others. **Physical Work Conditions:** Indoors; Using Hands on Objects, Tools, Controls; Hazardous Equipment; Hazardous Situations; Standing.

49-9064.00 Watch Repairers

Repair, clean, and adjust mechanisms of timing instruments such as watches and clocks. **Education:** Long-term O-J-T. **Occupational Type:** Realistic. **Job Zone:** 3. **Average Salary:** $24,580. **Projected Growth:** –4.2%. **Occupational Values:** Moral Values; Independence; Working Conditions; Ability Utilization; Security; Autonomy; Compensation. **Skills Required:** Repairing. **Abilities:** Finger Dexterity; Near Vision; Arm-Hand Steadiness. **Interacting with Others:** Communicating with Persons Outside Organization. **Physical Work Conditions:** Indoors; Using Hands on Objects, Tools, Controls; Sitting; Making Repetitive Motions.

51-9082.00 Medical Appliance Technicians

Construct, fit, maintain, or repair medical supportive devices such as braces, artificial limbs, joints, arch supports, and other surgical and medical appliances. **Education:** Work experience in a related occupation. **Occupational Type:** Realistic. **Job Zone:** 2. **Average Salary:** $23,260. **Projected Growth:** 1.7%. **Occupational Values:** Moral Values; Independence; Achievement; Working Conditions; Recognition; Security; Compensation. **Skills Required:** Technology Design; Operations Analysis. **Abilities:** Oral Expression; Manual Dexterity. **Interacting with Others:** Assisting and Caring for Others; Teaching Others. **Physical Work Conditions:** Indoors; Using Hands on Objects, Tools, Controls; Hazardous Equipment; Making Repetitive Motions; Sitting.

51-9083.00 Ophthalmic Laboratory Technicians

Cut, grind, and polish eyeglasses, contact lenses, or other precision optical elements. Assemble and mount lenses into frames or process other optical elements. No other data currently available.

51-9083.02 Optical Instrument Assemblers

Assemble optical instruments such as telescopes, level-transits, and gunsights. **Education:** Long-term O-J-T. **Occupational Type:** Realistic. **Job Zone:** 4. **Average Salary:** $19,530. **Projected Growth:** 4.7%. **Occupational Values:** Moral Values; Independence; Working Conditions; Supervision, Human Relations; Supervision, Technical; Company Policies and Practices; Security. **Skills Required:** Equipment Selection; Mathematics. **Abilities:** Arm-Hand Steadiness; Manual Dexterity; Near Vision. **Interacting with Others:** Performing Administrative Activities. **Physical Work Conditions:** Indoors; Using Hands on Objects, Tools, Controls; Sitting; Standing.

05.03.04 Mechanical Work: Musical Instrument Fabrication and Repair

49-9063.01 Keyboard Instrument Repairers and Tuners

Repair, adjust, refinish, and tune musical keyboard instruments. **Education:** Long-term O-J-T. **Occupational Type:** Realistic. **Job Zone:** 3. **Average Salary:** $23,010. **Projected Growth:** 6.5%.

Occupational Values: Moral Values; Independence; Working Conditions; Autonomy; Security; Responsibility; Company Policies and Practices. **Skills Required:** Repairing; Problem Identification; Testing; Equipment Selection. **Abilities:** Manual Dexterity; Wrist-Finger Speed; Arm-Hand Steadiness. **Interacting with Others:** Communicating with Persons Outside Organization. **Physical Work Conditions:** Indoors; Using Hands on Objects, Tools, Controls; Making Repetitive Motions.

49-9063.02 Stringed Instrument Repairers and Tuners

Repair, adjust, refinish, and tune musical stringed instruments. **Education:** Long-term O-J-T. **Occupational Type:** Realistic. **Job Zone:** 3. **Average Salary:** $23,010. **Projected Growth:** 6.5%. **Occupational Values:** Moral Values; Independence; Working Conditions; Ability Utilization; Autonomy; Security; Responsibility. **Skills Required:** Repairing; Product Inspection; Problem Identification. **Abilities:** Wrist-Finger Speed; Manual Dexterity. **Interacting with Others:** Communicating with Other Workers. **Physical Work Conditions:** Indoors; Using Hands on Objects, Tools, Controls; Sitting.

49-9063.03 Reed or Wind Instrument Repairers and Tuners

Repair, adjust, refinish, and tune musical reed and wind instruments. **Education:** Long-term O-J-T. **Occupational Type:** Realistic. **Job Zone:** 4. **Average Salary:** $23,010. **Projected Growth:** 6.5%. **Occupational Values:** Moral Values; Independence; Working Conditions; Autonomy; Security; Responsibility; Ability Utilization. **Skills Required:** Repairing; Testing. **Abilities:** Manual Dexterity; Finger Dexterity; Information Ordering; Wrist-Finger Speed. **Interacting with Others:** Establishing and Maintaining Relationships. **Physical Work Conditions:** Indoors; Using Hands on Objects, Tools, Controls; Sitting.

49-9063.04 Percussion Instrument Repairers and Tuners

Repair and tune musical percussion instruments. **Education:** Long-term O-J-T. **Occupational Type:** Realistic. **Job Zone:** 3. **Average Salary:** $23,010. **Projected Growth:** 6.5%. **Occupational Values:** Moral Values; Independence; Working Conditions; Autonomy; Security; Responsibility; Ability Utilization. **Skills Required:** Repairing; Testing. **Abilities:** Hearing Sensitivity; Manual Dexterity; Near Vision. **Interacting with Others:** Monitoring and Controlling Resources. **Physical Work Conditions:** Using Hands on Objects, Tools, Controls; Indoors; Sitting; Standing.

05.04.01 Hands-on Work in Mechanics, Installers, and Repairers

47-3013.00 Helpers—Electricians

Help electricians by performing duties of lesser skill. Duties include using, supplying, or holding materials or tools, and cleaning work area and equipment. **Education:** Short-term O-J-T. **Occupational Type:** Realistic. **Job Zone:** 2. **Average Salary:** $19,440. **Projected Growth:** 7.3%. **Occupational Values:** Moral Values; Supervision, Technical; Advancement; Activity; Coworkers; Supervision, Human Relations; Security. **Skills Required:** Equipment Selection. **Abilities:** Manual Dexterity; Arm-Hand Steadiness; Static Strength. **Interacting with Others:** Assisting and Caring for Others. **Physical Work Conditions:** Using Hands on Objects, Tools, Controls; Common Protective or Safety Attire; Hazardous Conditions; Standing; Hazardous Equipment; High Places; Outdoors.

49-3093.00 Tire Repairers and Changers

Repair and replace tires. **Education:** Short-term O-J-T. **Occupational Type:** Realistic. **Job Zone:** 1. **Average Salary:** $16,810. **Projected Growth:** 10.4%. **Occupational Values:** Moral Values; Independence; Security; Activity; Responsibility; Supervision, Technical; Supervision, Human Relations. **Skills Required:** Repairing. **Abilities:** Information Ordering. **Interacting with Others:** Performing for/Working with Public. **Physical Work Conditions:** Using Hands on Objects, Tools, Controls; Standing; Special Uniform; Indoors; Kneeling, Crouching, or Crawling; Outdoors; Distracting Sounds and Noise Levels.

49-9098.00 Helpers—Installation, Maintenance, and Repair Workers

Help installation, maintenance, and repair workers in maintenance, parts replacement, and repair of vehicles, industrial machinery, and electrical and electronic equipment. Perform duties such as furnishing tools, materials, and supplies to other workers; cleaning work area, machines, and tools; and holding materials or tools for other workers. **Education:** Short-term O-J-T. **Occupational Type:** Realistic. **Job Zone:** 1. **Average Salary:** $18,230. **Projected Growth:** 13.4%. **Occupational Values:** Moral Values; Advancement; Activity; Supervision, Technical; Coworkers; Supervision, Human Relations; Security. **Skills Required:** Equipment Maintenance; Repairing; Installation. **Abilities:** Information Ordering; Extent Flexibility; Manual Dexterity; Near Vision; Arm-Hand Steadiness; Static Strength. **Interacting with Others:** Assisting and Caring for Others. **Physical Work Conditions:** Indoors; Using Hands on Objects, Tools, Controls; Standing; Hazardous Equipment; Bending or Twisting the Body.

06 Construction, Mining, and Drilling

06.01.01 Managerial Work in Construction, Mining, and Drilling

11-9021.00 Construction Managers

Plan, direct, coordinate, or budget, usually through subordinate supervisory personnel, activities concerned with the construction and maintenance of structures, facilities, and systems. Participate in the conceptual development of a construction project and oversee its organization, scheduling, and implementation. **Education:** Bachelor's degree. **Occupational Type:** Enterprising. **Job Zone:** 4. **Average Salary:** $47,610. **Projected Growth:** 14%. **Occupational Values:** Authority; Autonomy; Responsibility; Variety; Compensation; Ability Utilization; Company Policies and Practices. **Skills Required:** Coordination; Judgment and Decision Making; Management of Personnel Resources; Problem Identification; Product Inspection; Critical Thinking; Time Management. **Abilities:** Oral Comprehension; Written Comprehension; Oral Expression; Problem Sensitivity; Written Expression. **Interacting with Others:** Coordinating Work and Activities of Others; Guiding, Directing, and Motivating Subordinates. **Physical Work Conditions:** Sitting; Outdoors; Indoors; Distracting Sounds and Noise Levels; Standing.

47-1011.01 First-Line Supervisors and Manager/Supervisors—Construction Trades Workers

Directly supervise and coordinate activities of construction trades workers and their helpers. Manager/Supervisors are generally found in smaller establishments where they perform both supervisory and management functions such as accounting, marketing, and personnel work and may also engage in the same construction trades work as the workers they supervise. **Education:** Work experience in a related occupation. **Occupational Type:** Enterprising. **Job Zone:** 4. **Average Salary:** $36,766. **Projected Growth:** 8.9%. **Occupational Values:** Authority; Responsibility; Autonomy; Activity; Coworkers; Variety; Moral Values. **Skills Required:** Coordination; Time Management; Product Inspection; Management of Personnel Resources; Active Listening; Instructing; Speaking. **Abilities:** Oral Expression; Problem Sensitivity; Oral Comprehension; Information Ordering; Written Comprehension; Number Facility; Written Expression. **Interacting with Others:** Communicating with Other Workers; Coordinating Work and Activities of Others; Guiding, Directing, and Motivating Subordinates. **Physical Work Conditions:** Common Protective or Safety Attire; Outdoors; Standing; Using Hands on Objects, Tools, Controls; Hazardous Equipment; Contaminants; High Places.

47-1011.02 First-Line Supervisors and Manager/Supervisors—Extractive Workers

Directly supervise and coordinate activities of extractive workers and their helpers. Manager/Supervisors are generally found in smaller establishments where they perform both supervisory and management functions such as accounting, marketing, and personnel work and may also engage in the same extractive work as the workers they supervise. **Education:** Work experience in a related occupation. **Occupational Type:** Enterprising. **Job Zone:** 3. **Average Salary:** $36,766. **Projected Growth:** 8.9%. **Occupational Values:** Authority; Responsibility; Autonomy; Coworkers; Achievement; Activity; Variety. **Skills Required:** Management of Personnel Resources; Time Management; Coordination; Judgment and Decision Making; Speaking; Problem Identification; Critical Thinking. **Abilities:** Oral Expression; Near Vision; Deductive Reasoning. **Interacting with Others:** Coordinating Work and Activities of Others; Communicating with Other Workers; Guiding, Directing, and Motivating Subordinates. **Physical Work Conditions:** Common Protective or Safety Attire; Standing; Outdoors; Indoors; Sitting; Using Hands on Objects, Tools, Controls.

06.02.01 Construction: Masonry, Stone, and Brick Work

47-2021.00 Brickmasons and Blockmasons

Lay and bind building materials such as brick, structural tile, concrete block, cinder block, glass block, and terra-cotta block with mortar and other substances to construct or repair walls, partitions, arches, sewers, and other structures. **Education:** Long-term O-J-T. **Occupational Type:** Realistic. **Job Zone:** 3. **Average Salary:** $35,570. **Projected Growth:** 12.3%. **Occupational Values:** Moral Values; Compensation; Independence; Ability Utilization; Achievement; Security; Company Policies and Practices. **Skills Required:** Mathematics; Equipment Selection. **Abilities:** Manual Dexterity; Visualization; Information Ordering; Dynamic Strength; Extent Flexibility. **Interacting with Others:** Communicating with Other Workers. **Physical Work Conditions:** Using Hands on Objects, Tools, Controls; Standing; Outdoors; Making Repetitive Motions; Contaminants; Common Protective or Safety Attire; Kneeling, Crouching, or Crawling.

47-2022.00 Stonemasons

Build stone structures such as piers, walls, and abutments. Lay walks, curbstones, or special types of masonry for vats, tanks, and floors. **Education:** Long-term O-J-T. **Occupational Type:** Realistic. **Job Zone:** 4. **Average Salary:** $32,220. **Projected Growth:** 12.3%. **Occupational Values:** Moral Values; Compensation; Independence; Ability Utilization; Achievement; Security; Company Policies and Practices. **Skills Required:** Equipment Selection. **Abilities:** Wrist-Finger Speed; Static Strength; Dynamic Strength; Visualization. **Interacting with Others:** Assisting and Caring for Others. **Physical Work Conditions:** Using Hands on Objects, Tools, Controls; Outdoors; Common Protective or Safety Attire; Kneeling, Crouching, or Crawling; Making Repetitive Motions; Standing; Bending or Twisting the Body.

47-2042.00 Floor Layers, Except Carpet, Wood, and Hard Tiles

Apply blocks, strips, or sheets of shock-absorbing, sound-deadening, or decorative coverings to floors. **Education:** Moderate-term O-J-T. **Occupational Type:** Realistic. **Job Zone:** 3. **Average Salary:** $26,900. **Projected Growth:** 11%. **Occupational Values:** Moral Values. **Skills Required:** Installation. **Abilities:** Extent Flexibility. **Interacting with Others:** Communicating with Other Workers. **Physical Work Conditions:** Indoors; Using Hands on Objects, Tools, Controls; Kneeling, Crouching, or Crawling; Standing; Bending or Twisting the Body.

47-2044.00 Tile and Marble Setters

Apply hard tile, marble, and wood tile to walls, floors, ceilings, and roof decks. **Education:** Long-term O-J-T. **Occupational Type:** Realistic. **Job Zone:** 2. **Average Salary:** $33,810. **Projected Growth:** 8.7%. **Occupational Values:** Moral Values; Independence; Company Policies and Practices; Compensation; Achievement; Activity; Ability Utilization. **Skills Required:** Installation. **Abilities:** Arm-Hand Steadiness. **Interacting with Others:** Monitoring and Controlling Resources. **Physical Work Conditions:** Using Hands on Objects, Tools, Controls; Hazardous Situations; Standing; Indoors; Bending or Twisting the Body; Contaminants; Hazardous Equipment.

47-2051.00 Cement Masons and Concrete Finishers

Smooth and finish surfaces of poured concrete, such as floors, walks, sidewalks, roads, or curbs, using a variety of hand and power tools. Align forms for sidewalks, curbs, or gutters; patch voids; use saws to cut expansion joints. **Education:** Long-term O-J-T. **Occupational Type:** Realistic. **Job Zone:** 3. **Average Salary:** $25,770. **Projected Growth:** 6.1%. **Occupational Values:** Moral Values; Company Policies and Practices; Ability Utilization; Achievement; Compensation; Coworkers. **Skills Required:** Equipment Selection; Idea Evaluation; Product Inspection. **Abilities:** Manual Dexterity; Arm-Hand Steadiness; Information Ordering; Multilimb Coordination; Trunk Strength. **Interacting with Others:** Communicating with Other Workers. **Physical Work Conditions:** Outdoors; Using Hands on Objects, Tools, Controls; Standing; Kneeling, Crouching, or Crawling; Bending or Twisting the Body; Making Repetitive Motions.

47-2053.00 Terrazzo Workers and Finishers

Apply a mixture of cement, sand, pigment, or marble chips to floors, stairways, and cabinet fixtures to fashion durable and decorative surfaces. **Education:** Long-term O-J-T. **Occupational Type:** Realistic. **Job Zone:** 3. **Average Salary:** $25,770. **Projected Growth:** 6.1%. **Occupational Values:** Moral Values; Compensation; Company Policies and Practices; Achievement; Ability Utilization; Coworkers. **Skills Required:** Equipment Selection; Idea Evaluation; Product Inspection. **Abilities:** Manual Dexterity; Arm-Hand Steadiness; Information Ordering; Multilimb Coordination; Trunk Strength. **Interacting with Others:** Communicating with Other Workers. **Physical Work Conditions:** Outdoors; Using Hands on Objects, Tools, Controls; Standing; Kneeling, Crouching, or Crawling; Bending or Twisting the Body; Making Repetitive Motions.

51-9195.03 Stone Cutters and Carvers

Cut or carve stone according to diagrams and patterns. **Education:** Long-term O-J-T. **Occupational Type:** Realistic. **Job Zone:** 3. **Average Salary:** $19,847. **Projected Growth:** 12.3%. **Occupational Values:** Moral Values; Independence; Achievement; Autonomy; Ability Utilization; Recognition. **Skills Required:** Equipment Selection. **Abilities:** Arm-Hand Steadiness; Visualization. **Interacting with Others:** Coaching and Developing Others. **Physical Work Conditions:** Indoors; Using Hands on Objects, Tools, Controls; Common Protective or Safety Attire; Standing; Contaminants; Distracting Sounds and Noise Levels.

06.02.02 Construction: Construction and Maintenance

47-2011.00 Boilermakers

Construct, assemble, maintain, and repair stationary steam boilers and boiler house auxiliaries. Align structures or plate sections to assemble boiler frame tanks or vats, following blueprints. Use hand and power tools, plumb bobs, levels, wedges, dogs, or turnbuckles. Assist in testing assembled vessels. Direct cleaning of boilers and boiler furnaces. Inspect and repair boiler fittings such as safety valves, regulators, automatic-control mechanisms, water columns, and auxiliary machines. **Education:** Long-term O-J-T. **Occupational Type:** Realistic. **Job Zone:** 4. **Average Salary:** $38,380. **Projected Growth:** 1.6%. **Occupational Values:** Moral Values; Company Policies and Practices; Supervision, Human Relations; Compensation; Activity; Supervision, Technical; Ability Utilization. **Skills Required:** Repairing; Product Inspection; Installation; Equipment Maintenance; Troubleshooting; Testing; Equipment Selection. **Abilities:** Manual Dexterity; Static Strength. **Interacting with Others:** Communicating with Other Workers. **Physical Work Conditions:** Using Hands on Objects, Tools, Controls; Hazardous Equipment; Indoors; Standing; Common Protective or Safety Attire; Hazardous Situations; Distracting Sounds and Noise Levels.

47-2031.01 Construction Carpenters

Construct, erect, install, and repair structures and fixtures of wood, plywood, and wallboard using carpenter's hand tools and power tools. **Education:** Long-term O-J-T. **Occupational Type:** Realistic. **Job Zone:** 4. **Average Salary:** $28,740. **Projected Growth:** 6.9%. **Occupational Values:** Moral Values; Compensation; Activity; Achievement; Ability Utilization; Variety; Responsibility. **Skills Required:** Installation. **Abilities:** Visualization; Arm-Hand Steadiness; Manual Dexterity; Explosive Strength; Extent Flexibility; Dynamic Strength; Information Ordering. **Interacting with Others:** Monitoring and Controlling Resources. **Physical Work Conditions:** Using Hands on Objects, Tools, Controls; Standing; Common Protective or Safety Attire; Hazardous Equipment; Contaminants; Indoors; Kneeling, Crouching, or Crawling.

47-2031.02 Rough Carpenters

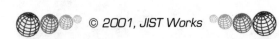

Build rough wooden structures (such as concrete forms; scaffolds; tunnel, bridge, or sewer supports; billboard signs; and temporary frame shelters) according to sketches, blueprints, or oral instructions. **Education:** Long-term O-J-T. **Occupational Type:** Realistic. **Job Zone:** 3. **Average Salary:** $28,740. **Projected Growth:** 6.9%. **Occupational Values:** Moral Values; Activity; Compensation; Ability Utilization; Variety; Achievement; Security. **Skills Required:** Installation. **Abilities:** Manual Dexterity; Information Ordering; Visualization. **Interacting with Others:** Communicating with Other Workers. **Physical Work Conditions:** Using Hands on Objects, Tools, Controls; Outdoors; Standing; Common Protective or Safety Attire; Hazardous Equipment; Climbing Ladders, Scaffolds, Poles, etc.; High Places.

47-2031.04 Ship Carpenters and Joiners

Fabricate, assemble, install, or repair wooden furnishings in ships or boats. **Education:** Long-term O-J-T. **Occupational Type:** Realistic. **Job Zone:** 3. **Average Salary:** $28,740. **Projected Growth:** 6.9%. **Occupational Values:** Moral Values; Activity; Independence; Supervision, Human Relations; Compensation; Ability Utilization; Variety. **Skills Required:** Information Gathering. **Abilities:** Manual Dexterity; Visualization. **Interacting with Others:** Communicating with Other Workers. **Physical Work Conditions:** Using Hands on Objects, Tools, Controls; Standing; Common Protective or Safety Attire; Hazardous Equipment; Kneeling, Crouching, or Crawling; Outdoors; Hazardous Situations.

47-2031.05 Boat Builders and Shipwrights

Construct and repair ships or boats according to blueprints. **Education:** Long-term O-J-T. **Occupational Type:** Realistic. **Job Zone:** 4. **Average Salary:** $28,740. **Projected Growth:** 6.9%. **Occupational Values:** Moral Values; Ability Utilization; Achievement; Compensation; Activity; Independence; Variety. **Skills Required:** Equipment Selection. **Abilities:** Manual Dexterity; Information Ordering; Visualization; Arm-Hand Steadiness; Extent Flexibility; Near Vision; Wrist-Finger Speed. **Interacting with Others:** Communicating with Other Workers. **Physical Work Conditions:** Using Hands on Objects, Tools, Controls; Standing; Outdoors; Common Protective or Safety Attire; Hazardous Equipment; Kneeling, Crouching, or Crawling; Making Repetitive Motions.

47-2041.00 Carpet Installers

Lay and install carpet from rolls or blocks on floors. Install padding and trim flooring materials. **Education:** Moderate-term O-J-T. **Occupational Type:** Realistic. **Job Zone:** 4. **Average Salary:** $26,480. **Projected Growth:** 3.6%. **Occupational Values:** Moral Values. **Skills Required:** Installation; Information Organization; Mathematics; Problem Identification; Product Inspection. **Abilities:** Static Strength; Extent Flexibility; Multilimb Coordination; Manual Dexterity; Number Facility; Arm-Hand Steadiness; Explosive Strength. **Interacting with Others:** Communicating with Persons Outside Organization. **Physical Work Conditions:** Indoors; Kneeling, Crouching, or Crawling; Using Hands on Objects, Tools, Controls; Bending or Twisting the Body; Making Repetitive Motions; Hazardous Situations.

47-2043.00 Floor Sanders and Finishers

Scrape and sand wooden floors to smooth surfaces, using floor scraper and floor sanding machine. Apply coats of finish. **Education:** Short-term O-J-T. **Occupational Type:** Realistic. **Job Zone:** 2. **Average Salary:** $23,360. **Projected Growth:** 7.3%. **Occupational Values:** Moral Values; Independence. **Skills Required:** Installation. **Abilities:** Manual Dexterity; Trunk Strength. **Interacting with Others:** Communicating with Other Workers. **Physical Work Conditions:** Using Hands on Objects, Tools, Controls; Contaminants; Indoors; Standing; Making Repetitive Motions; Common Protective or Safety Attire; Walking or Running.

47-2081.01 Ceiling Tile Installers

Apply plasterboard or other wallboard to ceilings or interior walls of buildings. Apply or mount acoustical tiles or blocks, strips, or sheets of shock-absorbing materials to ceilings and walls of buildings to reduce or reflect sound. Materials may be of decorative quality. Includes lathers who fasten wooden, metal, or rockboard lath to walls, ceilings, or partitions of buildings to provide support base for plaster, fire-proofing, or acoustical material. **Education:** Moderate-term O-J-T. **Occupational Type:** Realistic. **Job Zone:** 4. **Average Salary:** $31,750. **Projected Growth:** 8.9%. **Occupational Values:** Moral Values; Independence; Supervision, Human Relations; Activity; Company Policies and Practices; Compensation. **Skills Required:** Product Inspection. **Abilities:** Manual Dexterity. **Interacting with Others:** Monitoring and Controlling Resources. **Physical Work Conditions:** Using Hands on Objects, Tools, Controls; Indoors; Standing; Common Protective or Safety Attire; Hazardous Situations; Hazardous Equipment; Bending or Twisting the Body.

47-2081.02 Drywall Installers

Apply plasterboard or other wallboard to ceilings and interior walls of buildings. **Education:** Moderate-term O-J-T. **Occupational Type:** Realistic. **Job Zone:** 2. **Average Salary:** $29,150. **Projected Growth:** 7.5%. **Occupational Values:** Moral Values; Supervision, Human Relations; Company Policies and Practices; Activity; Independence. **Skills Required:** Installation; Equipment Selection. **Abilities:** Explosive Strength. **Interacting with Others:** Communicating with Other Workers. **Physical Work Conditions:** Indoors; Using Hands on Objects, Tools, Controls; Standing; Contaminants.

47-2111.00 Electricians

Install, maintain, and repair electrical wiring, equipment, and fixtures. Ensure that work is in accordance with relevant codes. May install or service street lights, intercom systems, or electrical control systems. **Education:** Long-term O-J-T. **Occupational Type:** Realistic. **Job Zone:** 3. **Average Salary:** $35,310. **Projected Growth:** 10.3%. **Occupational Values:** Moral Values; Ability Utilization; Compensation; Activity; Responsibility; Security; Authority. **Skills Required:** Installation; Repairing; Troubleshooting; Testing; Equipment Selection; Equipment Maintenance; Product Inspection. **Abilities:** Manual Dexterity; Near Vision; Finger Dexterity; Arm-Hand Steadiness; Problem Sensitivity; Visual Color Discrimination; Wrist-Finger Speed. **Interacting with Others:** Communicating with Other Workers. **Physical Work Conditions:** Using Hands on Objects, Tools, Controls; Indoors; Common Protective or Safety Attire; Hazardous Conditions; Hazardous Equipment; Standing; Sitting.

47-2121.00 Glaziers

Install glass in windows, skylights, store fronts, and display cases, or on surfaces such as building fronts, interior walls, ceilings, and tabletops. **Education:** Long-term O-J-T. **Occupational Type:** Realistic. **Job Zone:** 3. **Average Salary:** $25,612. **Projected Growth:** 3.9%. **Occupational Values:** Moral Values. **Skills Required:** Installation; Product Inspection; Mathematics; Information Organization; Equipment Selection. **Abilities:** Arm-Hand Steadiness; Static Strength; Information Ordering;

Extent Flexibility; Manual Dexterity; Multilimb Coordination; Wrist-Finger Speed. **Interacting with Others:** Communicating with Persons Outside Organization. **Physical Work Conditions:** Standing; Using Hands on Objects, Tools, Controls; Hazardous Situations; Common Protective or Safety Attire; Indoors; Kneeling, Crouching, or Crawling; Outdoors.

47-2131.00 Insulation Workers, Floor, Ceiling, and Wall

Line and cover structures with insulating materials. May work with batt, roll, or blown insulation materials. **Education:** Moderate-term O-J-T. **Occupational Type:** Realistic. **Job Zone:** 3. **Average Salary:** $25,490. **Projected Growth:** 7.5%. **Occupational Values:** Moral Values; Independence. **Skills Required:** Installation. **Abilities:** Control Precision. **Interacting with Others:** Communicating with Other Workers. **Physical Work Conditions:** Standing; Indoors; Using Hands on Objects, Tools, Controls; Common Protective or Safety Attire; Contaminants.

47-2132.00 Insulation Workers, Mechanical

Apply insulating materials to pipes, ductwork, or other mechanical systems in order to help control and maintain temperature. **Education:** Moderate-term O-J-T. **Occupational Type:** Realistic. **Job Zone:** 3. **Average Salary:** $24,669. **Projected Growth:** 7.5%. **Occupational Values:** Moral Values; Independence. **Skills Required:** Installation. **Abilities:** Control Precision. **Interacting with Others:** Communicating with Other Workers. **Physical Work Conditions:** Standing; Indoors; Using Hands on Objects, Tools, Controls; Common Protective or Safety Attire; Contaminants.

47-2141.00 Painters, Construction and Maintenance

Paint walls, equipment, buildings, bridges, and other structural surfaces, using brushes, rollers, and spray guns. May remove old paint to prepare surface prior to painting. May mix colors or oils to obtain desired color or consistency. **Education:** Moderate-term O-J-T. **Occupational Type:** Realistic. **Job Zone:** 4. **Average Salary:** $25,110. **Projected Growth:** 8.6%. **Occupational Values:** Moral Values; Independence; Activity; Company Policies and Practices; Achievement. **Skills Required:** Equipment Selection. **Abilities:** Visual Color Discrimination; Dynamic Strength. **Interacting with Others:** Communicating with Other Workers. **Physical Work Conditions:** Standing; Using Hands on Objects, Tools, Controls; Making Repetitive Motions; Contaminants; Indoors; High Places; Climbing Ladders, Scaffolds, Poles, etc.

47-2142.00 Paperhangers

Cover interior walls and ceilings of rooms with decorative wallpaper or fabric, or attach advertising posters on surfaces such as walls and billboards. Duties include removing old materials from surface to be papered. **Education:** Moderate-term O-J-T. **Occupational Type:** Realistic. **Job Zone:** 2. **Average Salary:** $25,110. **Projected Growth:** 8.6%. **Occupational Values:** Moral Values; Activity; Independence. **Skills Required:** Product Inspection. **Abilities:** Extent Flexibility. **Interacting with Others:** Monitoring and Controlling Resources. **Physical Work Conditions:** Standing; Indoors; Climbing Ladders, Scaffolds, Poles, etc.; Making Repetitive Motions; Using Hands on Objects, Tools, Controls.

47-2152.01 Pipe Fitters

Lay out, assemble, install, and maintain pipe systems, pipe supports, and related hydraulic and pneumatic equipment for steam, hot water, heating, cooling, lubricating, sprinkling, and industrial production and processing systems. **Education:** Long-term O-J-T. **Occupational Type:** Realistic. **Job Zone:** 4. **Average Salary:** $34,670. **Projected Growth:** 5.3%. **Occupational Values:** Moral Values; Independence; Activity; Company Policies and Practices; Ability Utilization; Security; Responsibility. **Skills Required:** Installation; Equipment Selection; Product Inspection; Operation and Control. **Abilities:** Visualization; Near Vision; Finger Dexterity; Information Ordering; Manual Dexterity; Arm-Hand Steadiness; Control Precision. **Interacting with Others:** Monitoring and Controlling Resources. **Physical Work Conditions:** Using Hands on Objects, Tools, Controls; Common Protective or Safety Attire; Indoors; Kneeling, Crouching, or Crawling; Standing; Bending or Twisting the Body; Contaminants.

47-2152.02 Plumbers

Assemble, install, and repair pipes, fittings, and fixtures of heating, water, and drainage systems according to specifications and plumbing codes. **Education:** Long-term O-J-T. **Occupational Type:** Realistic. **Job Zone:** 3. **Average Salary:** $34,670. **Projected Growth:** 5.3%. **Occupational Values:** Compensation; Moral Values; Responsibility; Achievement; Authority; Autonomy; Ability Utilization. **Skills Required:** Installation. **Abilities:** Manual Dexterity; Finger Dexterity; Visualization; Multilimb Coordination; Arm-Hand Steadiness; Extent Flexibility; Information Ordering. **Interacting with Others:** Communicating with Other Workers. **Physical Work Conditions:** Using Hands on Objects, Tools, Controls; Indoors; Standing; Kneeling, Crouching, or Crawling; Bending or Twisting the Body; Cramped Work Space, Awkward Positions.

47-2161.00 Plasterers and Stucco Masons

Apply interior or exterior plaster, cement, stucco, or similar materials. May also set ornamental plaster. **Education:** Long-term O-J-T. **Occupational Type:** Realistic. **Job Zone:** 4. **Average Salary:** $29,390. **Projected Growth:** 17.1%. **Occupational Values:** Moral Values; Company Policies and Practices; Coworkers; Achievement; Compensation. **Skills Required:** Product Inspection. **Abilities:** Manual Dexterity; Wrist-Finger Speed. **Interacting with Others:** Communicating with Other Workers. **Physical Work Conditions:** Using Hands on Objects, Tools, Controls; Climbing Ladders, Scaffolds, Poles, etc.; Contaminants; Indoors; Standing; Common Protective or Safety Attire; High Places.

47-2181.00 Roofers

Cover roofs of structures with shingles, slate, asphalt, aluminum, wood, and related materials. May spray roofs, sidings, and walls with material to bind, seal, insulate, or soundproof sections of structures. **Education:** Moderate-term O-J-T. **Occupational Type:** Realistic. **Job Zone:** 3. **Average Salary:** $25,340. **Projected Growth:** 12%. **Occupational Values:** Moral Values. **Skills Required:** Equipment Selection. **Abilities:** Gross Body Equilibrium; Static Strength. **Interacting with Others:** Communicating with Other Workers. **Physical Work Conditions:** Outdoors; High Places; Using Hands on Objects, Tools, Controls; Kneeling, Crouching, or Crawling; Keeping or Regaining

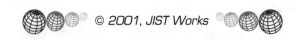

Balance; Bending or Twisting the Body; Common Protective or Safety Attire.

47-2211.00 Sheet Metal Workers

Fabricate, assemble, install, and repair sheet metal products and equipment such as ducts, control boxes, drainpipes, and furnace casings. Work may involve setting up and operating fabricating machines to cut, bend, and straighten sheet metal; shaping metal over anvils, blocks, or forms, using hammer; operating soldering and welding equipment to join sheet metal parts; inspecting, assembling, and smoothing seams and joints of burred surfaces. **Education:** Moderate-term O-J-T. **Occupational Type:** Realistic. **Job Zone:** 3. **Average Salary:** $28,030. **Projected Growth:** 14.1%. **Occupational Values:** Moral Values; Supervision, Human Relations; Company Policies and Practices; Activity; Independence; Compensation; Advancement. **Skills Required:** Installation; Operation and Control. **Abilities:** Information Ordering. **Interacting with Others:** Monitoring and Controlling Resources. **Physical Work Conditions:** Indoors; Hazardous Equipment; Using Hands on Objects, Tools, Controls; Common Protective or Safety Attire; Standing; Distracting Sounds and Noise Levels; Sitting.

49-2098.00 Security and Fire Alarm Systems Installers

Install, program, maintain, and repair security and fire alarm wiring and equipment. Ensure that work is in accordance with relevant codes. No other data currently available.

06.02.03 Construction: General

47-2031.06 Brattice Builders

Build doors or brattices (ventilation walls or partitions) in underground passageways to control the proper circulation of air through the passageways and to the working places. **Education:** Long-term O-J-T. **Occupational Type:** Realistic. **Job Zone:** 2. **Average Salary:** $33,900. **Projected Growth:** 6.9%. **Occupational Values:** Moral Values; Supervision, Human Relations; Company Policies and Practices; Activity. **Skills Required:** Installation; Product Inspection. **Abilities:** Extent Flexibility. **Interacting with Others:** Communicating with Other Workers. **Physical Work Conditions:** Standing; Using Hands on Objects, Tools, Controls; Common Protective or Safety Attire; Cramped Work Space, Awkward Positions; Outdoors.

47-2071.00 Paving, Surfacing, and Tamping Equipment Operators

Operate equipment used for applying concrete, asphalt, or other materials to road beds, parking lots, or airport runways and taxiways; or equipment used for tamping gravel, dirt, or other materials. Includes concrete and asphalt paving machine operators, form tampers, tamping machine operators, and stone spreader operators. **Education:** Moderate-term O-J-T. **Occupational Type:** Realistic. **Job Zone:** 2. **Average Salary:** $24,510. **Projected Growth:** 10.6%. **Occupational Values:** Moral Values; Independence; Supervision, Human Relations; Supervision, Technical. **Skills Required:** Operation and Control; Equipment Selection. **Abilities:** Control Precision; Multilimb Coordination. **Interacting with Others:** Communicating with Other Workers. **Physical Work Conditions:** Outdoors; Using Hands on Objects, Tools, Controls; Hazardous Equipment; Sitting; Distracting Sounds and Noise Levels; Contaminants; Whole Body Vibration.

47-2072.00 Pile-Driver Operators

Operate pile drivers mounted on skids, barges, crawler treads, or locomotive cranes to drive pilings for retaining walls, bulkheads, and foundations of structures such as buildings, bridges, and piers. **Education:** Moderate-term O-J-T. **Occupational Type:** Realistic. **Job Zone:** 2. **Average Salary:** $42,870. **Projected Growth:** 8.3%. **Occupational Values:** Moral Values; Independence. **Skills Required:** Operation and Control; Operation Monitoring. **Abilities:** Control Precision; Multilimb Coordination; Depth Perception. **Interacting with Others:** Communicating with Other Workers. **Physical Work Conditions:** Outdoors; Using Hands on Objects, Tools, Controls; Hazardous Equipment; Sitting; Distracting Sounds and Noise Levels; Whole Body Vibration; Common Protective or Safety Attire.

47-2073.01 Grader, Bulldozer, and Scraper Operators

Operate machines or vehicles equipped with blades to remove, distribute, level, or grade earth. **Education:** Moderate-term O-J-T. **Occupational Type:** Realistic. **Job Zone:** 2. **Average Salary:** $26,920. **Projected Growth:** 5.7%. **Occupational Values:** Moral Values; Independence; Supervision, Human Relations. **Skills Required:** Operation and Control. **Abilities:** Control Precision; Trunk Strength; Manual Dexterity. **Interacting with Others:** Communicating with Other Workers. **Physical Work Conditions:** Outdoors; Using Hands on Objects, Tools, Controls; Hazardous Equipment; Sitting; Whole Body Vibration; Distracting Sounds and Noise Levels; Common Protective or Safety Attire.

47-2073.02 Operating Engineers

Operate several types of power construction equipment such as compressors, pumps, hoists, derricks, cranes, shovels, tractors, scrapers, or motor graders to excavate, move, and grade earth, to erect structures, or to pour concrete or other hard surface pavement. May repair and maintain equipment in addition to other duties. **Education:** Moderate-term O-J-T. **Occupational Type:** Realistic. **Job Zone:** 3. **Average Salary:** $35,260. **Projected Growth:** 7.9%. **Occupational Values:** Moral Values; Independence; Supervision, Technical; Company Policies and Practices. **Skills Required:** Operation and Control; Repairing; Equipment Maintenance. **Abilities:** Multilimb Coordination. **Interacting with Others:** Communicating with Persons Outside Organization. **Physical Work Conditions:** Hazardous Equipment; Using Hands on Objects, Tools, Controls; Common Protective or Safety Attire; Outdoors; Standing; Whole Body Vibration; Distracting Sounds and Noise Levels.

47-2082.00 Tapers

Seal joints between plasterboard or other wallboard to prepare wall surface for painting or papering. **Education:** Moderate-term O-J-T. **Occupational Type:** Realistic. **Job Zone:** 2. **Average Salary:** $32,060. **Projected Growth:** 7.5%. **Occupational**

Values: Moral Values; Independence; Supervision, Human Relations; Activity; Company Policies and Practices. **Skills Required:** Equipment Selection. **Abilities:** Manual Dexterity. **Interacting with Others:** Communicating with Other Workers. **Physical Work Conditions:** Using Hands on Objects, Tools, Controls; Indoors; Standing; Common Protective or Safety Attire; Contaminants; Bending or Twisting the Body; Climbing Ladders, Scaffolds, Poles, etc.

47-2151.00 Pipelayers

Lay pipe for storm or sanitation sewers, drains, and water mains. Perform any combination of the following tasks: grade trenches or culverts, position pipe, or seal joints. **Education:** Moderate-term O-J-T. **Occupational Type:** Realistic. **Job Zone:** 2. **Average Salary:** $24,880. **Projected Growth:** 4.9%. **Occupational Values:** Moral Values. **Skills Required:** Product Inspection. **Abilities:** Trunk Strength; Stamina; Dynamic Strength; Static Strength; Dynamic Flexibility; Explosive Strength; Extent Flexibility. **Interacting with Others:** Communicating with Other Workers. **Physical Work Conditions:** Outdoors; Using Hands on Objects, Tools, Controls; Standing; Making Repetitive Motions; Common Protective or Safety Attire; Hazardous Equipment; Contaminants.

47-2152.03 Pipelaying Fitters

Align pipeline section in preparation of welding. Signal tractor driver for placement of pipeline sections in proper alignment. Insert steel spacer. **Education:** Moderate-term O-J-T. **Occupational Type:** Realistic. **Job Zone:** 2. **Average Salary:** $34,290. **Projected Growth:** 4.9%. **Occupational Values:** Moral Values; Company Policies and Practices. **Skills Required:** Product Inspection. **Abilities:** Manual Dexterity; Extent Flexibility. **Interacting with Others:** Communicating with Other Workers. **Physical Work Conditions:** Outdoors; Standing; Using Hands on Objects, Tools, Controls; Common Protective or Safety Attire; Kneeling, Crouching, or Crawling; Bending or Twisting the Body; Hazardous Equipment.

47-2171.00 Reinforcing Iron and Rebar Workers

Position and secure steel bars or mesh in concrete forms in order to reinforce concrete. Use a variety of fasteners, rod-bending machines, blowtorches, and hand tools. **Education:** Long-term O-J-T. **Occupational Type:** Realistic. **Job Zone:** 3. **Average Salary:** $32,850. **Projected Growth:** 8%. **Occupational Values:** Moral Values; Independence; Company Policies and Practices; Activity. **Skills Required:** Equipment Selection. **Abilities:** Manual Dexterity. **Interacting with Others:** Monitoring and Controlling Resources. **Physical Work Conditions:** Using Hands on Objects, Tools, Controls; Common Protective or Safety Attire; Hazardous Situations; Outdoors; Standing; Bending or Twisting the Body; Contaminants.

47-2221.00 Structural Iron and Steel Workers

Raise, place, and unite iron or steel girders, columns, and other structural members to form completed structures or structural frameworks. May erect metal storage tanks and assemble prefabricated metal buildings. **Education:** Long-term O-J-T. **Occupational Type:** Realistic. **Job Zone:** 3. **Average Salary:** $32,890. **Projected Growth:** 8%. **Occupational Values:** Moral Values; Company Policies and Practices; Activity; Coworkers; Supervision, Human Relations; Compensation. **Skills Required:** Installation. **Abilities:** Depth Perception; Static Strength; Dynamic Strength; Extent Flexibility; Visualization; Gross Body Equilibrium; Information Ordering. **Interacting with Others:** Communicating with Other Workers. **Physical Work Conditions:** Common Protective or Safety Attire; Standing; Using Hands on Objects, Tools, Controls; Outdoors; Distracting Sounds and Noise Levels; Bending or Twisting the Body; Climbing Ladders, Scaffolds, Poles, etc.

47-4031.00 Fence Erectors

Erect and repair metal and wooden fences and fence gates around highways, industrial establishments, residences, or farms, using hand and power tools. **Education:** Moderate-term O-J-T. **Occupational Type:** Realistic. **Job Zone:** 2. **Average Salary:** No Data Available. **Projected Growth:** 5.7%. **Occupational Values:** Moral Values. **Skills Required:** Repairing. **Abilities:** Manual Dexterity. **Interacting with Others:** Communicating with Persons Outside Organization. **Physical Work Conditions:** Outdoors; Using Hands on Objects, Tools, Controls; Standing; Common Protective or Safety Attire; Hazardous Situations; Kneeling, Crouching, or Crawling; Distracting Sounds and Noise Levels.

47-4041.00 Hazardous Materials Removal Workers

Identify, remove, pack, transport, or dispose of hazardous materials, including asbestos, lead-based paint, waste oil, fuel, transmission fluid, radioactive materials, contaminated soil, etc. Specialized training and certification in hazardous materials handling or a confined entry permit are generally required. May operate earth-moving equipment or trucks. No other data currently available.

47-4061.00 Rail-Track Laying and Maintenance Equipment Operators

Lay, repair, and maintain track for standard or narrow-gauge railroad equipment used in regular railroad service or in plant yards, quarries, sand and gravel pits, and mines. Includes ballast cleaning machine operators and roadbed tamping machine operators. **Education:** Moderate-term O-J-T. **Occupational Type:** Realistic. **Job Zone:** 1. **Average Salary:** $34,330. **Projected Growth:** 8.3%. **Occupational Values:** Moral Values; Supervision, Human Relations; Company Policies and Practices; Supervision, Technical. **Skills Required:** Operation and Control; Product Inspection; Operation Monitoring. **Abilities:** Control Precision; Depth Perception. **Interacting with Others:** Establishing and Maintaining Relationships. **Physical Work Conditions:** Outdoors; Using Hands on Objects, Tools, Controls; Hazardous Equipment; Sitting; Distracting Sounds and Noise Levels; Common Protective or Safety Attire; Contaminants.

47-4091.00 Segmental Pavers

Lay out, cut, and paste segmental paving units. Includes installers of bedding and restraining materials for the paving units. No other data currently available.

47-5031.00 Explosives Workers, Ordnance Handling Experts, and Blasters

Place and detonate explosives to demolish structures or to loosen, remove, or displace earth, rock, or other materials. May perform specialized handling, storage, and accounting procedures. Includes seismograph shooters. **Education:** Long-term O-J-T. **Occupational Type:** Realistic. **Job Zone:** 2. **Average Sal-**

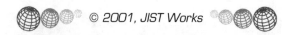

ary: $30,910. **Projected Growth:** –19.1%. **Occupational Values:** Moral Values; Supervision, Technical; Compensation. **Skills Required:** Equipment Selection; Mathematics. **Abilities:** Information Ordering; Multilimb Coordination; Arm-Hand Steadiness; Reaction Time; Manual Dexterity; Mathematical Reasoning; Number Facility. **Interacting with Others:** Communicating with Other Workers. **Physical Work Conditions:** Hazardous Conditions; Outdoors; Common Protective or Safety Attire; Distracting Sounds and Noise Levels; Using Hands on Objects, Tools, Controls; Hazardous Equipment; Standing.

49-9045.00 Refractory Materials Repairers, Except Brickmasons

Build or repair furnaces, kilns, cupolas, boilers, converters, ladles, soaking pits, ovens, etc., using refractory materials. **Education:** Long-term O-J-T. **Occupational Type:** Realistic. **Job Zone:** 1. **Average Salary:** $29,600. **Projected Growth:** 4.4%. **Occupational Values:** Moral Values; Independence; Company Policies and Practices; Security; Activity; Supervision, Human Relations; Compensation. **Skills Required:** Equipment Selection; Installation; Repairing; Operation and Control; Equipment Maintenance. **Abilities:** Dynamic Strength; Information Ordering; Extent Flexibility; Trunk Strength; Explosive Strength. **Interacting with Others:** Establishing and Maintaining Relationships. **Physical Work Conditions:** Using Hands on Objects, Tools, Controls; Common Protective or Safety Attire; Hazardous Equipment; Indoors; Standing; Very Hot; Contaminants.

49-9092.00 Commercial Divers

Work below surface of water, using scuba gear to inspect, repair, remove, or install equipment and structures. May use a variety of power and hand tools such as drills, sledgehammers, torches, and welding equipment. May conduct tests or experiments, rig explosives, or photograph structures or marine life. **Education:** Unknown. **Occupational Type:** Realistic. **Job Zone:** 2. **Average Salary:** $28,309. **Projected Growth:** 14.3%. **Occupational Values:** Moral Values; Ability Utilization; Responsibility; Achievement; Variety; Compensation; Coworkers. **Skills Required:** Problem Identification. **Abilities:** Gross Body Coordination; Manual Dexterity; Spatial Orientation; Stamina; Far Vision; Control Precision; Flexibility of Closure. **Interacting with Others:** Communicating with Other Workers. **Physical Work Conditions:** Common Protective or Safety Attire; Outdoors; Specialized Protective or Safety Attire; Using Hands on Objects, Tools, Controls; Extremely Bright or Inadequate Lighting; Kneeling, Crouching, or Crawling; Very Hot.

49-9095.00 Manufactured Building and Mobile Home Installers

Move or install mobile homes or prefabricated buildings. **Education:** Long-term O-J-T. **Occupational Type:** Realistic. **Job Zone:** 2. **Average Salary:** $21,420. **Projected Growth:** 14.3%. **Occupational Values:** Moral Values; Variety; Security; Company Policies and Practices; Activity; Supervision, Technical; Supervision, Human Relations. **Skills Required:** Installation; Repairing; Troubleshooting; Problem Identification. **Abilities:** Control Precision. **Interacting with Others:** Communicating with Persons Outside Organization. **Physical Work Conditions:** Standing; Using Hands on Objects, Tools, Controls; Indoors; Outdoors.

49-9096.00 Riggers

Set up or repair rigging for construction projects, manufacturing plants, logging yards, ships and shipyards, or the entertainment industry. **Education:** Long-term O-J-T. **Occupational Type:** Realistic. **Job Zone:** 3. **Average Salary:** $31,770. **Projected Growth:** 0.5%. **Occupational Values:** Moral Values; Company Policies and Practices; Responsibility; Supervision, Human Relations; Coworkers; Supervision, Technical; Authority. **Skills Required:** Testing; Coordination; Repairing; Equipment Maintenance; Equipment Selection; Operation and Control; Operation Monitoring. **Abilities:** Extent Flexibility; Manual Dexterity; Static Strength; Multilimb Coordination; Arm-Hand Steadiness; Information Ordering; Trunk Strength. **Interacting with Others:** Communicating with Other Workers; Coordinating Work and Activities of Others. **Physical Work Conditions:** Using Hands on Objects, Tools, Controls; Outdoors; Standing; Climbing Ladders, Scaffolds, Poles, etc.; High Places; Bending or Twisting the Body; Common Protective or Safety Attire.

06.03.01 Mining and Drilling

47-5011.00 Derrick Operators, Oil and Gas

Rig derrick equipment and operate pumps to circulate mud through drill hole. **Education:** Moderate-term O-J-T. **Occupational Type:** Realistic. **Job Zone:** 2. **Average Salary:** $26,060. **Projected Growth:** 0%. **Occupational Values:** Moral Values; Supervision, Human Relations; Company Policies and Practices; Supervision, Technical. **Skills Required:** Operation and Control; Repairing. **Abilities:** Manual Dexterity. **Interacting with Others:** Communicating with Other Workers. **Physical Work Conditions:** Outdoors; Hazardous Equipment; Standing; Using Hands on Objects, Tools, Controls; Common Protective or Safety Attire; Contaminants; Distracting Sounds and Noise Levels.

47-5012.00 Rotary Drill Operators, Oil and Gas

Set up or operate a variety of drills to remove petroleum products from the earth and to find and remove core samples for testing during oil and gas exploration. **Education:** Moderate-term O-J-T. **Occupational Type:** Realistic. **Job Zone:** 3. **Average Salary:** $31,940. **Projected Growth:** 0%. **Occupational Values:** Moral Values; Company Policies and Practices; Compensation; Supervision, Human Relations. **Skills Required:** Operation and Control; Repairing; Operation Monitoring. **Abilities:** Control Precision. **Interacting with Others:** Communicating with Other Workers. **Physical Work Conditions:** Outdoors; Hazardous Equipment; Using Hands on Objects, Tools, Controls; Common Protective or Safety Attire; Contaminants; Hazardous Situations; Standing.

47-5013.00 Service Unit Operators, Oil, Gas, and Mining

Operate equipment to increase oil flow from producing wells or to remove stuck pipe, casing, tools, or other obstructions from drilling wells. May also perform similar services in mining exploration operations. **Education:** Moderate-term O-J-T. **Occupational Type:** Realistic. **Job Zone:** 4. **Average Salary:** $22,390. **Projected Growth:** 0%. **Occupational Values:** Moral

Values; Supervision, Human Relations; Compensation; Supervision, Technical; Company Policies and Practices; Coworkers; Responsibility. **Skills Required:** Operation and Control; Equipment Selection; Operation Monitoring; Problem Identification; Judgment and Decision Making; Speaking; Identification of Key Causes. **Abilities:** Control Precision. **Interacting with Others:** Communicating with Other Workers. **Physical Work Conditions:** Outdoors; Hazardous Equipment; Using Hands on Objects, Tools, Controls; Standing; Hazardous Conditions; Distracting Sounds and Noise Levels; Common Protective or Safety Attire.

47-5021.01 Construction Drillers

Operate machine to drill or bore through earth or rock. **Education:** Long-term O-J-T. **Occupational Type:** Realistic. **Job Zone:** 2. **Average Salary:** $27,890. **Projected Growth:** –19.1%. **Occupational Values:** Moral Values. **Skills Required:** Operation and Control. **Abilities:** Control Precision; Static Strength; Information Ordering; Manual Dexterity; Reaction Time; Response Orientation; Depth Perception. **Interacting with Others:** Communicating with Other Workers. **Physical Work Conditions:** Outdoors; Hazardous Equipment; Common Protective or Safety Attire; Contaminants; Distracting Sounds and Noise Levels; Standing; Using Hands on Objects, Tools, Controls.

47-5021.02 Well and Core Drill Operators

Operate machine to drill wells and take samples or cores for analysis of strata. **Education:** Long-term O-J-T. **Occupational Type:** Realistic. **Job Zone:** 3. **Average Salary:** $27,890. **Projected Growth:** –19.1%. **Occupational Values:** Moral Values; Independence. **Skills Required:** Operation and Control; Equipment Selection; Operation Monitoring. **Abilities:** Control Precision; Multilimb Coordination; Depth Perception; Near Vision; Static Strength; Information Ordering; Manual Dexterity. **Interacting with Others:** Communicating with Other Workers. **Physical Work Conditions:** Common Protective or Safety Attire; Outdoors; Distracting Sounds and Noise Levels; Standing; Hazardous Equipment; Using Hands on Objects, Tools, Controls; Very Hot.

47-5041.00 Continuous Mining Machine Operators

Operate self-propelled mining machines that rip coal, metal and nonmetal ores, rock, stone, or sand from the face and load it onto conveyors or into shuttle cars in a continuous operation. **Education:** Long-term O-J-T. **Occupational Type:** Realistic. **Job Zone:** 2. **Average Salary:** $34,740. **Projected Growth:** –19.1%. **Occupational Values:** Moral Values; Supervision, Human Relations; Company Policies and Practices; Supervision, Technical; Activity. **Skills Required:** Operation and Control; Repairing; Equipment Maintenance. **Abilities:** Control Precision. **Interacting with Others:** Communicating with Other Workers. **Physical Work Conditions:** Outdoors; Using Hands on Objects, Tools, Controls; Common Protective or Safety Attire; Hazardous Equipment; Distracting Sounds and Noise Levels; Contaminants; Extremely Bright or Inadequate Lighting.

47-5042.00 Mine Cutting and Channeling Machine Operators

Operate machinery such as longwall shears, plows, and cutting machines to cut or channel along the face or seams of coal mines, stone quarries, or other mining surfaces to facilitate blasting, separating, or removing minerals or materials from mines or from the earth's surface. **Education:** Long-term O-J-T. **Occupational Type:** Realistic. **Job Zone:** 2. **Average Salary:** $32,920. **Projected Growth:** –19.1%. **Occupational Values:** Moral Values; Supervision, Technical; Supervision, Human Relations; Activity; Company Policies and Practices; Coworkers. **Skills Required:** Operation and Control; Coordination; Operation Monitoring. **Abilities:** Control Precision. **Interacting with Others:** Communicating with Other Workers. **Physical Work Conditions:** Outdoors; Common Protective or Safety Attire; Using Hands on Objects, Tools, Controls; Distracting Sounds and Noise Levels; Contaminants; Hazardous Conditions; Hazardous Equipment.

47-5051.00 Rock Splitters, Quarry

Separate blocks of rough dimension stone from quarry mass using jackhammer and wedges. **Education:** Long-term O-J-T. **Occupational Type:** Realistic. **Job Zone:** 2. **Average Salary:** $22,030. **Projected Growth:** –19.1%. **Occupational Values:** Moral Values; Independence. **Skills Required:** Operation and Control. **Abilities:** Dynamic Strength. **Interacting with Others:** Communicating with Other Workers. **Physical Work Conditions:** Outdoors; Common Protective or Safety Attire; Using Hands on Objects, Tools, Controls; Distracting Sounds and Noise Levels; Standing; Hazardous Equipment; Contaminants.

47-5061.00 Roof Bolters, Mining

Operate machinery to install roof support bolts in underground mine. **Education:** Long-term O-J-T. **Occupational Type:** Realistic. **Job Zone:** 2. **Average Salary:** $36,420. **Projected Growth:** –19.1%. **Occupational Values:** Moral Values; Supervision, Human Relations; Supervision, Technical; Company Policies and Practices. **Skills Required:** Operation and Control; Product Inspection. **Abilities:** Extent Flexibility. **Interacting with Others:** Communicating with Other Workers. **Physical Work Conditions:** Outdoors; Using Hands on Objects, Tools, Controls; Common Protective or Safety Attire; Standing; Extremely Bright or Inadequate Lighting; Contaminants; Specialized Protective or Safety Attire.

47-5071.00 Roustabouts, Oil and Gas

Assemble or repair oil field equipment using hand and power tools. Perform other tasks as needed. **Education:** Short-term O-J-T. **Occupational Type:** Realistic. **Job Zone:** 2. **Average Salary:** $19,780. **Projected Growth:** –21.1%. **Occupational Values:** Moral Values; Supervision, Human Relations; Company Policies and Practices; Supervision, Technical. **Skills Required:** Repairing; Troubleshooting. **Abilities:** Manual Dexterity. **Interacting with Others:** Communicating with Other Workers. **Physical Work Conditions:** Outdoors; Using Hands on Objects, Tools, Controls; Hazardous Equipment; Standing; Distracting Sounds and Noise Levels; Common Protective or Safety Attire; Contaminants.

53-7032.01 Excavating and Loading Machine Operators

Operate machinery equipped with scoops, shovels, or buckets to excavate and load loose materials. **Education:** Moderate-term O-J-T. **Occupational Type:** Realistic. **Job Zone:** 2. **Average Salary:** $27,090. **Projected Growth:** 15.3%. **Occupational Values:** Moral Values; Supervision, Human Relations; Company

Policies and Practices; Activity; Compensation. **Skills Required:** Operation and Control. **Abilities:** Oral Comprehension; Written Comprehension; Control Precision. **Interacting with Others:** Communicating with Other Workers. **Physical Work Conditions:** Outdoors; Using Hands on Objects, Tools, Controls; Whole Body Vibration; Hazardous Equipment; Distracting Sounds and Noise Levels; Sitting; Bending or Twisting the Body.

53-7033.00 Loading Machine Operators, Underground Mining

Operate underground loading machine to load coal, ore, or rock into shuttle or mine car or onto conveyors. Loading equipment may include power shovels, hoisting engines equipped with cable-drawn scraper or scoop, or machines equipped with gathering arms and conveyor. **Education:** Moderate-term O-J-T. **Occupational Type:** Realistic. **Job Zone:** 2. **Average Salary:** $29,990. **Projected Growth:** 21.5%. **Occupational Values:** Moral Values; Supervision, Human Relations; Independence; Supervision, Technical; Company Policies and Practices; Activity. **Skills Required:** Operation and Control; Repairing. **Abilities:** Control Precision. **Interacting with Others:** Communicating with Other Workers. **Physical Work Conditions:** Common Protective or Safety Attire; Outdoors; Using Hands on Objects, Tools, Controls; Hazardous Equipment; Contaminants; Extremely Bright or Inadequate Lighting; Hazardous Situations.

53-7111.00 Shuttle Car Operators

Operate diesel or electric-powered shuttle car in underground mine to transport materials from working face to mine cars or conveyor. **Education:** Moderate-term O-J-T. **Occupational Type:** Realistic. **Job Zone:** 2. **Average Salary:** $35,090. **Projected Growth:** 21.5%. **Occupational Values:** Moral Values; Independence; Supervision, Human Relations; Company Policies and Practices; Supervision, Technical. **Skills Required:** Operation and Control. **Abilities:** Control Precision; Multilimb Coordination. **Interacting with Others:** Communicating with Other Workers. **Physical Work Conditions:** Outdoors; Using Hands on Objects, Tools, Controls; Common Protective or Safety Attire; Distracting Sounds and Noise Levels; Contaminants; Extremely Bright or Inadequate Lighting; Hazardous Equipment.

06.04.01 Hands-on Work in Construction, Extraction, and Maintenance

47-2031.03 Carpenter Assemblers and Repairers

Perform a variety of tasks requiring a limited knowledge of carpentry, such as applying siding and weatherboard to building exteriors or assembling and erecting prefabricated buildings. **Education:** Long-term O-J-T. **Occupational Type:** Realistic. **Job Zone:** 2. **Average Salary:** $28,740. **Projected Growth:** 6.9%. **Occupational Values:** Moral Values; Activity; Security; Achievement; Coworkers; Supervision, Human Relations; Variety. **Skills Required:** Installation; Repairing. **Abilities:** Manual Dexterity; Arm-Hand Steadiness; Static Strength; Explosive Strength; Extent Flexibility; Control Precision; Depth Perception. **Interacting with Others:** Communicating with Other Workers. **Physical Work Conditions:** Using Hands on Objects, Tools, Controls; Standing; Hazardous Equipment; Kneeling, Crouching, or Crawling; Common Protective or Safety Attire; Indoors; Making Repetitive Motions.

47-2061.00 Construction Laborers

Perform tasks involving physical labor at building, highway, and heavy construction projects, tunnel and shaft excavations, and demolition sites. May operate hand and power tools of all types: air hammers, earth tampers, cement mixers, small mechanical hoists, surveying and measuring equipment, and a variety of other equipment and instruments. May clean and prepare sites; dig trenches; set braces to support the sides of excavations; erect scaffolding; clean up rubble and debris; and remove asbestos, lead, and other hazardous waste materials. May assist other craft workers. **Education:** Moderate-term O-J-T. **Occupational Type:** Realistic. **Job Zone:** 2. **Average Salary:** $27,890. **Projected Growth:** 5.7%. **Occupational Values:** Moral Values; Coworkers; Activity. **Skills Required:** Equipment Selection. **Abilities:** Static Strength; Trunk Strength. **Interacting with Others:** Communicating with Other Workers. **Physical Work Conditions:** Outdoors; Standing; Using Hands on Objects, Tools, Controls; Common Protective or Safety Attire; Contaminants; Hazardous Equipment; Hazardous Situations.

47-3011.00 Helpers—Brickmasons, Blockmasons, Stonemasons, and Tile and Marble Setters

Help brickmasons, blockmasons, stonemasons, or tile and marble setters by performing duties of lesser skill. Use, supply, or hold materials or tools; clean work area and equipment. **Education:** Short-term O-J-T. **Occupational Type:** Realistic. **Job Zone:** 1. **Average Salary:** $21,450. **Projected Growth:** 7.3%. **Occupational Values:** Moral Values; Coworkers; Activity; Advancement; Supervision, Technical. **Skills Required:** Installation. **Abilities:** Static Strength. **Interacting with Others:** Assisting and Caring for Others. **Physical Work Conditions:** Outdoors; Using Hands on Objects, Tools, Controls; Kneeling, Crouching, or Crawling; Common Protective or Safety Attire; Making Repetitive Motions; Standing; Walking or Running.

47-3012.00 Helpers—Carpenters

Help carpenters by performing duties of lesser skill. Use, supply, or hold materials or tools; clean work area and equipment. **Education:** Short-term O-J-T. **Occupational Type:** Realistic. **Job Zone:** 1. **Average Salary:** $19,550. **Projected Growth:** 7.3%. **Occupational Values:** Moral Values; Coworkers; Advancement; Supervision, Technical; Activity. **Skills Required:** Equipment Selection. **Abilities:** Static Strength; Dynamic Strength; Explosive Strength; Extent Flexibility; Arm-Hand Steadiness; Manual Dexterity; Multilimb Coordination. **Interacting with Others:** Communicating with Other Workers. **Physical Work Conditions:** Using Hands on Objects, Tools, Controls; Common Protective or Safety Attire; Standing; Hazardous Equipment; Indoors; Kneeling, Crouching, or Crawling; Making Repetitive Motions.

47-3014.00 Helpers—Painters, Paperhangers, Plasterers, and Stucco Masons

Help painters, paperhangers, plasterers, or stucco masons by performing duties of lesser skill. Use, supply, or hold materials or tools; clean work area and equipment. **Education:** Short-term O-J-T. **Occupational Type:** Realistic. **Job Zone:** 1. **Average Salary:** $18,260. **Projected Growth:** 7.3%. **Occupational Values:** Moral Values; Supervision, Technical; Activity; Advancement; Coworkers. **Skills Required:** Equipment Selection. **Abilities:** Static Strength. **Interacting with Others:** Assisting and Caring for Others. **Physical Work Conditions:** Using Hands on Objects, Tools, Controls; Common Protective or Safety Attire; Contaminants; Indoors; Standing; Climbing Ladders, Scaffolds, Poles, etc.; Making Repetitive Motions.

47-3015.00 Helpers—Pipelayers, Plumbers, Pipefitters, and Steamfitters

Help plumbers, pipefitters, steamfitters, or pipelayers by performing duties of lesser skill. Use, supply, or hold materials or tools; clean work area and equipment. **Education:** Short-term O-J-T. **Occupational Type:** Realistic. **Job Zone:** 2. **Average Salary:** $19,520. **Projected Growth:** 7.3%. **Occupational Values:** Moral Values; Supervision, Technical; Activity; Coworkers; Advancement; Security; Supervision, Human Relations. **Skills Required:** Equipment Maintenance. **Abilities:** Manual Dexterity; Extent Flexibility; Arm-Hand Steadiness; Trunk Strength; Static Strength. **Interacting with Others:** Assisting and Caring for Others. **Physical Work Conditions:** Using Hands on Objects, Tools, Controls; Indoors; Standing; Common Protective or Safety Attire; Hazardous Equipment; Bending or Twisting the Body; Contaminants.

47-3016.00 Helpers—Roofers

Help roofers by performing duties of lesser skill. Duties include using, supplying, or holding materials or tools, and cleaning work area and equipment. No other data currently available.

47-4051.00 Highway Maintenance Workers

Maintain highways, municipal and rural roads, airport runways, and rights-of-way. Duties include patching broken or eroded pavement, repairing guard rails, highway markers, and snow fences. May also mow or clear brush from along road or plow snow from roadway. **Education:** Short-term O-J-T. **Occupational Type:** Realistic. **Job Zone:** 1. **Average Salary:** $24,490. **Projected Growth:** 11.1%. **Occupational Values:** Moral Values; Supervision, Human Relations; Company Policies and Practices. **Skills Required:** Repairing. **Abilities:** Trunk Strength. **Interacting with Others:** Communicating with Other Workers. **Physical Work Conditions:** Outdoors; Standing; Using Hands on Objects, Tools, Controls; Common Protective or Safety Attire; Contaminants; Very Hot; Walking or Running.

47-4071.00 Septic Tank Servicers and Sewer Pipe Cleaners

Clean and repair septic tanks, sewer lines, or drains. May patch walls and partitions of tank, replace damaged drain tile, or repair breaks in underground piping. **Education:** Long-term O-J-T. **Occupational Type:** Realistic. **Job Zone:** 2. **Average Salary:** $25,410. **Projected Growth:** 5.3%. **Occupational Values:** Moral Values; Independence. **Skills Required:** Operation and Control; Problem Identification; Equipment Selection; Mathematics; Installation. **Abilities:** Manual Dexterity. **Interacting with Others:** Communicating with Other Workers. **Physical Work Conditions:** Outdoors; Using Hands on Objects, Tools, Controls; Standing; Common Protective or Safety Attire; Contaminants; Kneeling, Crouching, or Crawling; Bending or Twisting the Body.

47-5081.00 Helpers—Extraction Workers

Help extraction craft workers such as earth drillers, blasters and explosives workers, derrick operators, and mining machine operators by performing duties of lesser skill. Duties include supplying equipment or cleaning work area. **Education:** Short-term O-J-T. **Occupational Type:** Realistic. **Job Zone:** 1. **Average Salary:** $20,660. **Projected Growth:** 14.1%. **Occupational Values:** Moral Values; Supervision, Technical; Advancement; Supervision, Human Relations; Activity; Coworkers. **Skills Required:** Operation Monitoring. **Abilities:** Oral Expression. **Interacting with Others:** Communicating with Other Workers. **Physical Work Conditions:** Outdoors; Using Hands on Objects, Tools, Controls; Contaminants; Distracting Sounds and Noise Levels; Standing; Whole Body Vibration; Common Protective or Safety Attire.

53-7062.02 Grips and Set-Up Workers, Motion Picture Sets, Studios, and Stages

Arrange equipment; raise and lower scenery. **Education:** Short-term O-J-T. **Occupational Type:** Realistic. **Job Zone:** 2. **Average Salary:** $17,860. **Projected Growth:** 13.4%. **Occupational Values:** Moral Values; Company Policies and Practices; Supervision, Human Relations; Supervision, Technical; Coworkers; Activity; Working Conditions. **Skills Required:** Operation and Control; Active Listening; Coordination; Equipment Selection. **Abilities:** Visualization; Information Ordering; Manual Dexterity. **Interacting with Others:** Communicating with Other Workers. **Physical Work Conditions:** Using Hands on Objects, Tools, Controls; Standing; Indoors.

07 Transportation

07.01.01 Managerial Work in Transportation

11-3071.01 Transportation Managers

Plan, direct, and coordinate the transportation operations within an organization or the activities of organizations that provide transportation services. **Education:** Work experience, plus degree. **Occupational Type:** Enterprising. **Job Zone:** 4. **Average Salary:** $52,810. **Projected Growth:** 19.3%. **Occupational Values:** Autonomy; Authority; Ability Utilization; Security; Activity; Company Policies and Practices; Supervision, Human Relations. **Skills Required:** Management of Material Resources; Coordination; Speaking; Reading Comprehension; Problem Identification; Critical Thinking. **Abilities:** Oral Expression; Problem Sensitivity; Oral Comprehension; Written Comprehension; Speech Clarity; Mathematical Reasoning. **Interacting with Others:** Communicating with Other Workers; Guiding, Directing, and Motivating Subordinates; Monitoring and Controlling Resources; Resolving Conflict, Negotiating with Others. **Physical Work Conditions:** Indoors; Sitting; Standing.

53-1031.00 First-Line Supervisors/Managers of Transportation and Material-Moving Machine and Vehicle Operators

Directly supervise and coordinate activities of transportation and material-moving machine and vehicle operators and helpers. **Education:** Work experience in a related occupation. **Occupational Type:** Enterprising. **Job Zone:** 3. **Average Salary:** $36,730. **Projected Growth:** 8.9%. **Occupational Values:** Authority; Responsibility; Autonomy; Variety; Activity; Coworkers; Moral Values. **Skills Required:** Speaking; Active Listening; Coordination; Mathematics; Reading Comprehension; Writing; Instructing. **Abilities:** Oral Expression; Written Comprehension. **Interacting with Others:** Communicating with Other Workers; Coordinating Work and Activities of Others; Guiding, Directing, and Motivating Subordinates; Establishing and Maintaining Relationships. **Physical Work Conditions:** Indoors; Sitting.

53-4031.00 Railroad Conductors and Yardmasters

Conductors coordinate activities of train crew on passenger or freight train. Coordinate activities of switch-engine crew within yard of railroad, industrial plant, or similar location. Yardmasters coordinate activities of workers engaged in railroad traffic operations, such as the makeup or breakup of trains; coordinate yard switching; and review train schedules and switching orders. **Education:** Work experience in a related occupation. **Occupational Type:** Realistic. **Job Zone:** 4. **Average Salary:** $38,500. **Projected Growth:** –6.7%. **Occupational Values:** Security; Company Policies and Practices; Supervision, Technical; Authority; Autonomy; Supervision, Human Relations; Responsibility. **Skills Required:** Coordination; Active Listening; Speaking; Operation and Control. **Abilities:** Oral Expression; Deductive Reasoning; Problem Sensitivity; Near Vision; Oral Comprehension; Speech Clarity; Written Comprehension. **Interacting with Others:** Coordinating Work and Activities of Others; Communicating with Other Workers; Communicating with Persons Outside Organization; Performing for/Working with Public. **Physical Work Conditions:** Outdoors; Special Uniform; Standing; Walking or Running; Indoors; Using Hands on Objects, Tools, Controls.

07.02.01 Vehicle Expediting and Coordinating

53-2021.00 Air Traffic Controllers

Control air traffic on and within vicinity of airport. Control movement of air traffic between altitude sectors and control centers according to established procedures and policies. Authorize, regulate, and control commercial airline flights according to government or company regulations to expedite and ensure flight safety. **Education:** Long-term O-J-T. **Occupational Type:** Conventional. **Job Zone:** 4. **Average Salary:** $64,880. **Projected Growth:** 2.3%. **Occupational Values:** Authority; Security; Ability Utilization; Responsibility; Achievement; Company Policies and Practices; Supervision, Human Relations. **Skills Required:** Speaking; Operation and Control; Active Listening; Coordination; Operation Monitoring; Critical Thinking; Idea Evaluation. **Abilities:** Speech Clarity; Oral Comprehension; Written Comprehension; Near Vision; Oral Expression; Selective Attention; Problem Sensitivity. **Interacting with Others:** Communicating with Other Workers; Assisting and Caring for Others. **Physical Work Conditions:** Indoors; Sitting; Using Hands on Objects, Tools, Controls.

53-2022.00 Airfield Operations Specialists

Ensure the safe takeoff and landing of commercial and military aircraft. Duties include coordination between air-traffic control and maintenance personnel; dispatching; using airfield landing and navigational aids; implementing airfield safety procedures; monitoring and maintaining flight records; and applying knowledge of weather information. No other data currently available.

53-4021.00 Railroad Brake, Signal, and Switch Operators

Operate railroad track switches. Couple or uncouple rolling stock to make up or break up trains. Signal engineers by hand or flagging. May inspect couplings, air hoses, journal boxes, and hand brakes. No other data currently available.

53-6041.00 Traffic Technicians

Conduct field studies to determine traffic volume, speed, effectiveness of signals, adequacy of lighting, and other factors influencing traffic conditions, under direction of traffic engineer. **Education:** Associate degree. **Occupational Type:** Realistic. **Job Zone:** 4. **Average Salary:** $34,290. **Projected Growth:** 4.1%. **Occupational Values:** Moral Values; Independence; Supervision, Human Relations; Security; Company Policies and Practices; Variety; Achievement. **Skills Required:** Information Gathering; Mathematics; Problem Identification; Information Organization; Idea Generation; Idea Evaluation; Critical Thinking. **Abilities:** Number Facility. **Interacting with Others:** Communicating with Other Workers. **Physical Work Conditions:** Standing; Indoors; Using Hands on Objects, Tools, Controls.

07.03.01 Air Vehicle Operation

53-2011.00 Airline Pilots, Copilots, and Flight Engineers

Pilot and navigate the flight of multi-engine aircraft in regularly scheduled service for the transport of passengers and cargo. Requires Federal Air Transport rating and certification in specific aircraft type used. **Education:** Long-term O-J-T. **Occupational Type:** Realistic. **Job Zone:** 4. **Average Salary:** $91,750. **Projected Growth:** 5.9%. **Occupational Values:** Compensation; Ability Utilization; Company Policies and Practices; Recognition; Achievement; Responsibility; Social Status. **Skills Required:** Operation and Control; Judgment and Decision Making; Operation Monitoring; Coordination; Active Listening; Identification of Key Causes; Monitoring. **Abilities:** Control Precision; Spatial Orientation; Problem Sensitivity; Near Vision; Oral Expression; Depth Perception; Far Vision. **Interacting with Others:** Communicating with Other Workers; Coordinating Work and Activities of Others; Teaching Others. **Physical Work Conditions:** Special Uniform; Sitting; Using Hands on Objects, Tools, Controls; High Places; Indoors; Hazardous Equipment; Whole Body Vibration.

53-2012.00 Commercial Pilots

Pilot and navigate the flight of small fixed or rotary winged aircraft, primarily for the transport of cargo and passengers. Requires Commercial Rating. **Education:** Long-term O-J-T. **Occupational Type:** Realistic. **Job Zone:** 4. **Average Salary:** $91,750. **Projected Growth:** 5.9%. **Occupational Values:** Ability Utilization; Company Policies and Practices; Compensation; Recognition; Achievement; Social Status; Responsibility. **Skills Required:** Operation and Control; Judgment and Decision Making; Operation Monitoring; Coordination; Active Listening; Identification of Key Causes; Instructing. **Abilities:** Control Precision; Spatial Orientation; Problem Sensitivity; Near Vision; Oral Expression; Depth Perception; Far Vision. **Interacting with Others:** Communicating with Other Workers; Coordinating Work and Activities of Others; Teaching Others. **Physical Work Conditions:** Special Uniform; Sitting; Using Hands on Objects, Tools, Controls; High Places; Indoors; Hazardous Equipment; Whole Body Vibration.

07.04.01 Water Vehicle Operation

53-5011.01 Able Seamen

Stand watch at bow or on wing of bridge to look for obstructions in path of vessel. Measure water depth. Turn wheel on bridge or use emergency equipment as directed by mate. Break out, rig, overhaul, and store cargo-handling gear, stationary rigging, and running gear. Chip rust from and paint deck or ship's structure. Must hold government-issued certification. Must hold certification when working aboard liquid-carrying vessels. **Education:** Short-term O-J-T. **Occupational Type:** Realistic. **Job Zone:** 2. **Average Salary:** $26,790. **Projected Growth:** 5.1%. **Occupational Values:** Moral Values; Coworkers; Supervision, Technical; Advancement; Supervision, Human Relations; Activity. **Skills Required:** Monitoring. **Abilities:** Far Vision; Control Precision; Oral Expression; Spatial Orientation. **Interacting with Others:** Communicating with Other Workers. **Physical Work Conditions:** Standing; Outdoors; Special Uniform; Using Hands on Objects, Tools, Controls; Common Protective or Safety Attire; Indoors; Keeping or Regaining Balance.

53-5011.02 Ordinary Seamen and Marine Oilers

Stand deck department watches and perform a variety of tasks to preserve the painted surface of the ship and to maintain lines and ship equipment, such as running and cargo-handling gear. May oil and grease moving parts of engines and auxiliary equipment. Must hold government-issued certification. Must hold certification when working aboard liquid-carrying vessels. **Education:** Short-term O-J-T. **Occupational Type:** Realistic. **Job Zone:** 2. **Average Salary:** $22,160. **Projected Growth:** 5.1%. **Occupational Values:** Moral Values; Supervision, Technical; Advancement; Activity; Coworkers; Supervision, Human Relations. **Skills Required:** Equipment Maintenance; Repairing. **Abilities:** Far Vision; Spatial Orientation; Manual Dexterity; Trunk Strength. **Interacting with Others:** Communicating with Other Workers. **Physical Work Conditions:** Outdoors; Special Uniform; Standing; Using Hands on Objects, Tools, Controls; Common Protective or Safety Attire; Hazardous Equipment; Hazardous Situations.

53-5021.01 Ship and Boat Captains

Command vessels in oceans, bays, lakes, rivers, and coastal waters. **Education:** Work experience in a related occupation. **Occupational Type:** Enterprising. **Job Zone:** 4. **Average Salary:** $41,420. **Projected Growth:** 3%. **Occupational Values:** Authority; Responsibility; Autonomy; Achievement; Ability Utilization; Compensation; Recognition. **Skills Required:** Operation and Control; Operation Monitoring; Coordination; Management of Personnel Resources; Speaking; Mathematics; Judgment and Decision Making. **Abilities:** Control Precision; Problem Sensitivity; Far Vision; Spatial Orientation; Glare Sensitivity; Near Vision; Night Vision. **Interacting with Others:** Communicating with Other Workers; Coordinating Work and Activities of Others; Monitoring and Controlling Resources; Developing and Building Teams; Guiding, Directing, and Motivating Subordinates. **Physical Work Conditions:** Outdoors; Standing; Using Hands on Objects, Tools, Controls; Making Repetitive Motions.

53-5021.02 Mates—Ship, Boat, and Barge

Supervise and coordinate activities of crew aboard ships, boats, barges, or dredges. **Education:** Work experience in a related occupation. **Occupational Type:** Realistic. **Job Zone:** 3. **Average Salary:** $29,310. **Projected Growth:** 7.9%. **Occupational Values:** Authority; Coworkers; Advancement; Moral Values; Company Policies and Practices; Autonomy; Activity. **Skills Required:** Coordination; Operation and Control; Management of Personnel Resources; Problem Identification; Operation Monitoring; Mathematics; Speaking. **Abilities:** Control Precision; Oral Comprehension; Far Vision; Oral Expression. **Interacting with Others:** Communicating with Other Workers;

Coordinating Work and Activities of Others. **Physical Work Conditions:** Outdoors; Standing; Using Hands on Objects, Tools, Controls; Indoors; Very Hot.

53-5021.03 Pilots, Ship

Command ships to steer them into and out of harbors, estuaries, straits, and sounds, and on rivers, lakes, and bays. Must be licensed by U.S. Coast Guard with limitations indicating class and tonnage of vessels for which license is valid and route and waters that may be piloted. **Education:** Work experience in a related occupation. **Occupational Type:** Realistic. **Job Zone:** 5. **Average Salary:** $41,650. **Projected Growth:** 3%. **Occupational Values:** Responsibility; Autonomy; Authority; Achievement; Ability Utilization; Social Status; Security. **Skills Required:** Operation and Control; Operation Monitoring; Monitoring; Judgment and Decision Making; Systems Perception; Identification of Key Causes; Critical Thinking. **Abilities:** Far Vision; Oral Expression; Spatial Orientation. **Interacting with Others:** Communicating with Other Workers. **Physical Work Conditions:** Using Hands on Objects, Tools, Controls; Special Uniform; Standing; Indoors; Keeping or Regaining Balance; Outdoors; Sitting.

53-5022.00 Motorboat Operators

Operate small motor-driven boats to carry passengers and freight between ships or from ship to shore. May patrol harbors and beach areas. May assist in navigational activities. **Education:** Short-term O-J-T. **Occupational Type:** Realistic. **Job Zone:** 2. **Average Salary:** $24,750. **Projected Growth:** 5.1%. **Occupational Values:** Autonomy; Independence; Moral Values; Recognition; Responsibility. **Skills Required:** Operation and Control; Repairing; Equipment Maintenance. **Abilities:** Control Precision; Far Vision. **Interacting with Others:** Performing for/Working with Public. **Physical Work Conditions:** Outdoors; Common Protective or Safety Attire; Using Hands on Objects, Tools, Controls; Hazardous Equipment; Standing; Hazardous Situations; Keeping or Regaining Balance.

53-7031.00 Dredge Operators

Operate dredge to remove sand, gravel, or other materials from lakes, rivers, or streams and to excavate and maintain navigable channels in waterways. **Education:** Moderate-term O-J-T. **Occupational Type:** Realistic. **Job Zone:** 2. **Average Salary:** $27,340. **Projected Growth:** 21.5%. **Occupational Values:** Moral Values; Supervision, Human Relations; Independence. **Skills Required:** Operation and Control; Operation Monitoring. **Abilities:** Control Precision. **Interacting with Others:** Communicating with Other Workers. **Physical Work Conditions:** Outdoors; Using Hands on Objects, Tools, Controls; Hazardous Equipment; Sitting; Distracting Sounds and Noise Levels; Hazardous Situations; Standing.

07.05.01 Truck Driving

53-3032.01 Truck Drivers, Heavy

Drive truck with capacity of more than three tons to transport materials to specified destinations. **Education:** Short-term O-J-T. **Occupational Type:** Realistic. **Job Zone:** 1. **Average Salary:** $27,980. **Projected Growth:** 16.6%. **Occupational Values:** Independence; Compensation; Company Policies and Practices; Supervision, Human Relations; Security; Autonomy; Activity. **Skills Required:** Operation and Control. **Abilities:** Static Strength; Spatial Orientation; Reaction Time; Far Vision; Response Orientation; Extent Flexibility. **Interacting with Others:** Performing Administrative Activities. **Physical Work Conditions:** Sitting; Using Hands on Objects, Tools, Controls; Indoors; Outdoors.

53-3032.02 Tractor-Trailer Truck Drivers

Drive tractor-trailer truck to transport products, livestock, or materials to specified destinations. **Education:** Short-term O-J-T. **Occupational Type:** Realistic. **Job Zone:** 2. **Average Salary:** $27,980. **Projected Growth:** 16.6%. **Occupational Values:** Compensation; Company Policies and Practices; Supervision, Human Relations; Activity; Independence; Autonomy; Security. **Skills Required:** Operation and Control. **Abilities:** Far Vision; Near Vision; Reaction Time; Response Orientation; Static Strength; Spatial Orientation; Depth Perception. **Interacting with Others:** Communicating with Other Workers. **Physical Work Conditions:** Sitting; Using Hands on Objects, Tools, Controls; Indoors; Outdoors; Standing.

53-3033.00 Truck Drivers, Light or Delivery Services

Drive a truck or van with a capacity of under 26,000 GVW, primarily to deliver or pick up merchandise or to deliver packages within a specified area. May use automatic routing or location software. May load and unload truck. **Education:** Short-term O-J-T. **Occupational Type:** Realistic. **Job Zone:** 1. **Average Salary:** $19,980. **Projected Growth:** 16.6%. **Occupational Values:** Independence; Compensation; Company Policies and Practices; Activity; Supervision, Human Relations; Security. **Skills Required:** Operation and Control. **Abilities:** Far Vision; Spatial Orientation; Reaction Time; Static Strength; Extent Flexibility. **Interacting with Others:** Communicating with Persons Outside Organization. **Physical Work Conditions:** Sitting; Outdoors; Indoors; Using Hands on Objects, Tools, Controls; Standing.

07.06.01 Rail Vehicle Operation

53-4011.00 Locomotive Engineers

Drive electric, diesel-electric, steam, or gas-turbine-electric locomotives to transport passengers or freight. Interpret train orders, electronic or manual signals, and railroad rules and regulations. **Education:** Work experience in a related occupation. **Occupational Type:** Realistic. **Job Zone:** 4. **Average Salary:** $39,800. **Projected Growth:** 4.8%. **Occupational Values:** Security; Company Policies and Practices; Supervision, Human Relations; Moral Values; Supervision, Technical; Compensation; Achievement. **Skills Required:** Operation and Control; Speaking; Reading Comprehension; Systems Perception; Active Listening; Operation Monitoring. **Abilities:** Control Precision. **Interacting with Others:** Communicating with Other Workers. **Physical Work Conditions:** Using Hands on Objects, Tools, Controls; Hazardous Equipment; Special Uniform; Contaminants; Sitting; Distracting Sounds and Noise Levels; Hazardous Conditions.

53-4012.00 Locomotive Firers

Monitor locomotive instruments and watch for dragging equipment, obstacles on rights-of-way, and train signals during run. Watch for and relay traffic signals from yard workers to yard engineer in railroad yard. **Education:** Work experience in a related occupation. **Occupational Type:** Realistic. **Job Zone:** 3. **Average Salary:** $37,290. **Projected Growth:** 4.8%. **Occupational Values:** Moral Values; Company Policies and Practices; Supervision, Human Relations; Security; Supervision, Technical. **Skills Required:** Operation Monitoring; Systems Perception; Coordination; Problem Identification; Operation and Control; Product Inspection. **Abilities:** Far Vision; Near Vision; Problem Sensitivity. **Interacting with Others:** Communicating with Other Workers. **Physical Work Conditions:** Hazardous Equipment; Outdoors; Distracting Sounds and Noise Levels; Special Uniform; Common Protective or Safety Attire; Contaminants; Standing.

53-4013.00 Rail Yard Engineers, Dinkey Operators, and Hostlers

Drive switching or other locomotive or dinkey engines within railroad yard, industrial plant, quarry, construction project, or similar location. **Education:** Work experience in a related occupation. **Occupational Type:** Realistic. **Job Zone:** 2. **Average Salary:** $35,720. **Projected Growth:** –47.8%. **Occupational Values:** Moral Values; Supervision, Human Relations; Supervision, Technical; Company Policies and Practices; Security; Compensation. **Skills Required:** Operation and Control. **Abilities:** Control Precision; Problem Sensitivity; Oral Comprehension. **Interacting with Others:** Communicating with Other Workers. **Physical Work Conditions:** Outdoors; Using Hands on Objects, Tools, Controls; Distracting Sounds and Noise Levels; Making Repetitive Motions; Sitting; Standing.

53-4041.00 Subway and Streetcar Operators

Operate subway, elevated suburban train with no separate locomotive, or electric-powered streetcar to transport passengers. May handle fares. **Education:** Moderate-term O-J-T. **Occupational Type:** Realistic. **Job Zone:** 2. **Average Salary:** $43,330. **Projected Growth:** 7.1%. **Occupational Values:** Supervision, Human Relations; Moral Values; Supervision, Technical; Security; Independence; Company Policies and Practices; Activity. **Skills Required:** Operation and Control; Operation Monitoring. **Abilities:** Reaction Time. **Interacting with Others:** Performing for/Working with Public. **Physical Work Conditions:** Special Uniform; Indoors; Sitting; Using Hands on Objects, Tools, Controls.

07.07.01 Other Services Requiring Driving

53-3011.00 Ambulance Drivers and Attendants, Except Emergency Medical Technicians

Drive ambulance or assist ambulance driver in transporting sick, injured, or convalescent persons. Assist in lifting patients. **Education:** Short-term O-J-T. **Occupational Type:** Social. **Job Zone:** 1. **Average Salary:** $16,960. **Projected Growth:** 35%. **Occupational Values:** Social Service; Security; Moral Values; Variety; Achievement; Supervision, Human Relations; Coworkers. **Skills Required:** Identification of Key Causes; Judgment and Decision Making; Active Listening. **Abilities:** Reaction Time; Wrist-Finger Speed; Spatial Orientation. **Interacting with Others:** Assisting and Caring for Others. **Physical Work Conditions:** Special Uniform; Diseases/Infections; Using Hands on Objects, Tools, Controls; Outdoors; Sitting; Common Protective or Safety Attire; Contaminants.

53-3021.00 Bus Drivers, Transit and Intercity

Drive bus or motor coach, including regular route operations, charters, and private carriage. May assist passengers with baggage. May collect fares or tickets. **Education:** Moderate-term O-J-T. **Occupational Type:** Realistic. **Job Zone:** 1. **Average Salary:** $24,370. **Projected Growth:** 15.8%. **Occupational Values:** Supervision, Technical; Supervision, Human Relations; Company Policies and Practices; Security; Independence; Moral Values; Activity. **Skills Required:** Operation and Control. **Abilities:** Far Vision; Reaction Time; Night Vision; Control Precision. **Interacting with Others:** Performing for/Working with Public. **Physical Work Conditions:** Sitting; Special Uniform; Using Hands on Objects, Tools, Controls; Indoors; Outdoors.

53-3022.00 Bus Drivers, School

Transport students or special clients such as the elderly or persons with disabilities. Ensure adherence to safety rules. May assist passengers in boarding or exiting. **Education:** Short-term O-J-T. **Occupational Type:** Realistic. **Job Zone:** 2. **Average Salary:** $18,820. **Projected Growth:** 17.6%. **Occupational Values:** Supervision, Human Relations; Supervision, Technical; Company Policies and Practices; Moral Values; Independence; Security; Social Service. **Skills Required:** Operation and Control; Operation Monitoring. **Abilities:** Response Orientation; Depth Perception; Reaction Time; Far Vision; Multilimb Coordination; Night Vision; Peripheral Vision. **Interacting with Others:** Assisting and Caring for Others. **Physical Work Conditions:** Sitting; Distracting Sounds and Noise Levels; Outdoors; Using Hands on Objects, Tools, Controls; Making Repetitive Motions.

53-3031.00 Driver/Sales Workers

Drive truck or other vehicle over established routes or within an established territory; sell goods such as food products, including restaurant take-out items; or pick up and deliver items such as laundry. May also take orders and collect payments. Includes newspaper delivery drivers. **Education:** Short-term O-J-T. **Occupational Type:** Enterprising. **Job Zone:** 1. **Average Salary:** $19,330. **Projected Growth:** 4.7%. **Occupational Values:** Independence; Moral Values; Supervision, Human Relations; Activity. **Skills Required:** Time Management. **Abilities:** Oral Expression. **Interacting with Others:** Performing for/Working with Public; Selling or Influencing Others; Communicating with Persons Outside Organization; Establishing and Maintaining Relationships. **Physical Work Conditions:** Outdoors; Standing; Using Hands on Objects, Tools, Controls.

53-3041.00 Taxi Drivers and Chauffeurs

Drive automobiles, vans, or limousines to transport passengers. May occasionally carry cargo. **Education:** Short-term

O-J-T. **Occupational Type:** Realistic. **Job Zone:** 1. **Average Salary:** $15,540. **Projected Growth:** 20%. **Occupational Values:** Independence; Social Service; Moral Values. **Skills Required:** Operation and Control; Service Orientation. **Abilities:** Oral Comprehension; Number Facility; Multilimb Coordination; Reaction Time; Written Comprehension; Depth Perception; Far Vision. **Interacting with Others:** Communicating with Other Workers. **Physical Work Conditions:** Outdoors; Sitting.

53-6021.00 Parking Lot Attendants

Park automobiles or issue tickets for customers in a parking lot or garage. May collect fee. **Education:** Short-term O-J-T. **Occupational Type:** Realistic. **Job Zone:** 1. **Average Salary:** $13,930. **Projected Growth:** 31.2%. **Occupational Values:** Moral Values; Independence; Social Service. **Skills Required:** Mathematics. **Abilities:** Control Precision. **Interacting with Others:** Performing for/Working with Public. **Physical Work Conditions:** Outdoors; Standing; Special Uniform; Using Hands on Objects, Tools, Controls; Walking or Running.

07.08.01 Support Work in Transportation

53-4021.01 Train Crew Members

Inspect couplings, airhoses, journal boxes, and handbrakes on trains to ensure that they function properly. **Education:** Work experience in a related occupation. **Occupational Type:** Realistic. **Job Zone:** 2. **Average Salary:** $36,550. **Projected Growth:** –47.8%. **Occupational Values:** Moral Values; Supervision, Human Relations; Supervision, Technical; Security; Company Policies and Practices; Social Service; Coworkers. **Skills Required:** Product Inspection. **Abilities:** Oral Expression; Information Ordering; Problem Sensitivity; Manual Dexterity; Oral Comprehension. **Interacting with Others:** Communicating with Other Workers. **Physical Work Conditions:** Standing; Using Hands on Objects, Tools, Controls; Special Uniform; Walking or Running; Indoors; Outdoors; Distracting Sounds and Noise Levels.

53-4021.02 Railroad Yard Workers

Perform a variety of activities such as coupling railcars and operating railroad track switches in railroad yard to facilitate the movement of rail cars within the yard. **Education:** Work experience in a related occupation. **Occupational Type:** Realistic. **Job Zone:** 1. **Average Salary:** $36,550. **Projected Growth:** –47.8%. **Occupational Values:** Moral Values; Company Policies and Practices; Supervision, Technical; Security; Supervision, Human Relations; Coworkers. **Skills Required:** Operation and Control. **Abilities:** Control Precision; Reaction Time; Far Vision; Oral Comprehension; Written Comprehension. **Interacting with Others:** Communicating with Other Workers. **Physical Work Conditions:** Outdoors; Using Hands on Objects, Tools, Controls; Standing; Hazardous Equipment.

53-6051.00 Transportation Inspectors

Inspect equipment or goods in connection with the safe transport of cargo or people. Includes rail transport inspectors, such as freight inspectors, car inspectors, rail inspectors, and other nonprecision inspectors of other types of transportation vehicles. No other data currently available.

53-6051.06 Freight Inspectors

Inspect freight for proper storage according to specifications. **Education:** Work experience in a related occupation. **Occupational Type:** Conventional. **Job Zone:** 2. **Average Salary:** $39,560. **Projected Growth:** –3.2%. **Occupational Values:** Moral Values; Supervision, Technical; Company Policies and Practices; Activity; Security; Supervision, Human Relations; Independence. **Skills Required:** Mathematics; Speaking; Product Inspection; Problem Identification; Writing; Information Gathering; Reading Comprehension. **Abilities:** Oral Expression; Problem Sensitivity. **Interacting with Others:** Coordinating Work and Activities of Others. **Physical Work Conditions:** Standing; Outdoors; Using Hands on Objects, Tools, Controls.

53-7062.01 Stevedores, Except Equipment Operators

Manually load and unload ship cargo. Stack cargo in transit shed or in hold of ship using pallet or cargo board. Attach and move slings to lift cargo. Guide load lift. **Education:** Short-term O-J-T. **Occupational Type:** Realistic. **Job Zone:** 1. **Average Salary:** $41,400. **Projected Growth:** 13.4%. **Occupational Values:** Moral Values; Supervision, Technical; Company Policies and Practices; Supervision, Human Relations. **Skills Required:** Active Listening. **Abilities:** Dynamic Strength; Trunk Strength; Static Strength; Stamina. **Interacting with Others:** Communicating with Other Workers. **Physical Work Conditions:** Outdoors; Standing; Using Hands on Objects, Tools, Controls; Bending or Twisting the Body; Walking or Running; Hazardous Equipment.

08 Industrial Production

08.01.01 Managerial Work in Industrial Production

11-3051.00 Industrial Production Managers

Plan, direct, or coordinate the work activities and resources necessary for manufacturing products in accordance with cost, quality, and quantity specifications. **Education:** Bachelor's degree. **Occupational Type:** Enterprising. **Job Zone:** 4. **Average Salary:** $56,320. **Projected Growth:** -0.9%. **Occupational Values:** Authority; Autonomy; Responsibility; Company Policies and Practices; Activity; Creativity; Compensation. **Skills Required:** Coordination; Judgment and Decision Making; Product Inspection; Problem Identification; Implementation Planning; Management of Personnel Resources; Speaking. **Abilities:** Oral Expression; Written Comprehension; Oral Comprehension; Inductive Reasoning; Written Expression; Deductive Reasoning; Problem Sensitivity. **Interacting with Others:** Coordinating Work and Activities of Others; Communicating with Other Workers; Resolving Conflict, Negotiating with Others; Monitoring and Controlling Resources; Providing Consultation and Advice to Others; Developing and Building Teams; Establishing and Maintaining Relationships. **Physical Work Conditions:** Indoors; Sitting.

51-1011.00 First-Line Supervisors/Managers of Production and Operating Workers

Supervise and coordinate the activities of production and operating workers such as inspectors, precision workers, machine setters and operators, assemblers, fabricators, and plant and system operators. **Education:** Work experience in a related occupation. **Occupational Type:** Enterprising. **Job Zone:** 3. **Average Salary:** $36,320. **Projected Growth:** 8.9%. **Occupational Values:** Authority; Responsibility; Coworkers; Variety; Autonomy; Achievement; Activity. **Skills Required:** Coordination; Speaking; Reading Comprehension; Critical Thinking; Information Gathering; Time Management; Product Inspection. **Abilities:** Oral Expression; Written Comprehension; Oral Comprehension; Deductive Reasoning; Mathematical Reasoning; Problem Sensitivity; Speech Clarity. **Interacting with Others:** Communicating with Other Workers; Coordinating Work and Activities of Others; Guiding, Directing, and Motivating Subordinates; Establishing and Maintaining Relationships. **Physical Work Conditions:** Indoors; Sitting; Standing; Walking or Running.

53-1021.00 First-Line Supervisors/Managers of Helpers, Laborers, and Material Movers, Hand

Supervise and coordinate the activities of helpers, laborers, or material movers. **Education:** Work experience in a related occupation. **Occupational Type:** Enterprising. **Job Zone:** 3. **Average Salary:** $30,320. **Projected Growth:** 8.9%. **Occupational Values:** Authority; Responsibility; Coworkers; Autonomy; Activity; Moral Values; Variety. **Skills Required:** Management of Personnel Resources; Problem Identification; Instructing; Critical Thinking; Coordination; Systems Perception. **Abilities:** Oral Expression; Information Ordering; Oral Comprehension; Problem Sensitivity. **Interacting with Others:** Communicating with Other Workers; Guiding, Directing, and Motivating Subordinates; Teaching Others. **Physical Work Conditions:** Indoors; Sitting.

08.02.01 Production Technology: Machine Set-up and Operation

51-4021.00 Extruding and Drawing Machine Setters, Operators, and Tenders, Metal and Plastic

Set up, operate, or tend machines to extrude or draw thermoplastic or metal materials into tubes, rods, hoses, wire, bars, or structural shapes. **Education:** Moderate-term O-J-T. **Occupational Type:** Realistic. **Job Zone:** 2. **Average Salary:** $24,100. **Projected Growth:** 7.7%. **Occupational Values:** Moral Values; Independence; Activity; Supervision, Human Relations; Company Policies and Practices; Supervision, Technical. **Skills Required:** Operation and Control; Testing; Product Inspection; Operation Monitoring. **Abilities:** Control Precision. **Interacting with Others:** Communicating with Other Workers. **Physical Work Conditions:** Indoors; Common Protective or Safety Attire; Standing; Using Hands on Objects, Tools, Controls; Hazardous Equipment; Distracting Sounds and Noise Levels.

51-4022.00 Forging Machine Setters, Operators, and Tenders, Metal and Plastic

Set up, operate, or tend forging machines to taper, shape, or form metal or plastic parts. **Education:** Moderate-term O-J-T. **Occupational Type:** Realistic. **Job Zone:** 2. **Average Salary:** $35,910. **Projected Growth:** 7.7%. **Occupational Values:** Moral Values; Company Policies and Practices; Activity; Supervision, Human Relations; Independence; Supervision, Technical; Coworkers. **Skills Required:** Operation and Control; Operation Monitoring; Installation; Product Inspection; Equipment Selection. **Abilities:** Control Precision; Visualization; Information Ordering. **Interacting with Others:** Communicating with Other Workers. **Physical Work Conditions:** Using Hands on Objects, Tools, Controls; Indoors; Standing; Common Protective or Safety Attire.

51-4023.00 Rolling Machine Setters, Operators, and Tenders, Metal and Plastic

Set up, operate, or tend machines to roll steel or plastic (forming bends, beads, knurls, rolls, or plate) or to flatten, temper, or reduce gauge of material. **Education:** Moderate-term O-J-T. **Occupational Type:** Realistic. **Job Zone:** 2. **Average Salary:** $27,000. **Projected Growth:** 7.7%. **Occupational Values:** Moral Values; Activity; Supervision, Human Relations; Independence; Company Policies and Practices; Supervision, Technical; Coworkers. **Skills Required:** Operation Monitoring; Product Inspection; Operation and Control; Mathematics; Installation; Speaking. **Abilities:** Manual Dexterity; Arm-Hand Steadiness; Control Precision; Information Ordering; Extent Flexibility; Problem Sensitivity; Rate Control. **Interacting with Others:** Communicating with Other Workers. **Physical Work Conditions:** Indoors; Using Hands on Objects, Tools, Controls; Hazardous Equipment; Standing; Distracting Sounds and Noise Levels; Common Protective or Safety Attire.

51-4031.01 Sawing Machine Tool Setters and Set-Up Operators, Metal and Plastic

Set up, or set up and operate, metal or plastic sawing machines to cut straight, curved, irregular, or internal patterns in metal or plastic stock or to trim edges of metal or plastic objects. Involves the use of such machines as band saws, circular saws, friction saws, hacksawing machines, and jigsaws. **Education:** Moderate-term O-J-T. **Occupational Type:** Realistic. **Job Zone:** 2. **Average Salary:** $23,630. **Projected Growth:** –19.9%. **Occupational Values:** Moral Values; Independence; Company Policies and Practices; Activity; Supervision, Human Relations; Supervision, Technical; Security. **Skills Required:** Equipment Selection; Equipment Maintenance; Product Inspection. **Abilities:** Manual Dexterity; Arm-Hand Steadiness; Control Precision; Visualization; Written Comprehension. **Interacting with Others:** Communicating with Other Workers. **Physical Work Conditions:** Indoors; Hazardous Equipment; Using Hands on Objects, Tools, Controls; Standing; Distracting Sounds and Noise Levels; Common Protective or Safety Attire; Hazardous Situations.

51-4031.02 Punching Machine Setters and Set-Up Operators, Metal and Plastic

Set up, or set up and operate, machines to punch, crimp, cut blanks, or notch metal or plastic workpieces between preset dies, according to specifications. **Education:** Moderate-term O-J-T. **Occupational Type:** Realistic. **Job Zone:** 2. **Average Salary:** $23,270. **Projected Growth:** –7.5%. **Occupational Values:** Moral Values; Activity; Independence; Supervision, Human Relations; Company Policies and Practices; Supervision, Technical. **Skills Required:** Operation and Control. **Abilities:** Control Precision; Manual Dexterity; Near Vision; Information Ordering. **Interacting with Others:** Assisting and Caring for Others. **Physical Work Conditions:** Indoors; Using Hands on Objects, Tools, Controls; Standing; Hazardous Equipment; Common Protective or Safety Attire; Making Repetitive Motions.

51-4031.03 Press and Press Brake Machine Setters and Set-Up Operators, Metal and Plastic

Set up, or set up and operate, power-press machines or power-brake machines to bend, form, stretch, notch, punch, or straighten metal or plastic plate and structural shapes, as specified by work order, blueprints, drawing, templates, or layout. **Education:** Moderate-term O-J-T. **Occupational Type:** Realistic. **Job Zone:** 2. **Average Salary:** $24,150. **Projected Growth:** 7.7%. **Occupational Values:** Moral Values; Activity; Independence; Company Policies and Practices; Supervision, Human Relations; Supervision, Technical. **Skills Required:** Product Inspection; Operation Monitoring; Operation and Control; Mathematics; Installation; Science; Information Organization. **Abilities:** Information Ordering; Visualization; Control Precision; Arm-Hand Steadiness; Manual Dexterity; Multilimb Coordination; Static Strength. **Interacting with Others:** Communicating with Other Workers. **Physical Work Conditions:** Indoors; Hazardous Equipment; Using Hands on Objects, Tools, Controls; Common Protective or Safety Attire; Standing; Distracting Sounds and Noise Levels; Hazardous Situations.

51-4031.04 Shear and Slitter Machine Setters and Set-Up Operators, Metal and Plastic

Set up, or set up and operate, power-shear or slitting machines to cut metal or plastic material such as plates, sheets, slabs, billets, or bars to specified dimensions and angles. **Education:** Moderate-term O-J-T. **Occupational Type:** Realistic. **Job Zone:** 2. **Average Salary:** $24,290. **Projected Growth:** –19.9%. **Occupational Values:** Moral Values; Activity; Independence; Company Policies and Practices; Supervision, Human Relations; Supervision, Technical. **Skills Required:** Operation Monitoring; Product Inspection; Operation and Control; Testing; Installation; Mathematics; Reading Comprehension. **Abilities:** Information Ordering; Written Comprehension; Control Precision. **Interacting with Others:** Communicating with Other Workers. **Physical Work Conditions:** Indoors; Hazardous Equipment; Using Hands on Objects, Tools, Controls; Common Protective or Safety Attire; Standing; Hazardous Situations; Making Repetitive Motions.

51-4032.00 Drilling and Boring Machine Tool Setters, Operators, and Tenders, Metal and Plastic

Set up, operate, or tend drilling machines to drill, bore, ream, mill, or countersink metal or plastic work pieces. **Education:** Moderate-term O-J-T. **Occupational Type:** Realistic. **Job Zone:** 2. **Average Salary:** $25,630. **Projected Growth:** –18.3%. **Occupational Values:** Moral Values; Independence; Activity; Company Policies and Practices; Supervision, Human Relations; Supervision, Technical; Security. **Skills Required:** Product Inspection; Operation Monitoring; Installation; Mathematics; Equipment Selection; Operation and Control; Reading Comprehension. **Abilities:** Written Comprehension; Arm-Hand Steadiness; Control Precision; Visualization. **Interacting with Others:** Communicating with Other Workers. **Physical Work Conditions:** Indoors; Using Hands on Objects, Tools, Controls; Hazardous Equipment; Standing; Common Protective or Safety Attire; Distracting Sounds and Noise Levels; Hazardous Situations.

51-4033.01 Grinding, Honing, Lapping, and Deburring Machine Set-Up Operators

Set up and operate grinding, honing, lapping, or deburring machines to remove excess materials or burrs from internal and external surfaces. **Education:** Moderate-term O-J-T. **Occupational Type:** Realistic. **Job Zone:** 3. **Average Salary:** $24,740. **Projected Growth:** –9.6%. **Occupational Values:** Moral Values; Independence; Activity; Supervision, Human Relations; Company Policies and Practices; Supervision, Technical; Security. **Skills Required:** Operation and Control; Equipment Selection; Product Inspection; Operation Monitoring. **Abilities:** Control Precision; Near Vision; Manual Dexterity; Visualization. **Interacting with Others:** Monitoring and Controlling Resources. **Physical Work Conditions:** Indoors; Using Hands on Objects, Tools, Controls; Hazardous Equipment; Standing; Common Protective or Safety Attire; Making Repetitive Motions; Distracting Sounds and Noise Levels.

51-4033.02 Buffing and Polishing Set-Up Operators

Set up and operate buffing or polishing machine. **Education:** Moderate-term O-J-T. **Occupational Type:** Realistic. **Job Zone:** 2. **Average Salary:** $24,740. **Projected Growth:** –9.6%. **Occupational Values:** Moral Values; Independence; Activity; Supervision, Human Relations; Company Policies and Practices; Supervision, Technical. **Skills Required:** Operation and

Control. **Abilities:** Control Precision. **Interacting with Others:** Communicating with Other Workers. **Physical Work Conditions:** Using Hands on Objects, Tools, Controls; Indoors; Standing; Hazardous Equipment; Common Protective or Safety Attire; Making Repetitive Motions; Distracting Sounds and Noise Levels.

51-4034.00 Lathe and Turning Machine Tool Setters, Operators, and Tenders, Metal and Plastic

Set up, operate, or tend lathe and turning machines to turn, bore, thread, form, or face metal or plastic materials such as wire, rod, or bar stock. **Education:** Moderate-term O-J-T. **Occupational Type:** Realistic. **Job Zone:** 3. **Average Salary:** $26,036. **Projected Growth:** –8.4%. **Occupational Values:** Moral Values; Company Policies and Practices; Independence; Activity; Supervision, Human Relations; Supervision, Technical; Security. **Skills Required:** Equipment Selection; Installation. **Abilities:** Visualization; Written Comprehension; Information Ordering; Control Precision. **Interacting with Others:** Assisting and Caring for Others. **Physical Work Conditions:** Indoors; Using Hands on Objects, Tools, Controls; Hazardous Equipment; Standing; Common Protective or Safety Attire; Distracting Sounds and Noise Levels.

51-4035.00 Milling and Planing Machine Setters, Operators, and Tenders, Metal and Plastic

Set up, operate, or tend milling or planing machines to mill, plane, shape, groove, or profile metal or plastic work pieces. **Education:** Moderate-term O-J-T. **Occupational Type:** Realistic. **Job Zone:** 3. **Average Salary:** $28,920. **Projected Growth:** –3.9%. **Occupational Values:** Moral Values; Independence; Company Policies and Practices; Supervision, Human Relations; Activity; Supervision, Technical; Security. **Skills Required:** Equipment Selection; Mathematics. **Abilities:** Number Facility. **Interacting with Others:** Communicating with Other Workers. **Physical Work Conditions:** Indoors; Using Hands on Objects, Tools, Controls; Standing; Common Protective or Safety Attire; Hazardous Equipment; Making Repetitive Motions; Distracting Sounds and Noise Levels.

51-4072.01 Plastic Molding and Casting Machine Setters and Set-Up Operators

Set up, or set up and operate, plastic molding machines (such as compression or injection molding machines) to mold, form, or cast thermoplastic materials to specified shape. **Education:** Moderate-term O-J-T. **Occupational Type:** Realistic. **Job Zone:** 2. **Average Salary:** $21,920. **Projected Growth:** 14.7%. **Occupational Values:** Moral Values; Independence; Company Policies and Practices; Activity; Supervision, Human Relations. **Skills Required:** Operation and Control; Product Inspection. **Abilities:** Control Precision; Manual Dexterity. **Interacting with Others:** Communicating with Other Workers. **Physical Work Conditions:** Indoors; Using Hands on Objects, Tools, Controls; Hazardous Equipment; Standing; Common Protective or Safety Attire; Contaminants; Distracting Sounds and Noise Levels.

51-4072.02 Plastic Molding and Casting Machine Operators and Tenders

Operate or tend plastic molding machines (such as compression or injection molding machines) to mold, form, or cast thermoplastic materials to specified shape. **Education:** Moderate-term O-J-T. **Occupational Type:** Realistic. **Job Zone:** 1. **Average Salary:** $17,840. **Projected Growth:** 14.7%. **Occupational Values:** Moral Values; Company Policies and Practices; Independence; Supervision, Human Relations; Activity; Supervision, Technical. **Skills Required:** Operation and Control; Operation Monitoring; Product Inspection. **Abilities:** Control Precision; Problem Sensitivity; Manual Dexterity. **Interacting with Others:** Communicating with Other Workers. **Physical Work Conditions:** Indoors; Using Hands on Objects, Tools, Controls; Standing; Hazardous Equipment; Distracting Sounds and Noise Levels; Common Protective or Safety Attire.

51-4072.03 Metal Molding, Coremaking, and Casting Machine Setters and Set-Up Operators

Set up, or set up and operate, metal casting, molding, and coremaking machines to mold or cast metal parts and products such as tubes, rods, automobile trim, carburetor housings, and motor parts. Use die casting and continuous casting machines and roll-over, squeeze, and shell molding machines. **Education:** Moderate-term O-J-T. **Occupational Type:** Realistic. **Job Zone:** 2. **Average Salary:** $25,240. **Projected Growth:** –3.9%. **Occupational Values:** Moral Values; Independence; Company Policies and Practices; Activity; Supervision, Human Relations; Supervision, Technical. **Skills Required:** Product Inspection; Operation and Control. **Abilities:** Arm-Hand Steadiness; Control Precision; Manual Dexterity; Near Vision. **Interacting with Others:** Communicating with Other Workers. **Physical Work Conditions:** Indoors; Using Hands on Objects, Tools, Controls; Hazardous Equipment; Common Protective or Safety Attire; Standing; Hazardous Situations; Contaminants.

51-4072.04 Metal Molding, Coremaking, and Casting Machine Operators and Tenders

Operate or tend metal molding, casting, or coremaking machines to mold or cast metal products (such as pipes, brake drums, and rods) and metal parts (such as automobile trim, carburetor housings, and motor parts). Use centrifugal casting machines, vacuum casting machines, turnover draw-type coremaking machines, conveyor-screw coremaking machines, and die casting machines. **Education:** Moderate-term O-J-T. **Occupational Type:** Realistic. **Job Zone:** 1. **Average Salary:** $24,640. **Projected Growth:** –3.9%. **Occupational Values:** Moral Values; Company Policies and Practices; Activity; Independence; Supervision, Human Relations. **Skills Required:** Operation and Control; Product Inspection; Operation Monitoring; Mathematics; Problem Identification; Equipment Selection; Repairing. **Abilities:** Arm-Hand Steadiness; Manual Dexterity; Information Ordering; Multilimb Coordination; Number Facility; Static Strength. **Interacting with Others:** Communicating with Other Workers. **Physical Work Conditions:** Indoors; Using Hands on Objects, Tools, Controls; Standing; Common Protective or Safety Attire; Hazardous Equipment; Contaminants; Hazardous Situations.

51-4072.05 Casting Machine Set-Up Operators

Set up and operate machines to cast and assemble printing type. **Education:** Moderate-term O-J-T. **Occupational Type:** Realistic. **Job Zone:** 3. **Average Salary:** $24,093. **Projected Growth:** 4.1%. **Occupational Values:** Moral Values; Independence; Activity; Supervision, Human Relations; Company Policies and Practices; Supervision, Technical. **Skills Required:** Operation and Control; Operation Monitoring. **Abilities:** Manual Dexterity; Control Precision. **Interacting with Others:** Communicating with Other Workers. **Physical Work Conditions:** Indoors; Using Hands on Objects, Tools, Controls; Standing; Hazardous Equipment; Distracting Sounds and Noise Levels.

51-4081.01 Combination Machine Tool Setters and Set-Up Operators, Metal and Plastic

Set up, or set up and operate, more than one type of cutting or forming machine tool such as gear hobbers, lathes, press brakes, shearing, and boring machines. **Education:** Moderate-term O-J-T. **Occupational Type:** Realistic. **Job Zone:** 3. **Average Salary:** $26,330. **Projected Growth:** 13.8%. **Occupational Values:** Moral Values; Activity; Company Policies and Practices; Independence; Supervision, Human Relations; Supervision, Technical. **Skills Required:** Operation and Control; Product Inspection; Operation Monitoring; Testing; Mathematics; Installation; Reading Comprehension. **Abilities:** Control Precision; Information Ordering; Written Comprehension; Number Facility; Manual Dexterity; Mathematical Reasoning; Near Vision. **Interacting with Others:** Teaching Others. **Physical Work Conditions:** Indoors; Hazardous Equipment; Using Hands on Objects, Tools, Controls; Standing; Common Protective or Safety Attire; Distracting Sounds and Noise Levels; Hazardous Situations.

51-4122.01 Welding Machine Setters and Set-Up Operators

Set up, or set up and operate, welding machines that join or bond together components to fabricate metal products or assemblies, according to specifications and blueprints. **Education:** Moderate-term O-J-T. **Occupational Type:** Realistic. **Job Zone:** 3. **Average Salary:** $26,470. **Projected Growth:** 5.4%. **Occupational Values:** Moral Values; Independence; Company Policies and Practices; Supervision, Human Relations; Activity; Security; Supervision, Technical. **Skills Required:** Operation and Control; Equipment Selection; Product Inspection; Testing; Operation Monitoring; Mathematics. **Abilities:** Control Precision; Manual Dexterity; Information Ordering; Arm-Hand Steadiness; Near Vision; Problem Sensitivity. **Interacting with Others:** Coordinating Work and Activities of Others. **Physical Work Conditions:** Indoors; Using Hands on Objects, Tools, Controls; Standing; Hazardous Equipment; Common Protective or Safety Attire; Distracting Sounds and Noise Levels.

51-4122.03 Soldering and Brazing Machine Setters and Set-Up Operators

Set up, or set up and operate, soldering or brazing machines to braze, solder, heat treat, or spot weld fabricated metal products or components as specified by work orders, blueprints, and layout specifications. **Education:** Moderate-term O-J-T. **Occupational Type:** Realistic. **Job Zone:** 2. **Average Salary:** $21,530. **Projected Growth:** 8.2%. **Occupational Values:** Moral Values; Company Policies and Practices; Independence; Supervision, Human Relations; Activity; Supervision, Technical. **Skills Required:** Operation and Control. **Abilities:** Control Precision. **Interacting with Others:** Teaching Others. **Physical Work Conditions:** Indoors; Common Protective or Safety Attire; Using Hands on Objects, Tools, Controls; Hazardous Conditions; Hazardous Equipment; Distracting Sounds and Noise Levels; Standing.

51-4191.01 Heating Equipment Setters and Set-Up Operators, Metal and Plastic

Set up, or set up and operate, heating equipment such as heat-treating furnaces, flame-hardening machines, and induction machines that anneal or heat-treat metal objects. **Education:** Moderate-term O-J-T. **Occupational Type:** Realistic. **Job Zone:** 3. **Average Salary:** $24,340. **Projected Growth:** -4.1%. **Occupational Values:** Moral Values; Company Policies and Practices; Activity; Independence; Supervision, Human Relations; Supervision, Technical. **Skills Required:** Operation and Control; Product Inspection; Operation Monitoring. **Abilities:** Control Precision; Information Ordering; Arm-Hand Steadiness; Manual Dexterity. **Interacting with Others:** Communicating with Other Workers. **Physical Work Conditions:** Indoors; Using Hands on Objects, Tools, Controls; Hazardous Equipment; Standing; Common Protective or Safety Attire; Hazardous Situations; Distracting Sounds and Noise Levels.

51-4191.02 Heat Treating, Annealing, and Tempering Machine Operators and Tenders, Metal and Plastic

Operate or tend machines such as furnaces, baths, flame-hardening machines, and electronic induction machines to harden, anneal, and heat-treat metal products or metal parts. **Education:** Moderate-term O-J-T. **Occupational Type:** Realistic. **Job Zone:** 2. **Average Salary:** $25,160. **Projected Growth:** -4.1%. **Occupational Values:** Moral Values; Independence; Company Policies and Practices; Supervision, Human Relations; Activity; Supervision, Technical. **Skills Required:** Operation Monitoring; Product Inspection; Operation and Control; Reading Comprehension; Testing. **Abilities:** Control Precision. **Interacting with Others:** Communicating with Other Workers. **Physical Work Conditions:** Indoors; Using Hands on Objects, Tools, Controls; Hazardous Equipment; Standing; Hazardous Conditions; Hazardous Situations; Common Protective or Safety Attire.

51-5011.01 Bindery Machine Setters and Set-Up Operators

Set up, or set up and operate, machines that perform some or all of the following functions in order to produce books, magazines, pamphlets, catalogs, and other printed materials: gathering, folding, cutting, stitching, rounding and backing, supering, casing-in, lining, pressing, and trimming. **Education:** Moderate-term O-J-T. **Occupational Type:** Realistic. **Job Zone:** 2. **Average Salary:** $24,330. **Projected Growth:** 11.5%. **Occupational Values:** Moral Values; Activity; Company Policies and Practices; Supervision, Human Relations; Independence; Supervision, Technical. **Skills Required:** Operation and Control; Reading Comprehension; Product Inspection. **Abilities:** Control Precision; Information Ordering. **Interacting with Others:** Teaching Others. **Physical Work Conditions:** Indoors; Using Hands on Objects, Tools, Controls; Standing; Making Repetitive Motions.

51-5023.06 Screen Printing Machine Setters and Set-Up Operators

Set up, or set up and operate, screen printing machines to print designs onto articles and materials such as glass or plasticware, cloth, and paper. **Education:** Moderate-term O-J-T. **Occupational Type:** Realistic. **Job Zone:** 3. **Average Salary:** $18,880.

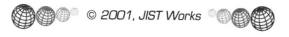

Projected Growth: 3%. **Occupational Values:** Moral Values; Company Policies and Practices; Activity; Independence; Supervision, Human Relations; Supervision, Technical; Achievement. **Skills Required:** Product Inspection; Operation Monitoring; Operation and Control; Reading Comprehension; Troubleshooting; Problem Identification; Repairing. **Abilities:** Near Vision. **Interacting with Others:** Teaching Others. **Physical Work Conditions:** Indoors; Using Hands on Objects, Tools, Controls; Hazardous Equipment; Standing; Common Protective or Safety Attire; Contaminants; Distracting Sounds and Noise Levels.

51-6062.00 Textile Cutting Machine Setters, Operators, and Tenders

Set up, operate, or tend machines that cut textiles. **Education:** Moderate-term O-J-T. **Occupational Type:** Realistic. **Job Zone:** 3. **Average Salary:** $19,371. **Projected Growth:** –9.6%. **Occupational Values:** Moral Values; Supervision, Human Relations; Activity; Independence; Company Policies and Practices; Supervision, Technical; Security. **Skills Required:** Product Inspection; Testing; Operation and Control; Repairing; Operation Monitoring; Installation; Equipment Maintenance. **Abilities:** Control Precision; Arm-Hand Steadiness; Information Ordering; Written Comprehension; Manual Dexterity; Problem Sensitivity; Finger Dexterity. **Interacting with Others:** Communicating with Other Workers. **Physical Work Conditions:** Indoors; Using Hands on Objects, Tools, Controls; Standing; Hazardous Equipment; Common Protective or Safety Attire; Hazardous Situations; Making Repetitive Motions.

51-6063.00 Textile Knitting and Weaving Machine Setters, Operators, and Tenders

Set up, operate, or tend machines that knit, loop, weave, or draw in textiles. **Education:** Moderate-term O-J-T. **Occupational Type:** Realistic. **Job Zone:** 3. **Average Salary:** $19,371. **Projected Growth:** –9.6%. **Occupational Values:** Moral Values; Activity; Company Policies and Practices; Independence; Supervision, Human Relations; Supervision, Technical; Security. **Skills Required:** Product Inspection; Testing; Operation and Control; Operation Monitoring; Repairing; Installation; Equipment Maintenance. **Abilities:** Control Precision; Arm-Hand Steadiness; Information Ordering; Written Comprehension; Manual Dexterity; Problem Sensitivity; Finger Dexterity. **Interacting with Others:** Communicating with Other Workers. **Physical Work Conditions:** Indoors; Using Hands on Objects, Tools, Controls; Standing; Hazardous Equipment; Common Protective or Safety Attire; Hazardous Situations; Making Repetitive Motions.

51-6064.00 Textile Winding, Twisting, and Drawing Out Machine Setters, Operators, and Tenders

Set up, operate, or tend machines that wind or twist textiles or draw out and combine sliver such as wool, hemp, or synthetic fibers. **Education:** Moderate-term O-J-T. **Occupational Type:** Realistic. **Job Zone:** 3. **Average Salary:** $19,752. **Projected Growth:** –9.6%. **Occupational Values:** Moral Values; Activity; Company Policies and Practices; Independence; Supervision, Human Relations; Supervision, Technical; Security. **Skills Required:** Product Inspection; Repairing; Operation and Control; Operation Monitoring; Testing; Equipment Maintenance; Installation. **Abilities:** Control Precision; Arm-Hand Steadiness; Information Ordering; Written Comprehension; Manual Dexterity; Problem Sensitivity; Finger Dexterity. **Interacting with Others:** Communicating with Other Workers. **Physical Work Conditions:** Indoors; Using Hands on Objects, Tools, Controls; Standing; Hazardous Equipment; Common Protective or Safety Attire; Hazardous Situations; Making Repetitive Motions.

51-7042.01 Woodworking Machine Setters and Set-Up Operators, Except Sawing

Set up, or set up and operate, woodworking machines such as lathes, drill presses, sanders, shapers, and planing machines to perform woodworking operations. **Education:** Moderate-term O-J-T. **Occupational Type:** Realistic. **Job Zone:** 2. **Average Salary:** $20,310. **Projected Growth:** –12.5%. **Occupational Values:** Moral Values; Independence; Activity; Supervision, Human Relations; Company Policies and Practices; Supervision, Technical. **Skills Required:** Operation and Control; Equipment Selection. **Abilities:** Control Precision. **Interacting with Others:** Communicating with Other Workers. **Physical Work Conditions:** Hazardous Equipment; Using Hands on Objects, Tools, Controls; Common Protective or Safety Attire; Indoors; Hazardous Situations; Standing; Making Repetitive Motions.

51-9041.01 Extruding, Forming, Pressing, and Compacting Machine Setters and Set-Up Operators

Set up, or set up and operate, machines such as glass forming machines, plodder machines, and tuber machines to manufacture any of a wide variety of products such as soap bars, formed rubber, glassware, food, brick, and tile, by means of extruding, compressing, or compacting. **Education:** Moderate-term O-J-T. **Occupational Type:** Realistic. **Job Zone:** 2. **Average Salary:** $24,330. **Projected Growth:** 5%. **Occupational Values:** Moral Values; Company Policies and Practices; Independence; Activity; Supervision, Human Relations; Supervision, Technical. **Skills Required:** Operation and Control; Operation Monitoring. **Abilities:** Information Ordering. **Interacting with Others:** Communicating with Other Workers. **Physical Work Conditions:** Indoors; Using Hands on Objects, Tools, Controls; Hazardous Equipment; Standing; Distracting Sounds and Noise Levels.

51-9121.01 Coating, Painting, and Spraying Machine Setters and Set-Up Operators

Set up, or set up and operate, machines to coat or paint any of a wide variety of products such as food products, glassware, cloth, ceramic, metal, plastic, paper, and wood products with lacquer, silver and copper solution, rubber, paint, varnish, glaze, enamel, oil, or rust-proofing materials. **Education:** Moderate-term O-J-T. **Occupational Type:** Realistic. **Job Zone:** 2. **Average Salary:** $22,750. **Projected Growth:** 8.7%. **Occupational Values:** Moral Values; Activity; Independence; Supervision, Human Relations; Company Policies and Practices; Supervision, Technical; Security. **Skills Required:** Operation and Control. **Abilities:** Control Precision; Manual Dexterity. **Interacting with Others:** Performing Administrative Activities. **Physical Work Conditions:** Indoors; Using Hands on Objects, Tools, Controls; Standing; Common Protective or Safety Attire; Contaminants; Hazardous Conditions; Hazardous Equipment.

51-9196.00 Paper Goods Machine Setters, Operators, and Tenders

Set up, operate, or tend paper goods machines that perform a variety of functions such as converting, sawing, corrugating, banding, wrapping, boxing, stitching, forming, or sealing paper or paperboard sheets into products. **Education:** Moderate-term O-J-T. **Occupational Type:** Realistic. **Job Zone:** 2. **Average Salary:** $25,990. **Projected Growth:** -4.1%. **Occupational Values:** Moral Values; Company Policies and Practices; Independence; Activity; Supervision, Human Relations; Supervision, Technical. **Skills Required:** Installation; Operation Monitoring; Operation and Control. **Abilities:** Control Precision; Manual Dexterity. **Interacting with Others:** Communicating with Other Workers. **Physical Work Conditions:** Indoors; Standing; Using Hands on Objects, Tools, Controls; Hazardous Equipment; Distracting Sounds and Noise Levels; Common Protective or Safety Attire.

08.02.02 Production Technology: Precision Hand Work

51-2011.01 Aircraft Structure Assemblers, Precision

Assemble tail, wing, fuselage, or other structural sections of aircraft, space vehicles, and missiles from parts, subassemblies, and components; install functional units, parts, or equipment such as landing gear, control surfaces, doors, and floorboards. **Education:** Work experience in a related occupation. **Occupational Type:** Realistic. **Job Zone:** 3. **Average Salary:** $38,400. **Projected Growth:** 19.3%. **Occupational Values:** Moral Values; Independence; Company Policies and Practices; Activity; Supervision, Human Relations; Compensation; Ability Utilization. **Skills Required:** Installation; Product Inspection; Equipment Selection; Mathematics. **Abilities:** Arm-Hand Steadiness; Extent Flexibility; Visualization; Manual Dexterity; Finger Dexterity; Information Ordering. **Interacting with Others:** Communicating with Other Workers. **Physical Work Conditions:** Using Hands on Objects, Tools, Controls; Standing; Outdoors; Bending or Twisting the Body; Common Protective or Safety Attire; Hazardous Equipment; Indoors.

51-2011.02 Aircraft Systems Assemblers, Precision

Lay out, assemble, install, and test aircraft systems such as armament, environmental control, plumbing, and hydraulic. **Education:** Work experience in a related occupation. **Occupational Type:** Realistic. **Job Zone:** 3. **Average Salary:** $38,400. **Projected Growth:** 19.3%. **Occupational Values:** Moral Values; Independence; Company Policies and Practices; Compensation; Supervision, Human Relations; Activity; Ability Utilization. **Skills Required:** Equipment Maintenance; Testing; Installation; Equipment Selection; Troubleshooting; Product Inspection; Repairing. **Abilities:** Arm-Hand Steadiness; Visualization; Manual Dexterity; Written Comprehension; Information Ordering. **Interacting with Others:** Communicating with Other Workers. **Physical Work Conditions:** Using Hands on Objects, Tools, Controls; Indoors; Hazardous Equipment; Standing; Kneeling, Crouching, or Crawling; Distracting Sounds and Noise Levels; Common Protective or Safety Attire.

51-2011.03 Aircraft Rigging Assemblers

Fabricate and assemble aircraft tubing or cable components or assemblies. **Education:** Work experience in a related occupation. **Occupational Type:** Realistic. **Job Zone:** 3. **Average Salary:** $38,400. **Projected Growth:** 19.3%. **Occupational Values:** Moral Values; Independence; Company Policies and Practices; Supervision, Human Relations; Activity; Achievement; Ability Utilization. **Skills Required:** Mathematics. **Abilities:** Manual Dexterity; Arm-Hand Steadiness; Written Comprehension; Control Precision; Near Vision. **Interacting with Others:** Communicating with Other Workers. **Physical Work Conditions:** Using Hands on Objects, Tools, Controls; Standing; Hazardous Equipment; Making Repetitive Motions; Outdoors; Sitting; Hazardous Situations.

51-2022.00 Electrical and Electronic Equipment Assemblers

Assemble or modify electrical or electronic equipment such as computers, test equipment telemetering systems, electric motors, and batteries. **Education:** Work experience in a related occupation. **Occupational Type:** Realistic. **Job Zone:** 3. **Average Salary:** $20,117. **Projected Growth:** 6%. **Occupational Values:** Moral Values; Company Policies and Practices; Activity; Compensation; Supervision, Human Relations; Working Conditions; Ability Utilization. **Skills Required:** Equipment Selection; Product Inspection; Installation; Equipment Maintenance; Testing; Instructing; Science. **Abilities:** Finger Dexterity; Wrist-Finger Speed; Manual Dexterity; Arm-Hand Steadiness; Information Ordering. **Interacting with Others:** Communicating with Other Workers; Communicating with Persons Outside Organization; Providing Consultation and Advice to Others. **Physical Work Conditions:** Indoors; Using Hands on Objects, Tools, Controls; Sitting; Standing.

51-2023.00 Electromechanical Equipment Assemblers

Assemble or modify electromechanical equipment or devices such as servomechanisms, gyros, dynamometers, magnetic drums, tape drives, brakes, control linkage, actuators, and appliances. **Education:** Work experience in a related occupation. **Occupational Type:** Realistic. **Job Zone:** 3. **Average Salary:** $23,250. **Projected Growth:** 5.7%. **Occupational Values:** Moral Values; Independence; Company Policies and Practices; Supervision, Human Relations; Activity; Supervision, Technical; Advancement. **Skills Required:** Product Inspection; Installation; Equipment Selection; Testing. **Abilities:** Manual Dexterity; Arm-Hand Steadiness; Visualization; Finger Dexterity; Near Vision. **Interacting with Others:** Communicating with Other Workers. **Physical Work Conditions:** Indoors; Using Hands on Objects, Tools, Controls; Hazardous Equipment; Standing; Distracting Sounds and Noise Levels; Common Protective or Safety Attire; Making Repetitive Motions.

51-2031.00 Engine and Other Machine Assemblers

Construct, assemble, or rebuild machines such as engines, turbines, and similar equipment used in such industries as construction, extraction, textiles, and paper manufacturing. **Education:** Work experience in a related occupation. **Occupational Type:** Realistic. **Job Zone:** 3. **Average Salary:** $21,554. **Projected Growth:** 1.7%. **Occupational Values:** Moral Values; Independence; Company Policies and Practices; Activity; Supervision, Human Relations; Achievement; Supervision, Technical. **Skills Required:** Product Inspection; Operation Monitoring; Testing; Installation; Troubleshooting; Repairing; Operation and Control. **Abilities:** Information Ordering; Manual Dexterity; Control Precision; Visualization; Written Comprehension; Finger Dexterity; Near Vision. **Interacting with Others:** Coaching and Developing Others. **Physical Work Conditions:** Hazardous Equipment; Using Hands on Objects, Tools, Controls; Indoors; Standing; Hazardous Situations; Common Protective or Safety Attire; Kneeling, Crouching, or Crawling.

51-2093.00 Timing Device Assemblers, Adjusters, and Calibrators

Perform precision assembling or adjusting, within narrow tolerances, of timing devices such as watches, clocks, or chronometers. **Education:** Work experience in a related occupation. **Occupational Type:** Realistic. **Job Zone:** 2. **Average Salary:** $23,941. **Projected Growth:** 3.7%. **Occupational Values:** Moral Values; Independence; Ability Utilization; Achievement; Working Conditions; Company Policies and Practices; Activity. **Skills Required:** Repairing; Equipment Selection; Testing; Installation. **Abilities:** Finger Dexterity; Arm-Hand Steadiness; Near Vision; Manual Dexterity; Visualization. **Interacting with Others:** Monitoring and Controlling Resources. **Physical Work Conditions:** Indoors; Using Hands on Objects, Tools, Controls; Sitting.

51-4071.00 Foundry Mold and Coremakers

Make or form wax or sand cores or molds used in the production of metal castings in foundries. **Education:** Moderate-term O-J-T. **Occupational Type:** Realistic. **Job Zone:** 2. **Average Salary:** $23,372. **Projected Growth:** 2.5%. **Occupational Values:** Moral Values; Supervision, Human Relations; Company Policies and Practices; Supervision, Technical; Independence; Activity; Coworkers. **Skills Required:** Operation and Control; Product Inspection. **Abilities:** Manual Dexterity; Information Ordering. **Interacting with Others:** Communicating with Other Workers. **Physical Work Conditions:** Indoors; Common Protective or Safety Attire; Using Hands on Objects, Tools, Controls; Standing; Hazardous Equipment; Hazardous Situations; Very Hot.

51-5012.00 Bookbinders

Perform highly skilled hand finishing operations such as grooving and lettering to bind books. **Education:** Moderate-term O-J-T. **Occupational Type:** Realistic. **Job Zone:** 4. **Average Salary:** $20,690. **Projected Growth:** –15.2%. **Occupational Values:** Moral Values; Supervision, Technical; Independence; Working Conditions; Company Policies and Practices; Supervision, Human Relations; Security. **Skills Required:** Operation and Control. **Abilities:** Manual Dexterity; Near Vision. **Interacting with Others:** Communicating with Other Workers. **Physical Work Conditions:** Indoors; Using Hands on Objects, Tools, Controls; Contaminants; Hazardous Situations; Sitting; Standing.

51-9071.01 Jewelers

Fabricate and repair jewelry articles. **Education:** Long-term O-J-T. **Occupational Type:** Realistic. **Job Zone:** 4. **Average Salary:** $24,130. **Projected Growth:** –6%. **Occupational Values:** Working Conditions; Ability Utilization; Independence; Responsibility; Autonomy; Variety; Achievement. **Skills Required:** Product Inspection; Equipment Selection. **Abilities:** Finger Dexterity; Arm-Hand Steadiness; Near Vision; Manual Dexterity; Visualization; Wrist-Finger Speed; Visual Color Discrimination. **Interacting with Others:** Interpreting Meaning of Information to Others. **Physical Work Conditions:** Indoors; Using Hands on Objects, Tools, Controls; Sitting; Making Repetitive Motions.

51-9071.02 Silversmiths

Anneal, solder, hammer, shape, and glue silver articles. **Education:** Long-term O-J-T. **Occupational Type:** Realistic. **Job Zone:** 3. **Average Salary:** $24,130. **Projected Growth:** –6%. **Occupational Values:** Independence; Autonomy; Moral Values; Working Conditions; Variety; Achievement; Ability Utilization. **Skills Required:** Product Inspection; Equipment Selection. **Abilities:** Manual Dexterity; Visualization; Arm-Hand Steadiness; Finger Dexterity; Wrist-Finger Speed. **Interacting with Others:** Communicating with Other Workers. **Physical Work Conditions:** Indoors; Using Hands on Objects, Tools, Controls; Standing; Hazardous Equipment.

51-9071.03 Model and Mold Makers, Jewelry

Make models or molds to create jewelry items. **Education:** Long-term O-J-T. **Occupational Type:** Realistic. **Job Zone:** 3. **Average Salary:** $22,488. **Projected Growth:** –6%. **Occupational Values:** Independence; Moral Values; Working Conditions; Security; Ability Utilization; Achievement; Variety. **Skills Required:** Product Inspection. **Abilities:** Arm-Hand Steadiness; Near Vision; Manual Dexterity; Information Ordering; Wrist-Finger Speed; Finger Dexterity. **Interacting with Others:** Performing Administrative Activities. **Physical Work Conditions:** Indoors; Using Hands on Objects, Tools, Controls; Sitting; Common Protective or Safety Attire; Hazardous Situations; Hazardous Equipment.

51-9071.04 Bench Workers, Jewelry

Cut, file, form, and solder parts for jewelry. **Education:** Long-term O-J-T. **Occupational Type:** Realistic. **Job Zone:** 3. **Average Salary:** $22,378. **Projected Growth:** –6%. **Occupational Values:** Independence; Moral Values; Working Conditions; Activity; Ability Utilization; Security; Variety. **Skills Required:** Product Inspection; Operations Analysis. **Abilities:** Finger Dexterity; Arm-Hand Steadiness; Near Vision; Visualization; Manual Dexterity. **Interacting with Others:** Communicating with Persons Outside Organization. **Physical Work Conditions:** Indoors; Using Hands on Objects, Tools, Controls; Sitting; Making Repetitive Motions.

51-9071.05 Pewter Casters and Finishers

Cast and finish pewter alloy to form parts for goblets, candlesticks, and other pewterware. **Education:** Long-term O-J-T. **Occupational Type:** Realistic. **Job Zone:** 4. **Average Salary:** $19,060. **Projected Growth:** –6%. **Occupational Values:** Moral Values; Independence; Ability Utilization; Creativity; Working Conditions; Achievement; Autonomy. **Skills Required:** Product Inspection; Operation and Control; Operations Analysis.

Abilities: Information Ordering; Arm-Hand Steadiness; Originality; Manual Dexterity; Near Vision; Visualization. **Interacting with Others:** Communicating with Persons Outside Organization. **Physical Work Conditions:** Indoors; Using Hands on Objects, Tools, Controls; Hazardous Situations; Very Hot; Common Protective or Safety Attire; Standing; Sitting.

51-9071.06 Gem and Diamond Workers

Split, saw, cut, shape, polish, or drill gems and diamonds used in jewelry or industrial tools. **Education:** Long-term O-J-T. **Occupational Type:** Realistic. **Job Zone:** 2. **Average Salary:** $18,800. **Projected Growth:** 14%. **Occupational Values:** Independence; Moral Values; Ability Utilization; Working Conditions; Compensation; Supervision, Technical; Autonomy. **Skills Required:** Product Inspection. **Abilities:** Near Vision; Manual Dexterity; Arm-Hand Steadiness; Control Precision; Finger Dexterity; Wrist-Finger Speed. **Interacting with Others:** Communicating with Other Workers. **Physical Work Conditions:** Indoors; Using Hands on Objects, Tools, Controls; Sitting; Hazardous Equipment; Hazardous Situations.

51-9081.00 Dental Laboratory Technicians

Construct and repair full or partial dentures or dental appliances. **Education:** Long-term O-J-T. **Occupational Type:** Realistic. **Job Zone:** 3. **Average Salary:** $25,660. **Projected Growth:** 1%. **Occupational Values:** Moral Values; Independence; Working Conditions; Achievement; Security; Ability Utilization; Supervision, Human Relations. **Skills Required:** Product Inspection; Reading Comprehension; Science; Testing; Information Gathering; Operations Analysis; Problem Identification. **Abilities:** Arm-Hand Steadiness; Written Comprehension; Finger Dexterity; Near Vision; Manual Dexterity; Visualization; Wrist-Finger Speed. **Interacting with Others:** Communicating with Other Workers. **Physical Work Conditions:** Indoors; Using Hands on Objects, Tools, Controls; Sitting; Common Protective or Safety Attire.

51-9083.01 Precision Lens Grinders and Polishers

Set up and operate variety of machines and equipment to grind and polish lens and other optical elements. **Education:** Long-term O-J-T. **Occupational Type:** Realistic. **Job Zone:** 3. **Average Salary:** $19,530. **Projected Growth:** 4.7%. **Occupational Values:** Moral Values; Independence; Working Conditions; Security; Compensation; Ability Utilization; Achievement. **Skills Required:** Product Inspection; Equipment Selection; Operation and Control. **Abilities:** Arm-Hand Steadiness; Manual Dexterity; Finger Dexterity; Near Vision; Control Precision; Written Comprehension. **Interacting with Others:** Communicating with Other Workers. **Physical Work Conditions:** Indoors; Using Hands on Objects, Tools, Controls; Sitting.

51-9195.01 Precision Mold and Pattern Casters, except Nonferrous Metals

Cast molds and patterns from a variety of materials except nonferrous metals, according to blueprints and specifications. **Education:** Moderate-term O-J-T. **Occupational Type:** Realistic. **Job Zone:** 3. **Average Salary:** $19,847. **Projected Growth:** 2.5%. **Occupational Values:** Moral Values; Supervision, Human Relations; Independence; Activity; Supervision, Technical; Company Policies and Practices. **Skills Required:** Mathematics. **Abilities:** Visualization. **Interacting with Others:** Communicating with Other Workers. **Physical Work Conditions:** Indoors; Standing.

51-9195.02 Precision Pattern and Die Casters, Nonferrous Metals

Cast metal patterns and dies, according to specifications, from a variety of nonferrous metals such as aluminum or bronze. **Education:** Moderate-term O-J-T. **Occupational Type:** Realistic. **Job Zone:** 4. **Average Salary:** $19,847. **Projected Growth:** 2.5%. **Occupational Values:** Moral Values; Independence; Supervision, Human Relations; Company Policies and Practices; Activity; Security. **Skills Required:** Operation and Control. **Abilities:** Manual Dexterity. **Interacting with Others:** Communicating with Other Workers. **Physical Work Conditions:** Indoors; Common Protective or Safety Attire; Using Hands on Objects, Tools, Controls; Very Hot; Contaminants; Hazardous Equipment; Standing.

08.02.03 Production Technology: Inspection

45-4023.00 Log Graders and Scalers

Grade logs or estimate the marketable content or value of logs or pulpwood in sorting yards, millpond, log deck, or similar locations. Inspect logs for defects or measure logs to determine volume. **Education:** Short-term O-J-T. **Occupational Type:** Realistic. **Job Zone:** 2. **Average Salary:** $22,950. **Projected Growth:** –6%. **Occupational Values:** Moral Values; Independence; Activity; Responsibility; Supervision, Human Relations; Company Policies and Practices. **Skills Required:** Product Inspection; Judgment and Decision Making; Mathematics. **Abilities:** Number Facility. **Interacting with Others:** Communicating with Other Workers. **Physical Work Conditions:** Outdoors; Standing; Using Hands on Objects, Tools, Controls; Common Protective or Safety Attire.

51-9061.00 Inspectors, Testers, Sorters, Samplers, and Weighers

Inspect, test, sort, sample, or weigh nonagricultural raw materials or processed, machined, fabricated, or assembled parts or products for defects, wear, and deviations from specifications. May use precision measuring instruments and complex test equipment. No other data currently available.

51-9061.01 Materials Inspectors

Examine and inspect materials and finished parts and products for defects and wear and to ensure conformance with work orders, diagrams, blueprints, and template specifications. Usually specialize in a single phase of inspection. **Education:** Work experience in a related occupation. **Occupational Type:** Realistic. **Job Zone:** 3. **Average Salary:** $23,411. **Projected Growth:** –3.2%. **Occupational Values:** Responsibility; Moral Values; Independence; Company Policies and Practices; Activity; Security; Supervision, Human Relations. **Skills Required:** Product Inspection; Operation Monitoring; Testing; Operation and Control; Problem Identification; Information Gathering. **Abilities:** Information Ordering; Perceptual Speed; Near Vision; Problem Sensitivity; Selective Attention; Visualization. **Interacting with Others:** Communicating with Other Workers; Performing Administrative Activities; Providing Consultation and Advice to Others. **Physical Work Conditions:** Indoors; Standing; Using Hands on Objects, Tools, Controls; Common Protective or Safety Attire.

51-9061.02 Mechanical Inspectors

Inspect and test mechanical assemblies and systems such as motors, vehicles, and transportation equipment for defects and wear, to ensure compliance with specifications. **Education:** Work experience in a related occupation. **Occupational Type:** Realistic. **Job Zone:** 4. **Average Salary:** $23,411. **Projected Growth:** –3.2%. **Occupational Values:** Responsibility; Moral Values; Independence; Autonomy; Activity; Security; Company Policies and Practices. **Skills Required:** Product Inspection; Problem Identification; Testing; Science; Operation Monitoring; Troubleshooting; Reading Comprehension. **Abilities:** Near Vision; Problem Sensitivity; Written Comprehension; Perceptual Speed; Number Facility; Deductive Reasoning; Flexibility of Closure. **Interacting with Others:** Communicating with Other Workers; Communicating with Persons Outside Organization. **Physical Work Conditions:** Indoors; Standing; Using Hands on Objects, Tools, Controls; Distracting Sounds and Noise Levels.

51-9061.03 Precision Devices Inspectors and Testers

Verify accuracy of and adjust precision devices such as meters and gauges, testing instruments, clock and watch mechanisms, to ensure operation of device is in accordance with design specifications. **Education:** Work experience in a related occupation. **Occupational Type:** Realistic. **Job Zone:** 3. **Average Salary:** $27,670. **Projected Growth:** –3.2%. **Occupational Values:** Moral Values; Independence; Responsibility; Autonomy; Activity; Company Policies and Practices; Security. **Skills Required:** Product Inspection; Operation Monitoring; Testing; Problem Identification. **Abilities:** Problem Sensitivity; Finger Dexterity; Control Precision; Near Vision; Information Ordering; Perceptual Speed; Number Facility. **Interacting with Others:** Communicating with Other Workers. **Physical Work Conditions:** Indoors; Using Hands on Objects, Tools, Controls; Sitting; Making Repetitive Motions; Standing.

51-9061.04 Electrical and Electronic Inspectors and Testers

Inspect and test electrical and electronic systems such as radar navigational equipment, computer memory units, and television and radio transmitters, using precision measuring instruments. **Education:** Work experience in a related occupation. **Occupational Type:** Realistic. **Job Zone:** 3. **Average Salary:** $22,178. **Projected Growth:** –3.2%. **Occupational Values:** Moral Values; Responsibility; Activity; Security; Company Policies and Practices; Coworkers; Supervision, Technical. **Skills Required:** Testing; Operation Monitoring; Product Inspection; Problem Identification; Operation and Control. **Abilities:** Near Vision; Perceptual Speed; Deductive Reasoning; Visual Color Discrimination; Control Precision; Visualization; Oral Expression. **Interacting with Others:** Communicating with Other Workers; Providing Consultation and Advice to Others. **Physical Work Conditions:** Indoors; Using Hands on Objects, Tools, Controls; Standing; Common Protective or Safety Attire; Sitting.

51-9061.05 Production Inspectors, Testers, Graders, Sorters, Samplers, Weighers

Inspect, test, grade, sort, sample, or weigh nonagricultural raw materials or processed, machined, fabricated, or assembled parts or products. Work may be performed before, during, or after processing. **Education:** Work experience in a related occupation. **Occupational Type:** Realistic. **Job Zone:** 1. **Average Salary:** $27,670. **Projected Growth:** –3.2%. **Occupational Values:** Moral Values; Activity; Security; Responsibility; Company Policies and Practices; Supervision, Technical; Supervision, Human Relations. **Skills Required:** Product Inspection; Problem Identification; Testing. **Abilities:** Category Flexibility; Problem Sensitivity; Near Vision; Visual Color Discrimination; Perceptual Speed; Written Comprehension; Control Precision. **Interacting with Others:** Communicating with Other Workers. **Physical Work Conditions:** Indoors; Using Hands on Objects, Tools, Controls; Sitting; Standing.

53-6051.05 Motor Vehicle Inspectors

Inspect automotive vehicles to ensure compliance with governmental regulations and safety standards. **Education:** Work experience in a related occupation. **Occupational Type:** Realistic. **Job Zone:** 2. **Average Salary:** $39,560. **Projected Growth:** –3.2%. **Occupational Values:** Moral Values; Responsibility; Security; Autonomy; Activity; Independence; Company Policies and Practices. **Skills Required:** Product Inspection; Problem Identification; Testing; Troubleshooting; Science; Operation Monitoring; Equipment Maintenance. **Abilities:** Problem Sensitivity; Hearing Sensitivity; Near Vision; Manual Dexterity; Oral Expression; Written Expression. **Interacting with Others:** Communicating with Persons Outside Organization. **Physical Work Conditions:** Standing; Outdoors; Using Hands on Objects, Tools, Controls; Bending or Twisting the Body; Kneeling, Crouching, or Crawling.

08.03.01 Production Work: Machine Work, Assorted Materials

51-4011.01 Numerical Control Machine Tool Operators and Tenders, Metal and Plastic

Set up and operate numerical control (magnetic- or punched-tape-controlled) machine tools that automatically mill, drill, broach, and ream metal and plastic parts. May adjust machine feed and speed, change cutting tools, or adjust machine controls when automatic programming is faulty or if machine malfunctions. **Education:** Moderate-term O-J-T. **Occupational Type:** Realistic. **Job Zone:** 2. **Average Salary:** $27,110. **Projected Growth:** 22.6%. **Occupational Values:** Moral Values; Activity; Company Policies and Practices; Independence; Supervision, Human Relations; Supervision, Technical. **Skills Required:** Operation and Control; Product Inspection; Operation Monitoring; Equipment Selection. **Abilities:** Control Precision; Problem Sensitivity. **Interacting with Others:** Communicating with Other Workers. **Physical Work Conditions:** Indoors; Standing; Using Hands on Objects, Tools, Controls; Hazardous Equipment; Common Protective or Safety Attire.

51-4081.02 Combination Machine Tool Operators and Tenders, Metal and Plastic

Operate or tend more than one type of cutting or forming machine tool which has been previously set up. Use such machine tools as band saws, press brakes, slitting machines, drills, lathes, and boring machines. **Education:** Moderate-term O-J-T. **Occupational Type:** Realistic. **Job Zone:** 2. **Average Salary:** $21,740. **Projected Growth:** 13.8%. **Occupational Values:** Moral Values; Company Policies and Practices; Activity; Supervision, Human Relations; Independence. **Skills Required:** Operation and Control; Operation Monitoring; Product Inspection. **Abilities:** Manual Dexterity; Information Ordering; Control Precision; Problem Sensitivity. **Interacting with Others:** Coordinating Work and Activities of Others. **Physical Work Conditions:** Indoors; Using Hands on Objects, Tools, Controls; Hazardous Equipment; Standing; Common Protective or Safety Attire; Distracting Sounds and Noise Levels; Hazardous Situations.

51-6031.01 Sewing Machine Operators, Garment

Operate or tend sewing machines to perform garment sewing operations such as joining, reinforcing, or decorating garments or garment parts. **Education:** Moderate-term O-J-T. **Occupational Type:** Realistic. **Job Zone:** 1. **Average Salary:** $14,740. **Projected Growth:** –30.3%. **Occupational Values:** Moral Values; Activity; Company Policies and Practices; Independence; Supervision, Human Relations; Supervision, Technical; Security. **Skills Required:** Product Inspection; Equipment Selection; Operation and Control; Operation Monitoring. **Abilities:** Arm-Hand Steadiness; Near Vision; Manual Dexterity; Wrist-Finger Speed. **Interacting with Others:** Communicating with Other Workers. **Physical Work Conditions:** Indoors; Using Hands on Objects, Tools, Controls; Sitting; Making Repetitive Motions; Hazardous Equipment; Distracting Sounds and Noise Levels; Common Protective or Safety Attire.

51-6031.02 Sewing Machine Operators, Non-Garment

Operate or tend sewing machines to join together, reinforce, decorate, or perform related sewing operations in the manufacture of nongarment products such as upholstery, draperies, linens, carpets, and mattresses. **Education:** Moderate-term O-J-T. **Occupational Type:** Realistic. **Job Zone:** 1. **Average Salary:** $16,990. **Projected Growth:** 2.5%. **Occupational Values:** Moral Values; Activity; Independence; Supervision, Human Relations; Company Policies and Practices; Security; Supervision, Technical. **Skills Required:** Product Inspection. **Abilities:** Arm-Hand Steadiness; Visualization; Manual Dexterity; Finger Dexterity; Control Precision; Near Vision; Problem Sensitivity. **Interacting with Others:** Performing Administrative Activities. **Physical Work Conditions:** Indoors; Using Hands on Objects, Tools, Controls; Sitting; Hazardous Equipment; Making Repetitive Motions.

51-6042.00 Shoe Machine Operators and Tenders

Operate or tend a variety of machines to join, decorate, reinforce, or finish shoes and shoe parts. **Education:** Moderate-term O-J-T. **Occupational Type:** Realistic. **Job Zone:** 1. **Average Salary:** $16,230. **Projected Growth:** –35.8%. **Occupational Values:** Moral Values; Independence; Activity; Supervision, Human Relations; Company Policies and Practices; Security. **Skills Required:** Operation and Control; Product Inspection. **Abilities:** Arm-Hand Steadiness; Finger Dexterity. **Interacting with Others:** Communicating with Other Workers. **Physical Work Conditions:** Indoors; Sitting; Using Hands on Objects, Tools, Controls; Making Repetitive Motions; Hazardous Situations.

51-6091.01 Extruding and Forming Machine Operators and Tenders, Synthetic or Glass Fibers

Operate or tend machines that extrude and form continuous filaments from synthetic materials such as liquid polymer, rayon, and fiberglass, preparatory to further processing. **Education:** Moderate-term O-J-T. **Occupational Type:** Realistic. **Job Zone:** 1. **Average Salary:** $27,940. **Projected Growth:** 7.9%. **Occupational Values:** Moral Values; Company Policies and Practices; Supervision, Human Relations; Activity; Independence; Supervision, Technical; Security. **Skills Required:** Operation and Control; Equipment Maintenance; Operation Monitoring. **Abilities:** Control Precision; Near Vision. **Interacting with Others:** Communicating with Other Workers. **Physical Work Conditions:** Indoors; Using Hands on Objects, Tools, Controls; Standing; Common Protective or Safety Attire; Making Repetitive Motions.

51-7041.01 Sawing Machine Setters and Set-Up Operators

Set up, or set up and operate, wood-sawing machines. Examine blueprints, drawings, work orders, and patterns to determine size and shape of items to be sawed, sawing machines to set up, and sequence of sawing operations. **Education:** Moderate-term O-J-T. **Occupational Type:** Realistic. **Job Zone:** 2. **Average Salary:** $20,240. **Projected Growth:** –5.7%. **Occupational Values:** Moral Values; Independence; Company Policies and Practices; Supervision, Human Relations; Activity; Supervision, Technical. **Skills Required:** Equipment Selection; Operation and Control. **Abilities:** Manual Dexterity. **Interacting with Others:** Assisting and Caring for Others. **Physical Work Conditions:** Hazardous Equipment; Indoors; Using Hands on Objects, Tools, Controls; Common Protective or Safety Attire; Hazardous Situations; Standing; Distracting Sounds and Noise Levels.

51-7041.02 Sawing Machine Operators and Tenders

Operate or tend wood-sawing machines such as circular saws, band saws, multiple blade sawing machines, scroll saws, ripsaws, equalizer saws, power saws, and crozer machines. Saw logs to specifications; cut lumber to specified dimensions. **Education:** Moderate-term O-J-T. **Occupational Type:** Realistic. **Job Zone:** 2. **Average Salary:** $18,940. **Projected Growth:** –5.7%. **Occupational Values:** Moral Values; Independence; Activity; Supervision, Human Relations; Company Policies and Practices; Supervision, Technical. **Skills Required:** Operation and Control. **Abilities:** Control Precision; Arm-Hand Steadiness; Manual Dexterity. **Interacting with Others:** Communicating with Other Workers. **Physical Work Conditions:** Hazardous Equipment; Using Hands on Objects, Tools, Controls; Standing; Common Protective or Safety Attire; Contaminants; Hazardous Situations; Distracting Sounds and Noise Levels.

51-7042.02 Woodworking Machine Operators and Tenders, Except Sawing

Operate or tend woodworking machines such as drill presses, lathes, shapers, routers, sanders, planers, and wood-nailing machines to perform woodworking operations. **Education:** Moderate-term O-J-T. **Occupational Type:** Realistic. **Job Zone:** 1. **Average Salary:** $18,780. **Projected Growth:** –12.5%. **Occupational Values:** Moral Values; Independence; Activity; Supervision, Human Relations; Company Policies and Practices; Supervision, Technical. **Skills Required:** Operation and Control; Product Inspection; Operation Monitoring; Equipment Selection; Equipment Maintenance; Testing; Monitoring. **Abilities:** Arm-Hand Steadiness; Manual Dexterity; Control Precision; Near Vision; Written Comprehension; Information Ordering. **Interacting with Others:** Communicating with Other Workers. **Physical Work Conditions:** Indoors; Using Hands on Objects, Tools, Controls; Common Protective or Safety Attire; Hazardous Equipment; Standing; Hazardous Situations; Distracting Sounds and Noise Levels.

51-9021.00 Crushing, Grinding, and Polishing Machine Setters, Operators, and Tenders

Set up, operate, or tend machines to crush, grind, or polish materials such as coal, glass, grain, stone, food, or rubber. **Education:** Moderate-term O-J-T. **Occupational Type:** Realistic. **Job Zone:** 1. **Average Salary:** $23,350. **Projected Growth:** 2.8%. **Occupational Values:** Moral Values; Company Policies and Practices; Independence; Supervision, Human Relations; Activity; Supervision, Technical; Security. **Skills Required:** Operation and Control; Operation Monitoring. **Abilities:** Control Precision; Written Expression; Problem Sensitivity. **Interacting with Others:** Communicating with Other Workers. **Physical Work Conditions:** Indoors; Common Protective or Safety Attire; Using Hands on Objects, Tools, Controls; Standing; Hazardous Equipment; Distracting Sounds and Noise Levels; Contaminants.

51-9032.01 Fiber Product Cutting Machine Setters and Set-Up Operators

Set up and operate machine to cut or slice fiber material such as paper, wallboard, and insulation material. **Education:** Moderate-term O-J-T. **Occupational Type:** Realistic. **Job Zone:** 2. **Average Salary:** $22,360. **Projected Growth:** 6.4%. **Occupational Values:** Moral Values; Activity; Independence; Supervision, Human Relations; Company Policies and Practices; Supervision, Technical. **Skills Required:** Operation and Control; Operation Monitoring; Product Inspection. **Abilities:** Control Precision; Manual Dexterity. **Interacting with Others:** Communicating with Other Workers. **Physical Work Conditions:** Indoors; Using Hands on Objects, Tools, Controls; Hazardous Equipment; Standing; Hazardous Situations; Distracting Sounds and Noise Levels; Common Protective or Safety Attire.

51-9032.02 Stone Sawyers

Set up and operate gang saws, reciprocating saws, circular saws, or wire saws to cut blocks of stone into specified dimensions. **Education:** Moderate-term O-J-T. **Occupational Type:** Realistic. **Job Zone:** 2. **Average Salary:** $21,696. **Projected Growth:** 6.4%. **Occupational Values:** Moral Values; Company Policies and Practices; Activity; Supervision, Human Relations; Independence; Supervision, Technical. **Skills Required:** Product Inspection; Operation and Control; Equipment Selection. **Abilities:** Control Precision; Manual Dexterity; Information Ordering; Problem Sensitivity; Static Strength; Depth Perception; Multilimb Coordination. **Interacting with Others:** Communicating with Other Workers. **Physical Work Conditions:** Using Hands on Objects, Tools, Controls; Standing; Hazardous Equipment; Common Protective or Safety Attire; Indoors; Distracting Sounds and Noise Levels; Contaminants.

51-9032.03 Glass Cutting Machine Setters and Set-Up Operators

Set up and operate machines to cut glass. **Education:** Moderate-term O-J-T. **Occupational Type:** Realistic. **Job Zone:** 1. **Average Salary:** $22,360. **Projected Growth:** 6.4%. **Occupational Values:** Moral Values; Activity; Company Policies and Practices; Coworkers; Authority; Supervision, Human Relations; Supervision, Technical. **Skills Required:** Product Inspection; Operation and Control. **Abilities:** Arm-Hand Steadiness; Control Precision; Manual Dexterity; Near Vision. **Interacting with Others:** Communicating with Other Workers. **Physical Work Conditions:** Indoors; Using Hands on Objects, Tools, Controls; Hazardous Equipment; Hazardous Situations; Standing; Common Protective or Safety Attire; Making Repetitive Motions.

51-9032.04 Cutting and Slicing Machine Operators and Tenders

Operate or tend machines to cut or slice any of a wide variety of products or materials such as tobacco, food, paper, roofing slate, glass, stone, rubber, cork, and insulating material. **Education:** Moderate-term O-J-T. **Occupational Type:** Realistic. **Job Zone:** 1. **Average Salary:** $21,420. **Projected Growth:** 6.4%. **Occupational Values:** Moral Values; Activity; Independence; Supervision, Human Relations; Company Policies and Practices; Supervision, Technical. **Skills Required:** Product Inspection; Operation Monitoring; Operation and Control. **Abilities:** Written Comprehension; Extent Flexibility; Control Precision. **Interacting with Others:** Performing Administrative Activities. **Physical Work Conditions:** Indoors; Hazardous Equipment; Using Hands on Objects, Tools, Controls; Hazardous Situations; Standing; Common Protective or Safety Attire.

51-9041.02 Extruding, Forming, Pressing, and Compacting Machine Operators and Tenders

Operate or tend machines to shape and form any of a wide variety of manufactured products such as glass bulbs, molded food and candy, rubber goods, clay products, wax products, tobacco plugs, cosmetics, or paper products, by means of extruding, compressing or compacting. **Education:** Moderate-term O-J-T. **Occupational Type:** Realistic. **Job Zone:** 1. **Average Salary:** $22,750. **Projected Growth:** 5%. **Occupational Values:** Moral Values; Independence; Activity; Supervision, Human Relations; Company Policies and Practices; Supervision, Technical; Security. **Skills Required:** Operation and Control; Operation Monitoring; Product Inspection; Equipment Maintenance. **Abilities:** Manual Dexterity; Perceptual Speed; Control Precision; Problem Sensitivity; Reaction Time. **Interacting with Others:** Performing Administrative Activities. **Physical Work Conditions:** Using Hands on Objects, Tools, Controls; Indoors; Standing; Hazardous Equipment; Making Repetitive Motions; Distracting Sounds and Noise Levels.

51-9111.00 Packaging and Filling Machine Operators and Tenders

Operate or tend machines to prepare industrial or consumer products for storage or shipment. Includes cannery workers who pack food products. **Education:** Moderate-term O-J-T. **Occupational Type:** Realistic. **Job Zone:** 1. **Average Salary:** $20,060. **Projected Growth:** 12.9%. **Occupational Values:** Moral Values; Independence; Activity; Supervision, Human Relations; Company Policies and Practices; Supervision, Technical. **Skills Required:** Operation and Control; Operation Monitoring; Product Inspection. **Abilities:** Manual Dexterity; Near Vision; Information Ordering; Perceptual Speed; Control Precision; Extent Flexibility; Static Strength. **Interacting with Others:** Monitoring and Controlling Resources. **Physical Work Conditions:** Indoors; Standing; Using Hands on Objects, Tools, Controls; Hazardous Equipment; Distracting Sounds and Noise Levels; Making Repetitive Motions.

51-9121.02 Coating, Painting, and Spraying Machine Operators and Tenders

Operate or tend machines to coat any of a wide variety of items, such as coating food products with sugar, chocolate, or butter, or coating paper and paper products with chemical solutions, wax, or glazes. **Education:** Moderate-term O-J-T. **Occupational Type:** Realistic. **Job Zone:** 1. **Average Salary:** $21,360. **Projected Growth:** 8.7%. **Occupational Values:** Moral Values; Company Policies and Practices; Independence; Supervision, Human Relations; Activity; Supervision, Technical. **Skills Required:** Operation and Control; Operation Monitoring. **Abilities:** Control Precision. **Interacting with Others:** Communicating with Other Workers. **Physical Work Conditions:** Indoors; Using Hands on Objects, Tools, Controls; Standing; Common Protective or Safety Attire; Contaminants; Making Repetitive Motions; Hazardous Conditions.

51-9191.00 Cementing and Gluing Machine Operators and Tenders

Operate or tend cementing and gluing machines to join items for further processing or to form a completed product. Processes include joining veneer sheets into plywood, gluing paper, and joining rubber and rubberized fabric parts, plastic, simulated leather, or other materials. **Education:** Moderate-term O-J-T. **Occupational Type:** Realistic. **Job Zone:** 1. **Average Salary:** $20,720. **Projected Growth:** –15.6%. **Occupational Values:** Moral Values; Supervision, Human Relations; Company Policies and Practices; Activity; Independence; Supervision, Technical. **Skills Required:** Operation and Control; Product Inspection; Operation Monitoring. **Abilities:** Arm-Hand Steadiness; Manual Dexterity; Control Precision; Problem Sensitivity. **Interacting with Others:** Communicating with Other Workers. **Physical Work Conditions:** Indoors; Using Hands on Objects, Tools, Controls; Hazardous Equipment; Common Protective or Safety Attire; Standing; Distracting Sounds and Noise Levels; Contaminants.

08.03.02 Production Work: Equipment Operation, Assorted Materials Processing

51-3011.02 Bakers, Manufacturing

Mix and bake ingredients according to recipes to produce breads, pastries, and other baked goods. Produce goods in large quantities for sale through establishments such as grocery stores. Use high-volume production equipment. **Education:** Moderate-term O-J-T. **Occupational Type:** Realistic. **Job Zone:** 3. **Average Salary:** $22,030. **Projected Growth:** 8.5%. **Occupational Values:** Moral Values; Company Policies and Practices; Supervision, Technical; Supervision, Human Relations; Independence; Activity; Security. **Skills Required:** Operation and Control. **Abilities:** Information Ordering. **Interacting with Others:** Communicating with Other Workers. **Physical Work Conditions:** Indoors; Hazardous Situations; Standing; Using Hands on Objects, Tools, Controls.

51-3022.00 Meat, Poultry, and Fish Cutters and Trimmers

Use hand tools to perform routine cutting and trimming of meat, poultry, and fish. **Education:** Short-term O-J-T. **Occupational Type:** Realistic. **Job Zone:** 1. **Average Salary:** $16,270. **Projected Growth:** 24.2%. **Occupational Values:** Moral Values; Activity; Independence; Supervision, Technical. **Skills Required:** Product Inspection. **Abilities:** Information Ordering; Static Strength; Wrist-Finger Speed; Arm-Hand Steadiness; Manual Dexterity. **Interacting with Others:** Communicating with Other Workers. **Physical Work Conditions:** Indoors; Using Hands on Objects, Tools, Controls; Standing; Making Repetitive Motions; Common Protective or Safety Attire; Contaminants; Hazardous Situations.

51-3023.00 Slaughterers and Meat Packers

Work in slaughtering, meat packing, or wholesale establishments performing precision functions involving the preparation of meat, including specialized slaughtering tasks, cutting standard or premium cuts of meat for marketing, making sausage, or wrapping meats. **Education:** Long-term O-J-T. **Occupational Type:** Realistic. **Job Zone:** 2. **Average Salary:** $18,790. **Projected Growth:** –7.1%. **Occupational Values:** Security; Independence; Activity; Company Policies and Practices; Moral Values. **Skills Required:** Product Inspection. **Abilities:** Manual Dexterity; Static Strength; Information Ordering; Wrist-Finger Speed. **Interacting with Others:** Communicating with Other Workers. **Physical Work Conditions:** Common Protective or Safety Attire; Using Hands on Objects, Tools, Controls; Standing; Indoors; Hazardous Situations; Making Repetitive Motions; Special Uniform.

51-3091.00 Food and Tobacco Roasting, Baking, and Drying Machine Operators and Tenders

Operate or tend food or tobacco roasting, baking, or drying equipment, including hearth ovens, kiln driers, roasters, char kilns, and vacuum drying equipment. **Education:** Moderate-term O-J-T. **Occupational Type:** Realistic. **Job Zone:** 1. **Average Salary:** $21,661. **Projected Growth:** -8.5%. **Occupational Values:** Moral Values; Company Policies and Practices; Independence; Supervision, Human Relations; Activity; Supervision, Technical; Security. **Skills Required:** Product Inspection; Operation and Control; Testing; Operation Monitoring; Installation; Reading Comprehension; Problem Identification. **Abilities:** Control Precision; Manual Dexterity; Information Ordering. **Interacting with Others:** Communicating with Other Workers. **Physical Work Conditions:** Indoors; Using Hands on Objects, Tools, Controls; Standing; Hazardous Situations; Common Protective or Safety Attire; Hazardous Equipment.

51-3093.00 Food Cooking Machine Operators and Tenders

Operate or tend cooking equipment such as steam cooking vats, deep fry cookers, pressure cookers, kettles, and boilers, to prepare food products. **Education:** Moderate-term O-J-T. **Occupational Type:** Realistic. **Job Zone:** 1. **Average Salary:** $21,350. **Projected Growth:** -8.5%. **Occupational Values:** Moral Values; Company Policies and Practices; Supervision, Human Relations; Independence; Security; Activity; Supervision, Technical. **Skills Required:** Operation Monitoring; Operation and Control. **Abilities:** Written Comprehension; Information Ordering. **Interacting with Others:** Communicating with Other Workers. **Physical Work Conditions:** Indoors; Standing; Using Hands on Objects, Tools, Controls; Common Protective or Safety Attire; Hazardous Situations; Very Hot.

51-4051.00 Metal-Refining Furnace Operators and Tenders

Operate or tend furnaces such as gas, oil, coal, electric-arc or electric induction, open-hearth, or oxygen furnaces, to melt and refine metal before casting or to produce specified types of steel. **Education:** Moderate-term O-J-T. **Occupational Type:** Realistic. **Job Zone:** 2. **Average Salary:** $25,870. **Projected Growth:** –5%. **Occupational Values:** Moral Values; Independence; Activity; Supervision, Human Relations; Company Policies and Practices; Supervision, Technical. **Skills Required:** Operation Monitoring; Operation and Control. **Abilities:** Control Precision; Static Strength; Problem Sensitivity. **Interacting with Others:** Communicating with Other Workers. **Physical Work Conditions:** Indoors; Using Hands on Objects, Tools, Controls; Hazardous Equipment; Contaminants; Hazardous Situations; Standing; Very Hot.

51-4052.00 Pourers and Casters, Metal

Operate hand-controlled mechanisms to pour and regulate the flow of molten metal into molds to produce castings or ingots. **Education:** Moderate-term O-J-T. **Occupational Type:** Realistic. **Job Zone:** 1. **Average Salary:** $24,350. **Projected Growth:** 9%. **Occupational Values:** Moral Values; Independence; Company Policies and Practices; Activity; Supervision, Human Relations; Supervision, Technical. **Skills Required:** Operation and Control; Equipment Selection; Operation Monitoring; Product Inspection. **Abilities:** Manual Dexterity; Control Precision; Arm-Hand Steadiness; Information Ordering. **Interacting with Others:** Communicating with Other Workers. **Physical Work Conditions:** Indoors; Using Hands on Objects, Tools, Controls; Common Protective or Safety Attire; Standing; Hazardous Situations; Very Hot; Hazardous Equipment.

51-4191.03 Heaters, Metal and Plastic

Operate or tend heating equipment such as soaking pits, reheating furnaces, and heating and vacuum equipment, to heat metal sheets, blooms, billets, bars, plates, and rods to a specified temperature for rolling or processing, or to heat and cure preformed plastic parts. **Education:** Moderate-term O-J-T. **Occupational Type:** Realistic. **Job Zone:** 2. **Average Salary:** $24,510. **Projected Growth:** -4.1%. **Occupational Values:** Moral Values; Supervision, Human Relations; Company Policies and Practices; Supervision, Technical; Activity; Independence. **Skills Required:** Operation and Control. **Abilities:** Control Precision. **Interacting with Others:** Communicating with Other Workers. **Physical Work Conditions:** Indoors; Using Hands on Objects, Tools, Controls; Standing; Hazardous Equipment; Common Protective or Safety Attire; Hazardous Situations; Hazardous Conditions.

51-6021.02 Pressing Machine Operators and Tenders—Textile, Garment, and Related Materials

Operate or tend pressing machines such as hot-head pressing, steam pressing, automatic pressing, ironing, plunger pressing, and hydraulic pressing machines, to press and shape articles such as leather, fur, and cloth garments, drapes, slipcovers, handkerchiefs, and millinery. **Education:** Moderate-term O-J-T. **Occupational Type:** Realistic. **Job Zone:** 1. **Average Salary:** $15,140. **Projected Growth:** -4%. **Occupational Values:** Moral Values; Independence; Company Policies and Practices; Supervision, Human Relations; Activity; Supervision, Technical; Security. **Skills Required:** Operation and Control; Operation Monitoring; Product Inspection; Equipment Selection; Installation. **Abilities:** Control Precision; Arm-Hand Steadiness; Near Vision; Manual Dexterity; Information Ordering. **Interacting with Others:** Communicating with Other Workers. **Physical Work Conditions:** Indoors; Using Hands on Objects, Tools, Controls; Hazardous Situations; Standing; Making Repetitive Motions; Very Hot; Hazardous Equipment.

51-6061.00 Textile Bleaching and Dyeing Machine Operators and Tenders

Operate or tend machines to bleach, shrink, wash, dye, or finish textiles or synthetic or glass fibers. **Education:** Moderate-term O-J-T. **Occupational Type:** Realistic. **Job Zone:** 1. **Average Salary:** $19,350. **Projected Growth:** -9%. **Occupational Values:** Moral Values; Company Policies and Practices; Supervision, Human Relations; Supervision, Technical; Activity; Independence; Security. **Skills Required:** Operation and Control. **Abilities:** Control Precision; Problem Sensitivity; Wrist-Finger Speed; Visual Color Discrimination. **Interacting with Others:** Communicating with Other Workers. **Physical Work Conditions:** Indoors; Using Hands on Objects, Tools, Controls; Hazardous Equipment; Standing; Contaminants; Making Repetitive Motions; Common Protective or Safety Attire.

51-9011.01 Chemical Equipment Controllers and Operators

Control or operate equipment to control chemical changes or reactions in the processing of industrial or consumer products. Use equipment such as reaction kettles, catalytic converters, continuous or batch treating equipment, saturator tanks, electrolytic cells, reactor vessels, recovery units, and fermentation chambers. **Education:** Moderate-term O-J-T. **Occupational**

Type: Realistic. **Job Zone:** 2. **Average Salary:** $32,740. **Projected Growth:** 11.4%. **Occupational Values:** Moral Values; Company Policies and Practices; Activity; Supervision, Human Relations; Supervision, Technical; Security; Independence. **Skills Required:** Operation and Control; Product Inspection; Science; Testing; Operation Monitoring; Reading Comprehension; Equipment Maintenance. **Abilities:** Information Ordering; Control Precision; Written Comprehension; Near Vision; Oral Expression; Problem Sensitivity. **Interacting with Others:** Coordinating Work and Activities of Others. **Physical Work Conditions:** Indoors; Using Hands on Objects, Tools, Controls; Hazardous Conditions; Common Protective or Safety Attire; Standing; Hazardous Situations.

51-9011.02 Chemical Equipment Tenders

Tend equipment in which a chemical change or reaction takes place in the processing of industrial or consumer products. Use equipment such as devulcanizers, batch stills, fermenting tanks, steam-jacketed kettles, and reactor vessels. **Education:** Moderate-term O-J-T. **Occupational Type:** Realistic. **Job Zone:** 2. **Average Salary:** $28,280. **Projected Growth:** 11.4%. **Occupational Values:** Moral Values; Company Policies and Practices; Activity; Independence; Supervision, Human Relations; Supervision, Technical; Advancement. **Skills Required:** Operation Monitoring; Science; Operation and Control. **Abilities:** Problem Sensitivity; Information Ordering; Control Precision; Reaction Time. **Interacting with Others:** Communicating with Other Workers. **Physical Work Conditions:** Indoors; Hazardous Conditions; Common Protective or Safety Attire; Using Hands on Objects, Tools, Controls; Contaminants; Standing; Hazardous Equipment.

51-9012.00 Separating, Filtering, Clarifying, Precipitating, and Still Machine Setters, Operators, and Tenders

Set up, operate, or tend continuous flow or vat-type equipment filter presses; shaker screens; centrifuges; condenser tubes; precipitating, fermenting, or evaporating tanks; scrubbing towers; or batch stills. Use these machines to extract, sort, or separate liquids, gases, or solids from other materials to recover a refined product. **Education:** Moderate-term O-J-T. **Occupational Type:** Realistic. **Job Zone:** 1. **Average Salary:** $29,600. **Projected Growth:** –7.2%. **Occupational Values:** Moral Values; Company Policies and Practices; Supervision, Human Relations; Supervision, Technical; Activity; Independence; Security. **Skills Required:** Product Inspection; Operation and Control; Operation Monitoring. **Abilities:** Control Precision; Near Vision. **Interacting with Others:** Communicating with Other Workers. **Physical Work Conditions:** Using Hands on Objects, Tools, Controls; Indoors; Standing; Common Protective or Safety Attire; Contaminants; Making Repetitive Motions.

51-9023.00 Mixing and Blending Machine Setters, Operators, and Tenders

Set up, operate, or tend machines to mix or blend materials such as chemicals, tobacco, liquids, color pigments, or explosive ingredients. **Education:** Moderate-term O-J-T. **Occupational Type:** Realistic. **Job Zone:** 1. **Average Salary:** $23,350. **Projected Growth:** 2.8%. **Occupational Values:** Moral Values; Independence; Company Policies and Practices; Supervision, Human Relations; Activity; Supervision, Technical; Security. **Skills Required:** Operation and Control; Operation Monitoring. **Abilities:** Control Precision; Written Expression; Problem Sensitivity. **Interacting with Others:** Communicating with Other Workers. **Physical Work Conditions:** Indoors; Common Protective or Safety Attire; Using Hands on Objects, Tools, Controls; Standing; Hazardous Equipment; Distracting Sounds and Noise Levels; Contaminants.

51-9051.00 Furnace, Kiln, Oven, Drier, and Kettle Operators and Tenders

Operate or tend heating equipment other than basic metal, plastic, or food processing equipment, to anneal glass, dry lumber, cure rubber, remove moisture from materials, or boil soap. **Education:** Moderate-term O-J-T. **Occupational Type:** Realistic. **Job Zone:** 1. **Average Salary:** $25,110. **Projected Growth:** –5.6%. **Occupational Values:** Moral Values; Company Policies and Practices; Security; Independence; Supervision, Human Relations; Activity; Supervision, Technical. **Skills Required:** Reading Comprehension. **Abilities:** Written Comprehension. **Interacting with Others:** Communicating with Other Workers. **Physical Work Conditions:** Indoors; Standing; Using Hands on Objects, Tools, Controls; Hazardous Equipment; Distracting Sounds and Noise Levels; Common Protective or Safety Attire; Very Hot.

51-9141.00 Semiconductor Processors

Perform any or all of the following functions in the manufacture of electronic semiconductors: load semiconductor material into furnace; saw formed ingots into segments; load individual segment into crystal growing chamber and monitor controls; locate crystal axis in ingot using x-ray equipment and saw ingots into wafers; clean, polish, and load wafers into series of special purpose furnaces, chemical baths, and equipment used to form circuitry and change conductive properties. **Education:** Moderate-term O-J-T. **Occupational Type:** Realistic. **Job Zone:** 1. **Average Salary:** $24,810. **Projected Growth:** 45.2%. **Occupational Values:** Moral Values; Independence; Company Policies and Practices; Supervision, Human Relations; Activity; Working Conditions; Security. **Skills Required:** Operation and Control; Equipment Selection; Operation Monitoring; Science; Product Inspection. **Abilities:** Control Precision; Near Vision; Information Ordering. **Interacting with Others:** Performing Administrative Activities. **Physical Work Conditions:** Indoors; Using Hands on Objects, Tools, Controls; Standing; Common Protective or Safety Attire; Making Repetitive Motions.

51-9192.00 Cleaning, Washing, and Metal Pickling Equipment Operators and Tenders

Operate or tend machines to wash or clean products such as barrels or kegs, glass items, tin plate, food, pulp, coal, plastic, or rubber, to remove impurities. **Education:** Moderate-term O-J-T. **Occupational Type:** Realistic. **Job Zone:** 1. **Average Salary:** $20,910. **Projected Growth:** 15.2%. **Occupational Values:** Moral Values; Independence; Company Policies and Practices; Supervision, Human Relations; Activity; Supervision, Technical. **Skills Required:** Operation and Control; Operation Monitoring. **Abilities:** Control Precision. **Interacting with Others:** Performing Administrative Activities. **Physical Work Conditions:** Indoors; Standing; Using Hands on Objects, Tools, Controls; Common Protective or Safety Attire; Hazardous Equipment; Making Repetitive Motions; Distracting Sounds and Noise Levels.

51-9193.00 Cooling and Freezing Equipment Operators and Tenders

Operate or tend equipment such as cooling and freezing units, refrigerators, batch freezers, and freezing tunnels, to cool or freeze products, food, blood plasma, and chemicals. **Education:** Moderate-term O-J-T. **Occupational Type:** Realistic. **Job Zone:** 1. **Average Salary:** $19,400. **Projected Growth:** 15.2%. **Occupational Values:** Moral Values; Independence; Company Policies and Practices; Security; Supervision, Human Relations; Supervision, Technical; Activity. **Skills Required:** Operation and Control; Repairing; Operation Monitoring; Equipment Maintenance; Product Inspection; Science; Testing. **Abilities:** Information Ordering; Control Precision; Finger Dexterity; Near Vision; Manual Dexterity; Wrist-Finger Speed. **Interacting with Others:** Communicating with Other Workers. **Physical Work Conditions:** Indoors; Using Hands on Objects, Tools, Controls; Standing; Very Hot; Hazardous Equipment.

51-9198.01 Production Laborers

Perform variety of routine tasks to assist in production activities. **Education:** Short-term O-J-T. **Occupational Type:** Realistic. **Job Zone:** 1. **Average Salary:** $17,860. **Projected Growth:** 13.4%. **Occupational Values:** Moral Values; Activity. **Skills Required:** Product Inspection. **Abilities:** Manual Dexterity; Static Strength; Extent Flexibility; Trunk Strength; Dynamic Strength; Explosive Strength; Multilimb Coordination. **Interacting with Others:** Assisting and Caring for Others. **Physical Work Conditions:** Using Hands on Objects, Tools, Controls; Standing; Indoors; Making Repetitive Motions; Bending or Twisting the Body; Hazardous Equipment; Common Protective or Safety Attire.

51-9198.02 Production Helpers

Perform variety of tasks requiring limited knowledge of production processes in support of skilled production workers. **Education:** Short-term O-J-T. **Occupational Type:** Realistic. **Job Zone:** 1. **Average Salary:** $17,860. **Projected Growth:** 13.4%. **Occupational Values:** Moral Values; Activity; Supervision, Human Relations; Supervision, Technical. **Skills Required:** Equipment Maintenance. **Abilities:** Manual Dexterity; Control Precision. **Interacting with Others:** Communicating with Other Workers. **Physical Work Conditions:** Using Hands on Objects, Tools, Controls; Indoors; Standing; Hazardous Equipment; Hazardous Situations; Common Protective or Safety Attire; Walking or Running.

08.03.03 Production Work: Equipment Operation, Welding, Brazing, and Soldering

51-2041.01 Metal Fabricators, Structural Metal Products

Fabricate and assemble structural metal products such as frameworks or shells for machinery, ovens, tanks, and stacks, and metal parts for buildings and bridges, according to job order or blueprints. **Education:** Moderate-term O-J-T. **Occupational Type:** Realistic. **Job Zone:** 4. **Average Salary:** $24,070. **Projected Growth:** 7.5%. **Occupational Values:** Moral Values; Company Policies and Practices; Activity; Supervision, Human Relations; Independence; Security; Supervision, Technical. **Skills Required:** Operation and Control; Mathematics; Product Inspection; Equipment Selection. **Abilities:** Manual Dexterity; Control Precision. **Interacting with Others:** Communicating with Other Workers. **Physical Work Conditions:** Indoors; Using Hands on Objects, Tools, Controls; Standing; Hazardous Equipment; Common Protective or Safety Attire.

51-2041.02 Fitters, Structural Metal—Precision

Lay out, position, align, and fit together fabricated parts of structural metal products preparatory to welding or riveting. **Education:** Work experience in a related occupation. **Occupational Type:** Realistic. **Job Zone:** 4. **Average Salary:** $26,180. **Projected Growth:** –13%. **Occupational Values:** Moral Values; Company Policies and Practices; Independence; Activity; Supervision, Human Relations; Supervision, Technical. **Skills Required:** Mathematics; Equipment Selection. **Abilities:** Deductive Reasoning. **Interacting with Others:** Communicating with Other Workers. **Physical Work Conditions:** Using Hands on Objects, Tools, Controls; Common Protective or Safety Attire; Hazardous Equipment; Hazardous Situations; Distracting Sounds and Noise Levels; Standing; Bending or Twisting the Body.

51-4121.01 Welders, Production

Assemble and weld metal parts on production line, using welding equipment. Requires only limited knowledge of welding techniques. **Education:** Postsecondary vocational training. **Occupational Type:** Realistic. **Job Zone:** 1. **Average Salary:** $25,810. **Projected Growth:** 8.3%. **Occupational Values:** Moral Values; Activity; Company Policies and Practices; Supervision, Human Relations; Security; Independence; Supervision, Technical. **Skills Required:** Operation and Control; Product Inspection; Equipment Selection. **Abilities:** Arm-Hand Steadiness; Near Vision; Manual Dexterity; Control Precision; Dynamic Strength; Trunk Strength. **Interacting with Others:** Communicating with Other Workers. **Physical Work Conditions:** Indoors; Using Hands on Objects, Tools, Controls; Standing; Common Protective or Safety Attire; Hazardous Equipment; Distracting Sounds and Noise Levels; Contaminants.

51-4121.02 Welders and Cutters

Use hand welding and flame-cutting equipment to weld together metal components and parts or to cut, trim, or scarf metal objects to dimensions, as specified by layouts, work orders, or blueprints. **Education:** Postsecondary vocational training. **Occupational Type:** Realistic. **Job Zone:** 2. **Average Salary:** $25,810. **Projected Growth:** 8.3%. **Occupational Values:** Moral Values; Activity; Company Policies and Practices; Independence; Supervision, Human Relations; Security. **Skills Required:** Product Inspection; Equipment Maintenance; Operation and Control. **Abilities:** Arm-Hand Steadiness; Manual Dexterity; Control Precision; Near Vision. **Interacting with Others:** Communicating with Other Workers. **Physical Work Conditions:** Using Hands on Objects, Tools, Controls; Indoors; Common Protective or Safety Attire; Hazardous Equipment; Hazardous Situations; Standing; Contaminants.

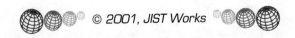

51-4121.03 Welder-Fitters

Lay out, fit, and fabricate metal components to assemble structural forms such as machinery frames, bridge parts, and pressure vessels, using knowledge of welding techniques, metallurgy, and engineering requirements. Includes experimental welders who analyze engineering drawings and specifications to plan welding operations where procedural information is unavailable. **Education:** Postsecondary vocational training. **Occupational Type:** Realistic. **Job Zone:** 4. **Average Salary:** $25,810. **Projected Growth:** 8.3%. **Occupational Values:** Moral Values; Activity; Company Policies and Practices; Supervision, Human Relations; Independence; Security; Compensation. **Skills Required:** Product Inspection; Equipment Selection. **Abilities:** Arm-Hand Steadiness; Written Comprehension; Manual Dexterity. **Interacting with Others:** Communicating with Other Workers. **Physical Work Conditions:** Using Hands on Objects, Tools, Controls; Indoors; Common Protective or Safety Attire; Hazardous Equipment; Hazardous Situations; Making Repetitive Motions; Standing.

51-4121.04 Solderers

Solder together components to assemble fabricated metal products, using soldering iron. **Education:** Short-term O-J-T. **Occupational Type:** Realistic. **Job Zone:** 1. **Average Salary:** $17,600. **Projected Growth:** 14.4%. **Occupational Values:** Moral Values; Activity; Company Policies and Practices; Supervision, Human Relations; Independence; Security. **Skills Required:** Equipment Selection; Product Inspection; Operation and Control; Monitoring. **Abilities:** Arm-Hand Steadiness; Near Vision; Manual Dexterity; Wrist-Finger Speed; Finger Dexterity. **Interacting with Others:** Monitoring and Controlling Resources. **Physical Work Conditions:** Using Hands on Objects, Tools, Controls; Indoors; Common Protective or Safety Attire; Standing; Making Repetitive Motions; Contaminants; Hazardous Equipment.

51-4121.05 Brazers

Braze together components to assemble fabricated metal parts, using torch or welding machine and flux. **Education:** Short-term O-J-T. **Occupational Type:** Realistic. **Job Zone:** 2. **Average Salary:** $17,600. **Projected Growth:** 14.4%. **Occupational Values:** Moral Values; Activity; Company Policies and Practices; Supervision, Human Relations; Independence; Security. **Skills Required:** Operation and Control; Product Inspection. **Abilities:** Near Vision. **Interacting with Others:** Communicating with Other Workers. **Physical Work Conditions:** Using Hands on Objects, Tools, Controls; Common Protective or Safety Attire; Indoors; Standing; Hazardous Conditions; Hazardous Equipment; Making Repetitive Motions.

51-4122.02 Welding Machine Operators and Tenders

Operate or tend welding machines that join or bond together components to fabricate metal products and assemblies according to specifications and blueprints. **Education:** Moderate-term O-J-T. **Occupational Type:** Realistic. **Job Zone:** 2. **Average Salary:** $24,400. **Projected Growth:** 5.4%. **Occupational Values:** Moral Values; Independence; Company Policies and Practices; Supervision, Human Relations; Activity. **Skills Required:** Operation and Control; Operation Monitoring; Product Inspection. **Abilities:** Control Precision; Manual Dexterity. **Interacting with Others:** Coordinating Work and Activities of Others. **Physical Work Conditions:** Indoors; Using Hands on Objects, Tools, Controls; Hazardous Equipment; Standing; Common Protective or Safety Attire; Distracting Sounds and Noise Levels; Contaminants.

51-4122.04 Soldering and Brazing Machine Operators and Tenders

Operate or tend soldering and brazing machines that braze, solder, or spot weld fabricated metal products or components as specified by work orders, blueprints, and layout specifications. **Education:** Moderate-term O-J-T. **Occupational Type:** Realistic. **Job Zone:** 1. **Average Salary:** $20,490. **Projected Growth:** 8.2%. **Occupational Values:** Moral Values; Independence; Company Policies and Practices; Supervision, Human Relations; Activity. **Skills Required:** Operation Monitoring; Product Inspection; Operation and Control; Equipment Selection; Equipment Maintenance. **Abilities:** Control Precision; Near Vision. **Interacting with Others:** Performing Administrative Activities. **Physical Work Conditions:** Indoors; Using Hands on Objects, Tools, Controls; Common Protective or Safety Attire; Standing; Hazardous Equipment.

08.03.04 Production Work: Plating and Coating

51-4193.01 Electrolytic Plating and Coating Machine Setters and Set-Up Operators, Metal and Plastic

Set up, or set up and operate, electrolytic plating or coating machines such as continuous multistrand electrogalvanizing machines, to coat metal or plastic products electrolytically with chromium, copper, cadmium, or other metal to provide protective or decorative surfaces or to build up worn surfaces. **Education:** Moderate-term O-J-T. **Occupational Type:** Realistic. **Job Zone:** 3. **Average Salary:** $21,560. **Projected Growth:** 9.6%. **Occupational Values:** Moral Values; Independence; Activity; Company Policies and Practices; Supervision, Human Relations; Supervision, Technical. **Skills Required:** Operation and Control; Operation Monitoring; Product Inspection. **Abilities:** Control Precision. **Interacting with Others:** Communicating with Other Workers. **Physical Work Conditions:** Indoors; Using Hands on Objects, Tools, Controls; Common Protective or Safety Attire; Standing.

51-4193.02 Electrolytic Plating and Coating Machine Operators and Tenders, Metal and Plastic

Operate or tend electrolytic plating or coating machines such as zinc-plating machines and anodizing machines, to coat metal or plastic products electrolytically with chromium, zinc, copper, cadmium, or other metal to provide protective or decorative surfaces or to build up worn surfaces. **Education:** Moderate-term O-J-T. **Occupational Type:** Realistic. **Job Zone:** 2. **Average Salary:** $21,060. **Projected Growth:** 9.6%. **Occupational Values:** Moral Values; Independence; Activity; Supervision, Human Relations; Company Policies and Practices; Supervision, Technical. **Skills Required:** Operation and Control. **Abilities:** Control Precision. **Interacting with Others:** Communicating with Other Workers. **Physical Work Conditions:** Indoors; Using Hands on Objects, Tools, Controls; Common Protective or Safety Attire; Hazardous Conditions; Standing.

51-4193.03 Nonelectrolytic Plating and Coating Machine Setters and Set-Up Operators, Metal and Plastic

Set up, or set up and operate, nonelectrolytic plating or coating machines such as hot-dip lines and metal-spraying machines, to coat metal or plastic products or parts with metal. **Education:** Moderate-term O-J-T. **Occupational Type:** Realistic. **Job Zone:** 3. **Average Salary:** $21,300. **Projected Growth:** 11.9%. **Occupational Values:** Moral Values; Independence; Company Policies and Practices; Activity; Supervision, Human Relations; Supervision, Technical. **Skills Required:** Operation and Control; Product Inspection; Operation Monitoring. **Abilities:** Control Precision; Written Comprehension; Manual Dexterity; Visual Color Discrimination. **Interacting with Others:** Communicating with Other Workers. **Physical Work Conditions:** Using Hands on Objects, Tools, Controls; Indoors; Common Protective or Safety Attire; Standing; Hazardous Equipment; Hazardous Situations.

51-4193.04 Nonelectrolytic Plating and Coating Machine Operators and Tenders, Metal and Plastic

Operate or tend nonelectrolytic plating or coating machines such as metal-spraying machines and vacuum metalizing machines, to coat metal or plastic products or parts with metal. **Education:** Moderate-term O-J-T. **Occupational Type:** Realistic. **Job Zone:** 1. **Average Salary:** $21,500. **Projected Growth:** 11.9%. **Occupational Values:** Moral Values; Independence; Activity; Company Policies and Practices; Supervision, Human Relations; Supervision, Technical. **Skills Required:** Operation Monitoring. **Abilities:** Control Precision. **Interacting with Others:** Communicating with Other Workers. **Physical Work Conditions:** Indoors; Using Hands on Objects, Tools, Controls; Standing; Common Protective or Safety Attire.

08.03.05 Production Work: Printing and Reproduction

51-5011.02 Bindery Machine Operators and Tenders

Operate or tend binding machines that round, back, case, line stitch, press, fold, trim, or perform other binding operations on books and related articles. **Education:** Moderate-term O-J-T. **Occupational Type:** Realistic. **Job Zone:** 1. **Average Salary:** $19,290. **Projected Growth:** 11.5%. **Occupational Values:** Moral Values; Independence; Activity; Company Policies and Practices; Supervision, Human Relations; Supervision, Technical; Security. **Skills Required:** Product Inspection. **Abilities:** Manual Dexterity; Control Precision. **Interacting with Others:** Communicating with Other Workers. **Physical Work Conditions:** Indoors; Using Hands on Objects, Tools, Controls; Standing; Hazardous Equipment; Making Repetitive Motions; Distracting Sounds and Noise Levels; Contaminants.

51-5021.00 Job Printers

Set type according to copy; operate press to print job; order and read proof for errors and clarity of impression; and correct imperfections. Job printers are often found in small establishments where work combines several job skills. **Education:** Long-term O-J-T. **Occupational Type:** Realistic. **Job Zone:** 5. **Average Salary:** $24,100. **Projected Growth:** 4.3%. **Occupational Values:** Moral Values; Independence; Activity; Working Conditions; Security; Autonomy. **Skills Required:** Product Inspection; Monitoring; Operation and Control; Equipment Selection; Reading Comprehension. **Abilities:** Finger Dexterity; Manual Dexterity; Near Vision; Control Precision; Wrist-Finger Speed. **Interacting with Others:** Communicating with Other Workers. **Physical Work Conditions:** Indoors; Hazardous Equipment; Using Hands on Objects, Tools, Controls; Contaminants; Standing; Hazardous Conditions; Common Protective or Safety Attire.

51-5022.01 Hand Compositors and Typesetters

Set up and arrange type by hand. Assemble and lock setup of type, cuts, and headings. Pull proofs. **Education:** Long-term O-J-T. **Occupational Type:** Realistic. **Job Zone:** 4. **Average Salary:** $22,560. **Projected Growth:** –18.9%. **Occupational Values:** Moral Values; Independence; Supervision, Human Relations; Working Conditions; Supervision, Technical; Activity; Security. **Skills Required:** Product Inspection; Information Organization; Monitoring; Solution Appraisal. **Abilities:** Finger Dexterity; Near Vision. **Interacting with Others:** Communicating with Other Workers. **Physical Work Conditions:** Indoors; Using Hands on Objects, Tools, Controls; Sitting; Standing.

51-5022.05 Scanner Operators

Operate electronic or computerized scanning equipment to produce and screen film separations of photographs or art for use in producing lithographic printing plates. Evaluate and correct for deficiencies in the film. **Education:** Long-term O-J-T. **Occupational Type:** Realistic. **Job Zone:** 4. **Average Salary:** $33,560. **Projected Growth:** –31.4%. **Occupational Values:** Moral Values; Independence; Autonomy; Security; Working Conditions. **Skills Required:** Product Inspection; Testing; Operation and Control; Monitoring. **Abilities:** Near Vision. **Interacting with Others:** Communicating with Other Workers. **Physical Work Conditions:** Using Hands on Objects, Tools, Controls; Indoors; Sitting.

51-5022.06 Strippers

Cut and arrange film into flats (layout sheets resembling a film negative of text in its final form) which are used to make plates. Prepare separate flat for each color. **Education:** Long-term O-J-T. **Occupational Type:** Realistic. **Job Zone:** 4. **Average Salary:** $32,300. **Projected Growth:** –33%. **Occupational Values:** Moral Values; Independence; Responsibility; Working Conditions; Autonomy; Activity; Compensation. **Skills Required:** Product Inspection. **Abilities:** Near Vision; Visualization; Visual Color Discrimination; Arm-Hand Steadiness; Finger Dexterity. **Interacting with Others:** Communicating with Other Workers. **Physical Work Conditions:** Indoors; Sitting; Using Hands on Objects, Tools, Controls.

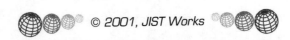

51-5022.07 Platemakers

Produce printing plates by exposing sensitized metal sheets to special light through a photographic negative. May operate machines that process plates automatically. **Education:** Long-term O-J-T. **Occupational Type:** Realistic. **Job Zone:** 3. **Average Salary:** $28,600. **Projected Growth:** –5.2%. **Occupational Values:** Moral Values; Independence; Responsibility; Autonomy; Working Conditions; Creativity; Activity. **Skills Required:** Product Inspection; Testing; Operation and Control. **Abilities:** Arm-Hand Steadiness. **Interacting with Others:** Communicating with Other Workers. **Physical Work Conditions:** Using Hands on Objects, Tools, Controls; Indoors; Sitting; Standing.

51-5022.10 Electrotypers and Stereotypers

Fabricate and finish electrotype and stereotype printing plates. **Education:** Long-term O-J-T. **Occupational Type:** Realistic. **Job Zone:** 5. **Average Salary:** $24,510. **Projected Growth:** 0.2%. **Occupational Values:** Moral Values; Independence; Supervision, Human Relations; Supervision, Technical; Activity; Company Policies and Practices; Working Conditions. **Skills Required:** Operation and Control. **Abilities:** Arm-Hand Steadiness; Near Vision; Manual Dexterity. **Interacting with Others:** Coordinating Work and Activities of Others. **Physical Work Conditions:** Using Hands on Objects, Tools, Controls; Indoors; Hazardous Equipment; Common Protective or Safety Attire; Making Repetitive Motions; Standing; Sitting.

51-5022.11 Plate Finishers

Set up and operate equipment to trim and mount electrotype or stereotype plates. **Education:** Moderate-term O-J-T. **Occupational Type:** Realistic. **Job Zone:** 5. **Average Salary:** $23,736. **Projected Growth:** 4.1%. **Occupational Values:** Moral Values; Independence; Activity; Supervision, Human Relations; Company Policies and Practices; Supervision, Technical. **Skills Required:** Product Inspection; Operation and Control. **Abilities:** Manual Dexterity; Near Vision; Arm-Hand Steadiness. **Interacting with Others:** Communicating with Other Workers. **Physical Work Conditions:** Using Hands on Objects, Tools, Controls; Indoors; Standing; Hazardous Equipment; Making Repetitive Motions; Common Protective or Safety Attire; Distracting Sounds and Noise Levels.

51-5022.13 Photoengraving and Lithographing Machine Operators and Tenders

Operate or tend photoengraving and lithographing equipment such as plate graining, pantograph, roll varnishing, and routing machines. **Education:** Moderate-term O-J-T. **Occupational Type:** Realistic. **Job Zone:** 2. **Average Salary:** $23,960. **Projected Growth:** –14.7%. **Occupational Values:** Moral Values; Independence; Activity; Supervision, Human Relations; Company Policies and Practices; Supervision, Technical; Security. **Skills Required:** Product Inspection. **Abilities:** Information Ordering. **Interacting with Others:** Monitoring and Controlling Resources. **Physical Work Conditions:** Indoors; Using Hands on Objects, Tools, Controls; Sitting; Standing.

51-5023.01 Precision Printing Workers

Perform variety of precision printing activities, such as duplication of microfilm and reproduction of graphic arts materials. **Education:** Long-term O-J-T. **Occupational Type:** Realistic. **Job Zone:** 2. **Average Salary:** $29,386. **Projected Growth:** 0.2%. **Occupational Values:** Moral Values; Independence; Supervision, Technical; Security; Company Policies and Practices; Ability Utilization; Achievement. **Skills Required:** Product Inspection; Operation and Control. **Abilities:** Visual Color Discrimination; Information Ordering; Near Vision; Visualization. **Interacting with Others:** Communicating with Persons Outside Organization. **Physical Work Conditions:** Indoors; Using Hands on Objects, Tools, Controls; Standing; Making Repetitive Motions.

51-5023.02 Offset Lithographic Press Setters and Set-Up Operators

Set up, or set up and operate, offset printing press, either sheet or web fed, to print single and multicolor copy from lithographic plates. Examine job order to determine press operating time, quantity to be printed, and stock specifications. **Education:** Moderate-term O-J-T. **Occupational Type:** Realistic. **Job Zone:** 5. **Average Salary:** $31,000. **Projected Growth:** –14.7%. **Occupational Values:** Moral Values; Independence; Activity; Supervision, Human Relations; Company Policies and Practices; Supervision, Technical; Security. **Skills Required:** Operation and Control; Operation Monitoring. **Abilities:** Written Comprehension; Control Precision. **Interacting with Others:** Coordinating Work and Activities of Others. **Physical Work Conditions:** Indoors; Standing; Using Hands on Objects, Tools, Controls.

51-5023.03 Letterpress Setters and Set-Up Operators

Set up, or set up and operate, direct relief letterpresses, either sheet or roll (web) fed, to produce single or multicolor printed material such as newspapers, books, and periodicals. **Education:** Moderate-term O-J-T. **Occupational Type:** Realistic. **Job Zone:** 3. **Average Salary:** $28,620. **Projected Growth:** –18.2%. **Occupational Values:** Moral Values; Independence; Activity; Supervision, Human Relations; Company Policies and Practices; Supervision, Technical; Achievement. **Skills Required:** Operation and Control; Operation Monitoring; Product Inspection; Installation. **Abilities:** Near Vision. **Interacting with Others:** Communicating with Other Workers. **Physical Work Conditions:** Indoors; Using Hands on Objects, Tools, Controls; Standing; Hazardous Equipment; Common Protective or Safety Attire; Making Repetitive Motions.

51-5023.04 Design Printing Machine Setters and Set-Up Operators

Set up, or set up and operate, machines to print designs on materials. **Education:** Moderate-term O-J-T. **Occupational Type:** Realistic. **Job Zone:** 3. **Average Salary:** $18,880. **Projected Growth:** 8.3%. **Occupational Values:** Moral Values; Independence; Company Policies and Practices; Supervision, Human Relations; Activity; Supervision, Technical. **Skills Required:** Operation and Control; Operation Monitoring. **Abilities:** Visual Color Discrimination; Control Precision. **Interacting with Others:** Performing Administrative Activities. **Physical Work Conditions:** Indoors; Using Hands on Objects, Tools, Controls; Hazardous Equipment; Standing; Making Repetitive Motions.

51-5023.05 Marking and Identification Printing Machine Setters and Set-Up Operators

Set up, or set up and operate, machines to print trademarks, labels, or multicolored identification symbols on materials. **Education:** Moderate-term O-J-T. **Occupational Type:** Realistic. **Job Zone:** 1. **Average Salary:** $25,894. **Projected Growth:**

8.3%. **Occupational Values:** Moral Values; Independence; Company Policies and Practices; Supervision, Human Relations; Activity; Supervision, Technical. **Skills Required:** Operation and Control; Product Inspection. **Abilities:** Visual Color Discrimination. **Interacting with Others:** Communicating with Other Workers. **Physical Work Conditions:** Using Hands on Objects, Tools, Controls; Indoors; Standing; Making Repetitive Motions.

51-5023.07 Embossing Machine Set-Up Operators

Set up and operate embossing machines. **Education:** Moderate-term O-J-T. **Occupational Type:** Realistic. **Job Zone:** 3. **Average Salary:** $24,812. **Projected Growth:** 4.1%. **Occupational Values:** Moral Values; Independence; Activity; Supervision, Human Relations; Company Policies and Practices; Supervision, Technical. **Skills Required:** Operation and Control. **Abilities:** Manual Dexterity. **Interacting with Others:** Communicating with Other Workers. **Physical Work Conditions:** Indoors; Using Hands on Objects, Tools, Controls; Standing; Common Protective or Safety Attire; Hazardous Equipment; Making Repetitive Motions.

51-5023.08 Engraver Set-Up Operators

Set up and operate machines to transfer printing designs. **Education:** Moderate-term O-J-T. **Occupational Type:** Realistic. **Job Zone:** 4. **Average Salary:** $26,327. **Projected Growth:** 4.1%. **Occupational Values:** Moral Values; Independence; Activity; Supervision, Human Relations; Company Policies and Practices; Supervision, Technical. **Skills Required:** Operation and Control. **Abilities:** Arm-Hand Steadiness; Control Precision; Manual Dexterity; Information Ordering; Near Vision. **Interacting with Others:** Performing Administrative Activities. **Physical Work Conditions:** Indoors; Using Hands on Objects, Tools, Controls; Hazardous Equipment; Standing; Hazardous Situations.

51-5023.09 Printing Press Machine Operators and Tenders

Operate or tend various types of printing machines such as offset lithographic presses, letter or letterset presses, flexographic or gravure presses, to produce print on paper or other materials such as plastic, cloth, or rubber. **Education:** Moderate-term O-J-T. **Occupational Type:** Realistic. **Job Zone:** 1. **Average Salary:** $26,020. **Projected Growth:** 8.3%. **Occupational Values:** Moral Values; Company Policies and Practices; Activity; Compensation; Supervision, Human Relations; Achievement; Independence. **Skills Required:** Operation and Control; Product Inspection; Operation Monitoring; Equipment Selection. **Abilities:** Control Precision; Near Vision; Visual Color Discrimination; Oral Comprehension; Manual Dexterity; Visualization. **Interacting with Others:** Coordinating Work and Activities of Others. **Physical Work Conditions:** Indoors; Using Hands on Objects, Tools, Controls; Common Protective or Safety Attire; Standing.

51-9131.01 Photographic Retouchers and Restorers

Retouch or restore photographic negatives and prints to accentuate desirable features of subject, using pencils, watercolors, or airbrushes. **Education:** Long-term O-J-T. **Occupational Type:** Artistic. **Job Zone:** 3. **Average Salary:** $21,620. **Projected Growth:** 7%. **Occupational Values:** Moral Values; Independence; Working Conditions; Autonomy; Achievement; Ability Utilization; Creativity. **Skills Required:** Product Inspection. **Abilities:** Arm-Hand Steadiness; Finger Dexterity; Visual Color Discrimination; Near Vision; Visualization; Manual Dexterity. **Interacting with Others:** Communicating with Other Workers. **Physical Work Conditions:** Using Hands on Objects, Tools, Controls; Indoors; Sitting.

51-9131.02 Photographic Reproduction Technicians

Duplicate materials to produce prints on sensitized paper, cloth, or film, using photographic equipment. **Education:** Long-term O-J-T. **Occupational Type:** Realistic. **Job Zone:** 3. **Average Salary:** $21,620. **Projected Growth:** 7%. **Occupational Values:** Independence; Moral Values; Working Conditions; Autonomy; Supervision, Technical; Supervision, Human Relations; Achievement. **Skills Required:** Equipment Selection; Mathematics; Product Inspection. **Abilities:** Information Ordering; Visual Color Discrimination; Near Vision; Arm-Hand Steadiness; Written Comprehension. **Interacting with Others:** Communicating with Other Workers. **Physical Work Conditions:** Indoors; Using Hands on Objects, Tools, Controls; Hazardous Conditions; Standing; Extremely Bright or Inadequate Lighting; Sitting.

51-9131.03 Photographic Hand Developers

Develop exposed photographic film or sensitized paper in series of chemical and water baths to produce negative or positive prints. **Education:** Long-term O-J-T. **Occupational Type:** Realistic. **Job Zone:** 2. **Average Salary:** $21,620. **Projected Growth:** 7%. **Occupational Values:** Moral Values; Independence; Security; Working Conditions; Supervision, Technical. **Skills Required:** Mathematics. **Abilities:** Visual Color Discrimination; Information Ordering. **Interacting with Others:** Communicating with Other Workers. **Physical Work Conditions:** Indoors; Using Hands on Objects, Tools, Controls; Standing; Hazardous Conditions; Extremely Bright or Inadequate Lighting; Contaminants.

51-9131.04 Film Laboratory Technicians

Evaluate motion picture film to determine characteristics such as sensitivity to light, density, and exposure time required for printing. **Education:** Long-term O-J-T. **Occupational Type:** Realistic. **Job Zone:** 4. **Average Salary:** $21,620. **Projected Growth:** 7%. **Occupational Values:** Moral Values; Independence; Working Conditions; Supervision, Technical; Autonomy; Security; Supervision, Human Relations. **Skills Required:** Product Inspection. **Abilities:** Near Vision; Number Facility; Information Ordering. **Interacting with Others:** Interpreting Meaning of Information to Others. **Physical Work Conditions:** Indoors; Using Hands on Objects, Tools, Controls; Sitting.

51-9132.00 Photographic Processing Machine Operators

Operate photographic processing machines such as photographic printing machines, film developing machines, and mounting presses. **Education:** Short-term O-J-T. **Occupational Type:** Realistic. **Job Zone:** 2. **Average Salary:** $17,800. **Projected Growth:** –11.4%. **Occupational Values:** Moral Values; Independence; Working Conditions; Supervision, Human Relations; Company Policies and Practices; Activity; Supervision, Technical. **Skills Required:** Operation and Control; Product Inspection. **Abilities:** Near Vision. **Interacting with Others:** Performing Administrative Activities. **Physical Work Conditions:** Using Hands on Objects, Tools, Controls; Standing; Contaminants; Indoors; Hazardous Conditions.

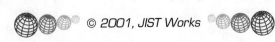

08.03.06 Production Work: Hands-on Work, Assorted Materials

45-2041.00 Graders and Sorters, Agricultural Products

Grade, sort, or classify unprocessed food and other agricultural products by size, weight, color, or condition. **Education:** Short-term O-J-T. **Occupational Type:** Realistic. **Job Zone:** 1. **Average Salary:** $13,400. **Projected Growth:** 1.7%. **Occupational Values:** Moral Values; Independence; Supervision, Human Relations; Company Policies and Practices; Activity; Supervision, Technical; Responsibility. **Skills Required:** Product Inspection. **Abilities:** Category Flexibility. **Interacting with Others:** Monitoring and Controlling Resources. **Physical Work Conditions:** Using Hands on Objects, Tools, Controls; Indoors; Making Repetitive Motions; Standing.

51-2021.00 Coil Winders, Tapers, and Finishers

Wind wire coils used in electrical components such as resistors and transformers and in electrical equipment and instruments such as field cores, bobbins, armature cores, electrical motors, generators, and control equipment. **Education:** Short-term O-J-T. **Occupational Type:** Realistic. **Job Zone:** 2. **Average Salary:** $18,660. **Projected Growth:** 2.5%. **Occupational Values:** Moral Values; Company Policies and Practices; Activity; Supervision, Human Relations; Independence; Supervision, Technical; Security. **Skills Required:** Operation Monitoring; Product Inspection; Operation and Control; Equipment Maintenance. **Abilities:** Manual Dexterity; Control Precision. **Interacting with Others:** Communicating with Other Workers. **Physical Work Conditions:** Indoors; Using Hands on Objects, Tools, Controls; Standing; Hazardous Equipment; Common Protective or Safety Attire; Distracting Sounds and Noise Levels.

51-2091.00 Fiberglass Laminators and Fabricators

Laminate layers of fiberglass on molds to form boat decks and hulls, bodies for golf carts, automobiles, or other products. No other data currently available.

51-2092.00 Team Assemblers

Work as part of a team having responsibility for assembling an entire product or component of a product. Team assemblers can perform all tasks conducted by the team in the assembly process and rotate through all or most of them rather than being assigned to a specific task on a permanent basis. May participate in making management decisions affecting the work. Includes team leaders who work as part of the team. No other data currently available.

51-3092.00 Food Batchmakers

Set up and operate equipment that mixes or blends ingredients used in the manufacturing of food products. Includes candy makers and cheese makers. **Education:** Long-term O-J-T. **Occupational Type:** Realistic. **Job Zone:** 3. **Average Salary:** $23,060. **Projected Growth:** 8.5%. **Occupational Values:** Moral Values; Company Policies and Practices; Supervision, Technical; Security; Supervision, Human Relations; Activity; Authority. **Skills Required:** Product Inspection; Mathematics. **Abilities:** Information Ordering; Near Vision; Manual Dexterity. **Interacting with Others:** Monitoring and Controlling Resources. **Physical Work Conditions:** Indoors; Standing; Using Hands on Objects, Tools, Controls; Making Repetitive Motions.

51-6051.00 Sewers, Hand

Sew, join, reinforce, or finish, usually with needle and thread, a variety of manufactured items. Includes weavers and stitchers. **Education:** Short-term O-J-T. **Occupational Type:** Realistic. **Job Zone:** 1. **Average Salary:** $15,520. **Projected Growth:** -14.8%. **Occupational Values:** Moral Values; Independence; Activity; Supervision, Human Relations. **Skills Required:** Equipment Selection. **Abilities:** Arm-Hand Steadiness; Near Vision; Wrist-Finger Speed; Finger Dexterity; Visual Color Discrimination. **Interacting with Others:** Communicating with Other Workers. **Physical Work Conditions:** Indoors; Using Hands on Objects, Tools, Controls; Making Repetitive Motions; Sitting; Common Protective or Safety Attire.

51-6092.00 Fabric and Apparel Patternmakers

Draw and construct sets of precision master fabric patterns or layouts. May also mark and cut fabrics and apparel. **Education:** Long-term O-J-T. **Occupational Type:** Realistic. **Job Zone:** 2. **Average Salary:** $21,580. **Projected Growth:** –3.8%. **Occupational Values:** Moral Values; Independence; Working Conditions; Security; Achievement; Company Policies and Practices; Supervision, Human Relations. **Skills Required:** Information Organization; Operations Analysis; Monitoring. **Abilities:** Arm-Hand Steadiness; Near Vision; Wrist-Finger Speed; Visualization; Information Ordering; Number Facility. **Interacting with Others:** Communicating with Other Workers. **Physical Work Conditions:** Indoors; Using Hands on Objects, Tools, Controls; Sitting.

51-9022.00 Grinding and Polishing Workers, Hand

Grind, sand, or polish, using hand tools or hand-held power tools, a variety of metal, wood, stone, clay, plastic, or glass objects. **Education:** Short-term O-J-T. **Occupational Type:** Realistic. **Job Zone:** 1. **Average Salary:** $20,450. **Projected Growth:** 4.3%. **Occupational Values:** Moral Values; Independence; Activity; Company Policies and Practices; Supervision, Technical. **Skills Required:** Equipment Selection. **Abilities:** Manual Dexterity. **Interacting with Others:** Performing Administrative Activities. **Physical Work Conditions:** Using Hands on Objects, Tools, Controls; Common Protective or Safety Attire; Indoors; Standing; Making Repetitive Motions; Hazardous Equipment; Distracting Sounds and Noise Levels.

51-9031.00 Cutters and Trimmers, Hand

Use hand tools or hand-held power tools to cut and trim a variety of manufactured items such as carpet, fabric, stone, glass, or rubber. **Education:** Short-term O-J-T. **Occupational Type:** Realistic. **Job Zone:** 1. **Average Salary:** $17,130. **Projected Growth:** –8.3%. **Occupational Values:** Moral Values; Independence; Company Policies and Practices; Activity. **Skills Required:** Operation and Control. **Abilities:** Manual Dexterity; Wrist-Finger Speed; Visualization; Near Vision. **Interacting with Others:** Performing Administrative Activities. **Physical Work

Conditions: Indoors; Using Hands on Objects, Tools, Controls; Hazardous Equipment; Standing; Common Protective or Safety Attire; Making Repetitive Motions; Hazardous Situations.

51-9123.00 Painting, Coating, and Decorating Workers

Paint, coat, or decorate articles such as furniture, glass, plateware, pottery, jewelry, cakes, toys, books, or leather. **Education:** Short-term O-J-T. **Occupational Type:** Realistic. **Job Zone:** 1. **Average Salary:** $19,121. **Projected Growth:** 17.7%. **Occupational Values:** Moral Values; Independence; Activity; Ability Utilization; Company Policies and Practices; Supervision, Human Relations. **Skills Required:** Product Inspection. **Abilities:** Manual Dexterity; Near Vision; Information Ordering; Visual Color Discrimination. **Interacting with Others:** Communicating with Other Workers. **Physical Work Conditions:** Indoors; Using Hands on Objects, Tools, Controls; Standing; Common Protective or Safety Attire; Contaminants; Making Repetitive Motions; Sitting.

51-9195.06 Mold Makers, Hand

Construct or form molds from existing forms for use in casting objects. **Education:** Moderate-term O-J-T. **Occupational Type:** Realistic. **Job Zone:** 2. **Average Salary:** $18,920. **Projected Growth:** 3.7%. **Occupational Values:** Moral Values; Independence; Supervision, Human Relations; Supervision, Technical; Company Policies and Practices; Security. **Skills Required:** Product Inspection; Equipment Selection. **Abilities:** Manual Dexterity; Wrist-Finger Speed. **Interacting with Others:** Communicating with Other Workers. **Physical Work Conditions:** Indoors; Using Hands on Objects, Tools, Controls; Common Protective or Safety Attire; Contaminants; Making Repetitive Motions; Sitting; Standing.

51-9195.07 Molding and Casting Workers

Perform a variety of duties such as mixing materials, assembling mold parts, filling molds, and stacking molds, to mold and cast a wide range of products. **Education:** Moderate-term O-J-T. **Occupational Type:** Realistic. **Job Zone:** 2. **Average Salary:** $19,847. **Projected Growth:** 3.7%. **Occupational Values:** Moral Values; Independence; Company Policies and Practices; Activity; Supervision, Human Relations; Supervision, Technical; Security. **Skills Required:** Operation and Control; Operation Monitoring; Product Inspection; Equipment Selection. **Abilities:** Manual Dexterity; Near Vision. **Interacting with Others:** Performing Administrative Activities. **Physical Work Conditions:** Indoors; Using Hands on Objects, Tools, Controls; Standing; Making Repetitive Motions.

51-9197.00 Tire Builders

Operate machines to build tires from rubber components. **Education:** Moderate-term O-J-T. **Occupational Type:** Realistic. **Job Zone:** 1. **Average Salary:** $36,430. **Projected Growth:** –1.4%. **Occupational Values:** Moral Values; Independence; Company Policies and Practices; Activity; Supervision, Human Relations; Security; Supervision, Technical. **Skills Required:** Operation and Control. **Abilities:** Manual Dexterity. **Interacting with Others:** Communicating with Other Workers. **Physical Work Conditions:** Indoors; Using Hands on Objects, Tools, Controls; Hazardous Equipment; Standing; Hazardous Situations; Common Protective or Safety Attire; Contaminants.

08.04.01 Metal and Plastics Machining Technology

51-4041.00 Machinists

Set up and operate a variety of machine tools to produce precision parts and instruments. Includes precision instrument makers who fabricate, modify, or repair mechanical instruments. May also fabricate and modify parts to make or repair machine tools or maintain industrial machines, applying knowledge of mechanics, shop mathematics, metal properties, layout, and machining procedures. **Education:** Long-term O-J-T. **Occupational Type:** Realistic. **Job Zone:** 4. **Average Salary:** $28,860. **Projected Growth:** 6.2%. **Occupational Values:** Moral Values; Company Policies and Practices; Security; Autonomy; Supervision, Human Relations; Compensation; Activity. **Skills Required:** Testing; Operation and Control; Product Inspection; Mathematics; Operations Analysis; Operation Monitoring; Equipment Selection. **Abilities:** Visualization; Near Vision; Control Precision; Manual Dexterity; Written Comprehension; Information Ordering; Arm-Hand Steadiness. **Interacting with Others:** Communicating with Other Workers; Providing Consultation and Advice to Others. **Physical Work Conditions:** Indoors; Using Hands on Objects, Tools, Controls; Common Protective or Safety Attire; Hazardous Equipment; Distracting Sounds and Noise Levels; Standing; Making Repetitive Motions.

51-4061.00 Model Makers, Metal and Plastic

Set up and operate machines such as lathes, milling and engraving machines, and jig borers to make working models of metal or plastic objects. **Education:** Moderate-term O-J-T. **Occupational Type:** Realistic. **Job Zone:** 4. **Average Salary:** $31,590. **Projected Growth:** –9.6%. **Occupational Values:** Moral Values; Ability Utilization; Company Policies and Practices; Supervision, Human Relations; Achievement; Compensation; Activity. **Skills Required:** Operations Analysis; Product Inspection; Technology Design; Information Organization; Problem Identification; Testing; Information Gathering. **Abilities:** Information Ordering; Written Comprehension; Visualization; Arm-Hand Steadiness; Near Vision; Control Precision; Finger Dexterity. **Interacting with Others:** Communicating with Other Workers. **Physical Work Conditions:** Indoors; Using Hands on Objects, Tools, Controls; Hazardous Equipment; Standing; Common Protective or Safety Attire; Hazardous Situations; Sitting.

51-4062.00 Patternmakers, Metal and Plastic

Lay out, machine, fit, and assemble castings and parts to metal or plastic foundry patterns, core boxes, or match plates. **Education:** Long-term O-J-T. **Occupational Type:** Realistic. **Job Zone:** 4. **Average Salary:** $31,590. **Projected Growth:** –1.5%. **Occupational Values:** Moral Values; Independence; Company Policies and Practices; Ability Utilization; Supervision, Human Relations; Security; Activity. **Skills Required:** Product Inspection; Information Organization; Mathematics; Equipment Selection; Monitoring; Operation and Control; Technology Design. **Abilities:** Arm-Hand Steadiness; Visualization; Information Ordering; Manual Dexterity; Near Vision; Wrist-Finger Speed; Written Comprehension. **Interacting with Others:** Communicating with Persons Outside Organization. **Physical Work Conditions:** Indoors; Using Hands on Objects, Tools, Controls; Common Protective or Safety Attire; Hazardous Equipment; Standing; Hazardous Situations; Distracting Sounds and Noise Levels.

51-4111.00 Tool and Die Makers

Analyze specifications, lay out metal stock, set up and operate machine tools, and fit and assemble parts to make and repair dies, cutting tools, jigs, fixtures, gauges, and machinists' hand tools. **Education:** Long-term O-J-T. **Occupational Type:** Realistic. **Job Zone:** 4. **Average Salary:** $37,250. **Projected Growth:** –1.5%. **Occupational Values:** Moral Values; Company Policies and Practices; Activity; Independence; Supervision, Human Relations; Security; Compensation. **Skills Required:** Product Inspection; Equipment Selection; Operation and Control. **Abilities:** Control Precision; Manual Dexterity; Near Vision; Wrist-Finger Speed. **Interacting with Others:** Communicating with Other Workers. **Physical Work Conditions:** Indoors; Using Hands on Objects, Tools, Controls; Hazardous Equipment; Standing; Common Protective or Safety Attire; Making Repetitive Motions.

51-4192.00 Lay-Out Workers, Metal and Plastic

Lay out reference points and dimensions on metal or plastic stock or workpieces such as sheets, plates, tubes, structural shapes, castings, or machine parts, for further processing. Includes shipfitters. **Education:** Long-term O-J-T. **Occupational Type:** Realistic. **Job Zone:** 3. **Average Salary:** $29,390. **Projected Growth:** –1.5%. **Occupational Values:** Moral Values; Company Policies and Practices; Independence; Supervision, Human Relations; Ability Utilization; Achievement; Security. **Skills Required:** Mathematics; Product Inspection. **Abilities:** Number Facility; Visualization; Mathematical Reasoning. **Interacting with Others:** Communicating with Other Workers. **Physical Work Conditions:** Indoors; Using Hands on Objects, Tools, Controls; Standing.

51-4194.00 Tool Grinders, Filers, and Sharpeners

Perform precision smoothing, sharpening, polishing, or grinding of metal objects. **Education:** Moderate-term O-J-T. **Occupational Type:** Realistic. **Job Zone:** 3. **Average Salary:** $26,660. **Projected Growth:** –9.6%. **Occupational Values:** Moral Values; Company Policies and Practices; Supervision, Human Relations; Activity; Independence; Security. **Skills Required:** Operation and Control; Operation Monitoring; Product Inspection; Testing; Equipment Maintenance; Mathematics; Equipment Selection. **Abilities:** Information Ordering; Written Comprehension; Manual Dexterity; Control Precision; Near Vision; Arm-Hand Steadiness; Wrist-Finger Speed. **Interacting with Others:** Communicating with Other Workers. **Physical Work Conditions:** Indoors; Hazardous Equipment; Using Hands on Objects, Tools, Controls; Common Protective or Safety Attire; Hazardous Situations; Standing; Sitting.

08.05.01 Woodworking Technology

51-7011.00 Cabinetmakers and Bench Carpenters

Cut, shape, and assemble wooden articles or set up and operate a variety of woodworking machines such as power saws, jointers, and mortisers to surface, cut, or shape lumber or to fabricate parts for wood products. **Education:** Long-term O-J-T. **Occupational Type:** Realistic. **Job Zone:** 3. **Average Salary:** $22,390. **Projected Growth:** 5.2%. **Occupational Values:** Moral Values; Independence; Activity; Ability Utilization; Achievement; Autonomy; Compensation. **Skills Required:** Operation and Control; Installation; Equipment Selection. **Abilities:** Written Comprehension. **Interacting with Others:** Communicating with Other Workers. **Physical Work Conditions:** Using Hands on Objects, Tools, Controls; Indoors; Standing; Kneeling, Crouching, or Crawling; Hazardous Equipment.

51-7021.00 Furniture Finishers

Shape, finish, and refinish damaged, worn, or used furniture or new high-grade furniture to specified color or finish. **Education:** Long-term O-J-T. **Occupational Type:** Realistic. **Job Zone:** 2. **Average Salary:** $19,880. **Projected Growth:** –1%. **Occupational Values:** Moral Values; Independence; Autonomy; Achievement. **Skills Required:** Equipment Selection. **Abilities:** Manual Dexterity; Finger Dexterity; Wrist-Finger Speed. **Interacting with Others:** Monitoring and Controlling Resources. **Physical Work Conditions:** Indoors; Using Hands on Objects, Tools, Controls; Contaminants; Kneeling, Crouching, or Crawling; Standing; Hazardous Conditions; Hazardous Situations.

51-7031.00 Model Makers, Wood

Construct full-size and scale wooden precision models of products. Includes wood jig builders and loft workers. **Education:** Long-term O-J-T. **Occupational Type:** Realistic. **Job Zone:** 4. **Average Salary:** $30,490. **Projected Growth:** 3.2%. **Occupational Values:** Moral Values; Independence; Ability Utilization; Security; Company Policies and Practices; Working Conditions; Achievement. **Skills Required:** Product Inspection. **Abilities:** Written Comprehension. **Interacting with Others:** Communicating with Other Workers. **Physical Work Conditions:** Indoors; Using Hands on Objects, Tools, Controls; Standing; Hazardous Situations.

51-7032.00 Patternmakers, Wood

Plan, lay out, and construct wooden unit or sectional patterns used in forming sand molds for castings. **Education:** Long-term O-J-T. **Occupational Type:** Realistic. **Job Zone:** 4. **Average Salary:** $30,490. **Projected Growth:** 3.2%. **Occupational Values:** Moral Values; Independence; Company Policies and Practices; Working Conditions; Ability Utilization; Security; Achievement. **Skills Required:** Product Inspection. **Abilities:** Written Comprehension. **Interacting with Others:** Communicating with Other Workers. **Physical Work Conditions:** Indoors; Using Hands on Objects, Tools, Controls; Standing; Hazardous Situations.

08.06.01 Systems Operation: Utilities and Power Plant

51-8011.00 Nuclear Power Reactor Operators

Control nuclear reactors. **Education:** Long-term O-J-T. **Occupational Type:** Realistic. **Job Zone:** 4. **Average Salary:** $53,180. **Projected Growth:** 3.1%. **Occupational Values:** Moral Values; Supervision, Technical; Supervision, Human Relations; Security; Company Policies and Practices; Activity; Compensation. **Skills Required:** Operation Monitoring; Coordination; Operation and Control; Problem Identification; Speaking; Reading Comprehension; Judgment and Decision Making. **Abilities:** Oral Expression; Written Comprehension. **Interacting with Others:** Communicating with Other Workers. **Physical Work Conditions:** Indoors; Using Hands on Objects, Tools, Controls; Hazardous Conditions; Standing.

51-8012.00 Power Distributors and Dispatchers

Coordinate, regulate, or distribute electricity or steam. **Education:** Long-term O-J-T. **Occupational Type:** Realistic. **Job Zone:** 4. **Average Salary:** $45,690. **Projected Growth:** –12.2%. **Occupational Values:** Security; Moral Values; Authority; Supervision, Human Relations; Company Policies and Practices; Activity; Supervision, Technical. **Skills Required:** Operation and Control; Equipment Maintenance; Operation Monitoring; Repairing; Management of Personnel Resources. **Abilities:** Information Ordering. **Interacting with Others:** Coordinating Work and Activities of Others; Communicating with Other Workers; Guiding, Directing, and Motivating Subordinates. **Physical Work Conditions:** Indoors; Using Hands on Objects, Tools, Controls; Sitting; Standing.

51-8013.01 Power Generating Plant Operators, Except Auxiliary Equipment Operators

Control or operate machinery such as steam-driven turbogenerators to generate electric power, often through the use of panelboards, control boards, or semi-automatic equipment. **Education:** Long-term O-J-T. **Occupational Type:** Realistic. **Job Zone:** 4. **Average Salary:** $44,040. **Projected Growth:** 3.1%. **Occupational Values:** Moral Values; Security; Supervision, Technical; Independence; Supervision, Human Relations; Company Policies and Practices; Activity. **Skills Required:** Operation and Control; Testing; Operation Monitoring; Repairing; Troubleshooting; Equipment Maintenance; Equipment Selection. **Abilities:** Perceptual Speed. **Interacting with Others:** Performing Administrative Activities. **Physical Work Conditions:** Indoors; Using Hands on Objects, Tools, Controls; Common Protective or Safety Attire; Standing; Sitting.

51-8013.02 Auxiliary Equipment Operators, Power

Control and maintain auxiliary equipment, such as pumps, fans, compressors, condensers, feedwater heaters, filters, and chlorinators, that supplies water, fuel, lubricants, air, and auxiliary power for turbines, generators, boilers, and other power-generating plant facilities. **Education:** Long-term O-J-T. **Occupational Type:** Realistic. **Job Zone:** 2. **Average Salary:** $43,640. **Projected Growth:** 3.1%. **Occupational Values:** Moral Values; Supervision, Human Relations; Security; Company Policies and Practices; Supervision, Technical; Activity. **Skills Required:** Operation Monitoring; Equipment Maintenance; Operation and Control. **Abilities:** Control Precision. **Interacting with Others:** Communicating with Other Workers. **Physical Work Conditions:** Indoors; Using Hands on Objects, Tools, Controls; Standing; Hazardous Equipment.

51-8021.01 Boiler Operators and Tenders, Low Pressure

Operate or tend low pressure stationary steam boilers and auxiliary steam equipment such as pumps, compressors and air conditioning equipment, to supply steam heat for office buildings, apartment houses, or industrial establishments or to maintain steam at specified pressure aboard marine vessels. **Education:** Moderate-term O-J-T. **Occupational Type:** Realistic. **Job Zone:** 2. **Average Salary:** $30,320. **Projected Growth:** –11%. **Occupational Values:** Moral Values; Company Policies and Practices; Independence; Supervision, Human Relations; Security; Supervision, Technical. **Skills Required:** Operation and Control. **Abilities:** Control Precision; Problem Sensitivity; Manual Dexterity. **Interacting with Others:** Communicating with Other Workers. **Physical Work Conditions:** Using Hands on Objects, Tools, Controls; Standing; Indoors; Very Hot; Contaminants; Hazardous Equipment; Making Repetitive Motions.

51-8021.02 Stationary Engineers

Operate and maintain stationary engines and mechanical equipment to provide utilities for buildings or industrial processes. Operate equipment such as steam engines, generators, motors, turbines, and steam boilers. **Education:** Long-term O-J-T. **Occupational Type:** Realistic. **Job Zone:** 3. **Average Salary:** $38,270. **Projected Growth:** –5.7%. **Occupational Values:** Moral Values; Supervision, Human Relations; Autonomy; Independence; Supervision, Technical; Security; Activity. **Skills Required:** Operation and Control; Operation Monitoring; Equipment Maintenance; Troubleshooting; Problem Identification; Testing; Repairing. **Abilities:** Problem Sensitivity. **Interacting with Others:** Communicating with Other Workers. **Physical Work Conditions:** Indoors; Using Hands on Objects, Tools, Controls; Distracting Sounds and Noise Levels; Standing.

51-8031.00 Water and Liquid Waste Treatment Plant and System Operators

Operate or control an entire process or system of machines, often through the use of control boards, to transfer or treat water or liquid waste. **Education:** Long-term O-J-T. **Occupational Type:** Realistic. **Job Zone:** 2. **Average Salary:** $29,660. **Projected Growth:** 14.2%. **Occupational Values:** Moral Values; Security; Company Policies and Practices; Activity; Supervision, Human Relations; Coworkers; Supervision, Technical. **Skills Required:** Operation and Control; Information Organization; Operation Monitoring; Mathematics; Testing; Problem Identification; Information Gathering. **Abilities:** Information Ordering; Near Vision; Problem Sensitivity. **Interacting with Others:** Coordinating Work and Activities of Others. **Physical Work Conditions:** Using Hands on Objects, Tools, Controls; Contaminants; Indoors; Common Protective or Safety Attire; Standing; Hazardous Conditions; Hazardous Equipment.

53-5031.00 Ship Engineers

Supervise and coordinate activities of crew engaged in operating and maintaining engines, boilers, deck machinery, and electrical, sanitary, and refrigeration equipment aboard ship. **Education:** Work experience in a related occupation. **Occupational Type:** Realistic. **Job Zone:** 5. **Average Salary:** $40,150. **Projected Growth:** 4.3%. **Occupational Values:** Authority; Responsibility; Compensation; Company Policies and Practices; Ability Utilization; Autonomy; Achievement. **Skills Required:** Operation and Control; Repairing; Operation Monitoring; Equipment Maintenance; Product Inspection; Writing; Problem Identification. **Abilities:** Problem Sensitivity. **Interacting with Others:** Coordinating Work and Activities of Others. **Physical Work Conditions:** Indoors; Standing; Using Hands on Objects, Tools, Controls.

08.06.02 Systems Operation: Oil, Gas, and Water Distribution

51-8091.00 Chemical Plant and System Operators

Control or operate an entire chemical process or system of machines. **Education:** Long-term O-J-T. **Occupational Type:** Realistic. **Job Zone:** 2. **Average Salary:** $39,030. **Projected Growth:** 11%. **Occupational Values:** Moral Values; Security; Company Policies and Practices; Compensation; Supervision, Human Relations; Activity; Supervision, Technical. **Skills Required:** Operation Monitoring; Problem Identification; Operation and Control; Information Gathering; Systems Perception; Science; Reading Comprehension. **Abilities:** Control Precision; Information Ordering. **Interacting with Others:** Communicating with Other Workers. **Physical Work Conditions:** Indoors; Standing; Sitting; Using Hands on Objects, Tools, Controls; Common Protective or Safety Attire.

51-8092.01 Gas Processing Plant Operators

Control equipment such as compressors, evaporators, heat exchangers, and refrigeration equipment to process gas for utility companies and for industrial use. **Education:** Long-term O-J-T. **Occupational Type:** Realistic. **Job Zone:** 2. **Average Salary:** $41,160. **Projected Growth:** –12.6%. **Occupational Values:** Security; Moral Values; Supervision, Human Relations; Activity; Company Policies and Practices; Coworkers; Supervision, Technical. **Skills Required:** Operation and Control; Mathematics; Operation Monitoring; Information Gathering; Testing. **Abilities:** Control Precision. **Interacting with Others:** Communicating with Other Workers. **Physical Work Conditions:** Indoors; Using Hands on Objects, Tools, Controls; Common Protective or Safety Attire; Standing; Contaminants; Hazardous Conditions.

51-8092.02 Gas Distribution Plant Operators

Control equipment to regulate flow and pressure of gas for utility companies and industrial use. May control distribution of gas for a municipal or industrial plant or a single process in an industrial plant. **Education:** Long-term O-J-T. **Occupational Type:** Realistic. **Job Zone:** 3. **Average Salary:** $41,160. **Projected Growth:** –12.6%. **Occupational Values:** Moral Values; Security; Supervision, Human Relations; Activity; Company Policies and Practices; Independence; Supervision, Technical. **Skills Required:** Operation and Control; Equipment Maintenance; Operation Monitoring. **Abilities:** Control Precision. **Interacting with Others:** Performing Administrative Activities. **Physical Work Conditions:** Indoors; Contaminants; Hazardous Conditions; Using Hands on Objects, Tools, Controls; Common Protective or Safety Attire; Standing.

51-8093.01 Petroleum Pump System Operators

Control or operate manifold and pumping systems to circulate liquids through a petroleum refinery. **Education:** Long-term O-J-T. **Occupational Type:** Realistic. **Job Zone:** 3. **Average Salary:** $44,730. **Projected Growth:** –12.6%. **Occupational Values:** Moral Values; Security; Supervision, Human Relations; Supervision, Technical; Company Policies and Practices; Compensation; Activity. **Skills Required:** Operation and Control; Operation Monitoring. **Abilities:** Oral Expression. **Interacting with Others:** Communicating with Other Workers. **Physical Work Conditions:** Indoors; Using Hands on Objects, Tools, Controls; Standing.

51-8093.02 Petroleum Refinery and Control Panel Operators

Analyze specifications and control continuous operation of petroleum refining and processing units. Operate control panel to regulate temperature, pressure, rate of flow, and tank level in petroleum refining unit, according to process schedules. **Education:** Long-term O-J-T. **Occupational Type:** Realistic. **Job Zone:** 4. **Average Salary:** $45,470. **Projected Growth:** –12.6%. **Occupational Values:** Moral Values; Security; Company Policies and Practices; Activity; Supervision, Human Relations; Supervision, Technical; Independence. **Skills Required:** Operation Monitoring; Product Inspection; Operation and Control; Reading Comprehension. **Abilities:** Problem Sensitivity; Written Comprehension; Number Facility. **Interacting with Others:** Interpreting Meaning of Information to Others. **Physical Work Conditions:** Indoors; Using Hands on Objects, Tools, Controls; Standing; Hazardous Conditions; Sitting.

51-8093.03 Gaugers

Gauge and test oil in storage tanks. Regulate flow of oil into pipelines at wells, tank farms, refineries, and marine and rail terminals, following prescribed standards and regulations. **Education:** Long-term O-J-T. **Occupational Type:** Realistic. **Job Zone:** 3. **Average Salary:** $38,300. **Projected Growth:** –12.6%. **Occupational Values:** Moral Values; Independence; Supervision, Human Relations; Company Policies and Practices; Supervision, Technical; Security. **Skills Required:** Operation and Control; Mathematics; Operation Monitoring; Science; Equipment Maintenance; Troubleshooting; Problem Identification. **Abilities:** Control Precision. **Interacting with Others:** Communicating with Other Workers. **Physical Work Conditions:** Hazardous Conditions; Using Hands on Objects, Tools, Controls; Contaminants; Standing; Common Protective or Safety Attire; Outdoors.

53-7071.01 Gas Pumping Station Operators

Control the operation of steam, gas, or electric-motor-driven compressor to maintain specified pressures on high- and low-pressure mains dispensing gas from gasholders. **Education:** Moderate-term O-J-T. **Occupational Type:** Realistic. **Job Zone:** 2. **Average Salary:** $27,170. **Projected Growth:** 0%. **Occupational Values:** Independence; Moral Values; Supervision, Human Relations; Security; Company Policies and Practices. **Skills Required:** Operation and Control; Operation Monitoring. **Abilities:** Control Precision. **Interacting with Others:** Performing Administrative Activities. **Physical Work Conditions:** Standing; Indoors; Using Hands on Objects, Tools, Controls.

53-7071.02 Gas Compressor Operators

Operate steam or internal combustion engines to transmit, compress, or recover gases such as butane, nitrogen, hydrogen, and natural gas in various production processes. **Education:** Moderate-term O-J-T. **Occupational Type:** Realistic. **Job Zone:** 4. **Average Salary:** $38,620. **Projected Growth:** 0%. **Occupational Values:** Moral Values; Supervision, Human Relations; Independence; Supervision, Technical; Security; Company Policies and Practices. **Skills Required:** Operation Monitoring; Operation and Control. **Abilities:** Control Precision. **Interacting with Others:** Performing Administrative Activities. **Physical Work Conditions:** Indoors; Contaminants; Standing; Using Hands on Objects, Tools, Controls; Common Protective or Safety Attire; Hazardous Conditions.

53-7073.00 Wellhead Pumpers

Operate power pumps and auxiliary equipment to produce flow of oil or gas from wells in oil field. **Education:** Moderate-term O-J-T. **Occupational Type:** Realistic. **Job Zone:** 4. **Average Salary:** $33,610. **Projected Growth:** 0%. **Occupational Values:** Moral Values; Independence; Supervision, Human Relations; Company Policies and Practices; Supervision, Technical. **Skills Required:** Operation and Control; Operation Monitoring. **Abilities:** Control Precision. **Interacting with Others:** Performing Administrative Activities. **Physical Work Conditions:** Common Protective or Safety Attire; Standing; Contaminants; Using Hands on Objects, Tools, Controls.

08.07.01 Hands-on Work: Loading, Moving, Hoisting, and Conveying

47-4041.01 Irradiated-Fuel Handlers

Package, store, and convey irradiated fuels and wastes, using hoists, mechanical arms, shovels, and industrial truck. **Education:** Moderate-term O-J-T. **Occupational Type:** Realistic. **Job Zone:** 2. **Average Salary:** $27,620. **Projected Growth:** 8.3%. **Occupational Values:** Moral Values; Supervision, Technical; Independence; Company Policies and Practices; Supervision, Human Relations; Security; Compensation. **Skills Required:** Reading Comprehension. **Abilities:** Control Precision; Information Ordering. **Interacting with Others:** Communicating with Other Workers. **Physical Work Conditions:** Contaminants; Outdoors; Radiation; Common Protective or Safety Attire; Standing; Specialized Protective or Safety Attire; Using Hands on Objects, Tools, Controls.

53-7011.00 Conveyor Operators and Tenders

Control or tend conveyors or conveyor systems that move materials or products to and from stockpiles, processing stations, departments, or vehicles. May control speed and routing of materials or products. **Education:** Moderate-term O-J-T. **Occupational Type:** Realistic. **Job Zone:** 1. **Average Salary:** $21,800. **Projected Growth:** 21.5%. **Occupational Values:** Moral Values; Supervision, Human Relations; Activity; Supervision, Technical; Company Policies and Practices; Independence; Coworkers. **Skills Required:** Operation Monitoring; Equipment Maintenance; Operation and Control; Repairing. **Abilities:** Perceptual Speed. **Interacting with Others:** Communicating with Other Workers. **Physical Work Conditions:** Indoors; Using Hands on Objects, Tools, Controls; Standing; Making Repetitive Motions.

53-7021.00 Crane and Tower Operators

Operate mechanical boom and cable, or tower and cable, equipment to lift and move materials, machines, or products in many directions. **Education:** Moderate-term O-J-T. **Occupational Type:** Realistic. **Job Zone:** 2. **Average Salary:** $30,510. **Projected Growth:** 0.5%. **Occupational Values:** Moral Values; Company Policies and Practices; Supervision, Human Relations; Activity; Supervision, Technical. **Skills Required:** Operation and Control; Product Inspection. **Abilities:** Multilimb Coordination; Depth Perception; Control Precision; Oral Expression. **Interacting with Others:** Communicating with Other Workers. **Physical Work Conditions:** Outdoors; Using Hands on Objects, Tools, Controls; Hazardous Equipment; Sitting; Standing.

53-7032.00 Excavating and Loading Machine and Dragline Operators

Operate or tend machinery equipped with scoops, shovels, or buckets, to excavate and load loose materials. No other data currently available.

53-7032.02 Dragline Operators

Operate power-driven crane equipment with dragline bucket to excavate or move sand, gravel, mud, or other materials. **Education:** Moderate-term O-J-T. **Occupational Type:** Realistic. **Job Zone:** 2. **Average Salary:** $27,960. **Projected Growth:** 21.5%. **Occupational Values:** Moral Values; Independence. **Skills Required:** Operation and Control. **Abilities:** Control Precision; Depth Perception; Far Vision; Multilimb Coordination. **Interacting with Others:** Communicating with Other Workers. **Physical Work Conditions:** Outdoors; Using Hands on Objects, Tools, Controls; Hazardous Equipment; Sitting; Whole Body Vibration; Common Protective or Safety Attire; Distracting Sounds and Noise Levels.

53-7041.00 Hoist and Winch Operators

Operate or tend hoists or winches to lift and pull loads using power-operated cable equipment. **Education:** Moderate-term O-J-T. **Occupational Type:** Realistic. **Job Zone:** 1. **Average Salary:** $28,030. **Projected Growth:** 6%. **Occupational Values:** Moral Values; Independence; Company Policies and Practices; Supervision, Technical; Supervision, Human Relations. **Skills Required:** Operation and Control; Repairing; Equipment Maintenance; Operation Monitoring; Equipment Selection. **Abilities:** Control Precision; Depth Perception; Multilimb

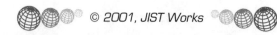

Coordination; Manual Dexterity; Trunk Strength. **Interacting with Others:** Performing Administrative Activities. **Physical Work Conditions:** Outdoors; Using Hands on Objects, Tools, Controls; Hazardous Equipment; Common Protective or Safety Attire; Distracting Sounds and Noise Levels; Standing; High Places.

53-7051.00 Industrial Truck and Tractor Operators

Operate industrial trucks or tractors equipped to move materials around a warehouse, storage yard, factory, construction site, or similar location. **Education:** Short-term O-J-T. **Occupational Type:** Realistic. **Job Zone:** 1. **Average Salary:** $23,360. **Projected Growth:** 9.2%. **Occupational Values:** Moral Values; Supervision, Human Relations; Company Policies and Practices; Supervision, Technical. **Skills Required:** Operation and Control; Equipment Selection. **Abilities:** Control Precision; Depth Perception; Multilimb Coordination; Manual Dexterity; Static Strength. **Interacting with Others:** Communicating with Other Workers. **Physical Work Conditions:** Using Hands on Objects, Tools, Controls; Common Protective or Safety Attire; Outdoors.

53-7062.00 Laborers and Freight, Stock, and Material Movers, Hand

Manually move freight, stock, or other materials or perform other unskilled general labor. Includes all unskilled manual laborers not elsewhere classified. No other data currently available.

53-7062.03 Freight, Stock, and Material Movers, Hand

Load, unload, and move materials at plant, yard, or other work site. **Education:** Short-term O-J-T. **Occupational Type:** Realistic. **Job Zone:** 1. **Average Salary:** $18,260. **Projected Growth:** 1.5%. **Occupational Values:** Moral Values; Supervision, Technical; Activity; Security; Supervision, Human Relations; Company Policies and Practices; Coworkers. **Skills Required:** Installation. **Abilities:** Extent Flexibility; Static Strength. **Interacting with Others:** Performing Administrative Activities. **Physical Work Conditions:** Using Hands on Objects, Tools, Controls; Indoors; Standing; Common Protective or Safety Attire; Walking or Running.

53-7063.00 Machine Feeders and Offbearers

Feed materials into or remove materials from machines or equipment that is automatic or tended by other workers. **Education:** Short-term O-J-T. **Occupational Type:** Realistic. **Job Zone:** 1. **Average Salary:** $18,810. **Projected Growth:** –0.9%. **Occupational Values:** Moral Values; Activity; Security; Coworkers; Supervision, Human Relations; Company Policies and Practices; Supervision, Technical. **Skills Required:** Product Inspection. **Abilities:** Manual Dexterity; Trunk Strength; Static Strength; Control Precision; Extent Flexibility. **Interacting with Others:** Performing Administrative Activities. **Physical Work Conditions:** Using Hands on Objects, Tools, Controls; Indoors; Standing; Hazardous Equipment; Making Repetitive Motions; Distracting Sounds and Noise Levels; Bending or Twisting the Body.

53-7064.00 Packers and Packagers, Hand

Pack or package by hand a wide variety of products and materials. **Education:** Short-term O-J-T. **Occupational Type:** Realistic. **Job Zone:** 1. **Average Salary:** $14,540. **Projected Growth:** 21.7%. **Occupational Values:** Moral Values; Activity; Supervision, Technical; Supervision, Human Relations; Company Policies and Practices; Coworkers; Independence. **Skills Required:** Operation and Control. **Abilities:** Manual Dexterity. **Interacting with Others:** Performing Administrative Activities. **Physical Work Conditions:** Indoors; Using Hands on Objects, Tools, Controls; Standing; Making Repetitive Motions.

53-7072.00 Pump Operators, Except Wellhead Pumpers

Tend, control, or operate power-driven, stationary, or portable pumps and manifold systems to transfer gases, oil, other liquids, slurries, or powdered materials to and from various vessels and processes. **Education:** Moderate-term O-J-T. **Occupational Type:** Realistic. **Job Zone:** 2. **Average Salary:** $26,740. **Projected Growth:** 21.5%. **Occupational Values:** Moral Values; Supervision, Human Relations; Supervision, Technical; Company Policies and Practices; Activity; Independence. **Skills Required:** Operation and Control; Operation Monitoring. **Abilities:** Control Precision. **Interacting with Others:** Communicating with Other Workers. **Physical Work Conditions:** Using Hands on Objects, Tools, Controls; Indoors; Hazardous Equipment; Standing; Common Protective or Safety Attire; Hazardous Conditions; Making Repetitive Motions.

53-7081.00 Refuse and Recyclable Material Collectors

Collect and dump refuse or recyclable materials from containers into truck. May drive truck. **Education:** Short-term O-J-T. **Occupational Type:** Realistic. **Job Zone:** 1. **Average Salary:** $21,860. **Projected Growth:** 3.9%. **Occupational Values:** Moral Values; Company Policies and Practices; Supervision, Human Relations; Activity; Security; Supervision, Technical. **Skills Required:** Operation and Control. **Abilities:** Static Strength. **Interacting with Others:** Communicating with Other Workers. **Physical Work Conditions:** Outdoors; Standing; Using Hands on Objects, Tools, Controls; Special Uniform; Contaminants; Very Hot; Distracting Sounds and Noise Levels.

53-7121.00 Tank Car, Truck, and Ship Loaders

Load and unload chemicals and bulk solids such as coal, sand, and grain into or from tank cars, trucks, or ships using material moving equipment. May perform a variety of other tasks relating to shipment of products. May gauge or sample shipping tanks and test them for leaks. **Education:** Moderate-term O-J-T. **Occupational Type:** Realistic. **Job Zone:** 3. **Average Salary:** $31,170. **Projected Growth:** 8.3%. **Occupational Values:** Moral Values; Independence; Supervision, Human Relations; Company Policies and Practices; Supervision, Technical. **Skills Required:** Operation and Control; Operation Monitoring. **Abilities:** Control Precision. **Interacting with Others:** Communicating with Other Workers. **Physical Work Conditions:** Hazardous Conditions; Standing; Contaminants; Outdoors; Common Protective or Safety Attire; Using Hands on Objects, Tools, Controls.

09 Business Detail

09.01 Managerial Work in Business Detail

09.02 Administrative Detail

09.03 Bookkeeping, Auditing, and Accounting

09.04 Material Control

09.05 Customer Service

09.06 Communications

09.07 Records Processing

09.08 Records and Materials Processing

09.09 Clerical Machine Operation

09.01.01 Managerial Work in Business Detail

11-3011.00 Administrative Services Managers

Plan, direct, or coordinate supportive services of an organization, such as recordkeeping, mail distribution, telephone operator/receptionist, and other office support services. May oversee facilities planning and maintenance and custodial operations. **Education:** Work experience, plus degree. **Occupational Type:** Enterprising. **Job Zone:** 4. **Average Salary:** $44,370. **Projected Growth:** 18.1%. **Occupational Values:** Working Conditions; Authority; Company Policies and Practices; Autonomy; Responsibility; Security; Activity. **Skills Required:** Writing; Management of Personnel Resources; Coordination; Judgment and Decision Making; Reading Comprehension; Speaking; Time Management. **Abilities:** Oral Expression; Speech Clarity; Oral Comprehension; Written Comprehension; Written Expression; Near Vision; Information Ordering. **Interacting with Others:** Communicating with Other Workers; Staffing Organizational Units; Coordinating Work and Activities of Others; Performing Administrative Activities; Providing Consultation and Advice to Others; Guiding, Directing, and Motivating Subordinates; Coaching and Developing Others. **Physical Work Conditions:** Indoors; Sitting.

43-1011.01 First-Line Supervisors, Customer Service

Supervise and coordinate activities of workers involved in providing customer service. **Education:** Work experience in a related occupation. **Occupational Type:** Enterprising. **Job Zone:** 3. **Average Salary:** $31,090. **Projected Growth:** 19.4%. **Occupational Values:** Authority; Autonomy; Activity; Achievement; Working Conditions; Responsibility; Creativity. **Skills Required:** Speaking; Coordination; Management of Personnel Resources; Active Listening; Critical Thinking; Time Management; Problem Identification. **Abilities:** Oral Expression; Near Vision; Oral Comprehension; Written Comprehension; Written Expression; Speech Clarity; Number Facility. **Interacting with Others:** Staffing Organizational Units; Guiding, Directing, and Motivating Subordinates; Communicating with Other Workers; Establishing and Maintaining Relationships; Resolving Conflict, Negotiating with Others; Coaching and Developing Others; Coordinating Work and Activities of Others. **Physical Work Conditions:** Indoors; Sitting; Standing; Walking or Running.

43-1011.02 First-Line Supervisors, Administrative Support

Supervise and coordinate activities of workers involved in providing administrative support. **Education:** Work experience in a related occupation. **Occupational Type:** Enterprising. **Job Zone:** 3. **Average Salary:** $31,090. **Projected Growth:** 19.4%. **Occupational Values:** Authority; Autonomy; Activity; Working Conditions; Responsibility; Ability Utilization; Security. **Skills Required:** Management of Personnel Resources; Time Management; Speaking; Monitoring; Reading Comprehension; Coordination; Critical Thinking. **Abilities:** Oral Expression; Written Expression; Oral Comprehension; Written Comprehension; Near Vision; Speech Clarity; Mathematical Reasoning. **Interacting with Others:** Coordinating Work and Activities of Others; Guiding, Directing, and Motivating Subordinates; Coaching and Developing Others; Establishing and Maintaining Relationships; Performing Administrative Activities; Communicating with Other Workers; Staffing Organizational Units. **Physical Work Conditions:** Indoors; Sitting.

09.02.01 Administrative Detail: Administration

43-4031.01 Court Clerks

Perform clerical duties in court of law; prepare docket of cases to be called. **Education:** Short-term O-J-T. **Occupational Type:** Conventional. **Job Zone:** 3. **Average Salary:** $22,960. **Projected Growth:** 10.8%. **Occupational Values:** Activity; Security; Company Policies and Practices; Supervision, Human Relations; Moral Values; Working Conditions; Coworkers. **Skills Required:** Information Organization; Active Listening; Reading Comprehension; Information Gathering. **Abilities:** Oral Comprehension; Written Expression; Wrist-Finger Speed; Near Vision; Oral Expression; Written Comprehension. **Interacting with Others:** Performing Administrative Activities. **Physical Work Conditions:** Sitting; Indoors; Using Hands on Objects, Tools, Controls.

43-4031.02 Municipal Clerks

Draft agendas and bylaws for town or city council; record minutes of council meetings. **Education:** Short-term O-J-T. **Occupational Type:** Conventional. **Job Zone:** 2. **Average Salary:** $22,810. **Projected Growth:** 11.9%. **Occupational Values:** Working Conditions; Moral Values; Supervision, Human Relations; Company Policies and Practices; Security; Activity; Independence. **Skills Required:** Writing; Active Listening; Reading Comprehension. **Abilities:** Oral Comprehension; Written Expression. **Interacting with Others:** Communicating with Persons Outside Organization. **Physical Work Conditions:** Indoors; Sitting.

43-4031.03 License Clerks

Issue licenses or permits to qualified applicants. Obtain necessary information; record data. **Education:** Short-term O-J-T. **Occupational Type:** Conventional. **Job Zone:** 2. **Average Salary:** $22,900. **Projected Growth:** 13.1%. **Occupational Values:** Moral Values; Activity; Supervision, Human Relations; Security; Company Policies and Practices; Working Conditions; Supervision, Technical. **Skills Required:** Active Listening; Information Gathering; Speaking; Reading Comprehension. **Abilities:** Speech Clarity. **Interacting with Others:** Performing for/Working with Public. **Physical Work Conditions:** Indoors; Sitting; Standing.

09.02.02 Administrative Detail: Secretarial Work

43-6011.00 Executive Secretaries and Administrative Assistants

Provide high-level administrative support by conducting research, preparing statistical reports, handling information requests, and performing clerical functions such as preparing correspondence, receiving visitors, arranging conference calls, and scheduling meetings. May also train and supervise lower-level clerical staff. **Education:** Bachelor's degree. **Occupational Type:** Conventional. **Job Zone:** 4. **Average Salary:** $23,550. **Projected Growth:** 20.9%. **Occupational Values:** Working Conditions; Company Policies and Practices; Moral Values; Supervision, Human Relations; Activity; Security; Social Service. **Skills Required:** Reading Comprehension; Writing; Coordination; Synthesis/Reorganization; Speaking; Time Management; Active Listening. **Abilities:** Near Vision; Information Ordering; Written Comprehension; Oral Comprehension; Written Expression. **Interacting with Others:** Performing Administrative Activities; Communicating with Other Workers; Coordinating Work and Activities of Others; Interpreting Meaning of Information to Others; Monitoring and Controlling Resources; Establishing and Maintaining Relationships. **Physical Work Conditions:** Indoors; Sitting.

43-6012.00 Legal Secretaries

Perform secretarial duties utilizing legal terminology, procedures, and documents. Prepare legal papers and correspondence such as summonses, complaints, motions, and subpoenas. May also assist with legal research. **Education:** Postsecondary vocational training. **Occupational Type:** Conventional. **Job Zone:** 3. **Average Salary:** $30,050. **Projected Growth:** 13%. **Occupational Values:** Working Conditions; Activity; Company Policies and Practices; Moral Values; Security; Compensation; Supervision, Human Relations. **Skills Required:** Information Organization; Time Management; Coordination; Information Gathering; Reading Comprehension; Product Inspection; Writing. **Abilities:** Oral Comprehension; Near Vision; Written Comprehension; Written Expression; Oral Expression; Wrist-Finger Speed. **Interacting with Others:** Communicating with Other Workers; Communicating with Persons Outside Organization; Performing Administrative Activities. **Physical Work Conditions:** Sitting; Indoors; Using Hands on Objects, Tools, Controls.

43-6013.00 Medical Secretaries

Perform secretarial duties utilizing specific knowledge of medical terminology and hospital, clinic, or laboratory procedures. Duties include scheduling appointments, billing patients, and compiling and recording medical charts, reports, and correspondence. **Education:** Postsecondary vocational training. **Occupational Type:** Conventional. **Job Zone:** 3. **Average Salary:** $22,390. **Projected Growth:** 12%. **Occupational Values:** Activity; Working Conditions; Company Policies and Practices; Security; Moral Values; Supervision, Human Relations; Compensation. **Skills Required:** Coordination; Synthesis/Reorganization; Writing. **Abilities:** Oral Comprehension; Wrist-Finger Speed; Oral Expression. **Interacting with Others:** Performing Administrative Activities. **Physical Work Conditions:** Indoors; Sitting; Using Hands on Objects, Tools, Controls.

43-6014.00 Secretaries, Except Legal, Medical, and Executive

Perform routine clerical and administrative functions such as drafting correspondence, scheduling appointments, organizing and maintaining paper and electronic files, or providing information to callers. **Education:** Postsecondary vocational training. **Occupational Type:** Conventional. **Job Zone:** 2. **Average Salary:** $23,550. **Projected Growth:** 0%. **Occupational Values:** Moral Values; Activity; Working Conditions; Supervision, Human Relations; Company Policies and Practices; Security; Coworkers. **Skills Required:** Coordination; Reading Comprehension; Active Listening; Writing; Information Organization. **Abilities:** Oral Expression; Written Comprehension; Oral Comprehension; Speech Clarity; Speech Recognition; Wrist-Finger Speed; Finger Dexterity. **Interacting with Others:** Communicating with Other Workers; Communicating with Persons Outside Organization; Establishing and Maintaining Relationships; Performing Administrative Activities; Performing for/Working with Public. **Physical Work Conditions:** Indoors; Sitting; Using Hands on Objects, Tools, Controls.

09.02.03 Administrative Detail: Interviewing

43-4061.01 Claims Takers, Unemployment Benefits

Interview unemployed workers and compile data to determine eligibility for unemployment benefits. **Education:** Moderate-term O-J-T. **Occupational Type:** Conventional. **Job Zone:** 2. **Average Salary:** $31,110. **Projected Growth:** 14.5%. **Occupational Values:** Security; Supervision, Human Relations; Social Service; Activity; Supervision, Technical; Working Conditions; Moral Values. **Skills Required:** Speaking; Active Listening; Reading Comprehension; Information Gathering. **Abilities:** Oral Expression; Written Comprehension; Oral Comprehension; Written Expression. **Interacting with Others:** Communicating with Persons Outside Organization. **Physical Work Conditions:** Indoors; Sitting.

43-4061.02 Welfare Eligibility Workers and Interviewers

Interview and investigate applicants and recipients to determine eligibility for use of social programs and agency resources. Duties include recording and evaluating personal and financial data obtained from individuals; and initiating procedures to grant, modify, deny, or terminate eligibility for various aid programs. **Education:** Moderate-term O-J-T. **Occupational Type:** Social. **Job Zone:** 2. **Average Salary:** $33,100. **Projected Growth:** –7.6%. **Occupational Values:** Social Service; Security; Achievement; Supervision, Human Relations; Activity; Company Policies and Practices; Coworkers. **Skills Required:** Speaking; Information Gathering; Judgment and Decision Making; Active Listening; Problem Identification; Service Orientation; Reading Comprehension. **Abilities:** Oral Expression; Written Comprehension; Oral Comprehension; Written Expression; Number Facility; Speech Clarity. **Interacting with Others:** Assisting and Caring for Others; Communicating with Persons Outside Organization; Interpreting Meaning of Information to Others; Monitoring and Controlling Resources. **Physical Work Conditions:** Indoors; Sitting.

43-4111.00 Interviewers, Except Eligibility and Loan

Interview persons by telephone, mail, in person, or by other means for the purpose of completing forms, applications, or questionnaires. Ask specific questions, record answers, and assist persons with completing form. May sort, classify, and file forms. **Education:** Short-term O-J-T. **Occupational Type:** Conventional. **Job Zone:** 1. **Average Salary:** $18,540. **Projected Growth:** 23.3%. **Occupational Values:** Moral Values; Independence; Working Conditions; Activity. **Skills Required:** Active Listening; Reading Comprehension; Speaking; Information Gathering. **Abilities:** Oral Expression; Speech Clarity; Oral Comprehension. **Interacting with Others:** Communicating with Persons Outside Organization. **Physical Work Conditions:** Indoors; Sitting.

43-4131.00 Loan Interviewers and Clerks

Interview loan applicants to elicit information; investigate applicants' backgrounds and verify references; prepare loan request papers and forward findings, reports, and documents to appraisal department. Review loan papers to ensure completeness; and complete transactions between loan establishment, borrowers, and sellers upon approval of loan. **Education:** Short-term O-J-T. **Occupational Type:** Conventional. **Job Zone:** 2. **Average Salary:** $22,629. **Projected Growth:** 11.8%. **Occupational Values:** Working Conditions; Moral Values; Activity; Company Policies and Practices; Supervision, Human Relations; Coworkers; Security. **Skills Required:** Mathematics; Reading Comprehension; Information Gathering; Active Listening. **Abilities:** Number Facility; Near Vision; Information Ordering; Oral Expression; Written Comprehension; Mathematical Reasoning; Written Expression. **Interacting with Others:** Communicating with Persons Outside Organization; Performing Administrative Activities; Establishing and Maintaining Relationships. **Physical Work Conditions:** Indoors; Sitting.

09.03.01 Bookkeeping, Auditing, and Accounting

13-2082.00 Tax Preparers

Prepare tax returns for individuals or small businesses, without having the background or responsibilities of an accredited or certified public accountant. **Education:** Moderate-term O-J-T. **Occupational Type:** Conventional. **Job Zone:** 2. **Average Salary:** $27,960. **Projected Growth:** 19.3%. **Occupational Values:** Working Conditions; Independence; Company Policies and Practices; Activity; Supervision, Human Relations; Compensation; Ability Utilization. **Skills Required:** Mathematics; Problem Identification; Information Gathering; Reading Comprehension; Active Listening. **Abilities:** Number Facility; Oral Comprehension; Mathematical Reasoning; Deductive Reasoning; Oral Expression; Written Comprehension; Information Ordering. **Interacting with Others:** Performing Administrative Activities. **Physical Work Conditions:** Sitting; Indoors.

43-3021.01 Statement Clerks

Prepare and distribute bank statements to customers, answer inquiries, and reconcile discrepancies in records and accounts. **Education:** Short-term O-J-T. **Occupational Type:** Conventional. **Job Zone:** 2. **Average Salary:** $18,630. **Projected Growth:** –22.3%. **Occupational Values:** Working Conditions; Moral Values; Activity; Security; Supervision, Human Relations; Company Policies and Practices; Independence. **Skills Required:** Mathematics; Active Listening. **Abilities:** Near Vision. **Interacting with Others:** Communicating with Persons Outside Organization. **Physical Work Conditions:** Indoors; Sitting; Using Hands on Objects, Tools, Controls.

43-3021.02 Billing, Cost, and Rate Clerks

Compile data, compute fees and charges, and prepare invoices for billing purposes. Duties include computing costs and calculating rates for goods, services, and shipment of goods; and posting data. **Education:** Short-term O-J-T. **Occupational Type:** Conventional. **Job Zone:** 2. **Average Salary:** $22,670. **Projected Growth:** 14.6%. **Occupational Values:** Working Conditions; Activity; Independence; Security; Company Policies and Practices; Supervision, Human Relations; Moral Values. **Skills Required:** Mathematics; Information Gathering; Reading Comprehension. **Abilities:** Number Facility; Written Comprehension; Mathematical Reasoning; Written Expression; Near Vision; Information Ordering; Wrist-Finger Speed. **Interacting with Others:** Communicating with Persons Outside Organization; Performing Administrative Activities. **Physical Work Conditions:** Indoors; Sitting.

43-3031.00 Bookkeeping, Accounting, and Auditing Clerks

Compute, classify, and record numerical data to keep financial records complete. Perform any combination of routine calculating, posting, and verifying duties to obtain primary financial data for use in maintaining accounting records. May also check the accuracy of figures, calculations, and postings pertaining to business transactions recorded by other workers. **Education:** Moderate-term O-J-T. **Occupational Type:** Conventional. **Job Zone:** 2. **Average Salary:** $23,190. **Projected Growth:** –3.9%. **Occupational Values:** Independence; Working Conditions; Company Policies and Practices; Autonomy; Activity; Security; Supervision, Human Relations. **Skills Required:** Mathematics; Information Gathering; Information Organization; Writing; Reading Comprehension. **Abilities:** Number Facility; Near Vision; Mathematical Reasoning; Written Comprehension; Information Ordering; Perceptual Speed; Written Expression. **Interacting with Others:** Communicating with Other Workers; Performing Administrative Activities. **Physical Work Conditions:** Indoors; Sitting.

43-3051.00 Payroll and Timekeeping Clerks

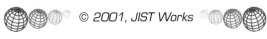

Compute wages and post wage data to payroll records. Keep daily records showing employees' times of arrival and departure from work. Compute earnings from time sheets and work tickets using calculator. Operate posting machine to compute and subtract payroll deductions. Enter net wages on earnings record card, check stub, and payroll sheet. **Education:** Short-term O-J-T. **Occupational Type:** Conventional. **Job Zone:** 2. **Average Salary:** $24,560. **Projected Growth:** -6.2%. **Occupational Values:** Working Conditions; Independence; Supervision, Human Relations; Company Policies and Practices; Security; Activity; Advancement. **Skills Required:** Mathematics; Information Gathering. **Abilities:** Number Facility; Mathematical Reasoning. **Interacting with Others:** Communicating with Other Workers. **Physical Work Conditions:** Indoors; Sitting.

43-4011.00 Brokerage Clerks

Perform clerical duties involving the purchase or sale of securities. Duties include writing orders for stock purchases and sales, computing transfer taxes, verifying stock transactions, accepting and delivering securities, tracking stock price fluctuations, computing equity, distributing dividends, and keeping records of daily transactions and holdings. **Education:** Short-term O-J-T. **Occupational Type:** Conventional. **Job Zone:** 2. **Average Salary:** $26,270. **Projected Growth:** 28.4%. **Occupational Values:** Working Conditions; Activity; Security; Coworkers; Moral Values; Supervision, Human Relations; Company Policies and Practices. **Skills Required:** Mathematics; Reading Comprehension; Writing; Speaking; Information Gathering; Active Listening. **Abilities:** Written Expression; Mathematical Reasoning; Number Facility; Oral Expression; Written Comprehension; Oral Comprehension. **Interacting with Others:** Communicating with Persons Outside Organization; Communicating with Other Workers. **Physical Work Conditions:** Indoors; Sitting.

09.04.01 Material Control

43-5041.00 Meter Readers, Utilities

Read meter and record consumption of electricity, gas, water, or steam. **Education:** Short-term O-J-T. **Occupational Type:** Conventional. **Job Zone:** 1. **Average Salary:** $25,380. **Projected Growth:** 0.4%. **Occupational Values:** Independence; Moral Values; Supervision, Human Relations; Security; Supervision, Technical; Company Policies and Practices. **Skills Required:** Information Gathering. **Abilities:** Near Vision. **Interacting with Others:** Performing Administrative Activities. **Physical Work Conditions:** Outdoors; Standing; Special Uniform; Walking or Running; Using Hands on Objects, Tools, Controls; Very Hot.

43-5061.00 Production, Planning, and Expediting Clerks

Coordinate and expedite the flow of work and materials within or between departments of an establishment according to production schedule. Duties include reviewing and distributing production, work, and shipment schedules; conferring with department supervisors to determine progress of work and completion dates; and compiling reports on progress of work, inventory levels, costs, and production problems. **Education:** Short-term O-J-T. **Occupational Type:** Conventional. **Job Zone:** 2. **Average Salary:** $29,270. **Projected Growth:** 0.4%. **Occupational Values:** Moral Values; Supervision, Human Relations; Activity; Security; Company Policies and Practices; Supervision, Technical; Coworkers. **Skills Required:** Problem Identification; Monitoring; Implementation Planning; Coordination; Reading Comprehension; Systems Perception; Time Management. **Abilities:** Number Facility; Near Vision; Information Ordering; Mathematical Reasoning; Oral Comprehension; Oral Expression; Written Expression. **Interacting with Others:** Communicating with Other Workers; Communicating with Persons Outside Organization. **Physical Work Conditions:** Indoors; Sitting; Using Hands on Objects, Tools, Controls.

09.05.01 Customer Service

41-2011.00 Cashiers

Receive and disburse money in establishments other than financial institutions. Use electronic scanners, cash registers, or related equipment. Process credit or debit card transactions and validate checks. **Education:** Short-term O-J-T. **Occupational Type:** Conventional. **Job Zone:** 1. **Average Salary:** $13,690. **Projected Growth:** 17.4%. **Occupational Values:** Coworkers; Supervision, Technical; Security; Supervision, Human Relations; Moral Values; Activity; Company Policies and Practices. **Skills Required:** Mathematics; Speaking; Service Orientation. **Abilities:** Oral Expression; Near Vision; Number Facility; Finger Dexterity; Oral Comprehension; Speech Clarity; Wrist-Finger Speed. **Interacting with Others:** Communicating with Persons Outside Organization; Performing for/Working with Public; Establishing and Maintaining Relationships; Performing Administrative Activities. **Physical Work Conditions:** Indoors; Standing; Sitting; Using Hands on Objects, Tools, Controls.

41-2012.00 Gaming Change Persons and Booth Cashiers

Exchange coins and tokens for patrons' money. May issue payoffs and obtain customer's signature on receipt when winnings exceed the amount held in the slot machine. May operate a booth in the slot machine area and furnish change persons with money bank at the start of the shift, or count and audit money in drawers. No other data currently available.

41-2021.00 Counter and Rental Clerks

Receive orders for repairs, rentals, and services. May describe available options, compute cost, and accept payment. **Education:** Short-term O-J-T. **Occupational Type:** Conventional. **Job Zone:** 1. **Average Salary:** $14,510. **Projected Growth:** 23.1%. **Occupational Values:** Working Conditions; Moral Values; Coworkers; Supervision, Human Relations; Supervision, Technical; Independence; Company Policies and Practices. **Skills Required:** Service Orientation; Mathematics; Speaking; Active Listening; Writing. **Abilities:** Oral Comprehension; Number Facility; Oral Expression. **Interacting with Others:** Communicating with Persons Outside Organization; Performing for/Working with Public; Establishing and Maintaining Relationships; Selling or Influencing Others. **Physical Work Conditions:** Indoors; Standing; Sitting.

43-3011.00 Bill and Account Collectors

Locate and notify customers of delinquent accounts by mail, telephone, or personal visit to solicit payment. Duties include receiving payment and posting amount to customer's account; preparing statements to credit department if customer fails to respond; initiating repossession proceedings or service disconnection; and keeping records of collection and status of accounts. **Education:** Short-term O-J-T. **Occupational Type:** Conventional. **Job Zone:** 2. **Average Salary:** $22,540. **Projected Growth:** 35.3%. **Occupational Values:** Supervision, Human Relations; Activity; Security; Company Policies and Practices. **Skills Required:** Speaking; Social Perceptiveness; Information Gathering; Active Listening. **Abilities:** Number Facility; Oral Expression; Oral Comprehension; Speech Clarity. **Interacting with Others:** Communicating with Persons Outside Organization; Performing for/Working with Public; Resolving Conflict, Negotiating with Others; Selling or Influencing Others. **Physical Work Conditions:** Indoors; Sitting.

43-3041.00 Gaming Cage Workers

In a gaming establishment, conduct financial transactions for patrons. May reconcile daily summaries of transactions to balance books. Accept patron's credit application and verify credit references to provide check-cashing authorization or to establish house credit accounts. May sell gambling chips, tokens, or tickets to patrons, or to other workers for resale to patrons. May convert gaming chips, tokens, or tickets to currency upon patron's request. May use a cash register or computer to record transaction. No other data currently available.

43-3071.00 Tellers

Receive and pay out money. Keep records of money and negotiable instruments involved in a financial institution's various transactions. **Education:** Short-term O-J-T. **Occupational Type:** Conventional. **Job Zone:** 2. **Average Salary:** $17,200. **Projected Growth:** –5.5%. **Occupational Values:** Working Conditions; Coworkers; Supervision, Human Relations; Supervision, Technical; Security; Company Policies and Practices; Moral Values. **Skills Required:** Mathematics; Speaking; Service Orientation. **Abilities:** Number Facility; Oral Expression; Near Vision; Speech Clarity; Information Ordering; Oral Comprehension; Perceptual Speed. **Interacting with Others:** Communicating with Persons Outside Organization; Monitoring and Controlling Resources; Performing for/Working with Public; Establishing and Maintaining Relationships; Performing Administrative Activities. **Physical Work Conditions:** Indoors; Sitting; Using Hands on Objects, Tools, Controls; Making Repetitive Motions; Standing.

43-4051.01 Adjustment Clerks

Investigate and resolve customers' inquiries concerning merchandise, service, billing, or credit rating. Examine pertinent information to determine accuracy of customers' complaints and responsibility for errors. Notify customers and appropriate personnel of findings, adjustments, and recommendations such as exchange of merchandise, refund of money, credit to customers' accounts, or adjustment to customers' bills. **Education:** Short-term O-J-T. **Occupational Type:** Conventional. **Job Zone:** 2. **Average Salary:** $22,040. **Projected Growth:** 34%. **Occupational Values:** Working Conditions; Supervision, Human Relations; Activity; Moral Values; Security; Company Policies and Practices; Coworkers. **Skills Required:** Problem Identification; Information Gathering; Active Listening; Writing; Reading Comprehension; Speaking. **Abilities:** Oral Comprehension; Written Comprehension; Oral Expression; Deductive Reasoning; Near Vision; Written Expression. **Interacting with Others:** Performing for/Working with Public; Resolving Conflict, Negotiating with Others; Communicating with Persons Outside Organization. **Physical Work Conditions:** Indoors; Sitting.

43-4051.02 Customer Service Representatives, Utilities

Interview applicants for water, gas, electric, or telephone service. Talk with customer by phone or in person and receive orders for installation, turn-on, discontinuance, or change in services. **Education:** Short-term O-J-T. **Occupational Type:** Conventional. **Job Zone:** 2. **Average Salary:** $28,030. **Projected Growth:** 16.5%. **Occupational Values:** Security; Supervision, Human Relations; Moral Values; Working Conditions; Company Policies and Practices; Supervision, Technical; Activity. **Skills Required:** Speaking; Problem Identification; Active Listening; Service Orientation. **Abilities:** Oral Comprehension; Speech Clarity; Oral Expression; Near Vision; Number Facility. **Interacting with Others:** Communicating with Persons Outside Organization; Performing for/Working with Public; Performing Administrative Activities. **Physical Work Conditions:** Indoors; Sitting; Using Hands on Objects, Tools, Controls.

43-4141.00 New Accounts Clerks

Interview persons desiring to open bank accounts. Explain banking services available to prospective customers and assist them in preparing application forms. **Education:** Work experience in a related occupation. **Occupational Type:** Conventional. **Job Zone:** 2. **Average Salary:** $21,340. **Projected Growth:** 14.7%. **Occupational Values:** Working Conditions; Supervision, Human Relations; Coworkers; Moral Values; Security; Company Policies and Practices; Supervision, Technical. **Skills Required:** Speaking; Information Gathering; Active Listening; Mathematics. **Abilities:** Oral Expression; Number Facility; Oral Comprehension; Written Comprehension. **Interacting with Others:** Communicating with Persons Outside Organization; Performing Administrative Activities; Performing for/Working with Public. **Physical Work Conditions:** Indoors; Sitting.

43-4151.00 Order Clerks

Receive and process incoming orders for materials, merchandise, classified ads, or services such as repairs, installations, or rental of facilities. Duties include informing customers of receipt, prices, shipping dates, and delays; preparing contracts; and handling complaints. **Education:** Short-term O-J-T. **Occupational Type:** Conventional. **Job Zone:** 2. **Average Salary:** $21,550. **Projected Growth:** 4.6%. **Occupational Values:** Moral Values; Activity; Supervision, Human Relations; Supervision, Technical; Company Policies and Practices; Working Conditions; Coworkers. **Skills Required:** Service Orientation; Writing; Active Listening; Mathematics; Speaking. **Abilities:** Oral Comprehension; Written Comprehension; Oral Expression; Mathematical Reasoning; Number Facility; Speech Clarity; Written Expression. **Interacting with Others:** Communicating with Persons Outside Organization; Communicating with Other Workers; Performing for/Working with Public; Performing Administrative Activities; Resolving Conflict, Negotiating with Others. **Physical Work Conditions:** Indoors; Sitting.

43-4171.00 Receptionists and Information Clerks

Answer inquiries and obtain information for general public, customers, visitors, and other interested parties. Provide information regarding activities conducted at establishment and regarding location of departments, offices, and employees within organization. **Education:** Short-term O-J-T. **Occupational Type:** Conventional. **Job Zone:** 1. **Average Salary:** $18,620. **Projected Growth:** 23.6%. **Occupational Values:** Company Policies and Practices; Activity; Moral Values; Supervision, Human Relations; Working Conditions; Security; Supervision, Technical. **Skills Required:** Speaking; Active Listening; Service Orientation. **Abilities:** Oral Expression; Oral Comprehension; Speech Clarity; Speech Recognition; Written Comprehension; Written Expression. **Interacting with Others:** Performing for/Working with Public; Communicating with Persons Outside Organization; Establishing and Maintaining Relationships; Interpreting Meaning of Information to Others. **Physical Work Conditions:** Indoors; Sitting.

43-4181.01 Travel Clerks

Provide tourists with travel information such as points of interest, restaurants, rates, and emergency service. Duties include answering inquiries, offering suggestions, and providing literature pertaining to trips, excursions, sporting events, concerts, and plays. May make reservations, deliver tickets, arrange for visas, or contact individuals and groups to inform them of package tours. **Education:** Short-term O-J-T. **Occupational Type:** Conventional. **Job Zone:** 2. **Average Salary:** $18,090. **Projected Growth:** 6%. **Occupational Values:** Working Conditions; Moral Values; Activity; Company Policies and Practices; Supervision, Human Relations; Social Service; Security. **Skills Required:** Service Orientation; Speaking; Active Listening; Mathematics; Reading Comprehension; Information Gathering; Coordination. **Abilities:** Oral Expression; Near Vision; Oral Comprehension; Written Comprehension. **Interacting with Others:** Communicating with Persons Outside Organization; Performing for/Working with Public; Assisting and Caring for Others; Establishing and Maintaining Relationships; Interpreting Meaning of Information to Others; Performing Administrative Activities. **Physical Work Conditions:** Sitting; Indoors; Using Hands on Objects, Tools, Controls.

09.06.01 Communications

43-2011.00 Switchboard Operators, Including Answering Service

Operate telephone business systems equipment or switchboards to relay incoming, outgoing, and interoffice calls. May supply information to callers and record messages. **Education:** Short-term O-J-T. **Occupational Type:** Conventional. **Job Zone:** 1. **Average Salary:** $18,220. **Projected Growth:** -13.9%. **Occupational Values:** Moral Values; Activity; Independence; Working Conditions; Supervision, Human Relations; Company Policies and Practices; Supervision, Technical. **Skills Required:** Active Listening; Writing; Speaking. **Abilities:** Oral Comprehension; Speech Clarity; Oral Expression; Speech Recognition. **Interacting with Others:** Communicating with Persons Outside Organization. **Physical Work Conditions:** Indoors; Sitting; Using Hands on Objects, Tools, Controls.

43-2021.00 Telephone Operators

Provide information by accessing alphabetical and geographical directories. Assist customers with special billing requests, such as charges to a third party and credits or refunds for incorrectly dialed numbers or bad connections. May handle emergency calls and assist children or people with physical disabilities to make telephone calls. No other data currently available.

43-2021.01 Directory Assistance Operators

Provide telephone information from central office switchboard. Refer to alphabetical or geographical reels or directories to answer questions or suggest answer sources. **Education:** Moderate-term O-J-T. **Occupational Type:** Conventional. **Job Zone:** 1. **Average Salary:** $30,530. **Projected Growth:** -31.1%. **Occupational Values:** Independence; Activity; Supervision, Technical; Moral Values; Supervision, Human Relations; Security; Company Policies and Practices. **Skills Required:** Speaking; Service Orientation; Active Listening; Reading Comprehension; Information Gathering. **Abilities:** Oral Expression; Oral Comprehension; Speech Clarity; Speech Recognition; Near Vision; Auditory Attention; Perceptual Speed. **Interacting with Others:** Communicating with Persons Outside Organization; Performing for/Working with Public. **Physical Work Conditions:** Indoors; Sitting; Using Hands on Objects, Tools, Controls; Making Repetitive Motions.

43-2021.02 Central Office Operators

Operate telephone switchboard to establish or assist customers in establishing local or long-distance telephone connections. **Education:** Short-term O-J-T. **Occupational Type:** Conventional. **Job Zone:** 1. **Average Salary:** $26,220. **Projected Growth:** -16.6%. **Occupational Values:** Moral Values; Supervision, Technical; Independence; Supervision, Human Relations; Activity; Company Policies and Practices; Security. **Skills Required:** Speaking; Active Listening. **Abilities:** Oral Expression; Speech Clarity; Oral Comprehension. **Interacting with Others:** Communicating with Persons Outside Organization; Performing for/Working with Public. **Physical Work Conditions:** Indoors; Sitting; Using Hands on Objects, Tools, Controls.

43-5031.00 Police, Fire, and Ambulance Dispatchers

Receive complaints from public concerning crimes and police emergencies. Broadcast orders to police patrol units in vicinity of complaint to investigate. Operate radio, telephone, or computer equipment to receive reports of fires and medical emergencies and relay information or orders to proper officials. **Education:** Moderate-term O-J-T. **Occupational Type:** Social. **Job Zone:** 2. **Average Salary:** $23,670. **Projected Growth:** 8%. **Occupational Values:** Supervision, Human Relations; Security; Authority; Social Service; Supervision, Technical; Company Policies and Practices; Moral Values. **Skills Required:** Active Listening; Service Orientation; Speaking; Problem Identification; Judgment and Decision Making; Information Gathering; Coordination. **Abilities:** Oral Comprehension; Speed of Closure; Speech Clarity; Oral Expression; Selective Attention; Auditory Attention; Speech Recognition. **Interacting with Others:** Communicating with Other Workers; Communicating with Persons Outside Organization; Assisting and Caring for Others; Coordinating Work and Activities of Others; Interpreting Meaning of Information to Others. **Physical Work Conditions:** Indoors; Sitting.

43-5032.00 Dispatchers, Except Police, Fire, and Ambulance

Schedule and dispatch workers, work crews, equipment, or service vehicles for conveyance of materials, freight, or passengers, or for normal installation, service, or emergency repairs rendered outside the place of business. Use radio, telephone, or computer to transmit assignments; compile statistics and reports on work progress. **Education:** Moderate-term O-J-T. **Occupational Type:** Conventional. **Job Zone:** 2. **Average Salary:** $26,370. **Projected Growth:** 14.4%. **Occupational Values:** Moral Values; Supervision, Technical; Security; Authority; Supervision, Human Relations; Company Policies and Practices; Independence. **Skills Required:** Active Listening; Speaking. **Abilities:** Oral Comprehension; Speech Clarity; Oral Expression. **Interacting with Others:** Communicating with Other Workers; Coordinating Work and Activities of Others; Communicating with Persons Outside Organization. **Physical Work Conditions:** Indoors; Sitting.

09.07.01 Records Processing: Verification and Proofing

43-4041.01 Credit Authorizers

Authorize credit charges against customers' accounts. **Education:** Short-term O-J-T. **Occupational Type:** Conventional. **Job Zone:** 1. **Average Salary:** $22,990. **Projected Growth:** –10.7%. **Occupational Values:** Working Conditions; Moral Values; Security; Supervision, Human Relations; Activity; Company Policies and Practices; Independence. **Skills Required:** Active Listening; Information Gathering. **Abilities:** Number Facility. **Interacting with Others:** Communicating with Persons Outside Organization. **Physical Work Conditions:** Indoors; Sitting; Using Hands on Objects, Tools, Controls.

43-4041.02 Credit Checkers

Investigate history and credit standing of individuals or business establishments applying for credit. Telephone or write to credit departments of business and service establishments to obtain information about applicant's credit standing. **Education:** Short-term O-J-T. **Occupational Type:** Conventional. **Job Zone:** 1. **Average Salary:** $21,550. **Projected Growth:** 1.5%. **Occupational Values:** Working Conditions; Activity; Supervision, Human Relations; Moral Values; Security; Company Policies and Practices; Coworkers. **Skills Required:** Information Gathering; Speaking; Active Listening; Reading Comprehension; Writing. **Abilities:** Oral Comprehension; Written Comprehension; Oral Expression; Problem Sensitivity; Speech Clarity. **Interacting with Others:** Communicating with Persons Outside Organization. **Physical Work Conditions:** Indoors; Sitting.

43-9041.01 Insurance Claims Clerks

Obtain information from insured or designated persons for purpose of settling claim with insurance carrier. **Education:** Short-term O-J-T. **Occupational Type:** Conventional. **Job Zone:** 2. **Average Salary:** $22,526. **Projected Growth:** 14.5%. **Occupational Values:** Moral Values; Supervision, Human Relations; Working Conditions; Activity; Company Policies and Practices; Independence; Security. **Skills Required:** Speaking; Information Gathering; Active Listening; Mathematics; Reading Comprehension. **Abilities:** Number Facility; Information Ordering; Written Comprehension; Near Vision; Oral Comprehension; Oral Expression; Speech Clarity. **Interacting with Others:** Communicating with Persons Outside Organization; Performing Administrative Activities. **Physical Work Conditions:** Indoors; Sitting.

43-9041.02 Insurance Policy Processing Clerks

Process applications for, changes to, reinstatement of, and cancellation of insurance policies. Duties include reviewing insurance applications to ensure that all questions have been answered, compiling data on insurance policy changes, changing policy records to conform to insured party's specifications, compiling data on lapsed insurance policies to determine automatic reinstatement according to company policies, canceling insurance policies as requested by agents, and verifying the accuracy of insurance company records. **Education:** Short-term O-J-T. **Occupational Type:** Conventional. **Job Zone:** 2. **Average Salary:** $23,960. **Projected Growth:** 7.9%. **Occupational Values:** Working Conditions; Moral Values; Supervision, Human Relations; Activity; Company Policies and Practices; Security; Coworkers. **Skills Required:** Reading Comprehension; Information Gathering. **Abilities:** Mathematical Reasoning; Number Facility; Written Comprehension; Speech Clarity; Oral Expression. **Interacting with Others:** Communicating with Other Workers. **Physical Work Conditions:** Indoors; Sitting.

43-9081.00 Proofreaders and Copy Markers

Read transcript or proof type setup to detect and mark for correction any grammatical, typographical, or compositional errors. **Education:** Short-term O-J-T. **Occupational Type:** Conventional. **Job Zone:** 2. **Average Salary:** $18,620. **Projected Growth:** –17.1%. **Occupational Values:** Moral Values; Working Conditions; Activity; Independence; Company Policies and Practices; Supervision, Human Relations; Security. **Skills Required:** Product Inspection; Monitoring; Reading Comprehension; Problem Identification; Solution Appraisal; Information Gathering. **Abilities:** Written Comprehension; Memorization; Near Vision. **Interacting with Others:** Communicating with Other Workers. **Physical Work Conditions:** Indoors; Sitting.

09.07.02 Records Processing: Preparation and Maintenance

23-2091.00 Court Reporters

Use verbatim methods and equipment to capture, store, retrieve, and transcribe pretrial and trial proceedings or other information. Include stenocaptioners who operate computerized stenographic captioning equipment to provide captions of live or prerecorded broadcasts for hearing-impaired viewers. No other data currently available.

29-2071.00 Medical Records and Health Information Technicians

Compile, process, and maintain medical records of hospital and clinic patients in a manner consistent with medical, administrative, ethical, legal, and regulatory requirements of the health care system. Process, maintain, compile, and report patient information for health requirements and standards. **Education:** Associate degree. **Occupational Type:** Conventional. **Job Zone:** 3. **Average Salary:** $20,590. **Projected Growth:** 43.9%. **Occupational Values:** Moral Values; Working Conditions; Activity; Supervision, Human Relations; Security; Independence; Company Policies and Practices. **Skills Required:** Information Organization; Information Gathering; Reading Comprehension; Synthesis/Reorganization. **Abilities:** Written Comprehension; Written Expression; Oral Comprehension; Near Vision. **Interacting with Others:** Performing Administrative Activities. **Physical Work Conditions:** Indoors; Sitting.

31-9094.00 Medical Transcriptionists

Use transcribing machines with headset and foot pedal to listen to recordings by physicians and other healthcare professionals dictating a variety of medical reports, such as emergency room visits, diagnostic imaging studies, operations, chart reviews, and final summaries. Transcribe dictated reports and translate medical jargon and abbreviations into their expanded forms. Edit as necessary and return reports in either printed or electronic form to the dictator for review and signature, or correction. No other data currently available.

43-3061.00 Procurement Clerks

Compile information and records to draw up purchase orders for procurement of materials and services. **Education:** Short-term O-J-T. **Occupational Type:** Conventional. **Job Zone:** 1. **Average Salary:** $22,630. **Projected Growth:** –14.8%. **Occupational Values:** Moral Values; Working Conditions; Company Policies and Practices; Activity; Independence; Supervision, Human Relations; Supervision, Technical. **Skills Required:** Active Listening; Reading Comprehension; Speaking; Mathematics; Writing; Information Gathering; Management of Material Resources. **Abilities:** Near Vision. **Interacting with Others:** Monitoring and Controlling Resources; Communicating with Persons Outside Organization; Establishing and Maintaining Relationships. **Physical Work Conditions:** Indoors; Sitting.

43-4021.00 Correspondence Clerks

Compose letters in reply to requests regarding merchandise, damage claims, credit and other information, delinquent accounts, incorrect billings, or unsatisfactory services. Duties may include gathering data to formulate reply and typing correspondence. **Education:** Postsecondary vocational training. **Occupational Type:** Conventional. **Job Zone:** 2. **Average Salary:** $22,270. **Projected Growth:** 12.2%. **Occupational Values:** Working Conditions; Moral Values; Company Policies and Practices; Supervision, Human Relations; Activity; Security; Compensation. **Skills Required:** Reading Comprehension; Information Gathering; Writing; Problem Identification; Information Organization. **Abilities:** Written Expression; Wrist-Finger Speed; Written Comprehension. **Interacting with Others:** Communicating with Persons Outside Organization; Performing Administrative Activities. **Physical Work Conditions:** Indoors; Sitting.

43-4071.00 File Clerks

File correspondence, cards, invoices, receipts, and other records in alphabetical or numerical order or according to the filing system used. Locate and remove material from file when requested. **Education:** Short-term O-J-T. **Occupational Type:** Conventional. **Job Zone:** 1. **Average Salary:** $16,830. **Projected Growth:** 9.6%. **Occupational Values:** Moral Values; Activity; Company Policies and Practices; Supervision, Human Relations; Working Conditions; Independence; Security. **Skills Required:** Information Organization. **Abilities:** Written Comprehension; Information Ordering. **Interacting with Others:** Performing Administrative Activities. **Physical Work Conditions:** Indoors; Sitting.

43-4161.00 Human Resources Assistants, Except Payroll and Timekeeping

Compile and keep personnel records. Record data for each employee, such as address, weekly earnings, absences, amount of sales or production, supervisory reports on ability, and date of and reason for termination. Compile and type reports from employment records. File employment records. Search employee files and furnish information to authorized persons. **Education:** Short-term O-J-T. **Occupational Type:** Conventional. **Job Zone:** 2. **Average Salary:** $24,360. **Projected Growth:** 2%. **Occupational Values:** Working Conditions; Moral Values; Company Policies and Practices; Activity; Supervision, Human Relations; Security; Compensation. **Skills Required:** Reading Comprehension; Speaking; Information Organization; Writing; Active Listening; Information Gathering. **Abilities:** Oral Comprehension; Written Comprehension; Speech Clarity; Oral Expression. **Interacting with Others:** Communicating with Other Workers; Communicating with Persons Outside Organization; Staffing Organizational Units; Performing Administrative Activities. **Physical Work Conditions:** Indoors; Sitting; Using Hands on Objects, Tools, Controls.

43-9061.00 Office Clerks, General

Perform duties too varied and diverse to be classified in any specific office clerical occupation, requiring limited knowledge of office management systems and procedures. Clerical duties may be assigned in accordance with the office procedures of individual establishments and may include a combination of answering telephones, bookkeeping, typing or word processing, stenography, office machine operation, and filing. **Education:** Short-term O-J-T. **Occupational Type:** Conventional. **Job Zone:** 1. **Average Salary:** $19,580. **Projected Growth:** 15.3%. **Occupational Values:** Moral Values; Activity; Working Conditions; Advancement; Supervision, Human Relations; Coworkers; Supervision, Technical. **Skills Required:** Reading Comprehension; Writing. **Abilities:** Information Ordering; Oral Comprehension; Number Facility; Oral Expression; Speech Clarity; Near Vision; Written Comprehension. **Interacting with Others:** Communicating with Persons Outside Organization; Performing Administrative Activities; Communicating with Other Workers. **Physical Work Conditions:** Indoors; Sitting.

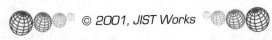

09.08.01 Records and Materials Processing

43-5011.00 Cargo and Freight Agents

Expedite and route movement of incoming and outgoing cargo and freight shipments in airline, train, and trucking terminals and at shipping docks. Take orders from customers and arrange pickup of freight and cargo for delivery to loading platform. Prepare and examine bills of lading to determine shipping charges and tariffs. **Education:** Short-term O-J-T. **Occupational Type:** Conventional. **Job Zone:** 2. **Average Salary:** $23,050. **Projected Growth:** 6.8%. **Occupational Values:** Moral Values; Company Policies and Practices; Supervision, Human Relations; Security; Supervision, Technical; Coworkers; Activity. **Skills Required:** Service Orientation. **Abilities:** Trunk Strength. **Interacting with Others:** Communicating with Other Workers. **Physical Work Conditions:** Special Uniform; Indoors; Standing; Using Hands on Objects, Tools, Controls; Distracting Sounds and Noise Levels; Walking or Running.

43-5021.00 Couriers and Messengers

Pick up and carry messages, documents, packages, and other items between offices or departments within an establishment or to other business concerns, traveling by foot, bicycle, motorcycle, automobile, or public conveyance. **Education:** Short-term O-J-T. **Occupational Type:** Realistic. **Job Zone:** 1. **Average Salary:** $16,680. **Projected Growth:** 8.8%. **Occupational Values:** Independence; Moral Values. **Skills Required:** Reading Comprehension; Writing; Active Listening; Idea Generation; Speaking; Equipment Maintenance. **Abilities:** Oral Comprehension; Written Comprehension. **Interacting with Others:** Communicating with Persons Outside Organization. **Physical Work Conditions:** Outdoors; Walking or Running; Hazardous Equipment; Indoors; Standing; Using Hands on Objects, Tools, Controls.

43-5052.00 Postal Service Mail Carriers

Sort mail for delivery. Deliver mail on established route by vehicle or on foot. **Education:** Short-term O-J-T. **Occupational Type:** Conventional. **Job Zone:** 1. **Average Salary:** $34,840. **Projected Growth:** 7.4%. **Occupational Values:** Independence; Security; Supervision, Human Relations; Company Policies and Practices; Moral Values; Compensation; Supervision, Technical. **Skills Required:** Service Orientation. **Abilities:** Written Comprehension; Perceptual Speed. **Interacting with Others:** Performing for/Working with Public. **Physical Work Conditions:** Special Uniform; Outdoors; Walking or Running; Standing; Using Hands on Objects, Tools, Controls; Very Hot.

43-5053.00 Postal Service Mail Sorters, Processors, and Processing Machine Operators

Prepare incoming and outgoing mail for distribution. Examine, sort, and route mail by State, type of mail, or other scheme. Load, operate, and occasionally adjust and repair mail processing, sorting, and canceling machinery. Keep records of shipments, pouches, and sacks and other duties related to mail handling within the postal service. Must complete a competitive exam. No other data currently available.

43-5071.00 Shipping, Receiving, and Traffic Clerks

Verify and keep records on incoming and outgoing shipments. Prepare items for shipment. Duties include assembling, addressing, stamping, and shipping merchandise or material; receiving, unpacking, verifying and recording incoming merchandise or material; and arranging for the transportation of products. **Education:** Short-term O-J-T. **Occupational Type:** Conventional. **Job Zone:** 1. **Average Salary:** $22,500. **Projected Growth:** 3.1%. **Occupational Values:** Moral Values; Supervision, Human Relations; Company Policies and Practices; Independence; Activity; Coworkers; Security. **Skills Required:** Problem Identification; Writing; Mathematics; Implementation Planning; Information Gathering; Product Inspection; Judgment and Decision Making. **Abilities:** Written Comprehension; Near Vision; Written Expression; Oral Expression. **Interacting with Others:** Communicating with Persons Outside Organization. **Physical Work Conditions:** Indoors; Sitting; Standing; Using Hands on Objects, Tools, Controls.

43-5081.02 Marking Clerks

Print and attach price tickets to articles of merchandise using one or several methods such as marking price on tickets by hand or using ticket-printing machine. **Education:** Short-term O-J-T. **Occupational Type:** Conventional. **Job Zone:** 1. **Average Salary:** No Data Available. **Projected Growth:** 6.8%. **Occupational Values:** Moral Values; Independence; Supervision, Human Relations; Activity; Working Conditions. **Skills Required:** Mathematics. **Abilities:** Category Flexibility. **Interacting with Others:** Performing Administrative Activities. **Physical Work Conditions:** Indoors; Using Hands on Objects, Tools, Controls; Standing; Making Repetitive Motions.

43-5081.03 Stock Clerks—Stockroom, Warehouse, or Storage Yard

Receive, store, and issue materials, equipment, and other items from stockroom, warehouse, or storage yard. Keep records and compile stock reports. **Education:** Short-term O-J-T. **Occupational Type:** Conventional. **Job Zone:** 2. **Average Salary:** $19,120. **Projected Growth:** 5.6%. **Occupational Values:** Moral Values; Independence; Supervision, Human Relations; Security; Company Policies and Practices; Supervision, Technical; Activity. **Skills Required:** Reading Comprehension; Active Listening; Information Organization. **Abilities:** Information Ordering; Extent Flexibility; Category Flexibility; Memorization; Written Comprehension. **Interacting with Others:** Monitoring and Controlling Resources. **Physical Work Conditions:** Indoors; Using Hands on Objects, Tools, Controls; Walking or Running; Standing; Sitting.

43-5081.04 Order Fillers, Wholesale and Retail Sales

Fill customers' mail and telephone orders from stored merchandise in accordance with specifications on sales slips or order forms. Duties include computing prices of items; completing order receipts; keeping records of outgoing orders; and requisitioning additional materials, supplies, and equipment. **Education:** Short-term O-J-T. **Occupational Type:** Conventional. **Job Zone:** 2. **Average Salary:** $19,030. **Projected Growth:** 5.6%. **Occupational Values:** Moral Values; Supervision, Human Relations; Independence. **Skills Required:** Mathematics. **Abilities:**

Number Facility. **Interacting with Others:** Performing Administrative Activities. **Physical Work Conditions:** Indoors; Standing; Making Repetitive Motions.

43-5111.00 Weighers, Measurers, Checkers, and Samplers, Recordkeeping

Weigh, measure, and check materials, supplies, and equipment for the purpose of keeping relevant records. Duties are primarily clerical by nature. **Education:** Short-term O-J-T. **Occupational Type:** Conventional. **Job Zone:** 1. **Average Salary:** $22,300. **Projected Growth:** 1.5%. **Occupational Values:** Moral Values; Supervision, Human Relations; Company Policies and Practices; Security; Supervision, Technical; Independence; Co-workers. **Skills Required:** Mathematics; Product Inspection. **Abilities:** Manual Dexterity; Information Ordering; Category Flexibility. **Interacting with Others:** Performing Administrative Activities; Communicating with Persons Outside Organization. **Physical Work Conditions:** Using Hands on Objects, Tools, Controls; Indoors; Standing; Making Repetitive Motions.

43-9051.02 Mail Clerks, Except Mail Machine Operators and Postal Service

Prepare incoming and outgoing mail for distribution. Duties include time stamping, opening, reading, sorting, and routing incoming mail; sealing, stamping, and affixing postage to outgoing mail or packages. **Education:** Short-term O-J-T. **Occupational Type:** Conventional. **Job Zone:** 1. **Average Salary:** $17,660. **Projected Growth:** 9.5%. **Occupational Values:** Moral Values; Security; Activity; Company Policies and Practices; Supervision, Human Relations; Supervision, Technical; Independence. **Skills Required:** Writing; Product Inspection; Mathematics; Information Organization; Problem Identification; Reading Comprehension; Service Orientation. **Abilities:** Perceptual Speed; Number Facility; Near Vision; Wrist-Finger Speed; Written Comprehension. **Interacting with Others:** Communicating with Persons Outside Organization. **Physical Work Conditions:** Indoors; Using Hands on Objects, Tools, Controls; Making Repetitive Motions; Standing; Sitting.

09.09.01 Clerical Machine Operation

43-3021.03 Billing, Posting, and Calculating Machine Operators

Operate machines that automatically perform mathematical processes such as addition, subtraction, multiplication, and division to calculate and record billing, accounting, statistical, and other numerical data. Duties include operating special billing machines to prepare statements, bills, and invoices; and operating bookkeeping machines to copy and post data, make computations, and compile records of transactions. **Education:** Short-term O-J-T. **Occupational Type:** Conventional. **Job Zone:** 1. **Average Salary:** $20,560. **Projected Growth:** -2.6%. **Occupational Values:** Independence; Moral Values; Supervision, Human Relations; Working Conditions; Activity; Security; Company Policies and Practices. **Skills Required:** Mathematics. **Abilities:** Number Facility; Wrist-Finger Speed; Mathematical Reasoning. **Interacting with Others:** Performing Administrative Activities. **Physical Work Conditions:** Indoors; Making Repetitive Motions; Sitting; Using Hands on Objects, Tools, Controls.

43-5051.00 Postal Service Clerks

Perform any combination of tasks in a post office, such as receive letters and parcels; sell postage and revenue stamps, postal cards, and stamped envelopes; fill out and sell money orders; place mail in pigeon holes of mail rack or in bags according to State, address, or other scheme; and examine mail for correct postage. **Education:** Short-term O-J-T. **Occupational Type:** Conventional. **Job Zone:** 2. **Average Salary:** $35,100. **Projected Growth:** 6.8%. **Occupational Values:** Security; Supervision, Human Relations; Supervision, Technical; Company Policies and Practices; Moral Values; Compensation; Activity. **Skills Required:** Service Orientation; Speaking; Active Listening. **Abilities:** Number Facility; Oral Expression; Oral Comprehension; Near Vision; Speech Clarity. **Interacting with Others:** Performing for/Working with Public; Assisting and Caring for Others; Communicating with Persons Outside Organization. **Physical Work Conditions:** Indoors; Standing; Making Repetitive Motions; Special Uniform.

43-9011.00 Computer Operators

Monitor and control electronic computer and peripheral electronic data processing equipment to process business, scientific, engineering, and other data according to operating instructions. May enter commands at a computer terminal and set controls on computer and peripheral devices. Monitor and respond to operating and error messages. **Education:** Moderate-term O-J-T. **Occupational Type:** Conventional. **Job Zone:** 3. **Average Salary:** $24,787. **Projected Growth:** -24.1%. **Occupational Values:** Moral Values; Working Conditions; Supervision, Human Relations; Company Policies and Practices; Independence; Security; Activity. **Skills Required:** Reading Comprehension; Problem Identification. **Abilities:** Near Vision; Information Ordering; Written Comprehension; Oral Comprehension; Oral Expression. **Interacting with Others:** Communicating with Other Workers. **Physical Work Conditions:** Indoors; Sitting; Using Hands on Objects, Tools, Controls.

43-9021.00 Data Entry Keyers

Operate data entry device such as keyboard or photo composing perforator. Duties may include verifying data and preparing materials for printing. **Education:** Postsecondary vocational training. **Occupational Type:** Conventional. **Job Zone:** 2. **Average Salary:** $19,186. **Projected Growth:** 9%. **Occupational Values:** Moral Values; Independence; Activity; Working Conditions; Supervision, Human Relations; Security; Company Policies and Practices. **Skills Required:** Product Inspection; Problem Identification. **Abilities:** Wrist-Finger Speed; Near Vision; Written Comprehension. **Interacting with Others:** Performing Administrative Activities. **Physical Work Conditions:** Indoors; Sitting; Making Repetitive Motions; Using Hands on Objects, Tools, Controls.

43-9022.00 Word Processors and Typists

Use word processor/computer or typewriter to type letters, reports, forms, or other material from rough draft, corrected copy, or voice recording. May perform other clerical duties as assigned. **Education:** Moderate-term O-J-T. **Occupational Type:** Conventional. **Job Zone:** 2. **Average Salary:** $22,590. **Projected Growth:** –20.4%. **Occupational Values:** Moral Values; Working Conditions; Company Policies and Practices; Supervision, Human Relations; Activity; Independence; Security. **Skills Required:** Reading Comprehension. **Abilities:** Wrist-Finger Speed; Oral Comprehension; Near Vision; Perceptual Speed; Written Comprehension. **Interacting with Others:** Performing Administrative Activities. **Physical Work Conditions:** Indoors; Sitting; Making Repetitive Motions; Using Hands on Objects, Tools, Controls.

43-9051.01 Mail Machine Operators, Preparation and Handling

Operate machines that emboss names, addresses, and other matter onto metal plates for use in addressing machines, or that print names, addresses, and similar information onto items such as envelopes, accounting forms, and advertising literature. **Education:** Short-term O-J-T. **Occupational Type:** Realistic. **Job Zone:** 1. **Average Salary:** $17,250. **Projected Growth:** 1.9%. **Occupational Values:** Moral Values; Independence; Supervision, Technical; Activity; Supervision, Human Relations; Company Policies and Practices; Security. **Skills Required:** Operation and Control. **Abilities:** Written Comprehension. **Interacting with Others:** Communicating with Other Workers. **Physical Work Conditions:** Indoors; Using Hands on Objects, Tools, Controls; Standing; Making Repetitive Motions.

43-9071.00 Office Machine Operators, Except Computer

Operate one or more of a variety of office machines, such as photocopying, photographic, and duplicating machines, or other office machines. No other data currently available.

43-9071.01 Duplicating Machine Operators

Operate one of a variety of office machines such as photocopying, photographic, mimeograph, and duplicating machines to make copies. **Education:** Short-term O-J-T. **Occupational Type:** Conventional. **Job Zone:** 1. **Average Salary:** $19,530. **Projected Growth:** 1.9%. **Occupational Values:** Moral Values; Independence; Supervision, Human Relations; Activity; Supervision, Technical; Company Policies and Practices; Working Conditions. **Skills Required:** Operation and Control. **Abilities:** Near Vision. **Interacting with Others:** Performing Administrative Activities. **Physical Work Conditions:** Indoors; Using Hands on Objects, Tools, Controls; Standing; Making Repetitive Motions.

49-2011.01 Automatic Teller Machine Servicers

Collect deposits and replenish automatic teller machines with cash and supplies. **Education:** Short-term O-J-T. **Occupational Type:** Realistic. **Job Zone:** 3. **Average Salary:** $28,498. **Projected Growth:** 9.4%. **Occupational Values:** Independence; Moral Values; Supervision, Human Relations; Security; Company Policies and Practices; Supervision, Technical; Working Conditions. **Skills Required:** Mathematics; Testing; Problem Identification; Reading Comprehension; Writing. **Abilities:** Number Facility; Information Ordering; Near Vision. **Interacting with Others:** Communicating with Other Workers. **Physical Work Conditions:** Standing; Using Hands on Objects, Tools, Controls; Indoors; Outdoors.

51-5022.12 Typesetting and Composing Machine Operators and Tenders

Operate or tend typesetting and composing equipment such as phototypesetters, linotype or monotype keyboard machines, photocomposers, linocasters, and photoletterers. **Education:** Moderate-term O-J-T. **Occupational Type:** Realistic. **Job Zone:** 2. **Average Salary:** $23,050. **Projected Growth:** –59.8%. **Occupational Values:** Moral Values; Independence; Activity; Supervision, Human Relations; Company Policies and Practices; Supervision, Technical. **Skills Required:** Operation and Control. **Abilities:** Control Precision; Manual Dexterity; Information Ordering; Arm-Hand Steadiness; Near Vision; Written Comprehension. **Interacting with Others:** Communicating with Other Workers. **Physical Work Conditions:** Indoors; Using Hands on Objects, Tools, Controls; Hazardous Equipment; Sitting; Standing.

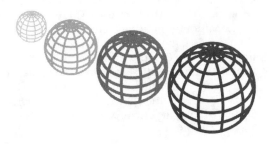

10 Sales and Marketing

10.01 Managerial Work in Sales and Marketing

10.02 Sales Technology

10.03 General Sales

10.04 Personal Soliciting

10.01.01 Managerial Work in Sales and Marketing

11-2011.00 Advertising and Promotions Managers

Plan and direct advertising policies and programs, or produce collateral materials such as posters, contests, coupons, or give-aways, to create extra interest in the purchase of a product or service for a department, an entire organization, or one account. **Education:** Work experience, plus degree. **Occupational Type:** Artistic. **Job Zone:** 4. **Average Salary:** $57,300. **Projected Growth:** 23%. **Occupational Values:** Working Conditions; Creativity; Authority; Achievement; Ability Utilization; Compensation; Company Policies and Practices. **Skills Required:** Coordination; Implementation Planning; Idea Generation; Speaking; Information Gathering; Idea Evaluation; Reading Comprehension. **Abilities:** Oral Expression; Originality; Fluency of Ideas; Written Expression; Oral Comprehension; Written Comprehension; Near Vision. **Interacting with Others:** Communicating with Other Workers; Selling or Influencing Others; Communicating with Persons Outside Organization; Coordinating Work and Activities of Others; Establishing and Maintaining Relationships; Developing and Building Teams; Guiding, Directing, and Motivating Subordinates. **Physical Work Conditions:** Indoors; Sitting; Standing.

11-2021.00 Marketing Managers

Determine the demand for products and services offered by a firm and its competitors and identify potential customers. Develop pricing strategies with the goal of maximizing the firm's profits or share of the market while ensuring customer satisfaction. Oversee product development or monitor trends that indicate the need for new products and services. **Education:** Work experience, plus degree. **Occupational Type:** Enterprising. **Job Zone:** 4. **Average Salary:** $57,300. **Projected Growth:** 23%. **Occupational Values:** Working Conditions; Creativity; Ability Utilization; Achievement; Autonomy; Activity; Compensation. **Skills Required:** Speaking; Active Listening; Visioning; Idea Generation; Critical Thinking; Reading Comprehension; Coordination. **Abilities:** Oral Comprehension; Originality; Oral Expression; Fluency of Ideas; Written Comprehension; Speech Clarity; Written Expression. **Interacting with Others:** Communicating with Other Workers; Communicating with Persons Outside Organization; Providing Consultation and Advice to Others; Selling or Influencing Others; Coordinating Work and Activities of Others; Performing Administrative Activities; Establishing and Maintaining Relationships. **Physical Work Conditions:** Indoors; Sitting.

11-2022.00 Sales Managers

Direct the actual distribution or movement of a product or service to the customer. Coordinate sales distribution by establishing sales territories, quotas, and goals; establish training programs for sales representatives. Analyze sales statistics gathered by staff to determine sales potential and inventory requirements; monitor the preferences of customers. **Education:** Work experience, plus degree. **Occupational Type:** Enterprising. **Job Zone:** 4. **Average Salary:** $57,300. **Projected Growth:** 23%. **Occupational Values:** Authority; Compensation; Activity; Working Conditions; Autonomy; Creativity; Company Policies and Practices. **Skills Required:** Speaking; Time Management; Coordination; Problem Identification; Critical Thinking; Service Orientation; Reading Comprehension. **Abilities:** Oral Comprehension; Written Comprehension; Oral Expression; Speech Clarity; Mathematical Reasoning; Deductive Reasoning; Fluency of Ideas. **Interacting with Others:** Selling or Influencing Others; Communicating with Other Workers; Communicating with Persons Outside Organization; Establishing and Maintaining Relationships; Staffing Organizational Units; Coordinating Work and Activities of Others; Guiding, Directing, and Motivating Subordinates. **Physical Work Conditions:** Indoors; Sitting.

41-1011.00 First-Line Supervisors/Managers of Retail Sales Workers

Directly supervise sales workers in a retail establishment or department. Duties may include management functions such as purchasing, budgeting, accounting, and personnel work in addition to supervisory duties. **Education:** Work experience in a related occupation. **Occupational Type:** Enterprising. **Job Zone:** 3. **Average Salary:** $29,570. **Projected Growth:** 10.2%. **Occupational Values:** Responsibility; Authority; Working Conditions; Activity; Autonomy; Ability Utilization; Creativity. **Skills Required:** Critical Thinking; Speaking; Information Gathering. **Abilities:** Oral Expression; Written Comprehension; Oral Comprehension; Written Expression. **Interacting with Others:** Monitoring and Controlling Resources; Communicating with Other Workers; Staffing Organizational Units; Coordinating Work and Activities of Others; Communicating with Persons Outside Organization; Selling or Influencing Others. **Physical Work Conditions:** Indoors.

41-1012.00 First-Line Supervisors/Managers of Non-Retail Sales Workers

Directly supervise and coordinate activities of sales workers other than retail sales workers. May perform duties such as budgeting, accounting, and personnel work in addition to supervisory duties. **Education:** Work experience in a related occupation. **Occupational Type:** Enterprising. **Job Zone:** 3. **Average Salary:** $29,570. **Projected Growth:** 10.2%. **Occupational Values:** Authority; Responsibility; Working Conditions; Ability Utilization; Autonomy; Activity; Creativity. **Skills Required:** Speaking; Information Gathering; Critical Thinking. **Abilities:** Oral Expression; Written Comprehension; Oral Comprehension; Written Expression. **Interacting with Others:** Monitoring and Controlling Resources; Communicating with Other Workers; Staffing Organizational Units; Coordinating Work and Activities of Others; Communicating with Persons Outside Organization; Selling or Influencing Others. **Physical Work Conditions:** Indoors.

10.02.01 Sales Technology: Technical Sales

41-4011.01 Sales Representatives, Agricultural

Sell agricultural products and services such as animal feeds,

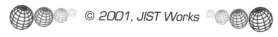

farm and garden equipment, and dairy, poultry, and veterinarian supplies. **Education:** Moderate-term O-J-T. **Occupational Type:** Enterprising. **Job Zone:** 2. **Average Salary:** $44,690. **Projected Growth:** 16.5%. **Occupational Values:** Achievement; Moral Values; Responsibility; Ability Utilization; Autonomy; Working Conditions; Company Policies and Practices. **Skills Required:** Speaking; Writing; Persuasion. **Abilities:** Oral Expression; Oral Comprehension; Speech Clarity; Written Expression. **Interacting with Others:** Selling or Influencing Others; Communicating with Persons Outside Organization. **Physical Work Conditions:** Indoors; Standing; Using Hands on Objects, Tools, Controls; Sitting.

41-4011.02 Sales Representatives, Chemical and Pharmaceutical

Sell chemical or pharmaceutical products or services such as acids, industrial chemicals, agricultural chemicals, medicines, drugs, and water treatment supplies. **Education:** Moderate-term O-J-T. **Occupational Type:** Enterprising. **Job Zone:** 3. **Average Salary:** $44,690. **Projected Growth:** 16.5%. **Occupational Values:** Compensation; Achievement; Moral Values; Recognition; Ability Utilization; Working Conditions; Autonomy. **Skills Required:** Speaking; Active Listening; Persuasion. **Abilities:** Oral Expression; Oral Comprehension. **Interacting with Others:** Communicating with Persons Outside Organization; Selling or Influencing Others; Establishing and Maintaining Relationships. **Physical Work Conditions:** Indoors; Sitting; Standing.

41-4011.03 Sales Representatives, Electrical/Electronic

Sell electrical, electronic, or related products or services such as communication equipment, radiographic-inspection equipment and services, ultrasonic equipment, electronics parts, computers, and EDP systems. **Education:** Moderate-term O-J-T. **Occupational Type:** Enterprising. **Job Zone:** 2. **Average Salary:** $44,690. **Projected Growth:** 16.5%. **Occupational Values:** Working Conditions; Moral Values; Achievement; Autonomy; Ability Utilization; Compensation; Recognition. **Skills Required:** Instructing; Negotiation; Persuasion; Information Gathering; Speaking. **Abilities:** Oral Expression; Speech Clarity; Oral Comprehension. **Interacting with Others:** Selling or Influencing Others; Communicating with Persons Outside Organization; Performing for/Working with Public; Resolving Conflict, Negotiating with Others. **Physical Work Conditions:** Indoors; Standing; Sitting.

41-4011.04 Sales Representatives, Mechanical Equipment and Supplies

Sell mechanical equipment, machinery, materials, and supplies such as aircraft and railroad equipment and parts, construction machinery, material-handling equipment, industrial machinery, and welding equipment. **Education:** Moderate-term O-J-T. **Occupational Type:** Enterprising. **Job Zone:** 2. **Average Salary:** $44,690. **Projected Growth:** 16.5%. **Occupational Values:** Autonomy; Achievement; Company Policies and Practices; Compensation; Variety; Working Conditions; Responsibility. **Skills Required:** Speaking; Active Listening; Instructing; Reading Comprehension; Persuasion; Operations Analysis; Negotiation. **Abilities:** Speech Clarity; Number Facility; Mathematical Reasoning; Oral Comprehension; Oral Expression; Written Comprehension; Written Expression. **Interacting with Others:** Selling or Influencing Others; Communicating with Persons Outside Organization; Establishing and Maintaining Relationships. **Physical Work Conditions:** Indoors; Standing; Sitting; Walking or Running.

41-4011.05 Sales Representatives, Medical

Sell medical equipment, products, and services. Does not include pharmaceutical sales representatives. **Education:** Moderate-term O-J-T. **Occupational Type:** Enterprising. **Job Zone:** 3. **Average Salary:** $44,690. **Projected Growth:** 16.5%. **Occupational Values:** Autonomy; Achievement; Company Policies and Practices; Working Conditions; Compensation; Supervision, Human Relations; Responsibility. **Skills Required:** Speaking; Persuasion; Active Listening. **Abilities:** Oral Expression; Written Comprehension; Oral Comprehension; Written Expression. **Interacting with Others:** Selling or Influencing Others; Communicating with Persons Outside Organization. **Physical Work Conditions:** Indoors; Standing.

41-4011.06 Sales Representatives, Instruments

Sell precision instruments such as dynamometers, spring scales, and laboratory, navigation, and surveying instruments. **Education:** Moderate-term O-J-T. **Occupational Type:** Enterprising. **Job Zone:** 3. **Average Salary:** $44,690. **Projected Growth:** 16.5%. **Occupational Values:** Autonomy; Achievement; Working Conditions; Company Policies and Practices; Supervision, Human Relations; Compensation; Responsibility. **Skills Required:** Persuasion; Speaking; Active Listening. **Abilities:** Oral Expression; Oral Comprehension. **Interacting with Others:** Selling or Influencing Others; Communicating with Persons Outside Organization; Establishing and Maintaining Relationships; Providing Consultation and Advice to Others. **Physical Work Conditions:** Indoors; Standing; Sitting.

10.02.02 Sales Technology: Intangible Sales

41-3011.00 Advertising Sales Agents

Sell or solicit advertising including graphic art, advertising space in publications, custom-made signs, or TV and radio advertising time. May obtain leases for outdoor advertising sites or persuade retailer to use sales promotion display items. **Education:** Moderate-term O-J-T. **Occupational Type:** Enterprising. **Job Zone:** 3. **Average Salary:** $31,850. **Projected Growth:** 16.5%. **Occupational Values:** Achievement; Working Conditions; Ability Utilization; Variety; Autonomy; Creativity; Social Status. **Skills Required:** Persuasion; Identification of Key Causes; Speaking; Active Listening; Social Perceptiveness; Reading Comprehension. **Abilities:** Oral Comprehension; Fluency of Ideas; Oral Expression; Written Expression. **Interacting with Others:** Communicating with Persons Outside Organization; Selling or Influencing Others; Establishing and Maintaining Relationships. **Physical Work Conditions:** Indoors; Sitting.

41-3021.00 Insurance Sales Agents

Sell life, property, casualty, health, automotive, or other types of insurance. May refer clients to independent brokers, work as independent broker, or be employed by an insurance company. **Education:** Long-term O-J-T. **Occupational Type:** Enterprising. **Job Zone:** 3. **Average Salary:** $34,370. **Projected Growth:** 2.2%. **Occupational Values:** Working Conditions; Responsibility; Advancement; Ability Utilization; Autonomy; Company Policies and Practices; Achievement. **Skills Required:** Speaking; Reading Comprehension; Persuasion; Active Listening. **Abilities:** Oral Expression; Oral Comprehension; Written Comprehension; Speech Clarity; Written Expression. **Interacting with Others:** Selling or Influencing Others; Communicating with Persons Outside Organization; Performing for/Working with Public; Interpreting Meaning of Information to Others; Establishing and Maintaining Relationships. **Physical Work Conditions:** Indoors; Sitting.

41-3031.01 Sales Agents, Securities and Commodities

Buy and sell securities in investment and trading firms; develop and implement financial plans for individuals, businesses, and organizations. **Education:** Long-term O-J-T. **Occupational Type:** Enterprising. **Job Zone:** 4. **Average Salary:** $48,090. **Projected Growth:** 41%. **Occupational Values:** Compensation; Recognition; Responsibility; Autonomy; Working Conditions; Ability Utilization; Social Status. **Skills Required:** Systems Perception; Management of Financial Resources; Identifying Downstream Consequences; Systems Evaluation; Judgment and Decision Making; Information Gathering; Critical Thinking. **Abilities:** Deductive Reasoning; Written Comprehension; Oral Comprehension; Written Expression; Mathematical Reasoning; Number Facility; Oral Expression. **Interacting with Others:** Providing Consultation and Advice to Others; Communicating with Persons Outside Organization; Monitoring and Controlling Resources; Establishing and Maintaining Relationships; Interpreting Meaning of Information to Others; Selling or Influencing Others. **Physical Work Conditions:** Indoors; Sitting.

41-3031.02 Sales Agents, Financial Services

Sell financial services such as loan, tax, and securities counseling to customers of financial institutions and business establishments. **Education:** Long-term O-J-T. **Occupational Type:** Enterprising. **Job Zone:** 3. **Average Salary:** $48,090. **Projected Growth:** 41%. **Occupational Values:** Compensation; Working Conditions; Autonomy; Responsibility; Recognition; Social Status; Activity. **Skills Required:** Persuasion; Judgment and Decision Making; Information Gathering; Speaking; Visioning; Systems Perception; Identification of Key Causes. **Abilities:** Oral Expression; Deductive Reasoning; Number Facility; Mathematical Reasoning; Speech Clarity; Written Comprehension; Near Vision. **Interacting with Others:** Communicating with Persons Outside Organization; Selling or Influencing Others; Interpreting Meaning of Information to Others; Establishing and Maintaining Relationships; Providing Consultation and Advice to Others. **Physical Work Conditions:** Indoors; Sitting.

10.03.01 General Sales

41-2022.00 Parts Salespersons

Sell spare and replacement parts and equipment in repair shop or parts store. **Education:** Short-term O-J-T. **Occupational Type:** Enterprising. **Job Zone:** 2. **Average Salary:** $22,730. **Projected Growth:** 1.2%. **Occupational Values:** Working Conditions; Coworkers; Supervision, Human Relations; Independence; Supervision, Technical; Advancement; Company Policies and Practices. **Skills Required:** Service Orientation; Social Perceptiveness; Speaking; Product Inspection. **Abilities:** Oral Comprehension; Written Comprehension; Oral Expression; Speech Clarity. **Interacting with Others:** Communicating with Persons Outside Organization; Performing for/Working with Public; Selling or Influencing Others. **Physical Work Conditions:** Indoors; Standing; Using Hands on Objects, Tools, Controls.

41-2031.00 Retail Salespersons

Sell merchandise such as furniture, motor vehicles, appliances, or apparel in a retail establishment. **Education:** Short-term O-J-T. **Occupational Type:** Enterprising. **Job Zone:** 2. **Average Salary:** $15,830. **Projected Growth:** 13.9%. **Occupational Values:** Working Conditions; Coworkers; Supervision, Technical; Advancement; Supervision, Human Relations; Achievement; Company Policies and Practices. **Skills Required:** Service Orientation; Social Perceptiveness; Speaking; Active Listening. **Abilities:** Oral Expression; Speech Clarity; Oral Comprehension; Number Facility. **Interacting with Others:** Selling or Influencing Others; Performing for/Working with Public; Communicating with Persons Outside Organization; Establishing and Maintaining Relationships. **Physical Work Conditions:** Indoors; Standing; Walking or Running.

41-3041.00 Travel Agents

Plan and sell transportation and accommodations for travel agency customers. Determine destination, modes of transportation, travel dates, costs, and accommodations required. **Education:** Postsecondary vocational training. **Occupational Type:** Enterprising. **Job Zone:** 2. **Average Salary:** $23,010. **Projected Growth:** 18.4%. **Occupational Values:** Working Conditions; Moral Values; Autonomy; Achievement; Social Service; Recognition; Activity. **Skills Required:** Speaking; Service Orientation; Coordination; Implementation Planning. **Abilities:** Oral Expression; Oral Comprehension. **Interacting with Others:** Performing for/Working with Public; Selling or Influencing Others; Communicating with Persons Outside Organization. **Physical Work Conditions:** Indoors; Sitting.

41-4012.00 Sales Representatives, Wholesale and Manufacturing, Except Technical and Scientific Products

Sell goods for wholesalers or manufacturers to businesses or groups of individuals. Work requires substantial knowledge of items sold. **Education:** Moderate-term O-J-T. **Occupational Type:** Enterprising. **Job Zone:** 2. **Average Salary:** $36,540. **Projected Growth:** 16.5%. **Occupational Values:** Autonomy; Achievement; Compensation; Supervision, Human Relations; Company Policies and Practices; Working Conditions; Responsibility. **Skills Required:** Speaking; Social Perceptiveness; Persuasion; Service Orientation; Negotiation; Active Listening; Identification of Key Causes. **Abilities:** Oral Expression; Oral Comprehension; Speech Clarity; Memorization; Written Expression; Written Comprehension; Fluency of Ideas. **Interacting with Others:** Selling or Influencing Others; Communicating with Persons Outside Organization; Establishing and Maintaining Relationships; Performing for/Working with Public; Communicating with Other Workers; Interpreting Meaning of Information to Others; Performing Administrative Activities. **Physical Work Conditions:** Indoors; Sitting; Standing.

41-9021.00 Real Estate Brokers

Operate real estate office or work for commercial real estate firm, overseeing real estate transactions. Other duties usually include selling real estate or renting properties and arranging loans. No other data currently available.

41-9022.00 Real Estate Sales Agents

Rent, buy, or sell property for clients. Perform duties such as studying property listings, interviewing prospective clients, accompanying clients to property site, discussing conditions of sale, and drawing up real estate contracts. Includes agents who represent buyer. **Education:** Postsecondary vocational training. **Occupational Type:** Enterprising. **Job Zone:** 2. **Average Salary:** $28,020. **Projected Growth:** 9%. **Occupational Values:** Responsibility; Compensation; Autonomy; Ability Utilization; Recognition; Working Conditions; Social Status. **Skills Required:** Speaking; Active Listening; Reading Comprehension; Information Gathering; Persuasion; Judgment and Decision Making; Social Perceptiveness. **Abilities:** Written Comprehension; Oral Comprehension; Oral Expression; Number Facility; Speech Clarity. **Interacting with Others:** Selling or Influencing Others; Establishing and Maintaining Relationships; Communicating with Persons Outside Organization; Performing for/Working with Public. **Physical Work Conditions:** Indoors; Sitting.

43-5081.01 Stock Clerks, Sales Floor

Receive, store, and issue sales floor merchandise. Stock shelves, racks, cases, bins, and tables with merchandise and arrange merchandise displays to attract customers. May periodically take physical count of stock or check and mark merchandise. **Education:** Short-term O-J-T. **Occupational Type:** Realistic. **Job Zone:** 1. **Average Salary:** $15,190. **Projected Growth:** 5.6%. **Occupational Values:** Moral Values; Activity; Independence; Supervision, Technical; Company Policies and Practices; Supervision, Human Relations. **Skills Required:** Service Orientation. **Abilities:** Extent Flexibility; Oral Expression; Oral Comprehension; Manual Dexterity; Static Strength; Number Facility; Category Flexibility. **Interacting with Others:** Establishing and Maintaining Relationships; Performing for/Working with Public; Communicating with Persons Outside Organization. **Physical Work Conditions:** Indoors; Standing; Walking or Running; Using Hands on Objects, Tools, Controls.

53-6031.00 Service Station Attendants

Service automobiles, buses, trucks, boats, and other automotive or marine vehicles with fuel, lubricants, and accessories. Collect payment for services and supplies. May lubricate vehicle, change motor oil, install antifreeze, or replace lights or other accessories such as windshield wiper blades or fan belts. May repair or replace tires. **Education:** Short-term O-J-T. **Occupational Type:** Realistic. **Job Zone:** 1. **Average Salary:** $14,310. **Projected Growth:** –1.2%. **Occupational Values:** Moral Values; Social Service. **Skills Required:** Service Orientation. **Abilities:** Number Facility; Oral Comprehension. **Interacting with Others:** Communicating with Persons Outside Organization; Performing for/Working with Public. **Physical Work Conditions:** Contaminants; Outdoors; Hazardous Conditions; Standing; Using Hands on Objects, Tools, Controls; Kneeling, Crouching, or Crawling; Special Uniform.

10.04.01 Personal Soliciting

41-9011.00 Demonstrators and Product Promoters

Demonstrate merchandise and answer questions for the purpose of creating public interest in buying the product. May sell demonstrated merchandise. **Education:** Short-term O-J-T. **Occupational Type:** Enterprising. **Job Zone:** 1. **Average Salary:** $16,930. **Projected Growth:** 13.9%. **Occupational Values:** Independence; Moral Values; Variety. **Skills Required:** Persuasion; Social Perceptiveness; Speaking; Active Listening; Instructing; Information Gathering; Writing. **Abilities:** Speech Clarity; Oral Comprehension; Oral Expression. **Interacting with Others:** Performing for/Working with Public; Selling or Influencing Others; Communicating with Persons Outside Organization; Establishing and Maintaining Relationships; Interpreting Meaning of Information to Others. **Physical Work Conditions:** Indoors; Standing; Outdoors; Using Hands on Objects, Tools, Controls; Walking or Running.

41-9041.00 Telemarketers

Solicit orders for goods or services over the telephone. **Education:** Short-term O-J-T. **Occupational Type:** Enterprising. **Job Zone:** 1. **Average Salary:** $17,090. **Projected Growth:** 13.9%. **Occupational Values:** Independence. **Skills Required:** Persuasion; Speaking. **Abilities:** Speech Clarity. **Interacting with Others:** Communicating with Persons Outside Organization; Selling or Influencing Others; Performing for/Working with Public; Establishing and Maintaining Relationships; Monitoring and Controlling Resources. **Physical Work Conditions:** Outdoors; Standing; Walking or Running; Indoors; Sitting.

41-9091.00 Door-To-Door Sales Workers, News and Street Vendors, and Related Workers

Sell goods or services door-to-door or on the street. **Education:** Short-term O-J-T. **Occupational Type:** Enterprising. **Job Zone:** 1. **Average Salary:** $17,090. **Projected Growth:** 13.9%. **Occupational Values:** Independence. **Skills Required:** Persuasion; Speaking. **Abilities:** Speech Clarity. **Interacting with Others:** Communicating with Persons Outside Organization; Selling or Influencing Others; Performing for/Working with Public; Establishing and Maintaining Relationships; Monitoring and Controlling Resources. **Physical Work Conditions:** Outdoors; Standing; Walking or Running; Indoors; Sitting.

11 Recreation, Travel, and Other Personal Services

11.01.01 Managerial Work in Recreation, Travel, and Other Personal Services

11-9051.00 Food Service Managers

Plan, direct, or coordinate activities of an organization or department that serves food and beverages. **Education:** Work experience in a related occupation. **Occupational Type:** Enterprising. **Job Zone:** 4. **Average Salary:** $26,700. **Projected Growth:** 16.3%. **Occupational Values:** Authority; Security; Autonomy; Creativity; Responsibility; Activity; Ability Utilization. **Skills Required:** Time Management; Management of Personnel Resources; Coordination; Problem Identification; Service Orientation; Implementation Planning; Critical Thinking. **Abilities:** Oral Comprehension; Near Vision; Oral Expression; Written Comprehension; Deductive Reasoning; Information Ordering; Mathematical Reasoning. **Interacting with Others:** Monitoring and Controlling Resources; Communicating with Other Workers; Guiding, Directing, and Motivating Subordinates; Coordinating Work and Activities of Others; Performing Administrative Activities; Staffing Organizational Units; Communicating with Persons Outside Organization. **Physical Work Conditions:** Indoors; Standing; Sitting; Walking or Running.

11-9071.00 Gaming Managers

Plan, organize, direct, control, or coordinate gaming operations in a casino. Formulate gaming policies for assigned area of responsibility. **Education:** Work experience, plus degree. **Occupational Type:** Enterprising. **Job Zone:** 3. **Average Salary:** $49,220. **Projected Growth:** 14.4%. **Occupational Values:** Responsibility; Authority; Working Conditions; Security; Autonomy; Ability Utilization; Compensation. **Skills Required:** Speaking; Management of Financial Resources; Management of Personnel Resources; Mathematics; Problem Identification; Time Management; Monitoring. **Abilities:** Number Facility; Mathematical Reasoning; Oral Expression. **Interacting with Others:** Coordinating Work and Activities of Others; Performing Administrative Activities; Communicating with Other Workers; Guiding, Directing, and Motivating Subordinates; Monitoring and Controlling Resources; Performing for/Working with Public; Staffing Organizational Units. **Physical Work Conditions:** Indoors; Sitting; Standing.

11-9081.00 Lodging Managers

Plan, direct, or coordinate activities of an organization or department that provides lodging and other accommodations. **Education:** Work experience in a related occupation. **Occupational Type:** Enterprising. **Job Zone:** 3. **Average Salary:** $26,700. **Projected Growth:** 16.3%. **Occupational Values:** Autonomy; Responsibility; Working Conditions; Security; Authority; Activity; Moral Values. **Skills Required:** Service Orientation; Coordination; Speaking; Management of Personnel Resources; Social Perceptiveness; Problem Identification; Active Listening. **Abilities:** Oral Expression; Speech Clarity; Number Facility; Oral Comprehension; Speech Recognition. **Interacting with Others:** Establishing and Maintaining Relationships; Monitoring and Controlling Resources; Performing for/Working with Public; Communicating with Other Workers; Communicating with Persons Outside Organization; Coordinating Work and Activities of Others; Staffing Organizational Units. **Physical Work Conditions:** Indoors; Standing; Sitting; Walking or Running.

13-1121.00 Meeting and Convention Planners

Coordinate activities of staff and convention personnel to make arrangements for group meetings and conventions. **Education:** Bachelor's degree. **Occupational Type:** Enterprising. **Job Zone:** 4. **Average Salary:** $37,060. **Projected Growth:** 20.9%. **Occupational Values:** Working Conditions; Autonomy; Achievement; Authority; Responsibility; Creativity; Recognition. **Skills Required:** Coordination; Management of Personnel Resources; Speaking; Implementation Planning; Problem Identification; Active Listening; Service Orientation. **Abilities:** Oral Expression; Written Comprehension; Oral Comprehension; Speech Clarity. **Interacting with Others:** Coordinating Work and Activities of Others; Communicating with Other Workers; Communicating with Persons Outside Organization; Establishing and Maintaining Relationships; Monitoring and Controlling Resources. **Physical Work Conditions:** Indoors; Sitting.

35-1012.00 First-Line Supervisors/Managers of Food Preparation and Serving Workers

Supervise workers engaged in preparing and serving food. **Education:** Work experience in a related occupation. **Occupational Type:** Enterprising. **Job Zone:** 3. **Average Salary:** $23,320. **Projected Growth:** 16.3%. **Occupational Values:** Authority; Responsibility; Coworkers; Autonomy; Moral Values; Activity; Ability Utilization. **Skills Required:** Time Management; Management of Personnel Resources; Coordination; Implementation Planning; Speaking; Systems Perception; Reading Comprehension. **Abilities:** Oral Expression; Written Comprehension; Oral Comprehension; Number Facility; Speech Clarity; Written Expression. **Interacting with Others:** Coordinating Work and Activities of Others; Communicating with Other Workers; Communicating with Persons Outside Organization; Guiding, Directing, and Motivating Subordinates; Monitoring and Controlling Resources; Performing Administrative Activities. **Physical Work Conditions:** Indoors; Standing; Using Hands on Objects, Tools, Controls; Walking or Running; Hazardous Situations.

37-1011.01 Housekeeping Supervisors

Supervise work activities of cleaning personnel to ensure clean, orderly, and attractive rooms in hotels, hospitals, educational institutions, and similar establishments. Assign duties, inspect work, and investigate complaints regarding housekeeping service and equipment; take corrective action. May purchase housekeeping supplies and equipment, take periodic inventories, screen applicants, train new employees, and recommend dismissals. **Education:** Work experience in a related occupation. **Occupational Type:** Enterprising. **Job Zone:** 4. **Average Salary:** $19,590. **Projected Growth:** 10.5%. **Occupational Values:** Authority; Coworkers; Moral Values; Working Conditions; Activity; Security; Responsibility. **Skills Required:** Coordination; Management of Personnel Resources. **Abilities:** Oral Expression; Oral Comprehension. **Interacting with Others:** Coordinating Work and Activities of Others; Communicating with Other Workers; Guiding, Directing, and Motivating Subordinates; Monitoring and Controlling Resources; Staffing Organizational Units. **Physical Work Conditions:** Indoors; Sitting.

37-1011.02 Janitorial Supervisors

Supervise work activities of janitorial personnel in commercial and industrial establishments. Assign duties, inspect work, and investigate complaints regarding janitorial services; take corrective action. May purchase janitorial supplies and equipment, take periodic inventories, screen applicants, train new employees, and recommend dismissals. **Education:** Work experience in a related occupation. **Occupational Type:** Enterprising. **Job Zone:** 3. **Average Salary:** $19,590. **Projected Growth:** 10.5%. **Occupational Values:** Authority; Activity; Autonomy; Security; Moral Values; Responsibility; Coworkers. **Skills Required:** Coordination; Time Management; Management of Personnel Resources; Speaking; Instructing. **Abilities:** Oral Expression. **Interacting with Others:** Coordinating Work and Activities of Others; Communicating with Other Workers. **Physical Work Conditions:** Standing; Indoors; Using Hands on Objects, Tools, Controls; Walking or Running.

39-1011.00 Gaming Supervisors

Supervise gaming operations and personnel in an assigned area. Circulate among tables and observe operations. Ensure that stations and games are covered for each shift. May explain and interpret operating rules of house to patrons. May plan and organize activities and create friendly atmosphere for guests in hotels/casinos. May adjust service complaints. **Education:** Work experience, plus degree. **Occupational Type:** Enterprising. **Job Zone:** 3. **Average Salary:** $23,320. **Projected Growth:** 14.4%. **Occupational Values:** Authority; Responsibility; Working Conditions; Security; Autonomy; Ability Utilization; Company Policies and Practices. **Skills Required:** Speaking; Management of Financial Resources; Management of Personnel Resources; Mathematics; Time Management; Problem Identification; Monitoring. **Abilities:** Number Facility; Mathematical Reasoning; Oral Expression. **Interacting with Others:** Coordinating Work and Activities of Others; Performing Administrative Activities; Communicating with Other Workers; Guiding, Directing, and Motivating Subordinates; Monitoring and Controlling Resources; Performing for/Working with Public; Staffing Organizational Units. **Physical Work Conditions:** Indoors; Sitting; Standing.

39-1021.00 First-Line Supervisors/Managers of Personal Service Workers

Supervise and coordinate activities of personal service workers such as flight attendants, hairdressers, or caddies. **Education:** Work experience in a related occupation. **Occupational Type:** Enterprising. **Job Zone:** 3. **Average Salary:** $23,320. **Projected Growth:** 16.3%. **Occupational Values:** Authority; Activity; Autonomy; Responsibility; Working Conditions; Moral Values; Coworkers. **Skills Required:** Problem Identification; Time Management; Coordination; Management of Personnel Resources; Identification of Key Causes; Service Orientation; Instructing. **Abilities:** Oral Expression; Information Ordering; Near Vision; Oral Comprehension. **Interacting with Others:** Coordinating Work and Activities of Others; Communicating with Other Workers; Guiding, Directing, and Motivating Subordinates; Performing for/Working with Public; Resolving Conflict, Negotiating with Others. **Physical Work Conditions:** Indoors; Standing; Sitting.

53-1011.00 Aircraft Cargo Handling Supervisors

Direct ground crew in the loading, unloading, securing, and staging of aircraft cargo or baggage. Determine the quantity and orientation of cargo and compute aircraft center of gravity. May accompany aircraft as member of flight crew and monitor and handle cargo in flight, and assist and brief passengers on safety and emergency procedures. No other data currently available.

11.02.01 Recreational Services

39-1012.00 Slot Key Persons

Coordinate/supervise functions of slot department workers to provide service to patrons. Handle and settle complaints of players. Verify and payoff jackpots. Reset slot machines after payoffs. Make minor repairs or adjustments to slot machines. Recommend removal of slot machines for repair. Report hazards and enforce safety rules. No other data currently available.

39-3011.00 Gaming Dealers

Assist operators or customers in conducting games of chance. **Education:** Short-term O-J-T. **Occupational Type:** Enterprising. **Job Zone:** 2. **Average Salary:** $12,860. **Projected Growth:** 30.2%. **Occupational Values:** Supervision, Technical; Activity; Working Conditions; Compensation; Coworkers; Independence. **Skills Required:** Mathematics; Service Orientation; Social Perceptiveness; Speaking. **Abilities:** Number Facility; Speech Clarity; Near Vision; Information Ordering; Oral Expression; Selective Attention; Time Sharing. **Interacting with Others:** Performing for/Working with Public; Communicating with Persons Outside Organization; Establishing and Maintaining Relationships; Interpreting Meaning of Information to Others. **Physical Work Conditions:** Indoors; Special Uniform; Standing; Making Repetitive Motions; Using Hands on Objects, Tools, Controls; Sitting.

39-3012.00 Gaming and Sports Book Writers and Runners

Conduct games of chance such as dice, roulette, or cards. Perform a variety of tasks such as collecting bets or wagers, paying winnings, and explaining rules to customers. **Education:** Short-term O-J-T. **Occupational Type:** Enterprising. **Job Zone:** 2. **Average Salary:** $14,472. **Projected Growth:** 30.2%. **Occupational Values:** Supervision, Technical; Activity; Working Conditions; Independence; Coworkers; Compensation. **Skills Required:** Mathematics; Service Orientation; Social Perceptiveness; Speaking. **Abilities:** Number Facility; Speech Clarity; Near Vision; Information Ordering; Oral Expression; Selective Attention; Time Sharing. **Interacting with Others:** Performing for/Working with Public; Communicating with Persons Outside Organization; Establishing and Maintaining Relationships; Interpreting Meaning of Information to Others. **Physical Work**

Conditions: Indoors; Special Uniform; Standing; Making Repetitive Motions; Using Hands on Objects, Tools, Controls; Sitting.

39-3021.00 Motion Picture Projectionists

Set up and operate motion picture projection and related sound reproduction equipment. **Education:** Short-term O-J-T. **Occupational Type:** Realistic. **Job Zone:** 2. **Average Salary:** $15,420. **Projected Growth:** –21.8%. **Occupational Values:** Moral Values; Independence; Working Conditions; Supervision, Human Relations; Company Policies and Practices; Supervision, Technical. **Skills Required:** Operation and Control; Operation Monitoring. **Abilities:** Arm-Hand Steadiness; Problem Sensitivity; Control Precision. **Interacting with Others:** Communicating with Other Workers. **Physical Work Conditions:** Indoors; Sitting; Using Hands on Objects, Tools, Controls; Distracting Sounds and Noise Levels.

39-3031.00 Ushers, Lobby Attendants, and Ticket Takers

Assist patrons at entertainment events by performing duties such as collecting admission tickets and passes from patrons, assisting in finding seats, searching for lost articles, and locating such facilities as rest rooms and telephones. **Education:** Short-term O-J-T. **Occupational Type:** Social. **Job Zone:** 1. **Average Salary:** $12,520. **Projected Growth:** 17.6%. **Occupational Values:** Moral Values; Coworkers; Social Service; Supervision, Technical; Working Conditions. **Skills Required:** Service Orientation; Speaking. **Abilities:** Oral Expression. **Interacting with Others:** Performing for/Working with Public; Communicating with Persons Outside Organization. **Physical Work Conditions:** Indoors; Special Uniform; Standing; Walking or Running.

39-3091.00 Amusement and Recreation Attendants

Perform variety of attending duties at amusement or recreation facility. May schedule use of recreation facilities, maintain and provide equipment to participants of sporting events or recreational pursuits, or operate amusement concessions and rides. **Education:** Short-term O-J-T. **Occupational Type:** Realistic. **Job Zone:** 1. **Average Salary:** $12,860. **Projected Growth:** 30.2%. **Occupational Values:** Moral Values; Coworkers; Supervision, Technical; Activity; Social Service. **Skills Required:** Speaking; Service Orientation. **Abilities:** Oral Expression; Control Precision; Speech Clarity; Oral Comprehension; Rate Control. **Interacting with Others:** Communicating with Persons Outside Organization; Establishing and Maintaining Relationships; Performing for/Working with Public. **Physical Work Conditions:** Outdoors; Standing; Walking or Running; Indoors; Special Uniform.

39-6021.00 Tour Guides and Escorts

Escort individuals or groups on sightseeing tours or through places of interest such as industrial establishments, public buildings, and art galleries. **Education:** Short-term O-J-T. **Occupational Type:** Social. **Job Zone:** 1. **Average Salary:** $15,500. **Projected Growth:** 17.6%. **Occupational Values:** Social Service; Variety; Moral Values; Working Conditions; Authority. **Skills Required:** Speaking; Active Listening; Service Orientation; Social Perceptiveness. **Abilities:** Oral Expression; Speech Clarity; Oral Comprehension; Memorization; Number Facility; Spatial Orientation; Speech Recognition. **Interacting with Others:** Communicating with Persons Outside Organization; Interpreting Meaning of Information to Others; Performing for/Working with Public; Establishing and Maintaining Relationships; Teaching Others; Assisting and Caring for Others. **Physical Work Conditions:** Walking or Running; Outdoors; Sitting; Standing; Indoors.

39-6022.00 Travel Guides

Plan, organize, and conduct long distance cruises, tours, and expeditions for individuals and groups. **Education:** Postsecondary vocational training. **Occupational Type:** Enterprising. **Job Zone:** 2. **Average Salary:** $15,500. **Projected Growth:** 18.4%. **Occupational Values:** Social Service; Variety; Autonomy; Responsibility; Moral Values; Creativity; Working Conditions. **Skills Required:** Service Orientation; Active Listening; Speaking; Implementation Planning; Time Management; Social Perceptiveness. **Abilities:** Oral Expression; Speech Clarity; Oral Comprehension; Written Comprehension. **Interacting with Others:** Performing for/Working with Public; Communicating with Persons Outside Organization; Assisting and Caring for Others; Establishing and Maintaining Relationships. **Physical Work Conditions:** Outdoors; Standing; Walking or Running; Indoors; Sitting.

39-9032.00 Recreation Workers

Conduct recreation activities with groups in public, private, or volunteer agencies or recreation facilities. Organize and promote activities such as arts and crafts, sports, games, music, dramatics, social recreation, camping, and hobbies, taking into account the needs and interests of individual members. **Education:** Bachelor's degree. **Occupational Type:** Social. **Job Zone:** 3. **Average Salary:** $16,500. **Projected Growth:** 19.2%. **Occupational Values:** Social Service; Autonomy; Coworkers; Activity; Creativity; Moral Values; Variety. **Skills Required:** Coordination; Service Orientation; Speaking; Social Perceptiveness; Implementation Planning; Management of Personnel Resources. **Abilities:** Oral Expression; Oral Comprehension; Speech Clarity; Fluency of Ideas. **Interacting with Others:** Coordinating Work and Activities of Others; Establishing and Maintaining Relationships; Communicating with Persons Outside Organization; Communicating with Other Workers; Performing Administrative Activities; Guiding, Directing, and Motivating Subordinates; Teaching Others. **Physical Work Conditions:** Indoors; Outdoors; Standing; Sitting; Walking or Running.

11.03.01 Transportation and Lodging Services

39-6011.00 Baggage Porters and Bellhops

Handle baggage for travelers at transportation terminals or for guests at hotels or similar establishments. **Education:** Short-term O-J-T. **Occupational Type:** Enterprising. **Job Zone:** 1. **Average Salary:** $13,330. **Projected Growth:** 13.7%. **Occupational Values:** Social Service; Moral Values; Independence; Coworkers; Working Conditions. **Skills Required:** Service Orientation. **Abilities:** Static Strength; Oral Comprehension; Oral

Expression. **Interacting with Others:** Assisting and Caring for Others; Performing for/Working with Public; Communicating with Persons Outside Organization. **Physical Work Conditions:** Special Uniform; Standing; Indoors; Using Hands on Objects, Tools, Controls; Walking or Running.

39-6012.00 Concierges

Assist patrons at hotel, apartment, or office building with personal services. May take messages, arrange or give advice on transportation, business services or entertainment, or monitor guest requests for housekeeping and maintenance. No other data currently available.

39-6031.00 Flight Attendants

Provide personal services to ensure the safety and comfort of airline passengers during flight. Greet passengers, verify tickets, explain use of safety equipment, and serve food or beverages. **Education:** Long-term O-J-T. **Occupational Type:** Enterprising. **Job Zone:** 2. **Average Salary:** $37,800. **Projected Growth:** 30.1%. **Occupational Values:** Social Service; Coworkers; Supervision, Technical; Moral Values; Company Policies and Practices; Supervision, Human Relations; Security. **Skills Required:** Service Orientation; Speaking. **Abilities:** Oral Expression; Oral Comprehension; Speech Clarity. **Interacting with Others:** Performing for/Working with Public; Assisting and Caring for Others; Communicating with Persons Outside Organization. **Physical Work Conditions:** Special Uniform; Indoors; Standing; Walking or Running.

39-6032.00 Transportation Attendants, Except Flight Attendants and Baggage Porters

Provide services to ensure the safety and comfort of passengers aboard ships, buses, or trains or within the station or terminal. Perform duties such as greeting passengers, explaining the use of safety equipment, serving meals or beverages, or answering questions related to travel. **Education:** Unknown. **Occupational Type:** Enterprising. **Job Zone:** 1. **Average Salary:** $17,620. **Projected Growth:** 19.3%. **Occupational Values:** Social Service; Moral Values; Security; Supervision, Technical; Coworkers; Company Policies and Practices; Supervision, Human Relations. **Skills Required:** Service Orientation; Social Perceptiveness; Speaking; Active Listening. **Abilities:** Oral Expression; Speech Clarity. **Interacting with Others:** Performing for/Working with Public; Assisting and Caring for Others; Communicating with Persons Outside Organization; Establishing and Maintaining Relationships. **Physical Work Conditions:** Indoors; Special Uniform; Walking or Running; Standing; Bending or Twisting the Body.

43-4081.00 Hotel, Motel, and Resort Desk Clerks

Accommodate hotel, motel, and resort patrons by registering and assigning rooms to guests, issuing room keys, transmitting and receiving messages, keeping records of occupied rooms and guests' accounts, making and confirming reservations, and presenting statements to and collecting payments from departing guests. **Education:** Short-term O-J-T. **Occupational Type:** Conventional. **Job Zone:** 2. **Average Salary:** $15,160. **Projected Growth:** 13.5%. **Occupational Values:** Working Conditions; Moral Values; Supervision, Human Relations; Company Policies and Practices; Social Service; Supervision, Technical; Security. **Skills Required:** Service Orientation; Speaking. **Abilities:** Oral Expression; Oral Comprehension. **Interacting with Others:** Assisting and Caring for Others; Communicating with Persons Outside Organization; Performing for/Working with Public. **Physical Work Conditions:** Special Uniform; Standing; Indoors.

43-4181.02 Reservation and Transportation Ticket Agents

Make and confirm reservations for passengers and sell tickets for transportation agencies such as airlines, bus companies, railroads, and steamship lines. May check baggage and direct passengers to designated concourse, pier, or track. **Education:** Short-term O-J-T. **Occupational Type:** Conventional. **Job Zone:** 2. **Average Salary:** $22,770. **Projected Growth:** 6%. **Occupational Values:** Supervision, Human Relations; Working Conditions; Moral Values; Activity; Company Policies and Practices; Social Service; Security. **Skills Required:** Service Orientation; Active Listening; Speaking; Reading Comprehension; Information Gathering; Coordination. **Abilities:** Oral Expression; Near Vision; Oral Comprehension; Speech Clarity; Memorization; Written Comprehension; Number Facility. **Interacting with Others:** Assisting and Caring for Others; Communicating with Persons Outside Organization; Establishing and Maintaining Relationships; Performing for/Working with Public; Interpreting Meaning of Information to Others. **Physical Work Conditions:** Indoors; Special Uniform; Standing; Sitting.

11.04.01 Barber and Beauty Services

39-5011.00 Barbers

Provide barbering services such as cutting, trimming, shampooing, and styling hair; and trimming beards or giving shaves. **Education:** Postsecondary vocational training. **Occupational Type:** Realistic. **Job Zone:** 3. **Average Salary:** $18,460. **Projected Growth:** –7.3%. **Occupational Values:** Social Service; Moral Values; Autonomy; Independence; Achievement; Security; Working Conditions. **Skills Required:** Active Listening. **Abilities:** Arm-Hand Steadiness; Finger Dexterity. **Interacting with Others:** Performing for/Working with Public; Communicating with Persons Outside Organization; Establishing and Maintaining Relationships. **Physical Work Conditions:** Indoors; Standing; Using Hands on Objects, Tools, Controls; Making Repetitive Motions; Hazardous Situations.

39-5012.00 Hairdressers, Hairstylists, and Cosmetologists

Provide beauty services such as shampooing, cutting, coloring, and styling hair; and massaging and treating scalp. May also apply makeup, dress wigs, perform hair removal, and provide nail and skin care services. **Education:** Postsecondary vocational training. **Occupational Type:** Enterprising. **Job Zone:** 3. **Average Salary:** $15,150. **Projected Growth:** 10.2%. **Occupational Values:** Social Service; Moral Values; Achievement; Independence; Autonomy; Recognition; Creativity. **Skills Required:** Service Orientation. **Abilities:** Manual Dexterity; Oral Expression; Arm-Hand Steadiness; Visualization; Oral Comprehension; Originality. **Interacting with Others:** Communicating with Persons Outside Organization; Performing for/Working with Public; Establishing and Maintaining Relationships; Assisting and Caring for Others. **Physical Work Conditions:** Indoors; Standing; Using Hands on Objects, Tools, Controls; Contaminants; Making Repetitive Motions.

39-5092.00 Manicurists and Pedicurists

Clean and shape customers' fingernails and toenails. May polish or decorate nails. **Education:** Postsecondary vocational training. **Occupational Type:** Enterprising. **Job Zone:** 1. **Average Salary:** $13,480. **Projected Growth:** 26%. **Occupational Values:** Social Service; Moral Values; Autonomy; Working Conditions; Independence. **Skills Required:** Product Inspection. **Abilities:** Wrist-Finger Speed. **Interacting with Others:** Performing for/Working with Public. **Physical Work Conditions:** Indoors; Sitting; Using Hands on Objects, Tools, Controls.

39-5093.00 Shampooers

Shampoo and rinse customers' hair. No other data currently available.

39-5094.00 Skin Care Specialists

Provide skin care treatments to face and body to enhance an individual's appearance. No other data currently available.

11.05.01 Food and Beverage Services: Preparing

35-1011.00 Chefs and Head Cooks

Direct the preparation, seasoning, and cooking of salads, soups, fish, meats, vegetables, desserts, or other foods. May plan and price menu items, order supplies, and keep records and accounts. May participate in cooking. **Education:** Work experience in a related occupation. **Occupational Type:** Enterprising. **Job Zone:** 4. **Average Salary:** $23,320. **Projected Growth:** 16.3%. **Occupational Values:** Authority; Responsibility; Moral Values; Achievement; Autonomy; Ability Utilization; Coworkers. **Skills Required:** Coordination; Implementation Planning; Management of Material Resources; Time Management; Management of Personnel Resources; Speaking; Instructing. **Abilities:** Oral Expression; Problem Sensitivity; Information Ordering; Deductive Reasoning; Wrist-Finger Speed; Manual Dexterity; Number Facility. **Interacting with Others:** Communicating with Other Workers. **Physical Work Conditions:** Indoors; Using Hands on Objects, Tools, Controls; Standing; Hazardous Situations; Hazardous Equipment; Making Repetitive Motions.

35-2011.00 Cooks, Fast Food

Prepare and cook food in a fast food restaurant with a limited menu. Duties are limited to preparation of a few basic items and normally involve operating large-volume, single-purpose cooking equipment. **Education:** Short-term O-J-T. **Occupational Type:** Realistic. **Job Zone:** 2. **Average Salary:** $12,480. **Projected Growth:** 18.4%. **Occupational Values:** Moral Values; Activity; Coworkers; Supervision, Human Relations; Security; Company Policies and Practices; Supervision, Technical. **Skills Required:** Active Listening. **Abilities:** Oral Comprehension. **Interacting with Others:** Performing for/Working with Public. **Physical Work Conditions:** Indoors; Standing; Special Uniform; Using Hands on Objects, Tools, Controls; Hazardous Situations; Making Repetitive Motions.

35-2012.00 Cooks, Institution and Cafeteria

Prepare and cook large quantities of food for institutions such as schools, hospitals, or cafeterias. **Education:** Long-term O-J-T. **Occupational Type:** Realistic. **Job Zone:** 2. **Average Salary:** $16,090. **Projected Growth:** 2.9%. **Occupational Values:** Moral Values; Security; Activity; Responsibility; Coworkers. **Skills Required:** Service Orientation. **Abilities:** Wrist-Finger Speed. **Interacting with Others:** Monitoring and Controlling Resources. **Physical Work Conditions:** Indoors; Standing; Using Hands on Objects, Tools, Controls; Special Uniform.

35-2014.00 Cooks, Restaurant

Prepare, season, and cook soups, meats, vegetables, desserts, or other foodstuffs in restaurants. May order supplies, keep records and accounts, price items on menu, or plan menu. **Education:** Long-term O-J-T. **Occupational Type:** Realistic. **Job Zone:** 3. **Average Salary:** $16,250. **Projected Growth:** 18.7%. **Occupational Values:** Moral Values; Responsibility; Coworkers; Creativity; Achievement; Ability Utilization; Activity. **Skills Required:** Equipment Selection. **Abilities:** Information Ordering; Manual Dexterity; Memorization; Wrist-Finger Speed; Written Comprehension; Near Vision; Oral Expression. **Interacting with Others:** Monitoring and Controlling Resources; Coordinating Work and Activities of Others; Guiding, Directing, and Motivating Subordinates. **Physical Work Conditions:** Indoors; Special Uniform; Standing; Using Hands on Objects, Tools, Controls; Hazardous Situations; Making Repetitive Motions.

35-2015.00 Cooks, Short Order

Prepare and cook to order a variety of foods that require only a short preparation time. May take orders from customers and serve patrons at counters or tables. **Education:** Long-term O-J-T. **Occupational Type:** Realistic. **Job Zone:** 1. **Average Salary:** $14,390. **Projected Growth:** 18.4%. **Occupational Values:** Moral Values; Activity; Coworkers; Security. **Skills Required:** Active Listening. **Abilities:** Oral Comprehension. **Interacting with Others:** Performing for/Working with Public. **Physical Work Conditions:** Indoors; Standing; Using Hands on Objects, Tools, Controls; Special Uniform; Hazardous Situations.

35-2021.00 Food Preparation Workers

Perform a variety of food preparation duties other than cooking, such as preparing cold foods and shellfish, slicing meat, and brewing coffee or tea. **Education:** Short-term O-J-T. **Occupational Type:** Realistic. **Job Zone:** 1. **Average Salary:** $13,700. **Projected Growth:** 10.4%. **Occupational Values:** Moral Values; Activity; Coworkers. **Skills Required:** Active Listening. **Abilities:** Wrist-Finger Speed; Information Ordering; Manual Dexterity; Arm-Hand Steadiness. **Interacting with Others:** Communicating with Other Workers. **Physical Work Conditions:** Indoors; Standing; Using Hands on Objects, Tools, Controls; Special Uniform; Making Repetitive Motions.

35-9021.00 Dishwashers

Clean dishes, kitchen, food preparation equipment, or utensils. **Education:** Short-term O-J-T. **Occupational Type:** Realistic. **Job Zone:** 1. **Average Salary:** $13,700. **Projected Growth:**

10.4%. **Occupational Values:** Moral Values; Coworkers; Activity; Independence. **Skills Required:** Equipment Maintenance. **Abilities:** Information Ordering; Trunk Strength. **Interacting with Others:** Communicating with Other Workers. **Physical Work Conditions:** Indoors; Standing; Walking or Running.

51-3011.01 Bakers, Bread and Pastry

Mix and bake ingredients according to recipes to produce small quantities of breads, pastries, and other baked goods for consumption on premises or for sale as specialty baked goods. **Education:** Moderate-term O-J-T. **Occupational Type:** Realistic. **Job Zone:** 3. **Average Salary:** $16,990. **Projected Growth:** 16.6%. **Occupational Values:** Moral Values; Independence; Supervision, Human Relations. **Skills Required:** Operation and Control. **Abilities:** Information Ordering. **Interacting with Others:** Communicating with Persons Outside Organization. **Physical Work Conditions:** Indoors; Standing; Special Uniform; Making Repetitive Motions; Using Hands on Objects, Tools, Controls.

51-3021.00 Butchers and Meat Cutters

Cut, trim, or prepare consumer-sized portions of meat for use or sale in retail establishments. **Education:** Long-term O-J-T. **Occupational Type:** Realistic. **Job Zone:** 3. **Average Salary:** $22,770. **Projected Growth:** –7.1%. **Occupational Values:** Moral Values; Independence; Security; Activity; Responsibility. **Skills Required:** Product Inspection. **Abilities:** Manual Dexterity. **Interacting with Others:** Performing for/Working with Public. **Physical Work Conditions:** Indoors; Standing; Special Uniform; Using Hands on Objects, Tools, Controls; Hazardous Situations; Hazardous Equipment; Making Repetitive Motions.

11.05.02 Food and Beverage Services: Serving

35-3011.00 Bartenders

Mix and serve drinks to patrons, directly or through waitstaff. **Education:** Short-term O-J-T. **Occupational Type:** Enterprising. **Job Zone:** 1. **Average Salary:** $12,990. **Projected Growth:** 1.9%. **Occupational Values:** Moral Values; Social Service; Coworkers; Working Conditions; Supervision, Technical. **Skills Required:** Service Orientation; Active Listening. **Abilities:** Memorization; Manual Dexterity; Information Ordering; Speech Recognition; Wrist-Finger Speed. **Interacting with Others:** Establishing and Maintaining Relationships; Performing for/Working with Public; Communicating with Persons Outside Organization; Monitoring and Controlling Resources. **Physical Work Conditions:** Indoors; Standing; Using Hands on Objects, Tools, Controls; Walking or Running; Extremely Bright or Inadequate Lighting; Distracting Sounds and Noise Levels.

35-3021.00 Combined Food Preparation and Serving Workers, Including Fast Food

Perform duties that combine both food preparation and food service, with no more than 80 percent of time being spent in either job area. **Education:** Short-term O-J-T. **Occupational Type:** Realistic. **Job Zone:** 1. **Average Salary:** $12,550. **Projected Growth:** 10.4%. **Occupational Values:** Moral Values; Activity; Coworkers. **Skills Required:** Service Orientation; Speaking; Active Listening. **Abilities:** Wrist-Finger Speed; Manual Dexterity. **Interacting with Others:** Communicating with Persons Outside Organization; Performing for/Working with Public; Establishing and Maintaining Relationships. **Physical Work Conditions:** Indoors; Standing; Walking or Running; Special Uniform.

35-3022.00 Counter Attendants, Cafeteria, Food Concession, and Coffee Shop

Serve food to diners at counter or from a steam table. Does not include counter attendants who also wait tables. **Education:** Short-term O-J-T. **Occupational Type:** Social. **Job Zone:** 1. **Average Salary:** $12,800. **Projected Growth:** 12.2%. **Occupational Values:** Moral Values; Coworkers; Social Service; Activity; Supervision, Technical. **Skills Required:** Service Orientation. **Abilities:** Wrist-Finger Speed. **Interacting with Others:** Performing for/Working with Public; Communicating with Persons Outside Organization. **Physical Work Conditions:** Indoors; Standing; Special Uniform; Using Hands on Objects, Tools, Controls; Walking or Running.

35-3031.00 Waiters and Waitresses

Take food orders and serve food and beverages to patrons in dining establishments. **Education:** Short-term O-J-T. **Occupational Type:** Social. **Job Zone:** 1. **Average Salary:** $12,200. **Projected Growth:** 15%. **Occupational Values:** Moral Values; Coworkers; Supervision, Technical; Activity; Social Service; Supervision, Human Relations. **Skills Required:** Service Orientation; Speaking; Active Listening; Writing. **Abilities:** Oral Expression; Manual Dexterity; Oral Comprehension; Memorization; Speech Clarity; Speech Recognition; Static Strength. **Interacting with Others:** Performing for/Working with Public; Establishing and Maintaining Relationships; Communicating with Persons Outside Organization; Monitoring and Controlling Resources. **Physical Work Conditions:** Indoors; Standing; Walking or Running; Special Uniform.

35-3041.00 Food Servers, Nonrestaurant

Serve food to patrons outside of a restaurant environment, such as in hotels, hospital rooms, or cars. **Education:** Short-term O-J-T. **Occupational Type:** Social. **Job Zone:** 1. **Average Salary:** $14,300. **Projected Growth:** 9.4%. **Occupational Values:** Moral Values; Social Service; Coworkers; Company Policies and Practices; Supervision, Technical. **Skills Required:** Service Orientation. **Abilities:** Number Facility. **Interacting with Others:** Performing for/Working with Public. **Physical Work Conditions:** Standing; Special Uniform; Using Hands on Objects, Tools, Controls; Indoors; Walking or Running; Outdoors.

35-9011.00 Dining Room and Cafeteria Attendants and Bartender Helpers

Facilitate food service. Clean tables; carry dirty dishes; replace soiled table linens; set tables; replenish supply of clean linens, silverware, glassware, and dishes; supply service bar with food; and serve water, butter, and coffee to patrons. **Education:** Short-term O-J-T. **Occupational Type:** Realistic. **Job Zone:** 1. **Average Salary:** $12,580. **Projected Growth:** 4%. **Occupational Values:** Moral Values; Coworkers; Supervision, Technical; Social Service. **Skills Required:** Service Orientation. **Abilities:**

Wrist-Finger Speed. **Interacting with Others:** Performing for/Working with Public. **Physical Work Conditions:** Indoors; Standing; Using Hands on Objects, Tools, Controls; Walking or Running; Special Uniform.

35-9031.00 Hosts and Hostesses, Restaurant, Lounge, and Coffee Shop

Welcome patrons, seat them at tables or in lounge, and help ensure quality of facilities and service. **Education:** Short-term O-J-T. **Occupational Type:** Enterprising. **Job Zone:** 3. **Average Salary:** $13,400. **Projected Growth:** 18.2%. **Occupational Values:** Moral Values; Coworkers; Supervision, Technical; Social Service; Activity; Working Conditions; Company Policies and Practices. **Skills Required:** Service Orientation; Time Management; Coordination; Mathematics. **Abilities:** Oral Expression; Oral Comprehension. **Interacting with Others:** Communicating with Other Workers; Establishing and Maintaining Relationships; Performing for/Working with Public; Coordinating Work and Activities of Others; Communicating with Persons Outside Organization. **Physical Work Conditions:** Indoors; Standing; Special Uniform; Walking or Running.

11.06.01 Apparel, Shoes, Leather, and Fabric Care

49-9093.00 Fabric Menders, Except Garment

Repair tears, holes, and other defects in fabrics such as draperies, linens, parachutes, and tents. **Education:** Long-term O-J-T. **Occupational Type:** Realistic. **Job Zone:** 1. **Average Salary:** $15,990. **Projected Growth:** 4.4%. **Occupational Values:** Moral Values; Independence; Activity; Security; Supervision, Technical; Supervision, Human Relations. **Skills Required:** Product Inspection; Operation and Control; Problem Identification. **Abilities:** Arm-Hand Steadiness; Finger Dexterity; Near Vision; Manual Dexterity; Wrist-Finger Speed. **Interacting with Others:** Communicating with Other Workers. **Physical Work Conditions:** Indoors; Sitting; Using Hands on Objects, Tools, Controls; Making Repetitive Motions.

51-6011.00 Laundry and Dry-Cleaning Workers

Operate or tend washing or dry-cleaning machines to wash or dry-clean industrial or household articles, such as cloth garments, suede, leather, furs, blankets, draperies, fine linens, rugs, and carpets. No other data currently available.

51-6011.01 Spotters, Dry Cleaning

Identify stains in wool, synthetic, and silk garments and household fabrics and apply chemical solutions to remove stains. Determine spotting procedures on basis of type of fabric and nature of stain. **Education:** Moderate-term O-J-T. **Occupational Type:** Realistic. **Job Zone:** 1. **Average Salary:** $16,790. **Projected Growth:** 9.8%. **Occupational Values:** Moral Values; Independence; Security; Supervision, Technical; Activity. **Skills Required:** Product Inspection; Problem Identification. **Abilities:** Wrist-Finger Speed. **Interacting with Others:** Assisting and Caring for Others. **Physical Work Conditions:** Indoors; Using Hands on Objects, Tools, Controls; Hazardous Conditions; Standing; Contaminants.

51-6011.02 Precision Dyers

Use dyes to change or restore the color of articles such as garments, drapes, and slipcovers, applying knowledge of the composition of the textiles being dyed or restored and the chemical properties of bleaches and dyes. **Education:** Short-term O-J-T. **Occupational Type:** Realistic. **Job Zone:** 3. **Average Salary:** $19,620. **Projected Growth:** 4.4%. **Occupational Values:** Moral Values; Independence; Security; Activity; Supervision, Technical; Supervision, Human Relations. **Skills Required:** Science; Product Inspection. **Abilities:** Visual Color Discrimination. **Interacting with Others:** Communicating with Other Workers. **Physical Work Conditions:** Indoors; Standing; Using Hands on Objects, Tools, Controls.

51-6011.03 Laundry and Drycleaning Machine Operators and Tenders, Except Pressing

Operate or tend washing or dry-cleaning machines to wash or dry-clean commercial, industrial, or household articles such as cloth garments, suede, leather, furs, blankets, draperies, fine linens, rugs, and carpets. **Education:** Moderate-term O-J-T. **Occupational Type:** Realistic. **Job Zone:** 1. **Average Salary:** $14,670. **Projected Growth:** 9.8%. **Occupational Values:** Moral Values; Company Policies and Practices; Supervision, Human Relations; Supervision, Technical; Activity; Independence; Security. **Skills Required:** Operation and Control; Product Inspection; Operation Monitoring. **Abilities:** Visual Color Discrimination. **Interacting with Others:** Communicating with Other Workers. **Physical Work Conditions:** Indoors; Using Hands on Objects, Tools, Controls; Hazardous Equipment; Standing; Contaminants; Making Repetitive Motions; Very Hot.

51-6021.01 Pressers, Delicate Fabrics

Press dry-cleaned and wet-cleaned silk and synthetic fiber garments by hand or machine, applying knowledge of fabrics and heat to produce high quality finish. Finish pleated or fancy garments, normally by hand. **Education:** Short-term O-J-T. **Occupational Type:** Realistic. **Job Zone:** 2. **Average Salary:** $15,460. **Projected Growth:** –11.4%. **Occupational Values:** Moral Values; Independence; Security; Supervision, Technical; Activity. **Skills Required:** Operation and Control. **Abilities:** Manual Dexterity. **Interacting with Others:** Monitoring and Controlling Resources. **Physical Work Conditions:** Indoors; Using Hands on Objects, Tools, Controls; Standing; Hazardous Situations; Very Hot.

51-6021.03 Pressers, Hand

Press articles to remove wrinkles, flatten seams, and give shape by using hand iron. Articles pressed include drapes, knit goods, millinery parts, parachutes, garments, slip covers, and textiles such as lace, rayon, and silk. May block (shape) knitted garments after cleaning. May press leather goods. **Education:** Short-term O-J-T. **Occupational Type:** Realistic. **Job Zone:** 1. **Average Salary:** $14,750. **Projected Growth:** –11.4%. **Occupational Values:** Moral Values; Independence; Activity. **Skills Required:** Product Inspection. **Abilities:** Manual Dexterity. **Interacting with Others:** Monitoring and Controlling Resources. **Physical Work Conditions:** Indoors; Using Hands on Objects, Tools, Controls; Hazardous Situations; Standing; Making Repetitive Motions.

51-6041.00 Shoe and Leather Workers and Repairers

Construct, decorate, or repair leather and leather-like products such as luggage, shoes, and saddles. **Education:** Long-term O-J-T. **Occupational Type:** Realistic. **Job Zone:** 2. **Average Salary:** $16,610. **Projected Growth:** –17.6%. **Occupational Values:** Moral Values; Independence; Ability Utilization; Autonomy; Working Conditions; Achievement. **Skills Required:** Product Inspection; Equipment Selection; Information Organization; Problem Identification; Information Gathering. **Abilities:** Arm-Hand Steadiness; Written Comprehension; Finger Dexterity; Wrist-Finger Speed; Information Ordering; Manual Dexterity; Near Vision. **Interacting with Others:** Communicating with Persons Outside Organization. **Physical Work Conditions:** Indoors; Using Hands on Objects, Tools, Controls; Sitting; Making Repetitive Motions.

51-6052.01 Shop and Alteration Tailors

Make tailored garments from existing patterns. Alter, repair, or fit made-to-measure or ready-to-wear garments. **Education:** Work experience in a related occupation. **Occupational Type:** Realistic. **Job Zone:** 3. **Average Salary:** $18,630. **Projected Growth:** –8.4%. **Occupational Values:** Moral Values; Independence; Working Conditions; Activity; Autonomy; Ability Utilization; Security. **Skills Required:** Product Inspection. **Abilities:** Arm-Hand Steadiness; Finger Dexterity. **Interacting with Others:** Performing for/Working with Public. **Physical Work Conditions:** Indoors; Sitting; Using Hands on Objects, Tools, Controls; Making Repetitive Motions.

51-6052.02 Custom Tailors

Design or make tailored garments, applying knowledge of garment design, construction, styling, and fabrics. **Education:** Work experience in a related occupation. **Occupational Type:** Realistic. **Job Zone:** 4. **Average Salary:** $18,630. **Projected Growth:** –8.4%. **Occupational Values:** Moral Values; Autonomy; Working Conditions; Responsibility; Ability Utilization; Independence; Achievement. **Skills Required:** Product Inspection. **Abilities:** Arm-Hand Steadiness; Finger Dexterity; Originality; Visualization. **Interacting with Others:** Communicating with Persons Outside Organization. **Physical Work Conditions:** Indoors; Using Hands on Objects, Tools, Controls; Sitting.

51-6093.00 Upholsterers

Make, repair, or replace upholstery for household furniture or transportation vehicles. **Education:** Long-term O-J-T. **Occupational Type:** Realistic. **Job Zone:** 3. **Average Salary:** $22,050. **Projected Growth:** 0.9%. **Occupational Values:** Moral Values; Autonomy; Independence; Achievement; Working Conditions; Responsibility; Security. **Skills Required:** Monitoring. **Abilities:** Finger Dexterity; Visualization; Manual Dexterity; Near Vision. **Interacting with Others:** Performing Administrative Activities. **Physical Work Conditions:** Indoors; Using Hands on Objects, Tools, Controls; Standing; Bending or Twisting the Body; Kneeling, Crouching, or Crawling; Making Repetitive Motions.

11.07.01 Cleaning and Building Services

37-2011.00 Janitors and Cleaners, Except Maids and Housekeeping Cleaners

Keep buildings in clean and orderly condition. Perform heavy cleaning duties such as cleaning floors, shampooing rugs, washing walls and glass, and removing rubbish. Duties may include tending furnace and boiler, performing routine maintenance activities, notifying management of need for repairs, and cleaning snow or debris from sidewalk. **Education:** Short-term O-J-T. **Occupational Type:** Realistic. **Job Zone:** 1. **Average Salary:** $15,920. **Projected Growth:** 11.5%. **Occupational Values:** Moral Values; Independence; Security; Activity; Company Policies and Practices; Supervision, Human Relations. **Skills Required:** Equipment Maintenance. **Abilities:** Static Strength; Multilimb Coordination; Manual Dexterity; Stamina; Trunk Strength; Dynamic Strength; Information Ordering. **Interacting with Others:** Communicating with Other Workers. **Physical Work Conditions:** Indoors; Standing; Contaminants; Using Hands on Objects, Tools, Controls; Walking or Running.

37-2012.00 Maids and Housekeeping Cleaners

Perform any combination of light cleaning duties to maintain private households or commercial establishments such as hotels, restaurants, and hospitals in a clean and orderly manner. Duties include making beds, replenishing linens, cleaning rooms and halls, and vacuuming. **Education:** Short-term O-J-T. **Occupational Type:** Realistic. **Job Zone:** 1. **Average Salary:** $14,230. **Projected Growth:** 11.5%. **Occupational Values:** Moral Values; Independence; Activity; Coworkers. **Skills Required:** Service Orientation. **Abilities:** Trunk Strength. **Interacting with Others:** Communicating with Other Workers. **Physical Work Conditions:** Standing; Indoors; Walking or Running; Making Repetitive Motions; Special Uniform; Using Hands on Objects, Tools, Controls.

39-3093.00 Locker Room, Coatroom, and Dressing Room Attendants

Provide personal items to patrons or customers in locker rooms, dressing rooms, or coatrooms. **Education:** Work experience in a related occupation. **Occupational Type:** Social. **Job Zone:** 1. **Average Salary:** $15,330. **Projected Growth:** 19.3%. **Occupational Values:** Social Service; Moral Values; Working Conditions; Security; Independence. **Skills Required:** Service Orientation; Active Listening; Speaking; Coordination; Social Perceptiveness. **Abilities:** Oral Expression; Speech Clarity; Oral Comprehension. **Interacting with Others:** Communicating with Persons Outside Organization; Assisting and Caring for Others; Performing for/Working with Public; Establishing and Maintaining Relationships. **Physical Work Conditions:** Indoors; Standing; Walking or Running; Outdoors; Using Hands on Objects, Tools, Controls.

11.08.01 Other Personal Services

35-2013.00 Cooks, Private Household

Prepare meals in private homes. No other data currently available.

39-4011.00 Embalmers

Prepare bodies for interment in conformity with legal requirements. **Education:** Long-term O-J-T. **Occupational Type:** Realistic. **Job Zone:** 4. **Average Salary:** $28,180. **Projected Growth:** 16.1%. **Occupational Values:** Independence; Security; Moral Values; Social Service; Autonomy; Supervision, Human Relations. **Skills Required:** Equipment Selection. **Abilities:** Finger Dexterity. **Interacting with Others:** Assisting and Caring for Others. **Physical Work Conditions:** Indoors; Contaminants; Using Hands on Objects, Tools, Controls; Common Protective or Safety Attire; Standing; Hazardous Conditions.

39-4021.00 Funeral Attendants

Perform variety of tasks during funeral, such as placing casket in parlor or chapel prior to service, arranging floral offerings or lights around casket, directing or escorting mourners, closing casket, and issuing and storing funeral equipment. **Education:** Work experience in a related occupation. **Occupational Type:** Social. **Job Zone:** 1. **Average Salary:** $15,260. **Projected Growth:** 19.3%. **Occupational Values:** Moral Values; Security; Social Service. **Skills Required:** Social Perceptiveness; Service Orientation. **Abilities:** Static Strength. **Interacting with Others:** Communicating with Persons Outside Organization; Assisting and Caring for Others. **Physical Work Conditions:** Indoors; Standing; Walking or Running.

39-9021.00 Personal and Home Care Aides

Assist elderly or disabled adults with daily living activities at the person's home or in a daytime nonresidential facility. Duties performed at a place of residence may include keeping house (making beds, doing laundry, washing dishes) and preparing meals. May provide meals and supervised activities at nonresidential care facilities. May advise families and elderly or disabled persons on such things as nutrition, cleanliness, and household utilities. **Education:** Short-term O-J-T. **Occupational Type:** Social. **Job Zone:** 2. **Average Salary:** $14,920. **Projected Growth:** 58.1%. **Occupational Values:** Social Service; Moral Values; Autonomy; Company Policies and Practices; Security; Independence; Variety. **Skills Required:** Service Orientation; Social Perceptiveness; Speaking; Active Listening; Instructing; Identification of Key Causes; Critical Thinking. **Abilities:** Oral Expression; Oral Comprehension. **Interacting with Others:** Assisting and Caring for Others; Establishing and Maintaining Relationships; Teaching Others. **Physical Work Conditions:** Indoors; Standing; Walking or Running.

53-7061.00 Cleaners of Vehicles and Equipment

Wash or otherwise clean vehicles, machinery, and other equipment, using materials such as water, cleaning agents, brushes, cloths, and hoses. **Education:** Short-term O-J-T. **Occupational Type:** Realistic. **Job Zone:** 1. **Average Salary:** $14,540. **Projected Growth:** 25%. **Occupational Values:** Moral Values; Independence; Activity. **Skills Required:** Equipment Selection. **Abilities:** Extent Flexibility; Manual Dexterity. **Interacting with Others:** Monitoring and Controlling Resources. **Physical Work Conditions:** Using Hands on Objects, Tools, Controls; Standing; Outdoors; Common Protective or Safety Attire; Making Repetitive Motions; Bending or Twisting the Body; Contaminants.

12 Education and Social Service

12.01.01 Managerial Work in Education and Social Service

11-9031.00 Education Administrators, Preschool and Child Care Center/Program

Plan, direct, or coordinate the academic and nonacademic activities of preschool and child care centers or programs. **Education:** Work experience, plus degree. **Occupational Type:** Social. **Job Zone:** 4. **Average Salary:** $60,400. **Projected Growth:** 13%. **Occupational Values:** Ability Utilization; Activity; Achievement; Authority; Company Policies and Practices; Security; Working Conditions. **Skills Required:** Coordination; Reading Comprehension; Speaking; Writing; Social Perceptiveness; Judgment and Decision Making; Information Gathering. **Abilities:** Oral Expression; Written Comprehension; Written Expression; Oral Comprehension; Speech Clarity; Near Vision; Fluency of Ideas. **Interacting with Others:** Communicating with Persons Outside Organization; Communicating with Other Workers; Providing Consultation and Advice to Others; Coordinating Work and Activities of Others; Teaching Others; Establishing and Maintaining Relationships; Staffing Organizational Units. **Physical Work Conditions:** Indoors; Sitting.

11-9032.00 Education Administrators, Elementary and Secondary School

Plan, direct, or coordinate the academic, clerical, or auxiliary activities of public or private elementary or secondary level schools. **Education:** Work experience, plus degree. **Occupational Type:** Social. **Job Zone:** 4. **Average Salary:** $60,400. **Projected Growth:** 13%. **Occupational Values:** Ability Utilization; Activity; Achievement; Authority; Security; Company Policies and Practices; Working Conditions. **Skills Required:** Coordination; Reading Comprehension; Speaking; Writing; Social Perceptiveness; Information Gathering; Critical Thinking. **Abilities:** Oral Expression; Written Comprehension; Written Expression; Oral Comprehension; Speech Clarity; Near Vision; Fluency of Ideas. **Interacting with Others:** Communicating with Persons Outside Organization; Communicating with Other Workers; Providing Consultation and Advice to Others; Coordinating Work and Activities of Others; Teaching Others; Establishing and Maintaining Relationships; Staffing Organizational Units. **Physical Work Conditions:** Indoors; Sitting.

11-9033.00 Education Administrators, Postsecondary

Plan, direct, or coordinate research, instruction, student administration and services, and other educational activities at postsecondary institutions, including universities, colleges, and junior and community colleges. **Education:** Work experience, plus degree. **Occupational Type:** Enterprising. **Job Zone:** 5. **Average Salary:** $60,400. **Projected Growth:** 13%. **Occupational Values:** Working Conditions; Social Status; Authority; Activity; Ability Utilization; Recognition; Achievement. **Skills Required:** Management of Personnel Resources; Management of Financial Resources; Coordination; Judgment and Decision Making; Speaking; Visioning; Information Gathering. **Abilities:** Written Expression; Oral Comprehension; Deductive Reasoning; Oral Expression; Written Comprehension; Inductive Reasoning; Near Vision. **Interacting with Others:** Performing Administrative Activities; Communicating with Persons Outside Organization; Establishing and Maintaining Relationships; Monitoring and Controlling Resources; Staffing Organizational Units; Communicating with Other Workers; Coordinating Work and Activities of Others. **Physical Work Conditions:** Sitting; Indoors.

11-9151.00 Social and Community Service Managers

Plan, organize, or coordinate the activities of a social service program or community outreach organization. Oversee the program or organization's budget and policies regarding participant involvement, program requirements, and benefits. Work may involve directing social workers, counselors, or probation officers. **Education:** Work experience, plus degree. **Occupational Type:** Social. **Job Zone:** 4. **Average Salary:** $49,220. **Projected Growth:** 14.4%. **Occupational Values:** Security; Social Service; Activity; Achievement; Autonomy; Authority; Company Policies and Practices. **Skills Required:** Speaking; Instructing; Coordination; Reading Comprehension; Social Perceptiveness; Visioning; Service Orientation. **Abilities:** Speech Clarity; Oral Expression; Oral Comprehension; Written Comprehension. **Interacting with Others:** Communicating with Persons Outside Organization; Communicating with Other Workers; Guiding, Directing, and Motivating Subordinates; Monitoring and Controlling Resources; Coordinating Work and Activities of Others; Establishing and Maintaining Relationships; Providing Consultation and Advice to Others. **Physical Work Conditions:** Indoors; Sitting.

19-1031.03 Park Naturalists

Plan, develop, and conduct programs to inform public of historical, natural, and scientific features of national, state, or local park. **Education:** Bachelor's degree. **Occupational Type:** Social. **Job Zone:** 4. **Average Salary:** $42,750. **Projected Growth:** 17.9%. **Occupational Values:** Autonomy; Responsibility; Moral Values; Ability Utilization; Achievement; Creativity; Activity. **Skills Required:** Speaking; Service Orientation; Information Gathering; Active Listening. **Abilities:** Oral Comprehension; Oral Expression; Speech Clarity; Written Expression. **Interacting with Others:** Communicating with Persons Outside Organization; Performing for/Working with Public; Teaching Others; Establishing and Maintaining Relationships; Interpreting Meaning of Information to Others. **Physical Work Conditions:** Outdoors; Walking or Running; Standing; Hazardous Situations; Special Uniform.

25-9031.00 Instructional Coordinators

Develop instructional material, coordinate educational content, and incorporate current technology in specialized fields that provide guidelines to educators and instructors for developing curricula and conducting courses. **Education:** Work experience, plus degree. **Occupational Type:** Social. **Job Zone:** 5. **Average Salary:** $38,870. **Projected Growth:** 13%. **Occupational Values:** Achievement; Autonomy; Responsibility; Authority; Creativity; Working Conditions; Activity. **Skills Required:**

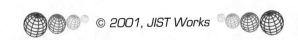

Speaking; Writing; Learning Strategies; Reading Comprehension; Instructing; Active Listening; Implementation Planning. **Abilities:** Oral Expression; Written Expression; Written Comprehension; Oral Comprehension. **Interacting with Others:** Communicating with Persons Outside Organization; Providing Consultation and Advice to Others; Communicating with Other Workers; Teaching Others. **Physical Work Conditions:** Indoors; Sitting.

12.02.01 Social Services: Religious

21-2011.00 Clergy

Conduct religious worship and perform other spiritual functions associated with beliefs and practices of religious faith or denomination. Provide spiritual and moral guidance and assistance to members. **Education:** First professional degree. **Occupational Type:** Social. **Job Zone:** 5. **Average Salary:** $28,850. **Projected Growth:** 13.4%. **Occupational Values:** Social Status; Achievement; Autonomy; Security; Social Service; Recognition; Ability Utilization. **Skills Required:** Speaking; Service Orientation; Social Perceptiveness; Active Listening; Writing; Reading Comprehension; Instructing. **Abilities:** Speech Clarity; Written Expression; Oral Expression; Written Comprehension; Oral Comprehension; Problem Sensitivity. **Interacting with Others:** Establishing and Maintaining Relationships; Assisting and Caring for Others; Interpreting Meaning of Information to Others; Performing for/Working with Public; Communicating with Persons Outside Organization; Providing Consultation and Advice to Others; Teaching Others. **Physical Work Conditions:** Indoors; Special Uniform; Standing; Sitting.

21-2021.00 Directors, Religious Activities and Education

Direct and coordinate activities of a denominational group to meet religious needs of students. Plan, direct, or coordinate church school programs designed to promote religious education among church membership. May provide counseling and guidance relative to marital, health, financial, and religious problems. **Education:** Bachelor's degree. **Occupational Type:** Social. **Job Zone:** 5. **Average Salary:** $24,970. **Projected Growth:** 25.1%. **Occupational Values:** Social Service; Social Status; Achievement; Working Conditions; Autonomy; Ability Utilization; Creativity. **Skills Required:** Speaking; Social Perceptiveness; Active Listening; Service Orientation; Reading Comprehension; Information Gathering; Coordination. **Abilities:** Oral Expression; Speech Clarity; Oral Comprehension; Written Expression; Problem Sensitivity; Written Comprehension. **Interacting with Others:** Communicating with Other Workers; Communicating with Persons Outside Organization; Assisting and Caring for Others; Establishing and Maintaining Relationships; Providing Consultation and Advice to Others; Teaching Others; Coordinating Work and Activities of Others. **Physical Work Conditions:** Indoors; Sitting.

12.02.02 Social Services: Counseling and Social Work

19-3031.02 Clinical Psychologists

Diagnose or evaluate mental and emotional disorders of individuals through observation, interview, and psychological tests, and formulate and administer programs of treatment. **Education:** Master's degree. **Occupational Type:** Investigative. **Job Zone:** 4. **Average Salary:** $48,050. **Projected Growth:** 11.4%. **Occupational Values:** Social Service; Autonomy; Responsibility; Creativity; Ability Utilization; Working Conditions; Achievement. **Skills Required:** Active Listening; Social Perceptiveness; Problem Identification; Reading Comprehension; Identification of Key Causes; Critical Thinking; Speaking. **Abilities:** Oral Comprehension; Written Comprehension; Oral Expression; Inductive Reasoning; Problem Sensitivity; Deductive Reasoning; Written Expression. **Interacting with Others:** Communicating with Persons Outside Organization; Establishing and Maintaining Relationships; Teaching Others; Assisting and Caring for Others; Communicating with Other Workers; Coordinating Work and Activities of Others; Performing for/Working with Public. **Physical Work Conditions:** Indoors; Sitting.

19-3031.03 Counseling Psychologists

Assess and evaluate individuals' problems through the use of case history, interview, and observation; provide individual or group counseling services to assist individuals in achieving more effective personal, social, educational, and vocational development and adjustment. **Education:** Master's degree. **Occupational Type:** Social. **Job Zone:** 5. **Average Salary:** $48,050. **Projected Growth:** 11.4%. **Occupational Values:** Social Service; Autonomy; Achievement; Creativity; Ability Utilization; Working Conditions; Security. **Skills Required:** Active Listening; Reading Comprehension; Social Perceptiveness; Critical Thinking; Active Learning; Problem Identification; Speaking. **Abilities:** Inductive Reasoning; Oral Expression; Oral Comprehension; Problem Sensitivity; Written Comprehension; Written Expression; Deductive Reasoning. **Interacting with Others:** Assisting and Caring for Others; Establishing and Maintaining Relationships; Communicating with Persons Outside Organization; Communicating with Other Workers; Interpreting Meaning of Information to Others; Performing for/Working with Public. **Physical Work Conditions:** Indoors; Sitting.

21-1011.00 Substance Abuse and Behavioral Disorder Counselors

Counsel and advise individuals with alcohol, tobacco, drug, or other problems such as gambling and eating disorders. May counsel individuals, families, or groups or engage in prevention programs. **Education:** Bachelor's degree. **Occupational Type:** Social. **Job Zone:** 4. **Average Salary:** $25,942. **Projected Growth:** 35.7%. **Occupational Values:** Social Service; Activity; Autonomy; Responsibility; Achievement; Ability Utilization; Security. **Skills Required:** Social Perceptiveness; Service Orientation; Judgment and Decision Making; Speaking; Active Learning; Learning Strategies; Active Listening. **Abilities:** Oral Comprehension; Problem Sensitivity; Oral Expression; Speech

Clarity; Written Comprehension; Fluency of Ideas; Speech Recognition. **Interacting with Others:** Communicating with Persons Outside Organization; Establishing and Maintaining Relationships; Assisting and Caring for Others; Providing Consultation and Advice to Others; Monitoring and Controlling Resources. **Physical Work Conditions:** Sitting; Indoors.

21-1013.00 Marriage and Family Therapists

Diagnose and treat mental and emotional disorders, whether cognitive, affective, or behavioral, within the context of marriage and family systems. Apply psychotherapeutic and family systems theories and techniques in the delivery of professional services to individuals, couples, and families for the purpose of treating such diagnosed nervous and mental disorders. No other data currently available.

21-1014.00 Mental Health Counselors

Counsel with emphasis on prevention. Work with individuals and groups to promote optimum mental health. May help individuals deal with addictions and substance abuse; family, parenting, and marital problems; suicide; stress management; problems with self-esteem; and issues associated with aging and mental and emotional health. **Education:** Bachelor's degree. **Occupational Type:** Social. **Job Zone:** 4. **Average Salary:** $25,942. **Projected Growth:** 35.7%. **Occupational Values:** Social Service; Autonomy; Achievement; Ability Utilization; Activity; Responsibility; Security. **Skills Required:** Judgment and Decision Making; Speaking; Social Perceptiveness; Active Learning; Service Orientation; Learning Strategies; Active Listening. **Abilities:** Oral Comprehension; Problem Sensitivity; Oral Expression; Speech Clarity; Written Comprehension; Fluency of Ideas; Speech Recognition. **Interacting with Others:** Communicating with Persons Outside Organization; Establishing and Maintaining Relationships; Assisting and Caring for Others; Providing Consultation and Advice to Others; Monitoring and Controlling Resources. **Physical Work Conditions:** Sitting; Indoors.

21-1015.00 Rehabilitation Counselors

Counsel individuals to maximize the independence and employability of persons coping with personal, social, and vocational difficulties that result from birth defects, illness, disease, accidents, or the stress of daily life. Coordinate activities for residents of care and treatment facilities. Assess client needs and design and implement rehabilitation programs that may include personal and vocational counseling, training, and job placement. No other data currently available.

21-1021.00 Child, Family, and School Social Workers

Provide social services and assistance to improve the social and psychological functioning of children and their families and to maximize the family well-being and the academic functioning of children. May assist single parents, arrange adoptions, and find foster homes for abandoned or abused children. In schools, address such problems as teenage pregnancy, misbehavior, and truancy. May also advise teachers on how to deal with problem children. **Education:** Bachelor's degree. **Occupational Type:** Social. **Job Zone:** 4. **Average Salary:** $29,960. **Projected Growth:** 36.1%. **Occupational Values:** Social Service; Activity; Autonomy; Achievement; Security; Ability Utilization; Variety. **Skills Required:** Social Perceptiveness; Speaking; Service Orientation; Active Listening; Problem Identification; Reading Comprehension; Information Gathering. **Abilities:** Oral Comprehension; Problem Sensitivity; Oral Expression; Written Expression; Written Comprehension. **Interacting with Others:** Establishing and Maintaining Relationships; Assisting and Caring for Others; Communicating with Persons Outside Organization; Providing Consultation and Advice to Others. **Physical Work Conditions:** Indoors; Sitting.

21-1022.00 Medical and Public Health Social Workers

Provide persons, families, or vulnerable populations with the psychosocial support needed to cope with chronic, acute, or terminal illnesses such as Alzheimer's, cancer, or AIDS. Services include advising family care givers, providing patient education and counseling, and making necessary referrals for other social services. **Education:** Bachelor's degree. **Occupational Type:** Social. **Job Zone:** 4. **Average Salary:** $31,620. **Projected Growth:** 35.7%. **Occupational Values:** Social Service; Autonomy; Activity; Responsibility; Achievement; Security; Ability Utilization. **Skills Required:** Judgment and Decision Making; Service Orientation; Social Perceptiveness; Active Learning; Speaking; Problem Identification; Learning Strategies. **Abilities:** Oral Comprehension; Problem Sensitivity; Oral Expression; Speech Clarity; Written Comprehension; Fluency of Ideas; Speech Recognition. **Interacting with Others:** Communicating with Persons Outside Organization; Establishing and Maintaining Relationships; Assisting and Caring for Others; Providing Consultation and Advice to Others; Monitoring and Controlling Resources. **Physical Work Conditions:** Sitting; Indoors.

21-1023.00 Mental Health and Substance Abuse Social Workers

Assess and treat individuals with mental, emotional, or substance abuse problems, including abuse of alcohol, tobacco, and/or other drugs. Activities may include individual and group therapy, crisis intervention, case management, client advocacy, prevention, and education. **Education:** Bachelor's degree. **Occupational Type:** Social. **Job Zone:** 4. **Average Salary:** $31,620. **Projected Growth:** 35.7%. **Occupational Values:** Social Service; Autonomy; Activity; Ability Utilization; Achievement; Security; Responsibility. **Skills Required:** Judgment and Decision Making; Speaking; Social Perceptiveness; Service Orientation; Active Learning; Solution Appraisal; Learning Strategies. **Abilities:** Oral Comprehension; Problem Sensitivity; Oral Expression; Speech Clarity; Written Comprehension; Fluency of Ideas; Speech Recognition. **Interacting with Others:** Communicating with Persons Outside Organization; Establishing and Maintaining Relationships; Assisting and Caring for Others; Providing Consultation and Advice to Others; Monitoring and Controlling Resources. **Physical Work Conditions:** Sitting; Indoors.

21-1092.00 Probation Officers and Correctional Treatment Specialists

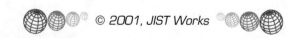

Provide social services to assist in rehabilitation of law offenders in custody or on probation or parole. Make recommendations for actions involving formulation of rehabilitation plan and treatment of offender, including conditional release and education and employment stipulations. **Education:** Bachelor's degree. **Occupational Type:** Social. **Job Zone:** 3. **Average Salary:** $25,971. **Projected Growth:** 36.1%. **Occupational Values:** Social Service; Security; Activity; Company Policies and Practices; Supervision, Human Relations; Autonomy; Ability Utilization. **Skills Required:** Speaking; Judgment and Decision Making; Active Listening; Service Orientation; Information Gathering; Social Perceptiveness; Reading Comprehension. **Abilities:** Oral Expression; Problem Sensitivity; Oral Comprehension; Speech Clarity. **Interacting with Others:** Communicating with Persons Outside Organization; Assisting and Caring for Others; Establishing and Maintaining Relationships; Communicating with Other Workers. **Physical Work Conditions:** Indoors; Sitting.

21-1093.00 Social and Human Service Assistants

Assist professionals from a wide variety of fields such as psychology, rehabilitation, or social work, to provide client services and support for families. May assist clients in identifying available benefits and social and community services and help clients obtain them. May assist social workers with developing, organizing, and conducting programs to prevent and resolve problems relevant to substance abuse, human relationships, rehabilitation, or adult daycare. **Education:** Moderate-term O-J-T. **Occupational Type:** Social. **Job Zone:** 2. **Average Salary:** $21,360. **Projected Growth:** 52.7%. **Occupational Values:** Social Service; Supervision, Human Relations; Company Policies and Practices; Variety; Working Conditions; Activity; Achievement. **Skills Required:** Speaking; Service Orientation; Social Perceptiveness; Active Listening; Problem Identification. **Abilities:** Oral Expression; Written Expression; Oral Comprehension. **Interacting with Others:** Assisting and Caring for Others; Communicating with Persons Outside Organization; Providing Consultation and Advice to Others. **Physical Work Conditions:** Indoors; Sitting; Standing.

39-9041.00 Residential Advisors

Coordinate activities for residents of boarding schools, college fraternities or sororities, college dormitories, or similar establishments. Order supplies and determine need for maintenance, repairs, and furnishings. May maintain household records and assign rooms. May refer residents to counseling resources if needed. **Education:** Bachelor's degree. **Occupational Type:** Social. **Job Zone:** 3. **Average Salary:** $18,840. **Projected Growth:** 46.3%. **Occupational Values:** Social Service; Supervision, Human Relations; Working Conditions; Achievement; Autonomy; Responsibility; Company Policies and Practices. **Skills Required:** Social Perceptiveness; Problem Identification; Active Listening; Critical Thinking; Speaking; Coordination; Solution Appraisal. **Abilities:** Oral Expression. **Interacting with Others:** Establishing and Maintaining Relationships; Assisting and Caring for Others; Providing Consultation and Advice to Others; Resolving Conflict, Negotiating with Others. **Physical Work Conditions:** Indoors; Sitting; Standing; Outdoors; Walking or Running.

12.03.01 Educational Services: Counseling and Evaluation

13-2052.00 Personal Financial Advisors

Advise clients on financial plans, utilizing knowledge of tax and investment strategies, securities, insurance, pension plans, and real estate. Duties include assessing clients' assets, liabilities, cash flow, insurance coverage, tax status, and financial objectives to establish investment strategies. **Education:** Work experience, plus degree. **Occupational Type:** Social. **Job Zone:** 3. **Average Salary:** $39,490. **Projected Growth:** 20.9%. **Occupational Values:** Working Conditions; Social Service; Security; Responsibility; Achievement; Coworkers; Company Policies and Practices. **Skills Required:** Speaking; Mathematics; Active Listening; Judgment and Decision Making; Service Orientation; Information Gathering. **Abilities:** Number Facility; Oral Comprehension; Mathematical Reasoning; Oral Expression; Problem Sensitivity; Speech Clarity. **Interacting with Others:** Communicating with Persons Outside Organization; Providing Consultation and Advice to Others; Assisting and Caring for Others; Establishing and Maintaining Relationships; Interpreting Meaning of Information to Others. **Physical Work Conditions:** Indoors; Sitting.

19-3031.01 Educational Psychologists

Investigate processes of learning and teaching; develop psychological principles and techniques applicable to educational problems. **Education:** Master's degree. **Occupational Type:** Investigative. **Job Zone:** 4. **Average Salary:** $48,050. **Projected Growth:** 11.4%. **Occupational Values:** Autonomy; Ability Utilization; Creativity; Social Service; Achievement; Security; Working Conditions. **Skills Required:** Reading Comprehension; Information Gathering; Writing; Active Listening; Critical Thinking; Mathematics; Speaking. **Abilities:** Oral Expression; Problem Sensitivity; Inductive Reasoning; Written Comprehension; Written Expression; Oral Comprehension; Near Vision. **Interacting with Others:** Communicating with Other Workers; Interpreting Meaning of Information to Others; Communicating with Persons Outside Organization; Providing Consultation and Advice to Others; Establishing and Maintaining Relationships. **Physical Work Conditions:** Indoors; Sitting; Using Hands on Objects, Tools, Controls.

21-1012.00 Educational, Vocational, and School Counselors

Counsel individuals and provide group educational and vocational guidance services. **Education:** Master's degree. **Occupational Type:** Social. **Job Zone:** 4. **Average Salary:** $38,650. **Projected Growth:** 25%. **Occupational Values:** Social Service; Achievement; Working Conditions; Autonomy; Responsibility; Authority; Creativity. **Skills Required:** Speaking; Active Listening; Problem Identification; Social Perceptiveness; Service Orientation; Critical Thinking; Identification of Key Causes. **Abilities:** Oral Expression; Written Expression; Oral Comprehension. **Interacting with Others:** Assisting and Caring for

Others; Establishing and Maintaining Relationships; Communicating with Persons Outside Organization; Interpreting Meaning of Information to Others; Performing for/Working with Public; Providing Consultation and Advice to Others; Coaching and Developing Others. **Physical Work Conditions:** Indoors; Sitting.

12.03.02 Educational Services: Postsecondary and Adult Teaching and Instructing

25-1011.00 Business Teachers, Postsecondary

Teach courses in business administration and management, such as accounting, finance, human resources, labor relations, marketing, and operations research. No other data currently available.

25-1021.00 Computer Science Teachers, Postsecondary

Teach courses in computer science. May specialize in a field of computer science such as the design and function of computers or operations and research analysis. **Education:** Doctor's degree. **Occupational Type:** Investigative. **Job Zone:** 5. **Average Salary:** $43,780. **Projected Growth:** 22.6%. **Occupational Values:** Ability Utilization; Achievement; Authority; Working Conditions; Autonomy; Social Status; Social Service. **Skills Required:** Instructing; Speaking; Learning Strategies; Reading Comprehension; Information Gathering; Mathematics; Information Organization. **Abilities:** Speech Clarity; Written Comprehension; Oral Expression; Written Expression. **Interacting with Others:** Teaching Others; Communicating with Persons Outside Organization. **Physical Work Conditions:** Indoors; Sitting; Using Hands on Objects, Tools, Controls.

25-1022.00 Mathematical Science Teachers, Postsecondary

Teach courses pertaining to mathematical concepts, statistics, and actuarial science and to the application of original and standardized mathematical techniques in solving specific problems and situations. **Education:** Doctor's degree. **Occupational Type:** Investigative. **Job Zone:** 5. **Average Salary:** $44,040. **Projected Growth:** 22.6%. **Occupational Values:** Achievement; Ability Utilization; Authority; Autonomy; Working Conditions; Social Service; Social Status. **Skills Required:** Mathematics; Reading Comprehension; Instructing; Learning Strategies; Speaking; Active Learning; Critical Thinking. **Abilities:** Mathematical Reasoning; Oral Expression; Written Comprehension; Written Expression; Speech Clarity; Number Facility; Oral Comprehension. **Interacting with Others:** Teaching Others; Interpreting Meaning of Information to Others; Communicating with Other Workers; Coaching and Developing Others; Communicating with Persons Outside Organization. **Physical Work Conditions:** Indoors; Sitting; Standing.

25-1031.00 Architecture Teachers, Postsecondary

Teach courses in architecture and agricultural design, such as architectural environmental design, interior architecture/design, and landscape architecture. **Education:** Doctor's degree. **Average Salary:** $46,600. **Projected Growth:** 23%. No other data currently available.

25-1032.00 Engineering Teachers, Postsecondary

Teach courses pertaining to the application of physical laws and principles of engineering for the development of machines, materials, instruments, processes, and services. Includes teachers of subjects such as chemical, civil, electrical, industrial, mechanical, mineral, and petroleum engineering. Includes both teachers primarily engaged in teaching and those who do a combination of teaching and research. **Education:** Doctor's degree. **Occupational Type:** Investigative. **Job Zone:** 5. **Average Salary:** $63,970. **Projected Growth:** 22.6%. **Occupational Values:** Ability Utilization; Achievement; Authority; Autonomy; Responsibility; Working Conditions; Creativity. **Skills Required:** Reading Comprehension; Instructing; Mathematics; Active Learning; Science; Critical Thinking; Speaking. **Abilities:** Oral Comprehension; Speech Clarity; Oral Expression; Written Comprehension; Written Expression; Mathematical Reasoning; Number Facility. **Interacting with Others:** Teaching Others; Communicating with Other Workers; Interpreting Meaning of Information to Others; Coaching and Developing Others. **Physical Work Conditions:** Indoors; Sitting; Standing.

25-1041.00 Agricultural Sciences Teachers, Postsecondary

Teach courses in the agricultural sciences. Includes teachers of agronomy, dairy sciences, fisheries management, horticultural sciences, poultry sciences, range management, and agricultural soil conservation. **Education:** Doctor's degree. **Occupational Type:** Investigative. **Job Zone:** 5. **Average Salary:** $60,790. **Projected Growth:** 22.6%. **Occupational Values:** Achievement; Ability Utilization; Authority; Creativity; Social Service; Working Conditions; Social Status. **Skills Required:** Reading Comprehension; Instructing; Speaking; Science; Active Learning; Writing; Critical Thinking. **Abilities:** Oral Expression; Written Expression; Speech Clarity; Written Comprehension; Oral Comprehension. **Interacting with Others:** Teaching Others; Coaching and Developing Others; Communicating with Other Workers. **Physical Work Conditions:** Indoors; Sitting; Standing.

25-1042.00 Biological Science Teachers, Postsecondary

Teach courses in biological sciences. **Education:** Doctor's degree. **Occupational Type:** Investigative. **Job Zone:** 5. **Average Salary:** $47,850. **Projected Growth:** 22.6%. **Occupational Values:** Achievement; Ability Utilization; Authority; Creativity; Responsibility; Social Service; Social Status. **Skills Required:** Reading Comprehension; Speaking; Instructing; Active Learning; Science; Writing; Critical Thinking. **Abilities:** Oral Expression; Written Expression; Speech Clarity; Written Comprehension; Oral Comprehension. **Interacting with Others:** Teaching Others; Coaching and Developing Others; Communicating with Other Workers. **Physical Work Conditions:** Indoors; Sitting; Standing.

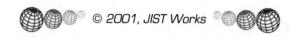

25-1043.00 Forestry and Conservation Science Teachers, Postsecondary

Teach courses in environmental and conservation science. **Education:** Doctor's degree. **Occupational Type:** Investigative. **Job Zone:** 5. **Average Salary:** $46,664. **Projected Growth:** 22.6%. **Occupational Values:** Achievement; Ability Utilization; Authority; Creativity; Autonomy; Responsibility; Social Service. **Skills Required:** Reading Comprehension; Instructing; Speaking; Active Learning; Science; Critical Thinking; Writing. **Abilities:** Oral Expression; Written Expression; Speech Clarity; Written Comprehension; Oral Comprehension. **Interacting with Others:** Teaching Others; Coaching and Developing Others; Communicating with Other Workers. **Physical Work Conditions:** Indoors; Sitting; Standing.

25-1051.00 Atmospheric, Earth, Marine, and Space Sciences Teachers, Postsecondary

Teach courses in the physical sciences, except chemistry and physics. No other data currently available.

25-1052.00 Chemistry Teachers, Postsecondary

Teach courses pertaining to the chemical and physical properties and compositional changes of substances. Work may include instruction in the methods of qualitative and quantitative chemical analysis. Includes both teachers primarily engaged in teaching and those who do a combination of teaching and research. **Education:** Doctor's degree. **Occupational Type:** Investigative. **Job Zone:** 5. **Average Salary:** $47,130. **Projected Growth:** 22.6%. **Occupational Values:** Achievement; Ability Utilization; Authority; Social Status; Autonomy; Social Service; Working Conditions. **Skills Required:** Instructing; Writing; Reading Comprehension; Speaking; Science; Critical Thinking; Mathematics. **Abilities:** Speech Clarity; Written Comprehension; Oral Expression; Oral Comprehension; Information Ordering; Written Expression. **Interacting with Others:** Teaching Others; Communicating with Persons Outside Organization; Interpreting Meaning of Information to Others; Coaching and Developing Others; Providing Consultation and Advice to Others. **Physical Work Conditions:** Indoors; Sitting; Standing; Hazardous Conditions; Using Hands on Objects, Tools, Controls.

25-1053.00 Environmental Science Teachers, Postsecondary

Teach courses in environmental science. No other data currently available.

25-1054.00 Physics Teachers, Postsecondary

Teach courses pertaining to the laws of matter and energy. Includes both teachers primarily engaged in teaching and those who do a combination of teaching and research. **Education:** Doctor's degree. **Occupational Type:** Investigative. **Job Zone:** 5. **Average Salary:** $52,450. **Projected Growth:** 22.6%. **Occupational Values:** Achievement; Ability Utilization; Authority; Responsibility; Autonomy; Working Conditions; Social Status. **Skills Required:** Instructing; Speaking; Reading Comprehension; Science; Writing; Critical Thinking; Mathematics. **Abilities:** Oral Expression; Written Comprehension; Speech Clarity; Deductive Reasoning; Number Facility; Oral Comprehension; Mathematical Reasoning. **Interacting with Others:** Teaching Others; Interpreting Meaning of Information to Others; Communicating with Persons Outside Organization; Providing Consultation and Advice to Others. **Physical Work Conditions:** Indoors; Sitting; Using Hands on Objects, Tools, Controls; Standing.

25-1061.00 Anthropology and Archeology Teachers, Postsecondary

Teach courses in anthropology or archeology. **Education:** Doctor's degree. **Occupational Type:** Social. **Job Zone:** 5. **Average Salary:** $47,230. **Projected Growth:** 22.6%. **Occupational Values:** Achievement; Ability Utilization; Authority; Autonomy; Responsibility; Working Conditions; Social Status. **Skills Required:** Instructing; Reading Comprehension; Speaking; Critical Thinking; Writing; Learning Strategies; Active Learning. **Abilities:** Oral Expression; Written Comprehension; Speech Clarity; Written Expression; Oral Comprehension. **Interacting with Others:** Teaching Others; Communicating with Other Workers; Coaching and Developing Others. **Physical Work Conditions:** Indoors; Sitting; Standing.

25-1062.00 Area, Ethnic, and Cultural Studies Teachers, Postsecondary

Teach courses pertaining to the culture and development of an area (e.g., Latin America), an ethnic group, or any other group (e.g., women's studies, urban affairs). **Education:** Doctor's degree. **Occupational Type:** Social. **Job Zone:** 5. **Average Salary:** $46,600. **Projected Growth:** 22.6%. **Occupational Values:** Achievement; Ability Utilization; Authority; Responsibility; Autonomy; Social Service; Creativity. **Skills Required:** Instructing; Reading Comprehension; Speaking; Critical Thinking; Active Learning; Writing; Learning Strategies. **Abilities:** Oral Expression; Written Comprehension; Speech Clarity; Written Expression; Oral Comprehension. **Interacting with Others:** Teaching Others; Communicating with Other Workers; Coaching and Developing Others. **Physical Work Conditions:** Indoors; Sitting; Standing.

25-1063.00 Economics Teachers, Postsecondary

Teach courses in economics. **Education:** Doctor's degree. **Occupational Type:** Social. **Job Zone:** 5. **Average Salary:** $54,350. **Projected Growth:** 22.6%. **Occupational Values:** Achievement; Authority; Ability Utilization; Responsibility; Autonomy; Working Conditions; Social Status. **Skills Required:** Instructing; Reading Comprehension; Speaking; Critical Thinking; Learning Strategies; Writing; Active Learning. **Abilities:** Oral Expression; Written Comprehension; Speech Clarity; Written Expression; Oral Comprehension. **Interacting with Others:** Teaching Others; Communicating with Other Workers; Coaching and Developing Others. **Physical Work Conditions:** Indoors; Sitting; Standing.

25-1064.00 Geography Teachers, Postsecondary

Teach courses in geography. No other data currently available.

25-1065.00 Political Science Teachers, Postsecondary

Teach courses in political science, international affairs, and international relations. **Education:** Doctor's degree. **Occupational Type:** Social. **Job Zone:** 5. **Average Salary:** $47,880. **Projected Growth:** 22.6%. **Occupational Values:** Achievement; Ability Utilization; Authority; Autonomy; Responsibility; Working Conditions; Creativity. **Skills Required:** Instructing; Reading Comprehension; Speaking; Critical Thinking; Writing; Learning Strategies; Active Learning. **Abilities:** Oral Expression; Written Comprehension; Speech Clarity; Written Expression; Oral Comprehension. **Interacting with Others:** Teaching Others; Communicating with Other Workers; Coaching and Developing Others. **Physical Work Conditions:** Indoors; Sitting; Standing.

25-1066.00 Psychology Teachers, Postsecondary

Teach courses in psychology, such as child, clinical, and developmental psychology, and psychological counseling. **Education:** Doctor's degree. **Occupational Type:** Social. **Job Zone:** 5. **Average Salary:** $48,750. **Projected Growth:** 22.6%. **Occupational Values:** Achievement; Authority; Ability Utilization; Autonomy; Responsibility; Social Service; Creativity. **Skills Required:** Instructing; Reading Comprehension; Speaking; Critical Thinking; Writing; Active Learning; Learning Strategies. **Abilities:** Oral Expression; Written Comprehension; Speech Clarity; Written Expression; Oral Comprehension. **Interacting with Others:** Teaching Others; Communicating with Other Workers; Coaching and Developing Others. **Physical Work Conditions:** Indoors; Sitting; Standing.

25-1067.00 Sociology Teachers, Postsecondary

Teach courses in sociology. **Education:** Doctor's degree. **Occupational Type:** Social. **Job Zone:** 5. **Average Salary:** $47,230. **Projected Growth:** 22.6%. **Occupational Values:** Achievement; Authority; Ability Utilization; Autonomy; Responsibility; Social Service; Working Conditions. **Skills Required:** Instructing; Reading Comprehension; Speaking; Critical Thinking; Active Learning; Learning Strategies; Writing. **Abilities:** Oral Expression; Written Comprehension; Speech Clarity; Written Expression; Oral Comprehension. **Interacting with Others:** Teaching Others; Communicating with Other Workers; Coaching and Developing Others. **Physical Work Conditions:** Indoors; Sitting; Standing.

25-1071.00 Health Specialties Teachers, Postsecondary

Teach courses in health specialties such as veterinary medicine, dentistry, pharmacy, therapy, laboratory technology, and public health. **Education:** Doctor's degree. **Occupational Type:** Investigative. **Job Zone:** 5. **Average Salary:** $47,650. **Projected Growth:** 22.6%. **Occupational Values:** Achievement; Ability Utilization; Authority; Autonomy; Responsibility; Social Service; Creativity. **Skills Required:** Instructing; Reading Comprehension; Science; Writing; Active Learning; Speaking; Critical Thinking. **Abilities:** Oral Expression; Written Comprehension; Written Expression; Speech Clarity; Oral Comprehension. **Interacting with Others:** Teaching Others; Communicating with Other Workers; Coaching and Developing Others. **Physical Work Conditions:** Indoors; Standing; Sitting.

25-1072.00 Nursing Instructors and Teachers, Postsecondary

Demonstrate and teach patient care in classroom and clinical units to nursing students. Includes both teachers primarily engaged in teaching and those who do a combination of teaching and research. **Education:** Doctor's degree. **Occupational Type:** Social. **Job Zone:** 5. **Average Salary:** $44,910. **Projected Growth:** 22.6%. **Occupational Values:** Achievement; Authority; Ability Utilization; Responsibility; Autonomy; Coworkers; Social Service. **Skills Required:** Instructing; Speaking; Learning Strategies; Management of Personnel Resources; Science; Reading Comprehension; Implementation Planning. **Abilities:** Oral Expression; Written Expression; Speech Clarity; Written Comprehension; Inductive Reasoning; Oral Comprehension; Deductive Reasoning. **Interacting with Others:** Teaching Others; Coaching and Developing Others; Interpreting Meaning of Information to Others; Communicating with Other Workers; Communicating with Persons Outside Organization; Establishing and Maintaining Relationships; Assisting and Caring for Others. **Physical Work Conditions:** Indoors; Special Uniform; Diseases/Infections; Standing; Common Protective or Safety Attire.

25-1081.00 Education Teachers, Postsecondary

Teach courses pertaining to education, such as counseling, curriculum, guidance, instruction, teacher education, and teaching English as a second language. No other data currently available.

25-1082.00 Library Science Teachers, Postsecondary

Teach courses in library science. No other data currently available.

25-1111.00 Criminal Justice and Law Enforcement Teachers, Postsecondary

Teach courses in criminal justice, corrections, and law enforcement administration. No other data currently available.

25-1112.00 Law Teachers, Postsecondary

Teach courses in law. No other data currently available.

25-1113.00 Social Work Teachers, Postsecondary

Teach courses in social work. No other data currently available.

25-1121.00 Art, Drama, and Music Teachers, Postsecondary

Teach courses in drama, music, and the arts, including fine and applied art such as painting and sculpture, or design and crafts. **Education:** Doctor's degree. **Occupational Type:** Artistic. **Job Zone:** 5. **Average Salary:** $41,870. **Projected Growth:** 22.6%. **Occupational Values:** Ability Utilization; Achievement; Authority; Working Conditions; Autonomy; Creativity; Responsibility. **Skills Required:** Instructing; Reading Comprehension; Speaking; Information Gathering; Writing; Learning Strategies; Idea Generation. **Abilities:** Oral Expression; Written Expression; Written Comprehension; Oral Comprehension; Speech Clarity; Fluency of Ideas; Near Vision. **Interacting with Others:** Teaching Others; Coaching and Developing Others; Communicating with Other Workers; Communicating with Persons Outside Organization. **Physical Work Conditions:** Indoors; Sitting; Using Hands on Objects, Tools, Controls; Standing.

25-1122.00 Communications Teachers, Postsecondary

Teach courses in communications, such as organizational communications, public relations, radio/television broadcasting, and journalism. No other data currently available.

25-1123.00 English Language and Literature Teachers, Postsecondary

Teach courses in English language and literature, including linguistics and comparative literature. **Education:** Doctor's degree. **Occupational Type:** Artistic. **Job Zone:** 5. **Average Salary:** $41,860. **Projected Growth:** 22.6%. **Occupational Values:** Achievement; Authority; Ability Utilization; Responsibility; Autonomy; Social Service; Working Conditions. **Skills Required:** Reading Comprehension; Instructing; Speaking; Writing; Learning Strategies; Information Gathering; Monitoring. **Abilities:** Oral Expression; Oral Comprehension; Speech Clarity; Written Comprehension; Written Expression; Speech Recognition. **Interacting with Others:** Teaching Others; Communicating with Other Workers. **Physical Work Conditions:** Indoors; Sitting; Standing.

25-1124.00 Foreign Language and Literature Teachers, Postsecondary

Teach courses in foreign (i.e., other than English) languages and literature. **Education:** Doctor's degree. **Occupational Type:** Artistic. **Job Zone:** 5. **Average Salary:** $41,690. **Projected Growth:** 22.6%. **Occupational Values:** Achievement; Ability Utilization; Authority; Working Conditions; Autonomy; Social Service; Responsibility. **Skills Required:** Reading Comprehension; Instructing; Speaking; Writing; Learning Strategies; Monitoring; Information Gathering. **Abilities:** Oral Expression; Oral Comprehension; Speech Clarity; Written Comprehension; Written Expression; Speech Recognition. **Interacting with Others:** Teaching Others; Communicating with Other Workers. **Physical Work Conditions:** Indoors; Sitting; Standing.

25-1125.00 History Teachers, Postsecondary

Teach courses in human history and historiography. **Education:** Doctor's degree. **Occupational Type:** Social. **Job Zone:** 5. **Average Salary:** $46,200. **Projected Growth:** 22.6%. **Occupational Values:** Achievement; Ability Utilization; Authority; Autonomy; Responsibility; Social Service; Working Conditions. **Skills Required:** Instructing; Reading Comprehension; Speaking; Critical Thinking; Active Learning; Learning Strategies; Writing. **Abilities:** Oral Expression; Written Comprehension; Speech Clarity; Written Expression; Oral Comprehension. **Interacting with Others:** Teaching Others; Communicating with Other Workers; Coaching and Developing Others. **Physical Work Conditions:** Indoors; Sitting; Standing.

25-1126.00 Philosophy and Religion Teachers, Postsecondary

Teach courses in philosophy, religion, and theology. No other data currently available.

25-1191.00 Graduate Teaching Assistants

Assist department chairperson, faculty members, or other professional staff members in college or university by performing teaching or teaching-related duties such as teaching lower level courses, developing teaching materials, preparing and giving examinations, and grading examinations or papers. Must be enrolled in a graduate school program. **Education:** Bachelor's degree. **Occupational Type:** Social. **Job Zone:** 5. **Average Salary:** $19,140. **Projected Growth:** 22.6%. **Occupational Values:** Coworkers; Working Conditions; Social Service; Authority; Achievement; Ability Utilization; Supervision, Human Relations. **Skills Required:** Instructing; Critical Thinking; Speaking; Reading Comprehension; Learning Strategies. **Abilities:** Oral Expression; Written Comprehension; Speech Clarity; Oral Comprehension; Written Expression. **Interacting with Others:** Teaching Others; Communicating with Other Workers. **Physical Work Conditions:** Indoors; Standing; Sitting.

25-1192.00 Home Economics Teachers, Postsecondary

Teach courses in child care, family relations, finance, nutrition, and related subjects as pertaining to home management. No other data currently available.

25-1193.00 Recreation and Fitness Studies Teachers, Postsecondary

Teach courses pertaining to recreation, leisure, and fitness studies, including exercise physiology and facilities management. No other data currently available.

25-1194.00 Vocational Education Teachers, Postsecondary

Teach or instruct vocational or occupational subjects at the postsecondary level (but at less than the baccalaureate level) to students who have graduated or left high school. Includes correspondence school instructors; industrial, commercial and government training instructors; and adult education teachers and instructors who prepare persons to operate industrial machinery and equipment and transportation and communications equipment. Teaching may take place in public or private schools whose primary business is education or in a school associated with an organization whose primary business is other than education. **Education:** Work experience in a related occupation. **Occupational Type:** Social. **Job Zone:** 4. **Average Salary:** $34,430. **Projected Growth:** 11%. **Occupational Values:** Authority; Achievement; Social Service; Responsibility; Working Conditions; Creativity; Autonomy. **Skills Required:** Instructing; Learning Strategies; Speaking; Active Listening; Reading Comprehension; Writing; Judgment and Decision Making. **Abilities:** Oral Expression; Speech Clarity; Oral Comprehension; Written Comprehension; Written Expression. **Interacting with Others:** Teaching Others; Interpreting Meaning of Information to Others; Assisting and Caring for Others; Communicating with Persons Outside Organization; Establishing and Maintaining Relationships. **Physical Work Conditions:** Indoors; Standing; Sitting; Walking or Running.

25-3011.00 Adult Literacy, Remedial Education, and GED Teachers and Instructors

Teach or instruct out-of-school youths and adults in remedial education classes, preparatory classes for the General Educational Development test, literacy, or English as a second language. Teaching may or may not take place in a traditional educational institution. **Education:** Work experience in a related occupation. **Occupational Type:** Social. **Job Zone:** 4. **Average Salary:** $24,790. **Projected Growth:** 20.9%. **Occupational Values:** Authority; Achievement; Social Service; Creativity; Responsibility; Ability Utilization; Working Conditions. **Skills Required:** Instructing; Active Listening; Speaking; Learning Strategies; Reading Comprehension; Writing; Information Gathering. **Abilities:** Oral Expression; Oral Comprehension; Speech Clarity; Written Comprehension; Written Expression. **Interacting with Others:** Teaching Others; Coaching and Developing Others; Communicating with Persons Outside Organization; Establishing and Maintaining Relationships; Assisting and Caring for Others; Interpreting Meaning of Information to Others; Communicating with Other Workers. **Physical Work Conditions:** Indoors; Sitting; Standing.

25-3021.00 Self-Enrichment Education Teachers

Teach or instruct courses other than those that normally lead to an occupational objective or degree. Courses may include self-improvement, nonvocational, and nonacademic subjects. Teaching may or may not take place in a traditional educational institution. **Education:** Work experience in a related occupation. **Occupational Type:** Social. **Job Zone:** 4. **Average Salary:** $24,790. **Projected Growth:** 20.9%. **Occupational Values:** Authority; Achievement; Social Service; Responsibility; Working Conditions; Creativity; Ability Utilization. **Skills Required:** Instructing; Learning Strategies; Speaking; Reading Comprehension; Active Listening; Writing; Information Gathering. **Abilities:** Oral Expression; Oral Comprehension; Speech Clarity; Written Comprehension; Written Expression. **Interacting with Others:** Teaching Others; Coaching and Developing Others; Communicating with Persons Outside Organization; Establishing and Maintaining Relationships; Assisting and Caring for Others; Interpreting Meaning of Information to Others; Communicating with Other Workers. **Physical Work Conditions:** Indoors; Sitting; Standing.

25-9021.00 Farm and Home Management Advisors

Advise, instruct, and assist individuals and families engaged in agriculture, agricultural-related processes, or home economics activities. Demonstrate procedures and apply research findings to solve problems. Instruct and train in product development, sales, and the utilization of machinery and equipment to promote general welfare. Includes county agricultural agents, feed and farm management advisers, home economists, and extension service advisors. **Education:** Bachelor's degree. **Occupational Type:** Social. **Job Zone:** 4. **Average Salary:** $37,200. **Projected Growth:** –2.2%. **Occupational Values:** Autonomy; Social Service; Achievement; Ability Utilization; Responsibility; Creativity; Authority. **Skills Required:** Instructing; Implementation Planning; Speaking; Learning Strategies; Information Gathering; Idea Evaluation; Writing. **Abilities:** Oral Expression; Mathematical Reasoning; Speech Clarity; Oral Comprehension; Written Expression; Problem Sensitivity. **Interacting with Others:** Communicating with Persons Outside Organization; Providing Consultation and Advice to Others; Teaching Others; Coaching and Developing Others; Establishing and Maintaining Relationships. **Physical Work Conditions:** Indoors; Standing; Sitting.

12.03.03 Educational Services: Preschool, Elementary, and Secondary Teaching and Instructing

25-2011.00 Preschool Teachers, Except Special Education

Instruct children (normally up to 5 years of age) in activities designed to promote social, physical, and intellectual growth needed for primary school, in preschool, day care center, or other child development facility. May be required to hold State certification. **Education:** Bachelor's degree. **Occupational Type:** Social. **Job Zone:** 4. **Average Salary:** $17,310. **Projected Growth:** 26.5%. **Occupational Values:** Authority; Social Service; Achievement; Responsibility; Creativity; Security; Autonomy. **Skills Required:** Instructing; Learning Strategies; Speaking; Social Perceptiveness; Active Listening. **Abilities:** Oral Expression; Speech Clarity; Oral Comprehension; Problem Sensitivity; Time Sharing; Near Vision; Speech Recognition. **Interacting with Others:** Teaching Others; Assisting and Caring for Others; Establishing and Maintaining Relationships; Communicating with Other Workers; Coordinating Work and Activities of Others; Resolving Conflict, Negotiating with Others; Communicating with Persons Outside Organization. **Physical Work Conditions:** Indoors; Standing; Sitting.

25-2012.00 Kindergarten Teachers, Except Special Education

Teach elemental natural and social science, personal hygiene, music, art, and literature to children from 4 to 6 years old. Promote physical, mental, and social development. May be required to hold State certification. **Education:** Bachelor's degree. **Occupational Type:** Social. **Job Zone:** 4. **Average Salary:** $33,590. **Projected Growth:** 13.4%. **Occupational Values:** Authority; Social Service; Achievement; Responsibility; Creativity; Autonomy; Security. **Skills Required:** Instructing; Speaking; Learning Strategies; Active Listening; Service Orientation; Social Perceptiveness; Time Management. **Abilities:** Oral Expression; Problem Sensitivity; Oral Comprehension; Written Comprehension; Fluency of Ideas; Speech Clarity; Written Expression. **Interacting with Others:** Teaching Others; Assisting and Caring for Others; Establishing and Maintaining Relationships; Communicating with Persons Outside Organization; Interpreting Meaning of Information to Others; Performing for/Working with Public; Resolving Conflict, Negotiating with Others. **Physical Work Conditions:** Indoors; Standing; Sitting.

25-2021.00 Elementary School Teachers, Except Special Education

Teach elementary-level pupils in public or private schools basic academic, social, and other formative skills. **Education:** Bachelor's degree. **Occupational Type:** Social. **Job Zone:** 4. **Average Salary:** $36,110. **Projected Growth:** 11.7%. **Occupational Values:** Authority; Achievement; Social Service; Creativity; Responsibility; Security; Autonomy. **Skills Required:** Instructing; Learning Strategies; Speaking; Reading Comprehension; Active Listening; Writing; Social Perceptiveness. **Abilities:** Oral Expression; Written Comprehension; Speech Clarity; Written Expression; Oral Comprehension; Number Facility; Mathematical Reasoning. **Interacting with Others:** Teaching Others; Establishing and Maintaining Relationships; Assisting and Caring for Others; Interpreting Meaning of Information to Others; Coaching and Developing Others; Communicating with Other Workers; Communicating with Persons Outside Organization. **Physical Work Conditions:** Indoors; Sitting; Standing.

25-2022.00 Middle School Teachers, Except Special and Vocational Education

Teach students in public or private schools in one or more subjects at the middle, intermediate, or junior high level, which falls between elementary and senior high school as defined by applicable State laws and regulations. **Education:** Bachelor's degree. **Occupational Type:** Social. **Job Zone:** 4. **Average Salary:** $37,890. **Projected Growth:** 22.6%. **Occupational Values:** Social Service; Authority; Achievement; Ability Utilization; Responsibility; Creativity; Working Conditions. **Skills Required:** Speaking; Learning Strategies; Instructing; Reading Comprehension; Social Perceptiveness; Active Listening; Monitoring. **Abilities:** Oral Expression; Written Comprehension; Oral Comprehension; Written Expression; Speech Clarity; Number Facility. **Interacting with Others:** Teaching Others; Communicating with Persons Outside Organization; Interpreting Meaning of Information to Others; Establishing and Maintaining Relationships. **Physical Work Conditions:** Indoors; Standing; Sitting.

25-2023.00 Vocational Education Teachers, Middle School

Teach or instruct vocational or occupational subjects at the middle school level. **Education:** Bachelor's degree. **Occupational Type:** Social. **Job Zone:** 4. **Average Salary:** $34,430. **Projected Growth:** 22.6%. **Occupational Values:** Social Service; Authority; Achievement; Creativity; Responsibility; Ability Utilization; Security. **Skills Required:** Instructing; Learning Strategies; Speaking; Reading Comprehension; Social Perceptiveness; Active Listening; Mathematics. **Abilities:** Oral Expression; Written Comprehension; Oral Comprehension; Written Expression; Speech Clarity; Number Facility. **Interacting with Others:** Teaching Others; Communicating with Persons Outside Organization; Interpreting Meaning of Information to Others; Establishing and Maintaining Relationships. **Physical Work Conditions:** Indoors; Standing; Sitting.

25-2031.00 Secondary School Teachers, Except Special and Vocational Education

Instruct students in secondary public or private schools in one or more subjects, such as English, mathematics, or social studies. May be designated according to subject matter specialty, such as typing instructors, commercial teachers, or English teachers. **Education:** Bachelor's degree. **Occupational Type:** Social. **Job Zone:** 4. **Average Salary:** $37,890. **Projected Growth:** 22.6%. **Occupational Values:** Social Service; Authority; Achievement; Ability Utilization; Responsibility; Creativity; Activity. **Skills Required:** Speaking; Learning Strategies; Instructing; Reading Comprehension; Active Listening; Social Perceptiveness; Monitoring. **Abilities:** Oral Expression; Written Comprehension; Oral Comprehension; Written Expression; Speech Clarity; Number Facility. **Interacting with Others:** Teaching Others; Communicating with Persons Outside Organization; Interpreting Meaning of Information to Others; Establishing and Maintaining Relationships. **Physical Work Conditions:** Indoors; Standing; Sitting.

25-2032.00 Vocational Education Teachers, Secondary School

Teach or instruct vocational or occupational subjects at the secondary school level. **Education:** Bachelor's degree. **Occupational Type:** Social. **Job Zone:** 4. **Average Salary:** $34,430. **Projected Growth:** 22.6%. **Occupational Values:** Social Service; Authority; Achievement; Ability Utilization; Responsibility; Creativity; Autonomy. **Skills Required:** Speaking; Learning Strategies; Instructing; Reading Comprehension; Social Perceptiveness; Active Listening; Information Gathering. **Abilities:** Oral Expression; Written Comprehension; Oral Comprehension; Written Expression; Speech Clarity; Number Facility. **Interacting with Others:** Teaching Others; Communicating with Persons Outside Organization; Interpreting Meaning of Information to Others; Establishing and Maintaining Relationships. **Physical Work Conditions:** Indoors; Standing; Sitting.

25-2041.00 Special Education Teachers, Preschool, Kindergarten, and Elementary School

Teach elementary school and preschool subjects to educationally and physically handicapped students. Includes teachers who specialize and work with audibly and visually handicapped students and those who teach basic academic and life processes skills to the mentally impaired. **Education:** Bachelor's degree. **Occupational Type:** Social. **Job Zone:** 4. **Average Salary:** $35,838. **Projected Growth:** 33.8%. **Occupational Values:** Social Service; Achievement; Authority; Ability Utilization; Responsibility; Creativity; Activity. **Skills Required:** Instructing; Speaking; Learning Strategies; Social Perceptiveness; Implementation Planning; Active Listening; Monitoring. **Abilities:** Oral Expression; Oral Comprehension; Written Comprehension; Problem Sensitivity; Speech Clarity; Written Expression. **Interacting with Others:** Teaching Others; Establishing and Maintaining Relationships; Interpreting Meaning of Information to Others; Communicating with Persons Outside Organization; Assisting and Caring for Others; Communicating with Other Workers. **Physical Work Conditions:** Indoors; Sitting; Standing.

25-2042.00 Special Education Teachers, Middle School

Teach middle school subjects to educationally and physically handicapped students. Includes teachers who specialize and work with audibly and visually handicapped students and those who teach basic academic and life processes skills to the mentally impaired. **Education:** Bachelor's degree. **Occupational Type:** Social. **Job Zone:** 4. **Average Salary:** $35,838. **Projected Growth:** 33.8%. **Occupational Values:** Social Service; Achievement; Authority; Ability Utilization; Responsibility; Activity; Creativity. **Skills Required:** Instructing; Social Perceptiveness; Learning Strategies; Speaking; Implementation Planning; Active Listening; Monitoring. **Abilities:** Oral Expression; Oral Comprehension; Written Comprehension; Problem Sensitivity; Speech Clarity; Written Expression. **Interacting with Others:** Teaching Others; Establishing and Maintaining Relationships; Interpreting Meaning of Information to Others; Communicating with Persons Outside Organization; Assisting and Caring for Others; Communicating with Other Workers. **Physical Work Conditions:** Indoors; Sitting; Standing.

25-2043.00 Special Education Teachers, Secondary School

Teach secondary school subjects to educationally and physically handicapped students. Includes teachers who specialize and work with audibly and visually handicapped students and those who teach basic academic and life processes skills to the mentally impaired. **Education:** Bachelor's degree. **Occupational Type:** Social. **Job Zone:** 4. **Average Salary:** $35,838. **Projected Growth:** 33.8%. **Occupational Values:** Social Service; Achievement; Authority; Ability Utilization; Responsibility; Activity; Creativity. **Skills Required:** Instructing; Social Perceptiveness; Learning Strategies; Speaking; Implementation Planning; Monitoring; Active Listening. **Abilities:** Oral Expression; Oral Comprehension; Written Comprehension; Problem Sensitivity; Speech Clarity; Written Expression. **Interacting with Others:** Teaching Others; Establishing and Maintaining Relationships; Interpreting Meaning of Information to Others; Communicating with Persons Outside Organization; Assisting and Caring for Others; Communicating with Other Workers. **Physical Work Conditions:** Indoors; Sitting; Standing.

25-9041.00 Teacher Assistants

Perform duties that are instructional in nature or deliver direct services to students and/or parents. Serve in a position for which a teacher or another professional has ultimate responsibility for the design and implementation of educational programs and services. **Education:** Short-term O-J-T. **Occupational Type:** Social. **Job Zone:** 3. **Average Salary:** $15,874. **Projected Growth:** 31.5%. **Occupational Values:** Social Service; Working Conditions; Achievement; Moral Values; Coworkers; Supervision, Human Relations; Activity. **Skills Required:** Instructing; Active Listening; Speaking; Learning Strategies; Reading Comprehension. **Abilities:** Oral Expression; Speech Clarity; Written Expression; Oral Comprehension; Written Comprehension. **Interacting with Others:** Teaching Others; Communicating with Persons Outside Organization; Establishing and Maintaining Relationships; Communicating with Other Workers; Assisting and Caring for Others; Interpreting Meaning of Information to Others. **Physical Work Conditions:** Indoors; Sitting; Standing.

39-9011.00 Child Care Workers

Attend to children at schools, businesses, private households, and child care institutions. Perform a variety of tasks such as dressing, feeding, bathing, and overseeing play. **Education:** Short-term O-J-T. **Occupational Type:** Social. **Job Zone:** 1. **Average Salary:** $13,750. **Projected Growth:** 26.1%. **Occupational Values:** Social Service; Activity; Security; Working Conditions; Moral Values; Coworkers; Company Policies and Practices. **Skills Required:** Social Perceptiveness; Service Orientation; Speaking; Active Listening. **Abilities:** Oral Expression; Oral Comprehension. **Interacting with Others:** Assisting and Caring for Others. **Physical Work Conditions:** Indoors; Standing; Sitting.

12.03.04 Educational Services: Library and Museum

25-4011.00 Archivists

Appraise, edit, and direct safekeeping of permanent records and historically valuable documents. Participate in research activities based on archival materials. **Education:** Master's degree. **Occupational Type:** Investigative. **Job Zone:** 5. **Average Salary:** $31,750. **Projected Growth:** 12.6%. **Occupational Values:** Working Conditions; Moral Values; Autonomy; Company Policies and Practices; Ability Utilization; Authority; Achievement. **Skills Required:** Information Gathering; Information Organization; Reading Comprehension; Product Inspection; Writing; Judgment and Decision Making. **Abilities:** Written Comprehension; Near Vision; Written Expression; Oral Expression; Speech Clarity. **Interacting with Others:** Providing Consultation and Advice to Others; Communicating with Other Workers; Interpreting Meaning of Information to Others. **Physical Work Conditions:** Indoors; Sitting.

25-4012.00 Curators

Administer affairs of museum and conduct research programs. Direct instructional, research, and public service activities of institution. **Education:** Master's degree. **Occupational Type:** Artistic. **Job Zone:** 4. **Average Salary:** $31,750. **Projected Growth:** 12.6%. **Occupational Values:** Working Conditions; Authority; Creativity; Ability Utilization; Responsibility; Security; Activity. **Skills Required:** Speaking; Writing; Active Listening; Reading Comprehension; Judgment and Decision Making; Coordination; Implementation Planning. **Abilities:** Oral Expression; Oral Comprehension; Written Expression; Speech Clarity; Written Comprehension; Category Flexibility; Information Ordering. **Interacting with Others:** Communicating with Persons Outside Organization; Establishing and Maintaining Relationships; Monitoring and Controlling Resources; Communicating with Other Workers; Performing for/Working with Public; Selling or Influencing Others; Coordinating Work and Activities of Others. **Physical Work Conditions:** Indoors; Sitting; Standing.

25-4013.00 Museum Technicians and Conservators

Prepare specimens such as fossils, skeletal parts, lace, and textiles for museum collection and exhibits. May restore documents or install, arrange, and exhibit materials. **Education:** Master's degree. **Occupational Type:** Artistic. **Job Zone:** 3. **Average Salary:** $31,750. **Projected Growth:** 12.6%. **Occupational Values:** Moral Values; Working Conditions; Ability Utilization; Coworkers; Achievement; Company Policies and Practices; Activity. **Skills Required:** Product Inspection; Equipment Selection; Judgment and Decision Making. **Abilities:** Visualization; Near Vision; Written Expression; Oral Expression; Visual Color Discrimination; Deductive Reasoning. **Interacting with Others:** Communicating with Other Workers. **Physical Work Conditions:** Indoors; Using Hands on Objects, Tools, Controls; Sitting; Standing.

25-4021.00 Librarians

Administer libraries and perform related library services. Work in a variety of settings including public libraries, schools, colleges and universities, museums, corporations, government agencies, law firms, nonprofit organizations, and healthcare providers. Tasks may include selecting, acquiring, cataloging, classifying, circulating, and maintaining library materials and furnishing reference, bibliographical, and readers' advisory services. May perform in-depth, strategic research and synthesize, analyze, edit, and filter information. May set up or work with databases and information systems to catalog and access information. **Education:** Master's degree. **Occupational Type:**

Artistic. **Job Zone:** 4. **Average Salary:** $38,470. **Projected Growth:** 4.8%. **Occupational Values:** Working Conditions; Moral Values; Autonomy; Security; Authority; Responsibility; Coworkers. **Skills Required:** Reading Comprehension; Information Gathering; Information Organization; Speaking; Service Orientation; Active Listening; Synthesis/Reorganization. **Abilities:** Category Flexibility; Oral Expression; Information Ordering; Written Comprehension; Near Vision; Written Expression; Oral Comprehension. **Interacting with Others:** Communicating with Persons Outside Organization; Performing for/Working with Public; Establishing and Maintaining Relationships; Providing Consultation and Advice to Others; Communicating with Other Workers; Interpreting Meaning of Information to Others; Monitoring and Controlling Resources. **Physical Work Conditions:** Indoors; Sitting; Standing.

25-4031.00 Library Technicians

Assist librarians by helping readers in the use of library catalogs, databases, and indexes to locate books and other materials and by answering questions that require only brief consultation of standard reference. Compile records, sort and shelve books, remove or repair damaged books, register patrons, and check materials in and out of the circulation process. Replace materials in shelving area (stacks) or files. Includes bookmobile drivers who operate bookmobiles or light trucks that pull trailers to specific locations on a predetermined schedule and assist with providing services in mobile libraries. **Education:** Short-term O-J-T. **Occupational Type:** Conventional. **Job Zone:** 2. **Average Salary:** $18,671. **Projected Growth:** 18.2%. **Occupational Values:** Working Conditions; Moral Values; Social Service; Company Policies and Practices; Coworkers; Supervision, Human Relations; Authority. **Skills Required:** Information Organization; Information Gathering; Reading Comprehension; Service Orientation; Active Listening. **Abilities:** Speech Clarity; Information Ordering; Category Flexibility; Oral Expression. **Interacting with Others:** Communicating with Persons Outside Organization; Communicating with Other Workers; Performing for/Working with Public; Interpreting Meaning of Information to Others. **Physical Work Conditions:** Indoors; Sitting; Using Hands on Objects, Tools, Controls; Standing; Walking or Running.

25-9011.00 Audio-Visual Collections Specialists

Prepare, plan, and operate audio-visual teaching aids for use in education. May record, catalog, and file audio-visual materials. **Education:** Short-term O-J-T. **Occupational Type:** Conventional. **Job Zone:** 4. **Average Salary:** $32,970. **Projected Growth:** 18.2%. **Occupational Values:** Working Conditions; Moral Values; Ability Utilization; Authority; Coworkers; Autonomy; Achievement. **Skills Required:** Idea Generation; Synthesis/Reorganization; Writing; Implementation Planning; Speaking; Idea Evaluation; Reading Comprehension. **Abilities:** Speech Clarity; Visualization; Oral Expression. **Interacting with Others:** Establishing and Maintaining Relationships; Teaching Others; Communicating with Other Workers; Coordinating Work and Activities of Others. **Physical Work Conditions:** Indoors; Using Hands on Objects, Tools, Controls; Sitting; Standing.

43-4121.00 Library Assistants, Clerical

Compile records, sort and shelve books, and issue and receive library materials such as pictures, cards, slides, and microfilm. Locate library materials for loan and replace material in shelving area, stacks, or files according to identification number and title. Register patrons to permit them to borrow books, periodicals, and other library materials. **Education:** Short-term O-J-T. **Occupational Type:** Conventional. **Job Zone:** 1. **Average Salary:** $24,900. **Projected Growth:** 16.5%. **Occupational Values:** Moral Values; Working Conditions; Supervision, Human Relations; Security; Supervision, Technical; Activity; Company Policies and Practices. **Skills Required:** Information Organization; Reading Comprehension. **Abilities:** Information Ordering; Oral Expression; Category Flexibility; Near Vision; Oral Comprehension; Written Comprehension. **Interacting with Others:** Communicating with Persons Outside Organization; Assisting and Caring for Others; Performing for/Working with Public. **Physical Work Conditions:** Indoors; Sitting; Bending or Twisting the Body.

13 General Management and Support

13.01.01 General Management Work and Management of Support Functions

11-1011.01 Government Service Executives

Determine and formulate policies and provide overall direction of Federal, State, local, or international government activities. Plan, direct, and coordinate operational activities at the highest level of management with the help of subordinate managers. **Education:** Work experience, plus degree. **Occupational Type:** Enterprising. **Job Zone:** 4. **Average Salary:** $55,030. **Projected Growth:** 2.8%. **Occupational Values:** Authority; Working Conditions; Autonomy; Activity; Ability Utilization; Responsibility; Security. **Skills Required:** Writing; Coordination; Speaking; Active Listening; Critical Thinking; Reading Comprehension; Problem Identification. **Abilities:** Oral Comprehension; Written Comprehension; Oral Expression; Written Expression; Inductive Reasoning; Speech Clarity; Deductive Reasoning. **Interacting with Others:** Communicating with Other Workers; Coordinating Work and Activities of Others; Communicating with Persons Outside Organization; Guiding, Directing, and Motivating Subordinates; Performing Administrative Activities; Establishing and Maintaining Relationships; Developing and Building Teams. **Physical Work Conditions:** Indoors; Sitting; Standing.

11-1011.02 Private Sector Executives

Determine and formulate policies and business strategies and provide overall direction of private sector organizations. Plan, direct, and coordinate operational activities at the highest level of management with the help of subordinate managers. **Education:** Work experience, plus degree. **Occupational Type:** Enterprising. **Job Zone:** 5. **Average Salary:** $55,890. **Projected Growth:** 16.4%. **Occupational Values:** Authority; Autonomy; Working Conditions; Responsibility; Social Status; Compensation; Activity. **Skills Required:** Coordination; Systems Perception; Judgment and Decision Making; Management of Financial Resources; Systems Evaluation; Identifying Downstream Consequences; Identification of Key Causes. **Abilities:** Oral Comprehension; Written Comprehension; Oral Expression; Speech Clarity; Written Expression; Deductive Reasoning; Number Facility. **Interacting with Others:** Monitoring and Controlling Resources; Communicating with Other Workers; Developing and Building Teams; Performing Administrative Activities; Providing Consultation and Advice to Others; Selling or Influencing Others; Communicating with Persons Outside Organization. **Physical Work Conditions:** Indoors; Sitting.

11-1021.00 General and Operations Managers

Plan, direct, or coordinate the operations of companies or public and private sector organizations. Duties and responsibilities include formulating policies, managing daily operations, and planning the use of materials and human resources, but are too diverse and general in nature to be classified in any one functional area of management or administration, such as personnel, purchasing, or administrative services. Includes owners and managers who head small business establishments whose duties are primarily managerial. No other data currently available.

11-1031.00 Legislators

Develop laws and statutes at the Federal, State, or local level. No other data currently available.

11-2031.00 Public Relations Managers

Plan and direct public relations programs designed to create and maintain a favorable public image for employer or client; or if engaged in fundraising, plan and direct activities to solicit and maintain funds for special projects and nonprofit organizations. No other data currently available.

11-3031.00 Financial Managers

Plan, direct, and coordinate accounting, investing, banking, insurance, securities, and other financial activities of a branch, office, or department of an establishment. No other data currently available.

11-3031.01 Treasurers, Controllers, and Chief Financial Officers

Plan, direct, and coordinate the financial activities of an organization at the highest level of management. Includes financial reserve officers. **Education:** Work experience, plus degree. **Occupational Type:** Enterprising. **Job Zone:** 5. **Average Salary:** $55,070. **Projected Growth:** 14%. **Occupational Values:** Working Conditions; Authority; Activity; Company Policies and Practices; Ability Utilization; Compensation; Advancement. **Skills Required:** Management of Financial Resources; Problem Identification; Mathematics; Information Gathering; Critical Thinking; Judgment and Decision Making; Systems Evaluation. **Abilities:** Deductive Reasoning; Oral Comprehension; Mathematical Reasoning; Written Comprehension; Number Facility; Oral Expression; Written Expression. **Interacting with Others:** Communicating with Other Workers; Providing Consultation and Advice to Others; Coordinating Work and Activities of Others; Interpreting Meaning of Information to Others; Monitoring and Controlling Resources; Establishing and Maintaining Relationships; Guiding, Directing, and Motivating Subordinates. **Physical Work Conditions:** Indoors; Sitting.

11-3031.02 Financial Managers, Branch or Department

Direct and coordinate financial activities of workers in a branch, office, or department of an establishment, such as a branch bank, brokerage firm, risk and insurance department, or credit department. **Education:** Work experience, plus degree. **Occupational Type:** Enterprising. **Job Zone:** 4. **Average Salary:** $55,070. **Projected Growth:** 14%. **Occupational Values:** Authority; Working Conditions; Company Policies and Practices; Ability Utilization; Activity; Responsibility; Autonomy. **Skills Required:** Critical Thinking; Reading Comprehension; Judgment and Decision Making; Management of Financial Resources; Information Gathering; Coordination; Problem Identification. **Abilities:** Written Expression; Oral Comprehension; Mathematical Reasoning; Written Comprehension; Oral Expression; Deductive Reasoning; Number Facility. **Interacting with Others:** Communicating with Other Workers; Performing Administrative Activities; Coordinating Work and Activities of Others; Guiding, Directing, and Motivating Subordinates; Monitoring and Controlling Resources; Providing

Consultation and Advice to Others; Communicating with Persons Outside Organization. **Physical Work Conditions:** Indoors; Sitting.

11-3040.00 Human Resources Managers

Plan, direct, and coordinate human resource management activities of an organization to maximize the strategic use of human resources and to maintain functions such as employee compensation, recruitment, personnel policies, and regulatory compliance. **Education:** Work experience, plus degree. **Occupational Type:** Enterprising. **Job Zone:** 4. **Average Salary:** $49,010. **Projected Growth:** 19.4%. **Occupational Values:** Working Conditions; Ability Utilization; Authority; Security; Autonomy; Activity; Responsibility. **Skills Required:** Management of Personnel Resources; Writing; Speaking; Reading Comprehension; Problem Identification; Idea Generation; Critical Thinking. **Abilities:** Written Comprehension; Oral Expression; Oral Comprehension; Speech Clarity; Written Expression; Deductive Reasoning; Problem Sensitivity. **Interacting with Others:** Communicating with Other Workers; Performing Administrative Activities; Resolving Conflict, Negotiating with Others; Staffing Organizational Units; Establishing and Maintaining Relationships; Guiding, Directing, and Motivating Subordinates; Interpreting Meaning of Information to Others. **Physical Work Conditions:** Indoors; Sitting.

11-3041.00 Compensation and Benefits Managers

Plan, direct, or coordinate compensation and benefits activities and staff of an organization. **Education:** Work experience, plus degree. **Occupational Type:** Enterprising. **Job Zone:** 4. **Average Salary:** $49,010. **Projected Growth:** 19.4%. **Occupational Values:** Working Conditions; Ability Utilization; Autonomy; Security; Authority; Responsibility; Activity. **Skills Required:** Management of Personnel Resources; Speaking; Writing; Reading Comprehension; Problem Identification; Critical Thinking; Idea Generation. **Abilities:** Written Comprehension; Oral Expression; Oral Comprehension; Speech Clarity; Written Expression; Deductive Reasoning; Problem Sensitivity. **Interacting with Others:** Communicating with Other Workers; Performing Administrative Activities; Resolving Conflict, Negotiating with Others; Staffing Organizational Units; Establishing and Maintaining Relationships; Guiding, Directing, and Motivating Subordinates; Interpreting Meaning of Information to Others. **Physical Work Conditions:** Indoors; Sitting.

11-3042.00 Training and Development Managers

Plan, direct, or coordinate the training and development activities and staff of an organization. **Education:** Work experience, plus degree. **Occupational Type:** Enterprising. **Job Zone:** 4. **Average Salary:** $49,010. **Projected Growth:** 19.4%. **Occupational Values:** Authority; Working Conditions; Achievement; Company Policies and Practices; Coworkers; Social Service; Supervision, Human Relations. **Skills Required:** Learning Strategies; Speaking; Instructing; Implementation Planning; Reading Comprehension; Critical Thinking; Active Listening. **Abilities:** Speech Clarity; Oral Comprehension; Deductive Reasoning; Oral Expression. **Interacting with Others:** Teaching Others; Coaching and Developing Others; Communicating with Other Workers; Providing Consultation and Advice to Others; Coordinating Work and Activities of Others; Establishing and Maintaining Relationships; Guiding, Directing, and Motivating Subordinates. **Physical Work Conditions:** Indoors; Sitting.

11-3061.00 Purchasing Managers

Plan, direct, or coordinate the activities of buyers, purchasing officers, and related workers involved in purchasing materials, products, and services. **Education:** Work experience, plus degree. **Occupational Type:** Enterprising. **Job Zone:** 4. **Average Salary:** $41,830. **Projected Growth:** 7.1%. **Occupational Values:** Working Conditions; Activity; Company Policies and Practices; Responsibility; Authority; Coworkers; Autonomy. **Skills Required:** Information Gathering; Speaking; Management of Personnel Resources; Critical Thinking; Judgment and Decision Making; Coordination; Mathematics. **Abilities:** Speech Clarity; Oral Expression; Mathematical Reasoning. **Interacting with Others:** Monitoring and Controlling Resources; Communicating with Other Workers; Communicating with Persons Outside Organization; Selling or Influencing Others; Coordinating Work and Activities of Others; Interpreting Meaning of Information to Others; Resolving Conflict, Negotiating with Others. **Physical Work Conditions:** Indoors; Sitting.

11-3071.02 Storage and Distribution Managers

Plan, direct, and coordinate the storage and distribution operations within an organization or the activities of organizations that are engaged in storing and distributing materials and products. **Education:** Work experience, plus degree. **Occupational Type:** Enterprising. **Job Zone:** 4. **Average Salary:** $52,810. **Projected Growth:** 19.3%. **Occupational Values:** Authority; Autonomy; Security; Responsibility; Company Policies and Practices; Activity; Creativity. **Skills Required:** Implementation Planning; Problem Identification; Speaking; Idea Generation. **Abilities:** Oral Comprehension; Written Comprehension; Oral Expression; Written Expression; Problem Sensitivity; Number Facility; Speech Clarity. **Interacting with Others:** Communicating with Other Workers; Coordinating Work and Activities of Others; Guiding, Directing, and Motivating Subordinates; Staffing Organizational Units; Coaching and Developing Others; Communicating with Persons Outside Organization; Resolving Conflict, Negotiating with Others. **Physical Work Conditions:** Indoors; Sitting; Standing.

11-9061.00 Funeral Directors

Perform various tasks to arrange and direct funeral services, such as coordinating transportation of body to mortuary for embalming, interviewing family or other authorized person to arrange details, selecting pallbearers, procuring official for religious rites, and providing transportation for mourners. **Education:** Long-term O-J-T. **Occupational Type:** Enterprising. **Job Zone:** 4. **Average Salary:** $35,040. **Projected Growth:** 16.1%. **Occupational Values:** Autonomy; Security; Social Service; Authority; Compensation; Achievement; Responsibility. **Skills Required:** Active Listening; Social Perceptiveness; Coordination; Speaking; Service Orientation; Implementation Planning; Time Management. **Abilities:** Oral Expression; Oral Comprehension. **Interacting with Others:** Communicating with Persons Outside Organization. **Physical Work Conditions:** Indoors; Sitting.

11-9131.00 Postmasters and Mail Superintendents

Direct and coordinate operational, administrative, management, and supportive services of a U.S. post office, or coordinate activities of workers engaged in postal and related work in assigned post office. **Education:** Work experience in a related occupation. **Occupational Type:** Enterprising. **Job Zone:** 4. **Average Salary:** $44,730. **Projected Growth:** 3%. **Occupational Values:** Security; Authority; Company Policies and Practices; Activity; Working Conditions; Compensation; Moral Values. **Skills Required:** Problem Identification; Coordination; Negotiation; Speaking; Critical Thinking; Management of Personnel Resources; Judgment and Decision Making. **Abilities:** Oral Expression; Oral Comprehension; Written Expression; Written Comprehension. **Interacting with Others:** Communicating with Other Workers; Coordinating Work and Activities of Others; Guiding, Directing, and Motivating Subordinates; Communicating with Persons Outside Organization; Resolving Conflict, Negotiating with Others. **Physical Work Conditions:** Indoors; Special Uniform.

11-9141.00 Property, Real Estate, and Community Association Managers

Plan, direct, or coordinate selling, buying, leasing, or governance activities of commercial, industrial, or residential real estate properties. **Education:** Bachelor's degree. **Occupational Type:** Enterprising. **Job Zone:** 4. **Average Salary:** $29,860. **Projected Growth:** 13.7%. **Occupational Values:** Autonomy; Activity; Responsibility; Working Conditions; Authority; Ability Utilization; Security. **Skills Required:** Speaking; Management of Personnel Resources; Judgment and Decision Making; Active Listening; Reading Comprehension; Coordination; Information Gathering. **Abilities:** Number Facility; Oral Expression; Oral Comprehension; Written Comprehension; Mathematical Reasoning; Speech Clarity; Written Expression. **Interacting with Others:** Communicating with Other Workers; Communicating with Persons Outside Organization; Coordinating Work and Activities of Others; Monitoring and Controlling Resources; Performing Administrative Activities; Staffing Organizational Units; Resolving Conflict, Negotiating with Others. **Physical Work Conditions:** Indoors; Sitting.

13.02.01 Management Support: Human Resources

13-1071.01 Employment Interviewers, Private or Public Employment Service

Interview job applicants in employment office and refer them to prospective employers for consideration. Search application files, notify selected applicants of job openings, and refer qualified applicants to prospective employers. Contact employers to verify referral results. Record and evaluate various pertinent data. **Education:** Bachelor's degree. **Occupational Type:** Social. **Job Zone:** 3. **Average Salary:** $36,482. **Projected Growth:** 12.9%. **Occupational Values:** Working Conditions; Social Service; Supervision, Human Relations; Company Policies and Practices; Activity; Security; Moral Values. **Skills Required:** Speaking; Judgment and Decision Making; Information Gathering; Active Listening; Reading Comprehension. **Abilities:** Oral Expression; Written Comprehension; Oral Comprehension; Speech Clarity. **Interacting with Others:** Communicating with Persons Outside Organization; Establishing and Maintaining Relationships. **Physical Work Conditions:** Indoors; Sitting.

13-1071.02 Personnel Recruiters

Seek out, interview, and screen applicants to fill existing and future job openings and to promote career opportunities within an organization. **Education:** Bachelor's degree. **Occupational Type:** Enterprising. **Job Zone:** 3. **Average Salary:** $36,482. **Projected Growth:** 17.9%. **Occupational Values:** Working Conditions; Company Policies and Practices; Supervision, Human Relations; Achievement; Activity; Responsibility; Security. **Skills Required:** Speaking; Information Gathering; Active Listening; Reading Comprehension; Idea Generation; Judgment and Decision Making; Management of Personnel Resources. **Abilities:** Oral Comprehension; Speech Clarity; Oral Expression; Written Comprehension; Written Expression; Mathematical Reasoning. **Interacting with Others:** Staffing Organizational Units; Communicating with Persons Outside Organization; Communicating with Other Workers; Establishing and Maintaining Relationships. **Physical Work Conditions:** Indoors; Sitting.

13-1072.00 Compensation, Benefits, and Job Analysis Specialists

Conduct programs of compensation and benefits and job analysis for employer. May specialize in specific areas such as position classification and pension programs. **Education:** Bachelor's degree. **Occupational Type:** Investigative. **Job Zone:** 3. **Average Salary:** $37,710. **Projected Growth:** 17.9%. **Occupational Values:** Working Conditions; Ability Utilization; Responsibility; Coworkers; Autonomy; Achievement; Activity. **Skills Required:** Information Gathering; Speaking; Systems Evaluation; Information Organization; Idea Generation; Active Listening; Writing. **Abilities:** Oral Comprehension; Oral Expression; Written Expression; Near Vision; Speech Clarity; Deductive Reasoning; Written Comprehension. **Interacting with Others:** Communicating with Persons Outside Organization; Providing Consultation and Advice to Others. **Physical Work Conditions:** Indoors; Sitting.

13-1073.00 Training and Development Specialists

Conduct training and development programs for employees. **Education:** Bachelor's degree. **Occupational Type:** Social. **Job Zone:** 4. **Average Salary:** $37,710. **Projected Growth:** 17.9%. **Occupational Values:** Working Conditions; Authority; Coworkers; Achievement; Responsibility; Company Policies and Practices; Creativity. **Skills Required:** Learning Strategies; Reading Comprehension; Time Management; Implementation Planning; Management of Personnel Resources; Speaking; Writing. **Abilities:** Oral Expression; Oral Comprehension; Speech Clarity; Written Expression; Near Vision; Written Comprehension; Originality. **Interacting with Others:** Staffing Organizational Units; Coaching and Developing Others; Communicating with Other Workers; Communicating with Persons Outside Organization; Guiding, Directing, and Motivating Subordinates; Establishing and Maintaining Relationships; Teaching Others. **Physical Work Conditions:** Indoors; Sitting; Standing.

13.02.02 Management Support: Purchasing

13-1021.00 Purchasing Agents and Buyers, Farm Products

Purchase farm products either for further processing or resale. **Education:** Bachelor's degree. **Occupational Type:** Enterprising. **Job Zone:** 4. **Average Salary:** $32,070. **Projected Growth:** 5%. **Occupational Values:** Responsibility; Coworkers; Autonomy; Ability Utilization; Achievement; Company Policies and Practices; Working Conditions. **Skills Required:** Negotiation; Writing; Judgment and Decision Making; Reading Comprehension; Speaking; Information Gathering; Mathematics. **Abilities:** Oral Expression; Oral Comprehension; Number Facility; Written Expression. **Interacting with Others:** Monitoring and Controlling Resources; Establishing and Maintaining Relationships; Communicating with Persons Outside Organization; Resolving Conflict, Negotiating with Others. **Physical Work Conditions:** Indoors; Sitting; Standing; Using Hands on Objects, Tools, Controls; Walking or Running.

13-1022.00 Wholesale and Retail Buyers, Except Farm Products

Buy merchandise or commodities, other than farm products, for resale to consumers at the wholesale or retail level, including both durable and nondurable goods. Analyze past buying trends, sales records, price, and quality of merchandise to determine value and yield. Select, order, and authorize payment for merchandise according to contractual agreements. May conduct meetings with sales personnel and introduce new products. **Education:** Bachelor's degree. **Occupational Type:** Enterprising. **Job Zone:** 3. **Average Salary:** $31,560. **Projected Growth:** -0.4%. **Occupational Values:** Working Conditions; Company Policies and Practices; Activity; Moral Values; Responsibility; Advancement; Coworkers. **Skills Required:** Critical Thinking; Information Gathering; Product Inspection; Speaking; Active Learning; Judgment and Decision Making; Social Perceptiveness. **Abilities:** Oral Expression; Oral Comprehension; Near Vision; Deductive Reasoning; Speech Clarity; Written Comprehension; Number Facility. **Interacting with Others:** Communicating with Other Workers; Monitoring and Controlling Resources; Teaching Others; Communicating with Persons Outside Organization; Establishing and Maintaining Relationships; Performing Administrative Activities. **Physical Work Conditions:** Indoors; Sitting; Standing.

13-1023.00 Purchasing Agents, Except Wholesale, Retail, and Farm Products

Purchase machinery, equipment, tools, parts, supplies, or services necessary for the operation of an establishment. Purchase raw or semi-finished materials for manufacturing. **Education:** Bachelor's degree. **Occupational Type:** Enterprising. **Job Zone:** 4. **Average Salary:** $38,040. **Projected Growth:** 10.8%. **Occupational Values:** Activity; Compensation; Ability Utilization; Achievement; Autonomy; Working Conditions; Authority. **Skills Required:** Negotiation; Persuasion; Active Listening; Management of Financial Resources; Judgment and Decision Making; Critical Thinking; Mathematics. **Abilities:** Oral Expression; Written Comprehension; Oral Comprehension; Mathematical Reasoning; Written Expression. **Interacting with Others:** Resolving Conflict, Negotiating with Others; Communicating with Other Workers. **Physical Work Conditions:** Indoors; Sitting.

13.02.03 Management Support: Accounting and Auditing

13-2011.00 Accountants and Auditors

Examine, analyze, and interpret accounting records for the purpose of giving advice or preparing statements. Install or advise on systems of recording costs or other financial and budgetary data. No other data currently available.

13-2011.01 Accountants

Analyze financial information and prepare financial reports to determine or maintain record of assets, liabilities, profit and loss, tax liability, or other financial activities within an organization. **Education:** Bachelor's degree. **Occupational Type:** Conventional. **Job Zone:** 4. **Average Salary:** $37,860. **Projected Growth:** 11.3%. **Occupational Values:** Working Conditions; Compensation; Security; Ability Utilization; Activity; Social Status; Autonomy. **Skills Required:** Mathematics; Information Gathering; Identifying Downstream Consequences; Problem Identification; Information Organization; Reading Comprehension; Judgment and Decision Making. **Abilities:** Number Facility; Near Vision; Mathematical Reasoning; Written Comprehension; Written Expression. **Interacting with Others:** Communicating with Other Workers; Providing Consultation and Advice to Others; Monitoring and Controlling Resources. **Physical Work Conditions:** Indoors; Sitting; Using Hands on Objects, Tools, Controls.

13-2011.02 Auditors

Examine and analyze accounting records to determine financial status of establishment and prepare financial reports concerning operating procedures. **Education:** Bachelor's degree. **Occupational Type:** Conventional. **Job Zone:** 4. **Average Salary:** $37,860. **Projected Growth:** 11.3%. **Occupational Values:** Working Conditions; Company Policies and Practices; Compensation; Ability Utilization; Security; Activity; Advancement. **Skills Required:** Information Gathering; Mathematics; Problem Identification; Information Organization; Critical Thinking; Systems Evaluation; Identification of Key Causes. **Abilities:** Near Vision; Written Comprehension; Number Facility; Mathematical Reasoning; Problem Sensitivity. **Interacting with Others:** Interpreting Meaning of Information to Others; Providing Consultation and Advice to Others; Communicating with Other Workers; Monitoring and Controlling Resources; Performing Administrative Activities; Communicating with Persons Outside Organization. **Physical Work Conditions:** Indoors; Sitting; Using Hands on Objects, Tools, Controls.

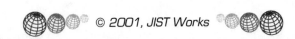

13-2081.00 Tax Examiners, Collectors, and Revenue Agents

Determine tax liability or collect taxes from individuals or business firms according to prescribed laws and regulations. **Education:** Bachelor's degree. **Occupational Type:** Conventional. **Job Zone:** 4. **Average Salary:** $39,540. **Projected Growth:** 5.4%. **Occupational Values:** Working Conditions; Security; Company Policies and Practices; Autonomy; Supervision, Human Relations; Responsibility; Ability Utilization. **Skills Required:** Mathematics; Information Gathering; Problem Identification; Reading Comprehension; Critical Thinking; Information Organization; Judgment and Decision Making. **Abilities:** Number Facility; Mathematical Reasoning; Written Comprehension; Oral Comprehension; Oral Expression; Deductive Reasoning; Problem Sensitivity. **Interacting with Others:** Communicating with Persons Outside Organization. **Physical Work Conditions:** Indoors; Sitting.

13.02.04 Management Support: Investigation and Analysis

13-1031.01 Claims Examiners, Property and Casualty Insurance

Review settled insurance claims to determine that payments and settlements have been made in accordance with company practices and procedures. Report overpayments, underpayments, and other irregularities. Confer with legal counsel on claims requiring litigation. **Education:** Bachelor's degree. **Occupational Type:** Conventional. **Job Zone:** 4. **Average Salary:** $40,110. **Projected Growth:** 12.5%. **Occupational Values:** Company Policies and Practices; Supervision, Human Relations; Working Conditions; Security; Advancement; Responsibility; Independence. **Skills Required:** Problem Identification; Reading Comprehension; Mathematics; Information Gathering; Solution Appraisal; Speaking. **Abilities:** Written Comprehension; Number Facility; Mathematical Reasoning; Problem Sensitivity. **Interacting with Others:** Communicating with Other Workers. **Physical Work Conditions:** Indoors; Sitting.

13-1031.02 Insurance Adjusters, Examiners, and Investigators

Investigate, analyze, and determine the extent of insurance company's liability concerning personal, casualty, or property loss or damages; attempt to effect settlement with claimants. Correspond with or interview medical specialists, agents, witnesses, or claimants to compile information. Calculate benefit payments and approve payment of claims within a certain monetary limit. **Education:** Long-term O-J-T. **Occupational Type:** Enterprising. **Job Zone:** 3. **Average Salary:** $38,290. **Projected Growth:** 20.4%. **Occupational Values:** Company Policies and Practices; Advancement; Supervision, Human Relations; Activity; Ability Utilization; Responsibility; Achievement. **Skills Required:** Speaking; Reading Comprehension; Judgment and Decision Making; Active Listening; Writing; Identification of Key Causes; Critical Thinking. **Abilities:** Written Comprehension; Oral Expression; Oral Comprehension; Written Expression; Inductive Reasoning; Near Vision; Number Facility. **Interacting with Others:** Communicating with Persons Outside Organization; Communicating with Other Workers. **Physical Work Conditions:** Indoors; Sitting; Standing.

13-1032.00 Insurance Appraisers, Auto Damage

Appraise automobile or other vehicle damage to determine cost of repair for insurance claim settlement and seek agreement with automotive repair shop on cost of repair. Prepare insurance forms to indicate repair cost or cost estimates and recommendations. **Education:** Long-term O-J-T. **Occupational Type:** Conventional. **Job Zone:** 4. **Average Salary:** $40,000. **Projected Growth:** 16%. **Occupational Values:** Company Policies and Practices; Supervision, Human Relations; Responsibility; Security; Advancement; Ability Utilization; Independence. **Skills Required:** Judgment and Decision Making; Information Gathering; Mathematics; Critical Thinking; Active Listening; Problem Identification; Writing. **Abilities:** Number Facility; Written Comprehension; Mathematical Reasoning. **Interacting with Others:** Performing Administrative Activities. **Physical Work Conditions:** Sitting; Indoors; Standing.

13-1051.00 Cost Estimators

Prepare cost estimates for product manufacturing, construction projects, or services, to aid management in bidding on or determining price of product or service. May specialize according to particular service performed or type of product manufactured. **Education:** Work experience in a related occupation. **Occupational Type:** Conventional. **Job Zone:** 4. **Average Salary:** $40,590. **Projected Growth:** 13%. **Occupational Values:** Working Conditions; Independence; Responsibility; Security; Autonomy; Ability Utilization; Company Policies and Practices. **Skills Required:** Information Gathering; Reading Comprehension; Mathematics; Information Organization; Active Learning; Writing. **Abilities:** Mathematical Reasoning; Written Comprehension; Number Facility; Oral Comprehension; Oral Expression; Deductive Reasoning. **Interacting with Others:** Providing Consultation and Advice to Others. **Physical Work Conditions:** Indoors; Sitting.

13-1081.00 Logisticians

Analyze and coordinate the logistical functions of a firm or organization. Responsible for the entire life cycle of a product, including acquisition, distribution, internal allocation, delivery, and final disposal of resources. No other data currently available.

13-1111.00 Management Analysts

Conduct organizational studies and evaluations, design systems and procedures, conduct work simplifications and measurement studies, and prepare operations and procedures manuals to assist management in operating more efficiently and effectively. Includes program analysts and management consultants. **Education:** Master's degree. **Occupational Type:** Enterprising. **Job Zone:** 4. **Average Salary:** $49,470. **Projected Growth:** 28.4%. **Occupational Values:** Achievement; Working Conditions; Creativity; Autonomy; Ability Utilization; Compensation; Social Status. **Skills Required:** Writing; Reading Comprehension; Identification of Key Causes; Speaking; Problem Identification; Information Gathering; Critical Thinking. **Abilities:** Oral Expression; Written Expression; Speech Clarity; Problem Sensitivity. **Interacting with Others:** Providing Consultation and Advice to Others; Communicating with Other Workers; Establishing and Maintaining Relationships. **Physical Work Conditions:** Indoors; Sitting.

13-2021.00 Appraisers and Assessors of Real Estate

Appraise real property to determine its fair value. May assess taxes in accordance with prescribed schedules. No other data currently available.

13-2021.01 Assessors

Appraise real and personal property to determine its fair value. May assess taxes in accordance with prescribed schedules. **Education:** Work experience in a related occupation. **Occupational Type:** Conventional. **Job Zone:** 4. **Average Salary:** $29,830. **Projected Growth:** 11.8%. **Occupational Values:** Responsibility; Independence; Security; Compensation; Autonomy; Moral Values; Working Conditions. **Skills Required:** Information Gathering; Writing; Product Inspection; Judgment and Decision Making; Reading Comprehension. **Abilities:** Number Facility; Mathematical Reasoning; Written Expression; Written Comprehension. **Interacting with Others:** Interpreting Meaning of Information to Others; Communicating with Other Workers. **Physical Work Conditions:** Outdoors; Standing; Indoors; Sitting; Walking or Running.

13-2021.02 Appraisers, Real Estate

Appraise real property to determine its value for purchase, sales, investment, mortgage, or loan purposes. **Education:** Work experience in a related occupation. **Occupational Type:** Enterprising. **Job Zone:** 4. **Average Salary:** $40,290. **Projected Growth:** 11.2%. **Occupational Values:** Responsibility; Independence; Autonomy; Ability Utilization; Working Conditions; Activity; Compensation. **Skills Required:** Information Gathering; Mathematics. **Abilities:** Oral Comprehension; Written Expression; Oral Expression; Deductive Reasoning; Written Comprehension; Number Facility; Speech Clarity. **Interacting with Others:** Communicating with Other Workers. **Physical Work Conditions:** Sitting; Standing.

13-2031.00 Budget Analysts

Examine budget estimates for completeness, accuracy, and conformance with procedures and regulations. Analyze budgeting and accounting reports for the purpose of maintaining expenditure controls. **Education:** Bachelor's degree. **Occupational Type:** Conventional. **Job Zone:** 4. **Average Salary:** $44,950. **Projected Growth:** 13.7%. **Occupational Values:** Working Conditions; Supervision, Human Relations; Advancement; Ability Utilization; Activity; Company Policies and Practices; Autonomy. **Skills Required:** Management of Financial Resources; Mathematics; Information Gathering; Problem Identification; Judgment and Decision Making; Solution Appraisal; Identification of Key Causes. **Abilities:** Number Facility; Written Comprehension; Mathematical Reasoning; Oral Comprehension; Oral Expression; Written Expression. **Interacting with Others:** Monitoring and Controlling Resources; Communicating with Other Workers; Providing Consultation and Advice to Others. **Physical Work Conditions:** Indoors; Sitting.

13-2041.00 Credit Analysts

Analyze current credit data and financial statements of individuals or firms to determine the degree of risk involved in extending credit or lending money. Prepare reports with this credit information for use in decision-making. **Education:** Bachelor's degree. **Occupational Type:** Conventional. **Job Zone:** 4. **Average Salary:** $35,590. **Projected Growth:** 19.9%. **Occupational Values:** Advancement; Activity; Company Policies and Practices; Supervision, Human Relations; Working Conditions; Responsibility; Security. **Skills Required:** Judgment and Decision Making; Problem Identification; Active Listening; Speaking; Information Gathering; Reading Comprehension; Critical Thinking. **Abilities:** Mathematical Reasoning; Written Comprehension; Near Vision; Number Facility; Problem Sensitivity; Deductive Reasoning; Oral Expression. **Interacting with Others:** Communicating with Persons Outside Organization. **Physical Work Conditions:** Indoors; Sitting; Using Hands on Objects, Tools, Controls.

13-2051.00 Financial Analysts

Conduct quantitative analyses of information affecting investment programs of public or private institutions. **Education:** Bachelor's degree. **Occupational Type:** Investigative. **Job Zone:** 5. **Average Salary:** $40,534. **Projected Growth:** 2.3%. **Occupational Values:** Autonomy; Compensation; Working Conditions; Company Policies and Practices; Ability Utilization; Security; Social Status. **Skills Required:** Reading Comprehension; Information Gathering; Mathematics; Critical Thinking; Information Organization; Active Learning; Identifying Downstream Consequences. **Abilities:** Number Facility; Deductive Reasoning; Written Comprehension; Mathematical Reasoning; Written Expression; Oral Comprehension; Oral Expression. **Interacting with Others:** Providing Consultation and Advice to Others; Communicating with Other Workers; Communicating with Persons Outside Organization; Interpreting Meaning of Information to Others; Establishing and Maintaining Relationships; Selling or Influencing Others. **Physical Work Conditions:** Indoors; Sitting.

13-2053.00 Insurance Underwriters

Review individual applications for insurance to evaluate degree of risk involved and determine acceptance of applications. **Education:** Bachelor's degree. **Occupational Type:** Conventional. **Job Zone:** 4. **Average Salary:** $38,710. **Projected Growth:** 2.7%. **Occupational Values:** Company Policies and Practices; Supervision, Human Relations; Working Conditions; Advancement; Responsibility; Security; Independence. **Skills Required:** Judgment and Decision Making; Mathematics; Reading Comprehension; Critical Thinking; Information Gathering. **Abilities:** Written Comprehension; Problem Sensitivity. **Interacting with Others:** Communicating with Other Workers. **Physical Work Conditions:** Indoors; Sitting.

13-2071.00 Loan Counselors

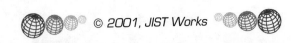

Provide guidance to prospective loan applicants who have problems qualifying for traditional loans. Guidance may include determining the best type of loan and explaining loan requirements or restrictions. **Education:** Bachelor's degree. **Occupational Type:** Enterprising. **Job Zone:** 4. **Average Salary:** $35,340. **Projected Growth:** 21.2%. **Occupational Values:** Working Conditions; Advancement; Coworkers; Company Policies and

Practices; Responsibility; Autonomy; Security. **Skills Required:** Judgment and Decision Making; Speaking; Mathematics; Information Gathering; Active Listening; Reading Comprehension. **Abilities:** Number Facility; Oral Comprehension; Written Comprehension; Oral Expression; Written Expression; Near Vision; Speech Clarity. **Interacting with Others:** Communicating with Other Workers; Performing Administrative Activities; Communicating with Persons Outside Organization; Establishing and Maintaining Relationships; Interpreting Meaning of Information to Others; Providing Consultation and Advice to Others. **Physical Work Conditions:** Indoors; Sitting.

13-2072.00 Loan Officers

Evaluate, authorize, or recommend approval of commercial, real estate, or credit loans. Advise borrowers on financial status and methods of payments. Includes mortgage loan officers and agents, collection analysts, loan servicing officers, and loan underwriters. **Education:** Bachelor's degree. **Occupational Type:** Enterprising. **Job Zone:** 4. **Average Salary:** $35,340. **Projected Growth:** 21.2%. **Occupational Values:** Working Conditions; Advancement; Coworkers; Responsibility; Company Policies and Practices; Security; Supervision, Human Relations. **Skills Required:** Judgment and Decision Making; Speaking; Mathematics; Information Gathering; Active Listening; Reading Comprehension. **Abilities:** Number Facility; Oral Comprehension; Written Comprehension; Oral Expression; Written Expression; Near Vision; Speech Clarity. **Interacting with Others:** Communicating with Other Workers; Performing Administrative Activities; Communicating with Persons Outside Organization; Establishing and Maintaining Relationships; Interpreting Meaning of Information to Others; Providing Consultation and Advice to Others. **Physical Work Conditions:** Indoors; Sitting.

19-3021.00 Market Research Analysts

Research market conditions in local, regional, or national areas to determine potential sales of a product or service. May gather information on competitors, prices, sales, and methods of marketing and distribution. May use survey results to create a marketing campaign based on regional preferences and buying habits. **Education:** Bachelor's degree. **Occupational Type:** Investigative. **Job Zone:** 4. **Average Salary:** $48,330. **Projected Growth:** 18.4%. **Occupational Values:** Autonomy; Working Conditions; Company Policies and Practices; Recognition; Ability Utilization; Achievement; Security. **Skills Required:** Identification of Key Causes; Mathematics; Information Gathering; Critical Thinking; Writing; Reading Comprehension; Solution Appraisal. **Abilities:** Mathematical Reasoning; Written Expression; Number Facility; Written Comprehension; Near Vision; Oral Expression; Deductive Reasoning. **Interacting with Others:** Interpreting Meaning of Information to Others; Communicating with Other Workers. **Physical Work Conditions:** Indoors; Sitting.

14 Medical and Health Services

14.01 Managerial Work in Medical and Health Services

14.02 Medicine and Surgery

14.03 Dentistry

14.04 Health Specialties

14.05 Medical Technology

14.06 Medical Therapy

14.07 Patient Care and Assistance

14.08 Health Protection and Promotion

14.01.01 Managerial Work in Medical and Health Services

11-9111.00 Medical and Health Services Managers

Plan, direct, or coordinate medicine and health services in hospitals, clinics, managed care organizations, public health agencies, or similar organizations. **Education:** Work experience, plus degree. **Occupational Type:** Enterprising. **Job Zone:** 4. **Average Salary:** $48,870. **Projected Growth:** 33.3%. **Occupational Values:** Working Conditions; Security; Authority; Autonomy; Responsibility; Social Status; Creativity. **Skills Required:** Management of Personnel Resources; Speaking; Judgment and Decision Making; Management of Financial Resources; Writing; Reading Comprehension; Coordination. **Abilities:** Oral Expression; Written Comprehension; Oral Comprehension; Written Expression; Speech Clarity; Mathematical Reasoning; Problem Sensitivity. **Interacting with Others:** Communicating with Other Workers; Guiding, Directing, and Motivating Subordinates; Communicating with Persons Outside Organization; Performing Administrative Activities; Staffing Organizational Units. **Physical Work Conditions:** Indoors; Sitting.

13-1041.06 Coroners

Direct activities such as autopsies, pathological and toxicological analyses, and inquests relating to the investigation of deaths occurring within a legal jurisdiction, to determine cause of death or to fix responsibility for accidental, violent, or unexplained deaths. **Education:** Work experience in a related occupation. **Occupational Type:** Investigative. **Job Zone:** 4. **Average Salary:** $36,820. **Projected Growth:** 10.5%. **Occupational Values:** Security; Autonomy; Responsibility; Authority; Ability Utilization; Company Policies and Practices; Compensation. **Skills Required:** Information Gathering; Reading Comprehension; Science; Active Listening; Writing; Critical Thinking; Coordination. **Abilities:** Inductive Reasoning; Near Vision; Oral Expression; Oral Comprehension; Problem Sensitivity; Written Expression; Deductive Reasoning. **Interacting with Others:** Communicating with Other Workers. **Physical Work Conditions:** Common Protective or Safety Attire; Using Hands on Objects, Tools, Controls; Indoors; Standing; Diseases/Infections; Contaminants.

14.02.01 Medicine and Surgery

29-1051.00 Pharmacists

Compound and dispense medications following prescriptions issued by physicians, dentists, or other authorized medical practitioners. **Education:** Bachelor's degree. **Occupational Type:** Investigative. **Job Zone:** 4. **Average Salary:** $66,220. **Projected Growth:** 7.3%. **Occupational Values:** Ability Utilization; Security; Achievement; Social Status; Working Conditions; Authority; Responsibility. **Skills Required:** Reading Comprehension; Mathematics; Science; Product Inspection; Information Gathering; Active Listening; Critical Thinking. **Abilities:** Written Comprehension; Oral Comprehension; Information Ordering; Oral Expression; Mathematical Reasoning; Written Expression. **Interacting with Others:** Communicating with Other Workers. **Physical Work Conditions:** Indoors; Special Uniform; Using Hands on Objects, Tools, Controls; Standing; Sitting.

29-1061.00 Anesthesiologists

Administer anesthetics during surgery or other medical procedures. **Education:** First professional degree. **Occupational Type:** Investigative. **Job Zone:** 5. **Average Salary:** $124,821. **Projected Growth:** 21.2%. **Occupational Values:** Social Service; Ability Utilization; Achievement; Social Status; Compensation; Responsibility; Security. **Skills Required:** Active Listening; Critical Thinking; Judgment and Decision Making; Monitoring; Speaking. **Abilities:** Problem Sensitivity; Near Vision; Control Precision; Speech Clarity. **Interacting with Others:** Assisting and Caring for Others; Communicating with Other Workers; Interpreting Meaning of Information to Others; Teaching Others. **Physical Work Conditions:** Indoors; Special Uniform; Common Protective or Safety Attire; Using Hands on Objects, Tools, Controls; Standing.

29-1062.00 Family and General Practitioners

Diagnose, treat, and help prevent diseases and injuries that commonly occur in the general population. **Education:** First professional degree. **Occupational Type:** Investigative. **Job Zone:** 5. **Average Salary:** $124,821. **Projected Growth:** 21.2%. **Occupational Values:** Social Status; Achievement; Ability Utilization; Responsibility; Social Service; Security; Autonomy. **Skills Required:** Reading Comprehension; Science; Identification of Key Causes; Judgment and Decision Making; Problem Identification; Critical Thinking; Solution Appraisal. **Abilities:** Inductive Reasoning; Manual Dexterity; Arm-Hand Steadiness; Near Vision; Oral Expression; Problem Sensitivity; Written Comprehension. **Interacting with Others:** Assisting and Caring for Others; Communicating with Persons Outside Organization; Communicating with Other Workers; Performing for/Working with Public; Providing Consultation and Advice to Others; Coordinating Work and Activities of Others; Interpreting Meaning of Information to Others. **Physical Work Conditions:** Indoors; Special Uniform; Diseases/Infections; Common Protective or Safety Attire; Using Hands on Objects, Tools, Controls; Standing; Walking or Running.

29-1063.00 Internists, General

Diagnose and provide nonsurgical treatment of diseases and injuries of internal organ systems. Provide care mainly for adults who have a wide range of problems associated with the internal organs. **Education:** First professional degree. **Occupational Type:** Investigative. **Job Zone:** 5. **Average Salary:** $124,821. **Projected Growth:** 21.2%. **Occupational Values:** Social Status; Ability Utilization; Social Service; Responsibility; Achievement; Security; Compensation. **Skills Required:** Reading Comprehension; Problem Identification; Identification of Key Causes; Judgment and Decision Making; Science; Critical Thinking; Active Listening. **Abilities:** Inductive Reasoning; Manual Dexterity; Arm-Hand Steadiness; Near Vision; Oral Expression; Problem Sensitivity; Written Comprehension. **Interacting with**

Others: Assisting and Caring for Others; Communicating with Persons Outside Organization; Communicating with Other Workers; Performing for/Working with Public; Providing Consultation and Advice to Others; Coordinating Work and Activities of Others; Interpreting Meaning of Information to Others. **Physical Work Conditions:** Indoors; Special Uniform; Diseases/Infections; Common Protective or Safety Attire; Using Hands on Objects, Tools, Controls; Standing; Walking or Running.

29-1064.00 Obstetricians and Gynecologists

Diagnose, treat, and help prevent diseases of women, especially those affecting the reproductive system and the process of childbirth. **Education:** First professional degree. **Occupational Type:** Investigative. **Job Zone:** 5. **Average Salary:** $124,821. **Projected Growth:** 21.2%. **Occupational Values:** Ability Utilization; Social Service; Social Status; Responsibility; Achievement; Security; Activity. **Skills Required:** Reading Comprehension; Judgment and Decision Making; Identification of Key Causes; Problem Identification; Science; Solution Appraisal; Critical Thinking. **Abilities:** Inductive Reasoning; Manual Dexterity; Arm-Hand Steadiness; Near Vision; Oral Expression; Problem Sensitivity; Written Comprehension. **Interacting with Others:** Assisting and Caring for Others; Communicating with Persons Outside Organization; Communicating with Other Workers; Performing for/Working with Public; Providing Consultation and Advice to Others; Coordinating Work and Activities of Others; Interpreting Meaning of Information to Others. **Physical Work Conditions:** Indoors; Special Uniform; Diseases/Infections; Common Protective or Safety Attire; Using Hands on Objects, Tools, Controls; Standing; Walking or Running.

29-1065.00 Pediatricians, General

Diagnose, treat, and help prevent children's diseases and injuries. **Education:** First professional degree. **Occupational Type:** Investigative. **Job Zone:** 5. **Average Salary:** $124,821. **Projected Growth:** 21.2%. **Occupational Values:** Ability Utilization; Achievement; Social Status; Responsibility; Social Service; Security; Compensation. **Skills Required:** Reading Comprehension; Judgment and Decision Making; Identification of Key Causes; Problem Identification; Science; Solution Appraisal; Information Gathering. **Abilities:** Inductive Reasoning; Manual Dexterity; Arm-Hand Steadiness; Near Vision; Oral Expression; Problem Sensitivity; Written Comprehension. **Interacting with Others:** Assisting and Caring for Others; Communicating with Persons Outside Organization; Communicating with Other Workers; Performing for/Working with Public; Providing Consultation and Advice to Others; Coordinating Work and Activities of Others; Interpreting Meaning of Information to Others. **Physical Work Conditions:** Indoors; Special Uniform; Diseases/Infections; Common Protective or Safety Attire; Using Hands on Objects, Tools, Controls; Standing; Walking or Running.

29-1066.00 Psychiatrists

Diagnose, treat, and help prevent disorders of the mind. **Education:** First professional degree. **Occupational Type:** Investigative. **Job Zone:** 5. **Average Salary:** $124,821. **Projected Growth:** 21.2%. **Occupational Values:** Ability Utilization; Achievement; Social Service; Autonomy; Responsibility; Social Status; Security. **Skills Required:** Active Listening; Speaking; Social Perceptiveness; Information Gathering; Problem Identification; Judgment and Decision Making; Identification of Key Causes. **Abilities:** Oral Comprehension; Oral Expression; Written Comprehension; Problem Sensitivity; Speech Clarity; Written Expression; Deductive Reasoning. **Interacting with Others:** Assisting and Caring for Others; Establishing and Maintaining Relationships; Communicating with Persons Outside Organization; Providing Consultation and Advice to Others; Interpreting Meaning of Information to Others; Communicating with Other Workers; Coaching and Developing Others. **Physical Work Conditions:** Indoors; Sitting.

29-1067.00 Surgeons

Treat diseases, injuries, and deformities by invasive methods such as manual manipulation or by using instruments and appliances. **Education:** First professional degree. **Occupational Type:** Investigative. **Job Zone:** 5. **Average Salary:** $124,821. **Projected Growth:** 21.2%. **Occupational Values:** Achievement; Ability Utilization; Social Status; Recognition; Social Service; Responsibility; Compensation. **Skills Required:** Reading Comprehension; Problem Identification; Critical Thinking; Judgment and Decision Making; Identification of Key Causes; Science; Management of Personnel Resources. **Abilities:** Arm-Hand Steadiness; Oral Expression; Manual Dexterity; Problem Sensitivity; Written Comprehension; Deductive Reasoning; Finger Dexterity. **Interacting with Others:** Assisting and Caring for Others; Communicating with Other Workers; Coordinating Work and Activities of Others; Communicating with Persons Outside Organization; Interpreting Meaning of Information to Others. **Physical Work Conditions:** Indoors; Special Uniform; Using Hands on Objects, Tools, Controls; Common Protective or Safety Attire; Standing; Diseases/Infections.

29-1071.00 Physician Assistants

Provide healthcare services typically performed by a physician, under the supervision of a physician. Conduct complete physicals, provide treatment, and counsel patients. May, in some cases, prescribe medication. **Education:** Bachelor's degree. **Occupational Type:** Investigative. **Job Zone:** 4. **Average Salary:** $47,090. **Projected Growth:** 48%. **Occupational Values:** Social Service; Achievement; Coworkers; Activity; Ability Utilization; Security; Social Status. **Skills Required:** Problem Identification; Speaking; Active Listening; Reading Comprehension; Science; Information Gathering; Critical Thinking. **Abilities:** Problem Sensitivity; Oral Expression; Oral Comprehension; Information Ordering; Near Vision; Written Expression; Inductive Reasoning. **Interacting with Others:** Assisting and Caring for Others; Communicating with Other Workers. **Physical Work Conditions:** Indoors; Special Uniform; Standing; Common Protective or Safety Attire.

29-1111.00 Registered Nurses

Assess patient health problems and needs, develop and implement nursing care plans, and maintain medical records. Administer nursing care to ill, injured, convalescent, or disabled patients. May advise patients on health maintenance and disease prevention or provide case management. Licensing or registration required. Includes advance practice nurses such as nurse practitioners, clinical nurse specialists, certified nurse midwives, and certified registered nurse anesthetists. Advanced practice nursing is practiced by RNs who have specialized formal, post-basic education and who function in highly autonomous and specialized roles. **Education:** Associate degree. **Occupational Type:** Social. **Job Zone:** 4. **Average Salary:**

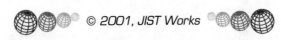

$40,690. **Projected Growth:** 21.7%. **Occupational Values:** Social Service; Coworkers; Activity; Achievement; Ability Utilization; Security; Social Status. **Skills Required:** Service Orientation; Social Perceptiveness; Speaking; Reading Comprehension; Judgment and Decision Making; Critical Thinking; Coordination. **Abilities:** Oral Expression; Problem Sensitivity; Oral Comprehension; Written Comprehension; Written Expression; Inductive Reasoning; Information Ordering. **Interacting with Others:** Communicating with Other Workers; Assisting and Caring for Others; Establishing and Maintaining Relationships; Performing Administrative Activities; Teaching Others; Communicating with Persons Outside Organization; Interpreting Meaning of Information to Others. **Physical Work Conditions:** Special Uniform; Indoors; Standing; Common Protective or Safety Attire; Diseases/Infections; Using Hands on Objects, Tools, Controls; Walking or Running.

29-2052.00 Pharmacy Technicians

Prepare medications under the direction of a pharmacist. May measure, mix, count out, label, and record amounts and dosages of medications. **Education:** Moderate-term O-J-T. **Occupational Type:** Conventional. **Job Zone:** 2. **Average Salary:** $15,850. **Projected Growth:** 15.7%. **Occupational Values:** Working Conditions; Coworkers; Moral Values; Activity; Security; Company Policies and Practices; Social Service. **Skills Required:** Reading Comprehension; Mathematics. **Abilities:** Information Ordering. **Interacting with Others:** Communicating with Other Workers. **Physical Work Conditions:** Indoors; Sitting; Standing; Using Hands on Objects, Tools, Controls.

29-2055.00 Surgical Technologists

Assist in operations, under the supervision of surgeons, registered nurses, or other surgical personnel. May help set up operating room; prepare and transport patients for surgery; adjust lights and equipment; pass instruments and other supplies to surgeons and surgeon's assistants; hold retractors; cut sutures; and help count sponges, needles, supplies, and instruments. **Education:** Postsecondary vocational training. **Occupational Type:** Realistic. **Job Zone:** 3. **Average Salary:** $25,780. **Projected Growth:** 41.8%. **Occupational Values:** Moral Values; Security; Social Service; Supervision, Human Relations; Company Policies and Practices; Coworkers; Working Conditions. **Skills Required:** Information Organization; Coordination; Active Listening. **Abilities:** Oral Comprehension. **Interacting with Others:** Assisting and Caring for Others. **Physical Work Conditions:** Indoors; Special Uniform; Standing; Common Protective or Safety Attire; Using Hands on Objects, Tools, Controls.

31-9092.00 Medical Assistants

Perform administrative and certain clinical duties under the direction of physician. Administrative duties may include scheduling appointments, maintaining medical records, billing, and coding for insurance purposes. Clinical duties may include taking and recording vital signs and medical histories, preparing patients for examination, drawing blood, and administering medications as directed by physician. **Education:** Moderate-term O-J-T. **Occupational Type:** Social. **Job Zone:** 3. **Average Salary:** $20,680. **Projected Growth:** 57.8%. **Occupational Values:** Moral Values; Social Service; Security; Supervision, Human Relations; Coworkers; Working Conditions; Compensation. **Skills Required:** Service Orientation; Active Listening; Writing; Information Organization; Speaking; Information Gathering; Social Perceptiveness. **Abilities:** Near Vision; Arm-Hand Steadiness; Oral Comprehension; Information Ordering; Control Precision; Oral Expression; Written Comprehension. **Interacting with Others:** Assisting and Caring for Others; Communicating with Other Workers; Establishing and Maintaining Relationships; Communicating with Persons Outside Organization; Performing Administrative Activities. **Physical Work Conditions:** Indoors; Special Uniform; Common Protective or Safety Attire; Diseases/Infections; Standing; Using Hands on Objects, Tools, Controls.

31-9095.00 Pharmacy Aides

Record drugs delivered to the pharmacy, store incoming merchandise, and inform the supervisor of stock needs. May operate cash register and accept prescriptions for filling. No other data currently available.

14.03.01 Dentistry

29-1021.00 Dentists, General

Diagnose and treat diseases, injuries, and malformations of teeth and gums and related oral structures. May treat diseases of nerve, pulp, and other dental tissues affecting vitality of teeth. **Education:** First professional degree. **Occupational Type:** Investigative. **Job Zone:** 5. **Average Salary:** $110,160. **Projected Growth:** 3.1%. **Occupational Values:** Responsibility; Social Service; Social Status; Achievement; Ability Utilization; Autonomy; Recognition. **Skills Required:** Reading Comprehension; Critical Thinking; Problem Identification; Science; Judgment and Decision Making; Active Learning; Information Gathering. **Abilities:** Arm-Hand Steadiness; Oral Comprehension; Control Precision; Problem Sensitivity; Finger Dexterity; Oral Expression. **Interacting with Others:** Assisting and Caring for Others. **Physical Work Conditions:** Indoors; Special Uniform; Common Protective or Safety Attire; Using Hands on Objects, Tools, Controls; Sitting; Standing.

29-1022.00 Oral and Maxillofacial Surgeons

Perform surgery on mouth, jaws, and related head and neck structure to execute difficult and multiple extractions of teeth, to remove tumors and other abnormal growths, to correct abnormal jaw relations by mandibular or maxillary revision, to prepare mouth for insertion of dental prosthesis, or to treat fractured jaws. **Education:** First professional degree. **Occupational Type:** Investigative. **Job Zone:** 5. **Average Salary:** $110,160. **Projected Growth:** 3.1%. **Occupational Values:** Social Service; Responsibility; Achievement; Social Status; Ability Utilization; Recognition; Compensation. **Skills Required:** Reading Comprehension; Judgment and Decision Making; Problem Identification; Critical Thinking; Science; Information Gathering; Solution Appraisal. **Abilities:** Arm-Hand Steadiness; Manual Dexterity; Near Vision; Finger Dexterity; Problem Sensitivity; Visualization. **Interacting with Others:** Assisting and Caring for Others. **Physical Work Conditions:** Indoors; Special Uniform; Using Hands on Objects, Tools, Controls; Common Protective or Safety Attire; Standing.

29-1023.00 Orthodontists

Examine, diagnose, and treat dental malocclusions and oral cavity anomalies. Design and fabricate appliances to realign teeth and jaws to produce and maintain normal function and to improve appearance. **Education:** First professional degree. **Occupational Type:** Investigative. **Job Zone:** 5. **Average Salary:** $110,160. **Projected Growth:** 3.1%. **Occupational Values:** Social Service; Responsibility; Social Status; Achievement; Ability Utilization; Autonomy; Recognition. **Skills Required:** Problem Identification; Science; Reading Comprehension; Judgment and Decision Making; Critical Thinking; Equipment Selection; Technology Design. **Abilities:** Arm-Hand Steadiness; Manual Dexterity; Control Precision; Problem Sensitivity. **Interacting with Others:** Assisting and Caring for Others; Communicating with Persons Outside Organization. **Physical Work Conditions:** Indoors; Special Uniform; Standing; Using Hands on Objects, Tools, Controls; Common Protective or Safety Attire; Sitting.

29-1024.00 Prosthodontists

Construct oral prostheses to replace missing teeth and other oral structures, to correct natural and acquired deformation of mouth and jaws, to improve appearance, and to restore and maintain oral functions such as chewing and speaking. **Education:** First professional degree. **Occupational Type:** Investigative. **Job Zone:** 5. **Average Salary:** $110,160. **Projected Growth:** 3.1%. **Occupational Values:** Responsibility; Social Service; Ability Utilization; Autonomy; Achievement; Security; Compensation. **Skills Required:** Problem Identification; Reading Comprehension; Science; Equipment Selection; Judgment and Decision Making; Technology Design; Solution Appraisal. **Abilities:** Arm-Hand Steadiness; Near Vision. **Interacting with Others:** Assisting and Caring for Others. **Physical Work Conditions:** Indoors; Special Uniform; Using Hands on Objects, Tools, Controls; Common Protective or Safety Attire; Sitting; Standing.

29-2021.00 Dental Hygienists

Clean teeth and examine oral areas, head, and neck for signs of oral disease. May educate patients on oral hygiene, take and develop X-rays, or apply fluoride or sealants. **Education:** Associate degree. **Occupational Type:** Social. **Job Zone:** 3. **Average Salary:** $45,890. **Projected Growth:** 40.5%. **Occupational Values:** Social Service; Moral Values; Security; Achievement; Ability Utilization; Coworkers; Activity. **Skills Required:** Reading Comprehension. **Abilities:** Arm-Hand Steadiness; Oral Expression. **Interacting with Others:** Assisting and Caring for Others; Communicating with Other Workers; Performing for/Working with Public. **Physical Work Conditions:** Indoors; Special Uniform; Common Protective or Safety Attire; Standing; Using Hands on Objects, Tools, Controls; Sitting.

31-9091.00 Dental Assistants

Assist dentist, set up patient and equipment, and keep records. **Education:** Moderate-term O-J-T. **Occupational Type:** Social. **Job Zone:** 3. **Average Salary:** $22,640. **Projected Growth:** No Data Available. **Occupational Values:** Social Service; Moral Values; Security; Coworkers; Working Conditions; Supervision, Human Relations; Compensation. **Skills Required:** Coordination. **Abilities:** Arm-Hand Steadiness; Near Vision. **Interacting with Others:** Assisting and Caring for Others; Communicating with Other Workers; Communicating with Persons Outside Organization. **Physical Work Conditions:** Indoors; Special Uniform; Using Hands on Objects, Tools, Controls; Common Protective or Safety Attire; Standing; Sitting.

14.04.01 Health Specialties

29-1011.00 Chiropractors

Adjust spinal column and other articulations of the human body to correct abnormalities caused by interference with the nervous system. Examine patient to determine nature and extent of disorder. Manipulate spine or other involved area. May utilize supplementary measures such as exercise, rest, water, light, heat, and nutritional therapy. **Education:** First professional degree. **Occupational Type:** Investigative. **Job Zone:** 5. **Average Salary:** $63,930. **Projected Growth:** 22.8%. **Occupational Values:** Responsibility; Social Service; Autonomy; Ability Utilization; Achievement; Compensation; Recognition. **Skills Required:** Problem Identification; Active Learning; Critical Thinking; Active Listening; Speaking; Judgment and Decision Making; Reading Comprehension. **Abilities:** Problem Sensitivity; Finger Dexterity; Manual Dexterity; Multilimb Coordination. **Interacting with Others:** Assisting and Caring for Others; Establishing and Maintaining Relationships. **Physical Work Conditions:** Indoors; Special Uniform; Standing; Using Hands on Objects, Tools, Controls; Bending or Twisting the Body; Common Protective or Safety Attire.

29-1041.00 Optometrists

Diagnose, manage, and treat conditions and diseases of the human eye and visual system. Examine eyes and visual system, diagnose problems or impairments, prescribe corrective lenses, and provide treatment. May prescribe therapeutic drugs to treat specific eye conditions. **Education:** First professional degree. **Occupational Type:** Investigative. **Job Zone:** 4. **Average Salary:** $68,480. **Projected Growth:** 10.6%. **Occupational Values:** Social Service; Ability Utilization; Responsibility; Autonomy; Achievement; Working Conditions; Social Status. **Skills Required:** Reading Comprehension; Speaking; Science; Active Listening; Problem Identification; Implementation Planning; Judgment and Decision Making. **Abilities:** Oral Expression; Near Vision; Written Comprehension; Oral Comprehension; Problem Sensitivity; Written Expression; Deductive Reasoning. **Interacting with Others:** Assisting and Caring for Others. **Physical Work Conditions:** Indoors; Sitting; Standing; Using Hands on Objects, Tools, Controls.

29-1081.00 Podiatrists

Diagnose and treat diseases and deformities of the human foot. **Education:** First professional degree. **Occupational Type:** Social. **Job Zone:** 4. **Average Salary:** $79,530. **Projected Growth:** 10.5%. **Occupational Values:** Responsibility; Social Service; Achievement; Ability Utilization; Autonomy; Compensation; Recognition. **Skills Required:** Active Listening; Reading Comprehension; Critical Thinking; Problem Identification; Speaking; Judgment and Decision Making; Solution Appraisal. **Abilities:** Deductive Reasoning; Oral Expression; Finger Dexterity; Problem Sensitivity; Inductive Reasoning; Manual Dexterity; Wrist-Finger Speed. **Interacting with Others:** Assisting and Caring for Others; Communicating with Persons Outside Organization; Interpreting Meaning of Information to Others;

Performing for/Working with Public. **Physical Work Conditions:** Indoors; Diseases/Infections; Common Protective or Safety Attire; Special Uniform; Using Hands on Objects, Tools, Controls; Sitting; Standing.

29-2081.00 Opticians, Dispensing

Design, measure, fit, and adapt lenses and frames for client according to written optical prescription or specification. Assist client with selecting frames. Measure customer for size of eyeglasses and coordinate frames with facial and eye measurements and optical prescription. Prepare work order for optical laboratory containing instructions for grinding and mounting lenses in frames. Verify exactness of finished lens spectacles. Adjust frame and lens position to fit client. May shape or reshape frames. **Education:** Long-term O-J-T. **Occupational Type:** Enterprising. **Job Zone:** 4. **Average Salary:** $22,440. **Projected Growth:** 13.8%. **Occupational Values:** Social Service; Achievement; Security; Responsibility; Social Status; Ability Utilization; Moral Values. **Skills Required:** Product Inspection; Active Listening; Problem Identification. **Abilities:** Oral Expression. **Interacting with Others:** Performing for/Working with Public; Assisting and Caring for Others; Communicating with Persons Outside Organization. **Physical Work Conditions:** Indoors; Sitting; Using Hands on Objects, Tools, Controls.

14.05.01 Medical Technology

29-2011.00 Medical and Clinical Laboratory Technologists

Perform complex medical laboratory tests for diagnosis, treatment, and prevention of disease. May train or supervise staff. **Education:** Bachelor's degree. **Occupational Type:** Investigative. **Job Zone:** 4. **Average Salary:** $37,280. **Projected Growth:** 17%. **Occupational Values:** Ability Utilization; Activity; Security; Working Conditions; Achievement; Moral Values; Coworkers. **Skills Required:** Science; Information Gathering; Reading Comprehension; Problem Identification; Critical Thinking; Active Learning; Information Organization. **Abilities:** Information Ordering; Oral Expression; Written Expression; Oral Comprehension; Written Comprehension; Near Vision; Problem Sensitivity. **Interacting with Others:** Communicating with Other Workers; Communicating with Persons Outside Organization; Interpreting Meaning of Information to Others; Performing Administrative Activities; Providing Consultation and Advice to Others. **Physical Work Conditions:** Common Protective or Safety Attire; Sitting; Indoors; Diseases/Infections; Using Hands on Objects, Tools, Controls; Standing; Special Uniform.

29-2012.00 Medical and Clinical Laboratory Technicians

Perform routine medical laboratory tests for the diagnosis, treatment, and prevention of disease. May work under the supervision of a medical technologist. **Education:** Bachelor's degree. **Occupational Type:** Realistic. **Job Zone:** 2. **Average Salary:** $26,300. **Projected Growth:** 17%. **Occupational Values:** Ability Utilization; Moral Values; Activity; Achievement; Security; Coworkers; Supervision, Human Relations. **Skills Required:** Science. **Abilities:** Information Ordering; Near Vision; Visual Color Discrimination; Arm-Hand Steadiness; Flexibility of Closure; Oral Comprehension; Written Comprehension. **Interacting with Others:** Communicating with Other Workers. **Physical Work Conditions:** Indoors; Common Protective or Safety Attire; Diseases/Infections; Sitting; Using Hands on Objects, Tools, Controls; Special Uniform; Standing.

29-2031.00 Cardiovascular Technologists and Technicians

Conduct tests on pulmonary or cardiovascular systems of patients for diagnostic purposes. May conduct or assist in electrocardiograms, cardiac catheterizations, pulmonary-functions, lung capacity, and similar tests. **Education:** Associate degree. **Occupational Type:** Investigative. **Job Zone:** 3. **Average Salary:** $31,125. **Projected Growth:** 39.4%. **Occupational Values:** Social Service; Moral Values; Company Policies and Practices; Achievement; Compensation; Security; Ability Utilization. **Skills Required:** Operation and Control; Operation Monitoring; Science; Reading Comprehension; Information Gathering; Speaking; Mathematics. **Abilities:** Written Comprehension; Oral Expression; Oral Comprehension. **Interacting with Others:** Assisting and Caring for Others; Communicating with Other Workers; Interpreting Meaning of Information to Others. **Physical Work Conditions:** Indoors; Special Uniform; Standing; Sitting; Specialized Protective or Safety Attire; Using Hands on Objects, Tools, Controls.

29-2032.00 Diagnostic Medical Sonographers

Produce ultrasonic recordings of internal organs for use by physicians. No other data currently available.

29-2033.00 Nuclear Medicine Technologists

Prepare, administer, and measure radioactive isotopes in therapeutic, diagnostic, and tracer studies utilizing a variety of radioisotope equipment. Prepare stock solutions of radioactive materials and calculate doses to be administered by radiologists. Subject patients to radiation. Execute blood volume, red cell survival, and fat absorption studies following standard laboratory techniques. **Education:** Associate degree. **Occupational Type:** Investigative. **Job Zone:** 4. **Average Salary:** $39,610. **Projected Growth:** 11.6%. **Occupational Values:** Moral Values; Ability Utilization; Security; Coworkers; Achievement; Social Service; Variety. **Skills Required:** Mathematics; Reading Comprehension; Operation and Control; Operation Monitoring; Science. **Abilities:** Oral Comprehension; Oral Expression; Written Comprehension; Problem Sensitivity; Written Expression. **Interacting with Others:** Communicating with Other Workers. **Physical Work Conditions:** Indoors; Radiation; Specialized Protective or Safety Attire; Special Uniform; Common Protective or Safety Attire; Using Hands on Objects, Tools, Controls; Diseases/Infections.

29-2034.01 Radiologic Technologists

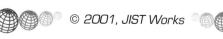

Take X-rays and CAT scans or administer nonradioactive materials into patient's blood stream for diagnostic purposes. Includes technologists who specialize in other modalities such as computed tomography, ultrasound, and magnetic resonance. **Education:** Associate degree. **Occupational Type:** Realistic. **Job Zone:** 4. **Average Salary:** $32,880. **Projected Growth:** 20.1%. **Occupational Values:** Ability Utilization; Security; Coworkers; Achievement; Moral Values; Social Service; Activity. **Skills Required:** Operation and Control; Operation Monitoring. **Abili-**

ties: Oral Expression; Control Precision. **Interacting with Others:** Assisting and Caring for Others. **Physical Work Conditions:** Indoors; Special Uniform; Radiation; Standing; Using Hands on Objects, Tools, Controls; Common Protective or Safety Attire; Sitting.

29-2034.02 Radiologic Technicians

Maintain and use equipment and supplies necessary to demonstrate portions the human body on X-ray film or fluoroscopic screen for diagnostic purposes. **Education:** Associate degree. **Occupational Type:** Realistic. **Job Zone:** 4. **Average Salary:** $32,880. **Projected Growth:** 20.1%. **Occupational Values:** Moral Values; Social Service; Coworkers; Company Policies and Practices; Security; Activity; Supervision, Human Relations. **Skills Required:** Operation and Control. **Abilities:** Oral Expression. **Interacting with Others:** Assisting and Caring for Others. **Physical Work Conditions:** Indoors; Radiation; Special Uniform; Specialized Protective or Safety Attire; Standing; Using Hands on Objects, Tools, Controls.

29-2091.00 Orthotists and Prosthetists

Assist patients who have disabling limb or spinal conditions or who have partial or total absence of limb, by fitting and preparing orthopedic braces or prostheses. **Education:** Associate degree. **Occupational Type:** Social. **Job Zone:** 3. **Average Salary:** $27,260. **Projected Growth:** 35%. **Occupational Values:** Social Service; Achievement; Ability Utilization; Company Policies and Practices; Moral Values; Compensation; Working Conditions. **Skills Required:** Active Listening; Instructing; Speaking; Product Inspection; Reading Comprehension; Technology Design; Equipment Selection. **Abilities:** Oral Expression; Speech Clarity; Oral Comprehension; Visualization; Written Comprehension; Manual Dexterity; Written Expression. **Interacting with Others:** Assisting and Caring for Others; Communicating with Persons Outside Organization. **Physical Work Conditions:** Indoors; Using Hands on Objects, Tools, Controls; Standing; Special Uniform; Sitting.

31-9093.00 Medical Equipment Preparers

Prepare, sterilize, install, or clean laboratory or healthcare equipment. May perform routine laboratory tasks and operate or inspect equipment. **Education:** Short-term O-J-T. **Occupational Type:** Realistic. **Job Zone:** 2. **Average Salary:** $20,077. **Projected Growth:** 22.3%. **Occupational Values:** Moral Values; Independence; Security; Supervision, Human Relations; Supervision, Technical; Working Conditions; Company Policies and Practices. **Skills Required:** Installation. **Abilities:** Problem Sensitivity. **Interacting with Others:** Monitoring and Controlling Resources. **Physical Work Conditions:** Indoors; Using Hands on Objects, Tools, Controls; Common Protective or Safety Attire; Diseases/Infections; Standing.

14.06.01 Medical Therapy

29-1121.00 Audiologists

Assess and treat persons with hearing and related disorders. May fit hearing aids and provide auditory training. May perform research related to hearing problems. **Education:** Master's degree. **Occupational Type:** Social. **Job Zone:** 4. **Average Salary:** $43,080. **Projected Growth:** 38.5%. **Occupational Values:** Social Service; Achievement; Ability Utilization; Authority; Coworkers; Creativity; Autonomy. **Skills Required:** Instructing; Writing; Speaking; Learning Strategies; Active Learning; Reading Comprehension; Active Listening. **Abilities:** Oral Expression; Written Comprehension; Oral Comprehension; Speech Clarity; Written Expression; Speech Recognition; Deductive Reasoning. **Interacting with Others:** Assisting and Caring for Others; Interpreting Meaning of Information to Others. **Physical Work Conditions:** Indoors; Sitting.

29-1122.00 Occupational Therapists

Assess, plan, organize, and participate in rehabilitative programs that help restore vocational, homemaking, and daily living skills, as well as general independence, to disabled persons. **Education:** Bachelor's degree. **Occupational Type:** Social. **Job Zone:** 4. **Average Salary:** $48,230. **Projected Growth:** 34.2%. **Occupational Values:** Social Service; Achievement; Ability Utilization; Social Status; Coworkers; Authority; Compensation. **Skills Required:** Instructing; Social Perceptiveness; Speaking; Implementation Planning; Solution Appraisal; Learning Strategies; Active Listening. **Abilities:** Oral Expression; Written Comprehension; Oral Comprehension. **Interacting with Others:** Assisting and Caring for Others; Providing Consultation and Advice to Others; Teaching Others. **Physical Work Conditions:** Indoors; Sitting; Special Uniform; Using Hands on Objects, Tools, Controls.

29-1123.00 Physical Therapists

Assess, plan, organize, and participate in rehabilitative programs that improve mobility, relieve pain, increase strength, and decrease or prevent deformity of patients suffering from disease or injury. **Education:** Bachelor's degree. **Occupational Type:** Social. **Job Zone:** 4. **Average Salary:** $56,600. **Projected Growth:** 34%. **Occupational Values:** Social Service; Achievement; Ability Utilization; Social Status; Coworkers; Autonomy; Authority. **Skills Required:** Judgment and Decision Making; Critical Thinking; Reading Comprehension; Active Listening; Speaking; Science; Service Orientation. **Abilities:** Oral Expression; Written Expression; Problem Sensitivity. **Interacting with Others:** Assisting and Caring for Others; Establishing and Maintaining Relationships; Coaching and Developing Others; Communicating with Persons Outside Organization. **Physical Work Conditions:** Indoors; Special Uniform; Standing; Using Hands on Objects, Tools, Controls.

29-1124.00 Radiation Therapists

Provide radiation therapy to patients as prescribed by a radiologist according to established practices and standards. Duties may include reviewing prescription and diagnosis; acting as liaison with physician and supportive care personnel; preparing equipment such as immobilization, treatment, and protection devices; and maintaining records, reports, and files. May assist in dosimetry procedures and tumor localization. **Education:** Associate degree. **Occupational Type:** Social. **Job Zone:** 4. **Average Salary:** $39,640. **Projected Growth:** 16.7%. **Occupational Values:** Moral Values; Social Service; Security; Ability Utilization; Coworkers; Activity; Achievement. **Skills Required:** Reading Comprehension; Operation and Control; Science; Operation Monitoring; Coordination; Writing; Speaking. **Abilities:** Problem Sensitivity; Written Comprehension. **Interacting with Others:** Assisting and Caring for Others; Communicating with Other Workers; Communicating with Persons Outside Organization; Performing Administrative Activities. **Physical Work Conditions:** Indoors; Common Protective or Safety Attire; Radiation; Special Uniform; Using Hands on Objects, Tools, Controls; Standing; Diseases/Infections.

29-1125.00 Recreational Therapists

Plan, direct, or coordinate medically-approved recreation programs for patients in hospitals, nursing homes, or other institutions. Activities include sports, trips, dramatics, social activities, and arts and crafts. May assess a patient condition and recommend appropriate recreational activity. **Education:** Bachelor's degree. **Occupational Type:** Social. **Job Zone:** 4. **Average Salary:** $27,760. **Projected Growth:** 13.4%. **Occupational Values:** Social Service; Achievement; Coworkers; Creativity; Ability Utilization; Social Status; Moral Values. **Skills Required:** Speaking; Active Listening; Learning Strategies; Service Orientation; Instructing; Social Perceptiveness; Critical Thinking. **Abilities:** Oral Comprehension. **Interacting with Others:** Assisting and Caring for Others; Establishing and Maintaining Relationships; Teaching Others; Coaching and Developing Others. **Physical Work Conditions:** Indoors; Diseases/ Infections; Standing; Outdoors; Sitting; Special Uniform; Walking or Running.

29-1126.00 Respiratory Therapists

Assess, treat, and care for patients with breathing disorders. Assume primary responsibility for all respiratory care modalities, including the supervision of respiratory therapy technicians. Initiate and conduct therapeutic procedures; maintain patient records; and select, assemble, check, and operate equipment. **Education:** Associate degree. **Occupational Type:** Investigative. **Job Zone:** 3. **Average Salary:** $34,830. **Projected Growth:** 42.6%. **Occupational Values:** Social Service; Achievement; Coworkers; Security; Ability Utilization; Activity; Moral Values. **Skills Required:** Operation and Control; Monitoring; Reading Comprehension; Active Listening; Operation Monitoring; Critical Thinking; Problem Identification. **Abilities:** Oral Comprehension; Oral Expression; Written Comprehension; Problem Sensitivity. **Interacting with Others:** Assisting and Caring for Others; Communicating with Other Workers; Establishing and Maintaining Relationships. **Physical Work Conditions:** Indoors; Special Uniform; Using Hands on Objects, Tools, Controls; Standing.

29-1127.00 Speech-Language Pathologists

Assess and treat persons with speech, language, voice, and fluency disorders. May select alternative communication systems and teach their use. May perform research related to speech and language problems. **Education:** Master's degree. **Occupational Type:** Social. **Job Zone:** 4. **Average Salary:** $43,080. **Projected Growth:** 38.5%. **Occupational Values:** Social Service; Achievement; Ability Utilization; Authority; Coworkers; Creativity; Social Status. **Skills Required:** Instructing; Writing; Speaking; Reading Comprehension; Active Learning; Learning Strategies; Critical Thinking. **Abilities:** Oral Expression; Written Comprehension; Oral Comprehension; Speech Clarity; Written Expression; Speech Recognition; Deductive Reasoning. **Interacting with Others:** Assisting and Caring for Others; Interpreting Meaning of Information to Others. **Physical Work Conditions:** Indoors; Sitting.

29-2054.00 Respiratory Therapy Technicians

Provide specific, well defined respiratory care procedures under the direction of respiratory therapists and physicians. No other data currently available.

31-2011.00 Occupational Therapist Assistants

Assist occupational therapists in providing occupational therapy treatments and procedures. May, in accordance with State laws, assist in development of treatment plans, carry out routine functions, direct activity programs, and document the progress of treatments. Generally requires formal training. **Education:** Moderate-term O-J-T. **Occupational Type:** Social. **Job Zone:** 2. **Average Salary:** $28,690. **Projected Growth:** 39.8%. **Occupational Values:** Social Service; Security; Moral Values; Supervision, Human Relations; Achievement; Coworkers; Working Conditions. **Skills Required:** Social Perceptiveness; Instructing; Service Orientation; Active Listening; Speaking; Reading Comprehension; Writing. **Abilities:** Problem Sensitivity. **Interacting with Others:** Assisting and Caring for Others; Communicating with Other Workers; Teaching Others. **Physical Work Conditions:** Indoors; Standing; Sitting; Using Hands on Objects, Tools, Controls.

31-2012.00 Occupational Therapist Aides

Under close supervision of an occupational therapist or occupational therapy assistant, perform only delegated, selected, or routine tasks in specific situations. Duties include preparing patient and treatment room. **Education:** Moderate-term O-J-T. **Occupational Type:** Social. **Job Zone:** 2. **Average Salary:** $28,690. **Projected Growth:** 39.8%. **Occupational Values:** Social Service; Security; Achievement; Supervision, Human Relations; Moral Values; Coworkers; Working Conditions. **Skills Required:** Active Listening; Instructing; Social Perceptiveness; Service Orientation; Speaking; Reading Comprehension; Technology Design. **Abilities:** Problem Sensitivity. **Interacting with Others:** Assisting and Caring for Others; Communicating with Other Workers; Teaching Others. **Physical Work Conditions:** Indoors; Standing; Sitting; Using Hands on Objects, Tools, Controls.

31-2021.00 Physical Therapist Assistants

Assist physical therapists in providing physical therapy treatments and procedures. May, in accordance with State laws, assist in the development of treatment plans, carry out routine functions, document the progress of treatment, and modify specific treatments in accordance with patient status and within the scope of treatment plans established by a physical therapist. Generally requires formal training. **Education:** Moderate-term O-J-T. **Occupational Type:** Social. **Job Zone:** 2. **Average Salary:** $21,870. **Projected Growth:** 43.7%. **Occupational Values:** Social Service; Moral Values; Security; Supervision, Human Relations; Achievement; Working Conditions; Coworkers. **Skills Required:** Speaking; Instructing. **Abilities:** Oral Expression; Oral Comprehension. **Interacting with Others:** Assisting and Caring for Others; Communicating with Other Workers; Establishing and Maintaining Relationships. **Physical Work Conditions:** Indoors; Special Uniform; Standing; Using Hands on Objects, Tools, Controls.

31-2022.00 Physical Therapist Aides

Under close supervision of a physical therapist or physical

therapy assistant, perform only delegated, selected, or routine tasks in specific situations. Duties include preparing the patient and the treatment area. **Education:** Moderate-term O-J-T. **Occupational Type:** Social. **Job Zone:** 2. **Average Salary:** $21,870. **Projected Growth:** 43.7%. **Occupational Values:** Social Service; Moral Values; Security; Supervision, Human Relations; Achievement; Coworkers; Working Conditions. **Skills Required:** Speaking; Instructing. **Abilities:** Oral Expression; Oral Comprehension. **Interacting with Others:** Assisting and Caring for Others; Communicating with Other Workers; Establishing and Maintaining Relationships. **Physical Work Conditions:** Indoors; Special Uniform; Standing; Using Hands on Objects, Tools, Controls.

31-9011.00 Massage Therapists

Massage customers for hygienic or remedial purposes. No other data currently available.

14.07.01 Patient Care and Assistance

29-2053.00 Psychiatric Technicians

Care for mentally impaired or emotionally disturbed individuals, following physician instructions and hospital procedures. Monitor patients' physical and emotional well-being and report to medical staff. May participate in rehabilitation and treatment programs, help with personal hygiene, and administer oral medications and hypodermic injections. **Education:** Associate degree. **Occupational Type:** Social. **Job Zone:** 3. **Average Salary:** $20,890. **Projected Growth:** 10.9%. **Occupational Values:** Social Service; Coworkers; Supervision, Human Relations; Company Policies and Practices; Security; Activity; Compensation. **Skills Required:** Social Perceptiveness; Service Orientation; Active Listening; Problem Identification; Speaking; Reading Comprehension. **Abilities:** Problem Sensitivity; Oral Expression; Oral Comprehension. **Interacting with Others:** Assisting and Caring for Others; Communicating with Other Workers; Establishing and Maintaining Relationships. **Physical Work Conditions:** Indoors; Special Uniform; Standing.

29-2061.00 Licensed Practical and Licensed Vocational Nurses

Care for ill, injured, convalescent, or disabled persons in hospitals, nursing homes, clinics, private homes, group homes, and similar institutions. May work under the supervision of a registered nurse. Licensing required. **Education:** Postsecondary vocational training. **Occupational Type:** Social. **Job Zone:** 3. **Average Salary:** $26,940. **Projected Growth:** 19.7%. **Occupational Values:** Social Service; Coworkers; Achievement; Ability Utilization; Activity; Security; Social Status. **Skills Required:** Service Orientation; Information Gathering; Active Listening; Reading Comprehension; Problem Identification. **Abilities:** Oral Expression; Oral Comprehension. **Interacting with Others:** Assisting and Caring for Others; Communicating with Other Workers. **Physical Work Conditions:** Indoors; Special Uniform; Standing; Using Hands on Objects, Tools, Controls; Diseases/Infections; Common Protective or Safety Attire.

31-1011.00 Home Health Aides

Provide routine, personal healthcare, such as bathing, dressing, or grooming, to elderly, convalescent, or disabled persons in the patient's home or in a residential care facility. **Education:** Short-term O-J-T. **Occupational Type:** Social. **Job Zone:** 1. **Average Salary:** $16,250. **Projected Growth:** 58.1%. **Occupational Values:** Social Service; Moral Values; Security; Achievement; Independence; Variety. **Skills Required:** Service Orientation; Social Perceptiveness. **Abilities:** Oral Comprehension; Static Strength; Oral Expression. **Interacting with Others:** Assisting and Caring for Others; Establishing and Maintaining Relationships. **Physical Work Conditions:** Indoors; Standing; Sitting.

31-1012.00 Nursing Aides, Orderlies, and Attendants

Provide basic patient care under direction of nursing staff. Perform duties such as feeding, bathing, dressing, grooming, or moving patients, or changing linens. **Education:** Short-term O-J-T. **Occupational Type:** Social. **Job Zone:** 2. **Average Salary:** $16,620. **Projected Growth:** 23.8%. **Occupational Values:** Social Service; Moral Values; Coworkers; Activity; Security; Supervision, Human Relations; Supervision, Technical. **Skills Required:** Service Orientation; Active Listening; Social Perceptiveness. **Abilities:** Oral Comprehension; Oral Expression; Static Strength; Arm-Hand Steadiness; Near Vision; Written Comprehension; Information Ordering. **Interacting with Others:** Assisting and Caring for Others; Establishing and Maintaining Relationships; Communicating with Other Workers. **Physical Work Conditions:** Indoors; Special Uniform; Diseases/Infections; Standing; Common Protective or Safety Attire; Walking or Running.

31-1013.00 Psychiatric Aides

Assist mentally impaired or emotionally disturbed patients, working under direction of nursing and medical staff. **Education:** Short-term O-J-T. **Occupational Type:** Social. **Job Zone:** 2. **Average Salary:** $22,170. **Projected Growth:** 7.7%. **Occupational Values:** Social Service; Coworkers; Security; Activity; Supervision, Human Relations; Moral Values. **Skills Required:** Active Listening; Speaking; Reading Comprehension; Social Perceptiveness; Judgment and Decision Making. **Abilities:** Oral Expression; Problem Sensitivity; Oral Comprehension. **Interacting with Others:** Assisting and Caring for Others; Establishing and Maintaining Relationships. **Physical Work Conditions:** Indoors; Special Uniform; Walking or Running; Standing; Using Hands on Objects, Tools, Controls; Diseases/Infections; Sitting.

14.08.01 Health Protection and Promotion

21-1091.00 Health Educators

Promote, maintain, and improve individual and community health by assisting individuals and communities in adopting healthy behaviors. Collect and analyze data to identify community needs prior to planning, implementing, monitoring, and evaluating programs designed to encourage healthy lifestyles, policies and environments. May also serve as a resource to assist individuals, other professionals, or the community; may administer fiscal resources for health education programs. **Education:** Master's degree. **Occupational Type:** Social. **Job Zone:** 5. **Average Salary:** $33,699. **Projected Growth:** 14.7%. **Occupational Values:** Social Service; Achievement; Working Conditions; Autonomy; Ability Utilization; Responsibility; Social Status. **Skills Required:** Active Listening; Speaking; Information Gathering; Writing; Implementation Planning; Active Learning; Reading Comprehension. **Abilities:** Oral Expression; Written Comprehension; Speech Clarity; Oral Comprehension; Written Expression. **Interacting with Others:** Communicating with Persons Outside Organization; Establishing and Maintaining Relationships; Teaching Others. **Physical Work Conditions:** Indoors; Sitting.

29-1031.00 Dietitians and Nutritionists

Plan and conduct food service or nutritional programs to assist in the promotion of health and control of disease. May supervise activities of a department providing quantity food services. May counsel individuals or conduct nutritional research. **Education:** Bachelor's degree. **Occupational Type:** Investigative. **Job Zone:** 4. **Average Salary:** $35,040. **Projected Growth:** 19.1%. **Occupational Values:** Social Service; Ability Utilization; Achievement; Authority; Working Conditions; Security; Creativity. **Skills Required:** Judgment and Decision Making; Instructing; Writing; Speaking; Reading Comprehension; Persuasion; Identification of Key Causes. **Abilities:** Oral Expression; Speech Clarity; Written Expression; Written Comprehension; Inductive Reasoning; Information Ordering; Near Vision. **Interacting with Others:** Communicating with Persons Outside Organization; Communicating with Other Workers; Interpreting Meaning of Information to Others; Teaching Others. **Physical Work Conditions:** Indoors; Sitting; Standing.

29-2051.00 Dietetic Technicians

Assist dietitians in the provision of food service and nutritional programs. Under the supervision of dietitians, may plan and produce meals based on established guidelines, teach principles of food and nutrition, or counsel individuals. **Education:** Associate degree. **Occupational Type:** Social. **Job Zone:** 4. **Average Salary:** $19,520. **Projected Growth:** 35%. **Occupational Values:** Social Service; Coworkers; Working Conditions; Moral Values; Security; Activity; Achievement. **Skills Required:** Speaking; Information Gathering; Active Listening; Reading Comprehension; Writing; Idea Generation; Active Learning. **Abilities:** Speech Clarity. **Interacting with Others:** Assisting and Caring for Others; Performing for/Working with Public; Teaching Others. **Physical Work Conditions:** Indoors; Sitting; Hazardous Situations; Special Uniform; Standing; Using Hands on Objects, Tools, Controls.

29-9091.00 Athletic Trainers

Evaluate, advise, and treat athletes to assist in recovery from injury, avoid injury, or maintain peak physical fitness. **Education:** Long-term O-J-T. **Occupational Type:** Social. **Job Zone:** 5. **Average Salary:** $25,157. **Projected Growth:** 27.9%. **Occupational Values:** Social Service; Autonomy; Ability Utilization; Variety; Achievement; Working Conditions; Supervision, Human Relations. **Skills Required:** Active Listening; Problem Identification. **Abilities:** Oral Expression; Problem Sensitivity. **Interacting with Others:** Assisting and Caring for Others. **Physical Work Conditions:** Standing; Indoors; Using Hands on Objects, Tools, Controls; Kneeling, Crouching, or Crawling; Outdoors; Walking or Running.

Part 3

Crosswalks to Careers

by Work Values, Leisure Activities, Home Activities, School Subjects, Work Settings, Skills, Abilities, and Knowledges

We mentioned the importance of these Crosswalks in the table of contents' Quick Summary as well as in the introduction. You can use these Crosswalks to help you identify GOE Work Groups that you should consider. In some cases, using the Crosswalks will help you identify options you had overlooked. There are eight Crosswalks:

Work Values with Corresponding Work Groups

Leisure Activities with Corresponding Work Groups

Home Activities with Corresponding Work Groups

School Subjects with Corresponding Work Groups

Work Settings with Corresponding Work Groups

Skills with Corresponding Work Groups

Abilities with Corresponding Work Groups

Knowledges with Corresponding Work Groups

Using the Crosswalks

Look at the first Crosswalk, "Work Values with Corresponding Work Groups," to see how the Crosswalks work. You will see a Work Value in bold, followed by a list of Work Groups. Only the Work Groups that most frequently incorporate a particular Work Value are included. Look at each bold Work Value and identify three or four that you most want to include in your long-term career plan. List these Work Values on a sheet of paper. (This book will probably be used by other people, so please don't mark in it.) Next, look at the Work Group numbers and names listed for each Work Value. Write down the Work Group information for the Work Values you chose. You can then refer to Part 1 to learn more about the Work Groups you have listed.

Crosswalk A: Work Values with Corresponding Work Groups

Ability Utilization: Making use of your individual abilities

01.01 Managerial Work in Arts, Entertainment, and Media

01.02 Writing and Editing

01.03 News, Broadcasting, and Public Relations

01.04 Visual Arts

01.05 Performing Arts

01.08 Media Technology

01.10 Sports: Coaching, Instructing, Officiating, and Performing

02.02 Physical Sciences

02.03 Life Sciences

02.04 Social Sciences

02.06 Mathematics and Computers

02.07 Engineering

02.08 Engineering Technology

07.03 Air Vehicle Operation

14.02 Medicine and Surgery

14.03 Dentistry

14.04 Health Specialties

14.08 Health Protection and Promotion

Achievement: Getting a feeling of accomplishment

01.01 Managerial Work in Arts, Entertainment, and Media

01.02 Writing and Editing

01.03 News, Broadcasting, and Public Relations

01.04 Visual Arts

01.05 Performing Arts

01.06 Craft Arts

01.08 Media Technology

01.09 Modeling and Personal Appearance

01.10 Sports: Coaching, Instructing, Officiating, and Performing

02.04 Social Sciences

04.01 Managerial Work in Law, Law Enforcement, and Public Safety

04.03 Law Enforcement

04.04 Public Safety

04.05 Military

07.03 Air Vehicle Operation

10.03 General Sales

10.04 Personal Soliciting

12.02 Social Services

12.03 Educational Services

14.02 Medicine and Surgery

14.03 Dentistry

14.04 Health Specialties

14.06 Medical Therapy

14.08 Health Protection and Promotion

Activity: Being busy all the time

03.02 Animal Care and Training

03.03 Hands-on Work in Plants and Animals

05.04 Hands-on Work in Mechanics, Installers, and Repairers

06.04 Hands-on Work in Construction, Extraction, and Maintenance

08.02 Production Technology

08.03 Production Work

08.07 Hands-on Work: Loading, Moving, Hoisting, and Conveying

09.02 Administrative Detail

09.03 Bookkeeping, Auditing, and Accounting

11.05 Food and Beverage Services

11.06 Apparel, Shoes, Leather, and Fabric Care

11.07 Cleaning and Building Services

Authority: Giving directions and instructions to others

02.01 Managerial Work in Science, Math, and Engineering

04.01 Managerial Work in Law, Law Enforcement, and Public Safety

05.01 Managerial Work in Mechanics, Installers, and Repairers

06.01 Managerial Work in Construction, Mining, and Drilling

07.01 Managerial Work in Transportation

08.01 Managerial Work in Industrial Production

09.01 Managerial Work in Business Detail

10.01 Managerial Work in Sales and Marketing

11.01 Managerial Work in Recreation, Travel, and Other Personal Services

12.01 Managerial Work in Education and Social Service

13.01 General Management Work and Management of Support Functions

Autonomy: Planning your work with little supervision

01.01 Managerial Work in Arts, Entertainment, and Media

01.02 Writing and Editing

02.01 Managerial Work in Science, Math, and Engineering

02.02 Physical Sciences

02.03 Life Sciences

02.04 Social Sciences

02.06 Mathematics and Computers

02.07 Engineering

03.01 Managerial Work in Plants and Animals

04.02 Law

05.01 Managerial Work in Mechanics, Installers, and Repairers

06.01 Managerial Work in Construction, Mining, and Drilling

07.01 Managerial Work in Transportation

07.04 Water Vehicle Operation

08.01 Managerial Work in Industrial Production

09.01 Managerial Work in Business Detail

10.02 Sales Technology

10.03 General Sales

11.01 Managerial Work in Recreation, Travel, and Other Personal Services

11.04 Barber and Beauty Services

12.01 Managerial Work in Education and Social Service

12.02 Social Services

13.01 General Management Work and Management of Support Functions

14.01 Managerial Work in Medical and Health Services

Coworkers: Having coworkers who are easy to get along with

04.01 Managerial Work in Law, Law Enforcement, and Public Safety

11.03 Transportation and Lodging Services

11.05 Food and Beverage Services

14.06 Medical Therapy

Company Policies and Practices: Being treated fairly by the company

04.01 Managerial Work in Law, Law Enforcement, and Public Safety

04.03 Law Enforcement

04.04 Public Safety

04.05 Military

05.02 Electrical and Electronic Systems

05.03 Mechanical Work

06.03 Mining and Drilling

07.02 Vehicle Expediting and Coordinating

07.05 Truck Driving

07.06 Rail Vehicle Operation

07.08 Support Work in Transportation

08.02 Production Technology

08.06 Systems Operation

09.02 Administrative Detail

09.04 Material Control

13.02 Management Support

Compensation: Being paid well in comparison with other workers

07.03 Air Vehicle Operation

07.05 Truck Driving

Creativity: Trying out your own ideas

01.02 Writing and Editing

01.04 Visual Arts

01.09 Modeling and Personal Appearance

02.07 Engineering

10.01 Managerial Work in Sales and Marketing

Independence: Doing your work alone

01.06 Craft Arts

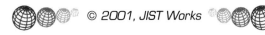

01.07 Graphic Arts

03.02 Animal Care and Training

03.03 Hands-on Work in Plants and Animals

05.03 Mechanical Work

06.02 Construction

07.05 Truck Driving

07.07 Other Services Requiring Driving

08.02 Production Technology

08.03 Production Work

08.05 Woodworking Technology

08.07 Hands-on Work: Loading, Moving, Hoisting, and Conveying

09.03 Bookkeeping, Auditing, and Accounting

09.06 Communications

09.08 Records and Materials Processing

09.09 Clerical Machine Operation

10.04 Personal Soliciting

11.06 Apparel, Shoes, Leather, and Fabric Care

11.07 Cleaning and Building Services

12.01 Managerial Work in Education and Social Service

Moral Values: Never being pressured to do things that go against your sense of right and wrong

01.05 Performing Arts

01.06 Craft Arts

01.07 Graphic Arts

01.08 Media Technology

01.09 Modeling and Personal Appearance

02.02 Physical Sciences

02.05 Laboratory Technology

02.08 Engineering Technology

03.01 Managerial Work in Plants and Animals

03.02 Animal Care and Training

03.03 Hands-on Work in Plants and Animals

05.02 Electrical and Electronic Systems

05.03 Mechanical Work

05.04 Hands-on Work in Mechanics, Installers, and Repairers

06.02 Construction

06.03 Mining and Drilling

06.04 Hands-on Work in Construction, Extraction, and Maintenance

07.02 Vehicle Expediting and Coordinating

07.03 Air Vehicle Operation

07.04 Water Vehicle Operation

07.06 Rail Vehicle Operation

07.07 Other Services Requiring Driving

07.08 Support Work in Transportation

08.02 Production Technology

08.03 Production Work

08.04 Metal and Plastics Machining Technology

08.05 Woodworking Technology

08.06 Systems Operation

08.07 Hands-on Work: Loading, Moving, Hoisting, and Conveying

09.04 Material Control

09.05 Customer Service

09.06 Communications

09.07 Records Processing

09.08 Records and Materials Processing

09.09 Clerical Machine Operation

10.03 General Sales

10.04 Personal Soliciting

11.02 Recreational Services

11.03 Transportation and Lodging Services

11.04 Barber and Beauty Services

11.05 Food and Beverage Services

11.06 Apparel, Shoes, Leather, and Fabric Care

11.07 Cleaning and Building Services

11.08 Other Personal Services

14.05 Medical Technology

14.07 Patient Care and Assistance

Recognition: Receiving recognition for the work you do

01.09 Modeling and Personal Appearance

01.10 Sports: Coaching, Instructing, Officiating, and Performing

Responsibility: Making decisions on your own

01.01 Managerial Work in Arts, Entertainment, and Media

02.02 Physical Sciences

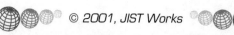

02.03 Life Sciences

03.01 Managerial Work in Plants and Animals

04.04 Public Safety

04.05 Military

05.01 Managerial Work in Mechanics, Installers, and Repairers

06.01 Managerial Work in Construction, Mining, and Drilling

07.01 Managerial Work in Transportation

08.01 Managerial Work in Industrial Production

11.01 Managerial Work in Recreation, Travel, and Other Personal Services

13.02 Management Support

Security: Having steady employment

02.05 Laboratory Technology

03.02 Animal Care and Training

04.02 Law

04.03 Law Enforcement

04.04 Public Safety

04.05 Military

05.02 Electrical and Electronic Systems

05.04 Hands-on Work in Mechanics, Installers, and Repairers

07.02 Vehicle Expediting and Coordinating

09.08 Records and Materials Processing

11.06 Apparel, Shoes, Leather, and Fabric Care

11.08 Other Personal Services

14.01 Managerial Work in Medical and Health Services

14.05 Medical Technology

14.07 Patient Care and Assistance

Social Service: Doing things for other people

07.07 Other Services Requiring Driving

11.02 Recreational Services

11.03 Transportation and Lodging Services

11.04 Barber and Beauty Services

11.07 Cleaning and Building Services

11.08 Other Personal Services

12.02 Social Services

12.03 Educational Services

14.02 Medicine and Surgery

14.03 Dentistry

14.04 Health Specialties

14.05 Medical Technology

14.06 Medical Therapy

14.07 Patient Care and Assistance

14.08 Health Protection and Promotion

Social Status: Being looked up to by others in your company and in your community

[No work group has a high average rating for this value.]

Supervision, Human Relations: Having supervisors who back you up with management

04.03 Law Enforcement

06.03 Mining and Drilling

07.02 Vehicle Expediting and Coordinating

07.06 Rail Vehicle Operation

07.07 Other Services Requiring Driving

07.08 Support Work in Transportation

08.04 Metal and Plastics Machining Technology

08.06 Systems Operation

08.07 Hands-on Work: Loading, Moving, Hoisting, and Conveying

09.04 Material Control

09.05 Customer Service

09.06 Communications

09.08 Records and Materials Processing

09.09 Clerical Machine Operation

11.03 Transportation and Lodging Services

Supervision, Technical: Having supervisors who train you well

05.04 Hands-on Work in Mechanics, Installers, and Repairers

07.08 Support Work in Transportation

Working Conditions: Having good working conditions

01.03 News, Broadcasting, and Public Relations

01.07 Graphic Arts

01.08 Media Technology

01.09 Modeling and Personal Appearance

02.01 Managerial Work in Science, Math, and Engineering

02.04 Social Sciences

02.06 Mathematics and Computers

04.02 Law

09.01 Managerial Work in Business Detail

09.02 Administrative Detail

09.03 Bookkeeping, Auditing, and Accounting

09.05 Customer Service

09.07 Records Processing

10.01 Managerial Work in Sales and Marketing

10.02 Sales Technology

10.03 General Sales

11.02 Recreational Services

12.03 Educational Services

13.01 General Management Work and Management of Support Functions

13.02 Management Support

Crosswalk B: Leisure Activities with Corresponding Work Groups

Acting in a play or amateur variety show

01.05 Performing Arts

01.09 Modeling and Personal Appearance

Addressing letters for an organization

09.01 Managerial Work in Business Detail

09.07 Records Processing

09.08 Records and Materials Processing

09.09 Clerical Machine Operation

Announcing or emceeing a program

01.03 News, Broadcasting, and Public Relations

11.02 Recreational Services

Applying first aid in emergencies as a volunteer

04.04 Public Safety

04.05 Military

14.01 Managerial Work in Medical and Health Services

14.02 Medicine and Surgery

14.03 Dentistry

14.04 Health Specialties

14.05 Medical Technology

14.06 Medical Therapy

14.07 Patient Care and Assistance

Applying makeup for amateur theater

01.09 Modeling and Personal Appearance

11.04 Barber and Beauty Services

Being a cheerleader

01.05 Performing Arts

01.09 Modeling and Personal Appearance

Being a member of the school safety patrol

04.03 Law Enforcement

04.04 Public Safety

04.05 Military

Belonging to a 4-H or garden club

03.01 Managerial Work in Plants and Animals

03.02 Animal Care and Training

03.03 Hands-on Work in Plants and Animals

Belonging to a computer club

01.07 Graphic Arts

01.08 Media Technology

02.02 Physical Sciences

02.06 Mathematics and Computers

02.07 Engineering

Belonging to a literary or book club

01.02 Writing and Editing

04.02 Law

Belonging to a political science club

02.04 Social Sciences

04.02 Law

Breeding animals

03.01 Managerial Work in Plants and Animals

03.02 Animal Care and Training

Building model airplanes, automobiles, or boats

05.01 Managerial Work in Mechanics, Installers, and Repairers

05.02 Electrical and Electronic Systems

05.03 Mechanical Work

05.04 Hands-on Work in Mechanics, Installers, and Repairers

06.03 Mining and Drilling

06.04 Hands-on Work in Construction, Extraction, and Maintenance

07.03 Air Vehicle Operation

07.04 Water Vehicle Operation

07.08 Support Work in Transportation

08.02 Production Technology

08.04 Metal and Plastics Machining Technology

08.05 Woodworking Technology

08.07 Hands-on Work: Loading, Moving, Hoisting, and Conveying

Buying large quantities of food or other products for an organization

09.04 Material Control

09.07 Records Processing

11.01 Managerial Work in Recreation, Travel, and Other Personal Services

13.02 Management Support

Campaigning for political candidates or issues

02.04 Social Sciences

04.02 Law

10.04 Personal Soliciting

14.08 Health Protection and Promotion

Camping, hiking, or engaging in other outdoor activities

03.03 Hands-on Work in Plants and Animals

07.04 Water Vehicle Operation

12.01 Managerial Work in Education and Social Service

Carving small wooden objects

01.06 Craft Arts

05.04 Hands-on Work in Mechanics, Installers, and Repairers

08.05 Woodworking Technology

08.07 Hands-on Work: Loading, Moving, Hoisting, and Conveying

14.03 Dentistry

Chauffeuring special groups such as children, older people, or people with disabilities

07.01 Managerial Work in Transportation

07.07 Other Services Requiring Driving

11.02 Recreational Services

11.03 Transportation and Lodging Services

11.08 Other Personal Services

14.06 Medical Therapy

14.07 Patient Care and Assistance

Coaching children or youth in sports activities

01.10 Sports: Coaching, Instructing, Officiating, and Performing

12.02 Social Services

Collecting and arranging stamps or coins

09.02 Administrative Detail

09.04 Material Control

09.05 Customer Service

09.07 Records Processing

Conducting experiments involving plants

02.01 Managerial Work in Science, Math, and Engineering

02.03 Life Sciences

02.05 Laboratory Technology

10.02 Sales Technology

Conducting house-to-house or telephone surveys for a PTA or other organization

02.04 Social Sciences

09.01 Managerial Work in Business Detail

09.05 Customer Service

10.01 Managerial Work in Sales and Marketing

10.04 Personal Soliciting

Constructing stage sets for school or other amateur theater

06.01 Managerial Work in Construction, Mining, and Drilling

06.02 Construction

06.04 Hands-on Work in Construction, Extraction, and Maintenance

Cooking large quantities of food for community events

08.03 Production Work

11.05 Food and Beverage Services

Creating a Web page for an organization

02.06 Mathematics and Computers

Creating dance steps for school or other amateur musicals

01.05 Performing Arts

Creating or styling hairdos for friends

01.09 Modeling and Personal Appearance

11.04 Barber and Beauty Services

Creating unusual lighting effects for school or other amateur plays

01.08 Media Technology

05.02 Electrical and Electronic Systems

Designing and making costumes for school plays, festivals, and other events

01.04 Visual Arts

01.06 Craft Arts

11.06 Apparel, Shoes, Leather, and Fabric Care

Designing stage sets for school or other amateur theater

01.01 Managerial Work in Arts, Entertainment, and Media

01.04 Visual Arts

06.02 Construction

Designing your own greeting cards and writing original verses

01.01 Managerial Work in Arts, Entertainment, and Media

01.02 Writing and Editing

Developing film

01.07 Graphic Arts

01.08 Media Technology

02.05 Laboratory Technology

Developing publicity fliers for a school or community event

01.01 Managerial Work in Arts, Entertainment, and Media

01.03 News, Broadcasting, and Public Relations

01.07 Graphic Arts

10.01 Managerial Work in Sales and Marketing

10.04 Personal Soliciting

14.08 Health Protection and Promotion

Directing school or other amateur plays or musicals

01.05 Performing Arts

Directing traffic at community events

04.01 Managerial Work in Law, Law Enforcement, and Public Safety

04.03 Law Enforcement

04.04 Public Safety

04.05 Military

07.02 Vehicle Expediting and Coordinating

07.07 Other Services Requiring Driving

Doing crossword puzzles

01.02 Writing and Editing

Doing desktop publishing for a school or community publication

01.02 Writing and Editing

01.03 News, Broadcasting, and Public Relations

01.07 Graphic Arts

08.03 Production Work

09.02 Administrative Detail

09.08 Records and Materials Processing

09.09 Clerical Machine Operation

Doing impersonations

01.05 Performing Arts

Doing needlework

01.06 Craft Arts

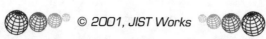

01.09 Modeling and Personal Appearance

11.06 Apparel, Shoes, Leather, and Fabric Care

14.03 Dentistry

Doing public speaking or debating

04.02 Law

09.06 Communications

10.02 Sales Technology

10.04 Personal Soliciting

12.03 Educational Services

14.08 Health Protection and Promotion

Doing volunteer work for the Red Cross

11.08 Other Personal Services

14.01 Managerial Work in Medical and Health Services

14.02 Medicine and Surgery

14.03 Dentistry

14.04 Health Specialties

14.05 Medical Technology

14.06 Medical Therapy

14.08 Health Protection and Promotion

Drawing posters for an organization or political campaign

01.01 Managerial Work in Arts, Entertainment, and Media

01.04 Visual Arts

Driving a bus as a volunteer for an organization

06.03 Mining and Drilling

07.01 Managerial Work in Transportation

07.02 Vehicle Expediting and Coordinating

07.04 Water Vehicle Operation

07.05 Truck Driving

07.06 Rail Vehicle Operation

07.07 Other Services Requiring Driving

Driving an ambulance as a volunteer

07.01 Managerial Work in Transportation

07.02 Vehicle Expediting and Coordinating

07.05 Truck Driving

07.06 Rail Vehicle Operation

07.07 Other Services Requiring Driving

14.07 Patient Care and Assistance

Editing or proofreading a school or organizational newspaper, yearbook, or magazine

01.01 Managerial Work in Arts, Entertainment, and Media

01.02 Writing and Editing

Entertaining at parties or other events

01.05 Performing Arts

Experimenting with a chemistry set

02.01 Managerial Work in Science, Math, and Engineering

02.02 Physical Sciences

02.03 Life Sciences

02.05 Laboratory Technology

02.07 Engineering

14.05 Medical Technology

Gardening

03.03 Hands-on Work in Plants and Animals

Handling equipment for a local athletic team

01.10 Sports: Coaching, Instructing, Officiating, and Performing

08.07 Hands-on Work: Loading, Moving, Hoisting, and Conveying

Helping conduct physical exercises for people with disabilities

11.08 Other Personal Services

14.04 Health Specialties

14.06 Medical Therapy

14.07 Patient Care and Assistance

Helping friends and relatives with their tax reports

09.03 Bookkeeping, Auditing, and Accounting

Helping in the school library or other library

09.05 Customer Service

12.03 Educational Services

Helping people with disabilities take walks

11.08 Other Personal Services

12.02 Social Services

14.04 Health Specialties

14.06 Medical Therapy

14.07 Patient Care and Assistance

Helping persuade people to sign petitions for a PTA or other organization

04.02 Law

10.01 Managerial Work in Sales and Marketing

10.02 Sales Technology

10.03 General Sales

10.04 Personal Soliciting

14.08 Health Protection and Promotion

Helping run a school or community fair or carnival

02.01 Managerial Work in Science, Math, and Engineering

09.01 Managerial Work in Business Detail

10.03 General Sales

11.02 Recreational Services

13.01 General Management Work and Management of Support Functions

14.01 Managerial Work in Medical and Health Services

Hunting or target shooting

04.03 Law Enforcement

04.04 Public Safety

04.05 Military

Illustrating the school yearbook

01.04 Visual Arts

01.07 Graphic Arts

Keeping score for athletic events

01.10 Sports: Coaching, Instructing, Officiating, and Performing

09.04 Material Control

Keying in text for a school or community publication

09.02 Administrative Detail

09.04 Material Control

09.08 Records and Materials Processing

09.09 Clerical Machine Operation

Making belts or other leather articles

11.06 Apparel, Shoes, Leather, and Fabric Care

Making ceramic objects

01.06 Craft Arts

Making sketches of machines or other mechanical equipment

05.03 Mechanical Work

06.03 Mining and Drilling

08.01 Managerial Work in Industrial Production

08.02 Production Technology

08.03 Production Work

08.04 Metal and Plastics Machining Technology

08.06 Systems Operation

Modeling clothes for a fashion show

01.09 Modeling and Personal Appearance

Operating a calculator or adding machine for an organization

09.03 Bookkeeping, Auditing, and Accounting

09.04 Material Control

09.08 Records and Materials Processing

09.09 Clerical Machine Operation

Operating a CB or ham radio

01.08 Media Technology

02.08 Engineering Technology

05.02 Electrical and Electronic Systems

07.03 Air Vehicle Operation

07.04 Water Vehicle Operation

07.08 Support Work in Transportation

09.06 Communications

Operating a model train layout

05.03 Mechanical Work

06.04 Hands-on Work in Construction, Extraction, and Maintenance

07.01 Managerial Work in Transportation

07.02 Vehicle Expediting and Coordinating

07.06 Rail Vehicle Operation

07.08 Support Work in Transportation

08.02 Production Technology

08.07 Hands-on Work: Loading, Moving, Hoisting, and Conveying

Operating a motor boat or other pleasure boat

07.01 Managerial Work in Transportation

07.04 Water Vehicle Operation

Painting landscapes, seascapes, or portraits

01.04 Visual Arts

Participating in gymnastics

01.10 Sports: Coaching, Instructing, Officiating, and Performing

Performing experiments for a science fair

02.02 Physical Sciences

02.03 Life Sciences

02.05 Laboratory Technology

02.06 Mathematics and Computers

02.07 Engineering

02.08 Engineering Technology

10.02 Sales Technology

14.05 Medical Technology

Performing magic tricks for friends

01.05 Performing Arts

Planning advertisements for a school or community newspaper

01.02 Writing and Editing

01.03 News, Broadcasting, and Public Relations

10.01 Managerial Work

Planning and arranging programs for school or community organizations

01.01 Managerial Work in Sales and Marketing

01.05 Performing Arts

12.01 Managerial Work in Education and Social Service

13.01 General Management Work and Management of Support Functions

Playing a musical instrument

01.05 Performing Arts

Playing baseball, basketball, football, or other sports

01.10 Sports: Coaching, Instructing, Officiating, and Performing

Posing for an artist or photographer

01.09 Modeling and Personal Appearance

Programming computer games

02.06 Mathematics and Computers

Racing midget or stock cars

01.10 Sports: Coaching, Instructing, Officiating, and Performing

07.03 Air Vehicle Operation

07.05 Truck Driving

07.07 Other Services Requiring Driving

Raising or caring for animals

03.01 Managerial Work in Plants and Animals

03.02 Animal Care and Training

Reading about technological developments such as computer science or aerospace

02.01 Managerial Work in Science, Math, and Engineering

02.02 Physical Sciences

02.05 Laboratory Technology

02.06 Mathematics and Computers

02.07 Engineering

02.08 Engineering Technology

08.06 Systems Operation

Reading airplane or boat magazines

05.03 Mechanical Work

07.01 Managerial Work in Transportation

07.02 Vehicle Expediting and Coordinating

07.03 Air Vehicle Operation

07.04 Water Vehicle Operation

07.08 Support Work in Transportation

Reading business magazines and newspapers

02.04 Social Sciences

09.02 Administrative Detail

10.01 Managerial Work in Sales and Marketing

10.02 Sales Technology

13.01 General Management Work and Management of Support Functions

13.02 Management Support

Reading detective stories and watching television detective shows

04.01 Managerial Work in Law, Law Enforcement, and Public Safety

04.03 Law Enforcement

04.04 Public Safety

Reading farm magazines

03.02 Animal Care and Training

Reading mechanical or automotive magazines

05.01 Managerial Work in Mechanics, Installers, and Repairers

05.03 Mechanical Work

06.03 Mining and Drilling

07.06 Rail Vehicle Operation

08.01 Managerial Work in Industrial Production

08.07 Hands-on Work: Loading, Moving, Hoisting, and Conveying

Reading medical or scientific magazines

02.02 Physical Sciences

02.03 Life Sciences

02.05 Laboratory Technology

02.07 Engineering

02.08 Engineering Technology

14.01 Managerial Work in Medical and Health Services

14.02 Medicine and Surgery

14.03 Dentistry

14.04 Health Specialties

14.05 Medical Technology

14.08 Health Protection and Promotion

Reading military stories and watching television shows and movies about the military

04.05 Military

Recruiting members for a club or other organization

09.06 Communications

10.03 General Sales

10.04 Personal Soliciting

Repairing or assembling bicycles or tricycles

05.03 Mechanical Work

05.04 Hands-on Work in Mechanics, Installers, and Repairers

07.08 Support Work in Transportation

08.01 Managerial Work in Industrial Production

08.04 Metal and Plastics Machining Technology

Selling advertising space in a school yearbook, newspaper, or magazine

10.01 Managerial Work in Sales and Marketing

10.02 Sales Technology

Serving as a leader of a scouting or other group

05.01 Managerial Work in Mechanics, Installers, and Repairers

06.01 Managerial Work in Construction, Mining, and Drilling

07.01 Managerial Work in Transportation

08.01 Managerial Work in Industrial Production

09.01 Managerial Work in Business Detail

10.01 Managerial Work in Sales and Marketing

11.01 Managerial Work in Recreation, Travel, and Other Personal Services

12.01 Managerial Work in Education and Social Service

12.02 Social Services

13.01 General Management Work and Management of Support Functions

Serving as a salesperson or clerk in a store run by a charity organization

09.05 Customer Service

10.03 General Sales

11.03 Transportation and Lodging Services

Serving as a volunteer aide in a hospital, nursing home, or retirement home

11.08 Other Personal Services

12.02 Social Services

14.01 Managerial Work in Medical and Health Services

14.02 Medicine and Surgery

14.03 Dentistry

14.04 Health Specialties

14.05 Medical Technology

Serving as a volunteer counselor at a youth camp or center

04.04 Public Safety

11.02 Recreational Services

12.02 Social Services

Serving as a volunteer in a fire department or emergency rescue squad

04.01 Managerial Work in Law, Law Enforcement, and Public Safety

04.03 Law Enforcement

04.04 Public Safety

04.05 Military

14.07 Patient Care and Assistance

Serving as a volunteer interviewer in a social service organization

09.05 Customer Service

09.06 Communications

13.02 Management Support

Serving as president of a club or other organization

02.01 Managerial Work in Science, Math, and Engineering

03.01 Managerial Work in Plants and Animals

04.01 Managerial Work in Law, Law Enforcement, and Public Safety

04.02 Law

09.02 Administrative Detail

13.01 General Management Work and Management of Support Functions

Serving as secretary of a club or other organization

09.02 Administrative Detail

Serving as treasurer of a club or other organization

09.03 Bookkeeping, Auditing, and Accounting

13.01 General Management Work and Management of Support Functions

13.02 Management Support

Setting tables for club or organizational functions

11.03 Transportation and Lodging Services

11.05 Food and Beverage Services

Singing in a choir or other group

01.05 Performing Arts

Soliciting clothes, food, and other supplies for needy people

10.03 General Sales

10.04 Personal Soliciting

Soliciting funds for community organizations

10.01 Managerial Work in Sales and Marketing

10.04 Personal Soliciting

Speaking on radio or television

01.03 News, Broadcasting, and Public Relations

09.06 Communications

Studying plants in gardens, parks, or forests

02.03 Life Sciences

02.05 Laboratory Technology

03.01 Managerial Work in Plants and Animals

Studying the habits of wildlife

02.03 Life Sciences

Taking ballet or other dancing lessons

01.05 Performing Arts

Taking lessons in singing or in playing a musical instrument

01.05 Performing Arts

Taking photographs

01.04 Visual Arts

01.07 Graphic Arts

01.08 Media Technology

Teaching dancing as a volunteer in an after-school center

01.05 Performing Arts

Teaching games to children as a volunteer aide in a nursery school

12.01 Managerial Work in Education and Social Service

12.03 Educational Services

Teaching immigrants or other individuals to speak, write, or read English

01.03 News, Broadcasting, and Public Relations

12.01 Managerial Work in Education and Social Service

12.03 Educational Services

Teaching in a religious school

12.02 Social Services

Training dogs or other animals to perform on command

03.02 Animal Care and Training

Tutoring pupils in school subjects

12.03 Educational Services

Umpiring or refereeing amateur sporting events

01.10 Sports: Coaching, Instructing, Officiating, and Performing

Ushering for school or community events

11.01 Managerial Work in Recreation, Travel, and Other Personal Services

11.02 Recreational Services

Using a pocket calculator or spreadsheet to figure out income and expenses for an organization

02.01 Managerial Work in Science, Math, and Engineering

09.01 Managerial Work in Business Detail

09.03 Bookkeeping, Auditing, and Accounting

09.08 Records and Materials Processing

09.09 Clerical Machine Operation

10.03 General Sales

13.02 Management Support

Visiting museums or historic sites

02.04 Social Sciences

Waiting on tables at club or organizational functions

11.05 Food and Beverage Services

Weaving rugs or making quilts

01.06 Craft Arts

11.06 Apparel, Shoes, Leather, and Fabric Care

Writing articles, stories, or plays

01.01 Managerial Work in Arts, Entertainment, and Media

01.02 Writing and Editing

01.03 News, Broadcasting, and Public Relations

04.02 Law

Writing songs for club socials or amateur plays

01.05 Performing Arts

Crosswalk C: Home Activities with Corresponding Work Groups

Advising family members on their personal problems

04.02 Law

14.02 Medicine and Surgery

Babysitting for younger children

11.08 Other Personal Services

12.02 Social Services

Baking and decorating cakes

11.05 Food and Beverage Services

Balancing checkbooks for family members

09.01 Managerial Work in Business Detail

09.03 Bookkeeping, Auditing, and Accounting

09.04 Material Control

13.01 General Management Work and Management of Support Functions

13.02 Management Support

Budgeting the family income

02.01 Managerial Work in Science, Math, and Engineering

02.06 Mathematics and Computers

09.01 Managerial Work in Business Detail

09.03 Bookkeeping, Auditing, and Accounting

11.01 Managerial Work in Recreation, Travel, and Other Personal Services

13.01 General Management Work and Management of Support Functions

13.02 Management Support

14.01 Managerial Work in Medical and Health Services

Building cabinets or furniture

05.01 Managerial Work in Mechanics, Installers, and Repairers

05.04 Hands-on Work in Mechanics, Installers, and Repairers

06.01 Managerial Work in Construction, Mining, and Drilling

06.02 Construction

06.04 Hands-on Work in Construction, Extraction, and Maintenance

08.01 Managerial Work in Industrial Production

08.05 Woodworking Technology

Building or repairing radios or television sets

01.08 Media Technology

02.08 Engineering Technology

05.01 Managerial Work in Mechanics, Installers, and Repairers

05.02 Electrical and Electronic Systems

05.04 Hands-on Work in Mechanics, Installers, and Repairers

Canning and preserving food

08.03 Production Work

11.05 Food and Beverage Services

Collecting rocks or minerals

02.02 Physical Sciences

06.01 Managerial Work in Construction, Mining, and Drilling

06.03 Mining and Drilling

Cutting and trimming hair for other members of the family

11.04 Barber and Beauty Services

Designing and building an addition or remodeling the interior of a home

02.07 Engineering

05.01 Managerial Work in Mechanics, Installers, and Repairers

06.01 Managerial Work in Construction, Mining, and Drilling

06.02 Construction

06.04 Hands-on Work in Construction, Extraction, and Maintenance

08.05 Woodworking Technology

Designing and landscaping a flower garden

03.01 Managerial Work in Plants and Animals

Doing electrical wiring and repairs in the home

02.08 Engineering Technology

05.01 Managerial Work in Mechanics, Installers, and Repairers

05.02 Electrical and Electronic Systems

05.04 Hands-on Work in Mechanics, Installers, and Repairers

06.01 Managerial Work in Construction, Mining, and Drilling

06.02 Construction

08.06 Systems Operation

Driving a truck and tractor to harvest crops on a family farm

03.03 Hands-on Work in Plants and Animals

07.05 Truck Driving

Helping members of the family with their English lessons

12.01 Managerial Work in Education and Social Service

12.03 Educational Services

Installing and repairing home stereo equipment

02.07 Engineering

02.08 Engineering Technology

05.01 Managerial Work in Mechanics, Installers, and Repairers

05.02 Electrical and Electronic Systems

14.05 Medical Technology

Instructing family members in observing traffic regulations

04.01 Managerial Work in Law, Law Enforcement, and Public Safety

04.03 Law Enforcement

04.04 Public Safety

04.05 Military

07.05 Truck Driving

07.07 Other Services Requiring Driving

12.01 Managerial Work in Education and Social Service

12.03 Educational Services

Making videos of family activities

01.01 Managerial Work in Arts, Entertainment, and Media

01.08 Media Technology

Mixing drinks for family or friends

11.03 Transportation and Lodging Services

11.05 Food and Beverage Services

Mounting and framing pictures

01.06 Craft Arts

Mowing the lawn with a riding lawnmower

03.03 Hands-on Work in Plants and Animals

06.03 Mining and Drilling

Nursing sick pets

02.03 Life Sciences

03.02 Animal Care and Training

Nursing sick relatives and friends

11.08 Other Personal Services

14.01 Managerial Work in Medical and Health Services

14.02 Medicine and Surgery

14.03 Dentistry

14.04 Health Specialties

14.05 Medical Technology

14.06 Medical Therapy

14.07 Patient Care and Assistance

Painting the interior or exterior of a home

06.02 Construction

06.04 Hands-on Work in Construction, Extraction, and Maintenance

Planning and cooking meals

11.05 Food and Beverage Services

14.08 Health Protection and Promotion

Planning family recreational activities

07.02 Vehicle Expediting and Coordinating

11.01 Managerial Work in Recreation, Travel, and Other Personal Services

11.02 Recreational Services

11.03 Transportation and Lodging Services

Preparing family income tax returns

09.03 Bookkeeping, Auditing, and Accounting

Raising vegetables in a home garden

03.01 Managerial Work in Plants and Animals

03.03 Hands-on Work in Plants and Animals

Refinishing or reupholstering furniture

08.05 Woodworking Technology

11.06 Apparel, Shoes, Leather, and Fabric Care

Repairing electrical household appliances

05.04 Hands-on Work in Mechanics, Installers, and Repairers

08.06 Systems Operation

Repairing plumbing in the home

05.03 Mechanical Work

06.01 Managerial Work in Construction, Mining, and Drilling

06.02 Construction

06.04 Hands-on Work in Construction, Extraction, and Maintenance

08.04 Metal and Plastics Machining Technology

08.06 Systems Operation

Repairing the family car

07.05 Truck Driving

08.02 Production Technology

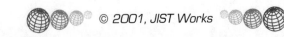

08.03 Production Work

Serving as a host or hostess for house guests

11.01 Managerial Work in Recreation, Travel, and Other Personal Services

11.02 Recreational Services

11.03 Transportation and Lodging Services

11.07 Cleaning and Building Services

11.08 Other Personal Services

Setting the table and serving family meals

11.01 Managerial Work in Recreation, Travel, and Other Personal Services

11.05 Food and Beverage Services

Trimming shrubs and hedges

03.03 Hands-on Work in Plants and Animals

Upgrading hardware in a personal computer

02.06 Mathematics and Computers

02.07 Engineering

05.02 Electrical and Electronic Systems

Washing and waxing the family car

11.07 Cleaning and Building Services

Crosswalk D: School Subjects with Corresponding Work Groups

Abnormal Psychology

12.02 Social Services

Abstract Writing

01.02 Writing and Editing

01.03 News, Broadcasting, and Public Relations

Accounting

01.01 Managerial Work in Arts, Entertainment, and Media

02.01 Managerial Work in Science, Math, and Engineering

04.01 Managerial Work in Law, Law Enforcement, and Public Safety

06.01 Managerial Work in Construction, Mining, and Drilling

07.01 Managerial Work in Transportation

08.01 Managerial Work in Industrial Production

09.02 Administrative Detail

09.03 Bookkeeping, Auditing, and Accounting

10.01 Managerial Work in Sales and Marketing

11.01 Managerial Work in Recreation, Travel, and Other Personal Services

12.01 Managerial Work in Education and Social Service

13.01 General Management Work and Management of Support Functions

13.02 Management Support

14.01 Managerial Work in Medical and Health Services

Acoustics

01.08 Media Technology

Acting Techniques

01.09 Modeling and Personal Appearance

Advertising

10.01 Managerial Work in Sales and Marketing

10.02 Sales Technology

10.03 General Sales

10.04 Personal Soliciting

Advertising Art/Production

01.07 Graphic Arts

01.08 Media Technology

10.02 Sales Technology

Aeronautical Charts

07.03 Air Vehicle Operation

Agribusiness

03.01 Managerial Work in Plants and Animals

Agricultural Systems

03.01 Managerial Work in Plants and Animals

Agriculture, Mechanized

03.01 Managerial Work in Plants and Animals

03.03 Hands-on Work in Plants and Animals

Agronomy

03.03 Hands-on Work in Plants and Animals

Aircraft Mechanics

05.03 Mechanical Work

Airport Safety

07.01 Managerial Work in Transportation

07.02 Vehicle Expediting and Coordinating

07.08 Support Work in Transportation

Anatomy

14.03 Dentistry

14.04 Health Specialties

14.05 Medical Technology

14.06 Medical Therapy

Anatomy, Specialized/Advanced

14.02 Medicine and Surgery

Anesthesia

14.02 Medicine and Surgery

14.03 Dentistry

14.04 Health Specialties

Animal Breeding

03.01 Managerial Work in Plants and Animals

Animal Grooming

03.01 Managerial Work in Plants and Animals

Animal Obedience Training

03.02 Animal Care and Training

Animal Science

03.01 Managerial Work in Plants and Animals

Arbitration/Negotiation

04.02 Law

13.01 General Management Work and Management of Support Functions

Archeology

02.04 Social Sciences

Architectural Drafting

02.08 Engineering Technology

Architectural History

02.07 Engineering

Art

01.04 Visual Arts

01.08 Media Technology

Arts and Crafts

01.04 Visual Arts

01.06 Craft Arts

01.07 Graphic Arts

Astronomy

02.02 Physical Sciences

Auditing Procedures

13.02 Management Support

Auditory Development

14.05 Medical Technology

Auto Body Repair/Shop

05.03 Mechanical Work

Auto Mechanics

05.03 Mechanical Work

Baking

11.05 Food and Beverage Services

Band

01.05 Performing Arts

Biochemistry

02.03 Life Sciences

Biology

02.01 Managerial Work in Science, Math, and Engineering

02.03 Life Sciences

02.05 Laboratory Technology

03.02 Animal Care and Training

12.03 Educational Services

14.02 Medicine and Surgery

14.03 Dentistry

Biostatistics and Epidemiology

14.08 Health Protection and Promotion

Blueprint/Schematic Reading

05.01 Managerial Work in Mechanics, Installers, and Repairers

05.02 Electrical and Electronic Systems

05.03 Mechanical Work

06.02 Construction

08.04 Metal and Plastics Machining Technology

08.05 Woodworking Technology

Bookbinding

08.02 Production Technology

11.06 Apparel, Shoes, Leather, and Fabric Care

Bookkeeping

09.03 Bookkeeping, Auditing, and Accounting

09.07 Records Processing

11.01 Managerial Work in Recreation, Travel, and Other Personal Services

Botany

02.03 Life Sciences

03.01 Managerial Work in Plants and Animals

Bricklaying

06.02 Construction

06.04 Hands-on Work in Construction, Extraction, and Maintenance

Broadcast Journalism

01.03 News, Broadcasting, and Public Relations

Business Analysis

09.01 Managerial Work in Business Detail

13.01 General Management Work and Management of Support Functions

13.02 Management Support

Business Computer Applications

09.01 Managerial Work in Business Detail

09.03 Bookkeeping, Auditing, and Accounting

09.04 Material Control

Business Law

01.01 Managerial Work in Arts, Entertainment, and Media

09.02 Administrative Detail

10.02 Sales Technology

13.01 General Management Work and Management of Support Functions

13.02 Management Support

Business Machine Operating

09.05 Customer Service

09.08 Records and Materials Processing

09.09 Clerical Machine Operation

Business Machine Repair

05.02 Electrical and Electronic Systems

Business Math

09.01 Managerial Work in Business Detail

09.02 Administrative Detail

09.04 Material Control

09.05 Customer Service

09.06 Communications

09.07 Records Processing

09.08 Records and Materials Processing

09.09 Clerical Machine Operation

10.02 Sales Technology

10.03 General Sales

10.04 Personal Soliciting

11.01 Managerial Work in Recreation, Travel, and Other Personal Services

Business Organization

09.01 Managerial Work in Business Detail

13.01 General Management Work and Management of Support Functions

13.02 Management Support

14.01 Managerial Work in Medical and Health Services

Business Writing

09.02 Administrative Detail

10.01 Managerial Work in Sales and Marketing

13.01 General Management Work and Management of Support Functions

13.02 Management Support

Cabinetmaking

08.05 Woodworking Technology

Cake Decorating

11.05 Food and Beverage Services

Calculating Machine Operating

09.03 Bookkeeping, Auditing, and Accounting

09.08 Records and Materials Processing

09.09 Clerical Machine Operation

Calculus

02.02 Physical Sciences

02.07 Engineering

Carpentry

06.02 Construction

06.04 Hands-on Work in Construction, Extraction, and Maintenance

Cashiering

10.03 General Sales

Ceramics

01.04 Visual Arts

Chemical Safety

02.05 Laboratory Technology

Chemistry

02.05 Laboratory Technology

Chemistry, Advanced/Specialized

02.02 Physical Sciences

Child Development/Care

11.08 Other Personal Services

12.03 Educational Services

14.03 Dentistry

Choir/Chorus

01.05 Performing Arts

Cinematography

01.01 Managerial Work in Arts, Entertainment, and Media

Clerical Practices/Office Practices

09.01 Managerial Work in Business Detail

09.02 Administrative Detail

09.03 Bookkeeping, Auditing, and Accounting

09.04 Material Control

09.05 Customer Service

09.06 Communications

09.07 Records Processing

Clothing

01.09 Modeling and Personal Appearance

11.06 Apparel, Shoes, Leather, and Fabric Care

Coaching

01.10 Sports: Coaching, Instructing, Officiating, and Performing

Commercial Art

01.06 Craft Arts

01.07 Graphic Arts

Computer Concept/Methods

01.07 Graphic Arts

01.08 Media Technology

02.06 Mathematics and Computers

Computer Graphics

01.04 Visual Arts

01.07 Graphic Arts

01.08 Media Technology

Computer Network Management

02.06 Mathematics and Computers

Computer Programming

02.06 Mathematics and Computers

Computer Science

02.07 Engineering

Computerized Drafting and Design

02.08 Engineering Technology

Construction Shop

06.02 Construction

06.04 Hands-on Work in Construction, Extraction, and Maintenance

Construction Technology

06.01 Managerial Work in Construction, Mining, and Drilling

Consumer Behavior

10.01 Managerial Work in Sales and Marketing

10.02 Sales Technology

10.03 General Sales

10.04 Personal Soliciting

11.01 Managerial Work in Recreation, Travel, and Other Personal Services

Contract Law

01.01 Managerial Work in Arts, Entertainment, and Media

Cookery, Quantity

11.05 Food and Beverage Services

Cooking

11.05 Food and Beverage Services

11.08 Other Personal Services

Copy Writing

01.02 Writing and Editing

10.04 Personal Soliciting

Cosmetology

01.09 Modeling and Personal Appearance

11.04 Barber and Beauty Services

Costuming

01.09 Modeling and Personal Appearance

11.06 Apparel, Shoes, Leather, and Fabric Care

Crafts Shop

01.06 Craft Arts

Creative Writing

01.01 Managerial Work in Arts, Entertainment, and Media

01.02 Writing and Editing

Criminal Investigating

04.03 Law Enforcement

Criminology

04.03 Law Enforcement

Culinary Arts

11.05 Food and Beverage Services

Customs Law

04.03 Law Enforcement

Dairy Science/Technology

03.01 Managerial Work in Plants and Animals

Dance

01.05 Performing Arts

Data Applications

09.09 Clerical Machine Operation

13.02 Management Support

Data Entry

09.08 Records and Materials Processing

09.09 Clerical Machine Operation

Data Retrieval Techniques

02.06 Mathematics and Computers

Database Theory/Design

02.06 Mathematics and Computers

Dental Anatomy

14.03 Dentistry

Design Graphics

01.06 Craft Arts

01.07 Graphic Arts

Design Media
01.06 Craft Arts
01.07 Graphic Arts

Diesel Mechanics/Diesels
05.03 Mechanical Work
07.04 Water Vehicle Operation
07.05 Truck Driving
07.06 Rail Vehicle Operation
08.06 Systems Operation

Diet and Therapy
14.08 Health Protection and Promotion

Directing
01.05 Performing Arts

Drafting
02.08 Engineering Technology

Drama
01.05 Performing Arts
01.09 Modeling and Personal Appearance

Driver Education
07.05 Truck Driving
07.07 Other Services Requiring Driving
11.08 Other Personal Services

Earth Science
06.03 Mining and Drilling

Ecology/Environmental Science
02.02 Physical Sciences

Economics
01.03 News, Broadcasting, and Public Relations
02.04 Social Sciences

Editing
01.01 Managerial Work in Arts, Entertainment, and Media
01.02 Writing and Editing
01.03 News, Broadcasting, and Public Relations

Education
12.01 Managerial Work in Education and Social Service
12.03 Educational Services

Educational Psychology
12.01 Managerial Work in Education and Social Service

Electric/Electronic Shop
05.02 Electrical and Electronic Systems

Electric/Electronic Theory
02.08 Engineering Technology
05.02 Electrical and Electronic Systems

Electrical Circuits
05.02 Electrical and Electronic Systems

Electrical Systems
05.02 Electrical and Electronic Systems

Electricity/Electronics
01.08 Media Technology
05.02 Electrical and Electronic Systems

Electronic Devices
05.02 Electrical and Electronic Systems

Emergency Care/Rescue
04.04 Public Safety
07.07 Other Services Requiring Driving

Engine Mechanics
07.04 Water Vehicle Operation
07.06 Rail Vehicle Operation
08.06 Systems Operation

Farm and Ranch Management
03.01 Managerial Work in Plants and Animals
03.02 Animal Care and Training

Fashion Illustration
01.04 Visual Arts
01.09 Modeling and Personal Appearance

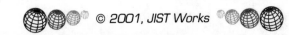

Fiction Writing
01.02 Writing and Editing

Finance

13.01 General Management Work and Management of Support Functions

Financial Information Systems

09.03 Bookkeeping, Auditing, and Accounting

Fire Fighting

04.01 Managerial Work in Law, Law Enforcement, and Public Safety

04.04 Public Safety

Fire Safety

04.04 Public Safety

First Aid

04.04 Public Safety

04.05 Military

Flight Safety

07.03 Air Vehicle Operation

11.03 Transportation and Lodging Services

Flight Training/Pilot Training

07.03 Air Vehicle Operation

Floral Arranging

01.04 Visual Arts

Food and Fiber Crops

03.03 Hands-on Work in Plants and Animals

Food Preparation/Service

11.05 Food and Beverage Services

Food Science

02.03 Life Sciences

Foreign Languages

12.03 Educational Services

Forestry

03.03 Hands-on Work in Plants and Animals

Genetics

02.03 Life Sciences

Geographic Information Systems

02.06 Mathematics and Computers

Geography

02.02 Physical Sciences

Geology

06.01 Managerial Work in Construction, Mining, and Drilling

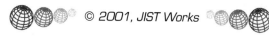

Geology, Specialized/Advanced

02.02 Physical Sciences

Government

04.01 Managerial Work in Law, Law Enforcement, and Public Safety

Grammar

01.02 Writing and Editing

01.03 News, Broadcasting, and Public Relations

04.02 Law

Graphic Arts

01.06 Craft Arts

01.07 Graphic Arts

Guidance

12.02 Social Services

12.03 Educational Services

Health

14.01 Managerial Work in Medical and Health Services

14.02 Medicine and Surgery

14.03 Dentistry

14.04 Health Specialties

14.05 Medical Technology

14.06 Medical Therapy

14.07 Patient Care and Assistance

14.08 Health Protection and Promotion

Health Law

14.01 Managerial Work in Medical and Health Services

14.08 Health Protection and Promotion

Heavy Equipment Operating

06.02 Construction

06.03 Mining and Drilling

Hematology

14.05 Medical Technology

History

02.04 Social Sciences

04.05 Military

Home Management

11.07 Cleaning and Building Services

11.08 Other Personal Services

Home/Consumer Economics

11.08 Other Personal Services

Horseshoeing

03.02 Animal Care and Training

Horticulture

03.03 Hands-on Work in Plants and Animals

Hotel Administration

11.01 Managerial Work in Recreation, Travel, and Other Personal Services

Human Growth and Development

02.04 Social Sciences

04.03 Law Enforcement

11.08 Other Personal Services

12.02 Social Services

12.03 Educational Services

14.02 Medicine and Surgery

14.03 Dentistry

14.05 Medical Technology

14.06 Medical Therapy

14.07 Patient Care and Assistance

Hydraulics/Hydraulic Shop

05.03 Mechanical Work

Industrial Arts

05.03 Mechanical Work

05.04 Hands-on Work in Mechanics, Installers, and Repairers

06.04 Hands-on Work in Construction, Extraction, and Maintenance

Industrial Distribution

07.02 Vehicle Expediting and Coordinating

Industrial Hygiene

14.08 Health Protection and Promotion

Industrial Materials

08.02 Production Technology

08.03 Production Work

Industrial Organization

05.01 Managerial Work in Mechanics, Installers, and Repairers

08.01 Managerial Work in Industrial Production

Industrial Safety

05.01 Managerial Work in Mechanics, Installers, and Repairers

08.01 Managerial Work in Industrial Production

08.02 Production Technology

08.03 Production Work

08.07 Hands-on Work: Loading, Moving, Hoisting, and Conveying

Industrial Shop

08.02 Production Technology

08.03 Production Work

08.07 Hands-on Work: Loading, Moving, Hoisting, and Conveying

Instrument Repair

05.03 Mechanical Work

Insurance

09.07 Records Processing

Insurance Law

09.02 Administrative Detail

Irrigation

08.06 Systems Operation

Jewelry

08.02 Production Technology

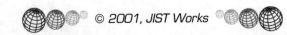

Journalism

01.03 News, Broadcasting, and Public Relations

Kinesiology

14.04 Health Specialties

14.06 Medical Therapy

Labor and Industry

13.01 General Management Work and Management of Support Functions

Laboratory Science

02.05 Laboratory Technology

Landscaping

03.03 Hands-on Work in Plants and Animals

Laser Electronics/Optics

02.08 Engineering Technology

Law Enforcement

04.03 Law Enforcement

Law, Comprehensive

04.02 Law

Leathercraft

11.06 Apparel, Shoes, Leather, and Fabric Care

Legal Terminology

04.02 Law

Literature

01.02 Writing and Editing

Lithography

08.03 Production Work

Locksmithing/Lock Repair

05.03 Mechanical Work

Locomotive Equipment/Operating

07.06 Rail Vehicle Operation

Machine Operating

08.02 Production Technology

08.03 Production Work

Management

01.01 Managerial Work in Arts, Entertainment, and Media

02.01 Managerial Work in Science, Math, and Engineering

03.01 Managerial Work in Plants and Animals

04.01 Managerial Work in Law, Law Enforcement, and Public Safety

05.01 Managerial Work in Mechanics, Installers, and Repairers

06.01 Managerial Work in Construction, Mining, and Drilling

07.01 Managerial Work in Transportation

08.01 Managerial Work in Industrial Production

09.01 Managerial Work in Business Detail

10.01 Managerial Work in Sales and Marketing

11.01 Managerial Work in Recreation, Travel, and Other Personal Services

12.01 Managerial Work in Education and Social Service

13.01 General Management Work and Management of Support Functions

14.01 Managerial Work in Medical and Health Services

Manufacturing Processes

08.01 Managerial Work in Industrial Production

08.02 Production Technology

Marketing/Merchandising

10.01 Managerial Work in Sales and Marketing

10.02 Sales Technology

10.03 General Sales

10.04 Personal Soliciting

Masonry

06.02 Construction

Math Computing, Advanced/Special

02.06 Mathematics and Computers

02.07 Engineering

02.08 Engineering Technology

Math Computing, Standard Formula

02.05 Laboratory Technology

05.02 Electrical and Electronic Systems

07.03 Air Vehicle Operation

09.03 Bookkeeping, Auditing, and Accounting

Mathematics

04.05 Military

Mechanical Drawing

02.08 Engineering Technology

Mechanics/Mechanics of Materials

02.07 Engineering

04.05 Military

Medical Record Science

09.07 Records Processing

Medical Terminology

09.07 Records Processing

14.01 Managerial Work in Medical and Health Services

Menu Planning

11.05 Food and Beverage Services

14.08 Health Protection and Promotion

Metal Forming and Fabrication/Technology

08.04 Metal and Plastics Machining Technology

Metallurgy/Metal Properties

02.07 Engineering

Meteorology

02.02 Physical Sciences

07.03 Air Vehicle Operation

Microbiology

02.03 Life Sciences

Mining Practices

06.03 Mining and Drilling

Model Making

08.03 Production Work

08.04 Metal and Plastics Machining Technology

Modeling, Personal

01.09 Modeling and Personal Appearance

Moldmaking

01.06 Craft Arts

Money and Banking

13.02 Management Support

Music: Theory and History

01.05 Performing Arts

Naval Architecture

02.07 Engineering

Navigation

07.03 Air Vehicle Operation

07.04 Water Vehicle Operation

News Writing

01.03 News, Broadcasting, and Public Relations

Newscasting

01.03 News, Broadcasting, and Public Relations

Nuclear Safety

14.05 Medical Technology

Nursing Care

14.02 Medicine and Surgery

14.07 Patient Care and Assistance

Nutrition

14.07 Patient Care and Assistance

14.08 Health Protection and Promotion

Officiating

01.10 Sports: Coaching, Instructing, Officiating, and Performing

Offset Printing

01.07 Graphic Arts

08.03 Production Work

Oilfield Practices

06.03 Mining and Drilling

08.06 Systems Operation

Operations Management

13.01 General Management Work and Management of Support Functions

Optics

14.04 Health Specialties

Oral Anatomy

14.03 Dentistry

Oral Communication

14.03 Dentistry

Oral Development

14.03 Dentistry

Oral Hygiene

14.03 Dentistry

Painting, Fine Arts and Applied

01.04 Visual Arts

01.06 Craft Arts

Pathology

14.01 Managerial Work in Medical and Health Services

14.02 Medicine and Surgery

14.05 Medical Technology

14.06 Medical Therapy

14.07 Patient Care and Assistance

Patient and Health Care

14.01 Managerial Work in Medical and Health Services

14.02 Medicine and Surgery

14.03 Dentistry

14.04 Health Specialties

14.05 Medical Technology

14.06 Medical Therapy

14.07 Patient Care and Assistance

Penology

04.03 Law Enforcement

Personal Grooming

01.09 Modeling and Personal Appearance

11.04 Barber and Beauty Services

Personnel Management

01.01 Managerial Work in Arts, Entertainment, and Media

02.01 Managerial Work in Science, Math, and Engineering

04.01 Managerial Work in Law, Law Enforcement, and Public Safety

05.01 Managerial Work in Mechanics, Installers, and Repairers

06.01 Managerial Work in Construction, Mining, and Drilling

07.01 Managerial Work in Transportation

08.01 Managerial Work in Industrial Production

10.01 Managerial Work in Sales and Marketing

11.01 Managerial Work in Recreation, Travel, and Other Personal Services

12.01 Managerial Work in Education and Social Service

13.01 General Management Work and Management of Support Functions

13.02 Management Support

14.01 Managerial Work in Medical and Health Services

Pharmacology

14.02 Medicine and Surgery

14.03 Dentistry

14.04 Health Specialties

Philosophy

12.02 Social Services

Photography

01.04 Visual Arts

01.07 Graphic Arts

01.08 Media Technology

02.05 Laboratory Technology

Physical Education

01.10 Sports: Coaching, Instructing, Officiating, and Performing

14.08 Health Protection and Promotion

Physical Science

02.01 Managerial Work in Science, Math, and Engineering

02.02 Physical Sciences

02.05 Laboratory Technology

02.07 Engineering

02.08 Engineering Technology

12.03 Educational Services

Physical Therapy

14.06 Medical Therapy

Physics

02.01 Managerial Work in Science, Math, and Engineering

02.02 Physical Sciences

02.07 Engineering

Physiology

02.03 Life Sciences

14.02 Medicine and Surgery

14.03 Dentistry

14.04 Health Specialties

14.05 Medical Technology

14.06 Medical Therapy

Plant Pest Management/Pathology

03.01 Managerial Work in Plants and Animals

03.03 Hands-on Work in Plants and Animals

Plumbing

06.02 Construction

06.04 Hands-on Work in Construction, Extraction, and Maintenance

Police Science

04.01 Managerial Work in Law, Law Enforcement, and Public Safety

04.03 Law Enforcement

Political Science

02.04 Social Sciences

04.05 Military

Power Systems/Technology

05.02 Electrical and Electronic Systems

08.06 Systems Operation

Print Shop/Printing

08.03 Production Work

Printmaking

08.03 Production Work

Production/Inventory Control

09.03 Bookkeeping, Auditing, and Accounting

Promotion

10.04 Personal Soliciting

Psychology

01.02 Writing and Editing

10.04 Personal Soliciting

12.03 Educational Services

14.07 Patient Care and Assistance

Psychology, Advanced/Specialized

02.04 Social Sciences

12.02 Social Services

14.02 Medicine and Surgery

Public Health

14.08 Health Protection and Promotion

Public Speaking

01.03 News, Broadcasting, and Public Relations

01.05 Performing Arts

04.02 Law

09.05 Customer Service

11.02 Recreational Services

12.02 Social Services

12.03 Educational Services

Pump Operation

06.03 Mining and Drilling

Quality Control

08.01 Managerial Work in Industrial Production

Radio/TV Operations

01.08 Media Technology

02.08 Engineering Technology

Railroad Safety

07.06 Rail Vehicle Operation

Real Estate Laws/Regulations

10.03 General Sales

Record Keeping

09.02 Administrative Detail

09.03 Bookkeeping, Auditing, and Accounting

09.04 Material Control

09.05 Customer Service

09.06 Communications

09.07 Records Processing

09.08 Records and Materials Processing

09.09 Clerical Machine Operation

10.03 General Sales

11.03 Transportation and Lodging Services

Recreation

11.01 Managerial Work in Recreation, Travel, and Other Personal Services

11.02 Recreational Services

Religion

12.02 Social Services

Rescue

12.02 Social Services

Research Methods

02.02 Physical Sciences

02.03 Life Sciences

02.04 Social Sciences

02.05 Laboratory Technology

Retailing

10.03 General Sales

Safety Regulations

04.04 Public Safety

07.06 Rail Vehicle Operation

07.08 Support Work in Transportation

Scheduling

07.02 Vehicle Expediting and Coordinating

Sculpture/Sculpting

01.04 Visual Arts

Selling

10.01 Managerial Work in Sales and Marketing

10.02 Sales Technology

10.03 General Sales

10.04 Personal Soliciting

Sewing

11.06 Apparel, Shoes, Leather, and Fabric Care

Ship Systems

07.04 Water Vehicle Operation

Shipping Regulations

07.02 Vehicle Expediting and Coordinating

07.04 Water Vehicle Operation

Shop Math

05.03 Mechanical Work

06.02 Construction

08.02 Production Technology

08.04 Metal and Plastics Machining Technology

08.05 Woodworking Technology

08.06 Systems Operation

Social Anthropology

02.04 Social Sciences

Social Problems

12.02 Social Services

Social Psychology

12.02 Social Services

Social Work

12.02 Social Services

Sociology

02.04 Social Sciences

Soil Science

02.03 Life Sciences

Spelling

01.02 Writing and Editing

01.03 News, Broadcasting, and Public Relations

Statistics

09.03 Bookkeeping, Auditing, and Accounting

Statistics, Advanced/Specialized

02.06 Mathematics and Computers

Surveying

02.08 Engineering Technology

Systems Analysis

02.06 Mathematics and Computers

Technical Writing

01.02 Writing and Editing

Theater Arts

01.01 Managerial Work in Arts, Entertainment, and Media

01.05 Performing Arts

01.08 Media Technology

Tool Design

08.02 Production Technology

08.04 Metal and Plastics Machining Technology

Traffic Control/Management

07.02 Vehicle Expediting and Coordinating

07.07 Other Services Requiring Driving

09.06 Communications

Transportation Engineering/Technology

07.02 Vehicle Expediting and Coordinating

Truck Mechanics

07.05 Truck Driving

Truck Operating

07.05 Truck Driving

Typing

09.08 Records and Materials Processing

09.09 Clerical Machine Operation

Veterinary Sciences

02.03 Life Sciences

03.02 Animal Care and Training

Vocational Agriculture

03.03 Hands-on Work in Plants and Animals

Voice

01.05 Performing Arts

Wastewater/Water Treatment Processes

08.06 Systems Operation

Watchmaking/Watch Repair Shop

05.03 Mechanical Work

Water Safety

07.04 Water Vehicle Operation

Welding

08.03 Production Work

Wood Machining

08.05 Woodworking Technology

Wood Shop/Woodworking

08.05 Woodworking Technology

X-Ray Technology

14.05 Medical Technology

Zoology

02.03 Life Sciences

Crosswalk E: Work Settings with Corresponding Work Groups

Airplanes

05.03 Mechanical Work

07.03 Air Vehicle Operation

11.03 Transportation and Lodging Services

Airports

04.03 Law Enforcement

04.04 Public Safety

04.05 Military

05.02 Electrical and Electronic Systems

06.02 Construction

07.01 Managerial Work in Transportation

07.02 Vehicle Expediting and Coordinating

07.03 Air Vehicle Operation

07.08 Support Work in Transportation

08.06 Systems Operation

08.07 Hands-on Work: Loading, Moving, Hoisting, and Conveying

09.05 Customer Service

11.07 Cleaning and Building Services

Amusement parks, circuses, and carnivals

01.05 Performing Arts

01.10 Sports: Coaching, Instructing, Officiating, and Performing

03.02 Animal Care and Training

11.02 Recreational Services

Animal hospitals, boarding kennels, and grooming parlors

02.03 Life Sciences

02.05 Laboratory Technology

03.02 Animal Care and Training

Artists' studios and craft workshops

01.01 Managerial Work in Arts, Entertainment, and Media

01.04 Visual Arts

01.06 Craft Arts

01.07 Graphic Arts

Auto service stations and repair shops

05.01 Managerial Work in Mechanics, Installers, and Repairers

05.03 Mechanical Work

05.04 Hands-on Work in Mechanics, Installers, and Repairers

09.01 Managerial Work in Business Detail

09.05 Customer Service

Barber shops and beauty salons

11.04 Barber and Beauty Services

Bowling alleys

01.10 Sports: Coaching, Instructing, Officiating, and Performing

05.03 Mechanical Work

11.02 Recreational Services

Bus and train stations

04.04 Public Safety

07.01 Managerial Work in Transportation

07.06 Rail Vehicle Operation

07.07 Other Services Requiring Driving

08.07 Hands-on Work: Loading, Moving, Hoisting, and Conveying

09.05 Customer Service

Buses and trolleys

05.03 Mechanical Work

07.06 Rail Vehicle Operation

07.07 Other Services Requiring Driving

Business offices

01.01 Managerial Work in Arts, Entertainment, and Media

01.02 Writing and Editing

01.03 News, Broadcasting, and Public Relations

01.04 Visual Arts

01.05 Performing Arts

01.07 Graphic Arts

02.01 Managerial Work in Science, Math, and Engineering

02.02 Physical Sciences

02.04 Social Sciences

02.06 Mathematics and Computers

02.07 Engineering

02.08 Engineering Technology

04.02 Law

05.01 Managerial Work in Mechanics, Installers, and Repairers

05.02 Electrical and Electronic Systems

05.03 Mechanical Work

06.01 Managerial Work in Construction, Mining, and Drilling

07.01 Managerial Work in Transportation

08.01 Managerial Work in Industrial Production

09.01 Managerial Work in Business Detail

09.02 Administrative Detail

09.03 Bookkeeping, Auditing, and Accounting

09.07 Records Processing

09.08 Records and Materials Processing

09.09 Clerical Machine Operation

10.01 Managerial Work in Sales and Marketing

10.02 Sales Technology

10.04 Personal Soliciting

11.01 Managerial Work in Recreation, Travel, and Other Personal Services

11.07 Cleaning and Building Services

12.01 Managerial Work in Education and Social Service

12.02 Social Services

13.01 General Management Work and Management of Support Functions

13.02 Management Support

14.01 Managerial Work in Medical and Health Services

14.08 Health Protection and Promotion

Colleges and universities

01.10 Sports: Coaching, Instructing, Officiating, and Performing

02.01 Managerial Work in Science, Math, and Engineering

02.02 Physical Sciences

02.03 Life Sciences

02.04 Social Sciences

02.05 Laboratory Technology

02.06 Mathematics and Computers

02.07 Engineering

09.01 Managerial Work in Business Detail

09.03 Bookkeeping, Auditing, and Accounting

09.07 Records Processing

12.01 Managerial Work in Education and Social Service

12.03 Educational Services

14.07 Patient Care and Assistance

14.08 Health Protection and Promotion

Computer centers

02.01 Managerial Work in Science, Math, and Engineering

02.02 Physical Sciences

02.06 Mathematics and Computers

05.02 Electrical and Electronic Systems

09.07 Records Processing

09.09 Clerical Machine Operation

12.03 Educational Services

Construction sites

02.07 Engineering

02.08 Engineering Technology

04.03 Law Enforcement

04.04 Public Safety

05.02 Electrical and Electronic Systems

05.03 Mechanical Work

05.04 Hands-on Work in Mechanics, Installers, and Repairers

06.01 Managerial Work in Construction, Mining, and Drilling

06.02 Construction

06.03 Mining and Drilling

06.04 Hands-on Work in Construction, Extraction, and Maintenance

Convention and trade show centers

01.09 Modeling and Personal Appearance

10.01 Managerial Work in Sales and Marketing

10.03 General Sales

11.07 Cleaning and Building Services

Country clubs and resorts

01.10 Sports: Coaching, Instructing, Officiating, and Performing

03.03 Hands-on Work in Plants and Animals

07.07 Other Services Requiring Driving

09.05 Customer Service

10.03 General Sales

11.01 Managerial Work in Recreation, Travel, and Other Personal Services

11.03 Transportation and Lodging Services

11.05 Food and Beverage Services

11.07 Cleaning and Building Services

Courthouses

01.03 News, Broadcasting, and Public Relations

04.02 Law

04.03 Law Enforcement

09.01 Managerial Work in Business Detail

09.02 Administrative Detail

09.08 Records and Materials Processing

09.09 Clerical Machine Operation

Doctors' and dentists' offices and clinics

02.04 Social Sciences

09.02 Administrative Detail

09.03 Bookkeeping, Auditing, and Accounting

09.05 Customer Service

09.07 Records Processing

10.02 Sales Technology

14.02 Medicine and Surgery

14.03 Dentistry

14.04 Health Specialties

14.05 Medical Technology

14.06 Medical Therapy

14.07 Patient Care and Assistance

Drug stores

09.02 Administrative Detail

09.05 Customer Service

14.02 Medicine and Surgery

Elementary schools

01.10 Sports: Coaching, Instructing, Officiating, and Performing

09.02 Administrative Detail

09.07 Records Processing

11.07 Cleaning and Building Services

12.01 Managerial Work in Education and Social Service

12.02 Social Services

12.03 Educational Services

14.05 Medical Technology

14.07 Patient Care and Assistance

Factories and plants

01.06 Craft Arts

01.07 Graphic Arts

02.01 Managerial Work in Science, Math, and Engineering

02.03 Life Sciences

02.04 Social Sciences

02.05 Laboratory Technology

02.06 Mathematics and Computers

02.07 Engineering

02.08 Engineering Technology

04.03 Law Enforcement

04.04 Public Safety

05.01 Managerial Work in Mechanics, Installers, and Repairers

05.02 Electrical and Electronic Systems

05.03 Mechanical Work

05.04 Hands-on Work in Mechanics, Installers, and Repairers

06.02 Construction

08.01 Managerial Work in Industrial Production

08.02 Production Technology

08.03 Production Work

08.04 Metal and Plastics Machining Technology

08.05 Woodworking Technology

08.06 Systems Operation

08.07 Hands-on Work: Loading, Moving, Hoisting, and Conveying

09.03 Bookkeeping, Auditing, and Accounting

09.04 Material Control

09.08 Records and Materials Processing

10.02 Sales Technology

10.03 General Sales

11.06 Apparel, Shoes, Leather, and Fabric Care

11.07 Cleaning and Building Services

12.02 Social Services

13.02 Management Support

14.07 Patient Care and Assistance

Farms

02.03 Life Sciences

02.05 Laboratory Technology

02.07 Engineering

02.08 Engineering Technology

03.01 Managerial Work in Plants and Animals

03.02 Animal Care and Training

03.03 Hands-on Work in Plants and Animals

04.04 Public Safety

05.01 Managerial Work in Mechanics, Installers, and Repairers

05.03 Mechanical Work

06.02 Construction

08.06 Systems Operation

10.02 Sales Technology

13.02 Management Support

Fire stations

04.01 Managerial Work in Law, Law Enforcement, and Public Safety

09.06 Communications

Fish hatcheries

02.01 Managerial Work in Science, Math, and Engineering

02.03 Life Sciences

02.05 Laboratory Technology

03.01 Managerial Work in Plants and Animals

03.02 Animal Care and Training

Foreign countries

04.05 Military

Forests

02.01 Managerial Work in Science, Math, and Engineering

02.03 Life Sciences

03.01 Managerial Work in Plants and Animals

03.03 Hands-on Work in Plants and Animals

04.01 Managerial Work in Law, Law Enforcement, and Public Safety

04.03 Law Enforcement

04.04 Public Safety

04.05 Military

Freight terminals

07.01 Managerial Work in Transportation

07.05 Truck Driving

07.08 Support Work in Transportation

08.07 Hands-on Work: Loading, Moving, Hoisting, and Conveying

09.03 Bookkeeping, Auditing, and Accounting

09.04 Material Control

09.06 Communications

09.08 Records and Materials Processing

09.09 Clerical Machine Operation

Gambling casinos and card clubs

01.05 Performing Arts

04.03 Law Enforcement

04.04 Public Safety

09.03 Bookkeeping, Auditing, and Accounting

09.05 Customer Service

11.01 Managerial Work in Recreation, Travel, and Other Personal Services

11.02 Recreational Services

11.05 Food and Beverage Services

11.07 Cleaning and Building Services

Golf courses and tennis courts

03.01 Managerial Work in Plants and Animals

03.03 Hands-on Work in Plants and Animals

Government offices

02.01 Managerial Work in Science, Math, and Engineering

02.04 Social Sciences

02.06 Mathematics and Computers

02.07 Engineering

04.01 Managerial Work in Law, Law Enforcement, and Public Safety

04.02 Law

09.01 Managerial Work in Business Detail

09.02 Administrative Detail

09.03 Bookkeeping, Auditing, and Accounting

09.07 Records Processing

09.08 Records and Materials Processing

09.09 Clerical Machine Operation

11.07 Cleaning and Building Services

12.01 Managerial Work in Education and Social Service

12.02 Social Services

13.01 General Management Work and Management of Support Functions

13.02 Management Support

14.01 Managerial Work in Medical and Health Services

14.08 Health Protection and Promotion

Gymnasiums and health clubs

01.10 Sports: Coaching, Instructing, Officiating, and Performing

11.01 Managerial Work in Recreation, Travel, and Other Personal Services

14.08 Health Protection and Promotion

High schools

01.10 Sports: Coaching, Instructing, Officiating, and Performing

09.02 Administrative Detail

09.07 Records Processing

11.07 Cleaning and Building Services

12.01 Managerial Work in Education and Social Service

12.02 Social Services

12.03 Educational Services

14.07 Patient Care and Assistance

Hospitals and nursing homes

02.03 Life Sciences

02.05 Laboratory Technology

02.06 Mathematics and Computers

04.04 Public Safety

05.02 Electrical and Electronic Systems

05.03 Mechanical Work

07.07 Other Services Requiring Driving

08.06 Systems Operation

09.02 Administrative Detail

09.03 Bookkeeping, Auditing, and Accounting

09.07 Records Processing

09.09 Clerical Machine Operation

10.02 Sales Technology

11.01 Managerial Work in Recreation, Travel, and Other Personal Services

11.07 Cleaning and Building Services

12.02 Social Services

14.01 Managerial Work in Medical and Health Services

14.02 Medicine and Surgery

14.05 Medical Technology

14.06 Medical Therapy

14.07 Patient Care and Assistance

14.08 Health Protection and Promotion

Hotels and motels

03.03 Hands-on Work in Plants and Animals

09.03 Bookkeeping, Auditing, and Accounting

09.05 Customer Service

11.01 Managerial Work in Recreation, Travel, and Other Personal Services

11.03 Transportation and Lodging Services

11.07 Cleaning and Building Services

Jails and reformatories

02.04 Social Sciences

04.03 Law Enforcement

09.07 Records Processing

11.01 Managerial Work in Recreation, Travel, and Other Personal Services

12.02 Social Services

Kindergartens and day care centers

11.08 Other Personal Services

12.01 Managerial Work in Education and Social Service

12.03 Educational Services

Laboratories

02.01 Managerial Work in Science, Math, and Engineering

02.02 Physical Sciences

02.03 Life Sciences

02.04 Social Sciences

02.05 Laboratory Technology

02.07 Engineering

02.08 Engineering Technology

03.02 Animal Care and Training

04.03 Law Enforcement

10.02 Sales Technology

12.01 Managerial Work in Education and Social Service

12.03 Educational Services

Laundries and dry cleaners

11.06 Apparel, Shoes, Leather, and Fabric Care

Libraries

04.02 Law

09.01 Managerial Work in Business Detail

09.07 Records Processing

12.03 Educational Services

Military bases

04.05 Military

Mines and quarries

02.02 Physical Sciences

02.07 Engineering

02.08 Engineering Technology

04.04 Public Safety

05.01 Managerial Work in Mechanics, Installers, and Repairers

05.03 Mechanical Work

05.04 Hands-on Work in Mechanics, Installers, and Repairers

06.01 Managerial Work in Construction, Mining, and Drilling

06.02 Construction

06.03 Mining and Drilling

08.07 Hands-on Work: Loading, Moving, Hoisting, and Conveying

Motion picture and recording studios

01.01 Managerial Work in Arts, Entertainment, and Media

01.02 Writing and Editing

01.04 Visual Arts

01.05 Performing Arts

01.08 Media Technology

01.09 Modeling and Personal Appearance

02.06 Mathematics and Computers

05.01 Managerial Work in Mechanics, Installers, and Repairers

05.02 Electrical and Electronic Systems

06.04 Hands-on Work in Construction, Extraction, and Maintenance

11.06 Apparel, Shoes, Leather, and Fabric Care

Nightclubs

01.05 Performing Arts

11.02 Recreational Services

11.05 Food and Beverage Services

Oil fields

02.01 Managerial Work in Science, Math, and Engineering

02.07 Engineering

02.08 Engineering Technology

05.01 Managerial Work in Mechanics, Installers, and Repairers

05.04 Hands-on Work in Mechanics, Installers, and Repairers

06.01 Managerial Work in Construction, Mining, and Drilling

06.02 Construction

06.03 Mining and Drilling

08.07 Hands-on Work: Loading, Moving, Hoisting, and Conveying

Parks and campgrounds

03.01 Managerial Work in Plants and Animals

03.03 Hands-on Work in Plants and Animals

06.04 Hands-on Work in Construction, Extraction, and Maintenance

12.01 Managerial Work in Education and Social Service

Photographers' studios

01.07 Graphic Arts

01.08 Media Technology

01.09 Modeling and Personal Appearance

Plant nurseries

03.01 Managerial Work in Plants and Animals

03.03 Hands-on Work in Plants and Animals

Police headquarters

04.01 Managerial Work in Law, Law Enforcement, and Public Safety

04.02 Law

04.03 Law Enforcement

09.06 Communications

Ports and harbors

04.03 Law Enforcement

04.04 Public Safety

04.05 Military

05.01 Managerial Work in Mechanics, Installers, and Repairers

06.02 Construction

07.01 Managerial Work in Transportation

07.04 Water Vehicle Operation

07.08 Support Work in Transportation

08.06 Systems Operation

08.07 Hands-on Work: Loading, Moving, Hoisting, and Conveying

Private homes

01.04 Visual Arts

03.03 Hands-on Work in Plants and Animals

04.03 Law Enforcement

06.04 Hands-on Work in Construction, Extraction, and Maintenance

09.04 Material Control

10.02 Sales Technology

10.03 General Sales

10.04 Personal Soliciting

11.08 Other Personal Services

Race tracks

01.10 Sports: Coaching, Instructing, Officiating, and Performing

09.03 Bookkeeping, Auditing, and Accounting

09.05 Customer Service

Radio studios

01.03 News, Broadcasting, and Public Relations

01.05 Performing Arts

01.08 Media Technology

05.01 Managerial Work in Mechanics, Installers, and Repairers

05.02 Electrical and Electronic Systems

Railroad tracks and yards

05.02 Electrical and Electronic Systems

06.04 Hands-on Work in Construction, Extraction, and Maintenance

07.01 Managerial Work in Transportation

07.02 Vehicle Expediting and Coordinating

07.06 Rail Vehicle Operation

07.08 Support Work in Transportation

Recreation centers and playgrounds

11.01 Managerial Work in Recreation, Travel, and Other Personal Services

11.02 Recreational Services

14.06 Medical Therapy

Restaurants, cafeterias, and other eating places

09.05 Customer Service

10.02 Sales Technology

11.01 Managerial Work in Recreation, Travel, and Other Personal Services

11.05 Food and Beverage Services

Schools and homes for people with disabilities

04.04 Public Safety

09.02 Administrative Detail

11.01 Managerial Work in Recreation, Travel, and Other Personal Services

11.07 Cleaning and Building Services

12.02 Social Services

12.03 Educational Services

14.01 Managerial Work in Medical and Health Services

14.02 Medicine and Surgery

14.06 Medical Therapy

14.07 Patient Care and Assistance

14.08 Health Protection and Promotion

Ships and boats

01.05 Performing Arts

01.10 Sports: Coaching, Instructing, Officiating, and Performing

02.02 Physical Sciences

03.01 Managerial Work in Plants and Animals

03.03 Hands-on Work in Plants and Animals

05.01 Managerial Work in Mechanics, Installers, and Repairers

05.03 Mechanical Work

07.01 Managerial Work in Transportation

07.04 Water Vehicle Operation

07.08 Support Work in Transportation

08.06 Systems Operation

11.03 Transportation and Lodging Services

11.05 Food and Beverage Services

Sports stadiums

01.01 Managerial Work in Arts, Entertainment, and Media

01.10 Sports: Coaching, Instructing, Officiating, and Performing

11.05 Food and Beverage Services

14.08 Health Protection and Promotion

Stores and shopping malls

01.04 Visual Arts

01.09 Modeling and Personal Appearance

04.03 Law Enforcement

09.01 Managerial Work in Business Detail

09.03 Bookkeeping, Auditing, and Accounting

09.05 Customer Service

10.01 Managerial Work in Sales and Marketing

10.02 Sales Technology

10.03 General Sales

10.04 Personal Soliciting

11.07 Cleaning and Building Services

14.04 Health Specialties

Streets and highways

02.07 Engineering

02.08 Engineering Technology

04.03 Law Enforcement

04.04 Public Safety

05.02 Electrical and Electronic Systems

05.04 Hands-on Work in Mechanics, Installers, and Repairers

06.02 Construction

06.03 Mining and Drilling

06.04 Hands-on Work in Construction, Extraction, and Maintenance

07.02 Vehicle Expediting and Coordinating

07.05 Truck Driving

07.07 Other Services Requiring Driving

09.02 Administrative Detail

Television studios

01.01 Managerial Work in Arts, Entertainment, and Media

01.02 Writing and Editing

01.03 News, Broadcasting, and Public Relations

01.04 Visual Arts

01.05 Performing Arts

01.08 Media Technology

01.09 Modeling and Personal Appearance

05.01 Managerial Work in Mechanics, Installers, and Repairers

05.02 Electrical and Electronic Systems

11.06 Apparel, Shoes, Leather, and Fabric Care

Theaters

01.01 Managerial Work in Arts, Entertainment, and Media

01.02 Writing and Editing

01.05 Performing Arts

01.08 Media Technology

09.05 Customer Service

11.02 Recreational Services

11.06 Apparel, Shoes, Leather, and Fabric Care

Trains

05.03 Mechanical Work

07.06 Rail Vehicle Operation

07.08 Support Work in Transportation

11.03 Transportation and Lodging Services

Travel agencies

09.01 Managerial Work in Business Detail

09.02 Administrative Detail

09.03 Bookkeeping, Auditing, and Accounting

09.05 Customer Service

10.03 General Sales

Warehouses

08.07 Hands-on Work: Loading, Moving, Hoisting, and Conveying

09.03 Bookkeeping, Auditing, and Accounting

Waterworks and light and power plants

02.01 Managerial Work in Science, Math, and Engineering

02.05 Laboratory Technology

02.07 Engineering

02.08 Engineering Technology

04.04 Public Safety

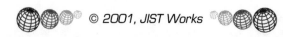

05.02 Electrical and Electronic Systems

05.03 Mechanical Work

05.04 Hands-on Work in Mechanics, Installers, and Repairers

06.02 Construction

08.06 Systems Operation

08.07 Hands-on Work: Loading, Moving, Hoisting, and Conveying

09.04 Material Control

Zoos and aquariums

02.03 Life Sciences

02.05 Laboratory Technology

03.02 Animal Care and Training

12.03 Educational Services

Crosswalk F: Skills with Corresponding Work Groups

Active Learning: Working with new material or information to grasp its implications

02.02 Physical Sciences

02.03 Life Sciences

Active Listening: Listening to what other people are saying and asking questions as appropriate

01.03 News, Broadcasting, and Public Relations

01.05 Performing Arts

01.08 Media Technology

03.02 Animal Care and Training

07.02 Vehicle Expediting and Coordinating

07.08 Support Work in Transportation

09.05 Customer Service

09.06 Communications

09.08 Records and Materials Processing

10.03 General Sales

11.04 Barber and Beauty Services

11.05 Food and Beverage Services

12.02 Social Services

14.01 Managerial Work in Medical and Health Services

14.02 Medicine and Surgery

14.04 Health Specialties

14.06 Medical Therapy

14.07 Patient Care and Assistance

14.08 Health Protection and Promotion

Coordination: Adjusting actions in relation to others' actions

01.01 Managerial Work in Arts, Entertainment, and Media

01.05 Performing Arts

01.09 Modeling and Personal Appearance

01.10 Sports: Coaching, Instructing, Officiating, and Performing

02.01 Managerial Work in Science, Math, and Engineering

03.01 Managerial Work in Plants and Animals

04.01 Managerial Work in Law, Law Enforcement, and Public Safety

05.01 Managerial Work in Mechanics, Installers, and Repairers

06.01 Managerial Work in Construction, Mining, and Drilling

07.01 Managerial Work in Transportation

07.08 Support Work in Transportation

08.01 Managerial Work in Industrial Production

09.01 Managerial Work in Business Detail

10.01 Managerial Work in Sales and Marketing

11.01 Managerial Work in Recreation, Travel, and Other Personal Services

13.01 General Management Work and Management of Support Functions

Critical Thinking: Using logic and analysis to identify the strengths and weaknesses of different approaches

02.01 Managerial Work in Science, Math, and Engineering

02.02 Physical Sciences

02.03 Life Sciences

02.06 Mathematics and Computers

02.07 Engineering

04.01 Managerial Work in Law, Law Enforcement, and Public Safety

04.04 Public Safety

04.05 Military

14.01 Managerial Work in Medical and Health Services

Equipment Maintenance: Performing routine maintenance and determining when and what kind of maintenance is needed

07.05 Truck Driving

07.07 Other Services Requiring Driving

Equipment Selection: Determining the kind of tools and equipment needed to do a job

01.07 Graphic Arts

01.08 Media Technology

03.03 Hands-on Work in Plants and Animals

05.03 Mechanical Work

05.04 Hands-on Work in Mechanics, Installers, and Repairers

06.02 Construction

06.04 Hands-on Work in Construction, Extraction, and Maintenance

08.05 Woodworking Technology

11.06 Apparel, Shoes, Leather, and Fabric Care

Idea Generation: Generating a number of different approaches to problems

01.04 Visual Arts

01.09 Modeling and Personal Appearance

Implementation Planning: Developing approaches for implementing an idea

02.01 Managerial Work in Science, Math, and Engineering

04.01 Managerial Work in Law, Law Enforcement, and Public Safety

Information Gathering: Knowing how to find information and identifying essential information

01.03 News, Broadcasting, and Public Relations

02.02 Physical Sciences

02.03 Life Sciences

02.04 Social Sciences

02.05 Laboratory Technology

02.08 Engineering Technology

04.02 Law

04.03 Law Enforcement

04.04 Public Safety

04.05 Military

07.03 Air Vehicle Operation

09.03 Bookkeeping, Auditing, and Accounting

09.07 Records Processing

10.01 Managerial Work in Sales and Marketing

13.01 General Management Work and Management of Support Functions

13.02 Management Support

14.01 Managerial Work in Medical and Health Services

14.02 Medicine and Surgery

14.08 Health Protection and Promotion

Information Organization: Finding ways to structure or classify multiple pieces of information

01.09 Modeling and Personal Appearance

02.04 Social Sciences

Installation: Installing equipment, machines, wiring, or programs to meet specifications

05.02 Electrical and Electronic Systems

06.04 Hands-on Work in Construction, Extraction, and Maintenance

Judgment and Decision Making: Weighing the relative costs and benefits of a potential action

02.01 Managerial Work in Science, Math, and Engineering

04.01 Managerial Work in Law, Law Enforcement, and Public Safety

07.03 Air Vehicle Operation

13.02 Management Support

14.01 Managerial Work in Medical and Health Services

Management of Personnel Resources: Motivating, developing, and directing people as they work; identifying the best people for the job

01.01 Managerial Work in Arts, Entertainment, and Media

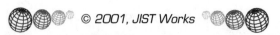

04.01 Managerial Work in Law, Law Enforcement, and Public Safety

05.01 Managerial Work in Mechanics, Installers, and Repairers

06.01 Managerial Work in Construction, Mining, and Drilling

08.01 Managerial Work in Industrial Production

09.01 Managerial Work in Business Detail

11.01 Managerial Work in Recreation, Travel, and Other Personal Services

13.01 General Management Work and Management of Support Functions

Mathematics: Using mathematics to solve problems

02.02 Physical Sciences

02.07 Engineering

02.08 Engineering Technology

09.03 Bookkeeping, Auditing, and Accounting

09.04 Material Control

09.08 Records and Materials Processing

Monitoring: Assessing how well one is doing when learning or doing something

01.05 Performing Arts

01.08 Media Technology

01.10 Sports: Coaching, Instructing, Officiating, and Performing

07.03 Air Vehicle Operation

Operation and Control: Controlling operations of equipment or systems

01.06 Craft Arts

01.07 Graphic Arts

01.08 Media Technology

03.03 Hands-on Work in Plants and Animals

06.02 Construction

06.03 Mining and Drilling

07.03 Air Vehicle Operation

07.04 Water Vehicle Operation

07.05 Truck Driving

07.06 Rail Vehicle Operation

07.07 Other Services Requiring Driving

08.02 Production Technology

08.03 Production Work

08.04 Metal and Plastics Machining Technology

08.06 Systems Operation

08.07 Hands-on Work: Loading, Moving, Hoisting, and Conveying

09.09 Clerical Machine Operation

11.06 Apparel, Shoes, Leather, and Fabric Care

11.07 Cleaning and Building Services

14.05 Medical Technology

Operation Monitoring: Watching gauges, dials, or other indicators to make sure a machine is working properly

06.03 Mining and Drilling

07.03 Air Vehicle Operation

07.04 Water Vehicle Operation

07.06 Rail Vehicle Operation

08.06 Systems Operation

08.07 Hands-on Work: Loading, Moving, Hoisting, and Conveying

Persuasion: Persuading others to approach things differently

10.02 Sales Technology

10.04 Personal Soliciting

Problem Identification: Identifying the nature of problems

03.01 Managerial Work in Plants and Animals

03.02 Animal Care and Training

04.01 Managerial Work in Law, Law Enforcement, and Public Safety

04.04 Public Safety

04.05 Military

07.03 Air Vehicle Operation

07.08 Support Work in Transportation

08.01 Managerial Work in Industrial Production

14.01 Managerial Work in Medical and Health Service

14.03 Dentistry

Product Inspection: Inspecting and evaluating the quality of products

01.04 Visual Arts

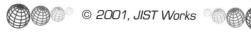

01.06 Craft Arts

01.07 Graphic Arts

01.08 Media Technology

03.01 Managerial Work in Plants and Animals

06.02 Construction

08.02 Production Technology

08.03 Production Work

08.04 Metal and Plastics Machining Technology

08.05 Woodworking Technology

11.06 Apparel, Shoes, Leather, and Fabric Care

Programming: Writing computer programs for various purposes

02.02 Physical Sciences

02.03 Life Sciences

02.04 Social Sciences

02.06 Mathematics and Computers

02.07 Engineering

02.08 Engineering Technology

Reading Comprehension: Understanding written sentences and paragraphs in work-related documents

01.01 Managerial Work in Arts, Entertainment, and Media

01.02 Writing and Editing

01.03 News, Broadcasting, and Public Relations

01.05 Performing Arts

02.01 Managerial Work in Science, Math, and Engineering

02.02 Physical Sciences

02.03 Life Sciences

02.04 Social Sciences

02.06 Mathematics and Computers

02.07 Engineering

04.02 Law

09.01 Managerial Work in Business Detail

09.02 Administrative Detail

09.03 Bookkeeping, Auditing, and Accounting

09.04 Material Control

09.07 Records Processing

09.08 Records and Materials Processing

09.09 Clerical Machine Operation

12.01 Managerial Work in Education and Social Service

12.03 Educational Services

13.01 General Management Work and Management of Support Functions

13.02 Management Support

14.01 Managerial Work in Medical and Health Services

14.02 Medicine and Surgery

14.03 Dentistry

Repairing: Repairing machines or systems using the needed tools

05.02 Electrical and Electronic Systems

05.03 Mechanical Work

05.04 Hands-on Work in Mechanics, Installers, and Repairers

Science: Using scientific methods to solve problems

02.02 Physical Sciences

02.03 Life Sciences

02.05 Laboratory Technology

02.07 Engineering

Service Orientation: Actively looking for ways to help people

07.07 Other Services Requiring Driving

10.03 General Sales

11.02 Recreational Services

11.03 Transportation and Lodging Services

11.04 Barber and Beauty Services

11.05 Food and Beverage Services

11.07 Cleaning and Building Services

11.08 Other Personal Services

14.07 Patient Care and Assistance

Social Perceptiveness: Being aware of others' reactions and understanding why they react the way they do

10.04 Personal Soliciting

11.08 Other Personal Services

12.02 Social Services

14.07 Patient Care and Assistance

Speaking: Talking to others to effectively convey information

01.01 Managerial Work in Arts, Entertainment, and Media

01.03 News, Broadcasting, and Public Relations

01.05 Performing Arts

01.08 Media Technology

01.09 Modeling and Personal Appearance

01.10 Sports: Coaching, Instructing, Officiating, and Performing

02.01 Managerial Work in Science, Math, and Engineering

03.01 Managerial Work in Plants and Animals

03.02 Animal Care and Training

04.01 Managerial Work in Law, Law Enforcement, and Public Safety

04.03 Law Enforcement

04.04 Public Safety

04.05 Military

07.01 Managerial Work in Transportation

07.02 Vehicle Expediting and Coordinating

09.01 Managerial Work in Business Detail

09.05 Customer Service

09.06 Communications

10.01 Managerial Work in Sales and Marketing

10.02 Sales Technology

10.03 General Sales

10.04 Personal Soliciting

11.02 Recreational Services

11.03 Transportation and Lodging Services

12.01 Managerial Work in Education and Social Service

12.02 Social Services

12.03 Educational Services

13.01 General Management Work and Management of Support Functions

14.04 Health Specialties

14.05 Medical Technology

14.06 Medical Therapy

14.08 Health Protection and Promotion

Time Management: Managing your own time and the time of others

05.01 Managerial Work in Mechanics, Installers, and Repairers

Writing: Communicating effectively with others in writing as indicated by their needs

01.01 Managerial Work in Arts, Entertainment, and Media

01.02 Writing and Editing

01.03 News, Broadcasting, and Public Relations

02.04 Social Sciences

04.01 Managerial Work in Law, Law Enforcement, and Public Safety

09.01 Managerial Work in Business Detail

09.02 Administrative Detail

09.04 Material Control

09.07 Records Processing

13.01 General Management Work and Management of Support Functions

Crosswalk G: Abilities with Corresponding Work Groups

Arm-Hand Steadiness: Keeping the hand and arm steady while making an arm movement or while holding the arm and hand in one position

01.04 Visual Arts

01.06 Craft Arts

01.07 Graphic Arts

01.09 Modeling and Personal Appearance

05.03 Mechanical Work

08.02 Production Technology

08.03 Production Work

08.04 Metal and Plastics Machining Technology

08.05 Woodworking Technology

11.04 Barber and Beauty Services

11.06 Apparel, Shoes, Leather, and Fabric Care

14.03 Dentistry

Control Precision: Quickly and repeatedly making precise adjustments in moving the controls of a machine or vehicle to exact positions

01.06 Craft Arts

01.07 Graphic Arts

01.08 Media Technology

02.05 Laboratory Technology

05.03 Mechanical Work

06.03 Mining and Drilling

07.03 Air Vehicle Operation

07.04 Water Vehicle Operation

07.06 Rail Vehicle Operation

08.02 Production Technology

08.03 Production Work

08.04 Metal and Plastics Machining Technology

08.05 Woodworking Technology

08.06 Systems Operation

08.07 Hands-on Work: Loading, Moving, Hoisting, and Conveying

14.03 Dentistry

Deductive Reasoning: Applying general rules to specific problems to come up with logical answers

02.01 Managerial Work in Science, Math, and Engineering

02.02 Physical Sciences

02.03 Life Sciences

02.04 Social Sciences

02.05 Laboratory Technology

02.06 Mathematics and Computers

02.07 Engineering

02.08 Engineering Technology

03.01 Managerial Work in Plants and Animals

04.02 Law

04.04 Public Safety

04.05 Military

05.01 Managerial Work in Mechanics, Installers, and Repairers

06.01 Managerial Work in Construction, Mining, and Drilling

07.01 Managerial Work in Transportation

12.01 Managerial Work in Education and Social Service

13.01 General Management Work and Management of Support Functions

14.06 Medical Therapy

Depth Perception: Judging which of several objects is closer or farther away from you, or judging the distance between an object and you

01.10 Sports: Coaching, Instructing, Officiating, and Performing

Extent Flexibility: Bending, stretching, twisting, or reaching out with your body, arms, and/or legs

01.06 Craft Arts

06.02 Construction

07.05 Truck Driving

07.08 Support Work in Transportation

Far Vision: Seeing details at a distance

01.10 Sports: Coaching, Instructing, Officiating, and Performing

07.02 Vehicle Expediting and Coordinating

07.03 Air Vehicle Operation

07.04 Water Vehicle Operation

07.05 Truck Driving

07.06 Rail Vehicle Operation

Finger Dexterity: Making precisely coordinated movements of the fingers of one or both hands to grasp, manipulate, or assemble very small objects

01.07 Graphic Arts

05.02 Electrical and Electronic Systems

05.03 Mechanical Work

11.04 Barber and Beauty Services

11.06 Apparel, Shoes, Leather, and Fabric Care

14.03 Dentistry

Fluency of Ideas: Coming up with a number of ideas about a given topic

01.02 Writing and Editing

01.04 Visual Arts

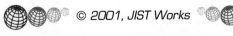

10.01 Managerial Work in Sales and Marketing

Glare Sensitivity: Seeing objects in the presence of glare or bright lighting

07.04 Water Vehicle Operation

Gross Body Coordination: Coordinating the movement of your arms, legs, and torso together in activities where your whole body is in motion

01.10 Sports: Coaching, Instructing, Officiating, and Performing

Hearing Sensitivity: Detecting or telling the difference between sounds that vary over broad ranges of pitch and loudness

01.05 Performing Arts

Inductive Reasoning: Combining separate pieces of information or specific answers to problems to form general rules or conclusions

02.01 Managerial Work in Science, Math, and Engineering

02.02 Physical Sciences

02.03 Life Sciences

02.04 Social Sciences

02.07 Engineering

04.01 Managerial Work in Law, Law Enforcement, and Public Safety

04.03 Law Enforcement

14.01 Managerial Work in Medical and Health Services

14.08 Health Protection and Promotion

Information Ordering: Correctly following a given rule or set of rules in order to arrange things or actions in a certain order

01.07 Graphic Arts

01.08 Media Technology

02.03 Life Sciences

02.05 Laboratory Technology

02.08 Engineering Technology

03.01 Managerial Work in Plants and Animals

05.01 Managerial Work in Mechanics, Installers, and Repairers

05.02 Electrical and Electronic Systems

05.03 Mechanical Work

05.04 Hands-on Work in Mechanics, Installers, and Repairers

06.01 Managerial Work in Construction, Mining, and Drilling

06.02 Construction

07.08 Support Work in Transportation

08.02 Production Technology

08.03 Production Work

08.04 Metal and Plastics Machining Technology

09.02 Administrative Detail

09.03 Bookkeeping, Auditing, and Accounting

11.05 Food and Beverage Services

14.02 Medicine and Surgery

14.05 Medical Technology

Manual Dexterity: Quickly making coordinated movements of one hand, a hand together with its arm, or two hands, to grasp, manipulate, or assemble objects

01.06 Craft Arts

03.03 Hands-on Work in Plants and Animals

05.02 Electrical and Electronic Systems

05.03 Mechanical Work

05.04 Hands-on Work in Mechanics, Installers, and Repairers

06.02 Construction

06.03 Mining and Drilling

06.04 Hands-on Work in Construction, Extraction, and Maintenance

08.02 Production Technology

08.03 Production Work

08.04 Metal and Plastics Machining Technology

08.05 Woodworking Technology

08.07 Hands-on Work: Loading, Moving, Hoisting, and Conveying

11.04 Barber and Beauty Services

11.05 Food and Beverage Services

11.06 Apparel, Shoes, Leather, and Fabric Care

11.07 Cleaning and Building Services

Mathematical Reasoning: Understanding and organizing a problem and then selecting a mathematical method or formula to solve the problem

02.02 Physical Sciences

02.06 Mathematics and Computers

02.07 Engineering

02.08 Engineering Technology

09.03 Bookkeeping, Auditing, and Accounting

13.02 Management Support

Memorization: Remembering information such as words, numbers, pictures, and procedures

01.05 Performing Arts

Multilimb Coordination: Coordinating movements of two or more limbs together

01.06 Craft Arts

01.10 Sports: Coaching, Instructing, Officiating, and Performing

06.03 Mining and Drilling

Near Vision: Seeing details of objects at a close range (within a few feet)

01.01 Managerial Work in Arts, Entertainment, and Media

01.02 Writing and Editing

01.03 News, Broadcasting, and Public Relations

01.04 Visual Arts

01.07 Graphic Arts

01.08 Media Technology

02.03 Life Sciences

02.04 Social Sciences

02.05 Laboratory Technology

02.08 Engineering Technology

03.01 Managerial Work in Plants and Animals

04.02 Law

04.03 Law Enforcement

04.04 Public Safety

04.05 Military

05.01 Managerial Work in Mechanics, Installers, and Repairers

05.02 Electrical and Electronic Systems

05.03 Mechanical Work

06.01 Managerial Work in Construction, Mining, and Drilling

07.02 Vehicle Expediting and Coordinating

07.03 Air Vehicle Operation

07.04 Water Vehicle Operation

07.05 Truck Driving

07.06 Rail Vehicle Operation

08.02 Production Technology

08.03 Production Work

08.04 Metal and Plastics Machining Technology

08.05 Woodworking Technology

09.01 Managerial Work in Business Detail

09.02 Administrative Detail

09.03 Bookkeeping, Auditing, and Accounting

09.04 Material Control

09.05 Customer Service

09.07 Records Processing

09.08 Records and Materials Processing

09.09 Clerical Machine Operation

10.03 General Sales

11.02 Recreational Services

11.04 Barber and Beauty Services

11.06 Apparel, Shoes, Leather, and Fabric Care

12.01 Managerial Work in Education and Social Service

13.02 Management Support

14.02 Medicine and Surgery

14.03 Dentistry

14.04 Health Specialties

14.05 Medical Technology

Number Facility: Adding, subtracting, multiplying, or dividing quickly and correctly

02.02 Physical Sciences

02.06 Mathematics and Computers

02.07 Engineering

02.08 Engineering Technology

09.01 Managerial Work in Business Detail

09.02 Administrative Detail

09.03 Bookkeeping, Auditing, and Accounting

09.04 Material Control

09.05 Customer Service

10.02 Sales Technology

10.03 General Sales

11.03 Transportation and Lodging Services

13.02 Management Support

Oral Comprehension: Listening to and understanding information and ideas presented through spoken words and sentences

01.01 Managerial Work in Arts, Entertainment, and Media

01.02 Writing and Editing

01.03 News, Broadcasting, and Public Relations

01.04 Visual Arts

01.05 Performing Arts

01.08 Media Technology

02.01 Managerial Work in Science, Math, and Engineering

02.02 Physical Sciences

02.04 Social Sciences

02.06 Mathematics and Computers

02.07 Engineering

03.01 Managerial Work in Plants and Animals

03.02 Animal Care and Training

04.01 Managerial Work in Law, Law Enforcement, and Public Safety

04.02 Law

04.03 Law Enforcement

04.04 Public Safety

04.05 Military

05.01 Managerial Work in Mechanics, Installers, and Repairers

06.01 Managerial Work in Construction, Mining, and Drilling

07.01 Managerial Work in Transportation

07.02 Vehicle Expediting and Coordinating

08.01 Managerial Work in Industrial Production

09.02 Administrative Detail

09.03 Bookkeeping, Auditing, and Accounting

09.05 Customer Service

09.06 Communications

09.07 Records Processing

10.01 Managerial Work in Sales and Marketing

10.02 Sales Technology

10.03 General Sales

10.04 Personal Soliciting

11.01 Managerial Work in Recreation, Travel, and Other Personal Services

11.02 Recreational Services

11.03 Transportation and Lodging Services

11.05 Food and Beverage Services

11.08 Other Personal Services

12.01 Managerial Work in Education and Social Service

12.02 Social Services

12.03 Educational Services

13.01 General Management Work and Management of Support Functions

13.02 Management Support

14.01 Managerial Work in Medical and Health Services

14.02 Medicine and Surgery

14.03 Dentistry

14.05 Medical Technology

14.06 Medical Therapy

14.07 Patient Care and Assistance

14.08 Health Protection and Promotion

Oral Expression: Communicating information and ideas in speaking so others will understand

01.01 Managerial Work in Arts, Entertainment, and Media

01.02 Writing and Editing

01.03 News, Broadcasting, and Public Relations

01.04 Visual Arts

01.05 Performing Arts

01.08 Media Technology

02.01 Managerial Work in Science, Math, and Engineering

02.04 Social Sciences

02.06 Mathematics and Computers

02.07 Engineering

03.01 Managerial Work in Plants and Animals

04.01 Managerial Work in Law, Law Enforcement, and Public Safety

04.02 Law

04.03 Law Enforcement

04.04 Public Safety

04.05 Military

05.01 Managerial Work in Mechanics, Installers, and Repairers

06.01 Managerial Work in Construction, Mining, and Drilling

07.01 Managerial Work in Transportation

07.02 Vehicle Expediting and Coordinating

07.03 Air Vehicle Operation

07.04 Water Vehicle Operation

07.07 Other Services Requiring Driving

08.01 Managerial Work in Industrial Production

09.01 Managerial Work in Business Detail

09.05 Customer Service

09.06 Communications

09.07 Records Processing

10.01 Managerial Work in Sales and Marketing

10.02 Sales Technology

10.03 General Sales

10.04 Personal Soliciting

11.01 Managerial Work in Recreation, Travel, and Other Personal Services

11.02 Recreational Services

11.03 Transportation and Lodging Services

11.04 Barber and Beauty Services

11.05 Food and Beverage Services

11.08 Other Personal Services

12.01 Managerial Work in Education and Social Service

12.02 Social Services

12.03 Educational Services

13.01 General Management Work and Management of Support Functions

13.02 Management Support

14.01 Managerial Work in Medical and Health Services

14.02 Medicine and Surgery

14.03 Dentistry

14.04 Health Specialties

14.05 Medical Technology

14.06 Medical Therapy

14.07 Patient Care and Assistance

14.08 Health Protection and Promotion

Originality: Coming up with unusual or clever ideas about a given topic or situation, or developing creative ways to solve a problem

01.01 Managerial Work in Arts, Entertainment, and Media

01.02 Writing and Editing

01.04 Visual Arts

01.05 Performing Arts

10.01 Managerial Work in Sales and Marketing

Peripheral Vision: Seeing objects or movement of objects to your side when your eyes are focused forward

01.10 Sports: Coaching, Instructing, Officiating, and Performing

Problem Sensitivity: Telling when something is wrong or is likely to go wrong

02.03 Life Sciences

03.01 Managerial Work in Plants and Animals

03.02 Animal Care and Training

04.01 Managerial Work in Law, Law Enforcement, and Public Safety

04.03 Law Enforcement

04.04 Public Safety

04.05 Military

05.02 Electrical and Electronic Systems

05.03 Mechanical Work

06.01 Managerial Work in Construction, Mining, and Drilling

07.01 Managerial Work in Transportation

07.03 Air Vehicle Operation

08.01 Managerial Work in Industrial Production

08.06 Systems Operation

12.02 Social Services

13.01 General Management Work and Management of Support Functions

14.01 Managerial Work in Medical and Health Services

14.02 Medicine and Surgery

14.03 Dentistry

14.04 Health Specialties

14.05 Medical Technology

14.06 Medical Therapy

14.07 Patient Care and Assistance

14.08 Health Protection and Promotion

Reaction Time: Quickly responding (with your hand, finger, or foot) to one signal (sound, light, picture, etc.) when it appears

01.10 Sports: Coaching, Instructing, Officiating, and Performing

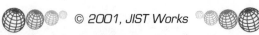

07.05 Truck Driving

07.06 Rail Vehicle Operation

07.07 Other Services Requiring Driving

Response Orientation: Choosing quickly and correctly between two or more movements in response to two or more signals

07.05 Truck Driving

Spatial Orientation: Knowing your location in relation to the environment, or knowing where other objects are in relation to yourself

07.03 Air Vehicle Operation

07.04 Water Vehicle Operation

07.05 Truck Driving

Speech Clarity: Speaking clearly so that what you say is understandable to a listener

01.01 Managerial Work in Arts, Entertainment, and Media

01.03 News, Broadcasting, and Public Relations

01.05 Performing Arts

02.01 Managerial Work in Science, Math, and Engineering

04.01 Managerial Work in Law, Law Enforcement, and Public Safety

04.02 Law

04.03 Law Enforcement

07.01 Managerial Work in Transportation

07.02 Vehicle Expediting and Coordinating

08.01 Managerial Work in Industrial Production

09.01 Managerial Work in Business Detail

09.02 Administrative Detail

09.05 Customer Service

09.06 Communications

10.01 Managerial Work in Sales and Marketing

10.02 Sales Technology

10.03 General Sales

10.04 Personal Soliciting

11.01 Managerial Work in Recreation, Travel, and Other Personal Services

11.02 Recreational Services

11.03 Transportation and Lodging Services

12.01 Managerial Work in Education and Social Service

12.02 Social Services

12.03 Educational Services

13.01 General Management Work and Management of Support Functions

14.06 Medical Therapy

14.08 Health Protection and Promotion

Speech Recognition: Identifying and understanding the speech of another person

01.03 News, Broadcasting, and Public Relations

09.06 Communications

Static Strength: Exerting maximum muscle force to lift, push, pull, or carry objects

03.03 Hands-on Work in Plants and Animals

06.02 Construction

06.04 Hands-on Work in Construction, Extraction, and Maintenance

07.05 Truck Driving

07.08 Support Work in Transportation

14.07 Patient Care and Assistance

Time Sharing: Efficiently shifting back and forth between two or more activities or sources of information

04.01 Managerial Work in Law, Law Enforcement, and Public Safety

11.02 Recreational Services

Trunk Strength: Using your abdominal and lower back muscles to support part of your body repeatedly or continuously over time

01.10 Sports: Coaching, Instructing, Officiating, and Performing

03.03 Hands-on Work in Plants and Animals

11.07 Cleaning and Building Services

Visual Color Discrimination: Matching or detecting differences between colors, including shades of color and brightness

01.09 Modeling and Personal Appearance

Visualization: Imagining how something will look after it is moved around or when its parts are moved or rearranged

01.04 Visual Arts

01.06 Craft Arts

01.07 Graphic Arts

01.08 Media Technology

01.09 Modeling and Personal Appearance

08.04 Metal and Plastics Machining Technology

08.05 Woodworking Technology

11.06 Apparel, Shoes, Leather, and Fabric Care

Wrist-Finger Speed: Making fast, simple, repeated movements of your fingers, hands, and wrists

01.06 Craft Arts

09.09 Clerical Machine Operation

11.04 Barber and Beauty Services

11.05 Food and Beverage Services

11.06 Apparel, Shoes, Leather, and Fabric Care

Written Comprehension: Reading and understanding information and ideas presented in writing

01.01 Managerial Work in Arts, Entertainment, and Media

01.02 Writing and Editing

01.03 News, Broadcasting, and Public Relations

01.05 Performing Arts

02.01 Managerial Work in Science, Math, and Engineering

02.02 Physical Sciences

02.03 Life Sciences

02.04 Social Sciences

02.05 Laboratory Technology

02.06 Mathematics and Computers

02.07 Engineering

02.08 Engineering Technology

03.01 Managerial Work in Plants and Animals

04.02 Law

04.04 Public Safety

04.05 Military

05.01 Managerial Work in Mechanics, Installers, and Repairers

06.01 Managerial Work in Construction, Mining, and Drilling

07.01 Managerial Work in Transportation

07.02 Vehicle Expediting and Coordinating

08.01 Managerial Work in Industrial Production

08.04 Metal and Plastics Machining Technology

09.01 Managerial Work in Business Detail

09.02 Administrative Detail

09.03 Bookkeeping, Auditing, and Accounting

09.05 Customer Service

09.07 Records Processing

09.08 Records and Materials Processing

09.09 Clerical Machine Operation

10.01 Managerial Work in Sales and Marketing

10.02 Sales Technology

10.03 General Sales

12.01 Managerial Work in Education and Social Service

12.02 Social Services

12.03 Educational Services

13.01 General Management Work and Management of Support Functions

13.02 Management Support

14.01 Managerial Work in Medical and Health Services

14.02 Medicine and Surgery

14.05 Medical Technology

14.06 Medical Therapy

14.07 Patient Care and Assistance

14.08 Health Protection and Promotion

Written Expression: Communicating information and ideas in writing so others will understand

01.01 Managerial Work in Arts, Entertainment, and Media

01.02 Writing and Editing

01.03 News, Broadcasting, and Public Relations

02.01 Managerial Work in Science, Math, and Engineering

02.02 Physical Sciences

02.03 Life Sciences

02.04 Social Sciences

02.05 Laboratory Technology

02.06 Mathematics and Computers

02.07 Engineering

02.08 Engineering Technology

04.01 Managerial Work in Law, Law Enforcement, and Public Safety

04.02 Law

04.03 Law Enforcement

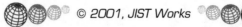

04.04 Public Safety

04.05 Military

07.01 Managerial Work in Transportation

08.01 Managerial Work in Industrial Production

09.01 Managerial Work in Business Detail

09.02 Administrative Detail

09.03 Bookkeeping, Auditing, and Accounting

09.04 Material Control

09.05 Customer Service

09.07 Records Processing

10.01 Managerial Work in Sales and Marketing

10.02 Sales Technology

10.03 General Sales

10.04 Personal Soliciting

12.01 Managerial Work in Education and Social Service

12.02 Social Services

12.03 Educational Services

13.01 General Management Work and Management of Support Functions

13.02 Management Support

14.01 Managerial Work in Medical and Health Services

14.02 Medicine and Surgery

14.05 Medical Technology

14.06 Medical Therapy

14.08 Health Protection and Promotion

Crosswalk H: Knowledges with Corresponding Work Groups

Administration and Management: Principles and processes involved in business and organizational planning, coordination, and execution

01.01 Managerial Work in Arts, Entertainment, and Media

02.01 Managerial Work in Science, Math, and Engineering

03.01 Managerial Work in Plants and Animals

04.01 Managerial Work in Law, Law Enforcement, and Public Safety

05.01 Managerial Work in Mechanics, Installers, and Repairers

06.01 Managerial Work in Construction, Mining, and Drilling

07.01 Managerial Work in Transportation

08.01 Managerial Work in Industrial Production

09.01 Managerial Work in Business Detail

10.01 Managerial Work in Sales and Marketing

11.01 Managerial Work in Recreation, Travel, and Other Personal Services

12.01 Managerial Work in Education and Social Service

13.01 General Management Work and Management of Support Functions

14.01 Managerial Work in Medical and Health Services

Biology: Plant and animal living tissue, cells, organisms, and entities, including their functions, interdependencies, and interactions with each other and the environment

01.10 Sports: Coaching, Instructing, Officiating, and Performing

02.03 Life Sciences

03.01 Managerial Work in Plants and Animals

03.02 Animal Care and Training

03.03 Hands-on Work in Plants and Animals

14.01 Managerial Work in Medical and Health Services

14.02 Medicine and Surgery

14.03 Dentistry

14.04 Health Specialties

14.05 Medical Technology

14.08 Health Protection and Promotion

Building and Construction: Materials, methods, and the appropriate tools to construct objects, structures, and buildings

06.02 Construction

06.04 Hands-on Work in Construction, Extraction, and Maintenance

08.05 Woodworking Technology

Chemistry: Composition, structure, and properties of substances and the chemical processes and transformations they undergo

02.03 Life Sciences

02.05 Laboratory Technology

Clerical: Administrative and clerical procedures and systems such as word processing systems, filing and records management systems, stenography and transcription, forms design principles, and other office procedures and terminology

09.02 Administrative Detail

09.03 Bookkeeping, Auditing, and Accounting

09.04 Material Control

09.05 Customer Service

09.07 Records Processing

09.08 Records and Materials Processing

09.09 Clerical Machine Operation

Communications: The science and art of delivering information

01.01 Managerial Work in Arts, Entertainment, and Media

01.02 Writing and Editing

01.03 News, Broadcasting, and Public Relations

01.08 Media Technology

Computers and Electronics: Electric circuit boards, processors, chips, and computer hardware and software, including applications and programming

02.06 Mathematics and Computers

05.02 Electrical and Electronic Systems

09.09 Clerical Machine Operation

Customer and Personal Service: Knowledge of principles and processes for providing customer and personal services

01.09 Modeling and Personal Appearance

07.07 Other Services Requiring Driving

09.01 Managerial Work in Business Detail

09.05 Customer Service

10.03 General Sales

11.01 Managerial Work in Recreation, Travel, and Other Personal Services

11.02 Recreational Services

11.03 Transportation and Lodging Services

11.04 Barber and Beauty Services

11.05 Food and Beverage Services

11.07 Cleaning and Building Services

11.08 Other Personal Services

14.07 Patient Care and Assistance

Design: Design techniques, principles, tools, and instruments involved in the production and use of precision technical plans, blueprints, drawings, and models

01.04 Visual Arts

01.07 Graphic Arts

02.07 Engineering

08.05 Woodworking Technology

11.06 Apparel, Shoes, Leather, and Fabric Care

Economics and Accounting: Economic and accounting principles and practices, the financial markets, banking, and the analysis and reporting of financial data

13.02 Management Support

Education and Training: Instructional methods and training techniques including curriculum design principles, learning theory, group and individual teaching techniques, design of individual development plans, and test design principles

01.10 Sports: Coaching, Instructing, Officiating, and Performing

12.01 Managerial Work in Education and Social Service

12.03 Educational Services

14.06 Medical Therapy

14.08 Health Protection and Promotion

Engineering and Technology: Equipment, tools and mechanical devices, and their uses to produce motion, light, power, technology, and other applications

02.07 Engineering

02.08 Engineering Technology

05.03 Mechanical Work

05.04 Hands-on Work in Mechanics, Installers, and Repairers

06.03 Mining and Drilling

08.06 Systems Operation

English Language: Structure and content of the English language including the meaning and spelling of words, rules of composition, and grammar

01.02 Writing and Editing

01.03 News, Broadcasting, and Public Relations

01.05 Performing Arts

02.04 Social Sciences

04.02 Law

04.04 Public Safety

04.05 Military

09.02 Administrative Detail

09.06 Communications

09.07 Records Processing

10.04 Personal Soliciting

11.02 Recreational Services

12.03 Educational Services

Fine Arts: Theory and techniques required to produce, compose, and perform works of music, dance, visual arts, drama, and sculpture

01.04 Visual Arts

01.05 Performing Arts

01.06 Craft Arts

01.07 Graphic Arts

01.09 Modeling and Personal Appearance

Geography: Various methods for describing the location and distribution of land, sea, and air masses including their physical locations, relationships, and characteristics

07.05 Truck Driving

Law, Government, and Jurisprudence: Laws, legal codes, court procedures, precedents, government regulations, executive orders, agency rules, and the democratic political process

04.02 Law

04.03 Law Enforcement

Mathematics: Numbers, their operations, and their interrelationships, including arithmetic, algebra, geometry, calculus, statistics, and their applications

02.01 Managerial Work in Science, Math, and Engineering

02.02 Physical Sciences

02.03 Life Sciences

02.04 Social Sciences

02.05 Laboratory Technology

02.06 Mathematics and Computers

02.07 Engineering

02.08 Engineering Technology

09.03 Bookkeeping, Auditing, and Accounting

09.04 Material Control

09.08 Records and Materials Processing

10.02 Sales Technology

11.05 Food and Beverage Services

13.01 General Management Work and Management of Support Functions

13.02 Management Support

Mechanical: Machines and tools, including their designs, uses, benefits, repair, and maintenance

03.03 Hands-on Work in Plants and Animals

05.01 Managerial Work in Mechanics, Installers, and Repairers

05.02 Electrical and Electronic Systems

05.03 Mechanical Work

05.04 Hands-on Work in Mechanics, Installers, and Repairers

06.02 Construction

06.03 Mining and Drilling

06.04 Hands-on Work in Construction, Extraction, and Maintenance

07.04 Water Vehicle Operation

07.06 Rail Vehicle Operation

07.08 Support Work in Transportation

08.02 Production Technology

08.03 Production Work

08.04 Metal and Plastics Machining Technology

08.06 Systems Operation

08.07 Hands-on Work: Loading, Moving, Hoisting, and Conveying

11.07 Cleaning and Building Services

Medicine and Dentistry: Information and techniques needed to diagnose and treat injuries, diseases, and deformities

03.02 Animal Care and Training

14.02 Medicine and Surgery

14.03 Dentistry

14.04 Health Specialties

14.05 Medical Technology

14.07 Patient Care and Assistance

Personnel and Human Resources: Policies and practices involved in personnel and human resource functions

06.01 Managerial Work in Construction, Mining, and Drilling

13.01 General Management Work and Management of Support Functions

Physics: Physical principles, laws, and applications including air, water, material dynamics, light, atomic principles, heat, electric theory, earth formations, and meteorological and related natural phenomena

02.02 Physical Sciences

07.03 Air Vehicle Operation

Production and Processing: Inputs, outputs, raw materials, waste, quality control, costs, and techniques for maximizing the manufacture and distribution of goods

01.06 Craft Arts

08.01 Managerial Work in Industrial Production

08.02 Production Technology

08.03 Production Work

08.04 Metal and Plastics Machining Technology

08.07 Hands-on Work: Loading, Moving, Hoisting, and Conveying

11.06 Apparel, Shoes, Leather, and Fabric Care

Psychology: Human behavior and performance, mental processes, psychological research methods, and the assessment and treatment of behavioral and affective disorders

11.08 Other Personal Services

12.02 Social Services

Public Safety and Security: Weaponry, public safety, and security operations, rules, regulations, precautions, prevention, and the protection of people, data, and property

04.01 Managerial Work in Law, Law Enforcement, and Public Safety

04.03 Law Enforcement

04.04 Public Safety

04.05 Military

Sales and Marketing: Principles and methods involved in showing, promoting, and selling products or services

10.01 Managerial Work in Sales and Marketing

10.02 Sales Technology

10.03 General Sales

10.04 Personal Soliciting

11.04 Barber and Beauty Services

Telecommunications: Knowledge of transmission, broadcasting, switching, control, and operation of telecommunications systems

01.08 Media Technology

07.02 Vehicle Expediting and Coordinating

09.06 Communications

Therapy and Counseling: Information and techniques needed to rehabilitate physical and mental ailments and to provide career guidance

12.02 Social Services

14.06 Medical Therapy

Transportation: Principles and methods for moving people or goods by air, rail, sea, or road, including their relative costs, advantages, and limitations

07.01 Managerial Work in Transportation

07.02 Vehicle Expediting and Coordinating

07.03 Air Vehicle Operation

07.04 Water Vehicle Operation

07.05 Truck Driving

07.06 Rail Vehicle Operation

07.07 Other Services Requiring Driving

07.08 Support Work in Transportation

11.03 Transportation and Lodging Services

Appendix: Information for Vocational Counselors and Other Professionals

The appendix is divided into three sections: the first provides information for individuals who want to use the revised GOE structure in other publications and databases; the second gives technical information on the GOE's development; and the third offers tips on how to use the GOE in counseling.

Much of the content in this appendix's second and third sections is adapted from information in earlier GOE editions. We used this material because much of the GOE's validity is based on the research conducted by the experienced labor market experts who worked on the original GOE's theory and structure.

Research studies done after the GOE's introduction have supported the validity of basing career and educational exploration on interests. We think this reinforces our collective common sense and our many years of practical experience in working with people who are making career decisions. If something interests you greatly, you will often be willing to overcome obstacles to get what you want. That is as true for choosing a career as it is for many other things in life. Even so, we'd like to include a review of recent research findings in our next GOE revision. If you know of research articles related to interest-based career exploration, please send copies to us. If you are a qualified researcher who wants to conduct formal research on the GOE, please contact us directly via e-mail or mail. Contact information is provided on the first few pages of this book.

Guidelines for Use of the GOE Structure by Other Developers

This new GOE revision obsoletes occupational information systems using or referring to the old GOE structure of Interest Areas, Work Groups, and Subgroups. Another major change is our cross-referencing the new O*NET jobs to the GOE rather than using the older DOT cross-reference. The U.S. Department of Labor does not plan to revise the GOE; therefore, our new GOE structure has become the de facto standard.

We know that many developers of occupational instruments, publications, software, and Internet systems will want to abandon the old GOE numbering references and replace them with the new ones presented in this revised GOE. To encourage this, we present the following answers to questions developers have asked us.

Who owns the new GOE structure and content?
The GOE was originally developed by the U.S. Department of Labor, and its content and structure were in the public domain. However, JIST's revised GOE incorporates many changes, and this allows us to copyright the revised structure and text, which we have done. What this means is that the new GOE structure and content are ***not*** in the public domain, and rights to this structure and content are protected under copyright laws.

Can others use the GOE structure in their own materials?
Yes. We encourage other developers and publishers to refer to and use the revised GOE structure in their materials and products. We want to do this because of the GOE's importance to other systems that have traditionally cross-referenced it. Also, we believe that allowing its use by others is in keeping with the GOE's original spirit and intent.

Is there a cost for using the new GOE structure in our products?
A small charge covers the costs of our negotiating and recording permissions. This is not a small matter, as we anticipate numerous inquiries regarding use of the new GOE structure. We also want to know who is using the new GOE structure and how it is being used—an essential requirement for protecting our copyrights. For those wanting to use the new GOE structure, there is a one-time fee of $250 for most printed products and an annual licensing fee of $200 for most software. These fees cover the use of the revised GOE Interest Area names, numbers, and brief descriptions; Work Group names and numbers; and related O*NET job title names arranged within the Work Groups. This fee does not cover use of the longer descriptive text for the Interest Areas, Work Groups, or job descriptions. Also, these fees do not include the use of the GOE structure in consumable items such as printed interest inventories. These other uses will be negotiated separately.

Are there other restrictions?
For the preceding uses, we require that a statement be included with each use, identifying JIST as the material's source and the copyright owner. We will provide you with this statement and will advise you of certain easy-to-follow guidelines for using the material in your product.

I work for the government. Why can't I use the new GOE structure for free?
JIST has invested a great deal of time and money in producing the new GOE structure. This material was not produced by any government agency. Even so, we will consider your special circumstances, particularly for uses by the good people at the U.S. Department of Labor.

Can we use the revised GOE text?
Perhaps, depending on the situation. It took us several years to develop this revised text, so we do not want someone to use it to create a product that directly competes with our products. Let us know what you want to do, and we will consider it. Additional fees would likely apply to these situations.

Can we arrange for custom variations of the text and database information?
Anything is possible, so you can ask; however, custom work depends on our resource availability. Programming and writing costs would be charged to you at an hourly rate, and these tasks are expensive due to the high skill levels required.

Will we have access to future changes to the GOE structure?
Sure. We expect to make improvements in all GOE elements over time, and these changes will be available to you as they are made. Note that it will be your responsibility to be aware of the newest changes because we have no mechanism to keep you informed. Check with us if you are creating or revising a product, and we'll give you the latest version.

Can we suggest changes to the GOE?
Of course. We are interested in any suggestions for improving the GOE. We prefer that you submit your suggestions via e-mail to editorial@jist.com, but we will be happy to take them via letter.

Are fees and other details subject to change?
Yes. As we gain experience with the various uses of the GOE, we will revise our licensing fees and restrictions. This means that the terms and conditions noted here are subject to change without notice. Check with us for the latest changes.

How do we contact you for permissions?
Please contact us in writing, providing clear information on the following:

- What GOE content or rights you want to use or obtain.
- The product in which you will be using our materials. A clear, complete description of your product or a sample draft would be helpful, if available.
- The nature and size of the population you expect to use your product.
- Any other information you think we should know.

Send your inquiry to Rights Editor, JIST Publishing, 8902 Otis Ave., Indianapolis, Indiana 46216-1033. Or contact us by e-mail at editorial@jist.com.

Technical Development of the GOE Interest Factors

Note: The material in this section comes with minimal changes from Appendix A of the 1984 revision of the *Guide for Occupational Exploration*. The information is presented here to help answer technical questions related to the development of the systems used to organize occupations in the original GOE. It may also refer to the older structures that existed prior to the 2001 revision of the GOE. For example, it mentions Subgroups of occupations, a system we eliminated in the 2001 revision.

Background

From 1939 to 1998, the *Dictionary of Occupational Titles* (DOT) was one of the basic sources of information about jobs in this country. The first edition (U.S. Department of Labor, 1939) reflected the job market situation of the time—a surplus of qualified workers and a shortage of jobs. Consequently, the book's content emphasized the work or tasks performed, with little attention to the requirements made of the worker.

With the advent of World War II, the economy—including the job market—radically changed: The surplus of qualified workers that had existed during the Depression years was replaced by a scarcity of workers, with many jobs to fill. Highly selective recruitment on the basis of training and/or experience was a thing of the past; acceptance of inexperienced or untrained workers with job potential became a common practice.

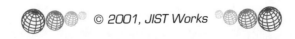

Recruitment and placement personnel needed to use every available source of workers, and to do this they needed to know what characteristics or traits a person should possess in order to learn to perform the job. Therefore, a system of evaluating jobs in terms of worker potential was developed, and this data was published for use in counseling and placement. The system appeared in Part IV of the second edition *Dictionary of Occupational Titles,* titled Entry Occupational Classification (U.S. Department of Labor, 1949). Groups of jobs were described in terms of the personal traits required of the worker—for example, ability to relate abstract ideas, ability to plan, memory for details, facility with language, dexterity and muscular control, persuasiveness, and liking for people.

In state employment service offices, Part IV soon became a basic tool for assisting the person who was not qualified for the job based only on his or her experience or training. It was also used to help in career exploration and choice, sometimes before the counselee entered college.

In 1949, the U.S. Employment Service initiated the Functional Occupational Classification project to develop a new classification system for jobs—one that would reflect not only what tasks were performed but also what worker traits were required. Some of the resulting data was released in the 1956 publication *Estimates of Worker Traits Requirements for 4,000 Jobs Defined in the Dictionary of Occupational Titles* (U.S. Department of Labor, 1956). This new methodology provided the basis for research and development of the Worker Traits Arrangement in Volume II of the third edition (1965) of the *Dictionary of Occupational Titles* (U.S. Department of Labor, 1965).

The Worker Traits Arrangement was intended for counselors, employment interviewers, curriculum planners, and others engaged in assisting persons in career exploration. The arrangement contained 22 areas of work. Within each area were 114 groups of jobs based on common worker traits requirements. The requirements, in profile form, appeared under the following headings: General Educational Development, Specific Vocational Preparation, Aptitudes, Temperaments, Interests, and Physical Capacities.

Despite the wealth of information contained in this arrangement, it was not used to any great extent by employment service personnel nor others involved in counseling and related activities. There were three reasons for this lack of use. First, no technique existed for obtaining information from the counselee in the same language as that used in describing the jobs, or for relating personal data to job data in the Worker Traits Arrangement. Second, the technical descriptive language could not be used to help people understand themselves or their actual potential to meet the requirements of a job. Third, because of its location between the Occupational Group Arrangement and the Arrangement of Titles by Industry, the Worker Traits Arrangement was difficult to use. The areas and groups were not identified by codes, and some of the titles were misleading. Researchers, however, found the Worker Traits Arrangement serviceable and have used the data in many different projects and studies.

The occupational interests of the trait qualifications profile were identified by Dr. William Cottle in research he conducted (Cottle, 1950). Dr. Cottle administered major interest and personality inventories then in use to 400 adult males. He scored the inventories with scales that had been developed for these instruments and factor-analyzed the intercorrelations of the scores. The 5 bipolar interest factors identified were adopted by the U.S. Employment Service for estimating interest requirements of occupations.

The Cottle-based interests, however, were of limited use in employment service operations, because counselors had no way of measuring interests of individuals in the same terms that interest requirements of occupations were shown in the DOT.

Some years ago, the Employment Service Division of Testing attempted to develop an interest inventory with scales corresponding to the Cottle factors. Though the attempt was unsuccessful, an extension of this research led to identification of measurable interest factors (Droege & Hawk, 1976). Further exploration indicated that these factors could also be used to form broad occupational interest areas for use in occupational exploration (Strohmenger & Padgett, 1979; Droege & Padgett, 1979). These Interest Areas eventually became the basis for the first edition of the *Guide for Occupational Exploration* (U.S. Department of Labor, 1979).

Procedure for Identification of Occupational Interest Factors

Three hundred occupational activity items were constructed by test development analysts in six state employment services: Mississippi, New York, North Carolina, Ohio, Pennsylvania, and Utah. All Worker Trait Groups and Occupational Groups in the third edition of the DOT were represented. As a result of item analysis studies, 192 of the 300 items were retained. A review of these items by test research and occupational analysis personnel for coverage of the Cottle factors revealed uneven distribution requiring additional item construction. The inventory that followed consisted of 307 items, providing apparently good coverage of the Cottle factors.

Occupational analysts from the Michigan, Florida, and Missouri Occupational Analysis Field Centers were asked to allocate the 307 activity items in the Interest Inventory to the Cottle factors used as the interest component in the third edition of the DOT. These allocations were reviewed by the national Employment Service Office, and the most relevant activity items were chosen to form the initial scales measuring the 10 Cottle factors.

The 307-item inventory was administered to 525 males and 590 females in nine states: Arizona, California, Georgia, Massachusetts, Minnesota, New York, Ohio, Oklahoma, and Wisconsin. About half of those tested were high school seniors and college students; the other half were local office applicants, trainees, and employed workers.

Analyses of the data were made to determine the extent to which the keys developed by the occupational analysts provided adequate measures of the 10 (5 bipolar) Cottle factors and to identify the most important interest factors underlying the 307 inventory items, without regard to the factors Cottle had found.

Results and Conclusions

The major finding with respect to the Cottle factor scales was that only half of the Cottle interest factors could be measured with any confidence. Another finding was that the marked bipolarity Cottle found in his research was not confirmed by the results of the present study, which showed positive intercorrelations among all of the factor scales. Thus, the attempt to develop interest inventory scales statistically and conceptually parallel to the Cottle factors was unsuccessful. To identify the interest factors that best represented responses to 307 items of the inventory, the items were factor analyzed. Principal components factor analyses with varimax rotation (Kaiser, 1958) were performed separately on the total male and female intercorrelation matrices. Results of the factor analyses led to these conclusions:

- Responses to the 307 activity items can be explained in terms of 11 basic occupational interest factors.
- These factors are readily interpretable.
- The factors are quite similar in meaning for males and females.

Development of Interest Areas

The last step in the development of the Worker Traits Arrangement in the third edition of the DOT was formation of Areas of Work. Occupational analysts allocated the 114 Worker Trait Groups in 22 Areas of Work, based on the similarity of work performed. These 22 Areas of Work were formed to help the counselor relate an individual's traits to a framework of occupational requirements broader than that provided by the 114 Worker Trait Groups.

The usefulness of the areas was limited, however, because the areas were not developed systematically according to well-defined principles and could not be described in trait-related terms. More sharply focused areas were needed that would be meaningful to counselors and interviewers, clients, applicants, and students as a beginning point in occupational exploration. This could be accomplished only if areas were formed first instead of last in the process of developing a structure for organizing the world of work and only if meaningful, well-defined, and measurable variables important for occupational success and satisfaction were used in relating occupations to areas.

The search for organizing principles coincided with the successful identification of measurable occupational interest factors referred to earlier. Further exploration into using the interest factors in the development of the new structure led to two decisions: (1) Cottle interest factors for identifying interest requirements were to be eliminated and replaced with the 11 new interest factors, and (2) the 11 interest factors were to be used as the basis for forming areas in the original *Guide for Occupational Exploration.*

These decisions, made in the summer of 1975, were critically important to the initial planning of the original *Guide for Occupational Exploration.* A specific, well-defined, and measurable variable (occupational interest) that was important in vocational counseling and in career exploration would be the prime organizing principle in the new structure to replace the Worker Traits Arrangement in the third edition of the DOT. The new Interest Areas would provide a much more meaningful and accessible entry into the structure than that provided in the DOT third edition's Areas of Work.

Procedure and Results

The critical first step in developing Interest Areas was to devise a suitable procedure that could be applied by occupational analysts.

Occupational analysts were given lists of interest inventory items with high factor loadings. These analysts were asked to develop concepts of the underlying nature of the factors.

The occupational analysts were then asked to apply these concepts to job descriptions for a standard sample of occupations. They were to do this by allocating the occupations to areas corresponding to the 11 factors. Differences existed among the analysts in how occupations were to be allocated to the various areas. These differences were discussed to achieve more uniform concepts of the interest factors.

Each analyst was assigned a set of occupations to allocate to Interest Areas. This was to be accomplished by reviewing job summaries and making judgments of the most prominent interest factors involved.

These allocations were reviewed by national office personnel. During the allocation process it became evident that there was a small group of occupations that could not be allocated to any of the 11 areas. To accommodate these occupations, it was necessary to establish a twelfth Interest Area, Physical Performing.

Relationship Between Holland's Occupational Categories and GOE Interest Areas

Many GOE readers use interest inventories or other techniques that relate an individual's interest or personality to Dr. John Holland's occupational categories (Holland, 1973). In recognition of the extensive research on the Holland model and its widespread use in vocational counseling today, the U.S. Employment Service Interest Areas were arranged according to the Holland categories. This was done without much difficulty because the two systems are closely related. The primary difference between the two is that the U.S. Employment Service system provides additional differentiation within the broader Holland Realistic and Social categories.

The relationship of the Holland Occupational Categories to the Employment Service's Interest Areas of Work is shown in the following table. For a detailed table relating the 66 Work Groups to Holland occupational codes, see Jones (1980).

Holland Occupational Category		**U.S. Employment Service Occupational Category**
Artistic	01	Artistic
Investigative	02	Scientific
Realistic	03	Plants and Animals
Realistic	04	Protective
Realistic	05	Mechanical
Realistic	06	Industrial
Conventional	07	Business Detail
Enterprising	08	Selling
Social	09	Accommodating[1]
Social	10	Humanitarian
Social	11	Leading–Influencing[2]
Social	12	Physical Performing

1 A relatively narrow area that includes a few occupations covered by Holland's Enterprising and Realistic categories in addition to those covered by the Social category.

2 A broad area including, in addition to occupations covered by Holland's Social category, business management and law/politics occupations covered by the Enterprising category, and social science occupations covered by the Investigative category.

Development of Groups and Subgroups

After the jobs were allocated to Interest Areas, the analysts in Occupational Analysis Field Centers were asked to group the jobs in each area. The criteria were the capabilities and adaptabilities required of the worker. Capabilities were such factors as general educational development, physical capacities, important aptitudes, and job knowledge. Adaptabilities were tolerances to job-worker situations including environment, routine, dealing with people, and working within precise limits and standards.

As a result, 66 discrete Work Groups were developed to further categorize the jobs in the 12 Interest Areas. The number of Groups per area ranges from 2 to 12. Some of the 66 Groups contained an unwieldy number of jobs; therefore, the jobs were divided into meaningful Subgroups. Criteria for Subgrouping varied from one Work Group to another. For example, in one Group, the Subgrouping might be based on differences in type of knowledge used. In another Group, it might be based on differences in industries where the workers are hired. The number of Subgroups per Work Group ranged from 1 to 40.

After the 66 Work Groups were formed, an empirical test was made of their homogeneity with respect to aptitudes required for successful performance of occupations within the Groups (Droege & Boese, 1984). This test was made by analyzing the results of the accumulated store of more than 450 occupational validation studies done on the General Aptitude Test Battery (GATB). The results showed that differences in job duties from one occupation to another within Work Groups are not associated with substantial differences in aptitude requirements for performing the job duties. This finding provides empirical support to the hypothesis that trained occupational analysts can group occupations into aptitude-homogeneous groupings.

A Final Comment on the GOE Occupational Structure

A unifying characteristic of the GOE's occupation-oriented Interest Areas and aptitude-oriented Work Groups is the homogeneous nature of the job duties involved. This fact is apparent from a review of Work Group titles and descriptions, for example:

Work Group 01.02, Writing and Editing. Workers in this group write or edit prose or poetry. Some use knowledge of a technical field to write manuals. Most work for publishers, in radio and television studios, and in the theatre and motion picture industries. Some are self-employed and sell their stories and plays directly to publishers.

Work Group 03.03, Hands-on Work in Plants and Animals. Workers in this group perform strenuous tasks with plants or animals, usually outdoors in a nonfactory setting. They work with their hands, use tools and equipment, or operate machinery. They work on farms or ranches, at logging camps or fish hatcheries, in forests or game preserves, or with commercial fishing businesses, onshore or in fishing boats. In cities and towns, they usually work in parks, gardens, or nurseries.

Work Group 05.02, Electrical and Electronic Systems. Workers in this group repair and install electrical devices and systems such as motors, transformers, appliances, and power lines, and electronic devices and systems such as radios, computers, and telephone networks. They work for manufacturers, utilities, and service companies. Since electrical and electronic equipment is used almost everywhere, they may work in almost any kind of location, as well as in repair shops.

Work Group 07.03, Air Vehicle Operation. Workers in this group pilot airplanes or helicopters, or train or supervise pilots. Most are hired by commercial airlines. Some find jobs piloting planes for private companies such as package delivery services or crop-dusting services or for individuals.

From a practical standpoint, the clear descriptions of work performed in the Interest Areas and Work Groups can be understood by lay persons. In addition, the homogeneous structure of the Interest Areas and Work Groups makes it possible to organize and present material from the original GOE in a manner that facilitates its use in occupational exploration by individuals who have limited or no access to counseling help.

The development of an occupational structure that can be described as both "human attribute-related" and "nature of work-related" is of some theoretical as well as practical importance. The GOE, which contains such a structure, provides at least an approximation of the goal of devising a unified taxonomy of work performance—that is, a taxonomy that addresses the relevant characteristics of people and jobs discussed in an exhaustive review of job family development (Pearlman, 1980).

The Counselee Assessment/ Occupational Exploration System

> **Important Reminder:** While some of the material in this section may be obsolete, it provides historical background on the development of the original GOE. We have included it here for the benefit of readers who may be interested.

As explained above, the GOE contains a psychologically meaningful occupational structure: the Interest Areas are homogeneous with respect to broad occupational interests, and the Work Groups within Interest Areas are homogeneous in occupational aptitude requirements. This means that appropriate interest and aptitude measures can be used with counselees and others to aid in occupational exploration that focuses on the Interest Areas and Work Groups where occupational aptitude and interest are strongest.

For this reason, the GOE is a keystone of the Counselee Assessment/Occupational Exploration System (Droege & Padgett, 1984) developed by the U.S. Employment Service. The checklists and worksheets found in chapter 2 of the 1984 Edition of the GOE provide a basis for assessment, occupational exploration, and planning. The other components of the system are listed here.

The U.S. Employment Service Interest Inventory and Interest Check List provide assessment links to the GOE based on occupational interests of counselees. The Interest Inventory is used to obtain a profile of scores on 12 scales measuring the same factors as those used to develop the GOE's Interest Areas. For counselors who prefer using a nonscored interviewing aid when discussing interests with the counselee, the Interest Check List provides a way of relating the interests of counselees in specific job activities to Work Groups within the Interest Areas and of exploring specific occupations within these Work Groups.

The General Aptitude Test Battery (GATB) is a second major assessment link to the GOE's occupational structure. The Occupational Aptitude Patterns were developed specifically to relate aptitude requirements for occupational success to Work Groups of the GOE. Administration of the GATB in a 2½-hour session makes it possible to determine a counselee's aptitude levels in comparison with requirements for 59 of the 66 Work Groups, covering 97 percent of nonsupervisory occupations in the U.S. economy. In addition to the GATB, the Bateria de Examenes de Aptitud General (BEAG) and a new edition of the Nonreading Aptitude Test Battery (NATB) are available for use with individuals who are Spanish-speaking and those who have limited literacy skills, respectively.

The Basic Occupational Literacy Test (BOLT) was developed to measure literacy skills of educationally deficient individuals. Since the BOLT is normed in terms of GED levels, it can be useful in determining the extent to which the individual has the literacy skills required to perform occupations in the various Work Groups.

It is important to recognize that assessment is only a preliminary step to occupational exploration by the counselee. Thus, in using the Counselee Assessment/Occupational Exploration System, the counselor should make a conscious attempt to help broaden the counselee's options for consideration and to encourage a maximum of occupational exploration in areas where application of the assessment techniques indicates potential. Specifically, counselees should be encouraged to think carefully about suitable occupational areas they may not have considered before because of lack of knowledge about the occupations or because of a misconception that the occupations were not open to members of the counselee's sex or ethnic group.

A related point is that all occupational options, not just those traditionally associated with one sex, should be considered within the broad areas covered by the assessment indicators. Thus, the counselee should be encouraged to consider the entire range of GOE Work Groups encompassed by an Interest Area being considered, rather than to narrow the area prematurely to those Work Groups traditionally associated with people of the counselee's sex.

The new system has considerable flexibility and can be applied in a variety of situations and circumstances. Ideally, the counselor should be in a position to select from the tools available the ones that are most appropriate for the particular counselee. Practically, because of time or other constraints, it may not be possible to use some of the tools in some situations. Following are examples of ways to apply the system:

In situations where counselees are available for extended assessment and occupational exploration over a one- or two-week period, the entire range of assessment techniques can be applied.

In counseling situations where there is limited time for test administration, self-assessment, and counseling interviews, it may be possible to administer only the GATB and either the Interest Check List or the Interest Inventory. Results can be interpreted according to the manuals for these tests. Self-scoring and interpretation in group sessions may be necessary in some instances.

Many job seekers are not prepared for effective job search because they lack knowledge about the kinds of jobs to look for. They have difficulty in relating their interests, skills, and potentials to appropriate occupations. The new Counselee Assessment/Occupational Exploration System based on the *Guide for Occupational Exploration* and related assessment tools can be of help in counseling such individuals.

Although designed primarily to meet the needs of employment service interviewers and counselors in their assessment of applicants, U.S. Employment Service tests are also useful to counselors in high schools, government-funded programs, rehabilitation agencies, etc. Because of the many requests for these tests, state employment services have developed procedures for making them available to other agencies, when warranted, for operational use or for research. As an alternative, cooperative arrangements are sometimes made whereby an agency's clients are referred to a local employment service office for testing. Organizations interested in exploring these possibilities should contact the local office of their state employment service.

References

Cottle, W. C. 1950. "A factorial study of the multiphasic," Strong, Kuder, and Bell Inventories using a population of adult males. *Psychometrica* 15:25-47.

Droege, R. C., and R. Boese. 1984. "Development of a new occupational aptitude pattern structure with comprehensive occupational coverage." *Vocational Guidance Quarterly.*

Droege, R. C., and J. Hawk. 1976. "Development of a U.S. Employment Service interest inventory." *Journal of Employment Counseling* 14:65-71.

Droege, R. C., and A. Padgett. 1979. "Development of an interest, U.S.-oriented occupational classification system." *Vocational Guidance Quarterly* 27:302-310.

Droege, R. C., and A. Padgett. 1984. "A new counselee assessment/occupational exploration system and its interest and aptitude dimensions." *The School Counselor.*

Holland, J. L. 1973. *Making Vocational Choices: A Theory of Careers.* Englewood Cliffs, New Jersey: Prentice-Hall.

Jones, L. K. 1980. "Holland's typology and the new *Guide for Occupational Exploration:* Bridging the gap." *Vocational Guidance Quarterly* 29:70-76.

Kaiser, M. E. 1958. "The varimax criterion for analytic rotation in factor analysis." *Psychometrica* 23:187-200.

Pearlman, K. 1980. "Job families: A review and discussion of their implications for personnel selection." *Psychological Bulletin* 87:1-27.

Strohmenger, C. T. and A. Padgett. 1979. "Guide to occupational exploration—a new approach in career planning." *Journal of Employment Counseling* 16:16-20.

U.S. Department of Labor. 1939. *Dictionary of Occupational Titles* (1st edition). Washington, D.C.: U.S. Government Printing Office.

U.S. Department of Labor. 1949. *Dictionary of Occupational Titles* (2nd edition). Part IV: Entry Occupational Classification. Washington, D.C.: U.S. Government Printing Office.

U.S. Department of Labor. 1965. *Dictionary of Occupational Titles* (3rd edition). Vol. II: Occupational Classification. Washington, D.C.: U.S. Government Printing Office.

U.S. Department of Labor. 1956. *Estimates of Worker Traits Requirements for 4,000 Jobs Defined in the Dictionary of Occupational Titles.* Washington, D.C.: U.S. Government Printing Office.

U.S. Department of Labor. 1979. *Guide for Occupational Exploration* (1st edition). Washington, D.C.: U.S. Government Printing Office.

Information for Vocational Counselors and Other Professionals

Note: This content comes, with few changes, from the original edition of the *Guide for Occupational Exploration,* published by the U.S. Department of Labor in 1979.

An essential ingredient of vocational counseling is providing occupational and labor market information. Although career decision making involves far more than just these elements, any instrument that organizes the world of work and provides information about occupational duties and requirements is valuable. Because vocational counseling services are not available to a large number of potential counselees, the *Guide for Occupational Exploration* was intended to help such persons make more informed vocational decisions.

The counselor who assists individuals in choosing a suitable occupational or vocational goal may function in any setting—the school, the college, the public employment service, the private employment service, the vocational rehabilitation agency, or the community or private vocational guidance center.

In virtually every setting in which such counselors operate, they wish to help the individual evaluate his or her occupational interests, skills, and potentials; relate them to occupational requirements and opportunities; arrive at a suitable occupational goal; and establish a plan for achieving it.

To assist the counselee in this analysis, the counselor uses various tools and sources of information. The counselor helps the applicant or client analyze his or her work experience (regular, casual, part-time, summer, military), education and training, volunteer and leisure-time activities, and other relevant experiences that may provide evidence of occupational preferences, skills, and potentialities. The counselor may administer or arrange the administration of interest inventories or checklists, aptitude tests, such as the U.S. Employment Service's General Aptitude Test Battery, or other tests and inventories.

Note: The GATB has been discontinued from widespread use as an assessment instrument.

Employment or vocational counseling, however, cannot be effective if it is limited to information about the counselee. The counselor and counselee must also have information about the world of work. Information about the counselee must be related to information about the world of work to help the individual determine a promising occupational choice.

For some time now, the counselor has had available sources of occupational information. Some sources published by the U.S. Department of Labor include the *Occupational Outlook Handbook,* the *Occupational Outlook Quarterly,* the *Dictionary of Occupational Titles,* and most recently the computer-accessed O*NET database. Other sources are state occupational guides and labor market reports prepared by state employment agencies. These and similar publications provide useful information about labor market trends and opportunities, and descriptions of occupations. However, a practical grouping of jobs in terms of occupational interest and work requirements did not exist until the development of the GOE in 1979. That publication and its revisions filled this long-expressed need of vocational counselors. The thousands of occupations in the world of work are now grouped by interests and traits required for successful job performance. Hence, the GOE provides a convenient connection between information about the counselee and potentially suitable fields of work.

Role of the GOE in Counseling and Guidance

Note: We have revised the text that follows to eliminate reference to the old GOE system that included Subgroups. We did this to avoid confusion, since this information can be helpful to career counselors, and the historical reference to the old GOE system is not useful here.

The GOE groups occupations into fields of work within 14 major Interest Areas, containing broad fields (four-digit Work Groups). The counselor and counselee can explore and relate occupationally significant information about the counselee. Rather than attempting to explore the entire world of work, the counselor and counselee can identify those areas of work in which the counselee has the strongest interest. They can also identify within the Interest Areas those Work Groups that are most closely related to the interests, skills, aptitudes, education and training, and physical abilities of the counselee.

The GOE may be used particularly (1) to give the counselee an overview of the world of work and thus widen his or her understanding of occupations and (2) to help the counselee determine his or her occupational goal by offering a choice of fields of work and occupations that best reflect the interests, abilities, and potentials of the counselee.

Widening the Understanding of the World of Work

If the counselee's experience and understanding of the world of work are limited, it will be desirable for him or her, during the early stages of the counseling process, to obtain an overview of the various Interest Areas and Work Groups covered in the GOE.

The counselor may review these sections with the counselee and suggest that the counselee review them independently. This will help the counselee become familiar with the various Interest Areas and the Work Groups covered in each area—especially those areas in which the counselee has a particular interest.

This overview should be helpful not only in giving the counselee an overall feel for the world of work but also in providing a background against which to relate elements of the counselee's work experience, education and training, leisure-time activities, and other experiences that point to possibly suitable fields of work and occupations.

Determining Occupational Goal

During the counseling process, the counselor assists the counselee in choosing an occupational field that best represents the counselee's interests, skills, and potential abilities, and that offers opportunity for employment. Analysis of occupation-related experiences, application of aptitude and interest tests, and relation of the resulting information to occupational groupings in the GOE are major steps in this process.

Analysis of Occupationally Related Experiences

The counselor assists the counselee in analyzing occupation-related experiences that may indicate the counselee's true occupational interests, aptitudes, acquired skills, personal traits, and any environmental and financial factors that may have vocational significance. Thus, the counselor explores with the counselee past work history, school courses, leisure-time activities, hobbies, volunteer activities, and other experiences for indications of the kinds of work the counselee particularly liked and seemed to do well in, and the types he or she disliked or did poorly in. From this analysis will emerge indications of types of work for the counselee either to consider seriously or avoid altogether.

When the counselee receives an overview of the world of work early in the counseling process, he or she will have an occupational information base for analyzing past experiences in light of their occupational significance.

Aptitude and Interest Testing

In addition to obtaining information about the counselee's background during the counseling interview, the counselor will often administer or arrange for the administration of assessment tests for further indications of interests and potential ability. The occupational preferences that derive from the interview(s) and the use of the interest tools will serve as entries to the 14 Interest Areas in the *Guide for Occupational Exploration.*

Uses of the GOE in Determining Occupational Goals

After occupationally significant information is obtained about the counselee through the counseling interview(s) and the use of the various tools, the counselor and the counselee can use the GOE to explore fields of work and help the counselee select a suitable occupational goal. The following steps are suggested:

STEP 1. Help the Counselee Identify Areas to be Considered. Information obtained about the counselee will reveal broad areas that are of particular interest to him or her. Making a list of these Interest Areas will ensure exploration of all pertinent areas. The counselee should be encouraged to read the description of the selected areas to further verify the relevance of his or her interests. Reviewing the descriptions of other Interest Areas will also identify possible areas to explore.

STEP 2. Help the Counselee Select and Explore Work Groups. When the counselee chooses further Interest Areas to explore, he or she may review all Work Group descriptions (indicated by the four-digit code) within these Interest Areas to decide which Work Groups to explore. Sometimes, glancing at the Work Group title may be enough to identify a type of activity the counselee does not wish to investigate further. The counselee may then turn to the next Group selected for further exploration. Alternatively, when the counselee reads a Group title and description and expresses interest in the Work Group, he or she may explore it immediately, before moving on to the next Work Group.

In the counselee's exploration of the Work Group, the counselor should help the counselee determine suitability of the Group from the standpoint of his or her true interests, aptitudes, skills and traits required, further preparation needed, and other relevant considerations.

To explore a selected Work Group, the counselee should review the information provided under the Work Group description. During the discussion of this information, the counselor should help the counselee try to relate occupationally significant information about himself or herself to the information in that Work Group.

- **ITEM 1. What kind of work would you do?** This item provides examples of some specific work tasks of occupations within the Group, such as "Prepare graphs or charts of data or enter data into a computer for analysis," or "Cultivate grass or lawn, using power aerator and thatcher." These examples, along with the description of the Work Group, will help the counselee get a feel for the kind of work involved and determine whether it is a type of activity in line with his or her interests, skills, and potentials. These activities may apply to just one occupation but usually are illustrative of the kind of work performed in various jobs in this Group.

- **ITEM 2. What things about you point to this kind of work?** This item mentions work experience, extracurricular activities, hobbies, and other activities and experiences, as well as work values, physical and mental abilities, and preferences for work settings relevant to occupations in this Work Group. This item provides clues concerning the counselee's possible ability to do or to learn to do this kind of work and his desire to do it.

  Included in this item are questions such as "Is it important for you to plan your work with little supervision?" "Have you enjoyed raising or caring for animals as a hobby or leisure-time activity?" "Have you liked and done well in Accounting as a school subject?" "Are you able to see details of objects at a close range (within a few feet)?" and "Would you work in places such as railroad tracks and yards?" These questions help the counselee think through whether he or she has the interest and ability to do or to learn to do types of work included in this Group. These questions also help the counselee think about certain issues of personal likes and dislikes that may affect the desirability of the occupations in this Group. The counselor should help the counselee relate these kinds of personal experiences and interests to the Work Groups being explored.

- **ITEM 3. What skills and knowledges do you need for this kind of work?** This item names the worker characteristics required to perform successfully in occupations in this Group. For example, it points to actual or potential abilities such as "Information Gathering–knowing how to find information and identifying essential information" and "Time Management–managing your own time and the time of others." It also points to actual or potential knowledges such as "Communications–the science and art of delivering information" and "Public Safety and Security–weaponry, public safety, and security operations; rules, regulations, precautions, prevention; and the protection of people, data, and property." This information should help the counselee determine whether these are the kind of work requirements that he or she is capable of handling.

- **ITEM 4. What else should you consider about this kind of work?** This item provides a number of other considerations that the counselee will want to weigh in making up his or her mind about the satisfactions and suitability of this kind of work. For example, the counselee may be advised "Most workers in these jobs are on call at all times to respond to emergencies," "There is keen competition for most jobs in this group," or "These workers are under considerable pressure to maintain passenger safety while keeping air traffic flowing on schedule, often at a brisk pace."

- **ITEM 5. How can you prepare for jobs of this kind?** This item describes the kind of training, work, and other experiences usually required by or acceptable to employers. It tells the counselee how to enter the field. Counselees who are interested in this Work Group should consider whether they have the kind of preparation usually needed or the willingness to take further training if needed.

The counselee should keep a simple record of all Work Groups he or she reviewed and those he or she identified for further exploration.

STEP 3. Help the Counselee Explore Specific Occupations. After exploring the Work Groups, the counselee will usually find either that he or she is not seriously interested in the type of work in the Group or will want to explore it still further. If the counselee is still interested in the Work Group, the counselor should help him or her examine specific occupations within the Work Group and choose one or more for further investigation.

The counselee should be encouraged to identify occupations that seem interesting and potentially suitable, based on all the information that the counselee now has about himself or herself. The counselee should be instructed how to look up information on occupations that seem particularly interesting in a print, software, or Internet source, such as this book, the *O*NET Viewer,* or the *O*NET Dictionary of Occupational Titles.* The counselee should then consider the specific occupations from the standpoint of opportunities available for placement or training, the counselee's interests and qualifications, and the occupational requirements.

STEP 4. Help the Counselee Select His or Her Vocational Goal. The counselee, working with the counselor, should compile a list of specific occupations that appear to be particularly interesting to the counselee. With the counselor's help, the counselee should weigh the pros and cons of each desirable and suitable Work Group or occupation.

STEP 5. Help the Counselee Develop a Plan for Attaining the Goal. As usual, the counselor will assist the counselee in developing a realistic vocational plan for reaching the goal. The plan should reflect actions to be taken by the counselee, by the counselor, or by other resources to enable the counselee to enter a training program, obtain suitable employment, or take some other step toward attaining the goal. A thoughtful plan will include a contingency plan for what to do if the intended goal proves unattainable or loses its appeal.

STEP 6. Assign Appropriate Occupational Titles. If the counselee's thinking remains at the Group level and the counselee does not select a specific occupational goal, the counselor should assign one or more occupational titles to the counselee. The assigned titles should reflect the counselee's goals and facilitate his or her selection for suitable employment.

Two or more counseling interviews are usually required to help the counselee make a suitable occupational choice and plan to implement that choice. The counselor may wish to suggest that, during one of the interviews or between interviews, the counselee review the GOE. The introduction provides helpful suggestions for reviewing the book.

The GOE thus serves as a useful reference tool in career exploration and can help the individual and the counselor develop a sound and realistic vocational goal for the counselee.

Index

of Interest Areas, Work Groups, and Jobs

A

B

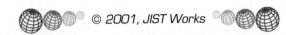

C

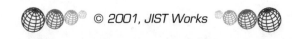

D

E

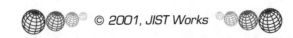

F

G

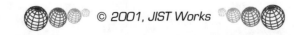

H

I

J

K-L

M

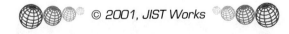

N

R

S

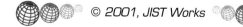

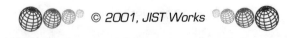

T

U-V

W-Z

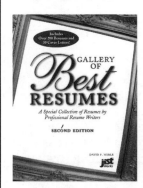

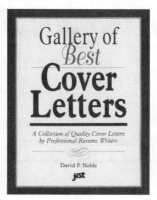

See us on the World Wide Web: www.jist.com

The Federal Resume Guidebook, Second Edition

Kathryn Kraemer Troutman

This resource leads you through the complexities of analyzing job announcements, writing federal resumes for both human and scanner "eyes," and packaging a resume to meet both federal and vacancy announcement criteria. Includes many helpful tips and examples.

ISBN 1-56370-545-1 / Order Code LP-J5451
$21.95

Career Success Is Color-Blind, Second Edition

Overcoming Prejudice and Eliminating Barriers in the Workplace

Ollie Stevenson

A veteran career counselor explains the basic rules of the "Business Mindset" that govern career success in America today. These guidelines have been used effectively by thousands of people to set career paths, move forward, and gain satisfaction at work.

ISBN 1-56370-733-0 / Order Code LP-J7330
$16.95

Quick Internet Guide to Career and Education Information, Third Edition

Anne Wolfinger

The author has researched thousands of career, job search, and education sites on the Web and includes only the very best places for solid information and advice. Saves you hours of time and frustration!

ISBN 1-56370-807-8 / Order Code LP-J8078
$16.95

Job Search Handbook for People with Disabilities

Daniel J. Ryan, Ph.D.

This book shows you how to prepare yourself for the overall job search. It helps you to best represent yourself to potential employers and to reassure them that you are a capable worker. Also covers employment laws and how they affect you.

ISBN 1-56370-665-2 / Order Code LP-J6652
$16.95

Call 1-800-648-JIST or FAX 1-800-JIST-FAX

See us on the World Wide Web: www.jist.com

Young Person's Occupational Outlook Handbook, Third Edition

Compiled by JIST Editors from U.S. government data

Based on the *Occupational Outlook Handbook,* this text is ideal for helping young people explore careers. This book covers 250 jobs–each on one page–held by 85 percent of the workforce. It clusters job descriptions, making it easy to explore job options based on interest. It also makes direct connections between school subjects and the skills needed for jobs.

ISBN 1-56370-731-4 / Order Code LP-J7314
$19.95

The College Majors Handbook

The Actual Jobs, Earnings, and Trends for Graduates of 60 College Majors

Neeta P. Fogg, Paul E. Harrington, and Thomas F. Harrington

Faced with the college decision? This book details what actually happened to more than 15,000 undergraduates from 60 college majors. This is the only college planning guide with the perspective of what actually happened to college undergraduates. It identifies jobs in which the graduates now work and their earnings on those jobs.

ISBN 1-56370-518-4 / Order Code LP-J5184
$24.95

The Kids' College Almanac, Second Edition

A first Look at College

Barbara C. Greenfeld and Robert A. Weinstein

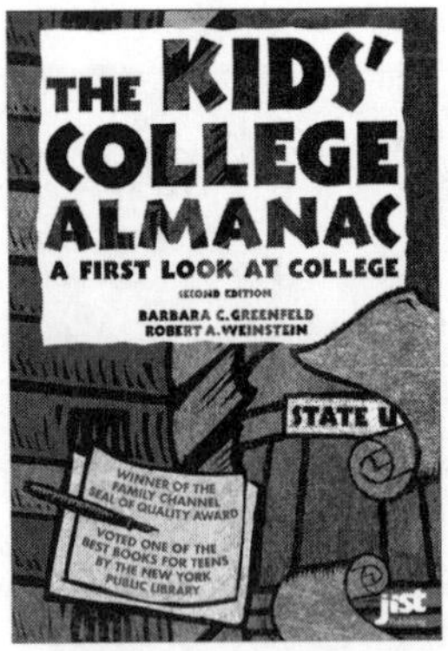

Selected by the New York Public Library as one of the best books for teens and preteens, it provides helpful information about going to college and encourages career and educational planning.

ISBN 1-56370-730-6 / Order Code LP-J7306
$16.95

Health-Care Careers for the 21st Century

Saul Wischnitzer, Ph.D., and Edith Wischnitzer

This three-in-one book is a career guidance manual, job description overview, and training program directory. It provides detailed descriptions of over 80 health-care careers, organized into five groups. It lists thousands of training programs with complete contact information. And it offers career guidance on everything from self-assessment to the interview process. Sample resumes and cover letters are included.

ISBN 1-56370-667-9 / Order Code LP-J6679
$24.95

Call 1-800-648-JIST or FAX 1-800-JIST-FAX

JIST Ordering Information

JIST specializes in publishing the very best results-oriented career and self-directed job search material. Since 1981 we have been a leading publisher in career assessment devices, books, videos, and software. We continue to strive to make our materials the best there are, so that people can stay abreast of what's happening in the labor market, and so they can clarify and articulate their skills and experiences for themselves as well as for prospective employers. **Our products are widely available through your local bookstores, wholesalers, and distributors.**

The World Wide Web

For more occupational or book information, get online and see our Web site at **www.jist.com**. Advance information about new products, services, and training events is continually updated.

Quantity Discounts Available!

Quantity discounts are available for businesses, schools, and other organizations.

The JIST Guarantee

We want you to be happy with everything you buy from JIST. If you aren't satisfied with a product, return it to us within 30 days of purchase along with the reason for the return. Please include a copy of the packing list or invoice to guarantee quick credit to your order.

How to Order

For your convenience, the last page of this book contains an order form.

Consumer Order Line:
Call toll free 1-800-648-JIST.
Please have your credit card (VISA, MC, or AMEX) information ready!

Mail your order:
JIST Publishing, Inc.
8902 Otis Avenue
Indianapolis, IN 46216-1033

Fax your order:
Toll free 1-800-JIST-FAX

Order online:
www.jist.com

Key Code: LP

JIST Order and Catalog Request Form

Purchase Order #: ______________________ (Required by some organizations)

Please copy this form if you need more lines for your order.

Billing Information

Organization Name: ______________________

Accounting Contact: ______________________

Street Address: ______________________

____

____

City, State, Zip: ______________________

Phone Number: (   ) ______________________

Phone: 1-800-648-JIST
Fax: 1-800-JIST-FAX
World Wide Web Address:
http://www.jist.com

Shipping Information with Street Address (If Different from Above)

Organization Name: ______________________

Contact: ______________________

Street Address: (We *cannot* ship to P.O. boxes) ______________________

____

____

City, State, Zip: ______________________

Phone Number: (   ) ______________________

Credit Card Purchases: VISA____ MC____ AMEX____

Card Number: ______________________

Exp. Date: ______________________

Name As on Card: ______________________

Signature: ______________________

Quantity	Order Code	Product Title	Unit Price	Total
	———	Free JIST Catalog	Free	———
			Subtotal	
			+5% Sales Tax *Indiana Residents*	
			+Shipping / Handling / Ins. (See left)	
			TOTAL	

jist Publishing
8902 Otis Avenue
Indianapolis, IN 46216

Shipping / Handling / Insurance Fees

In the continental U.S. add 7% of subtotal:

- Minimum amount charged = $4.00
- Maximum amount charged = $100.00
- FREE shipping and handling on any prepaid orders over $40.00

Above pricing is for regular ground shipment only. For rush or special delivery, call JIST Customer Service at 1-800-648-JIST for the correct shipping fee.

Outside the continental U.S. call JIST Customer Service at 1-800-648-JIST for an estimate of these fees.

Payment in U.S. funds only!

JIST thanks you for your order!